The Piano in Chamber Ensemble

MAURICE HINSON
and
WESLEY ROBERTS

The Piano in Chamber Ensemble

An Annotated Guide

SECOND EDITION

INDIANA UNIVERSITY PRESS

Bloomington and Indianapolis

This book is a publication of

Indiana University Press
601 North Morton Street
Bloomington, IN 47404-3797 USA

http://iupress.indiana.edu

Telephone orders   800-842-6796
Fax orders   812-855-7931
Orders by e-mail   iuporder@indiana.edu

Manufactured in the United States of America

Library of Congress Cataloging-in-Publication Data

Hinson, Maurice.
The piano in chamber ensemble : an annotated guide / Maurice Hinson and Wesley
Roberts. — 2nd ed.
p. cm.
Includes bibliographical references (p.) and indexes.
ISBN 0-253-34696-7 (cloth : alk. paper)
1. Piano with instrumental ensemble—Bibliography. 2. Chamber music—
Bibliography. I. Roberts, Wesley. II. Title.
ML128.C4H5 2005
016.785′2—dc22
2005021646

1 2 3 4 5   11 10 09 08 07 06

To Peggy and Sida

CONTENTS

Music for Four Instruments

Music for Five Instruments

Music for Six Instruments

Music for Seven Instruments

Music for Eight Instruments

Preface to the Second Edition

It may well be that the literature for piano in chamber ensembles is the most systematically diverse in style and quantity of all musical mediums. Maurice Hinson in his first edition to this guide a quarter century ago freely admitted that the quantity of literature available was far more than could be included in a single volume. No doubt with the rapid demise of many publishers in recent years and the rise of the independent online publisher we may never know the full resources which have been released, not to mention those which remain unpublished. While one would assume that the immense increase has been primarily in twentieth-century literature, this second edition contains a surprisingly large quantity of recent publications of works from composers of previous centuries, for the fascination with chamber music literature is steadily revealing many of its hidden resources.

The second edition of *The Piano in Chamber Ensemble* embraces the format and plan of the first edition in its identification of chamber music with piano. Key questions have been retained and addressed with each new entry: What is there? What is it like? Where can I get it? The criteria for selecting new entries remain unchanged and are thoroughly described in the Preface to the first edition.

Although every attempt to verify publishers' addresses and contact information has been made, some of this information will change with the passage of time. The reader is encouraged to search for updated information when this happens with well-established music sellers and on the Internet. In fact, scores available only through the Internet make their first appearance in the Hinson piano literature series with this volume.

The enthusiasm I encountered among performers and librarians for this new edition easily confirmed that chamber music interest and performance continues to wax among those who love music. In addition to those acknowledged for their contributions in the Preface to the first edition, I am deeply appreciative of many who have assisted me in the preparation of this newer edition. These include Karen Lynema and John Burch, Librarians of Campbellsville University; Karen Little, Music Librarian of the University of Louisville; Grace Baugh-Bennett of the Ceruti Chamber Players in Louisville, Kentucky, and of the piano faculty at Indiana University Southeast; Naomi Oliphant, Associate Dean of the School of Music and piano faculty at the University of Louisville; Rebecca Shockley of the piano faculty at the University of Minnesota; and Lisa McArthur, David McCullough, and Lisa Michaels, colleagues on the music faculty at Campbellsville University. In addition, many composers have supplied me with scores and recordings, for which I am graciously appreciative.

Generous assistance from many publishers made possible new entries which might otherwise have gone unnoticed. Grateful appreciation is expressed to Jill Newman of G. Henle USA; Ger van den Beuken of Muziekgroep Nederland; Larry McDonald of ECS Publishing; Kelly Gale of Neil A. Kjos Music Company; Lora Harvey of Dantalian, Inc.; Christopher McGlumphy of G. Schirmer; Alex Kuzyszyn of Duma Music; Cindy Broderick of Hal Leonard Corporation; Larry and Anne Schoenberg of Belmont Music; and Carl Fischer, LLC.

Last, special appreciation goes to my wife Sida for her linguistic skills, which often aided me in the review of materials, and for her encouragement throughout the preparation of this new edition.

Campbellsville, Kentucky   WESLEY ROBERTS
December 2004

Preface to the First Edition

The true spirit of chamber music, "the music of friends," has never been more eloquently expressed than by Henry Peacham, who stated it this way in 1622, in his book *The Compleat Gentleman:*

> Infinite is the sweete varietie that the Theorique of Musicke exerciseth the mind withal, as the contemplation of proportions, of Concords and Discords, diversitie of Moods and Tones, infiniteness of Invention, etc. But I dare affirme, there is no one Science in the world, that so affecteth the free and generous spirit, with a more delightfull and in-offensive recreation, or better disposeth the minde to what is commendable and vertuous.

Some of the most glorious literature written for the piano is found in the chamber music repertoire. Throughout the centuries composers have used chamber music to express their most intensely personal ideas. Surely Haydn, Mozart, and Beethoven gave Western culture some of their most sublime thoughts clothed in this medium, and contemporary composers are also using it for many of their most exciting expressions and avant-garde experiments.

In an attempt to make this vast literature more available to performers, teachers, librarians, music dealers, and all those interested in this rich area involving the piano, *The Piano in Chamber Ensemble* is here presented. As in *Guide to the Pianist's Repertoire* (Indiana University Press, 1973), which describes solo piano literature, answers will be found to the key questions: What is there? What is it like? Where can I get it?

Selection. Since the chamber music field is enormous, certain criteria had to be followed to make this volume manageable: 1. The listing includes compositions requiring no more than eight instruments (including piano). Larger ensembles would probably require a conductor, and this consideration suggested a logical and reasonable limitation. 2. The time span covered is mainly from 1700 to the present, but a few works dating from before 1700 are included because of their special musical interest. The listing contains some music composed before the invention of the piano, especially in the area of the trio sonata, for much of that literature is effective when performed on the piano. 3. In selecting composers an attempt was made to cover all standard composers thoroughly and to introduce contemporary composers of merit, especially those of the United States. 4. The guide includes only works that involve the piano on an equal basis. Even among trio sonatas, only those with well-developed keyboard realizations in good taste were chosen. 5. Transcriptions of music originally written for other instruments, as a rule, have been excluded, unless the arrangement has been made by the composer, or, in the view of the author, is highly effective. 6. Information on works listed but not described has been obtained from publishers' catalogs.

Special effort has been made to examine as many contemporary works as possible, both published and unpublished. Recent avant-garde pieces are difficult to judge since most of them have not met the test of time, although many avant-garde techniques of the 1950s and 1960s are becoming more refined and accepted into the compositional style of the 1970s. A number of contemporary composers use the piano strictly as a sonorous sound source in a chamber group, rather than identify the instrument with its past history. In any event, the piano is still being included in ensembles by almost all of our prominent and many of our less well-known composers.

A certain amount of subjectivity is unavoidable in a book of this nature, but I have attempted to be as fair and objective as possible. Composers who wish to submit compositions for possible inclusion in future editions are encouraged to do so.

Because of constant change in the publishing world it is impossible to list only music currently in print. Some works known to be out of print were listed because of their merit, and many of them can be located at secondhand music stores, in the larger university or municipal libraries, or, more especially, in the Library of Congress.

Acknowledgments. Many people in many places have generously given me their help. I gratefully acknowledge the assistance of Martha Powell, Music Librarian of the Southern Baptist Theological Seminary; Rodney Mill of the Library of Congress; David Fenske, Librarian of the Indiana University School of Music; Marion Korda, Music Librarian of the University of Louisville; Fernando Laires of the piano faculty of Peabody Conservatory of Music; Lee Luvisi, Professor of Piano at the University of Louisville; David Appleby, Professor of Music at Eastern Illinois University; my graduate assistant, Robert C. Smith; and the Southern Baptist Theological Seminary for making possible the typing of the manuscript and the aid of graduate assistants through the years. The American Composers Alliance Library and the Canadian Music Centre have been most helpful, as have the many composers who have graciously supplied me with scores and tapes.

Without the generous assistance of numerous publishers this volume would not be possible. Special appreciation goes to John Bice of Boosey and Hawkes, Inc.; Norman Auerbach of Theodore Presser Co.; Don Malin of Edward B. Marks Music Corp. and Belwin-Mills Publishing Corp.; Gertrud Mathys of C. F. Peters Corp.; Susan Brailove of Oxford University Press; Ronald Freed of Peer International Corp.; Ernst Herttrich of G. Henle Verlag; Barry O'Neal of G. Schirmer, Inc.; John Wiser of Joseph Boonin, Inc.; Robert Mabley of Galaxy Music Corp.; W. Ray Stephens of Frederick Harris Music Co., Ltd.; Mike Warren of Alphonse Leduc; Judy Carnoske and Almarie Dieckow of Magnamusic-Baton, Inc.;

Angelina Marx of McGinnis & Marx; Henson Markham and Michael Barnard of Editions Salabert; Arthur Ephross of Southern Music Co.; Howard Waterman of Western International Music, Inc.; Franz König of Tonos Verlag; B. J. Harrod of Alexander Broude, Inc.; Henri Elkan; and John Woodmason of Novello & Co., Ltd.

I also wish to express appreciation to my children, Jane and Susan, for living with the inconvenience necessarily caused by the preparation of this book.

As this volume has drawn to a close, I have been reminded of Dr. Samuel Johnson's request in the Preface to his great Dictionary: "In this work, when it shall be found that much has been omitted, let it not be forgotten that much likewise is performed."

Louisville, Kentucky   MAURICE HINSON
February 1977

Using the Guide

Arrangement of Entries. Instrumentation is indicated by categories, for example, "Music for Two Instruments: Duos for Piano and Double Bass." Within each category the composers are listed alphabetically. Under each composer's name, individual compositions are given by opus number, title, or musical form, or by a combination of the three.

In the scores of Baroque composers, *basso continuo* refers to the bass part that is to be performed by the keyboard, together with a viola da gamba or a cello. Sometimes only a figured bass is given, but frequently an editor has realized the part by writing in the required chords, passing tones, etc. *Continuo* literally means "continuing throughout the piece." The trio sonata, the most important type of Baroque chamber music, is written in 3 parts but is usually performed on 4 instruments—2 violins (or other treble instruments), a cello (viola da gamba) for the bass part, and a keyboard instrument for the bass part together with the realization of the keyboard accompaniment. Trio sonatas are listed in the Guide under "Music for Three Instruments."

Descriptions. Descriptions have been limited to general style characteristics, form, particular and unusual qualities, interpretative suggestions, and pianistic problems inherent in the music. Editorial procedures found in a particular edition are mentioned. The term "large span" is used when a span larger than an octave is required in a piece, and that occurs in many 20th-century chamber works. "Octotonic" refers to lines moving in the same direction one or more octaves apart. "Shifting meters" indicates that varied time signatures are used within the space mentioned (a few bars, a movement, the entire work). "Proportional rhythmic relationships," for instance, $\ulcorner 5"4\urcorner$, indicate 5 notes are to be played in the time space for 4. "3 with 2" means 3 notes in one voice are played with (against) 2 notes in another voice. "Chance music" (aleatory, aleatoric) is described or mentioned, not analyzed, since it has no definitely ordered sequence of events. "Synthetic scale(s)" are made up by the composer whose work is being discussed; the range may be less than one octave. "Stochastic techniques" refer to "a probabilistic compositional method, introduced by Iannis Xenakis, in which the overall contours of sound are specified but the inner details are left to random or chance selection" (DCM, p. 708). The term "multiphonics" concerns the wind-instrument technique in which one instrument plays 2 or even 3 pitches simultaneously. Reference to a work as "over-edited" means that an editor has imposed stylistic considerations from a time period other than that from which the piece comes.

Grading. An effort has been made to grade the piano part in representative works of each composer. Four broad categories of grading are used: Intermediate (Int.), for the above-average high school pianist; Moderately Difficult (M-D), for the above-average college pianist; Difficult (D), for advanced performers only. These categories must not be taken too strictly but are only listed for general indications of technical and interpretative difficulties.

Details of Entries. When known, the date of composition is given after the title of the work. Then, in parentheses, as many of the following are given as apply to the particular work: the editor, publisher, publisher's number, and copyright date. In principle, when more than one edition is available, editions are listed in order of preference, the most desirable first, though in some instances the authors may not have had access to each edition for a thorough evaluation. The number of pages and parts and the performance time are frequently listed. Spellings of composers' names and titles of the compositions appear as they do in the music being described. Details of the percussion parts are given only if the percussion ensemble is extensive. Specifically related books, dissertations or theses, and periodical articles are listed following individual compositions or at the conclusion of the discussion of a composer's work (a more extended bibliography appears at the end of the book).

Sample Entries and Explanation.

Music for Two Instruments: Duos for Piano and Cello

Johann Christoph Friedrich Bach. *Sonata* A 1770 (A. Wenzinger—Br 3970 1961) 15pp., parts. Larghetto; Allegro; Tempo di Minuetto.

A indicates the key of A major; 1770 is the date of composition; Wenzinger is the editor; Bärenreiter is the publisher; 3970 is the edition number; 1961 is the copyright date. The work is 15 pages long and has separate parts available. Larghetto, Allegro, and Tempi di Minuetto are the titles of the 3 movements.

Music for Six Instruments: Sextets for Piano(s) and Miscellaneous Instruments

Morton Feldman. *The Viola in My Life* (I) 1970 (UE 15395) 10pp., parts. 9½ min. For flute, violin, viola (solo), cello, piano, and percussion. M-D.

(I) means that this work is the first of a series of pieces by Feldman with the same title; 1970 is the date of composition; Universal Edition is the publisher; 15395 is the edition number. The work is 10 pages long and contains separate parts; the piece lasts 9½ minutes. The complete instrumentation is for flute, violin, viola (used in a solo capacity), cello, piano, and percussion; M-D means moderately difficult.

Other Assistance. See "Abbreviations" below for terms, publishers, books, and periodicals referred to in the text, and the directories, "Agents or Parent Companies of Music Publishers in the United States" and "Addresses of Music Publishers," to locate publishers. Two special indexes—"Works for Two or More Pianos and Other Instruments" and "Works by Female Composers"—direct the user to entries in the text for music in these categories, and the comprehensive index of composers represented in this volume gives birth and death dates, when known.

Abbreviations

AA	Authors Agency of the Polish Music Publishers	CCSCM	*Cobbett's Cyclopedic Survey of Chamber Music*
ABRSM	Associated Board of the Royal Schools of Music	CDMC	Centre de Documentation de la Musique Contemporaine
ACA	American Composers Alliance	CeBeDeM	CeBeDeM Foundation
ACA-CFE	American Composers Alliance—Composers Facsimile Edition	CF	Carl Fischer
		CFE	Composers Facsimile Edition
AL	Abr. Lundquist AB Stockholm	CFP	C. F. Peters
AM	*Acta Musicologia*	CLE	Composers Library Editions
AMC	American Music Center	CMC	Canadian Music Centre
AME	American Music Editions	CMP	Consolidated Music Publishers
AMP	Associated Music Publishers		
AMS	American Musicological Society	CPE	Composer/Performer Edition
AMT	*American Music Teacher*	D	Difficult
arr.	arranged, arranged by	DC	da capo
ASUC	American Society of University Composers	DCM	*Dictionary of Contemporary Music,* ed. John Vinton (New York: E. P. Dutton, 1974)
B&VP	Broekmans & Van Poppel		
BB	Broude Brothers	DDT	Denkmäler deutscher Tonkunst
BMC	Boston Music Co.		
BMI	Broadcast Music, Inc.	Der	Derry Music Co.
Bo&Bo	Bote & Bock	DM	Diletto Musicale (Dob)
Bo&H	Boosey & Hawkes	Dob	Doblinger
Br	Bärenreiter	DSS	Drustva Slovenskih Skladateljev
Br&H	Breitkopf & Härtel		
BS	Boccaccini and Spada	DTB	Denkmäler der Tonkunst in Bayern
ca.	circa	DTOe	Denkmäler der Tonkunst in Oesterreich
CAP	Composers' Autograph Publications	DVFM	Deutscher Verlag für Musik

EAM	Editorial Argentina de Música	IEM	Instituto de Extensión Musicale Calle Com-pañia
EAMC	European American Music Corporation	IMC	International Music Co.
EB	Editions J. Buyst	IMI	Israel Music Institute
EBM	Edward B. Marks	Int.	intermediate difficulty
EC	Edizioni Curci	IU	Indiana University School of Music Library
ECIC	Editorial Cooperativa Inter-americana de Composi-tores	JAMS	*Journal of the American Musicological Society*
ECo	Edition Cotta'sche	JF	J. Fischer
ECS	E. C. Schirmer	JITA	*Journal of the International Trombone Association*
EFM	Editions Françaises de Musique/Technisonor		
EGZ	Editore Gugliemo Zanibon	JWC	J. W. Chester
EHM	Edwin H. Morris		
Elem.	Elementary	K	Kalmus
ELK	Elkan & Schildknecht	K&S	Kistner and Siegel
EM	Edition Musicus	Ku	Kultura
EMA	European Music Archive		
EMB	Editio Musica Budapest	L	Longo, Alessandro
EMH	Editions Musikk-Huset	LAMC	Latin American Music Center, Indiana Univer-sity
EMM	Ediciones Mexicanas de Música		
EMR	Editions Marc Reift	LC	Library of Congress
EMT	Editions Musicales Transat-lantiques	LMP	Ludwig Music Publishers
		L'OL	L'Oiseau-Lyre
EPS	Eulenburg Pocket Scores		
ESC	Max Eschig	M&M	*Music and Musicians*
EV	Elkan-Vogel	MAB	Musica Antiqua Bohemica (Artia)
fl.	flourished	MCA	MCA Music (Music Corpo-ration of America)
FSV	Feedback Studio Verlag		
		M-D	Moderately Difficult
		Mer	Mercury Music Corp.
Gen	General Music Publishing Co.	MJ	*Music Journal*
GM	Gehrmans Musikförlag	MJQ	MJQ Music
GS	G. Schirmer	MK	Musikaliska Konstföreningen
GWM	General Words and Music Co.	ML	*Music and Letters*
GZ	Gugliemo Zanibon	m., mm.	measure, measures
		MM	*Modern Music*
HAM	*Historical Anthology of Music*	MMB	MMB Music Inc.
Hin	Hinrichsen	MMP	Masters Music Publications
HM	Hortus Musicus (Bären-reiter)	MMR	*Monthly Musical Record*
		MO	*Musical Opinion*
HV	Heinrichshofens Verlag	MQ	*Musical Quarterly*
HWG	H. W. Gray	MR	*Music Review*

M-S	*Music-Survey*		(Chapel Hill: University of North Carolina Press, 1963; 2nd ed., New York: W. W. Norton, 1972)
MS, MSS	manuscript(s)		
MT	*Musical Times*		
MVH	Musica Viva Historica (Artia)		
mvt.	movement	SCL	Southeastern Composers' League
Nag	Nagel's Musik-Archive	SDM	Servico de Documentacao Musical da Ordem dos Músicos do Brazil
NGD	*New Grove Dictionary of Music and Musicians, Second Edition*		
		SHV	Státní hudební vydavatelství
NME	New Music Edition	SM	Skandinavisk Musikförlag
NMO	Norsk Musikförlag	SP	Shawnee Press
NMS	Nordiska Musikförlaget	SPAM	Society for the Publication of American Music
Nov	Novello		
NV	Noetzel Verlag	SSB	*The Sonata since Beethoven*, by W. S. Newman (Chapel Hill: University of North Carolina Press, 1969; 2nd ed., New York: W. W. Norton, 1972)
OBV	Oesterreichischer Bundes- verlag		
OD	Oliver Ditson		
OUP	Oxford University Press		
		ST	Southern Music, San Antonio, Texas
PAU	Pan American Union		
PIC	Peer International Corporation	St&B	Stainer & Bell
		SUTE	Severinus Urtext Telemann Edition
PMP	Polish Music Publications		
PNM	*Perspectives of New Music*	SZ	Suvini Zerboni
PQ	*Piano Quarterly*		
PWM	Polskie Wydawnictwo Muzyczne	TP	Theodore Presser Co.
		trans.	transcribed, transcription
		TWV	*Telemann Werke Verzeichnis*
R&E	Ries & Erler		
Ric	Ricordi	UE	Universal Edition
Ric Amer	Ricordi Americana S.A.	UL	University of Louisville, Dwight Anderson Music Library
SA	Sonata-Allegro		
Sal	Salabert	UME	Unión Musical Española
SB	Summy-Birchard	UMKR	Unbekannte Meister der Klassik und Romantik (Boonin)
SBE	*The Sonata in the Baroque Era*, by W. S. Newman (Chapel Hill: University of North Carolina Press, 1959; rev. ed. 1966; 3rd ed., New York: W. W. Norton, 1972)		
		UMP	United Music Publishers
		USSR	Mezhdunarodnaya Kniga (Music Publishers of the USSR)
SCE	*The Sonata in the Classic Era*, by W. S. Newman	VKDR	*Violin and Keyboard: The Duo Repertoire*, by

| | Abram Loft, 2 vols.
(New York: Grossman
Publishers, 1973) | WH
WIM | Wilhelm Hansen
Western International Music |
| VU | Vienna Urtext Edition | ZV | Zenemükiadó Vállalat |

Agents or Parent Companies of Music Publishers in the United States

Bracketed numbers (e.g., **[1]**) are referenced in the following listing, "Addresses of Music Publishers." Every attempt has been made to verify the accuracy of this listing; however, the reader should be aware that some information may have changed since publication.

[1] Boosey & Hawkes, Inc.
35 East 21st Street
New York, N.Y. 10010-6212
Tel: (212) 358-5300
Fax: (212) 358-5301
www.boosey.com

[2] Brodt Music Company
P.O. Box 9345
Charlotte, N.C. 28299
Tel: (800) 438-4129; (704) 332-2177
Fax: (800) 446-0812; (704) 335-7215
www.brodtmusic.com

[3] Broude Brothers, Ltd.
141 White Oaks Road
Williamstown, Mass. 01267
Tel: (413) 458-8131
Fax: (413) 458-5242

[4] Concordia Publishing House
3558 South Jefferson Avenue
St. Louis, Mo. 63118-3968
Tel: (800) 325-3040; (314) 268-1055
Fax: (314) 268-1411
www.cph.org

[5] ECS Publishing (parent company to E. C. Schirmer Music)

138 Ipswich Street
Boston, Mass. 02215
Tel: (800) 777-1919; (617) 236-1935
www.ecspublishing.com

[6] Elkin Music International
128 N. Ocean Blvd.
Pompano Beach, Fla. 33062
Tel: (800) 367-3554; (954) 781-8082
Fax: (954) 781-8083
www.elkinmusic.com

[7] Carl Fischer, Inc.
65 Bleecker Street
New York, N.Y. 10012
Tel: (800) 762-2328; (212) 777-0900
Fax: (212) 477-6996
www.carlfischer.com

[8] Hal Leonard Publishing Corporation
P.O. Box 13819
Milwaukee, Wis. 53213
Tel: (414) 774-3630
Fax: (414) 774-3259
www.halleonard.com

[9] Oxford University Press
Order Department

2001 Evans Road
Cary, N.C. 27513
Tel: (800) 345-6296
Fax: (919) 677-1303
www.oup-usa.org

[10] C. F. Peters Corporation
70-30 80th Street
Glendale, N.Y. 11385
Tel: (718) 416-7800
Fax: (718) 416-7805
www.edition-peters.com

[11] Theodore Presser Company
588 N. Gulph Road
King of Prussia, Pa. 19406
Tel: (610) 592-1222
Fax: (610) 592-1229
www.presser.com

[12] Shawnee Press
P.O. Box 1250
Jay Park Plaza
9 Dartmouth Drive, Building 4
Marshall Creek, Pa. 18335
Tel: (800) 962-8584; (570) 476-0550
Fax: (800) 345-6842; (570) 476-5247
www.shawneepress.com

[13] Southern Music Company
P.O. Box 329
San Antonio, Tex. 78292
Tel: (800) 284-5443; (210) 226-8167
Fax: (210) 223-4537
www.southernmusic.com

[14] Location or American agent
unknown, despite our efforts to find
them; many of these publishers are
no longer in business.

Addresses of Music Publishers

A bracketed number (e.g., [1]) following the name of a publisher corresponds to that of its agent or parent company in the United States (see preceding listing, "Agents or Parent Companies of Music Publishers in the United States"). **Boldface** print is used to help the reader find items in the alphabetical sequence. Every attempt has been made to verify the accuracy of this listing; however, the reader should be aware that some information may have changed since publication. Unless otherwise noted, addresses are within the United States.

Accolade Musikverlag
Austraße 7
83607 Holzkirchen, Germany
Tel: (49) 08024-92143
Fax: (49) 08024-92146
www.accolade.de

Accura Music
P.O. Box 257
North Greece, N.Y. 14515-0257
Tel: (585) 227-1550
Fax: (585) 227-2829
www.accuramusic.com

Ahn & Simrock
Munich, Germany

Aibl [14]

Air-ev Productions
675 VFW Parkway
Suite 352
Chestnut Hill, Mass. 02167
www.air-ev.com

Akkord Music Publishers
Barackos út 28/a
1224 Budapest, Hungary
Tel: (36-1) 227-3447
Fax: (36-1) 226-7017
www.akkordmusic.hu

Alafia Publishing
P.O. Box 1441
Valrico, Fla. 33595-1441
www.alafia.com

Alfred Publishing Company, Inc.
P.O. Box 10003
Van Nuys, Calif. 91410-0003
Tel: (818) 891-5999
Fax: (818) 891-2369
www.alfred.com

Allegro Music
82 Suffolk Street
Queensway
Birmingham B1 1TA
United Kingdom

Tel: (44) 0121-643-7553
Fax: (44) 0121-633-4773
www.allegro-music.com

Alpeg Editions [**10**]

Editorial **Alpuerto**
Madrid, Spain

ALRY Publications
P.O. Box 36542
Charlotte, N.C. 28236
Tel: (704) 334-3413
Fax: (704) 334-1143
www.alrypublications.com

Alsbach [14]
Amsterdam, the Netherlands

Amadeus Verlag
Birkenweg 6
74579 Fichtenau, Germany
www.amadeus-verlag.com

Casa **Amarilla**
Santiago, Chile

American Composers Alliance–
Composers Facsimile Edition
170 West 74th Street
New York, N.Y. 10023
Tel: (212) 362-8900
Fax: (212) 362-8902
www.composers.com

American Institute of Musicology
c/o Tempo Music Publications
3773 West 95th Street
Leawood, Kans. 66206
www.tempomusic.com

American Music Center
30 West 26th Street, Suite 1001
New York, N.Y. 10010-2011
Tel: (212) 366-5260
www.amc.net

American Music Editions
263 East 7th Street
New York, N.Y. 10009-6049
Fax: (212) 420-9393

American Society of University Composers [**14**]

Gli **Amici** della Musica da Camera
Via Bocca di Leone 25
Rome, Italy

Amphion Editions Musicales [**8**]

Amsco Music Publishing Co. [**14**]

Johann **Andre**
Frankfurterstrasse 28
Offenback am Main, Germany

Anglo-French Music Co. [**14**]

Anglo-Soviet Press [**14**]

APR Publishers [**14**]

A-R Editions, Inc.
801 Deming Way
Madison, Wis. 53717
Tel: (800) 736-0070; (608) 836-9000
Fax: (608) 831-8200
www.areditions.com

Arcadia Music Publishing Co.
London, England

Groupe **Archambault**
500 Est, Rue Ste.-Catherine
Montreal, Quebec, H2L 2C6 Canada
Tel: (514) 849-6201
Fax: (514) 849-1481

Collection **Arion** [**14**]

Armelin Musica
Via dei Soncin, 42
35122 Padua, Italy
www.armelin.it

Armitage Press
9391 Kayenta Drive
Tucson, Ariz. 85749

Arno Press [14]

Arno Volk Verlag (*see* Universal
Music Publishing Group)

Arrow Music Press [1]

Editions **Ars Femina**
P.O. Box 7692
Louisville, Ky. 40257-0692

Ars Nova [14]

Ars Polona (*see* Polskie Wydawnictwo Muzyczne)

Ars Viva Verlag [14]

Arsis Press
1719 Bay Street, SE
Washington, D.C. 20003
Tel: (202) 544-4817

Artaria Editions [11]

Artia [1]

Ascherberg, Hopwood & Crew, Ltd.
Music Publishers
c/o Chappel International Music Publishing Group Ltd.
50 New Bond Street
London W1A 2BR, United Kingdom

Edwin **Ashdown,** Ltd. [1, 2]

**Associated Board of the Royal
School of Music** (England) [11]

Associated Music Publishers, Inc. [8]
Music Sales Group of Companies
257 Park Avenue South, 20th Floor
New York, N.Y. 10010
Tel: (212) 254-2100

Fax: (212) 254-2013
www.schirmer.com

Augener [5]

**Authors Agency of the Polish Music
Publishers**
ul. Hipteczna 2
00-950 Warsaw, Poland

Autograph Editions (*see* Philharmusica Company)

Bärenreiter Verlag [11] [works by
Schoenberg distributed in U.S. by
Belmont]

C. L. **Barnhouse** Co.

M. **Baron** Co. [14]

Barry & Cia (Argentina) [1]

Basheva Music [14]

M. P. **Belaieff** [10]

Belmont Music Publishers
P.O. Box 231
Pacific Palisades, Calif. 90272
Tel: (310) 454-1867
Fax: (310) 573-1925
www.geocities.com/belmontmusic90272

Belwin-Mills (*see* Alfred Publishing
Company)

Berandol Music Ltd. (Canada) [8]
(*see* Associated Music Publishers, Inc.)

Berben [11]

Edition **Bernoulli**
Basel, Switzerland

Biedermann [14]

Gérald **Billaudot [11]**

Editions **BIM**
P.O. Box 300

1674 Vuarmarens, Switzerland
Tel: (41) 21-909-1000
Fax: (41) 21-909-1009
www.editions-bim.com

Richard **Birnbach**
Lichterfelde, Germany

Les Editions **Bleu Blanc Rouge** (*see*
also Hansen House)
14-16, Rue de Faubourg Saint-Honoré
Paris, France

Boccaccini and Spada Editori [**11**]
Via Arezzo, 17
00040 Pavona di Albano Laziale
Rome, Italy
Tel: (39) 6-9310217
Fax: (39) 6-9311903
www.boccaccinispada.com

Boelke-Bomart Music Publications
(*see* Jerona Music Corp.)

Bongiovanni Frescesco Edizioni
Musicali
Via Ugo Bassi, 31/F
40121 Bologna, Italy
Tel: (39) 51-22-57-22
Fax: (39) 51-22-61-28

Bosse Edition
Postfach 417
Regensburg, Germany

Boston Music Co.
172 Tremont Street
Boston, Mass. 02111-1001
Tel: (800) 863-5150; (617) 528-6155
Fax: (617) 528-6199

Bosworth & Co. [**2, 12**]

Bote & Bock [8] (*see* Associated
Music Publishers, Inc.)

Bourne Company
5 West 37th Street, 6th Floor

New York, N.Y. 10018
Tel: (212) 391-4300
Fax: (212) 391-4306
www.internationalmusico.com

Bowdoin College Music Press
Bowdoin College
Brunswick, Maine 04011

Brass Music Ltd.
148 Eighth Avenue North
Nashville, Tenn. 37203

Bratti [**14**]
Florence, Italy

Fondazione Eugenio **Bravi**
Milan, Italy

Breitkopf & Härtel
Walkmühlstrasse 52
65195 Wiesbaden, Germany
Tel: (49) 6128 9663 20; 6128 9663 21
Fax: (49) 6128 9663 50

British and Continental Music Agencies Ltd.
64 Dean Street
London W1V 6AU, United Kingdom

Broadcast Music, Inc.
320 West 57th Street, 3rd Floor
New York, N.Y. 10019
Tel: (212) 586-2000

Broadcast Music Canada [**14**]

Broekmans & Van Poppel
van Baerlestraat 92-94
1071 BB Amsterdam, the Netherlands
Tel: (31) 20 679 65 75; 20 659 72 70
Fax: (31) 20 664 6759; 20 449 10 01

Aldo **Bruzzichelli,** Editore,
Italy [**14**]

Busch [**14**]
Lidingo, Sweden

Editions J. **Buyst**
76, Avenue du Midi
Brussels, Belgium

Calouste Gulbenkian Foundation
Av. de Berna, 45-A
1067-001 Lisbon, Portugal
Tel: (351) 21-782-3000
Fax: (351) 21-782-3041
www.musica.gulbenkian.pt

Carlanita Music **[8]** (*see* G. **Schirmer**)

Cameo Music
1527½ North Vine Street
Los Angeles, Calif. 90028

Canadian Music Centre
20 St. Joseph Street
Toronto, Ontario M4Y 1J9, Canada
Tel: (416) 961-6601
Fax: (416) 961-7198
www.musiccentre.ca

Carisch [1]

Leonard **Carroll**
204 West 55th Street
New York, N.Y. 10021

Carus Verlag
Sielminger Str. 51
70771 Lf.-Echterdingen, Germany
Tel: (49) 711-797-330-0
Fax: (49) 711-797-330-29
www.carus-verlag.com

Casa Amarilla
San Diego 128
Santiago, Chile

CeBeDeM (Centre Belge de Documentation Musicale)
Havenlaan 86C
Av. du Port 86C
1000 Brussels, Belgium
Tel: (32) 2-230-9430

Fax: (32) 2-230-9437
www.cebedem.be

Edições **Cembra**
São Paulo, Brazil

C.G.F. [14]

Chant du Monde (*see* Universal Music Publishing Group)

Chappell & Co. **[8]**

J. W. **Chester** Music **[8, 12]** (*see* also G. **Schirmer**)
8-9 Frith Street
London W1D 3JB, United Kingdom
Tel: (44) 20-7434-0066
Fax: (44) 20-7287-6329
www.chesternovello.com

Chopin Institute Edition (*see* Polskie Wydawnictwo Muzyczne)

Choudens [10, 11]

I Classici Musicali Italiani
Milan, Italy

M. M. **Cole** Co.
251 East Grand Avenue
Chicago, Ill. 60611

Collection Arion [14]

Collection Litolff [10]

Franco **Colombo** (*see* Alfred Publishing Company)

Columbia University Press
61 West 62nd Street
New York, N.Y. 10023
(212) 459-0600
www.columbia.edu/cu/cup

Editions **Combre [11]**

Composer/Performer Edition
330 University Avenue
Davis, Calif. 95616

Composers Facsimile Edition (*see* American Composers Alliance)

Composers Library Edition [11]

Composers Press (*see* Seesaw Music Corp.)

Edition **Compusic** [6]

Conners Publications
503 Tahoe Street
Natchitoches, La. 71457-5718
Tel: (318) 357-0924
www.coomansoftware.com/conners

The **Consort** Press [14]

Continuo Music Press, Inc. (*see* Plymouth Music Co., Inc.)

Consortium Musicale [11]

Costallat [11]

G. **Cotta'sche**
Stuttgart and Berlin, Germany

J. B. **Cramer** [1]

Cranz [14]

Edizioni **Curci**
4 Galleria del Corso
Milan, Italy

J. **Curwen** & Son [8]

Da Capo Press
10 East 53rd Street, 19th Floor
New York, N.Y. 10022
Tel: (800) 242-7737
Fax: (800) 822-4090
www.plenum.com
distributed by
Harper Collins Publishers
Order Department
1000 Keystone Park
Scranton, Pa. 18512

Dansk (*see* Dan **Fog** Musikförlag)

Dantalian, Inc.
11 Pembroke Street
Newton, Mass. 02458-2122
Tel/Fax: (617) 244-7230
www.dantalian.com

Deiss (*see* Editions **Salabert**)

Delevan
New York, N.Y.

Delkas (*see* Universal Music Publishing Group)

Georges **Delrieu** [6]

Dessain
Mallines, Belgium

Deutscher Verlag für Musik [14]

Oliver **Ditson** [11]

Editions **Doberman**-Yppan
C.P. 2021
Saint-Nicolas, Quebec QC G7A 4X5
Canada
Tel: (418) 831-1304
Fax: (418) 836-3645
www.dobermaneditions.com

Ludwig **Doblinger**
Vienna, Austria

Musikverlag Christoph **Dohr**
Kasselberger Weg 120
50769 Cologne, Germany
Tel: (49) 221-70-70-02
Fax: (49) 221-70-43-95
www.dohr.de

Donemus
Funenpark 1
1018 AK Amsterdam, the Netherlands
Tel: (31) 20-305-89-00
Fax: (31) 20-673-35-88
www.donemus.nl

Dorn Publications
P.O. Box 206
Medfield, Mass. 02052
Tel: (508) 359-1015
Fax: (508) 359-7988
www.dornpub.com

Dover Publications, Inc.
31 East Second Street
Mineola, N.Y. 11501-3582
Tel: (800) 223-3130; (516) 294-7000
Fax: (516) 742-6953

Dow [14]

A. **Drago**
Padua, Italy

Drei Masken Verlag
Mozartstrasse 18
80336 Munich, Germany
Tel: (49) 89-54456-909
Fax: (49) 89-53-81-99-52
www.dreimaskenverlag.de

Društvo Slovenskih Skladateljev
Trg francoske revolucije 6/1
1000 Ljubljana, Slovenia
Tel: (386) 1-241-5660
Fax: (386) 1-241-5666
www.drustvo-dss.si

Duma Music
557 Barron Avenue
Woodbridge, N.J. 07095
Tel/Fax: (732) 636-5406
www.dumamusic.com

Editions **Durand** & Cie. [8]
Paris, France
www.salabert.fr

Eastman School of Music Publications [7]

Ediciones Culturales Argentinas
Ayacucho 1578 Piso 2

1112 Buenos Aires, Argentina
Tel: 4803-6545 (local)

Editio Musica Budapest [11]
www.emb.hu

Edition d'Etat
Sofia, Bulgaria

Edition Modern [14]
Munich, Germany

Edition Musicus

Edition Russe de Musique [1]

Editions Alphonse **Leduc** (*see* **Leduc**)

Editions de la Sirène Musicale (*see* Editions Max **Eschig**)

Editions d'Etat pour la Litterature et l'Art **[14]**
Bucharest, Romania

Editions Française de Musique [11]

Editions International Music Diffusion (I.M.D.)
24, Rue Etex
75018 Paris, France
Tel: (33) 1-42-29-21-31

Editions Metropolis [14]
Antwerp, Belgium

Editions Musicales du Marais [14]

Editions Musicales Transatlantiques [11]
Paris, France

Editions **Salabert** (*see* **Salabert**)

Editions 75
75, Rue de la Roquette
75011 Paris, France
Tel: (33) 1.43.48.90.57
Fax: (33) 1.43.48.85.74
www.tom.johnson.org

Editorial Alpuerto
Madrid, Spain

Editorial Argentina de Música [11]

Editorial Cooperativa Interamericana de Compositores [14]
Montevideo, Uruguay

Editorial de Música Española Contemporánea
Alcalá, 70
28009 Madrid, Spain
Tel: (34) (91) 5770752
Fax: (34) (91) 5757645

Editorial Politonia
Buenos Aires, Argentina

Editorial Tritono
Lima, Peru

Editura de Stat Pentru Literatiră si Artă
Bucharest, Romania

Editura Muzicală Uniunii Compozitorilor din R.P.R.
Bucharest, Romania

Edizioni Musicali Mercurio
Rome, Italy

Elkan & Schildknecht
Kungsholmsgatan 15
11227 Stockholm, Sweden
Tel: (46) 8-6515421

Elkan-Vogel [11]

Elkin & Co., Ltd. **[6]**

E. H. **Elsberg [14]**

Emerson Edition (June Emerson) **[11]**
Windmill Farm
Ampleforth
North Yorkshire

England YO6 4HF
United Kingdom
Tel: (44) 1439-788324
Fax: (44) 1439-788715
www.juneemerson.co.uk

Muzeul George **Enescu**
Bucharest, Romania

Engstroem & Soedring (Denmark) **[10]**

Enoch & Cie. **[11]**
Paris, France

Ensemble Publications
P.O. Box 32
Ithaca, N.Y. 14851-0032
Tel/Fax: (607) 273-4655

Eres Edition
P.O. Box 1220
28859 Lilienthal/Bremen, Germany
Tel: (49) 04298-1676
Fax: (49) 04298-5312
www.eres-musik.com

Eriks Musikhandel
Stockholm, Sweden

Editions Max **Eschig [8]**
Paris, France
www.salabert.fr

Ethos Publications
P.O. Box 2043
Oswego, N.Y. 13126

Eulenburg Pocket Scores **[14]**

European Music Archive
52 Talfourd Road
London SE15 5NY
United Kingdom

Faber & Faber, Ltd. **[14]**

Faber Music **[8]**
3 Queen Square

London WC1N 3AU, United
Kingdom
Tel: (44) 20-7833-7900
Fax: (44) 20-7833-7939
www.fabermusic.co.uk

Facultad de Bellas Artes de la Universidad de Chile
Santiago, Chile

Fairfield, Ltd. (*see* Novello & Co., Ltd.)

Manuel de **Falla** Ediciones
Bretón de los Herreros 55
28003 Madrid, Spain
Tel: (34) 91-441-77-43
Fax: (34) 91-399-45-08
www.manueldefallaediciones.es

Fallen Leaf Press [14]

Fazer (*see* MMB Music)
Helsinki, Finland

Feedback Studio Verlag
Cologne, Germany

Fema Music Publications
Naperville, Ill.

Fentone Music
Fleming Road
Corby
Northants NN17 4SN
United Kingdom
Tel: (44) 1536.260981
Fax: (44) 1536.401075
www.fentone.com

Finnish Information Centre
Lauttasaarentie 1
00200 Helsinki, Finland
Tel: (358) 9-6810-1313
Fax: (358) 9-682-0770
www.fimic.fi

J. **Fischer** & Bro. [8] (*see* Associated Music Publishers, Inc.)

FJH Music Company
2525 Davie Road, Suite 360
Fort Lauderdale, Fla. 33317-7424
Tel: (800) 262-8744; (954) 382-6061
Fax: (954) 382-3073
www.fjhmusic.com

La **Flûte de Pan**
49, Rue de Rome
Paris, France
www.flutedepan.com

Foetisch Frères (Switzerland) [5]

Dan **Fog** Musikförlag
Graabrødretorv 1
1154 Copenhagen K, Denmark

Charles **Foley** Co. [7]

Fondazione Carminignani Rossini [14]
Pesaro, Italy

Fondazione Eugenio Bravi [14]
Milan, Italy

Forberg [10]

Föreningen Svenska Tonsättare
Stockholm, Sweden

A. **Forlivesi** & Cia
Via Roma, 4
50123 Florence, Italy
Tel: (39) (55) 78 44 76
Fax: (39) (55) 70 11 86

Arnaldo **Forni,** Editore
Via Gramsci 164, 40010 Sala
Bologna, Italy
Tel: (39) (51) 95 41 42; 95 41 98
Fax: (39) (51) 95 46 72

Forsyth Brothers, Ltd.
126-128 Deansgate

Manchester M3 2GR, United
Kingdom
Tel: (44) (161) 834-3281
Fax: (44) (161) 834-0630

Fortissimo Verlag
Vienna, Austria

Mark **Foster** Music Company
P.O. Box 4012
Champaign, Ill. 61824-4012
Tel: (800) 359-1386; (217) 398-2790
Fax: (217) 398-2791

Francis, Day & Hunter, Ltd. (England) **[14]**

H. **Freeman** & Co. **[14]**

Fundação Calouste Gulbenkian (*see*
Calouste Gulbenkian Foundation)

Furore Verlag
Naumburger Str. 40
34127 Kassel, Germany
Tel: (49) 561-89-73-52
Fax: (49) 561-8-34-72
www.furore-verlag.de

Adolph **Fürstner** **[14]**

Galaxy Music Corp. **[5]**

Galliard, Ltd. (England) **[14]**

Gamble Hinged Music Company **[14]**

Gaudioso
Buenos Aires, Argentina

Carl **Gehrmans** Musikförlag **[1]**
Stockholm, Sweden

General Music Publishing Company
(*see* Boston Music Co.)

General Words and Music Company
distributed by Neil Kjos Music Company

4380 Jutland Drive
San Diego, Calif. 92117-0894
Tel: (619) 270-9800
www.kjos.com

Gerard [14]

Musikverlag Hans **Gerig [14]**
Cologne, Germany

Gervan
Brussels, Belgium

Girolamo Musikverlag
Franz Müller-Busch e.k.
Poststr. 7
79098 Freiburg, Germany
Tel: (49) 7-61-285-28-98
Fax: (49) 7-61-285-28-99
www.girolamo.de

Gli Amici della Musica da Camera
Rome, Italy

Edition **Gravis**
Adolfstrasse 71
65307 Bad Schwalbach, Germany
Tel: (49) 6124-3719
Fax: (49) 6124-3472
www.editiongravis.de

H. W. **Gray** (*see* Alfred Publishing
Company)

Henri **Gregh**
129, Rue Montmartre
Paris, France

Gulbenkian Foundation
Parque de Sta. Gertrudes à Avda.
de Berna
Lisbon, Portugal

GunMar Music
167 Dudley Road
Newton Centre, Mass. 02159
Tel: (617) 332-6398
Fax: (617) 969-1079

Gutheil Edition [14]

Hamelle et Cie. [11]

Wilhelm **Hansen** [12, 13]
Copenhagen, Denmark

Hansen House
(Charles Hansen Publications)
1804 West Avenue
Miami Beach, Fla. 31139
Tel: (305) 672-8729
Fax: (305) 357-7768

Hänssler (*see* American Institute of Musicology)

The **Hardie** Press
17 Harrison Gardens
Edinburgh, United Kingdom
EH11 1SE
Tel/Fax: (44) 131-313-1388
www.hardiepress.co.uk

Hargail Music Press [14]

Harmonia Uitgave
Roeltjesweg 23-25
Hilversum, the Netherlands

T. B. **Harms** Company [14]

Frederick **Harris** Music Co., Ltd. (*see* FJH Music Company)

G. **Hartmann** [14]

Harvard University Press
79 Garden Street
Cambridge, Mass. 02138-1499
Tel: (800) 448-2242; (617) 495-2600
Fax: (800) 962-4983
www.hup.harvard.edu

Haslinger [14]

Heinrichshofens Verlag [10]

Helicon Music Corporation [14]

Helios Music Edition (*see* Plymouth Music Co., Inc.)

Hendon Music [1]

G. **Henle** USA, Inc.
P.O. Box 460127
St. Louis, Mo. 63146
Tel: (314) 514-1791
Fax: (314) 514-1269
www.henleusa.com

Henmar Press [10]

Editions **Henn**
P.O. Box 5476
1211 Geneva 11, Switzerland
Tel: (41) 22-311-51-85
Fax: (41) 22-311-18-52

Heugel & Cie. [11]
Paris, France

Editions **Heuwekenmeijer** [11]
Amsterdam, the Netherlands

Hidden Oaks Music Company
P.O. Box 47696
San Antonio, Tex. 78284
Tel/Fax: (210) 590-1689

Highgate Press [5]

Hildegard Publishing Co. [11]
www.hildegard.com

Hinrichsen Edition (England) [10]

Friedrich **Hofmeister** (Germany) [6]

Hovhaness-Fujihara Music Co.
P.O. Box 88381
Seattle, Wash. 98138-2381

Hudební Matice [14]
Prague, Czech Republic

Hug (Switzerland) [14]

Iceland Music Information Centre
Sidumuli 34
108 Reykjavik, Iceland
Tel: (354) 5683122
Fax: (354) 5683124
www.mic.is

Ichthys Verlag
Stuttgart, Germany

Imbault [14]

Indiana University Music
William and Gayle Cook Music
Library
Simon Music Library and Recital
Center
200 South Jordan Avenue
Bloomington, Ind. 47405
Tel: (812) 855-8541
Fax: (812) 855-3843
www.music.indiana.edu/muslib

Instituto di Alta Cultura
Conservatorio Statale di Musica
"Luisa D'Annunzio"
Via Leopoldo Muzii 5
65123 Pescara, Italy
Tel: (39) 85-421-9950
Fax: (39) 85-421-4341

Instituto Español de Musicología
(Renamed Departmento de Musi-
cología)
Consejo Superior de Investigaciones
Científicas (CSIC)
Serrano, 117
Madrid 28006, Spain
Tel: (34) 91-585-5000
Fax: (34) 91-411-3077
www.csic.es

Instituto de Extensión Musical
Calle Compañia 1274
Santiago, Chile
www.uchile.cl

Interlochen Press [14]

International Music Corporation (*see*
Bourne Company)

**International Musikgesellschaft für
Neue Musik** (International Society
for Contemporary Music)
Berlin, Germany

Internationale Stiftung Mozarteum
Schwarzstraße 26
5020 Salzburg, Austria
Tel: (43) 662-88940-30
Fax: (43) 662-88940-36
www.mozarteum.at

Ione Press, Inc. **[5]**

Íslensk Tónverkamidstöd (*see* Iceland Music Information Centre)

Israel Music Institute [11]

Israeli Music Publications [11]

Japan Federation of Composers
5th Sky Building, #310
3-3-8 Sendagaya Shibuya-Ku
Tokyo 151-0051, Japan
Tel: (81) 3-5474-1853
Fax: (81) 3-5474-1854
www.jfc-i.org/index_e.htm

**Japanese Society of Rights of
Authors & Composers**
3-6-12 Uehara
Shibuya Tokyo 151-8540, Japan
Tel: (81) 3-3481-2121
www.jasrac.or.jp/ejhp/index.htm

Jaymar Music Ltd.
P.O. Box 2191, Stn. B
London, Ontario N6A 4E3,
Canada
Tel: (519) 672-7369
Fax: (519) 672-0016

Jerona Music Corp.
P.O. Box 671
Englewood, N.J. 07631
Tel: (201) 568-8448
Fax: (201) 569-7023

JPM Music Publications
113 Glenfield Drive
Festus, MO 63028
Tel: (636) 933-2244
www.eppublications.com

Jean **Jobert** [11]

Joshua Corporation (*see* Boston
Music Co.)

Jost & Sander
Leipzig, Germany

P. **Jürgenson**
Moscow, Russia

C. F. **Kahnt** [10]
Lindau, Germany

Kallisti Music Press
810 South St. Bernard Street
Philadelphia, Pa. 19143
Tel: (215) 724-6511

Edwin F. **Kalmus** and Company
P.O. Box 5011
Boca Raton, Fla. 33431
Tel: (800) 434-6340 (outside Fla.);
(561) 241-6340
Fax: (561) 241-6347
www.kalmus-music.com

Edition **Kasparek**
Munich, Germany

KaWé
Amsterdam, the Netherlands

E. C. **Kerby** Ltd. [8]
Toronto, Canada

King's Crown Music Press [5]

Kistner & Siegel [4]
Cologne, Germany

Körlings Förlag
Stockholm, Sweden

L. **Krenn**
Vienna, Austria

Krompholz
Bern, Switzerland

Kultura [1]
Budapest, Hungary

Edition **Kunzelmann**
Hauptstrasse 35
79807 Lottstotten, Germany
Tel: (49) 7745-8020
Fax: (49) 7745-7221
www.edition-kunzelmann.com

Lacour (*see* Gérald **Billaudot**)

F. **Lauweryns**
Brussels, Belgium

Lea Pocket Scores [14]

Leblanc Publications [14]

Editions Alphonse **Leduc** [11]
175, Rue Saint-Honoré
75040 Paris, France
Tel: (33) 1-42-96-89-11
Fax: (33) 1-42-86-02-83
www.alphonseleduc.com

R. C. **Lee** [14]

Leeds Music Corporation (*see* Universal Music Publishing Group)

Leeds Music Ltd. (Canada; *see* Universal Music Publishing Group)

Henry **Lemoine** & Cie. [11]
Paris, France

Alfred **Lengnick** & Co., Ltd. **[8]** (*see*
G. **Schirmer**)

Lerolle
Paris, France

F. E. C. **Leuckart**
Munich, Germany

Liben Music Publishers
1191 Eversole Road
Cincinnati, Ohio 45230
Tel: (513) 232-6920
Fax: (513) 232-1866
www.liben.com

Lienau [14]

Lingua Press/Frog Peak Music
P.O. Box 1052
Lebanon, N.H. 03755
Tel/Fax: (603) 643-9037
www.frogpeak.org

Collection **Litolff**
Frankfurt, Germany

London & Continental Publishing
Company **[14]**

Ediciones **'Los Diez' [14]**
Santiago, Chile

Lottermoser S. A. C. I.
Buenos Aires, Argentina

Ludwig Music Publishers
1044 Vivian Drive
Grafton, Ohio 44044
Tel: (800) 851-1150; (440) 926-1100
Fax: (440) 926-2882
www.ludwigmusic.com

Harald **Lyche** & Co.
Oslo, Norway

Magni Publications
www.magnipublications.com

Magyar Kórus
Budapest, Hungary

Malcolm [14]

Marbot [14]

MarcoPaulo Publishing
1231 Barott Road
Lafayette, Calif. 94549
www.marco-paulo.com

Margun/Gunmar Music, Inc.
167 Dudley Road
Newton Center, Mass. 02459
Tel: (617) 332-6398
Fax: (617) 969-1079

John Markert & Co. **[14]**

Masters Music Publications
P.O. Box 810157
Boca Raton, Fla. 33481-0157
Tel: (561) 241-6340
Fax: (407) 241-6347
www.masters-music.com

Mathot (*see* Editions **Salabert**)

J. **Maurer**
Brussels, Belgium

Edizioni R. **Maurri**
Florence, Italy

McGinnis & Marx
236 West 26th Street, #11S
New York, N.Y. 10001-6736
Tel: (212) 243-5233
Fax: (212) 675-1630

McLaughlin & Reilly [14]

Media Press **[14]**

Mentor Music Inc. **[14]**

Mercury Music Corporation **[11]**

Meridian Music Publishing Co.,
Ltd. [11]

Merion Music Inc. [11]

Mersburger Verlag (Germany) [14]

Ediciones **Mexicanas de Música**
18 Avenida Juárez
Mexico City, Mexico

Mezhdunarodnaya Kniga
(USSR) [14]

Price **Milburn**
Wellington, New Zealand

Mills Music Inc. (*see* Alfred Publishing Company)

Minkoff Musique et Musicologie/
Editions Minkoff
8, Rue Eynard
1211 Geneva 12, Switzerland
Tel: (41) 22-310-46-60
Fax: (41) 22-310-28-57
www.minkoff-editions.com
distributed in U.S. by OMI
(*see* OMI)

Mitteldeutscher Verlag [14]

MJQ Music Inc.
1697 Broadway, Suite 503
New York, N.Y. 10019
Tel: (212) 582-6667
Fax: (212) 582-0627

MMB Music
Contemporary Arts Building
3526 Washington Avenue
St. Louis, Mo. 63103-1019
Tel: (800) 543-3771; (314) 531-9635
www.mmbmusic.com

Hermann **Moeck** Verlag [14]

Molenaar
Wormerveer, the Netherlands

Edwin H. **Morris**
39 West 54th Street
New York, N.Y. 10019

Möseler Verlag [14]
Wolfenbüttel, Germany

Mowbray Music Publishers [11]

Willy **Müller** [14]

Murdoch & Murdoch (London) [14]

Music Press [11]

Music Publishers of the USSR [14]

Music Sales
8-9 Frith Street
London W1D 3JB, United Kingdom
Tel: (44) 20-7434-0066
Fax: (44) 20-7287-6329
www.musicsales.com

Musica Rara Publications
Le Traversier
Chemin de la Buire
84170 Monteux, France
www.musicarara.com

Musikaliska Konstföreningen
Stockholm, Sweden

Musikhojskolens (Denmark) [14]

Musikk-Husets Forlag A/S
Storgaten 3
Postboks 822, Sentrum
0104 Oslo, Norway
Tel: (47) 22-82-59-00
Fax: (47) 22-42-55-41
www.musikk-huset.no

Musikus-Busch
Hamburg, Germany

Muziekuitgeverij
Amsterdam, the Netherlands

Muzychna Ukraina
Kiev, Ukraine

Muzyka
Moscow/Leningrad, Russia

Näckaus Vänner
1907 East Blaine Street
Seattle, Wash. 98112-2916

Nagel's Musik-Archive (*see* Bärenreiter Verlag)

Casa Arthur **Napoleão [14]**
Rio de Janeiro, Brazil

Nauka i Izkustvo
Sophia, Romania

Neue Musik Verlag
Berlin, Germany

New Music Edition **[11]**

New Valley Music Press
Smith College
Northampton, Mass.

New World Music Corporation (*see* Alfred Publishing Company)

Pierre **Noël** (*see* Gérard **Billaudot**)

Otto Heinrich **Noetzel** Verlag **[14]**

Nordiska Musikförlaget [8] (*see* G. **Schirmer**)
Stockholm, Sweden

Norsk Musikförlag (*see* MMB Music)
Oslo, Norway

Norwegian Information Service, c/o
Norsk Komponistforening
NOTAM
Nedre Gate 5
0551 Oslo, Norway
Tel: (47) 22-35-80-60
Fax: (47) 22-35-80-61
www.notam02.no

Novello & Co., Ltd. **[11]**

Johann **Oertel** Verlag **[14]**

Oesterreichischer Bundesverlag [14]

Editions de **l'Oiseau-Lyre**
B.P. 515
98015 Monaco
Tel: (377) 9330-0944
Fax: (377) 9330-1915
www.oiseau-lyre.com

Okra Music Corporation (*see* Seesaw Music Corp.)

Olivan Press
London, England

Omega Music Company **[11]**

OMI (Old Manuscripts and Incunabula)
P.O. Box 6019 FDR Station
New York, N.Y. 10150
Tel: (212) 758-1946
Fax: (212) 593-6186

Ongaku No Tomo Sha **[11]**

Orbis
Prague, Czech Republic

Orchesis Publications **[14]**

Oriana Publications Limited
33 Southminster Road
Penylan
Cardiff CF23 5AT
United Kingdom
Tel: (44) 029-2025-4768
Fax: (44) 029-2049-9970
www.orianapublications.co.uk

Orlando
Munich, Germany

Orphée [11]

Editions **Ouvrières** (*see* Editions Alphonse **Leduc**)

Musikverlag **Pan** [11]
Schaffhauserstraße 280
P.O. Box 176
8057 Zurich, Switzerland

Pan American Union Publication Division [14]

Panton [14]
Prague, Czech Republic

Papagena Press
Park West Station
Box 20484
New York, N.Y. 10025-1514
Tel: (212) 749-3012
Fax: (212) 316-2235
www.papagenapress.com

Paragon Music Publishers
c/o Benson Music Group
365 Great Circle Road
Nashville, Tenn. 37228
Fax: (615) 742-6911

Paterson's Publications, Ltd.
London, England

W. Paxton & Co., Ltd. [14]

Peer International, now known as Peermusic Classical [11]
www.peermusic.com

Pegasus [14]

Pelikan Musikverlag
Zurich, Switzerland

Pembroke Music [7]

Philharmusica Company
250 West 57 Street, Suite 1431
New York, N.Y. 10107

Philippo Editions (France) [14]

Pioneer Editions (*see* American Composers Alliance)

Pioneer Percussion
P.O. Box 10822
Burke, Va. 22009

Piper Press
P.O. Box 14038
Detroit, Mich. 48214

Piwarski Verlag [14]
Kraków, Poland

Hans **Pizka** Edition
P.O. Box 1136
85541 Kirchheim, Germany
Tel: (49) 89-903-9548
Fax: (49) 89-903-9414
www.pizka.de

Pizzicato Verlag Helvetia
Albisstrasse 57
8134 Adliswil, Switzerland
Tel: (41) 1-710-62-52
Fax: (41) 1-710-61-53
www.pizzicato.ch

Plymouth Music Co., Inc.
170 NE 33rd Street
Fort Lauderdale, Fla. 33334
Tel: (305) 563-1844
Fax: (305) 563-9006

Pocono Mountain Music Publishing
208 Drexel Road
Tobyhanna, Pa. 18466
Tel: 800-215-1880
www.poconomusic.com

Polish Music Publications (*see* Polskie Wydawnictwo Muzyczne)

Polskie Wydawnictwo Muzyczne [11]
al. Krasinskiego 11a

31-111 Krakow, Poland
Tel/Fax: (48) 12-422-71-71
www.pwm.com.pl

Friedrich **Portius** [14]

Pro Musica [14]

Pro Organo
Musikverlag Herbert Jess
7970 Leutkirch/Allgäu, Germany

Probst
Leipzig, Germany

Prosveta
Belgrade, Yugoslavia

Keith **Prowse** [14]
London, England

Quintard [14]
Paris, France

Radió Caracas, Editado por Radió
Caracas, Venezuela

Rahter [11]

Regina [14]

Editions Marc **Reift**
Route du Golf 122
3963 Crans-Montana, Switzerland
Tel: (41) 27-483-12-00
Fax: (41) 27-483-42-43
www.reift.ch

Reinhardt
Basel, Switzerland

Remick Music Corporation (*see*
Alfred Publishing Company)

Rhodes [14]

Richli [14]

G. **Ricordi** & Co. (International) [8]

Ricordi Americana (*see* G. **Ricordi**
& Co.)

Editions **Rideau Rouge** [14]

Ries & Erler (Germany) [1]

Robbins Music Corporation [14]

Rock Valley Music
800 Rock Valley Road
Long Eddy, N.Y. 12760

Ediciones Joaquín **Rodrigo**
General Yagüe 11, 4 J
28020 Madrid, Spain
Tel: (34) 91-555-2728
Fax: (34) 91-556-4335
www.joaquin-rodrigo.com

Winthrop **Rogers** Edition [1]
London, England

Rongwen Music [3]

Fondazione Carminignani **Rossini** [14]
Pesaro, Italy

E. **Rouart, Lerolle** & Co. (*see* Editions **Salabert**)

Rovnost [14]

Rózsavölgyi [14]
Budapest, Hungary

Russian State Publishers [14]

Ryûngihsha
Tokyo, Japan

Editions **Salabert** [8]
Paris, France
www.salabert.fr

**Samfundet til Udgivelse Af
Dansk Musik** (*see* Dan **Fog** Musikförlag)

Edizioni de **Santis**
Viale Mazzini 6
00195 Rome, Italy

Sassetti & Cia.
Lisbon, Portugal

Schauer [11]

G. **Schirmer [8]**
Music Sales Group of Companies
257 Park Avenue South, 20th Floor
New York, N.Y. 10010
Tel: (212) 254-2100
Fax: (212) 254-2013
www.schirmer.com

Schlesinger Schemusikhandlung **[14]**

Arthur P. **Schmidt** (*see* Alfred Publishing Company)

P. **Schneider [14]**

Editions Musicales de la **Schola Cantorum [8]**
Paris, France

Schott [6]

Schott Frères [14]

B. **Schott's Söhne**
Mainz, Germany

J. **Schuberth** & Co.
Wiesbaden, Germany

Schultheiss Musikverlag **[14]**
Stuttgart, Germany

Schwann Musikverlag **[10]**
Düsseldorf, Germany

Schweers & Haake
Bremen, Germany

Seesaw Music Corp.
2067 Broadway, Suite 58
New York, N.Y. 10023

Maurice **Senart** (*see* Editions **Salabert**)

Barthol **Senff [14]**

Serviço de Documentação Musical
da Ordem dos Músicos do Brasil
Rio de Janeiro, Brazil

Severinus Press
12 St. Ethelbert Close
Sutton St. Nicholas
Hereford HR1 3BF, United Kingdom
Fax: (44) 1432-880158
www.severinus.co.uk

Sidem Verlag
Geneva, Switzerland

Edition du **Siècle Musical [14]**

C. F. W. **Siegel**
Leipzig, Germany

Hans **Sikorski [8]** (*see* also G. **Schirmer**)
Johnsallee 23
20148 Hamburg, Germany
Tel: (49) 40-41-41-00-0
Fax: (49) 40-41-41-00-40

N. **Simrock**
Hamburg, Germany

La **Sirène Musicale** (*see* Editions Max **Eschig**)

Sirius Verlag **[14]**

Sisra Publications (*see* Arsis Press)

Skandinavisk Musikförlag **[14]**

Skandinavisk og Borups Musikförlag (*see* Dan **Fog** Musikförlag)

Smith College Music Archives
Northampton, Mass. 01063
Tel: (413) 584-2700
www.smith.edu

Smith Creek Music
3304 East Lake Drive

Nashville, Tenn. 37214
smithcreekmusic@aol.com

Smith Publications/Sonic Art
Editions
2617 Gwynndale Avenue
Baltimore, Md. 21207
Tel: (410) 298-6509
Fax: (410) 944-5113
www.smith-publications.com

Sociedade Portuguesa de Autores
Lisbon, Portugal

Società Anonima Notari
Milan, Italy

**Société des Auteurs, Compositeurs
et Editeurs de Musique** (SACEM)
225 av. Charles de Gaulle
92528 Neuilly-sur-Seine Cedex, France
Tel: (33) 1-47-15-47-15
www.sacem.fr

**Société pour la Publication de
Musique Classique et Moderne**
Paris, France

**Society for the Publication of
American Music** (SPAM) **[8]** (*see*
G. **Schirmer**)

Society for Publishing Danish Music
(*see* Dan **Fog** Musikförlag)

Southeastern Composers' League

Soviet Composer (Sovetskii Kom-
pozitor)
c/o Collet's Holdings Ltd.
Denington Estate
Wellingborough, Northants
NN8 2QT England
Tel: (44) 1933-224351
Fax: (44) 1933-276402

Rick **Sowash** Publishing Company
558 Liberty Hill

Cincinnati, Ohio 45210
Tel: (513) 721-1241
www.sowash.com

Leo **Sowerby** Foundation **[11]**

Spaeth/Schmid Blechbläsernoten
Lise Meitner Strasse 9
72202 Nagold, Germany
Tel: (49) 74-52-81-84-54
Fax: (49) 74-52-81-84-56
www.spaeth-schmid.de

Jack **Spratt [14]**

Staff Music Publishing Co.
Fort Lauderdale, Fla. 33334

Stainer & Bell [5]

Státní hudbení vydavatelskí (*see*
Supraphon)

**Státní Nakladtelstvi Krasne Lit-
eratury**
Prague, Czech Republic

Stockhausen Verlag
51515 Kürten, Germany
Fax: (49) 2268-1813
www.stockhausen.org

Süddeutscher Musikverlag (Willy
Müller) **[14]**

Supraphon
Palackeho 1
740 Prague, Czech Republic
Tel: (420) 221-966-666
Fax: (420) 221-966-631
www.supraphon.cz

Edizioni **Suvini Zerboni**
Galleria del Corso, 4
20122 Milan, Italy
Tel: (39) 02-770701
Fax: (39) 02-77070261
www.esz.it

Föreningen **Svenska** Tonsättare
Stockholm, Sweden

Swedish Society for Musical
Art (Musikaliska Konstföreningen) **[14]**

Symphonia Verlag **[14]**

Technisonor
Paris, France

Tenuto Publications **[11]**

Thames Music Publishing
London, England

Thesaurus Harmonicus (*see*
Severinus Press)

Tischler & Jangenberg [14]

To the Fore Publishers
c/o Paul Cohen
82 Copley Avenue
Teaneck, N.J. 07666
Tel: (201) 287-1872

Musikverlag P. J. **Tonger**
Auf dem Brand 10
50996 Cologne, Germany
Tel: (49) 221-935564-0
Fax: (49) 221-935564-11
www.tonger.de

Tonos Verlag (*see* Seesaw Music
Corp.)

Tritone Press **[11]**

Two-Eighteen Press (*see* also **Editions 75**)
12 Wolf Road, Room 218
Croton-on-Hudson, N.Y. 10520

**Udruženje Kompozitora Bosne i
Hercegovine**
Radiceva 15
71000 Sarajevo, Bosnia

Udruženje Kompozitora Hrvatske [14]
Zagreb, Croatia

Unión Musical Española [8] (*see*
G. **Schirmer**)

United Music Publishers [11]
London, England

Universal Edition [11]
Vienna, Austria

Universal Music Publishing Group
2440 Sepulveda Boulevard, Suite 100
Los Angeles, Calif. 90064-1712
Tel: (310) 235-4700
Fax: (310) 235-4900
www.universalmusicpublishing.com

Universidad Central de Venezuela
Caracas, Venezuela
www.ucv.ve/publicaciones

Universidade Federal do Rio de Janeiro
Rio de Janeiro, Brazil
www.ufrj.br

University College Cardiff Press
University College, Box 78
Cardiff CF1 1XL Wales
United Kingdom

University Music Press
Ann Arbor, Mich.

University of California Press
2120 Berkeley Way
Berkeley, Calif. 94720
Tel: (510) 642-4247
Fax: (510) 643-7127
www.ucpress.edu
Orders: California-Princeton
Fulfillment Services
1445 Lower Ferry Road
Ewing, N.J. 08618
Tel: (800) 777-4726; (609) 883-1759
Fax: (800) 999-1958

University of Pittsburgh Press
Eureka Building, Fifth Floor
3400 Forbes Avenue
Pittsburgh, Pa. 15260
Tel: (412) 383-2456
Fax: (412) 383-2466
www.pitt.edu/~press

University of Wales Press
10 Columbus Walk
Brigantine Place
Cardiff CF10 4UP
United Kingdom
Tel: (44) 29-2049-6899
Fax: (44) 29-2049-6108
www.uwp.co.uk

University of Washington Press
P.O. Box 50096
Seattle, Wash. 98145
Tel: (800) 441-4115; (206) 543-4050
Fax: (800) 669-7993; (206) 685-3460
www.washington.edu/uwpress

Urbánek (*see* Artia)

Ut Orpheus Edition
Palazzo de' Strazzaroli
Piazza di Porta Ravegnana, 1
40126 Bologna, Italy
Tel: (39) 051226468
Fax: (39) 051263720
www.utorpheus.com

Valley Music Press (*see* New Valley
Music Press)

Van Rossum
Utrecht, the Netherlands

Editions Ray **Ventura** [14]
Paris, France

Vienna Urtext Edition [11]
Vienna, Austria

Musikverlag C. F. **Vieweg** [14]

Viking Musikförlag
Lille Strandvej 3
2900 Hellerup
Copenhagen, Denmark
Tel: (45) 31-62-12-10

Vireo Press [5]

Viva Music [14]

E. **Vogel**
Basel, Switzerland

Arno **Volk** Verlag (*see* Universal
Music Publishing Group)
Cologne, Germany

Edition **Walhall**
Verlag Franz Biersack
Richard-Wagner-Straße 3
39106 Magdeburg, Germany
Tel: (49) 391-857820
Fax: (49) 391-8520079
E-mail: info-edition-walhall@freenet.de

Warner Brothers Publications (*see*
Alfred Publishing Company)

Warner/Chappell Music
10585 Santa Monica Boulevard
Los Angeles, Calif. 90025-4950
Tel: (310) 441-8600
Fax: (310) 470-1587
www.warnerchappell.com

Washington University Music Press
St. Louis, Mo.

Waterloo Music Company [3]

Weaner-Levant [14]

Josef **Weinberger** [1]
12-14 Mortimer Street
London W1T 3JJ, United Kingdom
Tel: (44) 20-7580-2827
Fax: (44) 20-7436-9616
www.josef-weinberger.com

Weintraub Music Company **[8]** (*see* G. **Schirmer**)

Wellesley College Edition
106 Central Street
Wellesley, Mass. 02481
Tel: (781) 283-1000
www.wellesley.edu

The **Well-Tempered Press** (*see* Masters Music Publications)

Wendigo Music **[14]**

Westerlund A. B.
Helsinki, Finland

Western International Music
3707 65th Avenue
Greeley, Colo. 80634-9626
Tel: (970) 330-6901
Fax: (970) 330-7738
www.wiminc.com

Western Music, Ltd. (Canada)
c/o Leslie Music Supply
198 Speers Road, Unit 2
Oakville, ON, L6K 2E9, Canada
Tel: (800) 291-1075; (905) 844-3109
Fax: (905) 844-7637
www.lesliemusicsupply.com

Wilder Music Incorporated (*see* Margun/Gunmar Music, Inc.)

Wilhelmiana [14]

Joseph **Williams** Editions **[14]**

Willis Music Company
P.O. Box 548

Florence, Ky. 41022-0548
Tel: (800) 354-9799; (859) 283-2050
Fax: (859) 283-1784
www.willismusic.com

Wingert-Jones Music
11225 Colorado
Kansas City, Mo. 64137-2502
Tel: (800) 258-9566
Fax: (800) 328-8250
www.wjmusic.com

M. **Witmark** and Sons **[14]**

Walter **Wollenweber** Verlag
Munich, Germany

Yorke Edition **[11]**
London, England

ZAIKS
Warsaw, Poland

Casa Musicale G. **Zanibon**
Via Salomone 77
20138 Milan, Italy
Tel: (39) 2-88811
Fax: (39) 2-5082280

Zenemükiado Vállalat (Editio Musica Budapest) **[11]**

Edizioni Suvini **Zerboni [6]**
Via Quintiliano, 40
20138 Milan, Italy

Wilhelm **Zimmermann [6]**
Frankfurt, Germany

Editions Aug. **Zurfluh [11]**

The Piano in Chamber Ensemble

Music for Two Instruments

Duos for Piano and Violin

Michel van der Aa. *Double* 1997 (Donemus 2000) 9pp., parts. 7 min. Requires preparing the piano by looping hairs from the bow of a stringed instrument through the piano strings of 6 notes with a rod above the instrument to bend their pitches. Pianist uses a plectrum and mallets, the latter with a thin wooden plate to prevent damage to piano. Score includes photographs to aid preparation. Avant-garde techniques of indeterminacy used to a mild extent with both instruments interacting in a complementary manner. A quartet version of this work exists as *Quadrivial*. An effective work which deserves to become a staple of late-20th-century avant-garde repertoire. M-D.

Evaristo Felice Dall'Abaco. *Six Sonatas* Op.1 (Kolneder—Schott 1956). Gamba or cello ad lib. Op.1/2, 4, 5, 6, 7, 11.
———. *Six Sonatas* Op.4 (Br&H). Cello ad lib.
———. *Sonatas* Op.1 and Op.4 are contained in DTB, Vol.I.
———. *Two Sonatas* (USSR).
———. *Sonata* a (Salmon—Ric R748).
———. *Sonata* F (Salmon—Ric R354).
See VKDR, I: pp.84–86.

Carl Friedrich Abel. *Sonatas* (Bacher, Woehl—Br). Vol.I: Sonatas e, D, G. Vol.II: Sonatas C, A, A. For viola da gamba (violin or flute) and basso continuo.
———. *Sonata* G (Broe—CFP B.330).
———. *Two Sonatinas* (Raphael—Hin) Op.5/4 C and 5/5 A. Cello ad lib.
———. *Sonata* Op.13/A (F. Piersig—Br&H 4165 1928) 11pp., parts. Editorial additions identified. Un poco moderato; Andante; Un poco vivace. Keyboard has a prominent part. Active melodic line in piano. M-D.
———. *Sonata* G (F. Brüggen—Br&VP 1960). For violin or flute.
———. *Sonata* B♭ (F. Piersig—Br&H 4104 1928) 9pp., parts. Editorial additions identified. Allegro moderato: large movement; piano part more important than violin; broken-chord figuration; trills; triplets; *p* closing. Tempo di Menuetto: tastefully edited. M-D.

Walter Abendroth. *Sonata* Op.26 (Simrock 1961) 20pp., parts. Moderato opening with piano providing punctuated rhythmic chords. Leads to Andante section, more free and rhapsodic. Attacca moves to Energico (Allegretto) with more rhythmic propulsion, triplets, and syncopated usage. Centers around g or G with chromatically altered harmony. M-D.

Jean Absil. *Sonata* Op.146 1970 (CeBeDeM) 28pp., parts. 18 min. Allegro Moderato; Andantino; Vivo leggiero; Lento mysterioso; Allegretto. Displays a novel language with subtle rhythms of Romanian folklore and varied artistry throughout. D.

Joseph Achron. *Suite* II Op.22 1906 (UE 7692 1925) 28pp., parts. En Passant; Menuet & Trio; Moulin; Intermezzo; Marionettes. Piano part very important. Colorful, post-Romantic writing. M-D.

———. *Sonata* Op.29 d 1910 (Belaieff 1914) 51pp., parts. Bewegt und ausgeregt; Hirtenliebe (Traümend); Interludium; Keck und sehr freudig. Highly chromatic, thick textures, first-rate pianism required. D.

———. *Deuxième Sonate* Op.45 A 1918 (UE 7561 1924) 72pp., parts. Giocondo; Misterioso e fantastico; Burla; Focoso. In Regerian harmonic style, virtuoso writing for both instruments. D.

John Adams. *Road Movies* 1995 (Hendon Music 1998) 37pp., parts. 17 min. Three movements: [untitled]; Contemplative; "40% Swing." Outer movements suggest perpetual mobiles in their motoric pace, punctuated with occasional syncopated interruptions. Middle movement introduces motivic idea in piano, a 7-note ascending sequence. Minimalist tendencies throughout. D.

Samuel Adler. *Sonata* II 1956 (OUP 1968) 23pp., parts. 14½ min. For piano or harpsichord. Allegro moderato; Lento espressivo; Allegro molto, ma non troppo. Neoclassic style. Numerous dynamic effects would not be possible on a harpsichord. M-D.

———. *Sonata* III 1965 (Bo&H 1974) 28pp., parts. In 6 episodes to be performed without interruption. Fast and intense: serial, atonal, dissonant. Very slowly: sustained, chordal, with sudden interruptions of fast short sections. Very lively: linear, staccato left-hand chords, octotonic, rhythmic melodies. Very slowly: requires large span, expressive. Like a waltz, gracefully: flowing lines, contains a few *ff* figuration surprises. Fast and intense: similar to opening episode, sparse textures. D.

———. *Sonata* IV 1989 (LMP 1999) 37pp., parts. Quite fast; Quiet and dreamlike; Fast and very rhythmic. Three dramatic movements, sometimes requiring 4 staves for piano. Intricate rhythmic patterns. Second movement is most successful in its spacious and contemplative sonority. Requires seasoned performers. D.

———. *Double Portrait* (ST 785 1989) 19pp., parts. Composed to honor the memory of 2 great artists and friends. In 2 attached sections: Slowly and serenely; Fast rhythmic, without letup. Wide span required as well as experienced performers. D.

Peter Stewart Adriaansz. *Lines, Dots, and Crosses* 1993 (Donemus 1993) 25pp., parts. 21 min. In 3 distinct sections as titled, meant to be played as one continuous movement. Includes notes to performers. Piano part extends to 4 staves. M-D.

Hans Ahlgrimm. *Sonata* g (Lienau 1938) 20pp., parts. 14 min. For violin or alto flute. Includes a separate part for alto flute. Moderato; Allegro non troppo. Chromatic, opening 3 bars in first movement contain thematic material for movement. Much alternating writing between hands in last movement. D.

Stephen Albert. *Tribute* 1988 (GS 3929 1988) 14pp., parts. 9 min. "*Tribute* revolves on a dual axis comprised of two lyrical themes that generate the other musical ideas appearing throughout this one movement work. The first theme is given to the piano in the opening and the second theme is announced by the violin on the heels of the opening piano section. Both themes are developed and elaborated on, woven in and around one another, until they are, at length, transformed into new themes that are more dramatic and rhythmic than their lyrical forebears. The end of the work is announced when a hymn-like section commences in the piano after a genuinely loud climactic section" (Composer's Note). D.

Tomaso Albinoni. *Six Sonatas* Op.4 (W. Kolneder—Eulenburg 1973–74). Cello part optional. Melodies have a fine sweep about them. Good realization of the figured bass.

———. *Trattenimenti Armonici per camera* 12 Sonatas Op.6 (M. Talbot—EMA 106 1981), parts. Vol.I (ISBN 0-906773-05-9): 1 C; 2 g; 3 B♭; 4 d. This group of solo Sonatas was the only one Albinoni himself prepared for publication. The collective title of *Trattenimenti Armonici* was translated as "An Entertainment of Harmony" in the Walsh edition. Informative Preface. Clean edition with fine realizations and editorial comments clearly indicated. M-D.

———. *Two Chamber Sonatas* Op.6/1 C, 2 A (W. Upmeyer—Nag 9).

———. *Three Sonatas* Op.6/4 d, 5 F, 7 D (Reinhart—Hug). Cello part optional. No.4 is perhaps the finest in the set. M-D.

———. *Sonata* g Op.6/2 (F. F. Polnauer—Schott 1967).

———. *Sonata* a Op.6/6 (B. Paumgartner—Hug 1951). See VKDR, I: p.83.

———. *Sonata* a (Schäffler—Nag). Cello part optional.

———. *Sonata* b (Scheck, Ruf—Symphonia SY502). Cello part optional.

Amalie, Princess of Prussia. *Sonata* F (G. Lenzewski—Vieweg 108 1975) 8pp., parts for flute or violin. See detailed entry under duos for piano and flute.

Rene Amengual. *Sonata* 1943–44 (IU) 26pp., parts. Moderato: SA, $\frac{7}{4}$, freely tonal, flowing, imitation, centers around B♭; harmonic 9ths require large span. Recitado, libremente: declamatory opening; leads to Andante espressivo; flowing; hemiola; returns to dramatic opening mood to close out; centers freely around F. Presto: rondo, built on opening idea in piano, contrasting episodes. The whole work has an attractive gentle flowing quality about it. M-D.

Jan van Amerongen. *Sonate* I 1981 (Donemus 1982) 17pp., parts. 15 min. Andante rubato; Adagio; Molto allegro. Conventional writing for the late 20th century. M-D.

———. *Sonate* II 1990 (Donemus 1991) 22pp., parts. 19 min. I. Fantasia: alternates between Adagio and Allegro non troppo in strongly contrasting characters. II. Largo: pensive with constantly repeated quarter notes. III. Scherzo: cast in $\frac{4}{4}$ with many passages of fleeting 16th notes in octaves. M-D.

William Ames. *Dust of Snow* (CF 1946) 5pp., parts for violin and/or cello. Chordal with left-hand figuration. Descriptive. M-D.

———. *Sonata* (CFE).

David Amram. *Sonata* 1960 (CFP 6686) 25pp., parts. 18 min. Allegro moderato; Andante espressivo; Theme and (8) Variations. Thoroughly 20th-century, much dissonance, expert handling of both instruments, eclectic. Effective alternation of contrasting moods. D.

Hendrik Andriessen. *Sonate* 1932 (Donemus 1948) 18pp., parts. 12 min. Allegro–Adagio–Allegro moderato; Adagio; Allegretto leggiero. Expressive writing often characterized by the contrast of lyric and dramatic qualities. M-D.

———. *Suite* 1950 (Donemus 1950) 29pp., parts. Preludio; Fughetta; Air Varié; Finale. Parallelism and planing techniques found in both block and broken chords. Imitative features in Fughetto become less technical as movement progresses. M-D.

Jurriaan Andriessen. *Sonate* 1946 (Donemus 1950) 22pp., parts. Allegro molto; Molto lento; Allegro. Neoclassic. M-D.

———. *Quattro Movimenti* 1992 (Donemus 1993) 14pp., parts. 8 min. Largo; Allegro; Largo; Allegro. M-D.

Louis Andriessen. *Disco* 1982 (Donemus 1982) 16pp., parts. 14 min. In one movement packed with changing meters in the outer sections of its ternary form. Octaves; harmonics; rhythmic complexities. Both instruments must be amplified. Performance notes included. M-D.

George Antheil. *Works for Violin and Piano* (R. Erickson—GS 3905 1995, ISBN 0-7935-5097-1) 207pp., parts. *Sonata I, II, III, IV, Sonatina*. Antheil entitled *Sonata IV* "No. 2" and apparently had in mind "to consolidate the *Sonata No. 1* with the Third and ignore the Second, so that all the violin and piano sonatas before 1940 would be known as one work, called *Sonata No. 1*" (from Preface). *Sonata I* (1923). One movement. Relentless ostinatos, much repetition of rhythmic cells. Antheil throws overboard most traditions of Western music in this jarring Stravinsky/Bartók–influenced work. *Sonata II* (1923). One movement. Music-hall dance rhythms permeate everything. Instruments exchange glissandi. Slow foxtrot, habanera, and Charleston are given to the melodic violin while the piano pounds out an ostinato. Stringent polytonality infuses some of the popular elements with sarcastic jolts. Percussion is brought in only at the end (à la Ives?) in an Oriental duet with the violin. Musical humor at its best. *Sonata III* (1924). 12 min. One movement. There is little development in this work; thematic and rhythmic material are frequently repeated, sometimes in polytonal layers. Generally more subdued and longer than the first 2 *Sonatas.* Stravinskyisms are lightly sprinkled everywhere. *Sonata IV* (1947–48). Retrospectively, Antheil fashioned 3 extensive movements from Baroque and Classical forms, the first a Scherzo: Sonata–Allegro; second: Passacaglia Variations; third: Toccata–Rondo. The composer's explosive qualities are still apparent in this later work but to a lesser extent with less strident harmonies in the post–World War II work. *Sonatina* (1945). Three movements. Shostakovich influence shows in the opening march, which returns at the conclusion of the last movement, as well as the "wrong" notes in opening theme. Contrapuntal dissonance, Neoclassic sophistication. Manuscripts for all except *Sonata IV* at Library of Congress. *Sonatas I, II, III, IV* D. *Sonatina* M-D.

Pietro Degli Antonii. *Three Sonatas* Op.5/1, 4, 6 (B. Paumgartner—Hug GH9339 1947) 31pp., parts. Preface in German, French, and English. 1. Con affetto; Vivace; Aria grave; Adagio; Allegro. 4. Grave; Aria–Vivace; Posato; Adagio; Vivace. 6. Adagio; Allegro; Grave; Vivace. These works have a personal physiognomy and an original style that date from the high Bolognese Baroque. They have a warm, pulsating, and dignified character about them and represent the finest type of chamber music from this period. Excellent edition. M-D.

Theodor Antoniou. *Lyrics* 1967 (Br 6103) 18pp., parts. These 7 short varied pieces present a free musical approach to forms of ancient lyric poetry. The verses are by the Greek poet Tassos Roussos and are based on ideas of the composer. If the verses are not recited during the performance, they should be printed in the program. Threnos; Epigram; Elegy; Nomos; Hymn; Ode; Skolion. Serial, some pointillistic treatment, harmonics, plucked strings, glissandi on strings, repetition as desired. A book is to be placed on strings covering specific pitches. Meaningful and expressive writing. M-D.

Attilio Ariosti. *Two Sonatas* (S. Renzo—DeSantis 982) 1 E♭, 2 A. From *Six Sonatas* for viola d'amore contained in "Six Lessons for Viola d'amore."
——. *Sonata* II transposed to D (Saint-George—Augener).
——. *Sonata* e (Salmon—Ric R346).
——. *Sonata* G (Salmon—Ric R347).

Thomas A. Arne. *Sonata* B♭ (Craxton—OUP 20.007 1931) 5pp., parts. 4 min. Transcribed for violin or cello. Poco largo: serves as introduction, with short cadenza to Gavotta: much 8th-note figuration for piano. Charming, with purity of style. M-D.

Richard Arnell. *Sonata* II Op.55 (Schott 10214 1950) 23pp., parts. 14½ min. Vivace: chromatic alternation of hands; opening motif is main idea and is thoroughly worked over. Andante: same chromatic idea is transformed; piano gets some lyric melodic interest; repeated octaves; wide skips; *ppp* ending. Allegro vivace: bitonal cover conceals chromatic motif but is present in a rocking $\frac{6}{8}$; Presto coda, movement ends abruptly. M-D.

Malcolm Arnold. *Sonata* I 1947 (Lengnick) 31pp., parts. Allegretto; Andante tranquillo; Allegro vivace. A large dramatic work. Third movement scampers lightly to provide contrast with the other weighty movements. Thorough pianistic equipment required. D.
———. *Sonata* II Op.43 (Paterson's 1953) 9pp., parts. 9 min. In one movement: Allegretto–Vivace–Andantino quasi allegretto–Adagio molto. Tonal, chromatic coloring, sweeping scales for piano in Allegretto. Somber, peaceful closing on G. M-D.

Claude Arrieu. *Sonate* 1949 (Leduc) 29pp., parts. 20 min. Risoluto maestoso: mildly dissonant chords, violin cadenza, a tempo sections contrasted with slower sections, big chordal C closing. Andante non troppo: chromatic inner voices of 2nds and 3rds provide unusual sonorities. Allegro vivo: very rhythmic, sweeping arpeggi. Più lento section concludes with opening figuration from first movement in stringendo fashion. Brilliant writing. D.

Tony Aubin. *Concertinetto* (Leduc 1962) 9pp., parts. 6 min. Driving rhythmic opening. Adagietto mid-section, some changing meters. Finale, Allegro, bounces along to a short violin cadenza. Scherzando character returns with both instruments contributing color and verve. A ritard appears just before the unexpected closing a tempo. M-D.

Georges Auric. *Sonata* G 1936 (Chant du Monde 1937) 32pp., parts. Assez lent et librement: varied tempos, textures, ideas. Vif: scherzo-like with clear figurations. Lent: chordal until Très calme et expressif, haunting melody. Vif: clear and light through most of movement, brilliant closing. D.

Menahem Avidom. *Concertino* (Israeli Music Publications 1951) 19pp., parts. Moderato; Andante quasi Allegro; Finale. Clear textures, lively color, and an Oriental atmosphere. The piano is treated equally and not as an orchestral substitute. M-D.

Emil Axman. *Sonata* (Hudební Matice 1924) 33pp., parts. Poetical, serious emotional quality, rustic strength. D.
———. *Capriccio* (Hudební Matice 1947).

Arno Babadjanian. *Sonata* b♭–B♭ (USSR 1970) 44pp., parts. Grave: frequent tempo changes, sweeping lines. Andante sostenuto: Presto mid-section, much interplay of ideas. Allegro risoluto: much alternation of $^6_8$ and $^4_8$ meters, driving, motoric, slows down to a brief Largo before an Andante sostenuto leads to the concluding Maestoso. Powerful writing. D.

Milton Babbitt. *Sextets* 1966 (CFP 66409 1975) 65pp., parts. 13 min. Total serialization, pointillistic, bristling with complicated intricacies, enormous dynamic range with more dynamic marks than notes, proportional rhythmic relationships. Great clarity with a certain amount of sterility, little or no emotional qualities present. Only for the most dedicated and experienced ensemble performers. D.

William Babell. *12 Sonatas* 4 vols. (M. Maute—Amadeus BP 334-7 1999), parts, including basso. For oboe, flute, or violin. See detailed entry under duos for piano and oboe.
——. *Sonata* g (M. Tilmouth—OUP 1963) 5pp., parts also for oboe or flute. See detailed entry under duos for piano and flute.

Grażyna Bacewicz. *Partita* (PWM 1957) 26pp., parts. Preludium: $^6_8$ alternating octaves and major 7ths between hands in Grave tempo. Toccata: large skips, highly rhythmic, glissandi. Intermezzo: widely spaced sonorities, hypnotic. Rondo: dancelike. D.
——. *Sonata da Camera* I (PWM 1945) 11 min.
——. *Sonata* II 1946 (Cofalik—PWM 2000, ISBN 83-224-0515-4) 34pp., parts. 21 min. Allegro: octotonic; biting harmonies; dramatic; furious. Andante: $^3_8$; both instruments develop own motivic patterns; lyric. Scherzo–Vivace: clever use of silences in individual parts to emphasize textural features; conventional, Neoclassic qualities. D
——. *Sonata* III 1947 (PWM) 33pp., parts, 18 min. Allegro moderato: much chromatic figuration, melodic and harmonic. Adagio: builds to climax in middle of movement, subsides. Scherzo: sprightly, colorful, dance rhythms, bitonal arpeggi at closing. Finale: a sustained Andante with a long crescendo; opening idea hammered out at conclusion. D.
——. *Sonata* IV 1949 (PWM, ISBN 83-224-1184-7) 35pp., parts. 20 min. A large work with clear textures. Piano part is expressive and contrasts with the violin. Pliability, unity, and homogeneity are all characteristic of the work. D.
——. *Sonata* V 1951 (PWM, ISBN 83-224-1075-1) 28pp., parts. 13 min. Moderato: sweeping chromatic lines. Nokturn: based on material from opening 2 bars. Finale: uneasy and constantly boiling. D.
——. *Theme with Variations* (PWM 1999) 16pp., parts. Allegro energico theme with 9 variations. Includes a menuetto and berceuse. Explores an assemblage

of pianistic techniques in 20th-century harmonies. Deserves to be better known. D.

———. *Easy Pieces I* (PWM, ISBN 83-224-2068-4) 11pp., parts. Contains 5 two-page pieces: *Preludium, Melodia, Marsz, Kołysanka,* and *Scherzino.* Int.

Carl Philipp Emanuel Bach. *Sonata* D 1731 W.71 (Ric SY570 1954) 14pp., parts. Adagio ma non molto; Allegro; Adagio: highly elaborate; Menuetto I and II. M-D.

———. *Sonata* d 1731 W.72 (Ruf—Ric SY571 1954) 14pp., parts. Editorial additions identified. Adagio ma non troppo: turn is prominently featured in melodic line; Allegro (Gigue); Allegro. M-D.

———. *Sonata* b 1763 (H. Sitt—CFP 3619A) 22pp., parts. Allegro moderato; Poco andante; Allegretto siciliano. D.

———. *Sonata* c 1763 (H. Sitt—CFP 3619b) 23pp., parts. Allegro moderato; Adagio ma non troppo; Presto. M-D. Keyboard part is highly prominent in both *Sonatas.*

———. *Sonata* C (Ruf—Ric SY572).

———. *Sonata* B♭ (Ruf—Ric SY576).

———. *Sonata* C (Klengel—Br&H). Originally for gamba.

———. *Sonata* D (Klengel—Br&H). Originally for gamba.

———. *Phantasy-Sonata* f♯ 1787 W.67 (A. Schering—Kahnt 1938) 16pp., parts. 13 min. Sehr traurig und ganz langsam: numerous tempo and mood changes. Allegro: heavily ornamented. D.

———. *Six Sonatas* (Kultura).

———. *Sonata* b (Ruf—Schott 1965).

———. *Sonata* B♭ (Scheck, Ruf—Symphonia SY503). Cello optional.

———. *Sonata* D (Scheck, Ruf—Symphonia SY505).

See G. Beechey, "C. P. E. Bach (1714–1788): His Solo Keyboard and Chamber Music," *The Consort* 44 (1988): 10–22.

Johann Christian Bach. *Five Sonatas* (Landschoff—Hin). Vol.I: Op.10/1, 2, 3. Vol.II: Op.10/4, 5.

———. *Sonata* Op.10/4 A (F. Piersig—Br&H 1928) 9pp., parts. Allegretto; Rondeau–Allegro moderato. Some tricky spots in last movement. M-D.

———. *Six Sonatas* Op.16 1779 (Heinrichshofen) 37pp., parts. Reprint of an early (first?) edition. Sonatas in D, G, C, A, D, F.

———. *Sonata* Op.16/1 A (F. Piersig—Br&H 4167 1928) 11pp., parts. Allegro assai; Andante grazioso. Charming and graceful. M-D.

———. *Two Sonatas* Op.16/1 D, 2 G 1779 (A. Küster—Nag 1 1927) 19pp., parts. Two movements each, ornamentation discussed in Preface. M-D.

———. *Sonata* Op.16/4 A (Küster—Nag 104 1933) 9pp., parts. For violin or flute. Allegretto; Pastorale. Charming and facile writing. Int. to M-D.

———. *Sonata* I d (Ruf—Schott).

———. *Sonata* E♭ (Zirnbauer—Schott 1951) 19pp., parts. Four movements. M-D.

Johann Sebastian Bach. *Sechs Sonaten* (H. Epstein—Henle 1971) 126pp., parts. Fingering added by Hans-Martin Theopold. Vol.I: S.1014 b, S.1015 A, S.1016 E. Vol.II: S.1017 c, S.1018 F, S.1019 G. Independent keyboard part so these are true Sonatas for 2 instruments. Two earlier versions of movements from No.6 are included in the Appendix. Editorial additions are printed in brackets. Contains comments on the individual works. D.

———. *Sechs Sonaten* (R. Gerber—Br 1967) 2 vols. S.1014–19. *Neue Ausgabe sämtlicher Werke.*

———. *Six Sonatas* (Stock, Müller—VU 1973) 2 vols. Keyboard part is frequently written out in full instead of using a figured bass. Critical commentaries and detailed performance directions. Also available from Jacobsen—CFP 232-3C; Naumann—Br&H; Debussy—Durand; David, Carse—Augener; Lea; David—IMC; De Guarnieri—Ric; K 03018-9.
Available separately: S.1014 b (Dyke—J. Williams; Kortschak, Hughes—GS). S.1015 A (Dyke—J. Williams; Kortschak, Hughes—GS; M. Reger—Simrock). S.1016 E (Dyke—J. Williams; Kortschak, Hughes—GS). S.1017 c (Kortschak, Hughes—GS). S.1018 f (Kortschak, Hughes—GS). S.1019 G (Kortschak, Hughes—GS).

———. *The Music for Violin and Cembalo/Continuo* (R. D. P. Jones—OUP) 2 vols., parts. S.1014–19. Includes first and second versions of S.1019 and an early version of S.1018, third movement. In a letter to Forkel, C. P. E. Bach writes: "The six clavier [and violin] trios . . . are amongst the best works of my dearly beloved father. Even now they sound very good and give me many delights, regardless of the fact that they are over fifty years old. There are several Adagios among them which even today could not be composed in a more singing style" (1744). Introductory notes in English and German, with critical commentary in English.

———. *Two Sonatas* (G. Kehr—VU 1973; H. Eppstein—Henle 1990) S.1021 G, S.1023 E. Figured bass in VU has been realized by Kurt-Heinz Stolze. Both works are in 4 movements. S.1023, with its toccata-like first movement, is especially interesting. S.1021 was discovered only in 1928 and includes 2 highly ornamented slow movements. Henle includes *Sonata* S.1020 g, now ascribed to C. P. E. Bach. Fine editions.

———. *Sonata* S.1021 G (F. Blume, A. Busch—Br&H 1929; Hausswald—Br).

———. *Sonata* S.1023 e (Hausswald—Br; Ferguson—Schott; W. Davisson—Br&H).

———. *Sonata* F (CFP 4464). Bach's arrangement of his *Trio G.*

———. *Toccata* S.1024 c (Herrmann—ESC). *Sonata* S.1024 c (David, Hermann—CFP).
See VKDR, I: pp.109–31.

Henk Badings. *Sonata* I (Schott 1933) 22pp., parts. 15 min. Dark, chromatic harmony, Germanic. M-D to D.

———. *Sonata* II (Schott 1940) 19pp., parts. 15 min. Allegro ma non troppo; Andante; Allegro. Neoclassic. Moderately thick textures. Thematic material mutually dispersed between instruments. M-D.

———. *Sonata* III 1952 (Donemus) 42pp., parts. 20 min. Hindemith-inspired. Allegro: dark. Adagio: foreboding. Rondo giocoso: delightful, but suffers somewhat from overuse of same melodic ideas. D.

———. *Sonata* IV 1931 (Donemus 1948) 22pp., parts. 15 min. Allegro; Adagio; Allegro molto ma legg. Intensely dramatic requiring a fine command of touch and foresight for successful performances. M-D.

———. *Sonata* V 1984 (Donemus 1985) 18pp., parts. 17 min. Introduzione–Lento; Presto; Adagio appassionato; Finale–Scherzando. Includes aleatoric passagework, trilled double stops, varying degrees of vibrato, and mixed meters. The most difficult of Badings's 5 Sonatas. D.

Leonardo Balada. *Sonata* I 1969 (Gen 1971) 35pp., parts. Moderato: short, freely chromatic, changing meters, varied figurations, moves directly to Lento molto: leisured pacing, mid-section Molto espressivo e dramatico provides contrast and extends to a short Largo coda that calms and lets the violin finish by itself. Allegro scherzando: fragmented chromatic thematic treatment, piano part moves over entire keyboard, attacca. Moderato energico: sweeping gestures in both instruments. Lento coda begins with solo violin and leads to Allegretto giocoso and "As fast as possible" conclusion. Requires experienced and first-rate players. Well written, imaginative, reveals a major developing talent. D.

Simon Balicourt. *Sonata* II 1750 (Les Editions Ouvrières 1967) 11pp., parts. For flute or violin and basso continuo. See detailed entry under duos for piano and flute.

Claude Ballif. *Sonate* Op.17 (Bo&Bo 1961) 26pp., parts. Three movements, uses tempo markings in lieu of terms. Expressionist, pointillistic. Carefully marked pedal indications. D.

Don Banks. *Sonata* (Schott 1954) 24pp., parts. 13 min. Allegro moderato, risoluto leads to Marcato e ritmato and pulls back to a more sustained Molto moderato section. The Maestoso section is broad and is quickly followed by a $\frac{9}{8}$ Scorrevole for 4 pages. The Càlmo section features a prominent left-hand punctuated figuration. Marcato e ritmato returns with chromatic unison passages 2 octaves apart in the piano that swell to a dramatic climax. Other contrasted tempo and character markings add to the turbulence and excitement before the final stringendo closes out breathlessly. D.

Granville Bantock. *Sonata* I G (OUP 1929) 44pp., parts. Allegro con moto; Andante sostenuto; Allegro vivo non tanto.

———. *Sonata* II D (Goodwin & Todd, through Belwin-Mills 1940) 43pp., parts.

31 min. Lentamente non troppo; A piacere, quasi recitativo; Andante con moto rubato.

George Barati. *Sonata* 1956 (Zimmermann) 28pp., parts. 16 min. Andantino tranquillo: 2 with 3, chromatic, close intervals preferred. Molto risoluto non troppo allegro: misterioso, flowing lines build to con fuoco before subsiding. A long crescendo leads to an imposing close with cascading octaves in the piano. Freely tonal, much chromatic usage throughout the entire composition, both instruments thoroughly exploited. Although this *Sonata* appears to be in only 2 movements, the considerable tempo and character changes in both movements suggest the idea of more movements. Piano part is pianistic at all times although difficult. This work has much to commend it. D.

——. *Two Dances* (PIC 1948) 17pp., parts. Slow Dance: Andantino e poco rubato. Centers around a, chromatic coloring. Calmando 16th-note figuration effectively used to close the piece. Fast Dance: Allegro vivo, Feroce opening. Piano propels rhythm. One bar of a quick crescendo rushes to the conclusion. M-D.

Emanuele Barbella. *Sonata* I A (F. F. Polnauer—Hug GH10723 1966) 14pp., parts. Allegretto; Andantino e gustoso; Allegro ma non poco. Editorial dynamic marks are placed in parentheses. Delightful and effective period writing. M-D.

Henry Barraud. *Sonatine* (Amphion 102 1943) 28pp., parts. 14 min. Moderato; Aria; Allegro. Piano is handled in a craftsmanlike manner throughout. Piece unfolds logically and efficiently in a mild 20th-century style for both instruments. M-D.

Lubor Bárta. *Sonata* II 1959 (Artia 1962) 39pp., parts. 17 min. Allegro, con larghezza: figurative, contrapuntal section; rich harmonies with some dissonance. Vivace: triplets exploited in various dynamic levels. Adagio: use of pedal provides overtones reinforcement for violin; sweeping gestures. Allegro vivo: metric accents between the hands do not coincide. Driving rhythms. D.

Béla Bartók. *Sonata* 1903 (Dille—Hungarian Academy of Sciences 1964) in a collection entitled *Documenta Bartókiana*. Dille was the curator at the Bartók Archives in Budapest.

——. *Sonata* I (Bo&H 1921; UE) 35 min. Three movements. Extreme tonal and formal freedom. The 2 instruments are completely independent, yet they are forced together by a unique expressive quality. Rough "edges" of the piece must be kept intact. Aggressively dissonant. Freely in C$\sharp$. D.

——. *Sonata* II (Bo&H 1922; UE) 20 min. Two parts. More concentrated and economical than *Sonata* I. Fantasy element permeates this work; individualistic in form. Rhythmic element is vital to this masterpiece. Freely in C. Both

Sonatas (I and II) show Bartók at his closest to Schoenbergian atonality and with leanings toward the 12-tone technique. D.

———. *Rhapsody* I (Bo&H 1928) 10 min. Two movements, slow-fast. Romanian folk music permeates this work and shows Bartók's use of this material in one of his least astringent moods. Also arranged for cello. M-D.

———. *Rhapsody* II (Bo&H 1928, rev. 1944) 12 min. Two movements, slow-fast. Florid, gypsy-like. M-D.

See Y. Hirota, "Past and Present Analytical Perspectives on Bartók's *Sonata for Violin and Piano No. 1* (1922): Intervallic Profiles in the Works of Experimentalism," AM 69 (July-Dec. 1997): 109–19. E. Y. Chung, "Bartók's *Sonata No. 2* for Violin and Piano: Structural Functions of Polymodal Combination," D.M.A. diss., University of Texas, Austin, 2000.

Leslie Bassett. *Sonata* 1959 (CFE) 33pp., parts. Allegro risoluto; Adagio, molto espressivo; Allegro brillante. Freely tonal, dissonant counterpoint, clear textures, deeply felt Adagio movement, superb craft, logical development. D.

———. *Sounds Remembered* (CFP 1975) 28pp., parts. 15 min. This is a homage to Roberto Gerhard (1896–1970), who was a friend of the composer's. Bassett recalls sounds from several of Gerhard's works—"a chord, a quickly-ascending line, an insistent high note, a characteristic manner of working a line. They are Gerhard-like in spirit, not exact quotations, and they serve as the generative basis for the four movements. The work is an unfolding of these key sounds, which become transformed, then return periodically to reassert themselves, as in memory" (from Program Notes). The pianist must stop notes by pressing the finger on the string. Clusters are used. Sections have no meter signature, and the pace remains essentially the same, but with slight freedom. Harmonics, bell-like sonorities, half pedaling, chromatic dramatic gestures. Since a preference for the upper register is noted, the piano should have this register bright and clear. Mature musicianship and pianism required. D.

Stanley Bate. *Sonata* I Op.47 (Lengnick 1951) 35pp., parts. Allegro; Lento; Tempo di marcia; Presto. Neoclassic, highly pianistic. Requires a large span. M-D.

Marion Bauer. *Fantasia quasi una Sonata* Op.18 (GS 1928) 35pp., parts. 16½ min. Moderato romantico; Ben ritmico e vivace; Lento espressivo–Allegro con moto e marcato. Strong post-Romantic writing with many dramatic moments. Always pianistic. D.

John Bavicchi. *Sonata* IV "Fantasy-Sonata on Lithuanian Folk Melodies" (OUP 1974) 15pp., parts. 10 min. Nine Lithuanian folk songs are woven into the 3 movements of this work. The first lines of each are given, along with the English translation. Moderato; Andante; Allegretto. Folk material is treated in a highly dissonant and individual yet effective style. Colorful Bartók-like idiom. D.

Arnold Bax. *Ballade* (Chappell) 8½ min.

———. *Legend* 1915 (Augener; MMP) 9 min.

———. *Mediterranean* (Heifitz—CF B2298).

———. *Sonata* I E 1915 (Chappell 1921, rev. 1945) 52pp., parts. 32 min. Moderate tempo–Idyllic and Serene; Allegro vivace; Moderate tempo–Smooth and Serene. D.

———. *Sonata* II D (Chappell 1923) 34pp., parts. 31 min. Fantasy–Slow and Gloomy; The Grey Dancer in the Twilight–Fast Valse measure; Very broad and Concentrated, but extremely expressive; Allegro feroce. D.

———. *Sonata* III g (Chappell 1929–43) 38pp., parts. 20 min. Moderato; Allegro moderato. D.

Antonio Bazzini. *La Ronde des Lutins: Scherzo Fantastique* Op.25 (Z. Francescatti—IMC 2733 1974; K 02180) 11pp., parts. Delightful piece packed with pyrotechnics and fun for all. M-D.

Mrs. H. H. A./Amy Marcy Cheney Beach. *Sonata* Op.34 a (Schmidt 1899; Da Capo 1986, ISBN 0-306-76250-1, 35pp.; B. Sonies, S. Glickman—Hildegard 9413 1994), parts. 30 min. Allegro moderato; Scherzo–Molto vivace; Largo con dolore; Allegro con fuoco. Strong writing for both instruments in an unabashedly mid-19th-century style. This work is slowly being recognized for its excellent quality. D.

———. *Music for Violin and Piano* (L. B. Plant—Hildegard 1994) 42pp., parts. Includes *Romance* (1893), *La Captive, Berceuse,* and *Mazurka,* Op.40/1–3 (1898), and *Invocation,* Op.50 (1904). These 5 short pieces were written during Beach's most prolific period and exhibit the intense emotional quality typically found in the late 19th century. M-D to D.

James Beale. *Sonata* Op.22 1956 (CFE) 36pp., parts. 23 min. Allegro: "Each bracketed grouping (in the violin) should be slightly hurried in the middle, and held back at the beginning and end, so as to coincide with the piano which remains in tempo" (from the score). Requires large span. Vivace: brusque rhythms and syncopations, octotonic, chromatic, tonal closing in D. Cantabile–Allegretto: added-note technique, free counterpoint, hand crossings, dance characteristics in the Allegretto, Neoclassic. M-D to D.

Arthur Conrad Beck. *Sonatine* (Schott 1928) 23pp., parts. Allegretto; Andantino; Allegro energico. Strongly chromatic. M-D.

———. *Sonatine* II (Heugel 1948) 15pp., parts. Lively rhythmic style, Neoclassic, preference for lush harmonies. M-D.

Jacques Beers. *Sonate* (Donemus 1950) 16pp. In one movement without tempo or dynamic indications. Suffers from an absence of basic performance information. M-D.

Ludwig van Beethoven. While best known as a pianist, Beethoven also studied the violin and knew the instrument well. Although he wrote for this instrumental combination between 1793 and 1812, all but the tenth *Sonata* appeared during his first creative period ending about 1803. The last *Sonata* appeared 9 years later as he entered that period of his life with the greatest emotional upheaval. Indeed, the final *Sonata* is the most sublime and profound, written in an intimate style not seen in the other *Sonatas.* While recordings and performances of the entire *Sonata* cycle are common, 3 enjoy the widest popularity: the "Spring"; the seventh *Sonata* in C Minor; and the famous warhorse nicknamed the "Kreutzer." Sadly, the remaining *Sonatas* do not always get the attention they deserve.

The first 8 *Sonatas* appeared in sets; it is believed that Opp.23 and 24 were initially introduced under the same opus number. Within these groupings, one observes wide character differentiation. Each set has at least one lyrical *Sonata* and one on a more robust scale. The first 4 are in the standard 3-movement form; an added scherzo appears for the first time in the fifth *Sonata.* Theme and variations are common, 2 such sets appearing in slow movements and 2 used as finales. Beethoven was a keen improviser, and those skills become apparent in his variation technique.

———. *Sonaten* Vol.I: Op.12, 23, 24. Vol.II: Op.30, 47, 96 (S. Brandenburg, H.-M. Theopold, M. Rostal—Henle 1975). From the new edition of Beethoven's Complete Works. Preface in German, English, and French describes sources consulted and editorial procedure. Includes valuable footnotes. Separate parts in this Urtext but also practical edition.

———. *Ten Sonatas* (Francescatti—IMC; Auer, Ganz—CF L789; Brodsky, Vogrich—GS L232; Fischer, Kulenkampff—Ric ER2295-6; Dover 1990 as *Complete Violin Sonatas,* ISBN 0-486-26277-4 236pp. no separate violin part). 2 vols.: (Joachim—IMC; Joachim—CFP 3031; Kreisler—Augener 8670; Kreisler—MC; Weiner—Kultura; Lea; Woytowicz—PWM 1973; Oborin, Oistrakh—CFP 1971; Oistrakh—IMC; K 02080-1).

———. *Sonatas for Violin and Piano* (J. Joachim—Dover 1996, ISBN 0-486-29142-1) 88pp., parts. Contains Op.24, 30/3, 47. Selected reprints from *Ten Sonatas* (CFP 3031).

———. *Sonata* Op.12/1 D 1797–98 (Kreisler—Augener). Allegro con brio; Tema con variazioni; Rondo–Allegro. Motivic manipulations, sudden dynamic and emotional contrasts, and unexpected modulations all add excitement. In the first movement there is scarcely a break as the melodic material continually passes in runs of 8ths, 16ths, and triplets between the 2 instruments and the 2 hands of the pianist. *Subito piano* is a prominent feature in the second movement, and the offering of a minor key variation darkens the graceful outlines of the theme. A vivacious and driving rondo is an infectious way to end.

———. *Sonata* Op.12/2 A 1797–98 (Kreisler—Augener). Allegro vivace; Andante più tosto allegretto; Allegro piacévole. The most lyrical *Sonata* of Op.12

is perhaps the most infrequently heard, perhaps due to a violin part often confined to the role of accompanist to the piano. The first movement, for example, opens with a graceful slurred figure in the piano while the violin merely offers a static chordal accompaniment. Much of the movement is made up of similar treatment, creating harmonic stability but not always challenging the violinist. Beethoven makes infrequent use of minor keys in these *Sonatas,* but does take advantage of a minor tonality for the second movement's sorrowful dialogue. The jaunty, concluding rondo is more relaxed and straightforward, with silences occurring in unexpected places. Overall, the work is youthful, lighthearted, and charming.

———. *Sonata* Op.12/3 Eb 1797–98 (Kreisler—Augener). Allegro con spirito; Adagio con molta espressione; Rondo–Allegro molto. Drama is introduced in the largest of the *Sonatas* from Op.12. Opening with concerto-like virtuoso passages, the piano seems to assume a large share of the musical activity in the first movement. Beethoven is at his sentimental best in the second movement. A whirling dance in rondo form, full of energy, gaiety, and frequent dynamic contrasts, brings the work to a thrilling ending, once again dominated by piano writing.

———. *Sonata* Op.23 a 1800–1801 (Kreisler—Augener). Presto; Andante scherzoso più allegretto; Allegro molto. A tarantella rhythm propels us through the passionate opening movement where thematic material is exchanged between the 2 instruments. Syncopations and dotted rhythms in the second movement produce an urgency rarely heard in a slow movement. The third movement, breathless and full of contrasts of color and intensity, finishes with a quiet ending.

———. *Sonata* Op.24 F 1800–1801 "Spring" (Lampe, Schäffer—Henle 162; Auer, Ganz—CF 03385; Brodsky, Vogrich—GS L468; Kreisler—Augener; Kreisler—Schott; Principe, Vitali—Ric ER1475; CFP 4066; Carisch). Allegro; Adagio molto espressivo; Scherzo–Allegro molto; Rondo–Allegro ma non troppo. The *Sonata* is immediately attractive and somewhat more relaxed. The lyrical, yet rhythmically powerful first movement is followed by a pensive and romantically profound slow movement whose statements of the principal theme all occur in the piano. Dancelike in character, the scherzo formed the basis for Schumann's "Soldiers' March," a popular children's work found in his set of piano pieces *Album for the Young.* The work ends in the spirit of Mozart, fresh and confident. This is the movement that earned the nickname "Spring."

———. *Sonata* Op.30/1 A 1802 (Kreisler—Augener). Allegro; Adagio molto espressivo; Allegretto con variazioni. It is hard not to recognize the equality of the instruments in the 3 *Sonatas* of Op.30, composed in 1802 and bearing a dedication to Czar Alexander I of Russia. Even so, they still bear the title "sonatas for piano with violin accompaniment"! This is the most lyrical *Sonata* of the 3 that make up Op.30. The themes of the opening movement contrast sensitivity and restraint with flashes of exuberance, while the tranquility of the beautiful and expressive second movement is punctuated by sudden *sforzandi* and the restlessness of dotted rhythms. The variations are studies in contrast, elegant versus virtuoso, delicate alternating with energetic.

———. *Sonata* Op.30/2 c 1802 (Brodsky, Vogrich—GS L467; Kreisler—Augener). Allegro con brio; Adagio cantabile; Scherzo–Allegro; Finale–Allegro. The most dramatic and extended *Sonata* of Op.30 is anything but relaxing. It is filled with abrupt emotional contrasts, wide dynamic ranges, striking modulations, contrapuntal textures, and lyrical melodies. The work is a testament to the excitement and exuberance of his youth. The piano range is increased, and the violin figurations made more brilliant.

———. *Sonata* Op.30/3 G 1802 (Kreisler—Augener). Allegro assai; Tempo di minuetto; Allegro vivace. The 8th *Sonata,* sometimes nicknamed the "Champagne" *Sonata,* is actually the shortest of the 10. Beethoven's writing is idiomatic for both instruments, but especially the violin with advantageous use of open strings and double stops. Perhaps the finest movement of the 3 is the slow one; a much more relaxed and thoughtful tempo is really needed to successfully achieve the meditative character. The work ends with an amusing and virtuoso-like perpetual motion.

———. *Sonata* Op.47 A 1802–1803 "Kreutzer" (Brandenburg, Theopold, Rostal—Henle 714; Auer, Ganz—CF 03758; Fischer, Kulenkampff—Ric ER 2506; Brodsky, Vogrich—GS L74; Kreisler—Augener; Kreisler—Schott). Adagio sostenuto–Presto; Andante con Variazioni; Presto. Beethoven's most famous chamber work, the "Kreutzer" is by far the most challenging for the performers. Beethoven noted in the title that the work was "written in a highly concerted style, just like a concerto" to be played by 2 instruments without orchestra. The work shows brilliant virtuosity with ample passagework for both instruments. Contrapuntal textures are common, and the violin figurations are much more brilliant than in the earlier *Sonatas.* The piano range is further extended, and the pianistic writing is similar to that found in the Piano Sonatas of his middle period. Originally intended as the finale of Op.31/1, the third movement is a sweeping tarantella in sonata form.

———. *Sonata* Op.96 G 1812 (Kreisler—Augener). Allegro moderato; Scherzo–Allegro; Poco allegretto–Allegro. After the wide range of emotions felt in the "Kreutzer" *Sonata,* Op.96 can seem at times austere and almost reserved; it is representative of Beethoven's later, more introspective period. While it contains some eloquent melodies, Beethoven has held a tight rein on his emotions. There is none of the flamboyance or extravagance of the "Kreutzer." In the opening bars, Beethoven gives us a reminiscence of the very early duo *Sonata* with the violin in an almost nonessential role that could easily have been omitted. While the second movement is expressive, the wonderful dialogue is said in a simple and clear way. There is no fuss. A more relaxed Trio follows the playful, minor-key Scherzo. His final movement again shows his skill and ingenuity in writing a set of variations.

———. *Duos mit Klavier* (Henle 1974) Band 2. viii + 184pp., facsimile. Urtext and practical edition.

———. *Variationen, Rondo, Tänze* WoO 40–42 (Brandenburg, Theopold, Röhrig— Henle 291) 24pp., parts. Early works in the composer's career. *Variations* (12) WoO 40 F 1793, based on "Se vuol ballare" from Mozart's *Nozze di Figaro;* *Rondo* WoO 41 G c.1794; *6 German Dances* WoO 42 F 1796. Available separately from Br&H; *Variations* also from K.

———. *Variations on Folk Songs* Op.105, 107 (A. Raab, K. Schilde—Henle 716 2001, ISMN M-2018-0716-4). For flute or violin. See detailed entry under duos for piano and flute. Op.105 available separately from VU and Br&H. Op.107 available separately from Br&H.

———. *Serenade* Op.41 D for flute or violin and piano (Rampal—IMC). Also arranged by composer from Op.25 for violin and piano (CFP 4663).

———. *Two Romances* Opp.40 & 50 (K 03150).

See Richard A. Kramer, "The Sketches for Beethoven's Violin Sonata, Op.30: History, Transcription, Analysis," Ph.D. diss., Princeton University, 1974, 659pp. Frederick Niecks, "Beethoven's Sonatas for Pianoforte and Violin," MMR 20 (1890): 145–47, 169–71, 193–97. Joseph Szigeti, *The Ten Beethoven Sonatas for Piano and Violin,* ed. Paul Rolland (Urbana, Ill.: American String Teachers Association, 1965). Laurence Daniel Greenfield, "A Study of the Characteristics and Performance Practices of the Beethoven Violin and Piano Sonata, Opus 24, No. 5," M. M. thesis, California State University, 1992. O. Jander, "The *'Kreutzer' Sonata* as Dialogue," *Early Music* 16/1 (1988): 34–49. Suhnne Ahn, "Genre, Style, and Compositional Procedure in Beethoven's 'Kreutzer' Sonata, Opus 47," Ph.D. diss., Harvard University, 1997. (The authors are indebted to Naomi Oliphant for introductory comments and notes on individual *Sonatas.*)

Filippo Carlo Belisi. *Sonata* C (A. Briner—Hug GH10425 1961) 3pp., parts. Preface in German and English. Poco Adagio; Allegro; Tempo di menuetto. This work excels in melodic spontaneity and in a strong sense of form. Fine keyboard realization by the editor. M-D.

Enzo de Bellis. *Sonata* (Zanibon 1948) 40pp., parts. Animato: splashing gestures, changing meters. Calmo, con tristezza: free, lyric, arpeggi coloration. Allegro giojoso: driving, enormous conclusion. D.

Vikter Belyi. *Sonata* 1953 (USSR) 19pp., parts. Allegro moderato; Andante cantabile; Allegro maestoso. Freely tonal but centers around d-D. More 20th-century-sounding than other comparable works from the former Soviet Union. D.

Franz Benda. *Sechs Sonaten* (S. Gerlach, K. Röhrig—Henle 455 1991) 61pp., parts, with basso. 1. A Lee III/114; 2. F Lee III/63; 3. G Lee III/83; 4. E Lee III/47; 5. c Lee III/9; 6. B♭ Lee III/130. Benda's *Sonatas* represent a transition from Baroque to Classical style and provide a fine documentation of the musical culture from which the great Viennese Sonata style emerged. Numbering uses Douglas A. Lee's *Franz Benda (1709–1786). A Thematic Catalogue of His Works.* Tasteful realization offers flexibility. Preface and critical notes in German, French, and English. M-D.

——. *Four Sonatas* (Štědroň—Artia 1962) MAB57.

——. *Sonata* VIII a (Jensen—Augener 7433).

——. *Sonata* XXVI (Chaumont—Senart 5396).

——. *Sonata* XXXI (Chaumont—Senart 5402 1925) 11pp., parts. Three movements, fast-slow-fast.

——. *Sonata* G (Ric R747).

——. *Sonata* F (CFP 3226 1909). See Arnold Schering, ed., *Alte Meister des Violinspiels.*

——. Adagio un poco Andante from *Sonata* A, in simple notation and 2 embellished versions of the violin part provided by the composer, in Ferand, *Improvisation,* a volume in the *Anthology of Music* series. For complete *Sonata* in facsimile with unrealized figured bass, see Hans-Peter Schmitz, *Kunst der Verzierung im 18. Jahrhundert: Instrumentale und vokale Musizierpraxis in Beispielen,* 2nd ed. (Kassel: Bärenreiter, 1965). For the complete *Sonata* with realization see the last of the *Four Sonatas* in MAB 57, listed above.

Georg Benda. *Sonata* G. See detailed entry under duos for piano and flute.

Arthur Benjamin. *Five Negro Spirituals* (Primrose—Bo&H).

——. *Sonatina* b (OUP). A 3-movement work rising to considerable heights of technique and expression. Final movement, a rondo, is compact and well knit with lively rhythms and melodic charm. Highly representative of the composer. M-D.

George Benjamin. *Sonata* 1976–77 (Faber Music 1998, ISBN 0-571-51758-7) 40pp., parts. 23 min. Composed at the age of 17 while studying with Messiaen. Molto adagio; Vivace; Adagio rubato (Tempo 1). The *Sonata* explores extremes of tempo and dynamics, incorporating harmonics, muted strings, and hints of birdsong. Frequently changes meters in a blend of stylistic influences not yet shaped into one distinctive voice. D.

Robert Russell Bennett. *A Song Sonata* (Chappell 1958) 43pp., parts. Quiet and Philosophic; Same tempo, but belligerent; Slow and lovely; Madly Dancing; Gracefully strolling. Movement titles give clue to moods. Mildly 20th-century with more emphasis on the melodic side. M-D.

Pascal Bentoiu. *Sonata* Op.14 (Editura Muzicala a Uniunii Compozitorilor din R. P. R. 1964) 21pp., parts. Lento, un poco rubato; Animato. Second movement uses white- and black-key clusters, flexible meters, glissandi, and displays a preference for harmonic 7ths and 9ths. M-D to D.

Arthur Berger. *Duo* I (ACA 1948) 13 min. One movement in 5 sections. Neoclassic in Stravinsky style, pandiatonic with chromatic elements. Main thematic material consists of a declamatory line and a scherzo-like series that bounces around frantically. The sonorous relation of the 2 instruments is carefully matched. Irregular-length ostinatos unfold during a tight development. A large piece for both instruments. D.

——. *Duo* II (ACA 1950) 12 min. Syncopated rhythms, disjunct melodic lines, and atonal harmonies in a sophisticated synthesis. A fine sense of taste and intellect comes through. Fluent and lyrical in Stravinsky's Neoclassicism. D.

Wilhelm Georg Berger. *Sonata* (Editura Muzicala 1963) 50pp., parts. Agitato: g, SA, freely tonal, 19th-century pianistic idioms in a more contemporary harmonic language. Broad sweeping gestures, frequent modulation. Larghetto: C pedal point, piano sustains but has some of its own melodic line against violin arpeggi. Allegro giocoso: B♭, strong rhythmic dance feeling, bitonal, big dramatic closing. D.

Rudolph Bergh. *Sonata* Op.20 (Birnbach 1905) 37pp., parts. Poco adagio–allegro risoluto; Allegretto desi deroso e mesto, molto moderato; Molto appassionato, come cercando invano. In Brahms idiom. D.

Charles de Bériot. *12 Airs Variés* (GS), parts. Published separately: 5 Op.7 E; 6 Op.12 A; 7 Op.15 E. Favors violin but requires skilled pianist. M-D.

Lennox Berkeley. *Sonatina* Op.17 A (JWC 1945) 17pp., parts. 14 min. Limpid writing with effective thematic treatment. Moderato; Lento; Allegretto (theme and 5 variations plus coda). M-D.

——. *Elegy* Op.32/2 A (JWC) 3 min.

——. *Toccata* Op.33/3 e (JWC) 2 min.

——. *Sonata* II D (JWC 1934) 25pp., parts. 15½ min. Allegro risoluto; Andante; Rondo–Allegro moderato. D.

Herman Berlinski. *Sonata* d (CFE 1949) 16 min. First movement is one of tempestuous expression and great rhythmic drive. The scherzo is a poignantly melodic trio. D.

Robert Bernard. *Sonata* D (Durand 1927) 45pp., parts. Allegro moderato: 14-bar piano introduction, Ravel's influence. Largo: 15-bar piano interlude. Très animé: dancelike, 20-bar piano interlude. More like a piano sonata. Clear textures and some delightful and charming writing. D, especially for piano.

Gérard Bertouille. *Sonata* I 1936 (CeBeDeM 1958) 37pp., parts. 18 min. Maestoso; Poco adagio; Allegro con fuoco. Chromatic, varied pianistic figurations.

————. *Sonata* III (CeBeDeM 1962) 11pp., parts. 13 min.

————. *Sonata* IV (CeBeDeM 1954).

Franz Berwald. *Duo* (GM 1946) Rev. by Sven Kjellström. 35pp., parts. Transparent form with clearly marked sections, some national traits, contrapuntal writing between parts, ingenious rhythms: Romantic harmonic tendencies including some surprising and bizarre effects. M-D to D.

Thomas Beversdorf. *Sonata* 1965 (ST 1967) 32pp., parts. Andantino ma non tanto: SA, freely tonal, black-key glissandi, large span required, interval of minor 9th plays important role. Attacca subito Andante: G pedal point, flowing, chromatic, broken octaves, sustained closing. Allegro con brio: syncopated idea; after hesitation finally gets going; repeated 16th notes in alternation of hands; sweeping scales; long trills; left-hand glissandi on white keys, right-hand on black keys. Sizzling conclusion punctuated by widely spread chords. D.

Philip Bezanson. *Sonata* II (CFE) 31pp., parts. Maestoso–Allegro molto: chordal introduction, chromatic, many 16th notes, octotonic, fast harmonic rhythm, very "busy." Intermezzo: octotonic and chromatic, thinner textures in outer parts. Vivace: $\frac{7}{8}$, toccata-like. Similarity of mood in all movements. D.

Günter Bialas. *Sonata Piccola* (Br 3471 1959) 23pp., parts. 13 min. Allegro vivo; Romanza; Kleiner Walzer; Nachtstück; Rondo. Thin textures, freely tonal, Neoclassic. $\frac{4}{8}$ alternates with $\frac{5}{8}$ in Allegro vivo, imitation in the Kleiner Walzer and Rondo. M-D.

Heinrich Ignaz Fran von Biber. *Fifteen Mysteries* (Rietz—UE 7283-84, 2 vols.; G. Lenzewski—Wilhelmiana 1954, 3 vols.). These are the *Mystery* or *Rosary Sonatas* intended to honor 15 sacred mysteries of the life of Christ and Mary. Each *Sonata* has a small engraving at the beginning depicting a New Testament scene. 1. The Annunciation of the Birth of Christ, 2. Mary Visits Elizabeth, 3. The Adoration of the Shepherds, 4. The Presentation of Christ in the Temple, 5. The Twelve-Year-Old Jesus in the Temple, 6. Christ on the Mount of Olives, 7. The Flagellation of Christ, 8. The Crowning with Thorns, 9. The Climbing of Calvary, 10. The Crucifixion, 11. The Resurrection of Christ, 12. The Ascent of Christ to Heaven, 13. The Coming of the Holy Ghost, 14. The Ascent of Mary to Heaven, 15. The Crowning of Mary, 16. An apocryphal scene, depicting the child Jesus, hand in hand with an angel, is represented by an extended Passacaglia for solo violin. *Sonatas* 14, 15, and 16 are the longest works. Each *Sonata* is made up of several short movements separated by short breaks. No.16 is one continuous movement. See VKDR, I: pp.26–38 for a discussion of the scordatura tunings Biber requested.

————. *Acht Violinsonaten* (G. Adler—DTOe Jahrgang V/2, Band 11).

————. *Sixteen Sonatas* (K 09194).

———. *Surrexit Christus hodie* from *Mysterien* Sonata No.11 in translated (non-scordatura) version, in HAM II, No.238.

———. *Sonata* c (CFP 4344). From *Acht (8) Violinsonaten.*

John Biggs. *Dialogue and Fugue* (Consort Press 1963) 18pp., parts. 8 min. Chromatic motifs contrast with open 5ths. A more sustained mid-section exploits lower register of the piano. Motif returns but subject is inverted, augmented, and brought to an exhilarating conclusion. Dialogue idea carefully worked out. M-D.

Henk Bijvanck. *Sonata* ca.1968 (Donemus 1968) 41pp., parts. Allegro non troppo; Andante con molto; Allegretto grazioso; Finale–Molto vivace. Conventional writing using traditional harmonic techniques in slightly Neoclassic mode. Last completed work by Bijvanck. M-D.

Christlieb Siegmund Binder. *Sonata* G (C. Hausswald—HM 62) 18pp., parts. Allegro; Adagio; Tempo di minuetto. Continuous flowing and expressive lines, keyboard part of equal interest. M-D.

Gordon Binkerd. *Sonata* 1974 (Bo&H). A conservative idiom, fine craftsmanship, strong ideas. Very effective first movement and a lively scherzo. Large-scale retrogradation is found in the first and third movements. Binkerd has something to say, and he says it eloquently in this work. D.

Johann Adam Birkenstock. *Sonata* Op.1/2 B♭ (Woehl—Nag). Cello optional.

———. *Sonata* Op.1/3 (M. Ettinger—CFP 4225) 4pp., parts. The Allegro movement only. A sunny SA movement. M-D.

———. *Sonata* Op.1/4 E (Polnauer—Schott). Cello optional.

———. *Sonata* e (Ruf—Schott). Cello optional.

———. *Sonata* e (J. Salmon—Ric 1918) 14pp., parts. Adagio; Courante; Largo; Gigue. A good deal of filling-in by the editor. M-D.

Chester Biscardi. *Tartini* 1972 (Merion 2000) 6pp., parts. 7 min. "*Tartini* ... employs a 12-tone row constructed from the melodies which make up the 'Allegro assai' movement of Giuseppe Tartini's *'Devil's Trill' Sonata*. This row in turn was used to create, along with melodic fragments from Tartini's work, the brief melodies and harmonies found in this piece. The 'fast-slow-fast' structure of this one-movement work is a miniature representation of the original and more expansive three-movement sonata" (from Program Notes). Twelve-tone row introduced in opening pitches. Allegro fantastico: abrupt; explosive; mixed meters; chordal slow section. D.

Marcel Bitsch. *Sonate* (Leduc 1959) 9pp., parts. One movement, contrasting tempos, sections, and moods. Mildly 20th-century. M-D.

Martino Bitti. *Sonata* c (H. Ruf—Schott OBB38 1997, ISMN M-001-11388-5) 11pp., parts, with basso. For oboe or violin. See detailed entry under duos for piano and oboe.

Boris Blacher. *Sonate* Op.18, 1941 (Bo&Bo 1947) 15pp., parts. Neoclassic, clear textures and form, terse and straightforward writing. M-D.

Easley Blackwood. *Sonata* Op.7 1960 (GS) 36pp., parts. Allegro rigoroso; Adagio; Allegro molto. Expansive writing, rich sonorities. D.
——. *Sonata* II (Library of Congress 1975). Three movements. Freely tonal; fairly straightforward, rhythmically speaking; and convincing. Opening movement strongest and most coherent of the 3. D.

Ernest Bloch. *Sonata* I 1920 (GS) 63pp., parts. 32 min. Agitato; Molto quieto; Moderato. More tightly constructed than *Sonata* II, all 3 movements interwoven thematically. When the material appears to be exhausted the work closes quietly. Proportions are similar to Bloch's *Piano Quintet.* D.
——. *Baal Shem* (Three Pictures of Chassidic Life) 1923 (CF 1924), parts. Original version. Published separately: 1. Vidu (Contrition; B1856); 2. Nigun (Improvisation; B1857); 3. Simchas Torah (Rejoicing; B1858). Requires experienced performers and much flexibility. M-D to D.
——. *Poème Mystique* (*Sonata* II) 1924 (Leuckart 1925) 31pp., parts. 22 min. Poetic style, freely rhapsodic, pedal points, open 5ths, modal melodies, bitonal spots but always euphonious. D.
——. *Mélodie* (CF 1924) 7pp., parts. Moderato. A pleasant melody cast in ternary form suitable for many occasions. Int.
——. *Music for Violin and Piano* (CF 2001). Includes *Baal Shem, Abodah, Mélodie,* and *Nuit Exotique.*

Luigi Boccherini. *Six Sonatas* Op.5 (E. Polo—Societă Anonima Notari 1919; A. Pasetti—Ut Orpheus 1998). B♭, C, B♭, D, g, E♭. Polo's greatly edited edition appears in Vol.4 of *I Classical Musicali Italiana.* Pasetti's edition is essentially Urtext. Sonatas are published separated by Ut Orpheus.
——. *Sonata* Op.5/3 B♭ (Borholz—CFP).
——. *Sonata* (Carisch).
——. *Sonata* G.570 E♭ (E. Bonelli—Zanibon 3555 1944) 14pp., parts. Allegro; Adagio; Allegro assai. Rather freely arranged, editorially heavy-handed. M-D.

Anatolii Vasilevich Bogatyrev. *Sonata* I Op.16 (USSR 1955) 62pp., parts. Allegro con fuoco; Largo; Allegretto. Effective writing in a late-19th-century idiom. Brahmsian, dark, foreboding in spots. D.

Rob du Bois. *Ad Libitum* 1965 (Donemus 1966) 7pp., parts. Indeterminate techniques with detailed performance indications. M-D.
——. *Seven Little Pieces* 1965 (Donemus 1971) 7pp., parts. Untitled pieces of

one to two pages with simply metronomic markings. Most are slow with frequent tempo changes. All determinate writing. M-D.

——. *Sonate* 1980 (Donemus 1980) 18pp., parts. 17½ min. Adagio–Allegro ma non troppo; Adagio molto; Scherzo–Molto allegro; Maestoso–Presto. Dramatic with extensive pedal effects in homophonic passages. Retreats from earlier experimentation. M-D.

René de Boisdeffre. *Sonata* I Op.12 f♯ (Hamelle) 45pp., parts. Allegro; Allegretto scherzando; Andante con moto; Final–Allegro vivace.

——. *Sonata* II Op.50 e (Hamelle) 45pp., parts. Allegro ma non troppo; Allegro grazioso; Lento e espressivo; Allegro con brio.

——. *Sonata* III Op.67 G (Hamelle) 43pp., parts. Allegro ma non troppo; Scherzando; Andante; Finale–Allegro vivace.

——. *Berceuse* Op.34 (K 9803). See detailed entry under duos for piano and viola.

Sonatas are written in late Romantic style, with broad and expansive gestures and long, unwinding themes. Full resources of the piano are realized. All 3 *Sonatas* D.

William Bolcom. *First Sonata* 1956, rev.1984 (EBM 1993, ISBN 0-634-00106-X) 46pp., parts. 19 min. This youthful work, conceived in 3 programmatic movements, bubbles with energy and rhythmic verve, foreshadowing the eclectic tastes of its composer which would soon become characteristic of his works. I. Legend: a lengthy movement with imitative ideas expressed lyrically in a wide range of textures and colors. II. Nocturne: reflective, delicate treatment of instruments with harmonics and special effects; *p* or softer in all except five measures. III. Quasi-Variations: Scenes from a Young Life: theme introduced by piano in chordal texture followed by variation-like treatment; restless with 25 tempo changes. The revised version eliminates over 200 measures from the original, mostly in the last movement. D.

——. *Duo Fantasy* 1973 (EBM) 10 min. An imaginative one-movement work suggesting aimlessness in its repetitive pursuits and contrasting sections. A musical casserole. Bolcom described it some 10 years later as "in the classic fantasy-form . . . I liken my *Duo Fantasy* to a passage through the layers of a musical onion. The outer layer, tightly organized on a four-note cell, gives way to a rhapsodic and more tonal passage. Another surprise leads us into a $\frac{3}{16}$ scherzoso section, which is succeeded by what is perhaps the 'onion's' center— a simple little waltz in E flat. Is the following ragtime meant as a contrasting section in the middle of the waltz, or is it part of the journey outward, through the other side of the 'onion' toward the end of the piece? All I know is that suddenly we come to the outer layer again, and it is time to leave" (by the Composer; liner notes for "William Bolcom: Second Sonata/Duo Fantasy/ Graceful Ghost," Nonesuch LP 79058, 1983). D.

——. *Second Sonata* 1978 (EBM) 16 min. "The first movement, 'Summer

Dreams,' is built on a modified blues format, with a contrasting middle section [à la Messiaen]. 'Brutal, fast,' which succeeds it, is constructed out of a small intervallic cell, and the following 'Adagio,' free and recitative in style, ends with a hymnlike passage, *segue*-ing directly into the final movement, 'In Memory of Joe Venuti'" (Composer's Notes on recording identified above). Venuti was a jazz violinist trained in classical technique. The *Sonata* is a study in contrast, serene and contemplative at times and rugged with jagged edges at others. It shows Bolcom's love for the blues with fun, relaxing episodes sure to win all audiences. M-D to D.

————. *Graceful Ghost* (Concert Variation) 1979 (EBM) 5 min. A paraphrased setting of Bolcom's famous rag for solo piano (which in itself was an arrangement from a Suite for clarinet, violin, and piano). Additionally influenced by Kreisler's famous adaptations for violin and piano. Bolcom intended it to be used as an encore. M-D.

————. *Third Sonata* (Sonata Stramba) 1992 (EBM 1994) 47pp., parts. 17 min. A piacere, drammatico–Allegro con fuoco; Andante; Like a shiver; Moderato, risoluto, all' arabesca. In stark contrast to the first 2 *Sonatas,* the range and depth of emotional and dramatic qualities in the Third reveal a new attitude toward the instruments and their capabilities. In every aspect of the work, whether from the opening a piacere and its subsequent march, to the detailed Andante and ensuing study of articulation in "Like a shiver," or the syncopated and resolved arabesque, Bolcom proceeds through a whirlwind of technical demands with unparalleled rhythmic drive and insistence. A colossal work requiring experienced performers. D.

————. *Fourth Sonata* 1994 (EBM 1998) 42pp., parts. 14 min. Composed for the 50th birthday of violinist Henry Rubin (who gave its premiere with the composer at the piano), Bolcom retreats herein to familiar forms of composition using both strong and harsh tonalities with melodies contrasted by angular and lyric qualities. Allegro brillante: modified SA; traces of Messiaen's influence; highly dramatic. White Night: (prefaced) "A fitful sleeper recalls an early tune, hoping it will soothe him to sleep. Instead it keeps him awake"; marked Slow–Faster, nervous–Grazioso, flowing and flexible; uses sustained chords in A of ternary form and lyric melody in B. Arabesque–Molto moderato: octotonic; special effects in violin. Jota–Vivo, risoluto: $\frac{3}{8}$; added-note and quartal chords; detailed articulation; rapid contrasts of dynamics; ends *fffz*. D.

Bolcom's love for the violin stems from seeing and hearing his grandfather's imitation Stradivarius and from friendships with violinists Gene Nastri and Sergiu Luca. Bolcom has become one of the most significant composers for the piano and violin of the 20th century.

Jacques Bondon. *Sonatine d'Eté* (EMT 1958) 15pp., parts. Promenade; Ronde Champêtre. Highly chromatic, flowing. Last movement has a special sprightly bounce made even more effective by some sudden dynamic changes. M-D.

Francesco Antonio Bonporti. *Ten Inventions* Op.10 "La Pace" (Giegling—Br HM 44, 45, 77) 3 vols. Cello optional. Vol.I: Inventions A, b, F. Vol.II: Inventions g, B♭, c. Vol.III: Inventions D, e, A, E.

———. *Four Inventions* (Grueters—CFP 2957). Cello optional.

———. *Sonata* Op.10/8 e (Barbian—Carisch).

Jo van den Booren. *Sonatine* I Op.47 1984 (Donemus 1984) 19pp., parts. 10 min. Allegretto; Largo; Allegro con brio. M-D.

———. *Sonata* I Op.75 1989 (Donemus 1992) 19pp., parts. 12 min. In one movement commencing Adagio and gradually accelerating with more motion. M-D.

———. *Sonata* II Op.83 1991–92 (Donemus 1992) 63pp., parts. 24 min. Andante; Scherzo; Adagio; Rondo–Allegro. A large-scale work with delectable melodies in a Neoclassic idiom. M-D.

Modesta Bor. *Sonata* 1963 (Universidad Central de Venezuela 1967) 44pp., parts. Allegro moderato; Andantino; Rondo–Allegro deciso. Mildly 20th-century, extensive first movement, some South American rhythms slightly suggested, freely tonal at times. M-D.

Luigi Borghi. *Sonata* a (Carisch).

———. *Sonata* A (Bonelli—Zanibon).

———. *Sonata* A (C. Barison—Carisch 1965) 16pp., parts. Allegro moderato; Adagio; Allegro. Pleasant and attractive. Int. to M-D.

———. *Sonata* E (Carisch).

———. *Sonata* IV Op.4 g (Jensen—Augener 7414).

———. *Sonata* f♯ (J. Salmon—Ric R740) 13pp., parts. Allegro brillante; Adagio; Allegretto grazioso. Piano part is effective but of secondary importance. M-D.

Pavel Bořkovec. *Sonata* 1934 (Panton 1973) 42pp., parts.

———. *Sonata* II 1956 (Artia 1959) 47pp., parts. 21 min. Poco allegro; Adagio; Allegro giusto; Grave–Agitato assai. Freely tonal; some changing meters; dance element present, especially in first and third movements. Broad range of pianistic devices used. Tonal D conclusion. D.

Siegfried Borris. *Sonate* II Op.30/2 (Sirius).

———. *Sonate* III Op.30/3 (Sirius).

———. *Sonatine* Op.65/2 (Sirius).

Sergei Bortkiewicz. *Sonata* Op.26 g (Simrock 1924) 39pp., parts. Sostenuto–Allegro dramatico; Andante; Allegro vivace e con brio. Big post-Romantic sounds and gestures but still rather effective with performers who readily identify with this idiom. D.

Roger Boutry. *Sonate* (Sal 1966) 35pp., parts. 20 min. Difficult ensemble and technical problems. Allegro con fuoco: opening marcato theme treated by both instruments, flexible meters, large span required. Adagio: treated in variation form with theme at opening and closing of the movement. Allegro vivace: spread out over entire keyboard, rhythmic motif developed, freely tonal with numerous bitonal implications, prestissimo coda. D.

York Bowen. *Sonata* Op.112 e (JWC 1946) 37pp., parts. 22 min. Maestoso con fuoco: SA, dramatic chordal opening interspersed with chromatic scalar passages, leads directly to Allegro commodo, with syncopated left-hand subject accompanied with right-hand tremolo, broken chordal figures in alternating hands, octotonic. Romantic second idea, 3 with 2, animated coda. Lento: recitative-like, double trills, arpeggi figuration, chromatic chords. Finale: quick skips, alternating contrary and parallel chords, hemiola, strong rhythms, arpeggi, concludes with a flourish. Very pianistic. M-D.

Johannes Brahms. Brahms's 3 *Sonatas* for piano and violin (notice priority given to piano by listing it first) have not yet been exceeded for ingenuity in combining the 2 instruments. *Sonata* I Op.78 G exhibits masterly and effective workmanship. A highly successful coherence is obtained by the thematic relationship between the first and last movements. *Sonata* II Op.100 A displays a more reflective mood. The piano is used effectively to suggest fragments of a theme after the theme has been exposed by the violin. *Sonata* III Op.108 d contains unusual rhythmic features and forceful use of pedal point. The slow movement is outstanding for its directness of expression.

————. *Sonaten* (H. O. Hiekel, H. M. Theopold, K. Röhrig—Henle 1967) rev. ed. Performance directions and notes. Excellent critical and practical edition. This edition also includes *Scherzo* c.

————. *Sonatas* (G. Kehr, J. Demus—VU). Contains a Preface, performance directions, and critical notes. Available separately.

————. *Complete Sonatas for Violin and Piano* (L. Auer, R. Ganz—Dover 1996, ISBN 0-486-29312-2) 88p., parts. Composite reprint of individual *Sonatas* published separately by CF.

————. *Sonatas* (IMC).

Available separately: Sonata Op.78 (Flesch, Schnabel—CFP 03715; Auer, Ganz— CF 03772; Corti—Ric ER1444; Br&H; Schnirlin—Schott; Kneisel, Bauer— GS L1310; Jacobsen—Augener 4761; K). Sonata Op.100 (same as listed for Op.78). Sonata Op.108 (same as listed for Op.78).

————. *F.A.E. (Frei aber einsam) Sonata* (Henle; CFP 6083; Br&H; Draheim— Heinrichshofen 2469 1999, ISMN M-2044-2469-6). This work, in honor of Joseph Joachim, was written by 3 composers: Allegro a by Albert Dietrich; Intermezzo F by Robert Schumann; Allegro (scherzo) c by Brahms; Finale a by Robert Schumann. FAE (*Frei aber einsam*—"Free, yet lonely") is the basic thematic material of the *Sonata* except for the third movement. Brahms did not use the FAE idea.

See Margaret Anne Notley, "Brahms's Chamber-Music Summer of 1886: A Study of Opera 99, 100, 101, and 108," Ph.D. diss., Yale University, 1992.

Helmut Bräutigam. *Sonate* Op.23 (Br&H 1951) 31pp., parts. Mit schwung: SA, freely tonal but centers around D. Langsam: ostinato-like treatment. Gemächlich: based on hunting song "O du wunderschöner Waldmann," alternating $\frac{4}{4}$, $\frac{3}{4}$, $\frac{2}{4}$ adds much bounce and freedom. D.

Jan Bresser. *Sonata* g (Donemus 426 1966) 51pp., parts. Allegro molto vivace ed appassionato; Allegretto ma non troppo (7 variations); Interludium; Allegro molto vivace e energico. Post-Romantic style, requires large span, Honegger influence, varied pianistic idioms and techniques. D.

Frank Bridge. *Sonata* 1932 (Augener) 45pp., parts. 23½ min. One large movement. Large span required for early-20th-century view of pianistic techniques. Expressive. D.

──────. *Four Short Pieces* 1912 (MMP) 12pp., parts. Meditation; Spring Song; Lullaby; Country Dance. Unabashedly influenced by mid-19th-century melodic and harmonic practices. Cute encore pieces without virtuosic demands. M-D.

Benjamin Britten. *Suite* Op.6 (Bo&H 1935). Cheerful, full of much virtuosity and invention. March; Moto perpetuo; Lullaby; Waltz. Brief introduction precedes March and is alluded to in Waltz. M-D to D.

──────. *Gemini Variations* Op.73 (Faber F014 1965). Quartet for 2 or 4 players for violin, flute, and piano 4-hands. If 2 players are used, it is performed by flute and piano or by violin and piano. Twelve variations and fugue on Epigram (musical piece) by Kodály. M-D.

František Brož. *Sonata* (Artia 1956) 48pp., parts. 20 min. Allegro moderato; Scherzo–Presto; Tema con (6) variazioni. Basically tonal around d-D, exploits resources of the piano in late-19th-century idioms. D.

Adolf Brunner. *Sonate* (Br 2691 1952) 32pp., parts. Neoclassic style. Allegro: numerous tempo changes. Adagio: much interplay between instruments. Allegro assai: "pressing on" feeling, wide chordal skips, fugal. D.

Michel Brusselmans. *Sonate* (Senart 1920) 34pp., parts. Modéré–Allegro non troppo; Lent; Vif. Romantic harmonies and melodies. Pianistic figuration explores most of keyboard. D.

Willy Burkhard. *Sonatine* Op.45 (Schott 1937) 11pp., parts. Allegro moderato: Poco adagio; Rondo–Allegretto. Outer movements are flowing and dancelike while the Poco adagio is in recitative style and more free in construction. M-D.

──────. *Sonata* Op.78 (Br 1949) 36pp., parts. Neoclassic style. Moderato, poco sostenuto; Lento; Intermezzo; Finale–Allegretto grazioso. Good octave technique required in Intermezzo. Five-eight meter and hemiola in Finale are especially effective. D.

Cecil Burleigh. *Sonata* Op.29 "From the Life of St. Paul" (CF 1926) 29pp., parts. With power and determination; With repose; Impetuously–threateningly. Colorful if somewhat dated. Programmatic concepts are self-evident. D.

Geoffrey Bush. *Sonata* (Augener 1959) 42pp., parts. One large movement with tempo and mood contrasts. Colorful writing with varied and extended 19th-century pianistic idioms and techniques. D.

Ferruccio Busoni. *Sonata* Op.29 e ca.1889 (Br&H; Rahter 1891) 39pp., parts. 25 min. Allegro deciso; Molto sostenuto; Allegro molto e deciso. This is a fine orthodox work with an intelligent design, but it is not a masterpiece. It fulfills all academic standards and is strongly influenced by Beethoven and Brahms. All elements appear to be exact, ordered, and precise. D.
——. *Sonata* Op.36a e 1898 (Br&H) 51pp., parts. 28 min. In one large movement with 4 contrasting sections. Written in a late-Romantic harmony, Neoclassic style, an embrace-everything type of piece. Reminiscent of Brahms in thematic materials and concludes with 9 variations in mixed Classical style on the Bach chorale "Wie wohl ist mir." Boldly dramatic, often impassioned writing. D.
——. *Variations on a Minnesinger Lied from the 13th Century* Op.22 (J. Draheim —Br&H 8686 1999) 18pp., parts. AABA design for theme in F as used by Busoni in chordal setting. Nine variations alternating between parallel major and minor keys in Classically based tonal setting. D.
——. *Albumblatt* e (MMP) 3pp., parts. For flute or violin. See detailed entry under duos for flute and piano.

Thomas Byström. *Trois Sonates* Op.1 (A. Ignatius—Fazer 1970). Editorial additions in parentheses. Preface in Finnish, German, and English. Bright and melodious, more like Sonatinas, in classic fluent style. Treatment of harmony and rhythm is often surprisingly original and stimulating. M-D. *Sonata* I B♭ 19pp., parts. Allegro; Adagio; Allegro vivace. *Sonata* II g 21pp., parts. Adagio–Allegro; Menuetto; Allegro. *Sonata* III E♭ 26pp., parts. Allegro; Adagio; Rondo.

Charles Wakefield Cadman. *Sonata* G (JF 1932) 36pp., parts. Allegretto con spirito (quasi recitativo); Andante grazioso; Allegro animato. Sweeping 19th-century-like gestures and pianistic techniques. Opening idea of first movement returns at conclusion of last movement. Mainly lyric but small influences of early-20th-century harmony creep in from time to time. D.

John Cage. *Nocturne* (CFP 1947) Shows Cage can write real music! According to Nicholas Slonimsky (*High Fidelity,* November 1975, p. 134) Cage said the purpose of this piece is "to dissolve the difference between string and piano sounds." Coloristic music before it was in fashion! M-D.

Hector Campos-Parsi. *Sonatina* II 1953 (PIC 1964) 27pp., parts. Vivo; Adagio; Comodo e gracioso. Freely tonal, centers around D. Adagio is more contrapuntally oriented. Wide skips, glissandi in last movement, clear textures throughout. Piano is handled as an equal. M-D.

John Alden Carpenter. *Sonata* G 1911 (GS 1913) 35pp., parts. Larghetto: widely spread figuration, sonorous arpeggi chords, chromatic inner voices; mood of repose is broken twice by greater intensity. Allegro: marcato driving theme; poco meno mosso section Db, lyric and dolce; tempo I and mood return, sonorous rolled chords, vivo ending; a happy contrast to the Larghetto. Largo mistico: contrasting mid-section, poco più mosso Eb; influence of Grieg and Franck. Presto giocoso: harmonic 4ths are important for piano part; tempo, key, and mood changes are numerous: con molto brio, largo, quasi ad lib, come cadenza, molto adagio, lento, molto più mosso, moderato; Appassionato conclusion dies away to *p* closing. Solid piece for both instruments. M-D to D.

Adam Carse. *Sonata* c (Augener 1921) 31pp., parts. Allegro appassionata; Andante; Allegro molto. Craftsmanlike writing for both instruments. Nineteenth-century idioms. M-D.
——. *Sonatina* A (Augener 11308).
——. *Sonatina* D (Augener 11306).
——. *Sonatina* g (Augener 11307).

Elliott Carter. *Duo* 1974 (AMP 7547 1976) 50pp., parts. "The composition draws its basic character primarily from the contrast between the sounds made by stroking the violin with a bow, that can be sensitively controlled during their duration and the sounds made by striking the piano that, once produced, die away and can only be controlled by being cut short. Deriving its various moods and its dramatic interplay from this contrast of stroking and striking—of variously inflected sounds as opposed to those that invariably fade away—the work starts with the violin's rugged recitative projected against an impassive background of slow piano sonorities. It continues with a series of episodes, each emerging from previously stated material—variations of the opening which present the violin as constantly changing in character while the piano follows its own path more systematically and regularly. This contrast between the two instruments is maintained throughout, while many different moods are expressed, some in quick succession, others in a more leisurely way" (Note from the score). The piano opens the work with long notes, while the violin has much activity. The roles alternate with aggression and withdrawal. Complete virtuosity required of both performers. Pointillistic, harmonics, unusual pedal effects, requires a large span, highly organized, uncompromisingly hewn timbres. D.

Robert Casadesus. *Sonata* II Op.34 (Durand 1950) 40pp., parts. Dedicated to Zino Francescatti. Allegro vivo; Allegretto a capriccio; Adagio; Allegro molto.

Piano part is beautifully laid out. Mildly 20th-century, easy to read, spread out on page. Excellent pianism required. Ensemble problems take care of themselves. A Neoclassic, peppery, and somewhat eclectic work. D.

Gaspar Cassado. *Sonata* 1926 (UE 8567) 24pp., parts. Fantaisie; Pastorale; Finale (dans le style populaire)–Allegro risoluto. Chromatic idiom, post-Romantic style. Cassado was a virtuoso cellist. D.

Dario Castello. *Two Sonatas* (F. Cerha—Dob 1965) 16pp., parts. No.37 in DM. Castello was concertmaster at St. Mark's in Venice around 1629. He wrote 2 books of "Sonate Concertate in stilo moderno" printed in 1621 and 1629. These 2 *Sonatas* are from the second book and display a soloistic and virtuoso spirit. The slow expressive sections look far into the future. Fast and slow tempos alternate in sections. Int. to M-D.

Mario Castelnuovo-Tedesco. *Concerto Italiano* g (Ric 119998).
——. *Humoresque on the Name of Tossy Spivakovsky* Op.70/81 1954 (Gen 1975) 11pp., parts. Clever handling of the letters assigned to specific pitches; freely tonal in a Romantic harmonic vocabulary. Name motto tossed between both instruments, quartal harmony, long lines in piano, large span required, parallel chords, glissando and pizzicato finish. M-D.
——. *Sonata—quasi una Fantasia* 1929 (Ric 1930) 36pp., parts. Prologo; Intermezzo–vivace e danzante; Epilogo. Colorful, even picturesque writing. Most of keyboard utilized. A vivid imagination displayed here. D.

René de Castéra. *Sonate* Op.13 e 1910 (Rouart, Lerolle) 48pp., parts. Modéré; Assez lent; Modéré. A large work with a short introduction to the opening movement. Second movement is a Lied in 5 sections based on a Basque folk song. The finale is a Sonata-rondo using elastic and varied rhythms. Post-Romantic techniques used throughout. Piano is given much prominence and displays a broad spectrum of pianistic styles. D.

Jacques Castérède. *Sonata* (Leduc 1956) 33pp., parts. Con moto; Intermezzo–Scherzando; Adagio; Allegro energico. Highly chromatic and complex writing, many changing meters, glissandi, metrical groupings of five 16ths to a pulse, rolled chords in contrary motion. Numerous ensemble problems for both performers; first-rate pianism required. D.

Alexis de Castillon. *Sonate* Op.6 1871–72 (Heugel) 61pp., parts. Allegro moderato–Allegro scherzando; Andante; Allegro molto. Written in Franck's idiom, symphonic proportions. D.
See CCSCM, I: pp.233–34 for a discussion of this work.

José María Castro. *Sonata Poética* 1957 (Library of Congress) 29pp., parts. 19 min. Allegro moderato: freely tonal around D; large span required; second theme has much rhythmic activity, flexible meters, Lento–Aria: E, chordal, sustained, chromatic. Allegro: b; toccata figuration given to violin and piano takes melody; chordal chromatic mid-section alternates with motoric activity. M-D.

Juan José Castro. *Intrata y Danza Rústica* 1946 (EAM 1946) 11pp., parts. Grave–Allegro rústico. Majestic opening with octotonic and chordal writing which yields to a cheerful dance of entertaining character. Castro's native Argentine flavor is easily heard in this endearing work. M-D.

Georgii L. Catoire. *Poem—Second Sonata* Op.20 1909 (USSR 1966) 51pp., parts. One expansive movement, in Rachmaninoff style; sometimes 4 bars take a complete page. Enormous technique necessary to bring off a successful performance. Piano part by far the more important. D.

Norman Cazden. *Suite* Op.43 1943 (ACA) 14½ min. Prelude: long lines, 2 contrasting ideas developed by both instruments. Gavotte: early-20th-century treatment similar to Ravel's and Prokofiev's approach to this genre. Sarabande: inventive. Reel: not merely background music for a square dance but balances out the "Classic" Suite idea in an up-to-date setting. D.

Friedrich Cerha. *Zwei Stücke/Two Pieces* 1948/51 (Dob 03 279 1999, ISMN M-012-18543-7) 21pp., parts. I. Mediation: in flowing triplet meters almost exclusively at p or softer dynamics; designed in curious ABCA′B′C′ form in which both C's feature bitonal 7th chords posed a major 7th apart at $pppp$. II. Altes Lied: ternary form requiring rubato character and rapid repeating notes in generally chordal A sections; staccatos off-beat figures in leaping patterns contrast scalar patterns in B; mixed meters. Large span required. D.

——. *Second Sonata* 1953 (Dob 1998) 35pp., parts. 18 min. Largo espressivo–Allegro molto; Fließend, sehr ebenmäß; Vivace. Conventional mid-20th-century work with daring passages in the first and third movements and facile writing in the second. M-D to D.

——. *Third Sonata* 1955 (Dob 1994) 14pp., parts. 10 min. Andante–Allegro non troppo; Interludium; Allegro. Miniature in scale to the *Second Sonata,* suggesting a Sonatina instead. Changing meters and harmonics in the violin give some interest to this largely academic exercise. The second movement would be a good first ensemble piece for less-experienced performers. Int. to M-D.

Giacomo Cervetto. *Sonata* C (Salmon—Ric R70 1914) 16pp., parts. Adagio; Allegro; Cantabile; Allegro.

——. *Sonata* G (Salmon—Ric R352) 14pp., parts. Siciliano; Allegro; Andante espressivo; Allegro. Both *Sonatas* seem more like Suites. The editor has added freely to the piano part. Int. to M-D.

Luciano Chailly. *Sonata Tritematica* No.8 Op.219 1955 (Forlivesi 1960) 22pp., parts. 16 min. One large movement with tempo changes generally delineating major sections. Subdivisions of the meter ($\frac{8}{8}$ = 3 + 2 + 3, etc.) are prominent. Stylistic mixture provides mainly mildly 20th-century sonorities. D.

———. *Sonatina Tritematica* No.12 (EC).

August Chapuis. *Sonate* g (Durand 1921). Strong Franckian influence. M-D.

Carlos Chavez. *Sonatina* 1924 (Belwin-Mills 1928) 11pp., parts. A one-movement work elemental in its primitivism, relentless rhythms, and harsh sonorities. Contrary glissandi, mechanistic, anti-Romantic, contrasted sections.

———. *Variations* (GS).

Charles Chaynes. *Sonate* (Leduc 1953) 27pp., parts. Risoluto; Lento–Molto sostenuto; Allegro giocoso. Thoroughly 20th-century. Some metrical subdivisions ($\frac{8}{4}$ = 5 + 3) among changing meters. Textural clarity in performance must match compositional textural clarity. D.

Camille Chevillard. *Sonata* Op.8 g (Durand 1894). Opening violin idea is basic for much of this work. The slow movement presents an expansive recitative on the subjects of the first movement. Franckian influence. D.

Mircea Chiriac. *Sonatina* (Editura Muzicala 1964) 23pp., parts. Allegro giocoso; Lento; Allegretto. Flexible meters, modal quality, preference for 4ths and 5ths in Lento, highly pianistic. M-D.

Osvald Chlubna. *Sonata* Op.66 1948 (Artia 1958) 59pp., parts. 25 min. Allegro energico; Molto lento consolante; Allegro burlescamento; Allegro risoluto. Sweeping lines, dissonantal treatment, well constructed, 19th-century pianistic treatment of 20th-century harmonic vocabulary. D.

Henning Christiansen. *Sonate* Op.13 1962 (Samfundet til Udgivelse Al Dansk Music 1965) 22pp., parts. Centrum; Elementer og varianter; Flader (Ritornel I) Episode I; Ritornel II; Episode II; Ritornel III; Episode III; Ritornel IV; Episode IV; Ritornel V; Oplösning. Aleatoric, numerous directions (in English and Danish) for the performers, clusters. Most precise pedal indications. D.

Giovanni Paolo Cima. *Three Sonatas* (Grebe—Sikorski 472). 1 g, 2 d, 3 a. *Sonatas* 2 and 3 are for violin or oboe and keyboard.

Muzio Clementi. *Sonata* Op.5/1 B♭ (Spada—BS 1219 1991) 17pp., parts. An elaborated, augmented version of the *Sonata* by its composer from the original publication in 1781, published here for the first time. For piano with violin accompaniment. M-D.

———. *Three Sonatas* Op.15 1786 (LC) 36pp. First edition. For the pianoforte, with an accompaniment obbligato for violin. M-D.

———. *Three Sonatas for the Piano or Harpsichord with the Accompaniment of a Flute or Violin* Op.2 (Hin 1971). See detailed entry under duos for piano and flute.

Louis-Nicolas Clérambault. *Sonate l'Impromptu* (B. Wahl—Ouvrières 1968) 11pp., parts. Largo; Allegro; Aria–gracioso; Maestoso. Attractive writing with keyboard part realized in excellent taste. M-D.

Ulric Cole. *Sonata* (SPAM 1930) 42pp., parts. Moderato; Scherzo; Intermezzo; Finale–Moderato. Big dramatic work with a few examples of 20th-century writing. Piece deserves looking into. D.

Samuel Coleridge-Taylor. *Sonata* Op.28 d (A. Sammons—Hawkes 1917) 27pp., parts. Allegro ma non tanto; Larghetto; Allegro vivo con fuoco. Big, strong, colorful 19th-century pianistic idioms and harmonies. Dvořák influence; more like a Suite than a Sonata. M-D to D.

Marius Constant. *Phantasma* 1990 (Sal 1990) 16pp., parts. 8 min. A broad multi-sectional one-movement fantasy in late-20th-century avant-garde style. Requires uniquely sonorous effects, especially with the violin played into the piano near the lowest strings while individual keys or the damper pedal is silently depressed. Frequently changing meters, sometimes asymmetric or no meter at all. Extremes of tempo and dynamics, the latter ranging from *pppppp* to *ffff,* as is expression, which ranges from calm, mediative qualities to pandemonium. All ends quietly in its broadly slow-fast-slow design on a B♭ chord at *pp.* See "Errata" sheet for corrections in printed score. D.

Dan Constantinescu. *Sonata* 1962 (Editura Muzicala 1965) 28pp., parts. 18 min. Adagio; Allegro. Unusual printing format—when either piano or violin does not play, the staff for that part is deleted—gives the appearance of many "empty" spaces in the score. Chromatic germ is inspiration for first movement. The Allegro is a scherzando with flexible meters and some unusual sonorities. D.

Paul Constantinescu. *Sonatina* (Editura Muzicala 1964) 15pp., parts. Allegro moderato; Andante; Allegro assai. Freely tonal, outer movements have dancelike qualities. Traditional pianistic techniques, mildly 20th-century. M-D.

Dinos Constantinides. *Landscape V* 1968, rev.2001 (Magni 2001) 19pp. In one movement, packed with repeated notes, mixed rhythms, and strong melodic features. "*Landscape V* . . . employs loosely serial procedures based on a 12-tone statement, which appears at the very beginning of the piece. As the title indicates, *Landscape V* describes various images of the land of the composer's birth place as crystalized in his mind over time. Changes of rhythms and special effects portray images of Greece's natural wild beauty" (Composer's Note). Principal theme introduced at opening easily lends itself to fragmentation and becomes the resource for considerable development. M-D.

———. *Patterns* 1989 (Conners 1995) 21pp., parts. 7½ min. In one movement, "based upon contrasting musical ideas organized within a tight framework. A

free slow section alternates with a fast rhythmic one leading to a frenzied ending" (Composer's Note). Technically challenging for both instruments. D.

———. *Idyll* 1994 (Conners 1995) 11pp. 7½ min. In one movement, "based upon
a three note figure which first appears at the beginning of the solo violin"
(Composer's Note). Melancholic, with much expression contrasting strong melodic and rhythmic development. The harmonic focus is on c at the opening
and the Lydian mode on C at the end. M-D.

Arnold Cooke. *Sonata* I G 1939 (OUP) 32pp., parts. 15 min. Allegro moderato;
Lento ma non troppo; Rondo–Allegro ma non troppo. Mildly 20th-century.
M-D.

———. *Sonata* II A 1951 (Nov 1961) 50pp., parts. 23 min. Allegro con brio; Andante con moto; Allegro vivace. Slightly more 20th-century-sounding than
No.I. More expansive, formal structure handled more logically than in No.I. D.

Paul Cooper. *Soliloquies* (JWC 1971) 6pp., parts. 9 min. Six short pieces, essentially a lyric set that requires no percussive effects from either player. The
work concentrates on more traditional pitch and technical demands in the violin and softer effects in the piano. Instructions on the meanings of new signs
are included. Rhythmic approximation through the spacing of signs rather
than by their individual detail of appearance is probably the most conspicuous
new technique used. Clusters, dampening of strings with left hand inside piano, harmonics, preparation with a ⅛″ bolt, and some improvisation are required. D.
See Edith Borroff, "A New Notation: *Soliloquies* for Violin and Piano (1971)
by Paul Cooper," in *Notations and Editions* (Dubuque, Iowa: Wm. C. Brown,
1974), pp.191–204. Also includes the score in MS and printed version.

———. *Variations* (JWC 1967) 19pp., parts. 12 min. Twelve-tone idiom makes
these variations within variations. Pianist has to read alto clef and pluck a few
strings inside the instrument. A few errors in the score. D.

Aaron Copland. *Sonata* 1942–43 (Bo&H) 33pp., parts. 19 min. A miniature lyric
and noble drama with excellent writing for both instruments. More robust and
taut than Copland's *Piano Sonata*. Andante semplice: austere but pensive
elegy with subjects evolving from motivic hinting; strong harmonic tension.
Lento: modal; sensitive; pedal points support cantabile line; slow-paced but effective evolution of theme. Allegretto giusto: dancelike; biting melodic leaps;
greatly contrasted rhythms and dynamics; opening idea of first movement returns to round off the work. D.

———. *Two Ballades* (Bo&H 1993). Reproduced from holograph.

———. *Two Preludes* (Bo&H 1993) Published separately. Reproduced from holograph.

Roque Cordero. *Sonatina* 1946 (PIC 1962) 20pp., parts. Adagio–Allegro con
spirito; Largo e recitativo–Andante, quasi adagio; Allegro moderato e burlesco.
Serially organized, terse atonal writing. D

Archangelo Corelli. *Sonatas* Op.5 (Paumgartner, Kehr, G. Jensen—Schott; Abbado—Ric ER2660; Dolmetsch—Nov; G. Jensen—IMC; B. Moosbauer, R. Goebel, M. Jira—VU 50235-6 2003, ISMN M-50057-249-7, M-50057-264-0, parts, including basso; K 04410-1), 2 vols.; (Gal), 4 vols. The 12 *Sonatas* in this opus are a summary of Corelli's style, taste, and technique. The first 6 are the more learned Sonata da Chiesa, while the last 6 are the Sonata da Camera type with their variety of dance movements.
Also available: *Six Sonatas* from Op.5 (Klengel—CFP) Vol.I: 1, 4, 8. Vol.II: 3, 5, 9. *Three Sonatas* from Op.5 (Jenson—Augener 7406) Nos.8, 9, 11. *Sonata* Op.5/5 g (Augener 11355; Salmon—Ric R721). *Sonata* 5/8 (Moffat—Simrock; PWM; Augener 11358). *Sonata* 5/9 A in Schering *Alte Meister,* pp.4ff. Complete and showing suggested additional ornamentation (PWM). *Sonata* Op.5/12 d "La Follia" (David, Auer—CF 03719; David, Petri—Br&H; Kreisler—Foley 1127; Leonard—CF B3288 with cadenza; Meyer—Schott; Salmon—Ric R720; Carish; Augener 7419; K 04409). This *Sonata* is the famous set of variations on "La Follia." It is a bowing textbook.

John Corigliano. *Sonata* 1964 (GS 1967) 47pp., parts. 22 min. Allegro: highly concentrated. Andantino: melodic peak of the work. Lento (quasi recitativo): brooding and moody. Allegro: not as focused as the other movements. Virtuoso Neoclassic writing of the highest order. Cadenza for the piano. Thoroughly 20th-century yet tonally based in the broadest sense of the term. D.

Michel Corrette. *Sonata* A (Lemoine 1924).
———. *Sonata* C (Ruf—Ric 1955).
———. *Sonate* D (Ruf—Schott 1968).
———. *Sonata* II 1735 (F. Petit—Ouvrières 1965) 6pp., parts. For violin or flute and keyboard. Allemanda–Aria; Minuetto 1 & 2. Charming period writing, tasteful realization. M-D.

Ramiro Cortés. *Elegy* (EV 1960) 5pp., parts. Serial, long lines, expressive, arpeggi gestures, repeated chords, atonal. M-D.

Jean Coulthard. *Duo Sonata* (BMI-Canada 1952) 36pp., parts. 18 min. Cyclic work developing from the opening theme given out by the violin. The 3 movements are connected by links. M-D.

François Couperin. The *Concerts Royaux* are "French" Suites of dances with much Italian influence, especially in their aria-like melodies. No instruments are specified except keyboard and whatever instruments are available. They come off well using violin and harpsichord or piano.
Concerts Royaux, Troisième Concert (F. Polnauer—Schott 1970). Nos.1, 2, and 4 available separately from Schott. Some movements are scored for keyboard and violin, others are in trio settings. *Les Goûts Réunis, Quatorzième Concert* (Boulay—EMT). *Concert* 5 F (Dukas—Durand); *Concert* 6 B♭ (Dukas—Durand); Concert 7 g (Dukas—Durand); *Concert* 9 E (Dukas—Durand).

Henry Cowell. *Homage to Iran* (CFP 6114 1959) 23pp., parts. 13 min. Andante rubato; Interlude; Andante rubato; Con spirito. Not based on actual ethnic material from Iran but written in the style and spirit of Persian music. "In the first and third movements, the piano strings may be muted by pressing the strings of the indicated notes near the bridge, while playing the keys. The resulting sound is somewhat similar to the sound of an Iranian drum" (from the score). M-D.

——. *Suite* (AMP 1926) 17pp., parts. Largo; Allegretto; Andante tranquillo; Allegro marcato; Andante calmato; Presto. Many clusters in piano part, tonal, 6 short contrasted movements. M-D.

——. *Sonata* I 1945 (AMP 1947) 24pp., parts. 17 min. Hymn; In Fuguing Style; Ballad; Jig; Finale. A few muted strings in Finale for the pianist are the clue to Cowell in this otherwise traditionally written but fresh-sounding work. M-D.

Paul Creston. *Suite* Op.18 (GS 1939) 9½ min. Prelude; Air; Rondo. Rhapsodic excitement, energetic rhythmic treatment, natural flowing melodic charm. M-D.

George Crumb. *Four Nocturnes. Night Music* II 1964 (CFP 1971) 9 min. Explores colorful sonorities, such as pianist rapping on metal frame of piano, sweeping strings with wire brush, scraping fingernail rapidly over metal winding of string. Numerous performance instructions. Extremes in dynamic range explored. Piano harmonics are exploited in this ethereal dialogue between instruments. D.

Ivo Cruz. *Sonata* (Sassetti 1956) 27pp., parts. Moderato; Lento; Con moto. Large, dramatic work in post-Brahms and Impressionist idiom. Much planing is used throughout. Well written for both parts, thoroughly integrated. D.

César Cui. *Sonate* Op.84 D 1911 (Jurgenson 1916) 26pp., parts. Allegro; Andante non troppo; Allegro. Not one of Cui's best works. M-D.

——. *Twelve Miniatures* (K 02178).

Luigi Dallapiccola. *Due Studi* 1947 (SZ 1950) 15pp., parts. 11 min. Very communicative serial writing. Sarabanda: ABA, based on a 12-tone series. Fanfare e Fuga: close and serious fugal treatment. Based on the same series as the B section of the Sarabanda; moves over keyboard. M-D to D.

——. *Tartiniana Seconda* 1956 (SZ) 12 min. A divertimento in 4 movements. Pastorale; Tempo di Boureo; Presto; Variazioni. Material by Tartini is freely adapted (as is the Paganini material in Dallapiccola's piano work *Sonatina Canonica*). Dissonant contrapuntal and accompaniment elements permeate the writing. M-D.

Jean-Michel Damase. *Sonate* 1974 (Lemoine 1975) 45pp., parts. 14 min. For flute or violin. See detailed entry under duos for flute and piano.

Gyula Dávid. *Sonata* 1968 (EMB 1969) 27pp., parts. Allegro molto; Andante, molto tranquillo; Allegro. Sparse textures, rhythmic vitality, fine lyric lines, outstanding sense of color, strong Bartók influence. M-D.

Claude Debussy. *Sonata* g 1917 (Durand, 33pp.; E.-G. Heinemann—Henle 410, 27pp.), parts. 12 min. Allegro vivo; Intermède (fantasque et léger); Finale. Refined workmanship and meticulous taste are characteristic of this last fully completed work. It is full of animated, melodious, and even vehement writing. Harmonic ambiguity is firmly put away with a brilliant G conclusion. D. See VKDR, II: pp.216–23.

Frederick Delius. *Sonata* B 1892 (Bo&H 1977) 44pp., parts. A passionately lyrical work.

———. *Sonata* I 1905–15 (Forsyth) 21pp., parts. This is the most extended of the violin *Sonatas.* Dreamy, rhapsodic, based on 5 descending notes. One expansive movement. In all 3 *Sonatas* the piano is used more for a harmonic background than for asserting its own independence. D.

———. *Sonata* II (Bo&H 1912) 12pp., parts. Lush and declamatory in style, somewhat Straussian but not knit together very strongly. An impassioned lyricism flows through this entire *Sonata.* M-D.

———. *Sonata* III (Bo&H 1931) 12pp., parts. Eloquently musical with most interest for the violin. Slow; Andante scherzando; Lento. Melancholy mood, most classical in structure of the 3 *Sonatas.* A certain longing beauty is characteristic of passages marked "slow and mysterious." M-D to D.

Norman Dello Joio. *Colloquies* (EBM 1966) 20pp., parts. 3 movements. 9 min.

———. *Fantasia on a Gregorian Theme* (CF 1949) 9pp., parts. Simple and mature style with plenty of distinctive and expressive power. M-D.

———. *Variations and Capriccio* (CF 1949) 19pp., parts. Imaginative, lucid, and poetic writing that makes musical sense. M-D.

Albert Delvaux. *Sonatine* 1956 (CeBeDeM) 8½ min.

———. *Sonate* 1962 (CeBeDeM) 41pp., parts. 17 min. Allegro con anima; Andante; Allegro vivo. Tonal but with much chromatic usage. Lines have a tendency to be short and corky. Much activity at all times. D.

David Diamond. *Sonata* 1943–46 (GS 1950) 48pp., parts. 22 min. Allegro moderato; Allegretto con moto; Adagio sospirando; Allegro con energia. Full battery of pianistic expertise required. Exciting transparent writing in a classical manner. Strong tonalities for each movement. D.

———. *Chaconne* 1948 (PIC 1951) 24pp., parts. 11½ min. Introduction, theme, 22 variations, and coda. Resources of both instruments exploited. D.

Emma Lou Diemer. *Sonata* 1949 (Seesaw) 25pp., parts. 10 min. Scherzo; Pastorale; Finale. Free dissonant counterpoint; octotonic; inner voice motives take on added significance; large span required; subtle syncopation in Pastorale;

driving rhythms; detached chords in Finale; intervals of 2nds and 3rds exploited; impressive conclusion. D.

Charles Dieupart. *Suite* IV e (J.-C. Veilhan, D. Salzer—Leduc 1974) 9pp., parts for flute or violin and basso continuo.

Karl Ditters von Dittersdorf. *Sonata* B♭ (Mlynarczky—Hofmeister 1929) 11pp., parts. Allegro; Adagio; Variationes–Tempo di Minuetto. M-D.
———. *Sonata* G (Mlynarczky—Hofmeister 1929) 11pp., parts. Adagio; Allegro molto; Tema con variazioni. M-D.
Clean editions with ornaments written out. Both *Sonatas* have final movements consisting of 4 variations and a coda.

Ernst Dohnányi. *Sonata* Op.21 c♯ 1912 (Simrock 1913) 30pp., parts. 18 min. Quiet first movement. Second movement (variation-scherzo) follows without a break and incorporates the second subject of the first movement in a variation and trio treatment. The finale opens with the motto figure (c♯–d♯–e) of the first movement, but in chords and develops into a free scherzo with a reflective trio in A. A long pedal point prepares for the return of the opening tempo of the first movement; finale concludes with much Romantic pathos. Requires thorough musicianship and pianistic expertise. D.

Samuel Dolin. *Sonata* (BMI-Canada 1968) 28pp., parts. 16½ min. Adagio; Allegro non troppo; Andante; Vivo. The second movement is marchlike and rhythmic. M-D.

Gaetano Donizetti. *Sonate* f (B. Paüler—Amadeus Verlag 1972) 12pp., parts. Short, graceful, more like a large-scale aria. A maestoso introduction leads to a SA section entitled Allegro, where both instruments toss off operatic themes in solo-tutti style. M-D.
———. *Impromptu* (P. Spada—BS 1991) 9pp., parts. In three sections: Larghetto–Andantino–Più mosso. Block chords; arpeggios; simple rhythms. M-D.

Jaroslav Doubrava. *Sonata* 1941 (Orbis 1949) 19pp., parts. Allegro moderato; Presto tenebroso; Adagio. Preference for bitonal sonorities with resolutions at cadence points. Second movement is toccata-like. Adagio is atmospheric. Folk sources are part of the style but never quoted directly. M-D.
———. *Sonata* II 1959 (Panton 1963) 43pp., parts. Turbulent, monothematic. Allegro: dramatic agitation evolves from folk ballades; SA design with secondary subject supplementing the main theme; a motive of diatonic seconds first heard at bar 22 becomes very important. Molto moderato: restless piano part in style of a cimbalom supports violin melody; ABA; balladic mood. Presto: turbulent idea of opening returns but is permeated by a lively and dancing rhythm; theme is varied and links up in mosaic fashion with first and second movements; ABA. Convincing and expressive work. D.

Franz Drdla. *Fantasie on Carmen by Bizet* Op.66 (UP). 11 min. Reissue of the 1909 publication.

Pierre Max Dubois. *Sonata* Op.91 (Leduc 1963) 36pp., parts. Allegro inquieto–ma non troppo vivo; Prestissimo comico; Andante cantabile; Impetuoso. Varied figurations, chordal, chromatic, textural clarity. Final movement with driving percussive chords is reminiscent of Bartók's style. D.

Théodore Dubois. *Cavatine* E♭ (P. Schmalfuss—Zimmermann 32190 1997) 8pp. 5 min. For flute, violin, or horn. See detailed entry under duos for piano and flute.

Vernon Duke. *Sonata* D (Ric 1960) 32pp., parts. Poco maestoso; Allegretto non troppo; Brilliante e tumultuoso. Mildly 20th-century, well crafted. The final movement is written in a $^{6}_{8}$ $^{3}_{4}$ meter and is delightfully lilting. M-D.

Petar Dumičić. *Sonata* Op.16 1939 (Udruženje Kompozitora Hrvatske 1966) 47pp., parts. Andante–Allegro moderato; Scherzo–Allegro molto; Andante tranquillo; Allegro. Freely tonal, individual style based on 19th-century compositional practices and pianistic concepts. M-D.

Marcel Dupré. *Sonate* Op.5 g (Leduc 1920) 36pp., parts. Allegro; Andantino; Presto. Tonal, Impressionist techniques, pianistic, requires large span. Toccata-like finale in $^{9}_{16}$. D.

Jan Ladislav Dussek. *Sonatas* Op.69/1 B♭, 2 G (Štědroň—Artia 1959) MAB 41. 72pp., parts. *Sonata* G is the more interesting of the 2. Colorful harmony coupled with youthful spirit makes it a favorite with audiences. Biographical and analytical notes in Czech, German, and English. M-D.

François Duval. *Two Sonatas* (Ruf—Schott 1953) 1 D, 2 G. From *Amusemens pour la Chambre,* Livre VI. Cello or viola da gamba optional.

Jiří Dvořáček. *Sonata Capriccioso* 1956 (Artia 1969) 44pp., parts. Con moto—Rubato–Allegretto; Rubato–Lento; Feroce; Allegro con fuoco. A capricious exuberant optimism pervades this work. Even the songful slow movement has a youthful spirit about it. D.

Antonín Dvořák. *Sonata* Op.57 F 1912 (Artia; Simrock; K 04343) 30pp., parts. 22 min. Allegro, ma non troppo; Poco sostenuto; Allegro molto. Idyllic, introspective, delicate, simple throughout. Outer movements are most original, while the Poco sostenuto shows the influence of Brahms. Has an irresistible zest about it. M-D.

———. *Romantische Stücke* Op.75 1887 (M. Pospíšil—Henle 466 1993) 16pp., parts. I. Allegro moderato; II. Allegro maestoso; III. Allegro appassionato; IV. Larghetto. Arranged from the original for strings, Dvořák "came to regard this arrangement as the final version, and completely suppressed the original." He

wrote his publisher in 1887, "At the moment I am composing little 'Miniatures', just imagine: for two viol[ins] and viola. The work gives me as much
pleasure as if I were writing a full-scale symphony . . . Admittedly they are intended more for dilettantes, but did not Beethoven and Schumann also sometimes compose music with quite limited means? And with what results!" (from
Preface). Rich lyric and harmonic writing in capsule forms. May be performed
separately or in small groups. M-D.

——. *Sonatina* Op.100 G (S. Gerlach, Z. Pilková—Henle 413 23pp.; D. Vorholz—
Litolff 32pp., parts; CFP; Kehr, Lechner—Schott; CF 03214; Stoessel—BMC;
Lengnick). Allegro risoluto; Larghetto; Scherzo–molto vivace; Finale–Allegro.
Stems from the composer's American visit and shows American Indian and
African American influences, which permeated his writing at that time. M-D.

——. *Ballade* Op.15/1 (Carus 1992) 12pp., parts. Preface in German with sum-
maries in English and French; critical commentary in German.
See Jinyoung Kim, "The Compositions for Violin and Piano by Antonín Dvořák," D.M.A. diss., Boston University, 1999.

Petr Eben. *Sonatina* (Artia 1957) 27pp., parts. 12 min. For violin or flute and piano. Separate part written when too low for flute. Allegro giusto: sprightly, broken octaves, chromatic. Moderato e cantabile: lyric and expressive. Vivace e accentato: freer tonal relationships, corky rhythms. M-D.

Helmut Eder. *Sonatine* Op.34/1 (Dob 1963) 12pp., parts. 5½ min. Lento espressivo–
Allegro; Andante; Allegro mobile. Small only in length. Expressionist, changing meters, intense. D.

Klaus Egge. *Sonata* I Op.3 1932 (Musikk-Huset 1946) 27pp., parts. 22 min. Moderato; Romanza–Adagio; Finale–Rondo, vivace. Slätter intervals, polyphonic
textures, freely tonal. D.

Gottfried von Einem. *Sonata* Op.11 1949 (UE) 16pp., parts. 12 min. Allegro moderato: in $\frac{7}{8}$, sustained, ingenious, much variety. Larghetto; Allegro. Neoclassic
style, tonally free, large span required, tight construction, clear textures, lively
rhythms. M-D.

Edward Elgar. *Sonata* Op.82 e 1918 (Nov 1919; MMP) 37pp., parts. 23 min. Allegro: rugged thematic material, freely treated, much vitality and fire. Romance:
ABA design with an element of mysticism in the A section; tender Romanticism; the broad B section provides a fine contrast; A section is recapped with
theme played con sordino. Allegro non troppo: tranquil opening to m.40,
where a new idea ushers in a wistful theme; large development of these ideas
leads to the recap, where a reference to the Romance, now in $\frac{3}{2}$ meter, appears;
short, strenuous coda rounds out the movement. D.

——. *Salut d'Amour* Op.12 1888 (D. Burrows—CFP 7429 1995) 11pp., parts.
Score contains 1st and 2nd versions of work, originally for piano and violin,

though later published in 20+ instrumental versions. Comparison of these 2 versions and later transcriptions reveals an interesting development in Elgar's concept of the piece. Extensive Preface and critical commentary. M-D.

———. *Chanson de Nuit* and *Chanson de Matin* Op.15 1897–99 (Burrows—CFP 1995) 14pp., parts. Urtext. Companion pieces which Elgar later arranged for chamber and orchestral ensembles. Strongly melodic and tonal qualities firmly rooted. *Chanson de Nuit:* Andante, calm, and expressive. *Chanson de Matin:* Allegretto in straightforward rhythms of $\frac{2}{4}$ with off-beat chords. Notes and critical commentary included. M-D.

———. *La Capricieuse* Op.17 1891 (AMP 1917) 7pp., parts. Favors the violin in virtuosic passagework though the piano is not without interest with occasional counter-melodies. Encore piece. M-D.

George Enesco. *Sonata* I Op.2 D (Enoch 1898; Editions d'Etat 1956 47pp., parts; Ashdown).

———. *Sonata* II Op.6 f (Enoch 1901 47pp., parts; Editions d'Etat 1956; Ashdown).

———. *Sonata* III Op.25 a (Enoch 1933 43pp., parts; Editions d'Etat 1956; Ashdown). Moderato malinconico; Andante sostenuto e misterioso; Allegro con brio, ma non troppo mosso.

Manuel Enríque. *Sonata* 1964 (IU) 16pp. Three atonal movements with only the first being entitled Tranquillo. Serial, violin opens by itself with piano joining at Deciso. Pointillistic, constantly moving over keyboard, dynamic extremes, Expressionist, cascading gestures. Piano used percussively; certain sonorities are maintained by timed seconds, a few avant-garde techniques, complex, abstract use, and abstract writing. Only for the most venturesome duo. D.

Donald Erb. *Three Poems* 1987–88 (Merion 1988) 32pp., parts. 17 min. Together Forever; Toccata (. . . rats' feet over broken glass—T. S. Eliot); Poem: "It is better to be a part of beauty for one instant and then cease to exist than to exist forever"—Don Marquis. Requires a guitar pick for pizzicati inside piano and two or three "pads" of masking tape to cover the top 2 octaves of piano strings. Pianist must dampen strings with hand while playing in Toccata. Octave hand clusters; random pitches; string strumming; indeterminacy; extremes of dynamics (niente to *ffff*). For musicians and audiences interested in novel effects. D.

———. *The Watchman Fantasy* (Merion 1992) 48pp., parts. For violin and 1 keyboard player (preferred) playing a piano and a synthesizer; 2 keyboard players may be used. Includes performance instructions.

Ivan Eröd. *Sonata* I 1969–70 (Dob) 36pp., parts. Allegro moderato: SA, freely tonal, clear textures, strong rhythms. Thema and (3) Variations: effectively contrasted variations, harmonics. Presto: triplets in 10ths, arpeggi figuration, Neoclassic. M-D.

Andrej Eschpaj. *Sonate* (Sikorski 1966 38pp., parts, composer's MS but easy to read; USSR 1967 27pp., parts). Broad expansive movement that effectively utilizes octaves, 4ths, and chromatics; varied tempos and moods. D.

Carlo Esposito. *Sonata* II (Edizioni Musicali Mercurio 1962) 30pp., parts. Tempo–Allegro Moderato; Tempo–Lentamente e accorato; Tempo–Rondo brillante. Fond of expanding intervals; chromatic; bitonal; long scalar passages for the pianist; pesante writing in coda. D.

Robert Evett. *Sonata* 1960 (ACA) 16pp., parts. 12 min. Andante–Allegretto: 2 basic tempos; changing meters; freely tonal around C; clear textures; quasi-recitativo section for violin; subtle lilting character permeates this movement. Allegro con brio: strong octave opening, dancelike, quartal harmony, short and brilliant coda; requires large span. Neoclassic. M-D.

Joseph Leopold Eybler. *Drei Sonaten* Op.9 (A. Weinmann—Amadeus/Päuler 1973) 46pp., parts.

Blair Fairchild. *Sonate* Op.43 (Durand 1919) 32pp., parts. Moderato; Allegretto vivo; Quasi adagio; Molto allegro. Impressionist. M-D.

Pietro Fasullo. *Sonata* f (Carrara 3519 1979) 48pp., parts. Allegro moderato; Andante tranquillo; Allegro vivace. Strongly tonal work using conventional compositional techniques. Lyric, tuneful melodies with expressive qualities. Ends in parallel major. D.
———. Sonata II A 1984 (Berben 2531 1985) 51pp., parts. A massive one-movement work in 3 sections by a composer unwilling to acknowledge 20th-century tonalities. Could have been written in the mid-19th century. D.

Gabriel Fauré. *Sonata* Op.13 A 1876 (Br&H; Francescatti, Casadesus—IMC; Loeffler—BMC; R. Howat—CFP 7487 1998, 87pp.; K 03484), parts. 27 min. Allegro molto: SA, piano opening followed by a dialogue that leads to the second tonal area; traditional development but beautiful working out of ideas. Andante: pure line juxtaposed with charming rocking $\frac{9}{8}$ theme in the piano. Allegro vivo: a light scherzo of darting passages, contrasted middle melodic section. Allegro quasi presto: declamatory, robust writing and formal experimentation; agitated, restless, Schumannesque. D.
———. *Sonata* Op.108 e 1916 (Durand) 44pp., parts. 25 min. Allegro non troppo; Andante; Final. Strange, austere melody, sustained by unconventional modal harmony (mainly Lydian). Metrical patterns avoid symmetry and squareness —typical of Fauré's late style. A work of great elegance, sympathetically written for both instruments, that deserves more frequent performances. D.
———. *Zwei Sonaten* (A. Amerongen—CFP 9891 1982) 126pp., parts. Contains both *Sonatas* Opp. 13 and 108. Valuable remarks and editorial notes in German, French, and English.
———. *Anthology of Original Pieces for Violin and Piano* (R. Howat—CFP 1999) 30pp., parts. Urtext. *Berceuse,* Op.16 (ca.1879); *Morceau de lecture* (1903);

Romance, Op.28 (1877); *Andante,* Op.75 (1897). Four delightful pieces revealing the charm and intense musical qualities of Fauré. First commercial publication of the *Morceau de lecture,* composed as the sight-reading piece for the
1903 Violin Concours at the Paris Conservatory. Extensive notes and critical
commentary. M-D to D.

See David Gene Tubergen, "A Stylistic Analysis of Selected Violin and Piano Sonatas of Fauré, Saint-Saëns, and Franck," Ph.D. diss., New York University,
1985.

Howard Ferguson. *Sonata* 1931 (Bo&H) 28pp., parts. 16 min. Molto moderato;
Allegro furioso; Quasi Fantasia. Preference for octaves and figuration noted.
Final movement surges and recedes. $\frac{3}{4}$ $\frac{6}{8}$ meter in the second movement adds
intensity. D.

See Ya-Chiao Lin, "The Two Sonatas for Violin and Piano by a Neglected Composer, Howard Ferguson: A Performer's Analysis," D.M.A. diss., Ohio State
University, 2000.

Giorgio Ferrari. *Sonata* I (Zanibon 1974) 29pp., parts, photostat.
———. *Sonata* II (Zanibon 1974) 30pp., parts, photostat.

Pierre Octave Ferroud. *Sonate* (Durand 1929) 33pp., parts. Allegro vivo e scherzando; Andante; Rondo vivace. Impressionist influences are felt but a virile
style is also present. Pianistic techniques are a continuation and expansion of
19th-century practice. D.

Willem de Fesch. *Sechs Sonaten* (W. Woehl—HM 127, 128) 2 vols. For violin,
flute, oboe or viola, and keyboard. Six *Sonatas* from the set of 12, Op.8. Vol.I:
D, c, e. Vol.II: G, A, b. Excellent Preface and performance notes. Short movements; appealing melodies. Provides excellent duo training; would be successful on recital programs. M-D.

Michael Christian Festing. *Two Sonatas* Op.4/2 c, 3 E 1736 (G. Beechey—OUP
1975) Musica da Camera 24. 16pp., parts. 8 min. Figured bass tastefully realized. Includes parts for bass instrument. Preface in English and German. Varied harmonies, imitation, attractive melodies. M-D.

———. *Sonata* Op.8/5 D 1744 (W. Bergmann—Schott 1955) 10pp., parts. Largo–
Spiritoso; Largo–Poco allegro, gratioso; Allegro spiritoso; Andante amoroso–
Più lento e dolce–Amoroso. Short attractive movements. A delightful Sonata.
Editorial marks indicated in brackets. M-D.

Paul Fetler. *Three Pieces* (SPAM 1953) 31pp., parts. I. Essay: Allegro moderato;
instrumental exchange of principal theme; even rhythms; ternary form. II. Air:
Adagio; $\frac{6}{8}$; contrasts ascending and descending phrases; contemplative. III. Caprice: Vivace; lengthy piano opening precedes main theme in violin in $\frac{5}{8}$; chords
played in staccato, block, and repeated patterns; finishes *pp.* Pieces may be performed separately. Mild 20th-century writing. M-D to D.

Zdenko Fibich. *Sonata* D (J. Zich—Orbis 1950; Artia).

——. *Sonatina* Op.27 d 1869 (Artia; Urbánek; BMC) 11pp., parts. Allegro moderato; Andante; Allegro molto. Colorful, folk elements present. M-D.

Jacobo Ficher. *Primera Sonata* Op.15 1929, rev. 1960 (IU) 38pp., parts. Allegro: SA; chromatic linear lines; syncopated chords; contrapuntal; 2 main ideas are synthesized and thoroughly worked out with a brilliant concluding coda. Lento: ABA; chromatic; chordal; violin has some lyric lines. Presto: syncopated chordal opening; arpeggi patterns divided between hands; contrasts with more tuneful meno mosso section; both main ideas return, and a coda combines elements of both for an exciting closing. Very difficult writing for both instruments. D.

——. *Sonata* II Op.56 1945–46 (IU) 48pp., parts. Allegro moderato: SA; undulating tonal (D) opening; second idea is dancelike; requires good octave technique. Lento: mistico octotonic subject; linear and chordal juxtaposed sections; effective ending in B. Allegro moderato: scalar passages serve as counterpoint to subject; imitation; thin and thick textures juxtaposed. Dramatic writing for both instruments. D.

——. *Tercera Sonata* Op.93 1959 (IU) 42pp., parts. Allegro agitato; Lento; Allegro molto. Many of the same techniques found in the first 2 *Sonatas* are used here. D.

Ficher is a colorist; his love of complex chromatic scalar passages and his unique manner of handling chordal textures shine through in all 3 works. All 3 require advanced pianism.

Irving Fine. *Sonata* (Warner Brothers 1948) 32pp., parts. In Stravinsky's Neoclassic style. Moderato; Lento con moto; Vivo. Thorny, chromatic. Large span required. Last movement has thinner textures and bouncing rhythms and seems to be the most successful. Strong tonal centers. D.

Izrail Borisovich Finkelshtein. *Sonata* (USSR 1968) 88pp., parts. Allegro moderato; Scherzo–Allegro; Aria–Lento assai in modo improvisato; Finale–Allegro risoluto. Expansive work, short lines, some contrapuntal usage, mildly 20th-century, long *pp* closing. Requires fortitude and plenty of reserve power. D.

Ross Lee Finney. *Sonata* II 1951 (AME 1954) 21pp., parts. Tranquilly; Capriciously; Tenderly, but with passion; Vigorously in march tempo; Tranquilly. Neoclassic tendencies, much interplay of ideas between instruments. M-D.

——. *Sonata* III 1955 (Valley Music Press 1957) 29pp., parts. Allegro caminando; Allegro scherzando; Adagio sostenuto con variazioni (9 variations). Beautiful balance between the 2 instruments. Serial with tonal implications. The set of variations is a tour de force in variation technique. D.

——. *Fiddle-Doddle-ad* 1945 (GS 1949) 15pp., parts. Eight American Folk-Tunes. Based on "Rosin the Bow, Rye Whiskey, Wayfaring Stranger, Cotton Eye Joe, Rippytoe Ray, The Nightingale, Oh, Lovely Appearance of Death, and Candy Girl." Short pieces requiring varying levels of skills. Could be performed individually or in smaller groups. Int. to D.

Giovanni Battista Fontana. *Sechs Sonaten* (F. Cerha—Dob) Nos.13, 14, and 15 in DM series. 3 vols., 2 *Sonatas* in each. Multimovement works. Valuable foreword. M-D.

Wolfgang Fortner. *Sonate* 1945 (Schott) 23pp., parts. Allegro; Adagio; Rondo–Vivace; Thema con Variazioni (5 variations and coda). Neoclassic, freely tonal, changing meters in Rondo, thin textures. M-D.

Lukas Foss. *Three American Pieces* 1944–45 (CF 05186 1994) 24pp., parts. Original version. 1. Early Song: Lento–Allegro; strongly contrasting sections; piano introduces main theme over broken-chord arpeggiation. 2. Dedication: Rather slow; large chordal structures; mixed meters. 3. Composer's Holiday: Allegro; a syncopated bouncy romp at breakneck speed. Large span required in 2 and 3. Available separately. D.

————. *Central Park Reel* 1987 (Pembroke 1993) 24pp., parts. A playful dance mimicking country fiddling with colorful pianistic sonority. Requires silently depressing keys and strumming strings. Straightforward to closing section, where instruments parts are notated separately and cannot be synchronized. Optional electronic tape addition for ending with synchronized instrumental parts. D.

Jean Françaix. *Sonatine* 1934 (Schott) 15pp., parts. 11 min. Vivace; Andante; Théme Varié (5 variations). Plenty of Gallic wit and humor are displayed. Chromatic, sprightly rhythms, light, Neoclassic style. M-D.

César Franck. *Sonata* A 1886 (M. Steegman—Henle 1975; E. Herttrich—VU 50174; Hamelle; Busch—Br&H; Francescatti, Casadesus—IMC; Lehmann—CF L766; Lichtenberg, Adler—GS L1235; Polo—Ric ER 2068; Sauret—Schott; Durand; M. Jacobsen—CFP 3742), parts. The Henle edition has a most informative Preface. One of the finest and most moving works in its form since Brahms. Graceful and tranquil first movement followed by the most important second movement, one of a troubled and searching nature. In place of an expected adagio or andante, the third movement is a Recitativo–Fantasia, with great sweep and freedom. The final movement, a rondo, displays the recurring theme in canonic fashion. Chromaticism and cyclic form add tautness and coherence to the entire unified work. Cello and flute versions of this *Sonata* are also available. The violin part appears to have been merely transposed in the cello version by Jules Delsart. See Henle Preface for more information concerning this edition. D.

See David Gene Tubergen, "A Stylistic Analysis of Selected Violin and Piano Sonatas of Fauré, Saint-Saëns, and Franck," Ph.D. diss., New York University, 1985.

François Francoeur. *Sonate* 6, Ier Livre E (Petit—Ouvrières 1968) 16pp., parts. Adagio; Allemande; Sarabande; Gavotte I, II; Gigue. Elements of both Sonata and Suite are present in this attractive work. Keyboard realization by the editor is in good taste. M-D.

Peter Racine Fricker. *Sonata* Op.12 (Schott 1950) 30pp., parts. Three movements of highly concentrated and engaging writing which becomes progressively slower. Allegro: SA; rich and full of material; extended development; melody varied in the recapitulation. Allegretto: begins muted "comme un valse distante"; formally it might be called a fantasy-rondo, with the mid-section of the opening idea serving as the refrain. The Adagio finale is in 3 sections, each followed by a brief decorative cadenza to a complex chord—a different resolution evolves each time, the last one to a C triad. D.

Géza Frid. *Sonate* Op.50 1955 (Donemus) Photostat of MS. 26pp., parts. 14½ min. Quasi-improvisando–Allegro marcato; Andante cantabile; Presto leggero. Sweeping lines opening the work are interrupted by a ruvido section. These alternate during the first movement. The lyric second movement erupts in maestoso chromatic chords before it signs itself out. The finale carries on a question-answer style until a meno mosso section becomes more intense. An a tempo moves quickly to the end. D.

Pierre Froidebise. *Sonate* 1938 (CeBeDeM 1956) 15pp., parts. 9 min. A one-movement work with contrasting sections. Highly Impressionist and pleasant. D.

Gunnar de Frumerie. *Sonata* I Op.27 (Nordiska Musikförlaget 1934, rev. 1962) Photostat of MS. 34pp., parts. Andante; Allegro molto rigoroso e energico; Siciliano; Andante espressivo–Molto vivo. D.
——. *Sonata* II 1944 (Nordiska Musikförlaget 1950) 46pp., parts. Allegro amabile; Andante espressivo; Scherzo, molto allegro misterioso; Allegretto grazioso. D.
Both *Sonatas* are conceived in a Neoclassic style and show a fine craft, with polished writing along lines of established tradition. A mildly 20-century flavor is present.

Sandro Fuga. *Sonata* 1938–39 (Ric) 34pp., parts. 25 min. Molto tranquillo; Molto allegro; Sostenuto espressivo. Sonorous use of piano, broad pianistic gestures. Large span required. D.
——. *Sonata* II (EC 1972) 38pp., parts.

Arthur Furer. *Sonate* Op.18 1954 (Krompholz) 32pp., parts. Allegro moderato; Molto tranquillo; Allegro con brio. Drive, color, and excitement, respectively, describe the 3 movements. Plenty of pianistic interest. Mildly 20th-century. D.

Wilhelm Furtwängler. *Sonate* I d (Br&H 1938) 96pp., parts. Ruhig beginnen; Sehr langsam, still; Moderato; Finale–Etwas breit. A work of enormous proportions. Reger-Strauss tradition underlined by Brahms. Virtuoso technique and plenty of reserve stamina required. D.

———. *Sonate* II D (G. Kulenhampff—Bo&Bo 1940).

Niels W. Gade. *Sonata* I Op.6 A 1842 (Lichtenberg—GS 1901) 31pp., parts. Allegro di molto; Andante con moto; Allegro con espressione. Composed around the time of the First Symphony when he was a young man and dedicated to Clara Schumann. Rhapsodic qualities in flamboyant style contrast with lyric, cantabile passagework imbedded in rich harmonic architectures. D.

———. *Sonata* II Op.21 d 1849 (Hoy-Draheim—Br&H 8457 1990) 36pp., parts. Adagio–Allegro di molto; Larghetto; Adagio–Allegro moderato; Allegro molto vivace. Owes much to Robert Schumann, to whom it is dedicated, with Romantic charm on every page. Sounds somewhat old-fashioned today but still has musicality to recommend it. M-D.

———. *Fantasias* Op.43 (JWC). See detailed entry under duos for piano and clarinet.

———. *Volkstänze* (im nordischen Charakter) Op.62 (Br&H) 29pp., parts. In 4 movements: Tempo moderato poco maestoso; Allegro scherzando; Allegro moderato, ma vivace; Menuetto. Strong 19th-century stylistic qualities permeate this set of folk dances in Norse character. Of particular interest is a Reel, which functions as the Trio of the Menuetto and is repeated at the end with an extension to conclude the work. D.

Blas Galindo. *Sonata* 1945 (EMM 1950) 45pp., parts. Allegro; Largo; Molto allegro. Freely tonal, flexible meters, folk influence, some driving rhythms, pandiatonic. D.

Francesco Geminiani. *Twelve Sonatas* Op.1 (a) (W. Kolneder—Schott) 4 vols. Cello part optional. Originally published in London in 1716. Indications of the revised edition of 1739 have been used for the articulation of the violin part in Kolneder's edition. Vol.I: A, d, e. Vol.II: D, g, g. Vol.III: c, b, F. Vol.IV: E, a, d. M-D.
Available separately: *Sonata* Op.1/1 A (Ruf—HM 173; Betti—GS) 11pp., parts. *Sonata* 1/4 D (Ruf—HM 174) 11pp., parts. *Sonata* Op.1/12 d "Impetuosa" (Moffat—Simrock 1929) 9 min. A "new concert version."

———. *Six Sonatas* Op.5 (W. Kolneder—CFP 9042). Cello part optional. Originally published in London in 1747 for cello and continuo but reappeared in this form almost immediately. The keyboard realization is somewhat thick but usable. Slow-fast-slow-fast movement order. Fast-moving harmonies, irregular phrase groups, unusual patterns, opportunities for many cadenza passages. Int. to M-D.

————. *12 Compositioni* (T. Orszagh, L. Böhm—EMB 1959) 2 vols. Thesaurus Musicus 7 & 8. Twelve movements included by the composer in his *The Art of Playing the Violin,* 1751. This treatise is available in a facsimile of the first edition (D. Boyden—OUP).

Harald Genzmer. *Sonata* I 1943 (Schott 3663) 15pp., parts. Mässig bewegt; Mit grosser ruhe; Sehr schwungvoll und lebendig vorzutragen.

————. *Sonata* II 1949 (Schott 4022, ISMN M-001-04805-7) 27pp., parts. Langsam: Breit strömend; Andante amabile; Finale: Sehr lebhaft.

————. *Sonatine* 1953 (Schott 4482, ISMN M-001-05243-6) 16pp., parts. Allegro; Adagio; Presto; Allegro.

————. *Sonata* III 1954 (Schott 5870) 12 min.

————. *Sonatine* II 1995 (Schott 8527 1997, ISMN M-001-11402-8) 23pp., parts. Allegro moderato; Andante tranquillo; Finale–Deciso. M-D to D.

————. *Sonatine* III 1995 (Schott 8529 1997) 22pp., parts. Moderato; Allegretto; Finale–Allegretto. M-D to D.

Roberto Gerhard. *Gemini: Duo Concertante* (OUP 1966) 12 min. The composer's note from the score states: "The work consists of a series of contrasting episodes, whose sequence is more like a braiding of diverse strands than a straight linear development. Except for the concluding episodes, nearly every one recurs more than once, generally in a different context. These recurrences are not like refrains, and do not fulfill anything remotely like the function of the classical refrain. Rather might they be compared to thought persistently on some main topic." The piano part uses clusters, widely spaced intervals, long trills, and other devices that help create sustained resonance. Strings damped by the hands; glissandi strummed on the strings with plectrum or nail file. An exciting experiment in duo sonority. D.

Felice Giardini. *Sonate* Op.3 (E. Polo—Fondazioni Eugenio Bravi 1941) *I Classici Musicali Italiani,* vol.3. For violin or flute and keyboard. 1 G, 2 C, 3 F, 4 A, 5 G, 6 D. "Elegant, balanced, and at many points of a delicate and original inspiration" (from the Preface by Polo). Two instruments are treated equally.

Joseph Gibbs. *Sonata* I d (Salter—Augener).

————. *Sonata* III G (D. Stone—Schott 1974) 12pp., parts. Continuo realization by Colin Tilney. Preface in English and German.

————. *Sonata* IV E (D. Stone—Schott 1974) 12pp., parts. Continuo realization by Colin Tilney. Preface in English and German.

————. *Sonata* V d (Moffat—Nov).

Walter Gieseking. *Variationen über ein Thema von Edvard Grieg* (Fürstner A8375 8358F 1938) 23pp., parts. For flute or violin and piano. See detailed entry under duos for piano and flute.

Alberto Ginastera. *Pampeana No. 1* Rhapsody Op.16 1947 (Barry 1954) 12pp., parts. Opens Lento e liberamente ritmato with violin in recitative style and piano with rolled or arpeggiated chords. Moves to an Allegro, the heart of the Rhapsody, in $\frac{6}{8} = \frac{3}{4}$. A rhythmic dance character follows with pianistic writing similar to that in the *Suite de danzas Criollas* composed the year before. Foreshadows the *Piano Sonata* (1952) with alternating chords between hands and percussive treatment. D.

Richard Franko Goldman. *Sonata* (Mercury 1964) 19pp., parts. Allegro moderato; Molto adagio; Molto allegro. Neoclassic. M-D.

Frederic Goossen. *Clausulae* 1971 (PIC 2276-17 1978) 17pp., parts. 12 min. In 7 continuous sections: I. Deliberato; II. Allegro vivo; III. Allegro; IV. Andante; V. Allegro vivo e feroce; VI. Andante; VII. Adagio. Score is copy of easy-to-read MS. M-D to D.

———. *Temple Music* 1972 (PIC 2275-28 1978) 28pp., parts. 16 min. In 3 movements: I. Allegro non troppo; II. Moderato; III. Pesante. Considerable octave work throughout. Score is copy of MS. D.

Eugene Goossens. *Sonata* I Op.21 e 1918 (JWC 321) 55pp., parts. Allegro con anima: contrary broken chordal figuration; inner and outer voice trills; freely tonal; syncopated chords; changing key signatures; arpeggi; parallelism; large span required. Molto adagio: 7th and 9th chords; chromatic; poetic; cantabile and expressive; broad arpeggi lines; 2 subjects are heard together with suggestions of a third. Con brio: dramatic gestures, glissando, light rocking motion, punctuated chords, 5 with 6 and 6 with 7 in arpeggi style, chords in contrary motion. Highly Romantic writing with a few mildly 20th-century sonorities. Second movement is probably the best of the 2 *Sonatas*. D.

———. *Sonata* II 1930 (JWC 370) 67pp., parts. Moderato con anima; Intermezzo–A la Sicilienne; Finale. Contains many of the devices found in *Sonata* I. Some of the French influences are retained, but there is also a German influence, especially that of Richard Strauss. Extreme chromaticism, large forms, textures with 3 individual layers, but firmly grounded in the Romantic tradition. D.

———. *Two Pieces* (MMP). Contains the *Romance* from the opera *Don Juan de Manara* and *Lyric Poem,* Op.35.

Henryk Górecki. *Sonatina in One Movement* 1956 (PWM 8332 1980) 7pp., parts. 2½ min. Allegro molto. An unpretentious work of playful quality suitable for less-experienced musicians. Int.

———. *Variazioni* Op.4 1956 (PWM 1980) 16pp., parts. 10 min. Introduction leads to a fluid theme in 8th and quarter notes with 9 variations and Finale. Clashing tonalities and bold writing contrasts quiet and smooth textures in rapidly changing characters. D.

———. *Little Fantasia* Op.73 1997 (Bo&H 1998) 11pp., parts. 13½ min. In one movement with considerable repetition and elements of minimalism. Most of the *Fantasia* is in slow tempos progressing in augmented values from 8ths to quarters to halves, and finally, to whole notes. Performers and audience must use much imagination to make this a fantasy. M-D.

Morton Gould. *Suite* 1945 (GS 3907 1947) 36pp., parts. 18 min. Warm Up: motoric; repeating patterns on large and small patterns. Serenade: alternating $\frac{3}{4}$, $\frac{2}{4}$ meters changing to $\frac{3}{4}$, $\frac{3}{8}$; grace notes; ternary form. March: "with rowdy gusto"; added-note and full tertian chords. Blues: rhapsodic; gentle rhythms; tremolos. Hoe Down: motoric; jumping patterns; broken and block chords; *sffz* finish. D.

Johann Gottlieb Graun. *Six Sonatas* (G. Müller—Sikorski 1957) published separately. Exciting and imaginative writing in most of the movements. Graun tried to incorporate all current trends and fashions in these pieces. See the Adagio of No.3 for highly unusual harmonic usage. There is plenty to keep both performers busy in these multimovement works. 1 D, 2 E, 3 A, 4 F, 5 g, 6 G. M-D.

Christoph Graupner. *Two Sonatas* (A. Hoffmann—HM 121) 19pp., parts. 1 g, 2 g. Treble line of keyboard part is written out, and the figured bass is abandoned. The 2 instruments are treated as equals, with the violin and the keyboard treble projected as the duetting solo lines. The editor points out in the Preface that these pieces are "an enrichment of our domestic player's estate." Excellent preparation for J. S. Bach's *Six Sonatas* with obbligato keyboard. M-D.

Giovanni Battista Grazioli. *Sei Sonate per Cembalo [od Organo] con Violino Obbligato* Op.3 (E. Zanovello—Armelin 120-1 1998), parts. Vol.I: g, G, D. Vol.II: F, C, A. Each *Sonata* is in 2 movements (except the first, in 3) and concludes with a Rondo. In a style similar to early Haydn though with greater dependence in left-hand octaves. Preface in Italian. M-D.

Edvard Grieg. *Sonata* I Op.8 F 1866 (C. Herrmann—CFP 1340 26pp., parts; Lichtenberg—GS L980; Spiering, Ganz—CF L271) 17 min. Opening graceful movement flows in Mendelssohn-Schumann style. Second movement shows charming Norwegian folk music influence. Third movement is fresh and scintillating. M-D.

———. *Sonata* II Op.13 G 1869 (CFP 2279 31pp., parts; Br&H; GS L525; Auer, Ganz—CF 03699; K 09206) 20 min. Called the "Dance Sonata"; rhapsodic in form. Full of youthful enthusiasm and vigor. Pleasing and refined with well-sustained interest throughout the relatively large form. M-D.

———. *Sonata* III Op.45 c 1887 (CFP 2414 45pp., parts; Spiering, Ganz—CF L786; GS L981) 24 min. Dramatic, Classical form, simple lines, the most fiery and important of the 3 *Sonatas*. The second movement, a romanza, is one of Grieg's most beautiful works. Of these 3 *Sonatas*, this one is closer to the level of other major Romantic violin Sonatas (such as those by Brahms, Fauré, and Franck). D.

See Rolf Christian Erdahl, "Edvard Grieg's Sonatas for Stringed Instrument and Piano: Performance Implications of the Primary Source Materials," 2 vols., D.M.A. diss., Peabody Institute of the Johns Hopkins University, 1994.

Louis Gruenberg. *White Lilacs* ca.1944 (GunMar 1989) 7pp., parts. 6 min. Third piece in the set *Four Silhouettes.* Probably composed around the time of Gruenberg's Violin Concerto. "*White Lilacs* is a miniature masterpiece, haunting and poignant in expression, elegant in style . . . located halfway between 'serious' recital and dazzling encore" (from Preface). M-D.

Camargo Guarnieri. *Sonata* 1/2 D 1930 (Ric BA 1957).

——. *Sonata* IV 1956 (Ric BA 11508) 36pp., parts. Energico ma espressivo; Intimo; Allegro appassionato. Flexible meters, freely tonal, much rhythmic drive in final movement along with splashing chords. D.

Gabriel Guillemain. *Sonata* Op.11/2 A (F. Polnauer—Sikorski 773 1972) 23pp., parts. Cello part optional. Allegro; Aria Gratioso; Presto. "The sonatas of Guillemain belong to the late epoch of the thoroughbass period and represent the galant style of the rococo" (from Preface). M-D.

Henry Hadley. *A Prayer* Op.86 (CF 1920) 5pp. parts. A brief, meditative work marked Andante with rich 19th-century harmonies and melodic writing. M-D.

George Frideric Handel. *Seven Sonatas* Op.1 (S. Sadie—Henle 1971). Based on the most reliable sources available. Clean edition, practical as well as scholarly. Also includes *Sonata* 1/6 g for oboe, marked for "Violino Solo" in Handel's autograph, which was left out of the Handel Halle edition (Br 1955). The keyboard part is simply realized, and the editor invites the more accomplished continuo player to feel free to elaborate. Editorial additions are shown in brackets. Textual commentary on each work is included. Also includes Op.1/10 g, 12 F, 13 D, 14 A, 15 E. Also available: *Six Sonatas* Op.1 (L. Bus, U. Haverkampf—Br&H 1974) 35pp., parts. Vol.I: Op.1/3 A, 10 g, 12 D. Vol.II: Op.1/13 D, 14 A, 15 E. *Sechs Sonaten* (J. P. Hinnenthal—Br 1955) Hallischer Händel-Ausgabe, Serie IV, Instrumentalmusik, Band 4. *Six Sonatas* from Op.1 (Sikorski, Wysocka-Ochiewska, Felinski—PWM) 2 vols. *Six Sonatas* from Op.1 (Auer, Friedberg—CF L846; Betti—GS L1545; Davisson, Ramin—CFP 4157A,B 2 vols.; Jacobsen—CFP 2475C,D 2 vols.; Doflein—Schott 2 vols.; Francescatti, Fuessl—IMC 2 vols.; Gevaert, Busch—Br&H 2 vols.; Maglioni—Ric ER2449; Augener 8668 2 vols.; Nov) includes Op.1/3 A, 10 g, 12 F, 13 D, 14 A, 15 E. *Four Sonatas* Op.1 (Hillemann—Schott). Available separately: Op.1/3 A (Auer, Friedberg—CF B3280; Hermann—Augener 7336; CFP). Op.1/10 g (Jensen—Augener 7426; Seiffert—Br&H; Wessely—J. Williams). Op.1/12 F (Riemann—Augener 7502; Wessely—J. Williams; Br&H). Op.1/13 D (Auer, Friedberg—CF B2703; Jensen

—Augener 7427; Wessely—J. Williams; Br&H). Op.1/14 A (Seiffert—Br&H; Wessely—J. Williams). Op.1/15 E (Br&H; Auer, Friedberg—CF B3325; Gibson—Augener 7377; Wessely—J. Williams).

——. *Sonata* d (R. Howat—OUP 1975) 15pp., parts. 8 min. Musica da Camera 25. A fresh and exciting work with a fine sense of proportion between the 4 movements. Impeccable edition. M-D.

Algot Haquinius. *Svit* (GM 1943) 7pp., parts. Andante moderato; Andante espressivo; Allegro moderato. Post-Romantic, tonal, Sibelius-like in style. Requires large span. M-D.

John Harbison. *Fantasy-Duo* 1988 (AMP 8008 1988) 48pp., parts. 14 min. In one extended movement. Opens Comodo ma preciso with dense chord structures spaced over 3 octaves, scalar runs in violin, and an impregnable melody emphasizing the tritone over an Alberti bass. Progresses into sections requiring more motion using repeated octaves or near octaves and chordal jumps as if arpeggios. An Allegro follows with a duet between instruments in multimeters of marcato nature. Sections allowing an expressive rubato give greater freedom and fantasy. Imitative elements abound as the work progresses to its penultimate section, a Perpetuum mobile marked Presto. Herein repeated notes are passed between instruments with sprinklings of arpeggiation, syncopation, and glissandos in constantly changing meters based on 8th and quarter notes. The work concludes with a return to the opening, transformed for a *pp* finish. Richly rewarding for experienced performers. Wide span required. D.

Roy Harris. *Sonata in Four Movements* 1942 (Belwin-Mills 1953) 41pp., parts. Rev.1974. Fantasy; Dance of Spring; Melody; Toccata. One of Harris's most impressive chamber works. The 4 large movements are freely tonal, with strong unities and bold contrasts. The movements are linked subjectively rather than thematically. The Toccata sizzles with excitement. D.

——. *Dance of Spring* (Belwin-Mills 1944) 8pp., parts. A succinct unpretentious dance in $\frac{6}{8}$ with hand crossings, sometimes awkward scalar patterns, and rich harmonies characteristic of early-20th-century tonality. M-D.

——. *Melody* (Belwin-Mills 1944) 9pp., parts. Extended opening in piano notated on 3 staves for spacing leads to songlike melody in violin. Full chords and octaves are characteristic as the intensity climbs to *fff* then subsides to a concluding chordal section marked Religioso. M-D.

——. *Fantasy* (Belwin-Mills 1945) 12pp., parts. Opens explosively as if bells are ringing. Full chords; arpeggiation traded between hands; 3 with 2; octotonic. Performers must be attentive to balance, especially on the last page where the violin finishes in its low register as the piano rings with sweeping chords at *ff.* D.

Moritz Hauptmann. *Six Sonatas* (CFP), parts. Vol.I: Op.5/1 g, 2 E♭, 3 D. Vol.II: Op.23/1 B♭, 2 G, 3 d. A violinist himself, Hauptmann wrote innately for the instrument, combining fluid and expressive qualities in a rich tapestry of early-19th-century pianistic techniques. These works deserve to be better known. M-D to D.

Miska Hauser. *Rhapsodie Hongroise* Op.43 (CFP 1891) 11pp., parts. An 11-measure piano introduction marked Adagio sets the rhapsodic character with marcato chords and melismatic flourishes. Proceeds with statement of theme and Allegro vivace, the heart of the work. Herein the emphasis is somewhat uneven with a leaning toward the violin for melodic concentration. The Adagio returns briefly near the end before a fiery finish with much animation. M-D.

Franz Joseph Haydn. The 8 or 9 *Sonatas* for violin and piano of this great composer in published editions are either transcriptions or arrangements. *Eight Sonatas* (CFP 190). *Sonata* 1 G is an arrangement of piano *Trio* Hob. (Hoboken) XV:32. 11 min. *Sonata* 2 D is an arrangement of piano *Sonata* Hob.XVI: 24. 10 min. *Sonata* 3 E♭ is an arrangement of piano *Sonata* Hob.XVI:25. *Sonata* 4 A is an arrangement of Piano Sonata Hob.XVI:26. 8 min. *Sonata* 5 G is an arrangement of Piano Sonata A♭, Hob.XVI:43. 10 min. *Sonata* 6 C is an arrangement of Piano Sonata Hob.XVI:15. *Sonata* 7 F is an arrangement of String Quartet Hob.III:82. 19 min. *Sonata* 8 G (for violin or flute) is an arrangement of String Quartet Hob.III:81.
——. *Nine Sonatas* (Betti—GS L1541). Includes an extra *Sonata* D.
——. *Eight Sonatas* (David—Augener 8672).
——. *Sonata* G Hob.XV:32 1794 (I. Becker-Glauch, J. Demus, K. Guntner—Henle 437 1987) 18pp., parts. Andante; Allegro. Composed near the end of the composer's career, this *Sonata* represents the fullest maturity of the composer in his approach to the instruments. Rich expressive qualities bubble from both movements with a colorful palette of imitative and homophonic resources. From the Haydn Complete Edition, minus a questionable cello part whose authenticity now leads scholars to believe the version for piano trio may not have been by Haydn after all. M-D.

Bernhard Heiden. *Sonata* 1954 (AMP 1961) 27pp., parts. Molto tranquillo, rubato; Molto vivace; Andante; Allegro deciso. Graceful and grateful in form and material, clear textures. Moves with ease in a Neoclassic style. M-D.

Paavo Heininen. *Sonata* Op.25 1970 (Finnish Music Information Center) 25 min. One movement. Moves from Tranquillo through a Tempo giusto (Allegro moderato) section before returning to a Tranquillo, misterioso and Tranquillo al fine to conclusion. Twelve-tone. Trill is exploited in both instruments. Large span required. Expressionist, pointillistic. D.

Anthony Philip Heinrich. *Scylla and Charybdis: Capriccio erratico* (Kallisti 1991) 36pp., parts. 15 min. A large one-movement design in 6 sections.

Everett Helm. *Sonata* (Schott 4047 1950) 28pp., parts. 19 min. Allegro; Lento ma non troppo; Presto. Contrasting movements, mildly 20th-century, impressive melodic treatment. The Presto is treated contrapuntally with interspersed chorale-like episodes. Large span required. D.

Fini Henriques. *Sonata* Op.10 g (WH). A large 4-movement post-Romantic work with some interest, although dated. M-D to D.

Fanny Hensel. *Adagio* E 1823 (R. Marciano—Furore 137 1989) 8pp., parts. "It is indeed a very simple piece of music which is charmingly designed as a dialogue. What makes the refinement of this composition is the way both instruments are 'exchanging thoughts.' Fanny seems here to become introspective in a highly sensitive way and to talk softly to herself" (from Preface). M-D.

Hans Werner Henze. *Sonata* 1946 (Schott 3859) 25pp., parts. 15 min. Prélude; Nocturne; Intermezzo; Finale. Neo-Romantic style, somewhat surprising for Henze. Finale uses fast chords in alternating hands. Large span required. D.
——. *Fünf Nachtstücke* 1990 (Schott 7825 1992) 16pp., parts. Elegie; Capriccio; First Shepherd's Song; Second Shepherd's Song; Ode. Economical writing showing Webern influence; bitonality; complex rhythms; *ppppp* to *fff* dynamics. D.

Lejaren A. Hiller. *Sonata* I 1949 (Kallisti 1992) 40pp., parts.
——. *Sonata* III (TP 1971) 40pp., parts. Furioso: clusters; serial; changing meters; pointillistic; spread out over entire keyboard; dynamic extremes; pianist has to play some clusters with the chin; outer notes in some chords must be played with elbows. Largo: long pedal effects with damper and sostenuto pedals; many repeated chords in low register; many strings of the bottom octave have to be hit inside piano with a large, soft tam-tam beater. Prestissimo: sweeping gestures in both instruments; sprawling layout; ends with a cluster chord; large span required. Requires virtuoso pianism throughout most of the work. D.

Paul Hindemith. *Sonata* Op.11/1 E♭ 1918 (Schott) 9 min. A short 2-movement work, one fast (Frisch), the other a slow dance (Im Zeitmass eines langsamer, feierlichen Tanzes) with much chromatic harmony. Extensive melodic development with harmonic barbs thrown in from time to time. M-D.
——. *Sonata* Op.11/2 D 1918 (Schott) 27pp., parts. 18 min. Lebhaft; Ruhig und gemessen; Im Zeitmasse und Charakter eines geschwinden Tanzes. Brahms and Reger influence. Linear development much more important than in Op.11/1. Third section is a fast dance movement. Lacks a uniformity of terse style but foreshadows later developments in the composer's career. D.
——. *Sonata* E (Schott 2455 1935) 15pp., parts. 9 min. Lusty strength and clear textures in these 2 short movements. Not nearly as difficult as the first 2 *Sonatas*. Ruhig bewegt: $\frac{9}{8}$, SA, subjects recapitulated in reverse. Langsam: slow–very

lively–slow–again lively; $^6_8$ seems to evolve from the $^9_8$ of the first movement; a lively dance contrasts with the slow sections. Connective principle binds the work formally. M-D.

———. *Sonata* C 1939 (Schott) 12 min. More elaborate and involved than *Sonata* E. Lebhaft: short, monothematic, prelude-like, athletic, cohesive stability. Langsam: deliberately paced ABA with the mid-section a rhythmically delightful scherzo in $^3_8$. Fugue: rondo form, complex triple fugue, combination of subjects especially difficult for the pianist, dynamic writing; C termination is most satisfying. D.

See VKDR, II: pp.267–77.

Alun Hoddinott. *Sonata* I Op.63 (OUP). 15 min.

———. *Sonata* II Op.73/1 (OUP). Not truly a Sonata, more a work for 2 to play. Cluster-like chords, cadenza, thin-textured moto perpetuo. Opening movement material returns in concluding Episodi e Coda. Plenty of technical problems for both instruments. D.

———. *Sonata* III Op.78/1 (OUP 1973) 24pp., parts. Intense organization, serial, homogeneous density, uncompromisingly dissonant at certain places, strong lyric writing. Works to a strong climax through the first movement and then unwinds palindromically. D.

———. *Sonata* IV Op.89 (OUP, ISBN 0-19-3571668). 18 min.

———. *Sonata* V (Oriana).

———. *Sonata* VI (Oriana). 18 min.

Sonatas I–III are now available through Archive Service, Allegro Music.

Franz Anton Hoffmeister. *Sonata* Op.13 C 1795–1805 (H.-P. Schmitz—Nag 236 1973) 40pp., parts. 20 min. with repeats. For flute or violin and piano. See detailed entry under duos for piano and flute.

Lee Hoiby. *Sonata* Op.5 1951, rev. 1979 (Rock Valley Music), parts. Allegro; Lento sostenuto; Allegro molto. A mid-20th-century work firmly rooted in the composer's preference for rich harmonies in a neo-Romantic manner. Octaves; full chords; expansive use of keyboard; agility. D.

Karl Höller. *Sonata* Op.4 (Litolff 1929, new ed. 1968) 26pp., parts.

———. *Vierte Sonate* Op.37 F♯ (CFP 5975 1965) 36pp., parts. Allegro appassionato: SA; chromatic; arpeggi figuration; develops logically. Andante sostenuto: more diatonic and linear; long, contoured lines; chordal mid-section. Agitato, tema con variazioni e fuga: quartal harmony; large arpeggiated chords; chromatic octaves and chords; theme and 6 contrasting variations lead to a highly chromatic fugue. Extension of Brahms-Reger tradition. D.

Heinz Hollinger. *Lieder ohne Worte* Vol.II 1985–94 (Schott 8430 1997, ISMN M-001-11238-3) 28pp., parts. 23 min. I. Frühlingslied (in memoriam Sándor Veress); II. Intermezzo I; III. (. . . fern . . .); IV. Intermezzo II; V. (. . . sam);

VI. (Flammen . . . Schnee); VII. Berceuse matinale (in memoriam Gertrud Demenga). Very complex rhythmic relationships in I, V, VI, including proportional structures requiring 4 staves for piano. Straightforward meters and note values in II, IV, VII. Uses extremes of instruments. Harmonies built on 2nds, 3rds, 4ths, and 5ths, with added notes. Novel effects for sonorous purposes. May be performed in different orders or as a selection of works as described in Preface. D.

Vagn Holmboe. *Sonata* II Op.16 1939 (WH 30146 1991) 29pp., parts. 16 min. Allegro moderato: SA; use of "germ" motive, expanded by fine craftsmanship in Neoclassic style; octotonic. Andante tranquillo: declamatory; large span required; expands on certain motivic features of previous movement. Allegro non troppo ma con brio: continues declamatory style; thick chordal writing; much interaction between instruments. M-D to D.

——. *Sonata* III Op.89 1965 (WH 30184 1992) 27pp., parts. 14 min. Moderato: recitative-like opening and conclusion contrasted by canonic treatment mixing duplets and triplets in middle. Allegro molto: triplet motive with detailed scalar writing in octaves; *pp* finish. Adagio ma non troppo: lyric; recitative-like opening followed by austere, terse writing. Allegro con forza: dramatic; expressive; mild use of cluster chords; forced finish on C's. M-D to D.

Arthur Honegger. *Sonate* I c♯ 1916–18 (Sal) 28pp., parts. 18 min. Andante sostenuto; Presto; Adagio–Allegro assai. Added-note technique, crossed hands, chromatic, glissandi, octotonic, subito dynamic changes. Multiple meters in finale— $\frac{10}{4}$: 4+2+4 in piano with 3+3+4 in violin. Ostinati, Impressionist, strong formal construction. Requires large span. D.

——. *Sonate* II B 1919 (Sal) 11½ min. Opening movement is sensuous and swinging in triple- and quadruple-pulse patterns. In place of a development a fugato section is substituted. A monothematic slow movement is constructed with figuration that twines around the main theme. The finale introduces 2 main ideas in the low register of the piano. D.

Alan Hovhaness. *Oror* Op.1 (CFP 1964) 6pp., parts. 3 min. A tonal, colorful lullaby. Int.

——. *Varak* Op.47 (CFP 1971) 9pp., parts. 5 min. Andante, noble and majestic: interplay between parts. Allegro: piano has many 16th-note figurations and much pattern repetition. Contrasted movements. M-D.

——. *Khirgiz Suite* Op.73 (CFP 1968) 9pp., parts. 4 min. Variations; A Khirgiz Tala; Allegro molto. Cumulative hypnotic effect. Each movement revolves around a few notes. Neither dissonant nor consonant. M-D.

——. *Three Visions of Saint Mesrob* Op.198 (CPF 1963) 7pp., parts. Celestial Mountain: broken and solid chords, cluster-like. Celestial Bird: freely measured; violin may begin at any time; piano part represents twittering of celestial birds; pandiatonic throughout. Celestial Alphabet: harmonic 7ths for piano. M-D.

——. *Saris* (CFP 1947) 16pp., parts. 8 min. Saris was the ancient Urarduan love goddess. Violin opening is followed by 3 pages of highly repetitious writing in the style of a *saz,* a long-necked, plucked string instrument from Turkey with a small, round, convex belly. Violin and piano merge with the 2 figurations heard first separately. Pedal is held for long sections. Written in the composer's international style. M-D.

Mary Howe. *Sonata* D (CFP 1962) 28pp., parts. The style is neo-Romantic, with the piano treated in a Brahmsian manner. Effective writing, if dated for the period. Allegro ma non troppo: SA. Lento recitativo: allegro scherzando midsection; opening idea returns before a final allegro vivo boldly ends the movement. Allegro non troppo: 2 basic ideas developed; *pp* coda, *ppp* closing. M-D.

Herbert Howells. *Sonata* I Op.18 E 1918 (Bo&H) 16 min. One movement with 4 designated sections. Fantasy-like with a kind of rhapsodic element, broad sweeping lines, contemplative, remote, shifting rhythms. M-D.

——. *Sonata* III Op.38 e 1923 (OUP) 20 min. Poco allegro, semplice; Allegro moderato, assai ritmico; Vivace, assai ritmico. Explores new (for Howells) tonal treatment and has more dissonance than *Sonata* I. D.

Johann Nepomuk Hummel. *Sonata* Op.5/1 B♭ 1798 (F. Samohyl—Dob 1963) 36pp., parts. Allegro moderato; Andante con variazioni; Rondo. Piano is most important, but much interplay takes place between the instruments. Delightful and grateful part writing; fun but difficult, especially for the pianist. Does not stand up too well with repeated hearings. A thorough stylistic understanding of the period is necessary to realize this work properly. M-D.

Karel Husa. *Sonatina* 1945 (AMP 8151 1999) 29pp., parts. 15 min. This youthful work on Classical models was composed before Husa studied with Honegger and Boulanger. Hints of Czech folk song are integrated into its musical language, strongly tonal with only mildly 20th-century dissonances. M-D to D.

——. *Sonata* 1972–73 (AMP) 20 min. A super-virtuoso showpiece full of spiccatos, double stops, scales, arpeggi. Twentieth-century sounding throughout. Difficult to follow thematic ideas in performance, but the work has much to recommend it. D.

Jacques Ibert. *Histoires* (Leduc 1931). 22 min. Effective transcription by Arthur Hoérée from the original for piano solo. Ten picturesque pieces on programmatic titles, including the famous "Le Petit âne blanc" (The Little White Donkey). M-D.

——. *Aria* (Leduc 1930), parts. 4 min. Transcription by the composer of the

original vocalise for voice and piano with the violin playing the voice part almost identically. Wide span required. M-D.

——. *Jeux: Sonatine* (Leduc 1925). See detailed entry under duos for piano and
flute.

Toshi Ichiyanagi. *Intercross* (Schott 1993), parts. 12 min. Performance instructions in English and Japanese.

Vincent d'Indy. *Sonata* Op.59 C (Durand 1905). A strong and original work even
though the opening and the rhythmic patterns owe much to Franck. The airy
and rather strange Scherzo movement is more chromatic than Franck's style
and leads to a tonally ambiguous feeling. D.

John Ireland. *Sonata* I d 1909 (Galliard) 28 min. Strong lyricism. Allegro leg-
giardo: SA, second tonal area in the relative major, 3 subsidiary themes. Romance: long melodic lines, chordal episode. Rondo: Grieg's influence, least satisfactory movement. M-D.

——. *Sonata* II a 1915–17 (Bo&H) 49pp., parts. 27 min. This is Ireland's masterpiece from this period. Exhibits fine craftsmanship throughout. Allegro:
dramatic, rugged, craggy. Poco lento quasi adagio: lyric, elegaic, suave theme.
In tempo moderato: lively popular-type melodies, releases tensions built up in
first 2 movements. D.

Charles E. Ives. *Sonata* I 1903–1908 (PIC 1953) 30pp., parts. 26 min. Andante–
Allegro vivace; Largo cantabile; Allegro. Abstract writing. The finely organized slow movement is extended, free, and noble, and filled with rich melodic
invention and contrapuntal texture. The hymn "Watchman, Tell Us of the
Night!" is used with dissonant accompanied treatment in the final movement. D.

——. *Sonata* II 1902–10 (GS 1951) 26pp., parts. Portraits are offered of: Autumn: thickest of the movements. In the Barn: a square dance, in effect the
scherzo; much snap and fun here with the improvising of a country-dance
fiddler; the tone-cluster "drum music" adds to the fantastic effect of the closing pages. The Revival: recalls the mounting intensity of a camp meeting and
works over thoroughly the hymn tune "Nettleton" in variation technique; the
closing is touchingly beautiful. D.

——. *Sonata* III 1902–14 (S. Babitz, I. Dahl—NME 1951) 26 min. Adagio
(verse 1) –Andante con moto (verse 2) –Allegretto (verse 3) –Adagio (last
verse); Allegro; Adagio. Abstract writing, grandly conceived, intense expression. All 3 movements evolve from the hymn "I Need Thee Every Hour," although the derivations are very obscure. The first movement is in reality variations with improvisatory excursions. Verse 3 is a fast, tricky, syncopated dance
tune with ragtime elements extravagantly thrown in. The Adagio is very beautiful with the hymn tune finally heard in its original form. D.

——. *Sonata* IV 1912–15, "Children's Day at the Camp Meeting" (AMP 1942)
20pp., parts. 10 min. Allegro; Largo; Allegro. The shortest of the 4 violin *Sona-*

tas, this work is based on the children's day at the outdoor summer camp meetings of the late 19th century in many farm towns of Connecticut. Its special American flavor is derived in part from commonly sung hymns of the day which Ives incorporated into the music, especially "Work for the Night Is Coming," "Jesus Loves Me," and "Shall We Gather at the River," found individually in the 3 respective movements. While the outer movements are rambunctious, the middle movement is particularly touching as it depicts elements of nature and religious expression in a quiet, tranquil setting broken only by an Allegro conslugarocko for piano solo depicting the boys throwing stones in the brook. The piano provides strongly dissonant chordal settings in all 3 movements, and weaker registers of the violin are occasionally pitted against a full piano part. D.

See Laurence Perkins, "The Sonatas for Violin and Piano by Charles Ives," Ph.D. diss., University of Rochester, Eastman School of Music, 1961.

Elizabeth-Claude Jacquet de la Guerre. *Sonates* 1707 (C. H. Bates—Furore 290; 350; 392), parts, with bass. Vol.I: 1 d; 2 D. Vol.II: 3 F; 4 G. Vol.III: 5 a; 6 A. "La Guerre's sonatas as a whole contain four to nine movements arranged on the basis of contrast but without adherence to any one pattern. Movements with tempo titles prevail, but arias and dances are also present . . . Although La Guerre's sonatas display a considerable variety of compositional techniques, they nonetheless exhibit several characteristic features, namely, simple yet artful melodies, repeated-note patterns, syncopations, major-minor inflections, and harmonic mutations. Frequent changes of mode and an occasional incorporation of contrasting keys attest to La Guerre's love of tonal contrast" (from Preface). Tasteful figured-bass realizations by editor. Occasional movements give the cello an independent voice apart from figured bass, resulting in a true trio as would later develop. Excellent Preface and critical commentary in English and German. M-D.

———. *Sonata* D (Borroff—University of Pittsburgh Press).

Leoš Janáček. *Ballada* (Philharmusica 1974) 8pp., parts. For violin, flute, or oboe and piano. Undulating passagework (32nd notes) interspersed with 2 chromatic chordal episodes. M-D.

———. *Dumka* 1880 (Hudební Matice 1947). More ballade-like than a true "dumka." Long lines. Not the best of this composer. M-D.

———. *Sonata* 1914, rev. during World War I, completed in 1921 (Artia 1966). Written in Janáček's nationalist and rugged style. Uses difficult keys (c♯, d♭, e♭, g♯) and broad deliberate tempos. Con moto: SA; mainly monothematic, second subject being an extension of the first (new theme in coda); tremolo in piano part accounts for atmospheric sonorities; abrupt tempo changes. Ballada: more tuneful; ABA design; exploits a folklike theme in B section with fluid chromatic runs in both instruments used to great effect. Adagio: almost mosaic-like in small sections; brings back some of the unusual figurations from the first movement. Fascinating rhythmic procedure, unusual texture and highly original writing, especially for the piano. Strong mood and texture continuity maintained in each movement. D.

———. *Compositions for Violin and Piano* (A. Němcová—Supraphon 1998) 118pp., parts. From the Complete Critical Edition of the Works of Janáček, Series E, Vol.2. *Romance* (1879); *Dumka* (1880); *Sonata* (1914–21); *Allegro* (1916). Introductory notes in Czech, German, English, French, and Russian. M-D to D.

Gustav Jenner. *Sonate* a 1893, rev. 1900 (H. Heussner—Schott VLB84 1993) 47pp., parts. Allegro; Andante–Allegro appassionato; Allegro energico. Jenner quotes material from his Lied "Hinter den Tannen" in the Allegro appassionato.

———. *Sonate* B♭ ca.1895 (H. Huessner—Schott VLB79 1990) 51pp., parts. 26 min. Allegro commodo; Adagio; Allegretto grazioso; Allegro non troppo.

———. *Sonate* E♭ 1899 (H. Heussner—Schott VLB80 1990) 32pp., parts. 20 min. Allegro moderato e grazioso; Adagio non troppo ed espressivo; Allegro non troppo.
Jenner's *Sonates* follow closely in Brahms's style, with whom he studied from 1888 to 1895, through an expansive compositional style process based upon Classical models. Informative Prefaces in German and English appear in each volume. These *Sonates* provide a fine alternative to those of Brahms but will never supersede them. D.

Ivan Jirko. *Sonata* 1959 (Artia) 61pp., parts. Con moto tranquillo; Allegro moderato; Andante–Allegro non troppo. Freely tonal, octotonic, broken chords in alternating hands, tertial harmonies. Second movement is toccata-like and contains arpeggi figuration. Strong rhythmic drive in the finale. Some nationalistic coloring. Large span required. M-D to D.

Lockrem Johnson. *Two Sonatas* (Dow 1955) 16pp., parts. Contains *Sonata Breve* Op.26 1948, rev.1949, 1953. 6 min. Lyrical, intensely expressive, rich in constructive melodic devices that give it an organic coherence and vitality. Unusual and well-calculated form. *Sonata Rinverdita* Op.38 1953. Similar to above. Both *Sonatas* are in one movement. M-D.

André Jolivet. *Sonate pour Piano et Violon* 1932 (D. Erlih—Sal 18744 1989) 37pp., parts. Ramassé; Librement (très lent); Bousculé. Intense writing in strong Neoclassic vein with blunt dissonances, sharp rhythmic features, and hints of Expressionism. Odd meters, such as 1+ ½ + 2 + ½ over 4, pop in and out in contrapuntal textures which are sometimes imitative. In spite of the innovative quality and stringent harmonies, the movements end on solid harmonic structures. Appropriately titled with piano listed first, though violin is only marginally easier. D.

———. *Aubade* E♭ 1932 (Billaudot 1991) 7pp., parts. 4 min. An unusually facile and richly harmonious depiction of dawn with lyric melody by a composer who would also engage brazen and austere harmonies in other works in a distinctive tonal language. Int.

Charles Jones. *Sonatina* 1942 (CFP 6019) 16pp., parts. 7 min. Allegro; Larghetto; Allegro deciso. Positive influence of Milhaud felt. Full of lyricism, sound structure, rhythmic vigor and brilliance. Imaginative and unique unconventional compositional language. Requires a firm rhythmic control. D.

Richard Jones. *Four Suites* (G. Beechey—OUP 1974) 1 A, 2 g, 3 D, 4 B♭. Each *Suite* has 5 movements: a Preludio, usually serious in character, followed by 4 dance movements. Fluently written, attractive entertainment music. The continuo player may realize his or her own bass part, for the continuo part contains only the bass line and the original figures. Int. to M-D.

Joseph Jongen. *Sonate* II Op.34 E 1909 (Durand 7704 1910) 50pp., parts. Assez lent–Animé; Assez lent; Finale: Assez animé. A large expansive work well grounded in late-19th-century harmonies without extensive chromaticism. Schumannesque and Brahmsian with full chords, octaves, arpeggiation, and intense expressivity. D.

Mihail Jora. *Sonata* Op.46 (Editura Muzicala 1964) 36pp., parts. Allegro brillante: SA, $\frac{5}{8}$, chromatic changing meters. Andante cantabile: ABA; long lines; chromatic; constant tonal insecurity; large span required. Allegro assai: duple with some triple interrupting from time to time; triplets; dancelike section has shifting rhythms; dramatic run from top to bottom of keyboard; thankfully ends on a D chord! A big "splashing" kind of work, colorful if a little contrived at spots. D.

Dmitri Kabalevsky. *Improvisation* Op.21/1 (Leeds 1945) 8pp., parts. Freely composed with expected early-20th-century flavor. Full chords, arpeggiation, chromaticism, 7 with 3 rhythmic relationships. M-D.

Pal Kadosa. *Suite* Op.6 (Bo&H) Five movements, no fingerings, piano part more effective than violin. M-D.

———. *Sonata* II Op.58 (EMB 1962). Preambule: rhapsodic. Scherzo: trio is most successful part. Finale: sustained sections contrasted with dancelike sections. M-D.

Heinrich Kaminski. *Hauskonzert* 1941 (Br 2050 1973) 28pp., parts. Praeludium; Opfertanz; Frühlingstanz; Finale. Neo-Baroque style with a few complex polyphonic entanglements set in a freely tonal framework. M-D.

Gija Kantscheli. *time . . . and again* 1996 (Sikorski 1980 2000, ISMN M-003-03037-1) 19pp., parts. Original version. Prefaced with biblical verse: "What I write is true, God knows I am not lying" (Gal. 1:20). In one sustained movement at very slow tempos. Sharply changing dramatic characters abound with frequent contrasts of loud passages moving to soft sustained chords. Harmonies range from traditional tertian structures to clusters. Atmospheric ending at *ppp*. Large span required. M-D.

Armin Kaufmann. *Sonatina* Op.53/1 (Dob 1974) 36pp., parts. Perky rhythms, tunes seem to be inspired by Bartók and Hindemith, mildly 20th-century-sounding. M-D.

Ulysses Kay. *Partita* A 1950 (ACA) 15 min.
———. *Sonatina* 1943 (ACA) 9 min. Easy flowing, warm sentiments. M-D.

Donald Keats. *Polarities* 1970 (AMC) 15pp., parts. Andante: serially influenced; intense; builds to dramatic climax; quiet ending; free cadenza for violin; piano part requires large span. Allegro: alternation of free and strict tempos, changing meters, fiery conclusion. Requires a first-rate pianist and experienced ensemble players. Can be stunning with the proper performers. D.

Milko Kelemen. *"good-bye my fancy!"* 1998 (Sikorski 1986 1999, ISMN M-003-03084-5) 26pp., parts. 15 min. Inspired by the poem by Walt Whitman. An extended single movement using conventional and nonconventional notation. Microtones, clusters, and chance elements are probed using the extremes of the instruments. D.

Robert Kelly. *Sonata* Op.22 1952 (ACA) 25pp., parts. 14 min. Vigorous; Slow; Moderate. Freely tonal around e, fluent rhythms, clear textures, traditional forms, spontaneous quality, forceful and distinctive style. M-D.

Aaron Jay Kernis. *Air* 1995 (AMP 8095 1995, ISBN 0-7935-5050-5) 13pp., parts. 11 min. "*Air* is songlike and melodic, and it is the 'purest' and sparest piece I've written in a few years. It contains many hymn- or chant-like elements, and though rooted in E♭ major, it retains a kind of plaintive quality more reminiscent of minor or modal tonalities. Formally, it combines a developing variation form with a simple song form" (Note by Composer). D.

Harrison Kerr. *Sonata* (Berben 1973) 28pp., parts. Large one-movement work. Dramatic gestures in the short Tempo liberamente introduction lead to a chromatic, secco, staccato Allegretto, in which there is much 16th-note motion. Changing tempos provide contrast for rest of work. Highly chromatic, but tonal. Requires first-rate pianistic equipment. D.

Willem Kersters. *Partita* Op.9 1956 (CeBeDeM) 24pp., parts. 9½ min. Intrada; Allemande; Courante; Sarabande; Gigue. Neoclassic structures, chromatic language. Relies heavily on octotonic technique. D.

Aram Khachaturian. *Two Pieces* 1926 (K 04403) 16pp., parts. 1. Dance; 2. Lyric Poem. Commanding writing rich with early-20th-century techniques and virtuosic qualities. D.

Karen Khachaturian. *Sonata* Op.1 1957 (USSR) 44pp., parts. Allegro; Andante; Presto. This work has a difficult time achieving its goal. Each movement has some interesting colorful material, but a tendency to wander prevents much direction. Large span required. M-D to D.

Friedrich Kiel. *Zwei Solostücke* Op.70 (C. Dohr—Dohr 98526 1998) 34pp., parts. 1. Andante con moto–Allegro; 2. Largo ma non troppo–Prestissimo. Mid-19th-century works reflecting compositional styles typical of the epoch. Extensive notes in German. M-D.

Gottfried Kirchhoff. *Zwölf Sonaten* (W. Serauky—Schott 5060-1 1960), parts, including bass. Vol.I: 1 d; 2 C; 3 G; 4 D; 5 E; 6 a. Vol.II: 7 A; 8 F; 9 e; 10 B♭; 11 b; 12 B♭. Follows late Baroque Sonata format of slow-fast-slow-fast, with additional 5th movement. Occasional dance movements. Tasteful figured-bass realizations. Preface in Vol.I in English, German, and French. M-D.

Leon Kirchner. *Duo* (Mercury 1947) 22pp., parts. 12 min. Aaron Copland wrote of this rhapsodic work: "Kirchner's best pages prove that he reacts strongly (to today's unsettled world); they are charged with an emotional impact and explosive power that is almost frightening in intensity. Whatever else may be said, this is music that is most certainly 'felt.' No wonder his listeners have been convinced." *Notes* 7 (1950): 434.

———. *Sonata Concertante* (Mercury 1952) 28pp., parts. 22 min. In one continuous intense and gloomy yet lyrical movement with "attacca" separating the Adagio molto from the Grazioso. Many metronome markings (30!). Varied musical texture, chromatic idiom, dissonant, driving rhythms. Many accelerations and ritardandos shift mood, texture, and rhythms; these are vital to successful performance. Separate cadenzas for both violin and piano provide a unique blending of the instruments. A complex, involved work requiring the best from experienced and highly sensitive performers. D.

Theodor Kirchner. *Romanze und Schlummerlied* Op.63 (H. Joelson—Amadeus 1998) 23pp., parts. Also includes 3 very short works: *Gedenkblatt* (from *Memorials,* Op.82/6); *Walzer* (Op.86/5); *Abendlied* (Op.59/2). These 5 pieces reveal Kirchner as a composer of intense expression, with thick chordal writing suggesting the influence of Schumann and Brahms. Introductory comments in English and German. M-D to D.

———. *12 Phantasiestücke* Op.90 (H. Joelson—Amadeus 2208 1998) 36pp., parts. Arnold Niggli described these pieces in the *Swiss Singers Paper* (July 31, 1895) as "Gems, like almost everything written by Robert Schumann's inspired disciple, are these Fantasy Pictures and Miniatures, in which a world of poetic feeling is concentrated into but a few measures. And yet each work sings and resounds the fragrance of consonance in a way so typical for Kirchner, executing an entrancing charm through its delicate musical nature" (from Preface). M-D to D.

Giselher Klebe. *Sonata* Op.14 (Schott 1953) 8½ min. Short, 3-movement work in Webernesque style, 12 tone. The piece is full-textured but delicate sounding, colorful and not contrived. Major and minor 2nds are in abundance both vertically and linearly. D.

————. *Sonate* Op.66 (Br 1973) 33pp., parts. Three movements. Written for Boris Blacher's 70th birthday and based on the letters B♭oriE♭(s) B♭lACB(h)Er from his name. Written in a lyric, neo-Impressionist, dodecaphonic-like texture. M-D.

Erland von Koch. *Rytmiska Bagateller* 1957–75 (GM 1976) 24pp., parts. Ten short pieces using fresh and unusual rhythms and meters. Originally written for solo piano. Violin part may also be played by a flute, oboe, recorder, clarinet, or other instrument. A fine introduction to 20th-century techniques. M-D.

Joonas Kokkonen. *Duo* 1955 (Finnish Music Information Center) 50pp., parts. 17½ min. Allegro moderato; Allegretto grazioso; Un poco adagio–Allegro. Neoclassic; much unison writing 2 octaves apart; serial overtones provide much chromatic usage; clear and consistent stylistic idiom. The 2 instruments are thoroughly integrated in an exciting manner. D.

Egon Kornauth. *Sonatine* Op.46a (Dob 1959) 16pp., parts. 11 min. Available for flute (violin) and piano as well as for viola and piano. Rondino; Intermezzo; Siciliano. Centers around e-E, chromatic, quartal harmony, thin textures, flowing, appealing Neoclassic writing. M-D.

Erich Wolfgang Korngold. *Sonata* Op.6 G 1912 (Schott 1913) 65pp., parts. Ben moderato, ma con passione: SA; massive; thick chords; 3 with 2; dramatic with much expression. Scherzo: Allegro molto (con fuoco): syncopation; imitation; scalar; hemiolas. Adagio: passionate, Brahmsian qualities; full use of both hands; octaves. Allegretto quasi Andante (con grazia): $\frac{3}{4}$; begins and finishes soft; agitato section crescendoing to *fff;* trills; staccato chords. A large late-19th-century stylized work requiring experienced performers. D.

György Kósa. *Gaba Szonáta* (Zenmükiado Vállalat 1964) 8pp., parts. Allegretto; Sostenuto tragico; Vivace. More like a short Hungarian dance Suite. Mildly 20th-century, attractive. Int.

Fritz Kreisler. *The Fritz Kreisler Collection* (CF ATF115 1990) 109pp., parts. Contains original compositions, transcriptions, and cadenzas. Original compositions include *Caprice Viennois*, Op.2: b; most famous of Kreisler's violin and piano compositions; requires good command of rhythm; passionate. *Tambourin Chinois,* Op.3: B♭; ternary form; percussive rhythmic interaction; harp-like arpeggios with wide stretches; said to have been "inspired by the bustling activity of a Chinese restaurant in San Francisco." *Liebesfreud:* C; waltz, full chords. *Liebesleid:* 3 min.; Tempo d'Ländler; sentimental; lyrical; alternates between parallel a/A. *Schön Rosmarin:* G; 3 min.; melody in violin with piano playing oom-pah-pah; not inspiring, though a charming waltz. *Rondino on a*

Theme by Beethoven: E♭; 4 min.; based on the opening 4 measures of Beethoven's *Rondo in G* for violin and piano (WoO 41); flowing passagework alternating between legato and staccato techniques. *La Gitana:* grandiose, but restless, changing tempos 4 times in short space; recitative opening, colorful and flashy; glissandos and Flamenco-like rhythms. *Variations on a Theme by Corelli: In the Style of Tartini:* F; based on Gavotte from Corelli's *Sonata,* Op.5/10; theme and 3 variations effectively written in Tartini's style; considerable doubling with chordal jumps of the octave in Var.II. *Chanson Louis XIII and Pavane: In the Style of Couperin:* in 2 movements, may be performed separately; Chanson is lyrical with thin textures at Andante; breaking tradition, the Pavane is lively, defying the customary slow dance style. *Sicilienne and Rigaudon: In the Style of Francoeur:* b; 2 movements in Baroque dance styles, may be performed separately; lyrical Sicilienne is graceful at quiet dynamics until the last 3 bars; lively Rigaudon with strong rhythmic flow and small chord changes; binary forms. *Praeludium and Allegro: In the Style of Pugnani:* e; 6 min.; most well-known of the series "in the style of . . . "; Praeludium set in a grand majestic style requiring careful balance of parts; Allegro is motoric with homophonic writing; ensemble playing is deceptively difficult and requires the utmost precision; cadenza-like passages offer attractive contrasting material; movements may be performed separately. M-D to D.

———. *Caprice Viennois and Other Favorite Pieces* (Dover 1995, ISBN 0-486-28489-1) 59pp., parts. Unabridged and unaltered reprints of 10 original works and arrangements previously published individually, most by Charles Foley and the others unknown. *Caprice Viennois, Liebesleid, Liebesfreud, Praeludium and Allegro (In the Style of Pugnani), Rondino (On a Theme by Beethoven), Schön Rosmarin, Sicilienne and Rigaudon (In the Style of Francœur), Slavonic Dance,* Op.46/2 (Dvořák), *Slavonic Dance,* Op.72/2 (Dvořák), and *Tambourin Chinois.* M-D to D.

———. *Berceuse Romantique* Op.9 (MMP).

———. *Three Pieces* (MMP). Contains the *Rondino on a Theme by Beethoven* and Kreisler's versions of Chaminade's *Serenade Espagnole* and Granados's *Spanish Dance.*

Ernst Křenek. *Sonata* Op.3 f♯ 1919 (Doblinger 1996) 59pp., parts. Allegro ma non troppo: an energetic SA with dramatically contrasting themes in strong tonal orientation. Adagio: $\frac{7}{8}$ meter with piano introducing principal theme, passionate detailed writing. Scherzo: lively A sections with dissimilar Trio in $\frac{6}{8}$. Allegro con [6] variazioni: marcato theme in $\frac{6}{8}$ followed by variations featuring imitation, folk song, dreamlike qualities, and scherzando ($\frac{12}{16}$) effects, concluding with a virtuosic finish. A noteworthy work by the 19-year-old composer revealing his liking for contrasting musical features in dramatic manners. D.

———. *Sonata* 1944–45 (UE 11839) 24pp., parts. 14 min. Andante con moto; Adagio; Allegro assai, vivace. Twelve-tone technique similar to serial method used in Křenek's Seventh Quartet. "The large figures in the staves refer to the rhythmic units (half-notes in the first and second, quarter-notes in the third movement). All trills end with the upper (auxiliary) note" (note in score). D.

Rodolphe Kreutzer. *Sonate* I C (J. Hardy—Sal 5243) 15pp., parts. Moderato; Andantino; Rondo. Comfortable if not the most idiomatic writing. M-D.

Karl Kroeger. *Sonata* 1952 (UL) 20pp., parts. Lento; Allegro Impetuoso; Lento e Sostenuto–Allegro non troppo. A challenging student work with clearly designed forms written in a mild 20th-century tonal style. Of special interest is the spry $\frac{7}{8}$ of the Allegro Impetuoso, and the fugue in the second part of the finale. Score is a copy of clean MS. D.

Gail Kubik. *Sonatina* 1941 (SPAM) 18pp., parts. Moderately fast, unhurried: contrary 3rds, flowing melody, triple meter divided in half, flexible meters, dance rhythms. Fairly slow, but with movement: long flowing lines, moving 3rds, Impressionist. In the manner of a Toccata—fast, briskly, with rough force: driving rhythms; subito dynamic changes; conclusion is to be played "savagely." M-D.

Meyer Kupferman. *Fiddle Energizer* 1971 (Gen 1973) 10pp., parts. Repeated harmonic 2nds, varied textures, freely tonal, 20th-century "Alberti bass" treatment, broad chords at conclusion. Mildly 20th-century. M-D.
——. *Fantasy Sonata* (Gen 1972) 29pp., parts. Commissioned by the Library of Congress. Rhapsodic, large gestures, repeated patterns and ostinati, grateful writing. Requires a few effects inside the piano. M-D.

Ladislav Kupkovic. *Souvenir* 1971 (UE) 16pp., parts. Explanations in German, French, and English. "'Souvenir' is the third part of the musical nonstop revue 'K-Rhapsodie.'"

György Kurtág. *Tre Pezzi* Op.14e 1979 (EMB 1996) 6pp., parts. The *Three Pieces* seem to be approached as if they are games, a trait common in the composer's works of the period. 1. Plays with grace notes and short melismas; piano entirely in bass clef. 2. Vivo: same "game" as 1., only contrasting staccato and legato at extremes of both instruments. 3. Experiments with suspended sound, suggesting ancient Chinese bells; piano restricted to staccato/tenuto whole notes; dynamic range is *pppp* to più *pppp*. Int. to M-D.

Paul Kurzbach. *Sonatine* 1962 (Litolff 5366) 18pp., parts. 12 min. Allegro moderato; Aria; Finale. Tonal, mildly 20th-century. Aria is Impressionist. M-D.

Toivo Kuula. *Sonata* e 1907 (Fazer) 42pp., parts. Allegro agitato; Adagio; Allegro molto. Overworked thematic treatment by use of imitation and sequences; lengthy, much decorative figuration; long phrases and climaxes well sustained; clear formal structure; Romantic harmonies. D.

Ezra Laderman. *Duo* (OUP 92.601 1971) 30pp., parts. 15 min. Three movements. Interval of minor 2nd is exploited. Dissonant, semi-serial. D.

——. *Sonata* 1958–59 (OUP 92.302) 22pp., parts. 15 min. Three movements, large gestures for both instruments. D.

Edouard Lalo. *Sonata* Op.12 D (Durand) 29pp., parts. Allegro moderato; Variations; Rondo. Classical influence is present in this striking and beautifully written work, from the Beethovenesque opening of the first movement to the Mendelssohnian second movement theme and variations. Even Brahms is present to assist when Lalo leans on more Romantic techniques, as in the finale rondo, a moto perpetuo with quasi-rhapsodic characteristics. D.

Philibert de Lavigne. *Six Sonatas* Op.2 ca.1740 (W. Hillemann—Noetzel). Published separately. Each work also includes a cello part ad lib. See detailed entry under duos for piano and flute.

Henri Lazarof. *Rhapsody* 1966 (AMP 1972) 13pp., parts. Written in a full-blooded and highly intense international style. A few harmonics, long pedals, quasi-cadenza passages, clusters. The rest uses traditional notation. Dynamic extremes, flexible tempos, pointillistic inspiration. Exciting, aggravating, and violent effects. D.

——. *Sonata* 1997–98 (Merion 1998) 23pp., parts. 23 min. Deciso: *ff* opening with marcato added-note and cluster chords; frequently changing meters; novel effects using conventional notation. [Untitled]: solemn character interrupted by repeated notes and rhythmic complexities; proportional relationships; tense dramatic passages contrast the otherwise quiet setting. Libero: ABA; functions as a continuation of previous movement, highlighting similar features with more austerity; concludes *p* on a surprising A♭ chord. D

Lojze Lebic. *Atelier* 1973 (Društva Slovenskih Skladateljev) 10pp. Two copies necessary for performance. Explanations in Croatian and English.

Franziska LeBrun. *Sechs Sonatas für Cembalo oder Klavier und Violine* (F. Zimmermann—Tonger 2964 1999), parts. Vol.I (ISMN M-005-29641): 1 B♭; 2 E♭; 3 F. Vol.II (ISMN M-005-29651-5): 4 G; 5 C; 6 D. All *Sonatas* are in 2 movements, generally an Allegro followed by a rondo or menuetto. Piano is emphasized more than violin. Interesting with character but not profound. Preface in German by Ingrid Helena Helmke. M-D.

Jean-Marie Leclair. *Zwölf Sonaten für Violine and Generalbass nebst einem Trio für Violine Violoncell und Generalbass* Op.2, *2. Buch der Sonaten* Paris ca.1732 (R. Eitner—Br&H 1903) Vol.XXVII, Publikation aelterer praktischer und theoretischer Musikwerke. Reprint (BB 1966). In spite of the title, there are 12 pieces in all; the trio is No.8 of the dozen.

——. *Sonatas* Op.5, Op.9, and Op.15 (R. E. Preston—A-R Editions) Recent Researches in the Music of the Baroque Era: Vol.IV: Op.5/I–V 1968; Vol.V:

Op.5/VI–XII 1969; Vol.X; Op.9/I–VI 1970; Vol.XI: Op.9/VII–XII, Op.15, post-humous *Sonata* 1971.

———. *Six Sonatas* (M. Pincherle, L. Boulay—l'OL 1952). Published separately: *Sonata* 1/8; *Sonatas* Op.2/1, 12; *Sonatas* Op.5/1, 4; *Sonata* Op.9/4.

———. *Sonata* 2/3 C (H. Ruf—Ric SY500) 10pp., parts.

———. *Sonata* Op.2/11 (H. Ruf—Ric SY501) 7pp., parts.

———. *Sonata* Op.5/5 (H. Ruf—Br 3414) 8pp., parts.

———. *Sonata* 5/6 c "Le Tombeau" (F. David—IMC 1945) 11pp., parts. Grave; Allegro ma non troppo; Gavotte; Allegro. M-D.

———. *Sonata* 5/7 a (H. Ruf—Br 3415) 12pp., parts. Largo; Allegro; Adagio; Tempo di Gavotta. Leclair's "personal style unites the best qualities of the Italian style, the nobility and pathos of the Corelli school, with the lively spirit of French composition" (from Preface). M-D.

———. *Sonata* Op.9/1 (F. Polnauer—CF B3347).

———. *Sonata* Op.9/2 e (F. Polnauer—JWC 1970) 20pp., parts. Continuo Series No. 3. For violin or flute and keyboard. Andante; Allemanda–Allegro ma non troppo; Sarabanda–Adagio; Menuetto–Allegro non troppo; fifth movement "Not for Flute" but for violin only. The dance movements in particular show the influence of Leclair's earlier profession as a dance master. M-D.

———. *Sonata* Op.9/4 A (F. Polnauer—CF B3348).

———. *Sonata* Op.9/5 a (F. Polnauer—Schott 1969) 31pp., parts. Andante; Allegro assai; Adagio; Allegro ma non troppo. Preface in German, English, and French. M-D.

———. *Sonata* Op.9/6 D (F. Polnauer—CF B3349).
See also detailed entries under duos for piano and flute.

Jacques Leduc. *Sonate* Op.27 1967 (CeBeDeM) 33pp., parts. 18 min. Moderato; Tempo Scherzando; Sostenuto; leads directly to Ritmico, ma non troppo, Vivo. Written in a colorful style that has characteristics of both Poulenc and Pro-kofiev. D.

Simon Le Duc. *Four Sonatas* 1767–71 (Doflein—Schott 1964), parts. 2 vols. Op.4/1 A; 6 f. Op.1/1 D. Op.4/4 c. Beautifully written, elegant and cultivated taste. Grateful to play. Preface in German, French, and English. M-D.

Noël Lee. *Dialogues* (TP 1958) 12pp., parts. Opens with an Adagio, recitative-like, chromatic, octotonic section. Moves to a Moderato syncopated section interspersed with linear lines. A sustained chordal section follows with thick but quiet sonorities. A fuguelike short section is followed by the sustained, chordal section but *ff*. These basic ideas are varied in further treatment with a coda that resembles the opening section. Chromatic style. D.

Benjamin Lees. *Sonata* I (Bo&H 1953) 20 min. Neoclassic style with Romantic influences. D.

———. *Sonata* II 1972–73 (Bo&H) 43pp., parts. Moderato; Adagio; Allegro. Interval of the 7th operates in various ways throughout this work. Treatment of thematic material suggests serial procedures, but closer inspection reveals this is not the case. Although no key signature is used the aura of tonality is present. Plenty of sequence is employed. The piano introduces the second movement with alternating bitonal harmonies; this movement is a series of crescendos and diminuendos with a bitonal conclusion. The final Allegro is toccata-like and moves to a brilliant assertive ending with the final chord built of major 7ths. A work of fine craft and confidence. D.

——. *Sonata* III 1989 (Bo&H) 32pp., parts. 19 min. "The work is in one movement and has three basic subjects. These are treated in a process of continuous development, a technique I have been utilizing for the past ten years. Instead of using a traditional presentation of thematic material followed by transitions and eventually a formal development section, I initiate development of ideas at the outset so that the listener can always be conscious of a continuous musical thread. The musical syntax is one whereby tonalities are not fixed and where one is aware merely of indefinite tonalities which cross one another, disappear, re-emerge and cross again. Piano and violin are to play equal roles in my sonatas for these instruments" (Composer's Program Note). D.

René Leibowitz. *Rhapsody Concertante* Op.36 1955 (Boelke-Bomart) 7 min.

——. *Sonata* Op.12 1944 (Boelke-Bomart) 6 min.

Kenneth Leighton. *Sonata* I a (Lengnick 1951) 35pp., parts. Allegro molto appassionata: arpeggi figuration; chords; ostinato-like right-hand treatment; freely centered around a. Attacca second movement–Lento e liberamente: Romantic chordal sonorities; builds to *fff* climax; returns to opening idea and diminishes to *ppp* closing. Attacca third movement–Presto energico: $\frac{6}{8}$; highly rhythmic; piano has second idea in G; cantabile; closes with reference from main idea of second movement; a rollicking good movement. M-D.

——. *Sonata* II Op.20 (Lengnick 1956) 41pp., parts. 18½ min. Fluent, neo-Romantic, large-scale work, eclectic idiom, some 12-tone themes and popular modernistic harmonic usage. D.

Technical craftsmanship with a tendency toward contrapuntal complexity permeates both *Sonatas*.

Guillaume Lekeu. *Sonata* G (Lerolle; IMC) 55pp., parts. 32 min. Reminiscent of Franck, with its restless chromaticism and bold sweeps. Beautiful if somewhat rambling music, especially the passionate finale. Piano part is highly challenging. Exemplifies many felicitous devices in expressing similar ideas with both instruments. D.

Isabella Leonarda. *Sonata Duodecima* Op.16/12 d ca.1693 (I. Grave-Müller—Furore 205 1995, ISMN M-50012-105-3) 19pp., parts, including bass. Adagio; Allegro, e presto; Vivace; (Adagio); Aria, allegro; Veloce. "Compared with contemporary composers (e.g. Corelli) her sonatas are longer, sometimes containing six movements rather than the usual four. She was also more generous than some with modulations, using a large number of related keys within the same sonata" (from Preface). Realization conceived for organ or harpsichord but could be successfully played on piano by informed pianists. Biography, Preface, and editorial notes in German, English, and Swedish. M-D.

Alfonso Letelier. *Sonatina* 1953 (IU) 18pp., parts. Adagio; Allegro moderato. Contemporary treatment of harmonies and melodies; interval of diminished octave plays an important part in opening movement. Neoclassic influence mixed with a personal style. M-D.

Peter T. Lewis. *Of Bells . . . and Time, a Dialogue for Violin and Piano* (Merion 1975) 11pp., 2 copies needed for performance.

Douglas Lilburn. *Sonata* 1950 (Price Milburn) 10 min. One continuous movement, diatonic with chromatic inflections. Well written for both instruments. M-D.

Malcolm Lipkin. *Sonata* (JWC 1957) 24pp., parts. 15½ min. Allegro; Adagio; Presto. Mildly 20th-century writing. Contains some especially dramatic gestures in the Presto. D.

Franz Liszt. *Duo Sonata* 1832–35 (T. Serly—PIC 1957) 52pp., parts. Four movements of broad sweeping lines, all based on Chopin's *Mazurka* c# Op.6/2, in cyclic form. The mazurka is subjected to a full range of sophisticated thematic metamorphoses. One theme, a folk song from Liszt's piano pieces *Glanes de Woronince,* appears in "Paganini harmonics." Chopin and Paganini influences are reflected throughout the complete work. Moderato: freely treated SA; brief introduction by piano; violin enters with mazurka theme; a clever fugue closes exposition; development contains varied treatment of the thematic segments; many pianistic passages point to Debussy and Impressionism 50 years later; movement ends attacca. Tema con Variazioni: theme is divided into 4 thematic sections; Paganini's influence clearly seen in piano part; bars 299–300 allude to Chopin's *Etude* E Op.10/3. Allegretto: a miniature concerto with syncopated jazzlike rhythms, strange-sounding chord sequences and modulations. Allegro con brio: a lively rondo, ends with a brilliant coda. D.
See Alan Walker, "Liszt's Duo Sonata," *MT* 1589 (July 1975): 620–21.
———. *Grand Duo über die Romance 'Le Marin' von Philippe Lafont* 1830s, rev.1852 and *Epithalam* (Hochzeitmusik) 1872 (Z. Gardonyi—EMB and Br 19112 1971) 36pp., parts.
———. *La Notte* 1864–66 (R. C. Lee). This work, in a Lento molto funèbre mood, is prefaced by a few verses by Michelangelo Buonarroti. The main body of the work is in ABA design. A 4-bar introduction in e is followed by a funeral march mood in c#, which leads directly into a soaring angelico theme in A. This theme gains in intensity and finally returns, in a dramatic way, to the opening

funèbre theme. The piano part has more interest than the violin part. Dotted rhythms with sustained chords make up much of the piano part. An effective character piece showing many characteristics of Liszt's later style. M-D.

Pietro Locatelli. *Sei Sonate da Camera per Violino e Basso dall'* Op.6 (G. Benvenuti, E. Polo, M. Abbado—Fondazione Eugenio Bravi 1956) *I Classici Musicali Italiani,* Vol.14. Includes *Sonatas* 1–6 of the 12 *Sonatas* in this opus. *Sonata* Op.6/12 (M. Abbado—Ric 1970).
——. *Sonata* D (Lemoine).
——. *Sonata* E (C. Barison—Casisch 1965). Overly realized.
——. *Sonata* f "Le Tombeau" (CFP Sch27).
——. *Sonata* G (Moffat, Mlynarczyk—Simrock).
——. *Sonata* g (Carisch).

Nikolai Lopatnikoff. *Fantasia Concertante* (MCA).
——. *Sonata* II Op.32 1948 (MCA 1951) 32pp., parts. 16 min. Risoluto–Allegro; Andante; Rondo: Allegro. Neoclassic with much dissonance, but strongly tonal. M-D.

István Lóránd. *Sonata* (EMB 1967). Appassionata: rhapsodic. Scherzando. Semplice, moderato: theme with 5 variations. Mildly 20th-century. Excellent choice for the professional duo. D.

Otto Luening. *Sonata* 1917 (Highgate; also published in Vol.II of the American Society of University Composers Journal of Musical Scores) 19pp., parts. Luening considers this to be his first professional composition. One movement with 2 contiguous sections: Allegro marcato; Allegro fugato. Freely tonal, tempo changes within large sections, dramatic gestures in strong disjunct octaves, rhythmic imitation. Presto coda. Effective. D.
——. *Sonata* II (Galaxy) 30pp., parts. Maestoso–Allegro vivace e con brio: chromatic runs in one hand; chords in the other; broken chordal figuration; sectional tempo contrasts; requires large span. Andante con moto: octotonic; piano has fine share of thematic material; varied tempos; strong pianistic figuration. D.
——. *Sonata* III 1950 (Galaxy) 24pp., parts. Andante tranquillo: flowing line with 16th-note broken figuration in piano; contrapuntal; freely tonal; works to expressive and broad closing; requires large span. Variations: Neoclassic 16-bar theme; variation treatment ranges from scherzo-like to Allegro, alla marcia; intense conclusion. A beautiful and effective work. M-D to D.

Witold Lutoslawski. *Partita* 1984 (JWC 1986) 31pp., parts. 15 min. In 5 movements. "The main movements are the first (Allegro guisto), the third (Largo), and the fifth (Presto). The second and fourth are but short interludes to be played ad libitum . . . Harmonically and melodically, *Partita* clearly belongs to the same group of recent compositions as *Symphony No. 3* and *Chain*" (Composer's Note). Mixes determinate and indeterminate compositional styles. D.

———. *Recitativo e Arioso* 1951 (JWC 1995) 4pp., parts. 3 min. In one continuous movement. "Although it was composed during the post-war years there is little trace in this piece of the folk sources that provided melodic and rhythmic material for many of his functional pieces of that time. Instead, it might be compared with later pieces of chamber music . . . albeit on a much simpler level" (from Preface). M-D.

———. *Subito* 1992 (JWC 1994) 12pp., parts. One of the composer's last works. In one movement at mostly fast tempos. Contrasts subito effects of dynamics, rhythms, meters, touch, drama, etc. Requires careful coordination. D.

Ernst Mahle. *Sonatina* 1955 (Ric 1972) 5pp., parts. Allegro moderato: SA, one basic thematic idea cleverly worked over. M-D.

———. *Sonata* 1968 (Tonos 1973) 24pp., parts. 12½ min. Allegro moderato: SA, serially organized. Andante: piano provides subtle chordal background for violin. Vivace: linear writing between the 2 instruments; some changing meters; chromatic; pianist must tap on wooden part of piano. D.

Riccardo Malipiero. *Sonata* 1956 (SZ) 23 min. Attractive, eclectic, fairly conservative idiom. M-D.

Francisco Manalt. *Sonatas* I–II (P. José A. de Donostia—Instituto Español de Musicología 1955) 27pp. I: E, Larghetto; Allegro; Tempo di Minuetto. II: F, Largo; Vivace grazioso. Both *Sonatas* are written in a classic Spanish style, somewhat similar to Soler's. M-D.

Francesco Mancini. *Zwölf Sonaten* (Michel—Amadeus 138-41 1999). See detailed entry under duos for piano and flute.

Frank Martin. *Sonata* Op.1 g (Hug 1914) 43pp., parts. Quasi-recitative–Allegro maestoso; Scherzo; Andantino piacevole; Allegro con fuoco. Written in a style that owes something to Franck, Richard Strauss, and Mahler. Reveals talent but not much originality. D.

———. *Sonata* E 1931–32 (UE 12874) 28pp., parts. 15 min. Très vif; Chaconne (Adagio); Finale (ben moderate). Dense and complex textures, extended. Each movement is written in a continuous nonsymmetrical form. The Chaconne embraces the Baroque style. D.

Jean Martinon. *Second Sonatine* Op.19/2 (Billaudot). One movement. Opens with an Adagio that briefly returns later. Main part of the work is fast and concludes with an extended Presto and Coda. M-D.

———. *Duo: Musique en Forme de Sonate* Op.47 (Schott 1959). Four large movements. Opening and closing movements are in SA design. Second movement, Molto vivace, is a scherzo with trio. The third, Lento, treats the instruments differently: the piano has more disjointed lines and rough rhythmic treatment, while the violin has more cantabile phrases. This work is for the concert ensemble, and both this work and the *Sonatine* treat the instruments equally. D.

Bohuslav Martinů. *Sonata* C 1919 (Schott P1215; Panton 1973, 71pp.), parts.

——. *Sonata* d 1926 (Schott P5032; Panton 1966). Allegro moderato; Andante moderato; Allegro.

——. *Sonata* I 1929 (Leduc) 29pp., parts. 19 min. Allegro: opens with long solo violin passage and has a longer violin solo before conclusion of movement; the duo sections are a fox-trot. Andante: more violin solos, slower dance rhythms. Allegretto–Allegro con brio: piano gets the solos here; that is the most interesting aspect of this movement. Plenty of lively rhythmic wit. M-D.

——. *Sonata* II 1931 (Sal) 23pp., parts. 11½ min. Allegro moderato: a bright tune in D opens the movement; much interplay between the instruments with the 2 main ideas. Larghetto: diffuse wanderings eventually arrive at a climax and wither away. Poco allegretto: flexible meters that seem to have no reason and weaken the perpetual-motion rhythmic drive. M-D.

——. *Rhymische Etüden* 1931 (Schott 2224 1932) 15pp., parts. 1. $\frac{2}{4}$; 2. $\frac{5}{8}$; 3. $\frac{7}{8}$, $\frac{10}{8}$, $\frac{11}{8}$; 4. mixed meters; 5. $\frac{3}{8}$; 6. Jazz Rhythmus; 7. mit Pausen. Piano part notated on one clef, sometimes requiring both hands. D.

——. *Sonatina* 1937 (V. Nopp—Gen 1970; Supraphon 1986; Br) 15pp., parts. 9 min. Moderato: folklike melodic ideas. Andante: much repetition of ideas, octotonic. Poco allegretto: lively dance rhythms make this the most successful movement. M-D.

——. *Five Madrigal Stanzas* 1943 (AMP) 26pp., parts. 10½ min. Dedicated to Albert Einstein. I. Moderato; II. Poco allegretto; III. Andante moderato; IV. Scherzando, poco allegro; V. Poco allegro. Strong rhythmic orientation. D.

——. *Sonata* III 1944 (AMP 1950) 21 min. Poco allegro; Adagio; Scherzo; Lento–Poco allegro.

——. *Rapsodie Tchèque* 1945 (ESC 1962) 17pp., parts. Lento opening is followed by other contrasting sections. Basically diatonic but contains a broad harmonic range encompassing simple progressions juxtaposed with more complex ones. Czech dance rhythms are present. M-D.

See John Clapham, "Martinů's Instrumental Style," MR 24 (1963): 158. Richart Kent, "The Violin and Piano Sonatas of Bohuslav Martinů," Ph.D. diss., University of Illinois, 1973, 126pp.

Jules Massenet. *Meditation* from *Thaïs* (CF 1950) 5pp., parts. 4 min. Transcription of the famous melody from Massenet's opera by M. P. Marsick. Flowing 8th-note arpeggiation. Delicate, contrasted by a passionate middle section, with a quiet beginning and ending. M-D.

William Mathias. *Sonata* Op.15 (OUP 1963) 24pp., parts. 14 min. Molto vivace: thin textures are juxtaposed against thicker ones; flexible meters; freely chromatic; bitonal implications; sweeping scales before coda; *pp* conclusion. Lento, ma con moto: long lines for the piano; sustaining quality of piano very important; rondo form; attacca senza pausa. Lento–Allegro ritmico: 4-bar flowing arpeggio introduction leads directly into Allegro ritmico section characterized by martial quality with subject in the violin soon tossed back and forth between the instruments. Second section keeps martial idea in violin while piano has leggiero 16th-note figuration. These 2 figurations lock in battle and eventually unwind with a final chord socked by the pianist. M-D.

Colin Matthews. *Omaggio* 1990–93 (Faber 1996, ISBN 0-571-51688-2) 8pp., parts. 4 min. In one movement, marked Seriamente. Proportional rhythmic relationships are found throughout the score. Impulsive and insistent, cutting its way to the end with little repose. D.

Charles McLean. *Sonata* Op.1/2 g (D. Johnson—OUP 1975) 6pp., parts. Musica da Camera 23. Preface in English and German. Adagio; Allegro; Adagio; Allegro. These movements show a slight influence of Corelli and Handel. In accordance with the practice of the time, the use of a cello or bassoon to reinforce the keyboard bass is desirable but not essential. Serviceable edition. Int. to M-D.

Nikolai Medtner. *Sonata* Op.21 b 1910 (USSR Complete Works, Vol.7; Edition Russe de Musique) 30pp., parts. 20 min. A serious if somewhat dry work of restrained contemplation, except in the final movement, where the clang of bells and jubilant sounds make this movement one of the most vivid and imaginative in the duo repertoire. D.
——. *Sonata* Op.44 G (Zimmermann 1924; USSR) 59pp., parts. Three movements. The first movement opens with a mood of concentrated and austere emotion and continues with a sustained academic artistry. The second movement is a grandiose set of variations. The whole work displays profound seriousness and requires enormous stamina from both performers (as well as the audience!). D.
——. *Sonata Epica* Op.57 e (Nov 1936; USSR) 84pp., parts. Four movements. Suffers from numerous motives that are not melodically distinctive and do not lend themselves to developmental technique. The problem of "heavenly length" is also present. D.
All 3 *Sonatas* are admirably laid out for both instruments.

Nelly Mele Lara. *Sonata* (PIC 1971) 62pp., parts. Neoclassic orientation. Allegro moderato: $\frac{4}{4}$, b, SA, serious opening, second idea more dancelike. Allegretto grazio: $\frac{2}{2}$, e–g, clear lines, chromatic, imitation; mid-section $\frac{4}{4}$, eb, more chordal; opening section returns. Allegro con brio: $\frac{4}{4}$, b, rondo with contrasting episodes; piano provides driving figuration punctuated with widespread chords; brilliant coda concludes work. D.

Alfred Mendelssohn. *Sonata Brevis* (Editura Muzicala 1964) 36pp., parts. Allegretto, affettuoso; Vivo, con fuoco; Lento, rubato–quasi recitative; Presto. Colorful mildly 20th-century writing with a middle-European flavor that adds interest. M-D.

Felix Mendelssohn. *Sonata* Op.4 f 1823 (F. Hermann—CFP No. 1732; Rietz—Br&H; Rauch—Litolff) 18 min. Three movements. Opening violin recitatives in first and third movements recall Beethoven's piano Sonata Op.31/2. Bold harmonies add interest. The simple melody of the slow movement has a bit more originality to it with hints of Weber present. Problems of balance occur but this impassioned, almost rhapsodic piece should not be overlooked by the aspiring young student and/or amateur. M-D.

——. *Sonata* F 1838 (Y. Menuhin—CFP 6075) 38pp., parts. 19 min. Contains a facsimile from the autograph and a Preface by Menuhin. This recently published *Sonata* contains similarities between the *String Quartet* Op.44/1 and the cello *Sonata* Op.45, all composed during the same year. Allegro vivace: excitement builds; suavity and refinement always present. Adagio: a simple, lovely, and elegiac movement full of the sentimental characteristics frequently associated with Mendelssohn; the performers can control some of this. Assai vivace: an elfin flight that constantly intertwines both piano and violin parts. The whole piece is a fine work and worthy of more performances.
See VKDR, II: pp.91–97 for more discussion.

Peter Mennin. *Sonata Concertante* 1956 (CF 04113) 31pp., parts. Sostenuto–Allegro con brio; Adagio semplice; Allegro con fuoco. Solidly crafted with clear and rugged melodic lines, transparent harmonic fabric, and insistent, propulsive rhythms. Vigorously energetic but logically developed and neatly structured. A dramatic tour de force for both players. D.

Olivier Messiaen. *Thème et Variations* 1932 (Leduc 1934) 14pp., parts. 8 min. A 28-bar melody constructed in AABA' design of 7, 7, 6, and 8 bars, respectively. Adheres somewhat closely to the shape of the theme in the 5 variations. A highly accomplished and effective work. M-D.

Krzysztof Meyer. *Misterioso* Op.83 1994 (Sikorski 1592 1994) 7pp., parts. Marked Sempre poco rubato throughout though with passages where rubato may be impractical for ensemble. Preference for competing rhythmic relationships, e.g., 3 with 5 and 4 with 5. Pianist must be able to reach a 10th. D.

——. *Capriccio Interrotto* Op.93 2000 (Sikorski 1563 2001, ISMN M-003-03240-5) 19pp., parts. 7 min. Commences Impetuoso, a brief section which reappears in altered forms twice, interspersed between contrasting sections of Adagio, Andante espressivo, and Precipitando. Some difficult rhythmic relationships, Neoclassic harmonies. Wide span required. D.

Paul Baudouin Michel. *Sonate* 1960 (CeBeDeM) 18 min.
——. *Serenade Concertante* 1962 (J. Maurer) 11½ min.
——. *Ballade—Jeu* (CeBeDeM 1976) 12pp., parts. 5 min.

Darius Milhaud. *Sonata* I 1911 (Durand) 35pp., parts. Lent et robuste: centers around d♯, chordal, arpeggiation, tremolo. Joyeux: très décidé et très large section before final 2 bars of Lent closes the movement. Très lent: $\frac{6}{8}$ rocking feeling, 4 sharps but feels more like B; mid-section in C, $\frac{5}{4}$, with piano taking much chordal figuration; B closing in rocking character. Très rhythmé, joyeux: C♯, arpeggiation in piano while violin supplies most melodic emphasis; contrasting section in Moins vite, très rhythmé; rhythmic activity is most important element in this movement. M-D.

———. *Sonata* II 1917 (Durand) 25pp., parts. Straightforward handling of polytonality, canonic writing, many "wrong-note" sounds. M-D.

Charles Mills. *Sonata* I (ACA) 17 min.
———. *Sonata* II 1941 (ACA) 20 min. Intense, aristocratic, reticent, strong melodies, exquisitely idiomatic writing. D.
———. *Sonata* III (ACA) 30 min.
———. *Sonatine* (ACA) 8 min.

Jean-Joseph Mondonville. *Pièces de Clavecin en Sonates avec Accompagnement de Violon* Op.3 ca.1734 (M. Pincherle, Publications de la Société Française de Musicologie, Première Série, Tome IX, 1969—Heugel). Sonatas 1 g, 2 F, 3 B♭, 4 C, 5 G, 6 A.
Available separately: *Sonata* 4 C (C. Saint-Saëns—Durand). *Sonata* 2 F (W. Höckner—Heinrichshofen 1963). Keyboard instrument is the dominant part; violin has supporting role but is never dispensable. Keyboard part is realized. "All sonatas in Op.3, except No. 1, have 3 movements each, typically in the order of a fugal or imitative allegro, an 'Aria' of moderate tempo in binary design with repeated 'halves,' and a similarly binary 'Giga' in compound or 'Allegro' in alla breve meter" (SCE, p. 619). Left hand mainly provides support. *Sonata* No.2 is an excellent example of the "accompanied sonata," which displays an equality between the violin and the keyboard. The violin seemingly has the bass line with numerous leaps. As Louis-Claude Daquin wrote in 1752, Mondonville "has so ably married the clavecin to his favorite instrument" (Lionel de la Laurencie, *L'Ecole française de violon de Lully à Viotti*, 3 vols., Paris: Delagrave, 1922–24).
———. *Sonata* Op.4/2 C ca.1735 (F. Polnauer—Heinrichshofen 1970) 19pp., parts. Andantino; Allegro; Aria; Giga. One of the earliest Sonatas to introduce harmonics. M-D.

Wolfgang A. Mozart. *Jugendsonaten I: Four Sonatas for Keyboard and Violin* K.6–9 (E. Reeser—Br 1967) 55pp., parts. Rev. separate edition, based on W. A. Mozart New Complete Edition. K.6 C, K.7 D, K.8 B♭, K.9 G. These *Sonatas* are for keyboard with optional violin accompaniment. Each has 3 movements and concludes with a double minuet. Keyboard part has more interest, and the violin part stays out of the way. Int. to M-D.

Available separately: K.6, 7, 8, 9 (Zeitlin, Levy—Markert).

———. *Jugendsonaten II: Six Sonatas for Keyboard and Violin* K.10–15 (W. Plath, W. Rehm—Br 1969) K.10 B♭, K.11 G, K.12 A, K.13 F, K.14 C, K.15 B♭. These Sonatas date from 1764 and mark the historical point at which the piano trio and the accompanied Piano Sonata began to diverge as musical forms. They are the first step in the transition from the keyboard Sonata accompanied ad lib to the later Classical Piano Trio. Valuable Preface. Int. to M-D.

———. *Jugendsonaten III: Six Sonatas for Keyboard and Violin* K.26–31 (E. Reeser —Br 1964). K.26 E♭, K.27 G, K.28 C, K.29 D, K.30 F, K.31 B♭. The title of this set, Op.4, indicates "with the accompaniment of the violin," so the violin is not ad lib even though the keyboard is still the dominant partner.

———. *Sonaten für Klavier und Violine* K.196–570 (E. F. Schmid, W. Lampe, K. Röhrig—Henle 1969) 2 vols. Vol.I: K.301 G, K.302 E♭, K.303 C, K.304 e, K.305 A, K.306 D, K.376 F, K.296 C, K.377 F, K.378 B♭, K.379 G, K.380 E♭. Vol.II: K.402 A, K.454 B♭, K.481 E♭, K.526 A, K.547 F, K.359 *Variations* G "La Bergère Célimène," K.360 *Variations* g "Hélas, j'ai perdu mon amant," K.403 C, K.570 B♭. Practical and scholarly edition. Excellent Preface includes a discussion of the chronology, background of each work, and sources consulted. Mozart brought the Violin Sonata to a successful birth and gave the equal partnership its first masterpieces. Note placement of the word "piano" before violin in these mature *Sonatas*.

Available separately: *Sonata* K.296 C (GS 8). *Sonata* K.301 G (PWM). *Sonata* K.304 e (Kehr, Schröter—Schott; W.-D. Seiffer, W. Lampe, K. Röhrig—Henle 728; GS 4). *Sonata* K.305 A (Kehr, Schröter—Schott). *Sonata* K.454 B♭ (Kehr, Schröter—Schott).

———. *Complete Sonatas and Variations* (Dover 1992, ISBN 0-486-27299-0, 0-486-27406-3) 2 vols. Separate violin part not provided. Vol.I: K.6–15, 26–31, 296, 301–306, 372. Vol.II: K.376–80, 402–404, 454, 481, 526, 547, 359, 360. Reprinted from the Br&H complete *Wolfgang Amadeus Mozart's Werke* (1879).

———. *20 Sonatas* (Br&H) 2 vols.

———. *20 Sonatas* (K 03735-6) 2 vols.

———. *19 Sonatas* (Flesch, Schnabel—CFP 3315; IMC; Nachrez—Augener 8669a, b) 2 vols. Peters includes K.296–547, except 404.

———. *18 Sonatas* (Schradieck—GS L836; Principe, Vitali—Ric ER59-60) 2 vols. Schirmer includes K.296–570, except 403, 404.

———. *18 Sonatas and Allegro* (K) 272pp., parts. Marked Urtext. Includes K.301– 547 and *Allegro* B♭ K.372.

———. *Sonatas for the Youth* (Szelényi—EMB) 2 vols.

———. *6 Sonatas* K.55–60 "Romantic" (Gärtner—Br&H; CFP 3329). Authenticity doubtful.

———. *Variationen für Klavier und Violine* K.359 (374a) G, 360 (374b) g c.1781 (E. F. Schmid, W. Lampe, K. Röhrig—Henle 181 1999) 15pp., parts. This is a new edition of the score previously issued from Henle's collected works for

piano and violin. "Recent research has revealed that Mozart took the themes of both sets from a French song collection of 1770 containing material of a much earlier date. Although he specifically cites the title of the theme underlying the G-major variations K.359/374a ('Variazioni sopra l'aria *La Bergére Célimene*' [*sic*]), there is no such indication for the g-minor set K.360/374b, which has become widely known under the title 'Hélas, j'ai perdu mon amant'. However, its theme survives in the aforementioned song collection as 'Au bord d'une fontaine' while the conventional title is not to be found there at all" (from Preface). The 12 variations of the former and 6 of the latter reveal all the fundamental qualities of Mozart's scores from the period. Highly recommended as an alternative to the *Sonatas.* M-D.
For a discussion of these works see: VKDR, I: pp.228–303.

Thea Musgrave. *Colloquy* 1960 (JWC) 16pp., parts. 11 min. A study in 4 untitled movements in the style of Webern. Short motifs, fragmented meters, irregular patterns with quick upbeat figurations. Eclectic writing with ideas appearing in various guises. Harmonics, some figures repeated ad lib. D.

Taro Nakamura. *Ballade* III (Mumyo) 1969 (Japan Federation of Composers 1973) 21pp., parts. Mumyo, a Buddhist term, means to be harassed by worldly and sinful desires. Moderato: opening section free and unbarred; 7th chords; moves into a steady $\frac{4}{4}$ with piano syncopation, 20th-century Alberti bass treatment, arpeggi figuration. Allegretto: interval of 2nd frequently used in left hand, syncopated melody in right hand; solo cadenza for violin leads to another Allegretto–Allegro: broken-chord figuration; Adagio free section uses tremolo in right hand over short figures in left-hand lower register; Allegretto returns and leads to più mosso coda, with much activity for both instruments. Mildly 20th-century. M-D.

Conlon Nancarrow. *Toccata* 1935 (Smith Publications) 7pp., parts. Version I for Violin and Piano. A perpetual mobile marked Molto presto (Fast as possible). Repeated notes; scalar patterns; octaves; full chords; synthetic arpeggiation. Version II is for violin and tape of player piano part. D.

Pietro Nardini. *Six Sonatas* (M. J. Johnson—GS 1967) 59pp., parts. 1 A; 2 F; 3 d; 4 C; 5 D; 6 B♭. Each *Sonata* is in Adagio–Allegro–Allegro format, some with slight modifications in last movement. All movements are binary or rounded binary, except No.5, where the final is a theme with 6 variations. M-D.
———. *Sonata* D (F. David—GS; Katims—IMC; K 09213), parts. Adagio–Allegro con fuoco; Larghetto; Allegretto grazioso. Edited in 19th-century manner. IMC is for viola (violin) and piano. M-D.

Carl Nielsen. *Sonata* Op.9 A 1895 (Telmányi—WH 3311) 22 min. Allegro glorioso: $\frac{4}{4}$; SA with snappy opening; second subject appears twice, in C and E in $\frac{3}{4}$, and in $\frac{4}{4}$ in the recapitulation. Andante: steady, cumulative effect; piano part is mainly chordal. Allegro piacevole e giovanile: strong writing, unusual harmonic resolutions. D.

——. *Sonata* II Op.35 1912 (WH 1982) 20 min. Allegro con tiepidezza: "tepidity" marking seems out of place in this heated and powerful movement; strong themes push forward in their intrinsic growth; brief interruptions provide contrast, but there is plenty of upheaval and excitement held tightly together by clear and concise control. Molto adagio: broad, rhapsodic writing of the highest order. Allegro piacevole: great rhythmic originality; final section stops on C when suddenly the piano gives forth with a series of thunderous B♭s, and both instruments quickly agree on C in the final diminishing bars of this weighty chamber music work. Difficult but worth the effort. D.

Per Nørgård. *Diptychon* Op.11 1954 (E. Z. Schneider, M. Schneider—WH 29775 1986) 17pp., parts. 9 min. In 2 sections: Adagio con affetto; Presto, molto leggiero. Strongly tonal and lyrical writing in a 20th-century vein. D.

——. *Fragment V* 1961 (WH 4101 1963) 3pp., no parts. May be performed separately or within a complete performance of *Fragments I–VI*. Based upon the song "Wie soll ich meine Seele halten." Webernesque writing in piano, composed just after attending 1960 ISCM Festival in Cologne, a revelation of avant-garde music for the composer. M-D.

Shōdai Okada. *Sonata* (Japan Federation of Composers 1972). Lento–Andantino–Allegretto–Moderato: uses extremes of instruments; trills; tremolos; rhythmic structure emphasized. Andantino: harmonics; shifting meters and tempos. Allegro: constantly shifting meters; energetic; emphasis on minor and major 2nd intervals; ends *pp* immediately after climatic *ff*. Score is facsimile of MS. D

Leo Ornstein. *Sonata* Op.26 (Br&H 1917).
——. *Two Russian Barcarolles* (Br&H).

Hans Osieck. *Sonatine* 1942 (Donemus), parts. 15 min. Neoclassic in spirit with influences from Impressionism. Tragic-like opening alternates with passagework in dark tones reflecting the era and conditions in which it was written. Long flowing lines in slow movement lead to a lively finale with detailed passagework. M-D.

Ignace Jan Paderewski. *Sonata* Op.13 1885 (Bo&Bo 1975) 39pp., parts. Allegro con fantasia; Intermezzo; Finale. Epilogue in Polish, English, and German. Fresh in its melodic appeal. Displays expert formal craftsmanship. The piano part, rich and effective, makes the most of the instrument's possibilities. The violin part, with a clear texture, affords the performer the opportunity of displaying graceful playing and good taste. The entire work encourages easy, natural playing from both performers. D.

Jean Papineau-Couture. *Dialogues* (PIC 1967) 29pp., parts. 15 min. Lourd; Très lent; Enjoué; Solennel. Serial organization, much use of staccato touch, kind of a stenciled style. M-D.

——. *Sonate en Sol* (CMC 1944) 24pp., parts. 11 min. Allegro: opening theme soft but energetic and characterized by great flexibility of meter; second theme in waltz rhythm; first theme returns after development, forte. Variations: opens with a lyrical theme followed by 3 variations in progressively faster tempo. Second movement linked to the third, a Rondo in the character of a scherzo in which some virtuosity is displayed, more in the violin than the piano. M-D.

——. *Trois Caprices* (CMC 1962) 11 min. Allegro; Adagio; Scherzando. Written to give the performers an opportunity to show their ability in a modern idiom. After this work was completed the composer noticed a definite relation between the character of the 3 movements and the personalities of his 3 children and gave the children's names as subtitles: Nadia, Ghilaine, and François. D.

Krzysztof Penderecki. *Sonate* 1953 (Schott 7797 1992) 18pp., parts. 9 min. A youthful work packed with energy and declamation. Allegro: SA; octotonic; full chords; marked rhythms; contrast of duplets and triplets. Andante: mixed meters based on 8th note; 2-voice single lines 2 octaves apart. Allegro vivace: syncopation; repeated notes; mixed meters. Precedes the well-known, nonconventional works the composer would later write and retains strong melodic and rhythmic emphases. M-D to D.

——. *Miniatury* 1959 (PWM 1962) 2pp., no parts. 2½ min. In 3 unmarked movements; piano plays on 1 and 3. Succinct arpeggiated runs either ascending or descending contrasted by sustained chords. Pressed nonsounding keys and pizzicato plucking of strings are required. M-D.

Charmine Pepe. *Sonata* 1965 (IU) 27pp., parts. Vivace; Dirge; Con spirito. Strong serial writing. Piano has full chords as well as being pointillistically spread over the keyboard. Ensemble problems in sheer rhythmic complexities. Last movement has long lines. D.

Johann Christoph Pepusch. *6 Sonate da Camera* (W. Kolneder—Schott 96 1999, ISMN M-001-12699-1) 31pp., parts, including bass. I b; II D; III C; IV d; V D; VI f. In the customary slow-fast-slow-fast format. Opening movements tend to be through-composed with remaining 3 generally binary. No dance titles appear except in VI with an Allemanda. Engaging realization enhances the overall facile requirements in original score. Preface in English, German, and French. M-D.

Giovanni B. Pergolesi. *Sonata* G (P. Oboussier—Schott 10504 1956) 12pp., parts. Largo; Allegro; Largo; Spiritoso. The only known Sonata for violin and figured bass by Pergolesi. Unencumbered realization. M-D.

Vincent Persichetti. *Serenade No. 4* Op.28 (EV 1982) 16pp., parts. 8½ min. Of the composer's 15 *Serenades,* this is the only one for violin and piano. Pastorale: lyrical, $^6_8$, occasional harmonics. Episode: decisive, triple stops, delayed imitation techniques. Interlude: delicate, songlike, large span required. Capriccio: brilliant, motoric, show piece for violin. The movements contrast folklike lyric qualities with marcato, technical concerns. M-D.

———. *Masques* Op.99 (DV 1965) 15pp., parts. Ten short pieces designed for less-experienced students. Int.–M-D.

Goffredo Petrassi. *Introduzione e Allegro* 1933 (Rico 1968) 13pp., parts. Originally for violin and 11 instruments. Has serial overtones but is strongly tonal. Chordal, rich sonorities, *pp* ending. M-D.

Hans Pfitzner. *Sonata* Op.27 e (CFP 3620 1922) 44pp., parts. Bewegt, mit empfindung; Sehr breit und ausdruckvoll; Ausserst schwungvoll und feurig. Expansive lyricism, chromatic richness, traditional cadences. Some dissonant counterpoint and involved rhythms all add up to a moving and expressive work. D.

Anne Danican Philidor. *Premier livre de pièces pour la flûte traversière ou la flûte a bec alto ou le violon et basse continue* (clavecin ou piano). Restitution de Maurice-Pierre Gourrier, realization de Colette Teniere (Ouvrières 1972) 10pp., parts. See detailed entry under duos for piano and flute.

Pierre Danican Philidor. *Suite* Op.I/6 b (H. Ruf—Schott OBB39 1997, ISMN M-001-11468-4). For oboe, flute, or violin. See detailed entry under duos for piano and oboe.

Burrill Phillips. *Sonata* C (GS). Dramatic gestures, clear harmonic content, incisive rhythms, and clear lines are found throughout this work. M-D.

Giovanni Antonio Piani. *Sonatas* Op.1 (B. G. Jackson—A-R Editions 1975) 122pp. Op.1/1 g, 2 e, 3 F, 4 G, 5 B♭, 6 G, 7 c, 8 b, 9 a, 10 D, 11 E♭, 12 A. These little-known works mix Sonata forms of the Style Gallant with dance forms from the Baroque. Extensive Preface and Notes. M-D.

Tobias Picker. *Invisible Lilacs* 1991 (Helicon 761 1991) 37pp., parts. I. Fast; II. Elegy; III. Very Fast. Inspired by a passage from *In Search of Lost Time* by Marcel Proust. Conventional end-of-the-century writing with mild harmonic dissonance and technical challenge. Wide span required. D.

Gabriel Pierné. *Sonate* Op.36 d 1900 (Durand) 33pp., parts. A large-scale work retaining Classical forms in a late-19th-century flavor with only inklings of chromaticism. Large Allegretto movement opens in $^{10}_{16}$ meter in piano and $^6_8$ in violin, later going to $^2_4$ in violin, the latter occasionally creating a disconcerting effect of 4 with 5. Expansive writing in keyboard with arpeggiation and scalar patterns, contrasted in development with introduction of a flowing third theme at Andante tranquillo to syncopated rhythms. Allegretto tranquillo movement follows in $\frac{3}{8}$ with rich lyricism and solid harmonic action. Andante non troppo–Allegro un poco agitato concludes with large chords in greater harmonic action and technical development. Requires agility, stamina, and experienced performers to realize exquisite musicality within the whole of the work. D.

Willem Pijper. *Sonata* I 1919 (JWC) 20pp., parts. 15 min. Mainly tonal but polytonal and polyrhythmic influences are felt. Commodo: sostenuto pedal usage, left-hand figuration based on broken 5ths, 3 with 4, quartal harmony, triplets. Tempo di menuetto tranquillo: 7th parallel chords, arpeggi and scalar figures, trills, cross-rhythms. Quasi scherzando: light, fast broken-4th figuration, mixture of chords and arpeggio Impressionist *ppp* ending. M-D.

———. *Sonata* II (Donemus 1922) 14 min. Short motifs provide the source or "germ-cell" from which the whole work develops. No elaborate themes, but much musical vitality is found here in spite of the pedestrian melodic writing. D.

Filipe Pires. *Sonatina* (EC 1975) 8pp., parts. Allegramente: rhythmic, syncopated, preference for major 7ths and minor 9ths noted. Andante con malinconia: $\frac{5}{8}$, equal and legatissimo, flowing lines, chromatic; large span required. Moto perpetuo: freely tonal, punctuated chords, many repeated notes in violin; piano provides chromatic chords as substructure. M-D.

Walter Piston. *Sonata* 1939 (Arrow 1940) 30pp., parts. 18 min. Austere, economical style with many devices of retrograde, passacaglia, and fugato. Moderato: $\frac{6}{8}$, mildly 20th-century and slightly dissonant; clear SA form in F-f. Andantino quasi Adagio: $\frac{5}{4}$, long lyric flowing lines, impressive episode, darkly expressive, in b. Allegro: clearly structured rondo, rhythmic patterns overworked, much activity, contrapuntal ingenuity in an episodic fugue. Piano is mostly treated linearly throughout the entire work. D.

See Ross Lee Finney, "Piston's Violin Sonata," MM 17/4 (May–June 1940): 210–13.

———. *Sonatina* (Bo&H) for violin and harpsichord or piano. Contains one of Piston's most moving and profound slow movements. M-D.

Ildebrando Pizzetti. *Sonata* A 1919 (JWC) 54pp., parts. 31 min. Inspired by the First World War. Tempestoso: in 4 parts, the last being a short coda; incisive and quick main theme in triple meter; violin has a melancholy subject in duple meter; both subjects develop independently and with one another; other ideas are heard in this dramatic movement; long flowing lines, large chords, hemiola effects, tremolo; though in the key of a, this movement has the signature of one flat. Preghiera per gl'innocenti ("Prayer for the Innocents"): strongly emotional; piano theme is chantlike; violin enters with a passionate idea; three separate episodes plus connecting material make up the movement; chordal, triplets, reiterated figures. Vivo e fresco: rondo; folk song–like lively theme intertwines with other melodies; tremolo; freely tonal figuration; parallel chords; all diverse elements pulled together to form a brilliant conclusion. D.

Robert Pollock. *First Duo* 1969 (Boelke-Bomart) 9 min.
———. *Second Duo* 1970 (Boelke-Bomart) 11 min.
———. *Third Duo* 1973 (Boelke-Bomart) 8 min.

Quincy Porter. *Sonata II* 1933 (SPAM 32) 28pp., parts. 15 min. A work of consummate skill and ingenuity. Problems of formal balance and motivic unity are thoroughly solved; writing of amplitude and intensity. D.
See Robert Eugene Frank, "Quincy Porter: A Survey of the Mature Style and a Study of the Second Sonata for Violin and Piano," Ph.D. diss., Cornell University, 1973, 128pp.

Francis Poulenc. *Sonata* (ESC 1942–43) 11pp., parts. Rev.1949. 19 min. Romantic harmonic and melodic writing full of "tragic" passion. Allegro con fuoco: much activity, Franckian sequences. Intermezzo—La guitare fait pleurer les songes (a quotation from Federico García Lorca [1899–1936] to whose memory the *Sonata* was written). Presto tragico: an overabundance of material in lyric style that seems to betray the title of this movement. All movements are free in form. A large-sized work with a smaller-sized impact. D.

John Powell. *Sonata Virginianesque* Op.7 (GS 1919) 38pp., parts. In the Quarters; In the Woods; At the Big House—Virginia Reel. A thoroughly charming and attractive work full of folk song inspiration. Requires mature pianism. Powell was an outstanding pianist, and his type of big technique is what is necessary here. D.

Sergei Prokofiev. *Sonata I* Op.80 f 1938–46 (D. Oistrakh—CFP 4718; Szigeti—MCA; D. Oistrakh—IMC; K 09216) 38pp., parts. 28 min. "In mood it is more serious than the Second [Sonata]. The first movement, Andante assai, is severe in character and is a kind of extended introduction to the second movement, a sonata allegro, which is vigorous and turbulent, but has a broad second theme. The third movement is slow, gentle, and tender. The finale is fast and written in complicated rhythm" (from an article by the Composer, "What I Am Working On," in I. V. Nestyev, *Prokofiev,* trans. Florence Jonas [Stanford, Calif.: Stanford University Press, 1960], p. 385). There is wonderful dialogue between the 2 instruments throughout the *Sonata.* Nestyev says concerning the second movement, Allegro brusco, that its "march-like phrases, with their rigid, clipped cadences and strident harmonies, create an image of brutal military power. This has much in common with the music of the Teutonic invasion in *Alexander Nevsky . . .* But later these coarse, mechanical images give way to a rich, soaring theme (marked 'eroico') sung out by the violin, which sounds particularly appealing after the harmonic and tonal harshness of the opening phrases"

(Nestyev, *Prokofiev,* p. 387). A serious foreboding quality permeates this entire work. D.

————. *Sonata* II Op.94 a 1944 (D. Oistrakh—IMC 36pp., parts; Szigeti—MCA 48pp., parts) 25 min. This lighter work was originally written for flute and piano, but David Oistrakh, to whom it is dedicated, inspired Prokofiev to arrange and rework it into its present form for violin and piano. The Szigeti edition gives both flute and violin versions, so quick comparison is a must! This *Sonata* differs greatly from *Sonata* Op.80 for violin and piano. Its main feature is a graceful melodic treatment, somewhat similar to the composer's "Classical" Symphony. The Moderato is transparent and serene. The Scherzo is elegance personified and is one of Prokofiev's most outstanding achievements in this style of writing. The Andante, with its emotional coolness and measured rhythm, and the lively and vivacious finale are both "Classically" fashioned. The flute and the violin versions are scored differently for the respective instruments and present an insight into Prokofiev's amazing instrumental scoring ability; such facility is seldom seen in his or other composers' works. D.
Both *Sonatas* are very difficult, and only the most skilled duo will do justice to them.

Héctor Quintanar. *Sonata* I (IU) 9pp. Commissioned by the Sociedad de Autores y Compositores de Música S. de A. Plucked and stopped strings, glissandi on strings, harmonics, serial, pointillistic, *pp* alternating clusters on white and black keys, long pedals, mainly soft. Interesting sonorities, avant-garde. D.

Sergei Rachmaninoff. *Two Pieces* Op.6 (MMP). Contains *Romance* and *Hungarian Dance,* 2 little-known works.

Behzad Ranjbaran. *Moto Perpetuo* 1998 (TP 114-41086 2001) 15pp., parts. 5 min. Almost nonstop 16th notes at Presto. Tertian and quartal harmonies provide support for challenging technical problems. D.

Einojuhani Rautavaara. *Dithyrambos* Op.55 (Fazer 1970) 7pp., parts. Toccatalike, using chords and 16th-note figuration; freely tonal. Contrasting midsection allows for violin acrobatics. Brilliant closing in upper register. M-D.

Maurice Ravel. *Sonate Posthume* 1897 (Sal 1975) 17pp., parts. The autograph of this one-movement work is dated April 1897. "The piece was probably performed at the Conservatoire by Georges Enesco and the composer who were classmates; for whatever reason, it was never heard of again. Consisting of an exposition, development and recapitulation, this *Sonata* points out the spiritual influence of Fauré's lyricism as well as that of Franck's harmonic language. The theme adumbrates the beginning of Ravel's *Trio,* and on occasion the themes are treated similarly (cf. bar 13 of the *Sonata* with bar 52 of the *Trio*). Thus, if the opening of the *Trio* is 'Basque in colour,' as the composer asserted, the same observation may be applied to the beginning of the *Sonata.* It turns out that this youthful composition is not a forerunner of the composer's well-known *Sonata* for violin and piano [listed below], but is rather an independent work, whose main theme foreshadows the opening of the *Trio*" (from the Introduction by Arbie Orenstein). M-D.

——. *Sonata* G 1923–27 (Durand 32pp., parts; USSR 1975 40pp., parts; EMB 1991 32pp., parts) 18 min. Allegretto; Blues; Perpetuum mobile. Clear textures; cool, colorful, and objective writing. Same material shared by both instruments, but they contrast it rather than cooperate with it. The Blues and finale lend themselves to virtuoso performances. M-D to D.

——. *Tzigane* Rapsodie de Concert 1924 (Durand 1924; CFP 10600 1990), parts. Original version. Long violin introduction leads to a cadenza-like series of rippling piano arpeggios and the body of the work. Typically clear, Neoclassic writing with coloristic qualities which without doubt inspired the composer to orchestrate the work. An emotionally charged piece for performers and audience alike. M-D.

See VKDR, II: pp.223–30.

Alan Rawsthorne. *Sonata* 1958 (OUP) 28pp., parts. 16 min. Adagio; Allegretto; Toccata (allegro di bravura); Epilogue (Adagio rapsodico). Cyclic, concise, and flexible formal treatment. Triads of D and e form the basis for motivating tonalities. The Toccata is by far the most difficult movement. D.

Gardner Read. *Sonata Brevis* (Seesaw).

——. *Sonoric Fantasia* II Op.123 1966 (TP 1974) 16pp., parts. 10½ min. Originally for violin and orchestra; piano reduction by the composer. Rhapsodic, broad gestures, some astringent dissonances, imitation, subtle dynamics, long pedals, effective trills in low register, pointillistic in spots, very slow and deliberate *ppp* closing. Large span required. D.

——. *Five Aphorisms* Op.150 1991 (Henmar 1998) 24pp., parts. 16 min. I. "Whom the gods would destroy they first make mad." Publilius Syros (First century B.C.): fierce; electrifying; stacked chords; arpeggiation. II. "Pains of love be sweeter far than all other pleasures are." John Dryden (1631–1700): much expression; fluid, with nearly continuous flow of 8th notes at slow tempos. III. "He that plants thorns must never expect to gather roses." Anonymous (ca.500 A.D.): Allegro scherzoso; principally staccato; mixed meters; playful. IV. "All that we see or seem is but a dream within a dream." Edgar Allan Poe (1809–1849): Lento e lontano; opening emphasizes chords of the 2nd; bitonality; mostly quiet dynamics. V. "Thou canst not stir a flower without troubling a star." Francis Thompson (1859–1907): allows much flexibility in a slower tempo; preference for building chords one note at a time; bitonality; *ppp* ending. M-D to D.

Max Reger. *Sonata* Op.1 d (Schott 1911) 18 min.

——. *Sonata* Op.3 D (Schott 1911) 22 min.

——. *Sonata* Op.41 A (UE 1208 1900) 43pp., parts. 23 min. Allegro con moto;

Intermezzo–Prestissimo assai; Largo con gran espressione; Allegro. Chromatic, exploits resources of both instruments. Intermezzo is highly effective. D.

——. *Sonata* Op.72 C (T. Prusse—Bo&Bo 1967) 51pp., parts. 32 min. Allegro con spirito; Prestissimo; Largo con gran espressione; Allegro con brio. In spite of some effective writing and colorful harmonies, the rhythmic procedure is repetitious. D.

——. *Sonata* Op.84 f♯ (T. Prusse—Bo&Bo 1965; UE No. 1968) 51pp., parts. 22 min. Allegro moderato, ma agitato; Allegretto; Andante sostenuto con variazioni. The finale, a large set of variations, is the most interesting movement. D.

——. *Suite im Alten Stil* Op.93 (CFP 1973; K04342) 27pp., parts. The Allegro commodo opens in the style of a Brandenburg concerto. The middle movement, Largo, has often been performed separately. Its expressive long lines are very beautiful. The closing Allegro con spirito is a fugue that opens quietly and builds to a brilliant contrapuntal movement. D.

——. *Suite* Op.103a (Bo&Bo) 28pp., parts. Präludium; Gavotte; Aria; Burleske; Menuet; Gigue. D.

Reger's study of Bach is seen in both these *Suites.* The ideas are more concentrated and clarified, while the thematic treatment is more plastic.

——. *Kleine Sonate* Op.103b/1 (Bo&Bo 1937) 17 min. Three movements. Easier than 103b/2. Concludes with appealing variations. M-D.

——. *Kleine Sonate* Op.103b/2 (Bo&Bo 1965) 19 min. Four smaller movements than usual. M-D.

These two shorter *Sonatas* are well suited to today's audiences.

——. *Sonate* Op.122 e (Bo&Bo 1971; UE 3429) 50pp., parts. 37 min. Moderato; Vivace; Adagio; Allegretto espressivo. D.

——. *Sonate* Op.139 c (CFP 1915) 51pp., parts. 36 min. Con passione; Largo; Vivace; Andantino con variazioni. There is great beauty in this work, especially in the soaring and passionate opening movement. Heavily chromatic with harmonic elaboration stretched almost to the breaking point. D.

See Paul Garvin Taylor, Jr., "Thematic Process and Tonal Organization in First Movement Sonata Forms of Max Reger's Nine Sonatas for Violin and Piano," Ph.D. diss., Catholic University of America, 1982.

Carl Reinecke. *10 Kleine Stücke* Op.213 1890 (B. Päuler—Amadeus 2634 1988) 23pp., parts. 1. Für die leeren Saiten; 2. Primula veris; 3. Serenata; 4. Bitte; 5. Air; 6. Unbekümmert; 7. Carillon; 8. Variationen; 9. Auf den Wellen; 10. Farandole. First-rate short pieces for less-experienced performers. Int. to M-D.

Albert Reiter. *Sonatina in Einem Satz* (Dob 1973) 8pp., parts. Neoclassic, mildly 20th-century. M-D.

Franz Reizenstein. *Sonata* g♯ 1945 (Lengnick) 52pp., parts. Tranquillo: undulating 6ths, flowing, chromatic, alternating octaves between hands, tremolo. Allegro ma non troppo: effective scherzo. Finale–Misterioso: sinewy chromatic figuration in 3rds with both hands, long lines, emphatic octaves. D.

Ottorino Respighi. *Sonata* b 1917 (Ric 117619) 33pp., parts. 18 min. Moderato; Andante espressivo; Passacaglia. Teutonic Romantic writing with some Impressionist influences. D.

Hermann Reutter. *Sonate* Op.20 (Schott 1932).
––––. *Rhapsodie* Op.51 (Schott 3690 1939) 24pp., parts. Contrasting sections use varied pianistic figuration with colorful rhythmic treatment. Freely tonal with opening and closing around f♯–F♯. D.

Roger Reynolds. *Aether* (J. Négyésy––CFP 66992 1988) 1 score. 21 min. Includes notes on performance techniques. Reproduced from holograph.

Phillip Rhodes. *Duo* 1965–66 (CFE 1968) 27pp., parts. 13 min. This work is to be played in its entirety without pause, but it is divided into 3 movements and 2 cadenzas as follows: Recitative: violin plays the leading role while the piano serves to comment and punctuate; a dialogue develops but is broken off by the violin. Cadenza: sums up preceding material. Aria: essentially monothematic and consists of varied repetition of the single theme in different tempos, registers, overlappings, etc., and leads to the piano Cadenza: ideas are worked through over the entire range of the keyboard. Ripresa: most of the musical material of the first 2 movements and the cadenzas reappears here. The names represent in general the character of the movements. Highly organized abstract writing, pointillistic. Complex ensemble problems but well worth the effort. A major work. D.

Marga Richter. *landscapes of the mind II* 1971 (CF 05075 1979) 25pp., parts. From a series of 3, each for different instrumentation. "The series owes its genesis to my encounter with two paintings by Georgia O'Keeffe, 'Sky above Clouds II' and 'Pelvis I'. The pieces seek to convey the spaciousness and serenity of the O'Keeffe paintings, contrasted with inner turbulence, urgency, and ultimate isolation. In addition to sharing thematic material, each piece also has music unique to itself. All are essentially one-movement works in many contrasting sections which paradoxically are closely interrelated, giving an overall impression of freedom and fantasy in construction and effect" (Composer's Note). D.

Wallingford Riegger. *Sonatina* Op.39 (EBM 1948) 15pp., parts. 7 min. Moderato; Allegro. Firm, clear structure, direct dialogue between the 2 instruments, lyric. Sounds like Brahms with wrong notes. Allegro has some effective toccata-like passages. Dolce *pp* ending. M-D.

Ferdinand Ries. *Introduzione e Gavotta* Op.26 (GM) 7pp., parts. Chordal and some interchange of ideas. M-D.
––––. *Drei Sonatinen* Op.30 C, a, F (R&E 1969) 30pp., parts. Light and brilliant

and not too difficult. Fine for the student duo. Each *Sonatina* has 3 movements, with the outside movements larger. Int. to M-D.

————. *Suiten* III Op.34 G (R&E) 41pp., parts. Moderato; Tempo di Bourrée; Adagio non troppo; Gondoliera; Perpetuum mobile. Written from an early-19th-century perspective. The Bourrée and Gondoliera are particularly effective. Perpetuum mobile makes a good encore. M-D to D.

————. *Grande Sonate* Op.83 D (R&E 1969) 24pp., parts. Allegro con brio; Andantino con moto; Rondo–Allegro vivace. Provides a good introduction and preparation for the middle Mozart Sonatas and the early Beethoven. Early Romantic traits are found here. M-D.

Vittorio Rieti. *Sonata Breve* 1967 (Gen) 20pp., parts. Allegretto mosso; Adagio cantabile; Allegro. Freely tonal but strong sense of key in this trim and attractive Neoclassic piece. M-D.

Wolfgang Rihm. *Antlitz: Zeichnung* 1992–93 (UE 30-122 1994) 6pp., parts. Piano holds silently pressed the lowest 9 notes with sostenuto pedal throughout the piece. Webernish, economical writing with chromatic changes of dynamics, all prolonged by harmonics from the sostenuto pedal. M-D.

Knudage Riisåger. *Sonate* (WH 2456 1923) 27pp., parts. Fresco con ritmo; Jocoso e risoluto. Virtuoso academic writing in Neoclassic style mixed with French influence. Large span required. D.

George Rochberg. *Sonata* 1988 (TP 1989) 39pp., parts. 28 min. Sarabande; Scherzo Capriccioso; Ardentemente; Poco sostenuto–Allegro, violentemente. An expressive late-20th-century work recalling forms of the Baroque and Classical periods in the context of a tonality threatened by stressed dissonances, quartal, and spatial features. Large span required. D.

————. *Rhapsody and Prayer* 1989 (TP 114-40510 1990) 16pp., parts. 9 min. Opens Liberamente; come una improvisazione as a multisectional, freely composed rhapsody. Prayer comes in the final 2 pages at Molto adagio with hymnlike chords finishing *ppp.* D.

Joaquín Rodrigo. *Dos Esbozos* (Two Sketches) 1923 (Schott 7916 1991) 11pp., parts. 5 min. 1. La enamorada junto al pequeño surtidor; 2. Pequeña ronda. Two Spanish-flavored short works with involved pianistic requirements. M-D to D.

————. *Rumaniana* 1943 (Ediciones Joaquín Rodrigo/UME), parts.

————. *Set Cançons Valencianes* 1982 (Schott), parts. 17 min. 1. Allegretto; 2. Andante moderato; 3. Allegro; 4. Andante moderato e molto cantabile; 5. Andantino; 6. Andante religioso; 7. Tempo di bolero–Moderato.

————. *Sonata Pimpante* 1966 (Ediciones Joaquín Rodrigo), parts. 16 min.

Bernard Rogers. *Sonata* 1962 (TP) 29pp., parts. Lento spirituale; Vivacissimo; Largo austero; Allegro. Colorful writing, strong craft, expert handling of both instruments. The Vivacissimo is built on *soave* sprightly arpeggi figures that are particularly effective. Keen and subtle sonorities are present in the Largo austero. A fine work that deserves more performances. M-D to D.

Ned Rorem. *Day Music* 1971 (Bo&H) 33pp., parts. Eight short sections with titles—i.e., "Wedge and Doubles," "A Game of Chess 4 Centuries Ago"—and comments by the composer. Dissonant and harsh sounds get some relief in the "Pearls" section with flowing polytonal layers of sonorities. Striking rhythmic and coloristic effects. D.

———. *Night Music* 1972 (Bo&H) 31pp., parts. 20 min. A sequel to *Day Music*. Eight short sections with titles—e.g., "Answers," "Mosquitos and Earthworms," "Gnats," "The Lighthouse," "Saying Goodbye Driving Off"—and comments by the composer. Similar idiom to *Day Music*. Colorful writing throughout. Requires first-rate performers on both instruments. D.

———. *Sonata* (CFP 6211) 19 min.

Hilding Rosenberg. *Sonata* I (NMS 1926).

———. *Sonata* II C (NMS 1941) 16 min.

Nino Rota. *Improvviso in re minore* 1947 (N. Scardicchio—Schott 95 1999, ISMN M-001-12622-9) 8pp., parts. 4 min. Taken from the film *D'amanti senza amore*. Passionate, titillating music alternating between slow and fast sections. Displays subtle as well as animated qualities in a brief rhapsodic setting. M-D.

Robert Steven Rouse. *Violin Sonata* 1992 (Henmar/CFP 67654 1995) 31pp., parts. 16 min. Energetic and rough—Driving forward—Very steady throughout: marked "with a swagger and an edge!"; requires careful pedaling, often sustained with blurred harmonies; dense chordal structures; SA. [Untitled]: austere, chromatic extremes back to back; independence of instruments emphasized; study in touch. Bright, Kicking: complex rhythms, splashes of awkward meters (e.g., $\frac{17}{16}$); performers may feel the sensation of the Kentucky Derby (held in the city of Louisville, where Rouse lives) as they deal with idiosyncrasies and character; finishes *sffffz*. Only for the most gifted performers. D.

Albert Roussel. *Sonata* I Op.11 d 1903, rev.1931 (Sal 1931) 60pp., parts. 32 min. Three long movements in cyclic form. Lent–Très animé; Assez animé; Très animé. The first movement is in SA design with a slow introduction that contains the cyclic theme. In the middle movement, a scherzo, a slow movement, Très lent, is inserted where the trio is usually placed. The lively finale is in Sonata-rondo form. D.

———. *Sonata* II Op.28 A 1925 (Durand) 16 min. More effective than No.I. Allegro con moto: SA, 3 themes carefully worked out. Andante: ABA with a violent B section. Presto: $\frac{6}{8}$ alternated with $\frac{4}{8}$, scherzo-like opening and closing, a dramatic and introspective mid-section. M-D.

Miklós Rózsa. *Variations on a Hungarian Peasant Song* Op.4 1929 (Br&H) 12 min.

————. *North Hungarian Peasant Songs and Dances* Op.5 (Br&H).

————. *Duo* Op.7 1931 (Br&H) 18 min. A theme in the second and fourth movements resembles the one used in the variation set listed above. Enormous rhythmic vitality and frequent climaxes are prevalent in both works.

All three works have a strong Hungarian flavor. They are colorful pieces that require energetic and polished performances. All are M-D.

Edmund Rubbra. *Sonata* II 1932 (OUP 23.410) 38pp., parts. 17 min. Allegretto liberamente e scorrevole; Lament; Allegro vivo e feroce (strident and very rhythmic). Displays Rubbra's early personal harmonic style infused with some counterpoint. Finale is toccata-like. Large span required. D.

————. *Sonata* III Op.133 (Lengnick 1968) 24pp., parts. Allegro: hemiola, broadly conceived themes, neo-Romantic. Andante poco lento e mesto: expressive; parallel chords; chromatic climax; requires a large span. Tema con Variazioni: rhythmic theme, 8 contrasting variations, coda (molto scherzando e leggiero) built on theme. Traditional writing in 20th-century clothes. D.

Anton Rubinstein. *Sonata* I Op.13 G (CFP; Hamelle) 39pp., parts. Moderato con moto; Theme and (2) Variations; Scherzo; Finale.

————. *Sonata* II Op.19 a (Hamelle).

————. *Sonata* III Op.98 b (Hamelle).

The 3 violin and piano *Sonatas* are perhaps Rubinstein's best chamber works. An eclectic-Romantic style is fed into Classic forms. All 3 *Sonatas* contain imaginative writing, but the piano part is treated in a more virtuoso manner in *Sonata* III.

Anton Ruppert. *Vorübergehen. 7 Stationen* (Orlando 1973) 12pp. Photostat. Two copies necessary for performance. Explanations in German only.

Antoni Rutkowski. *Sonata* Op.5 c (PWM 1975) 47pp., parts. Prepared for publication by Tadeusz Przybylski. Preface in Polish and English.

Charles V. Rychlík. *Caprice Boheme* Op.2 G (Urbánek 1930) 9pp., parts. ABA; Allegro con brio. M-D.

————. *Romance* Op.3 F (Urbánek 1929) 7pp., parts. Andante–Moderato. M-D.

————. *Intermezzo* Op.5 F (Urbánek 1933) 7pp., parts. Andante opening with multiple tempo changes following. M-D.

————. *Bohemian Fantasy* Op.6 D (Urbánek 1930) 20pp., parts. In one movement with multiple sections, including 5 variations. M-D.

————. *Humoresque* Op.7b D (Urbánek 1928) 4pp., parts. Allegretto. M-D.

————. *Andante Religioso* Op.13 C (Urbánek 1929) 7pp., parts. Solemn with intensive development according to the rule of Golden Proportion. M-D.

————. *Lullaby* Op.14 G (Urbánek 1929) 5pp., parts. Andante. M-D.

————. *Ballad* Op.17 B (Urbánek 1928) 11pp., parts. ABA'; Andante–Allegro moderato–Andante. D.

————. *Serenade* Op.20 D (Urbánek 1929) 7pp., parts. Moderato. M-D.

————. *Polka* Op.21 E (Urbánek 1933) 11pp., parts. ABA.D.

————. *Prelude and Fugue* Op.22(A) g (Urbánek 1929) 12pp., parts. Much emphasis on octaves and full chords; Mendelssohnian. M-D.

————. *Album Leaf—Song without Words* Op.22(B, C) (Urbánek 1929) 12pp., parts. Separate works published together. *Album Leaf:* ABA'; Moderato. *Song without Words:* ABA'; Allegro; flowing broken-chord figuration. M-D.

————. *Cogitation* e (Urbánek 1935) 8pp., parts. ABA'; Adagio–Andante–Tempo I. D.

————. *Dumka* (Urbánek 1931) 8pp., parts. ABA with coda. M-D.

————. *Etude* D (Urbánek 1931) 8pp., parts. Allegro con brio. D.

————. *Meditation* C (Urbánek 1929) 7pp., parts. Restless with frequent change of tempo and dynamics. M-D.

————. *Perpetuum Mobile* e/G (Urbánek 1930) 11pp., parts. M-D.

————. *Recollections* E♭ (Urbánek 1929) 5pp., parts. Continuous Allegro moderato without interruption. M-D.

————. *Regrets* C (Urbánek 1929) 7pp., parts. Passionate with many tempo changes. M-D.

————. *Remembrance* E (Urbánek 1930) 5pp., parts. Flowing broken-chord figurations contrasted by block chords. D.

————. *Reverie* a (Urbánek 1928) 6pp., parts. Modulatory effects. M-D.

Rychlík's considerable output for piano and violin was uneven at times, mixing subservient roles for both instruments with completely independent roles typical in character piece forms. Nevertheless his music is not without interest in many instances. His compositional style is strongly 19th century with large chords and octaves. Some pieces contain violin cadenzas. (All at UL).

Pedro A. Saenz. *Sonata* D (Ric Amer) 28pp., parts. Allegro con brio; Romanza; Allegro assai. Post-Romantic orientation with a few mildly 20th-century sonorities. D.

Joseph B. Chevalier de Saint-Georges. *Sonata* I 1781 (IU) 15pp., parts. Allegro; Tempo di menuetto. Delightful, simple, and straightforward Classical style. Int. to M-D.

Camille Saint-Saëns. *Sonata* I Op.75 d 1885 (Durand) 39pp., parts. 23½ min. Allegro agitato–Adagio: 2 main subjects; flowing and lyric; closing Allegro prepares for the Adagio, whose melody is contemplative. Allegretto moderato–Allegro molto: light, graceful interaction between the 2 parts. Finale: rich sonorities announced, dancelike and brilliant, strong accentuation. Difficult ensemble problems. D.

————. *Havanaise* Op.83 1887 (E. Ysaye—K 4369). Presented as an Urtext edition. This popular work makes effective use of a languorous Spanish melody set against the habanera rhythm. "Havanaise" is a French adaptation of the word "Habanera," a popular Spanish dance originating in Cuba in a slow $\frac{2}{4}$ meter. M-D.

———. *Sonata* II Op.102 E♭ 1896 (Durand). Allegretto: dreamy, poetical. Andante: aria style, somber pacing in piano. Allegretto scherzando: delicate, subtle, whimsical. Allegro: conceived in a Classical vein, pastorale. More accessible than *Sonata* I, shows great skill. M-D.

———. *Triptyque* Op.136 (Durand 1912; Walhall 136 1998) 29pp., parts. Prémice; Vision Congolaise; Joyeuseté. Spirited writing requiring well-seasoned performers. Movements could be performed separately. D.

See David Gene Tubergen, "A Stylistic Analysis of Selected Violin and Piano Sonatas of Fauré, Saint-Saëns, and Franck," Ph.D. diss., New York University, 1985.

Erkki Salmenhaara. *Trois Scènes de Nuit* 1970 (Finnish Music Information Center) 14pp., parts. 18 min. Oiseaux de nuit: 12-tone; row is frequently spread in arpeggio figuration; tonal implications; pictorial. Clair de lune: piano provides chromatic chordal accompaniment while the violin sings in a freely tonal decorative idiom. Chaconne: 10-note row is announced in bass of the piano; chordal; chromatic; atonal; tonal ending. Colorful and interesting writing in all 3 pieces. M-D.

Claudio Santoro. *Sonata* IV 1951 (Cembra 1956) 26pp., parts. Allegro: unison opening; piano provides syncopated accompaniment for first subject; violin has melody; leads to Meno ancora, where both instruments play syncopated thematic material; Meno e resuluto (Quasi recitativo) leads to recapitulation; short, quiet closing; centers around a–A. Lento: ABA, centers around g, melodic. Allegro: rondo form–ABCDABCD coda; highly rhythmical with a great deal of syncopation in both instruments; contains some slower sections (Meno; Lento); centers around C. M-D.

Andres Sas. *Cantos del Peru* Op.29 1935 (Flûte de Pan; UL) 12pp., parts. I. Siembra [sowing-time]: Molto moderato; uses Incan melody; octaves; block and broken chords. II. Keachampa [warlike dance]: Allegretto; off-beat chords requiring wide span; glissandi. III. La Nusta [concubine of the Inca king]: Andante; persuasive; rolled chords over much of keyboard. IV. Aire y Danza: recitative opening; rhythmic, with insistent patterns capturing the Latin spirit. M-D.

Erik Satie. *Deux Oeuvres* (R. Orledge—Salabert 1995) 20pp., parts. *Choses vues à Droite et à Gauche* (Sans Lunettes) 1914. Originally published by Rouart-Lerolle. Choral hypocrite: Grave; chordal. Fuge à tâtons: Pas vite; linear; salon-style mid-section; *ff* closing. [Autre Choral] Mouvement facultatif: marcato; strident. Fantaisie musculaire: Un peu vif; much staccato in piano part; short violin cadenza; kind of a spoof. *Embarquement pour Cythère* 1917. Probably inspired by Watteau's famous painting. "One of the most beautiful pieces of Erik Satie's maturity. One can compare it in its profundity with *Socrate;* in particular, its subtle evocations of an unforeseen and slightly sinister world suggest to us, from time to time, the second part of this symphonic drama, *Bords de l'Ilissus*" (from score). M-D.

Angel Sauce. *Sonata* (Radio Caracas 1944) 22pp., parts. Moderato: G. Andante: c. Rondó–Allegro: G. Classical style with a few Neoclassic characteristics. M-D.

Henri Sauguet. *Sonate Crépusculaire* (ESC 8706 1990) 20pp., parts.

A. Adnan Saygun. *Sonata* Op.20 1941 (PIC 1961) 38pp., parts. Andante: freely tonal, changing meters, arpeggio intense; requires large span. Molto vivo: $\frac{7}{16}$, repeated chords à la toccata style, quartal harmony, brilliant. Largo: parallel chords, full but quiet sonorities. Allegro: chordal punctuation combined with independent lines, contrasting sections, expressive E conclusion. D.
———. *Suite* Op.33 (PIC 1964) 27pp., parts. Lento: repeated octaves in syncopated triplets, ornamental Oriental melodic fioraturas. Horon: $\frac{7}{8}$, fast and exciting dance. Zeybek: slow, recitative-like, chordal. M-D.

Domenico Scarlatti. *Sonatas* (L. Salter—Augener 1950). Published separately. L.217 c, L.168 d, L.75 F, L.271 e, L.36 g, L.211 d, L.106 d, L.176 G. Of Scarlatti's 550-odd Sonatas, these 8 are the only ones for violin with figured bass; the rest are for solo keyboard. The violin *Sonatas* generally have good basso continuo realizations. They differ from the keyboard Sonatas in that the former have several movements and the latter usually have only one. In place of the active left-hand work normally found in the keyboard Sonatas there is substituted in the violin *Sonatas* what E. J. Dent has aptly termed a "table-leg bass," while the inner harmony is almost completely missing. M-D.
———. *Sonata* K.89 d (R. Bonucci—Boccaccini 1988) 9pp., parts.
See Lionel Salter, "Scarlatti's Violin Sonatas," *Listener* 38 (1947): 116.

Bogusław Schaeffer. *Gasab* 1983 (PWM 1992, ISBN 83-224-3082-5) 18pp., parts. 7 min. Violin may use alternate tuning. Prestissimo with traditional notation and indeterminacy. Uses extremes of both instruments. Requires much imagination to be effective. D.

Thomas Daniel Schlee. *Mouvement* Op.7C 1994 (Billaudot 1996) 12pp., parts. 3½ min. In the collection *L'Ecole du Violon,* published separately. Marked Molto vivo e leggiero. Completely independent instrumental parts, garnished with virtuosic and technical effects. D.

Johann Heinrich Schmelzer. *6 Sonatae Unarum Fidium* 1664 (F. Cerha—UE 1960) 2 vols. 1 C, 2 F, 3 g, 4 D, 5 c, 6 A.

Florent Schmitt. *Chant du Soir* (Rouart-Lerolle 1931) 7pp., parts. Has parts for violin or English horn and piano. Impressionist opening and closing. Builds to chordal climax in mid-section. Subtle rhythmic flexibility, expressive closing. M-D.

Artur Schnabel. *Sonata* (Bo&H 1961) 57pp., parts. Allegro ma non troppo (quasi moderato) e sempre semplice; Allegretto poco vivace; Adagio; Vivace. Extremely chromatic, complex Expressionist style, almost completely polyphonic. Idiom suggests Schoenberg and Sessions. Serious, meditative content. Roman numerals used to indicate length of the musical phrase. D.

Alfred Schnittke. *Sonata* I 1963 (USSR; CFP 5737 35pp., parts). "Adheres to neoclassic forms but uses serial structures as the source of thematic material" (DCM, p. 698).
——. *Quasi una Sonata* 1968 (UE 15826) 32pp., parts. Traditional and nontraditional chords, solid and tremolo clusters, graphic and proportional rhythmic notation, pointillistic, changing meters, quasi-cadenza passages for both instruments, sectional, dynamic extremes, same repeated chords over long period of time. Avant-garde. Large span required. D.
——. *Gratulationsrondo* (Congratulatory Rondo) 1973 (Sikorski 1914 1997) 19pp., parts. Allegro. Conventional writing in C with rondo theme introduced in piano. Strongly harmonic with clearly used form. Published score includes *Madrigal in Memoriam Oleg Kagan* for solo violin. Barely M-D.
——. *Sonata* III 1994 (M. Lubotsky—Sikorski 1936 1996) 23pp., parts. 12 min. Andante; Allegro (molto); Adagio; Senza tempo. Uses quarter tones within a context emphasizing intervals of the 2nd and 7th. Sparse piano textures, economical writing in Webernesque style. Senza tempo is recitative-like, concluding *Sonata* on cluster pitches of E, D, E♭. M-D.

Johann Schobert. *Ausgewählte Werke* (H. Riemann, rev. H. J. Moser—DDT, series 1, Vol.39). Contains *Sonatas* Op.2/1 B♭, Op.14/2 B♭, Op.14/3 c, Op.14/1 D, Op.14/5 A. Also contains Trios and Quartets.
——. *Sonata* A (W. Kramolisch—Nag 199 1962).

Othmar Schoeck. *Sonata* Op.16 D (Hug 1909) 17½ min. Neoclassic, melodious style, much spontaneity. M-D.
——. *Sonate* Op.46 1931 (Hug 1934).

Arnold Schönberg. *Phantasy* Op.47 1949 (CFP 1952) 8 min. A compact piece that contains the elements for several movements. The opening declamatory subject is followed by a contrasting lyrical second idea, which is developed with a lilting character. A 3-part scherzo follows, moving to an altered and condensed recapitulation. A highly effective work in 12-tone writing. Difficult and challenging but technically very playable. The piano part is frequently treated chordally and very complementarily to the violin. D.
——. *Stück* d ca.1893–94 (Belmont 1058 2001) 3pp. An early work by the composer showing mid-19th-century style characteristics. Conventional writing in 51 measures with flowing melody and traditional harmony. M-D.
See Allen Forte, *Contemporary Tone Structures* (New York: Da Capo Press, 1973).

Richard S. Hill, "Arnold Schoenberg: Phantasy for Violin, with Piano Accompaniment, Opus 47," *Notes* 9/4 (September 1952).

Ruth Schonthal. *Ode to a Departing Swan* 1964 (Furore 273 1996) 3 sheets, parts. 3 min. In $\frac{9}{8}$, marked Andante con moto. Possible encore piece with its gentle melodious quality. Score is copy of MS. M-D.

Franz Schubert. *Sonatas* (Sonatinas) D.384 D, D.385 a, D.408 g (Op.137), D.574 a (M. Holl, D. Oistrakh, H. Kann—VU 1973) 83pp., parts. Notes 28pp. The three *Sonatinas* of Op.137 appear here under Schubert's original title of *Sonatas for Piano and Violin.* This carefully researched version includes comparisons with the autographs and the earliest editions, but the violin part is printed in the piano score, and it is very difficult to distinguish original from editorial phrasings. Oistrakh provides helpful fingerings and bowing for the violin, while Hans Kann's fingerings for the piano are carefully thought out. M-D.

——. *Sonatinen* (G. Henle, K. Röhrig—Henle 1963) rev. ed. 48pp., parts. Contains the same works as listed above. Based on original Schubert MS; only fingering and signs for down-bow and up-bow have been added. Other editions are: Hermann—CFP 1561; Br&H; Kehr, Schröter—Schott; David—GS L921; Pessina—Ric BA11060; Augener 7571; K 09726. Available separately from CFP.

For a discussion of these pieces see VKDR, II: pp.67–77.

——. *Duos* (Ernst Herttrich—Henle 1976) 87pp., parts. Fingering by M. Rostal, H.-M. Theopold. Contains *Sonata* D.574, Op.Post. 162 A; *Rondo* D.895, Op.70 b; *Fantasie* D.934, Op.post. 159 C. Sources are identified and the most important variants between the sources are listed. Signs obviously missing in the sources are noted in parentheses. Outstanding Urtext-performing edition, superlative printing, informed editorial comment.

——. *Duos* (Carl Hennann—CFP 156B 1934). Includes the *Duos* listed above plus the *Introduction* and (7) *Variations* Op.160. The *Rondo* D.895 is magnificent salon music. The *Fantasie* D.934, in 7 connected sections, has Hungarian touches as well as brooding drama implicit in the development episodes. The song "Sei mir gegrüsst" is the basis for the slow section. A rousing march concludes the work. The *Duo* D.574 is gentle and charming.

Available separately: *Fantasie* D.934 Op.post.159 C 1827 (H. Wirth—Br 5620 1970 Urtext; C. Herrmann—IMC). *Rondo* D.895 (Br 5618 1992).

See P. McCreless, "A Candidate for the Canon? A New Look at Schubert's *Fantasie in C Major for Violin and Piano,*" *19th Century Music* 20/3 (1997): 205–30.

Robert Schumann. *Two Sonatas* Op.105, Op.121 (F. Hermann—CFP; Z. Francescatti —IMC). Op.105 a 1851 (W. Haug-Freienstein, H.-M. Theopold, K. Guntner— Henle 428 1994; Br&H; Bauer—GS L1696; Hamelle; K 04373). 19 min. Mit leidenschaftlichem Ausdruck; Allegretto; Lebhaft. A work of great depth and intensity, capped with an exquisite final movement of rhapsodic quality and meticulous detail. Op.121 d 1851 (Bauer—GS L1699) 39pp., parts. 28 min.

——. *Sonata* III a 1853 (O. W. Neighbour—Schott 1956) 30pp., parts. Ziemlich langsam; Lebhaft; Intermezzo; Finale. Valuable Preface, editorial notes. M-D.

——. *F.A.E. Sonata* 1853. See detailed entry under Brahms, this section.

——. *Fantasiestücke* Op.73 (W. Boetticher, E. Herttrich, H.-M. Theopold— Henle 421 1986, ISMN M-2018-0421-7) 15pp., parts. Originally for piano and clarinet, first published with ad lib parts for violin and cello. See detailed entry under duos for piano and clarinet. Excellent Preface. M-D.

——. *Three Romances* Op.94 (Henle 427). See detailed entry under duos for piano and oboe.

——. *Fünf Stücke im Volkston* Op.102 (Br&H 8473). See detailed entry under duos for piano and cello.

——. *Märchenbilder* ("Fairy-Tale Pictures") Op.113 (W. Haug-Freienstein, K. Schilde, K. Guntner—Henle 694 2000) 25pp., parts. See detailed entry under duos for piano and viola.

Joseph Schuster. *Sei Divertimenti da Camera* (W. Plath—Nag 1973 Vols.229, 232, 233). Vol.I: F, G. Vol.II: F, C. Vol.III: D, G. 6 separate volumes, score, and parts. Preface by editor. Date from around 1777 in Munich. No.V in D is the most important of the series. Delightful writing with keyboard part almost as important as the violin. M-D.

Eduard Schütt. *Suite* Op.44 d/D (Simrock 1894) 38pp., parts. Allegro risoluto; Scherzo–Vivace; Canzonetta con Variazioni; Rondo à la russe. Large-scale writing of Schumannesque character with no true historical relationship between the title and its movements. D.

Elliott Schwartz. *The Decline and Fall of the Sonata (A Fable)* 1972 (CF) facsimile. 14pp., parts. 11 min. Notation is generally proportional, each system (with a very few exceptions) being equal to 15 seconds. Also, many traditionally notated passages, aleatoric. Contains other performing instructions: pianist must play muted strings, pluck strings, make percussive sounds with palms or knuckles on wooden part of piano or metal cross-ribs inside, slap palms on strings, and needs a large wooden mallet. Two brief sections can use an optional tape, which heightens and intensifies theatrical tendencies. Tape directions are included for pianist to make tape. Pointillistic, serial influence, long pedals, arm clusters, extensive directions in score; theatrical tendencies should be played up as much as possible. Avant-garde. D.

——. *Memorial in Two Parts* 1988 (Fallen Leaf Press) 17 min. Performed from full score. "Dedicated to two friends who died in the 1980's, both musicians (one a pianist, the other a singer). Quoted fragments from works they loved to perform: Schumann, Gershwin, Schubert, Monteverdi, Mozart. Also other fragments[:] Ives, Elgar, and my own early *Patterns* (all concerned with death &

mortality). In two movements, with return to the opening at the work's conclusion" (from Composer's letter to authors).

Leif Segerstam. *At the Border* 1974 (Busch 1976) 8pp., parts. For violin or viola. Freely designed using proportional rhythmic relationships. Avant-garde with both instruments seemingly unaware of one another and functioning indeterminately. Dramatic use of sonorities with dynamics from *ffff* to *pppp possible*. Damper pedal to remain down with only occasional releases. Concludes ad lib whenever performers desire to stop. M-D.

Mátyas Seiber. *Sonata* (Schott 1963). First movement has complex percussive harmonic usage in the piano. Second movement is a kind of intermezzo, measured and dancelike. Finale is a lyrical slow movement, where the conflict between the instruments in the first movement is settled. M-D.

Jean Baptiste Senaillié. *Sonata* c (Lemoine).
———. *Sonata* d (J. A. Parkinson—OUP 1963).
———. *Sonata* E (Lemoine).
———. *Sonata* e (G. Beechey—OUP) 12pp., parts. A 4-movement work, typical of late-18th-century elegant style. This is No.5 of 10 *Sonatas* published in Paris in 1721. Last movement presents most challenge to the keyboard player. Figured bass is well realized. Excellent introductory note. M-D.
———. *Sonata* Op.5 G (Jensen—Augener 7405).
———. *Sonata* G (Moffat—Simrock).
———. *Sonata* G (Salmon—Ric).

Roger Sessions. *Duo* (EBM 1942) 42pp., parts. A strong and valuable work for the combination. Very difficult.

Harold Shapero. *Sonata* 1942 (PIC 1954) 32pp., parts. Moderato: incisive repeated chords, widely spread broken-chord figuration, independent lines, freely tonal; large span required. Adagio: short motivic ideas, chromatic, serious. Allegro preciso: marcato and secco contrasted with semi-legato style, repeated harmonic fourths, a few long lines interspersed, brilliant and pesante conclusion. D.

Ralph Shapey. *Fantasy* 1983 (UL) 22pp. 8 min. Two copies necessary for performance. In 3 movements: Variations (4); Scherzo; Song. Expressive within complex rhythmic relationships. D.

Rodion Shchedrin. *Menuhin-Sonata* 1999 (Schott 102 2001, ISMN M-001-12972-5) 19pp., parts. 20 min. Inspired by the artistry of Yehudi Menuhin, who died as the work was being composed. In one continuous movement, summarizing expressive musical features in contrasting sections. The timbre of both instruments is thoroughly explored within conventional writing. Occasionally folkloric. M-D.

Arthur Shepherd. *Sonate* (Senart 1927). Rich and plangent sonorities, long lines, chromatic, secondary 7th chords strung together, brief modal effects juxtaposed with disjunct intervals. All these elements are used for expressive purposes and lend an individual color to the work. M-D.

Seymour Shifrin. *Duo* (CFP 1968–69) 19pp., parts. 12 min. One movement of atonal writing, complex rhythmic problems, fragmentary melodic ideas equally shared by the 2 instruments. M-D.

Dmitri Shostakovich. *Sonata* Op.134 1968 (USSR 1970; Sikorski) 93pp., parts. A milestone of 20th-century chamber music. Opening theme in the piano is built around the 12 notes of the chromatic scale but is not a true tone row. This terse work moves closer to atonality than any previous works by Shostakovich. The entire compelling piece is built on a dependence-independence relationship between the 2 instruments that results in a continual musical tension, especially noticeable in the rhythmic and melodic elements. A gloomy Nachtmusik passage appears in the opening movement and returns cyclically to close the final movement, a tidy and effective unifying device. D.

Alan Shulman. *Suite Based on American Folk Songs* 1944 (www.capital.net/com/ggjj/shulman 2000) 38pp., parts. I. Fare Ye Well, My Darlin'; II. Little Bird; III. The Mermaid; IV. Cod Liver 'Ile; V. Johnny Stiles; VI. What Shall I Do with a Drunken Sailor? Picturesque settings of older folk songs with motivic and musical development suggestive of each song's character. Neoclassic writing with invigorating passagework for both instruments. M-D.

Jean Sibelius. *Suite* E 1888 (Fazer 08771 1994, ISMN M-042-08771-8) 27pp., parts. Four movements intended to be performed as a set: Allegro molto moderato–Allegro molto–Più lento quasi andantino–Allegro brillante. Composed while studying violin, the score favors this instrument though the piano part is not without interest. M-D.
——. *Sonata* 1889 (Fazer 8516 1996) 39pp., parts. [Unmarked]; Andante; Vivace. Of particular interest is the second movement, "a set of variations on a folk-like tune (intended to represent, he told Pehr, 'an authentic Finnish girl' singing with 'sadness and melancholy,' unaffected by flirtatious efforts to cheer her up), was his first explicitly 'nationalistic' piece" (NGD). Wide span required. D.
——. *Sonatine* Op.80 (J. A. Burt—WH 1921, reprint 1949).
——. *4 Stücke* Op.115 (Br&H) Published separately. Auf der Heide; Ballade; Humoreske; Die Glocken.
——. *3 Stücke* Op.116 (Br&H 1930) Published separately. Scène de danse; Danse caractéristique; Rondeau romantique.

Elie Siegmeister. *Sonata* I 1951–59 (CF) 54pp., parts. 22 min. Allegro con fuoco; Allegro ritmico; Adagio non troppo; Vivo, con spirito. Intense virtuoso writing of the highest order. Large span required. D.

——. *Sonata* II 1965–70 (CFP 1976) 38pp., parts. Lyric, long lines, poise, serene and elegant themes, conservative 20th-century idiom. D.

——. *Sonata* III 1965 (CFP) 15 min. Two seething movements. Long lyric lines, panchromatic, soaring expression. "Bartók pizzicati" used as an effective device, sinewy texture, astringent harmonies. D.

——. *Sonata* IV 1971 (CF) 36pp., parts. 18 min. Andante con moto; Andante; Allegro con spirito. A broad sweeping work. Many colorful ideas and dramatic moments. Large span required. D.

——. *Sonata* V 1972 (CF) 36pp., parts. 20 min. Andante: freely tonal and chromatic; varied tempos; harmonic 2nds are prevalent; subtle syncopation; texture thins at conclusion; requires large span. Andante: imitation, colorful and contrasting figuration. Allegro giocoso, molto ritmico: broken 9th figures in alternating hands, changing meters, strong rhythms and advanced eclectic style, firm control of the medium, bristling dissonance. D.

Christian Sinding. *Sonata* Op.12 C 1892 (WH 5) 41pp., parts. Allegro moderato; Andante; Finale. Nationalistic Norwegian melodic style coupled with Wagnerian technique. D.

——. *Sonata* Op.27 E (CFP 2826). Brilliant opening movement, Romantic second movement, lively finale with a delightful and flowing development. D.

Emil Sjögren. *Sonata* Op.19 g 1885 (CFP 2215) 27pp., parts. Allegro vivace; Andante; Finale. Exudes a youthful passion. Warm and some delicate melodies; strong Romantic and rich harmonies. Very fresh-sounding when written. M-D.

——. *Sonata* II Op.24 e 1888 (NMS 807) 35pp., parts. Allegro moderato; Allegretto scherzando; Andante sostenuto; Con fuoco. The most famous of Sjögren's piano and violin *Sonatas*. Form and construction are clearer than in first *Sonata*. M-D.

——. *Sonata* IV Op.47 1906 (Br&H) 31pp., parts.

——. *Five Sonatas* (GM 1956) 169pp., parts. Contains *Sonatas* Op.19, Op.24, Op.32 g (1900), Op.47, Op.61 a (1914). Reprints of the original editions.

Myroslav Skoryk. *Sonata* II (Duma 2000) 24pp., parts. Word: opens with considerable expressive freedom in violin and widely spaced chords in piano; strongly tonal with chromatic coloring as movement becomes more engaging. Aria: lyric with similar harmonic treatment; arpeggiated figures in both instruments generally follows tonal implications; repeated chords. Burlesque: lively $\frac{4}{4}$ setting with rhythmic emphasis; contrary motion used in harmonic intervals and melodic lines; dramatic ending loses its punch with Meno mosso tempo change. Large span required. M-D.

——. *A-RI-A* (Duma 1998). For cello or violin and piano. See detailed entry under duos for piano and cello.

Roger Smalley. *Capriccio* I 1966 (Faber) 14 min. Fantasia; Scherzo; Nocturne; Coda.

David Stanley Smith. *Sonata* Op.51 A 1923 (SPAM 1924) 63pp., parts. Allegro molto, tempestoso; Adagio; Allegretto, poi allegro; Epilogue: Andante maestoso. Large-scale neo-Romantic work requiring sensitive musicians with grandioso technique. Parts work together well. D.

Hale Smith. *Duo* Op.9 1953 (CFP) 33pp., parts. Energetic; Slow; Aggressively (Cadenza). Abstruse and dramatic writing, some Neoclassic characteristics, highly individual style. Rhythmic problems for pianist; large span required. D.

Leo Sowerby. *Sonata* H.165 B♭ 1922 (Sowerby 1996) 58pp., parts. Very slowly–Blithely and Merrily; Slowly and Moodily; With furious energy–Very fast. Richly neo-Romantic writing using Classical forms on a grand scale. Brahmsian and Schumannesque influences are unmistakable. Fully chordal writing requiring wide spans. Last movement pits the capabilities of the instruments and players at breakneck speed for a fiery finish. D.

———. *Fantasy-Sonata* H.281 1944 (Sowerby 1995) 53pp., parts. Quiet and tranquil: full chords; arpeggiation; octaves; frequent chromaticism. Bright and chipper: $\frac{5}{4}$; parallel 5ths; octaves; wide spans. Solemn: preference for downward chromaticism; octotonic; grand chordal gestures. Classical forms are used freely and imaginatively with clearly identifiable themes. D.

———. *Sonata in D* H.367 1959 (Sowerby 1996) 74pp., parts. Sprightly; Languorously; Agitated; With breadth. Octotonic; building blocks of chords; SA in first movement; wide spans required. Bartókian flavor in Agitated with $\frac{7}{8}$ meter and added notes. D.

These new editions are made available by the Leo Sowerby Foundation. Sowerby always maintained a late-19th-century approach to composition utilizing large concepts of form and pianistic technique.

Alojz Srebotnjak. *Sonatina* II (GS 1971) 32pp., parts. Andante, rapsodico: flexible meters; works to climax; subsides. Vivace: $3 + 2 + \frac{3}{8}$; thin textures, rhythmic propulsion, *pp* ending. Larghetto: serious dramatic gestures; leads to Andantino, pastorate then returns to Larghetto mood. Allegro molto: a fast dance, Bartóklike, glissandi, straightforward writing. Effective. M-D.

Johann V. Stamitz. *Sonata* Op.6a G (F. Brož—Artia 1956) MAB 28. 9pp., parts. Adagio; Allegro; Minuetto. More like a Sonata da Camera or a Suite. Musical expression and melodic lines show some characteristics of the Mannheim instrumental concertante style. Playful, folklike melodies with frequent embellishments. M-D.

John Stanley. *Six Solos for Flute, Violin or Oboe and Keyboard Instrument* (Concordia).

———. *Six Solos for a German Flute or Violin and Continuo* Op.4 (G. Pratt—JWC 1975) 44pp., parts for flute or violin and viola da gamba or cello. See detailed entry under duos for piano and flute.

Robert Starer. *Duo* 1988 (MCA 1988) 24pp., parts. In one continuous movement, treating the instruments "as equal partners in dialogue . . . The thematic ideas presented by the violin in the unaccompanied opening permeate the entire work, openly or in the guise of variation. Other sections have their own musical ideas and can be described as improvisatory, lyrical, energetic and noble. In the coda the mood of the opening returns, altered by the changes its material has gone through by the other musical themes it has encountered" (from the score). M-D.

Erich Walter Sternberg. *Sonata* 1955, rev. 1965 (IMI 1968) 39pp., parts. 17 min. Allegro sostenuto: SA, "full of vitality, giving expression to the exuberance of the adolescent rushing out into life to conquer it" (from the score). Variations on J. S. Bach's "Come Sweet Death": this movement "expresses an old man's feelings" (from the score); written in different canonic forms, one being a canon cancrizans; in Var.5 the theme of the first movement appears in counterpoint to the Bach chorale. M-D.

Edward Steuermann. *Improvisation and Allegro* 1955 (New Valley Music Press 1971) 26pp., parts. 12 min. "The violin piece is not a row composition, although it is 12-tone. The first 'statement' of the violin comprises six tones, the answer of the piano the other six tones. Then an inversion in the violin, which curiously, gives the same tones with this difference, that D appears instead of E. In this way each instrument has a reservoir of seven tones, and only these are used in the Improvisation. The form I see as a kind of sonata exposition (until bar 46). At bar 55 begins a kind of recapitulation, but as each instrument speaks in a different language, this is all, of course, only hinted (one feels it, however, very exactly in the form). Bar 74 begins the 'coda' of the Improvisation. The Allegro is a Rondo (it was first planned as a true 12-tone composition, but that would have sounded like milk after wine). The instruments simply exchange their 'keys.' The violin plays B for the first time in bar 99. Towards the end the instruments exchange more and more frequently; there are also small 'modulations.' The ending should have the effect of A minor in the violin and C minor in the piano" (from a letter by Edward Steuermann to Erwin Ratz, January 23, 1962). D.

Halsey Stevens. *Sonata* I (CFE 1947) 17 min. Allegro; Molto adagio; Allegretto ben accentato; Allegro. Expertly constructed; dissonance used dramatically yet warm and lyric writing permeates this fluent work. M-D.

———. *Sonatina Piacevole* 1956 (PIC 1968) 12pp., parts. 4½ min. For alto recorder or flute or violin, and piano or harpsichord. See detailed entry under duos for piano and flute.

———. *Sonatina* III 1959 (Helios) 15pp., parts. 8 min. Allegro: theme treated imitatively between instruments; dancelike; quartal and quintal harmony; freely centered around d. Adagio: expressive, overlapping sonorities, sustained, e tonal implications. Allegro: rhythmic drive, octotonic, imitation and diminution, 2 sustained episodes, repeated notes and octaves; the whole movement has much snap to it. Highly effective. M-D.

Karlheinz Stockhausen. *Sonatine* 1951 (UE 15170) 18pp., parts. 10 min. Schoenberg's influence noted; this was a "school work" written while Stockhausen was a student at the State Conservatory in Cologne. Lento espressivo: thin textures, trills are important. Molto moderato e cantabile: ostinato-like bass of broken octaves, chordal sonorities gradually added. Allegro scherzando: octotonic; repeated bitonal chords; 3 staves required to notate some parts; vigorous rhythms; large span required. M-D.

Richard Strauss. *Sonata* Op.18 E♭ 1888 (UE 1047; K 04353) 51pp., parts. 27 min. This scintillating work is indebted to Brahms and Schumann. Makes considerable technical demands on both players. Allegro ma non troppo: strongly rhythmic; beautifully contrasted second theme; brilliant piano writing but violin is not overpowered. Improvisation–Andante cantabile: nocturne-like, passionate mid-section. Finale—Andante-Allegro: piano has short solo introduction; main idea appears in the Allegro and is rhythmically unusual; expressive theme in the violin follows while the piano rustles through various arpeggi figurations; dancelike idea substitutes for a scherzo, and a climactic coda in $\frac{6}{8}$ brilliantly ends the work. D.

Igor Stravinsky. *Duo Concertante* 1931–32 (Bo&H 1947) 18 min. A kind of Sonata for piano and violin in 5 movements: Cantilène; Eglogues I & II; Gigue; Dithyrambe. Stravinsky said of this work in his autobiography, "The spirit and form of my 'Duo Concertante' were determined by my love of the pastorale poets of antiquity and their scholarly art and technique. The theme which I had chosen developed through all the five movements of the piece which forms an integral whole, and, as it were, offers a musical parallel to the old pastoral poetry." This writer can find no theme that is common to all 5 movements. There seems to be only a wonderful consistency of style exemplified by the avoidance of pure consonance and the use of 2 juxtaposed diatonic chords in one way or another. For a more thorough analysis of this work see VKDR, II: pp.257–61.

——. *Berceuse* (K 04339). Transcribed by the composer from *The Firebird*.

Joseph Suder. *Zweite Sonate* a 1949 (A. Suder—Amadeus 1079 1999) 35pp., parts. Allegro; Scherzo: Vivo; Adagio; Allegro moderato. "Contrary to many 20th Century composers—who seek to discover new acoustic perspectives or sound effects for the violin—in Suder the violin sings . . . The piano and violin are equal partners, whose genuine dialogue leads the thematic invention into different tonal realms . . . [It] dies contemplatively away at the end . . . confirm-[ing] the composition's lyrical attitude and, eschewing any triumphalism, leaves the listener in thoughtful mood" (from the score). D.

Karol Szymanowski. *Sonata* Op.9 d 1904 (UE; PWM 1984) 21 min. Allegro moderato; Andantino tranquillo e dolce; Finale: Allegro molto, quasi presto. A youthful work already showing the composer's willingness to break away from the prevailing late-19th-century mold. Large span required. D.

———. *Romans* Op.23 (T. B. Konarska, E. Umińska—PWM 1978, ISBN 83-224-1919-8) 8pp., parts. Large-scale, expansive writing with full chords, octaves, and arpeggiated figures. Marked Lento assai, poco rubato. Begins and ends very soft. D.

———. *Mythes* [Mity] Op.30 (UE 1915) 3 Poems. Available separately: "La Fontaine d'Arethuse" 14pp., parts. 6 min. "Narcissus" 12pp., parts. 7 min. "Dryads et Pan" 16pp., parts. 7 min. These pieces show a strong instrumental style with programmatic tendencies. They describe ancient legends using a refined harmonic hypersensitiveness that yields to a tendency to over-elaboration. The piano part is luminous and very independent of the violin, with a profusion of notes everywhere. D.

———. *La Berceuse d'Aïtacho Enia* Op.52 (UE 1925; PWM 1953) 5pp., parts. Mainly lyric, trill effectively used, tonal yet freely chromatic. M-D.

See Lisa Elizabeth Lantz, "The Violin Music of Karol Szymanowski: A Review of the Repertoire and Stylistic Features," D.M.A. diss., Ohio State University, 1994; Frank Kwantat Ho, "The Violin Music of Karol Szymanowski," M.A. thesis, University of Alberta, 2000.

Germaine Tailleferre. *Sonate* I c♯ 1921 (Durand) 39pp., parts. 17 min. Modéré sans lenteur: SA, polytonal, delightful and piquant writing. Scherzo: $\frac{5}{8}$, dainty, swaying rhythms in trio, spontaneous sounding. Assez lent: emotional, intense; builds to dramatic climax and leads directly to the Final: varied rhythmic and polytonal effects, effervescent closing in G. Beautifully balanced dialogue between the instruments. D.

———. *Pastorale* 1942 (EV 1946) 5pp., parts. 3 min. An uninterrupted pastorale setting marked Allegretto. Repeated chords and wide spans predominate. M-D.

———. *Sonate* II B♭ 1951 (Durand) 30pp., parts. Allegro non troppo: chordal, flowing second section, parallel chords; varied key signatures but ends in B♭. Adagietto: d, strongly Impressionist. Final: F, repeated notes and chords evolve into a toccata-like closing. M-D.

———. *Sonatina* 1973 (S. Weiner—Billaudot) 13pp., parts. Moderato; Andantino; Allegro–gaiement. In Poulencian style with a little more dissonance. Pianistic. M-D.

Toru Takemitsu. *Distance de Fée* 1951 (Schott Japan 1050 1989, ISBN 4-11-899577-8) 13pp., parts. 7½ min. Explores chordal structures in a setting marked Lentement mystérieux, à la Messiaen, whose works were an influence on Takemitsu. Contemplative. M-D.

———. *Hika* (Sal 1973) 6pp., parts. Serial, flexible meters, pointillistic, Expressionist, generally uses quiet dynamics, complex. Three staves required to notate most of the piece. Large span required. D.

————. *From Far beyond Chrysanthemums and November Fog* 1983 (Schott Japan 1014 1983, ISBN 4-11-899541-7) 12pp. Two copies required for performance. Entitled after a stanza from the poem *In the Shadow* by Japanese poet Makoto Ōoka. "The structure of the work is concise. It is a perspective drawing, based on the dominant six notes and with the remaining six notes used as 'shadows' " (from Preface). D.

See Miyako Tadokoro Zeng, "The Works for Piano and Violin by Toru Takemitsu: A Cultural and Stylistic Perspective," D.M.A. diss., University of Southern Mississippi, 1998.

Joseph Tal. *Sonata* (Israeli Music Publications 1952) 16pp., parts. 12 min. Moderato; Andantino; Moderato. Presents a 3-movement Sonata in the scheme of a Classical first movement, with the opening Moderato representing the first subject and exposition, the Andantino corresponding to an expressive development, and the final movement serving as the recapitulation and coda. Forceful and expressive writing. M-D.

Alexander Tansman. *Fantaisie* 1963 (ESC 8884 1995) 28pp., parts. 16 min. Divertimento: light and mechanical; frequent contrast of touch; wide span required. Elegie: expressive with rubato; emphasizes 7ths. Fuga: lively and resolved; linear throughout. Improvisazione: based upon previous thematic materials, esp. fugue. Canon: 3 voices; cantabile. Finale–Scherzo: strong marcato rhythms; detailed passagework, *ff* finish. To be performed as a set without pause. D.

————. *Sonata quasi una Fantasia* (Senart).

————. *Sonata* II (ESC).

————. *Sonatine* II (ESC 1991). 20pp., parts. 11 min.

————. *Cinq Pièces Faciles* (ESC 1991) 11pp., parts. Recreation; Marche; Aria; Air ancien; Finale in modo classico. Uses only first position for violinist. Int.

Simón Tapia Colman. *Sonata* "El Afilador" (EMM 1958) 28pp., parts. Poco recitativo–senza rigore–Andante mosso; Largo; Vivo. Many 7ths and 2nds add dissonance, parallel 4ths, chromatic, rhythmic push even in the espressivo cantabile section, spread-out quick figures. Arpeggi and chordal gestures in the Vivo, shifting rhythms, some strongly tonal sections. Short violin cadenza leads to a Presto coda. D.

Béla Tardos. *Sonate* 1965 (EMB Z.6157) 30pp., parts. Allegro con fuoco; Lento; Presto con bravura. Octotonic, 2 with 3, glissandi, full chords, chromatic arpeggi figuration, strong rhythms in finale, parallel chords, folk dance influence. Large span required. M-D to D.

Giuseppe Tartini. *Sonatas* Op.1 (E. Farina—Carisch) 2 vols., 12 *Sonatas*. Each *Sonata* has 3 or 4 movements; the second (slow) movement is often very short, only a few bars. Mature Tartini style even though Op.1. Careful editing, excellent introductory note. Cello part optional. M-D.

——. *Two Sonatas* from Op.1, e and G (Lichtenberg—GS L725).

——. *Six Sonatas* (Polo—Ric ER177). Includes Op.1/1 A, 2 C, 4 G, 5 e.

——. *Sonata* 1/5 (Lengnick).

——. *Sonata* Op.1/10 "Devil's Trill" (CFP 1099b; Auer—CF B2695; M. Abbado —Ric 132154; Joachim—Simrock; Nachez—Schott; Bo&H; Barison—Carisch; PWM; Kreisler—IMC; Jensen—Augener). 13 min. Adagio; Non troppo presto; Largo; Allegro commando.

——. *Sonata* Op.2/12 G (Schott; Polo—Ric).

——. *Six Sonatas* Op.5 (Bonelli—Zanibon 1951) 1 a, 2 B♭, 3 A, 4 G, 5 F, 6 B♭.

——. *Seven Sonatas* (CFP 1099A,B,C) 3 vols. Vol.I: 2 F, 4 G, 5 e. Vol.II: 10 g, Devil's Trill g. Vol.III: 6 D, Sonata C.

——. *Seven Sonatas* (K 02016)

——. *Three Sonatas* F, G, e (F. Hermann—CFP 1099C).

——. *Three Sonatas* (Artia).

——. *Sonata* Op.I/10 g "Didone Abbandonata" (M. Abbado—Ric 131799 1972, 11pp.; H. Marteau—Steingräber 1961, 7pp.), parts. One of the most famous of Tartini's nearly 200 *Sonatas* for violin and basso continuo. Tempo indications for the 3 movements differ in the 2 editions. Binary forms. Inspired by the final scene in the third act of Metastasio's opera by the same title, whose verses are printed in Ricordi edition. M-D.

——. *Sonata* 11 F (Nadaud, Kaiser—Senart 5264).

——. *Sonata* 13 B♭ (Nadaud, Kaiser—Senart 5265).

——. *Sonata* 18 A (Nadaud, Kaiser—Senart 5266).

——. *Sonata* 21 b (Nadaud, Kaiser—Senart).

——. *Sonata* 23 A (Nadaud, Kaiser—Senart).

——. *Sonata* 25 D (Nadaud, Kaiser—Senart 5269).

——. *Sonata* E (Nadaud, Kaiser—Senart 5208).

——. *Sonata* G (Corti—Carisch).

——. *Sonata* g (Auer—CF B2665).

——. *Sonata* g (Ric R429).

Bruce J. Taub. *Imported Crystal Cries* (CFP 67850 1999) 24pp., parts. 10 min. In one movement, inspired by stanzas from Dante's *Inferno*. Expressive sonorities which grow in intensity from the opening slow pace to rapid passages, and then alternate back and forth. Straightforward rhythms blaze toward the end with repeated notes at *ff*. D.

Alexander Tcherepnin. *Sonata* Op.14 F 1921 (Durand) 12 min. This youthful 3-movement cyclic work shows a strong Tchaikovsky-Rachmaninoff influence plus polychords and harmonic shifts à la Prokofiev. The outer movements (Allegro moderato; Vivace) have a motoric moto perpetuo rhythmic drive that also reminds one of Prokofiev. A limpid fugue makes up the middle movement (Larghetto). M-D.

————. *Romanze* A (J. Philipp—Simrock 1925) 3pp., parts. Peaceful, with flowing 8ths in piano alongside a facile violin melody marked Andante. A fine work for less advanced performers seeking first-time chamber music experience. Int.

————. *Elégie* Op.43 (Durand 1928) 5pp., parts. A quiet Andante expressively investigating the effects of trills and repeated notes. Wide span required. M-D.

————. *Mouvement Perpétuel* (Durand 1946) 19pp., parts. A stern whirlwind of motion presses forward in momentum as the instruments exchange patterns and musical ideas. Comes together quickly for experienced musicians. D.

Georg Philipp Telemann. *Sechs Sonaten* (W. Friedrich—Schott 4221 1954). Published by Telemann in Frankfurt in 1715.

————. *Zwölf Methodische Sonaten 1–6 für Violine oder Querflöte und Basso continuo, 7–12 für Querflöte oder Violine und Basso continuo,* Hamburg 1728 und 1732 (M. Seiffert—Br 2951 1955).

————. *Three Sonatas* for violin or flute and continuo (H. Kölbel—Heinrichshafen). The first 3 of a set of 12 *Sonatas* written in 1734. Continuo realizations are by Ernst Meyerolbersleben in a somewhat flamboyant but tasteful style. The other 9 *Sonatas* are available in 3 volumes from the same publisher.

————. [16] *Sonaten à Violino e Continuo* (I. Payne—SUTE), parts, with optional cello. Urtext/First edition from a MS in the Staatsbibliothek zu Berlin: Preußische Kulturbesitz, Musikabteilung mit Mendelssohn-Archive. Sonatas published separately. 5 C TWV41:C71 (SUTE 26 1996) 8pp., Adagio; Allegro; Grave; Vivace. 6 G TWV41:G10 (SUTE 27 1996) 8pp., [Andante]; [Allemanda:] Allegro; Adagio; [Giga:] Vivace. e TWV41:e8 (SUTE 28). 10 d TWV41: d6 (SUTE 29 1996) 8pp., Affettuoso; Allegro; Adagio; Allegro. c TWV41: c5 (SUTE 41 1997) 8pp., Adagio; Allegro; Adagio; [Vivace]. g TWV41:g11 (SUTE 42). A TWV41:A7 (SUTE 54 1997) 8pp., Adagio; Allegro; [Adagio]; Vivace. Preface and critical commentary in each score. M-D.

————. *Suite* g (B. Päuler, W. Hess—Amadeus 767 1992) 12pp., parts, with optional cello. Ouverture; Sans-Souci; Hornpipe; Gavotte; Passepied; Irlandoise. Tasteful continuo realization, completed in appropriate dance styles. Preface in German and English. M-D.

————. *Six Sonatas* (TP).

————. *Six Sonatinas* (Kauffman—Br&H).

————. *Sechs Sonatinen* (Schweickert, Lenzewski—Schott 2783) 24pp., parts, including bass. I G, II B♭, III D, IV A, V E, VI F.

————. *Sechs Sonatinen* (W. Maertens, W. H. Bernstein—CFP 9096 1967).

————. *Sonata* F (H. Ruf—Schott 5477 1965). This *Sonata* is Solo No.1 from the *Essercizii Musici.*

————. *Sonata* A (H. Ruf—Schott 5478 1965). This *Sonata* is Solo No.7 from the *Essercizii Musici.*

————. *Sonata* IV C (G. Frotscher—CFP 5644 1951).

———. *Sonata* IV C (Mitteldeutscher). Cello part optional.

———. *Sonata* C, from *Getreuer Musikmeister* (CFP 4550). Cello part optional.

———. *Sonata* c (Hinnenthal—Br&H 4176 1938).

———. *Sonata* I D (Mitteldeutscher). Cello part optional.

———. *Sonata* d (F. Brüggen—B&VP 557) 11pp. Andante; Allegro assai; Largo; Allegro. M-D.

———. *Sonata* F (F. Brüggen—B&VP 560).

———. *Sonata* II G (Mitteldeutscher). Cello part optional.

———. *Sonata* G (Schott).

———. *Sonata* III g (Mitteldeutscher). Cello part optional.

———. *Tafelmusik* II: Solo A-dur für Violine und Basso continuo (J. P. Hinnenthal— Br 3542 1966). Separate edition for practical use from *Georg Philipp Telemann, Musikalische Werke,* Vol.XIII (Gesellschaft für Musikforschung).

———. *Six Partitas* B♭, G, c, g, e, E♭ (W. Woehl—HM 47). For flute (violin or oboe) and continuo.

———. *Sonatas and Pieces* (D. Degen—HM 7). From *Der getreue Musikmeister.* For flute (violin or oboe) and continuo. Sonata a, Sonata g, L'hiver, Air Trompette, Niaise, Napolitana. M-D.

———. *Six Concerti* (Br 2961). See detailed entry under duos for piano and flute.

Frances Terry. *Sonata* Op.15 f♯/F♯ (SPAM 1931) 31pp., parts. Allegro moderato ma con passione; Scherzo non troppo presto; Largo; Allegro non troppo. Mildly 20th-century with strong expressive qualities and rich harmonies. D.

Virgil Thomson. *Sonata* I 1930 (Arrow 1941) 17pp., parts. 18 min. Allegro: diatonic, clear textures, free counterpoint, meticulous craft. Andante nobile: flowing lyric lines, parallel harmonies. Tempo di Valzer: Poulencian charm. Andante–Doppio movimento: linear introduction, arpeggi and chordal figuration, subtle charm; only strong chordal and tremolo conclusion seems out of character. Neo-Romantic. M-D.

Rudolf Tobias. *Durch die Nacht* ca.1914 (Eres 2728 2000, ISMN M-2024-2728-6) 7pp., parts. The only work by the Estonian composer for piano and violin. Night themes can be heard in many of his compositions, and these are expounded on here in a mysterious manner with repeated notes, tremolos, trills, sustained chords, and octaves in late-19th-century tonality. M-D.

Roy Travis. *Duo Concertante* 1967 (University of California Press 1970) 53pp., parts. Gakpa; Adagio; Allegro marcato; Adagio espressivo e rubato; Asafo. The rhythms of the first and last movements have been adapted from 2 Ewe dances (contained on pp.52–53). Complex, Expressionist, chromatic. Great sense of freedom must permeate fourth movement. Full resources of piano exploited. D.

Karl Ottomar Treibmann. *Sonata* 1967, rev. 1971 (DVFM 8114) 39pp., parts. Allegro; Adagio; Vivace. Octotonic treatment, flexible meters, toccata-like figuration spread between alternating hands, pointillistic, figures repeated ad lib, glissandi, mixture of avant-garde and traditional notation. Piano part uses clusters. Large span required. D.

George Tsontakis. *Three Sighs, Three Variations* 1981 (Merion 1993) 15pp., parts. 11 min. Six short distinctive pieces using sparse textures, constantly changing rhythmic patterns, pauses, and intervals greater than an octave for sonorous effect. D.

Joaquín Turina. *Sonata* I Op.51 d (Rouart-Lerolle 1930) 20pp., parts. 12 min. Lento; Aria–Lento; Rondeau–Allegretto. Tempo changes in outer movements add contrast. Colorful writing frequently employing Impressionist techniques. M-D.

————. *Sonata* II Op.82 "Sonata Espagnola" (Rouart-Lerolle 1934 24pp.; J. L. Turina—Schott VLB85 1993 54pp.), parts. Freely in C. Mainly Hispanic atmosphere with an abundance of charming themes. Violin sings in the opening movement with the piano providing harmonic and rhythmic contribution. Plucked sounds and a hushed ending to the variations movement provide some of the most colorful writing in the piece. The middle movement alternates scherzando with slower sections. Idiomatic writing. A sense of frustration at never arriving "anywhere." D.

Charles Turner. *Serenade for Icarus* (GS 1961) 16pp., parts. 10½ min. Freely tonal, varied sections, tempos, and moods, somewhat Impressionist, effective. M-D.

Galina Ustwolskaja. *Sonate* 1952 (Sikorski 1991 2001) 31pp., parts. In one continuous movement. Minimalist in nature with a 5-note motive as the germ idea. Little variety in a setting using quarter notes as the shortest duration; abundance of accidentals; very wide span required; imitation in a methodical pace. Conceptually conceived, but not for every audience. M-D.

Fartein Valen. *Sonata* Op.3 (Norsk 1916). Regerian style; chromatic with interlaced themes that produce a dissonant polyphony. Freely tonal. D.

Ralph Vaughan Williams. *Sonata* a 1954 (OUP 1968) 40pp., parts. 25 min. A substantial work that uses thick and heavy piano writing. Although a late work in the composer's career, it still has a fresh viewpoint. Fantasia: bi-thematic; unwinds its counterpoint dramatically. Scherzo: $\frac{4}{4}$ mixed with irregular accents. Variations: theme wanders into some interesting surroundings in the 6 variations. M-D.

————. *Romance and Pastorale* (Curwen/Faber 1994) 12pp., parts. Two pieces published together. *Romance* f♯/A 6 min. *Pastorale* e 3 min. Typical lyric quality and orchestral approach by the composer to these songlike, mid-career works.

Francesco Maria Veracini. *Twelve Sonatas* Op.1 (W. Kolneder—CFP 4937a–d 1958) 4 vols. No.1 g, No.2 a, No.3 b, No.4 c, No.5 d, No.6 e, No.7 A, No.8 B♭, No.9 C, No.10 D, No.11 E, No.12 F.

Available separately: No.1 (Jacobsen, Klengel—CFP 1060). No.2 (Salmon—Ric 1131), transposed to g. No.3, Largo and Rondo (Bonelli—Zanibon 2906). No.5, Giga all'antico (Elman—Schott). No.7 (Wotquenne, Cornelis—Schott 2788). *Three Sonatas* Op.1/1, 4, 8 (Albert Lazan—AMP), superb music but poorly edited.

——. *Sonate accademiche* Op.2 (W. Kolneder—CFP 9011-a-m 1961–71). Each *Sonata accademica*, Nos.1–12, appears in its own volume in this edition. Originally published in 1744.

Available separately: No.1 D (Br 316). Cello part optional. No.2 B (Br 317). Cello part optional. No.3 C (Br 318). Cello part optional. No.8 e (W. Kolneder—CFP). *Sonata* No.8, a Sonata-Concerto hybrid, serves as a good example of the set. All 3 movements have passages where the keyboard player is required to play only the written bass line. The absence of chords gives the impression of a solo-tutti effect. Continuo realization is in good taste. No.12 d (CFP 9011M). Cello part optional. Int. to M-D.

——. *Sonata* Op.3 a (Jensen—Augener 7416).

——. *Twelve Sonatas after Arcangelo Corelli* Op.5 (W. Kolneder—Schott 1961). 4 vols. (Nos.5157, 5158, 5170, 5171). These pieces are a reworking of the 12 Sonatas of Corelli's epochal Op.5 and will provide much interest for players already familiar with the Corelli Sonatas. They bear the same relationship to the original Sonatas as J. S. Bach's transcriptions do to the works of Vivaldi.

——. *Sonata* a (Salmon—Ric R726).

——. *Sonata* d (Moffat, Winn—CF B2726).

——. *Sonata* VI d (Respighi—Ric ER278).

——. *Sonata* d (Salmon—Ric R724).

——. *Sonata* e (David—IMC).

——. *Sonata* e (Salmon—Ric R727).

——. *Sonata* e (Carisch).

——. *Concert Sonata* e (CFP 4345).

——. *Sonata* g (Salmon—Ric R725).

——. *Sonata* VIII (Respighi—Ric ER279).

——. *Sonata* b (Jahnke—PWM with cadenza by R. Padlewski).

——. *Sonata* d (Br 349).

——. *Sonata* F (Br 347).

——. *Sonata* G (Br 348).

——. *Largo* f♯ (M. Katims—IMC 1945). For viola (or violin) and piano. See detailed entry under duos for piano and viola.

There is much fine music in these works.

Sándor Veress. *Sonatina* 1932 (SZ). Neoclassic, contrapuntal and dissonant, melodically attractive. M-D.

——. *Sonata* II 1939 (SZ 1943) 15 min. Nationalistic flavor. Written while Veress was assistant to Bartók in the folk music department at the Academy of Sciences, Budapest. D.

Giovanni Battista Viotti. *Six Sonates a violon seul et basse, 2ᵉ Livre.* Paris: Nader-mann, ca.1800. This edition is in the Music Division of the New York Public Library. This same collection also contains Viotti's *Six Sonates pour violon et basse... Oeuvre 4, Iᵉʳ Livre de Sonates.* Paris: Boyer, 17__?

———. *Ařtifici Musicali* Op.XIII 1689 (L. Rood, G. P. Smith—Smith College Music Archives, XII). Contains "Canons of various kinds, double counter-points, curious inventions, capricii and sonatas." There are 2 *Sonatas* at the end of this collection. The first is in 5 movements, slow, fast, slow, fast, slow, the sec-ond in 4, slow, fast, slow, fast. The second *Sonata* is thematically related. Excel-lent material for the less-experienced duo but also would work well in the re-cital program, placed in the proper context. M-D.

Heitor Villa-Lobos. *Sonata-Fantaisie* I "Désespérance" 1912 (ESC) 12pp., parts. 10 min. Four movements. Chromatic chordal figuration, 3 with 4. All move-ments lead into others; freely tonal. M-D.

———. *Sonata-Fantaisie* II 1914 (ESC 1953) 44pp., parts. 22 min. Allegro non troppo; Largo; Rondo Allegro Final. Bravura writing, colorful, chromatic, tremolos, octotonic, requires finesse and endurance. D.

———. *Sonata* III (ESC 1920) 40pp., parts. 22 min. Adagio non troppo; Allegro vivace scherzando; Molto animato e final. Final is 2 pages long and serves as coda. Pianistic figurations spread over keyboard; large span required. D.

———. *Sonata* IV (ESC 1923) 20 min. Four movements.

Tommaso Antonio Vitali. Son of Giovanni Battista Vitali. *Concerto di Sonate* Op.4 (D. Silbert, G. P. Smith, L. Rood—Smith College Music Archives, XII). Cello part optional. Twelve pieces in the set; the last is an ostinato work on the "folia" theme. Nos.8 C, 9 G, and 11 b are especially attractive and would be fine choices for the student duo.

———. *Sonate* Op.4/2 (J. P. Hinnenthal—Br 1959) HM 38. A delightful work with contrasting movements and some surprising harmonic procedure. Int. (except for the improvised ornamentation).

———. *Ciacona* g (F. David—Br&H) 15pp., parts. For violin or viola. See de-tailed entry under duos for piano and viola.

Antonio Vivaldi. *Sonatas* (Malipiero, unless otherwise indicated below—Ric). 41 *Sonatas* for violin and basso continuo, published separately. The F. number re-fers to the classification system devised by Antonio Fanna and used by the Instituto Italiano Antonio Vivaldi, under whose sponsorship the complete works of Vivaldi have been brought out. *Sonata* F.XIII/5 g (PR1006; Br&H). *Sonata* F.XIII/6 D (PR1014). *Sonata* F.XIII/7 d (PR1015; P. Everett, M. Tal-bot PR1253). *Sonata* F.XIII/8 C (PR1016; P. Everett, M. Talbot PR1250). *So-nata* F.XIII/9 d (PR1017). *Sonata* F.XIII/10 c (PR1018). *Sonata* F.XIII/11 C (PR1019). *Sonata* F.XIII/12 A (PR1020). *Sonata* F.XIII/13 G (PR1021). *So-nata* F.XIII/14 C (PR1022; PR1251). *Sonata* F.XIII/15 g (PR1023). *Sonata*

F.XIII/16 B♭ (PR1024). *Sonata* F.XIII/29 g (PR1069). *Sonata* F.XIII/30 A (PR1070). *Sonata* F.XIII/31 d (PR1071). *Sonata* F.XIII/32 F (PR1072). *Sonata* F.XIII/33 b (PR1073). *Sonata* F.XIII/34 C (PR1074). *Sonata* F.XIII/35 c (PR1075). *Sonata* F.XIII/36 G (PR1076). *Sonata* F.XIII/37 e (PR1077). *Sonata* F.XIII/38 f (PR1078). *Sonata* F.XIII/39 D (Ric). *Sonata* F.XIII/40 a (PR1080). *Sonata* F.XIII/41 F (Ric PR1105). *Sonata* F.XIII/42 A (Ric PR1106). *Sonata* F.XIII/43 B♭ (Ric PR1107). *Sonata* F.XIII/44 b (Ric PR1108). *Sonata* F.XIII/47 F (PR1166). *Sonata* F.XIII/49 G (PR1204). *Sonata* F.XIII/52 g (P. Everett, M. Talbot PR1243). *Sonata* F.XIII/53 D (P. Everett, M. Talbot PR1241). *Sonata* F.XIII/54 B♭ (P. Everett, M. Talbot PR1245). *Sonata* F.XIII/55 A (P. Everett, M. Talbot PR1244). *Sonata* F.XIII/56 G (P. Everett, M. Talbot PR1254). *Sonata* F.XIII/57 e (P. Everett, M. Talbot PR1252). *Sonata* F.XIII/58 b (P. Everett, M. Talbot PR1246). *Sonata* F.XIII/59 B♭ (P. Everett, M. Talbot PR1242). *Sonata* F.XIII/60 C (P. Everett, M. Talbot PR1240). *Sonata* F.XIII/61 C (PR1306). *Sonata* F.XIII/62 G (PR1350).

———. *12 Sonatas* Op.2 1709 (W. Hillemann—Schott 1953) 2 vols. (4212, 4213). (S. A. Luciani—Instituto di Alta Cultura). This edition is a miniature score with the figured-bass line unrealized. These works are fine and deserve playing even though they are closely related to Corelli's works. A preview of later things to come.

Available separately: No.1 g (Moffat—Simrock). No.2 A (Pierre—Ouvrières; Jensen—Augener 7423). No.3 d (IMC). No.7 c (Mompellio—Zanibon 3751).

———. *12 Sonatas* (O. Nagy—EMB) 2 vols. (40pp., 39pp.).

———. *4 Sonatas* Op.5 1716 (W. Upmeyer—Nag 162 1954). No.1 F, No.2 A, No.3 B♭, No.4 b. There is a good deal of rhythmic monotony in these *Sonatas;* No.4 is the finest of the group. This set also contains 2 Trio Sonatas. M-D.

———. *4 Sonatas for Maestro Pisendel* 1716–17 (H. Grüss, W. H. Bernstein—DVFM 8101 1965). These works are some of Vivaldi's best efforts.

Giovanni Buonaventura Viviani. *Capricci Armonici* ca.1678 (I. Kertész—EMB 14-252 2000) 52pp., parts, with optional cello. Urtext. This volume includes 8 works from the complete collection: *Symphonia prima* F; *Symphonia seconda* e; *Toccata prima* d; *Toccata seconda* a; *Sonata prima* g; *Sonata seconda* C; *Sonata da camera prima* a; *Sonata da camera seconda* g. "The first six three- or four-part compositions are, in spite of their designations (symphonia, toccata, sonata), church sonatas (sonate da chiesa)" (from Preface). These works show a variety of internal forms, most with a fugue or highly imitative passage. *Sonata prima* has an Aria with 5 variations. Preface in English, German, French, and Hungarian. M-D to D.

Václav Vodička. *Sei (6) Sonate* (C. Schoenbaum—Artia 1962) MAB 30. This set, Op.1, was published in Paris in 1739 and in London in 1745. The pieces have no great musical depths but are fresh and energetic throughout. No.1 B♭, No.2 C, No.3 d, No.4 G, No.5 A, No.6 F. No.6 is probably the best in the set. The opening Siciliana is followed by a virtuoso Allegro. A concluding Menuetto with variations gives very full chords to the keyboard part, adding a massive effect to the end of the set. Int. to M-D.

Jan Hugo Voříšek. *Sonata* Op.5 G (J. Štědroň, B. Štědroň—Artia 1956) MAB 30. 49pp., parts. Introduzione–Allegro moderato: poetic beginning; opening and closing sections of the movement are emphasized; the Allegro moderato (SA) consists of the main subject, which is progressively repeated with rising dramatic intensity. Scherzo: ranks among the most magnificent of Voříšek's writings; written in a scintillating, buoyant, and brilliant piano style; large ABA form in which B has an independent Trio; short coda. Andante sostenuto: violin pours out an ardent song supported by a basso ostinato in the piano; profoundly emotional writing; leads directly to Finale: SA; exciting; briskly flowing triplets alternate with lyrical song idea; short coda. A marvelous Romantic-type Sonata on a par with the Romantic Sonatas of the greatest masters. Has much audience appeal. D.

Bernard Wagenaar. *Sonata* D (SPAM 1928) 53pp., parts. Andante moderato; Vivace; Romanza; Finale: Allegro molto. Large-scale early-20th-century work showing Brahmsian influence with thick writing and sweeping figurations. Large span required. D.

George Walker. *Sonata in One Movement* 1958 (AMP 1097). 20pp., parts. 10 min. Lento–Allegro–Moderato–Meno mosso–Andante (senza mesura)–Molto Adagio. Key signatures of 2 flats and 3 sharps are encountered. Centers around Phrygian mode on D. A short introduction is followed by a fugue, a scherzo-like meno mosso (g♯), a recitative, and the final Molto Adagio reworks the opening introductory material. Pianistic. M-D.

Johann Jakob Walther. *Scherzi da Violino solo con il Basso Continuo* 1676 (Nag 1953). Unaltered reprint of *Das Erbe deutscher Musik,* Vol.17 (1941).
——. *Sonate* (E. Bethan—Nag 89 1931). This is *Sonata* No.4 of the *Scherzi* set. 9pp., parts.
——. *Sonate mit Suite* für Violine und Generalbass, Hortulus Chelicus 1688 No.2 (M. Seiffert—K&S 1930) No.28 Organum, Dritte Reihe.

William Walton. *Sonata* (OUP 1950) 42pp., parts. 26 min. Violin part edited by Yehudi Menuhin, for whom the piece was written. In 2 movements that are mainly lyric and with enough formal structure to produce clear designs. Allegro tranquillo: freely tonal and biting harmonies with rhythmic quirks add much interest. Variazioni: 7 variations with enough thematic variety so that square sectionalism is nicely avoided; the theme presents 2 statements of a 12-note series, which takes on more importance as the movement progresses but is never treated strictly. D.
See H. Murrill, "Walton's Violin Sonata," M&L 31/3 (July 1950): 208–15.

Robert Ward. *Sonata* I 1950 (PIC) 20pp., parts. Andante amabile: opens in a slow tempo with a sensitive lyric melody; fast part of this movement has much rhythmic vitality, changes in meter, quiet and relaxed closing. Allegro barbaro: much rhythmic activity, a cheerful second subject and an interesting fughetta add color. Demanding writing for both instruments, especially some of the complex rhythms. Requires a large span. D.

———. *Sonata* II (Vireo 1992) 32pp., parts. Lento–Doppio Movimento; Larghetto–Moderato; Allegro giocoso. An expressive work using cyclic principles. Preference for thin textures with occasional meter changes and multisectional movements. M-D to D.

———. *Appalachian Ditties and Dances* (ECS 7.0378 1991) 22pp., parts. 11½ min. Womenfolk, Just Chattin': "easy-going, relaxed" with imitative treatment contrasted by chordal Neoclassicism ending on 9th chord. A Lorn One, Grievin': "slow and sad" sentimentality, molto espressivo requiring intricate ensemble playing. Cloggin': "fast and energetic," the most demanding of the 3 as it imitates the popular dance style. These pieces can be played separately as well as a group. M-D to D.

Ben Weber. *Sonata* I Op.5 1939 (CFE) 10pp., parts. 8 min. One movement of bold gestures, bouncy rhythms, varied tempos, exhilarating, atonal, witty. Requires large span. D.

———. *Sonata* II Op.16 1940-2, rev.1943 (CFE) 19pp., parts. 8 min. Poco andantino; Allegro moderato. Strong tonal implications in this 12-tone ornate work, coloristic and brilliantly effective, well constructed. D.

———. *Sonata da Camera* Op.30 (Bo&H 1954) 20pp., parts. 9 min. Lento, con gran eleganza; Moderato; Allegro con spirito. Atonal melodic lines that produce mildly dissonant counterpoint. Light textures with successive movements that are noble, declamatory, graceful, meditative, and animated. Piano part is brilliant and difficult, but effective. D.

Carl Maria von Weber. *Six Sonatas* Op.10B 1810 (E. Zimmermann, H.-M. Theopold, K. Röhrig—Henle 1971 48pp., parts; David—CFP). Written for amateurs, with each *Sonata* supposedly more difficult, but the idea is scarcely evident. In the Henle edition editorial marks are printed in brackets, and some performance suggestions are included in the Preface. The piano part is much more interesting. *Sonata* I F (8 min.); *Sonata* 2 G "Carattere Espagnuolo" (8 min.); *Sonata* 3 d "Air russe" (4½ min.); *Sonata* 4 Eb, Variations. "Thema aus 'Silvana'"; *Sonata* 5 A; *Sonata* 6 C (8½ min.). M-D.
Available separately: Larghetto (Romance) from *Sonata* I (Kreisler—Schott).
See VKDR, II: pp.65–66.

Anton Webern. *Vier Stücke* Op.7 (UE 1922) 5½ min. 1. Sehr langsam; 2. Rasch; 3. Sehr langsam; 4. Bewegt. In his catalog of Webern's works, Friedrich Wildgans says of Op.7: "These highly concentrated pieces . . . already demonstrate the composer's conscious attempts to express every musical thought in the briefest possible form. They are, so to speak, the basis, as well as the point of departure, for those works of the middle period—without being built on the concept of a 12-note structure—that finally break with the old tonal connections; they also finally do away with traditional thematic form. In their place motivic working appears, with extremely brief motifs of only a few notes, sometimes only highly expressive, isolated single notes acting as motifs." *Anton Webern*, trans. Edith T. Roberts and Humphrey Searle (London: Calder and Boyars, 1966), "Critical Catalogue of Works," p.24. Ethereal music that requires the most careful attention to dynamic polarity. D.

Leo Weiner. *Sonata* Op.9 D (Rózsavölgyi 1911) 24 min.
——. *Sonata* II Op.11 f♯ (EMB 1918).

Stanley Weiner. *Sonata* IV Op.33 (Billaudot 1973) 56pp., parts. Andante miste-rioso: freely tonal around d, octotonic, 3 with 2, large rolled chords, arpeggi figuration in left hand under varied melodic line in right hand, passages in 3rds. Allegro feroce: percussive chords in low register, bitonal scales, extreme ranges exploited together, brilliant conclusion with glissando. Un poco lento: octotonic, shifting meters, chromatic, involved syncopated rhythmic passages, parallel chromatic chords. Allegro vivo: $\frac{3}{8}\frac{3}{8}\frac{2}{8}$, octaves, repeated chords in alter-nating hands, toccata-like, virtuoso writing à la Prokofiev. D.
——. *Sonatina* Op.69 (Bo&Bo 1977) 26pp., parts.

Adolph Weiss. *Sonata* 1941 (ACA) 16 min. A dynamic fabric of contrapuntal movement with cumulative activity produced through a structure of constant vitality. D.
——. *Five Fantasies Based on Gagaku* 1956 (CFE) 4–6 min. each.

Richard Wernick. *Violin Sonata* 1997 (TP 2000) 29pp., parts. 21 min. 1. ". . . in the grand manner": bold, assertive qualities in recitative-like opening with dra-matic figurations to follow. 2. ". . . in the manner of a chaconne": slow, me-thodical development of thin-textured spatial writing using contrasting touch and meters. 3. ". . . in the manner of a dance of death": rapid, fire-driven antics with mixed meters and extremes of keyboard. Requires experienced perform-ers. D.

Henri Wieniawski. *Capriccio-Valse* Op.7 (L. Auer—CF 1921) 13pp., parts. A sparkling waltz, packed with capricious whims sure to please any audience. M-D.
——. *Scherzo-Tarentelle* Op.16 (L. Luchtenberg—GS 1900; T. Spiering—CF; K 04401) 12pp., parts. A titillating romp in late-19th-century style. M-D.
Wieniawski favors the violin in his famous works as a showcase instrument yet provides effective piano parts.

Healey Willan. *Sonata* I e 1916 (BMI 1955).
——. *Sonata* II E (Bosworth 1928).

Ermanno Wolf-Ferrari. *Sonata* Op.10 a (Rahter 1902) Elite Edition 202. This is the second of 2 *Sonatas* for violin and piano, the other is Op.1. Two movements. Fast, intricate interweaving of both instruments in chromatic lines full of Romantic harmonies. Very difficult for both performers. D.

Stefan Wolpe. *Sonata* 1949 (McGinnis & Marx 1955) 71pp., parts. Un poco allegro; Andante appassionato; Lento; Allegretto deciso. Extreme dissonance, atonal melodic lines, complex rhythms. Special signs are used to indicate phrase units and focal points. Bar lines in piano and violin parts frequently do not coincide. Variation technique at work throughout. D.
——. *Sonata* (CFE). Uses electronic sounds.

Charles Wuorinen. *Duo* 1966–67 (CFP 66376) 39pp., parts. 15 min. Serial, pointillistic, frequently changing meters, proportional rhythmic relationships, harmonics. Stretches the sonic limits of both instruments with some incredible effects. Large gestures and form, extraordinary virtuoso vehicle for both pianist and violinist, strong avant-garde writing. Requires large span. D.
——. *Fantasia* (CFP) 15 min.
——. *Sonata* 1988 (CFP 1988) 57pp., parts. 20 min.

Yehudi Wyner. *Concert Duo* 1955–57 (AMP 1968) 38pp., parts. 19½ min. I. "The first movement is prevailingly dramatic, concerned with rhythmic energy and variation; the essential argument is often carried by the piano whose natural tendency to overbalance the violin is here deliberately indulged. The two instruments tend to carry forth their discourse on highly independent planes, and integrated exchange of material is practiced only at the end of the movement." Chromatic, atonal, serial influence, changing meters and tempos, tremolo, ferocious, optional number of repeated figures, Expressionist. II. "The second movement is prevailingly lyric. Here the two instruments pursue a less independent course than before and often share the same material; the violin, rather than the piano, tends to dominate. The climaxes, which arise with sudden and virulent intensity, may be seen as intrusions upon a foreground of sustained, introspective songfulness." Broad, slow, voicing problems, subtle bop style, discreetly irregular, many character and performance directions, maximum power required of piano, sudden dynamic changes, pointillistic, virtuoso writing for both instruments (from Composer's Notes, *Yehudi Wyner*, Composers Recording Inc. CD 701 1995, p. 6). D.
——. *Three Informal Pieces* 1961, rev.1969 (AMP). 8 min. I. Chromatic, dynamic extremes, pointillistic; parts sometimes play independently of each other. 2. Alternating hands, triplets spread over keyboard, tremolo, varied tempos, enormous climax; rhythmic notation is approximate at one place. 3. Subtle, sempre dolcissimo, highly expressive. "The word 'Informal' in the title was by no means an informal choice . . . I wanted to restore some elements of spontaneous improvisatory invention to the compositional process, to celebrate the power of the 'informal' even while acknowledging the organizing

power of rigor and formality" (from Composer's Note, *Yehudi Wyner: On This Most Voluptuous Night,* New World Records CD 80549-2 2000, p. 6). All 3 pieces fit both instruments uniquely and make a most effective grouping. M-D.

————. *Dances of Atonement* 1976 (AMP). 12 min. Kol Nidre: based upon an unfamiliar Kol Nidre chant from the music of Jews in Morocco. V'hakohanim: "and the priests entered." "Like much of my work, *Dances of Atonement* seeks to transform simple, even commonplace material into abstract, mystical, or otherwise unforeseen states of being" (from Composer's Note, *Yehudi Wyner: On This Most Voluptuous Night,* New World Records CD 80549-2 2000, p.7).

Isang Yun. *Sonata* I 1991 (Bote & Bote 23492 1992) 30pp., parts. 17 min. In one movement with 3 broad sections. Terse writing revealing influence of Darmstadt School in dramatic figurations, each slightly different, with jagged rhythms. Emphases on trills, melismatic patterns, repeated notes as embellishments, to create the heart of the work. Reflects traditional Korean musical qualities for contemplation. Makes use of "Haupttöne," melodic strands constituting "centres of gravity through which the musical form is generated" (NGD). Very D.

Julien-François Zbinden. *Sonata* Op.15 (SZ 5278 1956). Four movements; the first 2 are the most engaging. The opening Preludio shows off both instruments in dialogue, reaches numerous climaxes, then ends calmly. The lively Scherzo uses flexible meters and driving rhythms. A short Romanza precedes a sparkling finale, which features a brilliant display in the piano part. Thematic material from the opening movement returns to conclude the work. D.

Bernd Alois Zimmermann. *Kleine Suite* 1942 (Schott 7564 1988) 27pp., parts. 8 min. Capriccioso; Intermezzo; Rondino. "The individual movements of this work, characteristic of the 'early' Zimmermann, owe their departure to motor impulses. The prevailing theme generates new energy in its course, which is gradually used up as it becomes unspecific. This is a formal procedure which would not be untypical of the middle works of Hindemith. The expressive musical gesture, which still formed a central point in his compositorial efforts, was not, however, to be gained in this way. Zimmermann was henceforth to tread quite different paths" (from Preface). D.

————. *Sonata* 1950 (Schott 4485) 24pp., parts. 15 min. Sonata; Fantasia; Rondo. Freely tonal and dissonant; effective and thoroughly 20th-century writing throughout. D.

Ellen Taaffe Zwilich. *Sonata in Three Movements* 1973–74 (Merion 1978) 18pp., parts. 10½ min. Liberamente–Tempo giusto–Liberamente: recitative opening; constant meter changes; mostly thin texture; imitation. Lento e molto espressivo: extremes of instruments; acute dissonances; *pp* ending. Allegro vivo e con brio: parts juxtaposed, sometimes unrelated; imitation; pyrotechnics; *ff* finish on octave A's. D.

Duos for Piano and Viola

Carl Friedrich Abel. *Six Sonatas* 1759 (HM 39&40) 2 vols. For viola da gamba, continuo, and cello ad lib. Vol.I: (J. Bacher, W. Woehl) *Sonatas* e, D, G. Vol.II: (W. Woehl) *Sonatas* C, A, A. Excellent continuo realizations. M-D.

Samuel Adler. *Sonata* 1984 (TP 1987) 24pp., parts. 14 min. In one continuous movement with 2 broad sections: Gently moving–Very fast. Mild 20th-century stylistic features with frequently changing meters in opening section and cross-rhythms in closing. Wide span imperative. D.

Charles-Valentine Alkan. *Sonate de Concert* Op.47 1857 (H. MacDonald—Br 19122 1975) for cello (or viola) and piano. See detailed entry under duos for piano and cello.

William Ames. *Sonata* (CFE 1953) 51pp., parts. Moderately fast: chromatic, triplet chordal figuration, thick sonorities in middle keyboard range. Slow: extensive introduction in piano with melodic octaves, freely chromatic, span of 9th required. Fast: syncopation, piano introduction, similar chordal treatment as in first movement, fugal treatment; coda uses both instruments in a broad melodic presentation of main ideas. Requires stamina. D.

David Amram. *The Wind and the Rain* 1963 (CFP) 9pp., parts. 7 min. Based on the second movement of the "Shakespearean Concerto for Small Orchestra." A gentle opening featuring open 5ths builds to an intense and chromatic climax before subsiding. An effective and colorful character piece. M-D.

Thomas Jefferson Anderson. *Variations on a Theme by Alban Berg* 1977 (ACA) 8pp. 10 min. Two copies necessary for performance. Theme consists of sustained B's punctuated by a grand pause and tremolo. Ten variations contain cluster chords, glissandos, improvisatory features, harmonics, and dynamics from *ppp* to *fff*. Repeats theme at end. Score is copy of MS. M-D.

Jorges Antunes. *Microformóbiles I* 1971 (SZ) 4pp. Two scores required for performance. This work is formed by four *Microformóbiles*, A, B, C, and D. The violist arranges the 4 choosing 1 of the 24 possibilities listed. After choosing the combination, the performers play continuously without interruption. Diagrammatic notation in part, clusters, aleatoric, pointillistic, avant-garde. D.

Edward Applebaum. *Foci* (JWC 1973) 6pp., parts. 7½ min. Harmonics for both players, some spatial handling in piano part. A tour de force for viola. Serially oriented. D.

Michael J. Appleton. *Sonata* g 1967 (Thames 1973) 8pp., parts. The piano part is for left hand alone. M-D.

Attilio Ariosti. *Sonatas* 1, 2 (S. Renzo—DeSantis 981). From *Six Sonatas for Viola d'Amore* 1724.

————. *Stockholm Sonatas* (G. Weiss—HM 221) 19pp., parts. Continuo realized by Theodor Klein. Part I: *Sonatas* F, a, G. These *Sonatas* were among 15 discovered by the editor in a copy made by the Swedish composer Johann Helmich Roman (1694–1758), probably while Roman was studying with Ariosti in London. Attractive writing in the traditional style of the period, but the phrases are short, and some of the cadence treatment is not too exciting. *Sonatas* F and a are in 4 movements; *Sonata* G is in 3. Idiomatic continuo realization. M-D.
See David D. Boyden, "Ariosti's Lessons for Viola d'Amore," MQ 32 (1946): 545–63. Günther Weiss, "57 Unbekannte Instrumentalstücke (15 Sonaten) von Attilio Ariosti in einer Abschrift von Johan Helmich Roman," *Die Musikforschung* 33 (1970): 127–38.

Malcolm Arnold. *Sonata* Op.17 (Lengnick 1948) 20pp., parts. 13 min. Andante; Allegretto grazioso; Presto feroce. Tempo changes are integral parts of the outside movements. Effective tremolo writing for the piano. Span of 9th required in middle movement. Mildly 20th-century. M-D.

Jan Astriab. *Sonata* 1958 (PWM 1980) 20pp., parts. 12 min. Grave—Allegro moderato—Allegro assai; Lento; Allegro molto. A youthful work with early-20th-century tonal features. M-D.

Jacob Avshalomoff. *Sonatine* (Music Press 1947) 28pp., parts. Allegro appassionato: d; open 5th chords alternate between hands; arpeggio figuration coupled with melody at points; freely tonal. Lento: f♯; slow legato chords in outer sections; more movement in mid-section. Allegro con brio: d; driving rhythmic octaves in right hand over punctuated left-hand moving octaves; meno mosso, grazioso section flows freely before opening rhythmic idea returns. Neoclassically oriented. M-D.

Milton Babbitt. *Composition for Viola and Piano* 1950 (CFP 1972) 26pp., parts. 9½ min. Opening and closing sections use the viola muted and the piano una corda. The basic row series of the work is most easily heard in these sections. Fluid rhythmic treatment throughout this compelling and forceful work. D.

Carl Philipp Emanuel Bach. *Sonata* Wq88 g (B. Paüler, W. Hess—Amadeus 355 1996, 19pp.; Primrose—IMC), parts. Allegro moderato: SA; $\frac{2}{4}$ meter; playful imitation. Larghetto: c; $\frac{9}{8}$; lyrical. Allegro assai: $\frac{3}{4}$; scalar; motivic development. Well-conceived realization. M-D.

Johann Sebastian Bach. *Drei Gambensonaten* S.1027–29 (E.-G. Heinemann, K. Schilde, J. Weber—Henle 684 2000, ISMN M-2018-0684-6) 56pp., parts. S.1027 G: Adagio–Allegro ma non tanto; Andante; Allegro moderato. S.1028 D: Adagio–Allegro; Andante; Allegro. S.1029 g: Vivace: Adagio; Allegro. Arrangements by Bach of "works originally intended for other combinations of instruments" (from Preface). Extensive notes in German, English, and French. M-D.

Wilhelm Friedemann Bach. *Sonata* c (Y. Pessl—OUP 1945) 32pp., parts. 15 min. Adagio e mesto; Allegro non troppo; Allegro scherzando. Realization of the figured bass is set in small print. It follows good 18th-century style in bringing out the melodic possibilities of the keyboard, but it is only a suggestion. A charming and delightful work. M-D.

Henk Badings. *Sonata* 1951 (Donemus) 26pp., parts. Allegro: driving rhythms in viola, full pesante chords in piano, cluster-like sonorities, free dissonant counterpoint, many major 7ths, triplet and quadruplet figuration. Largo: repeated full chords, arpeggi figures. Vivace: many chords chromatically colored, long melodic lines broadly contoured, large span required. Milhaud and Hindemith influence noted. D.

Granville Bantock. *Sonata* F 1919 (JWC). Allegro: strong, stimulating writing; agitated syncopation. Slow movement: $\frac{5}{4}$, nocturne-like, emotional and melancholy, forceful climax before serene and wistful ending. Vivace: lilting like a Scottish jig, careful working out of ideas and development, 2 episodes, long coda constructed on opening theme. M-D.

George Barati. *Cantabile e Ritmico* 1947 (PIC 1954). Cantabile: broad lines with interesting contour and harmonic experiments; requires large span. Ritmico: more contrived but effective in its own way. M-D.

David Barlow. *Siciliano* 1958 (Nov) 6pp., parts. Freely tonal, flowing, mildly 20th-century, chromatic figuration. M-D.

Marion Bauer. *Sonata* Op.22 (SPAM 1951) 32pp., parts. Allegretto (rubato); Andante expressivo; Allegro. For viola or clarinet. Allegretto (rubato); Andante espressivo; Allegro. Some mixed rhythms in mildly 20th-century style. Large span required. M-D.

Arnold Bax. *Sonata* 1921–22 (Chappell). Heroic opening movement. "Satanic" scherzo with a cataclysmic climax is followed by a wistful closing section. Finale ends with opening theme from the first movement, although the work is not cyclic in form. M-D to D.

Irwin Bazelon. *Duo* 1970 (Novello 1981) 28pp., parts. 14 min. In one continuous movement of ternary design with broad range of thematic material. Asymmetric meters and rhythms requiring careful coordination of diverse parts. D.

Mrs. H. H. A. Beach. *Sonata* Op.34 (P. Hannay—Henmar 1984) 61pp., parts. 30 min. Transcribed from the original for piano and violin by Roger Hannay. Score is copy of excellent MS. See detailed entry under duos for piano and violin.

Gustavo Becerra-Schmidt. *Sonata* (IU) 41pp., parts. Allegro giusto; Andante; Allegro con brio. Movements complement one another. Mildly 20th-century. Rhythmic treatment in final movement is especially well handled. Large span required. M-D.

Conrad Beck. *Sonatine* 1976–77 (Schott 1981) 16pp., parts. 12 min. Allegro moderato: $^6_8$; linear; preference for thin textures. Adagio: lyrical; few expressive indications; lengthy piano solo. Vivace: straightforward rhythmic qualities; biting chords; octaves; dramatic ending. M-D.

Jack Beeson. *Sonata* 1953 (TP 1973) 28pp., parts. Cantando: large span required, changing meters; longer lines in piano part; freely tonal; viola has to play some pitches a quarter-tone sharp or flat; grace notes used to facilitate large intervals; large span required. Presto giocoso: light arpeggi figures, sprightly and bouncy, "clattering" at one spot near end. Andante moderato: chorale-like; more intense and involved un poco più largamente section; chorale-like opening returns to close movement in a Sereno and warmly rich mood. Written within the mainstream 20th-century tradition with formal and structural problems beautifully solved. M-D.

Arthur Benjamin. *Le Tombeau de Ravel* (Bo&H). A Suite of "Valse-Caprices."
——. *Sonata* 1942 (Bo&H) 36pp., parts. Elegy; Waltz; Toccata. Brilliant, entertaining, slight material. Idiomatic writing for the piano. M-D.

Erik Bergman. *Now* Op.126 ca.1995 (Fazer 1996, ISMN M-042-0851-0) 24pp., parts. 13 min. Four untitled movements at slow metronomic markings. Meant to be performed as a whole. "For man, 'now' is the very heart of existence lying between the events of the past and the dawning of a new day. The title of my work *Now* was chosen in order to describe the creative process itself—ideas vying with one another and colliding. In the midst of a violent outburst one may suddenly come upon an equally surprising moment of calm, a reflection on time's onward flow and the course taken by creation. The work's four movements make use of many similar thematic elements. Various motives appear and reappear like reminiscences or flashbacks. Different shades of illumination and playing techniques bring the content into relief, one contrast enhancing another . . . The viola and piano engage in a dialogue where the partners comment and answer in turn. Each has his or her own integrity, character and personality" (Composer's Note). M-D.

William Bergsma. *Fantastic Variations on a Theme from 'Tristan'* 1961 (Galaxy) 19pp., parts. 12 min. Theme drawn from Wagner's *Tristan und Isolde.* Neoclassic, strong tonal leanings, florid melody, dissonant. M-D.

Lennox Berkeley. *Sonata* d (JWC 1947) 28pp., parts. 17 min. Allegro ma non troppo; Adagio; Allegro. Neoclassic, expansive, lyric. Clear writing. M-D.

Sol Berkowitz. *Introduction and Scherzo (Blues and Dance)* (TP 1974) 24pp., parts. Piano slips back and forth between block chords, rhythmic motives, and imitative passages. Large span up to a 10th required. M-D.

Easley Blackwood. *Sonata* 1953 (EV 1959) 35pp., parts. 13 min. Adagio quasi senza misura ma non troppo rubato: freely chromatic; flexible meters; 6-note chords give cluster impression; lies in low or middle registers until closing, then moves up. Allegro motto: shifting rhythms in a brief introduction that leads to a Theme–Andante moderato e cantabile and 6 contrasting variations. Andante tranquillo: picks up mood and figuration of first movement opening for a short time, then moves to an Allegro molto e meccanico that drives to a brilliant conclusion. Neoclassic and Expressionist tendencies. D.

Arthur Bliss. *Sonata* 1933 (OUP 22.405) 60pp., parts. 28 min. Moderato: tonal, chromatic, arpeggi figuration, tremolo; requires large span. Andante: rich harmonies, buoyant melodies, ostinato-like, individual lines. Furiant: dancelike, brilliant, chordal punctuation, long trills. Coda: returns ideas from previous movements; cadenza for both instruments. Brilliant writing in the tradition of Liszt and Rachmaninoff. D.

Ernest Bloch. *Meditation and Processional* (GS 1954) 7pp., parts. Meditation: d, chromatic, serious, climax near end, *p* closing, long phrases, warm and impassioned with occasional Hebraic touches. Processional: modal, stately, well-pronounced bass line necessary, *p* closing. Colorful and imaginative writing using strong contrapuntal lines. Grateful to play. M-D.

René de Boisdeffre. *Berceuse* Op.34 (K 9803) 5pp., parts. Charming encore piece with flowing counter-melodies in piano. May also be played by violin or cello. M-D.

Mauro Bortolotti. *Combinazioni Libere* 1965 (Ric) 10pp., parts. "Improvvisazione per viola e pianoforte." Harmonics, plucked strings, clusters, pointillistic, mildly avant-garde. M-D.

Will Gay Bottje. *Fantasy Sonata* (CFE).

——. *Sonata* 2 (ACA).

Carlos Botto. *Fantasia* Op.15 1962 (IU) 9pp. Two copies necessary for performance. Opening Andante exploits interval of major 7th; mormoranto e rubato. Followed by an Adagio ma non troppo that works up more excitement with short motives and leads to a cadenza for the viola. Tempo I Adagio follows and moves directly into a highly rhythmic Allegro ma non troppo. Piano gets arpeggi figures before unwinding in a ben ritmato finish. Well written for both instruments. M-D.

York Bowen. *Sonata* I c 1909 (Tertis—Schott; K 4301). Virtuoso treatment of viola. Reflective opening movement, graceful and charming slow movement, strong introduction to finale that contains much dramatic writing. M-D.

Andries de Braal. *Introduzione ed Allegro Capriccio* 1969 (Donemus) 21pp., parts. Introduzione is free, recitative-like with dramatic gestures for both instruments, cadenza passages, tremolo. Leads directly to the Allegro Capriccio: driving rhythmic first part is juxtaposed with a meno allegro and alla cadenza section. Allegro driving rhythmic section returns and these 2 basic contrasts return again before the work seemingly evaporates. Mildly 20th-century. An effective "show piece" for both performers. M-D.

Johannes Brahms. *Sonatas* Op.120/1, 2 (M. Steegmann—Henle; H.-C. Müller—VU; Br&H; Jonas—Simrock; Katims—IMC; Augener; C. Herrmann—CFP; K 4310). These *Sonatas* were first published in 1895 together with an arrangement of the clarinet part for viola. Critical notes are given in the Henle and the VU editions. They also contain very good page turns in the piano part. These works show a fusion of melodic material and development procedures unrivaled in Brahms. D.

Frank Bridge. *Two Pieces* (MMP 1268) 12pp., parts. Includes *Pensiero* and *Allegro Appassionato*. Full chordal writing with much expression in a mild 20th-century tonality. M-D.

——. *Four Pieces* (Faber Music 1992) 18pp., parts. 9½ min. Berceuse; Serenade; Elegie; Cradle Song. Transcription from the original for cello and piano.

Benjamin Britten. *Lachrymae* "Reflections on a Song by John Dowland" Op.48 1950 (Bo&H 17817) 16pp., parts. Ten contrasting variations and a coda. Freely tonal. A catalog of Britten's eclectic techniques. The incorporation of another composer's music in his own style is an important characteristic of Britten. The writing uses some plain simple harmonies and falls under the fingers ingeniously. M-D.

Revol S. Bunin. *Sonate* Op.26 d 1955 (CFP 5735; USSR) 47pp., parts. Allegro appassionato; Andantino semplice; Sostenuto–Allegro spirituoso. Octotonic, achieves big sound without extreme effort. Dedicated to Shostakovich. A strongly tonal 20th-century work. D.

Eldin Burton. *Sonata* 1957 (CF 1960) 40pp., parts. 21 min. Moderato; Molto vivace; Lento drammatico; Allegro agitato. A well-crafted work with thoroughly 20th-century techniques and idioms. Piano writing is efficient and fits idiomatically with the viola. M-D.

Alan Bush. *Sonatina* Op.88 (Simrock 3181 1980) 28pp., parts. 16½ min. Introduzione–Allegro moderato; Quasi menuetto; Rondo–Epilogo. An extended use of the Sonatina form, complete with SA and standard forms of the Classical period in a gentle 20th-century context. M-D.

Claudio Carneyro. *Khroma* 1954 (Sociedade Portuguesa de Autores) 9pp., parts. This is the first known piece by a Portuguese composer using 12-tone technique. It is written in an atonal chromatic style in which the sporadic use of a 12-tone series does not fulfill the task of a structural base. ABA' design with A the exposition and expansion of the main theme, B a viola cadenza, and A' a reexposition of the initial theme by contrary motion with a concluding development. M-D.

Elliott Carter. *Pastorale* 1940 (TP) 15pp., parts. 12 min. Allegretto (Tempo I) serves as a unifying factor—tempos gradually increase until they return to Tempo I. Tricky rhythmic problems, quick octave grace notes in left hand. Piano part is very active and has some interesting sonorities. Experiments with texture and tone color. M-D.

———. *Elegy* 1943, rev. 1961 (PIC 1964) 4pp., parts. 5 min. Adagio sostenuto: chromatic; low register preferred; harmonics; exquisite legato required. M-D.

Robert Casadesus. *Sonata* Op.12 (IMC 1989) 30pp., parts. 15 min. Moderato; Vivo; Allegro molto. An early work by the composer firmly rooted in tonal and stylistic features of the past. Vivo functions as a scherzo. No slow movement. M-D.

Alexandre Cellier. *Sonate* G♭ (Senart 1923) 25pp., parts. Lento con molto fantasia; Allegro non troppo; Lamento; Allegretto simplice. Idiom of post-Franck, Dukas. Pianistic; all formal limitations are correct. D.

Friedrich Cerha. *Sonata* 1951 (Dob 03 588 1991) 14pp., parts. 13 min. Adagio espressivo; Allegro molto, leggiero; Largo; Allegro con brio. Much repetition; octaves; full chords; use of extended pedal point in opening movement; absence of bar lines in Largo. Little variety within movements. M-D.

Jacques Chailley. *Sonate* (Leduc 1950) 32pp., parts. 26 min. Semplice: SA; first and second themes are developed concurrently; first theme is in the nature of a folk song. Grave: meditative; somber; 2 themes alternate between the instruments. Scherzo: vigorous; contrasts with the supple songlike trio; somewhat reminiscent of the first idea in the Semplice. Final: various ideas treated in rondo fashion; brilliant conclusion. Freely tonal in a mildly 20th-century style, attractive. D.

Rebecca Clarke. *Sonata* 1919 (JWC 1921; Da Capo 1986), parts. Three imaginative rhapsodical movements, Impressionist. Impetuoso first movement in SA design. Fascinating scherzo of thin textures. A short introduction opens the finale, which has a pentatonic main theme combined with the introductory thematic material. Freely tonal. Instruments maintain equality throughout. May be performed by cello. M-D.
———. *Passacaglia on an Old English Tune* (GS 1943) 7pp. Uses a melody attributed to Thomas Tallis (though not the famous Canon by Tallis). For viola or cello. M-D.

Dinos Constantinides. *Sonata* 1971 (Seesaw). 24 min. For viola and/or cello and piano. Moderato: freely moving lines, flexible rhythms, freely tonal. Adagio: widely spread sonorities, dramatic gestures, sostenuto pedal effectively used. Allegro moderato: thin-textured opening section moves to a complex perpetual motion part that completely involves both performers. Distinctly modern in flavor. D.
———. *Grecian Variations* 1987 (Magni 1987) 43pp. Based upon a Greek folk tune, the work commences with the first variation and contains 8 in all. Employs modal scales and asymmetric rhythms in a wide range of musical settings. One of the few extended sets of variations from the late 20th century for viola and piano. Delightful. M-D.

Arnold Cooke. *Sonata* F 1937 (OUP 1040). Emotional reserve. Shows influence of Hindemith (Cooke's teacher).

Paul Cooper. *Variants II* (JWC 1975) 8pp., parts. 7 min. One bolt is required for piano preparation, and a few strings must be damped; strumming on strings. Six sections freely repeated, with some given number of seconds to repeat: Dramatic; Serene; Joyous; Calm; Resolute; Tranquil. Thoroughly 20th-century writing, somewhat avant-garde, but all put to the best musical use. Sensitive sonorities, clear indications. M-D.

Roque Cordero. *Tres Mensajes Breves* 1966 (LAMC). Allegro comodo: rhythmic orientation. Lento: viola has introduction; piano begins *pp*, works to a *ff* climax and recedes; Expressionist sonorities. Molto allegro: dramatic gestures over keyboard. Effective set. M-D.

Michel Corrette. *Sonata* ca.1780 (Schott VAB38 1972) 11pp., parts. Viola part has most bowings and some fingerings marked. Realized figured bass has an additional part for cello, which is to be used when a harpsichord is used, not with piano. M-D.

Henry Cowell. *Hymn and Fuguing Tune No. 7* (PIC 1953) 14pp., parts. Hymn: Larghetto, thin textures, imitation, diatonic. Fuguing Tune: con moto, corky rhythms, imitation; longer lines developed; left-hand octaves provide a "standing bass." M-D.

Arthur Custer. *Parabolas* 1970 (Gen 1972) 22pp., parts. I. Ah: serial; clusters; free sections synchronized only at bar lines, sustained notes are held for duration indicated, others are played at discretion of performers; tempo and dynamics ad lib; both performers are to sing "Ah" and play where indicated; octotonic. II. Block That Kick: opening similar to "Ah"; both performers sing "Block That Kick" in a dirgelike manner; if there is a page turner, he should rise and conduct this section; free sections; wide dynamic range. Mixture of avant-garde and traditional. Can be a fun piece. D.

Ingolf Dahl. *Divertimento* 1948 (SPAM) 48pp., parts. Sinfonia; Barcarolle; Variations on 'The Mermaid'; Finale and Coda. Combines serious and lighthearted qualities in tonal structure composed before Dahl's years of serial writing. D.

Edison Denisov. *Es ist genug* 1984 (Sikorski 1834 1989) 32pp., parts. Variations on a choral theme by J. S. Bach. One extended movement with variations flowing directly from one to another. Considerable proportional rhythmic relationships. D.

Karl Ditters von Dittersdorf. *Sonata* E♭ (H. Mlynarczyk, L. Lürmann—Hofmeister 7280, 14pp.; J. Vieland—IMC), parts. Allegro moderato; Menuetto I; Adagio; Menuetto II; Tema con [8] variazioni. Hofmeister provides bowings and fingerings with ornaments written out in full and a piano realization following the original bass. Haydn's influence noted in this charming work. M-D.
———. *Sonata* E♭ (Schroeder—Br&H). Cello ad lib.

Felix Draeseke. *Sonata* II WoO26 F 1901–1902 (A. Krueck—Coburg 1996) 32pp., parts. Bewegt; Langsam und gewichtig; Finale: mässig bewegt, leicht. Composed in a grand 19th-century tradition with sweeping figurations, full chords, and intense expression. Draeseke conceived of the *Sonata* for the viola alta, which "distinguished itself from the normal viola by its extended body and somewhat rounded top" (from Foreword). D.

Jean Durbin. *Mélancolic* 1979 (UL) 5pp. Includes a shepherd's theme. Score is photocopy of MS. M-D.
———. *Mélodie* 1971 (UL) 6pp. Très lent et lointain. Score is a photocopy of MS. M-D.
———. *Rapsodie* 1978 (UL) 7pp. Recitative-like opening progresses into Vif; *fff* conclusion. Score is a photocopy of MS. M-D.
Durbin is a little-known Parisian composer whose piano and viola miniatures are written in a Neoclassic vein.

Henry Eccles. *Sonata* g (Klengel—CFP 4326 1930) 7pp., parts. Largo; Courrente; Adagio; Allegro vivace. Late Baroque style with binary forms in all movements except Adagio. M-D.

———. *Sonata* g (Katims—IMC).

Helmut Eder. *Sonatina* Op.34/2 (Dob 1963) 12pp., parts. 5 min. Allegretto leggiero; Adagio molto, quasi recitativo; Allegro con spirito. Neoclassic orientation with Expressionist characteristics; dramatic gestures in finale. M-D.

Christopher Edmunds. *Sonata* D (Nov 1957) 21pp., parts. Andante comodo; Lento espressivo; Allegro moderato. Three pleasantly contrasted movements in a mildly 20th-century, flowing style. M-D.

Georges Enesco. *Concert Piece* 1906 (IMC; K 4311) 16pp., parts. Animation, intensity, and expressiveness are chief features with many changes of character and sections. D.

Manuel Enrique. *Cuatro Piezas* 1962 (IU) 11pp., parts. Serial. Lento: dramatic opening and closing, Expressionist. Con fuoco: impulsive, dynamic extremes, pointillistic. Allegretto: misterioso introduction leads to Allegro, other tempo changes; mainly quiet; all over keyboard. Moderato ritmico: a thorny maze. Requires experienced and fine performers. M-D to D.

Robert Evett. *Sonata* 1958 (CFE) 14 min. Based on intricate and ingenious thematic material, yet it is almost singable. The opening Allegro movement is one of concentrated power and spirit with humorous splashes here and there. The finale consists of an introduction and a minuet derived from the minuet in Mozart's *Don Giovanni,* but by moving harmonic devices and in other subtle ways Evett turns out an intriguing movement. M-D.

Morton Feldman. *The Viola in My Life* 1970 (UE 15402) 3pp., parts. 6 min. "There are four pieces by Morton Feldman with the title 'The Viola in My Life.' They are separate and independent pieces, not single movements. Feldman is not a violist, but a worshipper or admirer of Walter Trampler and Karen Phillips, who are violists—very good ones" (from a letter to Maurice Hinson from John D. Wiser, Vice President, Joseph Boonin, Inc., May 18, 1976). This writer has seen only the first 3 of these scores. The one listed here is metrically notated. The piano part consists of isolated 6- to 8-part chords. Tranquil, simple gestures, agreeable sounds. M-D.

Jacobo Ficher. *Sonata* Op.80 1953 (IU) 34pp., parts. Allegro moderato: C, SA, quixotic opening motive, longer idea for second tonal area. Lento: C, many 7th chords, chromatic. Allegro: rhythmic vitality, propulsive, C conclusion. M-D.

Juraj Filas. *Sonata* Op.1 (Panton 1984) 22pp., parts. 13 min. Moderato–Allegro assai; Adagio. Opens with viola glissando and piano single notes over 3 octaves apart, proceeding toward extended passages in octaves, quartal chords, repeated patterns, and sequencing. Ends contemplatively at *pp*. M-D.

Vivian Fine. *Lieder for Viola and Piano* 1979 (Sisra 1987) 23pp., parts. 17 min. In 6 movements: The Balcony; Moon-Stream; The Song of the Trout; Jewels; In the Garden of the Crucifixion; Transfiguring Night. "The inspiration for *Lieder for Viola and Piano* comes from Hugo Wolf, and, in 'The Song of the Trout', from Schubert. Motifs from these composers are used, but never literally. The intent was to convey the composer's involvement with the lyric and dramatic elements of traditional lieder in her own language" (from score). D.

Ross Lee Finney. *Sonata* a (R. Courte—Henmar 66254 1971) 27pp., parts. 13½ min. Allegro moderato con moto: octotonic, chromatic, free dissonant counterpoint, thin textures. Largo sostenuto: imitation, moving harmonic 3rds, more rhythmic Tranquillo section. Allegretto con spirito: vigorous rhythms contrasted with broad and sustained chords; strong traditional forms throughout. M-D.

———. *Second Sonata* (R. Courte—Henmar 1971) 35pp., parts. 15 min. Andante, teneramente; Permutations; Largo, teneramente; Allegro con moto. Clear textures, freely tonal, natural development of ideas. M-D.

William Flackton. *Sonata* C Op.2/4 (Bergmann—Schott; R. Sabatini—Dob DM62 1960, cello ad lib) 7pp., parts. Four short, contrasting movements: Largo grazioso; Allegro; Siciliano; Minuet I & II. Good simple, clean editing. M-D.

———. *Sonata* D Op.2/5 (Sabatini—Dob). Cello ad lib.

———. *Sonata* G Op.2/6 (Sabatini—Dob, cello ad lib; W. G. Bergmann—Schott 10115 1942). Andante; Allegro; Minuetto prima; Minuetto secondo. M-D.

———. *Sonata* c 1776 (A. Cullen—Lengnick 1955) 8pp., parts. Adagio; Allegro moderato; Siciliana; Minuetto (with one variation). Tasteful continuo realization. M-D.

Flackton's *Sonatas* Op.2 were the first original Sonatas for viola composed in England.

François Francoeur. *Sonata* IV E (Alard, Dessauer—IMC 820) 9pp., parts. Adagio; Courrente; Aria; Sarabande; Giga. In gallant style. Int. to M-D.

Robert Fuchs. *Sonata* Op.86 d 1909 (UMKR No. 5) 23pp., parts. Allegro moderato, ma passionate; Andante grazioso; Allegro vivace. Written in a Brahmsian idiom with expert craftsmanship. M-D.

Norman Fulton. *Sonata da Camera* 1945 (JWC 1952) 24pp., parts. 13½ min. Lento e appassionata; Poco lento, ma sempre ritmico; Poco Allegretto, con amore. Eclectic style, freely tonal, mildly 20th-century, interesting rhythmic treatment. M-D.

Paul Walter Fürst. *Sonatina* Op.13 (Dob 1966) 24pp., parts. Allegro, spielerisch; Scherzando, nicht zu schnell; Langsam, mit grossern Ausdruck; Bewegt, Übermütig. Freely tonal, octotonic, repeated notes in alternating hands, flowing quality, Neoclassic. M-D.
———. *Sonata* Op.33 (Dob).

Hans Gál. *Sonata* Op.101 (Simrock Elite Ed. 3150 1973) 25pp., parts. Adagio; Quasi menuetto, tranquillo; Allegro risoluto e vivace. Tonal, chromatic, Brahms influence noted, 19th-century pianistic idioms in a mildly 20th-century guise. M-D.
———. *Suite* Op.102a (Simrock Elite Ed. 3151 1973) 29pp., parts. Cantabile: large rolled chords support melody in viola; requires large span. Furioso: chordal, syncopated, octaves, contrasted tranquillo section, octotonic. Con grazia: chromatic, counterpoint between the 2 instruments. Buria: dancelike, chromatic, expressive inner voices, chromatic octaves, viola cadenza. M-D.

Maurice Gardner. *Micrologus* (Staff Music 1983) 24pp., parts. In 4 movements: Molto marcato; Intermezzo; Tranquillo; Allegro assai. Concentrates on tertian chord structures with the use of the major and minor 3rd, a practice described in Guido's famous treatise of the same name in the 11th century. D.

Fritz Geissler. *Sonatina* (Br&H 5818 1954) 11pp., parts. Kleiner Marsch; Elegie; Lebhaft bewegt. In style of Hindemith. Very expressive Elegie. M-D.
———. *Sonate* (CFP 9177 1971) 32pp., parts. Vivace; Adagio; Scherzando. Explores a cornucopia of early-20th-century techniques, including tones and chordal tremolos. Extensive expressive indications and directions (all in German). Performers searching for explorative uses of the instruments without overbearing emphasis will enjoy this work. D.

Harald Genzmer. *Sonata* D 1940 (R&E) 23pp., parts. 15 min. Fantasie; Thema mit (5) Variationen. Chromatic, large arpeggiated chords, secco and sustained styles contrasted, linear, strong traditional forms, Neoclassic. M-D.
———. *Sonate* II 1955 (Br 3223; Schott 58 1999, ISMN M-001-12643-4) 38pp., parts. Allegro; Adagio; Presto; Tranquillo–Vivace. Has many characteristics of solid Neoclassic style. Thorough musicianship required of both performers. Superb ensemble writing. M-D to D.
———. *Sonatine* (Litolff 1973) 15pp., parts. Short, 3 movements in a dissonant but mainly diatonic style. Effective finale alternates bars of $\frac{3}{4}$ with $\frac{7}{8}$. Int. to M-D.

Ottmar Gerster. *Sonate* (Hofmeister 7178 1956) 20pp., parts. 11½ min. Allegro; Andante (based on a Russian folk song); Finale. Tonal with chromatic coloring, traditional forms, post-Brahms style with fast harmonic rhythm in the finale. Large span required. M-D.

Emmanuel Ghent. *Entelechy* 1962–63 (OUP) 26pp. An early work by the composer in one continuous movement. Explores asymmetrical relationships, proportional rhythms, and alternation of scattering arpeggiated passagework with biting chords. Extremes of instruments are used. For experienced 20th-century performers with thorough mathematical understanding. D.

Miriam Gideon. *Sonata* (CFE 1957) 23pp., parts. Allegretto; Andante teneramente; Allegro furioso. Mixed meters within conventional notation and harmonic practices. M-D.

Tommaso Giordani. *Sonate* B♭ (H. Ruf—Schott 12 1968) 10pp., parts. Allegro; Largo; Rondo: Allegretto. Tasteful realization to complement the viola while suggesting creative motives in addition to Giordani's. M-D.

Aurelio Giorni. *Sonata* d 1917, rev.1924 (SPAM 1925). For cello or viola. See detailed entry under duos for piano and cello.

Alexander Glazunov. *Elegy* Op.44 g 1893 (IMC 1953; K 4299) 7pp., parts. Graceful stylistic features in $\frac{9}{8}$ meter using conventional harmonies and continuous lyricism. M-D.

Mikhail Glinka. *Sonata* d (Musica Rara 1961) 26pp., parts. Allegro moderato; Larghetto ma non troppo. This work was written between 1825 and 1828, but remained unfinished; in the present edition it has been completed by V. Borisovsky, who also edited the viola part. Those sections realized by the editor have been printed in small type. Glinka wrote several chamber works during his visit to Italy in the early 1830s. "As Glinka himself realized, the Viola Sonata is the most successful of his pre-Italian compositions; although intended primarily for domestic music-making, it contains, to use his own expression, 'some quite clever counterpoint.' Free from the Italianate mannerisms which mar some of his larger chamber works, it has a directness and charm which make it an important addition to the viola-piano repertoire" (from the score). Also exists in bassoon transcription; see entry under duos for piano and bassoon. M-D.

Alexander Goehr. *Sur terre, en l'air* Op.64 1997 (Schott 12619 1999, ISMN M-2201-1943-9) 19pp., parts. 10 min. Three movements: Andante; Vivo; " . . . kein Gedanke, nur ruhiger Schlaf" (in memoriam Olivier Messiaen). Linear, thin textures, uncomplicated rhythms, economic. Of special interest is the third piece, a slow, meditative remembrance of Messiaen containing surprising dramatic qualities. M-D.

Johann Gottlieb Graun. *Sonata* I B♭ (H. Wolff—Br&H 1937) 12pp., parts. Cello ad lib. Adagio (suggested cadenza included); Allegretto; Allegro non troppo. Creditable editing. M-D.

———. *Sonata* II F (H. Wolff—Br&H 1937) 21pp., parts. Cello ad lib. Adagio non molto (suggested cadenza included); Allegro; Allegro ma non tanto. M-D. Both *Sonatas* contain some lovely, if traditional, writing.

Giovanni Battista Grazioli. *Sonata* F (Marchet—Augener 5569) 9pp., parts. Allegro moderato; Adagio; Tempo di Minuetto. M-D.

Camargo Guarnieri. *Sonata* 1950 (IU) 30pp., parts. Tranquillo; Scherzomolo; Con intusiasmo. This work has all of Guamieri's characteristics: linear conception, dramatic writing for both instruments, plenty of rhythmic drive, well-developed ideas, a gift for knowing what works well at any given moment. D.

Karl Haidmayer. *Sonate* I 1964 (Br 6113 1971) 20pp., parts. Allegro spianato: mixture of homophonic and imitative writing; thin textures. Andante quasi adagio: recitative-like with extended ascending arpeggiation making 4-octave chords. Presto romîneasca: chains of triads and repeated chords; imitative motifs; octave formations spread over 4 octaves. Strongly tonal with slight Neoclassic flavor. M-D.

August Halm. *Sonate* f (R. Bierwald—Lienau 40470 1998) 25pp., parts. Andantino tranquillo: freely composed with busy 16th-note passagework. Allegro: fugal in nature with a subject in scalar motion. Larghetto: imitative exchange at opening between instruments in $\frac{4}{8}$ with triplets. Rondo Allegro: spirited rondo theme which yields to fragmentation and contrasting sections. The influence of Bach and Bruckner is evident. M-D.

Erich Hamann. *Sonata* Op.33 (Dob 1952) 16pp., parts. Allegro ma non tanto; Thema und [8] Variationen; Allegro molto. Chromatic, mixture of chordal and linear style, minor theme with contrasting variations, octotonic, pedal points, Presto closing. Mildly 20th-century. M-D.

Iain Hamilton. *Sonata* Op.9 1950 (Schott) 18 min. Three movements of aggressive writing, similar to the fierceness and intensity of early Bartók. Complex harmonies, propulsive rhythms, extremes of registers permeated with dissonance. The Alla marcia funèbre introduced in the last 30 bars of the finale has its counterpart in the stark Lento potente heard at the opening of the work. D.

George Frideric Handel. *Sonata* A (David, Hermann—IMC).
———. *Sonata* Op.1/15 A (Forbes, Richardson—OUP 22.007) 13pp., parts. Originally *Sonata* E for violin and figured bass. Adagio; Allegro; Largo; Allegretto. Generally a fine transcription with the exception of a few spots where the piano texture is too thick. M-D.
———. *Sonata* C (F. Längin—Br 1953 HM 112) 13pp., parts. Larghetto; Allegro; Adagio; Allegro. Beautifully contrasted movements. Outer movements are motoric. M-D.
———. *Sonata* e (Courte—H. Elkan).

————. *Sonata* 10 G (Alard, Meyer—IMC).

————. *Sonata* g (Katims—IMC).

Julius Harrison. *Sonata* ca.1945 (Lengnick 3474) 41pp., parts. 23 min. Allegro energico; Andante e cantabile sempre; Scherzo–Finale. Broadly planned, neo-Romantic style, traditional pianistic techniques and idioms. Requires large span. D.

Tibor Harsanyi. *Sonata* 1953–54 (Heugel 1958) 26pp., parts. 16 min. Harsanyi's last completed work. Allegro cantabile: SA, $\frac{5}{8}$, freely tonal around e–E, many sequences, lovely tranquillo coda. Adagio: ABA, $\frac{3}{4}$, chromatic, angular theme, long lines in piano part, almost atonal. Allegro giocoso con vivo: SA, vigorous rhythms, octotonic, highly chromatic, attractive but difficult and fluent writing with marked individuality, large span required. D.

Walter Hartley. *Sonata* 1953 (Interlochen Press). 14 min. Four movements, inspired by Bartók's Violin Sonatas.

Bernhard Heiden. *Sonata* 1959 (AMP 1968) 44pp., parts. Allegro moderato: flowing, linear conception. Andante sostenuto: unfolds naturally to an Adagio *ppp* closing. Vivace, ma non troppo: flexible meters, clear lines; a mistake is noted 6 bars after C in left hand of piano part—C♭ should be C♯. Lento: attention-getting, leads into Allegro molto: opening 2-note motif ingeniously develops throughout rest of movement; Lento idea returns (now extended) before an Allegro vivace brings this jaunty movement to a climactic conclusion. M-D.

Swan Hennessy. *Sonata Celtique* Op.62 E♭ (ESC 1924) 15pp., parts. More a fantasy than a Sonata. Allegro con brio: SA design, with popular tune "St. Patrick's Day in the Morning" used with counterpoint in the development section. Andante sostenuto: a simple and charming folk tune, treated chordally. Allegro: 2 contrasting themes are the basis for the finale, one (Celtic) syncopated in $\frac{2}{4}$, the other in $\frac{6}{8}$. Tuneful writing with a strong Irish idiom. M-D.

Hans Werner Henze. *Sonata* 1979 (Schott 6859 1980) 23pp., parts. 20 min. In one movement with multiple sections. Uses traditional and nontraditional notation, the latter more toward the end in a free style. Expanded score with 3–4 staves for piano. Some asymmetric rhythm patterns. D.

Heinrich Freiherr von Herzogenberg. *Legends* Op.62 1890 (Musica Rara 1975 27pp., parts, Preface in English by Harold Truscott; UWKR 34 1974 29pp., parts, Preface in German and English by W. Sawodny). Andantino: a slow minuet. Moderato: a dark ballade with a radiant tune. Andante: a set of variations on a simple folklike tune of the composer's invention. Brahms influence. These 3 well-contrasted pieces exhibit considerable formal and technical skill and are similar to Schumann's pieces as examples of the small form. M-D.

Kurt Hessenberg. *Sonate* Op.94 (Schott VAB45 1976) 35pp., parts. Allegro: SA; fluid, linear writing with a soaring first theme contrasted by a rhythmic, scalar second. Presto: $\frac{3}{8}$; opens and closes *pp;* hemiola effects. Adagio molto–Allegro: richly expressive, contrasting calmness with dramatic action; imitative; closes with return to Adagio molto and *ppp* finish. A rewarding work, well conceived and waiting to be rediscovered by performers. D.

Paul Hindemith. *Sonata* Op.11/4 F (Schott 1919) 26pp., parts. 18 min. Fantasie (Ruhig); Theme mit Variationen; Finale (mit Variationen). Opening movement quiet; shows some French influence in the whole-tone usage but is mainly a large Brahmsian melodic idea contrasted with more delicate moments. In spite of the second and third movements both being sets of variations, the variation techniques are different enough to provide contrast and still hold the work together. Forceful and vital writing by Hindemith for his principal instrument in a most Romantic vein. D.

———. *Sonata* Op.25/4 1922 (Schott 6740 1977) 27pp., parts. Sehr lebhaft. Markiert und Kraftvoll; Sehr langsome Viertel; Finale: Lebhafte Viertel. The final Sonata in a series of 4 for middle- to lower-pitched strings. Contains all the characteristics typical of the composer's distinctive individualist style. The slow movement, "using expressionistic techniques was more 'spatial' than emotional, resulting in a 'constructed subjectivism'" (David Neumeyer, *The Music of Hindemith* [New Haven, Conn.: Yale University Press, 1986], p. 13). D.

———. *Sonata* C 1939 (Schott) 48pp., parts. 23 min. Breit, mit Kraft–Ruhig–Lebhaft: aggressive and angular. Sehr lebhaft: shows some ragtime influence, ferocious climax. Phantasie: mysterious dialogue between the instruments. Finale (Mit 2 Variationen): opens in quixotic spirit and grows to weighty proportions with fugal overtones. Formidable and inexhaustible pianism required. D.

Sydney Hodkinson. *Introït, Elégie et Danse Macabre* 1981 (Merion 1983) 45pp., parts. 18 min. In one continuous movement with 3 parts corresponding to the title. "The opening—through measure 8—should sound like a continuation of the tuning procedure: leisurely, ad libitum. The viola may remain turned towards the piano: discreetly, privately; in an introverted manner" (from score). Numerous instructions as Introit progresses, including directions for page turner to assist by depressing a lower cluster chord silently. Elégie maintains similar spirit, with viola opening "*ppp* ghostly, 'white'." Dynamic and dramatic extremes personify the Danse Macabre, straightforward throughout with a molto crescendo from *ff* for the conclusion. A fascinating work, virtually unknown. D.

Lee Hoiby. *Ciaconetta* 1990 (TP 114-40645 1994) 4pp., parts. 3 min. A miniature work with large chord structures at Moderato tempo. M-D.

Karl Höller. *Sonate* Op.62 E (Schott 5847 1968) 47pp., parts. 25 min. Allegro moderato; Molto vivace; Larghetto affettuoso; Allegro con passione. A large-scale Sonata in linear, imitative writing with hints of Hindemith, in whose memory it was composed. Large span required. D.

Jean-Paul Holstein. 5 *Episodes de la Vie d'un Altiste* (Billaudot 1986), parts. Published separately. I. Enjouant à pousse-notes; II. En jouant à saute-croches; III. Cordes lisses et cordes à nœuds; IV. A contre-chant; V. A contre-chœur. In progressive levels of difficulty, written in a Neoclassic style. 2–3 min. each. Int. to D.

Arthur Honegger. *Sonata* (ESC 1921) 27pp., parts. Andante: sustained introduction leads into a Vivace section; these 2 ideas and contrasting moods are juxtaposed throughout this movement 3 times. Allegretto moderato: flowing 16ths in piano move into a Poco più allegretto with a grazioso marking; this movement is very "French"-sounding. Allegro non troppo: basically sectional; diatonic material contrasts with chromatic ideas; bold melodic line in viola; pianist's left hand must span a 10th. M-D.

Zoltán Horusitzky. *Sonata* (EMB 1974) 28pp., parts. Con passione; Andante; Presto con fuoco. Freely tonal, Neoclassic principles at work, parallel chords, strong and syncopated rhythms in finale, Hindemithian flavor. M-D.

Alexandru Hrisanide. *Sonata* 1965 (Gerig 1975) 15pp., parts. 8 min. Explanations in German and English.

Bertold Hummel. *Sonatina* (Simrock). Interesting rhythmic study. Int. to M-D.

Johann Nepomuk Hummel. *Sonata* Op.5/3 E♭ 1798 (Doktor—Dob 1960, 27pp., parts, Preface by editor; Louise Rood—McGinnis & Marx 1957, 36pp., parts, Preface by editor; W. Lebermann—Schott 1969, 39pp., parts). Allegro moderato; Adagio cantabile; Rondo con moto. This impressive work is written in a lyric and polished style that shows Mozartian elements logically infused with clear Romantic characteristics. Equal demands on both performers. M-D.

Karel Husa. *Poem* 1960 (Schott 1963) 19pp., parts. 13 min. Originally written for viola and orchestra; piano arrangement by the composer. Husa's style shows a fascinating combination of influences from his background and from his study with Arthur Honegger and Nadia Boulanger. Improvvisando; Misterioso; Dolce. Chromatic, harmonics, much rhythmic freedom, tremolo, individual style with lyric and dramatic elements. M-D.

Jacques Ibert. *Aria* 1930 (Leduc 1931), parts. 4 min. Transcription by Paul-Louis Neuberth of the original vocalise for voice and piano with the viola playing the voice part almost identically one octave lower. Wide span required. M-D.

John Ireland. *Sonata* (L. Tertis—Augener 1924) 24 min. See detailed entry under duos for piano and cello. Cello part arranged for viola and edited by Tertis.

Jean Eichelberger Ivey. *Music* (CF 1976) 2 scores, 11pp. each. Facsimile edition. 10 min. The pianist requires a grand piano with lid removed, and the following percussion accessories: metal beater, untuned finger cymbals, and soft timpani sticks. Partly avant-garde, effective. D.

Gordon Jacob. *Sonatina* (Nov 1949) 22pp., parts. 12 min. For viola or clarinet (in A) and piano. Allegro giusto; Andante espressivo; Allegro con brio. Octotonic, neo-Romantic with freely tonal tendencies, careful balancing of instruments throughout. Traditional forms. M-D.

——. *Air and Dance* (OUP 1957) 9pp., parts. In one movement with slow and fast sections. Commences Adagio espressivo with arpeggiated figures moving conversely at *pp*. Progresses to Allegro vivace where grace notes hop across the keyboard and sets the stage for a dance in $\frac{2}{4}$, perky and frivolous. M-D.

Wolfgang Jacobi. *Sonata* (Sikorski 387 1956) 31pp., parts. Allegro molto; Lento; Prestissimo, impetuoso–Allegro. Octotonic, varied textures but mainly thin, chromatic, low-register trills. Opening returns in the Prestissimo, impetuoso section. Final Allegro is fugal, brilliant ending. Large span required. D.

Maurice Jacobson. *Humoreske* (Lengnick 1948) 12pp., parts. For viola or cello and piano. A capricious character piece marked Allegro moderato with thick chords, scalar, and arpeggiated patterns. Fun to play. M-D.

Joseph Joachim. *Hebräische Melodien* Op.9 (Br&H) 16pp., parts. Three movements: Sostenuto; Grave; Andante cantabile–Poco più mosso. Rich, thick-textured writing common in the latter half of the 19th century with clearly defined Jewish melodies. The second is the most involved, requiring performers able to melt independent ideas into a cohesive whole. M-D to D.

——. *Variations* Op.10 E (Musica Rara 1975; Br&H 1855) 23pp., parts. Ten variations, with extended coda, on a theme by the composer. "The variations grow with a power similar to that found in later sets by Brahms, so that they form a single structure, not a collection of separate pieces" (from the score). Joachim's contrapuntal mastery is well in evidence in these variations. The whole set is crowned by the final variation and coda. "The music moves finally to a quiet restatement of the theme and a further part variation. Altogether the work is masterly and, in my opinion, is one of the two finest works ever written for viola and piano, the other being the Sonata by Arnold Bax" (from Notes in the score by Harold Truscott). M-D to D.

Betsy Jolas. *Quatre Duos* 1978–79 (Heugel 1979–81) 20pp., parts. L'Ardente; L'Interdite; La Toute-Vive; La Grande Irenée. Sparse textures, glissando effects, trills, and extreme sonoric play showing the influence of the Webern/ Boulez line of development. Pieces can be performed individually. D.

Douglas Jones. *Three Pieces* (Schott 11260 1977) 8pp., parts. Allegro; Andante cantabile; Allegro energico e sempre forte. Lighthearted works of contrasting nondescript character in traditional Western tonality with imitative motifs. Int.-M-D.

John Joubert. *Sonata* Op.6 (Nov 1954) 14 min. Although strongly influenced by William Walton, this is nevertheless a work of distinction showing first-rate craftsmanship and an appreciation of the need for "light and air" in a musical work. Transparent texture, tonal. All 3 movements are based on a single, 3-note melodic germ heard at the opening. Cyclic construction. Piano writing suggests the influence of Franck. The exuberant Prestissimo finale tends to overwork the unifying device. M-D.

Paul Juon. *Sonata* Op.15 D (Lienau; Katims—IMC; K 4302) 25pp., parts. Moderato; Adagio assai e molto cantabile; Allegro moderato. Strong Brahms influence mixed with Slavic themes and rhythms. D.

Sigfrid Karg-Elert. *Sonata* II Op.139B (Zimmermann) rev.1965, 27pp., parts. Ziemlich bewegt; Sehr rasch, mit Übermut. Constant chromatic sound full of technical difficulties; intense; great contrasts in mood, tempos, and dynamics. Requires large span. D.

Hugo Kauder. *Sonate* F 1918 (Seesaw 1987) 21pp., parts. Con moto tranquillo; Sostenuto e largamente–Allegro molto moderato–Andante. Score is copy of MS. M-D.

———. *Sonate* d 1953 (Seesaw 1987) 10pp., parts. Un poco sostenuto; Un poco presto, sempre sotto voce; Lento–Andante. Open 5th treatment in first movement is followed by single-note, plainchant style in the second and third with additional voices toward the end of the latter movements. Score is copy of MS. M-D.

———. *Sonate* D 1958 (Seesaw 1987) 12pp., parts. Molto tranquillo–Con molto moderato; Andante, un poco adagio–Allegretto molto moderato; Allegretto–Un poco meno mosso. Expanded use of open 5ths from 1953 *Sonate* for modal character. Lacks sustaining interest overall in its introspective demeanor. M-D.

Robert Keldorfer. *Sonata* 1964 (Dob 1966) 20pp., parts. Allegro moderato; Andante sostenuto; (7) Variationen über "Da steht ein Kloster in Österreich." Tonal, chromatic, sections in free counterpoint contrasted with more chordal sections, passacaglia-like treatment in middle movement. Variation movement is based on a tune from the *Antwerpner Liederbuch 1514.* M-D.

Robert Kelly. *Sonata* Op.16 1950 (CFE) 25pp., parts. 14 min. Moderately fast; Slow; Vigorously. Score is copy of MS. D.

Rudolf Kelterborn. *9 Momente* (Bo&Bo 1973) 9 leaves (partly folded), 2 copies necessary for performance. 12½ min. Explanations in German. Contrasting, proportional notation, glissandi, clusters, pointillistic, serial influence, Expressionist, unusual pedal effects, dynamic extremes, avant-garde. D.

Friedrich Kiel. *Variationen über ein schwedisches Volkslied* Op.37 f♯ (C. Dohr—Dohr 98545 1998, ISMN M-2020-0545-3), 38pp., parts. Based on a 16-measure

Swedish folk song, presented at Andante sostenuto, which leads to 16 variations and an extended Finale. Variations explore a myriad of performance styles and techniques. The 350+-mm. Finale, marked Presto, is over half the work. Clean, well-defined writing of exquisite quality. Extensive notes in German. M-D.

——. *Sonate* Op.67 g 1871 (Wollenweber 1972, 39pp., parts; UWKR 22 1972, 30pp., parts). Polished and tasteful writing. Allegro: broad theme, lyrical second group, full and rich harmonies. Scherzo: syncopated theme (Schumannesque), lively second subject. Andante con moto: colorful arpeggi; could be performed separately. Allegro molto: horn 5ths beginning; increased activity; interrupted by impassioned recitative; concludes quietly. Instruments equally balanced throughout. Thematic relationships between the movements. M-D.

——. *Three Romances* Op.69 ca.1870 (H. Truscott—Musica Rara 1972) 15pp., parts. Andante con moto (B♭); Allegretto semplice (G); Allegro con passione (e). Movements well contrasted; react on one another to form one work, not 3 separate pieces. Beautiful balance in style and texture between the large slow movement, which is the first piece, with its broad but restrained main melody and more impassioned minor middle part; the lighter mood of the second piece, the shortest of the 3; and the "appassionato" of the final one. Superb writing for both instruments. M-D.

Julius Klaas. *Sonata* Op.40 c (Heinrichshofen 1965) 40pp., parts. Bewegt; Langsam; Sehr geschwind; Mässig bewegt, aber energisch. Written in the Brahms tradition. D.

Franz Koczwara. *Sonate* Op.2/2 C (U. Drüner—Schott VAB18 1973) 11pp., parts, with basso. Moderato; Adagio; Rondo. Tasteful realization showing Rococo influences with binary forms in first 2 movements. Instruments complement one another well in largely facile writing. M-D.

Charles Koechlin. *Sonate* Op.53 (Senart) 30½ min. Dramatic first movement. Adagio is mainly an introduction that presents material and establishes mood for the rest of the work. Elfin but ominous Scherzo. Somber but restless opening section of the finale is followed by a restful episode that continues this mood to the end of the work. D.

Barbara Kolb. *Related Characters* 1980 (Bo&H 1985) 20pp. 12 min. I. Tranquillo; II. Ritmico; III. Lirico; IV. Esplosivo. Complex rhythmic relationships and indeterminacy are characteristic. Two copies of score necessary for performance. Parts also available for B♭ clarinet, trumpet, and E♭ alto sax.

Egon Kornauth. *Sonata* Op.3 c♯ (Dob 1913) 33pp., parts. 24 min. Allegro deciso; Andante, molto espressivo; Allegro feroce ed impetuoso. Highly chromatic, post-Brahms idiom. D.

——. *Sonatine* Op.46a (Dob 1959) 16pp., parts. 11 min. Available for flute (violin) and piano as well as for viola and piano. Rondino; Intermezzo; Siciliano. Centers around e–E, chromatic, much thinner textures than the *Sonata*. M-D.

Ernst Křenek. *Sonata* 1948 (Belwin-Mills) 15pp., parts. Andante; Allegro vivace; Andantino. Partial 12-tone technique; much academic, emotionally cold note-spinning. M-D.

Karl Kroeger. *Recitative and Allegro* 1966 (ACA-CFE). For cello or viola. See detailed entry under duos for piano and cello.

Ryszard Kwiatkowski. *Legenda* (PWM 1977) 12pp., parts. 7½ min. Angular melodies, mixed meters, extended trills, double stops, and use of the extremes of both instruments predominate. In ternary form with calm outer sections and a galloping rhythmic figuration in the middle. M-D.

Kenneth Leighton. *Fantasia on the Name BACH* Op.29 (Nov. 1957) 27pp., parts. 14 min. Neo-Romantic with some mildly 20th-century techniques. M-D to D.

Fritz Leitermeyer. *12 Episoden* Op.36 (Dob 1971) 23pp., parts. 14 min. Short pieces of 14–35 mm. exploring contrasting musical ideas in intense musical relationships. Mildly 20th-century. Wide span required. M-D to D.

Alfonso Letelier Llona. *Sonata* 1951 (IU) 35pp. Allegro: Bien en ritmo opening moves to a short Lento section before returning to Allegro; frenetic closing. Lentamente: repeated chords in piano, freely tonal, large span required. Vivace: elaborate movement well worked out; broad gestures moving over keyboard bring this piece to a stunning conclusion. D.

Lowell Liebermann. *Sonata* Op.13 1984 (TP 1988) 56pp., parts. 27½ min. Large-scale designs with dramatic features exploited in both instruments. Opens Allegro moderato at *pp* with rapid pianistic passagework contrasting sustained pitches in the viola and proceeds to cross-rhythms, double to quadruple stops, octotonic, repeated notes, and tremolo-like figures. A plain senza espressione melody introduces the Andante which follows and leads to intense repeated note/octaves and tremolo figuration in ternary form. The concluding movement commences in recitative style featuring the viola and soon follows with a rhythmic theme in $\frac{9}{8}$ marked Allegro feroce to challenge performing skills in a cornucopia of technical feats for both instruments. Concludes in a manner reminiscent of Beethoven with a quiet, slow reflection then a dash to the finish. Dynamics range from *ppppp* to *fff*. A major work for the ensemble from the late 20th century. D.

Franz Liszt. *Romance Oubliée* S.132 1880 (J. Temesváry, G. Balassa—EMB Z.1922 1955) 7pp., parts. An expressive late work by the Hungarian master with mostly soft dynamics and gentle character. Originally for piano and viola, violin, or cello. This edition is for piano and viola or clarinet (part included). M-D.

Pietro Locatelli. *Sonata* g (David, Hertmann—IMC). Largo; Allemanda; Adagio; Allegro moderato ed espressivo. Highly edited. M-D.

——. *Sonata* Op.6/12 (Doktor—IMC). Adagio cantabile; Allegro; Alla Siciliana; Allegro.

Jean-Baptiste Loeillet (of Lyons). *Sonata* B♭ (IMC).

——. *Sonata* f♯ (IMC).

Edwin London. *Sonatina* 1962 (New Valley Press) 30pp., parts. Allegro ma non troppo; Molto adagio; Allegro dondolamento. Serial, free rhythmic independence between parts (in piano), bold gestures, arpeggi figures, glissando, Expressionist, shifting meters in finale, thoroughly 20th-century idiom. Requires large span. D.

Otto Luening. *Suite* (Galaxy 1972) 23pp., parts. For cello or viola and piano. See detailed entry under duos for piano and cello.

Marin Marais. *Five Old French Dances* (JWC) 13pp., parts. L'Agréable; La Provençale; La Musette; La Matelotte; Le Basque. Short, contrasted, traditional treatment of piano part. Int.

——. *Suite* I d (G. Hunter—GS) for viola da gamba and basso continuo. No separate gamba part. From Book IV of *Pièces de Viole* 1717. Makes strong demands on the string player. Seven short movements, all in d. Imaginative realization of the continuo part. Several inaccuracies in notes and clefs. Facsimile included. M-D.

Benedetto Marcello. *Sonata* Op.2/2 e (Augener; Marchet—IMC) 7pp., parts. Adagio; Allegro; Largo; Allegretto. Augener edition is over-edited in dynamics and accent marks. M-D.

——. *Sonata* F (Sosin—USSR 4935).

——. *Two Sonatas* F, g (Katims, Piatti—IMC) 12pp., parts. Both *Sonatas* in slow-fast-slow-fast, mostly binary, forms. Can be performed on cello. M-D.

——. *Two Sonatas* G, C (Vieland—IMC) 8pp., parts. Slow-fast-slow-fast, mostly binary forms. M-D.

——. *Sonata* Op.2/6 G (Gibson—Schott).

——. *Sonata* Op.2/4 g (Piatti, d'Ambrosio—Ric 125328).

Carlo Marino. *Sonata* D (K. Stierhof—Dob 1973) DM 361. 11pp., parts. Grave; Allegro; Largo; Adagio; Allegro. A stylistically appropriate continuo realization has been added by F. A. Hueber. Originally for viola da gamba. Marino is considered the true founder of the Bergamo violin school.

Donald Martino. *Three Sad Songs* 1993 (Dantalian 509 1997) 16pp., parts. 14 min. I. Processional: cantabile melody contrasted by pointillistic staccatos and marcato figurations. II. Reflections: frequent tempo changes punctuated by metrical changes in nearly every measure; restless. III. Soliloquy and Cavatina: lyric

Soliloquy for viola solo connects directly into Cavatina with quiet atmospheric pianistic writing. Complex relationships in first 2 *Songs* balanced out in final. The score is a highly detailed performance guide. Pieces could be performed separately but work best as a collection. M-D.

Jean Martinon. *Rapsodie* 72 (Billaudot 1972) 15pp., parts. Sectional, numerous tempo changes, Expressionist, intense, based on opening broken-chord idea, freely dissonant, serial influence. Thorough musicianship required. D.

Bohuslav Martinů. *Sonata* I 1955 (Fuchs—AMP 1958) 32pp., parts. 17 min. Poco andante: changing meters; freely tonal around F; pedal points; full chords in introductory section; dance qualities present; varied textures and figurations; coda based on materials in introductory section; large span required. Allegro non troppo: free dissonant counterpoint; 16th-note patterns; octotonic; 3 with 4; broken-chord triplet figuration; varied tempos; syncopation; Allegro busy closing leads to final section that slows, thin textures, and ends on a restful C. D.

Jacques-Féréol Mazas. *Elegie* Op.73 c/C (B. Päuler—Amadeus BP887 2001) 16pp., parts. Opens Maestoso in c and proceeds through a recitative before settling into an Andante grazioso in C with rich melodic and harmonic qualities typical of the early 19th century. An attractive work which deserves to be better known in its version with piano.
———. *Le Songe: Fantaisie sur 'La Favorite'* Op.92 (F. Lainé—Billaudot 1995) 23pp., parts. 11 min. Based on a quotation from "Ange si pur" in the Fernand's Cavatina from Act IV of Donizetti's *La Favorite*. The quotation appears after a lengthy introduction marked Allegro moderato assai in a *gentil* setting at Larghetto. Colorful harmonic turns decorate the lyric quality in an orchestral conception which works well at the piano. The dream ends in a Più allegro "Réveil," with a dash to the finish in 7 mm. M-D.

Wilfrid Mellers. *Sonata* C 1946 (Lengnick 1949) 27pp., parts. 17 min. Lento; Rondo–Allegro agitato; Motto adagio. Mildly 20th-century; piano part has much activity; preference for tritone noted in the Lento. Large span required. M-D.

Jacques de Ménasce. *Sonate en un mouvement* 1955 (Durand) 17pp., parts. Adagio–Allegro–Fugato–Allegro–Adagio. Chromatic; verges on atonal writing; changing meters; chordal in Adagio sections; dance qualities in Allegro sections; logical thematic development; many rhythmic sequences. M-D.

Felix Mendelssohn. *Sonata* c 1823–24 (DVFM 1966, 36pp.; K 4297, 46pp.), parts. Adagio–Allegro: Introduction, SA, arpeggiated first subject, more diatonic second subject, extensive development; coda uses material from both subjects. Menuetto: Allegro molto, skilful writing, fleeting, contrasting chorale-like Trio. Andante con variazioni: theme is similar to theme in the *Variations Sérieuses*

Op.54; 8 extensive variations; recitativo section, Allegro molto, provides soaring conclusion. M-D.

Marcel Mihalovici. *Sonata* Op.47 E♭ 1942 (Heugel 1948) 58pp., parts. 25 min. Allegro serioso: SA, freely tonal around E♭, staccato rhythms, octotonic, wide dynamic range; requires large span. Agitato e vehemente: ABA, vigorous rhythmic drive, flowing chromatic mid-section, percussive. Andante espressivo: ostinato-like figures, misterioso section based on left-hand arpeggi figures and right-hand rolled semi-clusters, numerous tempo changes, Expressionist. Allegro tranquillo: low octaves, ostinato-like, full syncopated chords, 3 with 2, octotonic, appassionato closing. Neoclassic with influence of Enesco, Bartók, and Les Six. D.

——. *Textes* Op.104 1974 (Heugel) 20pp., parts. Notes in French.

Darius Milhaud. *Sonata* I 1944 (Heugel) 23pp., parts. 12 min. Based on 18th-century themes. Entrée; Française; Air; Final. Light and transparent writing. M-D.

——. *Sonata* II 1944 (Heugel) 18pp., parts. 12 min. Champêtre: pastoral. Dramatique: funeral march. Rude: vigorous. M-D.

——. *Quatre Visages* Op.238 1943 (Heugel 1946), parts. Published separately. I. La Californienne; II. The Wisconsonian; III. La Bruxelloise; IV. La Parisienne. Short musical portraits of individuals from 4 states and cities during World War II. M-D.

Philipp Mohler. *Concertante Sonate* Op.31 (Schott 1953) 44pp., parts. 22 min. Introduction; Vivace assai; Intermezzo a la recitativo; Allegro con brio. Mildly 20th-century. M-D.

Wolfgang Amadeus Mozart. *Sonata* E♭ (University Music Press).

——. *Sonatina* K.439b E♭ (Courte—H. Elkan; G. Piatigorsky—EV 1944), parts. Allegro; Menuetto; Adagio; Allegro. Transcribed from the Viennese Sonatinas for piano. Piatigorsky's score is in C. Piano parts differ in the 2 editions. Int.

——. *Sonatina* F (Courte—H. Elkan).

——. *Sonata* G (Courte—H. Elkan).

——. *Sonata* K.300c b (B. McWilliams—Armitage) 17pp., parts. Tasteful transcription. Score is copy of MS. M-D.

——. *Divertimento* K.334 D (M. Szaloski—PWM 6167, ISBN 83-224-1859-0) 8pp., parts. Andante with 6 variations. Transcription with editorial suggestions in brackets. M-D.

Pietro Nardini. *Sonata* I B♭ (Alard, Dessauer—IMC).

——. *Sonata* D (Katims—IMC) 15pp., parts. Adagio; Allegro con fuoco; Larghetto; Allegretto grazioso. Can be played on violin. M-D.

——. *Sonata* f (Zellner—IMC; Cranz), parts. 9½ min. Allegro moderato; Andante; Allegro. M-D.

Willi Niggeling. *Sonata* G (Mitteldeutscher Verlag 1057) 25pp., parts. Moderato; Adagio; Allegretto. Neoclassic in Hindemith tradition but slightly more tonally oriented. M-D.

G. G. Sparre Olsen. *Norwegian Love Song* [*Norsk Kjærleikssong*] Op.36/3 (Norsk Musikforlag 9339 1981) 4pp., parts. 2½ min. A succinct, colorful setting at Allegro con grazia of a simple melody in $^6_8$ meter with an engaging piano score requiring much more skill than the viola. Also for cello (part included). M-D.

Georges Onslow. *Sonata* Op.16/2 c (U. Wegner—Br 1972) 41pp., parts. For viola or cello and piano. Parts for viola and cello. Dates from before 1820. Allegro espressivo; Minuetto; Adagio cantabile; Finale–Allegretto. Written in Classical style (Beethoven); interesting if not innovative. M-D.
———. *Sonata* Op.16/3 A (Höckner—Simrock).

Juan Orrego-Salas. *Mobili* Op.63 1968 (PIC 1971) 22pp., parts. Flessibile: dramatic gestures. Discontinuo: syncopation; extreme ranges of keyboard used. Ricorrente: steady chordal movement; viola has cadenza-like section. Perpetuo: changing meters; large span required. Written in a 20th-century international style; well crafted. M-D.

Léon Orthel. *Sonata* Op.52 (Donemus 357 1965) 24pp., parts. 16 min. Lento non troppo; Allegro vivo; Lento non troppo–Allegro moderato. Strong emotional intensity, highly pianistic, mildly 20th-century in a Stravinskyesque, Neoclassic vein. D.

Hans Osieck. *Sonatine* 1952 (Donemus), parts. 13 min. Spirited opening movement with strongly willed development and insistence. Atmospheric slow movement of melodious texture gives way to an animated finale of acrobatic quality as pianist moves across the keyboard. May also be played on clarinet. M-D.

Hall Overton. *Sonata* 1960 (CFE) 58pp., parts. 18 min. One extensive movement. Serial influence, changing meters, syncopated chords, sonorous qualities, octotonic, percussive effects, fast chords in alternating hands; varied moods, tempos, textures, and idioms. Virtuoso writing for both instruments. Rich timbres and strongly emotional, flexible compositional technique; smoldering intensity. Large span required. D.

Niccolò Paganini. *La Campanella* (W. Primrose—Schott 1952) 10pp., parts. Transcription of the famous caprice from Paganini's own *24 Caprices*, Op.1. M-D.
———. *Moto Perpetuo* (J. Vieland—IMC 1951) 7pp., parts. Favors the viola. M-D.

Robert Palmer. *Sonata* 1951 (PIC 1962) 24pp., parts. Andante con moto e sempre cantabile: octaves, freely tonal, independent lines, syncopated triplets, emphatic chords at cadence points, intense. Allegro risoluto: short pungent motives, complex layers of rhythms, vigorous and rhythmic, octotonic, important inner voices, serious brilliant conclusion; large span required. D.

Robert Parris. *Sonata* 1957 (CFE) 16pp., parts. 10 min. Andantino: flowing chromatic contrapuntal texture; octotonic; large span required; coda leads directly to Canzona: dissonant linearity, gradual increase in tempo and intensity, dramatic Allargando closing. Unique impersonal and austere style. M-D.

Arvo Pärt. *Spiegel im Spiegel* 1978 (UE 31257 1998, ISMN M-008-05990-2) 8pp., parts. 10 min. Last work Pärt completed before leaving Estonia. The "mirror in mirror" image is seen primary in the use of contrary motion in the viola's dotted whole notes. Using a repeated second-inversion broken chord in the piano with widely spaced octaves and otherwise single notes, Pärt invokes the spirit of Beethoven's opening movement of the "Moonlight" Sonata in tintinnabuli style. Also in cello transcription. Int.

Johann C. Pepusch. *Sonata* d (F. Dinn—Schott 11262 1977) 8pp., parts. Largo; Allegro; Largo; Allegro. A fine edition of this transcription. M-D.

Vincent Persichetti. *Infanta Marina* Op.83 (EV 1960) 15pp., parts. 8 min. Reflections on a poem by Wallace Stevens. A lengthy Lento viola introduction gives way to chordal passages, imitation, octotonicism, synthetic arpeggiation, and changing tempos in a homespun form created by an unusual development. Returns to the opening section (abridged) to close *pp*. M-D.

Walter Piston. *Interlude* (Bo&H 1952) 4pp., parts. 4 min. An expressive Adagio character piece with soothing melody and calm character. M-D.

Nicola Porpora. *Sonata* G (David, Hermann, Vieland—IMC 1959) 11pp., parts. Grave sostenuto; Fuga; Aria; Allegretto moderato. Heavily edited with thick piano score. Challenging fugue for viola with occasional employment of 2 voices simultaneously. M-D.

———. *Sonata IX* E (Alard-Dessauer, Vieland—IMC 1960) 6pp., parts. Andantino; Lento; Allegro. Binary forms. M-D.

Quincy Porter. *Speed Etude* 1948 (Valley Music Press 1950) 4pp., parts. 3½ min. A perpetual mobile in $^{12}_8$ with scalar and arpeggiated figures. M-D.

———. *Poem* 1948 (Valley Music Press 1957) 3pp., parts. See detailed entry under duos for piano and cello.

William Presser. *Prelude and Rondo* (Tenuto) 8pp. 3¼ min. In one movement with a fragment of the rondo theme presented in the Prelude. Moves abruptly from slow to fast tempos for the Rondo proper. Clearly designed form with attractive writing in a mildly 20th-century style. Also for alto saxophone. M-D.

Sergei Prokofiev. *Field of the Dead* (J. Showell, P. Fan—Armitage 1984) 6pp., parts. Effective transcription from *Alexander Nevsky*. M-D.

Henry Purcell. *Suite* (J. Vieland—IMC 1973) 12pp., parts. Air; Contredance; Sarabande; Hornpipe; Air; Allemande; Jig; Canzonetta. M-D.

Priaulx Rainer. *Sonata* (Schott 1945) 15pp., parts. 12 min. Thin harmonies and textures. Melodic material extended and developed. First movement treats ricercar form freely. Slow movement uses linear writing. Last movement alternates $\frac{3}{8}$ and $\frac{5}{8}$ rhythms. Whole work looks toward the past for its inspiration. M-D.

Günther Raphael. *Sonata* Op.13 E♭ (Br&H).
——. *Sonata* II Op.80 1954 (Br&H 1957) 20pp., parts. 16 min. Con moto moderato; Scherzo–Allegro; Allegretto. Mildly 20th-century. M-D.

Karol Rathaus. *Rapsodia Notturna* Op.66 1950 (Bo&H 1968). For cello or viola. See detailed entry under duos for piano and cello.

Maurice Ravel. *Pièce en forme de Habanera* (Leduc 1926) 4pp., parts. Transcribed for "instrument" with piano from the *Sites Auriculaires*. Viola score adapted by P. L. Neuberth. Transcriptions are also available for other instruments with piano. M-D.

Alan Rawsthorne. *Sonata* (OUP 1937, rev.1954) 39pp., parts. 16 min. Sonata form individually approached with parts omitted and recapitulations compressed. Heavy and thick piano writing. First movement consists of a slow introduction followed by a toccata-like Allegro. A condensed form of the introduction and a fast coda round off the movement. Second movement consists of a scherzo and 2 trios. The serious and expressive slow movement is a short set of variations that leads directly to the finale, a delightful and vivacious rondo. M-D.

Carl Reinecke. *Phantasiestücke* Op.43 (UWKR 32 1974) 25pp., parts. Romanze; Allegro molto agitato; Humoreske. Three pieces Schumannesque in character. Melodious; make much use of arpeggi figuration and short motivic material. M-D.

Albert Reiter. *Sonata* (Dob 1962) 24pp., parts. Ruhig bewegt; Rasch; Langsam; Lebhaft. Harmonic 4ths, left-hand octaves, free counterpoint, freely tonal, octotonic, traditional forms, diatonic lines, Neoclassic. Large span required. M-D.

Franz Reizenstein. *Concert Fantasy* Op.42 (Hin 509 1967) 24pp., parts. 15 min. In one continuous movement with 14 broad tempo changes. Engaged writing founded primarily upon an imitative style in linear motion. A fascinating work which requires experienced performers with a keen insight into each instrumental part. Finally ends together on octave F's. M-D to D.

Hermann Reutter. *Musik* 1951 (Schott 4338) 21pp., parts. Sarabande; Pastorale mit Cantus Firmus; Variationen über "Es ist ein Ros' entsprungen"; Fuge. Baroque concepts in a 20th-century idiom. Movements can be performed individually. M-D.

Alan Richardson. *Sonata* Op.21 (Forbes—Augener 1955) 20 min. Four movements, pentatonic usage, well crafted, many sequences and clichés. M-D.

George Rochberg. *Sonata* 1979 (J. de Pasquale—TP 1979) 30pp., parts. 20 min. Allegro moderato; Adagio lamentoso; Fantasia–Epilogue. Largely chordal and intervallic structures built around the 2nd and 7th. Dramatic qualities permeate the opening movement where scalar octave patterns and well-accentuated chords are guideposts for development. Slow movement requires careful pedaling and balancing for expressive effect. The Fantasia is the shortest movement and hints at ideas heard in the first, closing with 3 pages at *pp* and atmospheric effects. M-D.

Alessandro Rolla. *Divertimento* (F. Sciannameo—Spratt 1974, ISBN 0-914568-03-5) 19pp., parts. Andante sostenuto; Allegro alla polacca. Reflects late Classical principles in composition. The work is a "combination of romantic inspiration and technical academism, due to the fact that the *Divertimento* was written to suit the talent of Signor G. Piglia (one of his pupils)" (from Foreword). M-D.

Nino Rota. *Sonata* C (Ric 1945) 30pp., parts. In one continuous movement: Allegretto scorrevole–Andante sostenuto–Allegro scorrevole. Tuneful melodies in a straightforward manner with only occasional animation, as at the end. M-D.

Anton Rubinstein. *Sonata* Op.49 f 1857 (Br&H 35pp., parts; USSR 1960). Moderato; Andante; Moderato con moto; Allegro assai. Rapturous melodies are seemingly present everywhere. Piano part inundates viola at times, especially in arpeggi sections. Effective piano writing. M-D to D.

Witold Rudzinski. *Sonata* 1946 (PWM 1946, ISBN 83-224-2364-0) 28pp., parts. 14 min. Masovienne; Aria; Gigue. Spirited outer movements surrounding a decorative aria. Deserves to be better known. M-D.

Friedrich Wilhelm Rust. *Sonata* F (W. Sawodny, C. Gevert—Amadeus 873 1999) 16pp., parts, including basso. [Unmarked]; Adagio; Minuetto I, II. Binary forms in outer movements. Realization is mostly chordal, not showing much originality. M-D.

Helmut Schiff. *Sonata* (Dob 1960) 28pp., parts. Allegro agitato; Andante; Vivace assai. Thin textures, freely tonal à la Hindemith, octotonic, long lines especially in the Andante, straightforward rhythms, Neoclassic. M-D.

William Schmidt. *Sonata* 1959 (WIM 1968) 30pp., parts. 11 min. In a lyrically expressive manner: spread-out broken chords, chromatic, varied tempos, independent lines; large span required. Slowly–agitated: expressive disjunct lines, faster and lighter section, dancelike, opening tempo and mood return to close work. M-D.

Anton Schoendlinger. *Sonata* (Br&H 5819 1955) 20pp., parts. Allegro, ma non troppo; Adagio; Allegro. Freely tonal, chromatic, thin textures, quartal and quintal harmony, toccata-like finale, Neoclassic. M-D.

Robert Schollum. *Sonata* Op.42/2 1950 (Dob 1963) 20pp., parts. 10 min. Ruhige, breite; Sehr rasch. Twelve-tone; timbres are related to styles of Debussy and Milhaud; austere writing. D.

Ruth Schonthal. *Sonata Concertante* 1973 (Furore 274 1997, ISMN M-50012-175-6). For cello, viola, or clarinet. See detailed entry under duos for piano and cello.

Franz Schubert. *Sonate 'Arpeggione'* Op.Post. D.821 a 1824 (W.-D. Seiffert, J. Weber, K. Schilde—Henle 612 1995, 29pp.; P. Doktor—GS 1968), parts. For viola or cello, transcribed from the original for the long-forgotten "guitar d'amour," a guitar-cello, and piano. Opens Allegro moderato with a gentle melody and rich harmonic qualities in the piano before passing the principal theme to the viola in what would become SA form. A quiet Adagio with delicate qualities follows in E with rocking motion in piano and sustained lyricism in viola. The concluding Allegretto invokes the spirit of the last movement from Mozart's Piano Sonata in a, only in the parallel major in an abridged rondo form. Published by Henle in separate editions for viola or cello in a manner preserving Schubert's ideas for the original instruments. Preface in German, English, and French. M-D.

———. *Sonatina* I Op.137 D (K 4327).

Robert Schumann. *Märchenbilder* ("Fairy-Tale Pictures") Op.113 1851 (W. Hang-Freienstein, K. Schilde, J. Weber—Henle 632; J. Draheim—Br&H; Litolff; H. Schradieck—GS; K 4323), parts. Nicht schnell: requires a cantabile style. Lebhaft: rhythmic, exuberant, joyful. Rasch: restless and agitated. Langsam, mit melancholischen Ausdruck: tender, wistful, and cantabile. May be performed on violin (Henle 694, GS, K include part). M-D.

Elliott Schwartz. *Suite* 1963 (ACA 1964) 13pp., parts. 9 min. Very slowly; Very spritely; Very slowly–Faster with motion; Very slowly. An expressive work showing many musical features in short space. Score is copy of MS. M-D.

Leif Segerstam. *At the Border* 1974 (Busch 1976) 8pp., parts. For violin or viola. See detailed entry under duos for piano and violin.

Albert Sendrey. *Sonata* (EV 1947) 30pp., parts. With Spirit; Slow Alla Breve; With Humor, fast. Mildly 20th-century with Impressionist and a few jazz influences. All directions are given in English; some very unusual but helpful. Requires well-developed technique and ensemble experience. M-D.

Ralph Shapey. *Duo* (CFE 1957) 17pp., parts. The Andante con espressivo section has many combined meters ($\frac{2}{4} + \frac{3}{16}$, $\frac{1}{8} + \frac{1}{4}$ ($\frac{3}{8}$), $\frac{2}{4} + \frac{3}{16}$, etc.), is highly Expressionist, with complex harmonies and rhythms and a quasi-cadenza for viola with piano participating. The segue to Leggiero section is pointillistic, while the segue to Andante con espressivo section accelerates to a Maestoso conclusion. Only for the most adventurous and highly qualified performers. D.

Judith Shatin. *Doxa* 1989 (Wendigo 1995) 10pp., parts. "*Doxa* is a Greek word meaning radiance; it is perhaps more familiar as the root of the word Doxology. The quality of [violinist] Rosemary Glides playing prompted the title; it also served as a springboard for the sweeping gestures that articulate the form" (Composer's Note). "Fiery," "relaxed," "expressive," "vigorous," "spirited," and "expansive" are descriptive words found in the score for performers. M-D.

Dmitri Shostakovich. *Viola Sonata* Op.147 (Bo&H; GS 1975) 44pp., parts. The composer's last completed composition. Sparse textures; piano frequently treated percussively; viola splurges with plenty of Russian cantabile. M-D.

Alan Shulman. *Theme and Variations* 1940 (www.capital.net/com/ggjj/shulman) 16pp., parts. 14 min. Based upon a theme in step movement in homophonic texture with alternating quarter-note meters in binary form. Initially at Andante moderato, the theme progresses through 7 variations at different tempos, a Finale–Chorale, 2 viola cadenzas, and Postlude. Also exists in orchestral adaptation. A standard of the repertoire which deserves publication by a major firm. M-D.
——. *A Piece in Popular Style* 1939 (www.capital.net/com/ggjj/shulman 1987) 5pp., parts. A fun-loving essay incorporating elements of blues and boogie-woogie. The composer was considered "a music master as comfortable with jazz as with the classical idiom" (Allan Kozinn, "Alan Shulman, Composer and Cellist," *New York Times*, July 13, 2002). Effective as an encore piece. M-D.
——. *Homage to Erik Satie* 1938 (www.capital.net/com/ggjj/shulman). For viola or cello and piano.

Otto Siegl. *Sonata* I Op.41 (Dob 1925) 20pp., parts. Molto vivace; Adagio espressivo; Allegro vivace. Bitonal, chromatic, traditional pianistic idioms, serious and intense. Requires large span. M-D to D.
——. *Sonata* II Op.103 E♭ (Dob).

Julia Smith. *Two Pieces* (P. Doktor—Mowbray 1966) 15pp., parts. 7 min. I. Nocturne: ABA′; preference for open chords; melismatic figurations within lyricism. II. Festival Piece: trills, harmonics, double stops; Maestoso finish at *ffz*. Neoclassic spirit within 20th-century framework. M-D.

Leland Smith. *Sonata* 1954 (CFE) 16pp., parts. For heckelphone or viola and piano. Three untitled movements. Chromatic, cluster-like sonorities, harmonics. Second movement to be played "as a waltz"; fast harmonic rhythm. Final movement is energetic, intense, Expressionist. Requires large span. D.

Jozsef Soproni. *Sonatina* 1964 (Zenemükiado Vállalat) 24pp., parts. Allegretto spirituoso; Aria–Lento ma non troppo; Burletta–Animato, molto agitato. This writing, of fairly thin textures, contains an attractive amount of Hungarian flavor. The chromatic triplet in the slow movement creates a strangely haunting effect. M-D.

Vladimir Soukup. *Sonata* 1961 (Český Hudební Fond Praha 1969) 28pp., parts. Adagio: quasi-recitativo opening for viola; gradually works in piano and rises to a Pesante *fff* before a subito Adagio, *ppp* closing. Allegro con brio: brilliant gestures for piano including tremolo chords between hands; martial, repeated, driving chords lead to an Allegro feroce, Pesante *fff* ending; an exciting movement. Mildly 20th-century with ample dissonance. M-D.

Leo Sowerby. *Sonata* H.240 1938 (SPAM 1944; Leo Sowerby Foundation 1996). For clarinet or viola and piano. See detailed entry under duos for piano and clarinet.

Norbert Sprongl. *Sonata* Op.115 (Dob 1958) 32pp., parts. Andante sostenuto; Lento; Vivace. Chromatic, Neoclassic, excellent craft. M-D to D.

Johann Stamitz. *Sonata* Op.6a G (V. Borissovsky—IMC 1972) 15pp., parts. Allegro risoluto; Adagio; Minuetto. Thick keyboard score. M-D.

Karl Stamitz. *Sonata* B♭ (G. Lenzewski—Vieweg V1678, 23pp.; U. Drüner—Amadeus 2268; K 4325; Primrose—IMC), parts. 14½ min. Allegro; Andante moderato; Rondo. Similar to Mozart's music but lighter in style. Contains some interesting dialogue between the instruments. M-D.
——. *Sonata* e (Borissovsky—IMC).

Roger Steptoe. *Three Pieces* (St&B 1983) 12pp., parts. 8 min. Narration: rhythmic flexibility in pastorale setting; large expansive chords formed melodically into block and arpeggiated fashions by use of pedal. Burlesque: frolicking repeated-note theme passed between instruments; spirited. Elegy: determinate and indeterminate techniques in recitative style. Added-note harmonies yield to transparent qualities in outer pieces. Can be performed separately or in pairs. M-D.

Halsey Stevens. *Serenade* 1944 (Music Press 1971) 4pp., parts. For viola or clarinet and piano. Piano provides rocking figure while viola soars melodically, then piano gets its own melody and, with the viola, produces a flowing duet. Sensitive chordal sonorities are used, and the work centers freely around e. Large span required. M-D.
——. *Three Hungarian Folk Songs* 1950 (Highgate 1968) 7pp., parts. 3 min. Short, snapshot portraits of folk songs found in Bartók's *A Magyar Népdal*: "Járjad pap a táncot," "Kertem alatt selyem rét," and "Bereslegény, jol meg-

rakd a szekeret." Facile with strong Hungarian qualities. May also be performed on clarinet, English horn, or cello (parts included). Int. to M-D.

———. *Suite* 1945, rev.1953 (CFP 1959) 16pp., parts for clarinet and viola. 9½ min.
See detailed entry under duos for piano and clarinet.

———. *Sonata* 1950 (CFE) 23 min. Mainly diatonic with chromatic surprises and
easily identifiable ideas. Chords in 4ths and sometimes double 3rds are suggested by the flow of melodic lines. Concentrated organic structure. Spontaneous and flowing. First movement: main idea (a 3-note motive) in the slow introduction returns many times in various disguises and is developed in an
urgent and vigorous movement. Second movement: slow, a leisurely siciliano;
darkly colored melody floats over rich sonorities in the piano. Third movement: exciting writing with a rhythmically complex subject; main idea from
first movement is brought back and treated in different ways and acts as a unifying device. M-D.

———. *Suite* 1959 (PIC 1969) 24pp., parts. 12 min. Poco andante: flowing lines,
freely centered around C, large span required. Allegro moderato: cross-rhythms,
mildly dissonant, hemiola, vigorous rhythmic thrust. Allegretto: octotonic, short
brittle figures contrasted with octave punctuation, imitation. Allegro moderato:
main theme treated percussively (quasi-campane), canon, effective voice leading, thin sonorities as in most of entire *Suite*. Neoclassic. M-D.

Robert Still. *Sonata* II (JWC 1956) 24pp., parts. 13½ min. One continuous movement with sectional markings such as: Moderato, Lentamente, Un poco posato
(with an element of the sedate), Ghiribizzoso, fuga libera. Thin textures, tonal,
Neoclassic, mildly 20th-century. M-D.

Toru Takemitsu. *A Bird Came Down the Walk* (Schott SJ1092 1995, ISBN
4-89066-392-4) 11pp., parts. 5 min. An example of Takemitsu's "garden form,"
based upon ideas drawn from *A Flock Descends*. The composer remarked: "the
bird theme goes walking through the motionless, scroll painting like a landscape, a garden hushed and bright with daylight" (Peter Burt, *The Music of
Toru Takemitsu* [Cambridge: Cambridge University Press, 2001], p. 173). M-D.

Josef Tal. *Duo* 1965 (IMI 1971) 16pp., parts. 8 min. In one movement cast in a
restlessness marked by continuous rhythmic intricacies. Sharp dissonances,
cluster tremolos, and independent lines shape this intense duo for experienced
performers. D.

Giuseppe Tartini. *Sonata* Op.10/1 c (Forbes, Richardson—OUP 22.808) 8 min.

———. *Sonata* D (Hermann—IMC).

———. *Sonata* II F (Alard, Dessauer—IMC).

Georg Philipp Telemann. *Sonata* a (W. Schulz, J. Vieland—IMC 1957) 9pp., parts.
Tasteful realization by Diethard Hellmann. Largo; Allegro; Soave (a flowing
Siciliano); Allegro. M-D.

———. *Sonata* B♭ (Ruf—Schott 5652 1966) 7pp., parts, with basso. Largo; Allegro; Largo; Vivace. Creative realization based upon thematic materials in viola part. M-D.

———. *Sonata* D 1734 (H. Leerink—B&VP 1948) 5pp., parts. 5 min. Vivace; Adagio; Allegro. M-D.

———. *Sonata* D (W. Upmeyer—IMC) 7pp., parts. Lento; Allegro; Largo; Allegro. Phrasing and dynamic markings added by editor. M-D.

———. *Sonata* G ca.1729 (H. Joelson—Amadeus BP818 1997) 9pp., parts, including basso. For viola da gamba or viola. See detailed entry under duos for piano and cello.

———. *Zwei Sonaten* ca.1739 (H. Joelson—Amadeus BP640 1997) 19pp., parts, including basso. For viola da gamba or viola. See detailed entry under duos for piano and cello.

Dimitri Terzakis. *Myrrhentropfen* 1993 (Gravis 410 1997) 9pp., parts. 6 min. Quarter-tone writing for viola in a slow, one-movement work of otherwise conventional 20th-century techniques. Emphasis entirely on linear construction with only resultant harmonies. M-D.

———. *Sonetto* 1993 (Gravis 409 1995) 19pp., parts. 11 min. Similar qualities to *Myrrhentropfen* though at much faster tempos and with greater development. The 2 works would make good companion pieces on recital programs. M-D.

Heuwell Tircuit. *Sonata (Homage to Mahler)* 1961 (AMP 1975) 22pp., parts. Material for this work is loosely drawn from the viola introduction to Mahler's *Tenth Symphony.* Allegro legato: chromatic, scalar, plucked strings, dynamic extremes, glissandi, pointillistic, *ppp* fist clusters; large span required. Five Canons in Rondo: thin textures; keyboard lid (shut) must be tapped; both hands are used flat on strings. Avant-garde mixed with traditional techniques. D.

George Tremblay. *For Viola and Piano* 1966 (ACA 1968) 23pp., parts. Straightforward one-movement design without tempo or descriptive comment outside dynamics and accentuation. Occasional double and triple stops ornament a largely sustained melody. Linear texture with wide spacing and chromatic tendencies. M-D.

Francesco Trevani. Trevani was possibly a product of the school of Alessandro Rolla (1757–1841), whose compositions for viola were exceedingly numerous and instructive. *Three Sonatas* (K. Stierhof—Dob 1967). Published separately. 1. E♭: 16pp., parts (DM 176). Andante; Allegro spiritoso. 2. c–C: 35pp., parts (DM 177). Allegro agitato; Allegretto (moves into an Adagio followed by a Tempo di waltz). 3. B♭: 39pp., parts (DM 178). Allegro; Adagio; Rondo; Allegretto. These works sound similar to middle-period Beethoven. Much greater demands on the pianist than on the violist. All are M-D and require solid pianistic equipment.

Lester Trimble. *Duo* (CFP 66076 1968) 24pp., parts. 12 min. Adagio; Allegro. "Mr. Trimble's *Duo for Viola and Piano* is cool in its lyrical aspects (they are none the less surely there) while its harmonic, contrapuntal and textural workmanship are refined, elegant and crystal clear. Its allegro movement is jet-propelled . . . the work is professionality itself" (William Flanagan, *New York Herald-Tribune*, [n.d.], quoted on inside cover of work).

Robert Valentine. *Sonata* a (F. Dinn—Schott 11263 1977) 6pp., parts. Adagio; Allegro; Adagio; Giga. Clean edition devoid of editorial markings. Imitative realization. Recommended. M-D.

Nancy van de Vate. *Sonata* 1965 (Tritone) 19pp., parts. 14½ min. Moderately slow; Brightly; Slowly. Reproduction of composer's MS. Well-crafted, mildly 20th-century, octotonic, free dissonant counterpoint, thin textures predominate, traditional forms, movements complement each other. M-D to D.

Johann B. Vanhal. *Sonata* E♭ after 1787 (A. Weinmann—Dob 1970) DM 544. 31pp., parts. Foreword in German and English. Allegro vivace; Poco adagio; Rondo–Allegro. Haydn-like (Vanhal moved among Haydn's circle) but interesting enough to stand on its own merits. The slow movement is especially poignant and is more involved than it appears. M-D.

Ralph Vaughn Williams. *Fantasia on Greensleeves* (W. Forbes—OUP 1947) 7pp., parts. 4 min. For viola or cello. Includes both "Greensleeves" and the folk tune "Lovely Joan." M-D.
———. *Romance* E♭ (B. Shore, E. Gritton—OUP 1962) 7pp., parts. Gently flowing character epitomizing the title in early-20th-century folkloric style. Stresses 7th chords and stepwise movement. "The manuscript was discovered with others, without any clue, among the composer's papers after his death" (Editor's Note). M-D.

Aurelio de la Vega. *Soliloquio* 1950 (IU) 13pp., parts. 7 min. Andante: viola alone. Sostenuto (Andantino tranquillo): $\frac{7}{8}$, *pp*, dolce, syncopated chords over punctuated left-hand octaves; builds to appassionato climax, then subsides. Poco piu mosso: cantabile. Animato (Allegro): two 8th-note seconds in right hand with triplet in left hand. Subito appassionato: full chords over scalar and arpeggi left-hand figuration. Poco meno mosso: chordal, long-short rhythm. Sostenuto (Andantino tranquillo): fuller treatment than similar opening Sostenuto. Andante: viola alone. Poco piu mosso: espressivo. Tempo I (Sostenuto): chromatic ostinato in left hand, chromatic chords in right hand. Well written for both instruments in a mildly 20th-century style. M-D to D.

Francesco Maria Veracini. *Sonata* e (IMC).
———. *Largo* f♯ (M. Katims—IMC 1945) 5pp., parts. Grandiose piano realization in over-edited score. May also be played on violin. M-D.

John Verrall. *Sonata* I 1942 (Dow 1956) 21pp., parts. Eclectic writing infused with dissonant angular counterpoint. Much use of major 7ths and minor 9ths, Expressionist, energetic Magyar rhythms in finale. Tight structure, emphatic sonorities. M-D.

———. *Sonata* II 1964 (CFP 6587) 18pp., parts. Allegro: freely tonal, much subtle syncopation, thin textures. Andante quasi adagio: free dissonant counterpoint, octotonic. Allegro: rocking figures, chromatic. M-D.

Henri Vieuxtemps. *Elégie* Op.30 (Amadeus 1976; R. Scholz—St&B), parts. An engaging score suggesting an appropriateness more as an encore rather than an elegy with persistent motion and technical challenge. M-D.

———. *Sonata* Op.36 B♭ 1863 (F. Beyer—Eulenburg GM181 1974) 25pp., parts. Maestoso; Barcarolla; Allegretto tranquillo–Animato; Finale scherzando. Thorough instrumental treatment but thematic material is uninteresting, and lack of contrapuntal usage adds to dullness. M-D.

———. *Etude* c (L. Mogill—GS 1975) 12pp., parts.

Tommaso Vitali. *Ciacona* g (F. David—Br&H) 15pp., parts. For violin or viola. Based upon 4-note descending bass pattern in step motion. Extensive development of melodic and harmonic materials exploring a variety of technical problems. Over-edited. M-D.

Antonio Vivaldi. *Sonata* A (David, Hermann—IMC) 7pp., parts. Preludio a Capriccio; Courrente; Giga. Over-edited. M-D.

———. *6 Sonatas* (L. Dallapiccola, W. Primrose—IMC 1955) 44pp., parts. For cello, transcribed for viola. Preface and realization by Dallapiccola. Realization infuses the notion of Romanticism to a score stylistically based upon the principle of imitation. See detailed entry under duos for piano and cello. M-D.

———. *Sonata* III a (Primrose—IMC).

———. *Sonata* B♭ (Primrose—IMC).

———. *Sonata* g (Katims—IMC).

Alexander Voormolen. *Sonata* 1953 (Donemus 87) 21pp., parts. Andante mosso–Allegro moderato; Elegia; Allegro. Impressionist influences mixed with Dutch humor and seriousness. Chromatic. The final Allegro alternates tempos (Allegro and Andante) effectively. Large span required. M-D.

George Walker. *Viola Sonata* 1989 (MMB 1989) 18pp., parts. In 2 untitled movements. Constantly changing meters, octotonic, imitation, harmonics, and double stops in an impulsive character define the *Sonata*'s compositional features. D.

Leopold Matthias Walzel. *Sonata Arioso* Op.30 1960 (Dob 1962) 22pp., parts. Allegro moderato: octotonic and chordal; tranquillo section requires 4 staves to notate; chromatic. Andante arioso: chromatic, disjunct melody, Expressionist. Allegretto scherzando: imitation, syncopated chords, parallel octaves, dance rhythms. D.

Robert Ward. *Arioso and Tarantelle* 1954 (Highgate 1960). Published separately: *Arioso* 7pp., parts, 5 min.; *Tarantelle* 17pp., parts, 6½ min. For viola or cello. Mildly 20th-century with musical qualities depicting the separate titles. M-D.

Paul W. Whear. *Sonata* (Ludwig 1981) 27pp., parts. 16 min. Subtitled "The Briefcase." Slow–Moving; Slow, expressive; Forceful–Driving. Opens majestically with full chords as an introduction to 2 contrasting themes in modified SA. In contrast, the second movement, a languishing elegy, may be performed alone (Composer's Note). Concludes with assertive open chords and marcato rhythms as it mounts to a *ff* finish. M-D.

Jan Michał Wieczorek. *Scherzo* (PWM 1972) 8pp., parts. A playful dance, chockfull of added-note chords, rapid figurations, and capriciousness, which boils to an explosive finish. M-D.

Henri Wieniawski. *Rêverie* (PWM 1973) 7pp., parts. Wieniawski's only known work for viola. Completed by H. Wieckmann, to whom Wieniawski dedicated the work, and first published by Rahter, Leipzig, in 1885.

Frank Wigglesworth. *Sonata* 1959 (ACA) 16 min.
——. *Sound Piece* 1948 (ACA) 12 min.

George Wilson. *Sonate* 1952 (Jobert 1969) 28pp., parts. 13 min. Lento Sostenuto–Allegro, con moto; Adagio ma non troppo; Prestissimo. Serial, atonal, thin textures, freely dissonant counterpoint. All movements end quietly. D.

Joseph Wood. *Sonata* 1940 (CFE) 32pp., parts. Allegro; Adagio; Finale–Allegro. Chromatic; bitonal; augmented 4th is prevalent; surplus of ideas, some very good but not well developed. M-D.

Isang Yun. *Duo* 1976 (Bo&Bo 1977) 16pp., parts. 12 min. Nearly devoid of expressive indications except for dynamics and articulation; however, these are so thoroughly included that the *Duo* becomes a highly expressive work. Uses extremes of the registers and dynamics, with indications *pppp* to *fff*. Finishes very soft and slow following occasional virtuosic passages for both instruments. M-D.

Efrem Zimbalist. *Sarasateana* (UL; in *The Virtuoso Violist*—GS 1995, see Collections for Piano and Viola), parts. A Suite of Spanish Dances: I. Tango; II. Polo; III. Malagueña; IV. Zapateado. For William Primrose, who also edited the score, a copy of the MS. Sparkling dances which deserve a first-rate publisher independent of collections. M-D.

Duos for Piano and Cello

Jean Absil. *Suite* Op.51 (CeBeDeM 1955) 27pp., parts. Introduction and Danse; Barcarolle; Intermezzo; Final. Dramatic gestures, chromatic, fluent pianistic treatment. D.

———. *2e Suite* Op.141 1968 (CeBeDeM) 20pp., parts. 17 min. Andante moderato; Allegretto poco scherzando; Andante; Vivo. Thinner textures than in Op.51; similar harmonic language and approach to the keyboard. D.

John Clement Adams. *Sonata* (ECS 1987) 17pp., parts. Three short movements in Sonatina style with mixed meters, biting dissonances, bitonality, repeated chords, soaring melodies, and complex rhythmic relationships. Score is nicely written facsimile of MS. D.

Jehan Alain. *Largo assai* 1935 (Leduc 1987) 8pp., parts. 5 min. To be performed with much rubato. One movement in concave shape which forms the basis for an expressive mediation. Complicated rhythmic values require detailed consideration. M-D.

Charles-Valentine Alkan. *Sonate de Concert* Op.47 1857 (H. MacDonald—Br 19122 1975) 77pp., parts. For cello (or viola) and piano. Cello and viola parts transcribed by Casimir Ney. "The bewildering variety of accents has been somewhat tempered, and fingerings in both parts and Alkan's tenuto markings (indicating exactitude, not prolongation) have been omitted. The pedal and metronome markings, on which Alkan was always insistent, are Alkan's own" (from Preface). Allegro; Allegrettino; Adagio; Finale alla Saltarelia. Highly effective Romantic virtuoso writing. The Adagio carries the following verse at the beginning: "As dew from the Lord, as showers upon the grass; that tarrieth not for man" (Micah 5:7). The finale was also published as a piano duet. D.

Gilbert Amy. *Mémoire: d'Après Shin'anim Sha'ananim* 1979–89 (UE 30 344 1989, ISMN M-008-05805-9) 12pp., parts. An extended one-movement design comprised of many sections using a style owing to the influences of Boulez and Dutilleux. Contains 3 cello cadenzas, including the ending, for which the piano is tacet for the final 60 mm. M-D.

Theodore Antoniou. *Commos* 1989 (GunMar Music 1993) 24pp., parts. Commences and concludes with solo cello in detailed but cadenza-like spirit. Mild avant-garde techniques. Quartal harmonies. Finishes with an Epilogue. M-D.

Edward Applebaum. *Shantih* (JWC 1969) 10pp. 7½ min. Two scores necessary for performance. Serial-like, harmonics for both instruments, tempo changes, much rubato, abstract. D.

José Ardévol. *Sonatina* 1950 (Ric BA10927) 16pp., parts. 10½ min. Andantino; Lento–Vivo; Allegretto. Neoclassic orientation with Spanish syncopations. M-D.

Attilio Ariosti. *Six Sonatas* (Carisch).
——. *Sonata* I E♭ (Schott).
——. *Sonata* II A (Piatti, Such—Schott).
——. *Sonata* III e (Salmon—Ric; Piatti—Schott).
——. *Sonata* IV F (Piatti—Schott).

Richard Arnell. *Four Serious Pieces* Op.16 (Hin 1958). Prelude; Toccata; Intermezzo; Recitative and Scherzo.

Bonifazio Asioli. *Sonata* C (F. Grützmacher—Simrock). 37pp., parts. Allegro moderato; Adagio; Waltz–Allegro; Finale–Vivace. Solidly rooted in Classicism with emphasis on melody, clarity, and a fluid pianist technique. M-D.

Tony Aubin. *Cantilène Variée* (Leduc 1946) 20pp., parts. Undulating theme is varied 5 times, extensive coda. Colorful and complex writing using numerous 20th-century techniques. Requires seasoned ensemble performers. D.

Georges Auric. *Imaginées* 1969 (Sal) 15pp., parts. One movement with varied tempos and moods. Percussive piano treatment is contrasted with soft Webernesque sonorities. Tremolo in inner and outer voices, syncopation, chromatic octaves, sonorities are allowed to sound for a long time. Dedicated to Mstislav Rostropovitch. D.

Victor Babin. *Sonata-Fantasia* G (Augener).
——. *Twelve Variations on a Theme of Purcell* (AMP).

Carl Philipp Emanuel Bach. *Sonata* W.136 D 1746 (P. Klengel—Br&H 4169) 13pp., parts. Andante; Allegro moderato; Allegretto. Originally for gamba. Not as fussy as some of C. P. E. Bach's works. Slightly heavy editing. M-D.
——. *Sonata* W.137 (Kiengel—Br&H; R. van Leyden—CFP; 13pp., parts). Originally for gamba.
——. *Six Sonatas* (Balassa—Artia).

Johann Christoph Friedrich Bach. *Sonata* A 1770 (A. Wenzinger—Br 3970 1961) 15pp., parts. Larghetto; Allegro; Tempo di Minuetto. "The nobility of the melodic line in the first movement and the freshness and grace of the quick movements mark it as one of the most charming pieces of the literature for cello between the periods of the baroque and classic" (from the Preface).

——. *Sonata* G (H. Ruf—Br 3745 1959) 12pp., parts. Allegretto; Rondeaux. Facile writing with a playful character. First publication of this Sonata. Int. to M-D.

——. *Sonata* D (J. Smith—Litolff).

Johann Sebastian Bach. *Three Sonatas* S.1027–29 1717–23 (E.-G. Heinemann, K. Schilde, R. Zipperling, C. Kanngiesser—Henle 676 2000, ISMN M-2018-0676-1; R. v. Leyden—CFP 4286; Naumann—Br&H; Grützmacher—CFP 239; Klengel—Br&H; Forbes—CFP; Naumann—IMC; L. Robinson—Faber Music 1987; J. Klengel—K 4428). S.1027 G: Adagio; Allegro, ma non tanto; Andante; Allegro moderato. S.1028 D: Adagio; Allegro; Andante; Allegro. S.1029 g: Vivace; Adagio; Allegro. Arrangements by Bach of "works originally intended for other combinations of instruments" (Henle). Henle and CFP include Prefaces in French, German, and English.

These 3 *Sonatas* are included in *Seven Sonatas* (Lea 10) for flute and clavier.

——. *Sonata* S.1017 G (Schroeder—Augener 5501).

Ernst Bacon. *A Life* (J. Krosnick, G. Kalish—King's Crown 1989) 31pp., parts. Birth: Rather slowly and with a shy, soft mystery; spatial harmonies. Light: Allegretto; piano predominance at times. Love: In a slow waltz tempo; imitation. Young Manhood: Maestoso; octotonic; secondary melody quotes Bloch. Departure: Andante con moto; lyric; hand crossings; finishes in a whisper. Large span required. M-D to D.

Henk Badings. *Four Concert Pieces* (Donemus 1947) 25pp., parts. Serenade; Scherzo pizzicato; Air triste; Rondo giocoso. Piece can stand alone, or together as a fine recital group. M-D.

——. *Sonata* II C (Alsbach 1935) 19pp., score. Allegro molto; Adagio; Allegro vivace. Freely tonal, dynamic extremes (*ppp* to *ffff*), sweeping gestures in last movement. M-D.

Robert Baksa. *Cello Sonata* 1980 (CLE 28 1993) 36pp., parts. Allegro; Adagio; Allegro. Strongly tonal for late 20th century. Scalar; imitative; repeated notes; octotonic; thin and thick textures contrasted. Last movement is the most demanding. M-D to D.

Filippo Banner. *Sonata* g (W. Upmeyer—Nag 160 1941) 7pp., parts. Grave; Allegro; Largo; Allegro. Tasteful realizations. M-D.

Granville Bantock. *Sonata* b (JWC 1941) 55pp., parts. Moderato assai; Largamente; Allegretto scherzando rubato; Allegro moderato non tanto. Post-Romantic pianistic writing. M-D to D.

Samuel Barber. *Sonata* Op.6 1932 (GS 1936) 27pp., parts. 18 min. Allegro ma non troppo; Adagio; Allegro appassionato. Sonorous, lyric melodic writing, expansive and Romantic in conception, freely tonal. D.

Jean Barrière. *Twelve Sonatas* (M. Chaigneau, W. M. Rummel—Senart 5246, 5394) 2 vols. Vol.I: Sonatas 1–6 (39pp., parts). Vol.II: Sonatas 7–12 (52pp., parts). There is much variety in these works. All require a certain maturity, both technically and interpretatively. *Sonata* 2 has a violin part in addition to cello and keyboard. *Sonata* 10 is for 2 solo celli. M-D.

Lubor Bárta. *Sonata* 1971 (J. Smolka—Panton 1973) 24pp., parts. Cello part rev. Josef Chuchro. Allegretto; Lento; Allegro vigoroso. "The composer has combined an expressive and individual melodic fund with a characteristic modern concision, expressiveness and contrasts within brief spaces" (from Preface).
———. *Balada a Burleska* (Artia).

Béla Bartók. *Rhapsody* I 1928 (UE). Bartók's own alternate setting of the *Rhapsody* I for violin and orchestra. See detailed entry under duos for piano and violin.

Robert Basart. *Variations* (Sal 1973) 21pp., parts. 14½ min. Part I: pointillistic; accidentals apply to single notes only; complex rhythms; fast-moving groups of notes; sudden dynamic shifts. Part II: linear, very few chords, dynamic mark on almost every note, serially influenced, long note groupings, nontonal throughout, tonal A final chord. D.

Leslie Bassett. *Music for Violoncello and Piano* (CFP 1971) 15pp., parts. Origin; Invention; Variation; Conclusion. Serial elements; widely spaced gestures; stopped and plucked strings in piano; harmonic 9ths in full chord require large span; tightly organized. D.
———. *Sonata* (CFE).

Jürg Baur. *Perpetuum Mobile* 1950, rev.1994 (Dohr 94175 1994, ISMN M-2020-0175-2) 15pp., parts. From *Musik für Violoncello und Klavier*. Races through several meter changes in a virtually nonstop cello part. Imitation is used in 2 passages suggestive of a fugue. M-D.
———. *Dialoge* 1962 (Br&H 6399) 22pp., parts. 16 min. Sostenuto rubato: low register exploited; shifting meters; clusters; large span required. Allegro con moto: toccata-like rhythms; glissandi; alternates with Grazioso section. Andante rubato: quasi-recitativo, contrary glissandi, tremolo. Presto: pointillistic, arpeggi figures, varied tempos, astringent dissonance, Expressionist, serial influence. D.

Arnold Bax. *Legend-Sonata* (Chappell 1944) 25 min.
———. *Sonata* E♭ (Murdoch 1925) 33 min. Much sensuous beauty. D.
———. *Sonatina* (Chappell 1934) 14 min.

Paul Bazelaire. *Deux Images Lointaines* Op.113 (Leduc 1930). 1. Yamilé. 2. Danse nonchalante: in $\frac{7}{4}$, lazy, indolent. M-D.

——. *Suite Française* Op.114 (Schott Frères 1934) 8½ min. Five movements.

——. *Funérailles* Op.120 (Durand).

——. *Variations sur une chanson naive* Op.125 (Schott Frères).

——. *Concertino* I Op.126 1957 (Durand) 8pp., parts. 5 min. Tonal, repeated chords, free counterpoint, witty, ends alla tarantella. M-D.

——. *Concertino* II Op.127 (Durand).

——. *Suite Italienne* (Consortium Musicale).

Irwin Bazelon. *Alliances* 1989 (TP 114-40708 1993) 27pp., parts. 17 min. In one extended movement of multiple sections. Both instruments play together and separately. Late-20th-century style with melodic features and mixed rhythms. Requires up to 4 staves for piano. Dramatically expressive. M-D.

——. *Five Pieces* (Weintraub).

Gustavo Becerra Schmidt. *3ª Sonata* 1957 (Sobre temas y a la memoria de Rene Amengual) (IU) 22pp., parts. Moderato; Allegro energico; Lento; Final–Allegro molto. Neoclassic, thin textures, freely tonal, rather tame rhythmically. M-D.

Conrad A. Beck. *Sonata* II (Schott 5062 1959) 23pp., parts. Allegro moderato; Intermezzo; Andante sostenuto; Allegro vivo. Linear, severe Neoclassic style, concise and highly taut fabric. Each movement freely centers around a tonality. No virtuoso display for either instrument, but D.

Ludwig van Beethoven. *Sonatas* Op.5/1 F, Op.5/2 g, Op.69 A, Op.102/1 C, Op.102/ 2 D (B. v. d. Linde—Henle 1971) 143pp., parts. Fingering and bowing added by André Navarra and Hans-Martin Theopold. Practical Urtext edition, same text as in the New Beethoven Collected Edition. Sources discussed in Preface. Fingering in italics comes from the sources. Other editions: (Tovey, Such— Augener 7660; CFP 748; Schulz—GS L810; Crepax, Lorenzoni—Ric ER2026; Lea, 2 vols.).
Available separately: *Sonata* Op.5/1 (Tovey, Such—Augener). *Sonata* Op.5/2 (Tovey, Such—Augener; Rose—IMC). Beethoven wrote the Op.5 *Sonatas* to feature himself at the keyboard. He was one of the most brilliant pianists of the day. The final movement of Op.5/1 is a catalog of outstanding examples of effective ways to combine the cello and piano. *Sonata* Op.69 (Tovey, Such— Augener; Rose—IMC). An excellent example of effective treatment of the cello in the bass range. *Sonata* Op.102/1 (Tovey, Such—Augener). Combines the 2 instruments with consummate artistry.

——. *Sonata* Op.17 F 1800 (A. Raab, A. Groethuysen, R. Ginzel—Henle 498, ISMN M-2018-0498-9) 24pp., parts. 13½ min. Originally for solo horn; see detailed entry under duos for piano and horn.

——. *Variations* (H. Münch-Holland, G. Henle—Henle; Stutschewsky—CFP

748B) 12 variations on a theme of Handel; 12 variations on a theme of Mozart; 7 variations on a theme of Mozart from *Die Zauberflöte.*

Available separately: *12 Variations on a Theme from Judas Maccabaeus* by Handel WoO 45 G (Such—Augener), *12 Variations on the Theme "Ein Mädchen oder Weibchen" from The Magic Flute* by Mozart Op.66 (Such—Augener; IMC). *7 Variations on "Bei Männern, welche Liebe fühlen" from The Magic Flute* WoO 46 EB (Stutschewsky—CFP 7048; Such—Augener; IMC).

———. *Complete Sonatas and Variations* (Dover 1990, ISBN 0-486-26441-6) 162pp. Contains all 5 *Sonatas* and *Variations* Op.66, WoO 45, WoO 46. This edition is a reprint of *Serie 13* in the Breitkopf and Härtel *Ludwig van Beethoven's Werke.*

———. *Sonatina* G (Belwin-Mills).

See S. R. Swift, "The Complete Works for Cello and Piano by Ludwig van Beethoven: A Performance Project," D.M.A. diss., University of Maryland, College Park, 2000; D. Blum, "Beethoven's *Cello Sonata* Opus 102, No. 2," *The Strad* 103 (May 1992): 418–22ff.; L. Lockwood, "Beethoven's Emergence from Crisis: The *Cello Sonatas* of Op.102," *Journal of Musicology* 16 (summer 1998): 301–22; Stephen Geoffrey Gates, "The Treatment of the Cello in Beethoven's Sonatas for Violoncello and Piano," D.M.A. diss., University of Texas, Austin, 1989.

Domenico Dalla Bella. *Sonata* C (W. Upmeyer—Nag 83) 6pp., parts. First printing of this work. Andante; Giga–Largo; Allegro. M-D.

Arthur Benjamin. *Five Negro Spirituals* (Bo&H).

———. *Sonatina* (Bo&H 1939) 11½ min. Preamble; Minuet; March.

Heinz Benker. *Two Part Inventions* (Br&H 1965) First Part (6478a). Second Part (6478b). Four short pieces, mainly linear, with No.4 more chordal. Imitation is prevalent, Hindemithian style, well-conceived instrumental writing. M-D.

William Sterndale Bennett. *Sonata-Duo* (G. Bush—St&B 1972). Included in "Musica Britannica," *Piano and Chamber Music,* Vol.37. The Duo is in 3 movements, of which the first is by far the best and should be played separately as a fine display piece for the cello. Expansive and lyrical writing. M-D.

Arthur Berger. *Duo* 1951 (J. Krosnick, G. Kalish—Columbia University Press 1988) 18pp., parts. 12 min. Like a heart-to-heart talk between two friends. The cello sounds off, and the piano responds with kindly and shrewd remarks. Neoclassic style. M-D.

Lennox Berkeley. *Andantino* (JWC 1955) 5pp., parts. 2½ min. A lovely, lyric character piece. In E but is freely tonal. Broken 3rds provide thematic germ. M-D.

———. *Duo* (JWC 1955) 14pp., parts. 9 min. One movement, Allegro moderato. Short, thin textures; opening turning figure is mainly used for development. D.

Franz Berwald. *Duo* Op.7 (GM 1946) 29pp., parts. Rev. Sven Kjellström. One large movement with varied sections, tempos, and textures. Written in a Classic style with numerous Romantic characteristics, mainly in harmony and pianistic idioms. M-D to D.

Bruno Bettinelli. *Sonata* (Drago) 12 min. Allegretto; Calmo pensoso; Allegro ritmico.

Thomas Beversdorf. *Sonata* 1967–69 (Indiana Music Center 1974) 17pp., parts. Andante con moto; Adagio con moto; Allegro Moderato. Expressionist; extremes of range exploited; sudden dynamic changes; stopped strings (for pianist); wide span required. D.

Gordon Binkerd. *Sonata* 1952 (Bo&H 1971) 56pp., parts. 25 min. Grave e con rubato; Andante; Allegro. Binkerd's only thoroughly dodecaphonic piece. Piano writing is concertante throughout. Relentless repetition of motivic germs, simultaneous statement of a line against its inversion, and tritone polarities are stylistic features found throughout the work. D.
See Rudy Shackelford, "The Music of Gordon Binkerd," *Tempo* 114 (September 1975): 1–13, for a more thorough discussion of this work.

Johann Adam Birkenstock. *Sonata* e (Moffat—Simrock; J. Salmon—Ric R384) 14pp., parts. Adagio; Courante; Largo; Gigue. The Salmon edition is over-edited and freely arranged but is somewhat effective. M-D.

Easley Blackwood. *Fantasy* Op.8 1960 (GS) 19pp., parts. 9 min. Expansive, Romantic, proclamatory, rich in sonorities. Octotonic, vigorous expressivity, austere dissonant idiom, strong thematic material. Large span required. D.

Ernest Bloch. *Music for Cello and Piano* (CF 05482 2000, ISBN 0-8258-4108-9) 24pp., parts. Contains: *Prayer* (From *Jewish Life* No.1); *Supplication* (From *Jewish Life* No.2); *Jewish Song* (From *Jewish Life* No.3); *Méditation Hébraïque; Nigun* (*Improvisation*) from *Baal Shem* (*Three Pictures of Chassidic Life*). *Méditation Hébraïque* (7 min.) is modal, cello has to play some tones a quarter tone above or below pitch. Allegro deciso mid-section adds contrast to the Moderato outer parts. Long C pedal point in piano closes this work with cello moving freely above. *Nigun* arr. Joseph Schuster. Each work is available separately from CF. M-D.

Waldemar Bloch. *Sonate* 1970 (Dob 1975) 36pp., parts. Vivace e con brio; Molto adagio; Presto. Freely tonal and well conceived for the medium. Writing is especially attractive in the warmly Romantic slow movement. Presto uses a French folk tune. Neoclassic orientation. M-D.

Luigi Boccherini. *Six Sonatas* (A. Bacon—GS L1874; Piatti, Crepax—Ric ER2461). 1 Bb, 2 Eb, 3 c, 4 G, 5 Eb, 6 C (GS numbering). Available separately: 1 A (Piatti—Ric). 2 C (Piatti—IMC). 3 G (Piatti—Ric; Schroeder—Augener; Schroeder,

Rapp—Schott). 6 A (Piatti—Ric; Piatti, Forino—IMC; Schroeder—Augener; Schroeder, Rapp—Schott). Schroeder and Piatti editions are over-edited.

——. *Sonata* VII (Spiegl, Bergmann, Duckson—Schott).

——. *Sonata* A (Moffat—Schott).

——. *Sonata* A (Stutschewsky—CFP 4283).

——. *Sonata* C (Crepax, Zanon—Ric).

——. *Sonata* A (Ticciati—Lengnick).

——. *Sonata* B♭ (Ewerhard, Storck—Schott 1965). 11pp., parts, with basso. Allegro moderato; Grave; Minuetto. M-D.

——. *Sonata* C (Feuillard—Delrieu).

——. *Sonata* c (Ewerhard, Storck—Schott).

——. *Sonata 'L'Imperatrice'* A (C. Speck—Schott CB152 1994) 23pp., parts, including basso. Allegro; Largo; Allegro. Binary forms with conventional realization. The only Boccherini Sonata to carry a descriptive title, probably composed while in the service of Empress Maria Theresa. Easy-to-read edition. Preface in German, English, and French. M-D.

León Boëllmann. *Sonate* Op.40 a (Durand 1897) 45pp., parts. Maestoso; Andante; Allegro molto. Modal influence; sombre Maestoso; Andante shows strong Franck influence; spirited finale. M-D.

René de Boisdeffre. *Berceuse* Op.34 (K 9803). See detailed entry under duos for piano and viola.

Joseph Bodin de Boismortier. *Sonata* Op.26/4 e (H. Ruf—Schott).

——. *Sonata* Op.26/5 g (H. Ruf—Schott).

——. *Sonata* Op.50/3 D (H. Ruf—Br 3963) 13pp., parts. Moderato; Corrente; Aria; Minuetto con Variazioni. Editorial additions have been limited to a minimum and are indicated by small print in brackets. Fine realizations. M-D.

——. *Sonata* G (Deirieu).

——. *Sonata* (Boulay—EMT).

William Bolcom. *Décalage* 1961–62 (Merion 2001) 16pp., parts. 9 min. Marked Con spirito, with humor. Intricate rhythms and the extremes of the instruments are explored in a wide variety of dynamics and touch. Meant to have a humorous quality. M-D.

——. *Capriccio* 1985 (EBM 1993, ISBN 0-7935-4255-3) 34pp., parts. 15 min. Allegro con spirito; Molto allegro; Like a Barcarolle; Gingando (Brazilian tango) Tombeau d'Ernesto Nazareth. "This four-movement work is very much like a sonata in outward form, although the proportions are unusual. There is a Brahms-cum-Milhaud urge behind the piece, including the Brazilian tango at its end, in the tradition of Ernesto Nazareth" (Composer's Note). Preserves the spirit and temperament of the Baroque capriccio with all its drama and glory in a late-20th-century eclectic manner. D.

——. *Sonata* 1989 (EBM 1993, ISBN 0-7935-1238-7) 35pp., parts. 16 min. Allegro inquieto; Adagio semplice; Allegro assai. "This *Sonata*, written for and dedicated to the duo of Yo-Yo Ma, cellist, and Emanuel Ax, pianist, is firmly based on classical and romantic models; it revels in the interplay between older music and modern sensibility, exactly as does the Ax-Ma Duo in my estimation" (Composer's Note). A bold and endearing work requiring careful attention to countless details and the ability to put these and frequently changing rhythmic features into musical expression. Triadic, quartal, and quintet chord structures; octotonic; *pppp* to *fff*. D.

Giovanni Battista Bononcini. *Aria* (CFP 4213).

———. *Sonata* a (H. Ruf—Schott CB101) 11pp., parts. Andante; Allegro; Grazioso (Minuett I & II). Attractive writing that shows why Bononcini, after 1720, was regarded in England, where he lived, as the leading composer next to Alessandro Scarlatti. M-D.

———. *Sonata* A (Schroeder—Augener 5509). With *Andante Cantabile* by Stiasni.

———. *Sonata* a (Salmon—Ric R386).

Siegfried Borris. *Kleine Suite* (Sirius).

———. *Sonate* Op.53 (Sirius).

Will Gay Bottje. *Sonata* 1 (ACA).

———. *Sonata* 2 (ACA).

———. *Sonata* 3 (ACA).

———. *Songs* (ACA).

York Bowen. *Sonata* Op.64 (Schott 1923) 25 min. Traditional form, rhapsodic in character, strong thematic material, full sonorities. D.

Johannes Brahms. *Sonate* Op.38 e (H. Münch-Holland—Henle; Müller, Kraus, Boettcher—VU; Br&H; Becker, Friedberg—Simrock; Klengel—CFP 3897A; Rose—IMC; Van Vliet, Hughes—GS L1411; Crepaz, Lorenzoni—Ric ER2101; K 9110). This work is an "homage to J. S. Bach." Brahms based the main theme of the finale on contrapunctus 13 of the *Kunst der Fuge*. The piano has been placed first by Brahms in the title; it should be a partner and should never assume a purely accompanying role. Somber and heavily saturated with mysticism. D.

———. *Sonata* Op.99 F (H. Münch-Holland—Henle; Müller, Boettcher—VU; Klengel—CFP; Rose—IMC; Becker, Friedberg—Simrock; Crepax, Lorenzoni— Ric ER2102; K 9111). Stern dignity, display studiously avoided, no sentimentality. D.

Darker tone qualities of the cello exploited in both *Sonatas* without overloading the lower register of the piano.

———. *Two Sonatas* with *Two Sonatas* for clarinet and piano (Lea 7).

See Margaret Anne Notley, "Brahms's Chamber-Music Summer of 1886: A Study of Opera 99, 100, 101, and 108," Ph.D. diss., Yale University, 1992.

Cesar Bresgen. *Zweite Sonata* (Litolff 5812 1962) 27pp., parts. Three untitled contrasting movements. Linear, freely tonal with much chromaticism. Requires large span as well as a fine left-hand octave technique. Neoclassic. M-D.

Jean-Baptiste Bréval. *Sonata* C (Schroeder—Augener 5502; Schroeder, Rose— IMC).

——. *Sonata* C (Stutschevsky—Schott).

——. *Sonata* G (Ernst Cahnbley—Schott 1918) 15pp., parts. Over-edited.

——. *Sonata* G (Cassado—IMC).

——. *Sonata* V G (E. Koch, B. Weigart—Schott CB67, 19pp.; A. Moffat—Simrock, 14pp.), parts. Brillante; Adagio; Rondo. Pleasant and fluent. M-D.

——. *Sonata* G (Salmon—Ric R809).

——. *Sonata* (Ric R498).

Frank Bridge. *Sonata* (Bo&H 1918) 23 min. Melody pours over everything; sings and builds to impassioned climaxes. Piano part is mainly improvisational and decorative in nature. D.

Benjamin Britten. *Sonata* Op.65 C (Bo&H 1961) 35pp., parts. 21½ min. Sonata and Suite principles combined although a monothematic basis controls most of the freely tonal 5 movements. Dialogo: SA, adjacent major and minor 2nds are important in thematic elements; 3 contrasting themes derive from opening material and are carefully worked over in the development. Scherzo–Pizzicato: Bartók's influence seen in the plucked timbre, especially in the Trio, where polymodality and minor inversions converge in stretto. Elegia: also uses minor inversion. Marcia: dry humorous march with a Trio; return of march is cleverly disguised. Finale, Moto Perpetuo: monothematic with all material arising from opening idea. D. See Peter Evans, "Britten's Cello Sonata," *Tempo* 58 (summer 1961): 8–16, 18–19; Hugh Wood, "Britten's Latest Scores" (refers to Cello Sonata), MT 103, no. 1429 (March 1962): 164–65.

Earle Brown. *Music for Cello and Piano* 1955 (AMP 1961) 15pp. Two copies needed for performance. Uses "time-notation" to represent sound relationships, independent of a strict pulse or metric system. "The durations are extended visibly through their complete space-time of sounding and are precise relative to the space-time of the score. It is expected that the performer will observe as closely as possible the 'apparent' relationships of sound and silence but act without hesitation on the basis of his perceptions . . . The vertical correspondences between instruments are composed relative to a concept of event-time flexibility. In performance it is best that each performer execute his own part as faithfully as possible relative to the notated time but not relative to the other part, and the correspondences will occur as intended" (from the Prefatory Note). Contains other performance directions. Piano techniques include plucking and damping strings, use of mallet to strike strings, as well as normal techniques. Avant-garde. D.

Max Bruch. *Adagio: On Celtic Melodies* Op.56 1891 (Simrock 5167 1930) 8pp., parts. Pensive melody introduced by piano is assumed by cello and developed in a passively expressive manner. Full chordal writing for piano to imitate original score for orchestra. M-D.

———. *Four Pieces* Op.70 1896 (Simrock 5168 1896) 16pp., parts. Aria; Finnish; Dance (Swedish); Scottish. Lyrical and richly harmonic in late-19th-century style with nationalist flavor. Pieces can be performed separately. M-D.

Victor Bruns. *Sonate* Op.35 1958 (Br&H 7531 1984) 40pp., parts. Allegro animato: SA; marchlike character; modal qualities; *pp* ending. Andante tranquillo: alternating $\frac{4}{4}$, $\frac{3}{4}$ meters; ternary; touches of bitonality. Allegretto grazioso: $\frac{7}{8}$; lyric, with snappy and contrasting rhythms; *ff* conclusion. Mildly 20th-century. D.

Gavin Bryars. *The South Downs* 1995 (Schott 12588 1996) 15pp., parts. 15 min. Minimalist with extensive arpeggiation and tremolo. A lyric melody emerges in the middle section as a contrast to the constant flow of the outer sections. Sonorous with dynamics ranging from only *mp* to *pppp* and occasional pizzicati at *mf*. M-D.

Willy Burkhard. *Sonate* Op.87 (Br 2685 1954) 24pp., parts. Introduzione; Scherzo Notturno; Finale. Octotonic, chromatic figures and scales, broken octaves, cello cadenza near conclusion of Introduzione. Second movement alternates moods and tempos; tremolo; Neoclassic; large span required. M-D to D.

Ferruccio Busoni. *Drei Stücke* (J. Draheim—Br&H EB8712 2000, ISMN M-004-18100-3) 38pp., parts. Contains: *Märchen* 1879 BV123; *Serenata* Op.34 BV196; *Kultaselle* (Variations on a Finnish Song) BV237. Of these 3 early works, Busoni revered *Kultaselle* throughout his life. It was composed while he was Professor of Piano at the Helsinki Conservatory and is a "dazzlingly virtuoso, succinctly cast and atmospherically dense variation cycle . . . imbued with a severe reserve that is far removed from all Scandinavian folkloristic romanticism" (from Preface). Excellent notes in German and English. *Kultaselle* is available separately. M-D.

———. Serenata Op.34 B♭ 1883 (Faber Music 1999, ISBN 0-571-51853-2) 12pp., parts. "Busoni's *Serenata* is therefore aptly titled with its singing cello line and discreet accompaniment in the calmer outer sections, and the chromatic central section features an oddly turbulent 'cantando', flanked by fanfares and briskly arpeggiated piano chords imitating a guitar. It is beautifully written for the cello, demanding tenderness, charm and the occasional spark of virtuosity, whilst the pianist is a sympathetic listener but at times even cheekier and more light-hearted than his partner" (from Introduction). M-D.

————. *Kleine Suite* Op.23 1886 (Br&H; Kahnt) 16½ min. Charming, combines graceful rococo spirit with mildly 20th-century harmonies.

Dietrich Buxtehude. *Sonata* D (F. Längin—Schott CB83) 7pp., parts. The only existing work by Buxtehude for a single stringed instrument with basso continuo. "Stylistically and formally this sonata is unparalleled in 17th century viola da gamba music" (from Postscript in score). The original manuscript contains no phrasing or tempo indications except "Allegro" (second movement, bar 44) and "Adagio" (bar 51). Written in a fast-slow-fast design. M-D.

Louis de Caix d'Hervelois. *Pièces de Viole avec Clavecin* (A. Chapuis—Durand) 2 vols. Has a part for cello and for viola. Vol.I: La Milanaise; Sarabande; Gavotte en Rondeau; L'Inconstant; La Gracieuse; Menuet I & II; Gavotte I & II. Vol.II: Les Petits Doigts; Sarabande; Menuet; La Napolitaine; Gavotte; Gigue; La Venitienne. Delightful character pieces, musical realizations. M-D.

————. *Sonata* a (Moffat—Simrock; Salmon—Ric R398).

————. *Suite* I A (Schroeder, Rapp—Schott) 12pp., parts. La Milanese; Sarabande; Menuett; L'Agreable; Gavotte. M-D.

————. *Suite* II D (Feuillard—Deirieu; K 9113).

————. *Suite* d (Kozalupova—USSR).

————. *Suite* (Béon—Costallat). For gamba or cello and keyboard.

————. *Trois Pièces* (Hamelle).

Andrea Caporale. *Sonata* d (J. Salmon—Ric R387) 12pp., parts. Largo amoroso; Allegro; Adagio motto espressivo; Allegro spiritoso. Over-edited. M-D.

————. *Sonata* d (Schott).

David Carlson. *Sonata* 1992 (TP 114-40742 1994) 37pp., parts. In one continuous movement of 485 measures with distinctive sections. Tonally conceived with a preference for developing rhythmic figures individually before moving on to the next. Contrasts lyric, expressive qualities with daring, bold statements. Large span required. D.

Elliott Carter. *Sonata* 1948 (SPAM 1953) 48pp., parts. 20 min. Corrected edition 1966. Moderato; Vivace, motto leggiero; Adagio; Allegro. Unusual time signatures such as $\frac{21}{32}$. This is Carter's first work to make extensive use of metrical modulation, an extremely flexible and subtle structuring of the time element. A Neoclassic formal framework is still present, but the rhythmic emphasis opens new directions. A strong work with ringing sonorities and possibly one of the most important compositions in the cello and piano repertoire. D.

See W. Glock, "A Note on Elliott Carter" (refers to the cello *Sonata* and *String Quartet I*), *The Score* 12 (June 1955).

Robert Casadesus. *Sonate* Op.22 1935–36 (Sal 1947). Lyrical, passionate, well-crafted in line, form, and texture. French neo-Romantic style. Brilliant virtuoso writing for the piano, great diversity of feeling. Cello is used melodically with the piano never overpowering. Allegro moderato: Dorian mode on c, diatonic Chopinesque figuration in piano, Aeolian on g for second subject. Scherzo: 2 subjects with one exclusively for the piano, gentle Trio, free paraphrase in recapitulation. Motto adagio: not a complete movement, fugal entries, ostinato figures; fades away on an inconclusive inverted dominant 11th and leads directly to the Allegro non troppo: C, a hybrid of SA and rondo; mysterious and exciting figuration in piano varied 6 times; bitonal hints; inverted 11th and 13th chords; closes brilliantly. M-D to D.

Alfredo Casella. *Sonata* C (UE 1927) Four movements in 2, each consisting of a slow section followed by a fast section. Preludio; Bourrée; Largo; Rondo quasi giga. Neoclassic style, clear tonal centers but with frequent diatonic harmonies overlapped. M-D.

Gaspar Cassadó. *Sonata nello stile antico spagnuolo* 1925 (UE 7931). 13½ min. Introduzione e Allegro: Warmly romanticized introduction yields to a spry Allegro packed with curiosities of melodic and harmonic invention. Grave: Dark, foreboding homophonic setting maintains a collective air of charm in spite of its title. Danza con Variazioni: Delightful dance takes on a playful character in several variations but ends surprisingly sentimentally and quietly. M-D.
———. *Sonate* a (Mathot) 22 min. Rapsodia; Arogonesa; Saeta; Paso-doble. A thorough work engaging both instruments in programmatic movements. Rapsodia is the longest, but the most unique is Saeta, a name which "literally translates as 'arrow' but here it represents a devotional song by that name— sung in Seville each year during Holy Week. Nightly processions carry floats depicting the scenes and sorrows of the Passion. At various points the processions halt for the singing of a Saeta from a balcony or window. The fervor and intensity of the occasion is beautifully captured by Cassadó in his own Saeta" (Thaddeus Brys, "Program Notes," *Music for Cello by Cassadó,* Thaddeus Brys, cello, Susan Brys, piano, Centaur 2381 1998, p.4). The nationalistic flavor of Cassadó's native Spain is unmistakable. M-D.
———. *La Pendule, La Fileuse et Le Galant* 1925 (UE).
———. *Sérénade* 1925 (UE).
———. *Lamente de Boabdil* 1931 (Schott).
———. *Requiebros* D 1931 (Schott 1562 1959, ISMN M-001-03375-6) 11pp., parts. 4½ min. A dramatic tour de force for the cellist with attractive writing for piano. Dedicated to Casals, who altered the key of the middle section from e to g, a change which has become common practice today. D.
———. *Partita* 1935 (Schott).
———. *Danse du diable vert* 1936 (UE).

Joaquin Cassadó. *Tres Composiciones* (UME 23760). 7 min. Serenata Española; Lo Fluviol, el Titil y l'Escarbat (The Brook, the Little Bird, and the Junebug);

Complanta. Picturesque pieces revealing a Spanish Romanticism of grace and elegance. May be performed separately but works best as a group. M-D.

Mario Castelnuovo-Tedesco. *I Nottambuli* 1927 (UE 8992) Variazioni Fantastiche. 28pp., parts. Preambolo and 5 long and contrasted complex variations. Colorful sonorities requiring advanced players for both parts. D.

———. *Sonata* E (Forlivesi 1929).

Giacomo Cervetto. *Sonata* Op.2/10 D (H.Ruf—Schott 1999, ISMN M-001-12139-2) 15pp., parts, including basso. Adagio: lyrical; dotted rhythms. Allegro: imitative; rounded binary with coda. Minuet: graceful; elegant, without excess. Clever figured-bass realization. Preface in English, German, and French. M-D.

———. *Two Sonatas* (Schroeder, Rapp—Schott).

———. *Sonata* C (Salmon—Ric R95).

———. *Sonata* G (Salmon—Ric 388).

Charles W. Chadwick. *Romanza* a (MMP) 4pp., parts. Ternary form with a charming Andantino contrasted by an Allegretto in the tempo of a Menuetto. Int. but requires full chord capabilities.

Carlos Chávez. *Madrigal* 1921 (M. Lifchitz—Carlanita 1983; Lifchitz—GS) 5pp., parts. Commences with a methodical Lento and a persuasive melody of sighs and repeated notes in step motion. Developed with colorful harmony and gradual animation into a *ff* ending. M-D.

———. *Sonatina* 1924 (Belwin-Mills).

Frédéric Chopin. *Grand Duo Concertant on Themes from Meyerbeer's Robert le Diable* composed with Auguste Franchomme E 1832 (PWM, *Complete Works,* Vol.XVI; Mikuli—K&S).

———. *Introduction et Polonaise Brillante* Op.3 C 1829–30 (PWM, *Complete Works,* Vol.XVI; Feuermann, Rose—IMC; Gendron—Schott; Graudan—GS L1803; Franchomme—Augener 7669; CFP, published with *Sonata* Op.65; Mikuli —K&S). 8½ min.

———. *Sonata* Op.65 g 1845–47 (E. Zimmermann, K. Schilde, C. Kanngiesser— Henle 495 1997; PWM, *Complete Works,* Vol.XVI; Pierre Fournier—IMC: Schulz—GS L64; Balakirew—CFP, published with *Polonaise Brillante* Op.3; Mikuli—K&S). 25 min. Allegro moderato; Scherzo; Largo; Finale–Allegro. For experts only. D.

See W. D. Sutcliffe, "Chopin's Counterpoint: The *Largo* from the *Cello Sonata, Opus 65,*" MQ 83 (spring 1999): 114–33.

Tichon Nikolajewitsch Chrennikow. *Sonate* Op.34 (CFP 8677 1991) 40pp., parts. Andantino maestoso; Andante molto espressivo; Allegro con fuoco. Packed with dramatic quality and a fondness for sudden shifts of harmony. Percussive, wide skips, scalar, and arpeggiated figures. Finale embodies a sportive character as it romps to the finish at *ff*. D.

Francesco Cilèa. *Sonata* Op.38 D (EC).
———. *3 Pezzi* (Ric 127934).

Rebecca Clark. *Passacaglia on an Old English Tune* (GS 4111 1943).
———. *Sonata* 1919 (JWC 1921; Da Capo 1986).
See detailed entry under duos for piano and viola.

Dinos Constantinides. *Sonata.* See detailed entry under duos for piano and viola.

Frederick Shepherd Converse. *Sonata* 1922 (IU) 42pp., parts. Adagio. Allegro giojoso: numerous changes of tempo and mood in this movement. Post-Romantic writing with ideas that are well developed but a little old-fashioned sounding today. M-D.

Arnold Cooke. *Sonata* 1941 (Nov 1960) 59pp., parts. 26½ min. Andante poco sostenuto–Allegro; Lento; Scherzo; Rondo. Accessible writing that displays an unfailing craft throughout. Mildly contemporary approach to tonality, clear lines, good sense of thematic symmetry and balance. M-D.

Aaron Copland. *Poème* (Bo&H 1993), parts. Reproduced from holograph.
———. *Lament* (Bo&H 1993). Reproduced from holograph.

Henry Cowell. *Sonata* ca.1915 (J. Krosnick, G. Kalish—Columbia University Press 1989) 24pp., parts. Allegro maestoso; Moderato espressivo; Larghetto maestoso. A largely conventional work based on harmonic principles of the past composed before Cowell began his musical experiments. Following its premiere, with Cowell at the piano, the work disappeared and was rediscovered by cellist Joel Krosnick after the composer's death. M-D.
———. *Four Declamations with Return* (CFE; AMP 7772).
———. *Hymn and Fuguing Tune* IX (AMP 1960) 11pp., parts. 6 min. Chordal Hymn, contrapuntal Fuguing Tune, freely tonal. Thin textures in Fuguing Tune to the coda, which becomes chordal. M-D.

Paul Creston. *Homage* Op.41 1947 (GS) 3 min.
———. *Suite* Op.66 1956 (GS) 16 min.

César Cui. *Orientale* Op.50/9 (E. Kurtz—IMC 3236 1989) 4pp., parts. 2½ min. From *Kaleidoscope* for violin and piano. M-D.

Carl Czerny. *Introduction Variations Concertantes* Op.248 1831 (F.-G. Hölÿ—Kunzelmann 589 1999) 34pp., parts. For horn or cello. See detailed entry under duos for piano and horn.

Noel Da Costa. *Five Verses with Vamps* (King's Crown 1976) 8pp. Requires 2 copies. Short colorful pieces packed with rhythmic energy. M-D.

Ingolf Dahl. *Duo* 1946 (J. Boonin) 25pp., parts. 17 min. Fantasia in Modo d'un Recitativo: complex rhythms, chromatic and freely tonal, varied tempos; concludes in C; requires large span. Capriccio: vigorous rhythms; free, dissonant counterpoint; 2 key signatures alternate. Corale: syncopated chords; cello line embellishes piano chorale; harmonized in unusual sonorities; *ppp* conclusion. D.

——. *Notturno* 1946 (J. Boonin) 9pp., parts. Originally the second movement of the *Duo* listed above. Short cello introduction leads immediately to vigorous but quiet repeated chords in $\frac{3}{8}$ $\frac{2}{8}$; chords become more chromatic and intense. Other sections have individual moods and tempos, including a highly embellished part. Uncompromising writing in a convincing but dissonant and polyphonic style. Requires large span. D.

Jean-Michel Damase. *Pavane Variée* (Lemoine 1956) 7pp., parts, also transcribed for horn. Slight hint of dance character in a melodic context defined primarily by diatonic steps and triads. Piano contrasts with intricate writing in an Andante setting that thickens in texture. Uses octave leaps in chord formations. Picturesque with colorful harmony. Ends *pp* on an added-note chord with dance step tapped out in low registers of the piano. M-D.

Franz Danzi. *Sonata* Op.62 F (K. Janetzky—Hofmeister 7336) 60pp., parts. For basset horn or cello. Larghetto–Allegretto; Larghetto sostenuto; Allegretto. Flowing melodies, fluent instrumental writing, more Classical than Romantic characteristics, traditional pianistic idioms. M-D.

Thomas Christian David. *Sonata* (Dob 1970) 40pp., parts. Energetic first movement (Beethoven inspired). Serious and somewhat tedious Andante. Finale alternates an Andante with a whimsical Vivace. An Allegro di molto coda concludes. Errors noted in clef changes and accidentals. Neoclassic. Athleticism required of both performers. D.

Claude Debussy. *Intermezzo* c (Piatigorsky—EV 1944). An early work in a broadly melancholy ABA form. Not Impressionist but well constructed and full of rich and opulent sonorities. M-D.

——. *Sonata* d 1915 (Durand 1915; P. Fournier—IMC 1997; E.-G. Heinemann, F. Lesure, R. Ginzel, K. Schilde—Henle 633 1998) 15pp., parts. 11 min. Prologue–Lent: centers around d; piano opens with straightforward statement; leads to a Poco animando section that is more sustained and uses parallel chords; gradually tempo and mood intensify and arrive at a climax before receding to a *ppp* D major close. Sérénade: light; has a seamless sense of unity about it; staccato with tempo changes; leads directly to the Finale–Animé: profuse triplet figuration; changes in tempo and mood. Even though this piece does not hold

together well, it is tersely crafted and the sonorities are fascinating. It is as
though Debussy is searching for a partially new style. Demanding writing. D.
See T. King, "A New Look at Debussy's *Cello Sonata*," *American String Teacher*
37/3 (1987): 38–40; S. Hong, "A Stylistic Analysis and Technical Consideration
of Debussy's *Sonata for Cello and Piano*," D.M.A. diss., City University of New
York, 2002.

Frederick Delius. *Sonata* (Bo&H 1919) 12½ min. One movement organized in a
3-part structure. Seems to be a more perfect piece than the Violin Sonatas.
Short, rhapsodic, melodious, and yearning. Geared more to a cantabile style
rather than to pyrotechnics. The 2 instruments are completely integrated. M-D.
See Julian Lloyd Webber, "Delius and the Cello," M&M (June 24, 1976): 22–23.

Norman Dello Joio. *Duo Concertato* (GS 1949) 10pp. parts. Slow introduction
and epilogue with a fast main section. Lyric, well written for both instruments,
clear textures, light harmonies. M-D.

Michael Denhoff. *Trace d'Etoile: Hommage à Wercollier* Op.87 1999 (Gravis EG
721 2000) 17pp., parts. 12 min. A broad, one-movement design at a slow tempo
with shifting meters. Preface gives performance suggestions. Dynamics are
primarily *pp* to *pppp* with only occasional moments over *mf.* M-D.

Edisson Vasil'evich Denisov. *Drei Stücke* 1967 (UE 19057 1992) 8pp., parts. 6½
min. Lento; Allegro; Lento. Displays similar qualities as the *Sonata,* only in
shorter, condensed forms. Extremes of instruments are exploited, often at very
soft dynamics. M-D.
——. *Sonata* 1971 (CFP 5746 1973) 16pp., parts. Recitativo: pointillistic; proportional rhythmic relationships; upper register exploited; grace-note chords;
requires large span. Toccata: chromatic 16th-note figures, chordal punctuation,
changing meters, bold gestures, freely dissonant. D.
——. *Variations on a Theme by Schubert* 1986 (Sikorski 1820 1988) 22p., parts.
Based upon the *Impromptu,* Op.142/2. Variations are developed continuously
without pause or designation. Straightforward writing, at once Schubertian,
then mildly 20th-century. Proportional rhythmic relationships provide the only
significant challenge. Barely hints at later 20th-century techniques heard in
Denisov's other cello and piano literature. M-D.
——. *Suite* 1995 (Leduc 1995) 19pp., parts. 9 min. Prélude; Menuet; Aria; Fugue.
More challenging for cellist with rapid arpeggiation and double stops. Harmonies built on tertian structures with occasional added notes and coloristic
treatment. Of special interest is the fugue, built upon a subject of half notes
which is developed and passed between instruments. M-D.

David Diamond. *Sonata* 1938 (TP) 36pp., parts. Tempo giusto e maestoso: develops emphatically; soaring melody; piano provides florid counterpoint. Lento
assai: a chant evolves into a decorative cantillation and is then followed by a

complex rhythmic section. Andante con grand espressione: a lyric interlude. Epilogo–Allegretto: a rhythmic jig. D.

———. *Sonata* II 1987 (Southern Music Publishing 1993) 26pp., parts. Allegro moderato: delicate and graceful; emphasizes sonority of both instruments; straightforward rhythms; frequent tempo changes; quadruple stops. Adagio cantabile: lyric, with much pathos; chordal with moving parts. Deciso: dance-like qualities; thematic ideas exchanged between instruments; concludes with race to finish. Some tricky elements here but deserves to be better known. M-D to D.

Hilda Dianda. *Estructuras* 1960 (PAU 1965) 18pp., 2 scores necessary. 12½ min. I. Andante, II. Andante, III. Untitled. Numerous directions for both perform-ers, e.g., strike the strings with the edge and/or palm of the hand, pluck strings with fingernails, harmonics, clusters. Avant-garde, pointillistic, meter change on almost every measure. D.

Josef Dichler. *Variationen über einen Song von Stephen Foster* 1964 (Dob) 27pp., parts. Four variations and Finale based on the tune "Swanee River." Refer-ences to the *New World Symphony* appear from time to time. A fun piece. M-D.

Martin Doernberg. *Variations* (Vieweg 6137 1974) 11pp., parts. No separation be-tween variations, serial influence, pointillistic, Expressionist, sparse textures, Webernesque. D.

Ernö Dohnányi. *Sonata* Op.8 B♭ (Schott; IMC; K 3378) 25 min.

Josef Friedrich Doppelbauer. *Sonata* I 1952 (Dob 1964) 23pp., parts. Fantasie: low octaves, large chords, dramatic, more chromatic second tonal area, rest-ful closing. Rondo: rhythmic drive, octotonic, choralelike episode, freely tonal around g. Fuga: restful and lyric; unfolds logically; coda is similar to opening of Fantasie; *pp* and relaxed closing. M-D.

Felix Draeseke. *Sämtliche Kompositionen* (W. Müller-Steinbach—Wollenweber WW302 2000) 59pp., parts. *Sonate* Op.51 D: Allegro moderato; Largo, molto espressivo; Finale–Allegro vivace, con fuoco. *Ballade* Op.7: a ternary slow-fast-slow form of richly expressive qualities. *Barcarole* Op.11: reflects its character designation in Lento tempo and meter. Full harmonic chords and lyric melo-dies predominate these works in a mid-19th-century style. M-D.

Johannes Driessler. *Fantasie* Op.24/2 (Br 2696 1953) 10pp., parts. Chordal open-ing; moves to chords in alternating hands; ostinato-like figuration; freely tonal; meter changes at formal sections. Requires large span. M-D.

———. *Sonate* Op.41/2 1959 (Br 3968) 22pp., parts. Sostenuto ma con brio; Ada-gio maestoso; Allegro vivace. Freely tonal, sudden dynamic changes, free dis-sonant counterpoint, octotonic, Neoclassic. Facile octave technique needed in finale. Requires large span. M-D to D.

Marcel Dupré. *Suite* Op.21 e (Heugel 1912) 25pp., parts. I. Meditation, II. Appassionato, III. Ganzonetta, IV. Final. Also exists in transcriptions for violin and piano, and cello and orchestra.

———. *Sonate* Op.80 (Heugel 1907) 49pp., parts. I. Allegro moderato, II. Andante con moto, III. Allegro vivace.

Antonín Dvořák. *Rondo* Op.94 g 1891 (M. Pospíšil, K. Schilde, R. Ginzel—Henle 698 2002, ISMN M-2018-0698-3) 16pp., parts. Originally for piano and cello, later orchestrated. Commences with a cheerful rondo theme in the cello at Allegretto grazioso and maintains the character with each repetition. A contrasting middle section in G at Allegro vivo hurries the work along with technical material testing the skill of both musicians. Finishes gracefully in an accelerando at *ppp*. Deserves to be better known. M-D.

———. *Waldesruhe* Op.68/5 D♭ 1884 (M. Pospíšil, K. Schilde, R. Ginzel—Henle 621 1999) 5pp., parts. Originally for piano, 4 hands, Dvořák arranged it for the present instrumentation and later orchestrated the piano part. A lyric work marked Lento e molto cantabile offering much expressiveness. M-D.
Both Henle scores contain detailed information regarding Dvořák's stormy relationship with Simrock and errors in the first publications.

Petr Eben. *Suita Balladica* (Artia 1957) 25 min. Introduzione e danza; Quazi mazurka; Elegia; Toccata.

Horst Ebenhöh. *Sonatina* Op.17/1 (Dob 1973) 13pp., parts. Molto vivace; Andante moderato; Allegro. Thin textures, rhythmic treatment varied, melodic poverty, freely tonal. M-D.

———. *Stücke* Op.17/2 (Dob 1973) 8pp., parts. Avant-garde extensions of technique. D.

George Enescu. *Sonata* I Op.26/1 f/F 1898 (C. L. Firca—Muzeul George Enescu ca.1988) 75pp., parts. Composed at the age of 17 under strong Brahmsian influence. Allegro molto moderato: SA; octotonic; 3 with 2; sweeping arpeggiation. Allegretto scherzando: $\frac{3}{8}$; scalar; 3rds; rhythmic influence of Scherzos in Beethoven's *5th Symphony* and Schubert's *8th* apparent. Molto andante: $\frac{12}{8}$; espressivo; repeated chords; quintuple tremolos; mixed meters within hands (e.g., mm. 65ff. have $\frac{4}{4}$ for top voice of each hand and $\frac{12}{8}$ for lower voice). Presto: $\frac{2}{2}$; cyclic ideas; imitation; octaves; 3rds; *ffff* finish. Detailed critical commentary in Romanian and French showing influences upon the young composer, his use of cyclic principles, and the use of rhythmic ostinatos in diminution and augmentation throughout the work. D.

———. *Nocturne et Saltarello* 1897 (S. Sensbach—Schott CB168 2000, ISMN M-001-12655-6) 19pp., parts. In separate movements, these recently discovered pieces reveal a youthful composer using strong lyricism and conventional harmonies with imagination and nerve. M-D.

———. *Sonate* II 1935 (Sal).

Lehman Engel. *Sonata* (SPAM 1948) 33pp., parts. Allegro ma non troppo; Andante misterioso; Allegro giocoso; Vivace. Dramatic gestures (fast running scale passages followed by sudden stops, repeated syncopated full chords in low register, etc.), clear ideas and textures. Deserves more performances. M-D.

Rudolf Escher. *Sonata* (Symphonia ST371).

——. *Sonate Concertante* Op.7 1943 (Alsbach 1947) 23 min.

Manuel de Falla. *Tres Obras* (M. Zanetti—Falla 1994) 23pp., parts. Three short works from the late 1890s. *Melodía* (1897): simple melody and chordal structures with facile writing at Andantino. *Romanza* (ca.1898): similar characteristics as *Melodía,* only more developed through repeated chords and arpeggios. [*Pieza en Do Mayor*] (ca.1898): facile piano writing with greater involvement in the cello at Molto vivo. These are charming pieces suitable for use in almost any setting. Revision notes and Prologue in Spanish. Int. to M-D.

Ferenc Farkas. *Sonatina Based on a Hungarian Folk Song* 1955 (Artia) 11pp., parts for double bass, bassoon, or cello. Allegro moderato; Andante espressivo; Allegro. Sparkling, attractive tunes cleverly worked out. A delight for performers and audience. M-D.

Renato Fasano. *Sonatina* 1942 (SZ 4099 1946) 19pp., parts. In one continuous movement comprised of numerous sections. Restless, with greater emphasis upon rhythm. Early-20th-century writing requiring skilled performers. M-D.

Johann Friedrich Fasch. *Sonata* C (J. Wojciechowski—CFP 5893) 12pp., parts. For bassoon (cello) and basso continuo; second cello part ad lib. See detailed entry under duos for piano and bassoon.

Gabriel Fauré. *Sonata* I Op.109 d 1918 (Durand; MMP) 19½ min. Allegro; Andante; Final–Allegro commodo. Shifting, irresolute harmonies; overlapping and uneven phrases; unpredictable rhythms. Piano and cello constantly echo and contrast with each other. M-D.

——. *Sonata* II Op.117 g 1921 (Durand) 36pp., parts. 18 min. Allegro: Fauré fuses the development and recapitulation in an unusual manner; this movement contains some ingenious melodic writing coupled with filigree harmonies. Adagio: an elegy; presents one theme after another with no transition; sustained lyricism. Allegro vivace: a persistent 3-bar rhythm, which in reality makes a $\frac{3}{4}$, gives a rich and warm effect; imitation, complex figuration, and syncopation build to triumphant conclusion. D.

Both *Sonatas* are a mixture of nostalgia and beauty.

——. *Elégie* Op.24; *Sicilienne* Op.78 (R. Howat—CFP 7385 1994; K 3485, 4431) 19pp., parts. The beautiful *Elégie* (1880) was originally for cello and piano, and only later orchestrated. By contrast the *Sicilienne* (1893) existed in several versions before Fauré transcribed it for cello and piano. "Cellist[s] may note in both pieces how carefully Fauré indicates phrasing in terms of bowing, an aspect previously obscured by the inaccuracy of the original editions" (from Preface). *Elegy* is also published by IMC. M-D.

Jindřich Feld. *Due Composizioni* (Panton).

——. *Sonate* (Schott 1972) 36pp., parts. Strongly contrasted materials. Plenty of technical difficulties for both players. Allegro agitato: lyric theme in dotted rhythms contrasts with an agitated theme; each is manipulated but not truly developed. Lento: ternary design; middle section recalls second subject from first movement. Allegro con brio: a moto perpetuo with a lyric theme appearing as a second subject. D.

Morton Feldman. *Durations 2* (CFP 1961) 1p. All pitches are in 8th notes. "The first sound with both instruments simultaneously. The duration of each sound is chosen by the performer. All beats are slow. Sounds should be played with a minimum of attack. Dynamics are very low" (from score). Score is photocopy of MS. Int.

Willem de Fesch. *Six Sonatas* Op.8 (W. Schultz—CFP 4989) Second cello ad lib. 31pp., parts. I D, II B♭, III d, IV C, V g, VI G. Excellent keyboard realizations by Eberhard Wenzel. Short colorful multimovements that display clarity in harmonic and contrapuntal writing. Contains some Style Galant characteristics. M-D. Available separately: III d (Ruf—Müller); IV C (Koch, Weigart—Schott); VI G (Koch, Weigart—Schott).

——. *Sonata* Op.13/1 D (Koch, Weigart—Schott).
——. *Sonata* Op.13/3 A (Koch, Weigart—Schott).
——. *Sonata* Op.13/4 d (Koch, Weigart—Schott).
——. *Sonata* Op.13/5 D (Koch, Weigart—Schott 1964) 8pp., parts. Siciliana; Allemanda; Minuetto I, II.
——. *Sonata* Op.13/6 a (Koch, Weigart—Schott).
——. *Sonata* d (Moffat—Schott).
——. *Sonata* F (Moffat—Simrock).
——. *Sonata* G (Salmon—Ric).

Ross Lee Finney. *Chromatic Fantasy* E (CFP).

——. *Sonata II* C (Valley Music Press 1953) 23pp., parts.

William Flackton. *Three Sonatas* from Op.2 (R. Sabatini—Dob 1962) Available separately: I C, 8pp., parts; II B♭; III F 8pp., parts. Three other Sonatas in Op.2 are for tenor violin and keyboard. Flackton points out in his Preface that he composed the "Solos" with the intention of activating the tenor violin. All are M-D.

Wolfgang Fortner. *Sonata* (Schott 1949) 21pp., parts. 17 min. Formally experimental. The first movement is a strange 2-part design with a complete Sonata followed by a scherzo-like episode; further development of the Sonata midsection is finally concluded with a restatement of the opening idea. The second movement is an ABA scherzo. First 2 movements make great use of ostinato-like progressions. The third movement—a Ballata: Variations on a theme of Guillaume de Machaut—makes harmonic references to the first 2 movements. M-D to D.

————. *Zyklus* 1964 (Schott) 21pp., parts. Mouvements; Variations; Etude; Prelude–Contrepoint–Epilogue. Serial, highly pointillistic, Expressionist. This work hops around all over the keyboard, almost constantly. D.

John Herbert Foulds. *Sonata* Op.6 1905 (Senart 1928). A startlingly impressive piece with virtuoso writing for both instruments. Expansive, late-Romantic idiom with rich figuration, Rachmaninoff-like melodic treatment, and daring harmonies that owe something to Debussy, Richard Strauss, and Mahler. Diatonic dissonance and huge pile-up of 3rds resemble Britten a little. D.

Auguste Joseph Franchomme. *Variations* Op.3 F (H. Best—Hofmeister FH2778 2001, ISMN M-2034-2778-9) 15pp., parts. Introduction, theme, and 5 variations. This early work by the composer shows the influence of Romanticism within a classically conceived context. Theme and variations are in binary form. M-D.

————. *Variations* Op.4 G (H. Best—Hofmeister FH 2774 2000, ISMN M-2034-2774-2) 15pp., parts. A Maestoso introduction with full chords leads to a theme in binary form and 4 variations with closing section. Similar to Op.3 except more daring and challenging for cellist. M-D.
Both scores contain Forewords in German.

César Franck. *Sonata* A 1886 (Hamelle). See detailed entry under duos for piano and violin.

Benjamin Frankel. *Sonata* Op.13 (Augener) 17 min. Sombre, distinctive harmonic style. D.

————. *Inventions in Major-Minor Modes* Op.31 (JWC 951 1960) 40pp., parts. 1. Moderato, 2. Allegro Fugato, 3. Andantino, 4. Appassionato, 5. Allegretto, 6. Improvisato, 7. Allegro Moderato, 8. Andante. Eight contrasting pieces that combine serial technique with Romantic expressiveness. Atonal chordal and broken octave figures. Major or minor per se are never felt except perhaps in a passing moment or at final cadences. Large span required. M-D.

Peter Racine Fricker. *Sonata* Op.28 (Schott 1957) 16 min. Four movements of well-wrought serious writing. Strong Schoenberg influence apparent. D.

Robert Fuchs. *Sonata* II Op.83 e♭ 1908 (UWKR 21 1973) 25pp., parts. Preface in German by Alfons Ott. Allegro moderato assai; Adagio con sentiments; Allegro vivace. Written in a Brahmsian style. Secure craft, fresh melodies. M-D.

Blas Galindo. *Sonata* (EMM 1962) 34pp., parts. Allegro; Lento; Allegro. Neoclassic, clear lines and phrases, lean textures, some hemiola treatment. M-D.

Johann Ernst Galliard. *Six Sonatas* 1726 (J. Marx, Weiss, Mann—McGinnis & Marx 1946) 2 vols. 1 a, 2 G, 3 F, 4 e, 5 d, 6 C.

——. *Sonata* a (Moffat, Whitehouse—Simrock).

——. *Sonata* e (Salmon—Ric R393).

——. *Sonata* IV e (Moffat—Schott 1911) 7pp., parts. Adagio; Allegro; Allemanda; Sarabanda; Corrente. Over-edited. M-D.

——. *Sonata* III F (Moffat—Simrock).

——. *Sonata* G (Ruf—Br 3964).

——. *Sonata* G (Salmon—Ric R392).

Janina Garścia. *Miniatures* Op.45 (PWM 7173 1971, ISBN 83-224-1860-4) 20pp., parts. For cello or double bass. A Dream; An Excursion; A Woodland Bird; Evening Song; Dance; Morning; In the Meadow; Bolero. Playful, childlike pieces of 2–3 pages each. May be played separately or in combinations. Int. to M-D.

Francesco Geminiani. *Six Sonatas* Op.5 1739 (CFP 9033) Second cello ad lib. Available separately: Sonata Op.5/2 d (Merrick, James—Schott); Sonata 5/6 a (Merrick, James—Schott).

——. *Sonata* C (Salmon—Ric R705).

——. *Sonata* G (Salmon—Ric R705).

Harald Genzmer. *Sonata* I 1953 (Schott 4603). M-D.

——. *Sonatine* 1967 (CFP 5943) 19pp., parts. 11 min. Allegro: SA, octotonic, freely tonal around D. Adagio: thicker textures, dotted rhythms, chromatic. Rondo: secco style, 7th chords, bitonal, changing meters, moves over keyboard; Neoclassic. M-D.

Roberto Gerhard. *Sonata* (OUP 1972) 30pp., parts. Three movements. Spanish rhythms and turns of phrases are evident. Much interplay between the instruments. Energetic opening movement. Slow movement displays versatile melodic writing, including exciting melismas. Finale evokes guitar and castanet sounds in an exuberant dance. D.

Miriam Gideon. *Fantasy on a Javanese Motive* (CFE).

——. *Sonata* (CFE).

Walter Gieseking. *Konzert Sonatine* (Oertel Jo8428 1948) 19pp., parts. Moderato; Presto. Freely tonal but centers around C. Prestissimo concluding coda. Effective pianistic writing. M-D.

Alberto Ginastera. *Pampeana* II "Rhapsody for Violincello and Piano" 1950 (Barry 1951, corrected ed. Bo&H 1994) 12pp., parts. 9 min. Three large sections, each displaying its own mood. Quartal harmonies predominate; full and complex texture; thematic ideas well unified. First 2 sections (Ricercare and Toccata) are somewhat fantasy-like, with cadenza passages, while the final section is more like a rondo with strong contrasting sections. Some frantic rhythms add color. The conclusion, full of heavy textures with added-note chords, is similar to the composer's *Piano Sonata*. D.

Aurelio Giorni. *Sonata* d 1917, rev.1924 (SPAM 1925) 43pp., parts. For cello or viola. Allegro con fuoco; Allegretto; Scherzo–Presto; Introduzione–Allegro–Allegro vivace. Large chordal structures and forms suggesting the influence of Brahms and MacDowell. M-D.

Reinhold Glière. *12 Album Leaves* Op.51 (Bo&H 1951) 45pp., parts. Untitled pieces, each displaying lyric qualities and early-20th-century compositional techniques. May be performed singly or in sets. Int. to M-D.

Radamés Gnattali. *Sonata* 1935 (IU) 32pp., parts. Movido; Lentamente; Allegremente. Post-Romantic writing with most interest residing in the free and flexible rhythmic treatment afforded various sections. M-D.

Morton Gould. *Suite* 1981 (L. Parnas—GS 3727 1981) 55pp., parts. 22½ min. I. Fantasy; II. Rag; III. Soliloquy; IV. Ostinato. Vividly imaginative with fierce individuality, Gould sets a challenging course for performers and listeners in this late-20th-century setting considerably removed from its historical designs. Score is copy of clean handwritten MS. D.

Carlo Graziani. *Sei Sonate* Op.3 (G. Benvenuti, G. Crepax—I Classici Musicali Italiani 1943) 163pp., parts. 1 G, 2 A, 3 B♭, 4 F, 5 D, 6 E♭. Realization slightly over-edited, but informed performers will be able to adjust accordingly. Extensive notes in Italian. M-D.

Giovanni Battista Grazioli. *Sonata* A (Ticciati—Lengnick).
———. *Sonata* F (Schroeder—Schott; Schroeder—Augener 5512 with *Sonata* e by Marcello) 8pp., parts. Allegro moderato; Adagio; Tempo di Minuetto. Heavily edited. M-D.
———. *Sonata* G (Salmon—Ric R395) 11pp., parts. Allegro moderato; Menuet. Over-edited. M-D.

Alexander T. Gretchaninov. *Sonata* Op.113 (Schott 1549) 31pp., parts. Mesto: chordal, melody woven into texture, chromatic, arpeggi figuration; large span required. Menuetto tragico: varied tempos and moods, Furiosamente midsection. Finale: cello cadenza introduction, chromatic octaves, much activity, rhythmic. D.

Edvard Grieg. *Sonata* Op.36 a 1883 (CFP 2157; L. Rose—IMC 1955; K 9118) 45pp., parts. 28 min. Allegro agitato; Andante molto tranquillo; Allegro. Norwegian folk material used in this graceful and charming work. Piano is given much prominence, while cello provides much rhythmic incisiveness. D.
———. *Intermezzo* a 1866 (F. Benestad—CFP 8694 1998) 3pp., parts. 3 min. Al-

legretto tranquillo. In flowing character with many expressive qualities in spite of its brevity. M-D.

See Rolf Christian Erdahl, "Edvard Grieg's Sonatas for Stringed Instrument and Piano: Performance Implications of the Primary Source Materials," 2 vols., D.M.A. diss., Peabody Institute of the Johns Hopkins University, 1994.

Cornelis Wilhelmus de Groot. *Invocation* (Donemus 1974) 6pp., parts, photostat.

————. *Solitude* 1968 (Donemus 1974) 5pp., parts, photostat.

Friedrich Grützmacher. *10 Morceaux en Style national* Op.9 1854 (H. Best—Friedrich Hofmeister 2769 2000), parts. 2 vols. Vol.I (ISMN M-2034-2769-8): 1. Melodie Chinoise; 2. Air Allemand; 3. Danse Espagnole; 4. Air Russe; 5. Tyrolienne. Vol.II (ISMN M-2034-2770-4): 6. Air Suedois; 7. Romance Française; 8. Alla Zingana; 9. Air Ecossais; 10. Tarantella. Picturesque gems of folklore in a 19th-century style. May be performed singly or in sets. M-D.

Philip Hahn. *Sonatine* 1995 (Dohr 99658 1999, ISMN M-2020-0658-0) 9pp., parts. Moderato rubato–Allegro marcato–Adagio; Allegro molto. A true Sonatina with easier parts and smaller forms. In Classical style only hinting at 20th-century compositional techniques. M-D.

Alexi Haieff. *Sonata* 1963 (Gen) 30pp., parts. Allegro, e con sentiments aperto; Andante; Vivo. Freely tonal; centers around e. Chords in alternating hands, octotonic, traditional forms. Vivo is mainly toccata-like, with *p* ending, Neoclassic. Wide span required. M-D.

Mihály Hajdu. *Hungarian Children's Songs* (Bo&H 1974) 23pp., parts. Charming settings of 15 tunes contained in *Corpus Musicae Popularis Hungaricae* (Collection of Hungarian Folk Music), Vol.I: *Children's Games* (Bartók, Kodály—Zenemükiado 1951). Int.

————. *Variations and Rondo* (Artia).

Rudolfo Halffter. *Sonata* Op.26 (EMM 1962) 36pp., parts. Allegro deciso; Tempo di Siciliana; Rondo–Allegro. Large, dramatic work. Strong opposition between major and minor 3rd is in part responsible for the tension felt throughout the entire first movement. Requires large span plus solid pianistic equipment and ensemble know-how. M-D.

Erich Hamann. *Sonata* Op.22 (Dob).

————. *Suite* Op.32 (Dob 1952) 12pp., parts. Andante; Allegro; Adagio ma non tanto; Presto; Andante. Tonal, mildly contemporary, bitonal spots, octotonic. Outer movements are similar. Requires large span. M-D.

Iain Hamilton. *Sonata* 1958 (Schott) 17 min. Serial technique, unusual form. Four cadenzas marked, respectively, bizarre, fantastic, passionate, and tempestuous, are separated by 3 "movements" of decreasing speed (allegro, con moto, placido). No thematic relationships between the 7 parts are obvious. Scoring includes unusual effects, thick and complex harmonies, with a post-Webernesque 12-tone texture. D.

George Frideric Handel. *Sonata* C (CFP 4903; Hoffmann—Schott; Jensen—IMC). Originally for gamba and cembalo. Adagio; Allegro; Adagio; Allegro. M-D.

Lou Harrison. *Suite* 1995 (Peermusic 2000) 12pp., parts. Moderato; Elergy; Allegro. Composed upon the request of a "piano-playing" physician for a "cello-playing" colleague using "two melodies in his notebooks from the late 1940's" (from score). Straightforward tuneful settings without complications. M-D.

Bernhard Heiden. *Siena* (A. Broude).
——. *Sonata* (A. Broude).
——. *Sonata* 1958 (AMP) 25pp., parts. For Janos Starker. Allegro; Andante poco sostenuto; Allegretto vivace. Neoclassic, clear lines and textures. In Hindemithian idiom but a solid work that can stand on its own merits; well crafted; contains attractive ideas that flow naturally. M-D.

Hans Henkemans. *Sonata* 1949 (Donemus 227) 26pp., parts. Allegro comodo: chordal, repeated thematic germ cells, chromatic; requires large span. Adagio: more sustained outer sections, chromatic 16ths in mid-section. Presto: marked and rhythmic, free dissonant counterpoint, many chords. Allegro ma non troppo: toccata-like, chordal punctuation, nervous emotionalism, all clothed in basically a post-Romantic pianistic idiom. M-D to D.

Fanny Hensel. *Two Pieces* (C. Lambour—Br&H 8575 1994) 25pp., parts. *Fantasia* g: Andante doloroso–Prestissimo. *Capriccio* A♭: Andante–Allegro di molto. Probably composed in the late 1820s, these works show the influence of Beethoven, whose Cello Sonatas were familiar to Hensel. Preface in German and English. M-D.

Julius Hijman. *Sonate* 1934 (IU) 34pp., parts. Allegretto; Adagio; Allegro con spirito, quasi presto. Fairly thick textures except for the final movement, which seems to scamper with many triplets. Neoclassic leanings. M-D.

Paul Hindemith. *Three Light Pieces* (Br&H 1917) 8pp., parts. Mässig schnell, munter; Langsam; Lebhaft. Contrasting, accessible. M-D.
——. *Three Pieces* Op.8 1917 (Schott 1938). Published separately. Capriccio A; Phantasiestücke B; Scherzo c. Sizable works, each complete in itself. M-D.
——. *Sonata* Op.11/3 a 1919 (Schott 1922) 26pp., parts. 22½ min. In 4 sections that make 2 movements: Mässig schnell, Viertel–Lebhaft; Langsam–sehr lebhaft. Twelve-note scale is used for thematic development but is independent of harmonic background. The third section serves as the slow movement. A central marchlike diatonic theme provides contrast to the outer sections. The interval of the augmented 4th dominates the finale and provides a special

character to the movement. Linear atonal polyphony permeates much of this striking and inventive work. D.

————. *Variations on an Old English Nursery Song "A Frog He Went A-Courting"* 1941 (Schott 1951) 5½ min. Thirteen charming variations based on the verses of the nursery song. Clever, attractive, not easy. M-D.

————. *Kleine Sonate* 1942 (Schott 8186 1990, ISMN M-001-08348-3) 12pp., parts. 12 min. First publication. Breit; Lebhaft; Langsam. Composed in the manner of a Sonatina with fewer technical difficulties and shorter forms. Wide span required. M-D.

————. *Sonate* 1948 (Schott 3839 1948) 38pp., parts. 22½ min. Three movements. Opens with a dramatic "Pastoral" with exposition and condensed recapitulation of 3 themes. Marchlike scherzo (moderately fast-slow) serves as the middle movement with a slow mid-section. A huge Passacaglia concludes the work. Weighty harmony full of strong dissonance recalls some of Hindemith's early daring works. D.

Alun Hoddinott. *Sonata* Op.73/2 (OUP 0-19-3571501 1972) 16pp., parts. The first movement is improvisatory in style. The second movement plays with metric subdivisions and fluctuating harmonies. D.

————. *Sonata II* Op.96/1 (OUP 0-19-357151X). 16 min.

————. *Sonata III* (Oriana). 20 min.

Arthur Honegger. *Sonata* 1920 (ESC 1922) 31pp., parts. 13½ min. Allegro non troppo; Andante sostenuto; Presto. Clever contrapuntalism coupled with varied rhythmic ideas and tonal independence are characteristic of this whole work. The first movement has 2 main ideas in duple meter; one drops and the other rocks. The slow movement is a large 3-part design with a fugal section in the middle. The Presto is whimsical in a kind of Stravinskian manner with a happy-go-lucky theme in E. D.

————. *Sonatine* A 1921–22 (Rouart Lerolle). A clarinet may be substituted for the cello. Three compressed but relaxed movements. A lazy kind of theme opens the work, followed by a short fugato and a recapitulation. The Lent et soutenu is in ABA form. Concluding movement is only 37 bars long and includes jazz effects. M-D. See further description under duos for piano and clarinet.

Katherine Hoover. *Aria and Allegro Giocoso* 1982–85 (Papagena Press 1982/5) 14pp., parts. "*Aria* was written in 1982 as the middle movement of a *Serenade* for clarinet and string quartet. This piece was originally intended for adult amateurs and its simplicity and lyricism have proven perfect for the cello. In 1985 a cellist friend requested a companion piece, so I added the *Allegro giocoso*. It is a light, quick movement with bantering between the two instruments, and a few effects that only a cello can make" (Composer's Note). Int. to M-D.

Joseph Horvath. *Sonata* Op.14 1951 (Belwin-Mills) 10 min. Common chords used in not-so-common progressions. Some original twists in a dry, witty, Neoclassic style. Pleasantly written and diversified with fluent invention apparent everywhere. M-D.

Alan Hovhaness. *Suite* Op.193 (CFP 6324 1962) 6pp., parts. 5 min. Andante: linear opening, chords in alternating hands, parallel and contrary motion chords. Largo: full bass chords, tremolo figures with moving chords, bitonal; requires large span. Moderato: moving inner lines, parallel chords, quartal harmonies. M-D.

———. *Sonata* Op.255 (PIC 1975) 18pp., parts.

Alexandru Hrisanide. *Volumes—Inventions* 1963 (Editura Muzical 1967) 18pp., parts. Three large sections, A, B, and C, can be arranged at the performer's discretion. Numerous directions for the pianist. Involves clusters, slamming piano lid closed *ffff*, plucking strings, scratching strings with the nails, stopping strings, knitting needles placed on strings. Complex ensemble problems. Playing of last note must continue for 25 seconds for volume C and 30 seconds for volume A. Avant-garde. D.

Johann N. Hummel. *Sonate* Op.104 A 1827 (UWKR 19 1971) 29pp., parts. Allegro amabile e grazioso: SA, interesting modulatory material. Romanza: expressive, melodic theme; parallel minor mid-section has much rhythmic and melodic appeal. Rondo: flowing, Maggiore and Minore sections, facile figuration. Piano is particularly favored. M-D.

Jacques Ibert. *Histoires* (Leduc 1931). Transcription of 4 pieces from the original collection for piano solo by Maurice Maréchal. La Meneuse de tortues d'or; La Cage de cristal; Le Vieux mendiant; Le Petit âne blanc. Picturesque, with typical Ibert wit and charm. M-D.

———. *Aria* (Leduc 1930). Transcription of the original vocalise, probably by Paul Louis Neuberth. Identical to original with cello playing the voice part. Wide span required. M-D.

Andrew Imbrie. *Sonata* 1966 (Malcolm 1970) 56pp., parts. Allegro; Andante con affetto; Andante–Allegro. Serial, thorny, well-developed rows. Textures are kept thin. Only for the finest players. D.

Vincent d'Indy. *Sonate* Op.84 D 1924–25 (Rouart Lerolle) 27pp., parts. Modéré; Gavotte et Rondeau; Air; Gigue. Warm Romantic writing that keeps the pianist constantly on the move. Chromatic usage sweeps into everything and opens brief tonal exercises into many keys. D.

John Ireland. *Sonata* g 1923 (Augener) 36pp., parts. 21 min. The metronome marks were revised by the composer in 1948. Moderato e sostenuto; Poco largamente; Con moto e marcato. Concise forms, close connection between movements accomplished by common thematic material (see first 6 bars of opening movement). Rhapsodic first movement in spirit of SA design if not in exact form. Lyric and elegaic slow movement. Strong finale. Freely tonal. Requires mature musicianship on the part of both performers. D.

Gordon Jacob. *Sonata* d (J. Williams 1957) 24pp., parts. 21 min. Allegro; Allegro vivace; Adagio; Allegro molto. Freely tonal, conservative writing. Chromatic side-slips in first movement add to much activity. M-D.

———. *Sonatina* (J. Williams).

Maurice Jacobson. *Humoreske* (Lengnick 1948) 12pp., parts. See detailed entry under duos for piano and viola.

Leoš Janáček. *Skladby pro Violoncello a Klavír* (*Compositions for Violincello and Piano*) (J. Fukač, B. Havlík—Supraphon/Br 8331 1988) 30/32pp., parts. Extracted from Series E, Vol.2 of the Complete Critical Edition of the works of Leoš Janáček. *Pohádka* (A Tale) 1910–23. 12 min. In 3 movements: Con moto; Con moto–Adagio; Allegro. Requires thorough understanding of the score and skilled performers for effective reading. Many accidentals in colorful writing. *Presto.* 2½ min. An exciting piece in ternary form with suggested hemiola effects. Supraphon includes extensive notes in Czech, German, English, French, and Russian. *Pohádka* is available separately, edited by Smetana (Supraphon, 28pp., parts).

Pál Járdányi. *Sonatina* (EMB) A diatonic 2-movement work with an especially attractive dancelike second movement. Int. to M-D.

Gustav Jenner. *Sonate* D (H. Heussner—Schott CB138 1990) 50pp., parts. 30 min. Allegro moderato; Andante con variazioni; Allegro. Commences with an expressive diatonic melody and an unmistakable Brahmsian influence. Large chordal structures, occasional cross-rhythms, and a late-19th-century signature characterize the work. Of particular interest are the 4 variations in the slow movement, where imitative features and distinctive rhythms soothe audiences and performers alike. M-D.

Otto Joachim. *Sonata* (BMI Canada) 8 min. Serial technique. D.

Lockrem Johnson. *Sonata* I Op.33 1949 (Dow 1956) 20pp., parts. 12 min. Molto moderato; Adagietto quasi andante–Allegro con spirito. M-D.

———. *Sonata* II Op.42 1953 (ACA) 17 min. Vigorous, full of complex linear writing contrasted with very transparent lyric, modal passages. M-D.

André Jorrand. *IIe Sonate* (Rideau Rouge 1970) 19pp., parts. 8½ min. Modéré; Calme; Enjoué. Vigorous and compelling writing in a freely tonal, animated style. Calme uses rich harmonic palette and is somewhat Impressionist. Enjoué is livened by a meter of $\frac{4}{4} + \frac{1}{8}$. A sure hand at work here. M-D.

Werner Josten. *Sonata* (AMP 1938) 16pp., parts. One movement, various tempos, Neoclassic characteristic, cello cadenza at end, freely tonal, centers around g, ends in D. A profusion of ideas. M-D.

John Joubert. *Kontakion* Op.69 (Nov 1974) 18pp., parts. Free fantasia, dramatic and expressive. Piano part as important as cello. Based on a fragment of a Russian traditional chant for the dead. M-D.

Dmitri Kabalevsky. *Sonata* Op.22 (USSR).
———. *Sonata* Op.71 B♭ 1962 (Rostropovich—IMC; Sikorski; USSR) 58pp., parts. Dedicated to Mstislav Rostropovich. Andante molto sostenuto; Allegretto; Allegro molto. The first movement is built on the contrast between the dramatic monologue in the cello and the lyrical secondary subject. Both the development section and the recapitulation are dramatically characterized. The second movement is a typical Russian waltz full of inner agitation. The waltz is repeatedly interrupted by melodic elements that are foreign to it, creating a feeling of incompleteness, of suspense and uneasiness. The finale presents a psychological conflict: The imperative toccata-like main subject is the most important element, but dramatic motifs intrude and create tension and agitation. The main subject from the first movement is brought in during the coda, re-establishing the atmosphere of that movement. All of Kabalevsky's stylistic characteristics are present. Large span required. D.

Donald Keats. *Diptych* 1974 (AMC) 23pp., parts. Allegro moderato: dissonant counterpoint, chromatic, well-developed ideas; large span required. Allegro: octotonic, dancelike, strong syncopation, proportional rhythmic relationships, thin textures. D.

Friedrich Kiel. *Reise-Bilder* Op.11 1858 (Dohr 97492 1997, ISMN M-2020-0492-0) 53pp., parts. A collection of 9 short pieces rich in harmonic development and packed with imagination. Reisebilder; Jagdszene; Rast; Intermezzo; Auf der Alpe; Sturm am Wasserfall; Romanze; Einkehr; Fremde Musikanten. Pieces not marked attacca may be performed separately. M-D to D.
———. *Sonate* D (C. Dohr—Dohr 21835 2001, ISMN M-2020-0835-5) 34pp., parts. Allegro; Allegretto siciliano; Allegro. A remarkable *Sonata* with extended outer movements and a charming siciliano. Shows influence of early-19th-century masters, especially Schubert and Weber, in its melodic features and prodigious fingerwork. Imitative techniques decorate its homophonic texture. The clean, well-laid-out edition makes it attractive for performers. Preface in German. M-D.

Zoltán Kodály. *Sonata* Op.4 1910 (UE 7130 1922) 23pp., parts. 17 min. Fantasia: SA, much tension created by agitated manipulating of themes from the exposition in the development section as well as emotional warmth and Hungarian character throughout. Allegro con spirito: SA, sweeps along with dance mobility using gutsy folk rhythms; concludes with a condensed return of the opening section of the first movement, which serves as a coda. Piano part is very important and requires plenty of "gusto." Debussyian harmony, Classical thematic outlines. D.

Peter Jona Korn. *Sonata* Op.6 1948–49 (Simrock Elite Edition 3336 1969) 55pp., parts. Allegro tranquillo; Introduzione (solo piano)—(15) Variationen über ein Deutsches Volkslied. Octotonic, freely tonal, some Romantic sonorities, trills in lower register, shifting rhythms. Contrasted variations treated fluently. Solid octave technique necessary; large span required. Virtuoso writing for both instruments. D.

Egon Kornauth. *Sonata* Op.28 (CFP 3771).
——. *Drei Stücke* Op.47 (Dob 1955) 23pp., parts. 15½ min. Elegie; Romanze; Dumka. In f#, D♭, f#, respectively, with engaging pianistic writing often emphasizing full chords. The distinctive character of each movement makes them attractive both individually and as a group. M-D.

Karl Kroeger. *Recitative and Allegro* 1966 (ACA-CFE) 12pp., parts. For cello or viola. In one extended movement cast in early-20th-century harmonies. The considerable rhythmic freedom of the Recitative yields to a spry Allegro and allows dialogue between the instruments and passing of musical ideas without interruption. Glissandos and double stops for cello. M-D.

Georg Kröll. *Erste Sonate* (Moeck 1967) 12 min.
——. *Zweite Sonate* (Moeck 1971) 15pp., 10 min.
——. *Sonata* (Moeck 5164 1975) 11pp., parts. 12 min. Explanations in German and English.

Robert Kurka. *Sonatina* Op.21 (Weintraub 1964) 16pp., parts. Fast; Slow, but flowing; Fast. Freely tonal with key signatures, parallel chords, syncopation, octotonic, à la Shostakovich, especially the last movement. M-D.

László Lajtha. *Sonate* Op.17 (Leduc 1933) 31pp., parts. Aria; Capriccio; Fantasia. The 3 movements can be played as separate pieces. Mildly 20th-century, freely tonal, parallel chords, octotonic; fine octave technique necessary. The Fantasia opens with a Lento introduction before moving on to an Allegro that provides the main body of the movement. M-D.

Edouard Lalo. *Sonata* a 1856 (Heugel; P. Cwojdzinski—Kunzelmann GM506 1996 32pp.), parts. Andante non troppo–Allegro moderato; Andante; Finale–Allegro. Unusual modulations, recapitulation treated originally in first movement (Allegro moderato). Great thematic beauty. D.

John La Montaine. *Sonata* Op.8 (EV 1966) 31pp., parts. 17 min. Allegro amabile: freely tonal around D, dancelike, parallel chords, vibrant figuration, octotonic. Scherzo:⅝, shifting meters, chordal punctuation, thicker textures in Trio. Soliloquy: for cello alone. Finale: graceful, cantabile section, elegant Neoclassic style; requires large span. M-D.

Armando Lavalle. *Sonata* (EMM 1973) 15pp., parts. Allegro, a piacere; Jarabe; Canto; Fuga. Serial; interesting writing, especially the animated Jarabe movement. Each movement provides fine contrast. Large span required. D.

Henri Lazorof. *Duo—1973* (TP) 12pp., parts. 12½ min.
——. *Intermezzi* 1998 (Merion 144-40378 2000) 16pp., parts. 14½ min. Five short, mostly untitled pieces exploring harmonies, sonority, and rhythmic features in a variety of late-20th-century techniques. Impulsive on one hand, yet free on the other. No.3 is an Homage to Debussy. M-D.

Kenneth Leighton. *Alleluia Pascha Nostrum* Op.85 1981 (Nov). 16 min. Plainchant-inspired, Romantic treatment, sustained spans.

John Lessard. *Sonata* 1956 (ACA). Neoclassic style, bright and crisp sonorities, marked textural contrasts. M-D.

David Lewin. *Classical Variations on a Theme by Schönberg* 1960 (University of California Press 1967) 18pp., parts. Theme, 9 variations, and finale. Based upon a dodecaphonic row spelled out at the opening in the cello. Lewin retains an Expressionist quality throughout the work in his Classical treatment of the theme. Var.2 is for piano solo and 4 is for cello solo. D.

Helene Liebmann. *Grande Sonate* Op.10 B♭ (F. Zimmermann—Tonger 2579 1994, ISMN M-005-25791-2) 32pp., parts. Andante sostenuto; Adagio ma non troppo; Andante con variazioni. A Classically conceived work clearly influenced by the Viennese School. Among its interesting qualities is the theme and 7 variations with its lyric melody and technical demands for both instruments. Var.5 is a study in octaves for solo piano. M-D to D.

Franz Liszt. *The Complete Music for Violoncello and Pianoforte* (Howard, Isserlis—Hardie Press 1992, ISBN 0-946868-11-5) 77pp., parts. Vol.10 of Liszt Society Publications. Urtext. Contains 6 works composed primarily toward the end of Liszt's career. *Elégie* S.130 (1874) contains optional parts for harp and harmonium/organ and is a transcription from the original for piano. *Zweite Elégie* S.131 (1877) is also transcribed from the original for piano and exists with violin solo. *Romance oubliée* S.132 (1880) originated in Liszt's song *O pourquoi donc* and went through numerous versions, including violin and viola. *La lugubre Gondola* S.134 (1882–85), perhaps Liszt's most significant work for this medium, is a transcription of the second piano version cast in $\frac{4}{4}$ meter. *Die Zelle in Nonnenwerth* S.382 (ca.1883) exists in many versions, the first for voice and piano from a poem by Felix Lichnowsky about Nonneworth, "an island in the river Rhine between Bonn and Koblenz, the site of a famous Benedictine abbey for 700 years, where Liszt, Marie d'Agoult and their children spent their summer holidays in 1841, 1842, and 1843" (Critical Notes). *6 Consolations* S.172, transcribed by Jules de Swert and approved by Liszt, offer fine alternatives to the original. *O du mein holder Abendstern*—Recitative and Romance from Wagner's *Tannhäuser* S.380 (1852), a missing work, is re-created here in a conjectural reconstruction by Leslie Howard (1991) based on Liszt's version for solo piano, S.444 (1849). Extensive critical notes by Howell. M-D to D.

Otto Luening. *Sonata* (CFE).

——. *Suite* (Galaxy 1972) 23pp., parts. For cello or viola and piano. Part also for viola. Recitative–Moderato: chordal opening, moves along freely; Moderato takes on many repeated notes in one hand with a subject in the other; broken octaves; short chromatic figures; large span required; mood of Recitative returns and Moderato material concludes movement. Scherzo: shifting meters, thin textures, one meter throughout for mid-section. Elegy: chordal, sustained, lyrical. Dance: octotonic, free dissonant counterpoint, much rhythmic vigor, bitonal ending. M-D.

——. *Variations on Bach's Chorale Prelude 'Liebster Jesu Wir Sind Hier'* (Galaxy) 17pp., parts. Piano alone plays chorale in A. Var.I: cello has chorale, piano counterpoints against it. Var.II: melody is in 16th-note figuration while cello has slow counterpoint. Var.III: piano has melody with slightly changed harmonies; cello moves along with its own separate melody. Var.IV: Bb, Alberti bass in piano with melody in octaves; cello has active counterpoint. Var.V: syncopated chordal treatment. Var.VI: varied melody in piano with counterpoint in cello similar to Var.IV. Var.VII: A, strong counter-melody in cello against chorale in piano. M-D.

Witold Lutoslawski. *Grave: Metamorphoses* 1981 (JWC 55413 1982) 10pp., parts. In one continuous movement at $\bullet$ = ca.152. Emphasizes dark, low tones at opening. Frequent changes of rhythmic groupings and meters which grow into one another, metamorphosing the flow into intricate developments.

James MacMillan. *Sonata* I (Bo&H 2000), parts. Two movements: Face, Image.

——. *Sonata* II (Bo&H 2001), parts. In one movement.

See John York, "The Makings of a Cycle? James MacMillan's Cello and Piano Sonatas," *Tempo* 221 (July 2002): 24–28.

Elizabeth Maconchy. *Divertimento* (Lengnick 1954) 22pp., parts. Serenade; Golubchik; The Clock; Vigil; Masquerade. Pastiche of technique and moods. A colorful Suite that employs the piano admirably. Freely tonal, least interesting in the metrical treatment. M-D.

Ernst Mahle. *Sonatina* 1956 (Ric Brazil 1968) 8pp., parts. Allegro moderato: harmonic staccatissimo 4ths and 5ths are prevalent in the piano part. Much rhythmic drive. M-D.

Enrico Mainardo. *Sonata* (Schott 1955).

——. *Sonata quasi Fantasia* (Schott 1962).

——. *Sonatina* (Schott).

Marin Marais. *Suite* I d 1717 (G. Hunter—AMP 1974). From *Pièces de Viole*, IV. Seven contrasting movements that cover a wide range of emotions, including a Prelude and a group of dances as well as 2 character pieces, "La Mignone" and "Caprice." Facile continuo realization. M-D.

Benedetto Marcello. *Six Sonatas* for cello or double bass and piano (GS 1973) 38pp., parts. Keyboard realization and cello part edited by Analee Bacon. Double bass part edited by Lucas Drew. M-D.

——. *Six Sonatas* Op.2 1712 (Bonelli, Mazzacurati—Zanibon).

——. *Six Sonatas* (W. Schulz, S. Pritsche—CFP 4647 1958) 31pp., parts. F, e, a, g, C, G. Second cello ad lib.

——. *Two Sonatas* C, G (J. Starker—IMC; Moffat, Whitehouse—Schott).

——. *Two Sonatas* G, C (Schroeder—Augener 5511).

——. *Two Sonatas* g, F (Piatti—IMC; Schroeder—Augener 5503).

——. *Sonata* A (Pollain—Senart 5370).

——. *Sonata* Op.2/1 F (Zanibon 4381).

——. *Sonata* Op.2/2 e (Zanibon 4382; Ric SY 644).

——. *Sonata* Op.2/3 (Zanibon 4383).

——. *Sonata* Op.2/4 g (Zanibon 4384).

——. *Sonata* 2/5 (Zanibon 4385).

——. *Sonata* Op.2/6 G (Zanibon 4386).

——. *Sonata* F (Zanibon 4167).

——. *Sonata* C (Ticciati—Lengnick).

——. *Sonata* D (Moffat, Whitehouse—Schott; Salmon—Ric R98).

——. *Sonata* e (Moffat, Whitehouse, Rapp—Schott; Salmon—Ric R403; Schroeder—IMC; Schroeder—Schott).

Some editions suggest the viola may be used in lieu of cello.

Tomás Marco. *Maya* (Moeck 1972) 16pp., parts (same as score but in loose leaves). 10 min.

Frank Martin. *Chaconne* 1931 (UE 12862) 10pp., parts. 6 min. Atonal bass line (row) plays against a tonal melody. Highly organized writing that presents an idea (statement) then treats it canonically. Martin "discovered" Schoenberg in 1930, and this work is partly an outgrowth of that discovery. Active *dux* and *comes*, beautifully crafted variation technique (6 variations and coda). M-D.

Bohuslav Martinů. *Sonata* I 1939 (Heugel 1949) 19 min. Poco allegro; Lento; Allegro.

——. *Sonata* II 1941 (AMP 1944) 46pp., parts. 18 min. Allegro; Largo; Allegro commodo. Many-faceted compositional style, thick and thin textures, Impressionist mixed with Expressionist characteristics. Freely tonal, chordal much of the time. D.

———. *Variations on a Theme of Rossini* 1942 (Bo&H 1949) 14pp., parts. Theme, 4 variations, and a brilliant coda. Eclectic style employed effectively. Spontaneous and cogent writing. D.

———. *Sonata III* 1952 (Artia 1957; MMP) 42pp., parts. 21 min. Poco andante–Moderato; Andante–Moderato–Allegro; Allegro, ma non presto. M-D to D.

———. *Variations on a Slovakian Theme* 1959 (Br ISBN 80-7058-052-6; Nov) 15pp., parts. Theme and 5 contrasting and highly colorful variations. M-D.

Giuseppe Martucci. *Sonata* Op.52 f♯ (P. Spada—Boccaccini 1275 1998) 55pp., parts. Allegro giusto; Scherzo–Allegro molto; Intermezzo–Andantino flebilo; Finale–Allegro. A large-scale work "which is generally ranked side by side with the two Brahms Sonatas of the same type and which occupies a unique position in Italian nineteenth-century instrumental music as no other composer has dedicated any like works to this instrument. The creative strain is of very high quality and a wide range of moods are expressed. The Brahmsian lesson is certainly evident in the overall style of the work, but not in the profound conception of the creative part, which is truly Martuccian and perhaps more reminiscent of Wagner than of the Maestro from Hamburg" (from Preface). D.

———. *2 Romanze* Op.72 (Boccaccini 1256).

———. *3 Pezzi* Op.69 (Boccaccini 1322).

Jules Massenet. *Thaïs (Méditation)* (A. Pejtsik—EMB Z13 635 1990) 4pp., parts. Trans. of the famous melody by J. Delsart. M-D.

Colin Matthews. *Three Enigmas* 1985 (Faber Music 1996, ISBN 0-571-51297-6) 16pp., parts. 10 min. Allegro–Con forza; Grave; Animato ed agitato. "To explain the title would, obviously, take away the enigma but there is nothing particularly mysterious intended, only an indication of the rather introverted, hermetic nature of the music (and the musical processes employed)" (from Composer's Note). Proportional rhythmic relationships, cluster chords, unison passagework, and extremes of dramatic character appear. For experienced performers. D.

Felix Mendelssohn. *Variations Concertante* Op.17 (Cahnbley—CFP; Br&H) 11pp., parts. Theme and 8 contrasting variations. Was extremely popular at one time. Piano is highly prominent in some of the variations. M-D.

———. *Sonata I* Op.45 B♭ 1838 (R. Elvers, E.-G. Heinemann, K. Schilde, C. Kanngiesser—Henle 667, ISMN M-2018-0667-9; Such—Augener; Cahnbley—CFP), parts. 24 min. Allegro vivace; Andante; Allegro assai. Well scored, themes are clearly and vigorously delineated. M-D.

———. *Sonata II* Op.58 D 1843 (R. Elvers, E.-G. Heinemann, K. Schilde, C. Kanngiesser—Henle 668, ISMN M-2018-0668-6; Such—Augener; Cahnbley—

CFP), parts. 26 min. Allegro assai vivace; Allegretto scherzando; Adagio; Molto allegro e vivace. Cello writing comes off better than does most of the piano part. D.

——. *The Collected Works* (MMP) 92pp., parts. Contains *Sonatas* I, II; *Variations Concertante*; *Lied ohne Worte*, Op.109.

Louis Mennini. *Sonatina* (Bo&H 1955) 15pp., parts. Allegro moderato; Largo; Allegro robusto. Straightforward and soaring melodic ideas, freely tonal, octotonic, strong rhythms and structures, shifting meters. Large span required. M-D.

Saverio Mercadante. *Fantasia su 'Il Reggente'* (P. Spada—Boccaccini 1266 1995) 9pp., parts. First publication. Based on themes from Mercadante's opera *Il Reggente*. "Although it can hardly be described as an exceptional work, Mercadante's sure musical qualities, his sense of euphony, measure and real expressiveness are all there, in a piece quite probably composed for some social occasion but which may take its own modestly dignified place beside the *Elegia* and *Serenata*" (from Preface). M-D.

——. *Elegìa* (Boccaccini 1155).

——. *Serenata* (Boccaccini 1156).

Krzysztof Meyer. *Canzona* Op.56 1981 (PWM 1983, ISBN 83-224-2152-4) 20pp., parts. 9½ min. In one movement with steady rhythms in constantly changing meters. Songlike, with quasi cadenzas for both instruments. Triple stops for cello. M-D.

——. *Sonata* Op.62 1983 (PWM/Sikorski 1986, ISBN 83-224-2572-4) 39pp., parts. 25 min. Misterioso; Furioso; Con moto. Avant-garde in character but retains well-defined melodies and customary technical designs. Frequent meter changes and writing which tests the capabilities of the instruments are commonplace. D.

Nikolai Miakovsky. *Sonata* I Op.12 D 1911–35 (USSR) 30pp., parts. Adagio; Allegro passionate. Numerous tempo changes and moods in finale. A remarkable work full of restrained austerity and at places great dynamism. Complex harmonic and contrapuntal writing. Awkward for piano at times, but the musical merits outweigh these few spots. Orchestrally conceived. M-D to D.

——. *Sonata* II Op.81 a 1948–49 (USSR). Three movements of clear melodic lines, lucid harmonic style, outstanding individual instrumental technique. M-D.

Hans Friedrich Micheelsen. *Suite* (W. Müller 1971). Chansonette (Allegretto grazioso); Arietta (Andante cantabile); Amouretta (Allegro). Well written. M-D.

Darius Milhaud. *Sonate* 1959 (Sal) 23pp., parts. Animé, Gai: $\frac{9}{8}$, independent lines, skipping left hand, chromatic, rocking figuration, tonal G ending; large span required. Lent, Grave: $\frac{4}{4}$, secco style, thin textures mixed with chords, rhythmic shifts, short motives. Vif et Joyeux: $\frac{3}{4}$, facile polytonal and free contrapuntal lines, vigorous rhythms, octotonic, d closing. M-D to D.

Albert Moeschinger. *Sonate* Op.61 (Br 2462 1949) 26pp., parts. Modéré; Allegro vivace; Lento; Presto. Freely tonal around E♭, Impressionist, broad gestures, expressive Lento, octotonic, quartal and quintal harmony. Large span required. M-D to D.

Xavier Bassols Montsalvatge. *Sonata Concertante* (UME 1974) 31pp., parts. Vigoroso: chromatic; large skips; parallel chords; flowing Allegretto senza rigore section; coda fades away; requires broad span. Moderato sostenuto: striking gestures open movement; chordal, including 3-note clusters in both hands; added-note technique. Scherzo: $\frac{5}{8}$, alternating hands, repeated octaves over open 5ths, short glissando, secco ending. Rondo–Allegro: piano alternates between chordal and linear style; declamatory ending. Very little influence noted. D.

Ignaz Moscheles. *Sonata* Op.121 E 1850–51 (J. Wolf—Lienau RL40630 2000) 80pp., parts. Opens Allegro espressivo e appassionato in $\frac{12}{4}$ with ascending ostinato in piano and duet melodic features between instruments. The movement quickly proceeds to patterns of repeated notes, trills, and tremolo effects along with modulatory sections far removed from E. An unusual feature of the Scherzo which follows is its setting in duple meter. Its vigorous melody and rhythmic patterns emphasize the dramatic quality of early Romanticism in music. A Ballade ensues in C with alternating sections of duple and triple rhythms before exploding into technically engaging passagework for experienced performers. The work concludes with a Finale and is packed with detail and pyrotechnical sections contrasted by dynamic and textual manipulation. A hint of Lisztian features is heard near the end in octave runs across the keyboard. D.

Joaquín Nin. *Chants d'Espagne* (P. Kochanski—ESC 1928) 16pp., parts. Adapted from the original for violin. Montañesa; Tonada Murciana; Saeta; Granadina. Picturesque pieces with popular themes from different regions of Spain. M-D.

Vítězslav Novák. *Sonata* Op.68 g (Artia 1941). Moravian and Slovak folk music influence felt throughout this work. M-D.

Lionel Nowak. *Sonata* I (CFE).
———. *Sonata* II (CFE).
———. *Sonata* III (CFE).

Jacques Offenbach. *Fantaisies Faciles* (W. Mengler—Bosworth BoE 7002 2000) 23pp., parts. Three easy *Fantasies* on famous operatic themes: *Fantasy on a Motive from Rossini's 'The Barber of Seville'* Op.71; *Fantasy on a Motive from Bellini's 'Norma'* Op.73; *Fantasy on a Motive from Mozart's 'The Marriage of Figaro'*

Op.72. The first 2 *Fantasies* emphasize the cello more than piano, whereas the last is more evenly handled. Int. to M-D.

——. *Danse Bohèmienne* Op.28 d/D (C. Dohr, M. Kliegel—Dohr 92038 1992) 16pp., parts. Commences Andante maestoso but soon turns to animated tempos for an exuberant dance. More difficult for cello, requiring double stops for a murderous finish. M-D.

——. *Deux Ames au Ciel* ca.1858 (P. Bruns—Hofmeister 2102 2000, ISMN M-2034-2102-3) 7pp., parts. Adagio maestoso. Dolce, lyric expressiveness juxtaposed to marked rhythms and tremolos. M-D.

——. in collaboration with **Friedrich von Flotow.** *6 Melodien* 1839 2 Books (J. Wolf—Zimmermann 30030/40 1995), parts. Bk.1: 1. Au bord de la mer; 2. Souvenir du bal; 3. La Prière du soir. Bk.2 (ISMN M-010-30040-5, 41pp.): 4. La Retraite; 5. La Ballade du Pâtre; 6. Danse norvegienne. "These little works are more than music for the salon, as they have a poetic style of their own. As an enlargement to the everyday romantic repertoire—as encores or single pieces for concerts—they enrich both the amateur's and the professional's musical repertoire" (from Preface). M-D.

Toshitsugu Ogihara. *Duet* (Japan Federation of Composers 1969) 40pp., parts. Andante; Introduction–Allegro. Bitonal, Neoclassic lines, some Japanese flavor, beautiful MS. M-D.

G. G. Sparre Olsen. *Norwegian Love Song* [*Norsk Kjærleikssong*] Op.36/3 (Norsk Musikforlag 9339 1981). See detailed entry under duos for piano and viola.

Georges Onslow. *Sonata* Op.16/2 C (U. Wegner—Br 1972) 41pp., parts for viola or cello and piano. See detailed entry under duos for piano and viola.

Juan Orrego-Salas. *Duos Concertante* Op.41 1955 (PIC 1963) 52pp., parts. Cantilena; Danza; Egloga; Ditirambo; Triskelion; Himno; Epoda. An impressive work with many features to recommend it. Requires thorough musicianship and technical accomplishment. Built along Neoclassic lines. Displays a catalog of pianistic techniques and idioms. Large span required. D.

Léon Orthel. *Kleine Burleske* Op.8/2 g 1926 (Albersen 1983) 8pp., parts. Begins and ends with a cheerful imitative exchange of motives between instruments. Scalar and arpeggio-like passagework occupy the larger portion of this short work while the cello soars with sustained melody and scalar figures of its own. M-D.

Hans Osieck. *Deux Pièces* 1991 (Donemus 1991) 13pp., parts. 10 min. *Intermezzo* pour Sida sur trois notes qui sont très aimables: based upon the 3 pitches comprised in the spelling of Sida [Roberts], to whom the work is dedicated—si [b], d, a. Ternary form with scherzando center section to balance the outer intermezzo sections. *Air et Mouvement Perpétuel:* introductory air in tranquil and poco rubato qualities leads to playful perpetual motion centered in the piano at a moderate pace. Pieces may be performed separately or together using a 3-mm. modulation provided by the composer. Individualist style with influences from early-20th-century French Neoclassicism. M-D.

Manuel Palau. *Cancion de Mar* (UME 1972) 4pp., parts.

———. *Coplas de mi Tierra* (UME 1972) 7pp., parts.

Paul Paray. *Sonate* B 1919 (Jobert) 40pp., parts. Andantino quasi allegretto; Andante; Allegro scherzando. Flowing melodies, undulating rhythms, flexible counterpoint, strong harmonies, Impressionist. D.

Robert Parris. *Cadenza, Caprice, Ricercare* 1961 (ACA) 32pp., parts. Cadenza: solo cello. Caprice: freely tonal, figuration divided between hands, fast half-pedals, dissonant counterpoint, dramatic arpeggi figuration, brilliant piano part, glissandi. Ricercare: octotonic, imitation, long lines, theme treated in various ways, pointillistic, expressive sustained conclusion; large span required. D.

Arvo Pärt. *Fratres* 1980 (UE 19563 1992) 12pp., parts. 9 min. Based on the version for instrumental ensemble. Spatial, uncomplicated writing for sonorous effects. Uses techniques from the composer's tintinnabuli style. The opening Bachian solo cello passage with its crescendo from *ppp* to *fff* is complemented by embellished harmonics at the end for a *ppp* finish by the piano. Numerous other versions for instrumental combinations exist. M-D.

———. *Spiegel im Spiegel* 1978 (UE 30336 1996, ISMN M-008-04339-0). For viola (cello) and piano. See detailed entry under duos for piano and viola.

Stephen Paulus. *Banchetto Musicale* (EAMC EA604 1981) 55pp., parts. 18 min. Intrada; Padouana; Gagliarda; Corrente; Air; Allemande/Tripla. Paulus's Suite is a late-20th-century, tonally based reflection on older historical forms. Occasional rhythmic figurations are awkward for the instruments but are rare in largely fluid contexts. Score is a copy of MS. M-D.

Stephen Paxton. *Sonata* Op.1/1 A (F. Dawes—Schott 1972) 20pp., parts. Allegro; Adagio; Rondo (tempo di minuetto). Bright and attractive work. M-D.

George Perle. *Concerto* (TP) 32pp., parts. Piano reduction by composer. Introduction and Allegro: a few harmonics called for in piano part. Andante espressivo: lyric, builds to climax, subsides. Finale: large span required; 5 different tempos indicated by metronome marks. The entire work has numerous Schoenbergian overtones. D.

———. *Sonata* 1985 (Galaxy 1.3086 1991) 32pp., parts. 16 min. I. Cadenza; II. Allegro; III. Variations. Conceived with an extensive cadenza of considerable demands for cellist. Conventional mid- to late-20th-century writing with frequent meter changes and biting dissonances. Variation techniques are used in the final movement in a continuously unfolding manner without clearly defined sections. M-D to D.

——. *Lyric Piece* 1946, rev.1949 (Galaxy 1.3054 1991) 6pp., parts. 3½ min. Andante con moto. Lives up to its name with contrasting repeated notes/chords and shifting rhythms in an early-20th-century style. M-D.

Wayne Peterson. *Rhapsody* 1976 (Henmar 67398 1992) 22pp., parts. In one extended movement with multiple sections. Detailed score with notation guide in late-20th-century style. Passionato, delicato, agitato, veloce, precipitando, and furioso are but a few indications for a work which tests the performance skills of musicians and listening ability of its audiences. D.

Ivo Petric. *Gemini Music* 1971 (Društva Slovenskih Skladateljev 1971) 7pp., plastic ring binder. Two copies necessary for performance. Explanations in Croatian and English. Reproduced from holograph.

Hans Pfitzner. *Sonata* Op.1 f♯ (Br&H 1892) 27 min. Shows influence of Schumann and Mendelssohn. The first movement treats 3 themes ingeniously, and the burlesque finale is especially effective. M-D to D.

Burrill Phillips. *Sonata* (Washington University Music Press 1957) 46pp., parts. Allegro; Adagio; Finale–Allegro assai e vigorosamente. Dramatic with contrasting reflective features in an early-20th-century style. M-D.

Gregor Piatigorsky. *Scherzo* (JWC 1939) 12pp., parts. Some changing meters, lyric mid-section, mildly 20th-century, tonal. M-D.
——. *Variations on a Theme of Paganini* (EV).

Alfredo Piatti. *The Race—La Corsa* 1894 (C. Bellisaro—Pizzicato 752 2001) 12pp., parts. A perpetual mobile for cello marked Allegro with light pianistic interaction. More difficult for the former. Preface in Italian and English. M-D.

Gabriel Pierné. *Sonata* Op.46 f♯ 1922 (Durand) 30pp., parts. A skillful technique and light touch are displayed in this one-movement work. It is well proportioned with original formal structure, has varied sonorities, is thoroughly French, and is full of charm and warmth. M-D.

Willem Pijper. *Sonata* I 1919 (JWC) 16 min. Strong dissonant writing with atonal and polytonal treatment. Themes from the opening movement are heard in the Habanera and Finale movements. Cyclic construction. D.

Mario Pilati. *Sonata* A (Ric 1931).
——. *Theme and Variations* (Ric 124428).

Ildebrando Pizzetti. *Sonata* F 1921 (Ric 119404 1933) 40pp., parts. 31 min. Largo; Molto concitato e angoscioso; Stanco e triste–Largo. Post-Romantic chromatic writing. Some unusual metrical treatment adds the most interest. Pianist is called on to move all over the keyboard with great facility. In the 1920s and 1930s this work was very popular. D.

David Popper. *Mazurka* Op.11/3 g (IMC 1946) 6pp., parts. Marked rhythms in keeping with the dance in its customary ternary form. Favors the cello. M-D.

———. *Gavotte* II Op.23 D (Hofmeister) 12pp., parts. Instruments are more thoroughly engaged than typical for Popper and complement one another effectively in the dance form. M-D.

———. *Barcarole* Op.38 G (Hofmeister) 13pp., parts. A fine setting of the character piece form for cello and piano. Reveals Popper as an effective composer for this combination with mutually developed parts. M-D.

———. *Elfentanz* Op.39 D (Rahter) 15pp., parts. Highlights the cello but contains effective pianistic writing. Also known in its orchestral form. M-D.

———. *Mazurka* Op.51 C (EMB Z13634 1990) 4pp., parts.

———. *Spinning Song* Op.55/1 (IMC) 9pp., parts. Concert study. Spinning effect realized by cello. Light piano. M-D.

———. *Hungarian Rhapsody* Op.68 D (L. Rose—IMC 1956) 12pp., parts. Distinctively nationalist in character with penetrating presence. Sectional differences in tempo and expression mark its features. M-D.

Quincy Porter. *Fantasy* (CFE).

———. *Poem* 1948 (Valley Music Press 1957) 3pp., parts. For cello or viola. A quiet, meditative essay in compound meters with only one crescendo beyond *mf*. M-D.

Francis Poulenc. *Sonata* 1948 (Heugel) 44pp., parts. 21 min. Allegro–tempo di marcia: strongly vigorous contrasted with charming and lyric writing. Cavatine: calm, lyric, elegant harmonies, Romantic lyricism, sweet. Ballabile–trés animé et gai: dancelike, brilliant, frivolity romps everywhere. Largo–Presto: refined sensuousness, witty, brisk, unpretentious, and thoroughly enjoyable writing in this large-scale work. D.

André Prevost. *Sonata* (Ric 1974) 23pp., parts.

———. *Sonata* II (Doberman). Elegiac and lyrical sections contrast with very assertive rhythmic sections. Beethovenian in inspiration.

Maria Teresa Prieto. *Adagio y Fuga* (EMM 1953) 13pp., parts. Adagio is freely tonal, chordal. Leads directly to the Fuga, which is properly treated with each instrument having its go with the subject. The Adagio intrudes near the middle of the fugue before the final fugue statement finishes in chordal fashion. M-D.

Sergei Prokofiev. *Ballade* Op.15 c 1912 (MCA). Shows a fine imagination with dramatic expression but is still a student work. M-D.

———. *Sonata* Op.119 1949 (Rostropovich—Sikorski 2286, rev.2001 47pp.; Rostropovich—IMC; Garbousova—MCA 55pp.; CFP 4710), parts. 21 min. Andante grave; Moderato; Allegro ma non troppo. Vigorous lyricism juxtaposed against a gently humorous setting. Three movements, respectively, of narrative, witty and biting diablerie (scherzo), and rather moody but lyric writing. D.

Sergei Rachmaninoff. *Sonata* Op.19 g 1901 (Bo&H; L. Rose—IMC) 49pp., parts. 32 min. Lento–Allegro moderato; Allegro scherzando; Andante; Allegro mosso. One of the most important Cello Sonatas of the 20th century. The 2 instruments are beautifully united in a ripe Romantic, expansive conception. It has much in common with the Second Piano Concerto, written about the same time, and is supremely grateful to the performers. D.

———. *Lied* (D. B. Cannata—Sikorski 1556 1992) 3pp. 2 min. First authorized edition. An early work of modest demands emphasizing songlike qualities at Andantino. Int.

See Clyde Edwin Beavers, "A Survey of Works for Violoncello and Piano by Sergei Rachmaninoff," D.M.A. diss., University of Kentucky, 1997.

Karol Rathaus. *Rapsodia Notturna* Op.66 1950 (Bo&H 1968) 10pp., parts. For cello or viola. A multisectional rhapsodic essay in early-20th-century style. M-D.

Alan Rawsthorne. *Sonata* 1949 (OUP 21.006) 15 min. Three closely linked movements. Main theme and secondary theme of the second movement come from the first-movement development section. New thematic material is introduced in the final movement; coda returns to the main subject of the first movement. D.

See M. Cooper, "Current Chronicle," MQ 35/2 (April 1949): 305–11. Refers to the Clarinet Quartet and the Cello Sonata.

Max Reger. *Caprice* a 1901 (UWKR 31 1973) 3pp., parts. Lively melody, accompanied punctuated chords. M-D.

———. *Sonata* Op.5 f (Schott 1911). One of Reger's finest early works, it beautifully displays his creative powers. D.

———. *Sonata* II Op.28 g (Br&H 1899; UE 1927) 33pp., parts. Agitato; Prestissimo assai; Intermezzo; Allegretto con grazia. Much activity for the pianist, whirlwinds of notes. D.

———. *Sonata* III Op.78 F (Bo&Bo 1934) 27 min. Arranged by Schulz-Furstenberg. Allegro con brio: rhapsodical, improvisatory. Scherzo: short and lively, effective. Andante con variazioni: simple theme, fluctuating harmonies. Finale: giguelike. D.

———. *Sonata* IV Op.116 a (CFP 1911) 30½ min.

Franz Reizenstein. *Sonata* A (Lengnick 1949) 60pp., parts. 27 min. Moderato; Allegro vivace; Adagio–Allegro amabile. Expansive writing requiring virtuoso technique. D.

Hermann Reutter. *Sonata Monotematica* (Schott 6424 1972) or for bassoon (6425) 19pp., parts. A one-movement work based on one subject. The exposition is contained in the Allegro appassionato section and is followed by a Vivace (Scherzo and Trio); the Adagio molto sostenuto section is a monody and is followed by an Allegro assai, a contrapuntal Finale in free fugato style. Freely tonal, Neoclassic. M-D.

Ivan Řezáč. *Sonata* 1956 (Artia) 62pp., parts. Allegro moderato; Andante con moto; Presto; Molto allegro. Freely tonal and modal with Hungarian folk music influence, octotonic, octaves in alternating hands, Neoclassic orientation. Requires large span. M-D.

George Rochberg. *Ricordanza: Soliloquy for Cello and Piano* (TP 1972) 8pp., parts. A surprising 3-section tonal work in post-Romantic tradition. Short cadenza for cello followed by an interesting closing for piano. Lovely Romantic sounds, pre-Wagnerian harmony. Rochberg describes it as a "commentary" on the opening of Beethoven's Cello *Sonata* in C, Op.102/1; and the opening of the central section is a direct quotation, transposed, of the Beethoven theme. A large piece of full-blown Romantic chamber music. M-D.

———. *Sonata-Aria* 1992 (TP 1994) 40pp., parts. 29 min. In one large movement suggestive of SA form with melodic material given primarily to cello. Piano does not merely accompany but juxtaposes the melody with dramatic features, widely spaced chords, and a host of technical figurations, including forceful tone clusters. Performers must have thorough knowledge of the other's part for successful performances. Large span required. D.

Joaquín Rodrigo. *Siciliana* 1929 (Ediciones Joaquín Rodrigo 1993, ISBN 84-88558-06-6) 11pp., parts. An extended setting of the siciliano style at a Lento tempo. Places cello in its strongest register, at times singing the gently rocking theme to marked and detailed passagework in the piano. Displays the germinating seeds to Rodrigo's nationalistic spirit. M-D.

———. *Sonata à la breve* 1977 (Schott), parts. 10 min. Adagietto; Scherzino; Allegro ma non troppo.

Bernhard Romberg. *Sonata* Op.38/1 e (IMC).
———. *Sonata* Op.38/2 G (IMC).
———. *Sonata* Op.38/3 B♭ (IMC).
———. *Sonata* Op.43/1 B♭ (IMC 10pp., parts; CF B3350; Billaudot; W. Jerel—UE 3472 16pp., parts). Allegro; Andante; Finale–Allegretto. Classic style, attractive. M-D.
———. *Sonata* Op.43/2 C (IMC; Billaudot; W. Jerel—UE 3473 23pp., parts). Allegro; Andante; Finale–Allegretto. M-D.
———. *Sonata* Op.43/3 G (IMC; Billaudot).

Joseph Guy Ropartz. *Sonata* I g 1904 (Durand) 34pp., parts. 28 min. Allegro moderato; Quasi lento; Allegro. Franckian influence is present in this well-constructed and expressive work. The slow movement is evocative of folk song usage. Piano writing is most effective. M-D.

———. *Sonata* II a 1918–19 (Durand).

Ned Rorem. *Dances* 1983 (Bo&H 1984) 24pp., parts. 15 min. Prelude; Valse Rappelée; Adagio; Pas de Deux; The Mirror Toccata; Scherzo; The Return. Attractive musical features abound in this Suite of modest requirements. Cheerfulness and gracefulness balance the serious and academic qualities found herein. Pieces may be played separately. Int. to M-D.

———. *Three Slow Pieces* 1978 (Bo&H). 10 min.

Nikolai Andreevich Roslavets. *Sonata* 1921 (Schott 1991) 32pp., parts.

———. *Sonata* II 1922 (Schott 8039 1991) 63pp., parts.

Miklos Rozsa. *Duo* Op.8 1932 (Br&H) 17 min. Romantic conception with musical and technical difficulties equally divided between the 2 instruments. Has much audience appeal. M-D.

Edmund Rubbra. *Sonata* Op.60 g 1946 (Lengnick) 31pp., parts. 22 min. Andante moderato: close to rondo form. Vivace flessible: a scherzo. Finale (Tema–Adagio) is a set of 7 contrapuntal variations ending with a fugue. Piano writing shows great variety in texture. M-D.

Marcel Rubin. *Sonata* 1928 (Dob 1974) 29pp., parts. 15 min. Molto vivace: octotonic, freely tonal around C, clear textures, linear. Grave: changing meters, mixture of chordal and linear textures, freely tonal around G. Allegro commodo: melodic counterpoint between the 2 instruments. Presto: dancelike (waltz), long lines, 2 contrapuntal lines between instruments, chordal coda. Neoclassic. M-D.

Anton Rubinstein. *Sonata* Op.18 D (Schulz—GS L63; USSR 70pp.; Augener 51pp.), parts. 26 min.

———. *Sonata* II Op.39 G (Br&H). Beautiful and grateful writing. Easily comprehended by lay audiences. M-D.

Armand Russell. *Jovian Sonatina* (Boume 1974) 9pp., parts. For solo bass clef instruments and piano.

Pierre Ruyssen. *Concertino* 1963 (Detrieu) 23pp., parts. Allegro moderato; Andante; Final. Conservative writing, operatic overtones. M-D.

Camille Saint-Saëns. *Sonata* I Op.32 C (Durand; IMC 2888; USSR). Allegro; Andante; Finale. An elegant and agitated work with clear Classical forms. One basic tempo per movement. Recapitulation always displays the ideas in their original order. Piano and cello are combined in intriguing configurations, but the independence of each instrument is never overlooked. The short, majestic Andante is treated in a full chorale style that contrasts effectively with the stormy and tempestuous Finale. A truly beautiful work that deserves to be heard more often. M-D.

———. *Sonata* II Op.123 F (Durand 1905). A rather serene and graceful opening movement leads to a classical scherzo followed by a Romantic Adagio and a disappointing finale. M-D.

———. *Romance* Op.36 F (K) 5pp., parts, also transcribed for horn. 4 min. Charming work in $\frac{3}{4}$ meter. Complementary instrumental parts require sensitivity for performance. M. D.

Aulis Sallinen. *Metamorfora* (Fazer 1974) 7pp., parts. Ideas evolve in a freely tonal style with a preference for 9th chords. Sustained sonorities in piano, sectionalized, mildly 20th-century. M-D.

———. *From a Swan Song* Op.67 (Novello 12-0728 1991) 20pp., parts.

Erkki Salmenhaara. *Sonata* 1960 (Fazer) 16pp., parts. Allegro; Adagio; Allegro. Neoclassic orientation. Clear textures, freely tonal, some changing meters, carefully crafted, much imitation in final movement. M-D.

Giovanni Battista Sammartini. *Sonata* G (N. Karjinsky—ESC 1963) 12pp., parts. 12 min. Allegro; Grave; Vivace. The realization contains some sonorities too heavy for this style. M-D.

———. *Sonata* G (Moffat—Schott).

———. *Sonata* G (Rose—IMC).

———. *Sonata* G (Salmon—Ric R101).

———. *Sonata* G (Stutschewsky—IMC).

———. *Sonata* G (Senart 5349).

———. *Sonata* G (Krane—Spratt).

———. *Sonata* g (Sal—Ric R703).

———. *Sonata* a (Ruf—Schott).

Some of these *Sonatas* may be duplicates.

Pierre Sancan. *Sonate* 1961 (Durand) 18pp., parts. Allegro deciso; Andante sostenuto; Vif. Disjunct octaves, freely tonal, chordal punctuation, toccata-like passages, octotonic, glissandi, melodic line superimposed in triplets. Expressive sonorities in Andante sostenuto; perpetual motion and toccata style in Vif. Superb piano writing. Large span required. D.

Luis Sandi. *Sonatina* (EMM 1965) 15pp., parts. Largo–Allegro comodo; Adagio non troppo; Allegro vivo. Colorful writing, some Latin American rhythmic treatment. M-D.

A. Adnan Saygun. *Sonata* Op.12 1935 (PIC 1961) 31pp., parts. Animato: broken-7th figures in ostinato style, freely tonal, tranquillo second section, modal; dramatic clusterlike sonority concludes movement. Largo: mixture of chordal and arpeggi texture, quartal harmony, recitative-like, brief Allegro and Vivace sections. Allegro assai: shifting meters, large span required, rhythmic, octotonic, brilliant conclusion; large span required. Turkish national flavor mixed with traditional forms. M-D to D.

Alessandro Scarlatti. *Tre Sonate* (G. Zanaboni—Zanibon 1967) 12pp., parts. Published for the first time. Unfigured bass realized. Introductory note in Italian and English. I d, II c, III C. M-D.

Christoph Schaffrath. *Sonate* A (H. Neemann—Br&H 1942) 11pp., parts. Allegretto; Adagio; Allegro. An attractive work; tasteful continuo realization. M-D.

Peter Schickele. *Mountain Music I* 1989 (EV 164-00203 1992) 16pp., parts. 10 min. 1. In Magic Meadow; 2. Stony Mountain Holler; 3. Jerome Evenings. "The music combines major and minor in a way that I associate with the singing and banjo playing of Dock Boggs, although Boggs' style is considerably less gentle. I chose the title 'Stony Mountain Holler' as a tribute to the best traditional bluegrass band record I've ever heard, performed by Earl Taylor and his Stony Mountain Boys. I am particularly fond of Bluegrass hollers, in which long, slow-moving notes are sung over an almost maniacally busy accompaniment and the central section of this movement certainly owes a debt to one of my favorite songs, 'In the Pines' " (from Program Note). M-D.

——. *Eagle Rock: Sonatina* 1996 (EV 164-00243 1999) 8pp., parts. 4½ min. 1. Song, for Armen; 2. Scherzo, for Luke and Cassie; III. Lullaby for Vanessa. Curiosity pieces, playful and songlike in colorful harmonic structures. Can be played separately. Int. to M-D.

Alfred Schnittke. *Sonate* II 1993–94 (Sikorski 1995 1997) 19pp., parts. 12 min. Senza tempo; Allegro; Largo; Allegro; Lento. Economical writing with a preference for thin textures. Outer movements are more contemplative with mostly single notes in piano. Widely divergent technical requirements between movements with double and triple stops in cello almost unplayable in fourth mvt. Wide span a must in second mvt. where cluster chords requiring full hand and arm are required. Mvts.4–5 must be played together while the others could be performed separately. Int. to M-D.

Othmar Schoeck. *Sonata* (Br 3960 1959) 21pp., parts. Fliessend; Schnell; Andantino. This work was intended by the composer to have 4 movements, but only 3 were completed when he died. Freely tonal with great doses of chromaticism in the Schnell movement especially. Neoclassic, thin textures. M-D.

Ruth Schonthal. *Sonata Concertante* 1973 (Furore 274 1997, ISMN M-50012-175-6) 40pp., parts. For cello, viola, or clarinet. Largo, ma molto rubato; Slow, calmly, with much expression; Allegro moderato. Bold, daring writing in characters ranging from calmness to agitatedness. "Ruth Schonthal's compositions, which reflect the concerns of today's world, display a unique blend of her deeply rooted European tradition, depth of feeling and masterful blending of traditional and contemporary techniques" (from Preface). M-D.

Franz Schubert. *Sonate 'Arpeggione'* Op.Post. D.821 a 1824 (W.-D. Seiffert, R. Ginzel, K. Schilde—Henle 611 1995, 29pp.; L. Rose—IMC 1953 23pp.; H. Wirth, K. Storck—Br 6970 1989 23pp.), parts. Transcription for viola or cello. See detailed entry under duos for piano and viola.

Robert Schumann. *Fantasiestücke* Op.73 (W. Boetticher, E. Herttrich, H.-M. Theopold—Henle 422 1986, ISMN M-2018-0422-4) 15pp., parts. Originally for piano and clarinet, first published with ad lib parts for violin and cello. See detailed entry under duos for piano and clarinet. Excellent Preface. M-D.

——. *Fantasiestücke* Op.73; *Adagio und Allegro* Op.70; *Stücke im Volkston* Op.102 (F. Grützmacher—CFP 2373 1950) 47pp., parts, with play-along CD. *Adagio und Allegro* was originally for horn or cello; see detailed entry under horn and piano. *Stücke im Volkston* is an original work for cello and piano, consisting of 5 short pieces. Nos.I and V contain optional violin part written in full score. M-D.

——. *Fünf Stücke im Volkston* Op.102 (J. Draheim—Br&H 8456 1991 27pp.; GS 19pp.), parts. I. 'Vanitas Vanitatum', Mit Humor; II. Langsam; III. Nicht schnell, mit viel Ton zu spielen; IV. Nicht zu rasch; V. Stark und markiert. "'Im Volkston' refers less to the contents than to Schumann's intent to compose in a songful, unpretentious manner, without salon-like elegance and virtuoso rhetoric, in a manner that lets the instruments simply 'speak,' without having to make any kind of compromises in technique or substance" (from Preface). A charming set of pieces suggestive of folk styles which have subsequently been transcribed for many instruments, including violin (Br&H 8473).

Humphrey Searle. *Fantasy* Op.57 1972 (Faber) 7 min. Eight variations and cadenza. Requires a big technique. D.

Ralph Shapey. *Kroslish Sonate* 1985 (TP 114-40457 1987) 16pp., parts. 22 min. Maestoso: broad dramatic gestures; mixed rhythmic patterns; double and triple stops; cello tunes C string to A; some material borrowed from composer's *Double Concerto*. Delicato: $\frac{4}{4} + \frac{1}{16}$ meter alternates with conventional and other asymmetrical meters; uses full range of instruments; widely spaced chords. Maestoso–Quasi scherzo: marked rhythms; large gestures; *fff* ending. Large span required. M-D to D.

Rodion Shchedrin. *Sonate* 1996 (Schott CB160 1997, ISMN M-001-12045-6) 38pp., parts. 28 min. Allegretto; Moderato; Sostenuto assai. Colorful harmony in playful, rhythmic settings. Cellist will enjoy quadruple-stop pizzicato with glissandi on each string at end of Moderato. Wide span required. M-D.

Vissarion Shebalin. *Sonata* Op.51/3 C (USSR 2541). Versatile contrapuntal style. Slow movement most appealing with a highly individual technique. D.

Seymour Shifrin. *Sonata* (J. Krosnick, G. Kalish—Columbia University Press, 1990) 34pp., parts. Allegro agitato; Largo; Scherzo–Allegro. A 5-note motive announced at the outset by cello becomes the center of gravity for the first movement as permutations of its rhythmic and pitch patterns are explored in an agitated manner. The cantabile slow movement and Scherzo finale follow in restless spirit with contrasting features uniquely their own. M-D.

Dmitri Shostakovitch. *Sonata* Op.40 d 1934 (Piatigorsky—Leeds 48pp., parts; Rose—IMC 36pp., parts; CFP 4748; USSR) 26 min. One of the most important works in the 20th-century repertoire. Moderato: pliable thematic material, contemplative at first, more dramatic later. Moderato con moto: scherzolike, large structure, peasant humor. Largo: serious, concentrated texture. Allegretto: vivacious, witty. D.

Jean Sibelius. *Three Easy Pieces* (Warner/Chappel Music 1988, ISMN M-042-08784-8) 16pp., parts. *Andantino* C (1884?): ternary form; lyric, with facile writing. *Andante molto* f (1887): $^6_8$; rich harmonies in chordal texture. *Tempo di valse 'Lulu Waltz'* f♯ (1889): oom-pah-pah rhythm alongside flowing 8ths; wide span required. Wonderful early works by the composer, useful in many settings. Preface in Finnish and English. Int. to M-D.

Emil Sjögren. *Sonate* Op.58 A (WH 1409) 25pp., parts. Allegro agitato; Romanza; Allegro con spirito. Romantic writing in a Nordic Brahmsian style and idiom. D.

Nikos Skalkottas. *Largo* (UE 1965) 5pp., parts. Turgid, thick chromatic textures. M-D.

———. *Sonatina* 1949 (UE 12387 1955) 24pp., parts. 15½ min. Allegro moderato; Andante; Allegro molto vivace. Freely atonal but resembles the composer's 12-tone works in sonority. Long lyric lines lend themselves to linear treatment. Novel harmonic idiom. Requires a large span and firm rhythmic control. D.

———. *Tender Melody* 1949 (UE). Brooding, dark lyricism. Piano part consists of various figurations and is built on an ostinato of three 4-voice chords. Uses early Schoenberg techniques. M-D.

Lucijan Marija Skerjanc. *Capriccio* (Društva Slovenskih Skladateljev & Gerig 1974) 24pp., parts. Cello part edited by Ciril Skerjanc.

Myroslav Skoryk. *A-RI-A* (Duma 1998) 8pp., parts. Characteristic piece in ternary form marked Andante concentrating on the pitch "A" with colorful harmonies in chordal texture. Middle section calls for a little more motion and uses a dotted rhythm to an oom-pah bounce. May be played on violin (part included). M-D.

Rick Sowash. *Harvest Hymn and Harvest Dance* 1980, rev.1996 (Sowash 1996) 9pp., parts. 6 min. Homage to Willa Cather. The composer has noted that "since harvest is such an important image in her work, it seemed right to use harvest music—a hymn and a square dance—in my musical homage. Of course, the hymn in my homage isn't really usable by a congregation on Sunday morning and the harvest dance wouldn't go over at a barn dance (it's in $\frac{7}{8}$ time). I've stylized in somewhat the same way as Cather's prose stylizes the 'folk events' that comprise her stories. The formal outline of the piece is borrowed from Copland's Clarinet Concerto" (from Program Notes, *Rick Sowash: A Portrait at 50*, compact disc recording, Rich Sowash Publishing Co., 2000, p.3). Lyric in strongly tonal setting with vibrant rhythm. M-D.

———. *The Cliffs above the Clear Fork* 1980 (Sowash), parts. 6½ min. Majestic, picturesque essay on a geographical location near Bellville, Ohio, from which the title of this work is taken. Slower tempos with passionate writing in rich harmonic color. M-D.

Leo Sowerby. *Sonata* H.160 G 1921 (Sowerby 1996) 40pp., parts. Gently swinging, yet not slowly; Slowly and Rhapsodically; Fast and Breezily; Very rhythmically. Large-scale designs of deeply personal perspectives with rich, colorful harmonies and lyric melodies. Arpeggiated and repeated-note harmonics in cello in the finale will require special attention. Parts fit together well. M-D.

Zeev Steinberg. *Six Miniatures* (IMI 1973). A dodecaphony primer similar to Křenek's *Twelve Short Piano Pieces.* Int.

Halsey Stevens. *Hungarian Children's Songs* (PIC 1957) 10pp., parts. The tunes on which these charming pieces are based were chosen from a large collection of children's game songs (*Gyermekjátékok*) edited by Bartók and Kodály. Many of the games are similar to the round games played in England and America, such as "London Bridge," "Go in and out the Window," etc. The texts (which are included), like those of "Mother Goose" rhymes, are frequently obscure in meaning and defy literal translation. Six tunes are attractively set in clear textures with the piano having an equal share in the ensemble. Int. to M-D.

———. *Three Hungarian Folk Songs* 1950 (Highgate 1968). For viola (cello, English horn, or clarinet) and piano. See detailed entry under duos for piano and viola.

———. *Three Pieces* 1947 (CFP 1958) 9pp., parts. 4½ min. For bassoon (or cello) and piano. See detailed entry under duos for piano and bassoon.

———. *Intermezzo, Cadenza and Finale* 1949, rev.1950 (PIC) 12pp., parts. 7½ min. Adagio: *pp* dark, low, sustained chords in piano support a more active yet dolce cello line. A *forte* in piano interrupts briefly what is otherwise a hypnotic and hushed Intermezzo. The Cadenza is mainly for the cello, with the piano making a few chordal and melodic contributions derived from the opening movement. The strong Finale is rhythmically active with contrasting sections. A meno mosso coda returns the Intermezzo mood, and the work closes in delicate and mysterious shadings. Suitelike in many ways, this work also fulfils the aesthetics of a fine Sonata. M-D.

———. *Music for Christopher* 1953 (PIC 1968) 8pp., parts. 3 min. Four short contrasting movements (Andante; Con moto moderato; Andante con moto; Allegretto) based on folklike material. Appealing. M-D.

———. *Sonatina Giocosa* 1954 (ACA) 7 min. For double bass (or cello) and piano. See detailed entry under duos for piano and double bass.

———. *Sonatina I* 1957 (Helios) 11pp., parts. 8 min. Moderato con moto: syncopated chords under a basically diatonic melody, hemiola, ternary design. Poco adagio: octotonic, moving chromatic chords, choralelike; large span required. Allegro: opening rhythmic motif is worked through many guises; brittle and staccato sonorities are interlaced with longer melodic lines supported by sustained chords; contains augmentation, diminution, and a cracking good closing. M-D to D.

———. *Sonata* 1965 (PIC) 27pp., parts. 14½ min. Commodo: freely centered around b, octotonic, octaves, quintal and tertian harmonies mainly with some quartal sonorities, tritone important, free imitation. Poco adagio: piano introduction, subtle metrical shifts from $\frac{7}{8}$ to $\frac{6}{8}$ keep expressive line constantly alive. Allegro moderato: sprightly rhythmic figures are transformed; cantando, more sustained mid-section brings out longer lines developed from opening figures; moving 3rds in piano part; octotonic writing in 16th notes leads to closing. Large span required. M-D to D.

See Edward Ernest Dixon, "The Violoncello Works of Halsey Stevens," D.M.A. diss., University of Cincinnati, 1989.

Alan Stout. *Sonata* 1966 (CFP 1975) 25pp., parts. 18 min. Moderato ₒ = 60–63; Moderato ₒ = 100–104; Maestoso ♩ = 56, ₒ = 112. Each movement has other tempos than the one listed at the beginning. "In the Presto section of the second movement, notes without stems are to be played freely, as the visual pattern suggests—within the time stated. Black notes are to be played short, white notes long and somewhat marcato. The absolute duration of the notes depends on the pedal indications, which *must* be followed strictly ... It is my hope that a performance of this work will give a sense of improvisation and play (in the highest meaning of that word). The performers should not hesitate to 'bend' the tempo; i.e., use nineteenth-century style rubato to accomplish this expressive aim" (from the Performing Notes). Complex rhythmic procedure, pointillistic, dynamic extremes, expressionistic. Entire range of both instruments used. D.

Richard Strauss. *Sonata* Op.6 F (UE 1007; Rose—IMC). 27 min. The less theatrical slow movement seems to come off best in this youthful piece, although keen regard for the artistic balance of both instruments is shown. Masterly technical skill is revealed, and there are numerous inspired passages. D.

Igor Stravinsky. *Suite Italian* 1932 (Edition Russe de Musique 1934) 27pp., parts. Arr. from the ballet *Pulcinella* by the composer in collaboration with Gregor Piatigorsky. Introduzione; Serenata; Aria; Tarantella; Minuetto e Finale. M-D.

Soulima Stravinsky. *Sonata* (CFP 67366 1992) 26pp., parts. 15 min. Allegro moderato; Allegretto [theme with 12 variations]; Molto vivace. Opening theme placed on off-beats in staccato texture. Forms are not lengthy, including the variations where a compendium of designs spanning historical periods are introduced. M-D.

Howard Swanson. *Suite* (Weintraub 1951) 27pp., parts. Prelude; Pantomime; Dirge; Recessional. Fluent writing, flexible meters, freely tonal, clear lines, well worked out. Much facility is required for the Recessional. M-D to D.

Alexander Tansman. *Sonata* C 1930 (ESC) 27pp., parts. 15 min. Allegro moderato: parallel harmonies, chromatic, secco style in lower register; large span required. Largo: ostinato-like figures, tranquil and legato, rich harmonies, works to appassionato climax and subsides to *pp* ending. Scherzo: changing meters in signature: $\frac{3}{4}, \frac{3}{8}, \frac{4}{4}, \frac{3}{8}$; octotonic, bitonal, shifting rhythms, unusual conclusion. M-D to D.

——. *Quatre Pièces Faciles* (ESC 1991) 9pp., parts. Cavatine; Sicilienne; Rondine; Serenade. Uses only first position on cello. Int.

Simón Tapia Colman. *Sonata* (EMM 1961) 27pp., parts. Moderato; Largo; Giocoso; Vivo. Serial overtones, syncopation, parallel chordal shifts, some awkward arpeggi in final movement. M-D.

Alexandre Tcherepnin. *Sonata* Op.29 D 1924 (Hekking—Durand) 16pp., parts. 10 min. Allegro (SA); Cadenza; Allegretto (Rondo). Skilfully written, eclectic style, attractive, contrapuntal Cadenza. M-D.

——. *Sonata* II Op.30/1 1924 (UE 7349) 20pp., parts. 10 min. Moderato: SA, thin textures, chromatic, octotonic; recapitulation is transposed down a major 3rd. Lento: 3 free contrapuntal lines. Vivace: Rondo, triplet and duplet figuration, hemiola, unusual rhythmic vitality. M-D.

——. *Sonata* III Op.30/2 1919, rev.1926 (UE 9572 1928) 18pp., parts. 8 min. Allegro moderato; Andantino; Presto. Colorful writing with the piano part thoroughly exploited. Pianistic, as one would expect, since the composer is an outstanding pianist. M-D.

——. *12 Préludes* Op.38 (L. Fournier—Durand 1927) 36pp., parts. Based on a scale of 9 intervals. Untitled but picturesque with changing characters and requirements. May be played separately. Large span required for several. M-D.

——. *Songs and Dances* Op.84 (Belaieff 3476 1955) 19pp., parts. Georgian Song; Tartar Dance; Russian Song; Kazakh Dance. Strongly contrasting pieces in Tcherepnin's typically early-20th-century style. Kazakh Dance is the longest and most demanding. Wide span required. M-D to D.

Georg Philipp Telemann. *Sonata* G ca.1729 (H. Joelson—Amadeus BP818 1997) 9pp., parts, including basso. For viola da gamba or viola. Siciliana; Vivace; Dolce; Scherzando. Opening 3 movements are in binary form and the fourth in ternary. Fine edition with thoughtful realization. M-D.

————. *Zwei Sonaten* ca.1739 (H. Joelson—Amadeus BP640 1997) 19pp., parts, including basso. For viola da gamba or viola. First published in Telemann's *Essercizii musici.* 1 e: Cantabile; Allegro; Recitativo–Arioso; Vivace. 2 a: Largo; Allegro; Soave; Allegro. These 2 *Sonatas* show the influence of the Style Galant. Outstanding edition. M-D.

————. *Sonata* a (Ruyssen—Delrieu).

————. *Sonata* D from *Der getreue Musikmeister* (Degen—Br; Upmeyer—Nag 23 8pp., parts; Upmeyer—IMC) Lento; Allegro; Largo; Allegro. In the Upmeyer editions a few wrong notes are found in bars 15–16 in the first Allegro. M-D.

Several additional Sonatas and Sonatinas are available in editions for cello, viola da gamba, or bassoon. See detailed entries under duos for piano and bassoon.

Augusta Reid Thomas. *Chant* (TP 114-40635 1994) 20pp., parts. 15 min. Commences Majestic in a declamatory manner with added-note chords using the full range of the piano against a B♭ pedal point in the cello. A second contrasting movement marked Rubato is intensely expressive in its cantabile spirit and recitative qualities. Proportional rhythmic relationships. Performers must have a strong feeling for gravitational points in an otherwise independent scoring of parts. D.

Olav Thommessen. *Duo-Sonata* 1968 (IU) 32pp., parts. Adagio grandiose; Pastorale; Adagio serioso; Intermezzo. Strong, dramatic, unusual writing; unique personal style. Expressionist, intense. Clusters at conclusion. Complex and very difficult for both instruments. D.

Niso Ticciati. *Sonata* G "Homage to J. S. Bach" (OUP 1963) 12pp., parts. "This sonata is intended to serve as an introduction to the study of the early Italian sonatas and has therefore been composed in a corresponding style" (Note in the score). M-D.

Ernst Toch. *Sonata* Op.50 (Schott 1929) 20pp., parts. 12 min. Allegro commodo; Intermezzo: "Die Spinne"; Allegro. First movement opens pandiatonically but evolves into more chromaticism until almost every note has an accidental attached. This clears up and a brief return to the opening mood ends the movement. The last movement has a great dance exuberance about it. Infectious writing. M-D.

Giuseppe Torelli. *Sonata* G (F. Giegling—HM 69) 7pp., parts. Adagio; Allegro; Adagio; Allegro. Valuable Preface by the editor. Elegant and expressive writing. M-D.

Joan Tower. *Très Lent (Hommage à Messiaen)* (AMP 8080 1995, ISBN 0-7935-3856-4) 5pp., parts. 9 min. Spatial, contemplative musicality developed through sustained-note durations, inspired by the slowest movement in Messiaen's *Quatuor pour la Fin du Temps*. M-D.

Ernst Ludwig Uray. *Sonata* f (Dob 1969) 50pp., parts. Kraftvoll, energisch, mässig Schnell: highly chromatic; slower and more sustained second tonal area; numerous inner voices; concludes in A at a *ppp* level; requires large span. Nicht Schnell, humorvoll: B♭, parallel chords, a dry humor. Sehr langsam, ausdrucksvoll: c, legato, intense, rich harmonies, soaring line, widely spread chords. Rhapsodisch bewegt: f, broken-chord figuration, contrasting sections, dramatic gestures, much activity, closes in f on a *sfz*. D.

Ralph Vaughan Williams. *Six Studies in English Folksong* (Galaxy 1927; MMP) 13pp., parts. Adagio; Andante sostenuto; Larghetto; Lento; Andante tranquillo; Allegro vivace. Picturesque settings in snapshot views. Alternative versions for violin, viola, English horn, clarinet, and bassoon exist. M-D.

———. *Fantasia on Greensleeves* (W. Forbes—OUP 1947). For viola or cello. See detailed entry under duos for piano and viola.

Aurelio de la Vega. *Legend of the Creole Ariel* 1953 (PAU 1955) 13pp., parts. An invigorating work with demanding writing for both instruments. Flavored with Vega's native Cuban rhythms. M-D.

Heitor Villa-Lobos. *Grand Concerto* (ESC) 20 min.

———. *Pequena Suite* 1913 (Casa Arthur Napoleao 1913) 15pp., parts. In 6 short movements: Romancette, Legendária, Harmonias soltas, Fugato (all' antica), Melodia, Gavotte–Scherzo. Picturesque in a strongly lyric style with only mild harmonic dissonances. Can be performed as individual pieces though the Suite conception is preferable. M-D.

———. *Sonata* II Op.66 1916 (ESC 1930) 56pp., parts. 23 min. No folklore influences are found in this work. It is built on solid traditional structures. Allegro moderato: extensive piano introduction; freely tonal around a; bold gestures; triplet figure divided between hands; involved rhythms; Presto coda. Andante cantabile: flowing line in cello; subtle syncopation in piano; widely rolled chords require left hand to cross over right hand; some quartal harmony. Scherzo: strong accents; octotonic, hemiola, double glissandi, fast harmonic rhythm. Allegro vivace sostenuto: percussive sonorities; 3 with 4; free counterpoint; large chords; a maze of tonal flux creates a downpour of color; requires large span. D.

Antonio Vivaldi. *Six Sonatas* (D. Hellmann—CFP 4938 44pp., parts, second cello ad lib; N. Graudan—GS L1794; Kolneder—Schott; Chaigneau—Senart 5082 45pp., parts; L. Dallapiccola—IMC 44pp., parts) 1 B♭, 2 F, 3 a, 4 B♭, 5 e, 6 B♭. The CFP edition is clean and includes tasteful realizations. The Senart edition has some heavy-handed realizations. The GS edition has a Preface that describes the editor's procedure: 1. Tempo definitions have been made more specific, and some descriptive terms have been added. 2. Dynamic markings have been provided (Vivaldi left none). 3. Additional bowings have been indicated. "These [4-movement] sonatas deserve a high place in the cellists' concert repertoire, but they are also singularly well suited for teaching purposes because of the many technical and musical problems they offer" (from the Foreword). Tasteful realizations. M-D.

———. *Sonatas* (Ric). Nine Sonatas for cello and basso continuo, published separately. *Sonata* F.XIV/1 B♭ (PR1148). *Sonata* F.XIV/2 F (PR1149). *Sonata* F.XIV/3 a (PR1150). *Sonata* F.XIV/4 B♭ (PR1151). *Sonata* F.XIV/5 e (PR1152). *Sonata* F.XIV/6 B♭ (PR1153). *Sonata* F.XIV/7 a (PR1178). *Sonata* F.XIV/8 E♭ (PR1179). *Sonata* F.XIV/9 g (PR1205). Outstanding editions.

———. *Sonata* a (Rose—IMC).

———. *Sonata* B♭ (Rose—IMC).

———. *Sonata* VI B♭ (Ticciati—Hin).

———. *Sonata* c (Salmon—Ric R691).

———. *Sonata* e (Salmon—Ric R692).

———. *Sonata* V e (Rose—IMC "Concerto in e"; Ticciati—Hin).

Hans Vogt. *Elemente zu einer Sonate* 1973 (Bo&BO) 24pp., parts. 18 min. Contains 14 separate sections, each involving one or more of the following elements: clusters, pointillistic treatment, unmeasured sections, complex rhythms, changing meters, varied moods and textures, tremolo, percussive use of piano, Expressionist writing. D.

George Walker. *Sonata* 1957 (Gen 1972) 30pp., parts. 15 min. Allegro passionate: SA; most involved movement of the work; opens with undulating triplets; contrasting spiky second idea; worked-through development section; slightly varied recapitulation fades away to *pp*. Sostenuto: piano part mainly chordal. Allegro: uses syncopation in a highly dramatic fashion; some of the spiky idea from the opening movement returns; Presto coda adds a brilliant finishing touch. M-D to D.

Robert Ward. *Arioso and Tarantelle* 1954 (Highgate 1960). For viola or cello. See detailed entry under duos for piano and viola.

Ben Weber. *Five Pieces* Op.13 1941 (J. Krosnick, G. Kalish—Columbia University Press 1988) 11pp., parts. 7 min. Animato; Allegretto; Largo; Largamente, Misterioso; Alla marcia. Contrapuntal 12-tone idiom, declarative statements, jaunty rhythms, flexible meters, clever "oom-pah" basses in Alla Marcia. Requires large span. D.

———. *Sonata* Op.17 (ACA) 9 min. Relaxed 12-tone idiom; vocal melodic contours almost recall Schubert. D.

Anton Webern. *Two Pieces* 1899 (G. Piatigorsky—CF 1975) 7pp., parts. From the composer's autograph MS in the Moldenhauer Archives.

———. *Cello Sonata* 1914 (F. Cerha—CF 1966) 3pp., parts. Taken from Webern's autograph MS in the Moldenhauer Archives. One sketched-out movement, intense and Expressionist. D.

————. *Three Small Pieces* Op.11 1914 (UE) 3pp., parts. 2½ min. Thirty-two aphoristic bars of skeletal statements, distilled and delivered through instrumentalized veils. Webern's exclusive aesthetic, which balances between sound and its cessation, has reached the end. It is very difficult to make these pithy epigrams comprehensible. D.

Charles-Marie Widor. *Suite* Op.21 e (Heugel 1912), parts. I. Méditation, II. Appassionato, III. Canzonetta, IV. Final. Published separately and as a set. M-D.
————. *Sonata* Op.80 (Heugel).

Jean Wiener. *Sonate* 1968 (Sal) 38pp., parts. Dedicated to Mstislav Rostropovitch. Lent–Vif; Largo; third movement untitled. Freely tonal and chromatic, alternating hands, arpeggi figuration, dancelike rhythms in final movement, strongly bitonal. Large span required. D.

Robert Wittinger. *Polemica* Op.29 1974 (Br&H 5028) 30pp., parts. Reproduced from holograph. Instructions in German. Clusters, indefinite repetitions, pointillistic, proportional notation, glissandi, sectional changes in tempo and texture, intense, percussive, nervous, avant-garde. D.

Joseph Wölfl. *Sonate* Op.31 d (F. Längin—Br HM 111 1953) 28pp., parts. Largo; Allegro molto; Andante; Finale–Allegro. Pianistic, much in the Classical style (middle Beethoven). The Andante is very touching. A fine and little-known addition to the literature. M-D.

William Wordsworth. *Sonata* Op.9 e 1937 (Lengnick 1946) 47pp., parts. Poco adagio–Allegro moderato; Largamente e molto cantabile; Allegro con brio. Post-Romantic writing, interesting chromatic treatment, big climaxes. M-D to D.

Charles Wuorinen. *Adopting to the Times* (CFP 1968-9) 46pp., 16 min. A first-rate pianist is required to handle the complexities. D.
————. *Duuiensela* 1962 (ACA) 28pp., parts. 9 min. Conventional and tactus-style notation. "The basic principle involved (in tactus-style notation) is that a constant quantity of space (demarked by half-bar-lines) represents a constant quantity of time (in this score, one second). Within this time-space, notes are positioned visually, and must be played so that: their occurrence in time corresponds to their placement in space" (from the score). Contains other directions. Pointillistic, clusters, flexible meters, serial influence, glissandi, dynamic extremes, virtuoso writing for both performers. Mixture of traditional and avant-garde. D.
————. *Grand Union* (CF) 13 min.

Isang Yun. *Espace 1* 1992 (Bo&Bo 1993) 12pp., parts. 11 min. In one movement with an emphasis on sonorous relationships. Requires experienced performers. Dynamics constantly shift between *fff* and *pppp* in an ever-changing texture. D.

Bernd Alois Zimmermann. *Intercomunicazione* 1967 (Schott 6004) 40pp., 2 scores necessary. 12–24 min. Graphic notation; piano adds pitches and chords and other short passages. Only time points are given to indicate ensemble; dynamics are serialized. Avant-garde. For the venturesome only. D.

Johann Rudolf Zumsteeg. *Sonata* B♭ (F. Längin—CFP 4823 1961) 18pp., parts. Allegro; Adagio; Finale–Presto. This attractive work, published 2 years after Zumsteeg's death, is apparently incomplete, having only 2 movements and just a "basso" part for accompaniment. The editor has realized the bass part in a simple, early Classical style and has added a Finale, the last movement of another cello Sonata of Zumsteeg's, still in MS. This last movement may be omitted. M-D.

Ellen Taaffe Zwilich. *Lament* 2000 (Merion 144-40419 2000) 4pp., parts. 7 min. In one movement with frequently changing meters. The composer notes "the performer should feel free to 'sculpt' the rhythm and dynamics for expressive purposes in order to give a spontaneous, improvisatory quality to the piece. It would be ideal if no two performers were exactly alike" (from score). M-D.

Duos for Piano and Double Bass

Alain Abbott. *Fusions* 1973 (EMT 1309) 13pp., parts. 6½ min. Concours du Conservatoire National Supérieur de Musique de Paris 1974. Rocking chordal figuration of various intervals, chromatic, cluster-like sonorities, independent lines, some avant-garde notation, proportional rhythmic relationships, tremolo, complex. Requires large span. D.

André Ameller. *Concertino* (IMC 1953) 12pp., parts. One movement with varied tempos and moods, flexible meters, freely tonal, mildly 20th-century. Shows off both instruments to good advantage. M-D.
———. *Sonate* I Op.39 G (Durand 1948) 12pp., parts. Allegro; Lento espressivo; Vivace. Tonal, clear textures, Neoclassic. M-D.

Gustavo Becerra-Schmidt. *Sonata* 1964 (LAMC) 13pp., parts. Allegro giusto; Andante; Allegro tranquillo. Neoclassic, clear, light textures, on quiet side. M-D.

Lennox Berkeley. *Introduction and Allegro* (Yorke 1972) 10pp., parts. Short with freshness and a lack of complexity, Neoclassic. Problem of balance is beautifully solved, well crafted. M-D.

Johann Adam Birkenstock. *Sonate* g (E. Bigot, D. Boussagol—Leduc 1954) 16pp., parts. Adagio; Allegro; Largo cantabile; Allegro con spirito. Effective keyboard realization. M-D.

Chester Biscardi. *Companion Piece* 1989 (CFP 67493a 1995) 9pp., parts. 6½ min. A musical commentary on Morton Feldman's *Extensions 3* for solo piano, to whom the work is dedicated. Explores harmonic color through subtle shifting of chord members, sometimes in dense relationships. A slow tempo permeates though a rather flexible interpretation is recommended. Contains performance and accidental guide. M-D.

Giovanni Bottesini. *Complete Bottesini* (Slatford—Yorke 1974) Preface in English and German. Vol.I: 34pp., parts. Contains *Bolero; Romanza patética (mélodie); Gavotta;* "Ne cor più non mi sento," *Tema con variazione* Op.23. Vol.II:

52pp., parts. Contains *Allegretto capriccio; Romanza drammatica (élégie)* Op.20; *Fantasia "I Puritani"; Fantasia "Lucia di Lammermoor."*

———. *Fantasia Lucia* (G. Járdányi—Akkord 1046 1999) 16pp., parts. 11 min. Drawn from Donizetti's *Lucia di Lammermoor*. Favors double bass but contains a lengthy piano introduction. Preface in English, Hungarian, and Italian. M-D.

———. *Fantasia Beatrice di Tenda* (G. Járdányi—Akkord 1053 2000) 20pp., parts. 11 min. Uses themes from Bellini's *Beatrice di Tenda*. Thick chordal writing and tremolos in piano can create balance problems. Invigorating with some alternating between instruments. Preface in English, Hungarian, and Italian. M-D.

———. *Tarantella* a (F. Zimmermann-IMC 1707 1956) 8pp., parts. 6 min. A playful work commencing with piano introduction and double bass cadenza. M-D. A famous double bass virtuoso of his day, Bottesini wrote piano and orchestral scores for most of these works.

Auguste Chapuis. *Fantaisie Concertante* (Durand 1907) 11pp., parts. Contrasted sections, late-Romantic style, similar to an opera transcription, tuneful. M-D.

Alfred Désenclos. *Aria and Rondo* (Leduc 21070 1952) 15pp., parts. Two distinctive movements. Neoclassic with complementary interaction between instruments. M-D.

Klaus Dillmann. *Sonate* e (Hofmeister 1957) 18pp., parts. Allegro moderato; Adagio cantabile; Allegretto. Mildly 20th-century, quartal and quintal harmonies, clear lines. M-D.

———. *Introduktion und Allegro* c$\sharp$ (Hofmeister) 10pp., parts. Commences with a brief Introduction of sustained double stops and thin pianistic texture with restless rhythms, then settles into a straightforward melody in a homophonic setting. A lively Allegro–Allegro vivace assai follows which bounces back and forth between duple and triple meters in a spirited manner with marked motives. Comes together quickly for performers. M-D.

Domenico Dragonetti. *Adagio and Rondo* C (Yorke 1975) 26pp., parts.

———. *Concerto* A (E. Nanny—Leduc 1925) 19pp., parts. Allegro moderato; Andante; Allegro giusto. Generally well edited. M-D.

———. *Concerto* A (Nanny, Sankey—IMC).

———. *Three Waltzes* (R. Slatford—Yorke 1969) 3pp., parts. Very brief, binary forms. M-D.

Pierre Max Dubois. *Le Gal cascadeur* (Rideau Rouge 1973) 4pp., parts. Variations très faciles.

Henry Eccles. *Sonata* g (F. Zimmerman—IMC 1951) 8pp., parts. Largo; Corrente–Allegro con spirito; Adagio; Vivace. An effective transcription. M-D.

Ferenc Farkas. *Sonatina Based on a Hungarian Folk Song* 1955 (Artia) 11pp., parts for double bass, bassoon, or cello. See detailed entry under duos for piano and cello.

Willem de Fesch. *Übungssonate* (K. Siebach—Hofmeister) 9pp., parts. Same work in d and e. Siciliano; Allemande; Arietta; Menuett I & II. M-D.
——. *Sonata* Op.8/12 G (Sanky—IMC 1965) 8pp., parts. Prelude; Allemande; Sarabande. Effectively transcribed. M-D.

Robert Fuchs. *Sonata* Op.97 (McGinnis & Marx) 23pp., parts. Allegro moderato molto; Allegro scherzando; Allegro giusto. In a Brahmsian style. Good writing for the piano. M-D.

Johann E. Galliard. *Sonata* G (F. Zimmermann—IMC 1152 1949) 12pp., parts. Lento; Allegro; Andante teneramente; Allegro spiritoso. Over-edited. M-D.

Janina Garścia. *Miniatures* Op.45 (PWM 7173 1971, ISBN 83-224-1860-4). For cello or double bass. See detailed entry under duos for piano and cello.

Giovannini [no first name]. *Sonata* a (R. Statford, C. Tilney—Yorke 1970) 5pp., parts. Adagio; Aria staccato e allegro; Staccato e Arioso; Ballo Arioso e Presto; Sarabanda. M-D.

Reinhold Moritsevich Gliere. *Four Pieces* (Hofmeister; USSR 1952; K 4458) 39pp., parts. *Prelude* Op.32/1, *Scherzo* Op.32/2, *Intermezzo* Op.9/1, *Tarantella* Op.9/2. Fairly attractive writing. M-D. Available separately from IMC, Forberg, and Liben.
——. *Intermezzo* Op.9/1 (K 9786).

Sofia Gubaidulina. *Sonata; Pantomine* (Sikorski 1895 1991) 26pp., parts. *Sonata* (1975) is in one movement with extended solos for both instruments. Avantgarde, cluster chords, and indeterminate in compositional techniques. *Pantomine* (1966) opens with alternating solos at Largo and then proceeds into a straightforward Allegro. Surprising finish retrieves Largo after brilliant passagework with sustained pitches in the upper register of double bass and atmospheric chords in piano. M-D.

František Hertl. *Sonata* 1947 (Státní Nakladtelstvi) 36pp., parts. Allegro moderato; Andantino; Rondo–Alla Polka, Moderato. Freely tonal, centers around a, clear lines. Rondo is especially interesting. M-D.
——. *Vier Stücke* (Supraphon 1969) 30pp., parts. *Preludium, Burleska, Nokturno, Tarantella.* Contrasting, colorful, bitonal, dance rhythms, mildly dissonant. Would make an attractive recital group. Large span required. M-D.

Paul Hindemith. *Sonata* 1949 (Schott) 21pp., parts. 14 min. Allegretto: rondo-like. Scherzo: short. Molto adagio–Allegretto grazioso (Lied): simple theme is gradually thickened with more decoration until a sudden interruption of a free recitative leads to the last variation (Lied). D.

Sidney Hodkinson. *Sonata* (Columbia University Press) 68pp., parts. 14½ min. Prologue–Cadenzas: rhythmically free. Threnody: more introspective, slow. Scherzo: Perpetuum mobile, in a quick, unrelenting triple meter. Scordatura tuning a whole step higher is used for double bass. D.

Franz Anton Hoffmeister. *Concertino* II (Sankey—IMC).
———. *Concerto* II (Malaric—Schott).

Alan Hovhaness. *Fantasy* 1974 (Continuo Music Press) 16pp., parts. 10 min. Six varied sections in mood and tempo. Typical of composer's writing; straightforward with no major difficulties in either part with regard to technique or interpretation. Title completely expresses composer's intent. M-D.

Nicolaus A. Huber. *Ohne Höldevin* 1992 (Br&H 9091 1994) 13 sheets. 16½ min. Two copies necessary for performance. Avant-garde using both determinate and indeterminate compositional techniques with extensive notes in English and German on reading the score. Constantly changing meters with dramatic changes in dynamics ranging from *pppppp* to *ffffff*. Requires a minimum of 2 tables for accessories used during performance. Very D.

Rudolf Jettel. *Konzertante Sonate* (Eulenburg GM 36 1971) 32pp., parts. Moderato: syncopated left-hand octaves, parallel chords, freely tonal, chromatic. Allegro scherzando: octotonic, shifting rhythms, runs in major 2nds, sprightly, sudden dynamic changes; large span required. Andante moderato: opens with slow dissonant counterpoint between instruments; picks up tempo, and piano part becomes rhythmic and chordal. Allegro: treats piano octotonically and concludes with tremolo pesante chords. Neoclassic. M-D.

Joseph Jongen. *Prelude, Habanera and Allegro* Op.106 1938 (CeBeDeM) 15pp., parts. 16 min. Widespread arpeggiated chords open the Prelude in recitative style. Piano provides harmony and rhythm in the Habanera. The Allegro is mainly chordal with some scalar passages. Colorful and appealing writing. M-D.

Tibor Kazacsay. *Divertimento* (EMB 1968) 27pp., parts. Scordatura tuning for double bass. Preludium: chordal, chromatic. Scherzo: light, flowing. Ballo dell'orso: sustained, leads to an Allegro vivo with heavy chords. Finaletto: rubato opening moves to Allegro vivo with propulsive driving chords, strong ending, mildly 20th-century. M-D.

Milko Kelemen. *Concertino* 1959 (CFP 5876 1961) 14pp., parts. One movement, varied tempos, chromatic, propulsive Allegro vivo section, flexible meters. Large span required. M-D.

Jan Kolasiński. *Three Pieces* 1950 (PWM 6518, ISBN 83-224-2733-6) 6pp., parts. Moment Musical; In the Desert; The Cheerful Peasant. Miniature pieces exhibiting early-20th-century qualities in a harmless tonal language. Int. to M-D.

Serge Koussevitzky. *Four Pieces* (D. Walter—Liben). Includes *Andante, Valse Miniature, Chanson Triste,* and *Humoresque.* M-D.

———. *Valse Miniature* Op.1/2 A (F. Zimmermann—IMC 1154 1949) 6pp., parts. Lyric with passionate qualities holding true to the late-19th-century waltz tradition. M-D.

———. *Chanson Triste* Op.2 (F. Zimmermann—IMC 1155 1949) 4pp., parts. Succinct setting in ternary form with brief bass cadenza. M-D.

———. *Humoresque* Op.4 (IMC 2455; Liben 1984; K 4460) 4pp. A cute, frivolous piece with detail requiring careful coordination. M-D.

Serge Lancen. *Croquis* (Yorke 1978) 20pp., parts. 14 min. 1. Habanera; 2. Mais que se passe-t-il donc?; 3. Tilbury; 4. Tendresse; 5. Reminiscence; 6. Espagnolade. Short picturesque sketches in an early-20th-century vein with added-note harmonies. M-D.

———. *Sonate* (Billaudot 1984) 27pp., parts. 18½ min. Andante quasi recitativo; Moderato; Vivace; Allegro vivo. Colorful, Neoclassic writing with parts well suited to one another. M-D.

Aleksander Lasoń. *Music in Four Movements* 1997 (PWM 8285 1980, ISBN 83-224-1373-4) 16pp., parts. 11 min. Chorale Prelude: bass introduction with double stops, choral, touches of indeterminacy. Dance: piano introduction and interludes, quasi campanelli, much vibrato, cluster chords. Song: sustained notes in bass contrasted by mostly quiet tremolos in piano. Finale with Cadenza: repeated cluster chords at Presto possible, expressive bass cadenza, double stops. M-D.

Lowell Liebermann. *Sonata* Op.24 1987 (TP 114-40863 1999) 18pp., parts. 25 min. Comodo: open 5th chords contrast tertian structures, cantabile melody, harmonics. Adagio: downward broken chords in quartal structures, tender melody, trills, scalar passagework in quintuplets, soft dynamics (*mp* to *pppp!*). Presto: fiery, scherzo-like character in duple meter with repeated notes and marked accentuation. Tempo primo, ma un poco ritenuto: returns to principal themes of opening movement, finishing quickly at *pppp* on an E chord stretching from the bottom of the bass to the top of the piano. One of the most significant Sonatas for double bass of the 20th century. M-D.

Otto Luening. *Suite* (Galaxy 1958) 12pp., parts. Moderato con moto: freely tonal around A; linear; low register of piano cleverly used with double bass. Not too slow: chantlike, expressive melodies. Allegro moderato: syncopated chords mixed with linear sections, organum-like, bitonal. M-D.

Elisabeth Lutyens. *The Tides of Time: 'Sleep Navigates the Tides of Time'* Op.75 1969 (Yorke) 6pp., parts. 6 min. Serial, no bar lines, one pedal for long sections, dynamic extremes, wispy sonorities, ensemble problems. Grasps and holds the attention firmly. D.

Elizabeth Maconchy. *Music* 1970 (Yorke) 8pp., set of 2 performing scores. Contrasting tempos; fondness for quartal harmony noted; sustained qualities of piano emphasized; glissandi for double bass. Mildly 20th-century, fundamentally post-Impressionist. Exploits most of what the double bass can do best; a first-rate piece for this combination. M-D.

Jean Maillot. *Fantaisie* (EMT 1971) 13pp., parts. 7½ min. Freely tonal, frequent major 7th chord usage, tempos and mood changes, pedal points, 2 with 3, repeated bitonal chords, octotonic. M-D.

Benedetto Marcello. *Six Sonatas* Op.1 (A. Bacon, L. Drew—GS 1973) 38pp., parts. For cello or double bass and piano. 1 F, 2 e, 3 a, 4 g, 5 C, 6 G. Excellent literature, multimovements, "sounds" well for the combination. M-D. Available separately (Zimmennan—IMC).

Adolf Mišek. *Sonata* Op.5 A (Hofmeister 2256, ISMN M-2034-2256-3) 23pp., parts. Allegro; Andante religioso; Finale–Rondo. Written in a late-19th-century style owing much to Brahms. Rich melodies, full chords, cross-rhythms, and balanced phrasing are found throughout. Very enjoyable. M-D.
————. *Sonata* Op.6 e (G. Klaus—Hofmeister 2065 1992, ISMN M-2034-2065-1 33pp.; Liben 32pp.; E. Levinson—IMC 1995 32pp.), parts. Con fuoco; Andante cantabile; Furiant–Allegro energico; Finale–Allegro appasionato. Passionate writing with abundant expressive possibilities. M-D to D.
————. *Sonata* Op.7 F (M. Bunya—Hofmeister 2267 1997, ISMN M-2034-2267-9) 47pp., parts. Allegro ma non troppo; Dumka–Largo lamentabile; Scherzino–Tempo giusto; Finale–Quasi una fantasia. The largest and most thoroughly developed of Mišek's double bass Sonatas. Some use of cyclic techniques, seen most clearly in the return of the opening theme at the conclusion of the *Sonata.* Preface in German. M-D to D.

Vilmos Montag. *Sonate* e (Hofmeister 3109 1967) 40pp., parts. 17 min. Allegro moderato; Andante; Allegro. German Neoclassicism with a mixture of thin and thick textures. M-D.

Thomas Baron Pitfield. *Sonatina* (Yorke 1974) 16pp., parts. Poco allegro: ostinato figuration exploited. Quodlibet–Moderato grazioso: lyric, based on folk songs. Allegro grazioso: Classically oriented, mildly 20th-century. Int. to M-D.

Frank Proto. *A Carmen Fantasy* 1991 (Liben 1991) 30pp., parts. Prelude; Aragonaise; Nocturne–Micaela's Aria; Toreador Song; Bohemian Dance. A paraphrase of thematic materials from Bizet's *Carmen*. Prelude is for solo double bass. Originally with piano, later orchestrated. M-D.

———. *Four Rogues: A Mystery for Double Bass and Piano* (Liben 1989) 24pp., parts. Calm–Allegro agitato; Freely; Agitato; Calm–Allegro agitato; Epilogue– calm. Dramatic contrasts; proportional rhythmic relationships; harmonics; free improvisation; added-note harmonies. M-D.

———. *Sonata '1963'* (Liben).

Paul Ramsier. *Divertimento Concertante on a Theme of Couperin* 1965 (GS) 23pp., parts. Originally for double bass and orchestra. Piano version by the composer. Barcarolle; March; Dirge; Recitative; Valse Cinématique; Toccata Barocca (Passacaglia). Neoclassic style, fluent idioms, freely tonal, octotonic. Large span required. M-D.

Karel Reiner. *Sonata* (Panton) 54pp., parts. Preface in Czech, Russian, German, English, and French by Jiri Valek.

Lucie Robert. *Ostinato pour Contrabass et Piano* (Leduc 1973) 12pp., parts. The low registers in piano are exploited, and these, combined with low double bass sounds, produce rich blurred sonorities, which are not always interesting. Bravura writing for the double bass. M-D.

Heinz Röttger. *Concertino* 1962 (DVFM 8122) 14pp., parts. Andante; Allegro molto; Quasi Cadenza (piano tacet); Vivace. Freely tonal, shifting rhythms, short patterns, cluster-like chords, driving rhythms in alternating hands, repeated notes, Neoclassic. M-D.

Armand Russell. *Jovian Sonatina* (Boume 1974) 9pp., parts. For solo bass clef instruments and piano.

Camille Saint-Saëns. *Elephant* 1886 (T. Glöckler—Henle 730 2002, ISMN M-2018-0730-0) 5pp., parts. 1½ min. Miniature extracted from *Carnival of the Animals*. Score contains versions in 2 keys, E♭ and F, the latter making it possible for bass players to use solo tuning. M-D.

Finn Savery. *Sonata* (Dan Fog 1970) 20pp., parts. 13 min. In one movement with many sections. Knotty passagework. Cadenzas for both instruments. M-D.

Hans Schmid-Sekyt. *Sonata im Antiken Stil* Op.93 (Dob 1951) 13pp., parts. Allegro; Andante; Menuett; Rondo. Good imitation of older (Classical) style. M-D.

Victor Serventi. *Largo et Scherzando* (Leduc 1944) 9pp., parts. Opens with an expressive Largo in d built around a one-measure motive announced at the outset. The Scherzando ensues without interruption in the parallel major for a light and bouncy Neoclassic essay which finishes with a pizzicato/staccato bump on the final off-beat. M-D.

Fritz Skorzeny. *Sonatina* I 1961 (Dob 1963) 12pp., parts. One movement, various tempos and moods, mildly 20th-century, fairly chromatic. The Sehr lebhaft scherzando section is especially attractive. M-D.

———. *Sonatina* II 1961 (Dob) 20pp., parts. Kraftvoll bewegt; Langsam, quasi recitativo; Sehr lebhaft. Tightly constructed movements, greater mixture of style here than in *Sonatina* I. D.

Johann Matthias Sperger. *Sonata* E 1876 (R. Malarić—Dob 1956) 15pp., parts. Moderato; Chorale Croato; Menuetto; Rondo elegante. Thin keyboard textures allow the bass much clarity. M-D.

———. *Trinital-Sonaten* I-3 (R. Malarić—Dob 1959–60). Arranged by the editor.

Norbert Sprongl. *Sonata* Op.74 (UE 11683 1953) 28pp., parts. Allegro; Andante cantabile; Allegro molto. Highly chromatic idiom but key signatures are present. Flowing figuration in second movement. D.

———. *Sonata* II Op.132 (Dob 1973) 29pp., parts. Translucent and practical piano writing. Three well-balanced movements. Allegro: many melodic phrases with rhythmic character. Lento: builds to climax and subsides; includes fine dialogue writing between the 2 instruments. Rondo-like finale exploits a perky melody with fetching rhythm. Highly effective. D.

Halsey Stevens. *Arioso and Etude* (AME).

———. *Sonatina Giocosa* 1954 (ACA) 17pp., parts. 7 min. Also for cello and piano. Allegro moderato ma giusto; Poco lento; Allegro. Combines both cheerful and serious moods. Strong demands made on double bass player. Numerous quotations from other works—Schoenberg's *Gurrelieder,* the *Dies Irae,* Ravel's *Bolero*—may be discovered in the score. M-D.

Antonio Vivaldi. *Six Sonatas* (N. Grandan—GS 1959). Double bass part edited by Lucas Drew.

Leopold Matthias Walzel. *Sonata Burlesca* Op.37 (Dob 1964) 22pp., parts. Allegretto burlesco; Moderato cantabile; Allegro buriesco. Clever, attractive writing; chromatic; displays both instruments to best advantage. M-D.

Alec Wilder. *Sonata* (Margun 1981) 24pp., parts. Four contrasted movements of light, witty, clear, urbane writing. Last movement is a tour de force in changing meters. This is a fun piece to play and hear, but there is also enough serious musical matter to place it in the literature. M-D.

Duos for Piano and Flute

Komei Abe. *Sonata* I 1942 (Ongaku 1981) 31pp., parts. Allegro moderato; Andantino quasi allegretto; Presto. "In this piece I endeavored to compose a work characterized by simplicity. Of the 3 movements, the first and third are in Sonata form while the second consists of a short, simple theme and 4 variations" (Composer's Note). Early-20th-century in tonal structure with a strong tie to the past. M-D.

Carl Friedrich Abel. *Sonata* e Op.6/3 (Beechey—OUP 1972). Clean edition, interpretation of appoggiaturas. Slurring not indicated but required in keyboard part. A separate basso continuo part is provided. Int. to M-D.
——. *Sonata* D Op.6/6 (Beechey—Br).
——. *Sonatas* D, F, G (Sonntag—CFP).
——. *Sonata* C (Sonntag—CFP).
——. *Sonata* G (F. Brüggen—Br&VP 1960). For violin or flute.
——. *Sonatas* (Bacher, Woehl—Br). Vol.I: Sonatas e, D, G. Vol.II: Sonatas C, A, A. For viola da gamba (violin or flute) and basso continuo.

Tommaso Albinoni. *Sonata* a (L. Schaffler—Nag 74 1931) Grave; Allegro; Adagio; Allegro. First-rate keyboard realization. M-D.
——. *Sonata* b (Scheck, Ruf—Ric).

Joseph Alexander. *Sonata* (Gen). Available in facsimile blueprint on special order.

Anna Amalie of Prussia. *Sonata* F 1771 (G. Lenzewski—Vieweg 108 1975 8pp.; G. Quer, W. Michel—Amadeus BP1063 1999 12pp.), parts for flute or violin in Vieweg; parts with basso in Amadeus. Adagio; Allegretto; Allegro ma non troppo. Agreeable and effective writing, similar in style to J. C. Bach. M-D.

André Amellér. *Uranie: Triptyque* (Leduc 1987) 14pp., parts. Prélude; Adagio; Rondo. Inspired by the great butterfly of Madagascar and its brilliant colors. Neoclassic style with flute cadenza. M-D.

Caroline Ansink. *All Roads Are Good* 1997 (Donemus 1999) 19pp., parts. 20 min. In one movement of multiple sections and tempos. Proportional rhythmic relationships, biting harmonies, wide span requirements. Score is copy of MS. D.

George Antheil. *Sonata* (Weintraub 1965) 22pp., parts. Allegro: SA, centers freely around F; sudden dynamic changes; repeated notes and chords; flute cadenza; alternating hand passages, left hand over right, large span required. Adagio: ABA, expressive lyric lines, melody in left-hand octaves, lilting. Presto: bitonal, light and staccato, shifting meters, glissando, rhythmic, broken left-hand figuration similar to first movement. M-D.

Paul Arma. *Douze Danses Roumaines de Transylvanie* 1940 (Lemoine 1959) 27pp., parts. 20 min. 1. Danse funèbre des vieillards. 2. Danse des garçons. 3. Hora. 4. Danse des sages-femmes. 5. Chant d'Adieu; repetition of 4, Allegro molto. 6. Hora. 7. En buvant. 8. Chanson du vagabond. 9. Danse ruthène. 10. Ronde. 11. Danse des garçons. 12. En buvant. Colorful, much rhythmic emphasis, contrasted. A group or the entire collection could be performed. M-D.

Malcolm Arnold. *Sonatina* (Belwin-Mills).
——. *Sonatina* d Op.19 (Lengnick 1948) 16pp., parts. 8 min. Allegro; Andante; Allegretto languido.
Both works are in a light, witty vein and are effective. M-D.

Claude Arrieu. *Sonatine* G 1943 (Amphion 1946) 16pp., parts. Allegretto moderato; Andantino; Presto. Tonal, Impressionist, parallelism, charming, a fun piece for both performers and audience. Presto has figurations similar to those in the Ravel *Sonatine.* Large span required. M-D.

Georges Auric. *Imaginées* 1968 (Sal) 13pp., parts. One movement with varied tempos and character indications, many abrupt ones. In the opening and closing sections low sonorities are exploited, followed by trills and chromatic figuration in the upper register. One voice in one hand leads voice(s) in the other hand by a 16th of a beat. Chromatic 3rds, skipping chords. Opening material is recapped. Large span required. M-D.

William Babell. *Sonata* f (Tilmouth—OUP). See detailed entry under duos for piano and oboe.
——. *Sonata* g (Tilmouth—OUP 1963) 5pp., parts also for oboe or violin. Allegro; Air; Hornpipe, Giga. Seems best-suited for oboe but is effective also on flute or violin. Excellent keyboard realization. Int. to M-D.
——. *12 Sonatas* 4 vols. (M. Maute—Amadeus BP 334-7 1999), parts, including basso. For oboe, flute, or violin. See detailed entry under duos for piano and oboe.

Joseph Baber. *Divertimento* Op.32/2 (Alry 1988) 16pp., parts. Introduction–Allegro moderato; Waltz–Moderato; Intermezzo–Andante; Scherzo–Presto; Chorale–Adagio. Movements are to be played without pause. Composed when Baber wrote his opera *Frankenstein,* taking "on some of the character of that work, a certain hallucinatory or spectral quality" (Performance Notes). Some theatrical elements. M-D.

Carl Philipp Emanuel Bach. *11 Sonatas* 6 vols. (M. Zimmermann—Amadeus BP2301-6 1992), parts, with basso. I: W.123 G 1725; W.124 e 1737. II: W.125 B♭ 1738; W.126 D 1738. III: W.127 G 1739; W.128 a 1740. IV: W.129 D 1740; W.130 B♭ 1746. V: W.131 D 1747; W.134 G ca.1735. VI: W.133 "Hamburger Sonate" G 1786. Scholarly edition. Preface in German and English. M-D.

———. *Complete Sonatas* 6 vols. (U. Leisinger—Musica Rara 1993–94), parts. I (MR 2202): W.161.2/H.578 B♭ 1748. Allegro; Adagio ma non troppo; Allegretto. II (MR 2203): W.83/H.505 D 1747. Allegro un poco; Largo; Allegro. III (MR 2204): W.84/H.506 E 1749. Allegretto; Adagio di molto; Allegro assai. IV (MR 2205): W.85/H.508 G 1754. Allegretto; Andantino; Allegro. V (MR 2206): W.86/ H.509 G 1755. Andante; Allegretto; Allegro. VI (MR 2207): W.87/H.515 C 1766. Allegretto; Andantino; Allegro. The last *Sonata* was apparently the only one "conceived as a sonata for obbligato keyboard and flute right from the beginning, all the others being authentic adaptations of trio sonatas for flute, violin, and basso continuo" (from Preface for Vol.6). Each volume contains extensive notes.

———. *Six Sonatas* B♭, D, G, D, B♭, G (Walther—CFP; MMP). W.125–27, 129, 130, 134.

———. *Four Sonatas* 2 vols. (Walther—Br&H 5991/2; K 2146). I: W.83, 84. II: W.85, 86.

———. *Sonatas* 2 vols. (K. Walther—HM 71 & 72). I: W.123 G, W.124 e. II: W.128 a, W.131 D.

———. *Sonata* W.83 D (G. Scheck, H. Ruf—Ric Sy505 1954) 26pp., parts. Allegro un poco; Largo; Allegro. M-D.

———. *Sonata* W.85 G (G. Scheck, H. Ruf—Ric Sy634 1955) 16pp., parts. Allegretto; Andantino; Allegro. M-D.

———. *Sonata* W.87 C (Leeuwen—Zimmerman; J.-P. Rampal—IMC 1955, 11pp., parts; G. Scheck, H. Ruf—Ric). 9 min. Allegretto; Andantino; Allegro. M-D.

———. *Sonata* W.125 B♭ (G. Scheck, H. Ruf—Ric Sy503) 11pp., parts. Adagio; Allegro; Vivace. M-D.

———. *Sonata* W.127 G (G. Scheck, H. Ruf—Ric).

———. *Sonata* W.133 G, "Hamburg Sonata" (Walther—Schott 4651) 11pp., parts. Allegretto; Rondo–Presto. M-D.

———. *Sonata* (D. Waitman—AMP 1974) 24pp., parts. For alto recorder (flute and harpsichord or piano obbligato with cello or basso continuo).

Johann Christian Bach. *Six Sonatas* D, G, C, A, F, B♭ (Wittenbecher—CFP).
———. *Six Sonatas* Op.16 1 D, 2 G, 3 C, 4 A, 5 D, 6 F (Heinrichshofen) 37pp., parts. Facsimile reprint of the first edition (ca.1780). M-D.
———. *Sonata* Op.16/1 D (Küster—Nag).
———. *Sonata* Op.16/2 G (Küster—Nag).
———. *Sonata* Op.16/4 A (Küster—Nag 103).
———. *Sonata* (Schunemann—Concordia).

——. *Sonata* D (Ruf—Nag).

——. *Sonata* I d (Schott).

——. *Sonata* F (Maguerre—Moeck).

Johann Christoph Friedrich Bach. *Six Sonatas* D, G, C, A, F, Bb (O. Wittenbecher—Zimmermann 1125a-f 1925). Published separately. Keyboard realizations get a little heavy from time to time, but they are generally acceptable. M-D.

——. *Sonata* F (Hinnenthal—Br&H).

——. *Sonata* II D (Schott).

——. *Sonata* D (Hugo Ruf—Nag 192). For keyboard and flute or violin; cello ad lib. See detailed entry under trios for piano, violin, and cello.

Johann Sebastian Bach. *Flute Sonatas* 2 vols. (H. Eppstein—Henle 269 1978, ISMN M-2018-0269-5, Henle 328 1981, ISMN M-2018-0328-9), parts, including basso. I: The Four Authentic Sonatas: S.1034 e, S.1035 E, S.1030 b, S.1032 A. II: The Three Sonatas attributed to J. S. Bach: S.1033 C, S.1020 g, S.1031 Eb. "Realization of the figured bass [in this edition] has been restricted to basic essentials thus providing scope for individual elaboration" (from Preface in German, English, and French).

——. *Three Sonatas* S.1030–32 b, Eb, A (Soldan, Woehl—CFP; Stainer, Geehl—Br&H; Wummer—ST; L. Moyse—GS 3180; Barrère—BMC; Kincaid, Polin—TP; K 7131). GS also includes *Sonata* a for flute solo.

——. *Three Sonatas* S.1033–35 C, e, E (David—CFP; Geehl, Stainer—ST; Soldan, Woehl—Br&H; Wummer—Billaudot; Rampal—IMC; L. Moyse—GS 3181; Barrère—BMC; Barge, Spiro, Todt—Br&H; Kincaid, Polin—TP; K 7132). GS also includes S.1020 g.

——. *Three Sonatas* S.1033 C, S.1031 Eb, S.1020 g (A. Durr—Br 4418). 1031 and 1020 are for flute and obbligato keyboard, 1022 is for flute and basso continuo.

——. *Two Sonatas* S.1034–35 e, A (H.-P. Schmitz—Br 5022). Comes with *Sonata* S.1030 b and *Sonata* S.1032 A, and Sonata S.1039 G for 2 flutes and basso continuo.

——. *Six Sonatas* (CF; Rampal—IMC).

——. *Seven Sonatas* b, Eb, a, C, e, E, g (M. Moyse—Leduc). Published separately.

——. *Sonatas* 1, 2, 3 (LeRoy—Billaudot; Roth—Br&H).

——. *Seven Sonatas* (Lea 10). See detailed entries for 3 of these (S.1027–29) under duos for piano and cello.

——. *Sonatas* 2, 6 (K. Soldan—CFP). Two of Bach's most ingratiating works, with the Siciliano movements in each being little masterpieces. Clean Urtext edition.

——. *Sonata* S.1030 b (B. Kuijken—Br&H 8582 1995) 21pp., parts. Extensive Postface and notes in German and English.

——. *Sonata* S.1032 A (S. Baron—OUP 1975 27pp.; B. Kuijken, S. Henstra—Br&H 8583 1997 20pp.; K. Hampe—CFP 4461c 1997 11pp.), parts. Excellent Prefaces for each edition in English and German with Kuijken's the most detailed. Hampe includes only the first movement. This is the least known of Bach's Sonatas for flute and harpsichord, not for any lack of quality, but because at some stage approximately 46 bars were removed from the original manuscript of the first of the 3 movements. In these editions the missing bars are reconstructed in fine, musically convincing manners by their editors. M-D.

——. *Sonata* S.1034 e (B. Kuijken, S. Henstra—Br&H 8554 1991) 15pp., parts, with basso. Extensive notes in German and English.

——. *Sonata* S.1020 g (K 7134).

——. *Sonatas Based on Organ Trio Sonatas* 3 vols. (Gerhard, Waltraut, Kirchner—Br 6801–3), parts. I: S.525 E♭, S.526 c. II: S.527 d, S.528 e. III: S.529 C, 530 G.

——. *Suite* S.1067 b (L. Moyse—GS 1974) 24pp., parts.

Parker Bailey. *Sonata* Op.3 (SPAM 1928–29) 36pp., parts. Moderato; Allegro non troppo; Andante con moto–Allegro non troppo. Fluent writing with strong reliance on arpeggi and varied figurations. Mildly 20th-century but tonal. Ideas not well developed. Facile pianism required. M-D.

Robert Baksa. *Flute Sonata* 1976 (CLE 1993) 31pp., parts. Allegro; Cadenza I; Adagio; Cadenza II; Allegro. Both cadenzas are for flute. Straightforward, tonally based writing. M-D.

Simon Balicourt. *Sonata* II 1750 (Les Editions Ouvrières 1967) 11pp., parts. For flute or violin and basso continuo. Transcribed and realized by François Petit. Andante; Allegro assai; Andante; Allegro. Well written in the style of the period. M-D.

Michel de la Barre. *Suite* D (F. Nagel, W. Radeske—Sikorski 784 1973) 15pp., parts. Preface in German and English. Prelude; Allemande; Air (le Badin); Air (l'Espagnol); Gavotte; Air (la Coquette); Allemande; Gigue. M-D.

——. *Sonata* G (Ruf—Ric).

——. *Sonate dit l'Inconnue* (Baron).

Francesco Barsanti. *Two Sonatas* Op.1/2 C, 6 B♭ (G. Beechey—OUP) 24pp., parts. 13 min. For alto recorder and basso continuo. Each *Sonata* has 4 movements, alternately slow and fast. Skillful and imaginative writing. Continuo well realized by the editor. M-D.

——. *Three Sonatas* F, d, g (Bergmann—Schott).

——. *Sonata* B♭ 1727 (H. Ruf—HM 184) 12pp., parts. Adagio: non tanto allegro; Sostenuto; Allegro. M-D.

——. *Sonata* C 1727 (H. Ruf—HM 183) 14pp., parts. Adagio; Allegro; Largo; Presto. M-D.

——. *Sonata* c 1727 (H. Ruf—HM 184) 12pp., parts. Adagio; Con spirito; Siciliana; Gavotte. M-D.

Cecilia Maria Barthélemon. *Sonata* II (F. Zimmermann—Tonger 2852-1 1998, ISMN M-005-28521-2) 16pp., parts, with basso. Allegro moderato; Rondo vivace; Vivace. Mozartian with well-balanced phrases, scalar runs, broken-chord figurations. An interesting alternative from the Classical masters. M-D.

Béla Bartók. *Suite Paysanne Hongroise* (Bo&H 1956, ISMN M-051-59024-7) 18pp., parts. 13½ min. Trans. by Paul Arma from *15 Hungarian Peasant Songs and Dances* for solo piano. Works very well as an ensemble piece. M-D.

Robert Basart. *Fantasy* 1963 (Sal 1972) 15pp., parts. 7 min. Serial, pointillistic, sectional, many tempo changes, Expressionist, dynamic marks on many notes, complex. D.

Leslie Bassett. *Illuminations* 1989 (CFP 67332 1992) 18pp., parts. 13 min. Poignant; Flowing; Mysterious; Fast, driving. Uses stopped piano strings for effect. Odd rhythmic figures result from asymmetric meters (e.g., $\frac{17}{16}$, $\frac{13}{16}$); proportional rhythmic relationships. Not as difficult as MS score first appears. M-D.

Stanley Bate. *Sonata* (L'OL 1938).

————. *Sonatina* (Schott 10040 1950) 16pp., part for tenor recorder or flute and piano. Allegro; Lento; Presto. Piano is treated percussively; harmonic 2nds are prevalent; alternating hands. Mildly 20th-century, freely tonal around a. Presto is toccata-like with a surprising decrescendo *mp* ending. M-D.

Gustavo Becerra Schmidt. *Sonata* 1953 (LAMC) 17pp., parts. Mosso; Andante; Furioso presto. Neoclassic treatment, clear textures and lines. M-D.

Conrad Beck. *Sonatina* (Schott FTR 100 1961) 16pp., parts. Moderato–Allegro; Vivo–molto sostenuto; Allegretto; Sostenuto. Chromatic and freely tonal, cluster-like chords, octotonic, Neoclassic. Large span required. M-D.

Ludwig van Beethoven. *Sonata* B♭ Kinsky, Anhang 4 (W. Richter—Zimmermann 1975, 23pp., parts; van Leeuwen—CFP; Laube—CF; IMC; Hess—Br&H; K 3151). Authenticity doubtful. Possibly dates from ca.1790. Allegro moderato; Polonaise; Largo; Allegretto molto con Variazioni. Delightful Classical writing. M-D.

————. *Variations on Folk Songs* Op.105, 107 (A. Raab, K. Schilde—Henle 716 2001, ISMN M-2018-0716-4) 96pp., parts. For flute or violin, ad lib. Score extracted from the new complete edition entitled *Beethoven Werke* V/4 (Henle). Op.105 contains 6 sets of variations, 2 on Welsh themes, 3 Irish, and one on "A Schüsserl und a Reinderl," a tune believed to be by Johann Baptist Henneberg. Op.107 contains 10 sets of variations, 4 on Scottish themes, one Welsh, one Irish, one Ukraine, one Russian, and 2 on melodies by Friedrich Satzenhofen. The piano is the focal instrument in these sets; however, "there are few passages where the flute or violin could be omitted" (from Preface). Both flute and violin parts are juxtaposed in the full score. M-D.

————. *Variations* Op.105 (VU; Br&H). For flute or violin.

————. *Variations* Op.107 (VU; Br&H). For flute or violin.

Sadio Bekku. *Sonate* 1954 (Ongaku 1958) 22pp., parts. Allegro moderato; Vivace. Both movements are in SA design, freely tonal. Clear and orderly lines reveal a refreshing lyricism. Feeling of moving ahead is necessary in the first movement. M-D.

Franz Benda. *Two Sonatas* C, e (Janetzky—Hofmeister).
———. *Sonata* e (Schoenbaum—Br).
———. *Sonata* F (EM; M. Munclingen—IMC 2765), parts. Adagio; Allegro; Vivace. M-D.

Friedrich Wilhelm Heinrich Benda. *Sonata* Op.3/1 G (Ruetz—Nag; H. Ruf—Schott FTR 9 1966, ISMN M-001-09323-1), parts. From "Trois Sonates pour le Clavecin Avec l'Accompagnement d'une Flute ou Violin." Allegro; Cantabile; Scherzando. Solid Classical writing with attractive figuration for both instruments. M-D.
———. *Sonate* Op.5/2 C (H. Ruf—Schott FTR 176 1999, ISMN M-001-12277-1) 24pp., parts. Allegro; Andante; Allegro scherzando. Outer movements are in binary forms. First modern-day edition. M-D.

Georg Benda. *Sonata* G (M. Ruetz—Nag 154 1960) 15pp., parts. Allegro moderato; Andantino; Allegro. This work was published in 1942 under the name of Franz Benda, Georg's brother, his senior by 13 years. It also exists in a slightly different version for violin and keyboard. The quick movements are melodious and lively; the slow movement has a plaintive and tragic character. Keyboard is treated in a competitive melodic way with the flute. M-D.

Niels Viggo Bentzon. *Six Variations on an Original Theme* Op.17 (WH 3406 1943) 11pp., parts. Quartal and quintal harmonies, freely tonal, Neoclassic, syncopated theme. Strongly contrasted variations, tremolo, wide dynamic range, chromatic triplets. Var.4 is a flute solo. Perpetual motion idea in Var.5. Var.6 uses the piano percussively in alternating hands. Coda is quiet, with theme returning for a Molto tranquillo closing. M-D.

Jean Berger. *Suite* (BB 1955) 23pp., parts. Allegro commodo; Moderato; Molto moderato; Allegro. Clear lines and textures, chordal. Parallelism in second movement gives an Impressionist feeling. M-D.

Lennox Berkeley. *Sonatina* a (Schott 10015 1940) 12pp., parts. 10 min. Moderato, Adagio; Allegro moderato. Lyrical and sustained thematic beauty, clear, terse. Alternating chords between hands. Modest in scale. M-D.

Wallace Berry. *Duo* 1969 (ST) 19pp., parts. Includes performance directions. Elegiac throughout most of the piece, canonic, chromatic, melodious, large arpeggiated chords, flexible meters; keen sense of rubato necessary. A 20th-century tone poem. Pianist must tap knuckles on solid wood of the piano. Large span required. M-D to D.

Thomas Beversdorf. *Sonata* (ST 503 1966) 32pp., parts. Allegro con moto: dramatic marcato opening, canonic, broken octaves, large chords, extreme ranges, chromatic broken-chordal figuration. Andante: repeated notes and chords, long lines; large span required. Allegro ma non troppo energico: fast scales, pesante rhythmic chordal figures, trills, ideas effectively combined, reiterated patterns, broken octaves in alternating hands, brilliant conclusion. D.

Jean Binet. *Sonatine* (Foetisch 1952) 15pp., parts. Lent–Modérément animé; Lent; Assez vif. Chromatic, Impressionist tendencies. M-D.

Gordon Binkerd. *Sonatina* 1947 (Bo&H 1972) 15pp., parts. Allegro moderato: SA, free counterpoint, chromatic lines. Andantino: flowing piano has a more active mid-section; opening section mood returns. Allegro giocoso: $\frac{5}{8}$, 3 + 2 and reverse 2 + 3 provide basis for dancelike quality; effective scalar closing. M-D.

Marcel Bitsch. *Three Sonatines* (Leduc 1949) 19pp., parts. Andante pastorale; Sarabande; Vivo assai. Like a 3-movement work. Moves over keyboard, chromatic, not easy. M-D to D.

Boris Blacher. *Duo* (Bo&Bo 1972) 12pp., parts. Allegro moderato; Andante; Presto; Andante. Pointillistic, flexible meters, thin textures. M-D.

Michel Blavet. *Six Sonatas* Op.2 1731 2 vols. (W. Kolneder—Müller; Bo&H; W. Hess—Amadeus BP2474 1983; L. Moyse—GS), parts. Bk.I: 1. L'Henriette, 2. La Vibray, 3. La D'Hérouville. Bk.II: 4. La Lumague, 5. La Chauvette, 6. La Boucot. GS published each *Sonata* individually. These multimovement *Sonatas* show Blavet to be a composer of good taste with a profound command of musical phraseology. In a Preface he speaks of "character pieces," which are summed up in the titles of individual movements. First and family names are used as well as captions like "Gossip," "Goblins," "Regrets," etc., in accordance with French ballet practice of the day. Tasteful basso continuo realizations. M-D.

———. *Two Sonatas* Op.2/2 d, 3 E (Ruf—Schott).

———. *Sonata* Op.2/2 d (J.-C. Veihan, D. Salzer—Leduc 1978) 12pp. Published in Archives de la Musique Ancienne.

———. *Sonata* Op.3/2 b (Ruf—Br).

Ernest Bloch. *Suite Modale* 1956 (BB 1958) 14pp., parts. 12 min. Moderato; L'istesso tempo; Allegro giocoso; Adagio–Allegro deciso. Modality permeates the entire work, giving rise to interesting scales and chords. M-D.

Theobald Böhm. *Nel cor più* Op.4 G (R. Hériché—Billaudot 1972) 17pp., parts. 7 min. Introduction, theme, and 6 variations based on the famous aria from Paisiello's *La Molinara*. Virtuosic for flute. M-D.

———. *Grande Polonaise* Op.16 D (R. Hériché—Billaudot 1979) 20pp., parts.

11½ min. A dramatic introduction leads to the Polonaise proper, a grand romp for both instruments in military style. M-D.

——. *Larghetto* Op.35 A♭ (P. Paubon—Billaudot 1994) 8pp., parts. 8 min. Expressive with rich harmonic movement and lyrical lines. M-D.

J. Bodin de Boismortier. *Six Sonatas* Op.91 D, g, G, e, A, c (M. Pincherle—Heugel 1970) 81pp., parts. Le Pupitre 20. All are multimovement works that show marked originality. Some gracious and charming writing here. M-D.

François Borne. *Fantaisie Brillante on Themes from Bizet's Carmen* 1900 (ST 1972 20pp.; J. Galway, P. Moll—GS 3346 1980, ISBN 0-7935-9810-9 24pp.), parts. Begins with a dramatic piano introduction in $^6_8$, followed by a lyrical, dolce melody evolving into flowing 16th-note passagework. A metamorphosis of themes and direct quotes from Bizet's opera follow with much variety; 2 variations are based upon the famous Habanera theme. A delightful piece, fun for the audience and performers. M-D.

Helmut Bornefeld. *Choralsonate* I "Auf Meinen Lieben Gott" 1957 (Br 3481) 16pp., parts. Keyboard part can be played on piano, harpsichord, or organ. Zart und ruhig fliessend: quartal and quintal chromatic harmony, flowing lines, many sequences; chorale ingeniously worked into texture. In sehr ruhigen Achteln einleitend: fragmentary ideas, nonlegato figures in keyboard, 3 against 2, chromatic arpeggi figures, tremolo, chords in alternating hands; descending lines provide restful conclusion. Neoclassic. M-D.

Pierre Boulez. *Sonatine* 1946 (Amphion 1954) 31pp., parts. One serial movement of complex rhythmic and percussive writing. Series inspires similar thematic motives. Highly varied and fragmentary texture, pointillistic. Varied SA design; development section, beginning at the Scherzando, alludes to material from the exposition. Flexible meters, terribly involved. D.
See Carol K. Brown, "An Analysis of the Pitch Organization in Boulez's 'Sonatine' for Flute and Piano," *Current Musicology* 20 (1975): 87–95.

Eugène Bozza. *Agrestide* Op.44 (Leduc 1942) 12pp., parts. Opens with piano in the style of a pastorale with a flowing ostinato in the upper register, a sustained chord in the bass, and added-note chords in the middle. Soon yields to a lengthy flute cadenza and contrasting sections in Neoclassic harmonies which require considerable technical skill and coordination. Composed for the Concours at the Paris Conservatory. D.

Cesar Bresgen. *Sonata* (Schott 4111 1951) 23pp., parts. Fliessend, doch nicht rasch; Lebhaft und sehr leicht; Ruhige Viertel. Strong Neoclassic writing, on a par both musically and technically with some of the Hindemith duo chamber Sonatas. D.

——. *Sonatine* D (Heinrichshofen/Sirius). For soprano blockflöte (recorder) and piano.

——. *Studies* IV (Dob).

Thomas Briccetti. *Sonata* Op.14 (McGinnis & Marx 1962) 42pp., parts. Moderato: freely tonal, chromatic figuration involving broken octaves, shifting rhythms, flute cadenza, sudden dynamic changes. Andante cantabile: free dissonant counterpoint, effective use of trills, rich sonorities. Prestissimo: fast octotonic 16th-note writing; dramatic arpeggi gestures; subtle syncopation; extreme dynamic range; leads directly into an Andante section full of chromatic chords and arpeggi; prestissimo tempo and mood return to wrap up this large and important contribution to the literature. D.

Benjamin Britten. *Gemini Variations* Op.73 (Faber F014 1965). Quartet for 2 or 4 players for violin, flute, and piano 4-hands. If 2 players are used, it is performed by flute and piano or by violin and piano. Twelve variations and fugue on an epigram (musical piece) by Kodály. See the entry under quartets for piano, strings, and winds for further information. M-D.

Raynor Brown. *Sonata* I (WIM 107 1975) 25pp., parts. Prelude; Fugue; Rondo. Freely tonal, octotonic, quartal harmony, flowing imitative lines, thin textures, Neoclassic. M-D.

Adolf Brunner. *Sonata* (Br 1990) 23pp., parts. 15 min. Allegro leggiero; Adagio rubato; Allegro molto. Neoclassic tendencies but textures are thick at stress points. Freely tonal, long lines. M-D.

Eldin Burton. *Sonatina* 1946 (CF 03643 1949, ISBN 0-8258-1033-7) 24pp., parts. 10 min. Allegretto grazioso; Andantino sognando; Allegro giocoso–quasi fandango. An engaging work in early-20th-century tonality with detailed writing and development. Of special interest is the final movement with its rhythmic flavor and dance qualities. M-D.

Stephen Douglas Burton. *Stravinskiana, Concertino for Flute and Piano* (Sal 1974) 25pp., parts. Maresto: strongly rhythmic; more sustained mid-section; groups of four 16th notes spread out over interval of major 7th frequently used. Intensivo: cool upper-register sonorities; flute has a solo section; walking bass octaves under pungent chords make for unusual effect; *pppp* closing. Moto Perpetuo (bongo and snare indicated in piano part—unclear whether to use those instruments or to imitate the effect on the piano): varied figurations from chromatic scale passages to tremolo to long-held low register chords; percussion and timpani indications also seen. A frantic and hair-raising piece of writing. D.

Ferruccio Busoni. *Albumblatt* e (MMP) 3pp., parts. For flute or violin. A short work marked Andantino of delicate, sustained quality. M-D.

John Cage. *Two* 1987 (Henmar 1987) 2pp., parts. 10 min. Composed in 10 parts with "timed brackets, nine which are flexible with respect to beginning and ending, and one, the eighth, which is fixed. No sound is to be repeated within a bracket. In the piano part each ictus in a single staff is to be played in the order given, but can be played in any relation to the sounds in the other staff. Some notes are held from one ictus to the next. A tone in parentheses is not to be played if it is already sounding. One hand may assist the other" (from Preface). M-D.

Louis de Caix d'Hervelois. *Suite* Op.6/1 A (W. Waechter, S. Petrenz—UE 18668 1989) 11pp., parts, with basso. 12 min. Prélude; Allemande; Sarabande; Muzette; La Badine; Menuet I, II; Gracieusement; Vivement. Preface in German, English, and French. M-D.

Martin Friedrich Cannabich. *Sonata* Op.1/1 D (H. Ruf—Schott 8663 1999, ISMN M-001-12056-2) 16pp., parts, with basso. Allegro; Andante; Allegro. Cannabich composed in the manner of the Mannheim School. M-D.

André Caplet. *Rêverie; Petit Valse* (Kunzelmann GM607 2000) 13pp., parts. Two expressive works revealing both instruments' capacity for lyricism and rhythmic ingenuity. Mostly soft. M-D.

Robert Casadesus. *Sonata* Op.18 (Durand 1948) 43pp., parts. Allegro moderato: flowing, lusingando figuration, scalar, added-note technique used in second subject, 3 with 4, 7th chords, fast 3rds in right hand, large span required. Andante: $\frac{6}{8}$, berceuse-like rocking figures, short trills in inner voice joined by trills in bass line, quiet. Molto vivo: secco, fleeting, trills, shifting rhythms, hemiola, broken octaves, melody embedded in figuration; builds to climax; centers around E. D.

———. *Fantaisie* Op.59 1959 (Durand) 13pp., parts. Freely tonal around e–E, varied mood and tempos, clever use of grace notes, flowing and undulating lines. M-D.

Jacques Castérède. *Sonata en forme de Suite* (Leduc 1957) 20pp., parts. Prelude: chromatic alternating lines between hands, freely tonal, long phrases, mordents. Menuet: fifth note, first bar, in flute part should be a C♯, not A; contains some snappy rhythms for a menuet; expanding chordal intervals are frequent. Sarabande: lovely expressive lines over sustained chords. Rondo: dancelike, spirited, *pp* closing. Thorough treatment of both instruments. D.

Charles Chaynes. *Sonatine* (Leduc 1952) 12pp., parts. Très allant: one movement, varied tempos, light, clever but also well written, somewhat in the style of Poulenc. Large span required. M-D.

Frédéric Chopin. *Variations sur un Thème de Rossini* E (PWM Vol.XVI of Complete Works 1959 8pp.; Rampal—IMC; Belwin-Mills; P. Paubon—Billaudot 1993 8pp.), parts. PWM has commentary in English by Ludwik Bronarski.

Wen-Chung Chou. *Cursive* 1963 (CFP) 15pp., parts. 11 min. "'Cursive' refers to the type of script in which the joined strokes and rounded angles result in expressive and contrasting curves and loops. The cursive script represents the essence of Chinese calligraphy as its expressiveness depends solely upon the spontaneous but controlled flow of ink which, through the brush-strokes, projects not only fluid lines in interaction but also density, texture and poise" (from Preface). This piece has been influenced by the cursive concept, mainly in its use of specific but indefinite pitches and rhythm, in regulated but variable tempo and dynamics, as well as various timbres on the 2 instruments. Pianist must tap, stop, and pluck strings and play glissandi on the strings. Performance directions. Pointillistic fragmentary melodies, virtuoso display of effects. D.

Cesare Ciardi. *Solo* II Op.125 (M. Bignardelli—Zimmermann 31590 1997, ISMN M-010-31590-4) 14pp., parts. Mid-19th-century stylistic writing with full chords and dramatic qualities. M-D.

Muzio Clementi. *Three Sonatas for the Piano or Harpsichord with the Accompaniment of a Flute or Violin* Op.2 (Hin 1971). Unchanged facsimile of an Amsterdam edition of the 1780s. These are actually *Sonatas* Op.2/3, Op.5, and Op.4/4. Misprints from the original have not been corrected, but they are easy to spot. M-D.

———. *Sonata* Op.2/3 G (Jean-Pierre Rampal—IMC 1963) 7pp., parts. Moderato: Rondo–Allegretto. Straightforward writing with the 2 couplets in the Rondo being especially pleasant. M-D.

Dinos Constantinides. *Rhapsody II* 1977, rev.1998 (Conners 193 1998) 8pp., parts. 7 min. A deeply felt, personal statement by the composer incorporating considerable freedom in a late-20th-century tonal style. Emphasis on intervals of major 7th and perfect 4th. Flutter tonguing, extremes of instruments, proportional rhythmic relationships, largely soft dynamics. Inspired by Homer's *Iliad* (Notes, *Dinos Constantinides: The Dancing Turtle and Other Flute Works,* Sarah Beth Hanson, flute, Vestige CD GR 0001-2 2000). M-D.

———. *Grecianas Brasileiras* (Magni 2002) 10pp., parts. For flauto d'amore and piano; may be performed on flute or alto flute. "Based on Greek-like folk tunes and Brazilian rhythms. It is diatonic in nature and its various events are built upon the harmonic sonorities derived from the tones of the C major scale in the order of the following tones: CGFEFGC and CABDBAC, thus underlying the importance of palindromic motion in the piece" (from Preface). M-D.

Arnold Cooke. *Sonatina* 1956, rev.1961 (OUP 1964) 16pp., parts. Allegro moderato; Andantino; Allegro vivace. Cheerful, bright, witty. Clever syncopation in last movement. M-D.

Paul Cooper. *Sonata* 1964 (JWC 1967) 18pp., parts. 12 min. Strong 20th-century writing for both instruments. Pianist is required to play rapid glissandi with fingernail while sustaining keys silently to produce colorful sonorities. Firm rhythmic control necessary for proper ratios in some measures. Form and fabric are uniquely molded together. D.

Aaron Copland. *Duo* (Bo&H 1971) 21pp., parts. Three movements of wide-ranging intervals coupled with propulsive and additive rhythms. Reflective passages recall *Appalachian Spring,* but the harmonies and intervallic structure are obviously later vintage. M-D.

——. *Vocalise* (Bo&H 1974) 4pp., parts. Flute part edited by Doriot A. Dwyer.

Michel Corrette. *Sonata* d (Galaxy).

——. *Sonata* e (Ruf—Schott).

——. *Sonata* II (Petit—Galaxy).

——. *Sonatille* b (L. Boulay—EMT 1964) 10pp., parts, cello ad lib. Preface in French, English, and German. Allegro moderato; Largo; Allegro. "Sonatille" is a term Corrette invented to designate some short Sonatas each subtitled "Solo for the transverse flute or violin with bass . . . oeuvre XIX." Keyboard part is equal in importance to that of the flute. Somewhat Italian in style. Editorial additions indicated. M-D.

François Couperin. *Concert Royal* IV (Rampal, Vemon-Lacroix—IMC 1960) 11pp., parts. Prélude; Allemande; Courante Française; Courante à L'Italienne; Sarabande; Rigaudon; Forland en Rondeau. Mainly because of the ornamentation this work is listed as D.

Adrian Cruft. *Seven Pieces* Op.79 (Chappell 1975). Simple flute tunes progressing in technical and rhythmic problems. The final piece is in $\frac{5}{4}$. Int.

Carl Czerny. *Duo Concertante* Op.129 G (F. Vester—UE 1975) 51pp., parts. Allegro; Scherzo–Allegro molto; Andantino grazioso; Rondo–Allegretto. Both instrumental parts are equally difficult. Strong Beethoven influence, excellent structure. M-D.

Ingolf Dahl. *Variations on a French Folktune* 1935 (Boonin) 16pp., parts. 10 min. Based on "Au clair de la lune." Eight contrasting variations, the last one a fughetta. Tonal and graceful writing for both instruments. M-D.

——. *Variations on an Air by Couperin* 1965 (Boonin) 20pp., parts. 10 min. Theme is "Les graces naturelles." Five contrasting variations plus an interlude and a fughetta. Separate part for alto recorder. Eighteenth-century theme is incorporated tastefully into a mildly 20th-century style. M-D.

Jean-Michel Damase. *Sonata en Concert* Op.17 (Lemoine 1952).

——. *Scherzo* Op.25 (Lemoine 1957) 14pp., parts. 3½ min. Constant motion in $\frac{6}{8}$ and/or $\frac{9}{8}$ moves over entire keyboard. Some long lines. Must be sparkling clean to impress properly. Large span required. M-D.

——. *Sonate* 1974 (Lemoine 1975) 45pp., parts. 14 min. For flute or violin. Andante–Allegro; Moderato; Allegro vivo. Neoclassic in style with detailed passagework punctuated by occasional changes in meter. Slow sections allow atmospheric qualities. Performers must be imaginative to pull the most out of the music. Large span imperative. M-D to D.

Raphael Dannatt. *Sonata* Op.6 1968 (ST SS-931) 19pp., parts. A one-movement work with contrasting sections, tempos, and mood. Freely chromatic; linear and homophonic mixture; short motifs expanded and developed; inner voices take on added significance; large chords, 3 with 2; careful interplay between instruments; good octave technique necessary, *p* closing. Neoclassic orientation. M-D.

Franz Danzi. *Sonatine* D (W. Lebermann—Schott 6191 1970) 32pp., parts. Larghetto–Allegretto; Larghetto; Polacca. M-D.
——. *Sonatine* e Op.34 (Müller 82 1048 09). Classical features, linked movements. M-D.

Gyula David. *Sonata Fuvolara es Zongorára* 1954 (EMB z.1867) 27pp., parts. Allegro; Adagio; Vivace molto. Tonal, based on folklike tunes. Octotonic, parallel chords, thin textures. Adagio is quite free (poco rubato). A folk dance with strong rhythms is the basis for the finale. M-D.

Jack Delano. *Sonatina* (PIC 1965) 26pp., parts. Allegro; Adagio; Allegretto grazioso; Allegro. Freely tonal, varied textures, parallel chords, quick figuration alternating between hands, hemiola, Neoclassic. M-D.

Jules Demersseman. *6ᵉ Solo de Concert* Op.82 F (R. Hériché—Billaudot 1976) 20pp., parts. Grand dramatic gestures permeate with only a few moments of repose. Includes a Chanson Napolitaine and a Final Saltarelle. M-D to D.

François Devienne. *Sonata* I e (J. P. Rampal—IMC 1974).
——. *Sonata* II Op.58 D (C. Chéret, T. Vikatou—Editions I.M.D. 17 1996) 15pp., parts. Allegro poco assai; Largo; Andantino con [5] variazione. Complementary realization in clean edition. M-D.
——. *Sonata* VI Op.68 D (C. Chéret, H. Modzelewska—Editions I.M.D. 414 1997) 17pp., parts. Allegro poco moderato ma non troppo lento; Adagio; Andante grazioso con [6] variatione. M-D.

Robert Di Domenico. *Sonata* 1957 (EM) 19pp., parts. Facsimile of composer's MS. One movement, varied tempos, atonal, thin textures, cadenzas for both instruments. Requires large span. M-D.

Emma Lou Diemer. *Sonata* 1958 (ST 1973) 23pp., parts. 9½ min. Moderately fast, gracefully: imitative, trills in inner voices. Moderately slowly, expressively: pastoral, flowing. Joyfully, fast: thin textures, freely tonal. M-D.

Charles Dieupart. *Suite* I C (H. Ruf—Moeck 1084 1966) Ouverture; Allemande; Courante; Sarabande; Gavotte; Menuet; Gigue. This is the first of 6 Suites left by Dieupart. J. S. Bach was so impressed with these works that he copied out 2 of them. Tasteful keyboard realization. M-D.

———. *Suite* IV e (J.-C. Veilhan, D. Salzer—Leduc 1974) 9pp., parts for flute or violin and basso continuo.

Gaetano Donizetti. *Sonata* C 1819 (R. Meylan—CFP 1969) 15pp., parts. Largo–Allegro. Opening in c sets somber mood; Allegro is all bright and cheerful. Development section proceeds through some interesting tonalities. M-D.

Albert Franz Doppler. *Fantaisie Pastorale Hongroise* Op.26 (Schott FTR91, ISMN M-001-09396-5) 13pp., parts. Unmistakably nationalistic in character with virtuosic requirements in flute. M-D.

Pierre Max Dubois. *Sonate* (Leduc 1959) 25pp., parts. 19 min. Allegro: octotonic, freely tonal around C, shifting rhythms, glissando, chords in alternating hands, Gallic wit. Recitative–Andante nostalgico: bitonal, plaintive melody, musette-like mid-section, rich harmonies. Rondo: broken-chord patterns, glissandi, varied meters, subito martelé effects; large span required. The entire work has a kind of Poulencian charm about it. M-D to D.

Théodore Dubois. *Cavatine* E♭ (P. Schmalfuss—Zimmermann 32190 1997) 8pp. 5 min. For flute, violin, or horn; parts included for each. Andantino tempo in ternary form. M-D.

Henri Dutilleux. *Sonatine* (Leduc 1943) 16pp., parts. 8 min. One large movement of transparent and clear colors, charming writing. Sections are Allegretto, Andante, and Animé, molded together in a strong formal construction. Carefully controlled harmonic dissonance and melodic distortion. M-D.

Jiří Dvořáček. *Dialoghi* 1973 (Panton 1986) 19pp., parts. 8 min. Idylický: flute in low register with piano in loud dynamics creates balance difficulties, octotonic, scalar and repeated note patterns; becomes more involved as movement progresses. Dramatický: lively from start to finish with fast passagework in scales, trills, and arpeggios using the complete registers of both instruments. M-D to D.

Petr Eben. *Miniaturen* (Hofmeister 2611 1998, ISMN M-2034-2611-0) 7pp., parts. Six untitled short pieces of inquisitive nature. For flute or oboe (see also entry under duos for piano and oboe). The composer noted: "The *Miniatures* have a somewhat different origin to my other compositions: The idea for them dates back many years, when I was called upon to write short interludes for a series of lyric poems that were to be broadcast on radio: at the time I notated only the melodic line for the soloist, and improvised the piano accompaniment myself. Because it seemed to me that despite their brevity these pieces contained something of the poetic nature of the verses, I decided to return to them and to amplify them with a piano part. And so it was that this cycle, which is not excessively difficult to play, was brought back to life" (from Postface). M-D.

Günther Eisenhardt. *Aus dem Indianerleben. Eulenspiegeleien* (DVFM 1974). For recorder and piano.

——. *Sonatine* (Hofmeister 1972) 16pp., parts for soprano blockflöte (recorder) and piano.

Manuel Enriquez. *Diptico* I (IU) 3pp., parts. Diagrammatic notation. Numerous directions for performers. Strings to be plucked and struck. Clusters, tremolo clusters, stopped strings, aleatoric, avant-garde. D.

Heimo Erbse. *Sonata* Op.25 1967 (Bo&Bo) 32pp., parts. Con moto; Lento; ♩ = 138–44; Vivace assai. Serial, Expressionist. D.

Gabriel Fauré. *Fantaisie* Op.79 (Hamelle 17pp.; K 3448), parts. 5 min. Andantino; Allegro. Lovely, cool, flowing writing. M-D.

——. *Morceau de Concours* 1898 (A. H. Brieff—Bourne 1977, 1988) 4pp., parts. 3 min. First publication of this short work for the 1898 Flute Concours at the Paris Conservatory. The score has been tastefully enlarged through repetition as explained in the Preface. Unusual as a Concours piece in that it is not virtuosic in character. Int.

Jindřich Feld. *Sonatine Americaine* (Leduc 2000) 41pp., parts. 13 min. Allegro giocoso; Andante tranquillo; Scherzino–Presto; Allegro giusto. Syncopation, cluster chords, and close-knit intervallic relationships are scattered through this late-20th-century essay. M-D.

Jan Reindert Adriaan Felderhof. *Suite* (Donemus 1974) 18pp., 2 parts (flute and oboe), photostat of MS.

Giorgio Ferrari. *Sonata* 1957 (EC 1968) 34pp., parts. 10 min. Allegro moderato; Adagio; Allegro vivo. Chordal punctuation, chromatic, octotonic, thin textures. The last 2 movements contain contrasting tempos and moods. Effective treatment of both instruments. M-D.

Willem de Fesch. *Six Sonatas* (Woehl—HM 1949) Vol.I: 1 D, 2 c, 3 e. Vol.II: 4 G, 5 A, 6 b.

Ronald Finch. *Sonata* (Schott 10723 1959) 12pp., parts. For tenor recorder and piano. Andante piacevole; Presto; Moderato. Tonal, shifting meters, thin textures, Neoclassic, attractive. M-D.

Gottfried Finger. *Zwei leichte Sonaten* d, G (H. Ruf—Schott 5338 1964) 11pp., parts, including basso. For flute, recorder, oboe, or violin. Inspired by the Sonata da Chiesa. M-D.

Bernard Fitzgerald. *Four Gaelic Miniatures* (TP 114-40057 1963) 12pp., parts. Rinnce Fada (Meadow Dance); Ceo ne Maidne (Morning Mist); Port Coeil (Jig Tune); Piobaire (A Piper). Curiosities, musical delights with strong rhythmic emphases. M-D.

Nicolas Flagello. *Concerto Antoniano* 1953 (Gen 1964) 45pp., parts. Originally for flute and orchestra, piano reduction by the composer. Allegro moderato: freely tonal, synthetic scales, sudden dynamic changes, long trill, flute cadenza, large span required. Andante comodo: Ravel-like, triplets, repeated chords, 2 with 3, sinking conclusion. Allegro con brio: disjunct subject; octotonic; concludes with an Alla Fuga; requires good octave technique. Neoclassic. M-D.

Marius Flothuis. *Sonata da Camera* Op.17 1943 (Donemus D40 1951) 16pp., parts. Cadenza: piano part is chordal while flute moves about freely. Sonatina: freely tonal, dissonant counterpoint, broken triplet chord figuration in left hand. Lamento: repeated low notes in left hand, chords in right hand; flute has melody. Rondo alla Francese: octotonic, like a 2-part invention between the instruments, surprise *pp* closing; large span required. M-D.

Hendrik Focking. *Sonata* Op.1/2 (H. Schouwman—Heuwekemeijer 1956) 7pp., parts. Moderato; Allegro; Presto. A few unusual harmonic characteristics would place this in the Rococo period. M-D.
——. *Sonata* Op.1/6 G (Wisse—Br&VP 1949).

Jacqueline Fontyn. *Sonate* 1952 (CeBeDeM 1964) 18pp., parts. 15 min. Allegretto, Adagio; Vivo. A mixture of Neoclassic and Expressionist writing; becomes very involved at spots. D.

John Vaino Forsman. *Sonatina Divertante* (Br 3301 1955) 15pp., parts. Allegretto moderato; Andante mesto; Allegro animato. Neoclassic, clear textures, taut construction. M-D.

Wolfgang Fortner. *Sonata* 1947 (Schott). In Hindemith idiom. Light, tonal centers apparent. The fourth-movement rondo has an extensive second episode made up of a theme, 4 variations, and a coda. M-D.

Lukas Foss. *Three American Pieces* (C. Wincenc—CF 1993) 24pp., parts. *Early Song* (1944); *Dedication* (1944); *Composer's Holiday* (1945). Conventional mid-20th-century writing. Large span required. M-D.

Jean Françaix. *Divertimento* (Schott FTR96 1955) 23pp., parts. Toccatina; Notturno; Perpetuum mobile; Romanza; Finale. Delightful, refreshing, witty, much charm. M-D.
——. *Sonate* 1996 (Schott FTR174 1997, ISMN M-001-12098-2) 35pp., parts. Allegro; Scherzo; Andante; Finale–Allegro assai. One of the composer's last works. Maintains youthful spunk and vitality. M-D to D.

César Franck. *Sonata* (P.-L. Graf—Br&H 8260 1988) 42pp., parts. Edition for flute of the famous Violin Sonata. Fractional changes were made to accommodate the flute, all noted in the Preface and score.

Frederick the Great, King of Prussia. *Ten Sonatas* 2 vols. (C. Bartuzat—Br&H 5451-2) I: d, B♭, B♭, D, A. II: B♭, e, d, E♭, D. Stylistic keyboard realizations by Paul G. Waldersee and Günter Raphael. Multimovement works in Rococo style. M-D.
——. *2 Sonatas* e, e (F. Müller-Busch, E. Kuper—Girolamo 1996, ISMN M-50084-014-5) 21pp., parts, with basso.
——. *Sonata* A (Sonntag—Sikorski).

Hermann L. Freedman. *Sonata* (Thames 1973). Atonal, nonstrict serial. M-D to D.

Kurt Joachim Friedel. *Sonata* (Möseler).
——. *Sonatina* (Heinrichshofen/Sirius 1973) 13pp., parts. For alto recorder and piano.
——. *Suite* (Möseler 1973) 19pp., parts.

Kazuo Fukushima. *Three Pieces from 'Chū-u'* (CFP 1964) 2 copies required. 7½ min. Pointillistic, major 7ths preferred, dynamic extremes with more use of quieter sonorities. Flutter tonguing and quarter tones required for flute. Second piece is for solo flute. M-D.

Anis Fuleihan. *Pastoral Sonata* 1940 (PIC 1967) 26pp., parts. Allegro: main idea is generated from opening triplet; quartal harmony; second theme is heard in the piano in an octave melody; development utilizes alternating hands in harmonic 4ths; staccato style in right hand contrasts with legato flute line; altogether a flowing movement. Andante: ABA; main idea is imitated by both instruments; rocking quartal and quintal chords; octotonic writing and octaves lead to flute cadenza; abbreviated A section returns and concludes with widely spread piano texture. Prestissimo: light perpetual-motion idea in piano is interspersed with 16th-note pattern and syncopated chords; legato, flowing 6ths in piano may present a problem; melody, 16th-note pattern, and syncopated chords all distilled together in the piano part; chords in alternating hand patterns; brilliant crescendo, decorated arpeggio, and a subito chord conclude this work of gracious writing. M-D.

Niels W. Gade. *Sonata* Op.21/2 d (Br&H 1992). Originally for violin and piano, arr. for flute and piano by Karl Müller (1818–94). Extensive Preface. See detailed entry under duos for piano and violin.

Hans Gál. *Concertino* Op.82 (UE).
——. *Three Intermezzi* Op.103 (Schott 1074) 19pp., parts. For tenor recorder or flute and piano or harpsichord. Pieces are charming, pose no great technical

demands, yet they present a full score for sensitive performers. Romantic influence. Int. to M-D.

Johann Ernst Galliard. *Sonata* Op.1/1 C (G. Schenk, H. Ruf—Ric Sy521 1956) 8pp., parts. Largo; Allegro; Largo; Allegro. M-D.

——. *Sonata* Op.1/2 d (G. Schenk, H. Ruf—Ric Sy522 1956) 7pp., parts. Grave; Allegro; Largo; Vivace e affettuoso. M-D.

——. *Sonata* Op.1/3 e (G. Schenk, H. Ruf—Ric Sy533 1956).

Harald Genzmer. *Sonata* 1940 (R&E) 24pp., parts. 11½ min. Lebhaft; Ruhig fliessend; Lebhaft. Neoclassic, strong tonal implications, clear textures. M-D.

——. *Zweite Sonate* E 1945 (Schott 3881) 21pp., parts. 10 min. For alto blockflöte (recorder) and piano. Material well developed, nonlyrical in approach. M-D.

Vittorio Giannini. *Sonata* 1958 (Colombo NY2103 1964) 28pp., parts. Adagio (Introduction–Allegro; Sostenuto e cantabile; Rondo–Allegro con brio. Neo-Romantic style, long beautiful melodies, pianistic, a rather sunny work. M-D.

Felice Giardini. *Sonate* Op.3 (E. Polo—Fondazioni Eugenio Bravi 1941) I *Classici Musicali Italiani,* vol.3. For violin or flute and keyboard. See detailed entry under duos for piano and violin.

Walter Gieseking. *Sonatine* 1935 (Fürstner A8355F) 17pp., parts. Moderato; Allegretto; Vivace. Mildly 20th-century chromatic style, flowing, attractive. M-D.

——. *Variationen über ein Thema von Edvard Grieg* (Fürstner A8375 8358F 1938) 23pp., parts. For flute or violin and piano. Theme is from the "Arietta" Op.12/1 by Grieg. Twelve contrasting variations in a freely chromatic style. Attractive writing that almost spotlights the piano more than the other instrument. M-D.

Anthony Gilbert. *The Incredible Flute Music* Op.11 (Schott 1070) 14pp., parts. Pointillistic, dynamic extremes, aleatoric. Pianist whistles; flutist sings; title is true! Avant-garde. D.

Peggy Glanville-Hicks. *Sonatina* (Schott 10029 1941) 12pp., parts. Animato assai; Lento recitativo; Vivace. Neoclassic, clear lines and textures. Slow movement is slightly Impressionist. M-D.

Alexander Goehr. *Variations* Op.8 1959 (Schott) 15pp., parts. 10 min. Eleven variations. Serial, pointillistic, complex writing. D.

Ernest Gold. *Sonatina* (Simrock 1966) 28pp., parts. 12 min. Allegretto giocoso; Moderato grazioso; Animato. Vitality permeates this entire work, even the slow movement. Texture gets thick but for a short time only. There is nothing here an experienced pianist could not handle. M-D.

Henryk Mikołaj Górecki. *For You, Anne-Lill* Op.58 1986 (Bo&H 1994) 10pp., parts. 12 min. Ternary form with outer section in very slow tempos. Middle section is cadenza-like for solo flute. Piano is octotonic until final 3 pages. Contemplative, minimalist in concept. Int.

———. *Good Night* [= *Dobranoc*] 1990 (Bo&H 1994) 16pp., parts. 30 min. For alto flute, soprano, 3 tam-tams, and piano. Three movements, all marked Lento with slight modifications of approximately 10 min. each. Soprano enters only in the last movement, singing exclusively one phrase from Shakespeare's *Hamlet*, "Good night . . . flights of angels sing thee to thy rest," and a final intonation of the name Michael Vyner, to whom the work is dedicated. Tam-tams "molto profondo" play only in the final 5 mm. A deeply contemplative piece serving as a requiem to Vyner, director of the London Sinfonietta. Concept music. Int.

Harold Gramatages. *Duo* A♭ 1943 (ECIC 1946) 8pp., parts. Allegro moderato; Tranquillo e molto cantabile; Allegro. Imitative, syncopation, freely tonal, clear lines. M-D.

Charles T. Griffes. *Poem* 1922 (Barrère—GS ST30970). Originally for flute and orchestra.

Camargo Guarnieri. *Sonatina* 1947 (Mercury) 19pp., parts. 9½ min. Allegro: thin textures, bitonal, tart. Melancolico: linear, cantabile, staccato middle-voice usage. Saltitante: dance, staccato textures, freely chromatic. M-D.

Sofia Gubaidulina. *Allegro Rustico; Sounds of the Forest* (Sikorski 814 1978) 23pp., parts. *Allegro Rustico* (1963/93): close-knit intervallic relationships, large spans, contrasting articulation at a driving pace. *Sounds of the Forest* (1978): lyric at moderate tempos, proportional rhythmic relationships, extensive trills, *pp* finish. M-D.

Jean-Pierre Guignon. *Sonata* Op.1/8 A, ca.1737 (H. Ruf—Schott 5883 1971) 14pp., parts. Allegro, poco grazioso; Un poco andante; Allegro poco e grazioso; Allegro molto. Expert continuo realization. M-D.

Louis-Gabriel Guillemain. *Sonata* G 1734 (H. Ruf—Schott 5570 1968) 15pp., parts. Adagio; Allemanda; Sarabanda; Allegro assai. M-D.

Joaquín Gutiérrez Heras. *Sonata Simple* (Collecion Arion 1968) 17pp., parts. Allegro non troppo; Andante; Allegro. Thin textures, Neoclassic, hemiola, tremolo, effective. M-D.

Reynaldo Hahn. *Variations on a Theme by Mozart* (IMC 1796) 10pp., parts. Theme and 7 contrasting variations. Only Var.4 changes tonality. M-D.

Karl Haidmayer. *Flötensonate* 1962 (Dob 1971) 26pp., parts. Allegro; Andante espressivo; Animato. Tonal and centered around d, chromatic, repeated cluster-like chords, quartal and quintal harmony, toccata-like finale, mainly thin textures, Neoclassic. Punctuating left-hand octaves; large span required. M-D.

Iain Hamilton. *Sonata* 1966 (TP 1969) 21pp., 2 scores necessary. 14 min. One player uses piccolo, flute, alto flute, and bass flute. In 9 sections with no breaks. All pedaling is marked although some may be added at pianist's discretion. Serial influence, pointillistic, dynamic extremes, shifting meters (5, 2, 3½, etc.). Chords are increased up to clusters with both hands and arms; large span required. Section 4 is a cadenza for solo piano requiring 4 staves to notate; tremolo chords, Expressionist. D.

——. *Spring Days* 1996 (TP 114-40848 1996) 8pp., parts. 5 min. I. The Linnet; II. Primroses; III. Swifts. Thin textures in strongly tonal settings.

George Frideric Handel. *Eleven Sonatas* (H.-P. Schmitz, M. Schneider, T. Best—Br 4225 1995, ISMN M-006-44625-4) 73pp., parts, with basso. Separate edition from *Hallische Händel Ausgabe* IV/3 (BA 4057). Contains HWV 379 e, 359b e, 360 g, 362 a, 363 G, 365 C, 367b b, 369 F, 374 a, 375 e, 376 b. Extensive Prefaces in German and English. M-D.

——. *Flute Sonatas* 2 vols. (A. Bensieck, U. Scheideler—Henle 483 2000, ISMN M-2018-0483-5, Henle 638 1999, ISMN M-2018-0638-9), parts, with basso. Eight Sonatas. I: HWV 359b e, 363b G, 367b b, 378 D, 379 e. II: Halle Sonatas HWV 374 a, 375 e, 376 b. The editor notes that the 3 Halle *Sonatas* are of questionable authorship and were probably not composed in Halle as generally assumed. Extensive Prefaces in German, English, and French appear in both volumes. M-D.

——. *Chamber Sonatas* (Seiffert—Br&H) published separately. Op.1/1a e, 1b e, 2 g, 5 G, 6 g, 8 c, 10 g, 12 F, 13 D, 14 A, 15 E, 17 a.

——. *Ten Sonatas* 2 vols. (J.-P. Rampal, R. Veyron-Lacroix—IMC 1968), parts. I: HWV 359b [Op.1/1B] e, 360 [Op.1/2] g, 362 [Op.1/4] a, 363b [Op.1/5] G, 365 [Op.1/7] C. II: HWV 367b [Op.1/9Op.] b, 369 [Op.1/11] F, 374 [Halle 1] a, 375 [Halle 2] e, 376 [Halle 3] b. Overall reliable older edition.

——. *Ten Sonatas* 3 vols. (W. Woehl—CFP 4552-4). I: g, a, C, F. II: e, G, b. III: Halle *Sonatas* a, e, b.

——. *Eight Sonatas* (Bopp—CFP; Fleury—Bo&H).

——. *Eight Sonatas* (G. Barrère—BMC). Vol.I: 1, 2, 3, 4; Vol.II: 5, 6, 7, 8. A few liberties are taken in this edition.

——. *Seven Sonatas* (Cavally—ST; Schwedler—CFP).

——. *Sonatas* (L. Moÿse—GS 1817 1965) 64pp., parts. Contains 7 *Sonatas*: [HWV 359b] e, [360] g, [362] a, [363b] G, [365] C, [367b] b, [369] F. Excessive editorial markings.

——. *Sonatas* 1, 2, 3, 4, 5, 6, 7 (CF).

——. *Four Sonatas* Op.1 (Hillemann—Schott).

——. *Four Original Sonatas* (H.-P. Schmitz—Nag 122) Op.1/2 g, 1/4 a, 1/7 C, 1/11 F.

————. *Four Sonatas* (Bopp—CFP).

————. *Fitzwilliam Sonatas* (T. Dart—Schott 1948) B♭, d, d.

————. *Fitzwilliam Sonatas* 1 B♭, 2 D, 3 G (K. Hofmann—Hänssler). A good discussion of each piece is contained in the Foreword. M-D.

————. *Three Sonatas* (Dancker—Nag).

————. *Three New Sonatas* (Nag).

————. *Sonatas* Op.1/1, 2 (Heugel 1974) score and parts.

————. *Sonata* Op.1/7 (M. Sanvoisin—Heugel 1974) 14pp., 2 parts.

————. *Sonata* Op.1/4 a (Heugel 1974, 10pp., parts, figured bass realized by Michel Sanvoisin, includes part for viola da gamba; Helmut Mönkemeyer—Moeck). Larghetto; Allegro; Adagio; Allegro. M-D.

————. *Sonata* b (Fleury—Bo&H).

————. *Sonata* B♭ (Mann—Bo&H).

————. *Sonata* c (Scheck, Ruf—Ric).

————. *Sonata* D (W. Hinnenthal—HM 3) 7pp., parts. Adagio; Allegro; Adagio; Menuet. M-D.

————. *Sonata* e (Fleury—Bo&H).

————. *Sonata* Op.1/11 F (H. Mönkemeyer—Moeck 2012) 7pp., parts. Larghetto; Allegro; Siciliana; Allegro. M-D.

————. *Sonata* g (Scheck, Ruf—Ric).

HWV = *Händel-Handbuch, Band 3. Thematisch-systematisches Verzeichnis: Instrumentalmusik, Pasticci und Fragmente,* herausgegeben von Bernd Baselt. Kassel 1986.

See A. O. Gould, "The Flute Sonatas of G. F. Handel: A Stylistic Analysis and Historical Survey," thesis, University of Illinois, 1961.

John Harbison. *Duo* 1961 (AMP 7996 1989) 32pp., parts. I. Fanfare is a strident duet with wide phrases and imitative features. II. Lullaby makes use of octaves and cantabile qualities at Adagio. III. Intermezzo strikes out Presto with repeated notes and running passagework, contrasted twice by brief homophonic sections. IV. Dithyramb reveals more contrasting material between an insistent melody and soft mysterious passages. V. Sonata and Coda begins subdued at Allegro scherzando and slowly gains momentum before turning toward the Coda with an Andante sostenuto for a sonorous climax and surprising *pp* finish. Requires much collaboration. D.

Tibor Harsanyi. *Three Pieces* 1924 (Sal) 8pp., parts. Lento: recitative-like opening and closing; Impressionist chordal sonorities in mid-section. Scherzo: fleeting, short chords in piano with moving flute line are contrasted with legato flowing chords in a short mid-section. Lento: bitonal broken triplet arpeggi figuration throughout in piano with long sustained lines in flute. A lovely group. M-D.

Walter Hartley. *Fantasia* 1961 (Wingert-Jones). 5 min.

———. *Four Sketches* 1964 (TP). 7 min.

Johann Adolph Hasse. *Sonata* d Op.1 (B&VP).

———. *Sonata* D (Nag 99) 8pp., parts. Adagio; Allegro; Larghetto; Minuetto. M-D.

———. *Sonata* G (H. Ruf—Schott 5447 1966) 11pp., parts. Andante; Allegro, Largo; Tempo di Minuetto. M-D.

———. *Sonata* G (Englander—Hofmeister).

Johann Wilhelm Hassler. *Two Sonatas* (M. Glöfrt—Nag 11; Rucker—CFP), parts. *Sonata* I D 1786: Andantino gracioso; Allegro, quasi presto e scherzando. Keyboard part takes on much more importance than the flute. M-D. *Sonata* 2 G 1787: Allegro; Allegro scherzando. Much use of triplet figuration in the Allegro. M-D.

Hikaru Hayashi. *Sonata* 1967 (Ongaku No Tomo Sha) 26pp., parts. SA design in outer movements, ABA form in slow movement. The third movement is based on a Japanese folk tune. Freely tonal, thick sonorities, Impressionist techniques in slow movement, imitation, and thick repeated chords in finale. M-D to D.

Franz Josef Haydn. *Sonata* No.8 G (IMC; CFP).

———. *Sonata* G (Perry—Bo&H).

John Hebden. *Sonata* I D (J. Barlow—OUP 1979) 11pp., parts, with basso. 9 min. Published in Musica da Camera series. Largo e siciliana; Allegro; Largo; Allegro con spirito. Editorial suggestions clearly indicated. M-D.

Bernard Heiden. *Sonatina* 1958 (AMP 95935-19) 20pp., parts. Allegro: alternating chords in both hands are interrupted by chorale material, which is the basis for this movement. Andante sostenuto: flowing 8th-note motion. Allegretto: much dialogue between the instruments. Neoclassic. M-D.

Everett Helm. *Sonata* C (Schott 4193 1952; Bo&H) 13pp., parts. 12 min. Allegro; Lento; Aria; Vivo. Neoclassic, freely tonal, many 3rds in the Aria; Lento is most Expressionist with some dramatic gestures. M-D.

Hans Werner Henze. *Sonatina* (Schott 1951) Light, well crafted. The tune "The Miller of Dee" is cleverly and amusingly introduced in the finale. M-D.

Kurt Hessenberg. *Sonata* Bb Op.38 1947 (Schott) 15 min. Notturno; Rondo; Fantasia. Neoclassic. M-D.

———. *Suite* Op.77 1963 (Schott) 12 min. Sonatina; Ostinato; Fughetta; Andantino con variazioni. M-D.

Paul Hindemith. *Sonata* 1936 (Schott) 14 min. Heiter bewegt; Sehr langsam; Sehr lebhaft; Marsch. Clear textures and forms, light in style. Final 2 movements are more cheerful and outgoing than the first 2. Ends with a crisp march that alludes to the first movement. D.

——. *Echo* 1942 (Schott 1945) 2pp., parts. Inspired by a poem by Thomas Moore included as an epigram on the flute score. Marked "Rather fast," the title of the work is clearly enunciated by a canon in the theme. M-D.

Franz Anton Hoffmeister. *Sonata* Op.13 C 1795–1805 (H.-P. Schmitz—Nag 236 1973) 40pp., parts. 20 min. with repeats. For flute or violin and piano. Three movements. Almost a Piano Sonata with flute accompaniment. Excellent secondrate music, well written for both instruments. M-D.

Karl Höller. *Sonata* I Op.45 (CFP).

——. *Sonata* II Op.53 C (Schott 4546 1955) 21pp., parts. 11½ min. Con moto e leggiero ($^{4+2}_4$); Vivo capriccioso; Tranquillo cantabile; Presto e giocoso. Freely tonal, exploits resources of the piano. M-D to D.

James Hook. *Six Sonatas* Op.54 (G. Braun—Carus 17.099 1996) 27pp., parts. Nos.I. G, II. C, III. G, IV. F, V. C, VI. D. Most *Sonatas* contain a rondo, and No.VI consists entirely of 2 rondos. No.II contains an Aria with 4 variations. Chipper writing showing qualities of the early Classical period with an almost complete avoidance of minor tonality. M-D.

Katherine Hoover. *Masks* Op.56 1998 (Papagena 1998) 23pp., parts. 15 min. Six untitled and contrasting essays firmly rooted in tonality. No.III quotes the spiritual "Swing Low." M-D.

Jacques Martin Hotteterre. *4 Suites* Op.5 2 vols. (H. M. Kneihs—Kunzelmann 23a/b 1971), parts, with basso. This edition is intended for recorder but may be performed on flute. Vol.I 39pp.: B♭, E♭. Vol.II 24pp.: F, d. Uses both standard and optional Baroque dance movements. Foreword in German and English with table of ornaments. M-D.

Alexandru Hrisanide. *Sonata* II 1960–62 (Gerig 1973) 15pp., parts. 7 min. Vivo: one movement, serial, pointillistic, dynamic extremes, uses full keyboard range, some unusual notation. D.

George Adolphe Hüe. *Fantaisie* 1913 (MMP) 12pp., parts. Contains colorful harmonies and picturesque qualities. In 2 continuous parts, the first with recitative-like features and melismatic writing, mostly sustained by chords in piano, and the second with lively passagework outlining the harmonic settings. An effective work. M-D.

Luigi Hugues. *La Gioconda di Ponchielli: Fantasia* Op.110 A (A. Mancini, M. Vitale—Ut Orpheus ACC-17 1998, ISBN 88-8109-324-3) 19pp., parts. A fantasy in 3 sections based on Ponchielli's *La Gioconda*. Cheerful, delicate with touches of virtuosity, and tuneful. Preface in Italian. M-D.

Johann Nepomuk Hummel. *Sonata* Op.2/2 G (H. Riessberger—Dob 181 1967) 32pp., parts. Allegro; Romanza (2 different versions are included); Rondo–Allegro. Foreword in German and English. Sources and editorial additions identified. An utterly charming work. M-D.

——. *Sonata* Op.50 D (H. Riessberger—Dob 148, 27pp., parts; CFP). In Dob edition sources are identified in a Foreword in German, English, and French. A challenge to both instruments is presented by this solidly structured piece. Allegro con brio: SA, unconventional harmonic treatment in the development section. Andante: serene, quiet, Beethoven-like. Rondo: pastoral and swift. M-D.

——. *Sonata* Op.62 A (H. Riessberger—Dob 473 1973) 25pp., parts. Urtext; editorial additions identified. Allegro con garbo: especially attractive second subject. Menuetto moderato: effective pianistic figuration. Rondo–Vivace: spirited, appealing. M-D.

Jacques Ibert. *Jeux: Sonatine* 1923 (Leduc 1925) 15pp., parts. 5 min. Animé: highly chromatic, light, cheerful, feathery; tripartite form; bounces on quintuple pulse. Tendre: more Impressionist sounds; melodic line woven into figuration; canonic treatment; fades away into nothingness. M-D.

——. *Histoires* (Leduc 1933). Transcription of 6 pieces from the original for solo piano by Marcel Moÿse. La Meneuse de tortues d'or; Le Petit âne blanc; Dans la maison triste; La Cage de cristal; La Marchande d'eau fraîche; Le Cortège de Balkis. Picturesque, with typical Ibert wit and charm. M-D.

——. *Aria* (Leduc 1931). Transcription of the original vocalise with the flute playing the voice part a minor 2nd higher in F. M-D.

Desiré-Emile Inghelbrecht. *Sonatine en Trois Parties* (Leduc 1920) 23pp., parts. For flute and piano or harp. Préambule; Sicilienne; Rondes. Impressionist, chromatic, octotonic. Contains some lovely and attractive sonorities. Probably more effective on the harp. Requires large span. M-D.

Hidenao Ito. *Apocalypse* 1965 (SZ 1971) 10pp., parts. 10 min. Four movements consisting of brief fragments that can be rearranged in various formats by the performers. Serial, pointillistic, clusters, avant-garde. D.

Gordon Jacob. *Suite* (OUP 1959) 33pp., parts. 20 min. Originally for tenor recorder and string quartet. Piano reduction by the composer. Prelude; English Dance; Lament; Burlesca alla Rumba; Pavane; Introduction and Cadenza; Tarantella (optional sopranino recorder). Diatonic and straightforward writing in delightfully contrasted movements. M-D.

Philipp Jarnach. *Sonatina* Op.12 (Lienau 1920) 11pp., parts. One movement, varied tempos, serious mood, similar to early Schoenberg style. D.

Carlos Jiménez Mabarak. *Cinco Piezas* (Collecion Arion 1968) 20pp., parts. Alegoria del Perejil; La Imagen Repentina; Nocturno; El Ave Prodigiosa; Danza Magica. Serial, astringent style, flexible meters. M-D.

André Jolivet. *Fantaisie-Caprice* (Leduc 1954) 4pp., parts. Tranquil opening, works up to an incisive Allegro climax, drops back, and builds again to the conclusion. Freely tonal; half-step is an important unifying device. M-D.

——. *Sonata* 1958 (Heugel) 30pp., parts. Fluide; Grave; Violent. Complex, well-organized writing that will require mature pianism. Intense and taut style throughout. Large span necessary. Very D.

Klaus Jungk. *Sonata* (Br 3305 1956) 18pp., parts. Largo–Allegro (Thema) and 6 Variations; Con moto; Vivace. Mildly 20th-century Neoclassic style, careful formal construction. First movement presents the most problems, the greatest being holding it together with all the tempo changes. M-D.

Paul Juon. *Sonata* Op.78 (Zimmermann 1924) 27pp., parts. Gemächlich; Langsam, doch nicht schleppend; Straff, jedoch nicht zu schnell. Much rhythmic activity, post-Romantic writing, tonal with chromatic coloration, sweeping pianistic gestures. M-D to D.

Pal Kadosa. *Sonatina* Op.56 (EMB 1962) 27pp., parts. Poco allegro; Andante moderato; Molto vivo. No pause between movements. Freely tonal, chords in alternating hands, imitation. Sustained chords in Andante movement, dance-like rhythms in finale reminiscent of Bartók. Attractive. M-D.

László Kalmár. *Sonata* (Bo&H 1971) 5 min. Eight short linked-together sections—sounds like one movement. M-D.

István Kardos. *Scherzo Variato* (Gen 1970) 12pp., parts. 8 min. Scherzo–Tema is strongly rhythmic and is made up of 3 extensively developed variations. Freely tonal. Hungarian color and rhythms make this a worthwhile work with much involvement for both instruments. M-D.

Talivaldis Kenins. *Concertante* 1966 (Bo&H 1972) 13 min. Presto furioso–Cadenza; Vivace assai. Explores all the flute technique and sonority. In a concertante, dialogue with the piano develops different moods of expression described by the movement titles. Clear textures with much rhythmic vitality. D.

Harrison Kerr. *Suite* 1940–41 (Arrow 1943) 20pp., parts. 9 min. Prelude; Dance; Recitativo; Toccata. Twelve-tone, quartal harmonies, dissonant counterpoint, sudden dynamic changes. Large span required. D.

Piet Ketting. *Preludium e Fughetta* 1970 (Donemus) 12pp., parts. Chromatic; both pieces evolve into a complicated climax before ending quietly. Piano must be careful not to overbalance flute in climaxes, which is easy to do. Well crafted. M-D to D.

Aram Khachaturian. *Three Pieces* (J. Galway—GS 3598 1987) 16pp., parts. Short transcriptions by James Galway of the famous Waltz from *Masquerade*, Adagio from *Spartak*, and Sabre Dance from *Gayane*. Retains the orchestral quality in the piano with the principal melodies in the flute. Delightful, will please any audience. M-D to D.

Johann Philipp Kirnberger. *Two Sonatas* G, g (CFP).

——. *Sonata* G (B. Weigant—Schott 5571 1967) 13pp., parts. Adagio; Allegro; Allegro. M-D.

Jakob Friedrich Kleinknecht. *Four Sonatas* 2 vols. 1748 (N. Delius, M. Müller—Zimmermann 33760 2000, ISMN M-010-33760-9), parts, with basso. I: G, B♭. II: D, D. Overshadowed by the First Viennese School, Kleinknecht's *Sonatas* show originality and melodic interest worthy of revival. Fine edition with effective keyboard realization. Preface in French, English, and German. M-D.

——. *Sonata* D (G. Zahn—UE 18 674 1990) 16pp., parts. 18 min. First publication, may have been composed by Kleinknecht's brother Johann Stephan (Preface). Allegro ma non troppo; Andantino, ma grazioso; Tantino allegro. Marked rhythms and an invigorating piano score realized by the editor. M-D.

Charles Koechlin. *Sonata* Op.52 (Sal 1922) 26pp., parts. 15 min. Adagio molto tranquillo; Mouvement de Sicilienne; Final. The outer movements are connected with similar thematic material, while the middle movement provides contrast in the form of a lyrical intermezzo. Long, flowing, chromatic lines; parallel chords and broken-chord figuration used frequently. Large span required. M-D.

——. *14 Pieces* (Sal 1948) 16pp., parts. Short, contrasting, appealing, interesting counterpoint between the instruments. Appropriate for various occasions, including church use. Int. to M-D.

Heinrich Köhler. *Sonata* Op.49 C ca.1806 (A. Pasetti—Ut Orpheus MAG57 1999, ISMN M-2153-0444-4) 19pp., parts. Urtext. Allegro; Andante grazioso; Rondo–Allegretto. Preface in Italian. M-D.

——. *Sonata* Op.59 C ca.1806 (A. Pasetti—Ut Orpheus MAG58 1999, ISMN M-2153-0445-1) 21pp., parts. Urtext. Allegro con spirito; Romanza–Andantino; Andante con variazioni. Preface in Italian. M-D.

Barbara Kolb. *Figments* (CF 1969) 9 min. One movement. Both instruments are pointillistically oriented with much hopping about. D.

Mieczyslaw Kolinski. *Dahomey Suite* Op.31 (Hargail 1952) 16pp., parts. For flute or recorder. Two Dokpwe Songs to Work the Fields; Song Sung as the Body of a Dead Cult Follower is Prepared by Priests for Burial; Song of Illusion; Two Tohwiyo Cult Songs; Story Song. "[T]he fascinating vitality and amazing refinement in the rhythmic, metric, melodic and formal structure of this music is far from being 'primitive'. The present Suite is based upon seven Dahomey songs . . . and represents an attempt at merging African and European elements into a stylistic unit" (from Foreword). M-D.

Egon Kornauth. *Sonatine* Op.46a (Dob 1959) 16pp., parts. 10 min. Rondino; Intermezzo; Siciliano. Tonal, chromatic, quartal harmony, thin textures, flowing, appealing Neoclassic writing. M-D.

Leo Kraft. *Fantasy* 1963 (Gen 1971) 8pp., parts. Freely: changing tempos, harmonics, serial, long pedal effects with both una corda and sostenuto, clusters, plucked strings. Effective. M-D.

Johann Ludwig Krebs. *Six Chamber Sonatas* (B. Klein—CFP 1962) Vol.I: *Sonatas* A, G, C. Vol.II: Sonatas e, a, D. Multimovement works with the slow movements having more interest. M-D.
——. *Sonata* C (Scheck, Ruf—Ric).
——. *Sonata* D (Ermeler—CFP).
——. *Sonata* e (Ermeler—Br).

Julian Krein. *Sonata* 1957 (USSR) 46pp., parts. Moderato; Lento; Presto. Key signatures are used, but this work is freely tonal and moves through many keys. Suggests Prokofiev's style but with more Slavic flavor. Piano part is thoroughly developed. D.

Ernst Křenek. *Suite* 1954 (BB) 11pp., parts. Andante; Allegretto moderato; Andante con moto; Allegro vivace. Serial, sparse textures. M-D.
——. *Flute Piece* 1959 (Br 3330) 15pp., parts. In nine phases. "Sections A & B may be performed separately. If section A alone is played the piano part is omitted. If section B is played by itself, the piano starts four bars before B" (from the score). Harmonics, pointillistic, serial, complex writing. D.

Conradin Kreutzer. *Sonata* Op.35 G (Eulenburg GM33 1971) 32pp., parts. Andante maestoso–Allegro; Andantino grazioso; Rondo–Allegro molto. Straightforward Classical style. M-D.

Ton de Kruyf. *Pas de Deux* Op.22 1968 (Bo&Bo) 12pp., 10 min. Ostinato; Intermezzo; Giochi. Directions in German. Serial, pointillistic, avant-garde. D.

Friedrich Kuhlau. *Grand Sonate Concertante* A (UMP).
——. *Grand Sonate Concertante* E (UMP).
——. *3 Grand Solos* Op.57 (J. Boulze—Billaudot), parts. Published separately. I: F, 20pp. 15½ min.: in 3-movement format—Allegro con giusto; Adagio; Allegro vivace. II: a, 19pp: in one continuous movement with 2 broad sections, the second based upon a theme by Mozart. III: G, 16pp.: in 3-movement format— Allegro, con grazia; Adagio–Con molto espressione; Alla Polacca. Well-developed ideas and musical features exhibiting early Romanticism. M-D.
——. *Introduction and Variations on a Theme from Carl Maria von Weber's 'Euryanthe'* Op.63 1825 (H.-P. Schmitz—Br 19111 1971) 23pp., parts. Preface in French, German, and English. Sources identified. Requires a warm and genial

performance with elegance and verve. Tempos and dynamics can be treated very flexibly, and contrasts can be emphasized. M-D.

———. *Six Divertissements* Op.68 (P. Taffanel—IMC; K 3586) 44pp., parts. 1 G, 2 D, 3 B, 4 E♭, 5 G, 6 c♯. M-D.

———. *Sonata* Op.83/1 G (CFP).

———. *Sonata* Op.83/2 C (CFP).

———. *Variationen* Op.94 1829 (A. Mehring—Zimmermann 31200 1995) 23pp., parts. Based on "the aria 'Pour des filles si gentilles' from the now-forgotten opera *Le Colporteur* by Georges Onslow (1784–1835). Modeled almost completely on the original note text, this aria was arranged by Kuhlau in its original key for flute and piano, thus forming the basis for eight charming variations, in which equally satisfying roles are assigned to both instruments" (from Preface). M-D.

———. *Introduktion und Variationen* Op.99 1829 (A. Mehring—Zimmermann 31180 1995) 18pp., parts. Based upon the aria "Toujours de mon jeune âge" from Onslow's *Le Colporteur*. "This aria, with its surprising minor-major modulation, inspired Kuhlau to write a charming introduction with eight separate variations, in which equally satisfying roles are assigned to both the flute and the piano" (from Preface). M-D.

———. *Variations on a Scottish Song* Op.104 (Billaudot; Hanssler).

———. *Trois Duos Brillants* Op.110 (Jack Spratt 1960). 1 B♭, 18pp., parts. 2 e, 16pp., parts. 3 D, 18pp., parts.

Billaudot has a large selection of Kuhlau's works for flute and piano.

Felicitas Kukuck. *Sonata* (Möseler 1962) 16pp., parts. Bewegt; Ruhig; Sehr Schnell und leicht. Clear Neoclassic construction throughout. M-D.

Ivan Kurz. *Vitamíny I* 1977 (Panton 1981) 20pp., parts. 9 min. Allegro; Largo; Presto. Thin textures in a Neoclassic style with strong rhythmic patterns. M-D.

Ezra Laderman. *Sonata* 1957 (OUP) 24pp., parts. 12 min. Moderato; Allegro molto; Fugato; Allegro. Short chromatic figures are important in this freely tonal work. Idioms involved include octotonic writing, broken chords, imitation and syncopation, and sudden dynamic changes. Neoclassic orientation. D.

Yehoshua Lakner. *Sonata* 1948 (Israeli Music Publications 1951) 32pp., parts. 18 min. Allegro energico molto rubato; Adagio; Allegro. Striking instrumental texture with strong Oriental atmosphere, logically developed form, varied rhythmic structure, expressive melodic lines. Large span required. M-D to D.

Peter Lamb. *Sonatina* (Bo&H 1074) 16pp., parts. Three movements (fast, slow, fast). Graceful, Prokofiev-like, mainly diatonic with shifting harmonies. Effective Neoclassic writing for both instruments. M-D.

Jean Langlais. *Mouvement* 1907 (Pro Organo 2002 1990) 8pp., parts. For flute (oboe or violin) and keyboard (piano, harpsichord, or organ with pedal ad libitum). Primarily homophonic in nature with imitative features at Andante. M-D.

————. *Deux Pièces* Op.39 (Combre 5931 1998, ISMN M-2303-5931-3) 6pp., parts. I. Histoire vraie pour une Môn: a simple piece with a plaintive melody in g. II. Rondel dans le style médiéval: thin textures cast in a quick tempo with soft dynamics. M-D.

Santo Lapis. *Three Easy Sonatas* Op.1 ca.1710 (H. Ruf—Schott 4632) 15pp., parts for flute (violin or oboe, cello or bassoon ad lib). I. D, Affettuoso; Moderato; Allegro. II. A, Spiritoso; Andante e delicato; Allegro. III. e, Vivace; Largo; Allegro assai. Graceful, appealing, fluent keyboard realizations. M-D.

William P. Latham. *Fantasy Concerto* (Spratt 1950) 28pp., parts. Piano reduction by Joan Seyler. One continuous large movement in varied tempos, moods, and textures. Mainly neo-Romantic with mildly 20th-century flavor created by colorful rhythms. M-D.

————. *Sonata* II (Spratt 1965) 6pp., parts. Allegro moderato; Adagio; Vivace. Like Prokofiev's *Classical Symphony* in style. Int. to M-D.

Philibert de Lavigne. *Six Sonatas* Op.2 ca.1740 (W. Hillemann—Noetzel) Published separately. I. La Baussan, 7pp., parts (N3264); II. La d'Acut, 8pp., parts (N3265); III. La Dubois, 7pp., parts; IV. La Beaumont, 10pp., parts (N3272); V. La Persan, 7pp., parts (N3273); VI. La Simianne, 7pp., parts (N3274). The program descriptions of the individual *Sonatas* and some of the movements are characteristic of the period. These multimovement works can be performed on all of the woodwind instruments in use during the first half of the 18th century, and on the violin. Performance practices are discussed in the Preface by the editor. Each work also includes a cello part ad lib.

Henri Lazarof. *Sonatina* 1999 (Merion 144-40379 1999) 14pp., parts. 14 min. In 4 untitled movements of slow, fast, slow, fast design. Expressionist with close intervals, detailed rhythms, and introspective motivic schemes. Requires experienced performers. M-D to D.

Jean-Marie Leclair. *Sonata* b (Druilhe—Ric).
————. *Sonata* b (Ruf—Ric).
————. *Sonata* C (ESC).
————. *Sonata* C (H. Ruf—Ric).
————. *Sonata* C Op.1/2 (H. Ruf—Schott FTR47 1967, ISMN M-001-09356-9) 15pp., parts, with basso. For flute or violin. Adagio; Corrente; Gavotta, Giga. M-D.
————. *Sonata* e (Bouillard—ESC).
————. *Sonata* I e (CFP; K 7137).

———. *Sonata* G (Bouillard—ESC) 11pp., parts. Andante; Allegro ma non troppo; Aria; Giga. M-D.

———. *Sonata* Op.2/5 G (Ruf—Br).

———. *Sonata* Op.9/2 (Polnauer—JWC; J.-C. Veilhan, D. Salzer—Leduc 1977), parts. For flute or violin. Andante; Allemanda; Sarabanda; Minuetto. M-D.

———. *Sonata* Op.9/7 (H. Ruf—Schott FTR49 1996, ISMN M-001-09358-3) 16pp., parts. Dolce–Andante; Allegro ma non troppo; Aria–Affettuoso; Giga–Allegro moderato. Preface in German, English, and French. M-D.

See also duos for piano and violin.

Jacques Leduc. *Sonate* Op.21 1966 (CeBeDeM) 31pp., parts. 16 min. Maestoso; Andante amabile; Allegro ritmico. Mildly 20th-century with strong French influence. Finale is highly rhythmic with toccata-like sections. M-D.

Noël Lee. *Variations Antiques* (ST 684 1989) 47pp., parts. Consists of a lyric theme in $^6_8$ with 8 variations. Spatial and linear writing techniques spread over extremes of instruments; flute must play low B. Piano has significant role throughout requiring a thorough command of the instrument and careful attention to balance. Concludes *pp* with the final variation using double-dotted notes and flutter tonguing, and an abbreviated repeat of the theme. M-D to D.

Lowell Liebermann. *Sonata* Op.23 1987 (TP 114-40463 1988) 25pp., parts. 13½ min. In 2 movements, both with clear lines of development. Lento con rubato: mysterious, sharply contrasting dynamics, uses full keyboard, pulsating, lyric. Presto energico: vigorous passagework, mixed meters (including $^{15}_{16}$), astringent harmonies in tonal context. Instruments fit together well in spite of independent characters. D.

See Lisa Michelle Garner, "Lowell Liebermann: A Stylistic Analysis and Discussion of the Sonata for Flute and Piano, Op.23, Sonata for Flute and Guitar, Op.25, and *Soliloquy* for Flute Solo, Op.44," D.M.A. diss., Rice University, 1997.

Johann Georg Linicke. *Sonata* a (C. Ruckler—Mitteldeutscher) 12pp., parts. Allegro; Adagio; Villanella. M-D.

Pietro Locatelli. *Three Sonatas* (G. Scheck, W. Upmeyer—Br 626 1944) 19pp., parts. I. G, Adagio; Allegro; Largo; Allegro. II. D, Vivace; Largo; Allegro. III. g, Largo; Allegro; Largo; Allegro. All 3 are M-D.

———. *Three Sonatas* Op.2 (G. Braun, S. Petrenz—Carus 17.098/01 1997) 28pp., parts. I. E, Andante; Largo; Allegro. II. G, Largo; Allegro; Minuetto. III. A, Largo; Allegro; Largo; Allegro. Complementary realization. Preface in German. M-D.

———. *Sonata* B♭ (Ruf—Schott).

———. *Sonata* II D (Feltkamp—B&VP) 8pp., parts.

——. *Sonata* F (Alexander Kowalscheff—Hug GH9000 1947) 8pp., parts. Largo; Allegro; Cantabile; Allegro. M-D.

——. *Sonata* F (CFP).

——. *Sonata* G (CFP).

Edward Loder. *Sonata* E♭ (N. Temperley—OUP 1990) 41pp., parts. Allegro non troppo; Allegro moderato, 'The Somnambulist'; Adagio–Rondo: Allegro assai. "The form and style are traditional, with the clear influences of Weber and Mendelssohn, but there are many individual touches—not least the 'Gothic' tone of the second movement, to which Loder added the title 'The Somnambulist.' Coming from a period in which the great bulk of the flute repertory is empty display material, this *Sonata* shows a welcome seriousness and integrity. It is exceptionally well laid out for the two instruments: the piano writing is full and varied, but it never overwhelms the tone of the flute" (from Preface). M-D.

Jean Baptiste Loeillet (of London). *Sechs Sonaten* Op.3/1–6 (H. Ruf—Schott 5331-6 1964), parts, with basso. Published separately. 1. C, Largo; Allegro; Affettuoso; Allegro. 2. d, Largo; Allegro; Largo; Allegro. 3. F, Adagio; Allegro; Larghetto; Allegro. 4. a, Largo; Poco allegro; Adagio; Allegro; Presto. 5. g, Grave; Allegro; Affectuoso; Allegro. 6. d, Adagio; Allegro; Adagio; Allegro. Almost exclusively binary forms. Fine realizations. Preface in German, English, and French. M-D.

——. *Sonata* Op.3/7 e (P. Poulteau—Leduc 1974) 8pp., parts.

——. *Sonata* Op.3/11 D (P. Poulteau—Leduc 1974) 9pp., parts.

Jean-Baptiste Loeillet (of Lyons). *Three Sonatas* Op.1/1, 2, 3 (Hinnendial—HM 43).

——. *Sonata* Op.1/1 a (Stave—Moeck; Hinnenthal—Br 1952).

——. *Sonata* Op.1/2 d (Hinnenthal—Br 1952).

——. *Sonata* Op.1/3 G (Hinnenthal—Br 1952).

——. *Sonata* Op.1/4 F (Mönkemeyer—Moeck 1029) 11pp., parts. Largo; Allegro; Vivace; Giga. M-D.

——. *Sonata* Op.1/6 C (Stave—Moeck).

——. *Two Sonatas* Op.2/5 c, 4/6 g (Mönkemeyer—Moeck 1032) 15pp., parts.

——. *Sonatas* Op.3/2 B♭, 3 g, 4 G, 5 c, 6 e, 10 d (Schott). Available separately.

——. *Three Sonatas* Op.3/9, 4/9, 10 (Hinnenthal—HM 162).

——. *Three Sonatas* Op.3/12, 4/11, 12 (Hinnenthal—HM 165).

——. *Sonata* Op.3/8 G (Ruf—Schott).

——. *Sonata* Op.3/9 B♭ (Ruf—Ric).

——. *Sonata* Op.4/11 f (Hinnenthal—Br 1960).

——. *Sonata* V c (Feltkamp—CFP).

——. *Sonata* Op.5/1 e (Sadie—Musica Rara 1961).

——. *Sonata* X F (Feltkamp—CFP).

———. *Sonata* e (Lovering—Bo&H), not Op.5/1.

———. *Sonata* F (Beon—IMC).

———. *Sonata* G (Beon—IMC).

———. *Sonata* g (Beon—IMC).

———. *Sonata* 14 g (CF).

———. *Sonatas* (Heugel 1974). For recorder and basso continuo. Selections. Edited from the Roger edition, Amsterdam, 1705 and 1715. Includes part for viola da gamba. Vol.I: Sonata Op.1/1 a; Sonata Op.1/2 e; Vol.II: Sonata Op.3/2 B♭; Sonata Op.3/8 F.

See Brian Priestman, "Catalogue thématique des œuvres de Jean-Baptiste, John et Jacques Loeillet," *Revue Belge de Musicologie* VI/4 (1952): 219–74.

George Simon Löhlein. *Sonate* G 1765 (D. Sonntag—Heinrichshofen 1967) 16pp., parts. Allegro; Amoroso poco Andante; Vivace. The slow movement requires an even trill. M-D.

Otto Luening. *Fantasia Brevis* (Highgate 1974) 11pp., parts. Varied sections concluding with a quasi-cadenza. Mixture of diatonic and chromatic as well as chordal and linear style, asymmetric phrase structure. Strong F♯ conclusion. M-D.

———. *Sonatina* 1952 (New Valley Music Press 1976) 5pp., parts. Andante tranquillo: slight tempo changes, tonal and chromatic, inner voice is important. Mildly 20th-century. M-D.

———. *Short Sonata* 1952 (Galaxy) 16pp., parts. For flute and piano or harpsichord. Allegro Moderato: freely tonal, changing meters, mainly linear with thickened textures for emphasis. Theme and Variations: no break between variations, contrasting textures for each variation, more tonal than first movement. Neoclassic. M-D.

———. *Second Short Sonata* (New Valley Music Press 1976) 7pp., parts. Moderato: linear, imitation. Adagio: chordal, bitonal. Allegro: triplet figuration, melody part of triplet, bitonal. Int. to M-D.

———. *Third Short Sonata* (New Valley Music Press 1976) 7pp., parts. Slow and somewhat free in tempo: atonal, chromatic lines divided between hands, chords in low register. Interlude: free in tempo and dynamics, chordal for piano. With fantasy and freedom: opens with flute cadenza; chordal punctuation; widely spread textures; tremolo 7ths; bitonal close. M-D.

Bruno Maderna. *Divertimento in Due Tempi* 1953 (M. Baroni, R. Dalmonte—SZ 8994 1995) 12pp., parts. Critical first edition drawn from manuscript. Andante scorrevole; Allegro. Dodecaphonic techniques using 6 series. The editors note: "Although the work is clearly complete, the fact that it is written in pencil and that the manuscript contains copious signs of serial calculation (numbers, arrows and dotted lines connecting notes) convey[s] the impression that this version may not have been entirely definitive. On the back of the last sheet we also find notes by the composer, seemingly unrelated to the *Divertimento,* consisting of a schematic serial analysis of Schoenberg's Opus 33b. The form of Schoenberg's series, based almost entirely on seconds and thirds, as well as Maderna's highlighting of four nuclei of three notes each, might, however, suggest that this material may have given Maderna some insights about the composition of his own piece" (from Preface). Extensive notes in Italian and English, almost as long as the score. M-D to D.

Robert Maggio. *Fluano Pianute* 1992 (TP 114-40812 1996) 31pp., parts. 15 min. I. bounce-minimalize; II. float upspace-mediate; III. izimanlime-musical box; IV. beditate-mounce; V. musing boxical-spoatupflace. Rhythmically complex with a degree of minimalistic technique. Wide span required in IV. For determined performers willing to make "cheerful" music from an academically intuitive work. M-D to D.

Antoine Mahault. *Sonata* VI G (H.-P. Schmitz—Br 3307) 16pp., parts. Source identified. Adagio; Allegro; Largo; Menuetto (with 8 variations). Excellent basso continuo realization by Max Schneider. M-D.

Peter Mai. *Concertino* (Hofmeister 7468) 18pp., parts. For soprano blockflöte (recorder) or oboe and piano. Allegro risoluto; Adagio misterioso; Allegro. Thin textures, freely tonal, highly attractive Neoclassic style. M-D.
———. *Sonatina* (Hofmeister 1974) 12pp., parts. Mässig bewegt; Ruhig schwingend; Lebhaft. Mildly dissonant Hindemith style. Freely tonal around d. Finale is toccata-like. M-D.

Francesco Mancini. *Zwölf Sonaten* (Michel—Amadeus 138-41 1999), parts, including bass. Vol.I: 1 d; 2 e; 3 c; all in a late-Baroque Sonata form of slow-fast-slow-fast. Vol.II: 4 a; 5 D; 6 B♭; Nos.4, 5 in 5 movements, No.6 in Sonata form. Vol.III: 7 C; 8 g; 9 f; No.7 in 5 movements, 8, 9 in Sonata form. Vol.IV: 10 b; 11 g; 12 G; all in Sonata form. Mancini was a leading composer of the Neapolitan late Baroque and was closely associated with A. Scarlatti, whose influence is evident. In the first edition, the *Sonatas* were titled for violin or flute; most could be played on oboe as well. Mancini's experiments with harmony occasionally led to key signatures which were not the true center of harmonic structure. Exquisite realizations in present edition, well suited for present-day instruments in the hands of informed musicians. Preface in English and German. M-D.
———. *Sonata* (M. Castellanti—HM 220 1974) 14pp., parts. Amoroso; Allegro; Largo; Allegro. Forward-looking harmonies in the Amoroso. Combines contrapuntal with cantabile style. M-D.

Benedetto Marcello. *Twelve Sonatas* (Colombo).
———. *Sonata* Op.1/4 (Wisse—CFP), with Focking *Sonata.*
———. *Sonatas* Op.2/1 F, 2 d (J. Glode—HM 151 1958) 15pp., parts.

———. *Sonatas* Op.2/3 g, 4 e (J. Glode—HM 142 1956) 13pp., parts.

———. *Sonatas* Op.2/6 C, 7 B♭ (J. Glode—HM 152 1958) 14pp., parts.

———. *Sonata* Op.3/1 F (Veggetti, Martucci—De Santis 1948) 12pp., parts. Adagio; Allegro; Largo; Presto. M-D.

———. *Sonata* Op.3/2 G (Veggetti, Martucci—De Santis 1948; Slater—OUP 1950; Zanke—Zimmermann 1954).

———. *Sonata* Op.3/3 d (Veggetti, Martucci—De Santis 1948) 12pp., parts.

———. *Sonatas* a, B♭ (Ermeler—OUP).

———. *Sonata* B♭ (Pearson—OUP).

Frank Martin. *Ballade* 1939 (UE 11318 1944) 16pp., parts. 7 min. Originally for flute, string orchestra, and piano. Piano reduction by composer. Sections marked off by contrasts of rhythm with a cadenza in the middle. Fresh and graceful writing, strong melodic rhythms, asymmetric phrases, quasi-modal harmonies. M-D.

Bohuslav Martinů. *First Sonata* 1945 (AMP 1951) 34pp., parts. 19½ min. Allegro moderato: SA; chromatic triads add shimmering effect; complex rhythms; polyphonic lines. Adagio: free variation form, 3 variations, theme repeated, short coda. Allegro poco moderato: new material plus brief altered restatements of ideas from previous movements. Rhythmic drive and bubbling vitality. Virtuoso performers required. D.

———. *Scherzo (Divertimento)* (Panton 1966) 11pp., parts. 3 min. Straightforward writing at Allegro vivo for experienced performers. D.

Jožka Matěj. *Invence* [=*Invention*] 1982–83 (Panton 1986) 16pp., parts. Chromatic texture with melody alternating between duple and triple at Allegro molto. In ternary form with coda. Lengthy piano solo in mid-section. Dynamics range from *ppp* to *ffff.* M-D.

Johannes Mattheson. *Twelve Sonatas* (van Leeuwen—Zimmermann 1923) Bk.I: 1 D, 2 G, 3 A, 4 D, 5 D, 6 e. Bk.II: 7 A, 8 b, 9 e, 10 A, 11 d, 12 D.

———. *Sonata* A (Schott).

Nicholas Maw. *Sonatine* 1957 (JWC 1611) 12pp., parts. 9 min. Allegro con spirito: syncopated chords, changing meters, freely tonal, harmonic 7ths frequent; flute cadenza ends movement. Lento: 7ths are used again; syncopated rhythms; ostinato-like figures; widespread rolled chords; cross-rhythms; leads directly to Allegro vivo: alternating hands, octaves, martellato chords, fast repeated notes, octotonic writing, strongly rhythmic, *pp* closing. M-D.

Charles McLean. *Two Sonatas* Op.1/9, 10 1737 (D. Johnson—OUP Musica da Camera 22 1975) 13pp., parts. Parts to each *Sonata* published separately. Italian characteristics mixed with a backward glance at the 17th century. Charming, unpretentious short movements. Keyboard realization is very playable. Int.

———. *Sonata* Op.1/9 D (E. Bullock—OUP 1948).

Kirke Mechem. *Wedding Madrigal* Op.56 (GS 3997 1994, ISBN 0-7935-6294-5) 9pp., parts. 3 min. In 2 connected sections marked Allegretto ($\frac{12}{8}$) and Largo ($\frac{3}{2}$). "The music is built around the superimposition of the dominant and tonic chords. In every marriage—so learned doctors tell us—only one partner can be dominant. The other must obviously be a tonic. That the two can live together in harmony is the burden of this wedding song. But in the end—and I am sure the worthy doctors would agree—each must learn to be a tonic to the other. Accordingly, at the close of the piece, the dominant chord merges into the tonic" (from Composer's Note). M-D.

Olivier Messiaen. *Le Merle Noir* [*The Blackbird*] (Leduc 1952) 8pp., parts. 6 min. Exposition of 4 short sections is recapped with the last 2 sections transposed, à la Sonata idea. An extended birdlike coda follows with an elaborate 12-note series accompaniment and its retrograde inversion, repeated 4 times. Each repetition rises a half-step. The entire process is repeated with the 12-note series inverted. Pedal is to be held down throughout this section, thereby providing highly interesting sonorities. M-D.

Johann Georg Mezger. *Sonate* Op.6/2 G (H. Ruf—Schott 8664 1999, ISMN M-001-12141-5) 15pp., parts, with basso. Allegro; Adagio commodo; Allegro. Clean edition with thoughtful realization. M-D.

Donal Michalsky. *Partita Piccola* 1962 (WIM 1969) 9 min. The structure of each movement is indicated by its title. Preludio: quasi-rhapsodic, cautious, expository. Toccata: flighty, light, repeated notes, binary form. Variazioni: theme and 6 variations. Giga alla rondo: contrapuntal imitative rondo in fast triple meter. The title is a historical reference to the 4 movements of the pre-Classical Suite (or Sonata): slow, fast, slow, fast. The tonality is the result of using a c 12-tone row (C–E♭–D–A–B♭–F–D♭–A♭–E–F♯–B–G, progressing from tonic to dominant). It is limited to 2 transpositions and 2 forms (original and retrograde), except for the third movement, which uses the inversion form. M-D.

Georges Migot. *Sonata* (Leduc 1950) 24pp., parts. Prélude: upper register favored. Allant–Léger: thin and thicker textures judiciously mixed. Deploration: choralelike; large span required. Allègre: open harmonies, arpeggi figuration, fugal section. Conclusion: chordal and arpeggi figures and unusual chord progression provide colorful movement. M-D to D.

———. *Sonatine* II (Schott 5347 1964) 16pp., parts. Prélude; Allant, comme une danse; Grave; Finale–une danse. Simple; straightforward style; has much charm. Mildly 20th-century. M-D.

Darius Milhaud. *Sonatine* 1922 (Durand 1923) 17pp., parts. 9½ min. Tendre: smooth textures, chromatic, difficult skips; 2nds are important to piano motif. Souple: barcarolle-like; flowing rhythm is punctuated with jazz characteristics. Clair: brilliant and dramatic, infused with subtle humor, silken *ppp* ending. M-D to D.

Charles Mills. *Sonata* E (ACA) 12 min. For alto recorder and piano.

———. *Sonata* (ACA) 14 min. For tenor recorder and piano.

Louis Moyse. *Trois Hommages* (GS 4090 1999, ISBN 0-7935-9956-3) 22pp., parts.
I. *Hommage à Katsue* Op.59: grace notes, repeated patterns, octaves, 2 with 3.
II. *Hommage à Gulbransen* Op.56: Con moto, 3rds, linear writing. III. *Hommage à Czerny* Op.58: variable-pitch ostinato of ascending and descending
passagework, most difficult of the three. May be played individually. M-D.

———. *Sonata* I (GS 3310).

———. *Sonata* II Op.60 (GS 4139)

———. *Introduction, Theme and Variations* (GS 3351).

Franz Xaver Mozart. *Rondo* e (L. Moyse—GS 1917 1976) 14pp., parts. Engaging
in an early-19th-century sampling of Romanticism. M-D.

Wolfgang Amadeus Mozart. *Six Sonatas* (Bopp—Reinhardt 1959) K.10 B♭, K.11
G, K.12 A, K.13 F, K.14 C, K.15 B♭.

———. *Six Sonatas* (L. Moyse—GS 3174 1974) 65pp., parts. Same *Sonatas* as
listed above. These 2- and/or 3-movement *Sonatas*, written by Mozart when he
was 8 years old, are astonishingly mature works for one this age. "All that will
be found in Mozart later on is already potentially here in these works" (from
the Foreword). These *Sonatas* are more satisfactory on the violin than on the
flute. Most of the time the flute part is an accompaniment to the fuller piano
part. In this edition the editor has given the flute a more important role by
sometimes interchanging the right hand of the piano with the flute part, establishing what he feels is a fairer dialogue between the two instruments. Editorial dynamics are enclosed in parentheses. M-D.

———. *Andante* K.315 C (Henle 675; J. Galway—GS 3794).

Robert Muczynski. *Sonata* Op.14 (GS 3353 1965) 32pp., parts. Allegro deciso;
Scherzo; Andante; Allegro con moto. Skillful writing that is variously energetic, exhilarating, expressive, and convincing. Freely tonal and exceptionally
melodic. The entire work affords both performers fine opportunities for displaying musicianship and virtuosity. Requires large span. D.

———. *Moments* Op.47 (TP 114-40672 1993) 22pp., parts. 12 min. In 3 movements: Allegro; Andante sostenuto; Allegro con spirito. Neoclassic with energy
and motion. M-D.

Herbert Murrill. *Sonata* G (OUP 19511) 11pp., parts. 5½ min. Largo; Presto;
Recitativo; Finale. Tonal, Neoclassic, hemiola, parallel chords. M-D.

Johann Gottfried Müthel. *Sonata* D (J. P. Hinnenthal—Br 3322 1959) 12pp.,
parts. Adagio: Allegro ma non troppo; Cantabile. Charming and cheerful. Excellent keyboard realization. M-D.

Jean-Jacques Naudot. *Six Flute Sonatas* Op.1 (CFP 1973). Composer is called
Jacques-Christophe in this edition. First published in Paris in 1726. These var-

ied and imaginative works consist mainly of dance movements, melodic tunes, and frequent use of "Gracieusement." The figured bass, realized by A. M. Gurgel, provides balanced support. A cello/gamba part is included. Would make a good substitute for the overplayed Handel recorder Sonatas, which were not written for the flute traversière! Int. to M-D.

———. *Sonata* Op.9/5 G (H. Ruf—HM 182) 12pp., parts. Larghetto; Allegro; Sarabanda; Allegro, ma non presto; Giga I and II. This work could have been played on the *musette,* the fashionable instrument in upper French society of the time. M-D.

———. *Sonata* c (H. Ruf—Schott OFB185 1998, ISMN M-001-12157-6). For oboe, flute, or recorder. See detailed entry under duos for piano and oboe.

Nguyên-Thiên-Dao. *Tây Nguyên* (Sal 1969) 15pp., parts. Directions are given in French for preparing the piano. Clusters, timed notation ("play this for so many seconds," etc.), dynamic extremes, serial-like, tempo changes. Pianist must strike and pluck strings, improvise, and use assorted brushes and tools. Flutist has as many different requirements as pianist. Also uses untuned signals from a shortwave radio, which produces unusual atmospheric and coloristic possibilities. Avant-garde. D.

Per Nørgård. *Pastorale* (WH 4287 1975) 4pp., parts. Impressionist, quiet, rocking accompaniment figure, hemiola. Trills effectively used. Centers around f♯–F♯. Large span required. M-D.

Juan Orrego-Salas. *Sonata de Estio* Op.71 1972 (Zalo 1975) 24pp., parts. In one movement with multiple sections using flexible and strict tempos. Highly expressive with instructions in nearly every measure. Performance notes for multiphonics. M-D.

Hans Osieck. *Ballade (Eine Wanderung im Eifelgebirge)* 1970 (Donemus).
———. *Suite* 1977 (Donemus). 17 min.

Jean Papineau-Couture. *Suite* (CMC 1944–45) 46pp., parts. 18 min. All 3 movements begin with the same flute motif, each in a different mood. Prélude: bithematic, a sort of pastorate. Aria: da capo form; in the nature of a prolonged meditation; piano serves more as accompaniment to solo flute in this movement while the outer movements treat both instruments equally. Rondo: lively; complete rhythmic independence retained with each instrument. D.

Thomas Pasatieri. *Sonata* 1996 (TP 114-41032 2000) 23pp., parts. 15 min. Allegro moderato; Andante cantabile; Allegro vivace. Neoclassic writing with occasional cluster chords and glissandi. Outer movements end on octave C's. M-D.

Ernst Pepping. *Sonata* (Br 3320 1958) 19pp., parts. Allegro cantabile; Quieto; Animato. Clear Neoclassic treatment, freely tonal. M-D.

Johann Christoph Pepusch. *Sonatas* 1, 2, 3, 4, 7, 8 (Danckler, Langner—Moeck).
———. *Two Sonatas* (Ruf—Schott).

————. *Two Little Sonatas* G, a (Rucker—CFP).

————. *Sonata* d (Ruyssen—Delrieu).

————. *Sonata* G (C. Ruckler—Mitteldeutscher) with J. G. Linicke *Sonata* a, 12pp., parts. Adagio; Allegro; Adagio; Allegro. Linicke: Allegro; Adagio; Villanella. M-D.

Piotr Perkowski. *Sonata* 1954 (PWM 1969, ISBN 83-224-1910-4) 16pp., parts. 10 min. Allegro molto; Lento; Presto. Linear writing at opening contrasted by chordal figurations with occasional added notes. M-D.

Anne Danican Philidor. *Premier livre de pièces pour la flûte traversière ou la flûte a bec alto ou le violon et basse continue* (clavecin ou piano). Restitution de Maurice-Pierre Gourrier, realisation de Colette Teniere (Ouvrières 1972) 10pp., parts. This first book was published in 1712 and contains an overture and 6 dances, a reflection of contemporary chamber music taste. The continuo realization is excellent. No performance directions but contains information on Philidor's life. M-D.

————. *Sonata* d (H. Ruf—HM 139 1956) 11pp., parts. Lentement; Fugue; Courante; Gracieusement; Fugue. M-D.

Pierre Danican Philidor. *Suite* Op.1/6 b (H. Ruf—Schott OBB39 1997, ISMN M-001-11468-4). For oboe, flute, or violin. See detailed entry under duos for piano and oboe.

Willem Pijper. *Sonata* 1925 (Donemus 1952) 20pp., parts. 11½ min. Achieves a striking balance between the instruments; musical ideas beautifully expressed. Rhythmically and melodically the flute and piano go their own ways to form a dual unity of musical ideas. The opening chord in the piano is the nucleus from which the whole work evolves, and the flute theme develops immediately from this chord. Allegro: in 3 parts with a flute cadenza serving as transition before a short repetition of the opening part. Lento: most important movement, tranquil and poetic in 2 parts, insistent bass patterns. Presto: colorful polymetric and polytonal combinations bring the whole work to a brilliant conclusion. M-D.

Walter Piston. *Sonata* 1930 (AMP 1933) 27pp., parts. Allegro moderato e grazioso; Adagio; Allegro vivace. Neoclassic lines and treatment. Freely tonal, dissonant. M-D.

Giovanni Platti. *Sonata* A (Ruf—Ric).

————. *Sonata* A (P. Jarnach—Schott 2457) 12pp., parts.

————. *Sonata* D (Schenk, Ruf—Ric).

————. *Sonata* e (P. Jarnach—Schott 376) 11pp., parts. Allegro non tanto; Larghetto; Minuetto; Giga. Heavy-handed editing. M-D.

————. *Sonata* G (P. Jarnach—Schott 377) 10pp., parts. Grave; Allegro; Adagio; Allegro molto. M-D.

————. *Sonata* Op.3/6 G (Ruf—Schott).

Ignance Pleyel. *Sonata* III B♭ (I. Alberti—Eulenburg GM 44 1971) 22pp., parts. Allegro molto; Tema con (6) variazioni.

——. *Sonata* IV A (I. Alberti—Eulenburg GM 45 1971) 28pp., parts. Untitled first movement; Andante; Rondo.

——. *Sonata* VI D (I. Alberti—Eulenburg GM 46 1971) 29pp., parts. Allegro; Rondo.

All 3 *Sonatas* are written in a Mozartian style with uniquely individual melodic ideas. The rondos are especially full of charm and freshness. M-D.

Claire Polin. *First Flute Sonata* (ST SS26 1959) 20pp., parts. Andantino: lilting $\frac{6}{8}$ displays the virtuosity of the flute while retaining a freely expressive feeling in its cadenza and fantasia passages; chromatic broken-chordal figuration in piano is basic to the movement. Adagio ma non tanto: a study in the production of bell-like tones for both instruments. Presto: climaxes the preceding movements with a brisk march in SA design. Mildly 20th-century. M-D.

Wilhelm Popp. *La Traviata: Konzert-Walzer* Op.378 (Kunzelmann GM 586 1999) 18pp., parts. In 2 parts: Introduction and Valse. Light-hearted, zestful music inspired by the great opera. The editor notes that Popp composed more than 500 works for flute and piano! M-D.

Francis Poulenc. *Sonata* 1957 (C. Schmidt, P. Harper—JWC 1994) 23pp., parts. 12 min. Allegro malinconico; Cantilena–Assez lent; Presto giocoso. Neoclassic orientation, light and witty. The second movement is attractively sentimental. Final movement alludes to both subjects from opening movement. Delicate textures. New edition with extensive historical introduction and editorial commentary in English, German, and French. M-D.

Sergei Prokofieff. *Sonata* Op.94 (Rampal—IMC; Leeds; GS 1965, ISBN 0-634-03667-X). GS juxtaposes flute and violin parts with occasional differences clearly visible. See detailed entry under duos for piano and violin.

Daniel Purcell. *Drei Sonaten* (B. Päuler, W. Hess—Amadeus BP494 1988) 19pp., parts, with basso. For recorder, flute, or violin. 1. F, 2. d, 3. C. Effective realizations complementing the character of the flute part. M-D.

——. *Sonata* F (P. Jarnach—Schott 3693 1940) 10pp., parts. Andante cantabile; Moderato; Allegro; Adagio; Allegro. Simple realization. M-D.

Henry Purcell. *Sonata* F (Fleury—Ric).

——. *Sonata* F (Jarnach—Schott).

——. *Sonata* g (Forst—EM).

Johann Joachim Quantz. *Six Sonatas* Op.1 (D. Sonntag—Müller 1965) 34pp., parts. 1 D, 2 G, 3 e, 4 G, 5 D, 6 A. Helpful realizations. M-D.

——. *Sonatas* ca.1728 (H. Augsbach—Carus 17.004-6 2000), parts, with basso. Published separately. QV1:44 D, 13 min.: Un poco andante; Allegro assai;

Presto. QVi:110 G, 12 min.: Un poco andante; Allegro assai; Presto. QVi:147
a, 11 min.: Grave; Allegro; Vivace. "Conceived in the three-movement Neapolitan sonata da camera form . . . attractive because of its virtuosity" (from Preface). Detailed and engaging realizations of high quality. M-D.

———. *Sonata* Op.1/2 B♭ (Nagel—CFP).

———. *Sonata* Op.1/3 e (H. Schreiter—Br&H 4172) 11pp., parts. Adagio cantabile; Presto; Moderato. M-D.

———. *Sonatas* (Forberg—CFP) available separately: 1 a, 2 B♭, 3 c, 4 D, 5 e.

———. *Sonata* b (Ruf—Schott).

———. *Sonata* e (Ruf—Schott).

———. *28 Variations on 'As I Slept, I Dreamt'* (Br&H).

Bertin Quentin. *Sonata* Op.1/2 d (H. Ruf—HM 186 1964) 11pp., parts. Allemanda I & II; Corrente; Sarabanda; Giga. M-D.

Marcel Quinet. *Concertino* 1959 (CeBeDeM) 26pp., parts. 11 min. Allegro moderato; Canons; Rondoletto. Well structured, freely tonal with a highly chromatic vocabulary, long-held sonorities. Complex imitative writing in Canons;
Rondoletto sparkles and dances. M-D to D.

Irmfried Radauer. *Duo Concertante* 1954–55 (Litolff CF 5871 1960) 26pp., parts.
16½ min. Evolution I; Kontrast; Evolution II. Written in an astringent Neoclassic style. Kontrast is slower, recitative-like, while the outer movements are
more rhythmically conceived. Flexible meter; moves over keyboard. D.

Anton Reicha. *Sonata* Op.54 G (CFP).
———. *Sonata* Op.103 D (W. Lebermann—Schott 5573 1968) 51pp., parts. Lento–
Allegro non troppo: rocking $\frac{6}{8}$ introduction all on a dominant pedal point, SA
in D, colorful development section, numerous varied figurations. Lento: G, expressive, classic patterns, crossing hands; strong punctuated chords outline tonal
evolution; busy coda must remain calm and *a piacere*. Finale–Allegro vivace:
D, rondo, broken octaves, chromatic figuration, a fun movement to play. M-D.

Mathieu André Reichert. *Works for Flute and Piano* 2 vols. (N. Delius—Schott
8921-2, ISMN M-001-12439-3, M-001-12440-9), parts. I: *Fantaisie Mélancolique*
Op.1 is multisectional with theme and 3 variations. *Tarentelle: Etude de Salon*
Op.3 is virtually perpetual mobile at Vivace in A. *La Coquette à faceira* [Polka
de Salon] Op.4 gives primary emphasis to the flute with lightning-speed passagework. *L'Illusion: Introduction et Variations sur une Havanaise* Op.7 is modest
and surprisingly short with flowing lyricism before its habanera. *La Sensitive:
Petite Polka de Concert* Op.8 is an essay primarily for flute. II: *Souvenir du
Para: Andante élégiaque* Op.10 is in $\frac{12}{8}$ with long melodic lines. *Romance sans
paroles* Op.11 concentrates on a steady melody at Allegro in $\frac{3}{8}$. *Souvenir de
Bahia* Op.12 flows poetically in $\frac{12}{8}$. *Rondo Caractéristique* Op.14 bubbles with
brilliant passagework and a surprising habanera. *Melodie sans paroles* Op.16 is

a short work for less experienced performers. *Rêverie* Op.17 remains relatively quiet in its dreamlike character and finishes *ppp.* Reichert was one of the best-known flutists of the 19th century. His works tend to favor the flute but generally show a close relationship with the piano. Preface in German, English, and French. M-D to D.

Carl Reinecke. *Sonata 'Undine'* Op.167 (J. Galway—GS 3369; IMC 1757; K 3811), parts. Clarinet may be substituted for flute. Allegro: e,$\frac{6}{8}$, SA, overlapping broken-chord figuration between hands, chromatic runs. Intermezzo–Allegretto vivace: b, ABA; A sections scherzo-like, B section more cantabile and flowing. Andante tranquillo: G, ABA with final A section beginning on dominant, lyric, sentimental. Finale: e, SA, nontonic opening, chromatic, broken-chord patterns, arpeggio closing. M-D.

Franz Reizenstein. *Partita* (Schott 10041 1946) 20pp., parts. Entrada: marchlike, freely tonal, thin textures. Sarabanda: expressive, lyric, chordal. Bourée: spirited, Neoclassic. Jig: flowing chromatic lines, cheerful. M-D.
See Petrus Jacobus Krige, "The Published Chamber Music for Woodwinds and Piano by Franz Reizenstein (1911–1968)," M.M. thesis, University of South Africa, 1982.

Roger Reynolds. *Mosaic* (CFP 6620) 12 min. This work occasionally requires unconventional methods of sound production. It achieves effect as a tile mosaic does, through the Gestalt from many discrete elements of various dimensions, textures, and colors. Segments are characterized by instrumental techniques (grace notes, trills, repeated notes, etc.) as well as by tempo, dynamics, and pitch organization. The work is lyrical but of sparse texture. D.

Verne Reynolds. *Sonata* (CF 04457 1965, ISBN 0-8258-4733-8) 31pp., parts. 22 min. Andante sostenuto; Scherzo–Allegro non troppo; Adagio; Presto. Early-20th-century flavor. Wide span required.

Alan Ridout. *Three Nocturnes* (Chappell 1974) 11pp., parts. Short, attractive. M-D.

Ferdinand Ries. *Sonata* Op.169 E♭ 1814 (H.-P. Schmitz—Br 19107 1970) 53pp., parts. Allegro moderato; Adagio con moto; Rondo–Allegro. This is the last of Ries's 5 flute *Sonatas.* Schmitz suggests in the Preface that the work should be played with great expression—"Con sentiments," in fact—and that the dynamic contrasts should be strongly marked in accordance with the contemporary concert notice (*Harmonicon* II 1824, 35) of Ries's playing, which remarked on his powerful hand and Romantic wildness and praised his strong contrasts of loud and soft. All the cliché figurations and idioms of late-Classical and early-Romantic writing are present. M-D.

Jean Rivier. *Sonatine* (EMT 1956) 18pp., parts. Allegro moderato: many tempo changes, freely tonal. Lento affettuoso: chromatic, expressive. Presto jocando: jaunty, Gallic humor shows throughout. M-D.

See Julie Anne Stone, "The Life and Published Flute Compositions of Jean Rivier (1896–1987)," D.M.A. diss., University of Maryland, College Park, 1992.

George Rochberg. *Between Two Worlds (Ukiyo-e III)* 1982 (TP 414-41159 1983) 18pp., parts. 10 min. Five Images: Fantasia; Scherzoso (Fast dance); Night Scene (A); Sarabande (Slow dance); Night Scene (B). Dramatic, with fantasy and much rhythmic freedom. Night Scene (B) is without meter and brings the work to a close at *pppp*. Uses instruments in traditional manner with late-20th-century tastes. M-D.

Joaquín Rodrigo. *Aria Antigua* 1960 (Ediciones Joaquín Rodrigo 1995, ISBN 84-88558-47-3) 4pp., parts. 4 min. An expressive short essay marked Adagio with singing roles for both instruments. Original version. M-D.

Marguerite Roesgen-Champion. *Sonata* F (Leduc 1950) 15pp., parts. 13½ min. Introduction–Moderato; Adagio; Rondo Final. Impressionist, chords in alternating hands, flowing lines, chromatic, added 6ths. Final is cheerful and very rhythmic. M-D.

Johan Helmich Roman. *Two Sonatas* (K. W. Senn—HM 101 1952). *Sonata* G: 11pp., parts. Largo; Allegro; Larghetto; Andante; Vivace. *Sonata* b: 9pp., parts. Larghetto; Allegro; Non troppo allegro; Grave; Allegro. Clear realizations. M-D.

——. *Two Sonatas* 4 B♭, 7 B♭ (CFP).

——. *Two Sonatas* 5 B♭, 8 C (CFP).

——. *Sonata* b (Erdmann—CFP).

——. *Sonata* D (J. Brinckmann, W. Moor—Sikorski 218 1954) 11pp., parts. *Sonata* 12 of "XII Sonatas flauto traverso, violine e cembalo." Editorial suggestions in smaller print. Con spirito; Allegro; Con affetto; Allegro. Stylistically correct continuo realization. M-D.

Joseph Guy Ropartz. *Sonatine* 1930 (Durand) 26pp., parts. Très modéré; Très lent; Assez vif. Mildly Impressionist idiom. Colorful. M-D.

Thomas Roseingrave. *Two Sonatas* 1728 (R. Platt—OUP, Musica da Camera 21 1975) 14pp., parts, including cello ad lib. Parts to each *Sonata* published separately. Preface in English and German. *Sonata* 4 (g) and *Sonata* 7 (C) from a set of 12 solos. Italian in style with a few unexpected progressions. Range of solo part suggests an oboe would be as suitable as the flute. Contains some fine music. A certain rhythmic vitality is needed in the keyboard realizations and should be added by the performer. Int.

Albert Roussel. *Joueurs de flûte* Op.27 1924 (Durand 1925), parts. Four pieces, published separately. Pan; Tityre; Krishna; M. de la Péjaudie. Short picturesque essays in character forms drawn from Roussel's journey to India years earlier. Requires careful coordination for successful performances. M-D.

———. *Andante et Scherzo* Op.51 1934 (T. Roorda—Broekmans 1987) 10pp., parts. In one continuous movement reflecting the composer's rough individualist style. Fits well in the hands but requires a thorough technique. M-D.

See Mary Joanna White, "The Eclectic Style of Albert Roussel as Seen in His Chamber Music with Flute," A.D. diss., Boston University, 1991.

Howard Rovics. *Cybernetic Study* I (Okra 1968) 9pp., parts. For alto flute and piano. Harmonics, serial, chromatic clusters. Strings prepared with rubber or felt wedges, for plucked, stopped, and tapped strings. Colorful instrumental interaction. D.

———. *Sonata* (CFE).

Giovanni Battista Sammartini. *Six Sonatas* 2 vols. (G. Braun, S. Petrenz—UE 31129 1998, ISMN M-008-05978-0, M-008-06050-2), parts, with basso. I: G, C, G. II: D, G, a. Gems of the Style Galant, flowing with melody and uncomplicated rhythms. Fine realizations. Some possibility remains that these may not have been composed by Sammartini, as noted in the Preface. Int. to M-D.

———. *Sonata* G (CFP).

Giuseppe Sammartini. *2 Sonatas* Op.2/4, 6 (H. Ruf—Schott FTR 140 1988) 27pp., parts, with basso. For flute or oboe. Op.2/4 G Andante; Allegro affettuoso; Allegro assai. Op.2/6 a Adagio ma non tanto; Allegro; Andante; Allegro assai. These *Sonatas* are extracted from the collection of *12 Sonatas* originally published in Amsterdam. M-D.

Pierre Sancan. *Sonatine* (Durand 1946) 19pp., parts. One movement, Ravel-like in style. Flute cadenza; graceful flowing lines in piano. Three sections of contrasting moods and tempos. M-D.

Tibor Sárai. *Studio* (Zenemükiadó Vallalat 1965) 10pp., parts. Bitonal, dance rhythms, contrasting moods and tempos. M-D.

József Sári. *Contemplazione* (EMB 1971) 12pp., parts. In one continuous movement with multiple sections. Marked rhythms, proportional rhythmic relationships, and cluster chords are among the many features found in this contemplative, sometimes abrasive work. M-D.

István Sárközy. *Sonata da Camera* 1964 (EMB 1972) 16pp., parts. 8 min. Sostenuto: Chromatic chordal sonorities, short-long rhythmic germ. Andante: tonal, simple accompaniment style, interrupted short-long rhythmic germ of Sostenuto. Allegro: Hungarian folk dance–like, attractive writing. Some chords of 9th require large span. M-D.

Andres Sas. *Sonatina-Fantasia* (PIC 1953) 20pp., parts. Fantasia: staccato style, dancelike, changing key signatures, free-form movement. Elegia: expressive, lyric, nocturne-like piano style. Danza: short-long alternates with long-short rhythms, contrasting lyric andante section, coda is a juxtaposition between andante and vivace. Attractive. M-D.

Alessandro Scarlatti. *Zwei Sonaten* F, G (W. Hess—Amadeus BP 492 1988) 10pp., parts, with basso. For treble recorder, flute, oboe, or violin. In F: (Grave); Allegro; Largo; Minuet. In G: (Moderato); (Arioso); Allegro; Allegro; (Largo); (Presto); Gigue. Complementary realizations, binary forms. M-D.

Christoph Schaffrath. *Duetto* Op.1/4 G (G. Zahn—Zimmermann 32410 1998, ISMN M-010-32410-4) 19pp., parts. From a collection of 6 duets (Sonatas), 3 for violin and 3 for flute. Cast in a well-developed 3-movement design. Fine realization. M-D.

Peter Schickele. *Music for Mary* 1988 (EV 1990) 16pp., parts. 8 min. For alto recorder or flute. In 3 movements: Moderately slow, clear and simple–Fast; Fast and joyful; Moderately slow. "In much of my recorder music I approach the instrument more in the tradition of the Irish pennywhistle and the Irish and Scottish bagpipes than the Renaissance-Baroque recorder tradition. Although the outer sections of the second movement owe an obvious debt to medieval music, both this and the last movements feature melodies that to my ear have a distinctly Celtic character. The principal melody of the last movement in particular employs a sound that is much more common in bagpipe music: grace notes and other so-called ornamentation figures played without fresh articulations within a long, smooth phrase. In fact, I think it's safe to say that my interest in writing for the recorder began with my thinking of it as a folk instrument" (from Program Note). Much use of octaves. M-D.

———. *Spring Serenade* (EV 1987).

Gary Schocker. *Sonata* Op.32 1993 (TP 114-40752 1994) 36pp., parts. 20 min. Allegro molto moderato; Burlesque; Andante espressivo; Presto. A strongly tonal work at the end of the 20th century with broad forms and musical intentions. Imitative writing appears throughout with clearest designs in the opening two movements. The finale is a toccata-like dash to the finish in c♯. The composer has noted, "This piece is an extremely challenging work technically for the flutist, who has many notes per square inch . . . it is a virtuosic sonata reminiscent of Liszt in his diabolical mode" (www.academic.marist.edu/julie/programnotes, June 29, 2004). M-D to D.

———. *Three Minute Sonata* 1998 (TP 114-40945) 4pp., parts. 3 min. Two short, contrasting movements of lyricism and energy. The academic approach robs the playful title from becoming a jovial, tongue-in-cheek essay. M-D.

———. *Sleepsong* (TP 114-40954 1999) 3pp., parts. 3½ min. Marked Lazy. A homophonic poem with occasional canon effects. Large span required. M-D.

————. *Xynóglyko* 2001 (TP 114-41118 2001) 16pp., parts. 7 min. In one movement. Pulsing with songlike character, at once plain and simple, then bubbling with melismatic figurations. Ends with unison trills for both instruments on high A. Title means "sweet-sour" in Greek. M-D.

Karol Scholl. *Introduzione e Variazioni Brillanti* Op.20 (M. Martino—Ut Orpheus ACC24 1999, ISMN M-2153-440-6) 25pp., parts. For flute and piano or guitar. Brief introduction leads to plain theme and 6 variations of virtuosic quality for flute. Pianistic interludes become involved and require more skill than when ensemble plays together. Preface in Italian. M-D.

Robert Schollum. *Sonatine* (Dob 1958) 12pp., parts. Energisch: serial, mixed figuration, leads directly to Chaconne: with 16 variations. Well-constructed atonal writing. M-D.

Franz Schubert. *Introduction and Variations on a Theme from Die schöne Müllerin* Op.post.160 D.802 1824 (W.-D. Seiffert, K. Schilde—Henle 474 2000; W. Richter—CFP 1968; Br&H; IMC; K 9254). One of the most important works from the Romantic era for flute and piano. A virtuoso set of variations, based on the eighteenth song in the cycle, "Trockne Blumen" (Withered Flowers). Introduction is moody. The following variations alternate between great introspection and display figuration for the flute. A mock military march serves as the final variation. The pianist is a full partner throughout, and the second variation presents a whirlwind octave passage for the left hand. D in a few spots. M-D.

Erwin Schulhoff. *Sonata* (JWC 1928) 28pp., parts. 11½ min. Allegro moderato; Scherzo; Aria; Rondo–Finale. Diffusive Neoclassic chromatic writing. Requires fine pianistic equipment. D.

Bart Schurink. *Madrigali* 1968 (Donemus) 15pp., parts. 10 min. Seven pieces. Piano is tacet in No.7. Vertical lines are not bar lines but points for orientation in time. Clusters, plucked strings, pointillistic, percussive use of the piano, Expressionist and thorny writing for both instruments. D.

Cyril Scott. *Sonata* (Elkin 1961) 30pp., parts. Tempo molto moderato e sempre poco rubato; Andante tranquillo; Rondo frivolo. Scott was experimenting with a new style in this work. Quartal and quintal harmonies, serial-like in places. D.

Jean Baptiste Senaillé. *Sonata* I. livre, No.5 c (Dolmetsch—UE 1974) 10pp., parts. For tenor recorder and keyboard. Transposed to g and arranged for recorder in accordance with the composer's comment, "Cette sonate peut se jouer sur la flûte." Edited and arranged by Carl Dolmetsch, keyboard accompaniment by Arnold Dolmetsch. M-D.

Syoko Shida. *Sonata* (Japan Federation of Composers 1970) 29pp., parts. Based on a Japanese tea-picker's song. Moderato: chromatic patterns, quartal and quintal harmonies, free interplay of ideas between instruments. Allegro (ma non troppo): fast repeated chords interspersed with rolled chords, long pedal effects, chromatic; 2 lento sections provide contrast. Colorful if not always convincing writing. D.

Makoto Shinohara. *Kassouga* (Leduc 1960) 7pp., parts. 6 min. Lent, expressif et souple: quintal harmonies in piano, free wistful melodic line in flute. Vif et rythmé: descending chordal 7ths, repeated 8th-note chords, flute cadenza, driving rhythms, recitative ending. M-D.

————. *Relations* (Moeck 1973) 4pp., notes. 2 playing scores, each has 13 loose leaves, 8 min. Explanations in German and English. Kind of a brilliant catalog of avant-garde gestures, no development of any type, and short on dramatic sense. D.

Otto Siegl. *Sonate* 1968 (Dob 1971) 25pp., parts. 18 min. Allegro assai; Meditation; Allegro con moto. Strong craft, Neoclassic, appealing Ländler tempo and style in finale. Tonal with chromatic coloration, imitation, octotonic, hemiola. M-D.

Harvey Sollberger. *Music for Flute and Piano* 1963–64 (McGinnis & Marx) 26pp. Serial, pointillistic, clusters, highly organized, Expressionist, sumptuous sonorities. Requires large span. D.

Eliodoro Sollima. *Sonata* (Schott). For alto flute and piano.

————. *Sonata* (Schott). For tenor recorder and piano. 15 min. Three movements. Traditional writing in atonal style. Reminiscent of Bartók. Rewarding for both performers. D.

Giovanni Battista Somis. *Sonata* F (F. Nagel—Möseler 1973) 8pp., parts. Fine realized figured bass. M-D.

József Soproni. *Sonata* (EMB 1971) 18pp. 2 copies necessary for performance. Andante, senza misura; Sostenuto; Allegro vivace. Serial, repeated notes, pointillistic, clusters, many tempo changes, sudden dynamic changes, rhythmic proportional relationships, strings plucked, strong glissandi, avant-garde. Large span required. D.

Rick Sowash. *Une Pavane Americaine: Homage à Ravel* 1990 (Sowash 1997) 14pp., parts. 7½ min. Inspired by and uses a structure similar to Ravel's *Pavane pour une infante défunte* with echoes of Gershwin and jazz, aspects of Americana which Ravel admired. M-D.

Norbert Sprongl. *Suite* Op.98 (Dob 1973). Four movements, somewhat reminiscent of Carl Nielsen's late style. M-D.

Edward Staempfli. *Fünf Stücke* (Bo&Bo 1960) 20pp., parts. 1. Ziemlich lebhaft, 2. Langsam, 3. Leicht bewegt, 4. Nicht zu langsam, 5. Mässig. Serial, atonal, severe writing. D.

Henk Stam. *Sonata* 1972 (Donemus 1974) 19pp., parts. Photostat of MS.

John Stanley. *Complete Works for Flute and Basso Continuo* Op.1 (J. Caldwell—UP 1974). These 8 solos are really Sonatas. Usually one dance is included within the general pattern of 4 movements. Well-balanced phrases, functional bass lines. Fine introduction in English and German as well as notes on performance, editorial method, and critical commentary. A wealth of varied material. Nos.3, 5, and 7 are available separately.
———. *Complete Works for Flute and Basso Continuo* Op.1 (G. Pratt—CFP 7108 1971). Each of the 8 works is available separately. Contains discreet use of legato and interesting keyboard realizations, tuneful. Excellent Preface.
———. *Six Solos for Flute, Violin or Oboe and Keyboard Instrument* (Concordia).
———. *Six Solos for a German Flute or Violin and Continuo* Op.4 (G. Pratt—JWC 1975) 44pp., parts for flute or violin and viola da gamba or cello. Excellent Preface. Solo I: Siciliana; Menuet. Solo II: Adagio; Poco Allegro; Adagio; Menuet. Solo III: Adagio; Allegro; Menuet with 3 variations. Solo IV: Adagio; Poco allegro; Gigg. Solo V: Adagio; Allegro; Gigg. Solo VI: Siciliana; Allegro; Menuet with 2 variations. Keyboard realization of these small Suites is a compromise between unimaginative chords and an over-ornate, contrived treatment. The performer may prepare or extemporize his own version. Int. to M-D.

Halsey Stevens. *Sonatina* 1943 (BB 1947) 15pp., parts. 6 min. Delicate, piquant. Two outer movements (Allegretto; Allegro) lively, contrasting warmth in the slow, middle movement (Andante quasi Siciliano). The Finale uses a 12-tone theme, but the movement is not organized along serial lines. M-D.
———. *Sonatina Piacevole* 1956 (PIC 1968) 12pp., parts. 4½ min. For alto recorder or flute or violin, and piano or harpsichord. With some modification, transposing the higher passages down an octave, it may also be played on the oboe. Allegro moderato; Poco lento, quasi ciaccona; Allegro. The chaconne is heard in 4 varied treatments. Neo-Baroque orientation. M-D.

Richard Stoker. *Sonatina* (CFP H526 1968) 12pp., parts. 8 min. Three untitled, contrasting movements with only tempo markings. Free dissonant counterpoint, Neoclassic style, attractive. Large span required. M-D.

Richard Strauss. *Introduction, Thema und Variationen* AV56 1879 (Schott FTR185 1999, ISMN M-001-12656-4) 19pp., parts. Composed at the age of 15; first publication. The editor notes the work "documents one of the early stages in the master's evolution, while at the same time demonstrating his unusual talent with regard to instrumental craftsmanship, and his 'familiarity with flute technique'" (Steinitzer). Follows after the work for horn and piano by the same title composed 6 months earlier. Contains 5 variations on an ordinary theme of 16 mm. Extensive Preface and critical notes in English, German, and French. M-D.

Endre Székely. *Capriccio* 1961 (Zenemükiadó Vállalat 1964) 20pp., parts. Lento rubato–(Animato) Andante–Allegro scherzando; Moderato; Allegro. In all outer forms a Sonata. Dancelike rhythms, enough Hungarian flavor to make the outside movements interesting. Mildly 20th-century. Percussive use of piano, much use of close intervals for rhythmic drive. Large span required. M-D to D.

Tadeusz Szeligowski. *Sonata* c (PWM 1955, ISBN 83-224-1111-1) 23pp., parts. Allegro moderato; Andante cantabile; Allegro con brio; Molto vivace. Strongly tonal in early-20th-century setting. Detailed passagework. Large span required. M-D.

Otar Taktakishvili. *Sonata* a/C 1968 (L. Moyse—AMP 7727 1977) 44pp., parts. Allegro cantabile; Aria–Moderato con moto; Allegro scherzando. A lyrical and expressive work thoroughly rooted in traditional tonality with a Neoclassic touch owing much to Kabalevsky and Khachaturian. Clear forms permeate the score, opening with SA and much lyricism. The Aria is pulsatile with homophonic structures and an operatic melody. A scherzo-like finale whirls to the end at breathtaking speed to bring the work to a triumphant conclusion. Overall, virtuosic flute is complemented by rhythmic piano of modest technical demands, closely following the flute in an optimistic and playful spirit in its outer movements and deep emotional pathos in the Aria. M-D to D.

Akira Tamba. *Sonata* 1957 (Rideau Rouge 1972) 21pp., parts. Originally for flute and string orchestra as a *Concerto da Camera*. A one-movement work in contrasting sections. Harmonic idiom based on 7ths; chromatic; sweeping gestures move over keyboard; full sonorities; imitation; much activity in both parts; Expressionist. D.

Alexandre Tansman. *Sonatine* (Sal 1926) 15pp., parts. Modéré; Intermezzo; Scherzo (Fox-Trot); Notturno; Finale. Charming and ingratiating Impressionist writing. Great fun for performers and listeners. M-D.

Alexander Tcherepnin. *Study* (Belaieff 1980) 3pp. Two copies necessary for performance. For voice or flute. Marked Lent throughout; monotonous character, offset by a slight increase in tempo in the middle of the ternary form.

Georg Philipp Telemann. *Six Partitas* B♭, G, c, g, e, E♭ (W. Woehl—HM 47). For flute (violin or oboe) and continuo.

———. *Twelve Method Sonatas* 1732 (M. Seiffert—Br 2951 1950). Each *Sonata* includes Telemann's own suggested ornamentation. Published separately: Bk.1: g, A. Bk.2: e, D. Bk.3: a, G. Bk.4: b, c. Bk.5: E, B♭. Bk.6: d, C.

———. *Four Sonatas* G, c, B♭, F (Wittgenstein, Wilt—GS).

———. *Four Sonatas* F, B♭, f, C (HM 6). From *Der getreue Musikmeister.*

———. *Sonatas and Pieces* (D. Degen—HM 7). From *Der getreue Musikmeister.* For flute (violin or oboe) and continuo. Sonata a, Sonata g, L'hiver, Air Trompette, Niaise, Napolitana. M-D.

———. *Two Sonatas* G, e (I. Payne—Thesaurus Harmonicus SUTE 34 1996) 24pp., parts, with basso. First modern-day edition. G [TWV 41:G11]: Lentement; Vite; Grave; Gay. e [TWV 41:e10]: Andante; Allegro; Largo; Vivace. Melody and realization foreshadow Rococo style. Uses both through-composed and binary forms. Preface and critical commentary in English. M-D.

———. *Two Sonatas* d, C (W. Woehl—CFP 1939) 13pp., parts, with basso. From *Essercizii Musici.*

———. *2 Sonatas* a, a (I. Payne—Amadeus BP794 1994) 20pp., parts, including basso. Known as the Stockholm *Sonatas,* published here for the first time. These *Sonatas* "display G. Ph. Telemann's elegant and varied melodic style, his rich harmonic language and his sure and unfailing sense of idiom in writing for the flute" (from Preface). Urtext. M-D.

———. *Sonata* D (H. Ruf—Schott 5719) 15pp., parts. No.2 from *Essercizii Musici.* Largo; Vivace; Dolce; Allegro. Excellent keyboard realization. M-D.

———. *Sonata* d (H. Ruf—Schott OFB104 1964) 11pp., parts, including basso. No.4 of *Essercizii Musici.* Affettuoso; Presto; Grave; Allegro. Passionate realization, well suited to flute. M-D.

———. *Sonata* B♭ (Concordia). From the continuation of the *Method Sonatas.*

———. *Sonata* b (CFP). From *Der getreue Musikmeister.*

———. *Sonata* C (CFP). From *Der getreue Musikmeister.*

———. *Sonata* F (E. Dohm—Nag 8 193) 7pp., parts. From *Der getreue Musikmeister,* Hamburg, 1728. Vivace; Largo; Allegro. Realization would be more effective if some of the thicker sonorities were pruned slightly. M-D.

———. *Sonata* a (ST).

———. *Sonata* b (M. Silver—JWC 1953) 12pp., parts. Continuo Series II. Cantabile; Allegro; Dolce; Allegro. Intelligent editing and realization. M-D.

———. *Sonata* C (M. Sanvoisin—Heugel 1974) 6pp., parts.

———. *Sonata* F (M. Sanvoisin—Heugel 1974) 5pp., parts.

———. *Four Sonatinas* e, D, G, E (W. Michel—Amadeus BP484 1987) 43pp., parts, including basso. Outstanding realizations in a fine edition. May be played by recorder or violin. M-D.

———. *Six Concerti* (J. P. Hinnenthal—Br 2961). For flute and harpsichord; cello ad lib. These concerti can also be played by the following combinations: flute, violin, and cello; violin and cello; or flute, violin, and continuo.
Published separately: *Concerto* D (Br 3341). *Concerto* g (Br 3342). *Concerto* A (Br 3343). *Concerto* e (Br 3344). *Concerto* b (Br 3345). *Concerto* a (Br 3346).

———. *Solo* b (J. P. Hinnenthal—Br 3537) from *Tafelmusik* I.

Carlo Tessarini. *Sonata* F (H.-P. Schmitz—Br 3303 1956) 8pp., parts. Largo; Allegro; Adagio; Vivace. Fine thorough-bass realization by Max Schneider. Attractive period writing. M-D.

Tôn Thât Tiêt. *Vision* II 1966 (Chan Anh 2) (EMT 1968) 17pp., parts. 10 min. Lento tranquillo; Allegro; Moderato; Lento tranquillo. Includes another realized version of the first piece. Strings are plucked; wooden case of piano has to be struck; brush is needed to stroke strings. Complex, pointillistic, Expressionist, avant-garde. D.

Michael Torke. *Sprite* 1996 (Bo&H WFB169 1997) 5pp., parts. 2 min. To be performed very fast, light, and effortlessly. For advanced performers. M-D.

Joan Tower. *Movements* (ACA 1970) 25pp., parts. Three untitled movements. Serial, pointillistic, stopped strings, dynamic extremes, varied tempos, Expressionist. D.

Johann Georg Tromlitz. *Sonata* C (H. Ruf—Schott 177 2000, ISMN M-001-12278-8) 30pp., parts. Allegro; Adagio; Tempo di minuetto alla ronda. Preface in English, German, and French. M-D.

Jean Louis Tulou. *Air varié* Op.22 G, Op.35 D (W. Riedel—Zimmermann 30100 1997, ISMN M-010-30100-6) 30pp., parts. Two Airs, both structured with an introduction, theme, and 4 and 5 variations respectively. Declamatory, spirited, and titillating. M-D.
———. *Fantaisie* Op.30 G, Op.36 C (W. Riedel—Zimmermann 30090 1999, ISMN M-010-30090-0) 32pp., parts. Similar in compositional style to the *Air varié* though Op.30 is through-composed, while Op.36 consists of an unmarked introduction and an animated, breakneck finish. These works deserve performances. Preface in English, French, and German. M-D.
———. *Solo* Op.82 A (Billaudot 1973) 17pp., parts. Rev. by Robert Heriche. Tulou was considered the leading French flutist of the early 19th century.

Erich Urbanner. *Acht Stücke* 1957 (UE 13026). Short, terse, atonal, serial, acerbic writing. No.4 is for solo flute. D.

Robert Valentine. *Three Sonatas* (H. Peter—Lienau 1956) 36pp., parts. Ornamentation table. I: d, Adagio; Allegro; Adagio; Allegro. II: G, Adagio; Allegro; Andante; Allegro. III: g, Adagio; Allegro; Andante; Allegro. Valentine worked for several decades in Italy, and these works, with their fertile themes, austere and formal structure, and typically English traits, also show the influence of the Italian school. Musical pieces of charming invention. M-D.

Giuseppe Valentini. *3 Sonate da Camera* (A. Bornstein, L. Corini—Ut Orpheus CSS-01 1994, ISMN M-2153-0060-6) 24pp., parts, with basso. All 3 *Sonatas* are in F. Engaging realization in slower movements, lighthearted in others. Urtext. Preface in Italian. M-D.

Johann Baptist Vanhal. *Sonata* Op.10/1 G (H. Ruf—Schott FTR172 1997, ISMN M-001-115261) 18pp., parts. Allegro; Adagio; Presto; Minuetto con [4] variazioni. Thin textures with Classically conceived harmonies. M-D.

David Van Vactor. *Sonata* (AME).
——. *Sonatina* 1975 (Rhodes) 11pp., parts.

Ralph Vaughan Williams. *Suite de Ballet* ca.1924 (R. Douglas—OUP 1961) 15pp., parts. 6 min. Improvisation; Humoresque; Gavotte; Passepied. Thin textures, folklike, charming. M-D.

Francesco Veracini. *Twelve Sonatas* (W. Kolneder—CFP) Vol.I: F, G, D. Vol.II: B♭, C, a. Vol.III: c, F, g. Vol.IV: d, F, c. Contrasting multimovements of great beauty. M-D.
——. *Sonata* I (Paumgartner—Bo&H).
——. *Sonata* II (Paumgartner—Bo&H).

John Verrall. *Sonata* (Tritone 1976) 16pp., parts. Excellent balance between flute and piano, 20th-century harmonic treatment, attractive and moving. M-D.

Leonardo Vinci. *Zwei Sonaten* D, G (K. Meier—Amadeus BP810 1998) 19pp., parts, with basso. In D: Adagio; Allegro; Largo; Presto; Pastorella. In G: Siciliana–Andante; Allegro; Aria–Cantabile; Gavotta–Vivace, Menuetto–Il gusto Italiano–Le Goût Français–Il gusto Italiano. Interesting writing with highly contrasting movements. Fine realizations. M-D.
——. *Sonata* D (J. Bopp—Reinhardt 1949) 12pp., parts.
——. *Sonata* G (J. Bopp—Reinhardt 1955) 14pp., parts.

Antonio Vivaldi. *Six Sonatas* "Il Pastor Fido" Op.13 (HM; IMC; T. Wye, R. Scott—Southern B330 1982) C, C, G, A, C, g. "Recent research has shown beyond reasonable doubt that most of these *Sonatas* are a pastiche, partly of Vivaldi concerto themes and partly of works by other composers, perhaps including work of the [original] publisher himself" (Wye, in Preface). M-D.
——. *Four Sonatas* (K. Meier—Amadeus BP 828 1999) 27pp., parts, with basso. [1.] C (RV 48): Affettuoso; Allegro assai; Larghetto; Allegro. [2.] g (RV 51): Largo; Allegro; Andante; Allegro. [3.] d (RV 49): Preludio–Largo; Siciliana–Adagio; Sarabanda; Allegro. [4.] e (RV 50): Andante; Siciliano; Allegro; Arioso. Preface in German and English. M-D.
——. *Sonatas* (Ric). 4 *Sonatas* for flute and basso continuo, published separately. *Sonata* F.XIV/3 C (PR1165). *Sonata* F.XIV/4 F (PR1176). *Sonata* F.XIV/5 d (PR1192). *Sonata* F.XIV/9 g (K. Heller PR1255). Outstanding editions.
——. *Sonata* C (M. Silver—JWC 1952) 11pp., parts. Affettuoso; Allegro assai;

Larghetto; Allegro. This work comes from a MS in the University Library, Cambridge. Vintage Vivaldi. Fine basso continuo realization. Int. to M-D.

———. *Sonata* C (G. Gatti—Br&H). A relatively simple work, efficient editing, large print, well spaced.

———. *Sonata* C (F. Nagel—Heinrichshofen 1970) 8pp., parts, cello ad lib. Affettuoso; Allegro; Larghetto; Allegro. Figured bass well realized by Winfried Radeke. M-D.

———. *Sonata* c (Schott).

———. *Sonata* d (F. Nagel—Heinrichshofen 1970) 7pp., parts, cello ad lib. Preludio; Siciliano; Sarabanda; Allegro. Basso continuo realized by Winfried Radeke. M-D.

———. *Sonata* e (D. Lasocki—Musica Rara 1973). Cello ad lib. Found in a Swedish MS. Andante; Siciliano; Allegro; Arioso. Editing and basso continuo realization are excellent. M-D.

———. *Sonata* F (F. Brüggen—Br&VP 517 1959) 8pp., parts. Siciliano; Allemanda; Allegro. Good realization of basso continuo. M-D.

———. *Sonata* g (J. Marx—McGinnis & Marx 1946) 20pp., parts. Vivace; Allabreve–Fuga da capella; Largo; Allegro ma non presto. Figured bass is finely realized by Erwin Bodky. M-D.

———. *Sonata* g (G. Zahn—Pan 880 1993) 11pp., parts, including basso. Largo; Allegro; Andante; Allegro. Complementary realization. M-D.

Roman Vlad. *Sonatina* (SZ 1956) 18pp., parts. Allegretto, con spirito: many tempo and texture changes, tremolo, dynamic extremes (*pppp*). Allegro comodo: rhythmic, thin textures, repeated notes, dancelike. D.

Georg Christoph Wagenseil. *Sonata* D ca.1765 (R. Scholz—Dob 1972) No.536 in DM. 14pp., parts. Allegro; Adagio; Allegro. "In its gallant-sentimental style, the work is typical of the Viennese Rococo: nimble, rippling triplets and sixteenth-note figures over a simple bass line, with an extremely economical use of harmony so that the solo instrument's preeminence is never endangered; melodic lines with florid embellishments and sighing suspensions; rhythmically pronounced sixteenth-note triplets and 32nd-note runs" (from Preface). M-D.

Karl Heinz Wahren. *Frétillement* (Bo&Bo 1972) 15pp., parts. Allegro con moto; Allegro agitato. Serial, atonal, complex rhythms, pointillistic. D.

Adam Walacinski. *Dichromia* (PWM 1970) 7pp. Clusters, harmonics, pointillistic, dramatic gestures, avant-garde. Directions in German and Polish. D.

Lloyd W. S. Webber. *Sonatina* D (Hin 76 1941) 15pp., parts. 8 min. Allegretto piacevole; Larghetto. Freely tonal but never moves too far from tonic. The Larghetto leads into a delightful Presto giocoso with arpeggi triplets and syncopated rhythms. A Larghetto e allargando section provides contrast with the final Presto giocoso, which is marchlike in character. M-D.

Jaromir Weinberger. *Sonatine* (CF W1811 1941) 13pp., parts. Con moto; Menuet; Rondo. Thin textures throughout, mildly 20th-century. Suggests a 20th-century Clementi Op.36 *Sonatina.* Int.

Jean Baptiste Wendling. *Sonata* G from Op.1 (E. Ade—Ichthys 231) 12pp., parts. Allegro; Adagio; Presto. Musical, worthy, cleanly realized figured bass. M-D.

Lawrence Widdoes. *Sonatina* 1963 (TP 1967) SPAM 46 12pp., parts. Two untitled movements. Serial, atonal, pointillistic, questioning conclusion. Presents some rhythmic ensemble problems. D.

Charles Widor. *Suite* Op.34 (Piper Press; K 2177) 27pp., parts. Moderato; Scherzo–Allegro vivace; Romance–Andantino; Final–Vivace. Large sweeping lines characteristic of the late 19th century infiltrate the work through busy instrumental parts. M-D.

Florian Wiefler. *Sonatine* Op.15/1 (Dob 1974) 15pp., parts. Fliessend; Sehr ruhig. Characteristics of Hindemith, frequent tempo changes, free serial treatment and triadic atonality make for an interesting style. The second movement is a combination of slow-fast sections. On p.10 and at the bottom of p.14 a treble clef should be added to the right hand of the piano part. M-D.

Alec Wilder. *Sonata* I 1964 (G. Schuller, V. Nanzetta—Margum) 25pp., parts. Untitled first movement; Andante; Scherzo; Rubato. Written in a light, clear, semi-Poulencian style. Freely tonal with flexible meters. May be performed by piccolo or alto flute. D.

——. *Sonata* II 1965 (Sam Fox [Margum] 1970) 20pp., parts. 12 min. Allegretto; Adagio ma non tanto; Scherzando; Molto cantabile. Foreword by Samuel Baron. A successful work that affords "a gratifying range of expressive possibilities to the performers." Each movement contains "leading clues to the interpretation, more from the emotional ramifications of a single mood than from a formalistic analysis of motives and keys . . . The restlessness of the first movement, the dreamlike introspection of the second, the humor of the third, and the full-throated outpouring of the fourth are all expressed in free forms, forms that have their unexpected twists and turns as well as modulations that seem to take us to the 'wrong' key" (from Preface). D.

Geoffrey Winters. *Sonatina* Op.28 (Thames 1965) 20pp., parts. Outer movements have humorous characteristics. Middle movement, Andante, utilizes chordal motion in the piano under the flute melody, which exploits the interval of a 4th. Int. to M-D.

Stefan Wolpe. *Piece in Two Parts for Flute and Piano* 1960 (McGinnis & Marx 1969) 72pp., parts. In 2 large movements, the first untitled, the second titled "Spirited." Complex writing that includes changing meters, sudden dynamic extremes, pointillistic treatment, proportional rhythmic relationships, serial organization, exploitation of extreme ranges, harmonics, fast chromatic figuration, tremolo chords. Intricate, requires a large span and thorough pianistic equipment as well as much ensemble experience. D.

Yehudi Wyner. *All the Rage* 1980 (AMP). 12 min.
——. *Sweet Consort* 1988 (AMP). 23 min.

Isang Yun. *Garak* 1963 (Bo&Bo) 11pp., parts. Cluster-like percussive chords, serial influence, Expressionist, complex atonal patterns, *ppppp* closing. D.

Luigi Zaninelli. *Canto* (EV 1973) 7pp., parts. Opens with a Con malinconia, row-like flute solo. At Con movimento, ma non troppo, the piano enters with full *pp* mildly dissonant chords. A Tranquillo section gives the piano more melodic flexibility. The full *pp* chords return, and these 2 basic ideas make up the form of the piece. The row seems to unwind gradually with assistance by the piano, and a calm a piacere settles over the concluding two bars. A true 20th-century extended character piece. D.

Julien François Zbinden. *Sonatina* Op.5 (Schott 1951).
——. *Fantaisie* Op.22 1954 (Br&H 6200) 11pp., parts. 6 min. Contrasting sections, flute cadenza, bitonal, octotonic, shifting meters, freely tonal, some jazz influence. M-D.

Hans Zender. *Musik für Flöte und Klavier* 1950 (Bo&Bo 1953) 27pp., parts. 20 min. Mässig schnell; Sehr langsam und ruhig; Scherzo; Ruhig und langsam; Rondo. This Suite follows Neoclassic lines, is somewhat more dissonant than Hindemith, and develops naturally. D.

Friedrich Zipp. *Au clair de la lune Variations* (CFP).
——. *Fantasia, Pastorale e Fuga* 1969 (W. Müller 1973) 12pp., parts. For tenor recorder (flute) and piano (harpsichord), cello or viol ad lib.
——. *Sonatine* Op.23a (Schott).
——. *Suite* Op.35a (Litolff 14011 1956) 20pp., parts. 15 min. Transcription by the composer of the original work for flute and string orchestra. Giocoso; Andante; Molto vivace; Introduction–Declamato e espressivo–Allegro ritmico. Spontaneous writing, Neoclassic orientation. M-D.

Duos for Piano and Oboe

Samuel Adler. *Sonata* (ST 784 1989) 23pp., parts. Slowly, expressively and very freely moving—Fast and rhythmic. Uses extremes of instruments, especially low B♭ on oboe. Dense chordal and proportional rhythmic relationships. Large span required. D.

Hendrik Andriessen. *Ballade* 1952 (Donemus) 10pp., parts. Bitonal, quasi-recitative sections, arpeggi figures. Romantic rolled-chord sonorities end this poetic tone poem *pp*. Requires large span. M-D.

Malcolm Arnold. *Sonatina* (Lengnick 1951) 15pp., parts. 8 min. Leggiero: Andante con moto; Vivace. Light, jocular style. M-D.

William Babell. *12 Sonatas* 4 vols. (M. Maute—Amadeus BP334-7 1999), parts, including basso. For oboe, flute, or violin. I: 1 F, 2 c, 3 f. II: 4 g, 5 E♭, 6 F. III: 7 B♭, 8 E♭, 9 B♭. IV: 10 E♭, 11 g, 12 c. "The compositional qualities of this group of *Sonatas* are an extraordinary testimony to Baroque musical culture: they reveal how strong an influence the Italian style had become in England. The ornaments in the slow movements are particularly interesting, providing an insight into the performance practices of the period" (from Preface). Babell, who seems to have lived his entire life in London, employed these new ideas from Italy and seems to have preferred a more improvisatory character in his ornaments. A welcome addition back into the repertoire. M-D.
——. *Sonata* f (Tilmouth—OUP 1963) 8pp., parts. For oboe, violin, or flute and keyboard. Adagio; Vivace; Largo; Presto. Slightly more difficult than the *Sonata* g. M-D.
——. *Sonata* g (Tilmouth—OUP 1963) 5pp., parts. For oboe, violin, or flute and keyboard, but best suited for oboe. Allegro; Air; Hornpipe; Giga. Int.
Both *Sonatas* are attractive to performers and listeners.

Grażyna Bacewicz. *Sonatina* (PWM 3855 1988, ISBN 83-224-2749-2) 19pp., parts. 9½ min. Allegretto; Kanon–Lento, Allegro non troppo. Sparkling, with unpredictable motive action. Lyric Kanon transpires with canonic techniques as expected. M-D.

Carl Philipp Emanuel Bach. *Sonata* W.135 g (K. Walther—Br&H 1953; G. Schreck, H. Ruf—Ric SY506 1954, 14pp., parts). Adagio; Allegro; Vivace (with 3 variations). Both editions have stylistically correct realizations. M-D.

Johann Sebastian Bach. *Sonate* g (R. Meylan—CFP 1972) 28pp., parts. This is probably the *Sonata* S.1030 b for flute and keyboard, transposed by Bach to the new key to suit the oboe's characteristics more adequately. It is an important addition to the oboe repertoire. M-D.

Simon Bainbridge. *Music for Mel and Nora* 1979 (UMP 1986) 16pp., parts. Commences *ppp* with repetitive triplets and minimalist ideas to yield an intenseness which grows in speed, rhythmic requirements, and repetitive patterns. Uses pitch-bending in oboe and frequent one-staff notation for piano. M-D.

Robert Baksa. *Oboe Sonata* 1988 (CLE 25 1993) 31pp., parts. Calm: large ternary design with sections linked by oboe cadenzas. Scherzo: commences with lengthy piano introduction hinting at the principal theme, introduced formally by the oboe. Theme and Variations: homophonic setting for theme built on quartal and step intervals which leads to a brief set of lyrical variations. Concludes with coda statement of theme at soft dynamics. M-D.

Wayne Barlow. *The Winter's Passed* 1938 (Eastman School of Music 1940) 7pp., parts. Effective trans. from the original for oboe and strings. Expressive with 2 haunting melodies in ternary form. Mildly 20th-century. M-D.

Christian Frederik Barth. *Sonate Brillant* (S. Ingerslev—Schott OBB35 1994) 32pp., parts. A fine addition to the limited repertoire for early Romantic solo oboe. Allegro: brilliant; Adagio sostenuto: expressive; Rondo–Scherzando: humorous and clever. M-D.

John Bavicchi. *Sonatina* Op.30 (OUP 1970) 12pp., parts. 10 min. Moderato: freely tonal around G; varied mood and tempo changes using different figuration; widely spread textures; octotonic; requires good octave technique. Poco Adagio: imitation; piano has more solo part. Con spirito: thin textures, repeated octaves, broken-chord figuration. Natural writing for both instruments. M-D.

Conrad Beck. *Sonatine* (Schott 4449 1957) 12pp., parts. 10 min. Allegro moderato; Larghetto; Allegro vivace. Freely tonal, Neoclassic. M-D.

Peter Benary. *Sonatine* (Möseler). Sensitive, clear Neoclassic lines, straightforward. Int. to M-D.

Richard Rodney Bennett. *Sonata* 1961 (Belwin-Mills) 26pp., parts. Vivace; Lento espressivo; Leggiero e ritmico; Agitato. Dissonant, careful thematic development. Requires large span. D.

——. *After Syrinx I* 1982 (Nov 120615 1989) 31pp., parts. 12 min. Based on Debussy's *Syrinx* for solo flute (1913). In one lengthy movement, initially marked

Adagio flessibile, with 2 scherzos and 2 cadenzas, one for each instrument. Asymmetrical rhythms and nonidiomatic writing. D.

Jean Berger. *Sonata da Camera* (BB 1037a 1957) 20pp., parts. 12 min. Moderato; Allegro; Lento; Animato. Parallel chords, changing meters, chromatic figuration, octotonic. Neoclassic with Impressionist influences. M-D.

Lennox Berkeley. *Sonatina* (JWC 1964) 16pp., parts. Molto moderato; Andante; Allegro. There are technical problems for both performers, but the piece wears well and is worth the effort. The outer movements are written in a mildly 20th-century flowing style, while the Andante is more sustained and serious. M-D.

Alessandro Besozzi. *Sonata* C (E. Rothwell—JWC 1956) 12pp., parts. Andante; Allegro; Larghetto; Allegretto. Delightful and interesting writing in Classical style. M-D.

Harrison Birtwistle. *An Interrupted Endless Melody* 1991–94 (Bo&H 10660 1996, ISMN M-060-106606) 9pp., parts. 3–9 min. "*An Interrupted Endless Melody* comprises one oboe part and three different piano accompaniments. A performance consists of a version for oboe with any one piano accompaniment, or all three in succession to form a three-movement piece. Alternatively, individual 'movements' might be interspersed between other pieces in a recital programme" (from Performance Note). Terse rhythmic patterns and harmonic structures. Large span required. M-D.

Martino Bitti. *Sonata* c (H. Ruf—Schott OBB38 1997, ISMN M-001-11388-5) 11pp., parts, with basso. For oboe or violin. Adagio; Allegro; Adagio; Allegro. Complementary realizations. M-D.

Edward Boguslawski. *Szkice* (Sketches) (PWM 1965) 10pp., parts. Preludium; Scherzino; Notturno; Postludium. Attractive 20th-century writing with subtle mood contrasts in each piece. A colorful and short Suite that would add interest to any program. M-D.

Edith Borroff. *Variations and Theme* (Sam Fox 1963) 15pp., parts. Introduction and Waltz Interlude; Romp; Story; Promenade; Interruption and Theme–Finale. Serial, thin textures, clever; contrasting movements that finally arrive at the attractive theme. M-D.

Roger Boutry. *Sonatine* 1958 (Sal) 20pp., parts. Allegro; Andante; Allegro. Freely tonal with much chromatic color, oboe cadenza in first and second movements. The finale is dancelike. Generally thin textures predominate. 3 with 2. Requires a large span. M-D.

Pierre de Bréville. *Sonatine* E♭ 1924 (Rouart-Lerolle) 20pp., parts. 10½ min. Allègre; Très calme; Vite. A well-crafted work that is pianistic and slightly 20th-century-sounding. Alternating hand usage and added-note technique seem to be favorite devices. Flowing, musical, careful attention to details, some Franck influence present. M-D.

Jacques Castèréde. *Sonate* 1959 (Leduc) 26pp., parts. 21 min. Moderato pastorate: chromatic figuration, varied tempos, basically pastoral mood throughout. Scherzando–Non troppo presto: broken left-hand octaves with right-hand chords, freely tonal, flexible meters, repeated notes, a few tricky spots. Adagio: repeated chords, some are 10ths; constant 8th-note pulsation. Moderato tranquillo: flowing, chromatic, French Neoclassic style. D.

Pietro Castrucci. *Sonata* I G 1720 (A. de Klerk—Broekmans 1617 1991) 6pp., parts, including basso.
———. *Sonata* V G 1720 (A. de Klerk—Broekmans 1613 1991) 6pp., parts, including basso.

Pierre Chédeville (the eldest). *Sonatille* Op.6/3 c (G. Favre—Siècle Musical 1949) 11pp., parts. Tendrement; Allemande; Rondeau; Gigue. Keyboard realization and oboe converse in a rhythmical and melodious counterpoint that is both charming and ingenious. M-D.

Brian Cherney. *Six Miniatures* 1968 (Doberman 1990) 16pp., parts. Allegro; Andante; Adagio; Allegro giocoso; Andante; Allegro giocoso. Brief musical essays in contrasting characters. Occasionally unconventional writing for oboe but largely straightforward for piano. Large span required. M-D.

Frédéric Chopin. *Variations on a Theme from Rossini's Cenerentola* 1824 (J. P. Rampal—IMC 1960) 5pp., parts. Finale of No.12 in the *Cenerentola* score serves as theme. Graceful, elegant; cleverly conceals a rather primitive harmonic scheme. M-D.

Johann Cilenšek. *Sonate* 1960 (Litolff 5248) 17pp., parts. Allegro; Lento assai; Molto vivace. Well-contrasted moods, dissonant style, ideas developed naturally, some Neoclassic characteristics, freely tonal. M-D.

Arnold Cooke. *Sonata* 1957 (Nov) 34pp., parts. 20 min. Andante: wistful quality; short cadenza leads to an Allegro vivace: martial opening idea contrasted with flowing sections. Andante: sustained, more rhythmical second idea. Rondo: dancelike, "patter" chords at Poco più mosso, chromatic coloration, long lines at closing. M-D.

Elizabeth Sprague Coolidge. *Sonata* (CF 1947) 35pp., parts. Introduction and Allegro; Reverie; Theme and (5 contrasted) Variations. Mildly 20th-century. Flowing quality with many triplets. Final movement has a different character for each variation: Gigue, Fugato, 3-voice Canon, etc. M-D.

Henry Cowell. *Three Ostinati with Chorales* (Music Press 1946) 16pp., parts. For oboe or clarinet and piano. Written for oboe and piano, but Cowell considered them equally suitable for clarinet and piano. Each chorale is followed by its ostinato, which is more elaborate. All have fresh and attractive ideas, simply conceived and containing melodic appeal. M-D.

Robert Cundick. *Turnabouts* (Bo&H 1964) 24pp., parts. Four contrasting pieces very effectively written for this combination. Ideas are well developed, and the entire Suite is attractive. Mildly 20th-century with flowing lines. M-D.

Martin Dalby. *Sonatina* 1969 (Nov 1975) 8pp., parts. 4½ min. Allegretto–molto rubato: atonal, pointillistic, chromatic. Adagio: piacevole, thin textures. Leggiero e quasi presto: serial influence, mainly secco style. M-D.

John Diercks. *Sonata* (TP 1966) 26pp., parts. Allegro: SA, flexible meters, buoyant themes; pianist uses light touches of pedal for color; arpeggiated chords contrast with a more transparent staccato section. Andante cantabile: ABA; diatonic theme in oboe treated in duet fashion with left-hand piano part; B section more active but mainly employs softer dynamic levels. Allegro con brio: changing meters, dancelike, more chromatic lines; Cantando section provides contrast before opening ideas return. A cracking good ending and an outstanding contribution to this literature. M-D.

Stephen Dodgson. *Suite* D (OUP 1974) 15pp., parts. 9 min. Prelude; Ground; Canzonet; Dance. Key signatures are no help. Instruments treated equally in thoroughly 20th-century Neoclassic settings; fairly relaxed moods. Keyboard writing is guitar-like at places, while the oboe is treated melodically (Dodgson is a guitarist). Experienced performers required. D.

Henri Dutilleux. *Sonata* (Leduc 1947) 23pp., parts. 11 min. Aria–Grave: curling ostinato-like chromatic figures underlie a more diatonic melody; 3 layers of sound; works up to cadenza-like conclusion. Scherzo: staccato chords, flexible meters, imitation, colorful; sustained chords fade away and movement ends *ppp*. Final–Assez allant: contrasting figurations and moods; requires firm rhythmic control and exact dynamics. Strong formal construction in all movements. D.

Petr Eben. *Amoroso* (Hofmeister 2302 1995) 9pp., parts. "The piece begins in a mood of lonely yearning, characterized by the constant repetition of the note 'A'. Trying to make contact, it finally succeeds in doing so with the harmonious interval of the third: as if feeling its way, it gradually makes its way in quarter-tone steps up to it. The quest builds in intensity to a desperate *fortissimo*, after which the redeeming 'love-third' is sounded *pianissimo*, now recurring in various guises and also inverted as a sixth. After playing around with these intervals the oboe, at first hesitatingly and constantly re-starting, finally plays the lyrical love-tune with which the piece ends" (from Preface). Uses quarter tones and indeterminacy. M-D.

——. *Miniaturen* (Hofmeister 2615 1998, ISMN M-2034-2615-8) 7pp., parts. Almost identical to *Miniaturen* for flute and piano with only slight changes to oboe part. See detailed entry under duos for piano and flute. M-D.

Alvin Etler. *Introduction and Allegro* 1952 (AMP 1958) 16pp., parts. 8 min. Sustained syncopated harmonies; piano bass line very important. The Allegro $\frac{5}{4}$ has much rhythmic mobility, is freely tonal, and contains a few dynamic surprises. M-D.

Peter Evans. *Sonata* (JWC 1953) 23pp., parts. 14½ min. Moderato; Variations; Rondo–Allegro con brio. Post-Romantic chromatic writing. Piano part contains much interest. M-D.

Jan Reindert Adriaan Felderhof. *Suite* (Donemus 1974) 18pp., 2 parts (flute and oboe). Photostat of MS.

Corey Field. *Rhapsody* (Helicon 1989) 12pp., parts. 6½ min. Pedal carefully marked for pianist, some clusters, contrasting sections, effective, well written for both instruments. D.

Félicien Foret. *Sonata* G (Lacour 1945) 25pp., parts. Allegro moderato; Andante, poco lento; Menuet; Vif. Witty and facile, à la Poulenc. Mildly 20th-century. M-D.

Christopher J. Freyer. *Sonata* 1986 (Duma 1995) 22pp., parts. In memoriam Brian Israel. Andante molto legato, with steady motion: facile, thin textures, reflective with quiet dynamics. Allegro marcato, violently: bitonal, dramatic, mixing homophonic and linear writing. Andante moderato, legato: contemplative, mostly facile except for extended piano solo, octotonic, *ppp* ending. M-D.

Géza Frid. *Caprices Roumains* Op.86 (Donemus 1975) 18pp., parts. 8½ min. Based on Romanian folk melodies, sectional, varied rhythms and moods, chromatic, modal, whole-tone scales used. Mildly 20th-century. M-D.

Friedrich Theodor Frohlich. *Pastorale and Rondo* 1824 (H. Steinbeck—Eulenburg 1974) 20pp., parts. Pastorale: gentle dotted rhythms; subdominant relationships; has some of the pseudo-qualities of Beethoven's *Pastorale Symphony*. Rondo: two episodes with three statements of the refrain, Chopinesque, syncopation, ornamental lines. M-D.

Pierre Gabaye. *Sonatine* (Leduc 1957) 19pp., parts. Assez vif: B, moving parallel chords, 20th-century Alberti-bass treatment, large span required (10ths). Lent, avec douceur: A♭, wistful, more active mid-section. Très vif: B, $\frac{6}{8}$, forward motion throughout, hemiola, chromatic in mid-section. Witty, pleasing, and attractive writing. M-D to D.

Francesco Geminiani. *Sonata* e (H. Ruf—Br HM 178 1961) 8pp., parts. Adagio; Allegro; Largo; Vivace. High notes, passages difficult for breath control, double fingerings avoided in this work. It is especially suitable for the oboe. Excellent keyboard realization. M-D.

Harald Genzmer. *Konzert* 1994 (Ries and Erler 11-513 1995, ISMN M-013-21008-4) 31pp., parts. Moderato; Tranquillo; Vivo; Improvisation–Molto tranquillo e poco rubato, dolcissimo!; Finale–Presto. Octotonic, wide chordal spacing, trills, scalar and arpeggiated figures predominate this large-scale commentary from the late 20th century. M-D.

Jaap Geraedts. *Jan Klaassen—Serenade* (Donemus 1953, rev.1973) 5pp., parts. Photostat. Quartal harmony exploited in an Allegro grazioso setting. M-D.

Cornelis Willhelmus De Groot. *Deux Figures* (Donemus 1974) 16pp., parts. 7 min.

John Hall. *Sonata* Op.19 (Chappell 1968–69). Three movements, changing meters, rhythmic problems. D.

George Frideric Handel. *Four Sonatas* B♭, c, F, g (W. Michel—Amadeus BP333 2001) 27pp., parts, including basso. Most *Sonatas* consist of a combination of Largo and Allegro movements, in both binary and through-composed forms. *Sonatas* c and F have Bourrées and Angloises. Fine realization. M-D.
——. *Sonata* Op.1/6 (Stade—CFP; Scheck, Ruf—Ric SY513 1954, 11pp., parts; Bleuzet—Costallat). Larghetto; Allegro; Adagio; Allegro. Ric edition gives original text in addition to the editor's suggested realization for the oboe. M-D.
——. *Sonata* Op.1/8 (Stade—CFP; Scheck, Ruf—Ric 1954; Bleuzet—Costallat).
——. *Fitzwilliam Sonata* B♭ (Dart, Bergmann—Schott 1948).
——. *Two Sonatas* (K 4513).

Howard Hanson. *Pastorale* Op.38 1949 (CF) 9pp., parts. 6 min. Freely tonal, Poco più mosso mid-section, molto espressivo ending, flowing, effective. M-D.

Michael Head. *Three Pieces* (E. Rothwell—Bo&H 1954), parts. Gavotte; Elegiac Dance; Presto. Published separately. Three of the most beautiful pieces in the repertoire for oboe and piano. Long flowing lines with uncomplicated rhythmic and harmonic languages which allow much expressiveness in an early-20th-century setting. Large span required. M-D.
——. *Three Hill Songs* (Emerson 80), parts. Int. to M-D.
——. *Siciliana* (Emerson 14), parts. Oboe and piano or harpsichord. M-D.

Christopher Headington. *Sonatina* 1960 (Bo&H 1973) 20pp., parts. Three movements in mildly 20th-century idiom that centers around E♭, triadic sonorities, not for beginners. M-D.

Willy Hess. *Drei Tonstücke* Op.71 (Eulenburg 1969) 12pp., parts.
——. *Sonate* Op.44 C (Amadeus 1975) 27pp., parts.

Paul Hindemith. *Sonata* 1938 (Schott) 23pp., parts. 12 min. Cheerful: short opening motive is thematic germ for entire work. Lively: same theme serves as basis for alternating slow and fast sections. Very slow: mid-section displays theme harmonized in a caricature of *Tristan*. Last 2 movements are telescoped into one. Fluctuating tonal polarity, clever rhythms, fugal textures. D.

Joseph Horvath. *Sonatina* Op.3 1949 (Belwin-Mills) 7½ min. Clean, transparent, concise, and economic in style. First movement bubbles over with high spirits and perky rhythms. A short slow movement leads directly to the extremely lively finale. Harmonic idiom has a sharp edge to it, and cross-accentuation of rhythms lends it a spicy and invigorating wit. M-D.

Jacques Ibert. *Tunis Nefta* from *Escales* 1922 (Leduc 1924) 5pp., parts. Arranged by the composer. Modéré, très rythmé: tritone is integral part of left hand; opens *pp*, builds to a climax, subsides, ends *ppp*. Colorful and attractive writing in a mildly 20th-century style. M-D.

Pierre Israel-Meyer. *Portrait d'un Masque* (Technisonor 1973) 7pp., 2 copies necessary. Notes in French only.

Gordon Jacob. *An 80th Birthday Card for Léon Goossens* 1977 (Emerson 124 1993) 2pp., parts. 2 min. A simple, musical tribute to Goossens marked tranquillo e semplice in homophonic texture. Int.

———. *Sonatina* (OUP 1963) 16pp., parts. 9½ min. For oboe and harpsichord (or piano). Adagio; Allegro giocoso; Lento alla Sarabanda; Allegro molto vivace. Coloristic qualities can be best achieved with piano. M-D.

Louis-Emmanuel Jadin/Charles Garnier. *6 Nocturnes* 2 vols. (F. Badol-Bertrand—Zimmermann 31240, 31250, 1998, ISMN M-010-31250-7) 53pp., parts. I: F, C, g. II: a, C, F. These *Nocturnes* are closer in style and spirit to the early-19th-century Sonata. Each is extended in length with multiple sections and varying tempos. Some popular and artistic songs of the day are quoted. "Although the extremely charming pieces published here are not regarded as great masterpieces of oboe music, they have nevertheless contributed to the continued existence of an instrument which was more or less doomed to be pushed aside by the clarinet after the Ancien Regime. Indeed, for several decades only oboe players wrote for their instrument, which did not appear to inspire any other great composers of the time. With hindsight it is easy to see the important role Louis Jadin and Charles Garnier played in ensuring that the oboe maintained a firm place in the compositions of French music and on the curriculum of the Paris Conservatory, even after the English horn had become increasingly popular" (from Preface). M-D.

André Jolivet. *Sérénade* 1945 (Billaudot 3153) 31pp., parts. Originally for wind quintet with oboe principal. Piano reduction by the composer. Cantilèna; Caprice; Intermède; March burlesque. Intense chromatic style, freely dissonant, atonal. M-D.

Johann Wenzel Kalliwoda. *Morceau de Salon* Op.228 g/G (K. Meier—Amadeus BP875 2001) 16pp., parts. In 2 lively sections meant to be performed together. Stylistically owes much to the early 19th century with pianistic writing alternating between salon and serious writing. M-D.

Willem Kersters. *Sonatina* Op.63 (CeBeDeM 1974) 12pp., parts. 5½ min. First 2 movements untitled; Scherzando. Thin textured, mild pointillistic technique, secco style, interesting pedal effects. M-D.

Johann Philipp Kirnberger. *Sonata* B♭ (H. Töttcher—Sikorski 269 1954). Fine keyboard realization. M-D.

Stefan Kisielewski. *Suita* (PWM 2384 1957, ISBN 83-224-1677-6) 25pp., parts. 18 min. Allegro molto energico; Andantino cantabile (quasi berceuse): Moderato (tempo di gavotte); Allegro veloce (quasi gavotte II); Presto agitato. Neoclassic with shifting harmonies. Large span required. M-D.

Charles Koechlin. *Sonata* 1915–16 (ESC), over 20 min. The longest of all oboe Sonatas. Moderato: pastoral, evokes a calm countryside where people work. Dance of the Fauns: a difficult scherzo. Evening in the Countryside: printed separately in *La Revue Musicale,* June 1923. A House in the Country: this was the original title, but in the definitive version there is no name for this movement. Popular songlike character. D.

———. *Quatorze Pièces* Op.179 1942 (ESC 1991), parts. For oboe, oboe d'amour, or English horn. Bk.1 (36pp.): I. Andante con moto, quasi allegretto moderato, II. Allegretto, pas vite (plutôt andantino), III. Andante (presque adagio à la blanche), IV. Allegro, assez animé, gai, solide, V. Très doux presque adagio, VI. Allegretto con moto, VII. Andante presque adagio. Bk.2 (31pp.): VIII. Allegretto, assez tranquille, presque andantino, IX. Lent, adagio, X. Allegro, très décidé, clair et gai, XI. Allegretto con moto, XII. [unmarked], XIII. Adagio à la blanche, XIV. Allegro con moto. Nos.1–3, 5, 12 are for oboe or oboe d'amour; 4, 6–11 for oboe; 13–14 for English horn. May be performed individually or in combinations. Int. to M-D.

Peter Jona Korn. *Sonata* Op.7 (Simrock Elite Edition 3230 1964) 39pp., parts. Moderato; Romanza; Rondo. Neoclassic style, fondness for triplets noted. Romanza uses many juxtaposed major and minor 3rds. Rondo concludes with a fugue plus a more chordal coda. D.

William Latham. *Sonata* I (Spratt 1949) 24pp., parts. Grave: quartal and quintal harmonies in piano support oboe melody and lead to Commodo section, which is more rhythmically oriented; piano has undulating quartal harmonies in left-hand triplets against two 8ths in right hand; chordal punctuation ends the movement. Andantino: pastoral feeling with both instruments contributing melodic ideas. Allegro: dancelike, broken octaves, bright closing. Mildly 20th-century. M-D.

Philibert de Lavigne. *Six Sonatas* Op.2 ca.1740 (W. Hillemann—Noetzel). Published separately. These multimovement works can be performed on all of the woodwind instruments in use during the first half of the 18th century, and on the violin. See detailed entry under duos for piano and flute.

Theodor Leschetizky. *Variationen über ein Thema van Beethoven* (Schott 1937). The theme is from Beethoven's "Andante Favori."

Jean-Baptiste Loeillet (of Lyons). *Sonata* Op.5/1 e 1717 (Sadie—Musica Rara 1961) 7pp., parts. Allemanda; Sarabanda (ornamented version, which may be used in repeats); Gavotta; Gigue. Dynamic marks have been added by the editor, and other editorial markings are identified. Excellent continuo realization. M-D.

Otto Luening. *Three Nocturnes* 1958 (Galaxy) 17pp., parts. Nights in the Garden of Chopin: E♭, flowing oboe line, chromatic broken chordal figuration in piano; B section has more elaboration in the piano line. Nights in the Garden of a "Night Club": blues and jazz influence, rich harmonies, full of chords, freely tonal around C. Nights in the Garden of Paganini: C, toccata-like and brilliant, dance influence, syncopated melody. A colorful set. M-D.

Witold Lutoslawski. *Epitaph* 1979 (JWC 55256 1981) 9pp., parts. Improvisational in spirit with relatively controlled indeterminacy. M-D.

Elizabeth Maconchy. *Three Bagatelles* (OUP 1974) 15pp., parts. 8 min. For oboe and harpsichord or piano. Allegro; Poco lento; Vivo. Imaginative writing, with the keyboard part mainly consisting of chromatic chords. Trills, broken chordal figures used for rhythmic punctuation, some melodic usage. Twentieth-century musical language throughout, eloquent gestures, tart dissonances, Neoclassic post-Stravinsky. M-D.

Peter Mai. *Concertino* (Hofmeister 7468) 18pp., parts. For soprano blockflöte (recorder) or oboe and piano. See detailed entry under duos for piano and flute.

Riccardo Malipiero. *Sonata* 1959 (SZ) 14pp., parts. Moderato: calm, sustained, ends with 9th chords. Veloce e grottesco: varied figures. Deciso: accented chords, Più tranquillo mid-section, *a tempo* Deciso returns. Neoclassic style. Thin textures never overbalance oboe. M-D.

Ursula Mamlok. *Five Capriccios* 1968 (CFP 1975) 7pp. 6½ min. Pointillistic, serial (including dynamics), plucked and stopped strings, clusters, long pedals in No.5, thorny. D.

Francesco Mancini. *Zwölf Sonaten* (Michel—Amadeus 138-41 1999). See detailed entry under duos for piano and flute.

Bohuslav Martinů. *Concerto* (ESC 1960) 27pp., parts. 16½ min. Originally for oboe and orchestra, piano reduction by the composer. Moderato; Poco Andante; Poco allegro. Chromatic style, some tremolo, rhythmic problems prevalent in first movement. Obviously comes off better with orchestra, but a fine pianist can make this a stunning-sounding piece. D.

Carl Ludewig Matthes. *Two Sonatas* C, E♭ (K. Meier—Amadeus BP856 1999) 19pp., parts, with basso. Engaging realization within stylistic expectations. M-D.

Robert McBride. *Workout* 1936 (AMP) 16 min. Fast; Slow; Medium. Both instruments collaborate in a carefree session of musical exercise, passing germinal themes from one to the other. Witty, jazzy, rhythmical construction. Virtuoso, idiomatic, and urbane writing. D.

John McCabe. *Dance—Prelude* (Nov 1971) 8pp., parts. 4 min. Bold piano part, expressive oboe treatment. Two bell-like sonorities worked over in numerous ways provide basis for this piece. Dissonant harmonic idiom. M-D.

Krzysztof Meyer. *Pezzo Capriccioso* Op.60 1982 (PWM 8584 1987, ISBN 83-224-2600-3) 11pp., parts. 7 min. Calculated with asymmetric rhythms and phrases. Alternates between less common traditional harmonic structures and small clusters. Finishes with F♯ in oboe and neighboring G in piano at *pp*. M-D.

Darius Milhaud. *Concerto* (Heugel 1958) 34pp., parts. 18½ min. Originally for oboe and orchestra, piano reduction by the composer. Animé; Avec sérénité; Animé. Large span required; difficult to make all parts sound. D.
———. *Sonatine* 1954 (Durand 1955) 20pp., parts. Charme et vivacité; Souple et clair; Entrain et gaité. Light, attractive to play and hear. M-D.

Otto Mortensen. *Sonata* (WH 1953) 19pp., parts. Moderato; Allegro vivace. In Poulencian style, light, witty, appealing. M-D.

Jacques Christophe Naudot. *Sonata* c (H. Ruf—Schott OFB185 1998, ISMN M-001-12157-6) 15pp., parts, with basso. For oboe, flute, or recorder. Adagio; Allegro; Aria–Affettuoso. Customarily outstanding realization by Ruf. M-D.

Carl Nielsen. *Fantasiestücke* Op.2 (WH 1959; K 4126) 11pp., parts. 5½ min. Romance; Humoresque. Contrasted, chromatic. These early works date from before Nielsen's mature style had developed, but they nevertheless make an attractive group. M-D.

Andrzej Nikodemowicz. *3 Cradle-Songs* [*Kołysanki*] (PWM 7425 1973) 7pp., parts. Lento assai; Moderato; Lento. Chromatic lyricism; occasionally compacted chords forming dense formations within an octave; awkward reaches. Large span required. M-D.

Peter S. Odegard. *Sonatina and Cadenza* 1965 (McGinnis & Marx) 8pp., parts. Very slowly: serial, tremolo, linear, attacca to Fast: shifting meters, rubato, many crescendi and decrescendi. Cadenza: each instrument has 12 fragments adding up to 52 beats at a given tempo; aleatoric, secco, ringing sonorities, Expressionist, thin but thorny textures; large span required. D.

Antonino Pasculli. *Fantasia sull'opera "Les Huguenots" di Meyerbeer* (S. Caldini— Musica Rara 2233 1998) 19pp., parts. Virtuosic for oboe, "the present composition of Pasculli is very complex and combines some of the best-known themes from Meyerbeer's opera with high technical demands requiring both expression and virtuosity. It is important to point out that the 'cadenza' of the central episode ('Adagio' in $\frac{12}{8}$) has a section resembling part of Pasculli's *Concerto sopra motivi dell'opera 'La Favorita'"* (from Preface). While not virtuosic, the piano score is M-D.

John Paynter. *Three Pieces* (OUP 1972) 7pp., parts. Estampie: chordal (quartal) for first part, linear and chordal for second part. Lamento: piano lid is opened, and the oboist directs his or her sound toward the strings to excite the sympathetic resonance; white-key clusters depressed silently. Saltarello: cluster-like chords in left hand with octaves in right hand, counter-melody with oboe. M-D.

Pierre Danican Philidor. *Suite* Op.I/6 b (H. Ruf—Schott OBB39 1997, ISMN M-001-11468-4) 15pp., parts, with basso. For oboe, flute, or violin. Lentement; Rondeau–Gavotte; Sarabande–Lentement; Rigaudon; Gigue. Unusually gay in spirit with compound meters in all except the 2 Lentements. M-D.

Karl Pilss. *Sonata* e (Dob 1974) 32pp., parts. In Richard Strauss and Pfitzner idiom, late-Romantic academicism. First movement: SA, coda joins opening material to second group material in an accelerando to the end. Second movement: slow, ABA; songlike A, agitated B section. Third movement: a terse scherzo. Fourth movement: aggressive tarantella. Well written for both players though it is no masterpiece. M-D.

Walter Piston. *Suite* 1931 (ECS 1934) 15pp., parts. Prelude; Sarabande; Minuetto; Nocturne; Gigue. Sure draftsmanship, fine sense of proportion, dry wit, simplicity of mood. M-D.

Amilcare Ponchielli. *Piccolo Concertino* Op.75 1848 (S. Caldini—Br&H MR2257 2000, ISMN M-004-48803-4) 11pp., parts. Composed at the age of 13. One continuous movement in 4 sections (Andantino, Allegro, Allegretto, Finale). Operatic, with drama. M-D.

Francis Poulenc. *Sonata* 1962 (JWC) 22pp., parts. 13 min. Elégie; Scherzo–Très animé; Déploration–Très calme. A mixture of moods with all the best-known Poulencian characteristics present, from lush harmonies to wistful tunes. A major work. D.

William Presser. *Sonata* 1966 (Tenuto) 20pp., parts. 13 min. Neoclassic style. Allegretto: opens with ostinato figures that evolve into a melody; Più mosso section with forward motion; opening idea returns to close movement. Adagio: sustained, active melodic lines in piano, ends *pp.* Allegro: hemiola, much rhythmic vitality; ends *pp.* M-D.

Filippo Prover. *Sonata* II C (J. Cuiller—Editions I.M.D.371 1996) 8pp., parts, with basso. Adagio; Allegro; Menuetto. Binary forms. M-D.

Pierre Prowo. *Sonata* A (H. Ruf—Schott OBB36 1997, ISMN M-001-11309-0) 14pp., parts, with basso. Allegro; Aria–Andante; Gigue; Sarabande; Bourrée; Menuet. Composed in the style of a late Baroque Suite. All binary movements. Preface in English, German, and French. M-D.

György Ránki. *Don Quijote y Dulcinea* (EMB 1961) 12pp., parts. For piano or harpsichord and oboe. Andantino espressivo e rubato: arpeggiated 7th chords, chromatic *pp* ending. Allegretto grazioso e capriccio: $\frac{5}{8}$, dancelike, mordents, turns, short oboe cadenza, extreme ranges of keyboard near conclusion; sprightly idea concludes this attractive piece. M-D.

Sam Raphling. *Sonata* (Spratt 1967) 16pp., parts. One continuous movement with varied tempos, moods, and idioms. The style is generally flowing, and the textures are clear and thin. Freely tonal around F♯. M-D.

Franz Reizenstein. *Sonatina* (Lengnick 1942) 21pp., parts. 12 min. Allegretto; Cantilène; Vivace. Attractive, effective, melodic charm, cheerful and sometimes witty (for Reizenstein!). Last movement requires a fine octave technique. M-D.
See Petrus Jacobus Krige, "The Published Chamber Music for Woodwinds and Piano by Franz Reizenstein (1911–1968)," M.M. thesis, University of South Africa, 1982.

Verne Reynolds. *Three Elegies* (MCA 1970) 11pp., parts. Contrasted, solid 20th-century style. Effective individually or as a group. No.2 needs much facility from the pianist. Large span required. M-D.

Alan Richardson. *Aria and Allegretto* (JWC 1965) 8pp., parts. 6 min. Contrasting, mildly 20th-century, tonal but highly colored style. M-D.
———. *French Suite* (OUP 1949) 26pp., parts. 14 min. Rendezvous; Les Peupliers; Passepied; Causerie; Les Moulins. Mildly 20th-century, careful balance between the instruments. M-D.

Thomas Roseingrave. *Two Sonatas* 1728 (R. Platt—OUP, Musica da Camera 21 1975) 14pp., parts. Range of solo part suggests an oboe would be as suitable as the flute. See detailed entry under duos for piano and flute.

Edwin Roxburgh. *Images* (UMP 1973) 10pp. Two playing scores necessary. Sectional, pointillistic, clusters, aleatoric, strings played inside the piano. D.

Edmund Rubbra. *Sonata* Op.100 C (Lengnick 1959) 12½ min. Three movements, the first 2 lyrical, with flowing harmonies and florid melodic line. The cheerful and witty finale is a brilliant Presto with dashing scales for the pianist. Key signatures of 3 flats for the first movement and 4 flats for the last movement in spite of the title page that proclaims this is a "Sonata in C"! M-D.

Marcel Rubin. *Sonatine* 1927 (Dob 1973) 12pp., parts. 11 min. Three movements, "Gallic" sounding, mildly 20th-century, flexible meters. Int.

Camille Saint-Saëns. *Sonata* Op.166 D (Durand 1921) 19pp., parts. 11 min. Andantino; Allegretto; Molto allegro. Facile writing throughout, graceful Andantino, beautifully flowing Allegretto introduced with an ad libitum oboe recitative. One of the most outstanding works in the repertoire, full of ingenious charm. M-D.

Giuseppe Sammartini. *2 Sonatas* Op.2/4, 6 (H. Ruf—Schott FTR140 1988). For flute or oboe. See detailed entry under duos for flute and piano.
——. *Sonata* G (E. Rothwell, A. Gibilaro—JWC 1951) 12pp., parts. 9 min. Andante; Allegro assai; Andante lento; Allegro. Tasteful figured-bass realization. A favorite of the repertoire, both for performers and listeners. M-D.

Peter Schickele. *Gardens* 1968 (A. Broude 1975) 8pp., parts. 6 min. Morning: "Because each player is to proceed independently at his own tempo, the score alignment of the oboe and piano parts has no bearing on how the instruments will sound together" (Note in score); diatonic and chromatic scale figuration in upper register with pedal held throughout; repeated notes and sequences. Noon: traditional rhythmic alignment, gentle, thin textures. Night: damper pedal held down throughout until final bar; shifting rhythms; left hand repeats low D in quarter notes throughout; varied 16th-note figuration in right hand for duration of the movement. M-D.

Gustav Schreck. *Sonata* Op.13 F (G. Angerhöfer—Hofmeister 2320 1995) 28pp., parts. Allegro; Andante quasi allegretto; Allegro di molto. Follows the Classical line of development in the latter half of the 19th century without thick textures. M-D.

Gunther Schuller. *Sonata* 1948–51 (McGinnis & Marx 1960) 33pp., parts. 22 min. An early work showing broad sweeping melodic lines. Some Schoenberg and Hindemith influence detected. Schuller is always aware of the performer and shows, even at this early stage, a personal language and fine sense of compositional judgment. M-D.

Robert Schumann. *Three Romances* Op.94 1849 (G. Meerwein, K. Börner—Henle 427 1988; Br&H; CFP 2387; GS; K 4128), parts. Nicht schnell; Einfach, innig; Nicht schnell. Exquisite long lines with deeply felt emotion. One of the oboe's finest works with piano. May also be performed on violin or clarinet, see entry under duos for piano and clarinet. M-D.

Elliott Schwartz. *Second Thoughts* 1984 (ACA) 8½ min. Players perform from full score. "Materials are all derived from an early *Sonata* for solo oboe (now withdrawn) . . . contrasts between tonal, triadic passages and angular modernist gestures. Oboist plays into open piano" (Composer's letter to authors).

David Stanley Smith. *Sonata* Op.43 e (SPAM 1925-6) 37pp., parts. Allegro moderato; Vivace; Andante sostenuto–Allegro giocoso. Fluent writing that is mainly conceived in Romantic idiom and style. A few mildly 20th-century sounds are encountered. M-D.

Leo Sowerby. *Suite* H.390 1963 (R. M. Huntington—Leo Sowerby Foundation 1996) 33pp., parts. I. Whimsey; II. Chorale; III. Rondo. Thick chordal writing requiring a judicious use of the damper pedal. Transforms the older Suite form into an early-20th-century style with forms normally found in other settings. M-D.

Halsey Stevens. *Sonatina Piacevole* 1956 (PIC 1968) 12pp., parts. 4½ min. For alto recorder or flute or violin, and piano or harpsichord. With some modification, transposing the higher passages down an octave, it may also be played on the oboe. See detailed entry under duos for piano and flute.

William Grant Still. *Incantation and Dance* (CF 1955) 9pp., parts. Recitative-like opening, arpeggiated chords. Dance: increased tempo and more rhythmic push; slower, sustained mid-section before rhythmic section returns. Attractive and conservative style. M-D.

William Sydeman. *Variations* 1959 (Ione 1969) 20pp., parts. 12 min. For oboe and harpsichord or piano. Dynamic indications for piano are included. Marchlike theme punctuated with chromatic chords. Var.I: frenetic motion, ends with punctuated chords from theme. Var.II: quietly, expressive, long lines with chromatic and rhythmic quirks. Var.III: dancelike, large span required. Var.IV: keyboard alone. Var.V: with energy, forceful, moves over keyboard. Theme returns extended. Concludes with a Presto coda. D.

Antoni Szalowski. *Sonatina* 1946 (Amphion 1948) 15pp., parts. 9 min. Allegro non troppo; Adagio; Allegro. Three characteristics describe this work: Neoclassic style, Impressionist, and a little Poulencian wit included. Attractive with much audience appeal. M-D.

Georg Philipp Telemann. *Sonata* a (Degen—Br; Bleuzet—Leduc 1955) 6pp., parts. From *Der getreue Musikmeister.* Siciliana; Spirituoso; Andante; Vivace. Tasteful keyboard realization by P. Ruyssen. M-D.

———. *Sonata* e (R. Lauschmann—Sikorski 1955) 12pp., parts. Largo; Allegro;

Grave; Vivace. Good realization although the Largo has almost too much activity. M-D.

——. *Sonata* g (Ruyssen, Bleuzet—Leduc 1952) 11pp., parts. 8 min. Ouverture; Vivo; Sans Souci; Hornpipe; Gavotte; Passepied; Iriandaise. Very attractive. M-D.

——. *Sonata* g (Degen—Br). From *Der getreue Musikmeister.*

——. *Sonata* g (Hinnenthal—Schott 1948).

——. *Sonatas and Pieces* (D. Degen—HM 7). From *Der getreue Musikmeister.* For flute (violin or oboe) and continuo. Sonata a, Sonata g, L'hiver, Air Trompette, Niaise, Napolitana. M-D.

——. *Six Partitas* B♭, G, c, g, e, E♭ (W. Woehl—HM 47). For flute (violin or oboe) and continuo.

Tôn Thât Tiêt. *Cinq Pièces* 1965 (EMT 1967) 16pp., parts. Lento tranquillo; Vivo giocoso; Allegro moderato; Lento; Allegro. Strong Expressionist style; moves over keyboard; serial overtones; complex spots; rhythmic problems. D.

Joan Tower. *Opa Eboni* 1967 (ACA-CFE 1967) 27pp. 8 min. In 5 untitled movements intended to be performed as a set. Angular melodies with almost unrealistic expectations for oboe. Uses full range of keyboard. Score is copy of MS. D.

Burnet Tuthill. *Sonata* Op.24 (Spratt 1946) 20pp., parts. Allegro: short motivic ideas in first section contrasted with more sustained theme in second tonal area; tonal with 3 different key signatures; requires large span. Slowly: expressive, linear with some harmonic 3rds and 6ths, flowing. Rondo: gaily, vivacious rhythms, freely tonal around D, *pp* ending. M-D.

Vladimir Ussachevsky. *Triskelion* 1982 (CFP 67112 1988) 27pp., parts. 15 min. In 3 movements, the first 2 marked by metronome and the last "In the spirit of the Blues." The second movement contains an incredibly difficult oboe part with special fingerings for 4-note chords, some pitches flattened and some sharpened, presumably to be approximated as overtones without arpeggiation. Idealistic. Large span required for pianist with good counting ability. D.

Robert Valentine. *Sonata* I F (Lefkovitch, Bergmann—Schott 1952).

——. *Sonata* VIII G 1730 (Lefkovitch, Bergmann—Schott 1951).

Antonio Vivaldi. *Sonata* c (K. Meier—Amadeus BP843 1998) 11pp., parts, with basso. Adagio; Allegro; Andante; Allegro. Active realization. M-D.

——. *Sonata* RV34 B♭ (S. Caldini, F. Caldini—Br&H MR2258 2001, ISMN M-004-48804-1) 8pp., parts, with basso. Adagio; Allegro; Largo; Allegro. M-D.

——. *Sonata* RV28 g (S. Caldini—Br&H MR2275).

Thomas Attwood Walmisley. *Sonatine* (R. J. Koch—Schott OBB34 1989) 20pp., parts. Andante mosso; Allegro moderato.

David Ashley White. *L'isola di S. Michele* 1990 (ECS 5378 2000) 14pp., parts. Designed to be a Nocturne, the work opens fast and agitated with furious dramatic statements in both instruments. Calms to slow, quieter dynamics with a lyric, nearly angular melody in contrasting linear and homophonic textures. Bitonal and added-note harmonies dot the musical landscape. Concludes mysterious at *ppp* with oboe in upper register and piano in lower. D.

Jacques Christian Michel Widerkehr. *Duo Sonata* (J. Brown—Musica Rara 1974) 29pp., parts. Transposed to e, taken from Widerkehr's *Trois duos pour piano et violin ou hautbois* (Paris: Erard, 1817). M-D.

Charles Marie Widor. *Pavane* (ST SS-127) 3pp., parts. A turn-of-the-century perspective on the older dance form marked Andante tranquillo.

Alec Wilder. *Sonata* (Wilder Music W107 1969) 24pp., parts. 11 min. Cast "in four movements, each having a distinct character. The first movement is rhythmic and marcato with a lyrical second theme. In the middle of the movement is a rhythmically intricate section in constantly changing eighth-note meters. The second movement is a 'blues'—plaintive and expressive. The third movement beautifully combines six-eight and three-quarter cross rhythms, technical passages in sixteenth-notes, and a long flowing melody. The finale is in the jazz style typical of much of Alec Wilder's music. The movement is built on a strongly syncopated opening theme, introduced at the beginning, and expanded in a contrapuntal texture that later introduces other more lyrical elements—a waltz fragment and a long melodic line" (from Preface by Ronald Roseman). M-D.

Stefan Wolpe. *Sonata* 1937–41 (J. Marx—McGinnis & Marx 1991) 48pp., parts. Score completed by Patricia Spencer (b. 1943).

Charles Wuorinen. *Composition for Oboe and Piano* (CFP 1965) 34pp., parts. 15 min. Durational serialization, canonic writing, qualitative notation, difficult demands on both performers. Extreme registers exploited, numerous tempo and expression markings. D.

———. *Cycle of Elaborations* I (ACA) 11 min.

Duos for Piano and English Horn

Niels Viggo Bentzon. *Sonata* Op.71 (WH 3976 1955) 16pp., parts. 10 min. Hinde-mithian influence, poetic, reflective writing. Moderato: moving chromatic chords with a pedal point, chromatic scales and figuration, flexible meters, strong com-positional gestures. Moderato: quasi-recitative; rhythmic freedom in both in-struments; serves as introduction to short Largo that closes the movement; large span required. Allegro molto: nonlegato triplets, dancelike, alternating hands; Moderato coda with sustained chords in piano moving underneath a flowing English horn line. M-D.

Elliott Carter. *Pastoral* (Merion 1982) 15pp., parts. For viola, English horn, or clarinet and piano. See detailed entry under duos for piano and viola.

George Frideric Handel. *Sonata* g (IMC).
———. *Sonata* 4 D (IMC).

Paul Hindemith. *Sonata* 1941 (Schott) 19pp., parts. 11 min. One movement with 6 sections: Langsam, Allegro pesante, Moderato, Schnell (scherzo), Moderato, Allegro pesante. These sections serve as alternating variations on themes, somewhat similar in construction to the Haydn f *Variations* (H.XVII:6) for pi-ano solo. Melancholy atmosphere balanced with a brighter outlook. D.

Hans Huber. *Romanze* 1919 (Eulenberg 1973) 4pp., parts. Romantic harmonies, flowing lines for both instruments, expressive dynamic usage. Int. to M-D.

Charles Koechlin. *Au Loin* Op.20 1896 (ESC 1989) 4pp., parts. First version (par-tial) of the symphonic poem by the same title. Calm, quiet, and reflective with atmospheric mystique. M-D.
———. *Quatorze Pièces* Op.179 (ESC 1991). For oboe, oboe d'amour, or English horn. See detailed entry under duos for piano and oboe.

Humphrey Searle. *Gondoliera* Op.19 (Schott 1950) 4pp., parts. A rocking left hand in $\frac{6}{8}$ broken-chord form provides the basic accompaniment. This idea is based on Franz Liszt's *La lugubre Gondola,* first version. Chords in the right hand are gradually added to the melody already provided by the English horn. The unresolved final sonority adds color to this enigmatic little work. M-D.

Halsey Stevens. *Three Hungarian Folk Songs* 1950 (Highgate 1968). For viola (cello, English horn, or clarinet) and piano. See detailed entry under duos for piano and viola.

Richard Stoker. *Three Epigrams* 1968 (Leeds 1971) 7pp., parts. Succinct, related pieces in atonal series idiom. Fast-changing dynamics, pointillistic. No.II is more cantabile and sustained. Large span required. M-D.

Johannes Paul Thilman. *Kleine Sonata* Op.34 (Müller 1959).
———. *Tristan-Kontemplationen* (CFP 1973).

Duos for Piano and Clarinet

Ella Adaievsky. *Sonata Greque* (Tischler & Jangenberg 1913). Greek atmosphere, effective. M-D.

Samuel Adler. *Sonata* (ST 860 1990) 17pp., parts. In 3 broad sections, opening with clarinet solo marked "Slowly, but freely and very expressively," followed by a second section similar in character with piano, before concluding with "Fast and energetic," the largest of the 3 sections. Mixed rhythms abound in the conclusion as both instruments race to the finish at *ff.* M-D.

Josef Alexander. *Sonata* (Gen 1972). Three movements. Available in facsimile blueprint on special order.

Maarten Altena. *Bemidei* 1997 (Donemus 2000) 12pp., parts. 6½ min. For bass clarinet and piano. Begin; Midden; Eind. Movements 1 and 3 are instructed to be played brutally, loud, and rhythmic. Uses paper and light weights to dampen the strings; includes instructions. Minimalist in notes but abundant in rhythms in opening and closing. Uses extremes of instruments. Cluster chords. M-D.

William Alwyn. *Sonata* 1962 (Bo&H 19145) 25pp., parts. 12 min. One movement. Varied tempos and moods, tertial and quartal harmonies, ideas carefully worked over, freely tonal around E♭, martellato octaves, instrumental color strongly emphasized. M-D.

Violet Archer. *Sonata* (Waterloo 1972). Neoclassic, challenging, convincing. D.

Paul Arma. *Divertimento VI* (Lemoine 1956) 17pp., parts. 11 min. Allegretto: much imitation, colorful "alla zappa" broken 7th sonorities. Poco lento e rubato: recitative-like with piano mainly in a sustaining role. Allegro ben ritmato: toccata-like motion is contrasted with 2 meno mosso sections. Colorful writing. M-D.

Thomas Arne. *Sonata* B♭ (Craxton—OUP 1950). Two movements, appealing. Arrangement of a harpsichord Sonata. M-D.

Malcolm Arnold. *Sonatina* Op.29 (Lengnick 1951) 16pp., parts. 8 min. Three short movements, some interesting areas, light and witty. M-D.

Larry Austin. *Current* (CPE 1967) 11 min. New notation, avant-garde. Durations of single notes and/or groups of notes are determined in general by the visual space between notational indications. Pitch symbols for quarter tone higher and lower, clusters on black and white keys. Pointillistic, indications where ensemble is simultaneous. D.

Jacob Avshalomoff. *Sonatina* (Music Press 1947) 28pp., parts. Originally for viola, separate part for clarinet. Allegro appassionato: alternating open 5ths, arpeggio mainly diatonic. Lento: moving chords, pochissimo più mosso mid-section. Allegro con brio: driving rhythms with repeated octaves and chords; broken chromatic figuration; Tempo II is più mosso. M-D.

Grażyna Bacewicz. *Easy Pieces* [*Łatweutwory*] (PWM, ISBN 83-224-2780-8) 14pp., parts. Five untitled pieces of 1–3 pages each. Despite the title, these pieces are M-D.

Eduard Bagdasarian. *Sonata* (Yerevan—USSR Epietrat 1953). Charming, tuneful, folklike. Int.

Jesus Bal y Gay. *Sonata* 1946–47 (EMM 1953) 33pp., parts. Allegro; Adagio; Adagio–Allegro. Contains some glittering writing. Freely tonal, imitation, Neoclassic orientation. Large span required, some left-hand octave technique necessary for finale. M-D.

Jacques Bank. *Last Post* (Donemus 1975). For bass clarinet and piano. 2 scores, each 13pp. Photostat of composer's MS. Based on a text from *The Observer Review,* June 15, 1975.

Don Banks. *Prologue, Night Piece and Blues for Two* 1968 (Schott 11092) 9pp., parts. A third-stream work (traditional composition and performance concepts combined with those of jazz). Banks has had much experience as a jazz pianist and arranger. Prologue: trills, repeated chords, atonal, thin textures. Night Piece: arpeggio figuration sustained by pedal, expressive, *pp* dissonant chords. Blues for Two: rhythmic with a jazz feeling, syncopated chords, clarinet cadenza, clever left-hand bass treatment. M-D.

Ramón Barce. *Siala* (Editorial de Música Española Contemporánea 1975) 15pp., parts.

Marion Bauer. *Sonata* Op.22 (SPAM 1951). For viola or clarinet. See detailed entry under duos for piano and viola.

Arnold Bax. *Sonata* (Murdoch 1935) 20pp., parts. 12½ min. Two movements with the second more interesting than the first. Thick piano scoring. M-D.

See Charles Howard Willett, "The Use of the Clarinet in the Solo and Chamber Music of Arnold Bax," D.Mus. diss., Florida State University, 1996.

Alban Berg. *Four Pieces* Op.5 (UE 1913) 10pp., parts. 8 min. Mässig–Langsam; Sehr langsam; Sehr rasch; Langsam. Highly sensitive Expressionist writing. Includes characteristics of Berg's mature style even though these are somewhat early works. A major work in this medium. D.

See L. East, "A Background Study and Extended Analysis of Alban Berg's *Four Pieces for Clarinet and Piano,* Op.5," thesis, King's College (London), 1971; D. S. Lefkowitz, "Alban Berg's Op.5 Clarinet and Piano Pieces," Ph.D. diss., Eastman School of Music, 1994.

Arthur Berger. *Duo* 1957 (CFP 66693 1979) 19pp., parts. 8 min. Freely transcribed by the composer from his *Duo* for oboe and clarinet (1952). Restless with a barrage of expressive terms. Score is photocopy of MS. D.

James Bernard. *Sonatina* (OUP 1958) 8 min. Mattinata; Notturno; Danza. Loose development but contains some clever ideas. M-D.

Leonard Bernstein. *Sonata* (Witmark 1943) 20pp., parts. 11 min. Two movements in Neoclassic idiom, both rhythmically interesting. $\frac{5}{8}$ meter in finale with shifting rhythms from bar to bar. Enough dissonance to produce a stimulating effect; catchy tunes; last movement is pandiatonic. M-D.

Wallace Berry. *Fantasy in Five Statements* (CF W2447 1971) 8pp., parts. Larghissimo, con affetto: serial, quiet dynamic range, Expressionist, harmonics, pointillistic, ethereal sonorities. Allegro molto e scorrendo: nimble fingers required for this fleeting piece. Come un imagio fantastico: expressive, changing tempos and meter. Scherzoso: quiet and quick except for some shocking interruptions. Agitato–tempestoso: dramatic gestures, climactic for entire work, dynamic extremes. All 5 are Webernesque in style. D.

Harrison Birtwistle. *Verses* (UE 1966) 6pp., parts. Piano part is sempre una corda throughout entire work, which consists of 8 very short pieces. No.1 is one line long, No.2 is 2 lines, No.3 is one line, while Nos.4–8 are also short, no more than one page each. Pointillistic, serial, abstract. D.

Bruno Bjelinski. *Sonata* (Gerig 1966). Thoroughly 20th-century, well organized, strong thematic material. D.

Vladimir Blok. *Sonatina* (USSR 1965). Two movements, shifting harmonies, facile writing, mildly 20th-century. M-D.

John Boda. *Sonatina* (Delevan 1966). Two expertly crafted movements for both instruments. M-D.

François-Adrien Boieldieu and Giovanni Battista Gambaro. *Sonata* (M. Schlesinger 1820; McGinnis & Marx 1965). The opera composer Boieldieu was assisted by the clarinetist Gambaro. Allegro; Theme and Variations. Effective period writing. M-D.

Dimitri Bortiniansky. *Sonata* (USSR 1955). One movement, pleasant. M-D.

Eugene Bozza. *Sonatine* Op.27 (Leduc 1955). A delightful work with plenty of *joie de vivre!* M-D.

Johannes Brahms. *Sonaten* für Klavier und Klarinette oder Viola, Op.120 (M. Steegman—Henle 1974). Fingering for piano by Hans-Martin Theopold. 55pp., parts. Preface in German, English, and French. (Br&H; Bo&H; GS; Augener; H. Bading—CFP).
Available separately: Op.120/1 f 21 min., Op.120/2 E♭ 20 min. (H.-C. Müller, J. Michaels, E. Seiler—VU 1973; K 3200, 9255).
First published in 1895 together with an arrangement of the clarinet part for viola. VU edition contains critical notes and corrections and explains the variations between the original edition and the engraver's copy. Unfortunately these corrections and variations are not similarly noted in the score. Very good page turns in the piano part. These are the greatest Sonatas in the repertoire for the instrument.
———. *Two Sonatas* (Lea 7).
See P. Fan, "The Unashamed, Unabashed Clarinet's Accompanist and the Brahms *Sonatas,* Part I," *The Clarinet* 9/4 (1982): 22–25, Part II, *The Clarinet* 10/1 (1982): 26–27; G. Dobree, "Breaking the Mold: Reflections on the *Opus 120 Sonatas* by Brahms," *The Clarinet* 23/4 (1996): 38–40; J. M. Hall, "Performance Practice Issues in Johannes Brahms's *Sonata for Clarinet and Piano in F Minor, Opus 120, No. 1,*" D.M.A. diss., University of California, Los Angeles, 2000.

Paul Brink. *Three Songs for Clarinet* (JPM Music WW109 2000) 12pp., parts. I. March, II. Blues, III. Chase. Thin textures, playful with sentiment. M-D.

Victor Bruns. *Sonata* Op.22 (E. H. Elsberg 1951). A well-written work that is brilliant if played quickly; lengthy. M-D.
———. *Vier Stücke* Op.44 (Br&H 1972). Serious, sincere writing. D. Bruns's career as a bassoonist gives him a special insight for writing for wind instruments.

Norbert Burgmüller. *Duo* Op.15 (W. Lebermann—Schott 6151 1970) 15pp., parts. Early-19th-century stylistic character piece in ternary form with rolling broken chords, octave scales, and dramatic development. M-D.

Francis Burt. *Duo* 1954 (UE 12946 1962) 12pp., parts. 8½ min. In 2 large sections: Adagio–Allegro moderato and Allegro molto with Adagio coda. Solid 20th-century writing with numerous 20th-century idioms and devices effectively used, such as quartal harmony and free dissonant counterpoint. Piano is treated as an equal partner. Requires large span. M-D.

Ferruccio Busoni. *Frühe Charakterstücke* [*Early Character Pieces*] (G. Meerwein, K. Schilde—Henle 467 1991) 51pp., parts. Contains: *Andante con moto* K.72, *Suite* K.88, *Solo Dramatique* K.101, *Andantino* K.107, *Serenade* K.108, *Novellette* K.116. The *Suite* consists of 6 movements: Improvvisata (Impromptu), Barcarola, Elegia, Danza campestre, Tema variato, Serenata. Youthful works revealing a fondness for the clarinet (Busoni's father was a clarinetist) with involved piano scores hinting at some of the massive works which would come later in life. (K = Jürgen Kindermann, *Thematisch-chronologisches Verzeichnis der Werke von Ferruccio Busoni,* Regensburg, 1980.) M-D.

——. *Elegie* BV.286 1920 (Br&H 5188 1921) 4pp., parts. 4½ min. Rocking piano part with a few runs, tremolo, tonal in E. M-D.

——. *Reverie Pastorale* (Ric).

Charles Camilleri. *Divertimento* II 1957 (Fairfield 1973) 35pp., parts. 16 min. Three movements, jazz idioms. Preface and notes for the performer are supplied by Jack Brumer, the dedicatee. D.

Frank Campo. *Kinesis* 1950 (WIM 1969) 20pp., parts. This work, divisible in 3 parts, is a rondo in spirit if not in form. The first part consists of several more or less closely related subsections; the second part is contrasting; the third consists of a modified return of the first followed by a coda. The title is very appropriate in view of the motoric force (almost moto perpetuo) that propels the music on its course. Thin textures, freely tonal figuration and chords. Large span required. M-D.

Elliott Carter. *Pastoral* (NME 1945) 15pp., parts. For viola, English horn, or clarinet and piano. See detailed entry under duos for piano and viola.

Romeo Cascarino. *Sonata* 1947 (Bo&H) 12pp., parts. For bassoon or clarinet in A. See detailed entry under duos for piano and bassoon.

Mario Castelnuovo-Tedesco. *Sonata* Op.128 (G. Garbarino—Ric 132287 1977, ISMN M-041-32287-2) 50pp., parts. Andante con moto; Scherzo–Mosso leggero; Lullaby–Calmo e semplice; Rondò alla Napolitana. Of special interest is the Scherzo and the Rondo with their elegant themes, playful nature, and imitative treatment. M-D.

Jacques Castérède. *Sonate* (Leduc 1956) 22pp., parts. Con Moto: excellently crafted counterpoint, freely tonal, tremolo chords between hands with melody riding in top voice, octotonic. Scherzo: $\frac{6}{8}\frac{2}{4}$, bitonal, profuse use of triplets. Elegie: wistful melody, full sonorities in mid-section, chromatic, large span required. Allegretto tranquillo: poetic, long lines, clear textures, *pp* closing on E. M-D to D.

Liviu Comes. *Sonata* (Editura Muzicală Uniunii Compozitorilor 1967) 18pp., parts. For clarinet in A or B and piano.

Dinos Constantinides. *Impressions II* 1975, rev.1998 (Conners 1998) 18pp., parts. Revised version of *Impressions I.* Slow introduction with the clarinet playing some indeterminate pitches. Piano part calls for harmonics, plucked strings, clusters. Cluster-like sonorities freely repeated; waltz tempo is important. Colorful, atonal. M-D.

———. *Transformations* 1993 (Conners 132 1997) 26pp., parts. 13 min. Originally for clarinet solo, this work itself was transformed into additional versions, including this one for clarinet and piano. I. Castles in the Air, II. Recollections, III. Tender Conversation, IV. On the Playground. It "is based upon personal experiences and associations of the composer. In all versions, the entire composition is a constant transformation of a single motive that the composer remembers from his youth when he did some work as a violinist for the Greek Cinema. Divided into four parts, the piece portrays four different scenes of simple everyday happenings" (from Preface). M-D.

Arnold Cooke. *Sonata* (Nov 1962). Mildly 20th-century, pleasant. May not wear well. M-D.

Henry Cowell. *Six Casual Developments for Clarinet and Piano* (Merion 1949) 16pp., parts. Nos.II, IV, V, and VI are versions of Cowell's *Suite for Woodwind Quintet.* I. Rubato: syncopated; single line in left hand juxtaposed against right-hand chords. II. Andante: flowing arpeggiated figuration with melodic line embedded in piano texture, hemiola. III. Andante: no dynamics indicated, flexible meters, jazz rhythms, chromatic chords. IV. Allegro: jiglike, chromatic, sustained left-hand octaves throughout. V. Adagio cantabile: chromatic chorale treatment; requires a fine legato; $\frac{7}{4} \frac{5}{4}$ alternating meters. VI. Allegretto con moto: fugal, thin textures throughout, changing meters cleverly concealed. M-D.

———. *Three Ostinati with Chorales* (Music Press 1946) 16pp., parts. See detailed entry under duos for piano and oboe.

See Bruce C. Trible, "The Chamber Music of Henry Cowell," thesis, Indiana University, 1952.

Bernhard Henrik Crusell. *Introduction et Air Suédois Varié* (Billaudot 1981, ISMN M-043-03230-4) 11pp., parts. Opens with full chords and rapid passagework to introduce a simple Swedish melody and 5 fully developed variations. Hints at early Beethoven and abounds in expressiveness. M-D.

Ingolf Dahl. *Sonata da Camera* 1967–70 (Alexander Broude 1973) 27pp., parts. Alla Marcia; Romanza; Intermezzo Nuvoloso; Introduzione e Giga Finale. Chromatic and freely tonal but tonalities firmly controlled. Chords in alternating hands, open textures, flexible rhythms. Virtuoso instrumental writing for both performers, glissandi on strings with fingernail, crossed hands, large span required. D.

Faraele D'Allessandro. *Sonatina* (Sidem Verlag 1956). Waltz; Habanera; Guagira; Rhumba. Four rhythmically interesting, light dance movements. M-D.

Franz Danzi. *Sonate* B♭ (J. Wojciechowski, H. Geuser—Simrock 3077 1960) 28pp., parts. Allegro; Andante sostenuto; Allegretto. Classical principles are applied for a well-balanced work of integrity and refinement. M-D.

Peter Maxwell Davies. *Sonata* 1956–57 (JWC 55902 1989) 30pp., parts. 25 min. A tightly knit composition where "the closely argued Moderato first movement leads to a great climax near the end. The succeeding Allegro, which includes a clarinet cadenza, is of scherzo character, while the final movement is a rhapsodic Allegro" (from Preface). Proportional rhythmic relationships. D.

———. *Hymnos 'Ymnos esperinos'* 1967 (Bo&H 1970) 2 scores, each 21pp. Nine sections in groups of 3. Dramatic treatment, pointillistic, avant-garde, complex, harmonics, dynamics and pitch serialized, bell-like sonorities. Palm and arm clusters splash around the keyboard; piano frequently overshadows clarinet; ensemble problems in No.4. Large span required. D.

Claude Debussy. *Première Rapsodie* (Durand 1910 12pp.; G. Garbarino—Ric 1989; K 9940), parts. 8 min. Flexible 2 with 3, tremolo octaves. Shimmering mood must be captured. Most complex problem is ensemble. Requires much experience of both players. K. edition includes *Petite Pièce*. M-D to D.
See D. Nygren, "Debussy's Works for Clarinet," *The Clarinet* 12/1 (1984): 40–42.

René Défossez. *Sonatina* (Editions Metropolis). Imaginative writing with a highly rhythmic finale. M-D.

Edison Denissow. *Sonate* 1993 (DVFM 8176 1995) 34pp., parts. 17 min. Agitato: rapid scalar passagework often set in proportional rhythmic relationships. Moderato: extensive use of repeated notes covering the full range of both instruments. Requires experienced performers to realize the composer's intentions. Ranges dynamically from *pppp* to *sff* but tends to stay at soft levels. D.

Ignacy Feliks Dobrzyński. *Duo* (A. Nowak-Romanowicz, L. Kurkiewicz—PWM 1197) 43pp., parts. "In this *Duet* Dobrzyński is still closely linked with the heritage of the classics. Each of the three movements is based in its structure on the classical model, yet it already reveals a quest for new solutions, both in form and means of expression" (from Preface). M-D.

Anthony Donato. *Sonata* (ST SS-766 1967) 20pp., parts. Allegro moderato: minor 2nds and major 7ths preferred, some imitation. Andante: pointillistic, rhythmic flexibility needed. Allegro: strong rhythmic writing. Twentieth-century dissonantal treatment. First-rate pianism required throughout. D.

Matt Doran. *Sonata* 1963 (WIM 1967) 43pp., parts. Allegretto: Andante; Allegro vivace. Doran writes about this work on WIM Records WIMR. I: "It develops along rather conventional lines—in contrast with many of today's trends—

and uses themes, motives, transitions, modifications of previously presented ideas and even such formal ideas of the old school as development sections and recapitulations." Freely tonal, shifting meters, quartal and quintal harmony, imitation. Bold, forceful writing. Large span required. D.

Pierre Max Dubois. *Sonatina* (Leduc 1956) 16pp., parts. Misterioso: much activity for the pianist, myriad notes! Vif et léger: humorous; triplets used profusely. Calmo: more Impressionist, parallel chords, *pp* closing. Witty and decorative chromatic writing. M-D to D.

Clyde Duncan. *Sonatina* (E. H. Morris 1955) 20pp., parts. Entertaining, fluent, bright and tuneful writing, a well-made piece. Int. to M-D.

Alvin D. Etler. *Sonata* 1952 (AMP) 15 min. Four well-written and contrasted movements. M-D.
——. *Sonata* No.2 (AMP 1960). Thoroughly 20th-century treatment with much dissonance, difficult ensemble problems. D.

Richard Faith. *Two Sea Pieces* (IU). Nocturne: flowing, arpeggio changing meters, Neo-Romantic. Capriccio: ABA design, 8th-note chordal figuration prominent in A section, B section more sustained; short "spurting" motive permeates A section; clever closing with long pedal and crescendo. M-D.

Václav Felix. *Sonata da Requiem* Op.30 1969 (Panton) 24pp., parts. For horn or bass clarinet and piano.

Gerald Finzi. *Five Bagatelles* (Bo&H 8903 1945) 21pp., parts. I. Prelude, II. Romance, III. Carol, IV. Forlana, V. Fughetta. Picturesque settings of modest durations. Can be technically involved though tends to flow gently. M-D.

Grant Fletcher. *Sonata* (AME 1958). Fluent 20th-century writing. M-D.

Arthur Roland Frackenpohl. *Sonatina* (GS 1970). Good structural sense, consistent musical style and substance. M-D.

Jean Françaix. *Tema con variazioni* (ESC 1974) 15pp., parts. 7 min. Delightful, clever, witty, successful. M-D.
See Margaret A. Donaghue, "The Chamber Music of Jean Françaix: A Clarinetist's Perspective," D.M.A. diss., University of Illinois at Urbana-Champaign, 1996.

Gunter Friedrichs. *Hommage à Anton Webern. Variationen* (Bo&Bo). Serious, intense, pointillistic, complex. D.

Witold Friemann. *Quasi una Sonata* (PWM 1953). Solid post-Romantic style with an expressive, lyric slow movement and a Polish dance finale. M-D.

Niels W. Gade. *Fantasias* Op.43 (JWC) 19pp., parts for clarinet and (violin). 13 min. Andantino con moto; Allegro vivace; Ballade–Moderato; Allegro molto vivace. Lush, Romantic writing for both instruments. M-D.

Hans Gál. *Sonata* Op.84 (Hin 1965). Post-Romantic with some mildly 20th-century sonorities. M-D.

Antony Garlick. *Sonata* (Seesaw 1970). Polytonal, clever, tart. M-D.

Harald Genzmer. *Sonatina* (Litolff 1968) 24pp., parts. 14 min. Introduction and 3 mildly 20th-century movements. Interesting melodic writing. M-D.
———. *Sonata* 1997 (Litolff/CFP 8971 1999) 32pp., parts. 15 min. Allegro; Tranquillo; Vivace leggiero; Presto. Coloristic with broadly changing rhythmic patterns. Requires fine command of both staccato and legato techniques in the Vivace, a movement almost exclusively quiet. M-D.

Edwin Gerschefski. *Sonatine* Op.18 (CFE 1935). Two short movements. Thin textures. M-D.

Anthony Gilbert. *Spell Respell* Op.14 (Schott 1973) 2 playing scores, 16pp. each. In 3 cycles. Long silences between chords characterize the first cycle; second is highly embellished; third is very thick in texture. Written for a clarinet with an extended lower range down to C, a "basset clarinet." Effective suggestions for amplification given. M-D.

Alexander Goehr. *Fantasias* Op.3 1952 (Schott 10509) 18pp., parts. 12 min. Three pieces in post-Schoenberg tradition. Concentrated, dense, many details, pointillistic, atonal, complex rhythms, dynamic extremes. Large span required. D.

Mikołaj Górecki. *Sonata* 1993–94 (PWM 2000, ISBN 83-224-3337-9) 44pp., parts. 25 min. Tranquillo; Molto energico; Lento–Poco più mosso. Dense chordal structure and asymmetric rhythms with unusual meters (e.g., $\frac{3}{8} + 5$) give the work thunderous quality in loud sections and nebulous uneasiness in quiet sections. Requires much experience for successful performances. D.

Percy Grainger. *Album for Clarinet and Piano* (GS 3866). Includes: Irish Tune from County Derry; Dublin Bay; Horkstow Grange; The Brisk Young Sailor; The Lost Lady Found; Australian Up-Country Tune; Country Gardens; Ye Banks and Braes O'Bonnie Doon; Molly on the Shore.

Alexander T. Gretchaninov. *Sonata* Op.161 (USSR).
———. *Sonata* Op.171 (USSR 1949). Delightful writing with a colorful set of variations. Satisfying conclusion. Facile pianism required. M-D.

Sofia Gubaidulina. *Dots, Lines, and Zigzag* [*Punkte, Linien und Zickzack*] 1976 (Sikorski 1870 1995, ISMN M-003-02733-3) 15pp., parts. 10 min. For bass clarinet and piano. "At the beginning the clarinettist sits at the piano instead of the pianist, and depresses the right pedal until fig. 15. At fig. 15 the pianist appears and plays on the piano strings. At fig. 24 the pianist sits down at the piano, and the clarinettist moves to his appointed place facing the audience" (from Preface). Determinate and indeterminate writing within a controlled environment. Imaginative. M-D.

Iain Hamilton. *Three Nocturnes* Op.6 (Schott 10194 1951) 19pp., parts. 12 min. Adagio mistico: bitonal, major 7th chords over moving octaves in left hand, arpeggi gestures, cadenza-like figuration; 20th-century Romantic idiom noted in the outer pieces. Allegro diabolico: syncopated chords in piano support unraveling chromatic fiorituras in clarinet; piano figuration includes melody line; chords in alternating hands; tremolo; percussive treatment of piano; large span required. Lento tranquillo: solo clarinet opening in a free style; low pedal-octaves in piano plus some melody ornamented with atonal figures; tranquil mood dominates. Strong sense of proportion and design. M-D.

Heinz Friedrich Hartig. *Sonata* Op.7 (Bo&Bo 1952) 12pp., parts. Praeambulum; Scherzo; Molto moderato; Rondo. Well-crafted Neoclassic writing throughout. M-D.

Walter Hartley. *Metamorphoses* 1975 (Ethos). 7½ min.
——. *Sonatina Romantica* 1994 (Ethos). 7 min.
——. *Sonorities IX* 1997 (Ethos). 4 min.

Bernard Heiden. *Sonatina* 1935 (AMP 1957) 17pp., parts. 10 min. Charming, straightforward, some brilliance. M-D.

Samuel Frederich Heine. *Sonata* Op.13 ca.1805 (L. Merriman—ST). One of the earliest Sonatas in the literature. Three movements, Classical style, lengthy. Solid keyboard writing. M-D.

Richard Hervig. *Sonata* II 1970 (Columbia University Press) 23pp. In 2 movements, both characterized by wide leaps and a restless quality. M-D to D.

Edward Burlingame Hill. *Sonata* Op.32 1927 (SPAM). Attractive and tuneful if somewhat dated writing. For A clarinet. M-D.

Paul Hindemith. *Sonata* 1939 (Schott) 28pp., parts. 18 min. Mässig bewegt; Lebhaft; Sehr langsam; Kleines rondo. Fine energetic writing in Hindemith's later expressive style. Strong mood contrasts. Each movement ends at a quiet dynamic level. D.

Alun Hoddinott. *Sonata* Op.50 1967 (OUP 0-19-3571447) 24pp., parts. 11 min. Cadenza; Aria; Moto Perpetuo. Complex rhythmically and technically. The finale involves fast chromatic octotonic writing, alternating hands, and long sustained chords. Large span required. D.
——. *Sonata* II (Oriana). 18 min.

Franz Anton Hoffmeister. *Sonata* (Musica Rara) for A clarinet. 27pp., parts. Allegro; Adagio ma non troppo; Allegretto. Charming and captivating. M-D.

Arthur Honegger. *Sonatine* A 1921–22 (Rouart Lerolle 1925) 11pp., part for A clarinet. Also available for cello and piano. Modéré: chromatic, well crafted. Lent et soutenu: intense individual writing. Vif et rythmique: uses jazz idioms;

fun to play. This work seems to be more effective in the piano-clarinet version. See further description under duos for piano and cello.

Katherine Hoover. *Ritual* 1989 (Papagena 1991) 24pp., parts. Inspired from studies of Greek folk music and the use of the clarinet in this tradition. "*Ritual* is in one movement with three distinct parts. The first consists mostly of isolated gestures; a sort of recitative. This moves into a mournful, measured duet that builds in steady motion to a climax that recalls some of these opening gestures. This is followed by a fast, at times almost frenzied dance, with a more obvious relationship to the Greek materials" (Composer's Notes). M-D.

Joseph Horovitz. *Sonatina* 1981 (Nov 120541 1982, ISBN 0-85360-287-5) 24pp., parts. 15 min. Allegro calmato; Lento, quasi andante; Con brio. The work "is lighthearted and follows a traditional pattern of the three movement division. The first, in classical sonata form, concentrates on the middle register of the clarinet, mainly lyrical against a rippling piano background. The second movement is an A-B-A song structure employing some of the lowest notes of the wind instrument in a long cantilena over a slow chordal accompaniment. The finale is a kind of rondo which alternates two themes in equal proportions, exploiting the upper register of the clarinet. The harmonic idiom of the whole work is obviously tonal, and . . . much influenced by Jazz and other popular music. It calls for equal virtuosity from both players" (from Programme Note). M-D.

Herbert Howells. *Sonata* 1946 (Bo&H 1954) 19 min. Con moto, dolce e con tenerezza; Allegro, ritmico, con brio. Brilliant writing for both instruments; requires imaginative projection. Fresh, attractive, spontaneous. Has a rhythmic springiness about it. D.

Karl Hoyer. *Sonata* Op.55 (Friedrich Portius 1934). A Romantic work worthy of performance.

Alexandru Hrisanide. *Sonata* (Editura Muzicală a Uniunii Compozitorilor din RPR 1964) 18pp., parts. Mosso: folk idiom influence felt in colorful rhythms and melodies, sprinkled with dissonance; pianist has the main workout. Calmo ma assai mosso: for solo clarinet; a virtuoso display. Lento, rubato molto precipitato: great freedom, musical sonorities; very short, only 2 pages. M-D.

Jacques Ibert. *Histoires* (G. Deplus—Leduc 29552 2004). 19 min. Arr. of the famous solo piano collection by Guy Deplus. Includes 8 of the original 10 pieces. M-D.

——. *Aria* (Leduc), parts. 4 min. Transcription preserving the parts identically to the original for voice and piano with only slight changes in phrasing. Large span required. M-D.

John Ireland. *Fantasy-Sonata* (Bo&H 1943) 22pp., parts. 14 min. One movement that exploits the wide range of the clarinet. Superb piano writing. M-D.

Gordon Jacob. *Sonatina* (Nov 1949) 22pp., parts. 12 min. For viola or clarinet (in A) and piano. See detailed entry under duos for piano and viola.

Gustav Jenner. *Sonata* Op.5 (Amadeus; Br&H 1900). For A clarinet. In tradition of Brahms, with whom Jenner studied. M-D.

Rudolph Jettel. *Sonata* (Hofmeister 1953) 30 min. Solid post-Romantic writing. M-D.

Thomas Arnold Johnson. *Scherzo* (British & Continental 1973) 8pp., parts. Bucolic, short, a good encore. Int.
———. *Pastorale* (British & Continental) 3 min. M-D.

Betsy Jolas. *Petites Musiques de Chevet* 1989 (Billaudot 1992) 7pp., parts. 4 min. For bass clarinet. In 9 short picturesque sections of bedside music connected by brief pauses. Colorful capsules of musical thought. M-D.

Paul Juon. *Sonata* Op.82 (Schlesinger 1925). One long movement of interesting but busy writing. M-D.

Mauricio Kagel. *Rrrrrrr—: Fünf Jazzstücke für Klarinette* (Litolff 8668 1992) 21pp., parts. 9 min. Five pieces in jazz style: Rackett; Rrrrrrr; Reeds; Rrrrrrr, old/new; Riff. May also be played on bass clarinet or alto saxophone.

Ivan Karabyts. *Disco—Round Dance* (Duma 1997) 16pp., parts. Flashy with a complete focus on rhythm. Opens with a penetrating syncopated pattern and melody at Allegro which is only briefly relaxed midway through. Some idiomatic problems for both instruments. Requires rhythmically apt performers. D.

Sigfrid Karg-Elert. *Sonata* Op.139b (Zimmermann 1924). Expressive, incisive writing, many notes! D.

Donald Keats. *Sonata* 1948 (AMC) 32pp., parts. Allegro con spirito; Andante; Presto. Freely tonal around C, octotonic, frequent use of harmonic 4ths and 7ths, songlike Andante, strong driving rhythms in Presto, quiet ending. M-D.

Talivaldis Kenins. *Divertimento* (Bo&H). Three movements of effective and imaginative writing. Piano part is reminiscent of Kabalevsky. D.

Stefan Kisielewski. *Sonata* 1972 (PWM) 26pp., parts.
———. *Intermezzo* (PWM 1955, ISBN 83-224-2111-7) 12pp., parts. 3 min. M-D.

Charles Koechlin. *Sonata* I Op.85 1923 (L'OL 1947; Billaudot 1993 16pp., parts). 9 min. Allegro bien décidé et rythmé; Andante quasi adagio; Final–Allegro moderato sans lenteur, bien allant mais sans précipiter le rythme. Distinctive and sensitive writing. D.

————. *Sonata* II Op.86 1923 (Billaudot 1991) 19pp., parts. 5½ min. Allegro bien moderato; Andante con moto; Allegro sans traîner. Expressive score with many descriptive indications. Sonorous ending with chords stretching nearly the full length of the keyboard. D.

————. *14 Pièces* Op.178 1942 (Billaudot 1992) 48pp., parts. 24 min. For B♭, C, or A clarinet. Fourteen untitled pieces of 1–3 min. in varying levels of difficulty, some consisting of a single line for the piano while others require 3 staves to notate. Elem. to M-D.

Both *Sonatas* were later orchestrated by the composer.

Ellis Kohs. *Sonata* (Mer 1956). For A clarinet. Excellently crafted, thoroughly 20th-century. M-D.

Barbara Kolb. *Related Characters* 1980 (Bo&H 1985). See detailed entry under duos for piano and viola.

Leo Kraft. *Five Pieces* 1962 (Gen 1970) 16pp., parts. Prelude; Intermezzo; Capriccio; Fantasia; Tarantella. Serial. Titles capture mood of individual pieces. Flexible meters, abstract serious style. Large span required. M-D.

Mikhail Krein. *Two Pieces* (MCA 1957) 16pp., parts. Nocturne: chromatic, serious cantabile style, freely tonal; large span required. Scherzo: outer sections mainly rhythmic; moderato mid-section gives some dynamic and melodic contrast. Style à la Prokofiev. M-D.

Ernst Křenek. *Sonatine* 1938–39 (Belwin-Mills). For bass clarinet.
————. *Suite* (BB 1955) 5 min.

A. F. Kropfreiter. *Aphorismen* (Dob 1970) 11pp., parts. Five pieces. Simultaneous seconds (major and minor) featured in piano part; free-flowing clarinet part. M-D.

Gail Kubik. *Sonatina* (MCA 1971). Mildly 20th-century, neo-Romantic characteristics, enchanting writing. Contains a few ensemble problems. M-D.

Jos Kunst. *No Time at All* (Donemus 1973). For bass clarinet and piano. 2 playing scores, 17pp. each. Reproduction of composer's MS. "My aim was to organize meanings and formal effects in such a way that these combinations would produce radical changes in as many elements, details and long-distance effects as possible" (composer in *Key Notes* 2 [1975]: 50).

Osvaldo Lacerda. *Valsa-Choro* 1962 (IU) 8pp., parts. A kind of tour de force treatment in waltz style, chromatic idiom, much hemiola, convincing writing. M-D.

Ezra Laderman. *Sonata* (OUP 1970) 11½ min. Strong formal structure, inventive thematic material, simultaneous major and minor triads. D.

Paul Ladmirault. *Sonate* (Leduc 1949) 18pp., parts. 14 min. Allegro: begins in f, other sections in C, e, F, and returns to f; flowing lines; free counterpoint between clarinet and upper voice of piano part. Andante: A♭, chorale-like, variations. Intermède: C, wistful melody, attacca. Finale: f–F, short motifs developed. Refined and poetic writing with folk song influence throughout. M-D.

Henri Lazarof. *Adieu* (Merion 1976) 11pp., parts. The first portion of the work is to be played on the bass clarinet, the remainder on the B♭ clarinet. D.

Roman Semenovich Ledenev. *Sonata* Op.1 (USSR 1960). Three movements of robust writing, special rhythmic treatment. M-D.

Jean Xavier Lefevre. *Sonata* B♭ Op.12/1 1804–1805 (G. Dobrée-OUP 1973) 16pp., parts. 12 min. Allegro moderato; Adagio; Rondo. Displays graceful bravura and melodic charm. M-D.

——. *Sonata* e (Edition du Siècle Musical 1949).

——. *Sonata* III B♭ (Borrel—Richli 1951).

——. *Sonata* V d (Viollier—Richli 1949) 5 min.

——. *Sonata* VII g (M. Claude—Billaudot 1974) 10pp., parts.

Victor Legley. *Sonata* Op.4/3 (CeBeDeM 1959). Well-developed writing with strong ideas. M-D.

Frank Levy. *Sonata* (Seesaw 1968). Emphasis on intervallic development. Strong dissonant writing. D.

Franz Liszt. *Romance Oubliée* S.132. See detailed entry under duos for piano and viola.

Otto Luening. *Fantasis Brevis* (Merion 1937) 6pp., parts. One movement, Neoclassic influence. Slowly, piano gives out rhythmic motif in chords, imitation. Più mosso section introduces repeated chords in piano. Varied tempos, pedal through last 4 bars diffuses closing. D.

Witold Lutoslawski. *Dance Preludes* (PWM 1956; JWC 1972) 19pp., parts. 7 min. Five contrasting dance pieces using many 20th-century compositional techniques. Effective writing for both instruments. An outstanding group. D.

Elisabeth Lutyens. *Valediction (Dylan Thomas, Dec. 1953)* Op.28 (Belwin-Mills 1958) 9pp., parts. 10 min. Lento appassionato, quasi fantasia: serial, heavy chords, atonal, changing dynamics, rhythmic and textural sonorities. Tema– Lento tranquillo, quasi variazione: intense, concentrated writing, tremolo, on the quiet side, ingenious and complex. M-D to D.

Donald Martino. *Sonata* 1951 (Dantalian 502 1979) 23pp., parts. 13 min. Allegro deciso; Grave; Andante cantabile–Con brio. Motivic development interchanged extensively between instruments in opening movement. Homophonic slow movement leads to lively conclusion. Mildly 20th-century style. M-D.

———. *Concertino: Fantasia per clarino nell' Opera 'Un Ballo in Maschera' di G. Verdi* (Dantalian 901 2000) 16pp., parts. Adaptation by Martino from the 1900 manuscript for clarinet and orchestra by Pietro Musone. M-D.

———. *Divertimento on G. Verdi's Opera 'La Forza del Destino' by E. Cavallini* (Dantalian 903 1999) 16pp., parts. Adaptation by Martino from an 1876 manuscript for clarinet and band. M-D.

Jean Martinon. *Sonatine* 1935 (Billaudot 1972) 16pp., parts. Allegro leggiero–Larghetto–Vivace; performed attacca. Spirited and well marked, with subtleties of expression marked by grace notes and touch. M-D.

Bohuslav Martinů. *Sonatine* 1956 (Leduc) 15pp., parts. 10½ min. Moderato; Allegro; Andante; Poco allegro. Well written in an accessible pleasant style, but there are difficult spots. French influence is strong; Czech dance rhythms appear in last section. Pandiatonic usage. D.

Daniel Gregory Mason. *Sonata* Op.14 c (SPAM 1920) 59pp., parts. Con moto, amabile; Vivace ma non troppo; Allegro moderato. Strong post-Romantic style, broad sweeping melodies, Brahmsian idiom with influence of d'Indy. Scherzo is based on the whole-tone scale. Effective writing for both instruments. D.

Felix Mendelssohn. *Sonata* E♭ 1824 (MCA 1941; Simon—GS 1951). Adagio–Allegro moderato; Andante; Allegro moderato. Good ensemble piece but not too exciting. M-D.

Paul-Baudouin Michel. *Delitation* I 1968 (CeBeDeM). For bass clarinet and piano. 11 min.

———. *Sonatine* 1960 (CeBeDeM) 10 min.

———. *Silhouette* (CeBeDeM 1991) 6pp., parts. 5 min.

Marcel Mihalovici. *Sonata* Op.78 (Heugel 1959) 16½ min. Hindemith influence. Requires fine rhythmic ensemble. D.

Darius Milhaud. *Sonatine* 1927 (Durand 1929) 15pp., parts. 9 min. Très rude: fiercely dissonant, terse and crisp. Lent: most appealing movement. Très rude: outer movements are thematically related. An exciting work for both performers. M-D.

———. *Duo Concertant* 1956 (Heugel) 11pp., parts. 7 min. A short one-movement work in basically a dry, humorous style. Parallel chords, scales in 6ths, freely tonal. M-D.

———. *Caprice* (Billaudot 1998) 4pp., parts. 2 min. Spry and witty with a capricious theme distinguished by scalar runs and "hiccup" skips. M-D.

See Robert Louis Petrella, "The Solo and Chamber Music for Clarinet by Darius Milhaud," D.M.A. diss., University of Maryland, College Park, 1979.

Albert Moeschinger. *Sonatina* Op.65 (Bo&H 1947). Finale is the strongest movement. M-D.

Wolfgang Amadeus Mozart. *Grande Sonate* A (F.-G. Hölÿ—Kunzelmann GM 503 1996) 30pp., parts. An arrangement of the *Quintet* K.581 published in 1809 which seems to have been made by the composer himself. Allegretto; Larghetto; Menuetto; Allegretto con variationi. Convincing. M-D.

Iwan Müller. *Serenade: 6 Easy Pieces* ca.1844 (D. Klöcker—Schott KLB46, ISMN M-001-12385-3) 20pp., parts. I. Valse, II. Amabile, III. Grazioso quasi andantino, IV. Romance, V. Rondo, VI. Troubadour. Miniatures reflecting early Romanticism in music. Nos.1–3 are in da capo form. These pieces were very popular during the 19th century. Preface in German, English, and French. M-D.

Vaclav Nelhybel. *Song for Kelley* 1985 (Pocono 2504 1998) 4pp., parts. Commissioned by a friend whose daughter Kelley died tragically at the age of 20, the work is a nostalgic remembrance. Adagio with deeply felt melodic lines and warm, sensitive harmonies. M-D.

Roger Nixon. *Music for Clarinet and Piano* (Fallen Leaf 1986) 26pp., parts. Five nondescript pieces reflecting a variety of 20th-century influences. I. Largo, poco rubato, II. Allegro, III. Quasi fantasia larghetto, IV. Adagio, V. Allegro scherzando. Intense, but expressive. M-D.

Roger North. *Sonata* 1951, rev.1953 (JWC 1959) 24pp., parts. 12 min. Allegro; Larghetto; Allegro di molto. Complex, rhythmic problems, flowing dissonant counterpoint. Thorough musicianship required in this Neoclassically oriented work. D.

Léon Orthel. 5 *Pezzettini* Op.46 (Donemus 1974) 11pp., parts. Photostat of MS.

Hans Osieck. *Sonatine* 1952 (Donemus), parts. For viola or clarinet and piano. See detailed entry under duos for piano and viola.

Juan Carlo Paz. *Composición en los 12 Tonos* Op.32 (NME 1943) 12pp., parts. 1. Toccata; 2. Tema con variaciones; 3. Canción; 4. Tempo di giga. Twelve-tone techniques explored; serious, taut construction. Tema contains the most interest. M-D.

Krzysztof Penderecki. *Three Miniatures* 1956 (PWM 1959/93, ISBN 83-224-1994-5) 10pp., parts. Allegro: scherzando, chromatic. Andante cantabile: flowing, large span required. Allegro ma non troppo: energetic, rhythmic, full chords, fast repeated chords, driving. M-D.

George Perle. *Sonata quasi una fantasia* (TP 1972) 23pp., 10½ min. 2 copies required. One continuous movement. Clarinetist required to use a mute at one place. A few multiple sounds are also indicated. Many meter changes. Beautifully printed score. Written in a kind of nonserial Stravinsky style. Tricky and brittle writing but not overly difficult for pianist. M-D.

Gabriel Pierné. *Canzonetta* Op.19 (Leduc) 5pp., parts, also transcribed for alto saxophone. A charming work of elegance and sophistication in ⁶⁄₈ at an Andantino moderato tempo. M-D.

Boris Pillin. *Sonata* 1965 (WIM 1968) 30pp., parts. Numerous high notes for clarinet, good linear writing, freely tonal, conceived along Classical lines. The principal element in the work, more salient than any individual theme, is the quasi-cyclic transformation in the outer movements of a "motto" consisting of an easily identified bitonal harmonic progression. Allegro: strict SA; second subject differs in tempo from the first. Adagio: ABA; first section broadly lyric, second more animated and dancelike. Allegro molto: combination of Scherzo–Finale, rondo, jagged and disjunct in character. Large span required. D.

Daniel Pinkham. *Sonata* (ACA 1946, rev.1952) 10 min. Allegro moderato; Adagio molto semplice; Allegro deciso. Contains an outstanding finale. D.

Paul A. Pisk. *Sonata* Op.59 1947 (CFE 1951). Serious, angular writing with much dissonance. D.

Ignaz J. Pleyel. *Sonata* Op.1 (Imbault 1801).
———. *Sonatas* Opp.2, 3 (Leduc 1791; Darmstadt Library).

Marcel Poot. *Sonatine* (Leduc 1965) 14pp., parts. 8 min. One movement, contrasting sections, octotonic, freely tonal, parallel chords, Concerto style, Neoclassic. M-D.

Francis Poulenc. *Sonata* (JWC 1962) 5th rev. ed. 1974. 24pp., parts. 13 min. Allegro Tristamente; Romanza; Allegro con fuoco. All of Poulenc's powers of charm and entertainment are brought together in this work. D.

William Presser. *Sonatina* 1978 (Tenuto T258 1984) 16pp., parts. 9½ min. Andante; Adagio; Allegro. Thin textures, translucent, some surprising harmonies. M-D.

Ebenezer Prout. *Sonata* Op.26 (Augener 1886). For A clarinet. Brilliant and graceful, late Classical style. M-D.

Francis J. Pyle. *Sonata* E♭ "From the Middle Border" (WIM 1969) 31pp., parts. Allegretto con Moto; Andante; Allegro e brilliante. Strong formal structure, serious and effective writing. Ensemble problems especially in the slow movement. Wide dynamic range, freely tonal, Neoclassic. Large span required. D.

Priaulx Rainier. *Suite* 1943 (Schott 1949). For A clarinet. 25pp., parts. 16 min. Vivace: harmonic 2nds, octaves in alternating hands, hemiola, freely tonal, cross-rhythms, repeated notes against quick rhythmic figures, octotonic, driving climactic close. Andante come da lontano: freely tonal melody in clarinet over repeated rhythmic patterns in piano used repetitively and cumulatively. Spiritoso: driving repeated patterns built on augmented 4ths and 5ths. Lento e tranquillo: individual use of triadic tonality, sustained low octaves under moving varied figuration. Allegro con fuoco: driving rhythmic repeated patterns, parallel chords, percussive piano texture. M-D.

Nicolai Rakov. *Sonata* 1956 (USSR 1958). Two movements, the first well developed, the second not as effective. Fast tempo helps second movement. M-D.

Gunther Raphael. *Sonata* Op.65/3 (Br&H 1951) 22pp., parts. Requires humor and strong projection. Final movement is preceded by a verse: "Not for the cat—but for a duck did I compose the final movement." M-D.

Max Reger. *Sonata* Op.49/1 A♭ (UE 1901; K 2158). For A clarinet.
——. *Sonata* Op.49/2 f♯ (UE 1903 35pp.; K 2158), parts. For A clarinet. Four movements.
——. *Sonata* Op.107 B♭ (Bo&Bo 1909; Well-Tempered Press) 35pp., parts. 28 min. Moderato; Vivace; Adagio; Allegretto con grazia (vivace).
Three outstanding works that deserve more hearing. In the class of the Brahms Sonatas. Advanced musicianship and pianism required. Kalmus edition includes both Op.49/1–2. D.

Hendrik de Regt. *Musica per clarinetto basso e pianoforte* Op.24 (Donemus 1973) 18pp., parts.

Carl Reinecke. *Sonata 'Undine'* Op.167 (IMC 1757) 31pp., parts. Clarinet may be substituted for flute. See detailed entry under duos for piano and flute.

Joseph Rheinberger. *Sonata* Op.105 e♭ (W. Stephan—Schott 1971) 36pp., parts. Allegro non troppo; Andante molto; Non troppo allegro. Late-19th-century style that requires advanced pianistic ability. Piece has a fine "sound" to it and is due to be heard again in the interest of 19th-century Romanticism. D.

Norman Richardson. *Sonatina* (Bo&H 1973) 16pp., parts. Three movements. Piano part slightly more difficult than clarinet part, slightly academic. M-D.

Ferdinand Ries. *Sonata* Op.29 g (Simrock 1820; W. Lebermann—Schott 5757 1967). Adagio–Allegro; Adagio con molto; Adagio–Allegro non troppo. Solid musical writing, brilliant piano part. M-D.

Johann Joseph Rainer Rudolph, Archduke of Austria. *Sonata* Op.2, A 1822 (H. Voxman—Musica Rara 1973) 35pp., parts. Written for Count Ferdinand Troyer (Schubert's clarinetist). Equal demands made on both performers. Long first movement has touches of Beethoven style, such as subito dynamics, quick key changes. Slow Minuet and Trio followed by an elaborate set of variations, varied mainly by harmonic changes. M-D.

Camille Saint-Saëns. *Sonata* Op.167 E♭ 1921 (Durand 1924) 23pp., parts. Allegretto; Allegro animato; Lento; Molto allegro. Effective concert work. Light attractive melodies, facile writing, interesting interplay in finale. M-D.

Pierre Sancan. *Sonatine* (Durand 1963) 7 min. Three connected movements. Excellent, light. D.

Henri Sauguet. *Suite* 1935 (ESC 8996 1995) 28pp., parts. 13 min. Vif; Minuet; Toccata–Allegro scherzando; Reverie–Pas vite (très expressif). Light, colorful harmonies in an early-20th-century setting of the older form. Especially noteworthy is the Toccata, a brilliant escapade with its scherzo-like qualities bound to please performers and listeners alike. All movements can be used individually for study and performance. M-D.

William Schmidt. *Rhapsody* I 1955 (WIM 1969) 16pp., parts. Two intransitive motifs are the germinating materials for this work: a 3-note figure suggesting a minor mode, and the leaping-upward interval of the minor 9th. After a slow introductory statement a basic 16th-note rhythm develops the music at a moderately fast tempo. The proportions of what has now become an A section are dissolved into a slower and more lyrically expressive B section characterized by a dialogue of the clarinet against an ever-descending tremolo in the piano. This crescendoes into a return of the 16th-note figures, and a short coda ends the work. Astringent dissonances, octotonic, cluster-like chords. Tremolando chords in alternating hands; large span required. D.
———. *Sonatina* (WIM 1969) 24pp., parts. Allegro; Adagio; Allegro con brio. Challenging dissonant and rhythmic writing, imitation, Neoclassic. Chords in alternating hands; large span required. M-D.

Gary Schocker. *Sonata* 1992 (TP 114-40707 1994) 20pp., parts. 13 min. Allegro moderato; Andante espressivo; Allegro. Commences with a 15-mm. introduction by piano with the main theme in octaves. Added-note harmonies, detailed passagework, and a tendency to write spatially are dominant factors in style. M-D.

Othmar Schoeck. *Sonata* Op.41 1928 (Br&H 1959). For bass clarinet and piano. 26pp., parts. Gemessen; Bewegt; moves directly into the third movement, which is untitled. Complex post-Romantic writing in a Regerian style. D.

Robert Schollum. *Sonatine* Op.42/1 (Dob 1969). Well crafted. M-D.
———. *Sonata* Op.55/4 (Dob 1956). Twelve-tone, complex. D.

Ruth Schonthal. *Sonata Concertante* 1973 (Furore 274 1997, ISMN M-50012-175-6). For cello, viola, or clarinet. See detailed entry under duos for piano and cello.

Robert Schumann. *Fantasiestücke* Op.73 1849 (W. Boetticher, E. Herttrich, H.-M. Theopold—Henle 416 1986, ISMN M-2018-0416-3; Bading, I. Barmas—CFP 2366 1950; Simon—GS 1951) 9 min. Zart und mit Ausdruck: tender, expressive melodies. Lebhaft, leicht: light, many triplets used in various ways. Rasch und mit Feuer: much motion and activity; Schneller: brilliant conclusion. Henle edition is for clarinet in A. First published with ad lib. parts for violin and cello, see entries under duos for piano and these instruments. M-D.

——. *Romanzen* Op.94 (G. Meerwein, K. Börner—Henle 442 1988, ISMN M-2018-0442-2) 16pp., parts. For clarinet in A. Originally for oboe and piano, the original publisher Simrock issued this work in violin and clarinet versions against the wishes of the composer. Extensive Preface details facts related to this event. See entry under piano and oboe for description of Romances.

Elliott Schwartz. *Souvenir* 1974 (GS/Margun) 7pp. 8½ min. Players perform from full score. "Performers [are] often un-synchronized with each other, in repetitive overlapping 'minimalist' patterns. Interior of piano used, clarinetist plays into open piano. Quasi-palindromic form. Seven pages (1 and 7 retrogrades of each other; page 4 serves as the midpoint, using materials first heard in earlier pages). Pages 2, 3, 5, and 6 have aleatoric elements" (Composer's letter to authors).

——. *Reading Session* 1983 (ACA) 8 min. Players perform from full score. "Both players 'read' (or speak, whisper, shout, etc.) from texts they have selected in advance. There are also specific words written into the composition, i.e. different permutations/re-orderings of the words in the famous John Cage sentence: 'I Have Nothing To Say and I Am Saying It and That Is Poetry'" (Composer's letter to authors).

Humphrey Searle. *Suite* Op.32 1956 (Schott 1957) 19pp., parts. 11 min. Prelude; Scherzo–fugue; Rhapsody; March; Hora. Mildly 20th-century throughout, well crafted. Hora is especially appealing. M-D.

——. *Cat Variations on a Theme from Prokofiev's Peter and the Wolf* 1971 (Faber Music 1974) 8pp., parts. For A clarinet and piano. Eight comic pieces. Growltiger's Serenade is a study of up-and-down glissandi. Tape is used in the Allegro molto Finale. Piano part not technically difficult but requires good chordal tremolos and fast off-beat chord leaps. D.

Giacomo Setacciola. *Sonata* Op.31 1921 (Ric 1958) 41pp., parts. Three movements. Well written with some unusual effects, similar in style to Respighi. M-D with a few spots D.

Mordecai Seter. *Elegy* 1954 (IMI 1968) 11pp., parts. This work "takes the form of a poem in 5 stanzas. Each stanza opens with a variation on the interval of the 3rd—a basic interval of the work—and develops into a free melodic recitative. The last stanza serves as an epilogue" (from the score). Colorful, effective. Hebraic modality permeates the piece. M-D.

Rodion Shchedrin. *Pastorale* 1997 (Schott KLB47 2000, ISMN M-001-12393-8) 11pp., parts. In one movement, combining traditional and nontraditional techniques for a calm opening and closing around a dramatic interior. Occasional proportional rhythmic relationships. Pianist must be able to reach 9th. M-D.

Leone Sinigaglia. *Twelve Variations on a Theme (Heidenröslein) by Franz Schubert* Op.19 (F.-G. Hölÿ—Kunzelmann GM591 1999) 15pp., parts. Delightful setting of this favorite theme with some variations composed purely in the manner of Schubert and others leaning toward the late 19th century. Deserves to be better known. M-D.

Dane Skerl. *Sonatina* (Društva Slovenskih Skladateljev 1972) 10pp. 2 copies necessary for performance.

Myroslav Skoryk. *Carpathian Rhapsody* (Duma 1997) 13pp., parts. Commences with an upward scalar pattern in the clarinet reminiscent of Gershwin's *Rhapsody in Blue* in a rubato tempo. An Allegretto follows with repetitive rhythmic patterns and mostly high-pitched melodic treatment. Concludes Presto with difficult full-chord bounce before settling in for an oompah finish in b♭. M-D to D.

———. *Fantasy on the Ukrainian Folk Song 'The Moon in the Sky'* (Duma 2003) 15pp., parts. Lyric with well-balanced phrases. Sportive in development with a march- and dancelike character. Large span required. M-D.

Leo Sowerby. *Sonata* H.240 1938 (SPAM 1944; Leo Sowerby Foundation 1996) 54pp., parts. For clarinet or viola and piano. A serious and superior work. Slow and sombre: generally quiet with straightforward rhythms and development; linear. Exuberantly, but not too fast: shifting harmonies in a spirited setting; chromaticism. Quietly flowing: 16th-note passagework with canonic theme in the B sections of this ABAB-coda design. Bright and merry: linear, imitative sections contrast with homophonic settings of lyric melody; mildly dissonant; arrives at an exciting musical climax finishing grand and glorious. Requires thorough musicianship and mature pianism. D.

Leopold Spinner. *Suite* Op.10 1955 (Bo&H 1962) 12pp., parts. Moderato; Allegro. Serial, frequent tempo changes, pointillistic, thin textures, Expressionist. M-D.

Charles Villiers Stanford. *Three Intermezzi* Op.13 1879 (C. Bradbury—JWC 55205 1979) 15pp., parts. Andante espressivo; Allegro agitato; Allegretto scherzando. Masterful use of instruments in a late-19th-century style. These *Intermezzi* predate Brahms's works for clarinet and piano and may have influenced him. M-D.

———. *Sonata* Op.129 1911 (St&B 1918) 40pp., parts. 18½ min. Allegro moderato; Caoine [an Irish lament]–Adagio (quasi Fantasia); Allegretto grazioso. Rich post-Romanticism with full chords, lyric melodies, and touches of spontaneity. One of the major works for the repertoire. D.

Walter Steffens. *Hommage* II Op.16 (Bo&Bo 1973) 6pp., parts. Persiflage; Akklamation; Konklusion.

Halsey Stevens. *Serenade* 1944 (Helios 1971) 4pp., parts. For viola or clarinet and piano. See detailed entry under duos for piano and viola.
——. *Suite* 1945, rev. 1953 (CFP 1959) 16pp., parts for clarinet and viola. 9½ min. Allegretto: terse, closely knit modal dialogue between the 2 instruments. Adagio: a broad-shaped movement, rich harmonies, alternates $\frac{2}{4}$ and $\frac{3}{4}$. Bucolico, pesante: subtle asymmetric rhythms $4 + \frac{7}{8}$, propulsive and well unified, more chordal than most of Stevens's writing. Moderato con moto: expressive long lines, recurring hemiola usage, flowing, develops naturally. M-D.
——. *Three Hungarian Folk Songs* 1950 (Highgate 1968). For viola (cello, English horn, or clarinet) and piano. See detailed entry under duos for piano and viola.
——. *Dittico* 1972 (Helios) 14pp., parts. 6 min. For sax (or clarinet) and piano. See detailed entry under duos for piano and saxophone.

Richard Stoker. *Sonata* (Leeds 1972) 9pp., parts. Allegretto; Largo mesto; Presto. Pleasant and freely tonal writing for both instruments. M-D.

Robert Suter. *Sonatina* 1937 (Henn 1957). One movement. Twelve-tone, clear, musical. D.

William Sydeman. *Duo* (PIC 1966) 32pp., parts. 11 min. Two abstruse (Adagio; Allegro) dissonant movements, excellent motivic development, unusual rhythmic divisions, tremolo, trills. Requires large span. D.

Antoni Szalowski. *Sonatina* (Omega 1948) 16pp., parts. 9 min. Allegro non troppo; Larghetto; Allegro. Attractive, clever but musical style, a modern classic. Has a great deal of audience appeal. M-D.

Jenö Takács. *Fantastic* Op.88a (Dob). For A clarinet. A one-movement work marked Andante, molto rubato. Free style, bar lines used only to cancel accidentals. M-D.

Louise Talma. *Three Duologues* 1967–68 (EM) 16pp., parts. 10½ min. Lento–Allegro: freely tonal, ornamental melody, Allegro section more rhythmic, repeated notes, long trills, linear; requires large span. Tranquillo: proportional rhythmic relationships, chromatic, harmonics, serious, Expressionist. Presto: pointillistic, left-hand skips, thin textures, independent lines. D.

Alexander Tcherepnin. *Sonata in One Movement* 1939 (Schott KLB22 1980) 11pp., parts. Dashing, with syncopated rhythms, rapid passagework, and challenging writing. Parts fit well but require experienced musicians. D.

Alec Templeton. *Pocket Size Sonata* (MCA 1949) 12pp., parts. Three short, attractive movements in jazz style. M-D.

———. *Pocket Size Sonata* II (SP 1964) 12pp., parts. Three brief movements in light, popular style. M-D.

Hector A. Tosar. *Sonata* (IU) 28pp., parts. 18 min. Allegro ma non troppo; Lento e mesto; Allegro vivace e scherzando. Chromatic, dense. Numerous layers of simultaneous sounds must be projected in the separate voices; "squirts" of notes in the Lento. A major work for the medium. Demands investigation and performance. D.

Donald F. Tovey. *Sonata* Op.16 B 1906 (Schott 1912). Three movements. A neglected late-Romantic work in the Brahms tradition. Virtuoso piano part. D.

Joan Tower. *Fantasy (. . . those harbor lights)* 1983 (AMP 8005 1983) 32pp., parts. 14 min. A somber opening by the piano yields to a quiet sustained melody in the clarinet, setting the tone for lightning-fast passagework and cadenzas in both instruments which follow. Multisectional; mixed meters, syncopation, and a boogie bass provide flavor in this recipe for musical invention. D.

Burnet C. Tuthill. *Fantasy Sonata* Op.3 (CF 1936) 9 min. Basically a 4-movement work distilled into one movement. Based mainly on materials of the first and second subjects. Rhapsodic and atmospheric, requiring thorough musicianship of both performers. M-D.

Jan Baptist Vanhal. *Sonata* B♭ 1806 (B. Tuthill—McGinnis & Marx 1948) 31pp., parts. 13½ min. Extensive Preface by Joseph Marx. Allegro moderato; Adagio cantabile; Rondo allegretto. This appears to be one of the earliest clarinet Sonatas available in a modern and carefully edited edition. Classical style, clear balance of parts. M-D.

———. *Sonata* II B♭ (Musica Rara 1973) 20pp., parts. Preface in English by Georgina Dobrée. Originally published in 1805. Charming, highly interesting musically, maintains stylistic consistency. M-D.

George Walker. *Perimeters* 1966 (Gen 1972) 14pp., parts. 9 min. Three untitled movements. Serial, terse, mainly linear with a few chordal sonorities that mainly function cadentially. D.

James Walker. *Sonatina* (GS 1974) 11pp., parts. Allegro moderato semplice; Andante Mesto; Allegro. Mildly 20th-century tonal writing that is full of charm, humor, and wit. In spite of its popular orientation the music has Classical structure and form. M-D.

Carl Maria von Weber. *Grand Duo Concertante* Op.48 E♭ (Schlesinger; Lemoine; Simon—GS 1951; Roth—Bo&H; P. Weston—Fentone 501 1989; G. Garbarino— Ricordi 1976; K 3358) 18 min. Brilliant, Sonata design. Tuthill says it is the "best show piece in the literature for both instruments, using all the resources of the clarinet. Weber's best music for clarinet" (*Journal of Research in Music Education* 20 [fall 1972]: 327).

———. *7 Variations* Op.33 B♭ (P. Hodgson—CFP 7015 1064; K 3359) 11pp., parts. An 18-mm. theme of marchlike quality serves as the basis for an engaging set of variations in a variety of tempos and characters. Vars.2 and 4 are for solo piano. M-D.

———. *Introduction, Theme and Variations* 1815 (Bo&Bo 1962) 9 min.

Jaromir Weinberger. *Sonatine* (CF 1940). Good teaching literature. Int.

Leo Weiner. *Ballade* Op.8 (Rozsavölgyi 1955) 15pp., parts. 10½ min. Sectionalized work in post–Brahms-Dohnányi idiom. Chromatic, tremolo, runs, and arpeggi figuration. M-D.

Egon Wellesz. *Zwei Stücke* Op.34 1922 (UE 1258) 5pp., parts. Moderato; Andante appassionato. Atonal, fluent writing, Expressionist, Schoenberg idiom. Requires large span. M-D.

Charles-Marie Widor. *Introduction et Rondo* Op.72 (MMP) 13pp., parts. Recitative-like opening leads to a winding rondo theme of alternating duple-triple rhythms. Sandwiches alternating sections with Rondo for flare and virtuosity. M-D.

Friedrich Wildgans. *Sonatina* b (Dob 1963). Three short movements, thin textures, folk influence. Delightful finale. M-D.

Yehudi Wyner. *Sonata* 1949 (ACA 1957). Energetic; Slow; Fast. Good ideas well worked out. M-D.

———. *Cadenza* 1969 (AMP). 13 min. For clarinet and harpsichord or piano. Cadenza; Canzona; Dodecadenza; Decadenza. D.

———. *Commedia* 2003 (AMP). 15 min. Commissioned by Emanuel Ax and Richard Stoltzman.

Isang Yun. *Riul* 1968 (Bo&Bo 1969) 21pp., parts. 14 min. Highly intense writing that sounds like a combination of late Berg and middle-period Stockhausen. Terribly involved for both performers. Great "spurts" of sound are contrasted with less activity. Only for the most adventurous. D.

Daniele Zanettovich. *Suite* (Leduc 1974) 13pp., parts. 10½ min. Preludio: freely tonal around b, parallel chords, subtle syncopation. Passepied: strong rhythms, staccato chords. Musette: added-note technique prevalent, Ravel-like. Rigaudon: toccata-like passages in alternating hands, ideas from Preludio appear, vigorous conclusion. Neoclassic. M-D.

Friedrich Zipp. *Sonatine* 1970 (Noetzel N3377) 15pp., parts. Allegro giusto; Andante con moto; Allegro energico. Strong quintal harmony, parallel chords, octotonic, more freely tonal second areas, vigorous finale, Neoclassic. Large span required. M-D.

Duos for Piano and Bassoon

Tadeusz Baird. *Four Preludes [Cztery Preludia]* 1954 (PWM 1799, ISBN 83-224-2055-2) 11pp., parts. 7 min. I. Moderato, II. Allegretto moderato, III. Adagio, con dolore, IV. Allegro giocoso. Miniature preludes with considerable descriptive performance techniques in a mild 20th-century vein. Int. to M-D.

Robert Baksa. *Bassoon Sonata* 1991 (CLE 64 1996) 34pp., parts. Ethereal-Earthy: bitonality, ABA'B'A'' form. Boisterous–Pensive: rambunctious, imitative, then calm, ABA' form. Contemplative and adventurous. M-D.

Warren Benson. *Song and Dance* 1953 (Bo&H 1955) 4pp., parts. 2½ min. In 2 connecting sections epitomizing the title. Fun. Int.

Antonio Bibalo. *Sonata* 1991 (Pizzicato 692 2000) 22pp., parts. In one movement, highly dramatic and restless with frequent changes. Repeated chords and an abundance of rhythmic patterns. Some ensemble difficulties. D.

Johann Ludwig Böhner. *Concertino für Pianoforte und Fagott in Form eines Duetts* Op.132 (G. Angerhöfer, W. Seltmann—Hofmeister 2809 2001, ISMN M2034-2809-1) 12pp., parts. 7½ min. Allegro non tanto con espressione in one-movement duet design. Early-19th-century concept. M-D.

Joseph Bodin de Boismortier. *Sonata II* a (R. Tyree—Musica Rara 1975) 8pp., parts.
———. *Sonata V* g (F. Oubradous—Siècle Musical 1950).
———. *Sonata* Op.26/2 a (R. Tyree—Musica Rara 1975) 14pp., parts.
———. *Two Sonatas* Op.50/4, 5 (K. Walker—Musica Rara MR 2169 1988) 15pp., parts, with basso. Op.50/4 d: Andante; Allegro; Sarabanda; Giga. Op.50/5 c: Largo; Gavotte; Largo; Allegro. M-D.

Eugène Bozza. *Récit, Sicilienne et Rondo* (Leduc 1936) 8pp., parts. Triptych form as implied by title. Récit allows much freedom for the bassoon in scalar and technically cadenza-like passages, while the Sicilienne features rolling broken chords with a dolce melody. The Rondo recalls a scherzando with a spirited romp. Not as demanding as usual for Bozza but requires alertness and preparation. Lovely themes. M-D.

———. *Fantaisie* (Leduc 1945) 8pp., parts. Commences with bassoon cadenza in the character of an improvisation. Homophonic structures follow as both instruments introduce the main theme. Chromaticism is prominent in the early-20th-century style and persists into the Allegro which ensues with a scherzo-like character and rapid passagework. Large span required. D.

Victor Bruns. *Sonata* Op.20 (Pro Musica 1952).

———. *Sonata* II Op.45 1969 (Br&H 1975) 29pp., parts.

Romeo Cascarino. *Sonata* 1947 (ST 646 1950) 12pp., parts. This work is equally adapted for clarinet and piano. Part for clarinet in A included. Allegretto Moderato: flexible meters, shifting rhythms. Andante Cantabile: broken 7th chords in left hand, flowing motion. Allegretto Giocoso: corky rhythms, delightful style. Mildly 20th-century, thoroughly pianistic. M-D.

Thomas Dunhill. *Lyric Suite* Op.96 (Bo&H 193 1941) 16pp., parts. I. Allegretto amabile, II. Scherzino–Allegro molto giocoso, III. Nocturne–Andante con moto, grazioso, IV. Intermezzo alla Gavotta–Animato, V. Vivace, capriccioso assai. Late-19th-century stylistic concepts. M-D.

Freiherr Thaddäus von Dürnitz. *Sechs Sonaten* 3 vols. (H.-P. Vogel—Accolade ACC4043-5 1999–2001), parts. I. 1 B♭, 2 E♭. II. 3 G, 4 F. III. 5 G, 6 C. Each *Sonata* is in 2 movements, the last typically a Rondo, with "the bassoon part avoid[ing] the very low register and concentrat[ing] on the upper register" (from Preface). Interesting with much musicality. M-D.

Henri Dutilleux. *Sarabande et Cortège* (Leduc 1942) 8pp., parts. Opens slowly, builds to a Mouvement de Marche. Moves over keyboard, chromatic. Cadenza for bassoon, coda for both instruments brings the piece to a blazing conclusion. M-D.

Alvin Etler. *Sonata* 1952 (AMP) 28pp., parts. 14 min. Moderately slow; Fast; Slow; Fast. Well-crafted, precise and deft Neoclassic writing. Resources of both instruments are thoroughly exploited. Ensemble experience required of both instruments. Salty and unsentimental style, moody atmosphere. M-D.

Ferenc Farkas. *Sonatina Based on a Hungarian Folk Song* 1955 (Artia) 11pp., parts for double bass, bassoon, or cello. See detailed entry under duos for piano and cello.

Johann Friedrich Fasch. *Sonata* C (J. Wojciechowski—CFP 5893) 12pp., parts. For bassoon (cello) and basso continuo; second cello part ad lib. Foreword in German and English. Largo; Allegro; Andante; Allegro assai. Virtuoso bassoon writing, more homophonic in style than most of Fasch's other works. Dynamics, phrasing, and ornamentation are editorial. Simple and effective keyboard realization. M-D. Another edition (B. Klitz, L. Seeber—McGinnis & Marx 1963) 14pp., parts. "Tempo, expression, and dynamic markings in this edition have been inserted simply as a guide for those who may need aid in formulating a finished performance within the musical idiom of the late Baroque" (from the score). Excellent keyboard realization.

Jindřich Feld. *Sonatine* (Schott 1971) 22pp., parts. 10 min. Allegro: clever syncopation, many harmonic 2nds, Impressionist. Andante tranquillo: close texture, cadenza for bassoon, intense melodies, colorful closing. Allegro molto: martial quality, figuration from first movement returns. Effective. M-D.

Jean Françaix. *Deux Pièces* 1996 (Schott FAG28 2000, ISMN M-001-12501-7) 12pp., parts. 6 min. I. Andante: homophonic texture with rolled chords in low register; melody alternates between instruments; *pppp* to *p*. II. Petit divertissement militaire: rapid splash chords, octaves, and repeated figurations; *ppp* to *ffff*. M-D.

Johann Ernst Galliard. *Six Sonatas* (E. Weiss-Mann—McGinnis & Marx 1946) Vol.I: *Sonatas* 1–3. Vol.II. *Sonatas* 4–6. Multimovements, more like Suites. Int. to M-D.

Noël Gallon. *Récit et Allegro* 1938 (L'OL 1938) 10pp., parts. Early-20th-century French character emphasizing clear melodies and balanced ensemble playing. Not too bold harmonically but with interesting ideas. M-D.

Harald Genzmer. *Introduktion und Allegro* 1966 (CFP 5920) 12pp., parts. 6½ min. Adagio opening with arpeggi and trills, chromatic figures, leads to Allegro molto: rhythmic, skipping left hand, intervals of 10ths between hands, bassoon provides melody. Adagio material returns briefly before the Allegro molto mood and a slowing-down chromatic chord sequence concludes the piece. M-D.

Mikhail Glinka. *Sonata* g/G (Sikorski 6787) 28pp., parts. Transcription and adaptation of the viola Sonata into a one-movement design of many sections. Rich harmonic and melodic expressiveness revealing a keen awareness and intuition toward early Romanticism. Enthralling writing with musical delights for performers and audiences. M-D.

Glenn Gould. *Sonata* 1950 (C. Morey—Schott FAG23 1996) 23pp., parts. Moderato; Vivace; Largo. This edition represents a resolution of 3 manuscripts Gould made of the *Sonata*. His style herein shows the influence of J. S. Bach and Schoenberg. "Gould used twelve-note organization to a limited extent, but for the most part the work is built on a free but motivically controlled chromatic technique" (from Preface). The middle movement includes a fugue. M-D.

Paul Hindemith. *Sonata* 1938 (Schott 3686) 12pp., parts. 8½ min. Leicht bewegt: short, pastoral, expressive, barcarolle-like. Langsam, Marsch, Pastorale: soon moves to march with trio, then to a coda that vaguely recalls the graceful pastoral opening. D.

William Hurlstone. *Bassoon Sonata* F 1904 (Emerson 75 1976) 31pp., parts. Vivace; Ballade–Moderato, ma sempre a piacere; Allegretto; Moderato–Animato–Vivace. Rich harmonies and cheerful melodies without a dependence on late-19th-century chromaticism. M-D.

Jacques Ibert. *Carignane* F 1953 (Pierre Noël 1953, in the collection *Les Contemporains Ecrivent pour les Instruments à Vent: Le Basson;* Billaudot 1998 ISMN M-043-06424-4) 4pp., parts. 1½ min. Expressive, with long sustained lines in carefully defined phrases at Moderato molto tempo. Repetitive figure mixes duples and triples. Concludes *ppp* with added-note F chord. Carignane is the name of a vine plant in France. M-D.
———. *Histoires* (Leduc 1939), parts. Le Petit âne blanc; La Cage de cristal; Le Vieux mendiant. Trans. by Fernand Oubradous from the original for solo piano. Int. to M-D.

Paul Jeanjean. *Prélude et Scherzo* (MMP) 16pp., parts. Expressive with much dynamic fluctuation. Scherzo has wit and brilliance. Deserves to be revived. M-D.

Ellis Kohs. *Sonatina* (Merrymount 1953) 20pp., parts. 10 min. I: $\quarternote$ = 76; II: $\eighthnote$ = 76; III: Alla marcia. The third movement consists of a theme, 3 variations, and a coda. Writing for the piano involves movement over the entire keyboard, mildly 20th-century, Neoclassic, effective combining of the instruments. M-D.

Nikolaus von Krufft. *Grande Sonate* Op.34 B♭ (B. Koenigsbeck—Accolade ACC1045 2000, ISMN M-50135-017-9) 55pp., parts. Allegro molto moderato; Adagio; Menuetto–Allegro; Presto. Large conceptual forms with unusually rich harmonies and modulations for its time. Discreet attention to balance is needed on occasion when full chords match bassoon's lowest pitches. One of the largest early Sonatas for bassoon and piano. M-D.

Otto Luening. *Sonata* (Highgate 1970) 11pp., parts. Andante: linear, chromatic, centers around C. Allegro: perpetual motion idea in 16th notes, like a 2-part invention. Larghetto: sustained, linear, a few chords. Fast: a quick 6 or a rollicking 2, broken octaves, quartal harmony, dancelike, ends firmly in C. M-D.

Benedetto Marcello. *Sonatas* (L. Sharrow—IMC), parts. Published separately. Op.1/2 e (IMC 2215 1967); Op.1/3 a (IMC 2286 1968); Op.1/5 C (IMC 3107 1970); Op.1/6 G (IMC 3106 1970). All are in 4 mvts.: Adagio (Andante in

Op.1/6); Allegro; Largo (Grave in 1/6); Allegro (Allegretto in 1/2). Over-edited. M-D.

———. *Sonata* (Bo&H).

Saverio Mercadante. 2 *Pezzi* g 1850, B♭ 1861 (G. Vernizzi—Boccaccini 1232 1997) 12pp., parts. First edition. Composed for competitions at the Naples Conservatory, where Mercadante was director. 1. Andante espressivo, 2. Andante cantabile. Lyric melodies with figured bass tastefully realized by the editor. M-D.

Ignace Moscheles. *Grand Duo Concertante* Op.34 (H. Voxman—Musica Rara 2157 1988) 52pp., parts. For bassoon or cello. Allegro moderato; Andante doloroso; Allegro molto. Fully developed piano score, virtuosic at times, requiring a thorough pianism to deal with technical and balance issues. Opening movement is in SA form with 2 invigorating themes. The work is so large that one 19th-century publisher released the score as a Sonata. Dedicated to J. N. Hummel. D.

Gabriel Pierné. *Solo de Concert* Op.35 (Leduc 1951) 12pp., parts. Composed for the Paris Conservatory Concours. Commences with a lively piano introduction announcing elements of the main theme to thick chords and octaves which the bassoon soon states in its entirety. Calmer, expressive sections follow, some to rolling chords over much of the keyboard. Then a scherzando ensues with a rollicking theme and receives both homophonic and imitative treatment, working its way to the end with grandeur and strength. D.

William Presser. *Suite* (TP 1967) 8pp., 2 scores required. 7 min. Fantasy: opening chord to be played when asterisk appears—"somewhere during that measure at the dynamic indicated." Waltz: à la Prokofiev. March: contrapuntal treatment. Habanera: piano provides rhythm, right hand plays only the final 3 bars. Scherzo: contrapuntal. Neoclassic, thoroughly convincing and entertaining. M-D.

André Previn. *Sonata* (GS 4065 1999, ISBN 0-7935-9272-0) 22pp., parts. With energy; Slowly; Vivace, very rhythmic. Syncopation, mixed meters, octaves, scalar passagework, and a rich variety of harmonic color spice this end-of-the-century essay. A slow waltzlike section is introduced in the middle movement and reappears near the end of the finale juxtaposing duple and triple rhythms sprinkled with melodic syncopation. A worthy work bound to become a favorite of the repertoire. Large span required. M-D to D.

Maurice Ravel. *Pièce en Forme de Habanera* (F. Oubradous—Leduc 1926) 4pp., parts. Transcription of the movement from Ravel's *Sites Auriculaires* for 2 pianos by Fernand Oubradous, the famous French bassoonist. M-D.

Hermann Reutter. *Sonata Monotematica* (Schott 6425 1972) 19pp., parts. See detailed entry under duos for piano and cello.

Alan Ridout. *Sonata* (Emerson 109 1978) 16pp., parts. In 3 untitled movements with only tempo markings. Opens with intensely dark dotted rhythms in the lower register of the piano and a marked theme in the upper register of the bassoon. Slow movement follows with a simple expressive melody in linear writing and leads to the finale, a roughed marchlike tromp in utmost seriousness. Wide span required. M-D.

Camille Saint-Saëns. *Sonata* Op.168 G 1921 (Durand) 21pp., parts. 10½ min. Allegretto moderato; Allegro scherzando; Molto adagio–Allegro moderato. Logical ideas developed to perfection in the Classical sense. Facile pianistic treatment throughout. M-D.
———. *Romance* Op.51 D 1877 (L. Sharrow—IMC 1977; K 9264) 6pp., parts. Trans. from the original for cello and piano. Richly melodic with strong undercurrent of pianistic interaction. M-D.

Peter Schickele. *Summer Serenade* 1983, rev.1989 (EV 164-00205 1993) 23pp., parts. 13 min. I. Dreams, II. Games, III. Songs and Dances. Thin textures, occasional doubling at the unison or third. Contrasts homophonic and imitative techniques, sometimes using the extremes of both instruments. Program Notes in English. M-D.

Gary Schocker. *Sonata* (TP 114-40754 1999) 19pp., parts. 12½ min. Allegro moderato; Andante; Tempo di minuetto. SA and rondo-like forms are found in the outer movements while the Andante floats along on a repetitive drone structure with lyric motivic materials in both instruments. M-D.

Joseph C. Schwantner. *Chronicon* (CFP 66283 1968) 9pp., parts. Mildly avant-garde with cluster chords, proportional rhythmic relationships, jagged melodies, extremes of instruments, and a novel "bassoon pizzicato." For artists dedicated (or willing to be dedicated) to unconventional late-20th-century techniques. D.

Elliott Schwartz. *Phoenix* 1995 (ACA) 13 min. Players perform from full score. "Materials have been drawn from familiar music related to 'fire' imagery: Wagner, Stravinsky, Jerome Kern. Wide stylistic shifts between triadic-tonal, minimalist, chromatic (Wagnerian), [and] angular-dissonant modernist" (Composer's letter to authors).
———. *Romance* 1961 (Gen 1968) 5pp., parts. Facile writing in a melodic context at a slow tempo. M-D.

Elie Siegmeister. *Contrasts* (MCA 1970) 8pp., parts. Lively, briskly: cheerful and vivacious. Slow, with sentiment: Tempo I (lively) returns and rushes to the closing, only to be met with a slow final 2 bars. Neoclassic style, flexible meters. The instruments complement each other. M-D.

Nikos Skalkottas. *Sonata Concertante* 1943 (G. Schuller, J. G. Papaiouannou— Margun 66 1984) 55pp., parts. 28 min. Allegro molto vivace; Andantino; Presto. "The first movement, earnest, concentrated and at times tenebrous in its first subject, is enlivened by the sprightly, sarcastic, dancing second subject. Highlighting this movement are such formal ideas as transposing the exposition with its dark, deep tones into eerie, dreamy high registers in the recapitulation. The heart-rending lyrical middle movement evolves in a grand symmetric pyramid form (ABCBA), reaching a climactic paroxysm in section C before the retrograded re-exposition. The quasi-gypsy finale starts in a spirited, humorous mood, but soon a cachinnating descending passage leads to the 'charming' and ironic second theme, followed by the already mentioned parodistic folk-like third theme. The writing for the bassoon throughout this work alternates successfully between abject gloom and witty charm in a rich kaleidoscope of moods. The piano writing is rich and highly varied" (from Notes by Papaiouannou). Monumental, bearing influences of Stravinsky and Schoenberg using Skalkottas's "nonserial" method. The final movement incorporates a Greek New Year's folk melody set in $\frac{7}{8}$. D.

Halsey Stevens. *Three Pieces* 1947 (CFP 1958) 9pp., parts. 4½ min. For bassoon (cello) and piano. Allegro moderato: ABA, flowing diatonic lines colored with chromaticism; in $\frac{3}{4}\frac{6}{8}$; metric divisions of $2 + \frac{3}{8} + 3$ add interest; pedal point. Andante: thin textures mixed judiciously with chords; inner voices important. Allegro: ABA; opening short thematic figure is inspiration for entire piece; rhythmic vigor, $3 + \frac{3}{8} + 3$. Functional dissonant harmonies. Large span required. M-D.

———. *Sonata* 1949 (ACA) 12½ min. Allegro: SA, linear, terse writing infused with highly effective rhythmic patterns. Lento moderato: passacaglia format uses flowing counterpoint against fixed figurations. Allegro: thematic germ of this rondo-like finale comes from the concluding idea of the second movement. Original rhythmic treatment, spontaneous. M-D.

Alexandre Tansman. *Sonatine* (ESC 1952) 11pp., parts. Allegro con moto: driving secco chords; some melodic answering by the right hand; bassoon quasi-recitative finishes the movement. Aria: large span required for numerous 9th chords. Scherzo–Molto vivace: rhythmic element is most important, secco chords, *pp* chromatic chords close out this colorful work. Wide span required. M-D.

———. *Suite* (ESC 1960) 12pp., parts. 7 min. I. Introduction et Allegro: slow cantabile melody with written-out grace notes followed by chit-chat with staccato chords and a syncopated melody in the Allegro. II. Sarabande: tranquil, expressive melody marked Adagio sostenuto within linear texture. III. Scherzo: rhythm is the central element as both instruments weave in and out of motivic and chordal figurations for a lively finish. Wide span required. M-D.

Alexandre Tcherepnin. *Sonatine Sportive* Op.63 1939 (Leduc) 10pp., parts. Lutte (Boxing); Mi-temps (Rest Period); Course (Race). Pits the instruments against one another in amusing competitively sportive essays. Short, effective; attempts to adapt to music the surprise elements of sports. Lengthy comments by the composer describe the musical commentary in the Preface. M-D.

Georg Philipp Telemann. *Sonata* f ca.1728 (W. Michel—Amadeus 665 1997 14pp.; R. Tyree—Musica Rara 1975 10pp.; S. Kovar, R. Veyron-Lacroix—IMC 1151 1949 10pp.), parts. Triste; Allegro; Andante; Vivace. "One could consider this Sonata . . . as one of the pioneer works of cultivated bassoon playing—a really 'adult' piece that doesn't give the bassoonist a comic role but mingles great expressiveness with a virtuosity perfectly suited to the instrument" (Michel in Amadeus). Amadeus edition includes photocopy of Telemann's MS. M-D.

——. *Sonata* E♭ (I. Rudas—EMB Z.4724 1965) 12pp., parts. For bassoon or cello. Cantabile; Allegro; Grave; Vivace giocoso (ma non troppo allegro) e staccato. Fine continuo realization by editor. M-D.

——. *Sonata* e ca.1720 (O. Oromszegi—EMB Z.5354 1969, ISMN M-080-05354-6) 15pp., parts. Originally for viola da gamba and continuo, presented here in a lovely transcription and realization for bassoon and piano. Cantabile; Allegro; Recitative–Arioso; Vivace. Judicious editorial comments added to score. Preface in English, German, and Hungarian. M-D.

——. *Two Sonatinas* c, a (W. Michel—Amadeus BP477 1993) 19pp., parts, with basso. For bassoon or cello. Nos.2, 5 of the 6 "New Sonatinas" published ca.1731–32. Only the solo part survives, and here Michel has created a basso continuo part with an engaging realization based upon Telemann's style. In Sonata da Camera form. M-D.

Jiří Teml. *Teatro Piccolo* 1983 (Panton 2442 1986) 25pp., parts. 13 min. A short theatrical portrait in mid-20th-century tonal style with an Introduction and 5 Acts. Act I. Drammatico, II. Recitativo, III. Scherzando, IV. Amoroso, V. Finale. M-D.

Heitor Villa-Lobos. *Ciranda das Sete Notas* 1933 (PIC 1961) 15pp., parts. Originally for bassoon and orchestra, but the composer made this highly effective arrangement for bassoon and piano. Varied figurations; tempo changes add contrast. Low broken 10ths provide unusual sonorities in a tempo do Andante section. Flowing chords of 4ths require facility. Large span required as 10ths must be played solidly. M-D.

Alec Wilder. *Sonata* I (Margun 105 1968) 27pp., parts. 11½ min. Giocoso; Andante; Con brio; Allegro. Colorful and imitative with mostly thin textures offset by passages of octaves or chords, particularly in outer movements. Dramatic and almost sportive. M-D.

————. *Sonata* II 1969 (ST 880) 23pp., parts. Four untitled movements with only tempos listed. Mvts.I and III are active with many chromatic runs and changing rhythmic patterns. Mvts.II and IV provide contrast in more restful moods; flowing open 5ths over ostinato-like figures; octotonic; chromatic chords; *p* ending. Appealing and well written for both instruments. Large span required. M-D.

Duos for Piano and Saxophone

Jean Absil. *Sonate* Op.115 (Lemoine 1963, ISMN M-2309-4063-4) 20pp., parts. For alto sax and piano. Allegro; Andantino; Vivo. Neoclassic with engaging technical requirements. For experienced performers. M-D to D.

Samuel Adler. *Pensive Soliloquy* 1997 (TP 114-40914 1998) 6pp., parts. 7 min. For alto sax and piano. Marked Slowly and expressively; contemplative with wide skips in melodic materials and mostly linear writing. M-D.

William Albright. *Sonata* 1984 (Henmar 1990) 34pp., parts. 20 min. For alto sax and piano. I. Two-Part Invention; II. La follia nuova: a lament for George Cacioppo; III. Scherzo 'Will o' the wisp'; IV. Recitative and Dance. Determinate and indeterminate writing using extremes of the instruments, cluster chords, biting harmonies, and driving rhythms. A challenge for performers and listeners alike. D.
See B. R. Utley, "William Albright's *Sonata for Alto Saxophone and Piano:* Analytical Insights and Performance Considerations," D.M.A. diss., Louisiana State University, 2001.

Garland Anderson. *Sonata* 1968 (ST SS-866 1974) 23pp., parts. For tenor sax and piano. Adagio–Allegro con brio; Scherzo–Presto; Andante con moto; Allegro ma non troppo. Misterioso opening, driving octotonic writing in the Allegro con brio. Tonal and Impressionist treatment in the Andante con moto. Pianistic, mildly 20th-century, attractive. M-D.
———. *Sonata* (ST 1968) 22pp., parts. For alto sax and piano. Allegro; Andante sostenuto (Chorale); Allegro agitato. Freely tonal, parallel chords, arpeggiation, subtle sonorities, colorful writing. M-D.

Robert Baksa. *Alto Sax Sonata* 1991 (CLE 24 1993) 37pp., parts. Moderato; Slow waltz; Quite fast. Colorful harmonic procedures though never drifting away from tonal centers. Rhythmic with some syncopation; movements mix homophonic and polyphonic techniques; generally thin textures; scalar. M-D.

Leslie Bassett. *Music for Saxophone and Piano* 1968 (CFP 66268 1969) 17pp., parts. 10 min. For alto sax and piano. Fast: dramatic gestures, extreme ranges exploited, tremolos, trills, "stopped" notes. Slow: more chordal, rhythmic problems, chromatic. Moderato: pointillistic, many dynamic marks, long pedals effective. Fast: chromatic, sweeping gestures, "stopped" notes, Presto coda; large span required. D.

————. *Duo Concertante* 1984 (CFP 67083 1988) 18pp., parts. 15 min. For alto sax and piano. Driving; Lyrical; Unhurried; Ascending; Dramatic. Instruments fit together well in pieces aptly described by their titles. M-D.

Marcel Bitsch. *Impromptu* (Leduc 1957) 5pp., parts. 4½ min. For bass sax, tuba, or bass trombone. Opens with quartal chord in piano and recitative-like writing marked "a piacere." An Andante follows with thematic material initially introduced by piano. Then a $\frac{5}{8}$ Vivo ensues with bouncy rhythms and colorful harmonies. Concludes Moderato with virtuosic-like writing and a contrary-motion bitonal cadence finishing in B♭. M-D.

————. *Villageoise* (Leduc 1953) 4pp., parts. For alto sax and piano. A joyful and lively character piece with chains of triads and much playfulness. M-D.

Paul Bonneau. *Suite* 1944 (Leduc 1944) 13pp., parts. 10 min. For alto sax and piano. Four relatively short movements reminiscent of early-20th-century French Neoclassicism with a strong dose of chromaticism: Improvisation, Danse des Démons, Plainte, and Espièglerie. An intriguing set of character pieces in Suite format with closely related instrumental parts. M-D.

Eugène Bozza. *Aria* 1936 (Leduc 1936) 3pp., parts. For alto sax and piano. Andante ma non troppo setting in ternary form. M-D.

————. *Pulcinella* Op.53/1 (Leduc 1944) 5pp., parts. For alto sax and piano. Playful character piece marked Allegretto vivo with a scherzando quality. M-D.

————. *Scaramouche* Op.53/2 (Leduc 1944) 7pp., parts. For alto sax and piano. Fantasy-like with wit and Gallic humor. M-D.

————. *Impromptu et Danse* (Leduc 1954) 7pp., parts. For alto sax and piano. Majestic piano introduction leads immediately to sax cadenza. An ornamented theme ensues to open 5th chordal treatment with melismatic features. The Dance follows at Allegro vivo with its own theme, a transformation of the opening theme from the Impromptu to alternating oompah and scalar treatment. Concludes with Bozza's typically fiery finish. M-D.

Timothy Broege. *Characteristic Suite* 1985 (Dorn) 20pp., parts. For tenor sax and piano. Fantasia; Aria; Canzona; Trio; German Dance; Round-O Jigg. Succinct essays in a variety of forms with straightforward rhythms in a mild late-20th-century style. Facile ensemble setting comes together quickly. M-D.

Rayner Brown. *Sonata Breve* 1970 (WIM M76) 24pp., parts. Allegro; Passacaglia; Vivace. Octotonic, thin textures, long lines, freely tonal, Neoclassic. M-D.

Ronald L. Caravan. *Quiet Time* (Ethos 1980) 4pp., parts. 4 min. For soprano (or tenor) sax and piano. A gentle essay in changing meters at mostly soft dynamics. M-D.

———. *Sonata* (Ethos 1984) 22pp., parts. 12 min. For soprano sax and piano. I. Prologue, II. Allegro, III. Song, IV. Dance-Finale. M-D.

———. *Soliloquy and Celebration* 1996 (Ethos 1996) 16pp., parts. 8 min. Subtitled "A tribute to the classic jazz saxophonist Paul Desmond (1925–1977)." For soprano (or tenor) sax and piano. In separate movements. M-D.

Jacques Castérède. *Fantaisie Concertante* (Leduc 1960). For bass trombone, tuba, or bass saxophone. See detailed entry under duos for piano and trombone.

Paul Creston. *Suite* Op.6 1935 (SP) 16pp., parts. 8 min. For E♭ alto sax and piano. Scherzoso; Pastorale; Toccata. Freely tonal, Pastorale meter is $\frac{9}{8}\frac{6}{8}\frac{9}{8}$. Toccata meter is $\frac{4}{4}\frac{3}{4}\frac{2}{4}\frac{3}{4}$. Metrical subdivision is effective in this well-contrasted work. M-D.

———. *Sonata* Op.19 (SP 1945) 35pp., parts. 13 min. For E♭ alto sax and piano. With vigor: freely chromatic; driving rhythms; juxtaposed against calmer lines; repeated short patterns; parallel chords; requires large span. With tranquility: expressive line over chordal substructure, arpeggi figuration, rich harmonies. With gaiety: like a 2-part invention for piano; dancing line in saxophone, shifting rhythms; fun for performers and listeners. M-D.

Michael Cunningham. *Trigon* Op.31 1969 (MMB 1987) 16pp., parts. For tenor sax and piano. Constant driving rhythm; Quiet and calm; Quite fast. Added-note harmonies, octotonic, glissandos, tremolos in mostly conventional writing. Uses extremes of instruments. Finale is a virtuosic toccata. M-D to D.

Claude Debussy. *Rapsodie* 1903–1905 (Durand 1919) 10 min. For alto sax and piano. Orchestral reduction for piano. A delectable morceau with syncopated Hispanic flavor, sensual languor, and a strange coda that seems to be inspired by Albéniz's *Iberia*. M-D.

Jules Demersseman. *Fantaisie sur un Thème Original* (I. Roth—Hug 11372 1988) 16pp., parts. For alto sax and piano. Multiple-section form of free design includes a lengthy introduction, cadenza, and theme and variation along with an orchestral-like use of the piano. One of the earliest works for this chamber ensemble combination. M-D.

Edisson Vasil'evich Denisov. *Sonate* (Leduc 1973) 34pp., parts. 12 min. For alto sax and piano. Both parts are difficult and highly organized. The character is one of agitation and up-beat rhythmic drive, especially in the faster outer movements, where increasingly faster passagework abounds. Half-steps, major

7ths, and minor 9ths are prevalent. Flexible meters—$\frac{6}{16}$, $\frac{9, 10, \text{or } 11}{32}$—require utmost rhythmic precision. In the middle movement the piano mainly has a few arabesques. The saxophonist is asked to play multiphonics, quarter tones, and unusual shakes. A valuable addition to the repertoire. D.

Alfred Désenclos. *Prélude, Cadence et Finale* (Leduc 1956) 15pp., parts. For alto sax and piano. In one continuous movement with virtuosic writing for sax. Lengthy solo piano passages allow the introduction and development of new thematic materials. Knotty fingering problems in an engaging score. M-D to D.

Paul Dessau. *Suite* 1935 (Bo&Bo 1989) 15pp., parts. For alto sax and piano. I. Petite Ouverture, II. Air, III. Serenade. Succinct movements with tuneful melodies and colorful harmony. Air requires large span. M-D.

David Diamond. *Sonata* 1984 (ST1993) 23pp., parts. For alto sax and piano. Allegro vivo; Andante molto, quasi adagio; Allegro vivo. Snappy rhythms in outer movements provide playful quality in intense ensemble settings. Cantando slow movement allows much expression in a mild late-20th-century context. M-D.

John Diercks. *Suite* (TP 1972) 12pp., parts. 6½ min. Chase; Barcarolle; Plaint; Gig. Beautifully contrasting movements in tempos and mood. Piano part is a joy to play and presents no major problems, but the Gig in particular needs plenty of projection to bring out the strepitoso character. Mildly 20th-century. M-D.

Henri Dillon. *Sonate* 1949 (Sal 1954) 12pp., parts. Allegro con brio; Andante; Vivace. Outer movements are strongly rhythmic, while the Andante is calm, legato, and melodious and makes interesting use of inner voices. Mildly 20th-century with Impressionist influences. M-D.

Pierre-Max Dubois. *Pièces Caractéristiques en Forme de Suite* Op.77 (Leduc 1962). Five pieces published separately. A l'Espagnole; A la Russe; A la Française; A la Hongroise; A la Parisenne. Attractive writing with resources of piano thoroughly used. M-D.
———. *Sonata* (Leduc 1956) 21pp., parts. 21 min. Allegro vivo: SA, scalar, chordal, tremolo, freely in C. Andante: chromatic chords; sax cadenza; midsection builds to vigorous climax before returning to opening mood and ideas. Tempo di Gavotto: piano part is mainly rhythmic. Rondo: giocoso, light Gallic humor, chromatic, scales, piquant conclusion. M-D.
———. *Sonatine* (Leduc 1966).
———. *Come Back* (Billaudot 1992) 19pp., parts. 16 min. For alto sax and piano. Lent et récité: recitative character assigned to saxophone who opens and closes the movement alone; ternary form with animated middle section to be played joyeux. Prestement: motoric with wide range of dynamics; glissandos; mixed meters; playful spirit. M-D.

——. *Mominettes* (Billaudot 1993) 16pp., parts. 13 min. For alto sax and piano. Prestissimo; Aimablement tranquille; Allegro giocoso ma tranquillo; Andante recitativo; Allegro. A busy collection of short pieces with thematic materials exchanged between instruments in a wide range of expressive contexts. M-D.

——. *La Gremellite* (Billaudot 1996) 7pp., parts. 3 min. Rag for alto sax and piano with title derived from the name Daniel Gremelle, to whom the work is dedicated. Virtuosic with witty charm and lightning speed. D.

——. *Bouquet d'Hommages* (Billaudot 1997) 32pp., parts. 21 min. For alto sax and piano. Six colorful movements dedicated to outstanding 20th-century composers. I. Prélude (to Albert Roussel), II. Barcarolle (Darius Milhaud), III. Rapsodie (Leonard Bernstein), IV. Aria (Jacques Ibert), V. Presto (Francis Poulenc), VI. Scherzo (Dmitri Shostakovich). Each movement hints at a well-known work by the respective dedicatee. May be performed separately or in groups. M-D.

Gabriel Fauré. Transcriptions and adaptations by Daniel Deffayet for piano and alto sax (Hamelle). Published separately. *Berceuse* Op.16 (HA 9313); *Elégie* Op.24 (HA 9315); *Fantaisie* Op.79 (HA 9312); *Pavane* Op.50 (HA 9314); *Sicilienne* from *Pelléas et Mélisande* Op.78 (HA 9292); *Après un rêve* (HA 9328). From the collection *Pièces Célèbres,* Deffayet has also transcribed the *Sérénade Toscane* Op.3/2, *Au Bord de l'eau* Op.8/1, *Les Berceaux* Op.23/1, *Les Roses d'Ispahan* Op.39/4, and *Clair de lune,* Op.46/2.

——. *Pièce* (Leduc). For alto sax and piano.

Jean Françaix. *Cinq Danses Exotiques* 1961 (Schott 4745) 15pp., parts. 5½ min. Pambiche; Baiao; Mambo; Samba lenta; Merengue. Clever rhythmic realizations of each characteristic dance. M-D.

Peter Racine Fricker. *Aubade* 1951 (Schott 10235) 4pp., parts. Elegant, freely tonal (almost atonal), grateful writing. M-D.

Hans Gál. *Suite* Op.102b (Simrock 1973) 29pp., parts. This work is identical to Gál's *Suite* Op.102a for viola and piano, except for transcribing the viola to the saxophone part. A long work in 4 movements in late-Romantic style and idiom. Rhapsodic phrases of the first movement and the playful theme of the finale are especially noteworthy. M-D.

Ida Gotkovsky. *Brillance* 1973 (Billaudot 1974) 22pp., parts. 12 min. For alto sax and piano. Déclamé; Désinvolte; Dolcissimo; Final. Mixes harmonic structures based on 2nds, 3rds, and 4ths. Dramatic, with frequent shifts in character and dynamics. Explores sonorous effects between instruments at slow and fast tempos in mixed meters. Always melodious. M-D.

John Harbison. *San Antonio (Sonata for Alto Saxophone and Piano)* 1994 (AMP 1995) 26pp., parts. 14 min. Three engaging movements reflecting a tourist's experience on a hot summer day in San Antonio, Texas: The Summons, Line

Dance, and Couples' Dance. A demanding work often pitting the 2 instruments against one another. Uses octotonic writing, extensive syncopation with touches of jazz, and a percussive approach to the piano. The 2 instruments often seem worlds apart in the first movement but come together at the end in a section marked "unforgivably crude." Rhythmic patterns are often dissimilar making ensemble playing difficult under breakneck tempos. Ends quietly after tornado-like activity. Commissioned by the World-Wide Concurrent Premières and Commissioning Fund, the *Sonata* received its premiere on December 3, 1995, by 100 pairs of saxophonists and pianists around the world. D.

Walter Hartley. *Duo* 1964 (Tenuto T10) 17pp., parts. 5½ min. For alto sax and piano. Octotonic; arpeggi figuration; toccata-like section; Lento section more chordal and sustained; Tempo I returns opening idea. Freely tonal, dramatic conclusion. M-D.

————. *Poem* 1967 (TP). 3½ min. For tenor sax and piano.

————. *Little Suite* 1974 (Dorn). 5½ min. For baritone sax and piano.

————. *Sonata* 1974 (Dorn 1975) 22pp., parts. 10½ min. For tenor sax and piano. Allegro moderato; Molto vivace; Lento. Dramatic, with full chordal writing, octotonicism, and extremes of instruments. Large span required. Score is easy-to-read copy of MS. M-D.

————. *Sonorities IV* 1976 (Dorn). 3 min. For alto sax and piano.

————. *Sonata* 1976 (Dorn). 10½ min. For baritone sax and piano.

————. *Valse Vertigo* 1978 (Dorn). 4 min. For alto sax and piano.

————. *Diversions* 1979 (Ethos 1979) 20pp., parts. 7½ min. For soprano sax and piano. I. Balkan Dance; II. Lines and Bells; III. Rigadoon. Mixed meters, octotonic, scalar, and syncopated techniques are all to be found in this spirited work. Multiphonics for sax with suggested fingerings and a forearm cluster for piano provide some of the diversions displayed in this character work. M-D.

————. *Sonorities VII* 1985 (Ethos). 2 min. For tenor sax and piano.

————. *Sonata Elegiaca* 1987 (TP). 14 min. For alto sax and piano.

————. *Sonatina Giocosa* 1987 (Tenuto 1988) 15pp., parts. 5 min. For bass sax and piano; "may be played by tuba or string bass (parts provided), but composer's first choice is bass saxophone" (from Note). Allegro molto; Allegretto grazioso; Quodlibet: Poco vivace, scherzando. Score is copy of MS. M-D.

————. *African Dance* 1994 (Dorn). 8 min. For alto sax and piano.

————. *Sonata* 1994 (Dorn). 8 min. For soprano sax (or oboe) and piano.

————. *Sonorities VIII* 1996 (Ethos). 1 min. For bass sax and piano.

————. *Romance* 1996 (Ethos). 2 min. For bass sax and piano.

————. *Elegy 2001* 2001 (TP). 3 min. For alto sax (or English horn) and piano.

————. *Sonatina* 2002 (Ethos). 6 min. For alto sax and piano.

An avid saxophonist, Dr. Hartley has probably composed more works for saxophone than any other composer. For a complete listing of his compositions, see www.walterhartley.com.

Bernhard Heiden. *Solo* (AMP 1969) 12pp., parts. For alto sax and piano. Slow introduction leads to a toccata-like main section interspersed with a lyrical interlude. Concludes with a recap of the slow material and a short coda based on the toccata material. Hindemithian in style with dissonant harmonies and angular melodies. Piano part is grateful to play; virtuoso approach avoided for sax. M-D.

———. *Sonata* 1937 (Schott) 32pp., parts. 15 min. Allegro; Vivace; Adagio–Presto. Written in a Neoclassic style, liberally sprinkled with chromaticism, freely tonal. Exciting writing for both instruments. D.

Paul Hindemith. *Sonata* 1943 (Schott) 11 min. For alto sax (or alto horn, or French horn) and piano. Four abbreviated movements, similar to a Handel violin Sonata. Ruhig bewegt: lyric, prelude-like. Lebhaft: SA, elaborate development section. Sehr langsam: ascends to a considerable climax (14 bars only) and leads to Das Posthorn (Zwiegespräch)–Lebhaft: a fairly extensive text outlines the mood of the movement, in 3 sections: a fast piano solo, a slower dancelike horn tune, and a recap of these 2 ideas simultaneously. D.

Jacques Ibert. *Mélopée* (Lemoine 1973) 4pp., parts. Transcribed from Ibert's *Vocalise* published in *L'Art du chant* by Rose Caron. Modal melody in the sax is supported by coloristic chords with inner voice in piano. Requires large span. M-D.

———. *Histoires* (Leduc 1939), parts. 20 min. Eight pieces transcribed from the original for piano by Marcel Mule. La meneuse de tortues d'or; Le petit âne blanc; Le vieux mendiant; Dans la maison triste; Le palais abandonné; Bajo la mesa; La cage de cristal; La marchande d'eau fraîche; Le cortège de Balkis. Effective transcription of this picturesque set. May be played separately or in groups. Int. to M-D.

———. *L'âge d'or* 1936 (Leduc 1956) 4pp., parts. 4 min. For alto sax and piano. Arranged from the ballet *Le chevalier errant.* Moderato assai: calm, serene, expressive. M-D.

———. *Aria* (Leduc), parts. 4 min. For alto sax and piano. Transcription from the original vocalise for voice and piano to D♭ with slight changes in phrasing. Large span required. M-D.

Gordon Jacob. *Variations on a Dorian Theme* (June Emerson 1972) 8pp., parts. 8 min. Piano part is in 3 flats and centers around F. Five variations: allegro, waltz, a rhapsodic variation, adagio, and a lively finale. Grateful writing. M-D.

Barbara Kolb. *Related Characters* 1980 (Bo&H 1985). See detailed entry under duos for piano and viola.

Gregory Kosteck. *Mini-Variations* (Media Press 1971) 6pp., parts. For tenor sax and piano. Harmonics, chromatic chords tossed between hands, detached scalar passages, sustained chords, pointillistic, Expressionist. M-D.

Hans Kox. *Sonata* 1983 (Donemus 1983) 34pp., parts. 17 min. For tenor sax and piano. I. [untitled], –Allegro molto, II. Presto misterioso, III. Adagio molto, IV. Allegro vivace. Conventional 20th-century techniques using the full range of both instruments. Score is copy of MS. M-D.

Bernhard Krol. *Sonate* Op.17 (Hofmeister) 23pp., parts. 13 min. Presto; Maestoso–Patetico; Allegro assai. Neo-Baroque writing in Hindemith style. Middle movement, with dramatic contrast, is most interesting. D.

Meyer Kupferman. *In Two Bits* (Gen 1969) 5pp., parts. For alto sax and piano. Lento: chromatic, pointillistic, dynamic extremes. Scherzando: same characteristics in faster tempo; complex rhythms. D.

John David Lamb. *Sonata* 1961, rev.1997 (Näckeus Vänner 1997) 34pp., parts. For soprano sax and piano. Andante; Adagietto; Scherzo (non affrettoso). Strongly tonal with facile writing. M-D.

Richard Lane. *Suite* (Bo&H 1962) 11pp., parts. For alto sax and piano. Prelude; Song; Conversation; Lament; Finale. Attractive, mildly 20th-century writing. Piano writing is handled in a polished manner. Int. to M-D.

Pierre Lantier. *Sicilienne* (Leduc 1944) 6pp., parts. For alto sax and piano. A lyrical, ternary work packed with accidentals, marked Andante. Charming re-creation of the historical form in Neoclassic style. D.

Libby Larsen. *Holy Roller* (OUP 1998) 27pp., parts. For alto sax and piano. In one movement: Very freely, slowly but with fierce energy—Fire and brimstone. "*Holy Roller* is inspired by classic revival preaching. To me, revival sermons are stunning musical masterpieces of rhythm, tempo, and extraordinary tension and release. The music flows directly from the language, cajoling, and incanting, at the same time magnetizing and mesmerizing the listener with its irresistible invocations. The music is the language, the language is the music and the result transports the spirit to other states of being. *Holy Roller* is a revival sermon captured in the sounds of the alto saxophone and piano" (from Preface). D.

Jean-Marie Londeix. *Tableaux Aquitains* (Leduc 1974) 2pp., parts for each volume. Quatre morceaux séparés (in 4 vols.). I. Bachelette, 2. La Gardeuse, 3. Le Traverseur de Landes, 4. Le Raconteur d'Histoires. Short colorful character pieces. Int. to M-D.

Lawson Lunde. *Sonata* 1959 (ST). For alto sax and piano. Allegro; Andantino cantabile; Allegro vivace. Well constructed, lots of excitement. M-D to D.
——. *Sonata* Op.37 "Alpine" (To the Fore). For soprano sax and piano.

Trygve Madsen. *Sonata* Op.95 (Musikk-Husets). For alto sax and piano.
——. *Sonata* Op.107 (Musikk-Husets). For soprano sax and piano.

Marcel Mihalovici. *Chant Première. Sonate* Op.103 1973 (Heugel) 26pp., parts. 15 min. For tenor sax and piano. One movement. Varied tempos, textures, and moods. Highly chromatic, atonal, octotonic, shifting meters, agitated and intense, Expressionist, complex writing. Nothing short of virtuoso performers will "bring this work off"! Requires large span. D.

Edvard Moritz. *Sonata* Op.96 1939 (ST) 44pp., parts. For alto sax and piano. Allegro molto; Molto andante; Scherzo–Presto; Finale–Quasi allegro. Mildly 20th-century style; 19th-century pianistic idioms. Well crafted. M-D.
——. *Sonata* II Op.103 1963 (ST) 32pp., parts. For alto sax and piano. Allegro; Molto Andante; Un poco presto: Vivace. Characteristics similar to those found in Sonata Op.96, plus more flexible meters. Solid writing. Requires large span. M-D.

Robert Muczynski. *Sonata* Op.29 (GS 1972) 15pp., parts. Andante: serious, effective. Allegro energico: virtuosic. D.

Claude Pascal. *Sonatine* b 1948 (Durand) 16pp., parts. A l'aise: syncopated figure in piano part moves over keyboard; cadenza for sax. Lent: chordal sonorities support line in sax; presses forward to Vif: freely tonal, much rhythmic vitality, arpeggi figuration for piano. M-D.

William Presser. *Prelude and Rondo* (Tenuto); see detailed entry under duos for piano and viola.

Sam Raphling. *Sonata* II (Gen 1968) 7pp., parts. One movement. Moderately slow, chromatic, bitonal, mysterious quasi-recitative opening, sudden dynamic changes. Moves through various tempos and figurations. Molto agitato leads to a rhythmic conclusion. Neoclassic. M-D.

Hermann Reutter. *Pièce Concertante* 1968 (Schott 5893) 16pp., parts. For alto sax and piano. Exposition; Berceuse; Combination. Highly disciplined Neoclassic writing. Fugal textures appear in the last movement. Thoroughly pianistic. M-D.

Lucie Robert. *Cadenza* (EFM 1974) 23pp., parts.
——. *Sonata* (EFM 1974) 23pp., parts. 11 min.
See John Stephen Bleuel, "A Descriptive Catalog of the Solo and Chamber Saxophone Music of Lucie Robert," D.M.A. diss., University of Georgia, 1998.

Albert Charles Paul Roussel. *Vocalise* (Lemoine 1973) 4pp., parts. For alto, tenor, or soprano sax and piano. Transcribed from Roussel's *Vocalise* published in *L'Art du chant* by Rose Caron.

William Schmidt. *Sonata* (WIM).
——. *Sonatina* (WIM 1967) 19pp., parts. March; Sinfonia; Rondoletto. Outer movements are more rhythmic in nature with strong syncopation, while the

Sinfonia is sustained and melodic. The written-out turn is important to the melody in the Sinfonia. Mildly 20th-century. M-D.

Albert D. Schmutz. *Sonata* (PIC 1969) 26pp., parts. Allegro; Andante sostenuto; Rondo. Freely tonal, with key signatures. Highly chromatic. The slow movement is especially lovely, with well-balanced textures in both instruments. Displays a facile craft. M-D.

Walter Skolnik. *Sonatina* 1962 (Tenuto 1971) 11pp., parts. 6½ min. Allegro molto; Lento; Allegretto. Linear, freely tonal. Chordal and linear textures combined in the Lento; flowing *pp* closing. Large span required. M-D.

Leon Stein. *Sonata* 1967 (ST) 28pp., parts. For tenor sax and piano. Allegro vivace; Adagio; Allegro. Strong chromatic and atonal writing, octotonic, highly organized. Requires large span. D.

Halsey Stevens. *Dittico* 1972 (Helios) 14pp., parts. 6 min. For sax (or clarinet) and piano. Notturno: flowing chromatic lines; interplay with melody between instruments; builds to climax then subsides to a dark *p* closing. Danza arzilla: a $\frac{6}{8}$ Allegro with hemiola intrusions propels this highly effective movement to a brilliant conclusion. This Suite is one of the finest works for the combination yet encountered by this writer. M-D.

Jenö Takács. *Two Fantastics* Op.88 (Dob 1972) 25pp., parts. 11 min. Tempo rubato: extreme-range sonorities created with long pedals; night music that is tranquil and expressive; certain parts do not necessarily need to be together; some rapid pedal changes; dramatic arpeggi gestures; cadenza-like. Tempo giusto: opening grows out of low-register secco sonorities; cadenzas for both instruments; repeated clusters. Both *Fantastics* make one musical entity. Bartók and jazz influences, strong rhythmic drive, imaginative writing. M-D.

Alexander Tcherepnin. *Sonatine Sportive* (Leduc 1943) 10pp., parts. "As its title indicates, this Sonatine attempts to adopt to music the surprise elements of Sports" (from Composer's Preface). Each movement has program notes. Boxing (Allegro); Mi-temps (Larghetto); Race (Vivace). Colorful writing for both instruments with a few surprises here and there. M-D.

Marshall W. Turkin. *Sonata* 1958 (TP 1969) 26pp., parts. Allegro con moto; Adagio; Allegro con spirito. Traditional forms, octotonic, freely tonal, hemiola, movements complement each other, ostinato-like figure in Adagio, large span required. M-D.

Burnet C. Tuthill. *Sonata* Op.20 (ST 1966) 24pp., parts. Allegro giocoso: SA; 16th-note figuration; Un poco tranquillo contrasting section has rocking quality and becomes more rhythmic; centers around c with a key signature of 2 flats. Andante, un poco adagio: highly Romantic, cantabile. Presto molto vivace: $\frac{6}{8}$, long arpeggi-like lines in piano, trills, chordal punctuation, Prestissimo closing. M-D.

Alec Wilder. *Sonata* (Sam Fox W110 1970) 23pp., parts. 11½ min. I: moving lines; freely tonal; changing meters; moves to a *pp* closing but final note is subito *ff*. II: chromatic chords, waltzlike. III: triplets frequent; syncopation in piano; thin textures mixed with chords. IV: piano part more chordal while the sax is melodically oriented; large span required. Neoclassic. M-D.

Duos for Piano and Trumpet (Cornet)

George Antheil. *Sonata* C (Weintraub 1953) 26pp., parts. Allegretto; Dolce–espressivo; Scherzo; Allegretto. Freely moving harmonies, chromatic, flowing lines, secco style, satiric, sardonic humor in Scherzo, refreshing with a mildly 20th-century flavor. Requires large span. M-D.

Mary Jeanne van Appledorn. *Incantations* 1991 (D. Kiser—Arsis 1992) 13pp., parts. 4 min. In 2 movements: Molto espressivo; Jubilantly. "The first incantation, marked Molto espressivo, conveys in free form the soulful, spiritual and emotional powers of chanting. At the Attacca, the second incantation is dramatically announced by the ostinato pattern of the accompaniment and immediately joined by the solo metamagicaltema, a short melodic series of notes occurring at times in double counterpoint against the ostinato, and marked by continuous development and variation. *Incantations* . . . also reflects upon the third Sunday after Easter—the Introit for the day begins 'Jubilate'" (from Preface). M-D.

Joseph Jean Baptiste Laurent Arban. *Arban's Twelve Celebrated Fantaisies and Airs Variés* (E. F. Goldman—CF 1912) 118pp. Cornet part found only in Arban's *Complete Method for Trumpet*. Collected edition of paraphrases and variations by the famous trumpeter. Includes *Fantaisie and Variations on a Cavatina from Beatrice di Tenda by V. Bellini* Bb, *Fantaisie and Variations on Acteon* D, *Fantaisie Brillante* bb/Bb, *Variations on a Tyrolean Song* Bb, *Variations on a Song 'Vois-tu la Neige qui brillé* Eb, *Cavatina and Variations* Bb, *Air Varié on a Folk Song 'The Little Swiss Boy'* g/Bb, *Caprice and Variations* Eb, *Fantaisie and Variations on a German Theme* Eb, *Variations on a Favorite Theme by C. M. von Weber* Bb, *Fantaisie and Variations on the Carnival of Venice* Eb, *Variations on a Theme from Norma by V. Bellini* Bb. M-D to D.

————. *Don Carlos di Verdi: Fantaisie Brillante* (I. Conforzi—Ut Orpheus TIB04 1998, ISMN M-2153-0417-8) 18pp., parts. Paraphrased setting of themes from *Don Carlos* in a grand and glorious style. Pompous and brilliant, showcasing the trumpet with pianistic writing alternating between soloistic and secondary roles. M-D.

Robert Baksa. *Trumpet Sonata* 1993 (CLE 27 1994) 31pp., parts. 15 min. Lively; Not too slow, singing; Very rhythmic, not too fast. Titles describe character of movements well. Refreshing literature, strongly tonal with a sense of destiny. Challenging but not overwhelming. M-D.

———. *Earth Elegy* 1994 (CLE 36 1994) 7pp., parts. 5 min. To be performed with much flexibility at a quick pace. Relatively soft throughout, finishing *pp* with added-note e chord. M-D.

Guillaume Balay. *Petite Pièce Concertante* (G. C. Mager, A. J. Andraud—ST SS-300 1958) 6pp., parts. For cornet. Initially in G♭ at Modéré, an elegant melody unfolds into a striking march in E♭ and a grand finish. M-D.

———. *Andante et Allegretto* (G. C. Mager, A. J. Andraud—ST SS-143 1958) 7pp., parts. Rich harmonic movement with chromaticism and vestiges of the late 19th century. Attractive. M-D.

———. *Pièce de Concours* (K 4539).

J. E. Barat. *Andante et Scherzo* (Leduc) 7pp., parts. Two contrasting sections with full chords, octotonic writing, and dramatic character. A thorough command of octaves is necessary. M-D.

———. *Fantaisie en mi bémol* (Leduc 1958) 7pp., parts. For cornet or trumpet. In 2 continuous sections: Andante; Scherzo Allegro. Lyric; opening yields to a playful scherzo in parallel major with chromatic passagework and flare. Large span required. M-D.

———. *Lento et Scherzo* (Leduc).

———. *Orientale* (Leduc)

Franz Benda. *Sonata* F (EM 1957) 7pp., parts. Andante con moto; Moderato; Presto. Flowing, graceful and appealing writing. M-D.

Niels Viggo Bentzon. *Sonata* Op.73 (WH 1970) 24pp., parts. Allegro moderato; Adagio; Allegro. Piano is thoroughly exploited, moving over entire keyboard. Neoclassic writing that requires complete pianistic equipment and ensemble experience. D.

Leonard Bernstein. *Rondo for Lifey* (Bo&H 20764 1977) 5pp., parts. 2½ min. Lifey was a friend's Skye terrier. Cute picturesque setting in multimeters suggestive of a dog running. Rondo theme in contrasting 8th notes followed by sustained values. Funlike with 2 brief episodic passages between the 3 statements of the theme. M-D.

Thomas Beversdorf. *Sonata* (ST SS-144 1963) 18pp., parts. Allegro decisivo: SA, chromatic, chordal; large gestures conclude movement. Largo: wide range of piano used; octaves employed melodically; strong climax; *ppp* closing; trumpet cadenza leads directly to Allegro: dancelike, much rhythmic figuration; arpeggi in final section; Neoclassic overtones throughout the entire work. M-D.

Marcel Bitsch. *Fantasietta* (Leduc 1950) 4pp., parts. Marked Allegro, this miniature fantasy is packed with marked rhythms, scalar and arpeggiated figurations, and a wide use of the keyboard. Driving rhythms. M-D.

————. *Quatre Variations sur un Thème de Domenico Scarlatti* B♭ (Leduc 1950) 14pp., parts. For trumpet or cornet. Commences with a martial-like theme in B♭, followed by 4 contrasting variations developing intervallic relationships heard in the theme with occasional asymmetric rhythm. Composed for the Paris Conservatory Concours. Large span required. M-D.

Ernest Bloch. *Proclamation* 1955 (BB 1959) 8pp., parts. 6 min. Piano reduction by Bloch. Stirring, attention-getting, sectionalized into Allegro energico, Poco meno mosso, Poco più animato, Andante, Più calmo ending. Freely tonal around C. Sections hold together, integral chromaticism. M-D.

Auguste de Boeck. *Allegro* (CF 1937) 14pp., parts. For cornet or trumpet. In late-19th-century style with chromaticism. Large chordal texture poses some problems at the lively tempo. M-D.

Eugène Bozza. *Caprice* Op.47 (Leduc 1943) 12pp., parts. Commences Assez lent with *pp* chords in piano and 2 recitative passages in trumpet serving as introductory material to the caprice proper. A pulsating Allegro of repeated chords and rhythmic ingenuity ensues and concludes with a scherzo-like dash to the finish. Large span required. M-D.

————. *Badinage* (Leduc 1950) 4pp., parts. Bang start with 3-mm. theme introduced in piano at Giocoso. Imitative, articulate, and well balanced for a picturesque essay in ternary form. M-D.

————. *Rustiques* (Leduc 1955) 8pp., parts. For cornet or trumpet. In one continuous movement with 3 distinct sections in Neoclassic vein. One of the easier Bozza scores for pianists though more difficult for trumpeters. Contains 4 cadenza-like passages for trumpet. Int.

————. *Rhapsodie* (Leduc 1957) 7pp., parts. Majestic, declarative opening with marked chords leads to a lyric melody at Moderato, followed by a blistering Allegro moderato marked scherzando. Animated conclusion. M-D.
Both *Caprice* and *Rustiques* were composed for the Paris Conservatory Concours.

Jacques Castérède. *Sonatine* (Leduc 1956) 15pp., parts. Allegro energico; Andantino; Rondo–Allegro giocoso. Chromatic with bold statements and detailed passagework. Andantino offers calmer melodic response with added-note harmonies. An individualist style blending eclectic techniques into a distinctly mid-20th-century approach. M-D.

Robert Clérisse. *Noce Villageoise* (Leduc) 3pp., parts. For cornet, trumpet, bugle, or baritone horn. Dancelike qualities assist in projecting a simple theme in a homophonic setting. M-D.

————. *Thème Varié* (Leduc). For cornet or trumpet.

David H. Cope. *Sonata* (CF) 12 min. Three movements. M-D.

Henry Cowell. *Triad* (PIC 1953) 8pp., parts. Concentrates on triadic formations, especially root position, treating them in parallel motion, bitonally, and as 7th chords. Strangely the melody makes little use of the structure. M-D.

Jean-Michel Damase. *Hymne* (Lemoine 1975) 7pp., parts. For cornet (or trumpet). Does little to invoke a hymn in the traditional sense. Could have been entitled using one of several character piece forms. Lyric, with chromaticism. M-D.

Peter Maxwell Davies. *Sonata* 1955 (Schott 11067 1969) 16pp., parts. Allegro moderato; Lento; Allegro vivo. Experiments with a rhythmic series. Full of motoric energy and clean, lean writing. M-D to D.

Eddy Debons. *A Bumble Bee's Fantasy* (EMR 6043 1996) 14pp., parts. For trumpet in C or B♭ (parts included). Picturesque with rapid scalar passagework at Vivace in chromatic and diatonic modes emulating the motion of the bumble bee. Lyric theme in central Andante espressivo section relieves the whirlwind motion momentarily. M-D.

Jean-Michel Defaye. *Sonatine* (Leduc 1956) 15pp., parts. Allegro; Aria; Rondo. Uses oompah rhythms with contrasting harmonic makeup extensively early on before yielding to repeating note and chord formations which visit neighboring tones. Soothing Aria is a bit repetitious, but the tension is quickly relieved by a rhythmic Rondo and its bullet-like theme. A dash to the finish leaves the trumpet on a sustained high C. M-D.

Marc Delmas. *Choral et Variations* Op.37 g/G (Billaudot) 8pp., parts. Choral of 16 mm. serves as theme for 4 variations and finale. The calmness and solemnity of the Choral is only slightly broken for a few mm. in the first 2 variations though the 3rd expands into louder dynamics and dramatic contrasts. The finale grows in animation for a sonorous ending at *fff*. Concours piece for Paris Conservatory. M-D.

Edison Denisov. *Con Sordino* (Leduc 1998) 19pp., parts. In one movement, mostly with mute, marked Tranquillo. Uses extremes of instruments, proportional rhythmic relationships, quartal chords, flurries of grace notes, and linear writing for a cornucopia of sonorous effects. Fascinating, though with almost impossible requirements for trumpet. Only once does the score exceed *p* in dynamics (*mf*) and only briefly at that. D.

Petr Eben. *Fantasia Vespertina* (Schott TR3 1969, ISMN M-001-10181-3) 8pp., parts. Contains solos for both instruments, commencing with trumpet at Andante. An Allegro doubles the tempo and rhythmically pushes its way forward with a series of double 8ths–quarters. Stays relatively quiet except for the approach to the end but diminishes away to *pp* in the final 3 mm. M-D.

Maurice Emmanuel. *Sonate* (Leduc 1951) 11pp., parts. For cornet or bugle in B♭ and piano. Adagio; Allemande; Aria; Gigue. Suitelike, facile writing with touch of humor. Mildly 20th-century. M-D.

Georges Enesco. *Légende* (Enoch) 7pp., parts. Lent et grave: chordal, chromatic, arpeggi, some tempo variation, sweeping lines in mid-section, builds to *fff* climax, *pppp* closing. Authoritative Romantic writing. M-D.

Eric Ewazen. *Sonata* (ST SU337 1997) 44pp., parts. Lento–Allegro molto; Allegretto; Allegro con fuoco. A constant beehive of passagework for piano using conventional writing techniques with little rest. Trumpet frequently reaches to its upper register in outer movements. Large span required. M-D.

Arthur Frackenpohl. *Sonatina* (GS 1974) 10pp., parts. Based on *Sonatinas* Opp.20 and 55 by Friedrich Kuhlau. Tempo di marcia; Adagio e sostenuto; Rondo. The piano part stays rather close to the original Kuhlau, with the trumpet line fitted in stylistically correctly. Int. to M-D.

Jean Français. *Sonatina* 1950 (ESC 1952) 12pp., parts. Prelude; Sarabande; Gigue. Light Neoclassic writing. Requires strong rhythmic emphasis. M-D.

George Friboulet. *Introduction et March* B♭ (Lemoine 1958) 6pp., parts. Brief introduction leads to traditional marchlike character in $\frac{2}{4}$ with mild 20th-century flavor. Requires extra attention in precision for effective reading. M-D.

Pierre Gabaye. *Boutade* F (Leduc 1957) 7pp., parts. 2½ min. Allegretto throughout with bouncy and driving rhythms, a melody spelling out the tonic triad, touches of chromaticism, broken-chord arpeggiation, and a surprise glissando at the end. Fun to hear and play. M-D.

Philippe Gaubert. *Cantabile et Scherzetto* (Leduc 1959) 11pp., parts. For cornet. A grand, sweeping introduction ushers in rich harmonic action and a melody to be played "avec charme." The Cantabile spirit of the section is very expressive and could very well stand on its own. High octave G's mark time as a Scherzetto marked Très vite commences with motivic play in the left hand announcing the theme and paving an introductory passage for the trumpet. Contrasting sections follow as the work dashes to the end at *ff* with majestic finesse. Composed for the Paris Conservatory Concours. M-D.

André Gédalge. *Pièce* (Leduc) 7pp., parts. Marked Molto allegro. Explores lively playing at extreme dynamic ranges. Paris Conservatory Concours piece. M-D.

Harald Genzmer. *Sonatine* 1965 (CFP 5989) 16pp., parts. 8 min. Allegro; Andante tranquillo; Saltarello. Octotonic, parallel chords, alternating hands, freely tonal, bitonal, vigorous finale. M-D.

Alexandre Glazounov. *Albumblatt* D♭ 1899 (T. Dokshitsen—EMR 643 1992) 6pp., parts. An expressive character piece embodying late-19th-century compositional techniques. M-D.

Alphonse Goeyens. *All'Antica* 1894 (ST SS-319) 6pp., parts. A concert piece in the olden style. Full textures with imitation, rhythmic vitality, and complementary writing. Challenging in places. M-D.

———. *Introduction and Scherzo* F (CF 1937) 11pp., parts. Brief introduction with rolled chords and melody leads to lively Scherzo of multiple sections and meters. Finishes as fast as possible. M-D.

Iain Hamilton. *Capriccio* (Schott 1952) 5 min.

———. *Five Scenes* 1966 (Schott) 13pp., parts. 10 min. Wild; Nocturnal; Declamato; Nocturnal; Brilliant. Strongly contrasted movements that use tremolo, pointillism (single notes and chords), long pedals, dynamic extremes, clusters. Large span required for these striking pieces. M-D.

Thorvald Hansen. *Sonata for Cornet and Piano* Op.18 E♭ 1915 (E. H. Tarr— Spaeth/Schmid [1998]) 19pp., parts. Allegro con brio; Andante con espressione; Allegro con anima. Conventional late-19th-century writing with charm and grace. Piano in slow movement is reminiscent of works by earlier masters. Comes together as an ensemble without much effort. M-D.

Walter Hartley. *Trumpet Sonatina* 1952 (Accura) 12pp., parts. 5½ min. Allegro alla marcia; Adagio; Presto. Miniature movements in a 20th-century tonal style with marked rhythms and considerable octaves. M-D.

———. *Caprice* 1967 (Ensemble). 3 min.

Willy Hess. *Sieben Tonstücke* Op.80 (Amadeus-Paüler 1974) 16pp., parts. Intrata; Impromptu; Ecossaise; Menuett; Siziliano; Trauermarsch; Fanfaren und Romanze. Short, well-written, attractive mildly 20th-century pieces for the young trumpeter and pianist. Int.

Paul Hindemith. *Sonata* 1939 (Schott) 24pp., parts. 11 min. Forceful; Moderately fast–Lively; Music of Mourning–Chorale. Similar in sturdy quality to the clarinet Sonata. Authoritative character. Second and third movements are based on alternating tempos with a tune in the second movement similar to "Ach du Lieber Augustin." The third movement is a funeral march. A middle section marked Ruhig bewegt provides contrast. The coda has the trumpet playing the chorale "Alle Menschen müssen sterben." D.

Alun Hoddinott. *Rondo Scherzoso* Op.12/1 (OUP 1958) 3½ min. Thin textures, freely tonal, glissando, colorful, *fff* closing. Would make an effective encore. M-D.

Theodore Holdheim. *Sonata* 1958 (IMI 1966) 43pp., parts. 10 min. Allegro con brio: SA, changing meters, percussive chords; Grave: ABA, expressive; Allegro vivace: rondo, strong rhythms, brilliant closing. Entire work is written in an extended or free tonality. Neoclassic characteristics. M-D to D.

Paul Holmes. *Sonata* (SP 1962) 11pp., parts. 10 min. Allegro: SA, ostinato-like treatment. Adagio: ABA, melodic emphasis in both instruments; Con moto mid-section has more activity. Allegro: rhythmic; opening idea from first movement returns; requires a good octave technique. Neoclassic orientation. M-D.

Arthur Honegger. *Intrada* 1947 (Sal 1947) 7pp., parts. Maestoso: chordal, low sonorities, melody in octaves, large span required. Allegro: vigorous rhythms, syncopation, repeated notes. Maestoso: uses material similar to that of beginning. Freely tonal and appealing writing. M-D.

Alan Hovhaness. *Haroutin* Op.71 (Resurrection) (CFP 6576a 1968) 11pp., parts. 10 min. Originally for trumpet and string orchestra. Piano reduction by the composer. Aria: diatonic, parallel moving 3rds and chords; trumpet has melodic emphasis with some embellishment. Fugue: long subject, extensive solo piano writing, scalar passages prevalent, *ppp* Largo misterioso conclusion on A. M-D.

Jean Hubeau. *Sonate* 1943 B♭ (Durand) 18pp., parts. 12½ min. Sarabande; Intermède; Spiritual. Chordal, added-note technique. Martellato brittle style in Intermède. Spiritual is written in a "Tempo di Blues," followed by a Tempo più animato section based on broken-octave figuration, *ffff* closing. Requires large span. M-D.

Jacques Ibert. *Impromptu* 1951 (Leduc 1951) 4pp., parts. 2 min. Commissioned by the Serge Koussevitzky Music Foundation, this short work consists of 4 lively capsule-like sections. Highly rhythmic with syncopation and a touch of boogie-woogie, a frolicking air is suggested within the work's complexity. Bitonality appears within the overall Neoclassic framework. D.

Kent Kennan. *Sonata* (Warner Brothers 1956) 24pp., parts. 13 min. With strength and vigor: a cracking good opening, has a more legato dolce contrasting second subject. Rather slowly and with freedom: varied sections and moods; ostinato-like treatment in Poco più mosso part; both performers need a good sense of feeling the bar line. Moderately fast, with energy: opens with a fugally conceived idea, followed by shifting rhythms in piano part while trumpet is mainly treated in rhythmic fashion; meno mosso (Simply, in the manner of a chorale) recalls second subject of first movement. Combination of ideas is worked through. Pianistic throughout. M-D.

Jan Koetsier. *Sonatina* Op.56 (EMR 238 1991) 15pp., parts. Larghetto con variazioni; Rondo Allegro. Opening movement has lilting theme in $\frac{6}{8}$ with 3 variations. Rondo bounces along with syncopated treatment and jovial quality. M-D.

Barbara Kolb. *Related Characters* 1980 (Bo&H 1985). See detailed entry under duos for piano and viola.

Alexander von Kreisler. *Sonatina* (ST SS-721 1966) 12pp., parts. Allegro moderato: quiet pianistic opening with heralding trumpet theme, contrasted by Poco più mosso in $\frac{6}{8}$; ternary form; linear writing. Andante: homophonic with subdued theme in ternary form. Allegro molto: shifting harmonies in largely chordal and broken-chord texture; brief coda finish. M-D.

Morten Lauridsen. *Sonata* (King 1973) 20pp., parts. 12½ min. Allegro vivace: markedly rhythmic, octaves, free dissonant counterpoint, trill important, linear, clear textures. Largo: legato and sustained, freely tonal, Allegro mid-section followed by solo cadenzas for both instruments, contrary synthetic scales. Presto con fuoco: vigorous, dancelike, changing meters, Adagio section recalls mood of Largo movement, Neoclassic orientation. M-D to D.

Otto Luening. *Introduction and Allegro* (CFP 66013 1972) 7pp., parts. 2½ min. For trumpet in C and piano. Short, 2-page atonal introduction, thin textures, requires large span. Allegro uses imitation; cadenza passage for trumpet; contrasting touches in each hand; chord and single note in alternating hands provide rhythmic drive. M-D.

Peter Mai. *Sonata Breve* (Philharmusica 1975) 12pp., parts. Rhythmisch bestimmt; Ruhig, gesangvoll; Lebhaft. Tonal in a mildly 20th-century way, thin textures, well-contrasted movements. M-D.

Bohuslav Martinů. *Sonatine* (Leduc 1957 15pp.; Supraphon 1989 17pp.), parts. Allegro moderato. A Poco andante brings the work to a close. Highly pianistic throughout with traditional keyboard idioms used in a mildly 20th-century fashion. M-D.

Mark Milman. *Sonata* (Philharmusica 1973) 23pp., parts. Allegro molto risoluto energico. This one-movement work contains many contrasts. Freely tonal, strong syncopation, toccata-like conclusion. Requires large span. M-D.

Jules Mouquet. *Légende Héroïque* Op.27 1908 (Leduc) 13pp., parts. For cornet. Picturesque setting in late-19th-century style with Lisztian techniques and Brahmsian harmonies. Commences Allegro con brio and maintains that tempo until close to the end while passing through multiple sections of key changes and technical development. Written for Paris Conservatory Concours. Allows the brilliance of both instruments to be heard. M-D.

Vaclav Nelhybel. *Golden Concerto on a Twelve Tone Row* (EM 1960) 12pp., parts. One sectionalized movement. Toccata-like figuration, expressive and sustained section, octotonic, broad conclusion. Row undergoes various treatment. M-D.

Andrzej Panufnik. *Concerto in Modo Antico* (Gothic Concerto) (Bo&H 1956) 20pp., parts. 15 min. Based on old Polish themes. Originally for trumpet and string orchestra, harp, and kettledrums. Piano reduction by the composer. M-D.

Flor Peeters. *Sonata* Op.51 (CFP 1961) 29pp., parts. 13 min. Allegro: B♭, freely flowing, colorful, con fuoco ending. Aria–Adagio: melodic emphasis, piano accompaniment in parallel chords. Finale–Toccata: motoric, alternation of hands in chords, piano has some melodic treatment but mainly provides rhythmic drive throughout. M-D.

Marcel Poot. *Etude de Concert* (ESC 3793 1933) 15pp., parts. For trumpet in C. Spirited concert étude in multiple sections at Allegro vivo. Specialized form which keeps unveiling as sections emerge, all with differing technical requirements rather than a general focus on one problem. M-D.

Henry Purcell. *Sonata* g (Lumsden—Musica Rara 1962) 7 min. Originally for trumpet and strings, but this is an effective keyboard arrangement. M-D.

Hermann Reutter. *Scherzo* (Leduc 1969) 6pp., parts. 3 min. Playful, snappy, and imitative with subtle harmonic changes. Briefly contrasting trio is homophonic. M-D.

Eric Richards. *Rocks; Gardens* 1970 ([Lingua Press/Frog Peak 1977]) 7 sheets, 2 copies needed for performance. For trumpet, cornet, or piccolo trumpet. Experimental; proportional notation; linear without chords. Contains detailed performance guide. D.

J. Guy Ropartz. *Andante et Allegro* E♭ (Salabert 1970 7pp.; CF CU572 6pp.), parts. In one movement cast in alternating slow-fast sections like the Baroque Sonata da Camera. Maintains clear harmonic progressions in early-20th-century tonality with engaging writing and a strong dependence of one instrument upon another. Written for Paris Conservatory Concours. Also available in trombone transcription by A. Shapiro. M-D.

Steve Rouse. *The Avatar* 1991 (MMB 1991) 24pp., parts. 11 min. For B♭ piccolo trumpet, flügelhorn, or B♭ trumpet, although the cornet or trumpet may be used if flügelhorn is not possible. Includes piano transposition of first mvt. in the event an A piccolo trumpet is used. I. Nativity, II. Enigma–Release, III. Rebirth. Roughed with energetic drive in outer movements. Added-note, parallel chords in slower middle movement with lengthy piano introduction. For experienced performers. D.

———. *More Light* 1995 (MMB) 3pp., parts. 4 min. "*More Light* contains familiar fragments of more than a dozen traditional Southern Baptist hymns. Some of these fragments can be clearly heard at the 'surface' of the music; others are more deeply embedded in the structure" (from Preface). Score is photocopy of MS. M-D.

Robert Russell. *Sonatina* Op.23 1967 (Gen) 11pp., parts. Lento–Allegro; Adagio; Vivo. Freely tonal around B♭, slow contrary octaves, figuration in alternating hands, fast repeated notes. The trumpet bell is placed inside the piano to produce harmonics at end of Adagio. Neoclassic orientation. M-D.

Peter Schickele. *Three Uncharacteristic Pieces* 1981 (EV 164-00184 1992) 23pp., parts. 10 min. 1. Dance of Uncertain National Origin, 2. Valse Enigmatique, 3.

Young Man Going West. The first piece "seemed to me to have echoes of various different cultures—middle European and Mexican, for instance—hence the titled 'Dance of Uncertain National Origin.' When an occasional piece turns out well, it frequently becomes part of a larger work . . . Much of the material in these pieces seemed somewhat atypical of my music, and this feeling led to the overall title of the work" (from Program Note). Favors trumpet. M-D.

William Schmidt. *The Turkish Lady: Variations on a Whaling Song* (WIM AV165 1969) 15pp., parts. Theme announced freely in robust character by trumpet followed by 5 variations of contrasting qualities, including a march and a recitative. Early-20th-century harmonies with occasional cluster chords. M-D.

Florent Schmitt. *Suite* Op.133 (Durand 1955) 23pp., parts. 16 min. Originally for trumpet and orchestra. Piano reduction by the composer. Gaiment: sprightly, scherzo, contrasting calmer section. Lent sans excès: parallel chords, melodic line worked into fabric, mildly Impressionist. Vif: chords in alternating hands, dancelike, chromatic. M-D.

Harold Shapero. *Sonata* 1940 (PIC 1956) 23pp., parts. For C trumpet. Slow; Fast. Strong rhythmic language, lyric element always present, logical formal treatment. Final section is marked Slower; Neoclassic. Large span required. M-D.

Nikos Skalkottas. *Concertino for Trumpet and Piano* 1941–43 (G. Schuller, J. G. Papaiouannou—Margun 67 1986) 10pp., parts. 6 min. "Although a highly virtuoso showpiece for the trumpet—the piano part is also rich in polyphony and massive chords—it makes no concessions in its high standard of creative invention. Fullness of sound, extreme melodic flexibility, and daring trumpet runs spanning the entire range of the instrument underscore the remarkable way in which these two highly dissimilar instruments are blended into a unified whole." In one movement, a "Lied-sonata form (exposition-recapitulation, without development section)" (from About the Music). M-D.

Walter Skolnik. *Sonata* 1971 (Tenuto T126) 23pp., parts. 10 min. Allegro moderato; Lento; Allegretto giocoso. Mildly 20th-century, formally well constructed, disjunct melodic material. M-D.

Harvey Sollberger. *Iron Mountain Song* 1971 (Columbia University Press 1974) 24pp., set of 2 scores. Changing meters, expanding intervals, proportional rhythmic relationships, tightly organized, atonal, pointillistic, linear, serial influence. Large span required. D.

Leo Sowerby. *Sonata* 1945 (Gamble Hinged 1948) 40pp., parts. Sprightly; Slow; In martial style. One of the largest 20th-century Sonatas in the repertoire. Ponderous in style with thick chords and extensive development. Treats instruments compatibly with closely entwined parts without sacrificing individuality. M-D to D.

Halsey Stevens. *Sonata* 1956 (CFP 1959) 23pp., parts. 15 min. Allegro moderato: incisive theme developed into a stimulating dialogue with the piano; thin piano part heightens brilliance of trumpet part with dissonance and lively rhythmic accents. Adagio tenero: slow, muted trumpet, broadly conceived theme, superimposed intervals, modal elements. Allegro: brilliant, variable meters, bouncy theme, Bartók influence. M-D.

Robert Suderburg. *Chamber Music VII: Ceremonies for Trumpet and Piano* 1984 (N. Gardener—TP 114-40402 1984) 24pp., parts. 16 min. 1. Calls and echoes, allegro; 2. Calls and echoes, adagio, andante; 3. Procession, closing-call. Commences with trumpet playing directly into piano with damper and sostenuto pedals down. Piano enters at m. 28 with rolled octave A's for lengthy solo using imitation between hands and rolled arpeggiation. Mixed meters predominate when both instruments play together. Reverberation techniques are explored in the middle movement and repeated notes in the last. Score is photocopy of MS. M-D.

William Sydeman. *The Affections* (AMP 1968) 30pp., parts. 14 min. For C trumpet. Determination; Frenzy; Quiet Dignity; Good Humour; Patriotism; Urgency; Yearning and Fulfillment. Complex, pointillistic writing throughout. Colorful sonorities. In the final piece the pianist is asked to play all extreme upper-register notes as hard as possible. Requires mature pianism and strong hands! D.

Jan Tausinger. *Sonatina Emancipata* 1968 (Panton 1973) 11pp., 2 copies necessary for performance. Explanations in Czech, German, and English.

Henri Tomasi. *Triptyque* (Leduc 1957) 7pp., parts. For trumpet in C or B♭. Scherzo; Largo; Saltarelle. Short essays in expressive technique and rhythmic fervor. Large span required. M-D.

Fisher Tull. *Sonata* (Bo&H 1988) 29pp., parts. 15 min. "The sonata is cast in four movements, the first being in the style of a recitative in bravura style. The second movement is in a modified sonata-allegro form with two contrasting thematic elements. The slow third movement features a gentle interplay between the trumpet and piano which culminates in a tender lament by the muted trumpet. The finale, in rondo form, features complex rhythmic activity by both instruments leading to a solo trumpet cadenza. The ensuing recapitulation exploits the extreme range of the trumpet in a dramatic fashion" (from Program Note). Score is photocopy of MS.

———. *Three Bagatelles* 1975 (Bo&H 1977) 15pp., parts. 6½ min. "The composer says, 'The three movements are designed to display three contrasting styles of trumpet performance: dramatic boldness, lyric expression and agile virtuosity.' This new work for trumpet and piano covers the gamut of trumpet technique and style for the entire range of the instrument is exploited. Various mutes are also utilized" (from Preface). M-D.

Burnet Tuthill. *Sonata* Op.29 (Warner Brothers 1951) 23pp., parts. Allegro ben marcato: E♭; dramatic chordal and octave opening; mid-section slower and more sustained, leads to an Agitato section, Tempo I, Slower, Agitato ending. Slowly: f; chromatic chords lead to a Vivace mid-section; Tempo I character and varied opening section returns. Rondo–Vivace: contrasting episodes in different keys and character; concludes in B♭. Mildly 20th-century. M-D.

David Uber. *Sonata* Op.34 (PIC 1969). For trumpet or trombone and piano. See description under duos for piano and trombone.

Paul Vidal. *Aria et Fanfare* C 1927 (Leduc 1927) 8pp., parts. 8½ min. For trumpet in C or B♭. In 2 movements of late-19th-century concept with prominent melodies and strongly harmonic structures. Lyrical with well-balanced phrases. M-D.

James Walker. *Sonatina* (GS 1974) 17pp., parts. Allegro moderato; Andante mesto; Allegro. Freely tonal; much charm, humor, and wit. Popular orientation but strong Classical structure and form. Pianist is kept busy. Neoclassic, phrases extended by irregular rhythmic interruptions. The middle movement is a highly expressive Passacaglia. M-D.

Donald H. White. *Sonata* (King 1967) 28pp., parts. Fast and Marked: octotonic, bitonal, undulating quartal and quintal harmonies, triplets, firm rhythms, freely tonal around B♭. Slow: expressive, free dissonant counterpoint, sustained chords in piano support melodic line in trumpet, chordal climax, relaxes and closes *pp*. Spirited: driving rhythms, many harmonic 2nds and 4ths, parallel chords, motivic generation, octaves in alternating hands, strong finish, freely tonal around B♭. M-D.

Alec Wilder. *Sonata* 1963 (G. Schuller—Margun 1978) 27pp., parts. Slowly, with feeling; Fast-in 2; Slowly rocking; Rhythmic (3 + 4). Expressive with good concept of lyric qualities and rhythms. M-D.

André Wormser. *Fantaisie Thème et Variations* f/F (Leduc 1937) 12pp., parts. For trumpet or cornet. In late-19th-century style with touches of chromaticism. Multisectional with variations easily discernible but not indicated. Complementary parts, sometimes exchanging ideas as question-answer. M-D.

Charles Wuorinen. *Nature's Concord* (CFP 66380 1969) 21pp., parts. 11 min. Serial, pointillistic, spatial relationships. D.

Duos for Piano and Trombone

Joseph Alexander. *Sonata* (Gen 1967) 20pp., parts. 12 min. Allegro moderato; Andante con moto; Vivace. A vigorous and robust work. The middle movement contains some expressive sonorities. Interplay of meters and rhythms is of special interest. Neoclassic orientation. M-D.

Ejvin Andersen. *Sonatina* (JWC 4135 1968) 16pp., parts. Allegro marziale; Nocturne legatissimo; Allegro assai. In early-20th-century style with added-note harmony. The flowing Nocturne is particularly noteworthy for its musical features. Large span required. M-D.

Anonymous. *St. Thomas Sonata* ca.1669 (K. Shifrin, J. Clarke—Virgo Music 1999) 4pp., parts. Believed to be the first work specifically written for trombone and basso continuo. I. [Dignitoso], II. Fuga, III. [Aria and Variations], IV. [Gigue]. Tasteful realizations for this mid-Baroque work. Found in the archives of the St. Thomas Church in Brno, Moravia. M-D.

J. Ed. Barat. *Andante et Allegro* (CF CU571) 7pp., parts. Rich chordal design in Andante continues into Allegro with a variety of compositional patterns. Rhythmic melodies. M-D.

Leslie Bassett. *Sonata* (King 1967) 24pp., parts. 9½ min. Three movements with first movement (Allegro moderato) SA, a small scherzo (Moderato cantabile) for the middle movement, and a marchlike extensive finale (Allegro marziale). Freely chromatic, flowing lines. Contrapuntal writing is beautifully exploited. M-D.

Bennie Beach. *Suite* (AMP 95666 1957) 8pp., parts. For trombone or baritone horn. Lento; Allegro giusto; Adagio. Colorful harmonic scheme built on conventional practices. Brief movements. M-D.

Niels Viggo Bentzon. *Sonata* Op.277 (WH 1971) 10 min. A large 3-movement work with well-developed material. Humor, wit, and satire are characteristic of the moods. D.

Marcel Bitsch. *Ricercare* (Leduc 1970) 8pp., parts. 6½ min. Twentieth-century setting of the Baroque form in Andante maestoso and Allegro sections. Chromaticism plays a significant role in the development. Large span required. M-D.

———. *Impromptu* (Leduc 1957). For bass saxophone, tuba, or bass trombone. See detailed entry under duos for piano and saxophone.

V. M. Blazewitch. *Concert Piece No. 5* (Belwin-Mills BWI57 1939) 15pp., parts. In 2 broad sections: Andante con afflizione; Allegro mosso. Early-20th-century flavor with rapidly contrasting dynamics, tertian chord structures, and melodic appeal. M-D.

John Boda. *Sonatina* 1954 (King) 14pp., parts. 7½ min. First movement is a moderate 2; fast, crisp, modified SA. The second movement is more linear and is in ABA design. Neoclassic style, freely tonal, pandiatonic at times. Mildly 20th-century. M-D.

Norman Bolter. *Arctic Emanations* 1997 (Air-ev 1998) 17pp., parts. 11 min. "This work is called *Arctic Emanations* because it seeks to connect not only to the fact of the Arctic itself but, more importantly, to *what* lives in the Arctic regions—not necessarily just the wildlife, but its *whole* life including what emanates from the land . . . The opening (piano solo) should take as much time as is needed to create the sense of the openness and starkness of an all-white landscape . . . Deeper into the piece, the pianist, at times, will encounter chords which will seem 'impossible' or nearly so. The pianist should decide which of the presented notes best capture the mood and essence of the piece according to his or her own feeling, registration and technical facility and, accordingly, should play those particular notes. The trombone solo utilizes a very full range of dynamics, mood, and high, mid and low registers. Also, cup mute and extensive Harmon mute techniques are used" (from Introduction). M-D.

———. *At Far, Brought Near* 1995 (Air-ev 1998) 4pp., parts. 4 min. This short work "was inspired by a very special kind of longing. Everyone has had the feeling, in some way, shape or form, of being distant from a loved one or a favourite place or circumstance . . . and the further experience of going through some seemingly necessary process or journey until one finds oneself no longer 'at far,' but rather 'brought near' to that longed for something else" (from Introduction). M-D.

———. *Dark Seas* 1997 (Air-ev 1998) 6pp., parts. 2½ min. Emulates the motion of the sea. "*Dark Seas* exemplifies the saying 'much in little.' While the trombone line is not technically demanding in the quick tempo'd sense, it nonetheless offers much both musically and technically in a short span of time. In addition to its dynamic contrasts and different tone colours, *Dark Seas* is rhythmically demanding in that it calls for the coordination of contrasting syncopated trombone and piano lines. Also, the trombonist is called upon to demonstrate skilled use of the Harmon mute in conjunction with subtle *glissandi*" (from Introduction).

———. *The Song of King David* 1997 (Air-ev 1998) 12pp., parts. 8 min. Ancient, Hebraic, noble. Inspired by the biblical account and writings of King David. "As well as requiring much feeling, *The Song of King David* calls for a great deal of physical stamina. Also, it is rhythmically testing in the 'battle scenes.' Here the pianist is met with repeated two against three patterns. A fast triple tongue is required of the trombonist, as well as the need to express large colour and dynamic contrasts. Throughout the score and trombone part, descriptive words and brief references to the Biblical story line are included to help connect you to the essences that caused this music" (from Introduction). M-D.
Bolter's compositions reveal a strong sense of tonality and considerable repetitive use of motivic devices.

Newel Kay Brown. *Sonata* (Brass Music 1977) 27pp., parts. With vigor–well marked; Tempo rubato; Theme and [6] Variations. Traditional to cluster-like harmonies spread several octaves. Rhythmic variations to the gentle theme include blues, march, and waltz tempos. Piano does not play on Var.5. Large span required. M-D.

Peter Cabus. *Fuga en Toccata* (Maurer 1958) 10pp., parts. Subject introduced by trombone at Grave to which the piano adds 2 voices, each in octaves, for fugal development. Octave treatment maintained until Toccata, whereupon a repeated note D in the piano forms a pedal point as the early-20th-century approach to the Baroque form evolves. Tonal centers shift as the figuration and harmonic development ensue at a rapid tempo just until the ending parallel-chord cadence. D.

Jacques Castérède. *Sonatine* (Leduc 1958) 18pp., parts. 13 min. Allegro vivo; Andante sostenuto; Allegro. Neoclassic with driving rhythms and detailed passagework. Octotonic; use of repeated static chords, chromaticism, and added-note harmonies prevail in finale. Large span required. D.
———. *Fantaisie Concertante* (Leduc 1960) 12pp., parts. 7½ min. For bass trombone, tuba, or bass saxophone. Neoclassic in concept with intricate rhythms and fingering. Slows occasionally for repose in an otherwise lively setting lightly spiced with wit and gaiety. For Paris Conservatory Concours. M-D.

Richard Coolidge. *Curves of Gold* 1973 (Kendor 6191A 1974) 12pp., parts. Uses a series of interlocking arches as structural design with 4 broad sections. Influenced by the poetry of Sara Teasdale, from whom a quote appears, and earlier vocal works by the composer. Passionate, with much expression, in an early-20th-century stylistic development. Large span required. M-D.

Henry Cowell. *Hymn and Fuguing Tune* No. 13 1960 (AMP 1960) 10pp., parts. 5½ min. Hymn: chordal, freely tonal around D, strong counterpoint between both instruments. Fuguing Tune: linear textures, freely tonal around C, chromatic runs, Poco più mosso final section leads to closing. M-D.

John Davison. *Sonata* 1957 (SP 1966) 23pp., parts. 12 min. First movement: monothematic, fantasia. Second movement: scherzo and song combination. Third movement: rondo using Advent carol "O Come, O Come, Emmanuel." Modal throughout. M-D.

Jean-Michel Defaye. *À la Manière de Schumann* (Leduc 2000) 8pp., parts. 4½ min. Long flowing lines and pianistic treatment reminiscent of Schumann composed at the end of the 20th century. M-D.

Wilhelm Domroese. *Sakura. Japanese Impressions for Trombone and Piano* (Leduc 1974) 12pp., parts. Theme and 5 variations plus coda. Includes all techniques of trombone playing including singing into mouthpiece. Freely tonal, quartal and quintal harmonies are exploited, octotonic, fast alternating hand passages. M-D.
——. *Les Ours* (The Bears) Metaphorical Suite for trombone and piano (Leduc 1974) 11pp., parts. 7 min. "This easy suite is a musical interpretation of the typical gestures of bears. For all the different movements the same material is used. The first movement symbolizes the clumsy walking of the bear which is glossed by continuous syncopation. The sorrowful resignation of the she-bear in the second movement changes into merry glee in the final dance of the third movement. A skilful distribution of musical tension and its culmination as well as a clear choice of glissandi will intensify the musical expression and place this work within easy reach of the young musician" (from the score). Mildly 20th-century. M-D.

Henri Dutilleux. *Choral, Cadence et Fugato* (Leduc 1950) 8pp., parts. Choral: E, Lent, good melodic line necessary over chordal accompaniment, chromatic. Cadence: piano provides tremolo and broken-octave gestures. Fugato: staccato, very rhythmic subject worked over and developed, sonorous closing. M-D.

Eric Ewazen. *Sonata for Trombone and Piano* (ST SU339 1998), parts. 20 min. "Written in the great nineteenth-century tradition of large scale sonatas" (from www.ericewazen.com).
——. *Ballade for Bass Trombone and Piano* (ST), parts. 12 min. May also be played on tenor trombone or tuba. In one movement. Lyrical.
See Ted Hale, "The Influence of Jazz on Eric Ewazen's *Sonata for Trombone and Piano,*" JITA 25/2 (spring 1997): 32–34.

Maurice Franck. *Fanfare, Andante et Allegro* 1958 (Sal) 15pp., parts. Parallel chords, bitonal, 7th chords, large skips, octotonic chromatic writing. M-D.

Henri Gagnebin. *Sarabande* (Leduc 1953) 2pp., parts. 3 min. Fine ensemble rapport in this 20th-century setting of the older dance form. Thick chords at Assez lent. M-D.

Harald Genzmer. *Sonata* (CFP 8194 1974) 19pp., parts. Allegro; Adagio; Finale. Genzmer continues the Neoclassic emphasis in his writing while gradually extending the harmonic resources. Cluster-like sounds are exploited in the slow movement while trills add effectively to the sonority. Traditional forms are still much in evidence, and a superb craft glows in every measure. M-D.

Walter Hartley. *Sonata Concertante* 1956–58 (Interlochen Press 1968) 23pp., parts. 10 min. Exposition followed by a chaconne with 7 variations and a scherzo that serves as a development, recapitulation, and coda. Synthetic scale, major and minor sonorities juxtaposed between instruments. Mature pianism required. D.

———. *Sonorities III* 1976 (TP). 3 min.

———. *Arioso* (Wingert-Jones 1992) 2pp., parts. 3½ min. Opens *pp* at Adagio molto with thick chordal writing in lower register. Trombone has majestic theme rising and falling which leads to a sudden crescendo to *ff* near the end, but closes *pp* on an added-note chord. M-D.

Otto Henry. *Passacaglia and Fugue* (King 1963) 12pp., parts. 7½ min. For bass trombone. Neo-Baroque with passacaglia theme introduced in piano and repeated several times in different keys; theme eventually is transformed from direct quotes into a variations treatment in the bass trombone with rhythmic open-5th chords in piano. Fugue also introduced by piano, first as a quiet, rhythmic subject with syncopated treatment, then developed into a frantic dash to the end with statically repeated open-5th chords and the subject in augmentation. M-D.

Paul Hindemith. *Sonata* 1941 (Schott 3673 1970, ISMN M-001-04395-3) 27pp., parts. 11 min. A direct thematic relationship links the heavy and festal opening Allegro moderato maestoso and the closing sections in this one-movement conception of quadruple parts. A light Allegretto grazioso, mainly for the piano, and the third part, entitled "Lied des Rauffolds" (Swashbuckler's Song), provide much contrast to the outer sections. Widely spaced intervals show off the trombone as a prancing instrument in this enthusiastic work. D.

Emil Hlobil. *Canto Emozionante* Op.43 1967 (Panton 1972) 15pp., parts.

———. *Sonata* Op.86 1973 (Panton No. 1821) 32pp., parts.

Arthur Honegger. *Hommage du Trombone exprimant la tristesse de l'auteur absent* H.59 1925 (Sal 1992) 1 page, parts. 1 min. Monothematic 9-mm. piece at Modéré with singing trombone melody and 16th-note piano passagework. Piano part placed in lower register for darker tone. M-D.

Warner Hutchinson. *Sonatina* (CF 1968) 12pp., parts. 8 min. For baritone horn or trombone and piano. See detailed entry under duos for piano and miscellaneous instruments.

Andrew Imbrie. *Three Sketches* 1967 (SP 1970) 20pp., parts. Con moto: opens with ascending leaps in both instruments stretching their full range; syncopated, rhythmic figurations; quasi-angular melody. Allegro: trombonist is to occasionally sing one pitch while playing a neighboring tone; biting dissonances; asymmetric. Andante: expressive with more lyricism; ternary form; open spacing of pitches and chords. M-D to D.

Frederick Jacobi. *Meditation* (ST 1953) 6pp., parts. Modified ternary form contrasting slow sections (A) and faster, agitated passages (B). Late-19th-century style with thick chords and dramatics. M-D.

Robert W. Jones. *Sonatina* 1958 (Fema 1970) 15pp., parts. Allegro molto; Lento–Allegro ma energico. Conventional early-20th-century writing, never far from strong tonal centers, yet tossing in coloristic harmonies as its strongest point of interest. M-D.

Robert Kelly. *Sonata* Op.19 1951 (Tritone T-103 1970) 22pp., parts. 10 min. For tenor trombone. Moderate: SA, spirited, with vigor and striking rhythmic character, freely tonal, octotonic. Moderately Slow: ABA, linear, some striking harmonies in rocking patterns, flowing, subtle syncopation. Fast: rondo variations, straightforward passagework in thin texture with occasional rhythmic bump, touches of imitation, ragtime and jazz influence. Concludes Presto with full chords at *ff.* M-D.

Jan Koetsier. *Sonatina* Op.58/1 1970 (Donemus 1970; EMR 1989), parts. 8 min. Allegro; Andante mesto; Molto vivace. Thematic material is not worked out, ABA design for each movement. Exciting short work. M-D.
——. *Allegro Maestoso* Op.58/2 (EMR 216 1990) 10pp., parts. 7 min. For bass trombone. Majestic and dramatic in ternary design with Schumannesque qualities in muscular writing of full chords, octaves, detailed figurations, and extensive passagework. D.
——. *Zürcher Marsch* Op.116 F (EMR 224 1990) 12pp., parts. March theme with 5 variations. Octotonic, use of neighboring keys in variations, pompous. M-D.
——. *Ludus Agonis* Op.118 (EMR 225 1990) 10pp., parts. Commences with rich harmonic chords and sustained melody, later contrasted by a fire drill Allegro molto with marked rhythms and constant activity. M-D.

Marek Kopelent. *Four Pieces* (M. Hejda—Supraphon/AMP 7792 1963) 8pp., parts. Ostinato; Scherzo; Aria; Finale. Early-20th-century concepts in expressive settings suggestive of movement titles. M-D.

Alexander von Kreisler. *Sonatina* (ST SS-742 1967) 12pp., parts. Allegro moderato; Larghetto; Presto. Abrupt harmonic shifts, added-note chords, the contrast of thin and thick textures, and a judicious use of damper pedal are found in this short triptych essay. M-D.

Ernst Křenek. *Five Pieces* Op.198 1967 (Br 6107 1969) 15pp., parts. 9 min. Short untitled pieces with metronomic tempo indications using avant-garde techniques. Glossary of signs included (2pp.) for indications ranging from random notes to shaking plastic handle in bell of trombone. Curiosity pieces. M-D.

György Kurtág. *Six Pieces [Hat Darab]* (EMB Z.14176 1999, ISMN M-080-14176-2) 15pp., 2 copies needed for performance. Six pieces with Appendix: Fanfare I, Dirge I, Beating I, Dirge II, Fanfare II, Hommage à Paganini (La nuova campanella), Beating II. Novel notational techniques for flexible, quasi-avant-garde score. Cluster notes with "circling" palm are used; "the palm on the white keys turns in the indicated direction. While doing so the fingers should attempt to remain on the same black keys" (from Signs Used). M-D.

W. Daniel Landes. *Sonata* (Smith Creek 2001) 36pp., parts. 19 min. Presto: majestic opening with full pianistic treatment; hemiolas; logical development of phrases with seamless flow from one to another; octotonic; frequently detailed passagework in one hand counterbalanced by sustained notes in other. Adagio: expressive within methodical pace; lengthy solo piano passages, sometimes using extremes of instrument; dark-boding harmonies, including quartal; *ppp* conclusion. Allegro: a tour de force for trombone, alternating between marcato and legato thematic materials; full chords with a variety of treatments in piano in a complementary manner; tuneful; furious finish at *ff*. A welcome addition to the repertoire from the final decade of the 20th century. M-D to D.

Pierre Lepetit. *Pièce de Concert* (Leduc 1955) 9pp., parts. Octotonic opening at Moderato yields to broad section at Très lent in $\frac{6}{4}$. An Allegro très modéré follows without interruption with invigorating piano passagework, chromatic coloring, and a full chordal finish. Composed for Paris Conservatory Concours. D.

Otto Luening. *Sonata* 1953 (Highgate) 15pp., parts. 8 min. Short movements. Introduction; Dance; Hymn; Lively–March tempo. Unusual sonorities; rhythmic treatment of melodic writing is of interest. Presents no difficult problems. Neoclassic. M-D.

George F. McKay. *Sonata* (Warner Brothers 1951) 18pp., parts. Allegro moderato–Joyfully expressive, with elasticity and animation: tempo and mood changes in con moto assai and Pastoral sections. Andante poetico: built around contrasting Andante cantabile and Un poco più moto sections; added 6ths and 7ths. Allegro ritmico e vigoroso: tempo changes are also present here; unison writing, parallel chords and some imitation for piano part provide limited interest. Mildly 20th-century. M-D.

Richard A. Monaco. *Sonata* 1958, 1964 (Philharmusica Editions 1969) 27pp., parts. Allegro: consists of contrasting thematic groups heard inverted, rhythmically altered, or augmented. Andante: loosely constructed and lyrical; rubato style in which both piano and trombone take the lead. Allegro molto: violence contrasted by flowing sections; both instruments work closely in a rhythmically unstable atmosphere. Neoclassic orientation. M-D.
See John A. Seidel, "The Trombone Sonatas of Richard Monaco," D.M.A. diss., University of North Texas, 1988.

Vaclav Nelhybel. *Suite* (Gen 1968) 15pp., parts. Allegro marcato; Quasi improvisando (very freely); Allegretto; Moderato espressivo; Allegro con brio. Short movements epitomizing boldness and energy with uncompromising expectations. M-D to D.

Paul Veronge de la Nux. *Solo de Concours* (Leduc) 7pp., parts. One movement design in slow and fast sections of modest difficulty. Wide span required. M-D.

Claude Pascal. *Pastorale Héroique* (Durand 1952) 12pp., parts. 6 min. Required piece for the 1952 Paris Conservatory competition. Strong chords, octaves, key changes, and freely tonal. Trombone cadenza, *ppp* closing. M-D.
———. *Sonate en 6 minutes 30* (Durand 1958). Bright French harmonic palette. M-D.

Richard Peaslee. *Arrows of Time* 1993 (Margun 116 1997) 36pp., parts. 12 min. I. Up-Jazz feeling, II. Slow-Freely, III. [untitled]. Virtuosic, with jazz influences, added-note chords, and mixed meters. Comes together well in spite of many technical difficulties. Later orchestrated. M-D to D.

William Presser. *Sonatina* 1961 (Tenuto) 16pp., parts. 11 min. Allegretto; Scherzo; Andante; Rondo. Simple folk-idiom style is more difficult than it looks. Musical, linear. *Dies Irae* is used in the scherzo; pianist required to tap on wood. M-D.

William H. Rivard. *Sonata* 1955 (Tenuto 1969) 26pp., parts. 15 min. Smoothly: SA, octotonic. Grave: aria and scherzo, requires large span. Presto agitato: toccata-like, changing meters, Neoclassic. M-D.

J. Guy Ropartz. *Andante et Allegro* (CF 6946-2). Originally for trumpet, trans. for trombone by A. Shapiro. See detailed entry under duos for piano and trumpet.
———. *Pièce* b♭ (K 4564).

Samuel Rousseau. *Pièce Concertante* (CF [1938]) 8pp., parts. Exploits concertante principle with equally challenging and important parts. Late-19th-century in concept with full chords and dramatic intensity. M-D.

Klaus George Roy. *Sonata* Op.13 1950–51 (King 1954) 19pp., parts. 10 min. Andante con moto: freely tonal, chromatic, terse, intense writing. Interludio–

Allegro scherzando: cheerful, ebullient, may be repeated without pause if desired. Passacaglia–Moderato, con brio assai: crafted in a masterful manner. Strong Neoclassic writing with the influence of Walter Piston and Paul Hindemith. M-D.

Anton Ruppert. *Vier Stücke für Posaune und Klavier über B A C H* (Orlando 1973) 13pp. Two copies necessary for performance. Photostat of MS. Explanations in German only.

Robert Russell. *Sonata* Op.24 1967 (Gen) 13pp., parts. 8 min. A one-movement work in 4 contiguous sections developed from a 3-note (opening) motive. Octotonic, thin textures, toccata-like figuration divided between hands. Contrasting moods and tempos Convincing and well-written work for both instruments. M-D.

Camille Saint-Saëns. *Cavatine* Op.144 D♭ 1915 (Durand 1915) 9pp., parts. Commences with ascending wide skips in both instruments. Octotonic, chordal tremolos, and arpeggiation are found throughout the ternary design. M-D.

Carlos Salzedo. *Pièce Concertante* Op.27 (Leduc 1958) 12pp., parts. Largo: f, chordal, arpeggi figuration. Molto più lento: more chromatic and melodic for piano. L'istesso tempo: $\frac{3}{4}$ then $\frac{6}{4}$, chromatic, closing in F major. M-D.

Robert L. Sanders. *Sonata* E♭ (Gamble Hinged/Warner Brothers 1948) 31pp., parts. 16 min. Rather fast: SA, rocking motion in first idea contrasted with more chordal and rhythmic second theme. Scherzo–Lively: a little slower midsection is more sustained. Chorale–Solemnly: chordal chorale in piano, poco movendo mid-section. Finale–Very fast: $\frac{5}{8}$ rondo, piano part treated thematically in unison and octaves. Ascending octaves to close out the movement. Mildly 20th-century. M-D.

Svend David Sandström. *Inside* (NMS 1975) 12pp. 2 copies necessary for performance. For bass trombone and piano.

Elliott Schwartz. *Archeopteryx* 1976 (ACA) 12pp. 11 min. Trombonist needs 3 mutes; pianist must prepare 10 notes with coins, rubber, or pencils and mark 6 strings for muting. Pianist also needs a large wooden mallet, i.e., the sort used for striking tubular chimes, and an ashtray (heavy glass) or coke bottle to press heavily on strings for shrill, ghostly, high overtones. Notation is spatial— each system equals 15 seconds, contains other performance directions. Pointillistic. Trombonist leans into piano and plays directly over strings; pianist has clusters, slaps under keyboard, finger tremolo on piano case. Strings are scraped, mallet is struck on different ribs of piano, etc. Unusual sonorities, avant-garde. D.

Kazimierz Serocki. *Sonatina* 1954 (PWM 1955) 12pp., parts. 7 min. Three movements with shifting meters and tonalities. M-D.

Noam Sheriff. *Piece for Ray* 1966 (Israel Music Institute 1966) 7pp., parts. 5 min. Transcription from the middle section of the larger *Music* for woodwinds, trombone, piano, and double bass. "The movement takes the form of a recitative for trombone and a dialogue between this instrument" and piano (from Postface). Exploits the outer registers of both instruments. M-D.

Halsey Stevens. *Sonatina* 1960 (PIC) 20pp., parts. 9 min. Moderato con moto; Andante affettuoso; Allegro. Rhythmic treatment is similar to the Sonata discussed below. Middle movement is chorale-like and needs an expressive legato; large span required. M-D.
————. *Sonata* 1965 (PIC 1969) 28pp., parts. 15 min. Allegro; Adagio; Allegro moderato ma giusto. Continuous development throughout all 3 movements. Diatonic, shifting meters, neo-Baroque style. Rhythmic subdivisions in last movement are most effective. M-D.

Sigismond Stojowski. *Fantaisie* E (Leduc) 9pp., parts. Larger multisectional one-movement design contrasting slow and expressive sections with animated dramatic episodes. Finishes quietly at Lento. Composed for Paris Conservatory Concours. M-D.

Franz Strauss. *Nocturno* Op.7 (MarcoPaulo 1996) 8pp., parts. Trans. and edited by Mark Lawrence from the original for horn and piano. See detailed entry under duos for piano and horn.

Robert Suderburg. *Chamber Music III: Night Set for Trombone and Piano* 1972 (TP 114-40267 1980) 32pp., parts. 13 min. I. cry, man, II. its been a long, long time, III. brother Devil. "Being the son of a jazz and club trombonist, one recalls a childhood filled with the coming and going of all types of musicians at all varieties of hour. Most of all, however, it guaranteed that the instrument itself and the way R. A. Suderburg played it would produce sound and sight images never to be forgotten. Thus when commissioned . . . the musical occasion was offered to let out those hot-licks and sliding styles which were the jazz trombonist's stock and trade during the thirties and forties as he wandered from indoor dance hall to outdoor bandstand and from club date to stage show. Hopefully . . . these styles and scenes can live again in *Night Set*" (from Composer's Note). Score is photocopy of easy-to-read MS. M-D.

Stjepan Šulek. *Sonata (Vox Gabrieli)* (Brass Press 1975) 16pp., parts. In one movement marked Andante moderato. Detailed passagework, full chords, octotonicism, and scalar patterns require considerable attention and ensemble preparation. Favors piano. D.

Alexander Tcherepnin. *Andante* Op.64 E♭ (Belaieff 223 1950). For tuba or trombone. See detailed entry under duos for piano and tuba.

Richard Trevarthen. *Sonata* 1966 (Autograph Editions) 12pp., parts. 8½ min. Three movements based on a light and popular style. Int. to M-D.

David Uber. *Sonata* Op.34 (PIC 1969) 24pp., parts. For trombone or trumpet and includes parts for both. Maestoso–Andante tranquillo; Poco lento e lamen-tando; Rondo. Freely tonal, rhapsodic, light popular style. Parallel chords, no development procedures, mildly 20th-century. M-D.

Walter Watson. *Sonatina* 1960 (SP) 8pp., parts. 6 min. Allegro; Adagio; Allegro. Three short movements displaying stylistic variety. Atmospheric with clearly designed motives. Lyric qualities are emphasized. Slow movement is richly harmonic with much expression. Frequent use of 7th chords. M-D.

Stanley Weiner. *Fantasia* Op.42 (Billaudot 1973) 21pp., parts.

Paul W. Whear. *Sonata* 1963 (King) 15pp., parts. 12 min. Moderately fast–Moving; Slow–Expressive; Rather fast. Quartal harmonies. Thematic material is re-arranged in the outer movements. M-D.

Donald H. White. *Sonata* (ST 1967) 27pp., parts. 14 min. Quietly and sustained: SA; potent tone-row opening subject with 8th- and 16th-note figuration fol-lowed by chords has many developmental possibilities; dramatic piano writing that uses most of the keyboard; meno mosso for second subject; well-worked-out movement; dissonance develops naturally. Andante sostenuto: ABA, low chords open followed by chromatic intervals (small and large); syncopated mid-section, opening ideas return; low chords close movement; Impressionist. Very spirited: rondo; strongly rhythmic and dissonant; low chords of second movement are here moved to the middle and upper registers. Highly effective for both instruments. D.

——. *Tetra Ergon* (Brass Music 7401 1975) 23pp., parts. For bass trombone and piano. 1. For Van, 2. In Memory of "The Boss," 3. In Memory of "The Chief," 4. In Memory of "Dottie." Composed "in memory of three renowned low-brass virtuoso performers and the commissioner" (from Preface). Explores harmonic relationships and sonorous features. For experienced performers. M-D to D.

See Robert Mullen, "Donald H. White's *Sonata for Trombone and Piano*," JITA 13/1 (January 1985): 40–43, and "*Tetra Ergon for Bass Trombone and Piano*," JITA 13/2 (April 1985): 24–26.

Alec Wilder. *Sonata for Bass Trombone and Piano* 1971 (G. Schuller—Margun Music 1983) 34pp., parts. 14 min. Energetically; [untitled]; [untitled]; Swinging. Linear, with appealing ensemble interaction and occasional surprises. M-D to D.

See Douglas Yeo, "A New Edition of the Alec Wilder *Sonata* for Bass Trom-bone and Piano," JITA 12/4 (October 1984): 38–41; Gunther Schuller, "Alec Wilder's *Sonata for Bass Trombone and Piano*," JITA 13/3 (July 1985): 6–9.

Duos for Piano and Horn

Samuel Adler. *Sonata* 1951 (King) 16pp., parts. 9½ min. Andante con moto: C, freely tonal, flowing melodies, linear writing. Allegro scherzando: C, $\frac{6}{8}$, much rhythmic vitality, harmonic interval of the 4th favored, invigorating contrary motion. Molto ma con appassionata: B♭, chromatic, lines always have motion. Allegro con fuoco: B♭, dancelike, ideas well developed. Linear conception that fits the hands. M-D.

Violet Archer. *Sonata* 1965 (CMC) 16pp., parts. 12½ min. Andante energico: serial, Largo cadenza for horn. Interlude–Largo, serioso: colorful sonorities. Arioso–Largo con poco moto: Expressionist. Serially organized, pointillistic treatment at places, difficult ensemble problems. Effective writing. D.

Robert Baksa. *Horn Sonata* D♭ 1983, rev. 1993 (CLE 26 1996) 30pp., parts. Boldly; Moderate, very fluid; Lively. Driving rhythms with repeated chords and ostinatos. Large span required for fast finale. M-D.

Leslie Bassett. *Sonata* 1952 (King) 20pp., parts. Allegro moderato: rhythmic opening subject followed by chorale-like second subject in Lento and Andantino espressivo mood and tempo; Tempo I returns; and movement closes *ppp*. Andante cantabile: freely tonal around e, nocturne-like. Allegro, ma non troppo: inspired by rhythm from first subject in opening movement; more sustained un poco meno mosso section provides contrast; *ppp* closing similar to first movement. M-D.

Ludwig van Beethoven. *Sonata* Op.17 F 1800 (A. Raab, A. Groethuysen, R. Ginzel—Henle 498 1994, ISMN M-2018-0498-9, 24pp.; B. Tuckwell—GS 3316 1978; Br&H; M. Wolff—Bo&H 1949; K 9269), parts. 13½ min. Allegro moderato; Poco adagio, quasi andante; Rondo–Allegro moderato. Shows great maturity and fine balance between horn and piano. Many Beethoven characteristics, such as muscular piano writing, distantly related key changes. Similar in style to the first and third Piano Concerti. Original edition included alternative cello score, a suggestion made to the publisher by Beethoven himself (part included in Henle). M-D.

Niels Viggo Bentzon. *Sonata* Op.47 (WH 1959) 27pp., parts. Moderato ma non troppo: rising and descending lines both chromatic and diatonic come to a *ppp* cadence; an Allegro employing triplet figuration brings the movement to a final sustained close. Quasi menuetto–allegretto: ABA, an active subject makes this movement very "busy"; mid-section in constant chromatic 16ths for piano adds much unrest. Rondo–Allegro ma non troppo: toccata-like until a sustained 11-bar Andante gives relief before toccata activity resumes. Written in an individual style that is strongly chromatic. D.

Leonard Bernstein. *Elegy for Mippy I* (Bo&H BHB-18 1950, ISMN M-060-07138-6) 2pp., parts. Largo, with soft dynamics. Mippy was a pet mongrel belonging to Bernstein's brother Burtie, to whom the work is dedicated. Int.

Thomas Beversdorf. *Sonata* 1949 (ST) 19pp., parts. Scherzo: freely centered around a–A. Andante sostenuto: E–e, horn sings, piano provides harmonic structure and rhythmic interest. Allegro moderato: a–A, upper register of piano effectively used; scales; most dramatic of the movements. Solid pianistic equipment required. M-D to D.

Marcel Bitsch. *Variations sur une Chanson Française* (Leduc 1954) 12pp., parts. Four variations and coda. Simple theme treated with mildly 20th-century harmonies. Var.III contains a cadenza for horn. Clever and appealing writing. M-D.
——. *Choral* D♭ (Leduc 1965) 11pp., parts. 6 min. Pompous theme introduced with full chords in a solemn marchlike character, followed by 5 distinct variations. Neoclassic with abundant added-note harmony. Composed for the Paris Conservatory Concours. M-D.

Edith Borroff. *Sonata* 1970 (King) 32pp., parts. 14 min. Rhapsody: Impressionist arpeggi figuration; syncopation; Agitato e più mosso section utilizes octaves in piano part against developing line in horn part; Tempo I returns to conclude movement. Scherzo–Allegro Vivo: triplet treatment, chordal syncopations between the hands. Sarabande: open chordal texture, melodic line tucked in inner voices, Impressionist. Estampie–Energico ma non presto: sprightly opening leads to a molto meno mosso espressivo section; opening idea returns to speed itself to a Più vivace closing. M-D.

Eugène Bozza. *En Forêt* Op.40 1941 (Leduc 1941) 8pp., parts. In one movement with 5 distinct sections: Allegro moderato–Recit–Andante espressivo–Allegro vivo–Allegro moderato. Marked rhythms with chromaticism, recitative, and planing techniques characterizing an essentially Neoclassic style. Quotes the plainchant *Victimae Paschali* in the middle section. Virtuosic and brilliant with marked rhythms, with horn glissandi, and dancing rhythms. Open 5th tonality in Andante creates contrasting atmospheric impressions. A standard in the repertoire. M-D.

———. *En Irlande* (Leduc 1951) 7pp., parts. Based on an old Irish melody. Programmatic with sectional titles and sharply contrasting materials. M-D.

———. *Chant Lointain* (Leduc 1957) 3pp., parts. 4 min. In 2 distinct sections contrasting slow and sustained qualities with fast and accented. Horn cadenza near end. M-D.

———. *Sur les Cimes* (Leduc 1960) 8pp., parts. 8 min. Commences with horn cadenza and brief piano comment before moving into an Andantino ma non troppo in $\frac{6}{8}$ with rocking rhythm and an expressive melody. An Allegro vivo ensues which reintroduces a motive from the opening page and boldly presents the principal theme heard earlier in a transformed version with rip and romp. A lengthy horn cadenza is heard near the end. M-D.

Margaret Brouwer. *Sonata* 1996 (Pembroke 139 2000, ISBN 0-8258-0767-0) 21pp., parts. 15 min. In 2 movements. The composer has written, "At the turn of a new century and after a century of atonality, I am eager to find paths in new harmonic directions. The Sonata for Horn and Piano is representative of explorations of mine done between 1995 and 1999 toward a personal expression in that new direction. It is also a very personal expression of searching prompted by the deaths of two loved ones within a year's time. *Hymn*, straightforward and melodic, expresses grief and faith. *Riding to Higher Clouds* deals with the complex struggle between the conflicting emotions of loss, hope, memories, and understanding" (from Performance Notes). M-D.

Henri Büsser. *Concert Piece* Op.39 D (ST) 10pp., parts. 5½ min. Fanfare opening at Moderato serves as introduction to an Andante poco lento in $\frac{9}{8}$ meter, the first of 2 extended sections. Sustained phrases offer many expressive possibilities in the context of late-19th-century harmonic writing. An Allegro vivo takes the piece to a rhythmic and flashy ending. M-D.

———. *Cantecor* Op.77 (Leduc 1961) 8pp., parts. Contrasts slower expressive passages with blistering virtuosity with a leaning toward an early-18th-century individualist style. Composed for the Paris Conservatory Concours. M-D.

———. *La Chasse de Saint Hubert* Op.99 (Leduc 1937) 11pp., parts. Likewise composed for Conservatory Concours, *La Chasse* requires a solid technique to navigate its multisectional design. Chromaticism is more evident here. Large span required. M-D.

Robert Clérisse. *Chant sans Paroles* F (Leduc 1952) 5pp., parts. Sustained songlike melody without words at Andante tempos in ABA' form. Five changes of key in restless harmonic patterns occasionally mix 2 with 3 while rolling arpeggiation decorates the harmony with color and stateliness. Gentle ending on F major chord. M-D.

Dinos Constantinides. *Reflections VI: The Tyger* 1996 (Conners 114 1996) 9pp., parts. 6 min. Inspired by William Blake's poem *The Tyger*. "First set for baritone and piano by the composer in 1994 . . . it [is] written for the composer's favorite cat "Tiger" and attempts to portray Tiger's personality . . . The piece employs a repeated note motive that pervades the entire work. A descending chromatic chord progression controls the harmonic structure of the composition and creates mood changes that were very much a part of every day with Tiger's life" (from Preface). Playful, jovial effects in character piece form. M-D.

David H. Cope. *Sonata* (Seesaw) 23pp., parts. 12 min. Three untitled movements. Freely tonal, changing meters. The second movement relies heavily on arpeggiation in the mid-section. The finale is a highly rhythmic giguelike conception. Strong thematic material that develops naturally. Large span required. D.

Bernard de Crepy. *Synopse* (EMT 1972) 10pp., parts. 6 min. Avant-garde idiom for horn. Piano part looks simple but contains difficult passagework. M-D to D.

Carl Czerny. *Introduction Variations Concertantes* Op.248 1831 (F.-G. Hölÿ— Kunzelmann 589 1999) 34pp., parts. For horn or cello. The title page for the first publication (in French) indicates that the work was jointly composed with Joseph Lewy, and that the principal theme is a Tyrol air. Lewy's contribution is acknowledged in this release only in the Preface. A majestic and virtuosic introduction leads to a flowing theme and a series of 4 variations, the last with piano cadenza, a separate Adagio, and then Finale alla Polacca. Every virtuosic technique of the early 19th century is found in this extended essay of ostentatious verbosity. D.

Jean-Michel Damase. *Berceuse* (Leduc 1951) 3pp., parts. 5 min. Calm lullaby atmosphere fits title in this homophonic, Neoclassic setting. Instruments complement each other well in rather noncontrasting material. Int.
———. *Pavane Variée* (Lemoine 1956) 7pp., parts. See detailed entry under duos for piano and cello.

Franz Danzi. *Sonate* Op.28 E♭ (G. Hausswald—Hofmeister 29pp.; J. Chambers— IMC 2110 1963 27pp.), parts. For waldhorn and piano. Critical commentary in German in Hofmeister. Adagio–Allegro; Larghetto; Allegretto. Classical style, attractive melodies. M-D.
———. *Sonate Concertante* Op.44 (J. Wojciechowski—Sikorski 458 1957) 28pp., parts. For waldhorn and piano. Allegro; Larghetto; Allegretto. A few glimpses of 19th-century harmony appear in this work. M-D.

Jean-Michel Defaye. *Alpha* (Leduc 1973) 10pp., parts. 6½ min. Slow and fast sections are contrasted. Lento section is recitative-like with arpeggi figuration and long pedals; octotonic. This leads to a faster section that is dancelike with large syncopated chords (needs a large span). A horn cadenza interrupts before dance idea continues. A colorful fantasy. M-D.

John Diercks. *Fantasy* 1952 (Tenuto 1962) 10pp., parts. Freely tonal, contrasting sections (flowing, poco marcato, with light bits of pedal, etc.), parallel chords, builds to large climax, mildly 20th-century, pianistic. M-D.

Anthony Donato. *Sonata* (Remick 1950) 23pp., parts. Briskly with abandon: clear textures, freely centered around b. Very slowly: piano part provides chords and contrasting counterpoint with horn. Boldly: ostinato figuration, chromatic chords, a faster section serves as coda. Writing for the piano is expert. D.

Théodore Dubois. *Cavatine* E♭ (P. Schmalfuss—Zimmermann 32190 1997) 8pp. 5 min. For flute, violin, or horn. See entry under flute and piano.

Gottfried von Einem. *Jeux d'Amour* Op.99 1993 (Dob 5659 1995, ISMN M-012-18168-2) 12pp., parts. 9 min. 3 Caprices: Ruhige Halbe; Allegretto; Allegretto. Playful and whimsical outer movements offset by a lyric and expressive middle movement. M-D.

Richard Faith. *Movements* 1965 (SP) 11pp., parts. 5½ min. Andante; Allegro; Andante espressivo. Short, relatively simple, melodic, rich harmonies. Each movement portrays a definite character or mood. Special care has been given to the idiomatic treatment of both instruments while preserving a coherence of sound and form. Mildly 20th-century. M-D.

Václav Felix. *Sonata da Requiem* Op.30 1969 (Panton) 24pp., parts. For horn or bass clarinet and piano.

Jean Françaix. *Divertimento* (EMT 1959) 12pp., parts. Introduzion: 16th-note figuration with embedded melody, staccato left hand, 20th-century Alberti bass, cadenza-like passages for horn at end of movement. Aria di cantabile: chromatic lines in piano with more diatonic melody in horn. Canzonetta: toccata-like with octaves and chords alternating between hands, chromatic chords and runs in mid-section. Witty, delightful, fun for performers and audience. M-D.
———. *Canon in Octave* (Pierre Noël; International 1385) 3pp., parts. 2 min. Uses a lively canon between piano and horn one beat apart. Canon supported by staccato chords in both hands while melody steps and skips in syncopation. Voices come together on the final beat. Ternary form. M-D.

Peter Racine Fricker. *Sonata* Op.24 1955 (Schott 10473) 27pp., parts. Con moto: SA, with short development section; leads directly to Presto: scherzo in ABABA design. Invocation: rondo-like form with extensive episodes. Versatile pianistic figuration throughout. M-D to D.

Jacques François Gallay. *Troisième Solo de Cor* Op.9 (Hans Pizka 1983) 12pp., parts. D.
———. *Neuvième Solo de Cor* Op.39 (Hans Pizka 1985) 14pp., parts. D.

Fully involved pianistic writing exhibiting early-19th-century Romanticism complements Gallay's horn solos.

Alexander Glazunov. *Reverie* Op.24 D♭ 1890 (J. Singer—Leeds 1945) 4pp., parts. Andantino in $\frac{3}{4}$ with triplet rhythms displaying a dolce theme and contemplative mood. M-D.

Reinhold Glière. *Nocturne* Op.35/10 F (J. Anderer—IMC 3159 1982) 6pp., parts.
———. *Intermezzo* Op.35/11 E♭ (J. Anderer—IMC 3158 1982) 3pp., parts.

Charles Gounod. *6 Pièces Mélodiques Originales* 3 vols. (E. Lelair—Billaudot 3367-9 1982–85), parts. I: g/G, D. II: F, B♭. III: A♭, c/C. Short pieces exemplifying mid-19th-century qualities. Preference given to horn but not without pianistic interest. Some adjustments to the original have been made by the editor. M-D.

Don Haddad. *Sonata* (SP 1966) 15pp., parts. 9 min. Allegro moderato; Largo; Allegro moderato. Written predominantly in the Lydian mode, which seems to lend itself particularly well to the unique character of the horn. Rehearsal suggestions included. Mildly 20th-century. Percussive treatment of piano in last movement. Large span required. M-D.
———. *Adagio and Allegro* (SP 1969) 12pp., parts. Adagio: orchestral-like introduction with bold harmonics at the piano leads to expressive melody of lyric quality. Piano interlude brings back the first half in a written-out repeat with changes in the homophonic piano part. Allegro: instrumental exchange of motives lends dramatic quality in this mildly 20th-century harmonic setting. Fanfare finish with both instruments complementing one another well. M-D.

Iain Hamilton. *Aria* 1951 (Schott) 5 min.
———. *Sonata Notturna* 1965 (Schott) 10pp., parts. 10 min. Lento: thick buildup of low chromatic sonorities; Allegro mid-section explodes with pointillistic chromatic chords and figuration; Lento returns with a Brutale hammered style, including a silent cluster in the lowest register for the harmonic effect. Largo: serial figuration collects into chords before unwinding again; Lento section concludes movement. Scherzando: similar procedures used in first 2 movements, *pp* closing. Unusual and hypnotic sonorities. M-D.

Walter S. Hartley. *Sonorities II* 1975 (Tenuto) 4pp., parts. 5 min. Has experimental features. M-D.
———. *Meditation* 1979 (TP). 3 min.

Bernhard Heiden. *Sonata* 1939 (AMP 1955) 23pp., parts. 12 min. Moderato; Tempo di Minuetto; Rondo–Allegretto. Centers freely around B♭, is Neoclassically oriented, has much attention-getting power and fascinating qualities. M-D.

Paul Hindemith. *Sonata* 1939 (Schott) 32pp., parts. 16 min. Three large movements: Moderately fast; With quiet motion; Allegro. Excellent fusion of the 2 instruments, lyrical. Piano part is especially thorny in the final movement, with 16th-note triplets embedded with inner voices. Thorough pianistic equipment required. D.

——. *Sonata* 1943 (Schott) 11 min. For alto sax (or alto horn, or French horn) and piano. See detailed entry under duos for piano and saxophone.

Alun Hoddinott. *Sonata* Op.78/2 (OUP 1972) 30pp., parts. 11 min. The first movement, lyrical and shaped with long lines, provides the thematic material for the complete *Sonata.* An elegiac second movement is followed by a 3-section scherzo. M-D.

Mark Hughes. *Sonata* (Tritone 1966) 16pp., parts. 16 min. Allegro: rhythmic, octotonic, bitonal, chromatic chords and runs, thinner sonorities in mid-section. Adagio: sustained, widely spread chords require large span; chromatic counterpoint between instruments. Fugue and Cadenza: well-developed fugal textures, chromatic runs in cadenza, Presto coda, *ppp* effective close. M-D.

Charles Koechlin. *Sonata* Op.70 (ESC 1970) 26pp., parts. 13 min. Moderato, très simplement et avec souplesse; Andante très tranquille, presque adagio; Allegro moderato, assez animé cependant. Cool flowing Impressionist sonorities, triplet figuration, parallel chords. M-D.

Jan Koetsier. *Sonatina* Op.59/1 (EMR 237 1991) 20pp., parts. Allegro moderato; Andantino grazioso, Presto. Capsule ideas expanded into fuller form using an early-20th-century flavor. Cluster chords are used judiciously in the buoyant finale. M-D.

——. *Romanza* Op.59/2 D♭ (EMR 240 1991) 7pp., parts. Ternary design with long flowing lines in outer sections and marcato, mostly repeated-note, middle section. Unabashedly tonal for late 20th century. M-D.

——. *Variationen* Op.59/3 F 1986 (EMR 268 1993) 11pp., parts. Commences Tempo giusto with rippling effect of 8th notes and cheerful melody. Four variations ensue emulating the essence of the theme. The fourth, a bouncy asymmetric diversion, is most interesting. Thematic material returns to reestablish the overall mood in a brief coda, concluding with a chordal stomp and stinging *sf.* M-D.

——. *Scherzo Brilliante* (EMR 267).

Peter Jona Korn. *Sonata* Op.18 (Simrock 3063 1959) 35pp., parts. Allegro tranquillo ma bene mosso: piano part is a study in various types of idiomatic Neoclassic figurations while the horn part continually unfolds. Andante con moto: a Hindemithian lullaby. Rondo à la Gigue: rhythmic drive in a unique manner, including a long stubborn and highly effective pedal point before closing. M-D.

Ernst Lévy. *Sonata* 1953 (Seesaw 1060) 23pp., parts. Adagio; Agitato; Andante; Tempo Giusto; Allegretto; Tempo Giusto. This 6-movement work has no meters and is written in a chromatic and linear freely tonal style. The fifth movement is for solo horn, while the sixth (with a key signature of 2 sharps) devotes about half of the movement to the piano in fugal textures; firm D tonal conclusion. D.

Ignaz Moscheles. *Duo* Op.63 (Introduction and Rondeau Ecossais) (H. Voxman—Musica Rara 1974) 20pp., parts. Ingratiating and convincing writing in a somewhat eclectic style of the day. Ample dexterous passagework for the pianist. M-D.

Thea Musgrave. *Music for Horn and Piano* 1967 (JWC 1967) 27pp., parts. 9½ min. Changing tempos, character. Unmeasured passages are to be played at the indicated speed. Arrows mark places where the ensemble should be exact. Piano part has frequent spidery figurations. First-rate ensemble players required. D.

Vaclav Nelhybel. *Scherzo Concertante* (Gen 400 1966) 8pp., parts. Intense with repeated notes, motivic development, and detailed expressive indications. Typical Nelhybel flare with bubbling rhythms, well-conceived interaction of instruments, and exuberant finish. M-D.

Carl Nielsen. *Canto Serioso* 1928 (SM 1944; MMP) 4pp., parts. ABA, centered freely around F, chordal and scalar figuration, chromatic chords, triplets singly and in harmonic 3rds and 4ths, tempo changes in mid-section. Lovely writing for both instruments. M-D.

Lucien Niverd. *Chant Mélancolique* (Billaudot) 2pp., parts. For horn, trombone, alto saxophone, bassoon, or trumpet. No.5 of *Six Petites Pièces de Style*. Cantabile melody treated dolce at Moderato. Homophonic texture of broken chords. Int.

Pieter Piacquadio. *Pavana e Rondo* (SP 1982) 12pp., parts. 7½ min. In one movement. Begins with a fiery opening and soon settles into a slow pace to imitate a pavane. Mixes duples and triples between instruments in frequently changing characters and tempos defying the traditional dance form qualities. The sense of a rondo is achieved through a rising 3-note motive heard at the beginning of nearly every section. An effective piece mistitled. Also available in chamber orchestra version. M-D.

Paul Pisk. *Sonata* Op.77 1953 (CFE) 30pp., parts. Allegro moderato; Adagio; Allegro, ma non tanto. Atonal, contrapuntal, rhythmic. D.

Marcel Poot. *Sarabande* (Leduc 1953) 4pp., parts. Stately rhythm at Lent throughout. Sonorous with a variety of touch and articulation for both instruments. M-D.

Quincy Porter. *Sonata* 1946 (King) 22pp., parts. Lento introduction leads to Allegro moderato followed by a Poco meno mosso before the Lento mood concludes the movement. Largo espressivo: unbarred, chromatic, rubato. Allegro molto: $\frac{2}{4}$, cross-phrasing in piano with driving rhythmic motif; Poco meno mosso section continues to rework the cross-phrasing idea; Poco più mosso returns to Tempo I in $\frac{6}{8}$; final statement of the opening motif unwinds to the end; this movement seems to have a difficult time settling down. M-D.

Hans Poser. *Sonate* Op.8 (Sikorski 312 1957) 30pp., parts. 17 min. A large work in 3 movements requiring thorough command of instruments. Ruhig fliessend: lyrical, constantly shifting harmonies. Larghetto: well-marked melody, pulsating rhythms. Etwas schnell Rhythmisch bewegt: intense, rhythmic, octaves in piano, fiery finish. D.

Francis Poulenc. *Elégie* 1957 (JWC 1958) 9pp., parts. 8 min. Technically and emotionally influenced by Benjamin Britten's *Canticle III*. Opening 12-note melody followed by a questioning theme with hammered 16th notes. Following a slightly varied repetition of these 2 short sections, a flowing melodic line based somewhat on the opening 12-note melody evolves and continues to the end. A final cadence states the 12-note theme again. This piece has some of the same flavor as Poulenc's opera *Dialogues des Carmélites*. Sweet but serious writing. M-D.

Primož Ramovš. *Sonatine* (Društvo Slovenskih Sktadateljev 1962) 23pp., parts. Allegro–Largo–Allegro vivace. Octotonic, chromatic, linear. Large span and fine octave technique required. M-D.

Hermann Reutter. *Theme Varié* (Leduc 1957) 3pp., parts. Andante theme E♭, 3 contrasting variations, theme returns slightly changed. Mildly 20th-century. M-D.

Verne Reynolds. *Sonata* (ST 1971) 31pp., parts. Moderately; Slow; Fast. Difficult but well written, serially oriented, broad gestures, Expressionist. D.

Joseph Rheinberger. *Sonate* Op.178 E♭ (M. S. Kastner—Schott 1967, ISMN M-001-02517-1) 40pp., parts. Con moto: SA, stately theme, rich harmonic language with thick texture. Quasi adagio: dolce and expressive, cantabile melody passed between instruments, strong dynamic contrasts. Con fuoco: spirited rhythmic treatment in rondo form, octaves, scalar passagework, with grand finish. M-D to D.

Ferdinand Ries. *Sonata* Op.34 F (W. Lebermann—Schott 5670 1969) 42pp., parts. Larghetto–Allegro molto; Andante; Rondo–Allegro. Built on many conventional figurations of the period, i.e., scales, octaves, arpeggi, extended Alberti basses, triplets, etc. Still has interest, and a stunning performance would be exciting for performers and listeners. M-D.

———. *Introduction and Rondo* Op.113/2 (G. Meerwein—Musica Rara 1973)

18pp., parts. Piano part requires fine and sensitive fingers if the work is not to sound labored. M-D.

Keith Roper. *Triptych* (Thames 1972) 19pp., parts. Photostat of MS. Both parts are difficult, atonal, fussy rhythmic and textural problems. Horn requires a few unusual effects. D.

Gioacchino Rossini. *Prelude, Theme and Variations* (R. de Smet—CFP 1972) 20pp., parts. 9 min. Available for horn in F (P-7173a) and for horn in E♭ (P-7173b). "Rossini composed this work in Paris in 1857 and dedicated it to his friend E. Leone Vivier (1817–1900), a famous horn soloist, who performed it at Rossini's famous Saturday evening parties, which were a feature of Parisian social and artistic life at that time" (from the score). Tuneful, pianistic, contains some interesting harmonies. M-D.

———. *Introduction, Andante et Allegro* (E. Leloir—Choudens 1970) 12pp., parts. This little-known work is presented in a revision and arrangement by Edmond Leloir. Subtitled Fantasia, it is operatic in nature and contains invigorating writing for piano. D.

Chretien Rummel. *Nocturne* (F.-G. Hölÿ—Kunzelmann GM 1355 1998) 8pp., parts. For horn in F or basset horn. One of the earliest nocturnes in the repertoire for this duo. Flowing structure shows Chopinesque influence with the horn using full range. Melismatic-like figures given to piano. Delayed entrance of theme provides ample anticipation following an entertaining opening. Fine interaction of instruments. M-D.

Camille Saint-Saëns. *Romance* Op.36 (K 4131) 5pp., parts. 4 min. See detailed entry under duos for piano and cello.

Robert L. Sanders. *Sonata* B♭ 1958 (King 1963) 32pp., parts. 11 min. Allegro cantabile; Tempo di Valse scherzando; Lento, leads directly into Vivace. Mildly 20th-century; most interesting sonorities occur in the Lento. The Valse has a kind of Richard Straussian chromatic coloring. M-D.

Peter Schickele. *What Did You Do Today at Jeffey's House?* 1988 (EV 164-00204 1992) 10pp., parts. 5 min. I. First we had a parade, II. After lunch Jeffey's mom made us take a nap, III. Then we did a carnival with a haunted house and dancing bears. Jazzy, sportive rhythms and frivolity in outer movements contrasted by a somber, muted middle movement. M-D.

Gunther Schuller. *Sonata* 1988 (Margun 7169 1989) 29pp., parts. Andante, with innermost expression; Allegro energico; Adagio mesto; Allegro giocoso. Strongly contrasting movements ranging from melancholic to highly energetic. Commissioned by the International Horn Society. Piano part is photocopy of MS; horn part is professionally printed. M-D.

Robert Schumann. *Adagio and Allegro* 1849 Op.70 (Br&H 11pp.; B. Tuckwell—GS 3298 1977 16pp.; CFP 2386 1925 11pp.; I. Philipp—IMC 1542 1952 15pp.; K 4530), parts. 10 min. Sharply contrasting movements rich in pathos and melodic invention. Originally entitled *Romance and Allegro.* M-D.

Halsey Stevens. *Sonata* 1953 (King) 23pp., parts. 12 min. Allegro moderato; Poco adagio; Allegro. Melodic and attractive linear writing. Tonalities are clear with pedal points in the Poco adagio. Hunting call references are heard in the finale. Neoclassic style with economy of thematic material. Thematic transformations are genuinely inspired. Has much audience appeal. M-D.

Franz Strauss. *Nocturno* Op.7 D♭ (UE 1368) 9pp., parts. One of the most significant nocturnes in music literature outside those for solo piano. Dolce melody in an Andante quasi Adagio with flowing 16th notes. Rich harmonic development makes this a delight for performers and audience alike. ABA′. M-D.
———. *Thema und Variationen* Op.13 E♭ (Zimmerman 12570 1957, ISMN M-010-12570-1) 15pp., parts. Introduction, theme, 2 variations, Andante cantabile, Rondo. Richly varied with simple theme, straightforward in character and motion. Andante cantabile is in C♭. M-D.

Richard Strauss. *Introduktion, Thema und Variationen* WoO AV.52 E♭ 1878 (Schott 1995) 16pp., parts. 12 min. Composed at age 14, this work is curiously in the same key and similar structure as his father's *Theme and Variations* noted above. Theme reveals a strong gift for lyricism, displayed in 5 distinctly rhythmic variations. M-D.
———. *Andante* Op. posth. C 1888 (Bo&H 1973) 5pp., parts. In rich, Romantic, Brahmsian style. M-D.

Henri Tomasi. *Chant Corse* (Leduc 1932) 3pp., parts. Neoclassic setting for a mournful Corsian melody. Mostly soft at an Andantino in cut time sprinkled with added-note harmonies and flowing patterns. M-D.
———. *Danse Profane* (Leduc 1960) 5pp., parts. 3 min. No.2 of *Cinq Danses Profanes et Sacrées* for horn and chamber orchestra. Effective reduction for solo piano (a piano part is actually part of the chamber orchestra). Commences with a one-phrase horn call which is also heard midway through and at the end. Scherzando with intriguing rhythmic interplay. M-D.

Alec Wilder. *First Sonata* 1964 (Margun) 23pp., parts. Allegro–Forcefully: a♭, strong, syncopated chordal gestures. Andante–Slow: G♭, "Rock it sweetly," light style writing. Allegro Giocoso: ostinato-like chordal figures evolve; most excitement is given to the piano; finally arrives at opening tonality of a♭. M-D to D.
———. *Suite* (Margun 111 1964) 20pp., parts. 11 min. Danse Quixotic; Slow and Suite; Song; Epilogue; Suitable for Dancing. A semi-light style permeates the

writing, but it is handled in a professional manner. Obviously Wilder knows the piano and its capabilities very well. M-D.

————. *Sonata No. 3* 1970 (J. Barrows—Wilder Music 109 1970) 24pp., parts. 15 min. Moderately fast; Slowly; With a solid beat and a jazz feeling; Tempo di Valse–Joyously. Colorful harmonies and rhythm with complementary instrumental parts. Modified SA in opening movement leads to bitonal second, jazzy third, and waltzlike fourth for a setting resembling a Suite rather than a Sonata. Effective. M-D.

See David Charles Calhoon, "The Horn Music of Alec Wilder: A Survey, With Analysis of His Sonata No. 1 for Horn and Piano," D.M.A. diss., University of Wisconsin, Madison, 1992.

Christian Wolff. *Duet* 2 1961 (CFP). Includes extensive instructions for performance. One page of diagrammatic notation. Avant-garde. D.

Duos for Piano and Tuba

Robert Baksa. *Tuba Sonata* 1993 (CLE 92 1998) 23pp., parts. Lively and flowing; Elegiac, somewhat freely; March. Thin textures, bitonality, and imitative. Refuses to end dramatically, choosing instead to fade away gently. M-D.

William Bardwell. *Sonata* 1968 (King) 12pp., parts. 10 min. Dialogue–Moderato, quasi recitativo: serial, piano part is mainly chordal with some melodic statement. Scherzo: mostly linear, some left-hand chordal activity. Passacaglia: piano part is in $\frac{30}{8}$, tuba in $\frac{5}{2}$, sonorous, chromatic, intense. D.

Bennie Beach. *Lamento* (ST SS-69 1961) 3pp., parts. In $\frac{5}{4}$ with ponderous chordal treatment. Lyric melody provides some relief to an otherwise heavily burdened lament. M-D.

Warren Benson. *Arioso* 1958 (EBM MS1249 1959) 2pp., parts. 3 min. Marked Slowly, in $\frac{3}{2}$, with melody cast in lower register of tuba. Homophonic, with counter-motivic presence. Int. to M-D.

Leonard Bernstein. *Waltz for Mippy III* (Bo&H 20763 1977) 5pp., parts. Named for a mongrel belonging to the composer's brother. Cheerful and cute, marked "As gracefully as possible under the circumstances." M-D.

Thomas Beversdorf. *Sonata* (ST 1962) 30pp., parts. 15 min. Allegro con moto; Allegretto grazioso e espressivo; Allegro con brio. A major work with dramatic gestures for both instruments. Flexibility, plenty of technique and interpretative abilities required. M-D.

Marcel Bitsch. *Impromptu* (Leduc 1957). For bass saxophone, tuba, or bass trombone. See detailed entry under duos for piano and saxophone.

John Boda. *Sonatina* 1967 (King) 15pp., parts. Two untitled movements. I: sustained chords in piano move gradually from upper to lower register; parts then switch and piano has active moving line against longer note values in tuba line; chromatic; short SA movement. II: ostinato-like chords; more linear section;

tuba has a solo Recitative; movement works to large climax, then quickly subsides to a closing *pp.* Neoclassic orientation. M-D.

Will Gay Bottje. *Concerto* 1973 (ACA) 21pp., parts. 15 min. Very Quietly: veiled and muffled sonorities, chromatic, chordal alternation between hands, *ppp* ending. Syncopated–Dance-Like, Generally Light in Character: dance variations, flexible meters, vigorous. Dramatic, but rubato: pointillistic tendencies, cadenza for tuba, changing meters, warm lyric mid-section followed by intense writing, very broad closing. A first-rate work that requires first-rate performers. One of the finest works in the medium. D.

Rayner Brown. *Diptych* (WIM 83 1970) 12pp., parts. Prelude and fugue in early-20th-century style. Clever use of piano's upper register against tuba's lowest pitches. M-D.

Jacques Castérède. *Sonatine* (Leduc 1963) 12pp., parts. 7½ min. For tuba or saxhorn. Défilé: robust and martial. Serenade: rocking $^6_8$, Fauré style. Final: figuration between alternating hands, repeated discords, trills, octotonic, martellato piano part. M-D.

———. *Fantaisie Concertante* (Leduc 1960). For bass trombone, tuba, or bass saxophone. See detailed entry under duos for piano and trombone.

Dinos Constantinides. *Mutability Fantasy* 1979 (Conners 61 1995). For euphonium or tuba and piano. See detailed entry under duos for piano and miscellaneous instruments.

———. *Landscape III* 1970, rev. (Magni 2001). For euphonium or tuba and piano. See detailed entry under duos for piano and miscellaneous instruments.

John Diercks. *Variations on a Theme of Gottschalk* (TP 1968) 12pp., parts. 4½ min. Theme is from *Le Bananier,* in C; opens with tuba playing it complete. Piano enters in low register followed by tuba in imitation. Opening motif of theme is expanded and leads to Var.II, in E♭, with more counterpoint in the piano and a *ff* climax to end this section. A tag emphasizing the raised 6th (A natural) moves into Var.III, which exploits the raised 6th degree in a cantando style in both instruments. Var.IV centers around C and becomes poco marcato and, for the piano, secco; motivic interplay makes this one of the most attractive variations. Var.V plays around d with more contrapuntal thrusts from the piano. A cadenza-coda utilizes both instruments and descends to a *ppp* before the final burst of activity that brilliantly concludes the piece. Highly attractive writing for both instruments. M-D.

Arthur R. Frackenpohl. *Variations* (The Cobbler's Bench) (SP 1973) 11pp., parts. 5½ min. After a short introduction the well-known theme is heard. Var.I: chordal, octaves. Var.II: legato, slower. Var.III: a fast waltz using cross-rhythms and the interval of the 3rd. Var.IV: a funeral march in minor. Var.V: syncopated and leads to a solo cadenza. Concludes with a codetta similar to the introduction. Clever, attractive writing. Int. to M-D.

Harald Genzmer. *Sonate* 1998 (Ries and Erler 28000 1999, ISMN M-013-28000-1) 21pp., parts. 11 min. Allegro; Lento–Andante; Finale–Vivace. Opens with fortitude as a *ff* chord and cascading passagework are heard in the piano to introduce ascending leaps of sustained pitches in tuba. Continues toward slow movement where modifications of this idea are heard amid added-note 2nds and spatial harmonies. The finale is a bubbling $^9_8$ essay in ternary form. M-D.

Don Haddad. *Suite* (SP 1966) 16pp., parts. 8 min. Allegro maestoso; Andante espressivo; Allegro con brio. Sensible and effective writing that displays the flexibility, sonority, and artistic capability of the instruments. Contains rehearsal suggestions. Mildly 20th-century. M-D.

Adolphus C. Hailstork. *Duo* 1973 (IU) 14pp., parts. Expressionist abstract writing, flexible meters, well structured. Moves over entire keyboard; exploits upper registers in unusual way that effectively blends with the tuba. M-D.

Walter Hartley. *Aria* 1967 (EV 1968) 7pp., parts. 2½ min. Expressive. M-D.
———. *Sonatina* 1957 (Interlochen Press) 9pp., parts. 6 min. Allegretto; Largo maestoso; Allegro moderato. Excellent piano writing that moves over the keyboard, requires much control and careful balance. M-D.
———. *Sonata* 1967 (Tenuto) 19pp., parts. 12 min. Andante–Allegro agitato; Allegretto grazioso; Adagio sostenuto; Allegro moderato, con anima. Mildly 20th-century writing in this major work for the instrument; chromatic vocabulary. Attacca between third and fourth movements. Thematic material lends itself readily to thorough development. M-D.
———. *Sonorities* [I] 1972 (Philharmusica) 4pp., parts. 4 min. Quartal and quintal harmonies, 9th chords, freely tonal. M-D.
———. *Largo* 1974 (Philharmusica). 4½ min.
———. *Tuba Rose* 1977 (TP). 3½ min.
———. *Sonata No. 2* 1993 (MMP 2377 1995) 13pp., parts. 10 min. Allegro; Adagio; Presto; Andante maestoso. Commences with a series of motivic exchanges between instruments to establish a compositional principle heard throughout the first 3 movements. Concludes with hymnlike setting using sustained chords and sonorous effects ranging from *pp* to *ff.* Brief movements. M-D.

Paul Hindemith. *Sonata* 1955 (Schott 1957) 20pp., parts. 11½ min. The bouncy piano part is animated with much harmonic wit as the composer plays with a 12-note idea. Allegro pesante: fantasy-like, develops freely, short recapitulation. Allegro assai: ABA, scherzo character, short passacaglia for trio. Variationen: ABA, 12-note idea announced by tuba then immediately by the piano; idea disappears for 2 variations but appears in the codetta that concludes the "exposition"; semi-development mid-section has a variation "Scherzando" for the piano; then the tuba has a recitative cadenza accompanied by chord progressions containing the 12-note idea; the "exposition" is repeated a 3rd lower with added decorations for the right-hand piano part. D.

Arthur Honegger. *Petite Suite.* See trios for piano and 2 violins.

Dumitru Ionel. *Rumanian Dances* Nos.1–6 (Editions BIM). Published separately. No.1: 1946 3 min.; 2: 1946 7 min.; 3: 1948 4 min.; 4: 1981 4½ min.; 5: 1972 3 min.; 6: 1982 2 min.

———. *Gluma Muzicala* 1948 (Editions BIM). 2 min.

———. *Fantezie Nocturna* 1956 (Editions BIM). 7½ min.

———. *Visare (Dreaming)* 1964 (Editions BIM 1996) 2pp., parts. 2½ min. An expressive cantabile essay at Andante with hardly a trace of 20th-century compositional styles. Firmly based in G with relatively quiet dynamics. Fits title well. M-D.

———. *Galop* 1976 (Editions BIM). 2 min.

Gordon Jacob. *Tuba Suite* (Bo&H 1973) 23pp., parts. Exploits the tuba's possibilities thoroughly without being difficult. In 9 short movements, one for solo piano. Another called "Jacob's Dream" is a ground bass in which the piano progresses step by step to heaven. The last movement is a Galop with cadenza. M-D.

———. *Bagatelles* (Emerson 146 1980) 5pp., parts. 1. In Tranquil Mood, 2. The Corsair Bold, 3. A Sprightly Dance, 4. After-Dinner Speech. Capsule-size character pieces with few technical difficulties. Suitable for less-experienced performers. M-D.

———. *Six Little Tuba Pieces* (Emerson 118 1978) 11pp., parts. 1. Restful Prelude, 2. Marching Tune, 3. Minuet, 4. Hungarian, 5. In Folk-Song Style, 6. Scottish. Picturesque, capsule settings of amusing dimensions. M-D.

Roger Kellaway. *The Westwood Song* 1975, rev.1997 (Editions BIM TU11 1997) 23pp., parts. 10 min. In one movement consisting of many short sections. Broadly divided into a slow-fast format, with much freedom of expression required. Proportional rhythmic relationships, octotonicism, large chord structures, arpeggiation stretching across the keyboard, and syncopation in sometimes biting harmonies are found within. Occasional indeterminacy. Loaded with expressive verbiage, ranging from "ad lib: with love" to "begin with 'fire,'" permeate the score. Large span required. M-D.

Jan Koetsier. *Sonatina* Op.57 1970 (Donemus) 7 min. Allegro; Tempo di minuetto; Allegro moderato. Piano overshadows tuba in the opening of the first movement. The last movement needs a strong sense of continuity between various sections. Solid writing for both instruments. Audience appeal. M-D.

Trygve Madsen. *Sonata* Op.34 (Musikk-Huset 2295 1980) 25pp., parts. Andante sostenuto; Allegro energico; Allegro moderato. Written in a late-19th-century style with strong harmonic centers and rarely a hint of the tonal challenges of the 20th century. Use of cyclic principles with the opening theme reappearing near the end of the final movement. Octotonic; large chord structures. M-D.

Jacques Murgier. *Concerstück* 1961 (Editions Transatlantiques 736 1961) 15pp., parts. Commences Andante con moto with a strongly rhythmic octotonic motive in the piano and sustained low pitches in tuba announce principal thematic materials. Gives way to an Allegro scherzando after two 4-mm. phrases of quiet hymnlike quality in the piano. Additional sections ensue contrasting slow-fast tempos with rhythmic drive and colorful French Neoclassic harmonies. A brief pause in intensity occurs near the end when the hymnlike passage returns in expanded form to set the stage for a Presto dance to the finish in $\frac{8}{8}$ (3+3+2). An attractive work which deserves to be better known. M-D.

Vaclav Nelhybel. *Concert Piece* (E. C. Kerby 1973) 7pp., parts. 4 min. Originally for tuba and band. Piano reduction by the composer. A dramatic dialogue between the 2 instruments. Three sections, tonal, much rhythmic thrust, repeated notes between hands, cluster-like sonorities, mildly 20th-century. M-D.
———. *Suite* (Gen 1966) 11pp., parts. 6 min. Allegro marcato; Quasi improvisando; Allegretto; Slow; Allegro con bravura. Syncopated and highly stylized, mildly 20th-century. M-D.

William Presser. *Sonatina* 1972 (Tenuto 1973) 20pp., parts. 10 min. Allegretto; Allegro; Adagio–Presto. A poem by Robert Herrick is included in the Adagio section, not to be sung but to help the players interpret the movement. The measure 3 bars before the end of the work is to be repeated several times. The pianist may play the last repetition one half-step higher. Thin textures. M-D.
———. *Second Sonatina* 1973 (Tenuto 1974) 16pp., parts. 8½ min. Three movements with a Neoclassic slant. Adagio movement is very poignant. M-D.

Verne Reynolds. *Sonata* (CF 1969) 13 min. Moderately fast; Slow; Variations. A large work requiring 2 experienced performers. M-D.

Peter Sacco. *Fantasy* (WIM 1971) 6 min. A one-movement work in contrasting lyric-dramatic sections; 12-tone. D.

Leonard Salzedo. *Sonata* Op.93 1980 (JWC 55464 1984) 22pp., parts. Allegro; Lentissimo; Allegretto; Vivace. Playful with snappy rhythms and imitative dialogue. Some bitonality in a mostly conventional harmonic idiom. The slow movement is particularly expressive in its long sustained tuba lines, while the last is scherzo-like with syncopated exchanges and a frolicking finish. M-D.

William Schmidt. *Sonata* (WIM AV235 1984) 36pp., parts. Moderately–Faster: thematic material easily developed through fragmentation; bitonality; quartal chords. Slowly: utilizes extremes of instruments; ABA′B′ Coda design. Moderately fast: quartal chords; emphasis on staccato technique; thin texture. Large span required. M-D

———. *Serenade* (WIM AV27 1962) 14pp., parts. Romanza; Waltz; Dirge; March. Short essays depicting their programmatic titles. Parts fit together well in spite of some uneven rhythms. M-D.

Robert Sibbing. *Sonata* 1963 (TP 1970) 32pp., parts. 11 min. Allegro moderato; Larghetto; Allegro giocoso. Thoroughly 20th-century writing in a mainly linear style with chordal punctuation used at important cadence and formal points. Solid pianism required. Easy-to-read MS. M-D.

Leo Sowerby. *Chaconne* (CF 1938). Concentrated writing in a mildly 20th-century style. M-D.

James Stabile. *Sonata* (WIM 1970) 22pp., parts. 8 min. Allegro vivace; Moderato; Più mosso. Many 7ths, chords in alternating hands, colorful. Last 2 movements are to be played attacca. First movement is not difficult to unravel. Large span required. M-D.

Halsey Stevens. *Sonatina* 1959–60 (PIC 1968) 20pp., parts. 9 min. Moderato con moto; Andante affettuoso; Allegro. Highly interesting rhythmic usage. Vitality permeates entire work. Extremely well written. Piano part requires thorough equipment. M-D.

Jeno Takács. *Sonata Capricciosa* Op.81 (Dob 1965) 18pp., parts. 9 min. Multisectional one-movement work. Mildly 20th-century, attractive. M-D.

Alexander Tcherepnin. *Andante* Op.64 E♭ (Belaieff 223 1950) 9pp., parts. For tuba or trombone. Important role given to the piano with introduction and interludes of moderate length. Octaves and motivic development are present throughout. Expressive. Large span imperative. M-D.

David Uber. *Sonata* (Edition Musicus 1978), parts. Allegro moderato: ternary, comprised of brisk, syncopated passagework. Andante, poco agitato: enchantingly melodic with chromaticism, expressive. Allegro: motivic development, pulsating with energy, virtuosic. M-D.

Rodger Vaughan. *Concertpiece No. 1* 1959 (Wingert-Jones 1992) 10pp., parts. Ternary form marked Allegro con fuoco in outer movements and Andante in center. Facile writing for tuba but more challenging for piano. Large span required. M-D.

Alec Wilder. *Sonata* I (Mentor Music 1963 19pp.; Margun), parts. 10 min. Four movements. Jazz influence, partial linear style, short motivic usage, chromatic. Blends the 2 instruments effectively. Solid musicianship and pianistic equipment required. M-D.

———. *Sonata* II (Margun).

———. *Suite No. 1 'Effie Suite'* (Margun).

———. *Suite No. 2 ('Jesse')* (G. Schuller—Margun 107 1993) 9pp., parts. 5 min. Four brief movements, the first 2 untitled, and remainder Brightly, Tenderly, respectively. Cheerful, facile writing. Large span required. M-D.

———. *Suite No. 3 'Suite for Little Harvey'* (Margun).

———. *Suite No. 4 'Thomas Suite'* (Margun).

———. *Suite No. 5 'Ethan Ayer'* 1963 (Margun AW128 1976) 17pp., parts. Lively; Slowly and sustained; Leisurely; Steadily. Short, serious essays with matter-of-fact character. M-D.

———. *Small Suite* 1968 (Margun).

———. *Song for Carol* 1970 (Margun).

———. *Encore Piece* (Margun).

Duos for Piano(s) and Miscellaneous Instruments: Audience, Baritone Horn, Euphonium, Guitar, Harp, Mandolin, Metronome, Ondes Martenot, Organ, Percussion, Unspecified

Paul Arma. *Deux Resonances* (Lemoine 1974) 25pp., parts. 12 min. For percussion (one player) and piano. I: serial; piano begins clangorously; clusters; very little melodic emphasis. II: impetuous skips plus chordal punctuation dominate this piece; clusters appear near conclusion. A tour de force for the percussionist. M-D.

Paolo Baratto. *Euphonissimo* 1996 (Editions BIM). 4 min. For euphonium and piano.

——. *Romanze in F* 1996 (Editions BIM). 4 min. For euphonium and piano.

Bennie Beach. *Suite* (AMP 95666 1957). For trombone or baritone horn. See entry under duos for piano and trombone.

Ludwig van Beethoven. *Works for Mandolin and Piano* 1796 (A. Raab, A. Groethuysen—Henle 499 1994, ISMN M-2018-0499-6) 17pp., parts. *Sonatina* WoO43a c, *Adagio ma non troppo* WoO43b E♭, *Sonatina* WoO44a C, *Andante con variazioni* WoO44b D. Short works of facile quality; the *Sonatinas* are in one movement each, the first Adagio and second Allegro. Of greater interest is the *Andante* with 6 variations and coda, a work requiring more dexterity and demonstrating greater development. M-D.

William Bolcom. *Frescoes* (EBM 1975) 32pp. For 2 pianos, harmonium, and harpsichord. Two performers. Each player has a piano; one also has a harmonium, the other a harpsichord. Wildly bombastic music; amazing handling of the 4 instruments. Bolcom draws on the *Book of Revelation, Paradise Lost,* and the *Aeneid* for visions of death, destruction, and apocalyptic war. Reminders of old battle pieces and rags are interspersed. In 2 parts: 1. War in Heaven, 2. The Caves of Orcus. D.

Robert Clérisse. *Noce Villageoise* (Leduc) 3pp., parts. For cornet, trumpet, bugle, or baritone horn. See entry under duos for piano and trumpet.

Dinos Constantinides. *Mutability Fantasy* 1979 (Conners 60 1995) 8pp., parts. 5 min. For euphonium and piano. Inspired by the poem *Mutability* by Percy Bysshe Shelley. Broadly ternary in form using repeated notes and patterns in a fantasy-like atmosphere to realize the title. Dramatic, ends on lowest A minor chord possible with added B♭, against a C♯ in euphonium. May also be performed on tuba (Conners 61). M-D.
————. *Landscape III* 1970, rev. (Magni 2001) 21pp., parts. 6 min. For euphonium or tuba and piano. "Employs thematic and harmonic materials derived from [the composer's] *20th Century Studies for Two Violins. Landscape III* is modal and lyrical in nature. Numerous polychords and sudden harmonic shifts highlight the entire piece. The solo part (Euphonium or Tuba) is full of ornamentations and virtuoso passages based on the sonorities of the Brass Ensemble" (from Preface). M-D.

Carlos Cruz de Castro. *Llámalo como quieras* (Editorial de Música Española Contemporánea 1974) 11pp. For piano and metronome. Includes performance instructions in Spanish, English, and French.

Anton Diabelli. *Sonatina* Op.68 (K. Scheit—OBV 1951) 7pp., parts. For guitar and piano. Andante sostenuto; Rondo–Allegro ma non troppo. Pianist must generally keep the dynamics down. Subtleties of the work must be followed. Int. to M-D.

François Dupin. *Myriades* (Leduc 1973) 27pp., parts. 10 min. For percussion and piano. Five pitches (timbales) are required for percussion. Lent: intense introduction, freely tonal, varied rhythmic figuration. Vif: shifting meters, chordal, repeated notes, chromatic runs, glissando 2-hand clusters, octave and chords in alternating hands. Lent: free, recitative-like. Vif: ostinato bass, chordal punctuation, waltz-like, bitonal, 2 linear lines, feverish finish. M-D.

Harold Farberman. *Variations for Percussion with Piano* (BB 1960) 8pp., parts. 5 min. 20th Century Composers Study Score Series, No.17. Percussion required: cymbal, tam-tam, timpani, snare drum, tambourine, triangle, glockenspiel, xylophone, 2 bongos, tom-tom, wood blocks, antique cymbal, bass drum, sleigh bells, congo drum. If 3 or 4 players are used, there are extra possibilities. Clusters; martial character to theme. Evolves through a waltz, glissandi, repeated chords, syncopated clusters. M-D.

César Franck. *Prelude, Fugue and Variation* Op.18 (JF 9733 1966) 20pp., 2 copies necessary for performance. 7 min. For piano and organ. Original version. In 3 sections with rich harmonic development, rhythmic vitality, and lyric melodies. Prelude introduces a single-line melody in organ at $\frac{9}{8}$ with countermelody and rhythm juxtaposed in piano. Fugue is led by organ throughout with octotonicism in piano. Variation is based on Prelude theme with flowing 16th-note passagework in piano. Soft and expressive. One of the finest works in the ensemble's repertoire. M-D.

Vinko Globokar. *Drama* 1971 (Litolff 1975) 17 leaves. 2 copies necessary for performance. For piano and percussion. Explanations in French, German, and English. Notes in the score are in German only. Each performer is equipped with microphones, a ring modulator, and amplifiers. Seven scenes, may be played in any successive order. Chance composition, avant-garde. D.

Walter Hartley. *Two Pieces* 1976 (TP). 3 min. For euphonium and piano.
——. *Sonata Euphonica* 1979 (TP). 11 min. For euphonium and piano.

Juan Hidalgo. *Milan Piano* (Editorial de Música Española Contemporánea 1974) 15pp. For piano and any kind of instruments or objects with which one can produce undetermined sounds. Avant-garde. M-D.

Warner Hutchinson. *Sonatina* (CF N4356 1966) 12pp., parts. 8 min. For baritone horn or trombone and piano. Moderately fast; Slowly; March style. Freely tonal, first movement requires a good left-hand octave technique. Slowly: colorful, tempo changes add interest. Attractive and flexible writing. M-D.

Tom Johnson. *Harpiano* 1983 (Two-Eighteen Press 1983) 13pp., 2 copies needed for performance. 16 min. For harp and piano. Ten short untitled movements using minimalist, sequential, and mathematical techniques to emphasize the subtle differences in color between the 2 instruments. Several movements require only one hand for performance. M-D.

Marcel Jorand and François Dupin. *Sept Pièces* (Leduc 1974) Bk.I: I. Pata-Caisse, II. Drôlerie (for snare drum and bass drum). Bk.2: III. Ta-ras-tata, IV. Danse (for 2 cymbals, 1 suspended cymbal, triangle, snare and bass drum, tambourine). Bk.3: V. Rapsodie, VI. La petite écossaise (for all percussion already listed plus timpani with pedals and kettledrum). Bk.4: VII. Variétés (for all percussion already listed plus woodblock, vibraphone, xylophone, 2 tom-toms, glockenspiel). Each book is more difficult than the last. All the piano writing is mildly 20th-century and helps display the percussion instruments. Large span required in Bk.4. M-D.

Mauricio Kagel. *Unguis Incarnatus Est* (UE 15621 1972) 7pp. For piano and ... (the choice of the second instrument is free). Based on a phrase from Franz Liszt's *Nuages Gris* (1881). Range of the second instrument is listed. Contains directions for the performers. Piano part is either a single line (Liszt melody) or chords based on the melody, or tremolo octaves. Silence is pedaled. Sudden dynamic changes; pianist must scream "Liszt" *fff* at conclusion. Avant-garde. Requires large span. M-D.

David Lumsdaine. *Kangaroo Hunt* 1971 (UE 29017A) 2 separate sheets, 1 for each player. For piano and percussion. Percussion required: 2 maracas, 2 bongos, 2 hi-hat cymbals, vibraphone, xylophone, bells, glockenspiel, pitched instruments ad lib. Includes directions for performance. A mobile work with the performers choosing from nine "blocks" of materials. Pointillistic, widely spread chords, repeated notes, glissando on strings, extreme ranges. Avant-garde, aleatoric. D.

Donald Martino. *Canon Ball* 1957 (Dantalian 802 1999) 4pp., parts. Two-Part Invention for vibraphone and piano. Jazzy with driving tempo in sportive manner. One part for each instrument. M-D.

Gilberto Mendes. *Blirium C9* 1965 (Ric Brazil) 7 sheets including one page of musical series. For one, 2, or 3 keyboard instruments: one organ, 3 pianos, harpsichord and accordion, etc. Or, for 3, 4, or 5 different instruments of the same family. Detailed instructions are given for the melodic plan or tessitura-pitch variations. Transitions between groups of notes, aleatoric. Instructions for fragmentation and mounting of the quotations. No two performances ever the same. Avant-garde. D.

Ignaz Moscheles and Mauro Giuliani. *Grande Duo Concertante* Op.20 1814 (S. Behrend—Simrock Elite Ed, 2709 1973) 68pp., parts. Moscheles added the piano accompaniment to Giuliani's guitar part. Allegro maestoso; Scherzo; Largo; Pastorale. This is the most elaborate work of this combination composed during the first half of the 19th century. Written by 2 outstanding virtuosi, the piano part is a charming catalog of Moscheles's style and idioms; consists of glittering runs, octaves, and generally facile writing throughout. This edition, when compared with the first edition, contains numerous errors (197 in the guitar part and 41 in the piano part). M-D.

Marlos Nobre. *Variações Rítmicas* Op.15 1963 (Tonos) 14 min. For piano and percussion.

———. *Sonancias* Op.37 1972 (Tonos) 12 min. For piano and percussion.

Tadeusz Paciorkiewicz. *Duet Concertante* (AA 1974) 43pp., 2 scores needed for performance. For piano and organ. General registration suggestions for the organ are listed. I. Comodo: melody in octaves, freely tonal, secco style, glissandi; requires fine octave technique. II. Largo quieto: imitative, chromatic undulating lines, *ppp* closing. III. Giocoso e scherzando: moving harmonies around pedal point, left-hand octave punctuation, many harmonic 2nds used in figuration. IV. Adagio deciso: melody in octaves, secco style with expanding and contrasting figures, brilliant passagework (in octaves ad lib) at conclusion. M-D to D.

Flor Peeters. *Concerto for Organ and Piano* Op.74 (HWG 1958) 58pp., 2 scores necessary for performance. Introduzione ed Allegro: forceful octaves; triplet figures lead directly to the Allegro (SA), which contains much octotonic writing; freely tonal around e; chords interspersed with figuration; recapitulation approached by a glissando; movement ends in a blaze of tremolo full chords in upper register. Arioso: ABA; rolled 7th and 9th chords in piano while organ has modal melody; second idea more chromatic; when A returns, piano has melody and organ the chords. Cadenza e Finale: chordal punctuation; trills in upper register; toccata figuration begins at the Allegro vivo e fermo; Andantino section uses rich harmonies; toccata figuration returns; brilliant scales and chords end movement. The success of this work (and any work in this combination) depends in part on the ability of the performers to allow for the time it takes the organ to "speak." The piano responds faster in most cases, and this ensemble problem can be solved only by familiarity with the room and the instruments involved. M-D.

Nicole Philiba. *Recit* 1973 (EMT) 16pp., parts. 7 min. For Ondes Martenot and piano. Sectionalized, varied tempos and moods, low register exploited, freely tonal, arch form, *pppp* closing. M-D.

Boris Pillin. *Duo* (WIM 1971). For percussion and piano. Allegro: SA except that the recapitulation and development are combined; 2 themes, both of which recur in various transformations in the second and third movements. Andante: roughly an arch form, i.e., it consists of several short sections which are recapitulated in (approximately) reverse order; general character of the movement is a gradual coalescence, out of sparse fragments, into a long-lined theme, followed by a return to fragmentation. Maestoso–Allegretto risoluto: overall AA′ form with coda; ironic and scherzo-like in character; at end of coda there is a return to material from beginning of the first movement. Primitivistic style, depending more upon rhythmic momentum and ostinato repetition than sophisticated material development. Dissonant but freely tonal; frequently uses clusters coloristically. M-D.

Marta Ptaszynska. *Little Mexican Phantasy* (PWM 1974) 10pp., parts. Percussion required: xylophone, 2 campanelli, 3 tom-toms, snare drum, triangle, small drum, suspended cymbal. M-D.

Sam Raphling. *Suite for Solo Percussion and Piano* 1968 (Bourne). In 2 parts, published separately. I: 1. Tambourine, 2. Wood Blocks, 3. Cymbals, 4. Castanets; Encore: Toccata (solo utilizing 4 instruments). II: 5. Triangle, 6. Bass Drum, 7. Temple Blocks, 8. Snare Drum; Encore: Theme and Variations (solo utilizing 8 instruments). Freely tonal style liberally laced with dissonance. Effective ensemble writing. M-D.

Carlos Salzedo. *Sonata* 1922 (SPAM) 37pp., 2 copies necessary for performance. For harp and piano. In one movement: Luminous–Lento subito–Languorously–Lento. Highly chromatic, tremolos, trills, Impressionist coloring throughout. Unusual combination produces some unusual sonorities. D.

Claudio Santoro. *Diagrammas Cíclicos* 1966 (Tonos 1971). For percussion and piano. 2 scores. Pianist has to play inside the piano. Clusters, improvisation, avant-garde. D.

Dieter Schnebel. *Abfälle I: Reactions* (Schott 1971) 7pp. 8 min. Concerto for one instrumentalist (piano) and audience, or instrumental group. Chance composition.
———. *Modelle* (Schott 1974) 4pp. of explanations in German and English, 13pp. on 6 folded loose leaves. For one pianist and audience. This is a worked-out version of the above *Abfälle I: Reactions*.

Fernando Schulmeier. *Micropiezas* 2001 (www.seiscuerdas.com/schulmeier). Copies obtainable directly from web site. For piano and guitar. Azar y nada; qfwfq; Brad's Illustrations (quasi aliator); Adán y raza (epilogo). Syncopated rhythms and colorful harmonies reveal Bartókian and late-20th-century influences. Indeterminate rhythms and clusters in Brad's Illustrations. Concludes on densely compacted added-note chord. M-D.

Karlheinz Stockhausen. *Mantra* 1970 (Stockhausen Verlag) 59pp. For 2 pianos, each with cymbals, wood blocks, and electronic modulators built to the composer's specifications (operated by the pianists). Includes prefatory notes and instructions for performance in German, English, and French. Avant-garde. D.

Koji Takeuchi. *Five Improvisations* 1965 (UE 14275) 19pp., parts. For piano and vibraphone. Allegro moderato; Andante; Vivace; Moderato; Presto, ma non troppo. Serial, atonal, contrasting, pointillistic, clusters. M-D.

Joaquín Turina. *Ciclo Plateresco—Tema y Variaciones* Op.100 (UME 1947) 17pp., 2 copies necessary for performance. For harp and piano. Lento introduction leads directly into the Theme (Andante). Three variations and a Majestuoso closing. Colorful and seductive sonorities that seethe with Spanish dance rhythms and cantando melodies. The 2 instruments complement each other. M-D.

Eugene J. Ulrich. *Sonata* (Tritone Press 1963) 12pp., parts. For baritone horn and piano. One movement. Chordal, freely tonal and dissonant, octotonic, basically same tempo throughout, Neoclassic. Requires large span. M-D.

Donald H. White. *Lyric Suite* (GS). For euphonium and piano. Four movements, supplied in both bass and treble clefs. Piano part is well written but difficult; preference for intervals of a 2nd and a 4th. Well laid-out with a good sense of climax and rhythmic drive. D.

Henri Zagwyn. *Mystère* 1942 (Donemus) 17pp., 2 copies required. For harp and piano. In 2 parts. I: Prélude; Evocation; Sabbat infernale. II: Intermède; Invocation; Apotheose. A chromatic and colorful style requiring fine pianistic ability. M-D.

———. *Van de Jaargetijden* 1945 (Donemus) 23pp., 2 copies required. For harp and piano. Zomer; Herfst; Winter; Lente. Same style as described above. D.

Music for Three Instruments

Trios for Piano, Violin, and Cello

Karl Friedrich Abel. *Six Sonatas* Op.5 (Reprint of the London edition: R. Bremmer 1764) 2 vols. For violin, cello, and harpsichord (piano). Nos.4 and 5 available from CFP. The slow movements are more weighty than many other slow movements from this time. Details of articulation, dynamics, and ornamentation show a definite polish. Keyboard parts range from Int. to M-D.

Jean Absil. *Trio* Op.7 1931 (CeBeDeM 1962) 43pp., parts. 30 min. Allegro energico; Nocturne; Intermezzo; Final. Bold pianistic gestures, chromatic, subtle sonorities in Nocturne, French influence. Requires facile octave technique. D.

Samuel Adler. *Trio* 1964 (OUP) 45pp., parts. 14½ min. Allegro con fuoco: rhythmic chromatic theme, changing meters, hemiola, flowing figuration, clear lines. Largo: the opening section consists of 2 contrasting ideas juxtaposed—brokenchordal sustained low harmonies and sprightly short motif in upper register— main idea is longer and treated 2 octaves apart in piano; *pp* closing. Allegro ma non troppo: syncopated opening motif, imitation. The whole work is built on Neoclassic lines and is freely tonal. Rhythmic vigor, flow of melodic ideas, and clarity of texture make this a distinctive work. M-D.

Tomaso Albinoni. *Tre Sonate* Op.6/4, 5, 7 (W. Reinhart—Hug 1959). Each *Sonata* is a unique piece in itself and contrasts with the others. M-D.

Alexander A. Aliabev. *Trio* E♭ 1817 (USSR 1952) 37pp., parts. Unfinished. Attractive writing in post-Mozart style. It is possible that Aliabev studied with John Field when Field was in Moscow. Allegro moderato: SA; opening idea shows Aliabev's indebtedness to Field; development moves through numerous keys, ending in E; a chromatic slide-slip returns to E♭ Cantabile style; movement is complete by itself and would make a delightful program opener. No evidence has been presented to contradict the possibility that Aliabev may have intended it to be only a one-movement work. M-D.
See Carol A. Green, "Style in the Instrumental Chamber Music of Alexander A. Aliabev," thesis, Indiana University, 1969, 72pp.

Jan van Amerongen. *Trio* 1986 (Donemus 1991) 23pp., parts. 14 min. Allegro; Adagio; Allegro con fuoco. Strongly tonal for the late 20th century. M-D.

David Amram. *Dirge and Variations* 1962 (CFP) 14 min. Tonal, skillfully conceived for each instrument. Quiet opening, full presentation of the extended Dirge, upper timbres explored in one variation for all instruments. Despite its title, there is much bright sound and motion. Fluent and natural lyric writing. M-D.

Volkmar Andreae. *Trio* Op.1 f (Schott 1901) 43pp., parts. Displays youthful sincerity and Romantic charm. Liszt and Wagner influence is strong. Three contrasting movements that were considered very modern when they appeared at the turn of the century. M-D.

Hendrik Andriessen. *Trio* b 1939 (Donemus 1947) 57pp., parts. 20 min. Andante con molto espr.; Presto, con spirito; Tempo sostenuto ma appassionato. Fully exploits the possibilities this combination offers. Written in a very personal style. Mildly 20th-century with the exception of some polytonal usage. M-D.

Caroline Ansink. *Skopós* 1988 (Donemus 1990) 25pp., parts. 20 min. Maestoso e mesto–Presto; Senza rubato; [untitled]. Strongly marked rhythms yield expressive energy. M-D.
——. *Crisalide* 1996 (Donemus 1997) 10pp., parts. 12 min. In one continuous movement at generally slow to moderate tempos. Piano cadenza near end yields to *ppp* ending. Some complicated rhythms emerge, especially in a "Con passione" passage where 7, 6, 4, and 3 notes per beat are heard among the instruments. M-D.

Violet Archer. *Trio* II 1956 (CMC) 50pp., parts. Allegro; Largo tranquillo; Allegro con brio, energico. Thin textures, thoroughly 20th-century treatment of all instruments. D.

Anton Arensky. *Trio I* Op.32 d 1894 (CFP 4315; USSR 1971: Augener; K; IMC) 51pp., parts. 29 min. Four movements that foreshadow Rachmaninoff's style, especially the subject of the last movement. Striking features include the arresting main theme of the first movement and the Scherzo with its fast scales in the piano part. Cyclic thematic material. M-D.
——. *Trio II* Op.73 f (USSR; Bosworth) 56pp., parts. Allegro moderato; Romance–Andante; Scherzo; Tema con (6) Variazioni. More characteristic of Arensky's mature style, but Schumann's spirit seems to hover over the first movement. The Romance also seems to come from the same origin that inspired Schumann's piano *Romances*. The Scherzo is a waltz in both tempo and style. Waltz influence is also seen in the third and fifth variations of the finale. M-D.

Isabel Aretz. *Trio* 1965 (IU) 28pp., parts. Andante: complex metric treatment, pointillistic, serial, barless. Theme and Variations: 7 variations, thorny. Allegretto: toccata-like in places. Final: bar lines, very advanced and difficult writing in a strongly dissonant style. Linear conception. D.

Richard Arnell. *Trio* Op.47 (Hin). Essentially diatonic writing but interlaced with 20th-century idioms. Pure melodic writing comes through in all parts. Music is effectively written and well laid-out for the medium. M-D.

Malcolm Arnold. *Trio* Op.54 (Paterson 2714). Basically diatonic style coupled with touches of humor and a direct simplicity. There is both a light and a serious quality about this piece. Transparent textures and clever handling of the piano part add to its attractiveness. Strong propulsive quality. M-D.

Claude Arrieu. *Trio* (Amphion 1958) 53pp., parts. Moderato; Lento; Scherzo; Toccata. Neoclassic style infused with seriousness of purpose and facile handling of all 3 instruments. The Lento especially has some beautiful sonorities. M-D.

Arno Babadjanian. *Piano Trio* f♯ 1952 (USSR) 36pp., parts. Largo–Allegro espressivo; Andante; Allegro vivace. Contains much Romantic excitement and dramatic pathos, sweeping lines, very colorful, Rachmaninoff influence but original idiom. Folk song tradition of Armenia, composer's native country, is also present. D.

Victor Babin. *Trio* (Augener 1956) 56pp., parts. Largo; Allegro ritmico e ben accentuato. Well written throughout, especially the piano part. Mainly in a diatonic style with some mildly 20th-century sonorities. M-D.

Carl Philipp Emanuel Bach. *Sonata* W.90/3 C 1776–77 (Oberdörffer—HM 46) 20pp., parts. This is a model for Haydn's Piano Trios. The piano part is completely emancipated from the strings. Allegro di molto: SA; piano part by far the most interesting, with runs, skips, and chords. Larghetto: A, second half moves to a, cadences on dominant of C. Allegretto: piano and violin are in duet much of the time; after much activity the movements ends in a *pp* whisper. M-D.

———. *Three Trios* Op.2 (Schmid—Br 305). Attractive if a little "cool" writing. Second ideas are often more appealing than the first. Keyboard part is completely involved. M-D.

Johann Christian Bach. *Trio* D (Riemann—IMC).

———. *Two Trios* A, C (Möseler). Charming and technically interesting. Clear homophonic textures with little or no imitation. Int. to M-D.

Johann Christoph Friedrich Bach. *Sonata* C (F. Oberdörffer—HM 46). Cello ad lib. Allegro di molto; Larghetto: Allegretto. Belongs to the same genre as the Piano Trios of Haydn, which developed later. In this *Sonata* the strings are only supplementary to the keyboard part, which is far more interesting, even if their participation does lend variety and a characteristic note to the sonority. M-D.

——. *Sonata* D (H. Ruf—Nag 192) 27pp., parts. Cello part ad lib. Allegro con spirito: much 16th-note figuration. Andante: elegant binary movement. Rondo Scherzo: delightful, invigorating. Charming and sometimes rather delicate writing. M-D.

——. *Trio Sonata* (Frotscher—Sikorski). Cello ad lib.

Henk Badings. *Trio I* 1934 (Schott 3169) 31pp., parts. 20 min. Allegro; Adagio; Scherzo; Allegro vivace. Broadly conceived melodies developed contrapuntally. Serious, almost tragic overtones permeate this work, especially the Adagio. Badings was a Romantic modern who continued the Brahms-Reger-Hindemith line. Polytonal writing a favorite harmonic device. Large span required. M-D to D.

Esther W. Ballou. *Trio* 1955 (CFE) 40pp., parts. Allegro con brio; Andante con moto; Allegro. Freely tonal, octotonic, changing meters, effective texture and dynamic contrasts within movements, bold figurative gestures, Neoclassic. Dissonant counterpoint creates strongly independent lines. D.

Josef Bartoš. *Piano Trio* (Hudební Matice 1947) 31pp., parts. One movement. ABA, chromatic, fast harmonic rhythm, varied pianistic idioms, contrasting più tranquillo mid-section with Allegro appassionato outer sections. M-D.

Arnold Bax. *Trio* B♭ (Chappell 1946) 41pp., parts. 22 min. Allegro con brio; Adagio; Tempo moderato e molto ritmico. Shows a mastery and grasp of this combination in Bax's Romantic style. Subtle sense of beauty. M-D.

Mrs. H. H. A. Beach. *Trio* Op.150 (Composers Press 1939) 41pp., parts. 15 min. Allegro con brio; Lento espressivo–Presto; Allegro. Finely adjusted sonorities make for an ideal balance in this work. The piano is not overly loaded and forms the binding partnership that is necessary for successful Trio writing. The work might be considered overly sweet by today's standards, but it is sincere writing by one of America's most outstanding women composers. It is well worth reviving. M-D.

James Beale. *Trio* Op.5 1947 (CFE) 55pp., parts. Reproduction of the MS. Adagio–Allegro–Adagio–Allegro; Allegro; Lento. A large-scale work that integrates the 3 instruments in a most efficient manner. Neoclassic style provides the framework. The piano is called upon to utilize most of the keyboard; arpeggi figuration. The composer makes suggestions in a preface concerning tempos in the Lento movement. Score is easy to read. Large span required. M-D.

Ludwig van Beethoven. *Piano Trios* (E. Planten—Henle 24, 26, 200) Vol.I: Op.1/1, 2, 3; Op.11. Vol.II: Op.70/1, 2; Op.97; Op.121. Vol.III (contains the less-known compositions): Op.44 E♭; WoO37 G for piano, flute, and bassoon; WoO38 E♭; WoO39 B♭; Op.38 E♭ for piano, clarinet (violin), and cello (Beethoven's own arrangement of *Septet* Op.20); and Hess-Verzeichnis 48 E♭. This last-named Trio movement is an integral work in itself found in a sketchbook of Beethoven containing compositional sketches made between 1784 and 1800. Beethoven did not specify the violin or the cello (but did specify the piano) in this movement, but he probably had them in mind. All sources in this edition were carefully checked. Practical and scholarly edition.

———. *Thirteen Trios* (C. Herrmann, P. Grümmer—CFP) Vol.I: Op.1/1, 2, 3; Op.11; Op.70/1, 2. Vol.II: Op.44; Op.97; Op.121a "Kakadu" Variations; Op. posth. *Trios* in B♭ and E♭. Vol.III: Op.36 after *Symphony No.2;* Op.38 after *Septet.* Lea has same volumes in study scores.

———. *Six Great Piano Trios* (Dover 1987, ISBN 0-486-25398-8) 202pp. Op.1/1, 2, 3; Op.70/1, 2; Op.97. Reprint from *Ludwig van Beethoven's Werke,* Series 11, Nos.79–84, originally published by Br&H, 1862–65.

———. *Six Celebrated Trios* (IMC). Op.1/1, 3; Op.11; Op.70/1, Op.97; Op.121a.

———. Available separately: *Trio* Op.1/1 E♭ (Br&H; Adamowski—GS L1421; Augener 7250a). *Trio* Op.1/2 G (Br&H; Adamowski—GS L1422; Augener 7250b); *Trio* Op.1/3 c (Br&H; Adamowski—GS L1423; Augener 7250c); *Trio* Op.11 B♭ (Br&H; Adamowski—GS L1424; Augener 7250d; IMC; CFP 7064). *Trio* Op.70/1 D (Br&H; Adamowski—GS L1425; Augener 7250e). The first movement is lively and outstanding for great clarity in the treatment of the 3 instruments. The second movement has a remarkable piano part with trills and runs but does not overbalance the strings. The third movement suggests a humorous folk song. *Trio* Op.70/2 (Br&H; Adamowski—GS L1426; Augener 7250f). A cheerful piece throughout with a set of variations for the second movement that display advances over earlier examples of this form. *Trio* Op.97 B♭ "Archduke" (Br&H; Adamowski—GS L1427; Augener 7250g). This symphonically conceived work makes great demands on both players and instruments. The first 2 movements are especially notable for their clarity, the scherzo in particular. The last 2 movements are a revelation of technical and expressive power. *Trio* Op.121a (Br&H) 10 Variations on "Ich bin der Schneider Kakadu." *Trio* Op.38 (IMC) arranged by the composer from the *Septet* Op.20. It should be remembered that Beethoven made his debut as a composer with the 3 Piano Trios Op.1, published in 1795. The Op.70 and the "Archduke" *Trio* Op.97 represent Beethoven's mature works in this form. Much territory is covered between Op.1 and Op.97, and the form must have been a favorite with the composer.

———. *Two Trios* Op. posth. B♭, E♭ (Augener 7250h).

———. *Allegretto* E♭ ca.1783 (Werner—Elkin 1955).

———. *Rondo* D (Werner—Chappell).

See Elfrieda F. Hiebert, "The Piano Trios of Beethoven: An Historical and Analytical Study," Ph.D. diss., University of Wisconsin, 1970.

Peter Benary. *Trio* (Möseler 1974) 15pp., parts. Hausmusik No.113. Adagio; Più mosso, molto agitato; Grazioso, non troppo allegro; Adagio. Free serial style, great variety of pianistic figuration, intense. M-D to D.

William Sterndale Bennett. *Piano and Chamber Music* (G. Bush—St&B 1972) Musica Britannica Vol.37. Introduction, facsimiles, 23pp.; commentary, 5pp. Includes *Chamber Trio* Op.26 of 1839, which is probably the finest work in the collection. It is slender but graceful. The second movement, a Serenade, provides pizzicato for both strings throughout while the piano supplies flowing lines in contrast. The entire work has many Mendelssohn characteristics. It is not known if this edition has separate parts. M-D.

Franz Berwald. *Trio* I E♭ 1849 (GM) 33pp., parts. Introduction–Allegro con brio; Andante grazioso; Finale. M-D.
——. *Trio* II f 1851 (GM) 41pp., parts. Introduzioni–Allegro molto; Larghetto; Scherzo. Conceived as one extensive movement. M-D.
——. *Trio* III d 1851 (GM) 45pp., parts. Allegro con molto; Adagio quasi largo; Finale. One extensive movement. M-D.
——. *Trio* IV C (GM). M-D.
Solid classical writing in all 4 *Trios* with Romantic characteristics appearing more frequently in the later works.

Boris Blacher. *Trio* (Belaieff 1973) 27pp., parts. Short rhythmic motifs, structurally integrated, thoroughly 20th-century style, variable meters, economy of texture, wiry, individual style. D.

Ernest Bloch. *Three Nocturnes* 1924 (CF 1925). Based on a Jewish theme, achieves interest through rhythmic vitality of short thematic elements.

Christopher Bochmann. *De Profundis—Meditation for Violin, Cello and Piano* 1970 (OUP) 14pp., parts. 6½ min. "The work takes its title from the opening of Psalm 130: 'Out of the deep have I called unto thee, O Lord: Lord, hear my voice'" (from Composer's Note). The work is an interaction of 4 separate arc forms: the minor 3rds in harmonics that mark the divisions between the 4 main sections form one of these arcs, the first and fourth main sections together form another, and the second and third each, another. All thematic material is derived more or less closely from a pattern of 7 notes and its combinations with itself. The title purposely avoids the designation "Piano Trio" because the way in which the instruments are used seems to be insufficiently close to that of the Piano Trio literature: here the violin and cello are treated nearly as one instrument in contrast to—almost in opposition to—the piano. Serial, proportional notation, dynamic extremes, changing meters, chords in tremolo, pointillistic, avant-garde. Large span required. D.

Leon Boëllmann. *Trio* Op.19 (Hamelle) 64pp., parts. An unusual form is used in this work: the first section comprises the introduction, allegro, and andante;

the second combines the scherzo and finale. Modal and Romantic harmonic characteristics. M-D.

René de Boisdeffre. *Trio II* Op.32 (Hamelle 1882) 45pp., parts. Prelude–Andante maestoso; Scherzo; Andante (with a grandiloquent conclusion); Finale–Allegro energico (rondo form). Boisdeffre wrote mainly chamber music. This piece is well written along traditional lines for all instruments. M-D.

Joseph Bodin de Boismortier. *Trio* Op.50/6 D 1734 (P. Ruyssen—Nag 143) 11pp., parts. Largo; Allegro; Larghetto; Allegro. Tuneful, technically simple, reflects the popular lighthearted and charming taste of the day. Tasteful keyboard realization. Int.

Bernard van den Boogaard. *Trio* 1983 (Donemus 1985) 41pp., parts. 20 min. Allegro vivace; Larghetto; Allegretto vivace. Restless with frequent changes of meters and indications urging agitation. M-D.

Lili Boulanger. *D'un Soir Triste* 1918 (GS).
——. *D'un Matin de Printemps* 1918 (GS).

Johannes Brahms. *Trios* (E. Herttrich—Henle 1972) 212pp., parts. Piano fingering added by H.-M. Theopold. Contains Op.8b (includes first and second versions with textual comparisons collated); Op.87 C; Op.101 c.
——. Op.9, first version (CFP; Br&H; GS; IMC). This early work already displays Brahms's consummate mastery of balance between the piano and strings. A complete revision took place in 1889, and this new version is the one usually heard. Shows slight influence of Schumann and Mendelssohn but displays supreme mastery of the chamber music idiom. A rich thematic, harmonic, and rhythmic substance is apparent from the broad opening lyrical theme. Crisp cross-rhythms come across in the Scherzo. This is the most Romantic of the first 3 *Trios*.
——. *Trio* Op.40 E♭ (Br&H; CFP 3899b; K; IMC; Augener 5117; EPS 249). For piano, violin, and horn or viola or cello. First movement is in ABABA rondo form. Similar themes quoted in third and fourth movements as a unifying device. D.
——. *Trio* Op.87 C (Br&H; CFP 3899C; GS L1768; Augener 9301; IMC). One of the great works in this form; full of inspiration; has perhaps the broadest appeal. Strong thematic relationship between the first (a good-humored, busy SA) and last movements. The separation of theme and development becomes less clear, especially in the opening of this work. Frequently the strings combine for vigorous chords alternating and contrasting with chords on the piano. The second movement is a set of variations on a melody of a vaguely Hungarian or gypsy character. The Presto section of the Scherzo is built on a large sweeping melodic arc. D.
——. *Trio* Op.101 c (Br&H; CFP 3899D, Adamowski—GS L1510; IMC). In the

intense and dramatic first movement, all exposition material is contained in bar 1. The nobility of the thematic material and the superlative manner in which it is developed are perfection exemplified. The second movement is light and delicate with an almost ghostly quality to it. The third movement, with its multiple rhythms, is mainly a dialogue between strings and piano. This is the greatest of the first 3 Trios. D.

——. Trio Op.114 a (Br&H; CFP 3899E; K; IMC; EPS 250). For clarinet or violin or viola, cello, and piano. Strong thematic relationships between the first and last movements. The third movement is in ABACA rondo form. D.

——. Trio A (Bücken, Haase—Br&H).

The Trio for piano, violin, and cello reached its full bloom with Brahms. See Fabio Roberto Gardenal da Silva, "Brahms' Piano Trio Op.8 in B Major: A Comparison between the Early (1854) and Late (1860) Versions," Ph.D. diss., New York University, 1993; Margaret Anne Notley, "Brahms's Chamber-Music Summer of 1886: A Study of Opera 99, 100, 101, and 108," Ph.D. diss., Yale University, 1992.

Cesar Bresgen. *Trio* 1972 (Dob 07217) 20pp., parts. Two short movements with chromatic harmonies and enormous rhythmic drive. The second movement makes much out of the interval of the 4th. Throughout there are continual changes of mood and tempo as well as of rhythm. Astringent dissonances abound, similar to middle-period Bartók. Piano textures are carefully handled. Ensemble will require much thought. D.

Tomás Bretón. *Four Spanish Pieces* (ESC). Also published separately. 1. Dance Orientale, 2. Boléro, 3. Polo Gitano, 4. Scherzo Andalou. These effective display pieces were very popular in the early part of the 20th century, but their brilliance has somewhat faded. M-D.

Frank Bridge. *Phantasie Trio I* (Augener 1908) 31pp., parts. The form corresponds to an SA design with an andante replacing the usual development and a scherzo providing a contrasting mid-section to the Andante. Abrupt ending. Main ideas treated in a broad, dignified manner. There are few ensemble problems in this well-crafted and highly Romantic work. M-D.

——. *Trio II* (Augener 1930) 75pp., parts. Allegretto ben moderato; Molto allegro; Andante molto moderato–Allegro ma non troppo. Post-Romantic writing of a high order. A catalog of pianistic clichés and idioms in this style. D.

Earle Brown. *Music for Violin, Cello and Piano* 1952 (UE 15443 1972) 7pp., parts. Explanations in English and German. One movement. Short, highly contrasted dynamics (serialized?), dissonant pointillism, post-Webernesque technique. Bar lines only indicate points at which all 3 parts have the same number of 16th-note units, for ensemble synchronization. The general conception of the work is of a kind of spontaneous "pulseless" energy. In rehearsing this piece it is more important to develop a sense of the time values of the durations and figurations at the various tempos than it is to count the rhythm in the usual way. Dynamic marks are attached to most notes. D.

Max Bruch. *Trio* Op.5 c 1857 (Br&H; Hamelle) 39pp., parts. Andante molto cantabile: broadly laid out and attractive. Allegro assai: same serious mood as the Andante. Presto: fiery, opening melody of the first movement returns in a short Andante section before the clangorous Prestissimo ending. Modeled on Classical lines. M-D.

Paul Bruinen. *Mano* 1990 (Donemus 1990) 42pp., parts. 17½ min. In 2 movements: Pollice, Indice. Intricate rhythms in complementary design. Performers must tap their instruments for nontraditional sounds. M-D.

———. *Anulare/Dito medio* 1995, rev.2002 (Donemus 1995) 34pp., parts. 22 min. In 2 movements with names taken from the title. Lengthy homophonic introduction in *Anulare* of 49 mm. for piano. Harmonics and cluster chords follow in a slow tempo as the movement progresses with few other changes. Syncopation abounds in *Dito medio* as the instruments press forward at a rapid tempo. Quadruple stops for strings make this a demanding work requiring experienced performers. M-D to D.

Willy Burkhard. *Trio* Op.43 (Br 2093) 20pp., parts. One movement. Extended, free design. A subtle rhythmic pulse is combined with a linear style. M-D.

Adolf Busch. *Trio* Op.15 a (Simrock 1920). Reger's influence shows through, but the writing is distinguished in many ways, in spite of its lack of motion and polyphony. The work gains by Busch's intimate knowledge of ensemble music. D.

Alan Bush. *Three Concert Studies* Op.31 1947 (Nov) 18 min. Sturdy pieces, vitality of No.1 and inventiveness of No.3 (in use of harmonics and rhythmic expertise) are of special interest. Impressive, inventive, and original.

Dietrich Buxtehude. *Trio Sonata* Op.1/1 F (B. Grusnick, A. Wenzinger—Br 1151; Peyrot, Rebuffat—Senart 2721) 15pp., parts. M-D.
———. *Trio Sonata* Op.1/2 G (Br 1152, 12pp., parts; Senart 2918). M-D.
———. *Trio Sonata* Op.1/3 a (Br 1153; Schott). M-D.
———. *Trio Sonata* Op.1/4 B♭ (Br 1154). M-D.
———. *Trio Sonata* Op.1/7 e (K&S; IMC) 15pp., parts. Allegro; Presto; Poco presto; Prestissimo. M-D.
———. *Trio Sonata* Op.2/2 D (Br&H; K&S; IMC). M-D.
———. *Trio Sonata* Op.2/6 E (Nag; IMC). M-D.
———. *Trio Sonata* D (Döbereiner—Br&H). M-D.
———. *Sonata à Trois* (Crussard—Foetisch). M-D.
These works have an average of 5 to 8 contrasting movements with the outer movements normally fast. The slow movements are usually short and transitional. For a more thorough discussion of these pieces see SBE, 250–54.

Charles Camilleri. *Trio* (Fairfield 1975) 60pp., parts. 23 min. Libero: serial movement; violin and cello open and are followed by piano in a Recitative section; all instruments come together in an Andante Sostenuto (calmo) section that works through the opening material. Allegro vivace: much rhythmic drive in all instruments. Lento: Impressionist sonorities with piano having a highly elaborate right-hand figuration. Allegro molto vivace: triplet figuration in all instruments leads to dramatically punctuated chromatic chords; these ideas continue to the second part of the movement, where we are told that "tempo is left to the discretion of each player. Familiarity with the material and style will eventually produce a serenity and depth of feeling surpassing the basic rhythmic excitement apparent at first"; Tempo I of this movement brings the work to a brilliant conclusion. D.

Alfredo Casella. *Sonata a Tre* Op.62 1938 (Ric 124383) 50pp., parts. Introduzione– Allegro ma non troppo; Andante cantabile, quasi Adagio; Finale (Tempo di Giga). The piano provides rhythmic and harmonic functions while the lyric strings are treated melodically. All movements are extensive. The second movement opens with a canonic 12-note idea, but it is not developed. D.

Mario Castelnuovo-Tedesco. *Piano Trio* G 1928 (Ric 121053) 78pp., parts. Allegro con baldanza; Litanie (Tema con 5 Variazioni); Allegretto; Rondo all'Ungherese. Strong melodies, rich harmonies, undulating lines, broad pianistic gestures. D.

René de Castéra. *Trio* Op.5 D (Rouart Lerolle 1904). Closely related themes in this 4-movement work. The first movement, in SA design, is overflowing with bold ideas. An introduction includes an important theme that returns in the slow conclusion of this movement. The second movement, a divertissement in rondo form, presents a Basque dance in $\frac{5}{8}$ meter. The third movement (assez lent) is a song in ABA design. The finale (très-animé) is in SA and glitters with color. The piano carries much of the interest in this piece, especially in the finale. M-D.

Alexis de Castillon. *Trio* Op.4 B♭ (Durand 1871) 45pp., parts. Prelude et Andante; Scherzo; Romance; Finale.
——. *Trio* II Op.17 d (Heugel 1872) 67pp., parts. Allegro moderato; Allegretto non vivo; Scherzando vivace; Adagio–Allegro con fuoco.

Auguste Caune. *Trio* (Hamelle) 57pp., parts. Allegro moderato; Scherzo; Adagio; Final. Fine sense of form, traditional harmonic and rhythmic vocabulary. M-D.

Sergio Cervetti. *Fünf Episoden* 1965 (Moeck 5032) 31pp., parts. 15 min. I. Molto agitato, II. Come improvvisando, III. Misterioso, IV. Molto lento con fantasia, V. Molto flessible e leggiero. Abstract, Expressionist, pointillistic, serial, avant-garde techniques such as damping strings with hands, clusters. D.

Cécile Chaminade. *Piano Trio I* Op.11 (Durand 1900) 45pp., parts. Allegro; Andante; Scherzo; Finale. The Scherzo shows off the piano in a Mendelssohnian brilliance. The outer movements are well written but not as spontaneous-sounding as the Scherzo. M-D.

———. *Piano Trio II* Op.34 (Enoch 189?) 61pp., parts. Allegro moderato; Lento; Allegro energico. D.

Auguste Chapuis. *Trio* G (Durand 1912). Animé, pas trop, et très espressif: vigorous, developed fugally then melodically with a big G conclusion. Assez vif, spiritual et chantant: scherzo, lively, light, flexible trio in G. Calme sans lenteur: a Lied; slow march rhythm of quasi-religious character; expressive theme that is developed in a calm, then strong manner. Gaiement, dans l'allure d'une ronde populaire: vivacious, joyful conclusion. Franck influence; solidly constructed. M-D.

Ernest Chausson. *Trio* a 1882 (Rouart Lerolle).

———. *Trio* Op.3 g 1882 (Rouart Lerolle 1919) 69pp., parts. 31 min. Pas trop lent; Vite; Assez lent; Animé. Strongly influenced by Franck, with some of Wagner's influence here and there. Great ingenuity in piano writing is coupled with a delicate and sensitive approach to the instrument. Long lines and lush sonorities provide much sensual beauty, but the individual movements leave a great deal to be desired with their loose formal construction. D.

See Yea-Shiuh Lin, "The Piano Trio in France, ca. 1880–1920: Debussy, Chausson, Fauré, and Ravel," D.M.A. diss., University of Cincinnati, 1998.

Camille Chevillard. *Trio* Op.3 F (Durand 1884). Franck influence seen here, but there is a certain amount of originality and a fine sense of form. The most unusual feature of this work is a piano cadenza, just before the finale coda, that incorporates not only the subjects of this finale but also the main idea from the first movement. The finale is brilliant and full of *joie de vivre.* M-D.

Frédéric Chopin. *Trio* Op.8 g 1828 (Br&H; Balakirev—CFP 48pp., parts; PWM, Vol.16 of *Complete Works;* Litolff; K&S) 25 min. Allegro con fuoco: SA; coda; tonic key is over-used. Scherzo–Con moto, ma non troppo: lively and flowing. Adagio sostenuto: nocturne-like, charming. Finale-Allegretto: cheerful and vivacious. "Its classicism may be disputed, nevertheless it contains lovely music" wrote Huneker. Chopin, in August of 1830, wrote: "Last Saturday I tried the trio, and, perhaps because I had not heard it for so long, was satisfied with myself. 'Happy man,' you will say, won't you? It then struck me that it would be better to use the viola instead of the violin, as the first string predominates in the violin, and in my trio it is hardly used at all. The viola would, I think, accord better with the cello." D.

Francesco Ciléa. *Trio* (EC 1963) 69pp., parts. Allegro sostenuto; Scherzo; Andante molto espressivo; Allegro con fuoco. Nineteenth-century style. M-D.

Rebecca Clarke. *Piano Trio* 1921 (Winthrop Rogers) 41pp., parts. Moderato ma appassionato; Andante molto semplice; Allegro vigoroso. The 3 movements are based on a central idea that is used in different forms throughout the work. A work of sweeping lines, unusual power, and passion; displays a great deal of brilliant writing for the piano. D.

Muzio Clementi. *Trio* Op.22/1 D. See detailed entry under trios for piano, one stringed instrument, and one wind instrument.
————. *Trio* Op.28/2 D 1791 or 1792 (Casella—EC; Casella—GS 1936) 23pp., parts. Allegro amabile; Polonaise; Rondo. Revised and elaborated on by Casella. The piano part is original, but the string parts have been completely reworked. This is a lustrous and delectable Trio with clear, limpid, and flowing musicality. The original edition is contained in the *Collected Works of Muzio Clementi* (New York: Da Capo Press, 1973), Vol.4, pp.65–75. M-D.

Reine Colaço Osorio-Swaab. *Trio* 1941 (Donemus 1949) 45pp., parts. Allegro energico; Scherzo; Lento; Rondo–Allegro. Neoclassic flavor with chromaticism. Tuneful melodies with occasional surprises. M-D.

Dinos Constantinides. *Trio* 1967 (Seesaw), parts. Allegro: frequent use of 2nds, varied figuration, octave tremolo in left hand, dramatic conclusion; large span required. Largo: ABA, sustained, repeated syncopated chords, works to broad climax, then subsides. Allegro vivo: driving rhythms, freely tonal, repeated chords, dissonant counterpoint, effective conclusion. M-D to D.
————. *Trio No. 2b* 1976, rev.2001 (Magni 2001) 55pp., parts. 18 min. In 3 movements, the first 2 untitled and the third a Scherzo. Pianist plays pizzicato and taps on wood of the piano; double stops and harmonics in strings. This Trio "is a revised and expanded re-composition of the composer's earlier piano Sonata. Its harmonic language makes use of the quartal system" (from Preface). M-D.

Aaron Copland. *Vitebsk* 1929 (Bo&H) 18pp., parts. Study on a Jewish Theme. Contains Copland's only use of quarter tones, which are used coloristically rather than structurally. The opening contains highly grating sonorities. A granitically conceived, expressive, and impressive work. D.

Henry Cowell. *Trio* 1964–65 (CFP) 29pp., parts. 19 min. Nine short movements based on common melodic and rhythmic materials. Largo tenuto; Allegretto; Andante; Allegro; Andante sostenuto; Allegro; Allegretto; Adagio cantabile; Allegro assai. "The piano functions by and large as an independent entity of the tonal texture with strings playing either soloistically or in duet. Musical material is treated in widely varied fashion—as sheer melody (1st movement), arpeggio etude (2nd and 7th movements), chromatic study in oblique motion (4th movement), chorale (5th movement), or fantastic scherzo (6th movement). The finale, of almost Webernian brevity, seems to break off almost before getting started, the intent being to create the feeling common to much Indian and Indonesian music of infinite continuity beyond the span of actual sound" (from Preface). Cowell's last completed work. M-D.

Ram Da-Oz. *Trio* 1963 (Israeli Music Publications) 36pp., parts. One serial movement divided into 3 parts. Opens slowly and meditatively; tempo increases to Allegro ma non troppo. Here begins a rondo-like section. Tempo and tension further increase until a climax is reached with the piano part having a percussive character, persistently repeating rhythmical figures. Second part opens with a piano subito (bar 226). Short introduction, then piano has a narrative theme. A series of free variations follow. Third part (begins at bar 311) presents rhythms that become more complex until the climax of the whole work is reached. Piano is here performing the task of several percussive instruments playing various rhythms. Tempo and tension decrease gradually, and the *Trio* closes as it began, Lento. D.

Ingolf Dahl. *Trio* 1962 (PIC 1971) 58pp., parts. Allegretto grazioso; Notturno I; Rondino Cantabile; Notturno II; Finale: Variazioni (5), Recitativo e Coda. Open textures, pointillistic, strong abstract writing. Well-controlled free tonal usage, supple rhythms, melodic and harmonic materials serialized, versatile writing for all instruments. Rhythmic problems, parts play together independently of each other. Large span required. D.

Mario Davidovsky. *Chacona* 1972 (EBM) 16pp., parts. 10 min. Pointillistic, flexible meters; at one point the pianist must pluck strings and strike the keys simultaneously. Abstract, Expressionist. Requires large span. D.

Claude Debussy. *Premier Trio en sol* 1880 (E. Derr, D. Blumenthal—Henle 379 1986, ISMN M-2018-0379-1) 35pp., parts. First edition, Urtext. Andantino con moto allegro; Scherzo–Intermezzo–Moderato con allegro; Andante espressivo; Finale–Appassionato. Composed in Italy at the age of 18, this early work shows "influences of César Franck and of Robert Schumann, whom Debussy especially admired" (from Preface). M-D.
See D. Tomatz, "*Piano Trio in G Major* by Claude Debussy: An Unknown Work Discovered," *American Ensemble* 6/4 (1983): 12–13; Yea-Shiuh Lin, "The Piano Trio in France, ca. 1880–1920: Debussy, Chausson, Fauré, and Ravel," D.M.A. diss., University of Cincinnati, 1998.

Helmut Degen. *Piano Trio* (Br 2095 1948) 39pp., parts. Andante espressivo–Allegro; Adagio cantabile; Allegro. Moderate modernism infused with a Hindemithian flavor, Neoclassic. M-D.

Lex van Delden. *Trio* I Op.95 1969 (Donemus 1969) 46pp., parts. 22 min. Allegro, con fierezza; Lento; Allegro frescamente. Conventional writing with complementary roles for each instrument. M-D.

———. *Trio* II Op.114 1988 (Donemus 1988) 22pp., parts. 13 min. Allegro energico; Lento; Allegro scorrevole. Strongly tonal even for its date in a most agreeable idiom.

Edisson V. Denisov. *Trio* Op.5 1954 (USSR C1755K) 60pp., parts. Moderato; Allegro; Largo; Allegretto. Freely tonal, colorful, pianistic, mildly 20th-century with a Russian flavor. M-D.

David Diamond. *Piano Trio* 1951 (PIC 1956) 46pp., parts. Clear structures, SA procedures, intense lyric writing tinged with Romantic feeling, freely chromatic harmonic usage. M-D.

Jan van Dijk. *Trio* I 1950 (Donemus 1951) 23pp., parts. 12 min. Preludio; Romance; Capriccio. Syncopated rhythms coupled with detailed passagework give the outer movements much interest. The Romance impatiently plays with musical ideas and never settles into place. M-D.

Gaetano Donizetti. *Trio* (B. Päuler—CFP 8116 1972) 20pp., parts. Largo–Allegro; Largo; Andantino. These movements have been merged into a Trio and published here for the first time. Preface by the editor describes editorial policy. Clear classic writing, tuneful. M-D.

Richard Donovan. *Trio* 1937 (Bo&H) 32pp., parts. One movement. One of Donovan's best works. Shows fine command of formal structure in particular. Mildly 20th-century. M-D.
———. *Trio* II 1963 (CFE) 45pp., parts. 23 min. Andante tranquillo; Variations; Allegro energico. Introspective, neo-Romantic, yet contains a certain kind of transparency. Freely tonal with varying harmonic pungency. Finale is especially vigorous and straightforward. D.

Sam Dresden. *Trio* 1942–43 (Donemus 1947) 71pp., parts. 29 min. Allegro, un poco agitato; Molto allegro–Poco adagio–Più andante; Molto allegro, quasi presto. An intriguing work with much originality considering its composition during World War II. Of special interest is the final movement, a fiery toccata-like whirlwind in $\frac{7}{8}$ which concludes with a surprising Lento at *ppp*. M-D.

Anton Dvořák. *Trio* Op.21 B♭ 1875 (Artia; Adamowski—GS L1524; Lienau) 58pp., parts. 29 min. Allegro molto; Adagio molto e maestro; Allegretto scherzando; Finale. An early work that does not reflect the true personal touch of the composer, but the form is most delightfully worked out. M-D.
———. *Trio* Op.26 g 1876 (Artia; IMC) 27 min. Displays an economy of thematic material plus a character of intense yearning. M-D.
———. *Trio* Op.65 f 1883 (Artia; Simrock; IMC) 41 min. All 3 instruments are well knit in their interaction. The music varies in character from grave and gloomy to passionate. The piano adds a symphonic grandeur. A peaceful resignation arrives only at the end of the work. D.

————. *Dumky Trio* Op.90 1890–91 (Artia; Mercury; Simrock; IMC) 44pp., parts. 30 min. Dvořák's most famous work in this combination; very typical of his chamber music; Bohemian in character. There are 6 *dumka* (alternation of yearning melancholy and wild gaiety) movements in this work, each thematically independent and separate from each other. Piano is accorded brilliant treatment; higher registers of cello exploited. Excellent counterpoint infuses all 3 parts; much vitality that comes from the national rhythms and melodic styles. D.

John Eaton. *Piano Trio* (SP) 18pp., parts. One extended movement. First string on the violin is tuned down a quarter step, and notes are written at sounding pitch. An arrow (accent) system is used in the piano part that means "bring out the notes preceded by the arrows." Expressionist, atonal, shifting meters and rhythms, irregular tremolo, spread-out sonorities, harmonics, large arpeggiated chords, clusters combined with melody. Pencil to be pressed into strings at one point; one large arpeggiated chord is given, and pianist is to improvise up the keyboard in similar arpeggios, splashing clusters around keyboard. Avant-garde, impressive sonorities and writing. Large span required. D.

Horst Ebenhöh. *Einigen Minuten für Klaviertrio* Op.32/1 1973 (Dob) 20pp., parts. All performers indulge in 20th-century techniques such as instrumental slides. New signs are explained (in German only). Varied piano writing includes short phrases of broken-chord figures, legato major 3rds in the bass, extended trills, much syncopation. Rhythmic complexities provide major ensemble problems. Many contrasting elements do not fit together well. D.

Anton Eberl. *Trio* (Sonata) c (Litolff). Formerly attributed to Mozart (K.291) but now considered to be the work of Eberl. M-D.

Klaus Egge. *Trio* Op.14 1941 (EMH). Dramatic, tender, and brutal sounds; strong emotional overtones. Written under the influence of the war between Finland and the former Soviet Union. D.

Ivo van Emmerik. *O—7 Pieces for 3 Instruments* 1990 (Donemus 1996) 5pp., parts. 15 min. "The title—*O*—not only refers to Odeon, but also may be read as a circle, thus being an indication of the many cyclic aspects of this composition. The structure of each piece, for example, is based on the regular reappearance of the same musical material, and harmonic details are influenced by cyclic processes. All possible combinations of the three instruments are used in the course of the composition. Beginning with a solo for violin, the piece gradually shifts the attention to the other instruments, to end with a solo for piano. As a whole the piece has a restful rather than exciting, a contemplative rather than contending character" (from score). The piano plays in Nos.3, 5, 6, 7.

Heimo Erbse. *Trio* Op.8 1953 (Bo&Bo) 57pp., parts. 16 min. Allegro; Scherzo; Larghetto; Vivace giocoso. Complex rhythmic treatment, Neoclassic melodic style, chromatic and freely tonal, effective handling of all 3 instruments. D.

Gabriel Fauré. *Trio* Op.120 d (Durand 1923) 40pp., parts. 21 min. Allegro, ma non troppo; Andantino; Allegro vivo. Three lofty movements filled with Fauré's incomparable grace and elegance. Thin textures (especially for the period), serene, tenderly persuasive, freely tonal. The second movement projects the piano cantando espressivo spontaneously. Requires more musicianship and refined sensibility than a brief look at the score would suggest. M-D.
See Yea-Shiuh Lin, "The Piano Trio in France, ca. 1880–1920: Debussy, Chausson, Fauré, and Ravel," D.M.A. diss., University of Cincinnati, 1998.

Václav Felix. *Trio* Op.5 C 1956 (Artia) 34pp., parts. Allegro; Lento; Moderato; Presto. Freely tonal, folk influence, dance qualities, colorful. M-D.

Oscar Lorenzo Fernández. *Trio Brasileiro* Op.32 1924 (Ric BA6113) 57pp., parts. Allegro maestoso; Cancao; Dansa; Final. Much Brazilian melodic inspiration (some folk themes, some original themes in folk song style) with 20th-century rhythmic vitality. This work won an international competition. Piano supplies much of the rhythmic interest. M-D.

Ross Lee Finney. *Trio II* A (CF 1958) 47pp., parts. 19½ min. Brightly colored opaque sounds, powerful rhythmic drive, strong tonal functions always freely present, idiomatic writing for all instruments. M-D.

Arthur Foote. *Trio* I Op.5 c 1882–83 (Schott) 55pp., parts. Allegro con brio; Allegro vivace; Adagio molto; Allegro commodo.
———. *Trio II* Op.65 Bb (Schmidt 1909) 39pp., parts. Allegro giocoso; Tranquillo; Allegro molto.
See Eugenia K. Hinson, "Arthur William Foote: His Contribution to Chamber Music in Boston and Analyses of Selected Piano Chamber Works (Massachusetts)," D.A. paper, Ball State University, 1994.

César Franck. *Trio* Op.1/1 F# 1840 (CFP 3745; Durand; Hamelle) 55pp., parts. Andante con moto (in 5 sections); Allegro molto (Scherzo and 2 trios); Finale–Allegro maestoso (SA design). The piano part is so massively scored that ensemble balance is almost impossible. Requires a fire-breathing virtuoso to handle the cascading octaves and numerous repeated chords. Cyclic in form and hints at the later Franck. This *Trio* is far superior to the other 2 in this opus number. D.
———. *Trio* Op.1/2 Bb 1840 (Hamelle; Schuberth).
———. *Trio* Op.1/3 b 1840 (Hamelle; Schuberth).
———. *Trio* Op.2 B 1842 (Hamelle; Schuberth). In one movement. This is the rewritten last movement of the Op.1/3, for Franz Liszt. Contains interesting mo-

ments (the recapitulation begins with the second subject), but it is nowhere near the equal of Op.1/1. M-D.

Géza Frid. *Trio* Op.27 1947 (Donemus 1948) 31pp., parts. 17 min. In one continuous movement of multiple sections, including a fugue, march, scherzo, passacaglia, and rondo. Frid's Hungarian origin can still be felt in the themes and spirit of this work, but French influence is also strong. The piano part is especially well written, in part because of Frid's outstanding ability as a concert pianist. May be performed in 3 different ways as described in the Preface. D.

James Friskin. *Phantasie* e 1908 (Nov) 15pp., parts. Serious intimacy of expression in this work, especially the melodic writing. Post-Romantic characteristics of the highest order are integrated into a well-crafted work. Contrasted sections. M-D.

Gunnar de Frumerie. *Trio II* (NMS). Brilliant Neoclassic writing showing strong free rhythms and brittle harmonies, freely tonal. A highly polished work of a fastidious craftsman who has contributed a composition of genuine substance; completely unostentatious. M-D.

Sandro Fuga. *Trio* 1941 (SZ) 52pp., parts. 28 min. Allegro con fuoco; Mosso, con semplitita; Grave–Sostenuto (Novembre 1939). Neoclassic, clear and transparent textures, freely tonal, colorful and idiomatic writing for the piano. M-D to D.

Niels W. Gade. *Trio* Op.42 F 1863 (Br&H; Augener) 35pp., parts. 20 min. Allegro animato; Allegro molto vivace; Andantino; Finale. A good work for amateurs who enjoy Romantic poetic sounds. Grateful writing for all instruments. M-D.
——. *Noveletten Trio* Op.29 a 1853 (Costallat) 35pp., parts. Allegro scherzando; Andante con moto; Moderato; Larghetto con moto; Finale. This Scandinavian pioneer of the Romantic school writes with an individual touch. Both Mendelssohn and Schumann influenced him, and a great deal of the former shows in both these *Trios*. The string writing appears to be more successful than that for the piano. M-D.

Renaud Gagneux. *Trio* (Jobert 1976) 6pp., parts. 7 min. Explanation of signs in French. One untitled movement. Long pedals, harmonics, repeated patterns, xylophone mallet used on piano strings, pointillistic, Expressionist. M-D to D.

Hans Gál. *Variations on a Viennese Popular Tune* Op.9 1921 (Simrock 843) 11pp., parts. Genuine Viennese music, although it is a little short on gaiety and sensuous charm. M-D.
——. *Trio* Op.49b 1948 (OBV) 16pp., parts. Violin can be replaced by an oboe or flute. Moderato e tranquillo; Pastorale; March Burlesque. Written in the best chamber music style with an ensemble of independent individuals whose

function of leading, counterpointing, accompanying parts is changing perpetually. Mildly 20th-century. M-D.

Fritz Geissler. *Trio* 1970 (DFVM) 55pp., parts. Trauermarsch: fluid rhythmic figures, serial influence, Expressionist dynamic extremes, cluster-like percussive chords, graphic and traditional notation, strongly chromatic. Intermezzo: scherzo, light and elegant, pointillistic, best-organized movement. Passacaglia: lugubrious subject built on tritone; 3 variations and reprises expose the subject to various treatment; thin textures. Finale: shifting meters; left hand is chordal; right hand has fluid figures similar to opening movement; accented chromatic chords; tremolo clusters; improvisation; short section in Walzer tempo; intense percussive ending. Mixture of Neoclassic and avant-garde techniques. D.

Armando Gentilucci. *Crescendo* (Ric 1971) 15pp. on 2 folded loose leaves. Photostat of MS. Three copies necessary for performance. 12 min. Pointillistic, takes the form of one long crescendo from *ppp* beginning to *fff* ending. D.

Harald Genzmer. *Trio* 1943 F (CFP 5025) 14 min. Hindemith influence is strong. This work is otherwise freely tonal, contains some polyrhythmic interpolations, and combines contrapuntal textures with expressive coloring. M-D.
——. *Trio* 1964 (CFP 5990) 33pp., parts. 20 min. Allegro con brio; Tranquillo; Burleske; Finale. Octotonic, shifting meters, repeated harmonic 2nds, alternating hand figuration, quartal and quintal harmony, effective trill usage, freely tonal with plenty of chromaticism, large arpeggiated chords. Large span required. Neoclassic. D.

Roberto Gerhard. *Trio* 1918 (Senart) 32pp., parts. 26 min. Modéré; Très calme; Vif. Attractive and accomplished tonal writing that shows strong French influences. M-D.

Edwin Gerschefski. *Rhapsody* Op.46 (CFE) 22pp., parts. Contrasting tempos, moods, and textures; freely tonal; tremolo; octotonic; figuration interestingly dispersed between hands; parallel chords; intense Andante cantabile section; bold gestures; dramatic conclusion. D.

Mikhail Gnessin. *Trio* Op.63 (USSR M18733G 1947) 34pp., parts. Draws on Arabic-Semitic sources, with their luxurious ornamentation, but at the same time preserves a strong bond with Russian musical culture. M-D.

Benjamin Godard. *Trio I* Op.32 G (Heugel) 49pp., parts. Allegro; Tempo di Minuetto moderato; Andante quasi adagio; Allegro vivace. M-D.
——. *Trio II* Op.72 F (Durand 1884) 59pp., parts. Allegro moderato; Adagio; Vivace; Allegro vivace. M-D.
Both works are delightfully written in the Romantic style of the day and are recommended to amateur performers. Godard knew how to turn a good melody, but there are places marked by an over-sentimentality.

Hugo Godron. *Trio* 1948 (Donemus 1948) 30pp., parts. 22 min. Allegro moderato; Andante mesto; Allegro. Written in an early-20th-century style with lyric melodies and clear harmonies. M-D.

———. *Nouvelles* 1963 (Donemus 1965) 42pp., parts. 25 min. Promenade; Berceuse pour Monique; La Chanson de Marion; Badinage pour Robert Clark; Le Tombeau à Paramarilo; Le Polichinel de Joep à Amsterdam. Difficult-to-read copy of MS. M-D.

Alexander Goehr. *Piano Trio* Op.20 1966 (Schott 11004) 20pp., parts. 20 min. Con anima: players required to play in different meters; in these places the relationship of meters is proportional and the bar lines (strong beats) do not synchronize; each player must express his or her own meter and not be hampered by the need of precise ensemble. Lento possibile e sostenuto: free, grace notes to be played as if anticipating (syncope) next indicated value; this long slow movement is the glory of this *Trio*. Free use of motivic elements; repetition employed to help clarify formal structures; concentrated dense idiom; unusual development of texture; Bartók influence. D.

Hermann Goetz. *Trio* Op.1 g 1863 (UWKR 14 1976) 40pp., parts. Langsam–Feurig; Sehr ruhig; Flüchtig, erregt; Mässig rasch–Ziemlich lebhaft. Influenced by Mendelssohn, Schumann, and Brahms. Even though this work is listed as Op.1, it displays expressive and effective writing for all instruments. M-D.

Carl Goldmark. *Trio* Op.4 B♭ (K&S) 57pp., parts. Schnell; Adagio; Scherzo; Finale. Pronounced Romanticism; lyric sections the most convincing. Spontaneous melodic and harmonic treatment is mainly diatonic. Abundant craft is evident in the conscientious development of this work. The Adagio is especially effective with its introductory improvisation that recalls Hungarian gypsy tunes. M-D.

———. *Trio* Op.33 (Schweers & Haake) 53pp., parts. Allegro con moto; Scherzo; Andante sostenuto; Allegro. One of Goldmark's finest works. D.

Enrique Granados. *Trio* Op.50 (UME 1996) 77pp., parts. Poco allegro con espressione; Scherzetto–Vivace molto; Duetto–Andante con molta espressione; Finale–Allegro molto. One of the major Spanish works for the repertoire. Follows Classical models with coloristic harmonics and lyric melodies. Instruments complement each other well. M-D.

Alexander Gretchaninov. *Trio I* Op.38 c 1906 (Belaieff) 59pp., parts. Allegro passionato; Lento assai; Finale–Allegro vivace. Nineteenth-century sweeping chromatic pianism throughout. The style is comparatively sustained and homophonic. D.

———. *Trio II* Op.128 G (Belaieff) 18 min.

Odd Grüner-Hegge. *Trio* Op.4 (WH 2288 1923) 51pp., parts. Allegro energico; Andantino, molto tranquillo; Allegro giocoso; Andante; Lugubre maestoso.

This youthful work exhibits a fine technique and sense of form. Nordic flavor cast in post-Wagnerian harmonic vocabulary. M-D to D.

Joseph Guy-Ropartz. *Trio* a (Durand 1919) 69pp., parts. Modérément animé; Vif; Lent–Animé. Somewhat austere writing with a Franckian tinge (Guy-Ropartz studied with Franck). The style is eclectic-Romantic with Breton folk tunes serving as some of the inspiration. Over-extended. M-D.

Elizabeth Gyring. *Trio Fantasy* 1954 (CFE) 11pp., parts. 9 min. One movement, sectionalized with contrasting tempos. Expressionist and intense, freely tonal and chromatic, many dynamic changes, short motivic lines, dramatic climax. D.

Adalbert Gyrowetz. *Sonata* F (M. Munclinger—Supraphon MVH No.30 1973) 25pp., parts. Preface in Czech and German. Allegro moderato; Andante con moto; Rondo. Classical style, clear forms, charming. M-D.

Karel Hába. *Trio* Op.24 1940 (Hudební Matice) 29pp., parts. Allegro moderato; Andante cantabile; Allegro scherzando. Written in a chromatic, Regerian style with strong lyrical elements. The piano is treated to many late-19th-century idioms. D.

John Hall. *Trio* (Chappell 1968) 21 min. Three movements; Presto coda concludes the work. Tonal feeling is present in a highly chromatic style. The piano writing is more difficult than the other parts. D.

Iain Hamilton. *Trio* Op.25 (Schott 10590 1956) 36pp., parts. 15 min. Allegro giojóso; Intermezzo; Presto. Neoclassic harmonic treatment although the scoring is dark-tinged and dense. Disciplined writing with serial influence. Technical and expressive capacities of individual instruments are explored. Large span required. M-D to D.

George Frideric Handel. *Chambertrio* XXIII g (M. Seiffert—McGinnis & Marx 1974) 12pp., parts. Largo andante; Allegro; Largo; Allemande; Allegro. This work has an interesting history, explained in an insert by Marx. In g tonality throughout with a key signature of one flat. A very beautiful and enduring work with fine keyboard realization. M-D.

Jan Hanuš. *Trio* (Frescos) Op.51 1961 (Artia) 53pp., parts. 23½ min. Andante mesto; Molto allegro, fantastico e feroce; Adagio non troppo; Allegro molto e tempestuoso. Designed in a formally Classical layout with alternating slow and quick movements, the finale being in SA form. The descriptive title indicates the composer's intention to create 4 musical pictures, but there is no definite extra-musical program. All are dramatic in character, and their essential mood or atmosphere is in keeping with the tempo and character indications of the individual movements. Mildly 20th-century with a certain Czech national flavor. D.

Roy Harris. *Piano Trio* 1934 (TP) 31pp., parts. Allegro con bravura: strong tonal elements embedded in polyharmonic structures; bold lines; imitation important; rhythmic canons with close-range entries prominent. Andante religioso: low descending slow octaves provide harmonic substructure; piano adds melodic and cross-phrasings. Fugue–Grave–poco più mosso: builds to enormous sonorous conclusion. D.

Tibor Harsanyi. *Trio* 1926 (Heugel 29665) 34pp., parts. Allegro; Lento; Presto; Allegro con fuoco. The first and last movements are in SA design, each with 3 subjects. Straightforward and clear writing throughout. Classical and national influences are at work in this freely tonal composition. The lyrical slow movement and the dramatic finale are especially effective for the piano. M-D.

Franz Joseph Haydn. *Piano Trios* (H. C. Robbins Landon—Dob 481-95, 501-14, 521-34) 45 *Trios*, published separately. Not fingered; editorial indications are in brackets. These *Trios* contain some of Haydn's most glorious music, and they cover most of his composing career. The large majority are unknown to most pianists, and only in recent years, with more complete editions becoming available, have we had the opportunity to become familiar with this great literature. A Piano Trio was, for Haydn, more an accompanied keyboard solo than a work for 3 independent instruments. Frequently the cello duplicates the bass of the keyboard part. H. C. Robbins Landon tells us in his Preface that Haydn's 45 *Trios* may be conveniently divided into 3 groups: the early works (Nos.1-16) composed in or before ca.1760, of which several were never published at all; the middle works (Nos.17-30), of which all except one (No.17, an arrangement made ca.1784 of a baryton piece composed about 1772) were composed between 1784 and 1790; and the London Trios (Nos.31-45) written in or for England between 1793/94 and 1796. This third group, especially, contains profundities and an imaginative, lean style.
——. *Piano Trios* (W. Stockmeier, I. Becker-Glauch, J. Demus—Henle 246, 277, 284, 411, 412) 5 vols., from the Complete Edition of the Joseph Haydn Institute (published by Henle). Fingered by Jörg Demus; preface in German, French, and English; critical commentary in German. Vol.I: Hob.XV:1, 2, 34-38, 40, 41, C1, fl. Vol.II: Hob.XV:5-14. Vol.III Flute Trios (flute or violin, cello, and piano): Hob.XV:15-17. Vol.IV: Hob.XV:18-26. Vol.V: Hob.XV:27-32.
——. *Trios* (F. Hermann—CFP) 3 vols. Vol.I: Hob.XV:3, 7, 14, 20, 24-30. Vol.II: Hob.XV:1, 9-11, 13, 18, 19, 21, 23, 31. Vol.III: Hob.XV:2, 4-6, 8, 15-17, 22.
——. *Great Piano Trios* (Dover 1995, ISBN 0-486-28728-9) 247pp. Hob.XV:12, 14, 18, 23-31. Reprinted from CFP edition.
——. *Trios* (David—Br&H) 29 trios, published separately.
——. *Divertimento* E Hob.XV:34 (Landon—Dob DM22).
——. *Divertimento* F Hob.XV:37 (W. Weismann—Leuckart) No.11 in Alte Musik. Cello ad lib.

Haydn's Keyboard Trios
As Numbered in Hoboken Catalog and Four Editions

Key	Doblinger (H.C. Robbins Landon) (Pub. Separately)	Henle/ Haydn Werke (Stockmeier– Becker- Glauch) (Vol./No.)	Hoboken Catalog	Peters (Hermann) (Vol./No.)	Breitkopf & Härtel (David) (Pub. Separately)
F	1	I/3	XV:37		
C	2	I/2	XV:C1		
G	3		XIV:6, XVI:6		
F	4		XV:39		
g	5	I/9	XV:1	II/19	16
F	6	I/8	XV:40		
G	7	I/7	XV:41		
D	8 (lost)	I/Appendix	XV:33		
D	9 (lost)	I/Appendix	XV:D1		
A	10	I/10	XV:35		
E	11	I/5	XV:34		
E♭	12	I/1	XV:36		
B♭	13	I/4	XV:38		
f	14	I/6	XV:f1		
D	15				
C	16		XIV:C1		
F	17	I/11	XV:2, XIV:2	III/26	25
G	18	II/1	XV:5	III/28	28
F	19	II/2	XV:6	III/25	23
D	20	II/3	XV:7	I/10	21
B♭	21	II/4	XV:8	III/24	22
A	22	II/5	XV:9	II/15	9
E♭	23	II/6	XV:10	II/20	17
E♭	24	II/7	XV:11	II/16	11
e	25	II/8	XV:12	I/7	10
C	26	II/9	XV:13	II/14	8
A♭	27	II/10	XV:14	I/11	24
D	28	Flute Trio III/1	XV:16	III/30	30
G	29	Flute Trio III/2	XV:15	III/31	31
F	30	Flute Trio III/3	XV:17	III/29	29
G	31	V/[6]	XV:32		
A	32	IV/[1]	XV:18	II/13	7
g	33	IV/[2]	XV:19	II/17	14
B♭	34	IV/[3]	XV:20	I/9	13

Key	Doblinger (H.C. Robbins Landon) (Pub. Separately)	Henle/ Haydn Werke (Stockmeier– Becker– Glauch) (Vol./No.)	Hoboken Catalog	Peters (Hermann) (Vol./No.)	Breitkopf & Härtel (David) (Pub. Separately)
C	35	IV/[4]	XV:21	II/21	18
E♭	36	IV/[5]	XV:22	III/23	20
d	37	IV/[6]	XV:23	II/22	19
D	38	IV/[7]	XV:24	I/6	6
G	39	IV/[8]	XV:25	I/1	1
f♯	40	IV/[9]	XV:26	I/2	2
e♭	41	V/[4]	XV:31	II/18	15
E♭	42	V/[5]	XV:30	I/8	12
C	43	V/[1]	XV:27	I/3	3
E	44	V/[2]	XV:28	I/4	4
E♭	45	V/[3]	XV:29	I/5	5

Appendix

Key			Hoboken Catalog	Peters (Hermann) (Vol./No.)	Breitkopf & Härtel (David) (Pub. Separately)
C			XV:3	I/12	26
F			XV:4	III/27	27

Hob.XV:3–4 are now ascribed to Ignaz Pleyel; see detailed entry later in this section.

———. *Divertimento* B♭ Hob.XV:38 (W. Weismann—Leuckart) No.10 in Alte Musik. Cello ad lib.

———. *Klaviertrio* F Hob.XV:40 (H. Heussner—Dob DM4).

———. *Capriccio* A Hob.XV:35 (EMB). Based on the National Széchényi Library Budapest copy.

See A. Craig Bell, "An Introduction to Haydn's Piano Trios," MR 16 (1955): 191–97; A. Peter Brown, "A Re-Introduction to Joseph Haydn's Keyboard Works," PQ 79 (fall 1972): 42–47; W. D. Sutcliffe, "Haydn's Piano Trio Textures," *Music Analysis* 6/3 (1987): 319–32; K. Komlos, "The Viennese Keyboard Trio in the 1780's: Sociological Background and Contemporary Reception," ML 68/3 (1987): 222–34.

Bernhard Heiden. *Trio* 1956 (AMP) 64pp., parts. 19 min. Allegro agitato; Adagio; Vivace; Allegretto. Cohesive writing with much variety that shows a masterful skill. In spite of the strong influence of Hindemith this work displays marked individuality, with much emotional power in the melodic inspiration. The piano carries no excessive weight and is used to advantage. Large span required. D.

Hans Werner Henze. *Kammersonate* 1948, rev.1963 (Schott 5382) 15pp., parts. 15 min. Allegro assai; Dolce, con tenerezza; Lento; Allegretto; Epilogo. Strong rhythmic style, lyric cantabile lines, intellectual refinement. Instrumental colors imaginatively explored in this serially influenced work. Henze reveals an expressive and direct 20th-century language. M-D.

———. *Adagio: Serenade* 1993 (Schott ED8131 1993), parts. 4 min.

Kurt Hessenberg. *Trio* Op.53 1950 (Wilhelmiana) 41pp., parts. 23 min. Allegro con fuoco; Adagio; Variationen. Classical leanings are present, but the work is mainly Romantic in style and conception and employs a mildly 20th-century harmonic and rhythmic setting that is freely tonal around F. A sense of humor comes through, especially in the finale, a large set of variations. M-D.

Alun Hoddinott. *Trio* I Op.77 (University College Cardiff Press 1984) 27pp. Schoenberg influence; written in a type of international style. The Andante has a kind of *Erwartung* mood. Twelve-tone; well worked out; anguished and nervous atmosphere about this piece. Ends *pp* on bitonal chords. D.

———. *Trio* II Op.111 1984 (OUP 1987, ISBN 0-19-357180-3) 28pp., parts. 14 min. Moderato: lyric with linear writing in octaves and octotonic passagework; occasional added-note chords in mostly thin texture. Presto: scherzo-like with strings functioning in duo juxtaposed to piano; repeated patterns. Adagio: initial *ff* entrance by all subsides in 10 mm. to *pp* where the dynamics remain for the remaining 36 mm.; concludes on unison C♯'s. Reverses traditional setting of slow and final fast movements for a quiet contemplative finish. M-D.

———. *Trio* III ca.1996 (Oriana) 32pp., parts. 15 min. In one continuous movement freely designed with sections marked Grave–Vivo–Grave–Moderato–Vivo–Presto–Grave (ABA′CB′DA″). Like Trio II, strings typically function in duo juxtaposed to piano. Linear with dramatic character; mixed meters in fast sections. Concludes *pp* on unison C's in same spirit as Trio II. M-D.

E. T. A. Hoffmann. *Trio* E (H. Schulze—DVFM 8303 1971) 49pp., parts. Allegro moderato: SA, very colorful development. Scherzo: ABA. Adagio: introductory, expressive, leads directly to Allegro vivace; straightforward writing with both Classical and Romantic overtones. M-D.

Vagn Holmboe. *Trio* Op.64 (Viking). Spontaneous eclectic style, thematically interesting, expansive yet concentrated and distinctive writing. Organically integrated; subtlety of motivic organization is superb. D.

Alan Hovhaness. *Trio* Op.3 e (CFP 1971) 18pp., parts. 9 min. Allegro moderato: SA, repeated figures, traditional development techniques. Adagio espressivo con doppio canone: sustained chordal opening followed by doppio canone treatment in mid-section; short coda uses imitation with sustained chordal closing. Fuga–Allegro ma non troppo: fugal textures. This early piece does not have the usual later Hovhaness characteristics but is written in a strictly Neo-classic style. M-D.

Johann Nepomuk Hummel. *Trio* Op.12 E♭ (CFP 24pp., parts; UE). Original ideas, piano is particularly favored. M-D.

——. *Trio* Op.22 F (Litolff 14pp., parts; Haslinger). Technique outweighs artistry. Contains some delightful variations on a pleasing theme. Unusual treatment of the cello. Concludes with a cheerful alla turca movement. M-D.

——. *Trio* Op.35 G (Litolff 18pp., parts; Haslinger). Influenced by Mozart.

——. *Trio* Op.65 G (Litolff) 18pp., parts.

——. *Trio* Op.83 E "Grand Trio" (CFP). Extremely well written; shows real progress in Hummel's technical ability. Much virtuosity displayed in brilliant passagework of the finale. D.

——. *Trio* Op.93 E♭ (CFP). This "Grand Trio" gives the piano highly preferential treatment. Brilliant opening movement, an emotional larghetto, and whirling rhythms are apparent in the rondo finale. M-D to D.

——. *Trio* Op.96 E♭ (Litolff). Catchy rhythms and spirit in opening movement. Slow movement is more Classically oriented, with some obvious defects. The Allegro vivo finale is a delightful piquant dance with much appeal. M-D.

Andrew Imbrie. *Trio* 1946 (SP 1963) 28pp., parts. Allegro energico: linear, octotonic, freely tonal around G, rich in ideas, cleverly proportioned; contains a section for solo piano; large span required. Lento: opens with cantabile section for solo piano; haunting in its strange and lyric appeal; freely tonal around E♭. Presto con fuoco: quasi-cadenza for solo piano, many chromatic harmonic 6ths, octaves in alternating hands, rhythmic drive. Colorful in its dynamic twists of rhythm and melody. Clear textures, parts balanced. D.

Vincent d'Indy. *Piano Trio II* Op.98 En forme de suite 1929 (Rouart Lerolle) 30pp., parts. 1. Entrée, en Sonate; 2. Air; 3. Courante; 4. Gigue en rondeau, sur une chanson Française. Written in a lighter, simpler, and more transparent style than d'Indy's earlier works. Economical use of material coupled with an intellectuality that sometimes overwhelms; expressive inspiration makes this an attractive but somewhat dated work. Rhythmic vitality displayed in the Gigue en rondeau gives this movement the most appeal. M-D.

John Ireland. *Phantasie* a 1908 (Augener 15202; MMP) 23pp., parts. 12½ min. An extended SA design in a Classical-Romantic style. M-D.

——. *Trio* II e 1917 (Augener 15219) 20pp., parts. 14 min. One movement. Martial atmosphere influenced by the period in which it was composed (World War I). Based on thematic material that is progressively metamorphosed in the manner of free variations. M-D.

——. *Trio* III E 1938 (Bo&H) 62pp., parts. 25 min. Allegro moderato; Scherzo; Andante cantabile; Finale. Written in a crisp Romantic idiom using material from 1913; reveals a happy balance between the 3 instruments. M-D.

Charles Ives. *Trio* 1904–11 (PIC 1955) 28pp., parts. 20 min. Andante moderato: no dynamic marks indicated; collage of polyrhythms and polyharmonies plus superimposed themes. Tsiaj: title signifies "This Scherzo Is a Joke"; contrasting tempos; traces of "Marching through Georgia," "Jingle Bells," "My Old Kentucky Home," "Long, Long Ago," and other tunes are embedded in the vigorous contrapuntal texture. Moderato con moto: varied tempos; last part of this movement quotes from "Rock of Ages." All the Ives trademarks are found in this work. It is one of the most important American chamber compositions. Meditative, richly lyric, one of Ives's most profound artistic statements. D.

Gordon Jacob. *Trio* (J. Williams 1959) 28pp., parts. Adagio; Scherzo allegro; Molto adagio e mesto; Allegro. Well crafted, clear lines, clever rhythms. Economy and astringent brusqueness of expression are characteristic of this work. Jacob knows how to exploit his musical materials and is a master at involving all instruments equally. M-D.

Tadeusz Jarecki. *Trio-Fugato e Aria* Op.11 (JWC 1943) 11pp., parts. 7½ min. See detailed entry under trios for piano, violin, and viola.

Joseph Jelinek. *Trio* Op.10 (Artia). Written in the accessible fashionable style of the day. Attractive and fluent melodies and harmonies pour forth at every turn. M-D.

Knud Jeppesen. *Little Summer Trio* 1957 (WH 4016) 26pp., parts. 15 min. See detailed entry under trios for piano, one stringed instrument, and one wind instrument.

Tom Johnson. *Predictables* 1984 (Editions 75 1984) 22pp., parts. 15 min. In 7 untitled movements, each establishing a rhythmic motive at the opening and expanding upon it by minimalist, sequential, and mathematical techniques, in effect making the work "predictable." M-D.

Paul Juon. *Trio I* Op.17 a (Schlesinger 1901) 35pp., parts. Allegro; Adagio non troppo; Rondo. Combines a blend of Russian and German influences with a Slavic character. Homogeneous thematic material. The Adagio is refreshing in its lyrical simplicity. M-D.

———. *Trio II* Op.39 D Trio Caprice on Selma Lagerlöf's *Gosta Berling* (Schlesinger) 55pp., parts. 27 min. Moderato non troppo; Andante; Scherzo; Risoluto. Inspired by the novel *Gösta Berling,* which made a profound impression on Juon. Brahmsian in treatment with well-developed melodic ideas and clever rhythmic treatment, this work is an adventure in highly colored tone painting. M-D.

———. *Trio* Op.60 (Zimmermann 1915) 35pp., parts. Moderato assai; Andante cantabile; Risoluto, ma non troppo allegro. M-D.

———. *Suite* Op.89 (Birnbach 1932) 24pp., parts. Moderato; Giocoso; Andantino;

Allegretto; Allegro giusto. Displays a fine sense of form and rhythmic power. M-D.

Pal Kadosa. *Trio* Op.49 1956 (Kultura) 24pp., parts. Moderato quasi andante, poco rubato; Vivo; Allegro ben marcato. Free metric treatment, strong accents, folk song influence present but not obvious, elaboration of short concise motifs. Sinewy contrapuntal textures and a percussive piano approach make this an exciting piece for performers and listeners. M-D.

Armin Kaufmann. *Trio* Op.57/2 (Dob 1958) 11pp., parts. 8 min. Andante; Allegro sereno. Striking thematic technique, Balkan folk influence, thin textures. A fresh-sounding and musicianly work; mildly 20th-century. M-D.

Donald Keats. *Revisitations* 1992 (AMC), parts. 16 min. Three movements, each "based on a theme by a noted composer of the past: Purcell, Monteverdi, and Mozart" (Composer).

Rudolf Kelterborn. *Fantasia a Tre* 1967 (Br 4138) 22pp., parts. One large movement with contrasting sections. Strong feelings of structure even in a piece entitled "Fantasia." An expanded tonal system and certain Neoclassic elements infuse this work with a sturdy, but at places lively, vitality. Large span required. M-D.

Harrison Kerr. *Trio* 1938, rev.1949–50 (CFE) 33pp., parts. 15 min. Allegro; Grave; Allegro. Vivid chromatic writing, freely tonal, austere, fine flow of ideas that unfold naturally. Highly active finale with only a short respite in a Meno mosso section. D.

Otto Ketting. *Trio* 1988, rev.1995 (Donemus 1994) 28pp., parts. 18 min. In 2 untitled movements. Special emphasis is given to the resonance of the piano pedal. Repetitive figurations and sustained pitches play important roles as well. M-D.

Leon Kirchner. *Trio* 1954 (AMP) 22pp., parts. 15 min. ♪ = 92; Largo. Strong Romantic lines and emotional excitement in all 3 instruments. Rhapsodic elements throughout, chromatic, violently dissonant, restless, clear design, strongly guided motion, unquenchable vitality, tempo fluctuations. Advanced pianism required. D.

Giselher Klebe. *Elegia Appassionata* Op.22 1955 (Bo&Bo) 22pp., parts. One movement. Tart vocabulary; 12-tone influence; various elements amalgamated into a personal harmonic system. Piano writing is thorny and uncompromising at spots. Varied moods and tempos; Expressionist. D.

Richard Rudolf Klein. *Fantasia* (Möseler 1974) 15pp., parts. Varied tempos and moods, sectionalized, shifting meters, Neoclassic orientation, thin textures preferred. M-D.

Jan Koetsier. *Klaviertrio* Op.70 1975 (Donemus 1978) 57pp., parts. Adagio–Allegro con brio; Romanza–Andante semplice; Scherzo–Presto; Rondo–Allegretto. Schumanesque writing in the late 20th century. A curious departure from the reality of the times. M-D.

Yuriko Hase Kojima. *Eclat du Soir* 1997 (Japan Federation of Composers JFC-9807) 9pp. 7 min. Indeterminate, using both metric and nonmetric notation, the latter based upon times in seconds. A character piece "inspired by my image of the Château de Fontainebleau [where the work was composed], whose color changes to a fascinating red at twilight and radiates its brightness as the light fades . . . This was the first time that I employed aleatoric elements in my music in an attempt to create unplanned, but well controlled, complex textures that allow the music to flow smoothly while maintaining a high level of intensity" (from Preface). Pianist must mute strings with fingers. D.

Joonas Kokkonen. *Trio* Op.1 1948 (Finnish Music Information Centre) 37pp., parts. 20 min. Un poco adagio leads to Allegro moderato, ma energico, SA: trills in piano move into a chromatically colored, rhythmically driving opening section; movement develops excitingly and closes sempre appassionato. Andante tranquillo e semplice: $\frac{5}{4}$; melodic treatment of all instruments; piano provides full chordal sonorities (10ths are used); chorale-like. Allegro molto e giocoso: rhythmic, changing meters, à la Prokofiev, 20th-century Alberti bass treatment, freely tonal. M-D.

Paul Kont. *Klaviertrio* 1964 (Dob 1974) 25pp., parts. 14 min. Based on the *Trio* 1948 for flute, harp, and cello and differs from it in character although the musical material is the same. The older work emphasized color and softness of the texture, whereas the 1964 trio emphasizes the rhythmic concertante element. Three movements (Vivace, Lento, Allegro) in a light Neoclassic style. The finale abounds in syncopations, arpeggi, and scales. A pleasurable piece for performers and listeners. M-D.

Hans Koolmees. *Niemandsland: A Very Satisfactory First Day* 1999 (Donemus 1999) 47pp., parts. 22 min. Concentrates on clarity of form, repeated patterns, and sustained notes in an extended one-movement design. All three instrumentalists sing near the end, "It's a Long Way to Tipperary." Surprisingly quiet and slow finish to the otherwise perpetual motion technique heard up to this point. A piece which desires to be heard. M-D.

Egon Kornauth. *Trio* Op.27 b (CFP 1921) 39pp., parts. Allegro moderato ma energico: piano has introduction alone, strings join in, and the piano then announces the first subject (Brahmsian); a short development follows. Andante molto rubato: follows attacca and uses the same ideas from the first movement; allegretto scherzando mid-section introduces new material. Allegro moderato ma energico: begins like the first movement but takes a different journey; theme from the scherzando (second movement), heard in piano, gently closes the movement while the strings hold the pedal note B for the last 11 bars. Mildly 20th-century style and fluent manipulation of the piano writing still make this an attractive piece today. D.

Erich Wolfgang Korngold. *Trio* Op.1 D 1909 (UE 2996) 51pp., parts. 26 min. Allegro non troppo, con espressione; Scherzo; Larghetto; Finale. The influence of Richard Strauss is very strong—complex modulatory procedure; strong contrasts; excessive changing of harmonic, rhythmic, and thematic direction—but characteristics of the future composer are seen even in this very early but astonishingly mature work of a 12-year-old. Over-elaborate writing with thick textures for the piano especially. M-D to D.

Hans Kox. *Piano Trio* 1976, rev.1991 (Donemus 1976) 36pp., parts. 12 min. Allegro con brio; Andante cantabile; Allegro capriccioso. Score is photocopy of fair MS. M-D.

Leopold Anton Koželuch. *Sonata* Op.12/1 B♭ (K&S) 35pp., parts. Organum series III/54. Mainly a piano Sonata with violin obbligato, as the piano carries most of the musical material. About the same difficulty as a Haydn or Mozart piano Sonata. A good introduction to Classic period style and form. M-D.

———. *Trio* Op.12/2 A (H. Albrecht—K&S) 35pp., parts. No.54 in Organum Series. Allegretto; Adagio; Allegro. Editorial tempo suggestions. Foreword in German.

———. *Trio* Op.12/3 g (K&S) 38pp., parts. No.41 in Organum Series. Allegro; Adagio: very florid; Allegro. Editorial tempo suggestions. Foreword in German. Pleasant and easy-flowing melodies with period harmony make these agreeable and attractive pieces. Effective instrumental idioms. M-D.

Jaroslav Křička. *Trio* Op.38 "Doma" (At Home) On a Czech Church Tune 1923–24 (Artia) 31pp., parts. 20 min. Sectionalized with such titles as: Prologo, Fuga, Intermezzo, Cantabile (Trio), Presto, Andante religioso, Epilogo. Influences of folk song, the Russian School (Rimsky-Korsakov in particular), and Vítězslav Novák are all felt in this work. Melodic lyricism, spontaneous invention, technical facility, fluent expression, and naiveté all shine through in various degrees. M-D.

Toivo Kuula. *Trio* Op.7 A 1908 (WH 1925) 72pp., parts. Moderato assai; Scherzo; Andante elegico; Finale. SA design; mechanical and over-extended developments; piano part highly decorative. Long lyrical phrases, broad climaxes, Romantic Brahmsian tradition. M-D.

Osvald Lacerda. *Trio* 1969 (IU) 27pp., parts. 10 min. Lento: SA, dissonant, linear construction. Movido: Rondo, ABA′CA″, hemiola, clusters, generally thin textures throughout. M-D.

Ezra Laderman. *Trio* 1959 (OUP) 38pp., parts. 14 min. Adagio espressivo; Andante con moto; Molto allegro, leggiero. Three contrasting movements evolve from one basic idea. Freely tonal. The "Come una danza" section from the first movement is especially appealing. M-D to D.

Edouard Lalo. *Trio* Op.7 c (Costallat) 45pp., parts. Allegro moderato; Romance; Scherzo; Final. M-D.

———. *Trio* II b (Hamelle 187?) 33pp., parts. Allegro maestoso: piano enters at the second section; opening theme treated canonically with piano; brilliant coda. Andante con moto: mainly 2 melodic ideas worked out. Menuetto allegretto: charming and fresh. Allegretto agitato: begins suddenly; 2 bold and sonorous ideas are mounted with restless rhythms. M-D to D.

———. *Trio* III Op.26 a 1880 (Durand 2740; Wollenweber 1991) 43pp., parts. 26 min. Allegro appassionato: a discussion of thematic material grows more heated to the end of the movement. Scherzo: d, all fire and vitality in a galloping $^6_8$ meter. Très lent: E, meditative and spiritual character. Allegro molto: A, explodes like a bomb in a furious marchlike character. Probably Lalo's finest and most finished chamber work. Intense rhythms and color. D.

Noël Lee. *Deux Mouvements* 1959, rev.1970 (AMC) 19pp., parts. Intermède: rhythmic and cantabile, chromatic, syncopation, short chordal sections, harmonics; large span required; effectively contrasts with Marche: low staccato bass versus upper register, clusters, misterioso *p* conclusion. Unusual endings for both movements. Neoclassic. M-D.

René Leibowitz. *Trio* Op.20 1950 (Boelke-Bomart) 12 min. Strict 12-tone writing with a dramatic quality that leans toward Berg. Complex rhythms, wide leaps, thin textures, and full harmonies in the piano writing. D.

Guillaume Lekeu. *Trio* 1890 (Rouart Lerolle) 59pp., parts. Lent–Allegro; Très lent; Très animé–Lent–Très vif–Lent–Très vif; Lent. Franck influence. Admirable ideas in long lines treated in a heroic and sometimes passionate manner. Romantic virtuoso approach. D.

John Lessard. *Trio in Six Parti* 1966 (Joshua). Strong Neoclassic lines. Well constructed. M-D.

Peter Tod Lewis. *Trio* 1960 (CFE) 16pp., parts. One movement. Expressionist, sectionalized, parallel sonorities, strong rhythms, tremolo, thin textures, freely tonal and serially influenced. Large span required. M-D.

Lowell Liebermann. *Trio* I Op.32 1990 (TP 114-40616) 26pp. 14 min.
———. *Trio* II (TP 114-41256).

Theo Loevendie. *Ackermusik* 1977 (Peer 1997) 16pp., parts. In one movement requiring experienced performers. D.

Otto Luening. *Trio* (Galaxy) 28pp., parts. One movement. Allegro agitato: strong asymmetrical melody, freely tonal, triplet broken-chord figuration and octaves, more chordal and sustained second tonal area, tremolo chords in alternate hands, imitation. Varied tempos, moods, and meters. Neoclassic. M-D to D.

Enrico Mainardi. *Trio* 1939 (SZ).

———. *Trio* 1954 (Schott 4770) 40pp., parts. Andante sostenuto; Intermezzo; Finale. Chromatic style, mildly Romantic. M-D.

Artur Malawski. *Trio* 1953 (PWM) 66pp., parts. 30 min. Lento–Allegro moderato: chromatic, alternating hands, many triplets, expansive lines; chordal sections contrast with linear sections. Andante sostenuto: right hand provides counterpoint with strings while the left hand provides a 20th-century Alberti bass; chromatic duplets and triplets; appassionato mid-section with trills moves to great climax before returning to opening mood and ideas. Scherzo: agitato and nonlegato alternating-hand figuration, parallel chords, octotonic. Rondo: octotonic, moving full-octave chords, hands crossing, chromatic runs; Andantino section is more chordal and sustained; strong dramatic conclusion. D.

Gian Francesco Malipiero. *Sonata a Tre* 1927 (UE 9519) 32pp., parts. 24½ min. Allegro impetuoso: for cello and piano alone. Ritenuto: for violin and piano alone. Lento–Allegro vivace: for all 3 instruments. All movements are sectional with varied tempos. Finale has a recapitulation of material from the first 2 movements. Colorful writing. M-D.

Frank Martin. *Piano Trio on Popular Irish Melodies* 1925 (Hug) 35pp., parts. 21 min. French influences seen in the harmonic and rhythmic treatment. Opening Allegro moderato is full of Gaelic spirit, while the more Impressionist Pastoral Adagio suggests an Irish landscape. The finale Gigue is more French than Irish and presents technical and interpretative problems for all instruments. M-D.

Maria de Lourdes Martins. *Trio* 1959 (Gulbenkian Foundation) 40pp., parts. Lento–Allegro–Lento: fluid rhythms that continually change; second theme is a canon between the violin and cello; development is divided into 2 parts. Tempo di Minuetto: 9 variations on Minuetto theme suggest an 18th-century atmosphere. Vif: rondo, strong rhythms, canon used, recitative-like wide arpeggiated chords. Neoclassic. M-D.

Bohuslav Martinů. *Bergerettes* (PIC 1963) 44pp., parts. Poco allegro: has a trio, Poco meno mosso. Allegro con brio: mid-section exploits alternating hands and tremolo. Andantino: A sections are more chordal; B section is more linear. Allegro: corky rhythms plus long phrases. Moderato: parallel chords, 16th-note triplets, Poco allegretto Trio contrasts. M-D.

———. *Trio* 1930 (Schott 2183) 20pp., parts. Five short pieces. Allegro moderato;

Adagio; Allegro; Allegro moderato; Allegro. Written in a highly chromatic style. No.5 has an extensive solo part for piano. M-D.

———. *Trio II* d 1950 (ESC) 39pp., parts. 16 min. Allegro moderato; Andante; Allegro. Contrast plus superb balance is the hallmark of this work with equally balanced outer movements and an Andante half again as long. It has a Czech folklike flavor with flowing themes and development. The finale evolves completely from the opening idea; this kinetic movement is one of the most exciting in all trio literature. D.

———. *Trio III* C 1951 (ESC) 51pp., parts. Allegro moderato; Andante; Allegro. Dissonant and polytonal setting with well-defined melodies. Sonorities are crucially important; climaxes underlined with strong densities. Motoric drive in the last section with asymmetric phrase divisions brings this significant Neoclassic work to a sonorous conclusion. D.

See Susan Lee Cable, "The Piano Trios of Bohuslav Martinů (1890–1959)," D.A. diss., University of Northern Colorado, 1984.

Joseph Marx. *Trio-Phantasie* g 1910 (UE) 74pp., parts. Four movements. Highly chromatic and rhapsodic idiom with some imaginative writing. Displays a well-developed craft. Seems long-winded today but does contain some inspired moments. See especially the Adagietto movement. For a full discussion of this work see CCSCM, II, 122.

Yori-aki Matsudaira. *Variazioni* 1957 (SZ) 31pp., parts. 14 min. Serial in dynamics and pitch, pointillistic, atonal, shifting meters, complex rhythms, solo variation for piano, involved and complicated. D.

Chiel Meijering. *Riot of the Mind* 1991 (Donemus 1991) 15pp., parts. 8 min. Minimalist in style with syncopation and proportional rhythmic relationships which could figuratively seem to drive the listener crazy. D.

Felix Mendelssohn. *Trios* (S. Grossmann—Henle 1972) 131pp., parts. Fingering for piano part added by H.-M. Theopold. Contains Trio Op.49 d (1839) 32 min.; Trio Op.66 c (1845) 27 min. The autograph of Op.49 differs greatly from the final printed version. This publication is based on the 2 earliest editions. Except for a youthful work from 1820, which so far has not been published, these are the only works of Mendelssohn in this category. Symbols placed in brackets are not in the sources, from which they have clearly been omitted through oversight. Preface contains other pertinent information. The piano is treated felicitously and pianistically and does not overpower the strings. Op.66 is especially well proportioned, and Op.49 is one of the treasures of the Romantic chamber literature. D.

Other editions: *Two Trios* (CFP 1740). *Trio* Op.49 (Br&H; Adamowski—GS L1458; Augener 7267a). *Trio* Op.66 (Adamowski—GS L1459).

Georges Migot. *Trio ou Suite à Trois* 1935 (Leduc) 46pp., parts. Prélude; Allègre; Danse; Final. Strong contrapuntal lines that develop their own modal harmony. Rhythm derives from an intertwining of melodic lines. Broad, expansive, individual style. D.

Darius Milhaud. *Trio* (Heugel 1968) 37pp., parts. Strong polytonal and contrapuntal lines with an overall supple feeling and spirited animation. The product is a brilliant and virtuosic-sounding work but does not require virtuosity from its performers. Solid and logical construction. M-D.

Charles Mills. *Trio* (ACA) 22 min. Mainly diatonic writing in a Neoclassic style, full of fine melodies and shifting chord progressions. Forceful and expressive writing, highly idiomatic, modern and imaginative. M-D.

Douglas Moore. *Trio* 1953 (Galaxy 1963) 48pp., parts. Allegro molto marcato; Adagio; Allegro vivace. Tonal with dissonant contrasts used to create tension; traditional formal schemes; fundamentally lyric. The musical substance explores with firm assurance the inherent possibilities of all 3 instruments. Mildly 20th-century. M-D.

Ennio Morricone. *Distanze* (Distances) 1958 (Sal 1973) 28pp., parts. 5 min. Pointillistic, sudden dynamic changes, wide dynamic range *pppp–ffff*, nontonal, frequent tempo changes, continuous development in a kind of variation technique, pedal used for sonority effects, Expressionist. Large span required. D.

Harold Morris. *Trio II* 1937 (SPAM 1952) 32pp., parts. Passacaglia: moderately slow. Scherzo: brisk and sprightly; slow–quick–Tempo I–very slow. Fugue: not too fast. Exploits much of the keyboard in a mildly 20th-century style. Deserves to be revived. M-D.

Wolfgang Amadeus Mozart. *Trios for Piano, Violin and Cello* (G. Lorenz—Henle 1972) 190pp., parts. Fingering for piano added by H.-M. Theopold. Includes K.254 B♭ (Divertimento), K.496 G, K.498 E♭, K.502 B♭, K.542 E, K.548 C, K.564 G. All but K.254 are sheer masterpieces. Most material is shared between the piano and the violin, although the cello does make a subtle and unique contribution. This excellent edition is based on autographs. Text is most carefully reproduced. The score for K.498 includes both the original clarinet part (from the autograph) and the violin arrangement of it. This *Trio* is available separately (Henle 344 1981, ISMN M-2018-0344-9).
———. *Klaviertrios* (W. Plath, W. Rehm—Br 4545). Includes K.10–15, K.254, K.496, K.498 "Kegelstatt," K.502, K.542, K.548, K.564, Fragment K.442, Anhang 52, 51.
———. *Seven Trios* (CFP 193; David—IMC). K.254, K.496, K.502, K.542, K.548, K.564, and K.498 for clarinet or violin, viola, and piano.
Available separately: *Trio* K.254 B♭ (Br&H; CFP; GS L1607; Augener 7268f) 16

min. *Trio* K.496 G (Adamowski—GS L1602; CFP; Br&H; Augener 7268a) 25 min. *Trio* K.502 B♭ (Br&H; GS L1603; Litolff; Augener 7268b). *Trio* K.542 E (Br&H; GS L1604; Augener 7268c; Litolff; Drei Masken Verlag—a facsimile of Mozart's MS). *Trio* K.548 C (Br&H; GS L1605; Litolff; Augener 7268d) 16½ min. *Trio* K.564 G (Br&H; GS L1606; Litolff, Augener 7268e). *Trio* K.498 E♭ (GS L1403) originally for piano, violin or clarinet, and viola.

———. *Trio* K.442 d (Br&H; Litolff; GS L1608).

Herman Mulder. *Trio* Op.137 1965 (Donemus 1965) 40pp., parts. Poco adagio–Allegro con fuoco; Allegro con spirito; Adagio; Allegro vivace. M-D.

———. *Sonata a tre* II Op.178 1978 (Donemus 1980) 49pp., parts. 24 min. Lento–Allegro risoluto; Adagio non troppo; Scherzo–Allegro vivace; Poco lento–Allegro. M-D.

Dika Newlin. *Trio* Op.2 1948 (CFE) 71pp., parts. Introduction; Largo; Liberamente; Quasi cadenza. A highly organized serial work, with contrasting tempos and moods and shifting meters. Intense and Expressionist. Includes 2 Trios. D.

Marlos Nobre. *Trio* Op.4 1960 (Tonos) 16 min. Influence of Villa-Lobos and Milhaud noted but serial tendencies are also evident; more in the "Latin" tradition of Dallapiccola and Berio. The piano part carries a great deal of the piece. In some instances it is more like a concerto for piano with string accompaniment. D.

Ib Nørholm. *Trio* Op.22 1959 (Samfundet til Udgivelse Af Dansk Musik) 20 min. Andante; Allegretto; Moderato; Adagio; Allegro. Fresh and subtle coloristic writing in serial style. D.

Vítězláv Novák. *Trio* Op.1 g (Urbanek 1187) 51pp., parts. Allegro moderato; Allegro giusto; Andante sostenuto e mesto; Allegro non troppo.

———. *Trio quasi una Ballata* Op.27 1902 (Artia; Simrock 31pp., parts; UE) 16 min. One movement with contrasting tempos and moods. In the Brahms-Dvořák tradition with Slovakian folk music inspiration. Contains 4 rhapsodic, linked movements in the manner of the ballad with monothematic treatment. M-D.

Andrezej Panufnik. *Trio* 1934 (PWM 1950) 40pp., parts. Three untitled movements. Freely tonal, mildly 20th-century, flowing lines, syncopation. Fine balance achieved between feeling and intellect, heart and brain, impulse and design. Large span required. M-D.

Vincent Persichetti. *Serenade III* Op.17 (PIC 1952) 14pp., parts. Moderato grazioso; Andante sostenuto; Moderato. Lyrical melodic lines based on seminal motivic materials rooted in diatonic harmony. A contrapuntal compactness and rhythmic drive combined with a personal and practical touch make this one of

Persichetti's most successful Serenades (he has written 8 Serenades for various instruments). Gratifying piano writing. M-D.

Rudolf Petzold. *Trio* Op.39 1961 (Gerig 435) 19pp., parts. 17 min. Introduzione; Adagio ben sostenuto; Prestissimo. Serial, intense, Expressionist, dynamic extremes, trills effectively used, short-long rhythmic idea prevalent, combination of linear and homophonic writing, brilliant and dramatic conclusion to entire work. D.

Hans Pfitzner. *Trio* Op.8 F (Simrock 1898) 67pp., parts. Movements are related with one fundamental theme serving as the basis of each. Kräftig und feurig, nicht zu schnell: begins in a high-spirited mood; cello has main theme, which is later fully developed. Langsam: Romantic, deeply expressive. Mässig schnell, etwas frei im Vortrag: piano opens with a vivacious and rhythmic idea; strings add their own dance theme, and the combination of these ideas provides the basis of the movement. Rasch und wild: fast and tempestuous, has the most pitfalls for the pianist. Strong dramatic contrasts add effectively to success of this piece. D.

Gabriel Pierné. *Trio* Op.45 (Durand 1922). One of Pierné's finest works; displays characteristics of clarity, elegance, and a fine sense of proportion. Color and variety permeate the harmonic language. Thoroughly French writing of a refined artistic nature. Highly pianistic. M-D.

Willem Pijper. *Trio* Op.7 e 1914 (Donemus 1956) 53pp., parts. 22 min. Poco agitato; Tranquillo; Adagio–Allegro. Diatonic themes, freely polyphonic, bitonal combinations, Mahler and Debussy influences noted. M-D.

———. *Trio II* 1921 (Donemus 1966) 24pp., parts. 12 min. Andante, molto rubato; Vivo; Allegretto giocoso. Polytonal treatment provides harsh dissonance; changing meters with overlapping contrapuntal lines; jolting dramatic gestures. Germ-cell provides most material for this strongly knit work. D.

Georg Pirckmayer. *Transition 56/71* 1956 (Dob 1975) 17pp., parts. Allegro moderato; Andante; Allegro vivace. Expressionist. Requires large span.

Filipe Pires. *Trio* (EC 1960) 23pp., parts. Lento assai: contains a mid-section Presto before returning to opening tempo and mood; leads directly into final movement, a Passacaglia with the cello taking the lead with the subject. Equal treatment of instruments throughout entire work. Freely tonal, mildly 20th-century. M-D.

Walter Piston. *Trio* 1935 (Arrow Press) 43pp., parts. 17 min. Allegro: SA unraveled in an almost Mendelssohnian circumspection. Adagio: short ABA. Allegro con brio: in a lively $\frac{6}{8}$, full of verve and inventiveness. Allegro moderato: much contrapuntal interplay between the 3 instruments. Tonality is in evidence throughout although it is not usually obvious. Simplicity of form and a highly finished contrapuntal texture are its main characteristics. M-D.

——. *Trio II* 1966 (AMP) 26pp., parts. Facsimile of composer's autograph. Molto leggiero e capriccioso; Adagio; Vigoroso. Displays a disciplined harmonic and contrapuntal technique with great manipulation of ideas. Freely dissonant, transparent textures, closely knit ensemble writing. D.

Ildebrando Pizzetti. *Trio* A (Ric 119896 1925) 71pp., parts. 30 min. Mosso e arioso; Largo; Rapsodia di Settembre. Sensitive writing in an expansively lyric character. The final movement has the two strings playing in $\frac{3}{2}$ (calmo e contemplativo) while the piano part has a $\frac{3}{4} \times 3$ time signature (Vivace–non presto). As the movement develops these rhythmic differences become less noticeable although the pianist retains the obvious opening 8th-note figuration throughout the movement. D.

Ignaz Pleyel. *Klavier-Trios* (W. Stockmeier—Henle 292 1976) 39pp., parts. Fingering for the piano part added by Jörg Demus. *Trios* in C, Hob.XV:3 and in F, Hob.XV:4. Both works have undergone a strange set of circumstances. There is now conclusive evidence that they were written by Haydn's pupil Pleyel, not by Haydn. This situation is discussed in the Preface. As regards form and style, both works deviate from the authentic Haydn trios to such an extent that if one ignores any philological consideration it would seem certain that they did not originate with Haydn. Editorial additions made to conform to analogous passages are distinguished by square brackets. Excellent Urtext and practical edition. M-D.

Marcel Poot. *Trois Pièces en Trio* (ESC 1935) 23pp., parts. 12 min. 1. Allegro Marziale, 2. Adagio in stilo antico, 3. Impromptu. Clever rhythmic treatment and arresting sonorities are mixed with gaiety, wit, and sophistication. Grateful piano writing; Impressionist influences felt in the second piece. M-D.

Sergei Rachmaninoff. *Trio Elégiaque I* g 1892 (USSR 1973; Bo&H) 34pp., parts.

——. *Trio Elégiaque II* Op.9 d 1893 (Gutheil; IMC) 64pp., parts. 43 min. Moderato–Allegro moderato; Quasi variazione–Andante; Allegro risoluto. Composed in the form of SA and a set of variations. The piano, as might be expected, dominates more than true chamber music style dictates. Written in honor of Tchaikovsky, who died while it was being composed. Strong emotional quality, melancholy. Sequences of hymnlike character are interspersed with brilliant piano passages. Powerful melodic gift already seen in this early and somewhat diffuse work. D.

Josef Joachim Raff. *Trio* Op.102 c (Schuberth 1864).

——. *Trio* II Op.112 G 1866 (Rieter—Biedermann).

——. *Trio* III Op.155 a "Grand Trio" (Bo&Bo 1872; Hamelle).

——. *Trio* IV Op.158 D (R&E 1871; Hamelle).

These works are not the best of Raff's compositions as they are somewhat diffuse and lack strong self-criticism. But there are good ideas and basically a fine understanding of the instruments. They are full of a special spirit of Central European Romanticism. No.III is the finest of those listed above. Raff demands a good deal from all the performers. M-D to D.

Erhard Ragwitz. *Trio* Op.10 1965 (DVFM 8311) 35pp., parts. Allegro; Lento appassionato; Allegro agitato. Freely tonal around d, generally thin textures, octotonic, toccata-like finale, Neoclassic. M-D.

Jean-Philippe Rameau. *Pièces de Clavecin en Concerts* 1742 (E. Jacobi—Br 1970) 63pp., parts. For violin or flute and viol (gamba) or a second violin and keyboard. Five concerts (suites), which are first and foremost keyboard pieces. They can all be played on the keyboard alone. "The term 'en concert' means 'for ensemble playing,' the ensemble being formed by the addition of parts for melodic instruments which 'accompany' the obbligato keyboard" (from Preface, which gives much more information). Includes Rameau's "Notice to Performers" and "Notice for the Harpsichord, Flute and Viole," all in French, German, and English. Beautiful Urtext and performing edition. D. (Saint-Saëns—Durand). Somewhat over-edited.
Each suite available separately (Peyrot, Rebuffat—Senart).

Maurice Ravel. *Piano Trio* a (Durand 1914) 35pp., parts. 28 min. Exudes warmth and is full of rich harmonic color, especially in the piano part. Long undulating melodic lines are often heard in octaves or double octaves in the violin and cello. All instruments are perfectly deployed. The rhythmically intricate Pantoum (second) movement requires a crispness in touch. All movements are closely related thematically. The opening movement (Modéré) has a broad sweeping melody in $\frac{8}{8}$ (3 + 2 + 3). By contrast, Pantoum is breathless and fast with a grand tune in the second middle section. Passacaille (Très large): a dignified passacaglia. The Final is elaborate and exciting. The outer movements are noble and highly expressive. D.
See Brian Newbould, "Ravel's Pantoum," MT 116 (March 1975): 228–31—clarifies the background of the title "Pantoum" used by Ravel in the Piano Trio; Yea-Shiuh Lin, "The Piano Trio in France, ca. 1880–1920: Debussy, Chausson, Fauré, and Ravel," D.M.A. diss., University of Cincinnati, 1998.

Alan Rawsthorne. *Trio* 1962 (OUP) 32pp., parts. 14 min. Introduction–poco lento: freely tonal, clear lines, subtle writing, leads directly to the Capriccio–Allegro deciso: theme is given out in octaves and quickly followed by a poco misterioso section in $\frac{5}{8}$; flowing chromatic triplets; large chordal gestures; movement unfolds fluently with these basic elements. Theme and Variations–Allegretto: no separation between variations; following the modal and mainly diatonic theme are 9 contrasting short variations; there is a consistency of texture and nervous intensity about the movement that is projected with lively figuration. The entire piece "communicates" well. M-D.

Max Reger. *Trio* Op.102 e (Bo&Bo 1908) 92pp., parts. Allegro moderato, ma con passione; Allegretto; Largo; Allegro con moto. Strong, sweeping and impassioned, influenced by J. S. Bach. Seriousness and expressive qualities in the outer movements are notable. The piquant and shapely scherzo and trio are masterfully crafted. D.

Carl Reinecke. *Trio* Op.188 a 1887 (Br&H; IMC) 33pp., parts. For oboe (violin), horn (cello), and piano. See detailed entry under trios for piano, one brass instrument, and one woodwind.

———. *Trio II* Op.230 (Br&H) 43pp., parts. Allegro; Adagio sostenuto; Scherzo; Finale. Reinecke's works have not withstood the test of time very well, but there is some solid musical writing in this *Trio* that should see it revived from time to time. M-D.

Otto Reinhold. *Piano Trio* (Br 1915 1952) 23pp., parts. Sehr heftig; Intermezzo; Sehr erregt. Freely tonal, repeated chords, quintal harmony. Outer movements have much rhythmic drive while the Intermezzo rides gracefully on flowing melodies. Neoclassic orientation. Requires large span. M-D.

Franz Reizenstein. *Trio* Op.34 1957 (Lengnick) 30pp., parts. 10 min. One movement. Reizenstein studied with Ralph Vaughan Williams, but there is not much English influence in this work. Reizenstein was a natural and fine pianist, and the piano part is idiomatically conceived in every aspect. Freely tonal, diffuse. M-D.

Josef Rheinberger. *Trio* III Op.121 B♭ (Forberg 1881) 59pp., parts. Allegretto amabile; Romanze; Scherzo; Finale.

———. *Trio* IV Op.191 F (Leuckart 1899) 47pp., parts. Moderato; Adagio molto; Tempo di minuetto; Finale.

Both of these works, while strongly Romantic, show the influence of Mozart, Beethoven, and Schubert. Formally and in developmental skill (his canonic weaving in particular), Rheinberger is a real craftsman. Hungarian influence is also heard in Op.121. Both *Trios* are highly recommended to amateur chamber groups. M-D.

Wallingford Riegger. *Trio* Op.1 1919 (SPAM 1933) 60pp., parts. Allegro moderato; Larghetto misterioso; Allegro. This early work is effective; leans toward a pre-Impressionist style with contrapuntal techniques, uses traditional formal schemes. M-D.

George Rochberg. *Piano Trio* 1963 (TP) 29pp., 3 scores necessary for performance. 18 min. Rochberg's last 12-tone work. Each instrument has a solo section that alternates with an ensemble section. These contrasting sections delineate the formal structure of the piece. Materials are passed from one part to another. The climax near the end displays the most instrumental interaction. All the techniques associated with 12-tone technique are present: pointillistic treatment, extreme dynamics that also appear to be serialized, Expressionist style. D.

————. *Summer 1990* (TP 1991) 73pp.

Ned Rorem. *End of Summer* 1985 (Bo&H). 22 min.

————. *Spring Music* 1990 (Bo&H). 27 min.

Albert Roussel. *Trio* Op.2 E♭ 1902, rev.1927 (Rouart Lerolle) 53pp., parts. 29 min. Modéré, sans lenteur; Lent; Très lent. Cyclic theme that appears in the Introduction and first movement takes on more importance in the slow movement and returns in the brisk and highly rhythmic finale. Varied tempos, especially in the finale. Fondness for triplet figuration and arpeggi is apparent. Lent movement is the most Impressionist. D.

Edmund Rubbra. *Piano Trio* Op.68 1950 (Lengnick) 27pp., parts. 20 min. Andante moderato, e molto flessibile; Episodio scherzando; Prima Meditazione–Seconda Meditazione–Terza Meditazione. One-movement form but actually in 3 without a break. Cyclic treatment, seems to prefer lower registers of the piano. Written for the Rubbra-Gruenberg-Pleeth Trio of which the composer was a member from 1945 to 1956. D.

————. *Piano Trio* II Op.138 1970 (Lengnick) 27pp., parts. Two movements, the second being a delightful scherzo with a syncopated main theme. Dignified writing showing development through the Brahms tradition. Solid craft, rich harmonies. D.

Anton Rubinstein. *Trio* I Op.15/1 F (Hofmeister) 47pp., parts. A good piece for amateurs looking for an accessible and M-D work, but there are many hurdles for the pianist.

————. *Trio* II Op.15/2 (Hamelle; Hofmeister; UE 49pp., parts). Moderato; Adagio; Allegro assai; Moderato.

————. *Trio* III Op.52 B♭ (Hamelle; Bartholf Senff) 51pp., parts. Moderato assai; Andante; Allegro moderato.

————. *Trio* IV Op.85 (Hamelle).

————. *Trio* V Op.108 (Hamelle).

As might be expected, the piano parts of all these works are effectively written in a Romantic-eclectic style and require fine technical facility.

Camille Saint-Saëns. *Trio* Op.18 F 1863 (Hamelle) 53pp., parts. 26 min. One of Saint-Saëns's most inspired early works. The opening movement is one of gaiety and alluring joy. The scherzo turns this gaiety into humor with pizzicato effects and cross-rhythms. The Andante is beautifully molded with an expressive theme in ballad style. M-D to D.

——. *Trio* Op.92 e 1892 (Durand) 32 min. Five movements that display great craft and inspiration. Unexpected episodes are introduced between the main subjects, and phrases return to the tonic in sinuous ways. At times all 3 instruments move with great freedom, then are heard in unison passages. $\frac{5}{4}$ interrupts $\frac{5}{8}$ at one point and adds interest. Logical development supports perfect balance. M-D to D.

These works display brilliant piano writing that does not overbalance the strings. They are models of style and have strong emotional appeal.

Karl Schiske. *Sonatine* Op.34 1952 (Dob) 20pp., parts. Andante; Allegro; Adagio. Constantly shifting meters, freely tonal around a, Neoclassic. M-D.

Johann Schobert. *Trio* Op.6/1 E♭ (A. Karsch—Nag 197) 18pp., parts. Allegro; Andante; Tempo di Menuetto. Schobert is one of the forefathers of modern chamber music for the piano. This trio is written in a style close to that of the Mannheim school. The keyboard part, with its figuration, is interesting on its own as well as combining effectively with the other instruments. The dark coloration of the Andante, with its extensive cantilena, looks forward to Beethoven. M-D.

Franz Peter Schubert. *Trios* (E. Badura-Skoda—Henle 1973) 156pp., parts. Fingering for the piano part added by H.-M. Theopold. Contains *Trio* Op.99 B♭, D.898, 31 min.; *Trio* Op.100 E♭, D.929, 39 min.; Sonata movement B♭, D.28; Adagio E♭, Op. posth.148, D.897. Preface in German, English, and French. Critical commentary in German. Beautifully printed and thoroughly reliable performing edition. Based on the most authentic sources. These and the background of all 4 works are discussed in the Preface. The inspiration and delicacy as well as restraint exhibited in the development of thematic material make D.898 and D.929 some of the most successful of this great lyricist's chamber music. See especially the exposition and development of the first movement of D.898. The scherzo of Op.100 is constructed from a canon that receives amazing treatment.

——. *Werke für Klavier und mehrere Instrumente* (A. Feil—Br 1975) 302pp., parts. 8 facsimilies. Contains *Trio* B♭, D.28 (1812); *Trio* E♭, D.929/Op.100 (1827); *Trio* B♭, D.898/Op.99 (1828?); *Trio* E♭, D.897/Op. posth.148 (1828?); *Quartett* F (Adagio e Rondo concertante), D.487 (1816); *Quintett* A, D.667/Op. posth.114 (1819?); Anhang: *Trio* E♭, D.929/Op.100 (Entwurf, 1827). Introduction, Preface, and critical commentary (with 23 musical examples) in German.

——. *Complete Chamber Music for Piano and Strings* (I. Brüll—Dover) 2 vols. A reprint of the Br&H complete edition. Includes *Quintet* Op.114 ("Trout"), *Quartet* (Adagio and Rondo Concertante F), and *Trios* Op.99, Op.100, Op.148 (a Notturno in B♭). Reasonably priced, but no mention is made of separate parts.

Available separately: *Trio* D.898/Op.99 (Br&H; CFP; UE 4851; Schott; Adamowski

—GS L1471; Augener 7277). *Trio* D.929/Op.100 (A. Feil—Br 5610 1988; Br&H; CFP; Adamowski—GS L1472; Augener 7278; EPS).
See T. A. Denny, "Articulation, Elision, and Ambiguity in Schubert's Mature Sonata Forms: The *Op. 99 Trio Finale* in Its Context," *Journal of Musicology* 6/3 (1988): 340–66.

Clara Schumann. *Piano Trio* Op.17 g (W. Wollenweber UWKR 16) 35pp., parts. Allegro moderato; Scherzo–Tempo di Menuetto; Andante; Allegretto. Shows influence of Haydn, Mendelssohn, Weber, and Robert Schumann, but the composer's own style displays interesting rhythms and fresh modulations that are sometimes abrupt and more delicate than forceful. The work is thoroughly musicianly and well crafted even if more imitative than innovative. Simple straightforward writing, charming. M-D.

Robert Schumann. *Three Trios* (CFP).
——. *Trio* Op.63 d 1848 (CFP; Adamowski—GS L1476; Augener) 28 min. Tumultuous opening movement, vivacious Scherzo, emotional intensity, anguished dynamism. Poetic and highly inspired with the piano part occasionally unduly overemphasized. All 3 instruments are called upon to supply virtuosic effects. Schumann's finest trio. D.
——. *Trio* Op.80 F 1847 (CFP; Adamowski—GS L1477; Augener) 26 min. Molto animato; Con espressione intima; In tempo moderato; Non troppo vivo. Although written at about the same time as the first *Trio*, in a letter to Carl Reinecke, Schumann said this work "makes a quicker and more ingratiating appeal." Has the warmth and Romantic style that characterize many of his other works. D.
——. *4 Phantasiestücke* Op.88 1842 (Br&H 25pp., parts; CFP 27pp., parts; IMC). Romanze a; Humoreske d; Duett d; Finale a. Highly sensitive writing. M-D.
——. *Trio* Op.110 g 1852 (CFP; Adamowski—GS L1478; Augener; Eulenburg) 25 min. Schumann is seen at his most dramatic in this work. Steady rise and fall of parts, contrary direction of lines, doublings not offensive. D.

Elliott Schwartz. *Tapestry* 1996 (GS/Margun) 10 min. Performed from full score. "This work is the expansion of an earlier piece for solo piano, commissioned to commemorate the successful Danish operation to save its Danish Jewish community during World War II. It uses quoted fragments from a Danish children's song, music by a Theresienstadt composer who perished, the Vaughan Williams 5th Symphony (serenity at the height of wartime), [and] musical spelling of the name Victor Borge, whose foundation commissioned the earlier piano piece" (Composer's letter to authors).

Ralph Shapey. *Trio* (CFE). Much internal play of energies that constantly sets up tension and release. Overlapping ideas in broad phrases. Shapey's own description of his compositional procedures is appropriate here: "imposed discipline by ritualistic reiteration." There is much expressive power and emotional impact in this complex music. D.

Seymour Shifrin. *Trio* 1974 (Boelke-Bomart) 11 min. Neoclassic, clear formal outlines, ambiguous tonal usage achieved by chromatic writing, fast harmonic motion. Strongly contrasted materials such as lyric and pointillistic lines; short dynamic upbeat figures combined with broad sustained downbeats. Dramatic and tense writing make for difficult listening. D.

Dmitri Shostakovich. *Trio* Op.67 e 1944 (CFP; MCA; USSR 63pp., parts; IMC) 27 min. First movement: strange opening in harmonics, unusual tonal quality, folklike melody, disquieting. Second movement: impetuous, frenetic, relentless. Third movement: somber, elegiac; piano carries harmonic color. Fourth movement: angular and menacing Jewish-flavored main subject; dancelike grotesquerie; moves with a contrapuntal mechanical, rhythmical motion; coda recalls theme of first movement. Anxious, tense, disturbing; achieves a profound result. Tragic moods of the time are reflected in this *Trio,* one of the most brilliant and effective Soviet chamber works. D.

Jean Sibelius. *Trio* C 1888 "Lovisa Trio" (A. Nybo—Fazer), parts. Nicknamed for the town where Sibelius composed the *Trio.* First publication; based on the manuscript at the Sibelius Museum.

Nikos Skalkottas. *Trio* 1936 (UE 14149). Light, transparent, introspective writing. Serial influence felt but not used in any strict manner. Long lyric lines lend themselves to contrapuntal development. D.
———. *Eight Variations on a Greek Folk Song* 1938 (UE 12735 1957) 21pp., parts. 12 min. Modal chromatic harmonic idiom; contrasting variations provide both interest and unity. Effective Expressionist treatment of folk material. M-D.

Bedřich Smetana. *Trio* Op.15 g 1855 (Artia; CFP 4238; UE 46pp., parts; IMC; Eulenburg 52pp., parts) 27 min. Moderato assai: SA; melancholy theme; piano has sustained chords until m. 17, when it gives out the main idea; octaves; vigorous but gloomy ending. Allegro, ma non agitato: has two contrasting alternativos (or trios): rhythmic motion of piano accompanies lament of strings; a doloroso scherzo. Finale–Presto: energetic; arpeggio figures; a grave martial quality gives idea of a funeral procession; Tempo I returns and brings the movement to a close. Written while Smetana was suffering from the loss of his first child, who was 4½ years old. Liszt appreciated this work. D.

Julia Smith. *Trio-Cornwall* (Mowbray 1966) 39pp., parts. 14½ min. Allegro giusto; Theme with (7) Variations; Allegro quasi rondo. The title refers to Cornwall-on-the Hudson, New York, where the composer first heard the birdcalls that provide thematic material for the first movement. The second movement presents a few outside glimpses, including Puerto Rico and the Virgin Islands. Third movement is back in Cornwall and uses the familiar street sound (c-eg-e auto horn call) as a first theme and a syncopated melody as a second theme. First and last movements are in SA design. Mildly 20th-century. M-D.

Leland Smith. *Trio* (CFE 1947) 25pp., parts. See detailed entry under trios for piano, one stringed instrument, and one wind instrument.

Jose Soler. *Trio* 1963 (Seesaw) 23pp., parts. Serial, pointillistic, broad atonal gestures, dynamic extremes, piano cadenza. One extended movement, varied tempos, moods, thorny and complex writing. D.

Rick Sowash. *Trio No. 1: Four Seasons in Bellville* 1977 (Sowash), parts. 25 min. I. Winter–Adagietto, II. Spring–Allegro moderato, III. Summer–Molto Allegro (segue), IV. Autumn–Largo. Inspired by the changing of seasons in Bellville, Ohio, the composer's residence at the time of composition. M-D.

——. *Trio No. 2: Orientale and Galop* 1980 (Sowash), parts. 10 min. I. Andante (segue), II. Presto. Cadenzas for violin and cello, as well as a gallop in the form of a rondo, are part of the unique musical landscape. Combines a multitude of styles, including "Gershwin-like blues cadenzas, quasi-Arabian modes, Jerome Kern–like ballad style, polkas, fight songs, Sousa marches, and Romanian rhapsody-like characteristics" (from Program Notes, *Rick Sowash: The Four Piano Trios,* Mirecourt Trio, compact disc, Gasparo 254, 1991). M-D.

——. *Trio No. 3: A Christmas Divertimento* 1983 (Sowash), parts. 21 min. I. Allegro, in one, II. Allegro, III. Moderato, IV. Allegro vigoroso, V. Lento, VI. Moderato espressivo, VII. Allegro moderato–Adagio–Presto (Variations on *The Boar's Head Carol*). Emulates Christmas exuberance in a divertimento setting. Shaker hymns appear in the fifth movement, but only the sixth actually quotes a melody associated with the Christmas season. M-D.

——. *Trio No. 4* 1983, rev.1989 (Sowash), parts. 9½ min. I. Presto tempesto (segue), II. Adagio, molto espressivo. The most succinct of the 5 *Trios* "presents anew the familiar Romantic pattern of peace attained through strife, an upward struggle through thorns to the view at the summit" (from Program Notes, *Rick Sowash: The Four Piano Trios,* Mirecourt Trio, compact disc, Gasparo 254, 1991). M-D.

——. *Trio No. 5: Eroica* 2000 (Sowash) 63pp., parts. 28 min. I. Allegro, II. Adagio, III. Presto. Inspired by the composer's father as he valiantly battled cancer, the work was begun nearly 20 years earlier as a Sonata for cello and piano but left incomplete. The composer returned to it in 2000 adding a violin and new themes, and adopting the title "Eroica" to symbolize the subject matter of the trio as "the courage of those who are afraid, who almost lose they way, but persist despite their fears and finally prevail" (from Program Notes, *Rick Sowash: Eroica,* compact disc, Rick Sowash Publishing Co., 2001 [p.6]). M-D.

Leopold Spinner. *Trio* Op.6 1955 (TP) 19pp., parts. Andante; Allegro moderato; Allegro poco vivace. Strong Webern influence, possibilities of 12-tone technique exploited. Changing tempos, pitch, and dynamics serialized; pointillistic. D.

Louis Spohr. *Trio* Op.119 e (Litolff) 27 min.
——. *Trio* Op.123 F 1843 (Br 48pp., parts; Litolff).
——. *Trio* Op.124 a 1844 (B. Mersson—KaWé 1973 43pp., parts; Litolff). Allegro moderato; Andante con Variazioni (highly figurative for the piano); Scherzo; Finale.
——. *Trio* Op.133 B♭ 1848 (F. Leinert—Br 19106 48pp., parts; Litolff). Br edition has a Preface and critical notes in German, French, and English. Allegro: shows a preference for chords in both hands and a full piano part, and even though Spohr was not a pianist, there is a remarkable versatility in the use of purely pianistic idioms. Menuetto–Moderato: sparkling passagework is required from the pianist in the trio. Poco Adagio: has the character of an Intermezzo; uses widely spread chords and harplike idioms, and serves as a link to the lively closing Rondo. Finale–Presto: pleasant lightness, transparency, and rhythmic pithiness; Spohr called this movement the *Sprudelsatz* (hot spring movement) as a facetious pun in remembrance of the Karlsbad hot springs, where he was staying when he composed the movement. One of the most grateful chamber works of the Romantic period. M-D to D.
——. *Trio* Op.142 g 1852 (Leinert—Br; Litolff).
These works are somewhat dated by today's standards, but there is a sturdy character streaked with tenderness that makes the writing highly interesting in places.

Patric Standford. *Trio* (Nov 1970) 34pp., parts. 25 min. Frequent octave passages and string tremolos provide much of the basic material for this one-movement work. Compelling and intense writing. D.

Christopher Steel. *Trio* Op.23 (Nov 1968) 34pp., parts. 10 min. Allegretto; Molto moderato; Presto. Freely tonal, flowing lines, octave imitation and syncopation, octotonic, parallel chords. Presto is toccata-like with harmonic 2nds, repeated chords; grand pause before coda leads to brilliant closing. Large span required. M-D.

Halsey Stevens. *Trio* III 1953–54 (ACA) 42pp., parts. 14½ min. Allegro non troppo, marcato; Con moto moderato; Vivace. Freely tonal, dissonant counterpoint, thin textures, modal, toccata-like finale with contrasting episodes. Material unfolds naturally. Large span required. M-D to D.

Georgy V. Sviridov. *Trio* Op.6 (USSR 1963) 79pp., parts. Allegro moderato; Allegro vivo; Andante; Allegretto. Has a full-blooded Russian Slavic sound. Large 19th-century pianistic gestures in a slightly 20th-century idiom. Thorough integration of all instruments. D.

Sergey Ivanovitch Taneyev. *Trio* Op.22 D (Simrock 101pp., parts; USSR). Allegro: condensed SA design, elegant and well-crafted writing. Allegro molto:

Scherzo with the addition of a theme and variations; returns to opening tempo. Andante espressivo: connected with a violin cadenza that leads directly to the Finale–Allegro con brio: animated and fast. Shows a masterful use of counterpoint coupled with unusual formal construction. D.

Alexandre Tansman. *Trio* II 1938 (ESC) 31pp., parts. Introduction et Allegro; Scherzo; Arioso; Finale. Strong lyric melodic inventiveness, rhythmic dynamism, subtle melancholy. Construction elements carefully worked out. Piano part displays complete understanding of the instrument. Chromatic; Impressionist tendencies. M-D.

Alexander Tcherepnin. *Trio* Op.34 (Durand 1925) 15pp., parts. 8 min. Moderato tranquillo; Allegretto; Allegro molto. Economic writing in all movements. The first movement, in SA design, has an extensive development section. The finale, highly rhythmic, is the most serious, and concludes with a perpetual motion idea. Lines are frequently passed from one instrument to another in the composer's "interpoint" approach. M-D to D.

———. *Triple Concertino* Op.47 1931 (UE 15772 trio version 1972) 36pp., parts. 15 min. Originally for violin, cello, piano, and orchestra. This version made by the composer. Allegro marciale: chordal with many seconds included, freely tonal, triplets, repeated notes; large span required. Lento: low register exploited; tremolo; rhythmic and melodic elements contrasted. Allegro: $\frac{7}{4}$, ostinato-like, alternating hands, heavy chords, chromatic figuration. Presto: quintal harmony, strong rhythms, 3 with 4; coda slows to a Lento closing. Colorful and pianistic writing. M-D.

Georg Philipp Telemann. *Six Concerti* (Br 2961). See detailed entry under duos for piano and flute.

Antoine Tisné. *Musique en Trio* (Billaudot 1973) 68pp., parts. Fervent; Hallucinant "Vision Fantastique"; Elégiaque; Violent. Chromatic, Expressionist, serial influence, wide dynamic range, octotonic, harmonics, pointillistic. The Elégiaque movement is made up of 12 contrasting "Structures" similar to variations. Percussive treatment of the piano in last movement. Virtuoso writing and instrumentation. Requires large span. D.

Donald Francis Tovey, *Trio* Op.1 b (Schott 28638 1910) 53pp., parts. Maestoso, quasi andante, ma con moto; Menuetto; Rhapsodie; Finale. M-D.

———. *Trio* Op.8 c (Schott 27833 1906). Originally for piano, clarinet, and horn. Separate parts for violin and cello. M-D.

———. *Trio* Op.27 D 1910 (Schott) 36pp., parts. Allegro con brio; Larghetto maestoso; Allegro energico, non presto. Spacious; broad writing; firm technical handling; influence of late Beethoven and Brahms discernible in the construction of this work. Classically oriented. M-D.

Joan Tower. *And . . . They're Off* 1997 (GS). 3 min.

———. *Big Sky* 2000 (GS). 7 min.

Peter I. Tschaikovsky. *Trio* Op.50 a 1882 (CFP 3777 91pp., parts; USSR; IMC; Augener 7285). Written in memory of Nicolas Rubinstein. Pezzo elegiaco: SA; melancholy opening idea; Russian Allegro giusto second subject; third idea brought in and worked out with the other 2 main ideas; concludes with heavy minor chords in the piano. Theme and Variations: beautiful swaying theme in Russian character is the basis for this movement with 11 variations; eighth variation, a fugue, is frequently omitted in performance; short coda (lugubre) brings back the elegiac main theme in the strings with a slow-rhythm funeral march in the piano. Strongly emotional and stirring. D.

Joaquín Turina. *Trio I* Op.35 d (Rouart Lerolle 1926) 32pp., parts. 23 min. In the nature of a 3-sectioned fantasy: Prélude et Fugue; Theme et (5) Variations; Sonata. Written in a style that blends Spanish and foreign elements. Has much charm and interesting timbre. The variations movement has the most interest, with each variation adapted to a different Spanish rhythm. M-D.

———. *Trio II* Op.76 b (Rouart Lerolle 1933) 28pp., parts. 14 min. Lento–Allegro molto moderato: much rhythmic drive, ideas contrasted, not developed. Molto vivace: $\frac{5}{8}$; a short Lento mid-section is chordal and Impressionist; $\frac{5}{8}$ returns. Lento: solid and broken-chordal figuration; moves to a dancelike Allegretto followed by a meno mosso that pulls it back to a Moderato before a quickening of pace continues to the end. Varied tempos could cause ensemble problems, cyclic. M-D.

———. *Círculo* Op.91 (Fantasia) 1936 (UME 1992) 19pp., parts. 9½ min. 1. Amanecer, 2. Mediodío, 3. Crespúsculo. Spanish color and glitter. M-D.

Alfred Uhl. *Kleines Konzert* (Dob 1975) 44pp., parts. Serially organized in a very personal style. D.

Fartein Valen. *Trio* Op.5 1924 (NMO) 37pp., parts. 22 min. Moderato; Scherzo; Largo; Finale. Harmonies occur in passing notes that are highly chromatic and treated in a linear fashion. Distinct, personal style that is complex, yet the music develops imaginatively. D.

Antonio Veracini. *Sonata à Tre* Op.1/10 (F. Polnauer—Hug 1973) 16pp., parts. Four movements—slow, fast, slow, fast—using same tonal vocabulary as Veracini's contemporary Corelli. Veracini is a careful craftsman. M-D.

———. *Sonata da Camera* Op.3/2 C (F. Polnauer—JWC 1970) 20pp., parts. Continuo Series No.1. Slow, fast, slow, fast outline; spacious printing. Int. to M-D.

Heitor Villa-Lobos. *Premier Trio* c 1911 (ESC 1956) 63pp., parts. 20 min. Allegro non troppo; Andante sostenuto; Scherzo; Allegro troppo e finale. Contains big splashes of color throughout. The finale anticipates Villa-Lobos's later experimentation with the blending of Bach's style and Brazilian musical elements in the *Bachianas Brasileiras.* D.

———. *Deuxième Trio* 1915 (ESC 1928) 64pp., parts. 20 min. Allegro moderato;

Berceuse–Barcarolla (in $^{10}_{16}$); Scherzo; Finale–Molto allegro. Requires enormous technique as well as stamina. Romantic-Impressionist sonorities with rather heavy-handed piano writing. D.

——. *Troisième Trio* 1918 (ESC 1929) 71pp., parts. 25 min. Allegro con moderato; Assai moderato; Allegretto spirituoso; Finale–Allegro animato. Requires virtuoso pianism with tremendous strength. D.

These 3 trios are almost a catalog of 20th-century pianistic techniques and idioms. D.

Ernst Vogel. *Trio* 1971 (Dob) 22pp., parts. 14 min. Three untitled contrasting movements. Written in a dissonant Neoclassic style. Thematic material is pale. D.

Robert Volkmann. *Trio* Op.3 F (Litolff 1917). Light in character. M-D.

——. *Trio* Op.5 b♭ (Litolff 1914; Br&H 44pp., parts). Three movements but gives the impression of having only 2, as the last 2 movements are connected. Opening movement is virile and passionate, while the second is pleasant with ritornello usage. A wild tempestuous finale ends rather quietly. Uses all the pianistic techniques common to the period. This work made Volkmann well-known. It was dedicated to Liszt, and he was fond of it. M-D.

——. *Musikalisches Bilderbuch* Op.11 (WH).

Alex Voormolen. *Trio* C 1918 (Rouart Lerolle) 26pp., parts. 13½ min. Lent; Pavane; Très modéré–Animé et spirituel. Strong Ravel and late Debussy influences. Aristocratic, picturesque writing combined with harmonic vitality. Voormolen studied with Ravel and Roussel. M-D.

George Walker. *Music for Three* 1970 (Gen) 7pp., parts. 5 min. Terse, abstract, serial, pointillistic, effective. Demands high level of ensemble experience from all players. D.

Louis Weingarden. *Things Heard and Seen in Summer* (OUP 1974) 17pp., parts. 7 min. Eleven short pieces: 1. Grazioso (violin, piano), 2. Andante (piano), 3. Andantino (cello, piano), 4. Lento (violin, piano), 5. Organum–Allegretto (violin, cello, piano), 6. Lento (cello), 7. Largo (violin, piano), 8. Ostinati (cello, piano), 9. Andante (violin, cello, piano), 10. Andantino (violin), 11. Vivace (violin, cello, piano). Expressionist writing. Piano employs clusters, plucked strings, glissandi with fingernail. Solid pianistic equipment required throughout. D.

Charles Marie Widor. *Trio* Op.19 B♭ (Hamelle 1875) 56pp., parts. Allegro: flexible writing, elegant second subject. Andante con moto quasi moderato: siciliano rhythm; contains some powerful moments; quiet ending. Scherzo–Vivace: piano announces well-marked theme; lively dialogue; a curious false entry of the trio before its normal appearance, then scherzo is repeated complete. Finale–Presto: rondo, followed by flowing and fresh writing; then all 3 instruments make strong statements before rondo returns. M-D.

Dag Wiren. *Trio* I Op.6 1933 (MG) 32pp., parts. 15 min. Allegro; Adagio; Fughetta. Fresh and lightly characterized melodic style; Nordic outlook but also shows influence of Prokofiev and Honegger. Freely tonal, centers around c♯. M-D.

——. *Trio* II Op.36 (MG 1963) 27pp., parts. 15 min. Andante–Allegro molto; Intermezzo; Lento espressivo; Molto allegro. Metamorphosis technique used (a musical motif derived from a basic theme forms the point of departure for the whole work). Lucid and polished tonal language. M-D.

Ermanno Wolf-Ferrari. *Trio* Op.7 F♯ 1901 (Rahter) 31pp., parts. Sostenuto; Largo; Lievemente mosso, e tranquillo sempre. Cobbett says this work "contains fine and interesting ideas, and there is an impression of independence in all three movements, the last of which is a very skillfully developed canon" (CCSCM, II, 590). Romantic writing that is heavily chromatic and sounds somewhat dated. Lyrical expression flows unchecked. D.

Russell Woollen. *Trio* Op.29 1957 (CFE) 77pp., parts. Andantino; Vivo; Adagio; Allegro deciso. Well-ordered and balanced forms, octotonic, freely tonal, poignant and expressive Adagio, dance influence in finale, Neoclassic. Requires large span. M-D.

Mario Zafred. *Trio* III 1955 (Ric 129607) 52pp., parts. Photo of composer's MS. Moderatamente mosso; Lento; Scherzando; Sostenuto. Neoclassic, clear textures, thorough use of all instruments. M-D.

Trios for Piano, Violin, and Viola

Carl Philipp Emanuel Bach. *Trio* I W.94 D (G. Picciolo—IMC 1955) 19pp., parts. Allegretto; Adagio; Allegro molto. M-D.

——. *Trio* II W.93 a (Piccioli—IMC 1955) 16pp., parts. Andantino; Largo e sostenuto; Allegro assai. M-D.

——. *Trio* III W.95 G (Piccioli—IMC 1955) 16pp., parts. Allegretto; Adagio; Presto. M-D.

These works were probably written for keyboard, flute, and viola but they sound equally well in the piano, violin, and viola combination. All 3 realizations border on the fussy.

Arnold Bax. *Trio* Op.4 1906 (JWC) 33pp., parts. 14½ min. In one movement. Strong Richard Strauss and Dvořák influence noted in this early work. Demonstrates high proficiency and facility in writing for this combination. Thick harmonic decoration; requires strong pianistic equipment to sort the more important from the less important. D.

Johannes Brahms. *Trio* Op.40 E♭. See detailed entry under trios for piano, violin, and cello.

——. *Trio* Op.114 a. See detailed entry under trios for piano, violin, and cello.

Johann Ladislav Dussek. *Notturno Concertante* Op.68. See detailed entry under trios for piano, one stringed instrument, and one wind instrument.

Hans-Georg Görner. *Concertino* Op.31 (Hofmeister). See detailed entry under trios for piano and 2 woodwinds.

Erich Hamann. *Trio* Op.38 (Dob 1964) 28pp., parts. Allegro con moto: SA, octotonic, broken octaves, freely tonal, linear; large span required. Allegro molto: ABA, imitation, repeated and chromatic octaves, chordal sonorities spread over keyboard. Thema con Variationi: folklike theme, 8 contrasting variations; Presto coda returns to opening idea of second movement; mildly 20th-century. M-D.

Tadeusz Jarecki. *Trio-Fugato e Aria* Op.11 (JWC 1943) 11pp., parts. 7½ min. For piano, violin, and cello or viola, includes viola part. Allegro agitato section centered around f♯ opens the work. Left-hand arpeggi figuration supports melodic full-chord octaves in right hand. Contrasting subdued material follows. Imitation is heard between the strings. The Aria centers around b and involves all instruments in contrapuntal melodic treatment. The opening fugato section returns to conclude the work con forza and *fff.* Mildly 20th-century. M-D.

Joseph Jongen. *Trio* Op.30 f♯ (Durand 1909) 51pp., parts. Prélude: 2 subjects intertwine in much chromatic figuration and chordal treatment; interlude leads to the Theme and Variations: freely developed in varied treatment; last variation serves as the Finale: expanded and further development of variation idea preceding brilliant conclusion. Cobbett says this work "is the first important contribution since Mozart to the repertoire for piano, violin and viola, and demonstrates convincingly the effectiveness of the combination" (CCSCM, II, p.40).

Robert Kelly. *Theme and Variations* Op.11 1947 (CFE) 29pp., parts. 14 min. Based on theme "Nobody Knows de Trouble I Seen." Nine variations of contrasting moods, textures, and tempos. Imaginative writing. Basically tonal with some chromaticism. The vigorous final variation is the most extensive and demanding. Effective and unpretentious. M-D.

Aram Khachaturian. *Trio* 1932 (CFP; Bo&H; MCA; Musica Rara; Anglo-Soviet Press) 41pp., parts. 16 min. See detailed entry under trios for piano, one stringed instrument, and one wind instrument.

Ignaz Lachner. *Trio* Op.37 B♭ (Hofmeister) 27pp., parts. Allegro moderato; Andante con moto; Scherzo; Finale.
———. *Trio* Op.45 G (Hofmeister) 62pp., parts. Allegro moderato; Andante; Allegretto; Finale.
———. *Trio* Op.58 D (Hofmeister) 50pp., parts. Allegro con spirito; Andante; Scherzo; Finale.
———. *Trio* Op.89 (Hofmeister) 35pp., parts. Allegro giusto; Andantino, quasi Allegretto; Scherzo; Allegro Molto.
———. *Grand Trio* Op.102 E♭ (Augener 5277) 27pp., parts. Andante con moto; Andante; Allegro con spirito.
These pieces are well constructed but sound old-fashioned today. Nevertheless, they are melodically charming and admirable for amateurs looking for works in this rather unusual combination. M-D.

Jean-Marie Leclair. *Sonata* D (David—IMC 1943) 11pp., parts. Adagio; Allegro; Sarabande–Andante; Allegro assai. Sarabande is especially attractive. M-D.

Georges Migot. *Trio* 1918 (Senart) 21pp., parts. Modéré; Un peu lent; Lent. Same theme is presented in each movement. Independent melodic lines produce polytonal and sometime strong dissonances (especially for 1918). Modéré is improvisational, has no virtuoso effects, uses syncopated octaves between hands. The whole work gives a static impression since all movements are somewhat slow. M-D.

Rudolf Moser. *Suite* Op.99 A (Gertrud Moser 1970) 26pp., parts. For violin, viola, and piano, or for flute, clarinet in A, and harpsichord.

Wolfgang Amadeus Mozart. *Trio* K.498 E♭ (Henle; CFP; Eulenburg; Adamowski —GS 31pp., parts) for piano, violin or clarinet, and viola. Andante; Menuetto and Trio; Allegretto. Perhaps the greatest masterpiece for this combination. M-D.

Max Reger. *Trio* Op.2 b (Schott 1004; Augener) 38pp., parts. Allegro appassionata ma non troppo; Scherzo; Adagio con variazioni. Not as chromatic as the late works, but Reger's personal style is already present. The variations (5) movement is the most effective. Technical problems are solved with great skill. M-D to D.

Robert Schumann. *Märchenerzählungen* (Fairy Tales) Op.132 (Br&H 27pp., parts; CFP 19pp., parts; IMC) for piano, violin or clarinet, and viola. 1. Lebhaft nicht zu schnell: scherzando, fast broken chords. 2. Lebhaft und sehr markiert: accented chords, some moving very quickly; more melodic mid-section; opening returns. 3. Ruhiges Tempo, mit zartem Ausdruck: restful, cantabile, 16th-note inner accompaniment figure difficult to control. 4. Lebhaft, sehr markiert: strong chords; good octave technique required; many repeated chords in mid-section; opening returns. An effective group. M-D.

Georg Philipp Telemann. *Six Trios* 1718 (K. Schultz-Hauser—Vieweg 1973) No.5 is for violin, viola da gamba (viola), and continuo. 14pp., parts. Some of Telemann's finest works. This fine set is richly contrapuntal with profound slow movements. No.5 is a good example from the set. The realization will probably need some elaboration. M-D.

———. *Triosonate* a (H. Ruf—Heinrichshofen 1973) 12pp., parts. No distinction between original and editorial additions. The simple continuo realization will need some elaboration. Both this work and No.5 above are first modern editions. Int. to M-D.

———. *Pyrmonter Kurwoche Scherzi Melodichi* 1734 (M. Ruhnke—Br 1974) 123pp., 8 facsimiles. Vol.XXIV of *Musikalische Werke*. For violin, viola, and continuo. Also contains the *Corellisierende Sonaten* for 2 violins or flutes and continuo. Preface and critical commentary in German.

———. *Scherzi Melodichi* (Hoffmann—Nag 246 1975) 2 vols. 62pp., parts.

Trios for Piano and Two Violins (including Trio Sonatas)

[Most of the trio Sonatas can be played by 2 violins and a keyboard instrument, with cello ad lib.]

Evaristo Felice dall' Abaco. *Trio Sonata* Op.3/2 (A. Egidi—Vieweg V34) 8pp., parts. Adagio; Allegro; Largo; Allegro. Charming writing, tasteful keyboard realization. M-D.

Henrico Albicastro. *XII Sonate a Tre* Op.1 (S. Kind—UE 1949) 4 vols., 3 *Sonatas* in each vol. Preface in German.

——. *12 Triosonaten* Op.8 (M. Zulauf—Br 1974) Schweizerische Musikdenkmaler, vol.10. Critical commentary in German.

——. *Dritte Sonate* b (R. Moser—Vieweg) 11pp., parts. Adagio; Allegro; Adagio; Allegro. Good keyboard realization. M-D.

Tomaso Albinoni. *Trio Sonata* Op.1/3 1694 (Upmeyer—Nag 34) 12pp., parts.

——. *Trio Sonata* Op.1/6 a (E. Schenk—Dob; OBV).

——. *Trio Sonatas* Op.1/10–12 (Kolneder—Schott). 2 vols.

——. *Trio Sonata* Op.8/4a 1720 (E. Schenk—Dob 1952) 19pp., parts. Allemanda: prelude-like. Giga: delightful. Sarabanda: quick; this type of sarabanda was frequently encountered in the middle Baroque period. This *Sonata da Chiesa* shows a more personal, intense kind of writing. Large leaps, more ornamentation, and some chromaticism appear. M-D.

——. *Trio Sonata* Op.8/4b B♭ (Schenk—OBV) 11pp., parts. Grave, Adagio: powerful, reminiscent of Handel. Allegro: active, motoric. Larghetto: subtle, siciliano-like. Allegro: delicate winding flourishes. Dynamics are editorial and are only suggestions. M-D.
Albinoni's earlier works are generally of the 4-movement, slow-fast-slow-fast design with fairly stereotyped harmonic schemes.

Thomas A. Arne. *Trio Sonata* Op.3/1 A (Langley, Seiffert—Br&H) 16pp., parts.

——. *Trio Sonata* Op.3/2 G 1739–40 (H. Murrill—Hin 1950) 13pp., parts. 8 min.

Largo; Con spirito; Largo; Allegro. Only the Con spirito movement might present problems, with its trills. M-D.

——. *Trio Sonata* Op.3/3 E♭ (H. Murrill—Hin 1950) 16pp., parts. 8 min. Grave; Allegro moderato; Giga. Int. to M-D.

——. *Trio Sonata* Op.3/4 f (H. Murrill—Hin 1960) 8pp., parts. 7 min. Largo; Vivace; Largo; Presto. Int. to M-D.

——. *Trio Sonata* Op.3/5 D (H. Murrill—Hin 1960) 7pp., parts. 6 min. Largo; Andante; Largo; Allegro. Int.

——. *Trio Sonata* Op.3/7 e (Hin).

——. *Trio Sonata* e (Nov).

All these pieces contain charming melodies in a variety of moods.

Charles Avison. *Trio Sonata* e (Moffat—Simrock 893) 8pp., parts. Adagio espressivo; Allegro ma non troppo; Largo; Allegro, ma grazioso. Effective writing in the style of the day. M-D.

Carl Philipp Emanuel Bach. *Trio Sonata* A (Dürr—Moeck 1073).

——. *Trio Sonata* a (Dürr—Moeck 1072).

——. *Trio Sonata* B♭ (Schumann—Leuckart).

——. *Trio Sonata* B♭ (IMC).

——. *Trio Sonata* B♭ (L. Landschoff—CFP 4237) 31pp., parts. Allegro; Adagio ma non troppo; Allegretto. Excellent realization. M-D.

——. *Two Trio Sonatas* F (CFP 4288).

——. *Trio Sonata* G (H. Riemann—Br&H 1829a/b) 17pp., parts. No.16 in Collegium Musicum series. Allegretto; Andantino; Allegro. Highly edited. M-D.

——. *Trio Sonata* G (IMC).

Most of these *Sonatas* are also suitable for flute and violin with keyboard.

Johann Sebastian Bach. *Four Trio Sonatas* (Landschoff—CFP 4203A,B). Vol.I: No.1, S.1037 C; No.2, S.1039 G. Vol.II: No.3, S.1038 G for flute, violin, and basso continuo; No.4, S.1079 c for 2 flutes and basso continuo (from *The Musical Offering*).

——. *Three Trio Sonatas* C, G, c (CFP 237) from *The Musical Offering*. No separate bass part.

Available separately: *Trio Sonata* c (Kirnberger—CFP 237 A).

——. *Two Trio Sonatas* S.1037, S.1038 (David—Br&H) 22pp., parts. S.1037: Adagio; Fuge; Canon; Gigue. S.1038: Largo; Vivace; Adagio; Presto. Highly edited.

——. *Trio Sonata* S.1036 d (Nag 49) 16pp., parts.

——. *Trio Sonata* S.1037 C (Schott; David—IMC), no separate bass part. Adagio; Fuge; Canon; Gigue.

——. *Konzert* S.1043 d (D. Oistrakh—CFP 9032) 23pp., parts. Piano reduction by Wilhelm Weismann. Foreword in German and Russian. Vivace; Largo, ma non tanto; Allegro. Excellent piano reduction; beautiful edition. M-D.

Wilhelm Friedemann Bach. *Trio Sonata* D (Zimmermann). No separate bass part.

———. *Trio Sonata* F (H. Buys—B&VP) 14pp., parts. Largo; Allegretto; Allegro assai e Scherzando. The Largo presents the most problems. M-D.

Giovanni Battista Bassani. *Sonata a tre* Op.5/2 d (Zanibon 4440).

———. *Sonata a tre* Op.5/7 A (Zanibon 4441).

———. *Sonata a tre* Op.5/9 C (Schenk—OBV 461) 10pp., parts. Cello ad lib. Presto; Grave; Allegro; Largo; Presto. In Corelli style. The 5 movements are bound to an earlier point of view. Imaginative writing. M-D.

Alfred von Beckerath. *Sonatine* 1937 (Moeck 1018) 11pp., parts. For 2 violins or other treble instruments and piano. Allegro moderato; Andante; Lento; Molto allegro. First 2 movements center around F although no key signature is present. Accidentals are added. Neoclassic, mildly 20th-century sonorities. Int. to M-D.

Jiri Antonin Benda. *Trio Sonata* E (V. Nopp—Artia MAB Vol.2) 11pp., parts. Moderato; Largo; Allegro. Imbued with a feeling of spontaneity and freshness. M-D.

Heinrich Ignaz Franz von Biber. *Sonata a tre* (Janetzky—Pro Musica).

———. *Sonata a tre* (Musica Rara).

Luigi Boccherini. *Sonata a tre* c (A. Moffat—Simrock Elite Edition 1143) 11pp., parts. Cello ad lib. Allegro; Andante espressivo; Allegro con spirito. Clear Classic style. M-D.

Giovanni Maria Bonocini. *Sonata a tre* Op.1/6 d (Schenk—OBV). Cello ad lib.

———. *Sonata a tre* C (Moffat—Simrock). Cello ad lib.

William Boyce. *Trio Sonata* II F (H. Murrill—Hin 55) 14pp., parts. Andante vivace; Adagio; Allegro; Allegro ma non troppo.

———. *Trio Sonata* III A (Jensen—Augener 7432).

———. *Trio Sonata* VI B♭ (Hin 733).

———. *Trio Sonata* VII d (Moffat—Nov).

———. *Trio Sonata* VIII E♭ (Hin 641).

———. *Trio Sonata* IX C (Hin 642).

———. *Trio Sonata* XI c (Moffat—Simrock) 11pp., parts. Adagio; Fuga; Andante affettuoso; Allegro.

———. *Trio Sonata* XII G (Hin 643).

These *Sonatas,* issued in 1747, are magnificent pieces, extraordinarily varied in dimensions and style.

Domenico Brasolini. *Sonata da Camera* g (K. Fellerer—Müller 33 1956) 6pp., parts. Balletto–Vivace; Corrente–Largo; Giga–Prestissimo. Dance quality permeates the entire piece. M-D.

Benedictus Buns. *Sonata* Op.8/3 d (Heuwekemeijer EH 803) 11pp., parts. Cello part ad lib. Foreword in Dutch. Adagio; Allegro; Adagio; Allegro. Continuo part well realized by Hans Schouwman. M-D.

Giovanni Battista Buonamente. *Sonata 'La Monteverde'* (D. Stevens, Y. Menuhin— Hin 680) 5pp., parts. Cello part ad lib. The 2 violins are in strict canon through-out. This is the first *Sonata* in Buonamente's Seventh Book of Sonatas and is dedicated to Monteverdi. M-D.

Antonio Caldara. *Sonata a tre* Op.1/4 B♭ (Upmeyer—Nag). Cello part ad lib.
——. *Sonata a tre* Op.1/5 e (Schenk—OBV). Cello part ad lib.
——. *Sonata a tre* Op.1/6 c (Upmeyer—Nag). Cello part ad lib.
——. *Sonata a tre* Op.1/9 (Schenk—OBV). Cello part ad lib.
——. *Sonata da Chiesa* b (Vieweg 99). No separate bass part.
——. *Sonata da Camera* g (UE 10677-8). Cello part ad lib.

Maurito Cazzati. *Trio Sonata* Op.18/9 1656 (W. Danckert—Br HM 34) 7pp., parts. Largo; Grave con Tremolo; Vivace; Allegro. In a Corelli-like style with freely flowing lines in the last 2 movements. Int.
——. *Capriccio* a 3 Op.50/29 "II Guastavilani" (E. Schenk—OBV DM 444) 9pp., parts. Preface in English and German. Cello part ad lib. Largo; Allegro; Grave; Allegro. Noble lines in the Largo. Moody and playful echoes occur in the Grave. Cazzati wrote 50 Capriccios for church and chamber music. Each one bears a name—in this case, that of a senator from Bologna. Int. to M-D.

Louis Nicolas Clérambault. *Sonate* VII e (Peyrot, Rebuffat—Senart 266). Cello part ad lib.
——. *Sonate* G (Lemoine). Cello part ad lib.

Arcangelo Corelli. *48 Sonatas* Op.1/4 (W. Woehl—Br 701-16 1939) 16 vols. bound as one or available separately. Sources are identified. Includes Pref-ace and a discussion of the ornaments. Vols.1–4: *12 Sonate da Camera,* Op.2. Vols.5–8: *12 Sonate da Camera,* Op.3. Vols.9–12: *12 Sonate da Camera,* Op.4. Vols.13–16: *12 Sonate da Camera,* Op.1.
——. *12 Sonatas* Op.1 (W. Woehl—IMC) rev. W. Lyman.
——. *12 Sonatas* Op.2 (L. Schaeffler—IMC) rev. W. Lyman, 3 vols. of 4 Sonatas each.
——. *12 Sonatas* Op.3 (Kolneder—Schott) 4 vols.
——. *6 Sonatas* Op.4 (H. Sitt—IMC).
These *Sonatas* are unrivaled as examples of the Trio Sonata. Most of them are short and occupy only 3 or 4 pages. The Sonata a tre occupies the same posi-tion in the chamber music of the thorough-bass period as the String Quartet did in the Classical period. Br&H, Schott, CFP, Augener, and Senart have a number of these *Sonatas* separately.

Paul Creston. *Partita* Op.12 1938. See detailed entry under trios for piano, one stringed instrument, and one wind instrument.

Hugo Distler. *Sonate on Old German Folksongs* Op.15a (Br 1091; MMP) 28pp., parts. I. Taglied: based on "Es Taget vor dem Walde." II. Legende: based on "Ach Elslein, Liebes Elslein." III. Maienkurante: based on "Wie schön blüht uns der Maien." Neoclassic, thin textures, imitation between all parts, delightful. M-D.

Karl Ditters von Dittersdorf. *Concerto* A 1779 (W. Upmeyer—Nag 41 1968) 43pp., parts. Allegro molto; Larghetto; Rondeau–Allegretto. The original score is intended for more than one string player to a part, but an intimate music-making session would require only one player to a part. Cadenzas are left to the discretion of the keyboard player. Charming period writing. Int. to M-D.

Thomas Alexander Eskine, Earl of Kelly. *Trio Sonata* IV C (D. Johnson—OUP 1973) 8pp., parts. 7 min. Musica da Camera No.5. First published in 1769. Editorial additions identified. Includes critical commentary. Andante; Minuetto. Adequate keyboard realization. Pianist could add more interest. M-D.

Johann Friedrich Fasch. *Trio-Sonata* c (CFP 1974) 14pp., parts. Cello ad lib. Preface in German and English. Critical commentary in German.
———. *Three Trio Sonatas* a, F, G (Br&H 1904).
———. *Trio-Sonata* D (F. Nagel—Eulenburg 1974) 12pp., parts. In 4 short movements like a Sonata da Chiesa. Affettuoso; Allegro; Largo; Allegro. Should be played as 2 pairs of movements: 1 and 2 together, and 3 and 4 together. Charming writing, rather plain continuo realization that should be added to. Int.
———. *Sonata a 3* (Kranz—Leuckart).
———. *Trio* a (Riemann—Br&H).
———. *Trio* D (Hausswald—Nag).
See David Alden Sheldon, "The Chamber Music of Johann Friedrich Fasch," Ph.D. diss., Indiana University, 1968, 243pp. Bach thought so highly of Fasch's music that he copied out 5 of his orchestral Suites.

Willem de Fesch. *X Sonata a Tre* (B&VP) 4 vols. For 2 flutes or 2 violins and keyboard. See detailed description under trios for piano and 2 flutes.
———. *Three Sonatas* Op.12 1748 (Heuwekemeijer 802 1957) 28pp., parts. Introduction by Willem Noske. 1 D: Largo; Allemanda; Menuetto I and II. 2 g: Largo; Alia Breve; Giga. 3 G: Largo; Allemanda; Menuetto. Outstanding melodies, splendid unbroken melodic lines. The allemandas are the most involved movements. M-D.

Johann Joseph Fux. *Sonata Pastorale* K.397 F (E. Schenk—Dob DM 420 1953) 4pp., parts. Preface in English and German. Adagio; Un poco Allegro. A lovely Christmas piece that symbolizes in a charming manner the Austro-Italian cultural synthesis of the Baroque period and clearly reflects Fux's style. Frequent dynamic changes and full harmony comply with the espressivo-style, pervaded by the deeply felt emotion related to the birth of Christ. M-D.

——. *Sonata a tre* d (Noetzel).

Christoph W. Gluck. *Eight Trio Sonatas* (F.-H. Neumann-Croll—Nag 205-208 1963). Vol.I: C, g. Vol II: A, B♭. Vol.III: E♭, F. Vol.IV: E, F. Gluck was Sammartini's pupil from 1737 to 1741. In these early works, Sammartini's influence is seen, especially in No.3. Short skipping motifs of a buffo character treated in canon and sentimental sighs add special interest to these works. They form a link between the instrumental music of the Baroque and Classical periods. Editorial additions are indicated by brackets and are printed in smaller type. Valuable Preface. Carefully realized bass but can be added to if desired. M-D.

——. *Triosonate* VI F (G. Beckmann—Br&H 1972). No.37 in Collegium Musicum series. Figured bass realized. Includes part for cello. M-D.

——. *Trio Sonata* F (Moffat—Simrock).

——. *Trio Sonata* g (Bouvet—ESC).

——. *Trio Sonata* g (Möbius—Nag).

George Frideric Handel. *Sonate en Sol Mineur* Op.2/2 (J. Peyrot, J. Rebufat—Sal 2723 11pp., parts; M. Seiffert—Br&H 15pp., parts). Andante; Allegro; Largo; Allegro. Tasteful realizations. M-D.

——. *Sonata* Op.2/4 B♭ (H. Sitt—IMC). Andante; Allegro; Larghetto; Allegro.

——. *Trio Sonata* Op.2/5 (S. Flesh—Nag 240 1974) 19pp., parts. Based on the Halle Handel Edition. Larghetto; Allegro; Adagio; Allegro. M-D.

——. *Sonata* Op.2/8 (H. Sitt—CFP). Andante; Allegro; Arioso; Allegro.

——. *Seven Sonatas* Op.5/1–7 (W. Serauky—Br 1973) 73pp. Vol.10, 2 in Series IV: Instrumentalmusik of the Halle Handel Edition. Continuo realization by Max Schneider. Based on the most reliable sources available.

——. *Sonata en Re* Op.5/2 (J. Peyrot, J. Rebufat—Sal 3116) 9pp., parts. Cello ad lib. Adagio; Allegro; Musette; Allegro; Musette; March; Gavotte. Careful realizations. M-D.

——. *Trio Sonata* C (Nag 230).

——. *Trio Sonata* g (S. Flesch—Nag 235).

——. *Trio Sonata* g (J. A. Parkinson—OUP 1969) 15pp., parts. Cello ad lib. See detailed entry under trios for piano and 2 flutes.

Josef Matthias Hauer. *Hausmusik* (F. Blasl, E. Stricz—UE 20031 1971) 15pp., 3 copies necessary for performance. Extensive introduction in German by Nikolaus Fheodoroff describes structure of the work. Twelve-tone, octotonic, cleverly worked out, tricky rhythms, does not contain a single rest. M-D.

Franz Joseph Haydn. *Six Sonatas* Op.8 (A. Gülzow, W. Weismann—CFP 4376A,B). Cello ad lib. Vol.I: 37pp., parts. 1 E♭: Allegro; Adagio; Presto. 2 G: Allegro; Menuetto; Presto. 3 b: Adagio; Allegro; Tempo di Menuetto. Vol.II: 39pp., parts. 4 E♭: Allegro; Menuetto; Presto. 5 G: Allegro, Menuetto; Presto. 6 A: Allegro moderato; Andante; Menuetto; Fuga. Most markings are editorial. These delightful early pieces, composed between 1750 and 1756, are interesting in style and full of charm. Int. to M-D.

Kurt Hessenberg. *Trio* Op.26 G 1942 (CFP) 17 min. Moderato; Menuetto; Introduktion und Finale. Neoclassic, mildly 20th-century. M-D.

Gustav Holst. *A Fugal Concerto* Op.40/2 (Nov 1923) 17pp., parts. See detailed entry under trios for piano and 2 miscellaneous winds.

Arthur Honegger. *Petite Suite* 1934 (Philharmusica 1974). 4 min. Le chant du Monde. Three short, somewhat whimsical tonal movements with only the first and third using the piano. French Gebrauchsmusik. Written for the Composer's niece and nephew and can be performed by any 2 treble instruments and piano. Int. to M-D.

Johann Ludwig Krebs. *Trio Sonata* b 1743 (L. H.-Erbrecht—K&S 1961) 19pp., parts. No.62 in Organum Series. Andante; Allegretto; Un poco allegro; Vivace. A fine example of Krebs's gallant style. M-D.

Jean-Marie Leclair. *Sonata* Op.4/1 d (H. Majewski—Heinrichshofen).
——. *Sonata* Op.4/2 Bb (H. Majewski—Heinrichshofen) 18pp., parts. Preface. Adagio; Allegro ma non troppo; Largo cantabile; Allegro assai.
——. *Sonata* Op.4/3 d (H. Majewski—Heinrichshofen) 22pp., parts. Preface. Adagio; Allegro; Aria; Sarabanda.
——. *Sonata* Op.4/4 F (H. Majewski—Heinrichshofen 1973) 22pp., parts. Preface.
——. *Trio Sonata* Bb (A. Moffat—Lengnick) 18pp., parts. Adagio; Allegro ma non troppo; Andante cantabile; Allegro.
These *Sonatas* unite French formal understanding with the German art of contrapuntal composition and the malleable Italian feeling for melody. Rich thematic invention, ingenious polyphonic arrangement, versatility in the forms, and a refined sense of harmony identify Leclair as one of the most important French composers of the 18th century. All these works are approximately M-D.

Pietro Locatelli. *Trio Sonata* Op.3/1 G (Riemann—Br&H).
——. *Trio Sonata* Op.5/1 G (H. Albrecht—K&S 1954) 23pp., parts. No.52 in Organum Series. Andante; Largo andante; Allegro; Vivace. Tempos and other suggestions contained in the Preface. M-D.
——. *Trio Sonata* Op.5/4 C (H. Albrecht—K&S 1951) 9pp., parts. No.46 in Organum Series. Largo; Allegro. Tempos and other suggestions contained in the Preface. M-D.
——. *Trio Sonata* Op.5/5 d (H. Albrecht—K&S 1953) 11pp., parts. No.50 in Organum Series. Largo; Vivace; Pastorale–Andante. Tempos and other suggestions contained in the Preface. M-D.
——. *Sonata* E (Ruf—Schott).

Jean-Baptiste Loeillet (of Lyons). *Sonata* Op.1/2 G (Ruf—Schott).
——. *Sonata* Op.1/4 D (Ruf—Schott).
——. *Sonata* Op.1/6 e (Ruf—Schott).

Bohuslav Martinů. *Sonata* (Deiss 1933) 24pp., parts. Allegro poco moderato: octotonic, chromatic, syncopated chords, thin textures prevail. Andante: scalar, staccato octotonic, tremolo; brief cadenza with all instruments participating leads directly to Allegretto: arpeggi and syncopated chordal gestures, trills, shifting accents; Allegro vivo coda. Freely tonal, Neoclassic. M-D.
——. *Sonatine* (Leduc).

Arthur Meulemans. *Sonata* 1954 (CeBeDeM) 25pp., parts. 18 min. Allegro non troppo; Adagio; Allegro. Extension of the Franck-Jongen style; chromatic and with varied idioms and devices. Lack of direction produces a "busy" quality, especially in the first movement. D.

Darius Milhaud. *Sonata* 1914 (Durand) 35pp., parts. Pastoral: easy-flowing, Impressionist, transparent. Vif: rhythmic and motoric; relieved by a Moins vif singing section; only 4 bars of the Vif section return before the Moins vif mood ends the movement. Lent: freely unwinding melodic line, parallelism in piano part, some ostinato treatment, elastic writing. Très vif: motoric opening leads to a dramatic (choral, arpeggi) intrusion; opening mood returns; 5 octave arpeggiated chords interspersed with broken octaves lead to a less active bridge to the coda; a rather strange movement that fortunately sounds better than it looks on the score. M-D.

Jean-Joseph Mondonville. *Sonatinas en Trio* Op.2 1734 (R. Blanchard—Heugel) 103pp., parts. No.3 in Le Pupitre series. Introduction in French. I e: Adagio; Allegro Aria; Presto. 2 B♭: Adagio; Fuga; Gratioso; Allegro. 3 G: Largo; Fuga; Cantabile; Giga. 4 F: Largo; Fuga; Gratioso; Presto. 5 D: Allegro; Fuga; Largo; Allegro. 6 c: Adagio; Fuga; Largo; Allegro.
——. *Sonata* Op.2/3 G (J. Peyrot, J. Rebuffat—Senart 2657) 9pp., parts. Frequent exchanges between all parts, idiomatic and resourceful writing. M-D.
See Edith Borroff, "The Instrumental Works of Jean-Joseph Casanéa Mondonville," 2 vols., Ph.D. diss., University of Michigan, 1958.

Leopold Mozart. *Sonata a 3* IV G (Schenk—OBV) 11pp., parts. Allegro; Adagio (g); Presto. Fine realization. M-D.

Andrzej Nikodemowicz. *Improvvisazione* (PWM 1973) 14pp., 6 min. Part for both violins in one score.

John Christopher Pepusch. *Six Trio Sonatas* 1710 (L. Hoffmann-Erbrecht— Br&H 2001 1954) Vol.I: 18pp., parts. 1 e, 2 g, 3 G. Vol.II: 20pp., parts. 4 B♭, 5 d, 6 F. Excellent keyboard realizations. M-D.

———. *Trio Sonata* C (G. Hausswald—Schott) 9pp., parts. Largo; Allegro; Adagio; Presto. Unobtrusive keyboard realization.

———. *Trio Sonata* D (L. Hoffmann-Erbrecht—K&S) 11pp., parts. No.57 in Organum Series. Preface in German. Largo; Allegro; Adagio; Allegro.

———. *Trio Sonata* F (K&S) 15pp., parts. No.56 in Organum Series. Preface in German. Largo; Allegro; Adagio; Allegro.

———. *Trio Sonata* G (K&S 1961) 8pp., parts. No.61 in Organum Series. Preface in German. Allegro; Adagio; Allegro.

All the *Sonatas* in the Organum Series have stylistically correct keyboard realizations.

———. *Trio Sonata* g (CFP 4556).

Giovanni Battista Pergolesi. *Sonate a Tre* (Gli Amici Della Musica da Camera 1940; Franco Columbo) 136pp. Preface in Italian by F. Caffarelli. 1 G, 2 B♭, 3 c, 4 G, 5 C, 6 E, 7 g, 8 E♭, 9 A, 10 F, 11 d, 12 E, 13 g, 14 C. Most of these *Sonatas* are in 3 movements: fast-slow-fast. Simple and tasteful realizations. M-D.

———. *2 Trio Sonatas* (T. W. Weiner—Nag 107) 16pp., parts. Preface in German. 5 c: Allegro; Adagio; Allegro. 10 E♭: Allegro non tanto; Andantino; Allegro fugato.

———. *Trio Sonata* I G (Riemann—Br&H).

———. *Trio Sonata* III G (CFP 4888A).

———. *Trio Sonata* IV B♭ (CFP 4888B).

———. *Trio Sonata* C (CFP 4557).

Henry Purcell. *Music for Strings and Keyboard* (Nov). Reprint from the complete edition published as a practical collection for the performer. This volume contains 3-part Pavans, a 4-part Pavan, 3 Overtures, Chacony, and a reconstruction of the *Suite* in G. Separate parts.

———. *Two Trio Sonatas* (H. David—Schott 2312) 20pp., parts. Preface in French, German, and English. 1 g, 2 B♭. Masterful contrapuntal skill, short themes, unique harmonic language with unusual harmonic progressions, deeply expressive. Excellent keyboard realizations. M-D.

———. *Trio Sonatas* (K. Schleifer—CFP 4649A) 1 g, 2 B♭.

———. *Trio Sonatas* (K. Schleifer—CFP 4649B) 3 a, 4 g, Chaconne.

———. *Trio Sonatas* (CFP 4242A) E♭, F ("The Golden Sonata").

———. *Trio Sonatas* (CFP 4242B) D, d.

Johann Joachim Quantz. *Trio Sonata* a (L. Hoffmann-Erbrecht—K&S) 19pp., parts. No.65 in Organum Series. Preface in German. Andante moderato; Allegro; Affettuoso; Vivace. Keyboard realization is stylistically outstanding. M-D.

———. *Trio Sonata* c (Zimmermann).

———. *Trio Sonata* d (Schroeder—Br&H).

———. *Trio Sonata* D (Forberg).

———. *Trio Sonata* D (Ruf—Symphonia SY650).

Jean-Philippe Rameau. *Pièces de Clavecin en Concerts* 1742 (E. Jacobi—Br 1970) 63pp., parts. For violin or flute and viol (gamba) or a second violin and keyboard. See detailed entry under trios for piano, violin, and cello.

Johan Helmich Roman. *Seven Trio Sonatas* (Vretblad—MG).
——. *Six Trio Sonatas* (Vretblad—MG).

Edmund Rubbra. *Fantasy* Op.16 1925 (Lengnick). Loose pastoral SA marked "flowing" in $\frac{6}{8}$ with 3 main subjects treated in a variety of ways. After a codetta the recapitulation begins with the third subject followed by the first 2 subjects. Music dies away to a close. M-D.

Giuseppe Sammartini. *Concerto* I A (H. Illy—Br 1971) No.196 in HM. 40pp., parts. Organ probably works best as solo instrument, but another continuo instrument could also be used. All parts written out. Andante spiritoso; Allegro assai; Andante; Allegro assai. M-D.
——. *Concerto* II (H. Illy—Br HM 197).
——. *Sonata* Op.1/3 E♭ (H. Riemann—IMC).

Cyril Scott. *Sonata* (Elkin 1964) 41pp., parts. Poco tranquillo: flowing, chromatic, rubato. Elegy: alternating chordal figure at beginning used frequently; haunting feeling; parallelism. Finale Frivolo–Energico: rhythmic push throughout; a few rhythmic tricky spots for the pianist; arpeggi figuration introduces the final romp. M-D.

Johann Wenzel Anton Stamitz. *Orchestral Trio* Op.1/1 C (H. Riemann—Br&H) 21pp., parts. Cello ad lib. Allegro; Andante ma non adagio; Menuet; Prestissimo. Over-edited. M-D.
——. *Orchestral Trio* Op.1/2 A (H. Riemann—Br&H) 19pp., parts. Cello ad lib. Allegro assai; Andante poco Adagio; Menuet; Prestissimo. Over-edited. M-D.
——. *Orchestral Trio* Op.1/3 F (H. Riemann—Br&H).
——. *Orchestral Trio* Op.1/4 D (H. Riemann—Br&H).
These pieces provide some interesting music.
——. *Sonata* a 3 G (Moffat—Simrock).

Giuseppe Tartini. *Trio Sonata* Op.8/6 D (E. Schenk—Dob DM 438 1954) 7pp., parts. Preface in German and English. Largo andante; Andante; Presto. A clean edition. M-D.
——. *Trio Sonata* D (H. Dameck—IMC 1943) 8pp., parts. Andante; Menuetto; Allegro assai. Octave bass line in last movement needs careful control. M-D.

Georg Philipp Telemann. *Six Trio Sonatas* (Kolneder—Schott) 2 vols.
——. *Corellisierende Sonaten* (A. Hoffmann—Nag 248 1975) Vol.I: Sonatas F, A, b. Score and parts.
——. *Trio Sonata* a (W. Woehl, rev. W. Lyman—IMC 1952) 12pp., parts. Cello ad lib. Largo; Vivace; Affettuoso; Allegro. M-D.

——. *Trio Sonata* c (W. Woehl, rev. W. Lyman—IMC 1952) 15pp., parts. Cello ad lib. Largo; Vivace; Andante; Allegro. M-D.

——. *Trio Sonata* e (Moffat—Simrock).

——. *Trio Sonata* g (Ruf—Schott).

Antonio Veracini. *Sonata* Op.1 c (Jensen—Augener 7415).

——. *Sonata* Op.1/10 (F. Polnauer—Schott 1973) 16pp., parts. Four movements, slow-fast-slow-fast, using same tonal vocabulary as Veracini's contemporary Corelli. Veracini is a careful craftsman. Distinction between original and editorial markings is shown. Simple continuo realization is effective. Int.

Antonio Vivaldi. *12 Sonate da Camera* Op.1 1705–1709 (W. Upmeyer—Br 351B2) Vol.I: Sonatas in g, e, C, E, F, D; 32pp., parts. Vol.II: Sonatas in E♭, d, A, B♭, b, d. Editorial additions indicated by brackets. Excellent realizations. M-D.

Available separately: Op.1/1 (Peyrot, Rebuffat—Senart 2717). Op.1/2 (Senart 2720). Op.1/3 (Senart 2913). Op.1/4 (Senart 3118).

——. *Two Sonatas* Op.5/5, 6 (Upmeyer—Nag).

——. *Sonata a tre* Op.5/6 g (E. Schenk—Dob DM 418 1949) 6pp., parts. Preface in German and English. Preludio: Rococo theme, rich and expressive harmony. Allemanda: powerful polyphony. Air menuet: profound, shows French spirit. Ternary form (written out) is unusual for the period. M-D.

George Christoph Wagenseil. *Sonata a Tre* Op.1/3 B♭ 1755 (E. Schenk—Dob DM 443 1953) 10pp., parts. Preface in German and English. Allegro; Allegro molto; Minuetto I, II: Molto Allegro. This work illustrates in a charming manner the style and spirit of Austrian Rococo music: graceful themes, preference for repetition of short motifs and for syncopated rhythms, concise form, and witty subtle harmonic language. M-D.

——. *Trio Sonata* F (K. Geiringer—UE 1067-8) 12pp., parts. Preface in German, English, and French. Allegro; Andante; Minuetto; Allegro assai. Editorial additions not indicated. M-D.

Gregorius Joseph Werner. *Sonatina* D (EMB with Dob DM 391 1974) 7pp., parts. Larghetto; Allegro.

——. *Sonatina* F 1759 (EMB with Dob DM 392 1974) 8pp., parts.

——. *Symphoniae sex Senaeque Sonatae* 1735 (R. Moder—Dob DM 401 1971) 20pp., parts. Foreword in German and English. A collection of 6 pairs of works, each pair consisting of a 3-movement *Symphonia* (Spirituoso; Larghetto e sempre piano; Allegro assai) and a 4-movement Sonata da Chiesa (Largo; Allegro; Largo; Allegro). In most of the pairs the *Symphonia* and the *Sonata* are related by key, but each can stand alone, as there is no other cyclic cohesion. The *Symphonias* are fresher sounding and more lively, while the *Sonatas* demonstrate more contrapuntal strictness. M-D.

Trios for Piano(s) and Miscellaneous Strings

Carl Philipp Emanuel Bach. *Six Sonatas* (G. Piccioli—IMC) 16pp., parts. For viola, cello, and piano or for clarinet, bassoon, and piano. I. E♭, Allegretto. 2. E♭, Allegro molto. 3. E♭, Allegro. 4. B♭, Allegro. 5. E♭, Andante. 6. B♭, Allegro. These short pieces sound more like the style of Johann Christian Bach than that of C. P. E. Bach. M-D.

——. *Trio* F (Piccioli—IMC) 12pp., parts. For viola, cello, and piano. Un poco andante; Allegretto; Allegro. Clear and neat realizations. M-D.

Arthur Berger. *Trio* 1972 (Boelke-Bomart) 27pp., parts. 10 min. For piano, guitar, and violin. Includes instructions for performance. One movement, Gentilmente e sotto voce: serial influence, pointillistic, shifting meters, long pedals, varied tempos and moods, repeated accented notes, silent clusters for harmonics, 2 notes prepared with a screw, removed from one pitch during the piece and another pitch is prepared. Grazioso section is dancelike. Final Calmo utilizes long pedals for spread-out sonorities; dolcissimo and *pp* conclusion. Contains some lovely and sensitive sonorities as well as being a thoroughly integrated piece of writing. M-D.

George Frideric Handel. *Double Concerto* C (F. Ronchini—ESC) 20pp., parts. For 2 cellos and piano. Originally for 2 cellos and orchestra. Allegro; Largo; Allegro. Interesting spacing of the cellos. Keyboard reduction is over-edited. M-D.

——. *Sonata* C (Delrieu). For 2 cellos and piano.

——. *Sonata* g (Feuillard—Delrieu). For 2 cellos and piano.

George Frederick McKay. *Suite* (B. Turetzky—McGinnis & Marx 1962) 7pp., parts. For 2 double basses and piano. Night Scene: Impressionist, melody in upper register of piano, thin chordal accompaniment. Canonic Capriccio: piano provides a delicate, thin-textured accompaniment to the 2 double basses in canon. Mother Elephant's Lullaby: moderato espressivo, chordal, added-note technique, unresolved final chord. Folk Dance: rhythmic, modal, clever. Attractive writing throughout entire *Suite*. Int. to M-D.

David Noon. *Fantasy* Op.28 (CF 1974) 26pp. 2 scores necessary for performance. For violin and piano 4-hands. Facsimile of MS.

Claudio Spies. *Viopiacem* 1965 (Bo&H) 12pp., parts. 9 min. For viola, piano, and 2-manual harpsichord. The title is derived from the first syllables of the names of each of the instruments in their order of entry. One player seated on a revolving piano stool can handle both the piano and the harpsichord parts. Twelve-tone, pointillistic, little barring, low registers exploited, complicated rhythms and ensemble problems, long pedals, fascinating sonorities. D.
For a full discussion of this work, see Paul Lansky, "The Music of Claudio Spies: An Introduction," *Tempo* 103 (1972): 38–44.

Antonio Vivaldi. *Six Sonatas* (CFP 4938). For 2 cellos and piano. Many basic patterns are similar but within the restricted framework Vivaldi constantly and delightfully varies the details. M-D.

Trios for Piano, One Stringed Instrument, and One Wind Instrument

Karl Friedrich Abel. *Trio Sonata* C (Möbius—Moeck). For flute, violin, and basso continuo. Weighty slow movement, concentrated treatment of ideas, polished craftsmanship, especially in the ornamentation and articulation. Basso continuo has interesting figurations and rich harmony for the period. M-D.

Dieter Acker. *Glossen, Trio* II (Bo&Bo 1974) 8pp., parts. For clarinet (flute), cello, and piano (harpsichord). Explanations in German and English. Austero; Animato, senza rigore; Faceto, senza rigore; Grave, senza rigore. Meter-free measures, duration in seconds of a section. Clusters, pointillistic, avant-garde.

Jurriaan Andriessen. *Trio* II 1955 (Donemus) 37pp., parts. 12 min. For flute, viola, and piano. Allegro moderato: octotonic 20th-century Alberti bass, chromatic sequence and figuration, repeated harmonic 3rds, dancelike character, bitonal, alternating hands. Andante cantabile con espressione: charming bitonal waltz, short motifs, à la Poulenc. Allegro vivace: expanding intervals, rhythmic, syncopation, running figures tossed from one hand to another, hemiola, acrobatic finish. Subtle French influence. M-D.

Edward Applebaum. *Montages* (JWC 1968) 16pp. 3 copies required for performance. 9 min. For clarinet, cello, and piano. Serial; piano part erupts then holds sustained chords. Thorny ensemble problems. D.

Paul Arma. *Divertimento* II 1951 (EMT 1967) 22pp., parts. 17 min. For piano, flute, and cello. Also available in a version for flute or violin, cello, and harp. Rubato; Con moto, scherzando; Poco lento; Robusto. Chromatic, secco, rhythmic finale, colorful. Certain sections feature 2 of the 3 instruments. M-D.

Richard Arnell. *Trio* Op.64 (Hin) 5 min. For flute, cello, and piano. Eclectic, efficient writing that communicates with its audience immediately. M-D.

Carl Philipp Emanuel Bach. *Trio* I D (IMC). For flute, viola, and piano.
———. *Trio* II a (IMC). For flute, viola, and piano.

——. *Trio* III G (IMC). For flute, viola, and piano.

——. *Trio* W.161 B♭ (L. Landshoff—CFP 4237) 31pp., parts. For flute, violin, and keyboard, or for 2 violins and keyboard; cello part ad lib. Allegro; Adagio ma non troppo (with ad lib cadenza); Allegretto. Tasteful realization. M-D.

——. *Trio* F (IMC). For viola, bassoon, and piano.

——. *Triosonata* D (G. Braun—Hänssler) 28pp., parts. For flute, violin, and piano.

——. *Trio* Sonata W.147 C (Ruf—Br). For flute, violin, and basso continuo.

——. *Trio Sonata* W.148 a (K. Walther—Zimmermann) 14pp., parts. For flute, violin (oboe), and continuo.

Also see listing of trios for piano and 2 violins.

——. *Quartett* W.93 a 1788 (E. F. Schmid—Nag 222; IMC) 19pp., parts. For piano, flute (violin), viola, and cello. Preface in German and English. Andantino; Largo e sostenuto; Allegro assai. In Viennese Classical style, Beethoven-like; keyboard writing has freed itself from thorough-bass principles and is fuller and richer than in earlier works of Bach. Delightful coloristic effects produced between interplay of instruments. M-D.

——. *Quartett* W.94 D 1788 (E. F. Schmid—Nag 223; IMC) 19pp., parts. For flute (violin), viola, cello, and harpsichord (piano). Usually listed as a Trio. Preface in German and English. A bright and ingenious piece. M-D.

——. *Quartett* W.95 D (Schmid—Br 2675). For piano, flute, viola, and cello. Usually listed as a Trio. M-D.

These 3 *Quartetts* are usually listed as Trios.

Johann Christian Bach. *Six Sonatas* Op.2 1764 (Smith—Dob). For flute, cello, and piano. Published separately. Nice runs, hands exchange, a few hand-crossings, fluent passagework. M-D.

——. *Sonata* C (Nagel—Schott). For flute, violin, and piano.

——. *Trio* B♭ (Nagel—WIM). For flute, violin, and basso continuo.

——. *Trio Sonata* B♭ (Koelbel—CFP). For flute, violin, and piano.

——. *Trio* II (Schünemann—K&S). For flute, violin, and piano.

Johann Sebastian Bach. *Three Trio Sonatas* (L. Moyse—GS 45815) 46pp., parts. For flute, violin, and piano; cello ad lib. I. G: Largo; Vivace; Adagio; Presto. II. c: Largo; Allegro; Andante; Allegro. III. G: Adagio; Allegro ma non presto; Adagio e piano; Presto. The fine realizations by the editor are aimed at performance on the piano. M-D to D.

——. *Two Sonatas* C, D (David—Br&H). For flute, violin, and piano.

——. *Trio Sonatas* III G, IV c (Landshoff—CFP). For flute, violin, and keyboard.

——. *Trio Sonata* G (IMC). For flute, violin, and basso continuo. No separate bass part.

——. *Trio Sonata* C (H. Eppstein—Br 1988) 24pp., parts. For flute, violin, and basso continuo. Based upon *Sonata* S.1032 A. Preface in German and English.

Wilhelm Friedemann Bach. *Sonata* B♭ (Seiffert—IMC). For flute, violin, and piano; cello ad lib. Strong motivic process at work; ideas fragmented. Ornaments, rests, and triplets present. M-D.

———. *Sonata* F (Br&VP). For flute, violin, and piano.

———. *Trio* B♭ (Br&H). For flute, violin, and piano; cello ad lib.

Sven-Erik Bäck. *Sentire* 1969 (WH) 7pp. 3 copies necessary for performance. For flute, cello, and piano. Explanations in English. Five short movements. Pianist uses soft vibraphone sticks, hand mutings, and some scratchings on strings. Cleverly put together. M-D.

Béla Bartók. *Contrasts* 1938 (Bo&H) 34pp., parts. 17½ min. For clarinet, violin, and piano. Three movements: 1. Verbunkos (Recruiting Dance), 2. Pihenö (Relaxation), 3. Sebes (Fast Dance). Piano part is antiphonally featured in the second movement. Composed for the combined talents of Benny Goodman and Joseph Szigeti. A display piece for the 3 instruments in a pure Hungarian idiom. Virtuosity required. D.

See K. Grant, "*Contrasts for Violin, Clarinet, and Piano* by Béla Bartók, *The Clarinet* 25 (Feb.-March 1998): 8–10.

Leslie Bassett. *Trio* 1953 (CFE) 36pp., parts. For clarinet, viola, and piano. Adagio: piano figuration serves as main thread of the movement while the other instruments counterpoint against it. Allegretto, ma ben marcato: syncopated dance movement, contrasting quiet sections. Adagio, ma non troppo: strong linear writing for all instruments, buildup of chords from time to time. Allegro moderato: ABA; outer sections use continuous 16th notes and dotted thematic ideas; mid-section employs 8th-note motion with legato themes. Neo-Baroque, freely tonal with chromatic texture, clear tonal centers. M-D.

———. *Trio* 1980 (CFP 66907) 17½ min. For clarinet, violin, and piano. Energetic; Assertive; Lyrical; Reflective; Affirmative. "Each movement picks up some aspect of the ending passage of its predecessor as its own point of departure" (Composer's Note). The work might be considered a duo for the violin and clarinet which often speak homogeneously in contrast to the piano. M-D.

Gustavo Becerra-Schmidt. *Trio* (PAU 1958) 23pp., parts. For flute, violin, and piano. Allegro moderato: octotonic, bitonal textures, open 5ths; large span required. Adagio: extreme registers used, repeated cluster-like chords in accompaniment, sequences. Allegro giusto: contrapuntal, chromatic lines, repeated harmonic 6ths, thin textures, Neoclassic orientation, mildly 20th-century. M-D.

Alfred von Beckerath. *Sonatine* 1937 (Moeck 1018) 11pp., parts. For 2 violins or other treble instruments and piano. See detailed entry under trios for piano and 2 violins.

Ludwig van Beethoven. *Clarinet Trios* (G. Raphael, F. Klugmann—Henle 342 1981, ISMN M-2018-0342-5) 68pp., parts. For clarinet or violin, cello, and piano. *Trio* Op.11 Bb 1798. Allegro con brio: extensive development of contrasting melodic fragments. Adagio: highly ornamented with piano providing the most atmosphere. Finale: 10 undistinguished variations based on a tune from Joseph Weigl's opera *The Corsair. Trio* Op.38 Eb 1802–1803. Arranged by Beethoven from his *Septet* Op.20. Adagio–Allegro con brio; Adagio cantabile; Tempo di Menuetto; Andante con [5] variazioni; Scherzo–Allegro molto e vivace; Andante con moto alla marcia–Presto. M-D. Available separately: Op.11 (Br&H; CFP 7064; GS L1424; CF; Augener 7250d; IMC). Op.38 (IMC).

———. *Trio* WoO37 G 1783 (F. Klugmann, H.-M. Theopold—Henle 343 1981, ISMN M-2018-0643-3) 27pp., parts. For flute, bassoon, and piano. Allegro; Adagio; Thema andante con [7] variazioni. A youthful work favoring the piano that shows a quickly developing concept of chamber music and instrumental interaction. Charming. M-D.

Richard Rodney Bennett. *Commedia* II 1972 (Nov) 16pp., parts. 8½ min. For flute, cello, and piano. Four related sections are bridged by duet or solo passages. D.

Alban Berg. *Adagio* from *Chamber Concerto* (UE 12242 1935) 24pp., parts. 13 min. For violin, clarinet, and piano, arranged by Berg. Full of 12-tone idioms, but technical adroitness is balanced with emotional perception. Heart as well as brain is present. M-D.

Wilhelm Reinhard Berger. *Trio* Op.94 g (Musica Rara 1974; CFP) 55pp., parts. For clarinet, cello, and piano. The pianist is overly worked, with Brahms being the model for this composition. An A clarinet is required for the slow movement, Bb for the other movements. M-D to D.

William Bergsma. *The Voice of the Coelacanth* (Columbia University Music Press 1995) 40pp. 13 min. For horn, violin, and piano. A theme and 10 variations. Solo, duo, and trio combinations are used. M-D.

Lennox Berkeley. *Trio* Op.44 1952 (JWC 1956) 33pp., parts. 26 min. For piano, horn, and violin. Allegro; Lento; Tema and (10) Variations. Neoclassic writing infused with lyrical and gentle, witty elements. Terse and clear forms. D.

Antonio Bertali. *Sonata a 3* a (R. Wigness, R. P. Block—Musica Rara 1975) 8pp., parts. For 2 violins, bassoon (or trombone), and basso continuo.

Thomas Beversdorf. *Suite* 1947 (IU) 30pp., parts. For clarinet, cello, and piano. Andante: piano opens in octotonic treatment of the main diatonic idea; triplets follow, interspersed with octaves; trills; open sonorities. Allemande: chromatic, 16th-note figuration, repeated octaves and patterns. Sarabande: piano provides chords that bind together the 2 other instruments; G closing. Menuetto I: fugal. Menuetto II: more imitation, DC Menuetto I. Gigue: rhythmic drive; chords and runs bounce along at a sprightly pace. A fine Neoclassic *Suite*. M-D.

Heinrich Ignaz Franz von Biber. *Sonata a 3* (Kanetzky—Musica Rara). For 2 violins, trombone, and continuo.

Karl-Birger Blomdahl. *Trio* (Schott 10508 1956) 36pp., parts. For clarinet, cello, and piano. Tranquillo: serial; opening quiet sonorities soon explode; leads to a moderato, fluente e grazioso that develops with thin textures, imitation, independent octave lines; spins itself out to a whisper. Tranquillo, ma non troppo lento: thicker sonorities for the piano with help of the pedal; chromatic lines unravel. Allegro giocoso: rhythmic and light; short repetitive patterns grow to climax and subito drop back to *pp;* same procedure is followed again freely reworked. Tranquillo: similar to opening; piano finishes alone. M-D to D.

Philipp Friedrich Böddecker. *Sonata* sopra "La Monica" 1651 (K&S). For violin, bassoon, and keyboard. Four variations on the binary tune "La Monica." Violin repeats tune while the bassoon creates elaborate variations. M-D.

Sebastian Bodinus. *Sonata* E♭ (Vieweg 193). For 2 oboes or flutes, cello, and basso continuo. Slow; Fast; Siciliana. Strong harmonies and lines, clear forms. M-D.

András Borgulya. *Trio* 1964 (EMB 1974) 15pp., parts. For piano, clarinet, and violin.
——. *Trio* (Gen). For flute, violin, and piano.

Johannes Brahms. *Trio* Op.40 E♭ 1865 (Br&H; CFP 3899b; Augener 5117; IMC; K). For horn, violin, and piano. Andante: quiet; in a 5-part form (not SA) with 2 contrasting themes that alternate; fluid and melancholy writing. Scherzo: wonderful energy and driving rhythm. Adagio mesto: sustained, deeply emotional; the recapitulation is one of Brahms's greatest. Finale–Allegro con brio: beautifully prepared for in the Adagio; has characteristics of a bouncing hunt. D.
——. *Trio* Op.114 a 1891 (M. Steegmann, H.-M. Theopold—Henle 322 1979, ISMN M-2018-0322-7; Br&H; CFP 3899E; K; IMC). For clarinet, cello, and piano. Allegro: SA; piano adds rhythmic punctuation along with thorough participation; broad Romantic writing. Adagio: elegiac theme; beautiful coloring of the instruments produces wonderful harmonies. Andantino: a minuet with 2 trios; ingenious scoring. Finale: SA, alternates $\frac{2}{4}$ and $\frac{6}{8}$ meter. D.

Benjamin Britten. *Gemini Variations* Op.73 (Faber F014 1965). Quartet for 2 or 4 players for violin, flute, and piano 4-hands. If 2 players are used, performed by flute and piano, or by violin and piano. Twelve variations and fugue on an Epigram (musical piece) by Kodály. M-D.

Max Bruch. *Eight Pieces* Op.83 (MMP), parts. For clarinet, viola (cello), and piano. In 2 volumes. I: 1. Andante, 2. Allegro con moto, 3. Andante con moto, 4. Allegro agitato. II: 5. Romanian Melody, 6. Nachtgesang (Nocturne), 7. Allegro vivace, ma non troppo, 8. Moderato. Delightful short works exploring worlds of tonal color and musicality. May be performed individually or in groups. Clarinet part may be performed by violin (part included). M-D.

Rudolph Bubalo. *Soundposts* (Ludwig 1975) 15pp., parts. 6½ min. For violin, clarinet, and piano. Part of the Cleveland Composers Guild publication series.

Barney Childs. *Trio* 1972 (Basheva Music). Also contained in Vol.4 of American Society of University Composers Journal of Music Scores. 10pp. For clarinet, cello, and piano. Cello opens, inflects quarter tones; piano enters lyric and drowsy with pedal; repeated patterns. Vertical alignment of parts is unimportant except where specifically cued: "Play your own tempo, ignore other players." "Stemless pitches once each only, in given order at any point during time of bar, any rhythms." Contains harmonics, long pedals. Piece fades out, and the performers all read listed poetry on cue. Avant-garde. M-D.

Muzio Clementi. *Trio* Op.22/1 D (I. Sauer, U. Hamest, H. Meier—Müller 1972) 21pp., parts. For flute, cello, and piano. Violin can replace flute. Based on an 1809 André edition. Allegro di molto: SA; piano shares greatly in melodic material in addition to providing rhythmic (broken octaves, triplets, etc.) interest. Allegretto innocente: charming ideas, Minore mid-section. Finale–Vivace assai: dancelike, unusual modulations, 3rd relationships, brilliant conclusion. Classical style with thin textures throughout. Int. to M-D.

Dinos Constantinides. *Trio No. 3* 1995 (Conners 26A 1995) 37pp., parts. 17 min. For violin, clarinet, and piano. I. Study III; II. Finale. "*Trio No. 3* is based on a folk-like modal tune that highlights the Greek heritage of the composer. This tune appears as a solo passage on the clarinet at the beginning. Parts of the tune and the intervals of fourths and fifths are worked out in various ways throughout the piece, thus creating new tonal possibilities . . . The first movement can be performed as a separate piece under the title *Study III*" (from Preface). M-D to D.

———. *The Oracle at Delphi (Study III)* 1994 (Conners 26 1994) 19pp., parts. 9 min. For violin, clarinet, and piano. Became Mvt.1 in the *Trio No. 3*. Also available for violin, flute or oboe, and piano (Conners 244).

———. *Dream* (Conners 78). For oboe, bassoon or cello, and piano. See detailed entry under trios for piano and 2 miscellaneous woodwinds.

François Couperin. *Concerts Royaux* 1722 (D. Lasocki—Musica Rara 1974). For flute (oboe), violin (viola da gamba), and basso continuo. Vol.I: 8pp., 3 parts. Vol.II: 11pp., 2 parts. Vol.III: 16pp., 3 parts. Vol.IV: 14pp., 3 parts. These pieces are really "French" Suites of dances with Italian influence seen in the lyrical structure of their melodies. No instruments were specified in the original editions. Contains groups of contrasting, charming airs and dances. Beautiful, pliant, and full of iridescent writing. This edition is helpful concerning problems of French ornamentation. Interesting continuo realizations.

Paul Creston. *Partita* Op.12 1938 (MCA) 46pp., parts. For flute, violin, and piano or for 2 violins and piano. Originally for flute, violin, and string orchestra. Piano reduction by Creston. Preamble; Sarabande; Burlesk; Air; Tarantella. Early 20th-century treatment of Baroque and dance forms. M-D.

———. *Suite* Op.56 1953 (SP 1972) 66pp., parts. 25 min. For flute, viola, and piano. Prelude; Quasi-Sarabande; Scherzino; Arioso; Rondo. A well-contrasted work written in a grateful, mildly 20th-century style that is extremely pianistic. Rich harmonies and strong melodic writing add to its effectiveness. Large span required. M-D to D.

George Crumb. *Vox Balaenae for Three Masked Players* 1971 (CFP) 10pp., parts. 18 min. For electric (electrically amplified) flute, electric piano, and electric cello. Vox Balaenae (Voice of the Whale) was inspired by the singing of the humpback whale. Performers should wear black half-masks throughout the performance of the work. They are intended to give a symbolic representation of the powerful impersonal forces of nature (nature dehumanized). All 3 instruments are electrically amplified with a minimum of distortion. Thorough performance directions are included. Pianist needs a paper clip, chisel, and solid glass rod, and harmonics are called for. A suggested form for program listing is: Vocalise (. . . for the beginning of time): flutist sings and plays the notes simultaneously; Variations on Sea-Time; Sea-theme; Archeozoic (Var.I) Proterozoic (Var.II); Paleozoic (Var.III); Mesozoic (Var.IV); Cenozoic (Var.V); Sea-Nocturne (. . . for the end of time). A tightly unified work with some incredible sonorities, slow pacing throughout. Avant-garde. D.

Nathan Currier. *Adagio and Variations* 1989 (TP). 33½ min. For clarinet, violin, and piano. Theme and 26 variations. The composer notes that the work derives its "formal and emotional thrust from the disparateness and relationships between two thematic areas—the first being an original movement, heard at the outset, and the second being Binchois' chanson, *De plus en plus,* finally presented near the work's end. The piece comprises, in fact, two simultaneous variation series, one treating of the original material, gradually dissected in its course, the second concerned with the Binchois, which comes into being—as the chanson's text would have it—*more and more*" (from Program Insert, *The Making of a Medium: Music Written for the Verdehr Trio,* Vol.3, Cristal CD743, 1994). M-D.

Thomas Christian David. *Schubertiade* 1987 (Dob). 13½ min. For clarinet, violin, and piano. Introduction, theme, and variations composed in the style of Schubert. Charming, melodic, and rhythmically stimulating. M-D.

Norman Dello-Joio. *Trio* 1944 (CF). For flute, cello, and piano. Unpretentious writing with spirit and grace and clear formal structures. Key signature for each movement but free modulation is frequent. Vivacious rhythmic usage. D.

Peter Dickinson. *American Trio (Hymns, Rags and Blues)* 1985 (Nov 120771 1995, ISBN 0-85360-525-4) 44pp., parts. For violin, clarinet, and piano. Commences "with three hymn-tunes, two remembered from my childhood and one invented. These hymn-tunes were converted unrecognisably into blues— one for each of the instruments involved—and the hymn-tunes also form (more recognisably) a section each of a classical rag, called Hymn-Tune Rag, in the pattern A-A-B-B-C-C-A. The rag style I chose is deliberately pre-jazz and follows quite closely the style of blind, white, Tennessee composer, Charles Hunter (1876–1906)" (from Composer's Note). The design of the *Trio* is in 8 sections mixing rags, blues, and cadenzas settings. M-D to D.

Friedheim Döhl. *Sotto Voce* 1973 (Gerig) 20pp. For flute, cello, and piano. 3 scores required for performance. Explanations in German and English. Avant-garde.

Pierre Max Dubois. *Suite* 1968 (Maurer) 28pp., parts. Photostat of MS. For piano, violin, and clarinet.

Maurice Duruflé. *Prélude, Récitatif et Variations* Op.3 1928 (Durand) 27pp., parts. 11 min. For flute, viola, and piano. Parallel chords, arpeggi figuration, subtle syncopation, crossed hands, varied tempos. Folklike tune is basis for the 4 variations and extensive closing section. In style of Fauré and Ravel; strong colors. M-D to D.

Johann Ladislav Dussek. *Grand Sonata* Op.65 F 1808 (D. Lasocki—Musica Rara 1975) 45pp., parts. For flute, cello, and piano. Preface in English. One of Dussek's finest chamber works. First movement presents a lovely melodious opening idea; a colorful and varied harmonic scheme in the development is especially unusual. The second movement, a Larghetto, is mainly notable for its lyrical beauty and versatile and imaginative use of small motifs. The opening four bars of the Rondo are based on dominant-7th harmony, which sounded very fresh at the time it was written; the rest of the movement unfolds naturally and effectively. Although built around the piano, the entire work shows a fine awareness of chamber music dialogue and counterpoint. M-D.

———. *Notturno Concertante* Op.68 (C. D. S. Field—Br 1972) 44pp., parts. 4pp. of notes. For piano, violin, and horn (viola). Mainly a brilliant duo for piano and violin with horn accompaniment. Long rondo (424 bars) is followed by a shorter minuet and trio. Broad cantabile melodies, arpeggiated accompaniment, colorful modulations—all molded into a lyrical and dramatic piece of Romantic writing. Viola part is provided by editor as an alternate to the horn. Articulation and dynamics are discussed in the Preface. D.

Anton Eberl. *Grand Trio* Op.36 E♭ (H. Voxman—Musica Rara 1973) 44pp., parts. For piano, clarinet, and cello. Dramatic, long lines, unusual harmonic shifts. Form is well developed; piano is the most important part. Probably one of the most valuable Trios in this combination written during the Classical period. M-D.

Halim El-Dabh. *Thulathiya* 1955 (CFP) 7½ min. For viola, oboe, and piano. Thoroughly original in its Eastern inflection, ingenious timbers, highly logical dissonance. M-D.

Richard Faith. *Trio* 1967 (IU) 65pp., parts. For piano, violin, and horn. Moderato: contrasted ideas, chromatic. Andante espressivo: piano treated more harmonically. Allegro scherzando: some meter changes, rhythmic subtleties. Presto: alternating hands, requires strong fingers. Neoclassically oriented. D.

———. *Fantasy Trio No. 1* (IU) 32pp., parts. 12 min. For piano, violin, and clarinet. Andantino, espressivo—Allegro: commences with solo clarinet to introduce the main theme, followed by lively $\frac{5}{8}$ in playful character; ternary form. Vivace: $\frac{3}{8}$ dancelike quality camouflaged by long flowing lines and motivic development. A reviewer for the *Washington Post* noted that the work is a "highly romantic piece of music, the success of which lies in the composer's evident understanding of the strengths of the individual instruments, and in his ability to create music that shows those strengths to the greatest advantage. The work is full of drama and tension, with beautifully etched phrases and sweeping lines. It is also based so solidly in the romantic tradition that you would think it has been part of the standard repertoire for many years" (from *The Ensemble da Camera of Washington,* Program Notes, Vernissage Records VR1019CD 1994 [p.3]). This is a work which deserves to be better known. M-D.

Morton Feldman. *Durations* III 1962 (CFP 6903) 6pp., parts. For piano, tuba, and violin. Instruments begin simultaneously and are then free to choose their own durations within a given general tempo. The sounds themselves are designated. Sonorities are thinned and thickened, thereby keeping the basic image intact. Avant-garde. M-D.

Benjamin Frankel. *Trio* Op.10 (Augener). For clarinet, cello, and piano. Written in a sustained and intensely introspective melancholy style. Has an affinity with Ernest Bloch. Displays great technical versatility and eclecticism. Freely tonal with much dissonance. D.

Paul Walter Fürst. *Petitionen* Op.51 (Dob 1975) 17pp., parts. For piano, clarinet, and viola. Allegro assai; Langsam; Improvisierend–Langsam; Vivace; Langsam–Allegro. Neoclassic, bitonal, parallel chords, cluster harmonics and clusters, glissando, mildly 20th-century. M-D.

Johann Joseph Fux. *Sonata a Tre* d (Hillemann—Heinrichshofen). For flute, violin, and piano. Polyphonic lines are beautifully woven into a fine texture for all 3 instruments. M-D.

Hans Gál. *Trio* Op.49b 1948 (OBV) 16pp., parts. See detailed entry under trios for piano, violin, and cello.

——. *Trio* Op.97 (Simrock Elite Edition 3145 1971) 32pp., parts. For piano, clarinet, and violin. Moderato assai; Andantino capriccioso poco sostenuto; Tema con Variazioni. Written in a fairly accessible style with no 20th-century "Second Viennese School" accoutrements. Freely tonal, mildly 20th-century, and "sounds" well. M-D.

Philippe Gaubert. *Serenade* F (R. Cavally—ST 649 1988) 15pp., parts. For flute, cello, and piano. No.3 of *Three Water Colors.* Spry, picturesque ternary setting in $\frac{3}{8}$ at Assez vif. Fluid middle section in f♯ gives harplike quality to piano with rapid 32nds in arpeggiated formations and imitative solo lines to others. A delightful piece which deserves to be better known. Large span required. M-D.

Mikhail Glinka. *Trio Pathétique* d 1832. For clarinet, bassoon or cello, and piano. See detailed entry under trios for piano and 2 miscellaneous woodwinds.

Joseph Goodman. *Trio* 1967 (AMP 96528-55) 55pp., parts. 20 min. For flute, piano, and violin. Moderato; Allegro molto; Lento (fugue). The first 2 movements are composed in such a way that formal structures and speeds of development unfold simultaneously on different levels. In the Moderato, 3 levels are formed in this way: flute: Introduction and Rhapsody; violin: SA design; piano: Etude and Trio. In the Allegro molto there are 2 levels, the flute and violin forming one (Rondo à la Tarantella), the piano another (Theme and Variations). Freely tonal, Neoclassic orientation. D.

Louis Haber. *Parade, Blues and Allegro* (Gen 1971) 16pp., parts. For flute, piano, and violin. Parade: clusterlike chords, martial rhythms, bitonal, chords in alternating hands; large span required. Blues: 7th and 9th chords, alternating octaves, octotonic. Allegro: syncopated, subito dynamic changes, imitation, octotonic, arpeggi figuration, contrary chromatic chords. M-D.

John Hall. *Trio* III 1970 (Chappell). 12 min. For violin, horn, and piano. Prelude; Scherzo; Night Interlude; Rondo. Equality of all parts achieved. Changing meters, effective 20th-century treatment. D.

George Frideric Handel. *Kammertrio* VII (M. Seiffert—Br&H). For flute, piano, and violin; cello ad lib. This is Trio-Sonata Op.2/1 c. Over-edited. M-D.

——. *Trio* (Kolneder—Schott). For oboe, violin, and basso continuo.

——. *Trio Sonata* Op.2/5 F (Hinnenthal—Br). For oboe, violin, and basso continuo. M-D.

Roger Hannay. *Fantôme* 1967 (CFP 66486 1976) 22pp., parts. 12 min. For clarinet, viola, and piano. The pianist requires the following auxiliary percussion: 2 xylophone sticks, 2 timpani sticks, 2 wire brushes, metal rod with blunt tip, claves.

Special piano notation indicates fingernail glissando on strings next to piano brace, arm clusters. Long pedals; strings must be struck with hands; sounding board must be tapped through sound hole. Pointillistic, harmonics, cadenza passage, improvisatory section, avant garde. Large span required. D.

John Harbison. *Variations* (AMP 7946-4 1987) 43pp., parts. 22 min. For clarinet in A, violin, and piano. Fifteen variations, finale, and epilogue; commences with Var.1 without a formal introduction of the theme. The composer alternates instrumental combinations, beginning with a duo for violin and clarinet, then piano solo (Var.2), clarinet and piano (Var.3), violin and piano (Var.4), all 3 (Var.5), etc. Includes variations in the form of a fughetta, waltz, passacaglia, and aria. Lengthy finale sums up many of the ideas expressed earlier as if a coda. The quiet, introspective epilogue functions as a final "amen," concluding with a C major chord at *pp*. Straightforward rhythms without complications, with clear lines of development. Harmonic features vary depending upon technical style from variation to variation but tend to be chromatic with a preference for intervals of 2nds, tritones, 6ths, 7ths, octaves, and added-note chords. Large span required. D.

Walter Hartley. *Dance Suite* 1985 (Ethos). 6½ min. For violin, alto sax, and piano.
——. *Lyric Suite* 1993 (To the Fore). 8 min. For viola, tenor sax, and piano.
——. *Reverie and Canonic Scherzo* 2001 (To the Fore). 6 min. For violin, tenor sax, and piano.
——. *Terzetto: Four Pieces for Three Players* 2002 (To the Fore). 9½ min. For violin, tenor sax, and piano.

Franz Joseph Haydn. *Cassation* D H IV: D2 (F. Nagel—Litolff 1973) 20pp., parts. For flute, violin, and piano.
——. *Trio* Op.2/4 (Bergmann—Schott). For flute, violin, and piano; cello ad lib.
——. *Three Trios* (Rampal—IMC). For flute, cello, and piano.
——. *Trio No.29* F (CF) 17pp., parts. For violin or flute, cello or bassoon, and piano. Allegro; Finale–Tempo di Menuetto. First movement contains elaborate figuration, while the last movement is an elegant menuetto. M-D.
——. *Klaviertrio* No.30 D (David—Br&H). For flute, cello, and piano.
——. *Trio No.31* G (CF) 25pp., parts. For flute or violin, cello or bassoon, and piano. Allegro; Andante; Finale–Allegro moderato. Contains some bold modulations. M-D to D.
Nos.29–31 are basically Sonatas for piano with an accompaniment by the other instruments.
——. *Trios* (W. Stockmeier—Henle 284 1976) Vol.III. 67pp., parts. For flute, cello, and piano. Contains *Trio* D Hob. XV:16, *Trio* G Hob. XV:15, *Trio* F Hob. XV:17. It is possible to play all 3 *Trios* replacing the flute part by the violin.

Fingering for the piano part has been added by Jörg Demus. Excellent Urtext and practical edition. M-D.

Paul Hindemith. *Trio* Op.47 1928 (Schott) 12½ min. For viola, heckelphone, and piano. Solo, Arioso, Duette (first movement): opens with a 3-part invention-like section; followed by a slow arioso for heckelphone and piano inspired by a fragment from the Solo; leads to the lively Duette: viola and heckelphone accompanied canonically by the piano. Potpourri: 4 sections all thematically independent. One of Hindemith's most important chamber works, too seldom heard. D.

Mogens Winkel Holm. *Transitions* II (WH 4256 1973) 43 loose leaves. 3 copies necessary for performance. For flute, cello, and piano. This entire work is to be played *pp.* It is a series of repetition and shifting principles, and the effects of these in interplay between the instruments. "The music could perhaps be compared to three sonorous whirls or spirals that move, quietly interlocking, by turning about themselves a couple of times in slow motion. This demands a certain amount of the performers. Perhaps first and foremost what one could call unshakable confidence in an 'a-personal' form of expression, a *non-espressivo,* in which the musician, instead of seeking solo brilliance, balances and interlaces the sound in order to achieve a perfect blend between the instruments (not more than *pp*), aiming at 'objective' phrasing without crescendo, stringendo, vibrato and other so-called expressive effects. I would like a great deal of the strength of the work to lie in these omissions" (from Foreword). Score is printed on separate pages to help solve page turning. Atonal, pointillistic, many repeated notes, tremolo, complex rhythms, alternating hands, avant-garde. Requires great control. D.

Arthur Honegger. *Petite Suite* 1934 (Philharmusica 1974). See detailed entry under trios for piano and 2 violins. Int. to M-D.

Katherine Hoover. *Images* 1981 (Papagena) 14 min. For clarinet, violin, and piano. Allegro; Variations on a Colonial Hymn; Allegro vivace. "*Images* . . . has to do with the way various images—or themes—are changed in the process of thinking. The first movement is concerned with two very distinct ideas that eventually interact and affect each other. The second movement is a set of six variations on a somewhat somber colonial American hymn, *God of My Justice.* The third begins with similar themes which eventually agree to a separation. It also contains hints of *It Ain't Necessarily So,* which is finally quoted at the end" (from Program Insert, *The Verdehr Trio: Trios for Violin, Clarinet and Piano,* Leonard CD LE326, 1988, p.7). M-D.

Alan Hovhaness. *Lake Samish* Op.415 1988 (Hovhaness-Fujihara). 17 min. For clarinet, violin, and piano. Andante–Fugue; Allegro; Andante maestoso; Adagio misterioso–Allegro giusto; Aria and Jhala. Contrasts peaceful, lyric qualities with polymodality, clashing harmonies, and a hymnlike character. Uses a wide variety of compositional techniques. Lake Samish is near Bellingham, Washington. M-D.

Klaus Huber. *Ascensus* (Ars Viva No.1979) 3 playing scores (piano has 31pp., flute and cello each have 23pp.). Instructions in German. Avant-garde.

Johann Nepomuk Hummel. *Adagio, Variations and Rondo on 'Schöne Minka'* Op.78 1819 (N. Delius—Musica Rara 1968; B. Pauler—Amadeus 1975) 30pp., parts. For flute, cello, and piano. Introduction; Thema, 7 Variations and Finale. Facile writing by a skilled hand, with the piano being especially favored. Treatment of the variations might be considered shallow, but it is at least superficially effective. M-D.

Jacques Ibert. *Aria* (Leduc 1930, 1931) 4 min. Two transcriptions from the original for voice and piano: (1) flute, violin, and piano, probably by Ibert himself, and (2) violin (flute or oboe), cello (or clarinet), and piano, by Arthur Hoérée. Uses imitation in a melodious setting. M-D.

Andrew Imbrie. *Serenade* 1952 (SP). 40pp. 20 min. For flute, viola, and piano. Lively ideas with clear shape and direction, chromatic, lyric and expressive. Rhythmic vitality, rich and inventive harmonic texture. Large-scale formal logic; clever interplay of motifs; concludes with a slow movement whose mood lives on after the music has ended. D.

———. *To a Traveler* 1971 (SP) 24pp., parts. 9 min. For piano, violin, and clarinet. Takes its title from Rexroth's translation of a poem by Su Tung P'o. "From a very quiet, transparently scored introduction, two chief melodic ideas soon emerge; the first for clarinet, the second, a little faster, for violin. This general rise in energy and pace is carried further by the passage which follows and moves to a rapid climax through the use of quickly moving figurations. The texture suddenly dissolves and the initial quiet motion is resumed. The much faster tempo and agitated figuration soon re-assert themselves, and they lead to an extended development. This culminates in a kind of brief cadenza for all three instruments at a still faster tempo. The effect of this is to consume most of the remaining energy, allowing for a final return to the peaceful character of the introduction, which is now combined with the reminiscent strains of the clarinet playing an expanded version of its original melody" (from the score). Long pedals, chromatic motifs, chords with four different dynamic levels, tremolando effects, cluster-like chord at conclusion. Large span required. D.

Vincent d'Indy. *Trio* Op.29 B♭ 1887 (Durand; Hamelle; IMC) 66pp., parts. For clarinet, cello, and piano. Ouverture: B♭; second section in F♯; third section in A♭; followed by a bridge theme with further modulations and then returns to B♭. Divertissement: E♭, has 2 Intermèdes with the second in e. Chant élégiaque:

Db, ABA, expressive melody. Finale: Bb, rondo, highly pianistic. D'Indy's first mature chamber work. The cyclic principle unifies the work remarkably well, and it is beautifully laid out for the pianist. D.

Charles E. Ives. *Largo* 1901–1902 (PIC 1953) 8pp., parts. For clarinet, cello, and piano. Broken chords over ostinato-like bass, freely tonal. Quasi allegretto section elaborates the bass line with cross-accents; full chords in right hand; climax; ritard; and returns to opening idea. Ends on a G triad with an added bb. M-D.

Wolfgang Jacobi. *Trio* 1946 (Edition Kasparek) 26pp., parts. 17 min. For flute, violin, and piano. Allegro; Larghetto; Fugue–Allegro. Neo-Baroque style, similar to Hindemith. M-D.

Knud Jeppesen. *Little Summer Trio* 1957 (WH 4016) 26pp., parts. 15 min. For flute, cello, and piano. Violin can be substituted for flute. Allegretto leggiero: sprightly, freely tonal, G key signature, passages in 10ths, contrasted lines, witty. Adagio: lyrical, centers around D, chromatic, syncopated pedal point closing. Allegro animato: jaunty rhythms, thin-textured opening, becomes more chordal, some imitation; a good-humored finale. Infused with Impressionist tendencies; mildly 20th-century harmonies. M-D.

Tom Johnson. *Composition with Descending Chromatic Scale in Eight-Voice Canon Played in Three Ways, Separated by Two Piano Interludes, Which Bring the Music Back Up to Its Starting Position* 1992 (Editions 75 1992) 9pp. 6 min. 3 copies necessary for performance. For clarinet, violin, and piano. Title says it all. The 2 piano interludes are actually one and the same, played twice, the ascending chromatic scale implied in the title, only expanding into chords and then returning to a single note. "From the concert of the London-based Balanescu-Heaton-Preuslin Trio, the 'Composition with descending . . . ' of Tom Johnson must be mentioned, because his minimalistic counting music always raises ones spirits in Darmstadt" (Gisela Gronemeyer and Reinhard Oehlschlägel, *MusikTexte*, December 1992, quoted in Postface). M-D.

Robert Kelly. *Introduction and Dialogue* Op.20 1951 (ACA) 20pp., parts. 8 min. For horn, cello, and piano. Tonal with touches of bitonality; no key signature. Introduction: uses a modified version of the spiritual *Were You There* and freely expressive rhythms with only one or 2 instruments playing at a time. Dialogue: uses themes reminiscent of early American folk material with strong rhythms in intense ensemble playing and sharply contrasting articulations; ends quietly on G major chord. D.

Harrison Kerr. *Trio* 1936 (Merion) 22pp., parts. For clarinet, cello, and piano. Allegro; Largo; Vivace–Scherzando; Allegro Vivace–quasi presto. Chromatic, quartal harmonies, dissonant counterpoint especially in the third movement, parallel chords, changing meters. Twelve-tone influence present but not used in a strict sense. Kerr is basically a Romantic, and that quality is never entirely lost in this work. M-D to D.

Aram Khachaturian. *Trio* 1932 (CFP; Bo&H; MCA; Musica Rara; Anglo-Soviet Press; IMC) 41pp., parts. 16 min. For clarinet (or viola), violin, and piano. Andante con dolore, con molto espressione: begins in g, ends in c; a poetic duet between the clarinet (imitating a *zurna,* a Transcaucasian wind instrument) and the violin while the piano mainly supports. Allegro: dance rhythms, transparent tonal coloring. Moderato: a set of variations based on an Uzbek folk tune; colorful harmonic and timbre contrasts. The composer's stylistic idiosyncrasies are already stamped on this early work, which explores most of the keyboard. M-D to D.

Karl Kohn. *Trio* 1972 (CF 1975) 26pp., parts. 16 min. For violin, horn, and piano. Corrente; Aria; Ripresa; Rondo. Facsimile edition.

Franz Koringer. *Sonata Profana 5:* quasi divertimento ungherese (L. Krenn 1974) 22pp., parts. 10 min. For clarinet, viola, and piano.

Johann Krebs. *Trio* e 1743 (F. Nagel—Müller). Four movements. For 2 flutes and piano; second flute part can be played on oboe or violin. M-D.

Ernst Křenek. *Trio* 1946 (AMP 1955) 15pp., parts. For violin, clarinet, and piano. Allegretto moderato comodo; Allegro agitato–Allegro deciso–Andante. Partial 12-tone technique incorporated into Křenek's spiky style; varied figuration and rhythmic treatment. Last movement is highly sectionalized. M-D.

Konradin Kreutzer. *Trio-Grande Sonate* Op.28/2 G (I. Sauer, U. Harnest, H. Meier —Müller 2064 SM 1972) 56pp., parts. For piano, flute, and cello. Allegro con moto; Adagio; Finale. Kreutzer had a distinguished reputation in Germany during the 19th century, but this work shows more skill and experience than inspiration. Traditional classic idioms and techniques are used. M-D.

Rudolphe Kreutzer. *Trio* Op.28/2 G (Müller). For flute, cello, and piano. Viennese Classical style, Beethoven influence noted, not especially idiomatic. M-D.

Friedrich Kuhlau. *Trio Concertante* Op.119 G (Simrock). For flute, cello, and piano. Strong melodies, reminiscent of Schubert and Weber, independent parts, forceful command of formal structures. M-D.

Kenneth Leighton. *Fantasy on an American Hymn Tune* Op.70 1974 (Nov). 18 min. For clarinet, cello, and piano. Contrasting mood changes, jazz influence, Ives-like sonorities in the simple melody and Impressionist chordal treatment. M-D.

John Lessard. *Trio* (Gen 1968) 31pp., parts. For flute, cello, and piano. Allegretto: freely tonal, serial influence, thin textures contrasted with fuller sonorities; large span required. Lento: chordal punctuation, dry staccato treatment in lower register. Andante: chordal, sustained, contrasted with short fragments. Presto: fugal textures, Neoclassic orientation. M-D.

Ernst Levy. *Trio* 1968 (Seesaw) 17pp., parts. For clarinet, viola, and piano. Andante: sustained octave syncopation, chromatic patterns. Moderato: octotonic, quartal and quintal harmonies, chromatic inner voices. Moderato: transfer of line between instruments, chromatic 16ths, sequence; gradually unwinds to a *ppp* conclusion. Moderato: solo piano elaborates previous ideas. Presto: similar to earlier material, upper register, fugal, left hand broken-octave pattern in low register. Mildly 20th-century. M-D.

———. *Second Trio* 1970 (MS at LC) 36pp., parts. For clarinet, cello, and piano. Four untitled movements in a freely tonal, highly chromatic style. Unusual symbols used are explained on final page. More dissonance here than in the first *Trio.* M-D to D.

Robert Hall Lewis. *Trio* 1966 (Dob 1974) 20pp., parts. 10 min. For violin, clarinet, and piano. "[My] earlier music was concerned with a basic linear-developmental process in the serial manner. In recent years I have abandoned this approach for a music embracing larger and more varied conceptual gestures. Hence, the interplay of continuity-discontinuity, subtle contrasts of timbre and rhythm, and structural flexibility are more characteristic of my present style" (DCM, 423). This atonal work is in one movement and contains cadenza-like passages for the 3 instruments. Similar texture throughout. Varied tempos, meters, melody, and rhythm do not display much continuity, and many notes have to be scrambled for! On p.13, right hand in piano part requires a bass clef, not a treble clef. D.

Lowell Liebermann. *Trio* I (TP 114-41253). For flute, cello, and piano.
———. *Trio* II Op.77 2001 (TP 114-41255). 15 min. For flute, cello, and piano. Opening Allegro requires an intense bundle of energy for dramatic and lyric exchange of musical ideas; canonic. Sicilienne juxtaposes ethereal-like piano to other instruments. Adagio opens with recitative which yields to a steady, marked pulse and extended crescendo; more explorative harmonically than preceding movements. Concluding Allegro-like finale is passionate with intense passagework resulting in a thrilling tour de force. D.

György Ligeti. *Trio* 1982 (Schott), parts. 21½ min. For horn, violin, and piano. Andantino con tenerezza; Vivacissimo molto ritmico; Alla marcia; Lamento–Adagio. "This trio bears the inscription 'Hommage à Brahms' and, given time and exposure, could possibly become the twentieth century equivalent of the Brahms trio in the literature for this ensemble. As part of the tribute to Brahms, Ligeti wrote numerous passages that are to be played without the use of valves in the manner of the waldhorn for which Brahms wrote. . . . although Ligeti's trio is one of great difficulty, it is a masterpiece and should be performed with much greater frequency" (from Patrick Miles, "A Bibliography of Trios for

Horn, Violin, and Piano Composed 1945–1985 with Selected Annotations," *Horn Call Annual* no. 6 [1994]: 24). D.

Otto Luening. *Trio* 1973 (CFP) 39pp., parts. For flute, cello, and piano. Shifting meters, freely tonal, pointillistic, 7 with 5, arpeggi figuration, clusters, tremolo, strong individual writing, some Neoclassic characteristics. M-D.

————. *Trio* II (Highgate 1974) 22pp., parts. For flute, violin, and piano; cello or bassoon, ad lib. Larghetto; Allegro; Largo; Allegro. Freely tonal, tertial harmony, shifting meters, free counterpoint, highly expressive Largo, interesting triplet use in finale. A very beautiful and flowing work. M-D.

Elisabeth Lutyens. *Horai* Op.67/4 1968 (Olivan Press 1968), parts. 16½ min. For violin, horn, and piano. Eclectic, in one extended movement.

Donald Martino. *Trio* 1959 (ECS 2069 1970; Dantalian 528 1998) 24pp., parts. 13 min. For violin, piano, and clarinet. Seven contrasting sections to be felt as a unit and played without pause. Six varied types of attack are included as well as a description of special signs. Also includes "Special Notes to the Pianist." Dynamic extremes, pointillistic, tightly organized, plucked and damped strings, clusters, Expressionist. D.

Bohuslav Martinů. *Madrigal Sonata* 1936 (AMP) 28pp., parts. 9 min. For piano, flute, and violin. Poco allegro; Moderato. Piano has largest share of the chromatic neo-Romantic writing. Syncopation in certain spots will require the most careful counting by all performers. Virtuosic and dramatic treatment. D.

————. *Sonata* 1936 (Br 3326 1959) 36pp., parts. For piano, violin, and flute. Allegro poco moderato: freely tonal, rhythmic drive, chromatic runs with chords, chordal syncopation, octotonic, cross-rhythms. Adagio: sustained and expressive; large span required. Allegretto (Scherzo): piano has rhythmic introduction with a bouncy left hand, chords in alternating hands, solo piano episode, varied gestures in coda. D.

————. *Trio* F 1944 (AMP) 44pp., parts. 19 min. For flute, cello (or viola), and piano. Poco allegretto; Adagio; Andante–Allegretto scherzando. Essentially conservative writing in a whimsical mood. Transparent and concentrated lyricism. D.

Karl Julius Marx. *Trio* Op.61 (Hänssler 16.014 1972) 36pp., parts. For flute, cello, and piano. Fantasia; Scherzo; Introduzione e Rondo. Coherent whole, mildly 20th-century writing, instruments treated equally. Scherzo would make a fine encore or short movement; a fine contribution to the limited repertoire. M-D.

Toshiro Mayuzumi. *Metamusic* (CFP 1964) 2pp., parts. For piano, violin, and saxophone. "This piece is to be performed *only on the stage,* as the piece has been written for both visual and acoustic effects. None of the parts (scores) is connected at any point with any of the other parts. Each performer is to play his part independently, though the performances should be started at the same time. The total duration of the performance may be decided freely by the performers. Namely, the piece can be played as a whole, in repetitions, or in part, according to the performers' desire" (from the Composer's Instructions for Performance). The pianist uses clusters; must shut the keyboard lid with a bang and get up, then sit down slowly and open it again. Everything must be performed as written *but only with animated gestures and without any sound!* Exceptions are the clusters, pizzicati, and the banging of the keyboard lid. Avant-garde.

John McCabe. *Dance Movements* 1967 (Nov 1967). For horn, violin, and piano. Plenty of dissonance in the piano part. A Lento moderato provides a quiet opening, followed by contrasting quick, slow, quick movements. A final upward rush of scale figuration concludes the piece. D.

——. *Sonata* (Nov 1969). For clarinet, cello, and piano. One continuous movement. Well constructed; very effective vivo section. Pianist is required to strike strings with rubber beaters and to pluck them. M-D.

Wilfred Mellers. *Trio* 1962 (Nov) 23pp., parts. For flute, cello, and piano. Eclogue: changing meters, freely tonal, skipping harmonic 6ths, chromatic figuration, trills. Estampie: quick and rhythmic, chords in alternating hands, melodic emphasis in sections, harmonics. Threnody: cantabile, chordal sonorities, involved rhythms, melodic *pp* closing. Mildly 20th-century style throughout. M-D.

Pavle Merkù. *Astrazioni* Op.23 1956 (Društvo Slovenskih Skladateljev 1963) 25pp., parts. For clarinet, cello, and piano. Introduzione Allegretto: short figures, freely tonal, sustained section leads to fugato textures, rhythmic conclusion. Contrasto–Allegro non troppo: chromatic harmonic 3rds in ostinato-like patterns in an 8-bar group; this grouping evolves through various (5) treatments. Distensione–Lento: further elaboration on Introduzione opening short figures. Conclusione–Allegro mosso: incisive rhythmic treatment, hemiola, chromatic triplets, marcato and crescendo to final *ff* conclusion. A folk flavor permeates this mildly 20th-century work. M-D.

Georges Migot. *Le Livre des Danceries* 1929 (Leduc) 37pp., parts. For flute, violin, and piano. Introduction; Gai; Religieux; Conclusion. Highly individual part writing that produces free counterpoint and strong dissonance with a profusion of polytonalities, all conceived in a modal harmonic vocabulary. Migot's techniques are inspired by Debussy. His mystic interests are reflected in the Religieux movement. Resources of all 3 instruments are thoroughly explored. M-D.

Darius Milhaud. *Suite* (Sal 1936) 20pp., parts. 12 min. For piano, violin, and clarinet. 1. Ouverture: light and cheerful, span of 10th required, centers freely around D, colorful textural shifts. 2. Divertissement: animated, $\frac{4}{4}$ Moins animé uses some 3 + 3 + 2 rhythms for clever effect. 3. Jeu: for violin and clarinet alone. 4. Introduction et Final: $\frac{5}{4}$ Modéré, chordal, leads to Vif, $\frac{6}{8}$, colorful light chords with added 2nds, glissandi, much vitality, *pp* ending. Charming and gracious writing. M-D.

Akira Miyoshi. *Sonate* (Ongaku No Toma Sha 1966) 29pp., parts. No.40 in Contemporary Japanese Music Series. For flute, cello, and piano. Modéré: octotonic, flexible meters, chromatic figuration, alternating hands; large span required. Passacaille: extensive gestures, repeated notes, subject fragmented. Finale: fast triplets, chordal punctuation interspersed with scalar and arpeggi figures, dramatic conclusion. Written in an international style with French influence noted. M-D.

Wolfgang Amadeus Mozart. *Trio* K.498 E♭ 1786 (G. Lorenz, H.-M. Theopold—Henle 344 1981, ISMN M-2018-0344-9; Br&H; Adamowski—GS L1403; Augener 7268g; Lienau; IMC). For piano, clarinet, and viola. Andante: monothematic; turn-figure of the opening bar is charmingly varied. Menuetto: contrapuntal, animated; highly interesting trio. Allegretto: a rondo that continually sings; melody and contrapuntal technique distilled toward end of the movement; an enchanting conclusion. Henle edition includes alternative violin score and an informative Preface. M-D.

Robert Muczynski. *Fantasy Trio* Op.26 (GS 1971) 24pp., parts. For clarinet, cello, and piano. Four movements. Well written, attractive but not easy, freely tonal with frequent bitonal clashes. Rhythmic variety is very adroit. The finale makes clever play out of changing meters. The piano part is very demanding in some places. Stravinskyesque. M-D.

Thea Musgrave. *Pierrot* 1985 (Novello 1990) 49pp., parts. 19 min. For clarinet, violin, and piano. In 8 short movements: Pierrot; Columbine; Pierrot's Serenade; Harlequin; Harlequin Attacks Pierrot; Columbine Rejects Pierrot; Harlequin's Serenade; Pierrot. Inspired by Debussy's *La Sérénade Interrompue*, the work is theatrical in nature with Pierrot represented by the violin, Columbine the clarinet, and Harlequin the piano. M-D.

Joseph Myslivecek. *Trio* Op.1/4 B♭ (H. Riemann—IMC) 11pp., parts. For flute, violin, and piano. Three contrasting movements with a minuet. Not difficult and very effective. This has become a popular and fairly well-known work. M-D.

Stefan Niculescu. *Triplum* 1971 (Sal) 15pp., parts. For flute, cello, and piano. Hétérophonie I, II, and III. Homophonie I, II. Polyphonie I, II. Contains elaborate performance directions. Improvisation, traditional and avant-garde notation, pointillistic, dynamic extremes, mobile form. Avant-garde. D.

Per Nørgård. *Trio* Op.15 (JWC 4033 1958) 35pp., parts. For clarinet, cello, and piano. Sostenuto–Allegretto: flexible meters, freely tonal, triplet usage, thin textures. Larghetto: sustained opening, expressive, widespread textures; half-step is thematically important; builds to chordal climax; tremolando; subsides; *pp* closing. Con moto: $^6_8$, trills, subito dynamic changes, chromatic, rhythmic drive, alternating hands, octotonic, 2 groups of four 8ths in $^6_8$; half-step still integral to motivic construction. Poco allegro, con affetto: intense; figures and patterns; grace notes used for rhythmic precision and color; *fff* climax; recedes; *pp* closing; half-step used constantly. This work shows a fine talent searching for a consistent style. M-D.

Toshitsugu Ogihara. *Concerto for Flute, Violin and Piano* 1961 (Japan Federation of Composers 1973) 51pp., parts. Allegro: SA; material well developed; pentatonic scale influence slightly felt. Andantino: ABA; triplet figure prominent; graceful chordal syncopations give a dance feeling. Allegro: free SA design; pentatonic influence mixed with chromatic usage; minor 2nds plentiful; bitonal; equal interest in all parts; calm, slow coda capped with a strong, lively finish. D.

Jean Papineau-Couture. *Trio en Quatre Mouvements* (CMC 1974) 20pp., parts. For clarinet, viola, and piano. Four movements have metronome marks. Directions for performers in French. Clusters, harmonics, contrary-motion glissandi. Virtuoso writing for all instruments. The framework for the piece is logical and well planned. D.

Gabriel Pierné. *Sonata da Camera* Op.48 (Durand) 32pp., parts. For violin, clarinet, and piano. Prélude; Sarabande et Finale. The sarabande is based on the name Louis Fleury, to whose memory the piece is dedicated. Well crafted; has qualities of grace, refinement, and sensitivity; supple writing that shows Pierné was well grounded in counterpoint. M-D.

Ignaz Pleyel. *Sonate* Op.16/1 C 1788 (H. Albrecht—K&S 35) 32pp., parts. For flute, cello, and piano. Allegro; Adagio; Rondo. Facile, charming. Especially lovely Adagio. M-D.

———. *Sonate* Op.16/2 G 1788 (H. Albrecht—K&S 36; K. Hoover, S. Lincoln—McGinnis & Marx 1990) 31pp., parts. For flute, cello, and piano. Allegro vivace; Rondo; Presto. Lively. M-D.

———. *Sonate* Op.16/5 e 1788 (H. Albrecht—K&S 37) 28pp., parts. For flute, cello, and piano. Allegro molto; Andantino; Rondo. Minor key is used to advantage. M-D.

———. *Grand Trio* Op.29 (Musica Rara; Simrock 15pp., parts). For flute, cello, and piano. Allegro; Andante; Rondo. Mozartian grace, high Classical style, fluent, melodious.

The general effect of all these pieces suggests a diffuse but harmonically rich Haydn style.

Elizabeth Posten. *Trio* (JWC 1960). For flute, clarinet (or viola), and harp (or piano). See detailed entry under trios for piano and 2 miscellaneous woodwinds.

Johann Joachim Quantz. *Trio Sonata* c (Schultz, Hauser—Schott). For flute, violin, and basso continuo.

———. *Trio Sonata* C (W. Bergmann, L. Lefkovitch—Schott 10652) 20pp., parts. For flute, violin, and continuo; cello ad lib. Allegro; Adagio; Allegro. Preface by editors. Tasteful realizations. M-D.

———. *Trio Sonata* D (M. Seiffert—K&S) 15pp., parts. For flute (oboe), violin, and basso continuo. Adagio; Allegro; Largo; Allegro. More appropriate realization than many of this editor's. M-D.

———. *Trio Sonata* D (Ruf—Ric). For flute, violin, and basso continuo.

———. *Trio Sonata* g (Br&H). For flute, violin, and continuo. Imaginative outer movements, Siciliana middle movement. M-D.

———. *Trio Sonata* G (Schott 11254). For oboe, cello (bassoon), and piano. See detailed entry under trios for piano and 2 miscellaneous woodwinds.

Jean-Philippe Rameau. *Pièces de Clavecin en Concerts* 1742 (E. Jacobi—Br 1970) 63pp., parts. For violin or flute and viol (gamba) or a second violin and keyboard. See detailed entry under trios for piano, violin, and cello.

Günther Raphael. *Trio-Suite* Op.44 (Müller WM1611SM 1968) 27pp., parts. For flute, cello, and piano. Praembulum; Courante; Sarabande; Menuett; Gigue. Neo-Baroque style, freely tonal. The Menuett is by far the most extensive movement. Requires solid pianism throughout. M-D.

———. *Trio* Op.70 1950 (Br&H 6206) 39pp., parts. 15 min. For clarinet, cello, and piano. Allegro: strong rhythms and syncopation; harmonic 2nds, 4ths, and 5ths; large span required. Andante: long lines with embellishments; sustained. Allegro molto: toccata-like, alternating hands, sustained and lyric episodes, driving coda. Neoclassic. M-D.

Hendrik de Regt. *Musica per flauto, violoncello e clavicembalo* Op.29 (Donemus 1973) 24pp., parts.

———. *Circe* Op.44 (Donemus 1975) 36pp., parts. For clarinet, violin (or viola), and piano. Photostat of MS.

Carl Reinecke. *Trio* Op.264 A 1904 (Br; Simrock 39pp., parts; IMC). For clarinet, viola, and piano. In a refined Mendelssohn style with an appealing Legend slow movement. M-D.

———. *Trio* Op.274 B♭ ca.1905 for Piano, Clarinet, and Horn (Viola). See detailed entry under trios for piano, one brass instrument, and one woodwind.

Karel Reiner. *Loose Leaves* (Panton 1972) 43pp., parts. For clarinet, cello, and piano. Free atonal style; melodic ideas varied by using mainly dissonant intervals— 2nds, 7ths, and 9ths. M-D.

Roger Reynolds. *Acquaintances* (CFP 6611 1963) 13pp., parts. 7 min. For flute, double bass, and piano. The disparate qualities of the flute and the double bass are combined through the mediation of the piano. Two atypical cadenzas separate the 3 characterized sections—Abrupt, Antic, and Acceptance. Short, continuous and freely developing, the work moves through a spectrum of moods from slapstick to severity. Plucked strings; pointillistic; in the Interlude the pianist is asked to ad lib if more support is necessary. Sense of humor will help the performance. D.

Ferdinand Ries. *Trio* Op.28 (D. Klöcher—Musica Rara 1969) 40pp., parts. For clarinet, cello, and piano. Allegro; Scherzo–Allegro vivace; Adagio; Rondo. Beethoven influence is obvious and reflects the transition from Classicism to early Romanticism. M-D.

Bernard Rogers. *Ballade* (PIC 1966) 15pp., parts. For piano, viola, and bassoon. Piano opens a long Vivace section alone, joined by the viola and bassoon at Deciso. Other sections are Deliberato, Andante moderato, ma agitato, Cadenza and Andante tranquillo, and Quasi adagio, all played without break. Lovely sonorities and excellent ensemble writing. M-D.

Ned Rorem. *Trio* 1960 (CFP 6430 1966) 26pp., parts. 18 min. For flute, cello, and piano. Largo misterioso—Allegro: interesting flute cadenza at beginning over sustained chords in the piano; Allegro section contrasts with running chromatic figuration. Largo: a melancholy, intermezzo-like, bittersweet slow movement. Andante: cello cadenza; piano part has repeated chords in left hand and melodic line that intertwines with cello and flute. Allegro molto: clear lines, French flavor, instruments used to fine advantage. M-D.

————. *The End of Summer* 1985 (Bo&H). 20 min. For clarinet, violin, and piano. In 3 movements: Capriccio, Fantasy, Mazurka. The composer has noted that "this trio follows in the wake of my septet, *Scenes from Childhood*. The pieces are about the same length and are formed from souvenirs. But while the septet contains twelve movements describing geographical landmarks of my youth, the trio is in but three movements, each suggested by musical works of yore. There are suggestions of Satie, Brahms, hopscotch ditties, and Protestant anthems" (from Program Insert, *The Making of a Medium: The Verdehr Trio*, Vol.2, Crystal Records CD742, 1991). M-D.

Archduke Johann Joseph Rainer Rudolph. *Trio* (Musica Rara). For clarinet, cello, and piano. A fine example of amateur composition; written in a pseudo-Beethoven style with some effective moments. M-D.

Dieter Salbert. *Kammermusik* 1971 (Möseler) 12pp. 3 copies are necessary for performance. For piano, clarinet, and violin.

László Sáry. *Image* (EMB 1974) 10pp. 3 copies necessary for performance. For clarinet, cello, and piano.

Herman Schroeder. *Zweites Klavier-Trio* Op.40 1967 (Schott 5651 1967) 35pp., parts. 13 min. For violin, horn, and piano. Andante sostenuto–Allegro; Adagio; Presto scherzando.

———. *Piano Trio* III Op.43 (Schott 6008 1969) 42pp., parts. For clarinet, cello, and piano. Allegro animato; Largo; Poco vivace.
Both works are written in an atonal and dissonant Neoclassic style based on the techniques of Hindemith. M-D.

Gunther Schuller. *A Trio Setting* 1990 (AMP). 16½ min. For clarinet, violin, and piano. Fast and Explosive; Slow and dreamy; Allegretto scherzando e leggero; Molto agitato. "My *Trio* . . . is in four contrasting movements, formally retaining the quite traditional classic sequence of fast-slow-scherzo-fast. This reflects my strong belief that the old classic and romantic forms are far from exhausted and obsolete, as many avant-gardists in recent decades have tried to make us believe. They are as appropriate today as they were 100 years ago, even when filled with the more rhythmically and chromatically complex tonal languages of today. It is also important that the contrasts of mood and character inherent in the classic symphonic forms—say, in a Mozart or Beethoven symphony—be reestablished, for we have had in the last 50 years too many multi-movement pieces in which, alas, every movement—whether marked *Adagio* or *Presto*—sounds alike" (from Program Insert, *The Making of a Medium: Music Written for the Verdehr Trio,* Vol.3, Crystal CD743, 1994). M-D to D.

Robert Schumann. *Fairy Tales* Op.132 1853 (Br&H; CF; IMC). For clarinet, viola, piano. See detailed description under trios for piano, violin, and viola.

Elliott Schwartz. *Trio* 1964 (CF 1972) 17pp., parts. 11 min. Facsimile edition. For flute, cello, and piano. Not too rapidly; Very slowly, but with tension; Very lively. Serial influence, wide skips, sudden dynamic changes, percussive use of piano. The sustained second movement uses only one piano stave. The exciting finale contains shifting meters and requires great agility on the part of the pianist. Large span required. D.

———. *Divertimento* IV 1980 (MMB/Norruth) 12 min. For flute, double bass, and piano. Performed from full score. "The piece has many brief movements, in the manner of a suite. All of them use the same melodic motive, which emerges at the end as a tonal, lyric, almost Mozartian passage. Ostinati and minimalism repetition figure heavily in all three parts" (Composer's letter to authors).

———. *A Garden for RKB* 1990 (ACA) 12 min. For violin, clarinet, and piano. Performed from full score. "Dedicated to the memory of a colleague who was both an opera scholar and an avid garden[er]. Each of the three movements is named after a flowering plant, and each is concerned with operatic repertoire: I. a single opera, *Otello,* II. a single composer, Wagner (*Tristan* and the Ring),

III. a grouping, Verdi *Traviata,* Mozart *Don Giovanni.* Minimalist repeated gestures in the rapid second movement" (Composer's letter to authors).

——. *Vienna Dreams* 1998 (ACA) 8½ min. For viola, clarinet, and piano. Performed from full score. "Much of this piece uses fragments of Mozart, Schubert, and Brahms—filtered through Mahler's *Das Lied von der Erde*—and sound[s] curiously like early Schoenberg. Often [uses] extreme contrasts in style and musical language" (Composer's letter to authors).

——. *Kaleidoscope* 1999 (ACA) 12½ min. For violin, contrabassoon, and piano. Performed from full score. "This work was designed to exploit the great contrasts in register between violin and contrabassoon. Paradoxically, it also focuses on the single octave they share in common. (As a result, there is a surprising amount of high contrabassoon writing.)" (Composer's letter to authors).

Bright Sheng. *Tibetan Dance* 2001 (GS). 15 min. For clarinet, violin, and piano. In 3 movements: Prelude; Song; Tibetan Dance.

Leland Smith. *Trio* (CFE 1947) 25pp., parts. For flute (or violin), cello, and piano. Fast, but not too much; Slowly, with expression; Scherzo–Fast; Very Fast. Freely tonal, octotonic. Fast movements are infused with dance qualities; slow movement is somewhat Impressionist but highly intense. Requires fine octave technique and large span. D.

Harvey Sollberger. *Divertimento* 1970 (ACA). For flute, cello, and piano. Unusual timbral and virtuosic writing. D.

Rick Sowash. *Trio No. 1: Voyage of the Spirit* (Sowash), parts. 18 min. For clarinet, cello, and piano. I. Moderato, II. Lento, III. Lento, poco mosso, andante, IV. Allegro. A work said to describe "a spirit journey in search of Certitude, of Joy, of God." Intones an Alleluia which the composer recalled from his boyhood church. Programmatic, with philosophical and spiritual influences imbedded in the music. M-D.

——. *Trio No. 2: Enchantment of April* (Sowash) 38pp., parts. 20 min. For clarinet, cello, and piano. I. Maestoso ma tranquillo, allegro, II. Lento, III. Allegretto. Based in part on melodies from songs written for a dear friend and from scenes in Elizabeth von Arnim's novel *Enchanted April.* Picturesque with deeply felt emotion. M-D.

——. *Trio No. 3: November Shadows* (Sowash), parts. 15 min. For clarinet, cello, and piano. I. Allegro, II. Lento, III. Allegretto. Re-creates the atmosphere of November, using strong dramatic gestures and musical figurations. M-D.

——. *Sunny Days* 1994, rev.1996 (Sowash), parts. 18 min. For clarinet, violin, and piano. I. Moderato, II. Allegretto, III. Moderato, IV. Vivo. Uses Belo-Russian folk songs in an Americanized treatment of "sunny" days, optimism, and wit. M-D.

Sowash composes in a strongly tonal style with eclectic influences endowed by personal experiences, friendships, philosophy, and nature.

Carl Stamitz. *Trio* Op.14/1 (W. Upmeyer—Nag 38) 13pp., parts. For flute, violin, and continuo. Moderato; Andante moderato; Rondo–Moderato. The last 2 movements contain minore sections. Keyboard part is mainly chordal. M-D.

———. *Triosonate* Op.14/5 F (Hillemann—Br&H). For flute, violin, and continuo.

Wolfgang Steffen. *Trio* Op.37 (Bo&Bo 1973) 19pp., parts. 12 min. For flute, cello, and piano. Directions for all instruments in German. Pointillistic, clusters, dynamic extremes, proportional rhythmic relationships, highly organized, complex. Strings are to be strummed. D.

Leon Stein. *Trio Concertante* 1961 (CFE) 49pp., parts. For piano, violin, and alto sax. Allegro con brio: SA, extensive development, Impressionist; sonorities handled in a Neoclassic style. Siciliano–Andante moderato: rocking mood in opening section; middle section has more activity (runs, arpeggi) but is generally kept subdued; opening mood returns briefly. Scherzoso–Allegro vivace: much rhythmic drive couched in a Gallic humorous style; clever ending. M-D.

Karlheinz Stockhausen. *Tierbreis [=Zodiac]* 1975/83 (Stockhausen Verlag 1993) 33pp. Trio version for clarinet, flute (piccolo), and trumpet/piano. Chance composition; trumpeter also plays piano. Includes text from the voice version of the work, and performance instructions in German and English, as well as photographs illustrating a rehearsal of the work with the original performers.

Igor Stravinsky. *Suite from L' Histoire du Soldat* (JWC 1918; IMC) 28pp., parts. For clarinet, violin, and piano. Arranged by the composer. March du Soldat; Le violon du Soldat; Petit concert; Tango-Valse-Rag; La danse du Diable. Highly effective arrangement. Retains the main ingredients and many of the sonorities from the original. D.

Richard Swift. *Trio* Op.14 (CFE). For clarinet, violin, and piano. Swift "describes his music as influenced by the Viennese twelve-tone school; by the work and thought of Stravinsky, Babbitt, Perle, and Sessions; and by the analytical methods of Heinrich Schenker" (DCM, 723).

William Sydeman. *Trio* 1961 (Seesaw). For oboe, viola, and piano. Sydeman describes himself as "a musical hybrid, split between the traditional urge to 'say something' and twentieth-century materials, which have so long been associated with impersonality and abstraction" (DCM, 725).

———. *Fantasy and Two Epilogues* 1964 (Okra) 17pp., parts. 9 min. Reproduced from holograph. For flute, cello, and piano. Serial; the flute and cello play together much of the time without the piano. When the piano enters in the Fantasy it is to play in a "wild" manner, grabbing low-pitched notes and chords.

About the middle of the first epilogue the following direction is given: "From here on to the end of the epilogue the piano dominates completely!" The second epilogue uses the piano in a "fleeting" manner and has figuration that is to be played "as if a three-note trill." Contains some stunning sonorities but is a very complex piece. D.

Phyllis Tate. *Air and Variations* 1957 (OUP) 29pp., parts. For violin, clarinet, and piano. 14 min. Air; Variations; Aubade; Tempo di Valse; Serenade; Tarantella; Fugal March (Finale). Piano is silent for the Tarantella variation. Strong Neoclassic style. M-D.

Georg Philipp Telemann. *Essercizii Musici. Trio Sonata* XII E♭ (H. Ruf—Schott 1974) 19pp., parts. For oboe, harpsichord (piano), and continuo. Sounds best when performed by oboe, harpsichord obbligato, a continuo instrument such as cello, viola da gamba, or bassoon, and a continuo chordal instrument such as another harpsichord or lute (guitar). The affecting mesto slow movement and the following brilliant Allegro are especially fine. M-D.

———. *Six Concerti* (Br 2961). See detailed entry under duos for piano and flute.

———. *Trio Sonata* e (K. Hofmann—HM 224) 10pp., parts. For oboe, violin, and basso continuo.

———. *Trio Sonata* g (Ruf—Ric). For oboe, violin, and basso continuo.

———. *Sonata* e (K. Hofmann—HM 219) 14pp., parts. For flute, oboe (or violin), and basso continuo. Largo; Allegro; Affettuoso; Vivace. Clean realization. M-D.

Numerous other Trios are available from Br, Heinrichshofen, Schott, and IMC.

Siegfried Thiele. *Proportionen* 1971 (DVFM) 27pp., parts. For oboe, cello, and piano. Explanations in German.

Alfred Uhl. *Kleines Konzert* (Dob 7744 1938) 32pp., parts. For clarinet, viola, and piano. Allegro con brio: chromatic, staccato style, chordal, octaves. Grave, molto tranquillo: ostinato-like figures, arpeggiated accompaniment, inner voices important. Vivo: scherzo-like, octotonic, sequences, secco style, chordal buildup, drops back, sudden *ff* closing. Neoclassic. M-D.

Hermann Josef Ullrich. *Trio-Fantasy* Op.20 1946 (Dob) 21pp., parts. 7 min. For horn, violin, and piano. One movement. Freely tonal with heavy doses of accidentals, frequent tempo changes, Expressionist. Some Impressionist influence noted in parallel chords and added 6ths. Arpeggi figuration, tonal conclusion. Piano part relies heavily on chords; large span required. M-D.

Jan K. Vanhall. *Trio* Op.20/5 E♭ (Weston, Bergmann—Schott). For clarinet, piano, and violin. Graceful and melodious writing. M-D.

———. *Trio* E♭ (Musica Rara). For clarinet, cello, and piano. Haydn and Mozart influence here. M-D.

Carl Maria von Weber. *Trio* Op.63 g 1813–19 (H. Wiese, K. Schilde—Henle 687 2000, ISMN M-2018-0687-7 30pp.; Musica Rara; CFP 1473; IMC). For flute, cello, and piano. Formal perfection and admirable contrapuntal treatment abound in this work, but the outer movements are over-worked with too much lively figuration. The scherzo has 2 sections; the concise Andante espressivo has the subtitle "Shepherd's Lament," an apt description probably based upon a text in common currency at the time and likely derived from an earlier Andante with Variations by Weber himself for cello and piano. Henle edition has excellent Preface and comments. M-D to D.

Dan Welcher. *Partita* 1979 (EV 164-00201 1990) 45pp., parts. For horn, violin, and piano. I. Prologue: Boldly, but freely; commencing with horn introduction to a Subito allegro for an action-packed exchange of motivic and rhythmic figures; includes notes sustained silently on piano for sonorous effect. II. Nocturne: Calmo; homophonic introduction in piano and later an extended solo; lyrical, yet with restlessness. III. Intermezzo: Agitato, frenetico; commences with violin but quickly intensifies with a 12-tone row in the piano; some development of the row takes place in this extended movement with a quasi-cadenza ending. IV. Aria: Lento; duet between horn and violin initially, then all 3 in a freely developed linear texture hinting at the use of a partial row. V. Toccata: Allegro energico in $\frac{5}{8} + \frac{4}{8}$ meter; 12-tone row, continuous rhythmic development in a lyrical expressionism. For experienced performers. Score is an easy-to-read copy of MS. D.

Stefan Wolpe. *Trio* 1963 (McGinnis & Marx) 63pp., parts. For flute, cello, and piano. Dense textures with much activity, but the work gives the feeling of great clarity! Similar to a high-speed virtuoso conversation. Exhilarating but complex writing. D.

Hugh Wood. *Trio* Op.3 (UB 12945 1961) 21pp., parts. 12 min. For flute, viola, and piano. Vivace; Tema and (8) Variations. The final variation is a cadenza. Serial, individual style, pointillistic, M-D.

Charles Wuorinen. *Trio* I 1961 (ACA) 4 min. For flute, cello, and piano.
———. *Second Trio: Piece for Stefan Wolpe* 1962 (CFP) 9 min. For flute, cello, and piano.
———. *Third Trio* (CFP) 16½ min. For flute, cello, and piano.
———. *Trio Concertante* (ACA) 12 min. For violin, oboe, and piano.

Trios for Piano and Two Flutes
(including Trio Sonatas)

Carl Philipp Emanuel Bach. *12 Little Pieces* W.81 (K. Walther—Zimmermann; Mitteldeutscher) 5pp., parts. Menuet; Polonaise; Allegro; Andantino, etc. Short, attractive. Int.

——. *12 Kleine Stücke* W.82 (Johnen—CFP).

——. *Trio* E♭ (Zimmermann).

Johann Sebastian Bach. *Sonatas* for 2 flutes and continuo arranged from *Sonatas* for viola da gamba and harpsichord, S.1028, S.1029 (J. Bopp, E. Müller—Reinhardt 1973) 40pp., parts. Preface in German and French.

——. *Trio* G (Müller).

——. *Trio Sonata* S.1039 (H.-P. Schmitz—Br 4403 25pp., parts; M. Seiffert—Br&H 23pp., parts; CFP). Adagio; Allegro ma non presto; Adagio e piano. The Seiffert edition is over-edited; the Schmitz edition is based on the *Neue Bach-Ausgabe* and has a Preface in French, German, and English. This work also exists in a version by Bach himself for viola da gamba, keyboard, and basso continuo (S.1027). There is a common denominator between the 4 movements: the 8th notes of the Adagio become the quarter notes of the Allegro ma non presto, and the 8th notes of the Adagio e piano become the half notes of the Presto. D.

Wilhelm Friedemann Bach. *Trio* I D (M. Seiffert—Br&H 5651 10pp., parts; IMC). Andante; Allegro; Vivace.

——. *Trio* II D (M. Seiffert—Br&H 5652 10pp., parts; IMC). Allegro ma non tanto; Larghetto; Vivace.

——. *Trio* III B♭ (M. Seiffert—Br&H 5653) 10pp., parts. Largo; Allegro ma non troppo; Vivace.

——. *Trio* IV a (M. Seiffert—Br&H 5654) 7pp., parts. Allegro; (Larghetto) unfinished.

Michel de la Barre. *Sonate* V G (R. Viollier—Pegasus PE 1069 1964) 12pp., parts. Preface in French and German. Prelude; Gigue; Gavotte; Fugue. Beautiful realization, many opportunities for ornamentation. M-D.

Joseph Bodin de Boismortier. *Trio Sonata* F (Ruf—Schott).

——. *Trio Sonata* G (Ruf—Schott).

Ferruccio Busoni. *Duo* (J. Theurich—Musica Rara). Composed at the age of 14. First publication. Charming.

William Corbett. *Sonata* C 1705 (H. Ruf—HM 216 1973) 10pp., parts. In Vol.I of the 2-volume collection *Trio Sonatas by Old English Masters*. Largo; Fuga; Adagio; Jigga. Fine clean realizations. M-D.

Archangelo Corelli. *Sonate da Camera* Op.2 (D. Degen—CFP 4567 1943) 12pp., parts. 1 F: Adagio; Allemanda; Corrente; Gavotta. 5 B♭: Adagio; Allemanda; Sarabanda; Tempo di Gavotta. 7 F: Adagio; Allemande; Corrente; Giga. All 3 *Sonatas* have short movements. Fine edition. M-D.

——. *Sonata* II (Moeck—Schott).

Veit Erdmann. *Mobile* I, II, III (Möseler 1973) 16pp. 3 copies necessary for performance. Avant-garde.

Willem de Fesch. *3 Sonaten* Op.7 (J. R. Le Cosquino de Bussy—B&VP 1947) 23pp., parts. 2 D: Largo; Allemanda. 4 g: Largo; Presto. 8 e: Andante; Tempo di Gavotte.

——. *Sonaten* Op.12 (W. Noske, H. Schouwman—Br 802 1957) 28pp., parts. 1 D: Largo; Allemanda; Menuetto 1 and 2. 2 g: Alle breve; Giga. 3 G: Largo; Allemanda; Menuetto. Strong melodic lines, a kind of instrumental bel canto. M-D.

——. *X Sonata a Tre* (B&VP) 4 vols. For 2 flutes or 2 violins and keyboard. II D: Largo; Allemanda; Giga. 8pp., parts. IV g: Largo; Presto. 9pp., parts. VIII e: Andante; Allemanda; Tempo di Gavotte. 6pp., parts. All are M-D.

Harald Genzmer. Sonate 1954 (Schott 4091) 12pp., parts. For 2 alto blockflöten and piano. Allegro molto; Andante; Vivace. All 3 movements are freely centered around C, with the Andante more chromatically colored. Superb Neoclassic writing, appealing. M-D.

Carl Heinrich Graun. *Triosonate* D (L. Stadelmann—Leuckart 1973) 12pp., parts. Leuckartiana No.41. Probably intended for Graun's master, Frederick the Great. A somewhat run-of-the-mill work but worth looking at. Int. to M-D.

——. *Sonata* E♭ (H. Kölbel—HM 211) 21pp., parts. Continuo realized by Ernst Meyerolbersleben. Preface in German and English. Adagio; Allegro non molto; Allegro. "The musical grandeur of the sonata is technically easy to achieve, thanks to the motto of the composer: 'One must not, without special cause, make unnecessary difficulties'" (from Preface). M-D.

——. *Triosonate* F (Moeck).

George Frideric Handel. *Trio Sonata* e (Nagel—Schott).

——. *Chamber Trio* XIII g (M. Seiffert—Br&H).

——. *Chamber Trio* IXX (M. Seiffert—Br&H).

——. *Trio Sonata* g (J. A. Parkinson—OUP 1969) 15pp., parts; cello ad lib. 11

min. This work is attributed to Handel. Editorial additions are identified. Adagio; Allegro; Siciliano; Allegro. Suitable for violins or oboes or treble recorders. Excellent keyboard realization. M-D.
——. *Triosonaten* Op.5 (Schneider—Barnhouse).
All these pieces remain an unalloyed delight.

Johann Adolph Hasse. *Trio Sonata* Op.3/6 D (E. Schenk—Dob DM 435 1973)
12pp., parts. Preface in German and English. Allegro moderato; Andante amoroso; Fuga. "Our work has all the musical charm of the Rococo; in it, Hasse
proves himself to be a mediator between Pergolesi (in the three-movement
formal scheme with fugal finale) and the Classic era, the tonal language of
which is present in elements of unmistakably Mozartian nature" (from Preface). M-D.
——. *Trio Sonata* e (Ruf—Schott).

Arthur Honegger. *Petite Suite.* See detailed entry under trios for piano and 2
violins.

Johann Krebs. *Triosonate* b (Erbrecht—K&S).
——. *Triosonate* b (Ruf—Schott).
——. *Trio* D (H. Riemann—Br&H No.1 865a/b) 17pp., parts. Ouverture à la
française; Rejouissance; Menuet; Bourrée; Gigue. Over-edited. M-D.
——. *Trio* e 1743 (F. Nagel—Müller). Four movements. Second flute part can
be played on oboe or violin. M-D.

Jean-Marie Leclair. *Sonate à trois* (Harmonia Uitgave). The keyboard part is im-
pressively integrated into the ensemble. M-D.

Pietro Locatelli. *Trio* Op.3/1 G (Riemann—Br&H; IMC).
——. *Trio Sonata* Op.5/1 G (H. Albrecht—K&S; H. Kolbel—Heinrichshofen
1261 16pp., parts; C. Crussard—Foetisch 7784 19pp., parts). Andante; Largo;
Andante; Allegro; Vivace. The Kolbel realization is more stylistically accept-
able. M-D.
——. *Trio Sonata* Op.5/3 E (Ruf—Schott).
——. *Trio Sonata* Op.5/4 C (H. Albrecht—K&S 1951) 9pp., parts. No.46 in Or-
ganum Series. Foreword in German includes tempo suggestions. Largo; An-
dante; Allegro. Clean edition. M-D.
——. *Trio Sonata* Op.5/5 d (H. Albrecht—K&S 1952) 11pp., parts. No.50 in Organum Series. Foreword in German includes tempo suggestions. Largo; Vivace;
Pastorale. Clean edition. M-D.

Jean-Baptiste Loeillet (of Lyons). *Trio Sonata* Op.1/2 (Ruf—Schott).
——. *Trio Sonata* Op.1/4 D (Ruf—Schott).
——. *Trio Sonata* Op.1/6 (Ruf—Schott).
——. *Trio Sonata* Op.2/12 (Ruf—Schott).

———. *Trio Sonata* e (A. Beon—IMC 1511) 15pp., parts. Largo; Allegro; Largo; Allegro. M-D.

———. *Sonata* g (A. Beon—IMC 1265) 12pp., parts. Adagio molto sostenuto; Allegro con brio; Largo; Allegro. Realization is somewhat heavy. M-D.

———. *Sonata* g (A. Beon—IMC).

Daniel Purcell. *Sonata* F ca.1710 (H. Ruf—HM 217 1973) 9pp., parts. In Vol.II of the 2-volume collection *Trio Sonatas by Old English Masters.* Largo; Allegro; Vivace. Fine and clean realization. M-D.

———. *Trio-Sonate* d (Ruf—Schott).

Johann J. Quantz. *Sonata* D (O. Fischer, O. Wittenbecher—Forberg 1921) 9pp., parts. Andante; Allegro; Affettuoso; Vivace. Over-edited. M-D.

———. *Sonata* G (Fischer, Wittenbecher—Forberg).

———. *Trio* a (Koch—Mösler).

———. *Trio Sonata* D (Ruf—Ric).

———. *Trio Sonata* a (Erbrecht—K&S).

———. *Trio Sonata* G (Ruf—Br).

———. *Trio Sonata* C (W. Birke—HM 60 1959) 16pp., parts. Affettuoso; Alla breve; Larghetto; Vivace. All editorial additions identified. Clean realization. M-D.

———. *Trio Sonata* c (C. Blumenthal—Zimmermann 11495) 15pp., parts. Andante moderato; Allegro; Larghetto; Vivace. Over-edited. M-D.

Giovanni Battista Sammartini. *Six Sonatas* Op.6 (Rampal—IMC) 2 vols. Bright, engaging, beautifully inventive writing. M-D.

———. *12 Sonatas* (Giesbert—Schott) 3 vols.

Georg Philipp Telemann. *Sonata* A (H. Schreiter—Br&H No.1970) 12pp., parts. Cantabile; Alla breve; Lento; Allegro. M-D.

———. *Sonata* F (Fussan—Schott).

———. *Sonata* g (Monkemeyer—Schott).

———. *Sonata* (Schreiter—IMC).

Robert Valentine. *Sonata* c 1721 (H. Ruf—HM 217 1973) 7pp., parts. In Vol.II of the 2-volume collection *Trio Sonatas by Old English Masters.* Adagio; Allegro; Adagio; Giga. Fine, clean realization. M-D.

Samuel Wesley. *Trio* F (H. Cobbe—OUP 1973) 33pp., parts. This work dates from 1826. Two long movements; the first in SA design is preceded by an Andante somewhat in the style of J. S. Bach. The second movement is a set of graceful variations in the style of Mozart. M-D.

William Williams. *Sonata* a 1703 (H. Ruf—HM 216 1973) 10pp., parts. In Vol.I of the 2-volume collection *Trio Sonatas by Old English Masters.* Adagio; Vivace; Allegro. Fine, clean realization. M-D.

Trios for Piano and
Two Miscellaneous Woodwinds

John Addison. *Trio* (Augener 18167R 1952) 30pp., parts. 13 min. For flute, oboe, and piano. Allegro; Lento con moto; Scherzo. Light film style, added-note technique frequently used, mildly 20th-century, octotonic, linear, witty. M-D.

Jurriaan Andriessen. *Trio* I 1955 (Donemus) 39pp., parts. 16 min. For flute, oboe, and piano. Allegro giusto; Andante; Allegro giocoso. Freely tonal with chromaticism, scales in 9ths, octotonic, generally thin textures, Neoclassic. Large span required. D.

Carl Philipp Emanuel Bach. *Six Sonatas* W.92 (G. Piccioli—IMC 1955) 16pp., parts. For clarinet, bassoon, and piano. Six short one-movement pieces. Allegretto; Allegro di molto; Allegro; Allegro; Andante; Allegro. In Johann Christian Bach style! Acceptable realizations. M-D.
——. *Six Pieces* (E. Simon—ST 1972) 20pp., parts. For clarinet, bassoon, and piano.
——. *Trio* I D (IMC). For flute, clarinet, and piano.
——. *Trio* II a (IMC). For flute, clarinet, and piano.
——. *Trio* III G (IMC). For flute, clarinet, and piano.
——. *Trio Sonata* W.148 a (K. Walther—Zimmermann) 14pp., parts. For flute, violin (oboe), and continuo.

Johann Sebastian Bach. *Trio Sonata* S. 1079 c (from *The Musical Offering*). For 2 flutes and basso continuo. In Vol.II of *Four Trio Sonatas* (Landschoff—CFP 42038).

Jacques Bank. *Die Ouwe* (Donemus 1975) 13pp. 3 copies required for performance. For bass recorder, bass clarinet, and piano. Photostat of composer's MS. Note in Dutch.

Ludwig van Beethoven. *Trio* G Kinsky37 ca.1786–90 (P. Badura-Skoda—Br&H 6604 1970) 27pp., parts. For piano, flute, and bassoon. Allegro; Adagio; Thema andante variazioni. Early and delightful writing. Piano has more than its share of the action. M-D.

——. *Trio* Op.38 (Musica Rara; IMC) 40pp., parts. For clarinet, bassoon or cello, and piano. Arranged by Beethoven from his *Septet* Op.20. Adagio–Allegro con brio; Adagio cantabile; Tempo di menuetto; Tema con (5) Variazionen; Scherzo; Andante con moto–Alla marzia–Presto. M-D.

Andras Borgulya. *Trio for Flute, Bassoon and Piano* (Gen 1973) 14pp., parts. Moderato: serial influence, thin textures, broken *ppp* secco octaves. Allegretto giocoso: piano mainly punctuates with chords and broken chordal figuration. Lento: sustained, changing meters, percussive grace notes. Allegro, ma non troppo: octotonic chromatic chords treated in ostinato-like fashion; Meno mosso section uses pesante chords and short figures; coda returns to opening idea of the movement. Neoclassic style. M-D.

Geoffrey Bush. *Trio* (Nov 1955) 11 min. For oboe, bassoon, and piano. Many 3rds, many octaves, little development; much repetition but contains some interesting harmonic usage. M-D.

Dinos Constantinides. *Dream* 1983 (Conners 78 1995) 7pp., parts. 2 min. For oboe, bassoon or cello, and piano. "*Dream* is derived from the third movement of an earlier work by the composer for solo piano. It depicts the story of a young artist and his efforts to acquire a place in the pantheon of the arts. As the title indicates, the artist is seeing in his unconsciousness images and colors of no definite shape" (from Postscript). Facile writing in a straightforward manner. M-D.

David Diamond. *Partita* 1935 rev.1956 (PIC 1961) 16pp., parts. 8 min. For oboe, bassoon, and piano. Neoclassic orientation, mildly 20th-century, most effective part is for the piano. Allegro vivo; Adagio espressivo; Allegro molto. M-D.

Pierre Max Dubois. *Les Tréteaux* (Choudens 1966) 29pp., parts. For flute, sax, and piano. Prologue en Fanfare: piano punctuates with chords; runs and passages for alternating hands. Romantica: nocturne-like style; broken triadic chords in left hand spread over interval of a 10th. Valse Vulgaire: piano provides rhythmic push and some melodic answering; somewhat like style of Jean Françaix. All glitter and fun. M-D.

Maurice Emmanuel. *Sonata* 1907 (Lemoine 1929) 23pp., parts. For flute, clarinet, and piano. Allegro con spirito; Adagio; Molto allegro e leggierissimo. A rousing and, at times, romping, fun-filled work in a pre-Poulenc style. Requires a large span and facile pianism. M-D to D.

Peter Racine Fricker. *Trio* (Serenade II) Op.35 1959 (Schott 10739) 26pp., parts. For flute, oboe, and piano. Andante moderato; Scherzo–Allegro; Slow–Poco allegro. Free and occasional use of serialism. This work shows that involved processes are part of Fricker's musical thinking, which has strong emotional qualities. Textures generally clear. Piano writing, even though serialistic, fits the hand appropriately. M-D.

Baldassare Galuppi. *Triosonate* G (Ruf—Br). For flute, oboe, and basso continuo. Lyrical and tuneful writing, skillful but traditional harmony with occasional chromatic inflection. A few ideas are thoroughly treated. M-D.

Mikhail Glinka. *Trio Pathétique* d 1832 (Musica Rara 1957; EMT; IMC 29pp., parts). For clarinet, bassoon or cello, and piano. Allegro moderato; Scherzo–Vivacissimo; Largo; Allegro con spirito. An attractive period piece from Glinka's early years in Italy. Full piano treatment in Romantic style with a preference displayed for external refinement and outward polish. M-D.

Hans-Georg Görner. *Concertino* Op.31 (Hofmeister 7246) 20pp., parts for all instruments. For 2 saxophones (alto and tenor) and piano, or for violin, viola, and piano. Allegro moderato; Moderato, all' antico; Rezitativo cantando. Freely tonal, traditional forms, Hindemith style, careful balancing of all parts. M-D.

Elizabeth Gyring. *Trio* 1951 (CFE) 40pp., parts. For oboe, clarinet, and piano. Allegro con fuoco–Molto vivace: driving rhythms, intense, Poco andante second tonal area, chromatic. Larghetto: chordal, syncopated accompaniment in left hand, serious and somber. Scherzo: lively but expressive; highly chromatic; canon appears in Trio; extensive coda. Finale–Rondo: vigorous, complex figures, strong, colorful, unique style. D.

———. *Trio* (CFE). For clarinet, bassoon, and piano.

George Frideric Handel. *Trio Sonata* g (J. A. Parkinson—OUP 1969) 15pp., parts; cello ad lib. 11 min. Attributed to Handel. Editorial additions identified. Adagio; Allegro; Siciliano; Allegro. Suitable for violins or oboes or treble recorders. Excellent keyboard realization. M-D.

Walter Hartley. *Trio for Reeds* 1987 (Dorn). 10½ min. For soprano sax (oboe), tenor (heckelphone), and piano.

———. *Trio Estatico* 1991 (Ethos). 9 min. For alto sax, tenor sax, and piano.

———. *Pastorale and Tarantella* 2000 (Ethos). 4 min. For soprano sax, alto sax, and piano.

———. *Trio-Miniatures* 2003 (TP). 5 min. For alto sax, baritone sax, and piano.

Franz Joseph Haydn. *Trio* No.29 F (CF). For flute, bassoon, and piano.

———. *Trio* No.31 G (CF). For flute, bassoon, and piano.

See detailed entry under trios for piano, one stringed instrument, and one wind instrument.

Michael Head. *Trio* 1935 (Emerson 83 1977) 29pp., parts. For oboe, bassoon, and piano. Allegro, crisp and lively; Andantino quasi allegretto; Allegro vivace.

Clear motivic development in multisectional forms, punctuated by snappy rhythms with ornamented melodies and colorful harmonies. Witty and playful. M-D.

Johann D. Heinichen. *Trio Sonata* F (Nov). For flute, oboe, and continuo. Four movements. Int. to M-D.
——. *Trio Sonata* F (Janetzky—Müller).
——. *Sonata* G (Hausswald—Br&H).

Alun Hoddinott. *Masks* Op.109 1983 (OUP 1987, ISBN 0-19-357178-1) 33pp., parts. 11 min. Subtitled Five Theatre Abstracts. For oboe, bassoon, and piano. I. Allegro e vivace, II. Moderato, III. Allegro, IV. Andante, V. Allegro molto. Mildly 20th-century in style with occasional strong dissonance and bitonality. No.III consists of separate cadenzas for oboe and bassoon framed by a brief piano statement. No.V sprints across the keyboard with 16th-note chromatic passagework in octaves. Curiosity pieces for double reeds and piano which deserve more attention. M-D.

Gustav Holst. *A Fugal Concerto* Op.40/2 (Nov 1923) 17pp., parts. For flute, oboe, and piano, or for 2 violins and piano. Moderato: octotonic, secco style, in D. Adagio: cantabile line in all 3 instruments, wistful melody. Allegro: staccato; shifting accents; old English dance tune "If All the World Were Paper" appears near conclusion; jiglike; good left-hand octave technique required; short cadenza passages for woodwinds. M-D.

Arthur Honegger. *Concerto da Camera* 1948 (Sal) 22pp., parts. 16½ min. For flute, English horn, and piano. Originally for flute, English horn, and string orchestra. Piano reduction by composer. Allegretto amabile; Andante; Vivace. Conceived in the Classical sense, virtuosity of all 3 instruments is intertwined in a refined polyphony. All movements are related to the 18th century in their natural rhythms and flowing pulses. Repeated chords, driving rhythms in outer movements, parallelisms. Large span required. M-D.
——. *Petite Suite.* See detailed entry under trios for piano and 2 violins.

Hunter Johnson. *Trio* 1954 (J. Kirkpatrick—Galaxy 1972) 28pp., parts. 23 min. For flute, oboe, and piano. Allegro con fuoco: main idea is the syncopated figure announced in octotonic fashion by the piano; freely tonal and centers around d; shifting meters; textures thicken at the coda. Adagio serioso: flexible meters; independent lines evolve; entire closing section is chordal and sustained for the piano; utilizes most of keyboard; requires large span. Allegro molto: chromatic lines begin in low register and work up the keyboard; imitation; reworks ideas from the other movements into one gigantic maelstrom. First-rate writing throughout. Deserves more hearings. D.

Piet Ketting. *Sonata* 1936 (Donemus) 41pp., parts. 26 min. For flute, oboe, and piano. Praembulum: dramatic skipping chords open movement; freely tonal;

thin textures; short-long motif is frequent. Ciaconna: piano opens with 8-bar subject; other instruments provide counterpoint; varied treatment evolves into complex figuration before thinning out near closing. Fuga: short-long idea is integral to subject; flute and oboe open with piano announcing subject in octaves; asymmetrical phrasing; *pp* closing. Neoclassic orientation. M-D.

Johann Krebs. *Trio* e 1743 (F. Nagel—Müller). Four movements. For 2 flutes and piano; second flute part can be played on oboe or violin. M-D.

Jean Baptiste Loeillet (of London). *Sonata* c (EV; A. Beon—IMC) 11pp., parts. For flute, oboe, and piano. Grave; Poco largo; Adagio–Andante; Allegro. Highly edited. M-D.
———. *Sonata* d (EV; IMC). For flute, oboe, and piano.
———. *Trio Sonata* Op.1/1 F 1722 (Ruf, Bergmann—Schott; Moeck 1076 11pp., parts). For flute, oboe, and piano. Grave; Allegro; Adagio; Gavotte; Aria; Allegro. M-D.
———. *Trio Sonata* Op.2/2 F (Ermeler, Kluge—Heinrichshofen).
———. *Trio Sonata* Op.2/4 d (Ruf—HM 181; A. Mann—Music Press MPI 513) 12pp., parts. Largo; Allegro; Adagio; Allegro.
———. *Trio Sonata* Op.2/6 c (Ruf—Br).

Elisabeth Lutyens. *Fantasie Trio* Op.55 1963 (Olivan Press) 19pp., parts. 10½ min. For flute, clarinet, and piano. Three untitled contrasting movements. Serial, pointillistic, shifting meters, Expressionist. Photostat of composer's MS, not easy to read. D.
———. *Music for Three* Op.65 (Olivan Press 1966). For flute (alto flute), piccolo, oboe, and piano.

William Mathias. *Divertimento* Op.24 (OUP 07.022 1966) 23pp., parts. 10 min. For flute, oboe, and piano. Allegretto: contrary-motion arpeggi, short buoyant motifs, fast repeated chords. Andante comodo: longer lines, chordal texture mixed with 16th-note staccato figuration with pedal, written-out trills. Allegro ritmico: fugal; varied textures; bimodal passage concludes work on D. A lighthearted work, crafted with great skill and imagination. M-D.

Felix Mendelssohn. *Konzertstück* I Op.113 f 1832 (Br&H 9pp., parts; McGinnis & Marx; Sikorski; IMC). For clarinet and basset horn or 2 clarinets and piano.
———. *Konzertstück* II Op.114 d (Br&H 11pp., parts; McGinnis & Marx; Sikorski; IMC). For clarinet and basset horn or 2 clarinets and piano.
Each work has 3 movements played without a break. The Br&H edition gives no alternative part for a second clarinet in lieu of the basset horn; has good page turns and cues. M-D.

Thea Musgrave. *Trio* (JWC 1960) 19pp., parts. 10 min. For flute, oboe, and piano. One movement. Short motif appears in various guises; serialism used to investigate textural problems and sonorities. Displays intelligence, resolution, and clarity of purpose. D.

Hans Osieck. *Variations on the Dutch Song 'De Vier Weverkens'* 1968 (Donemus). For flute, oboe (English horn), and piano. A lighthearted, straightforward work with incidental melancholy variations and Osieck's characteristic charm. M-D.

Elizabeth Posten. *Trio* (JWC 1960) 29pp., parts. 12½ min. For flute, clarinet (or viola), and harp (or piano). Piacevole; Pastorale nostalgica–Molto moderato; Fileuse–Dolce delicato; Vivace scherzando. Tonal; clear, concise writing. More effective, separate parts written for piano at a few spots. Colorful, programmatically conceived. D.

Francis Poulenc. *Trio* (JWC 1926) 34pp., parts. 12 min. For oboe, bassoon, and piano. Lent–Presto; Andante; Rondo–Très vif. A thoroughly effective work; dry humor marvelously exploited in the 2 wind instruments. Limpid style, except for final part of the last movement, which is a merry gigue. M-D.

Johann Joachim Quantz. *Trio Sonata* C (Bergmann—Schott). For flute, oboe, and basso continuo.
———. *Trio Sonata* c (C. Blumenthal—Zimmermann ZM95) 15pp., parts. For flute, oboe, and piano. Andante moderato; Allegro; Larghetto; Vivace. M-D.
———. *Trio Sonata* D (Ruf—Ric). For flute, oboe, and basso continuo.
———. *Trio Sonata* G (Ruf—Heinrichshofen). For flute, oboe d'amore, and continuo. The oboe d'amore part is alternately for violin. (Schott 11254) For oboe, cello (bassoon), and piano. An attractive Italian-style Trio with lively outer movements and a gracious middle Largo movement. Int. to M-D.

Alan Rawsthorne. *Sonatina* 1936 (OUP 1968) 30pp., parts. 11 min. For flute, oboe, and piano. Allegretto: no time signature, flexible number of counts in each bar; dotted bar lines, with regular bar lines at structural points; freely tonal; varied textures; large span required. Lento ma non troppo: thin chromatic lines; *ppp* triplet figure adds unusual sonority. Presto: like a 2-part invention in texture; shifting accents; octotonic; con brio quasi cadenza for piano near conclusion; strong rhythmic ending. Neoclassic. M-D.

Franz Reizenstein. *Trio* Op.25 A 1945 (Lengnick 1953) 61pp., parts. 21 min. For flute, oboe, and piano. Allegro tranquillo; Andante; Scherzando–Fughetta; Allegro vivo. Hindemith influence is strong. Various tonal centers are present, giving a kind of Romantic polytonal effect. Tune of "Daisy Bell" is used in the last movement. Superb pianistic writing. D.

Norbert Rosseau. *Rapsodie* Op.81 1958 (CeBeDeM) 23pp., parts. 12 min. Lento; Presto; Lento; Presto; Lento. Strong broken-octave gestures and quiet sonorities represent the Lento, while the Presto parts utilize shifting rhythms in octotonic style. Flowing triplet figuration. Neoclassic style. M-D.

Howard Rovics. *Cybernetic Study* II 1968 (Okra) 9pp., parts. For clarinet, bassoon, and piano. Serial, changing meters, pointillistic, Expressionist dramatic gestures, harmonics, abstract. Large span required. D.

Florent Schmitt. *Sonatine en Trio* Op.85 1934–35 (Durand) 13pp., parts. For flute, clarinet, and piano. Assez animé; Assez vif; Très lent; Animé. Post-Romantic rhetoric with a few Impressionist mannerisms; technically coherent if diffuse. Strong chromatic usage in the second movement presents a few complex pianistic problems. M-D.

Georg Philipp Telemann. *Sonata* a (IMC). For flute, oboe, and piano; cello part ad lib.

——. *Sonata* c (IMC). For flute, oboe, and piano; cello part ad lib.

——. *Sonata* c (K. Hofmann—HM 195) 12pp., parts. For flute, oboe, and basso continuo. Adagio; Allegro; Adagio; Allegro. Preface in English and German. M-D.

——. *Sonata* d (Ruf—Br 3332) 14pp., parts. For flute, oboe, and basso continuo. Trio XI from the *Essercizii Musici.* Largo; Allegro; Affettuoso; Presto. Excellent basso continuo realization. M-D.

——. *Sonata* e (K. Hofmann—HM 219) 14pp., parts. For flute, oboe (or violin), and basso continuo. Largo; Allegro; Affettuoso; Vivace. Clean realization. M-D.

——. *Trio Sonata* e (M. Ruetz—HM 25) 16pp., parts. For flute, oboe, and keyboard; cello ad lib. Affettuoso; Allegro; Grave; Allegro. Intelligent realization. M-D.

——. *Trio Sonata* XII E♭. See detailed entry under trios for piano, one stringed instrument, and one wind instrument.

Heitor Villa-Lobos. *Fantaisie Concertante* 1953 (ESC) 34pp., parts. 15 min. For piano, clarinet in C, and bassoon. Allegro non troppo; Lento; Allegro impetuoso. Colorful chordal sonorities chromatically enriched; entire keyboard utilized; 7th chords in triplets; inner lines to be brought out; syncopation; 3 with 2; contrary scales. Large span and stamina required! D.

Antonio Vivaldi. *Trio* a F.XV/1 (N. Deluis—Musica Rara 1967) 16pp., parts. For treble recorder (flute), bassoon (cello), and basso continuo; cello ad lib. Largo; Allegro; Largo cantabile; Allegro molto. The realization is a little plain and regular. M-D.

——. *Trio Sonata* g (Musica Rara). For 2 oboes and continuo.

Trios for Piano and Two Brass Instruments

Richard Benger. *Miniature Suite* (JWC 1972) 22pp., parts. For 2 B♭ trumpets and piano. Moderato: much ostinato in piano. Andante: complementing melodies in trumpets. Presto: staccato technique used in all parts. Maestoso: piano part is chordal, under syncopated trumpets. Allegro: broad dramatic sweeps in piano while trumpets are more rhythmically treated. Thin textures, Neoclassic influence, mildly 20th-century. M-D.

Boris Blacher. *Divertimento* Op.31 (Bo&Bo 1958) 18pp., parts. For trumpet, trombone, and piano. Allegro: chordal, span of 9th required. Andantino: rocking $\frac{6}{8}$ quality. Presto: triplets, chromatic chords. Moderato: melody interspersed with chords. Allegretto: for trumpet and trombone alone. No.6 (no title) for piano alone; melody punctuated with chords in left hand; quiet. Presto: $\frac{5}{8}$, flowing, *ppp* ending. M-D.

Eric Ewazen. *Pastorale* (ST), parts. 10 min. For trumpet, trombone (tenor or bass), and piano. "A beautiful, lyrical duet for the two brass instruments, supported by a rich impressionistic piano accompaniment" (from www.ericewazen.com).

Helge Jung. *Concertante Suite* Op.9 (Hofmeister 1972) 20pp., parts. For 2 trumpets and piano. Five movements of challenging writing for all 3 players. A complete trumpet score is provided both trumpet performers. M-D.

Roger Kellaway. *Dance of the Ocean Breeze* 1979 (Editions BIM). For horn, tuba, and piano.
———. *Sonoro* 1979 (Editions BIM). For horn, tuba, and piano.

Vaclav Nelhybel. *Suite* (Gen 1966) 12pp., parts. For 2 trumpets and piano. Vivo; Molto espressivo; Marcato con bravura; Slow; Allegro marcato. Effective, mildly 20th-century Neoclassic writing. M-D.

Johann Pezel. *Sonatinas* (Bicinia) (R. P. Block—Musica Rara 1972) Nos.63, 64, 67, 69, 70, 72, 73. For 2 cornetti and continuo. Score and parts for each *Sonatina*.
———. *Sonatinas* 1675 (Bicinia) (R. P. Block—Musica Rara 1969) 6pp., parts.

Nos.71, 74. For 2 clarini (trumpets) and basso continuo. Playable on C trumpet. Short pieces in binary form. Attractive; excellent foreword. Int.

Primoz Ramovs. *Con Sordino* (Društva Slovenskih Skladateljev 1974). 3 copies necessary for performance. For trumpet, trombone, and piano. Explanations in Croatian and English.

Alec Wilder. *Suite* I 1968 (Sam Fox 1971; Margun) 31pp., parts. 14 min. For horn, tuba, and piano. Maestoso; Pesante; In a Jazz manner; Berceuse; Alla caccia. Distinctive jazz idioms and chamber music are blended with a restrained nonchalance. Strong melodies, excellent balance between all instruments, a valid combination. The style is close to Neoclassic and results in some mildly 20th-century and unusual sonorities. M-D.

———. *Suite* II 1974 (Margun). For horn, tuba, and piano.

Trios for Piano, One Brass Instrument, and One Woodwind

Jacobo Ficher. *Sonatina* Op.21 1932 (NME) 19pp., parts. For piano, alto sax, and trumpet. Allegro, quasi alla breve: SA, linear style punctuated with chromatic chords, moves directly to Lento: chromatic harmonic 3rds in right hand move over broken triplet augmented octaves in left hand; moves immediately to Presto: more linear than opening movement but chromatic chords are still present; rhythmic drive. M-D.

Godfrey Finger. *Sonata* C (R. L. Minter—Musica Rara 1974) 10pp., parts. For trumpet, oboe, and keyboard. Preface in English. M-D.

Walter Hartley. *Double Concerto* 1969 (J. Boonin/Philharmusica) 16pp., parts. 7 min. For alto sax, tuba, and piano. Originally for alto sax, tuba, and wind octet. Piano reduction by the composer. Allegro con brio: piano has counterpoint to other parts and provides rhythmic punctuation. Andante: unfolding linear lines. Presto: integrally and equally related to the other parts with fine balance between all 3 instruments. Interesting sonorities. M-D.
———. *Suite* 1984 (Ethos). 5 min. For clarinet, trumpet (C), and piano.
———. *Two Dances* 1984 (ECS). 5 min. For clarinet, trumpet (C), and piano. Rag Tango; Slow Drag.

Heinrich von Herzogenberg. *Trio* Op.61 D (H. Truscott—Musica Rara 1972) 38pp., parts. For oboe, horn, and piano. Allegretto; Presto; Andante con moto; Allegro. Written in a general Brahmsian style, but independent thought is present at all times. Expert handling of the 3 instruments, especially in the thoughtful Allegretto and the final rondo. Worthwhile music that deserves reviving. Valuable Preface by the editor. M-D.

Arthur Honegger. *Petite Suite.* See detailed entry under trios for piano and 2 violins.

Noël Lee. *Commentaries on a Theme from Aaron Copland* 1966 (AMC) 19pp., parts. For trumpet, clarinet, and piano. Slow and Tranquil; With Motion; Very

Slow and Majestic; Moderate and Rhythmic; Slow and Tranquil. "This work, based on the opening measures of the third movement of the *Quartet* for piano and strings by Copland, is designed for moderately-advanced performers. If the pianist's hands are small, the notes in brackets may be omitted; certain octaves may be split between the two hands" (from the score). Written in a Neoclassic style that is chromatic and generally thin-textured. Clear formal structures. Effective balancing of the instruments. M-D.

Carl Reinecke. *Trio* Op.188 a 1887 (Br&H; IMC 2398) 33pp., parts. For oboe (violin), horn (cello), and piano. Flowing passagework at *pp* ushers in an 8-measure theme in the oboe to introduce the opening Allegro moderato and Reinecke's unmistakably conventional mid-19th-century harmonics. The SA form found here with a recapitulation in A/a stays close to the customary design and places the instruments in complementary roles. An energetic Scherzo–Molto Vivace follows with a theme centering around repeated notes in the winds and a countermelody in the piano. A richly expressive Adagio in ternary form ensues with contrasting solo and duet roles. The Trio concludes with a Finale–Allegro ma non troppo of cheerful spirit and slight acknowledgment of late-19th-century chromaticism. For all its glory and finely tuned design the composer refuses to move beyond the early-mid-century concept of Romanticism and plants his tonal palette firmly in the past. Nonetheless, it offers soloistic variety and musical features which make it a pleasure for performers and audiences alike. M-D.

———. *Trio* Op.274 B♭ ca.1905 (Br&H; Musica Rara, 51pp.; WIM), parts. For clarinet, horn (viola), and piano. Commences with a sparkling Allegro announced by imitative entrances and rich harmonies which reveals a descending scalar melody to become the principal thematic devices in this SA form. An Andante follows entitled "A Tale," with flowing passagework at mostly soft dynamics and passionate melodic qualities accentuated by dotted rhythms. Herein each instrument takes turns unveiling the treasures of Reinecke's compositional style. Then the piano announces a Scherzo in the relative minor, and an engaging exchange of motivic development ensues as the instruments weave back and forth through a dance form featuring 2 trios. The Finale starts modestly with rhythmic bounce, requiring careful coordination, and intensifies into a fiery presence for a surprise finish in the final bars by restating the *Trio*'s opening theme. Sweeping lines, full chords, and rhythmically charged writing predominate from the outset and the unmistakeable presence of Mendelssohn and Brahms can be felt in this Classically conceived work composed at the opening of the 20th century. Highly recommended. M-D.

Elliott Schwartz. *Divertimento* 1963 (Gen) 15pp., parts. 10 min. For clarinet, horn, and piano. Humoreske; Dirge; Dance (piano tacet); (4) Variations. Neoclassic, mildly 20th-century. Instruments are well integrated. M-D.

Trios for Piano(s), Percussion, and Another Instrument

Zbigniew Bargielski. *Servet* (AA 1975) 14pp., parts. 7 min. For violin, viola, or cello; or for violin and viola; or for viola and cello; or for all 3 stringed instruments, percussion, and piano. The pianist performs some of the percussion parts. Avant-garde.

Henry Brant. *5 and 10¢ Store Music* 1932 (ACA) 5 min. For violin, piano, and kitchen hardware. As early as 1921 Brant was playing homemade instruments in a backyard orchestra for which he composed his first experimental music. *5 and 10¢ Store Music* is an extension of this experiment. M-D.

———. *Ice Age* (NME 1954) 18pp., parts. For piano, clarinet, and glockenspiel. Sparkling. Aleatoric (called "independent" by Brant) and "coordinated" writing. Piano plays in upper or lower registers through much of the piece. Key signatures are present. "Glistening" sounds reinforce the title. M-D.

Henry Cowell. *Set of Five* (CFP 1968) 43pp., parts. 18 min. For piano, violin, and percussion. One skilled player can handle all the percussion instruments. Largo sostenuto: requires 5 muted gongs of various sizes; has a definite Oriental flavor (open 5ths); octotonic; chromatic lines. Allegro: xylophone in staccato passages with piano produces parallel moving 3rds. Andante: lyrical; requires 5 small-to-medium tom-toms. Presto leggiero: perpetual motion; a modern "Flight of the Bumble Bee"; 6 glass, metal, or porcelain bowls of different pitches may be used. Vigoroso: arpeggiated tone clusters using forearm; glissando harmonics on the strings; uses the same set of drums as in third movement. Skill and virtuosity, both intellectual and technical, are called for from all 3 performers. M-D to D.

Harold Farberman. *Trio* (Gen 1966) 20pp., parts. For piano, violin, and percussion. Two percussion players are preferred, but one can play the part with the proper setup. Requires large percussion complement; directions for percussion setup included. Five movements. Serial construction, pointillistic, clusters, plucked and stopped strings, fingers must be rubbed over strings. Piano cadenza follows the third movement. Fourth movement requires everyone to play *pp;* parts may be played in whatever rhythm the players wish, but notes must follow the order given. Each player selects his or her own tempo. Avant-garde. D.

Ross Lee Finney. *Two Acts for Three Players* (CFP 1975) 46pp., parts. 15½ min. For piano, clarinet, and percussion. Act I, Scene 1: Sweet and Low, Scene 2: The Plot Thickens; Intermezzo; Act II, Scene 1: Romance, Scene 2: The Chase. Clever treatment of all instruments. The pianist, by careful pedaling, contrasts rich sonorities with "dry." "Memory of the silent films that gave so many hours of pleasure in the early decades of this century—figures such as Buster Keaton, Fatty Arbuckle and Charlie Chaplin—forms the basis of this work . . . *Two Acts for Three Players* should sound as though accompanying a film, reflecting the pacing, the humor and the bathos. The performers are also actors to be watched by the audience as well as heard" (from Preface). Extensive directions, unmetered spatial sections, special instrumental notation explained. Traditional techniques mated with avant-garde. D.

Werner Heider. *Musik im Diskant* 1970 (Hänssler 11.403) 13pp., parts. 5½ min. For piccolo, piano (or harpsichord), and percussion. Traditional and proportional notation, dynamic extremes, clusters, glissando on strings, pointillistic, highly organized. To be spoken at conclusion: "genug" (enough). Avant-garde. D.

Alan Hovhaness. *Suite* Op.99 (CFP 6047 1957) 20pp., parts. 14 min. For piano, violin, and percussion (celesta, tam-tam, xylophone). Prelude: pedal held throughout; low-register sonorities. Pastoral: pedal held throughout; a low-register harmonic 2nd is to be played on the strings with a timpani stick. Allegro: repeated scale figures in upper register divided between the hands. Pastoral: same requirements as first Pastoral. Canon: octotonic writing 2 octaves apart. Allegro: pedal held throughout; figure consisting of triplet in left hand with alternating B♭ A♭ is repeated almost continuously; rests and a low C♯ sounding for 2 measures break it up; *ppp* conclusion. Effective if a little monotonous. M-D.

Toshi Ichiyanagi. *Trio Interlink* (Schott SJ1068 1992, ISMN M-65001-105-1) 25pp. 3 copies needed for performance. 13 min. For violin, piano, and percussion. Performance instructions included.

Nikolai Lopatnikoff. *Sonata* Op.9 1926 (Edition Russe de Musique) 35pp., parts. For piano, violin, and snare drum. Allegro Energico: parallel chords coupled with melodic elements, staccato octaves, repeated 4th, 7th, and 9th chords, freely tonal. Andante: Impressionist, asymmetrical phrase lengths, large span required. Allegro vivace: octotonic, driving rhythmic 16ths, syncopated chords, contrary-motion triplets, melodic emphasis in episode; vigorous rhythmic element returns to close out movement in a brilliant display for all instruments. M-D to D.

Alain Louvier. *Houles* (Leduc). For piano, percussion, and Ondes Martenot. Stormy, free in construction. Frantic explosions of quotes from Beethoven and Chopin intrude from time to time. Avant-garde. D.

Paul-Baudouin Michel. *Colloque* 1967 (CeBeDeM) 54pp., parts. 16 min. For piano, trumpet, and percussion. Performance instructions in French, including placement of instruments. Introduzione–Adagio–Allegretto; Lento; Allegretto. Freely tonal, tremolando, octotonic, percussive treatment of piano, secco style. Lento is intense, and dramatic gestures are important; octaves in alternating hands; contrast in tempo changes are part of this movement. The finale uses contrary chromatic runs and brilliant chordal skips, breathtaking finish. Solid craft is demonstrated in this mildly 20th-century, Neoclassic work. Large span required. D.

Marcel Mihalovici. *Improvisations* Op.83 1961 (Heugel) 20pp., parts. 8 min. For 2 percussionists and piano. Varied sections, tempos, and moods. Added-note technique, shifting meters, freely tonal style, mildly 20th-century. Percussion required: gong, vibraphone, timbales, marimba, 3 tom-toms, tambour militaire, kettle drum with pedals, 3 Chinese blocks. M-D.

Ödön Partos. *Agaga* (A Legend) (IMI 1962) 33pp., parts. 12 min. For piano, violin, and percussion. Serial, Oriental character. Source for the work is the Oriental technique of improvisation based on developing variations. In 5 movements to be played without a break. The first movement is an image-cadenza; the second, a quasi-theme; the third, a set of variations in accelerating tempo; the fourth, a reprise of the theme in modal variation; the fifth, a variant of the third movement. Pointillistic, flexible meters. Row dictates development. Contains a diagram and performance directions. D.

Francis Pyle. *Sonata for Three* (Leblanc 1964) 22pp., parts. 10 min. For piano, clarinet, and percussion. Aria; Quasi pastorale; Quasi recitativo; Vivo. One sectionalized movement that is played without stop. Key signatures are present; mildly dissonant and mainly linear style; wide dynamic range. Requires a large span. M-D.

William Schmidt. *Septigrams* 1956 (WIM AVI 28 1967) 34pp., parts. For flute, piano, and percussion. Percussion required: snare drum, medium tom-tom, low tom-tom, and suspended cymbal. Written in the form of a Suite with 7 short movements. Introduction: a fife and drum march. Quartal Blues: slow, brooding "blues" style that uses piano harmonics and soft brushes. Syncophrases: lively, syncopated $\frac{12}{8}$. Polyjazz: a mid-20th-century interpretation of American jazz. Improvisational Variant: a cadenza in free, unbarred style, without percussion. The Percussive Fugato: rondo, a 3-bar motif imitated in a quasi-fugal style using all 3 instruments. Finale: a slow chorale. The piano is handled in numerous ways, including percussive syncopated chords, figuration in alternating hands, bitonal octaves, "blues" 7th chords, harmonics, contrary chromatic triads. Many jazz sonorities. Requires a large span. M-D.

Robert Schollum. *Mosaik* Op.75 1968 (Dob) 15pp., 3 copies necessary for performance. For piano, oboe, and vibraphone. Rasch; Rasch, im Charakter etwa eines Geschwindmarsches; Ruhig fliessende; Rausch und leicht. Free 12-tone usage. Clusters, pointillistic, dynamic extremes, glissandi on white and black keys together, free repetition. "His use of timbres derived originally from Debussy and Milhaud. The later austerity in his style is related in part to his interest in the world's folk musics" (DCM, p.662). D.

Giora Schuster. *Accenti* (IMI 1965) 31pp. 3 copies required for performance. For 2 pianos and percussion. One player can handle all the percussion parts. First section untitled; Intermezzo; Andante–molto ritmico. Includes notes for performance and diagram for grouping the instruments. Percussion required: 3 timpani, xylophone, side drum with snares, suspended cymbal, bass drum, triangle, tam-tam, 3 tom-toms, 2 temple blocks, claves. Major 7ths are important; freely serial, pointillistic, some strings prepared by rubber wedges. Abstract. Requires seasoned ensemble players. D.

Kazimierz Serocki. *Fantasmagoria* (PWM 1971) 18 unnumbered leaves. 11–14 min. Instructions for performance (7pp.). 3 scores required for performance. Diagrammatic notation in part. Aleatoric. D.

Ralph Shapey. *Evocation* 1959 (IU) 37pp. For piano, violin, and percussion. Recitative–with intense majesty; With humor; With tenderness; With intense majesty. Serial, profound writing. The slow movement (With tenderness) and finale are unusually haunting and moving. Contains placement instructions for the percussion battery. Percussion required: low gong, high, medium, and low tom-toms, bass drum, cymbals high and low, high wood block, medium gamelan, snare drum, 3 different kinds of sticks. Bar lines are used only as visual aids to the performers; they do not refer to any conception of metric or phrase division. Clusters, pointillistic. D.

Wolfgang Steffen. *Triplum* 72 Op.39 (Bo&Bo 1973) 23pp. 4 copies required for performance. 14 min. For flute (alto recorder ad lib), piano, and percussion. Performance directions in German. Pointillistic, dynamic extremes, harmonics, improvisation, cluster tremolos, avant-garde. D.

Karlheinz Stockhausen. *No. 11 Refrain* (UE 13187 1961) 3pp., including one of instructions. For piano, celesta, and vibraphone. Pianist needs 3 wood blocks; celesta player requires 3 antique cymbales; vibraphonist needs 3 cowbells and 3 glockenspiel plates. Six systems (each consisting of 2 or 3 staves) are to be read from left to right and from top to bottom. An extensive set of rules is given. Six degrees of loudness are indicated by the thickness of the dots and lines. There are 6 different signs for durations and 5 different types of pauses. Performers, on indication, produce a click with the tip of the tongue on the upper inside gum; 5 different pitches are to be made by changing the position of the mouth. Shouted syllables, glissandi, clusters, etc. A quiet and spaciously composed continuity of sounds is disturbed 6 times by a short refrain consisting of glissandi and clusters, trills, bass notes (in the piano), and brief snatches of melody. Players choose the points at which the refrain is played, and these change from one performance to the next. Avant-garde. D.

Roger Tessier. *Vega* (EFM 1973) 16pp., parts. For piano, percussion, and Ondes Martenot. Part of series "Hommage à Copernic." Reproduced from holograph. Graphic notation in part. Avant-garde. D.

Alain Weber. *Variantes* (Leduc 1972) 16 min. For piano and 2 percussionists. Eleven variations of highly complex writing, severe chromaticism, some avant-garde notation, aleatoric sections. Only for the most adventurous with plenty of pianistic equipment and perseverance. D.

Charles Wuorinen. *Trio* III (CFP 1974) 52pp., parts. For piano, flute, and percussion. D.

Music for Four Instruments

Quartets for Piano and Strings

[Piano, violin, viola, and cello, unless otherwise noted.]

Jean Absil. *Quartet* Op.33 1938 (CeBeDeM 1962) 47pp., parts. 22 min. Allegro moderato: chromatic chordal opening, alternating hands, fleet 32nd-note arpeggi and scales, emphatic octaves. Intermezzo: broken octaves, 3 with 2, arpeggi triplet patterns; piano has a quasi-cadenza. Fileuse: an unending stream of steady 16ths in one instrument or another. Recit et Final: piano opens with a rising dramatic gesture; important inner voices; hand crossings; chromatic 3rds; exciting closing; large span required. D.

——. *Fantaisie* Op.40 1939 (CeBeDeM) 22pp., parts. 10 min. Chromatic vocabulary, arpeggi and scalar gestures, short cadenza for piano, octaves in alternating hands. M-D.

William Alwyn. *Rhapsody* 1939 (OUP) 20pp., parts. 10 min. Romantic and well-crafted writing with Impressionist touches. The outer, driving rhythmic Moderato e deciso sections are contrasted with a più tranquillo mid-section. Freely tonal, strong conclusion. M-D.

Carl Philipp Emanuel Bach. *Quartets* W.93 a, W.94 D, W.95 G 1788 (Schmid—Nag 222, 223, 224). See detailed entry under quartets for piano(s), strings, and winds.

Johann Christian Bach. *Quartet* G (W. Bergmann—Schott 4151) 34pp., parts. Allegro; Rondo: piano part is obbligato except for the places (indicated by figures) that have been supplemented by the editor. Because of the pianistic style and Bach's preference for the piano, the use of that instrument, rather than a harpsichord, is historically justified. M-D.

Henk Badings. *Quartet* 1973 (Donemus) 40pp., parts. 18 min. Lento–Presto; Adagio; Allegro molto. Badings favors an intense, chromatic harmony more in tune with German thinking than with French. A distant similarity to Hindemith. Reproduced from MS. D.

Leonardo Balada. *Cuatris for Four Instruments* (Gen 1970) 18pp., parts. 8½ min. For flute or violin, clarinet or viola, trombone or cello or bassoon, with prepared piano or harpsichord. Five movements that involve clusters, *pp* chromatic figuration, prepared strings using chains or metal, improvisation with clusters ad lib in bravura fashion, repeated notes, crossed hands, pointillistic treatment, striking strings and glissandi on strings. Large span required. Avant-garde. D.

Arnold Bax. *Quartet* (Murdoch 1924) 27pp., parts. In one movement, Allegro moderato. Dramatic, impulsive, explosive mood, chromatic. M-D to D.

Ludwig van Beethoven. *Quartets* (S. Kross—Henle 1973) 110pp., parts. Op.16, WoO36/1–3. Piano part fingered by H.-M. Theopold. The 3 piano *Quartets* WoO36 were written when Beethoven was 15 years old. The style of these works and the fact that he reached back into these *Quartets* for thematic material for his first piano Sonatas (Op.2/1 and 3) speak strongly for their genuineness. While not comparable with his later string Quartets, they are lovely compositions and have much to teach about ensemble work. The pianist needs to be able to handle octaves with some facility. Op.16 E♭ (1796–97) was originally written for piano, oboe, clarinet, bassoon, and horn. All the following publishers have Op.16 for violin, viola, cello, and piano as arranged by Beethoven: Br&H; F. A. Roitzsch—CFP 8431 54pp., parts; GS L1623; Augener 7198; EPS; IMC. Both versions have the same opus number.
———. *Quartet* II D Op. posth. (Br&H).
———. *Quartet* III C Op. posth. (Br&H).

Sebastian Bodinus. *Sonata* E♭ (H. Fischer—Vieweg 1939) 11pp., parts. For 2 oboes or violins, bassoon or cello, and piano. Adagio; Allegro; Siciliana; Allegro assai. Attractive, good realization. M-D.

Léon Boëllmann. *Quatuor* Op.10 (Hamelle). Four movements: spirited allegro, delicate scherzo, somber andante, breezy and cheerful finale. Mildly 20th-century modal harmonies, Franckian influence. M-D.

René de Boisdeffre. *1er Quatuor* Op.13 g (Hamelle) 82pp., parts. Allegro ma non troppo; Scherzo; Andante espressivo; Finale. M-D.
———. *2me Quatuor* Op.91 E♭ (Hamelle) 91pp., parts. Andante espressivo–Allegro con brio; Scherzo; Andante; Finale. M-D to D.
Both works display above-average Romantic writing.

Mélanie Bonis. *Quatuor* Op.72 1905 (Hamelle) 70pp., parts. Moderato; Intermezzo; Adagio; Final. Chromatic, numerous key signatures. Franck influence present; traditional late-turn-of-the-century pianistic treatment. M-D to D.

Johannes Brahms. *Quartet* Op.25 g 1861 (H. Krellmann—Henle 79pp., parts; Schumann—CFP 3939A; Br&H; GS L1624; Simrock; Schroeder—Augener;

EPS; IMC) 39 min. The Henle edition is based on the autograph and the most reliable sources. Allegro; Intermezzo–Allegro (ma non troppo); Andante con moto; Rondo alla Zingarese. Full of contrasts and majestic themes, this *Quartet* is one of the most exciting pieces in all chamber music literature. It is probably the most popular of the 3 piano *Quartets* because the Rondo is reminiscent of Brahms's *Hungarian Dances*. The Intermezzo displays unusual coloring and delicacy. D.

———. *Quartet* Op.26 A 1861–62 (H. Krellmann—Henle 67pp., parts; Br&H; CFP 3939C; GS L1626). The Henle edition has fingering for the piano part added by H.-M. Theopold and also contains a Preface in German, English, and French. Allegro non troppo; Poco adagio; Scherzo–Poco allegro; Finale–Allegro. The first movement demonstrates Brahms's fine contrapuntal skill with a theme easily expressed by strings or piano. Serene melodies in the slow movement, the finest in this work, plus a flowing scherzo (with the trio written in canon) and the sustained drive of the finale show Brahms at his best. D.

———. *Quartet* Op.60 c 1874–75 (H. Krellmann—Henle 55pp., parts; CFP 3939C; Br&H; GS L1626; IMC). 31 min. The Henle is an excellent practical Urtext with a Preface in French, German, and English. Allegro non troppo; Andante–Allegro commodo. This piano *Quartet* was the earliest one conceived, but Brahms reworked it later, hence the completion date of 1874–75. It shows youthful impulsiveness as well as characteristics of the mature, poised master. Displays great despair and is gloomier than Op.25 and Op.26. D.

See Henry Cope Colles, *The Chamber Music of Brahms* (New York: AMS Press, 1975; reprint of London, 1933 edition); Henry S. Drinker, *The Chamber Music of Brahms* (New York: AMS Press, 1974; reprint); Ivor Keys, *Brahms Chamber Music* (London: BBC Music Guides, 1974); Robert Pascall, "Ruminations on Brahms's Chamber Music," MT 1590 (August 1975): 697–99; J. Webster, "The C Sharp Minor Version of Brahms's Op. 60," MT 121 (Feb. 1980): 89–93.

Frank Bridge. *Phantasy* f♯ (Augener 1911) 32pp., parts. Many contrasted sections in an extended andante con moto enclosing a central allegro vivace and followed by a concluding retrospective tranquillo. Much arpeggiation, somber, reflective mood. M-D.

Edvard Hagerup Bull. *Sonata con spirito* 1970 (Editions Française de Musique, Technisonor) 87pp., parts.

Clement Calder. *Quartett* 1968 (Bo&Bo) 12pp., parts. Three untitled movements with metronome indications only. Serial, flexible meters, pointillistic, abstract writing. D.

Alexis de Castillon. *Quatuor* Op.7 g 1871–72 (Hamelle). Larghetto–Allegro deciso: SA; introduction plays an important part in the movement. Scherzando: a minuet with curious rhythmic effects. Larghetto, quasi marcia religiosa: ABA. Allegro: rondo, dancelike, flowing Romantic writing for all instruments. M-D.

Ernest Chausson. *Quartet* Op.30 A 1897 (Rouart Lerolle; IMC 95pp., parts). Animé: SA. Très calme. ABA. Simple et sans hâte: AB. Animé: SA. A mature work that presents an unusually fine balance in the motivic interplay between piano and strings. Superb piano writing, sweeping gestures, cyclic constituents. D.

Aaron Copland. *Quartet* 1950 (Bo&H) 36pp., parts. 21 min. Adagio serio: 11-note row, 2 mutually exclusive whole-tone groups; expressive polyphony. Allegro giusto: great rhythmic variety of the row, but steady meter throughout; witty, appealing. Non troppo lento: soliloquy-like; linked to original row by whole-tone scales; near the conclusion 10 notes of the row are heard in descending whole-tone scales in parallel major 6ths. This was Copland's first attempt at serial technique, and the motivic and rhythmic organization is almost too tight and stiff in places. Sonata and fugue elements are synthesized. D.

Arcangelo Corelli. *Trio Sonata* Op.1/1 F (E. P. Biggs—Music Press MPI 30-12). For 2 violins, cello, and organ or piano. Grave; Allegro; Adagio; Allegro; Adagio. Graceful and flowing ideas organized into perfect structural designs; unity of musical logic and beauty of melody. Excellent keyboard realization. A perfect example of the Sonata da Chiesa. M-D.

————. *Trio Sonata* Op.3/2 D (E. P. Biggs—Music Press MPI 34-10). For 2 violins, cello, and organ or piano. Grave; Allegro; Adagio; Allegro. M-D.

Ingolf Dahl. *Quartet* 1957 (J. Boonin) 50pp., parts. 18½ min. Melodic and harmonic materials are serialized. Fantasia Appassionata: pointillistic, martellato passage work, capricious and molto staccato, dry and brittle writing. Antiphon: flexible meters; more lyric and longer lines; section for solo piano; contrast range from dolcissimo, misterioso to energico and feroce; tremolo. Rondo alia Campanella: piano is mainly used percussively, with strongly accented sonorities colored with grace notes; alternating hands; fragmented ideas; effective arpeggio figures pedaled; widely spread gestures; solo piano part; harmonics. Melodic and harmonic materials are serialized. D.

Albert Delvaux. *Vijf Stukken* (Five Pieces) 1964 (CeBeDeM) 51pp., parts. Allegro spiritoso: freely serial, melodic, duplet and triplet figuration, alternating hands. Adagio: molto espressivo, chordal, syncopated melody, broken-chord figuration. Allegretto scherzando: dancelike; antiphonal writing between piano and strings. Larghetto: mainly chordal and sustained. Vivo: rocking triplet pulsation, punctuated chords. Mildly 20th-century serial treatment throughout. D.

Emma Lou Diemer. *Quartet* 1954 (Seesaw) 23pp., parts. 12 min. Agitated: freely tonal, repeated octaves and quartal harmonies, dialogue between strings and piano, octotonic, shifting rhythms in repeated patterns. Rather slow, pensive:

trills and long unfolding lines. Jocose: uses sharp, precise, and staccato figures; bouncing motifs, effective coda. M-D.

Théodore Dubois. *Quartet* a (Heugel 1907) 61pp., parts. Allegro agitato; Andante molto espressivo; Allegro leggiero; Allegro con fuoco. The last movement is based on thematic ideas from the other movements and serves as a summary of the whole work. M-D.

Antonín Dvořák. *Quartet* Op.23 D 1875 (Artia; Litolff; Schlesinger) 26 min. Clarity of style, vitality of thematic material. Treatment of piano fairly simple but highly effective, in spite of some obvious sequential modulation. Much short-sectioned exchange between instruments. The third and final movement, in 2 sections, combines the functions of scherzo and finale. M-D.

————. *Quartet* Op.87 E♭ 1889 (Artia; Simrock; IMC) 28 min. More commanding, with rich style, yet concise and expressive with greater emotional intensity than Op.23. The first theme of the opening movement (SA) is heard with great clarity and power. Later the cello maintains pedal points augmented by the viola (both playing, pizzicato) while the violin follows the piano figurations. The Lento is one of Dvořák's loveliest lyrical and atmospheric movements. The melodious first and last sections of the scherzo enclose a monotonously harmonized motif, Oriental in character. An energetic finale in clear SA design closes the work. D.

Anne Eggleston. *Piano Quartet* (Jaymar 1954–55) 38pp., parts. 22 min. Moderately with expression; Allegro scherzando; Lento; Allegro. The 4 movements, although not connected thematically, have in common the relationship between the piano as an individual and the strings as a group. All movements have passages in which these 2 elements are either united or contrasted. Influences of Bloch are evident in the first and third movements; of Bartók in the alternating rhythms of the Scherzo; and of Hindemith in the first movement, written in concerto grosso form, which builds to a 4-part fugue before the final statement of the theme. M-D.

Georges Enesco. *Quartet II* Op.30 d 1944 (Editura Muzicală Uniunii Compozitorilor din Republica Socialista Romania) 79pp., parts. Allegro moderato; Andante pensieroso ed espressivo; Con moto moderato. Unusual harmonic vocabulary, fluid and complex rhythms, surprising sonorities. D.

Gabriel Fauré. *Quartet I* Op.15 c 1879 (Hamelle 85pp., parts; IMC) 32 min. Allegro molto moderato: opens with an unusual unison passage for strings accompanied by syncopated piano chords. Scherzo–Allegro vivace: piano states the main theme, in $^6_8$; remarkably original writing that treats the piano like a harp. Adagio: breathes long lines and is of great intrinsic beauty. Allegro molto: flows ever forward. D.

————. *Quartet II* Op.45 g 1886 (Hamelle 91pp., parts; IMC) 36 min. Allegro molto moderato; Allegro molto; Adagio non troppo; Allegro molto. One of Fauré's most powerful works; combines highly interesting thematic material with a more closely woven texture. The fiery Scherzo has more sharply defined outlines than does *Quartet I*. A noble slow movement is followed by an impetuous finale, and the whole work reveals an intensity and a diversity of sentiment infrequently heard in Fauré's writing. D.

Morton Feldman. *Four Instruments* 1975 (UE 16501). 6 min.
———. *Piano, Violin, Viola, Cello* 1987 (UE 18751). 75 min.

Zdeněk Fibich. *Quartet* Op.11 e 1874 (Artia; Urbanek 51pp., parts). In 3 movements, with only 5 themes in the entire piece. Allegro moderato: 2 themes, rolled chords, tremolo, octave runs, alternation of hands. Tema con variazioni: one theme, 8 contrasting variations, coda. Finale–Allegro energico: 2 themes with all 5 themes from the entire work combined at the end. Romantic, nationalistic, flowing piano writing. Fibich's chef d'oeuvre is notable for its closely woven ensemble technique. M-D to D.

Benjamin Frankel. *Quartet* Op.26 (Nov 1962) 24pp., parts. Moderato: declamatory; fast chordal skips; 2nds prevalent; octotonic; moves over entire keyboard; atonal. Allegretto: octaves and chords in alternating hands; poco meno mosso mid-section contrasts secco and sustained writing; large span required. Lento: freely dissonant; cantando; many harmonic 7ths; intense buildup; *pp* closing. Sensitive writing throughout. D.

Isadore Freed. *Triptych* (SPAM 1945) 63pp., parts. Risoluto: chordal, some melodic emphasis. Andante sostenuto: ostinato treatment; Animato mid-section. Allegro, ben ritmato: rhythmic emphasis with chords, brief melodic sections for piano. Mildly 20th-century, mainly treated in homophonic style. M-D.

Gunnar de Frumerie. *Quartet* 1942 (NMS). Rich sonorities tinged with Romanticism; firm formal control; flowing counterpoint between instruments; broad gestures. Piano writing effective throughout. M-D to D.

Hermann Goetz. *Quartet* Op.6 E (Wollenweber UWKR 15 1974) 60pp., parts. Rasch und feurig; Langsam (theme and 4 variations); Scherzo; Sehr langsam–Frisch und lebendig. Shows a mastery of style. Instances of profound sadness and inspiring energy permeate the work. Emotional theme of the variations and the melancholy introduction to the finale show Goetz at his best. A 3-part canon in the trio of the scherzo points up the composer's fine craft. Brahmsian in style. Worth reviving. D.

Francesco de Guarnieri. *Quartetto* (Carisch 1942) 68pp., parts. 34 min. Allegro moderato; Cantabile; Finale. Chromatic, sequences, traditional pianistic approaches, mildly 20th-century. M-D.

Reynaldo Hahn. *Quartet III* G (Heugel 1946) 53pp., parts. Allegretto moderato; Allegro assai; Andante; Allegro assai. Flexible and light writing, clear harmonies, numerous easy-flowing melodies. Gallic clarity in the tradition of Saint-Saëns mixed with style of Massenet, Hahn's teacher. The slow movement is especially melodious and beautiful. M-D.

Franz Joseph Haydn. *Quartet* Op.5/4 G (W. Upmeyer—Nag 129) 12pp., parts. For 2 violins, viola, and piano; cello ad lib. Originally a Divertimento for woodwinds, strings, and basso continuo. Hob.II:1. This arrangement here can also be performed by flute, violin, viola, and piano. Vivace; Andante moderato; Menuetto; Fantasia (with 5 variations). Delightful writing, appealing format. M-D.

——. *Divertimenti* (H. Walter—Henle 453 1989, ISMN M-2018-0453-8) 57pp., parts. For 2 violins, cello, and piano. Contains 6 divertimentos: Hob.XIV:4 C 1764, [Allegro]; Menuet; Finale [Allegro]. Hob.XIV:3 C, Allegro moderato; Menuet; Finale–Allegro molto. Hob.XIV:7 C, Allegro moderato; Menuet; Finale–Presto. Hob.XIV:9 F, Allegro; Menuet; Finale–Allegro molto. Hob.XIV:8 C, Allegro moderato; Menuet; Finale–Scherzo. Hob.XIV:C2 C, Allegro moderato; Menuet. Each of these is short and facile without complication, "dominated by the keyboard part, with the subordinate string instruments generally serving to augment the volume of sound" (from Preface). This edition is extracted from the Complete Edition of Haydn, *Joseph Haydn Werke,* also published by Henle. Int. to M-D.

——. *Divertimento* Hob.XIV:2 C ca.1760 (H. C. Robbins Landon—Dob DM 325 1966) 5pp., parts. A genuine miniature in 2 tiny movements; charming and gracefully written. Int.

——. *Divertimento* Hob.XIV:8 C (G. Balla—Litolff). Written before 1766. The finale (Scherzo) is by far the best movement, truly vintage Haydn wit. Int. to M-D.

——. *Divertimento* Hob.XIV:9 F (L. Kalmar—Litolff 1972) 10pp., parts.

——. *Concertini* (H. Walter—Henle 1969) 47pp., parts. Fingering for piano added by H.-M. Theopold. From the Complete Edition of the Joseph Haydn Institute. Contains 4 concertinos: 1. Hob.XIV:11 C, Moderato; Adagio; Allegro. 2. Hob.XIV:12 C, Allegro; Adagio; Finale. 3. Hob.XIV:13 G, Allegro moderato; Adagio; Finale. 4. Hob.XVIII:F2 F, Moderato; Adagio; Allegro assai. These all date from the early 1760s when Haydn wrote concerted music with keyboard within the technical range of amateur performers. Contains Preface and remarks about the individual sources. An excellent practical and Urtext edition. Int. to M-D.

Kurt Hessenberg. *Quartett* Op.10 C 1935 (Müller) 21 min. Written in a mildly 20th-century style with a Hindemith flavor. Full of admirable individual traits that show that Hessenberg was a superb craftsman. M-D.

Emil Hlobil. *Quartette* Op.23 1943 (Hudební Matice 1948) 59pp., parts. 22 min. Allegro vivace: C, SA, bitonal usage; piano provides figuration and harmonic structure. Lento: E♭, ABA, lyric with B section more lively. Allegro assai: C,

SA; piano has short ostinato-like figurations and stays busy but has little or no melodic emphasis. Piano or harpsichord can be used, but the work seems to be conceived more for the piano since numerous crescendo and decrescendo marks are used. M-D.

Arthur Honegger. *Rhapsody* 1917 (Sal 1923) 13pp., parts. For 2 flutes, clarinet, and piano, or for 2 violins, viola, and piano. See detailed entry under quartets for piano and 3 woodwinds.

Herbert Howells. *Piano Quartet* Op.21 a 1916, rev.1936 (St&B). 27 min. Allegro moderato, tranquillo: the hill is reflected at dawn. Lento, molto tranquillo: hill seen during a day in mid-summer. Allegro molto, energico: the hill in the month of March. Programmatic references "to the Hill at Chosen and Ivor Gurney who knows it." Intensely moving and gripping; one of the finest works of the period. "English" style, modal, inspired by folk tunes. M-D.

Johann N. Hummel. *Quartet* Op. posth. G (K. Stierhof—Dob DM 538 1976) 37pp., parts. Two movements. Over-elaborate figuration in the piano part, somewhat superficial and showy. Not easy. M-D.

Karel Husa. *Variations* 1983–84 (AMP). Explores alternations of sound, intervals, chords, and forms in permutations, mirroring, and other techniques. Virtuosic.

Vincent d'Indy. *Quartet* Op.7 a 1878 (Durand). Opening movement: SA design with some interesting modulations in the second tonal area, but the style is mainly reserved and conservative. Andante: an expressive ballade, no complexities. Rondo: main idea not used at the conclusion, but principal subject from the second episode assumes supremacy. Clever rhythmic inventiveness adds to the interest of this work. D.

Gordon P. Jacob. *Quartet* (Nov 1972) 64pp., parts. 22 min. Opens majestically with a short Andante that leads to a lively Allegro section. Eight tempo changes are encountered in the Scherzo, in which the pianist has fast octave passages. The third movement is an expressive Variations and Epilogue. The pianist needs plenty of agility. D.

Joseph Jongen. *Quatuor* Op.23 E♭ 1902 (Durand). Cyclic in form, close affinity to Franck. Themes have a sustained beauty and are expressed in a unique way. Classical format, with the different parts of each movement built on 2 themes with traditional development procedure. No over-exuberant display in any of the instruments. Lengthy work. M-D to D.

Léon Jongen. *Divertissement en forme de variations sur un thème de Haydn* 1955 (CeBeDeM 1962) 32pp., parts. 11 min. Moderato; Nocturnal Pastoral; Tempo di Marcia; Vivamente. Based on tune from finale of Haydn's *"Surprise" Symphony.* Clever and effective, mildly 20th-century writing. M-D.

Jan Kapr. *Rotazione 9* (Supraphon 1967) 27pp. Full score required for each player. Includes passages in indeterminate notation. Three series used create a 9-angled crystal for Kapr to manipulate. Some controlled improvisation by prescribed pitches. Requires much rehearsal time. D.

Willem Kersters. *Quatuor* Op.53 1970 (CeBeDeM) 28pp., parts. 12½ min. Moderato; Andante (in memoriam Henri Koch); Allegro molto. Octotonic, chromatic, thin textures, eclectic style. Photostat of MS is difficult to read. M-D.

Ellis B. Kohs. *Quartet* 1962 (Cameo Music) 20 min. Studies in Variation, Part II. This is part of a larger work: Part I, for woodwind quintet; Part III, for piano; Part IV, for solo violin. "The grand design . . . is that the four compositions are variations of each other and have a measure-for-measure correspondence. That is to say, if we understand it correctly, the basic material remains the same and recurs in the same order, but on each appearance is varied in texture, dynamics, rhythm, melodic direction and special effects. In style, according to the composer, he has 'attempted a synthesis or reconciliation of certain elements of newer compositional techniques with traditional concepts of tonal order and structure.' As an ambitious project Mr. Kohs' work is probably unique. Countless composers have produced variations of one kind or another, but we can think of none who has utilized the variation principle on such a large and complicated scale" (Albert Goldberg in the *Los Angeles Times,* May 7, 1963).

Egon Kornauth. *Quartet* Op.18 c (Dob). Written in a mildly 20th-century idiom with strong Romantic influences, such as those of Brahms, Schumann, and Reger. M-D to D.

Hans Kox. *Quartet* 1959 (Donemus 1959) 30pp., parts. Allegro; Adagio; Allegro assai. Thematic material is developed in a convincing and conscious manner. Striking rhythmic procedure. M-D to D.

———. *Quartet* II 1968 (Donemus 1968) 22pp., parts. 6 min. A dramatic one-movement design of multiple sections. M-D.

Guillaume Lekeu. *Quartet* (Rouart Lerolle 1909). Unfinished; revised by Vincent d'Indy, who added an admirable conclusion to the second movement (lento e con passione), a highly expressive nocturne. Lengthy development in first movement, rich sonorities. Contains some moving and impassioned pages from a strong Romantic personality. D.

Daniel Lesur. *Suite* 1943 (Amphion 140) 29pp., parts. Nocturne; Ricercara; Berceuse; Tarantella. Elegant writing, modal. Some Impressionist influences and a little dissonance produce some subtle harmonies. The work shows Lesur to be a composer whose refined style displays both lyrical and poetic qualities. M-D.

Jean-Baptiste Loeillet (of Lyons). *Sonata* Op.2/11 D (H. Ruf—Schott 5393) 12pp., parts. For 2 violins, cello, and keyboard. Adagio; Allegro; Largo; Allegro. Excellent and stylistic realization. M-D.

Gustav Mahler. *Quartet* g 1876 (P. Ruzicka—Sikorski 800 1973) 31pp., parts, facsimile. First edition. Introduction in German and English, critical commentary in German. This 234-bar movement was written when Mahler was a student in Vienna, but the thematic ideas already have a personal profile. The form and treatment clearly show the influence of Brahms, Schumann, and Schubert on the young Mahler. Triplet figuration is relied on heavily in the exposition and recapitulation. An agitato-like development works to a suspenseful climax. The subdued, muted, intermezzo-like section just before the recapitulation is very moving, and the melancholy, sinking closing in a negates any conventional exterior one might expect to find in a 16-year-old. An Appendix contains a 24-bar sketch for a scherzo movement. D.

Bohuslav Martinů. *Quartet I* 1942 (AMP) 52pp., parts. 22 min. Poco allegro; Adagio; Allegretto poco moderato. Spontaneous pulse patterns produce a strong and virile rhythmic fabric. Wide harmonic range includes simple progressions as well as biting dissonance. Fluid and transparent polyphony plus vivid tonal sonorities add to the integral unity. Great variety of traditional pianistic techniques and idioms in a 20th-century setting. D.

Felix Mendelssohn. *Quartet* Op.1 c 1822 (CFP; Br&H) 25 min. M-D.
———. *Quartet* Op.2 f 1823 (CFP; Br&H) 22 min. The melody in the Adagio movement is especially fervent, and its bold enharmonic modulations as well as the melodic invention in the intermezzo (Allegro moderato) show great originality for a 14-year-old. M-D.
———. *Quartet* Op.3 b 1825 (CFP; Br&H) 30 min. In this compelling piece, the piano part requires lightness and transparency to balance the string writing. The Adagio is in the nature of an expressive "Song without Words." A noble quality permeates both outside movements. With this work, Mendelssohn finishes his apprenticeship and becomes a composer in his own right. M-D.
These 3 early *Quartets,* modeled on Weber and early Beethoven, show an extraordinary precocity. The strings are skillfully pitted against the piano in some places, but the piano part is much more important than the string complement in Opp.1 and 2. All 3 *Quartets* consist of 4 movements and contain scherzi in duple meter.
See John Horton, *The Chamber Music of Mendelssohn* (London: Oxford University Press, 1946), pp. 10–15.

Darius Milhaud. *Quartet* 1966 (Durand) 29pp., parts. Strongly characterized melodies in both shape and rhythm; chords of 9ths, 11ths, and 13ths are present and enrich the harmony. Milhaud utilizes maximum capacities for colorful sonorities in all 4 movements. M-D.

Wolfgang Amadeus Mozart. *Quartets* K.478 g 1785, K.493 E♭ 1785 (E. Herttrich—Henle 1974) 67pp., parts. This edition is based on the autograph, the first edition (1787), and the André edition (1809). Fingering for the piano part has been added by H.-M. Theopold. Clear printing, high Urtext standards continued here as in other Henle editions. Preface in German, English, and French. Most authorities seem to agree that K.478 is the finer of the 2 *Quartets.* Its passionate first movement, melancholy Andante, and exuberant finale with exquisite melodies make it a catalog of Mozart's finest art. D.

Available separately: *Quartet* K.478 (H. Federhofer—Br 1957) 52pp., parts. A fine Preface includes background on the work as well as editorial procedures and sources used. Allegro; Andante; Rondo–Allegro moderato. Virtuoso demands are made on the pianist, but the strings are completely integrated into the texture. This work is unjustly neglected. A facsimile of the MS is available (F. Ferguson—Internationale Stiftung Mozarteum Salzburg 1991, ISBN 3-9500072-0-2). *Quartet* K.493 (H. Federhofer—Br). Critically revised edition based on the *Neue Mozart Ausgabe.*

Other editions of both *Quartets* by CFP; Br&H; Augener; BMC.

——. *Chamber Concertos—Piano Quartets* 1765 (A. Hoffmann—Möseler) K.107/1 D (Corona 121); K.107/2 G (Corona 122); K.107/3 E♭ (Corona 123). For 2 violins, cello, and continuo. The continuo part is the solo piano. These are early concerto arrangements after Johann Christian Bach's *Sonatas* Op.5. Mozart played K.107/1, 2 not only in his prodigy days but also in later years. M-D.

——. *Chamber Concerto—Piano Quartet* K.246 C (Corona 125) (Möseler). M-D

Wolfgang Amadeus Mozart (The Son). *Quartett* Op.1 g 1802 (H. Riessberger—Dob 1966) 43pp., parts. Molto vivace; Adagio, ma non troppo; Thema con Variazioni (9 variations and coda). Reveals a noteworthy musical talent. Classical style with traditional pianistic idioms and figurations. M-D.

Herman Mulder. *Kwartet* Op.138 1965 (Donemus 1966) 42pp., parts. Allegro moderato; Allegro vivace; Adagio–Allegro vivace. Closely knit writing with occasional imitation between instruments. Quiet ending at *ppp.* M-D.

Vítězslav Novák. *Quartet* Op.7 c 1894, rev.1899 (Artia; Simrock 39pp., parts). Andante; Scherzino; Rondo. In the Brahms-Dvořák tradition; expert writing with Slovak folk materials making a distinguished contribution to this work. M-D.

Robert Palmer. *Piano Quartet* 1947 (J. Kirkpatrick—SPAM 1950) 80pp., parts. Allegro e molto energico: Oriental scale of half- and whole steps is used for main subject while contrasting subject is constructed on wide intervals. Andante con moto e semplice: chromatic possibilities exploited from alternating major and minor triads. Molto allegro e dinamico: tonal, pandiatonic. Presto: clean lines, driving rhythms, cross-rhythms; evolves from small motifs. Neoclassic, modal, unusual scales. D.

Walter Piston. *Quartet* 1964 (AMP 1974) 28pp., parts. 18 min. Facsimile of composer's autograph. Leggero e scorrevole; Adagio sostenuto; Allegro vivo. Classical sonata form is the basis for this work. Baroque polyphonic textures are welded together with harmony, key relationships, and rhythms of the 20th century. Neoclassic qualities permeate every bar of this work by a master craftsman. D.

Marcel Poot. *Quartet* 1932 (ESC) 39pp., parts. 24 min. Allegro giocoso; Menuetto; Finale. Stravinsky-like in rhythms and dissonance with some Prokofiev influence noted. Finale is especially dancelike with the exception of one Impressionist episode (Quasi moderato). D.

Marcel Quinet. *Quartet* 1957 (CeBeDeM) 52pp., parts. 16 min. Allegro moderato; Adagio; Allegramente. Neoclassic in structure and atonal harmonic treatment. Frequent alternation of hands. Large span required. D.

Max Reger. *Quartet* Op.133 a 1914 (CFP 3977; Simrock) 51pp., parts. Allegro con passione; Vivace; Largo con gran espressione; Allegro con spirito. This autumnal work is an impressive masterpiece. It contains a passionate first movement, a genial scherzo à la Beethoven, and a festive, lighthearted finale. Rich polyphonic lines and abrupt changes of mood underlie its construction. D.

Josef Rheinberger. *Quartet* Op.38 E♭ 1870 (Hamelle; Augener). This work sounds dated today, but in its time it proved to be interesting to pianists and string players. "This is one of those quartets which has provided amateurs, who are not all high-brows (myself among the number), with a transition stage, and for that reason alone deserves to be rated highly" (CCSCM, II, p.294).

Ferdinand Ries. *Quartet* Op.13 f (Wollenweber 1992) 55pp., parts. Published in the series *Unknown Works of the Classical and Romantic Period.* Preface in German and English.
——. *Quartet* Op.17 E♭ (Kunzelmann 1992) 65pp., parts. Preface in German and English.

Jean Roger-Ducasse. *Quatuor* g 1910 (Durand). First movement: ternary and binary rhythm alternated; second theme has a Fauré flavor; powerful coda, abrupt ending. Andantino ma scherzando: fantasy-like theme, with variations. Third movement: dark, mysterious, connected by a pedal point to the Finale: main ideas are combined with themes from previous movements; strong movement. M-D to D.

José Rolón. *Cuarteto* E♭ (EMM 1967) 82pp., parts. Allegro molto con brio; Adagio; Molto vivace; Allegro giocoso vivace. Post-Romantic writing, style of late-19th-century French school. A little Impressionist in places. Might be mistaken for Dubois or his contemporaries. M-D.

Anton Rubinstein. *Quatuor* Op.55 (Hamelle). Also published as a quintet for piano, flute, clarinet, horn, and bassoon. Eclectic writing with very little contra-

puntal development. Most interesting are the melodies with a hint of Russian melos. Beautiful musical writing (for its day) but not terribly original. M-D.
———. *Quatuor* Op.66 (Hamelle; Simrock).

Camille Saint-Saëns. *Quartet* Op.41 B♭ (Durand). Allegretto: serene, with a slow march entering near the end. Andante: effective melodic and contrapuntal writing, great variety of figuration and devices. Scherzo: $\frac{6}{8}$; a nocturnal dance with $\frac{2}{4}$ meter intruding near the conclusion; 2 recitatives also interrupt the movement. Finale: vigorous, thematics from previous movements are brought together to unify the work. Ingenious treatment of the subjects. M-D to D.

Franz Schubert. *Quartet* D.487 F, Adagio and Rondo Concertante 1816 (CFP 1347; Br&H) 35pp., parts. 14 min. The Adagio serves as an introduction and builds anticipation and suspense. The Rondo is a brilliant and colorful movement built on a number of contrasting ideas in different tonalities. An unusual pattern of ABCD–development–ABCD–coda is the result. Schubert incorporates all his unique pianistic idioms into this highly effective work, which is in many ways a miniature Concerto for piano with strings. D.
Also available in the Dover reprint of the I. Brull—Br&H edition in *Complete Chamber Music for Pianoforte and Strings*. This volume also contains the "Trout" Quintet and the 3 *Trios* for piano, violin, and cello.

Robert Schumann. *Quartet* Op.47 E♭ 1842 (A. Dörffel—CFP 53pp., parts; Henle 737; Br&H; Bauer—GS L1711; Augener; IMC). 27 min. Sostenuto assai–Allegro ma non troppo; Scherzo–molto vivace; Andante cantabile; Vivace. One of the most important works in the literature for this combination. Equal division of interest between the 4 instruments. Unsurpassed in Romantic fervor and beauty. D.

Elliott Schwartz. *Dream Music with Variations* 1983 (TP) 16 min. "Two structural ground-plans proceeding simultaneously: (1) a series of variations on a tone-row, which unfolds at the beginning of the piece, and (2) a narrative of quotation fragments, all related to images of night. Mendelssohn, Schoenberg, Debussy, Liszt, Chopin, Schumann. Accordingly, the music has tonal romantic elements and dissonant modernist ones, often overlapping simultaneously. In two movements, with return to the opening at the work's conclusion" (Composer's letter to authors).

Richard Strauss. *Piano Quartet* Op.13 c 1884 (Aibl; UE 65pp., parts; IMC) 35min. Requires a taut and lively performance with a good sense of Romantic stylistic traditions. All 4 movements effective. Striking and sweeping lyrical melodies; post-Brahmsian in its exuberant musical language. Brilliant coda in first movement (Allegro) and the spirited Scherzo require virtuosity of all interpreters. The Andante has an expressive melody and concludes like a delicate serenade. A syncopated Schumannesque opening announces the finale in which the themes are ingeniously combined and the coda is as effective as the one in the opening movement. D.

Rezsö Sugár. *Quartetto* (Zenmükiadó Vállalat 1964) 28pp., parts. For 2 violins, cello, and piano. Allegro; Andante; Vivo. Colorful Hungarian flavor, mildly 20th-century. M-D.

Carlos Surinach. *Quartet* (PIC 1944) 56pp., parts. 20 min. Three movements that are full of Spanish color and rhythmic vitality. Fresh and evocative writing. Little development and unashamed tunes, but the splashes of color and passionate treatment add up to a direct and charming work. The cross-rhythms of the third and final movements are intoxicating. M-D.

Sergei I. Taneiev. *Quartet* Op.20 E 1902–1906 (USSR 1974) 94pp., parts. First published by Belaieff in 1907. Brilliant and sonorous Romantic writing for the piano. Cobbett considers the work "profound and sublime in conception" (CCSCM, II, p.487). Three movements with the outer movements written in SA design while the second, an Adagio tosto largo, is in ABA form. D.

Alexander Tansman. *Suite-Divertissement* (ESC 1930). Neoclassic approach and construction; strong rhythmic emphasis does not detract from the lyricism of the work. Lightness and charm shine through at all times, even when textures become complex. M-D.

Joaquín Turina. *Quatuor* Op.67 a 1931 (Rouart Lerolle). Iberian poetic style throughout with strong rhythmic and coloristic effects. Chromatic idiom, some cyclic elements. Thematic opposition with repetition varied by timbre is preferred over large structures with organic development. D.

Antonio Vivaldi. *Sonata* g (G. F. Ghedini—IMC 1240) 19pp., parts. For flute (violin I), oboe (violin II), bassoon (cello), and piano. Allegro ma cantabile; Largo; Allegro molto. Unencumbered realizations. M-D.

William Walton. *Piano Quartet* 1918–19 (St&B 1924; rev. ed. OUP 1976) 74pp., parts. 26 min. Allegramente; Allegro scherzando; Andante tranquillo; Allegro molto. This early work displays stylistic distinctiveness and great technical assurance for a 16-year-old. Modal flavor, transparent textures. Ravel's influence is noted especially in the second movement, a rhythmic scherzo and rustling fugati. Noble and effective writing. Large span required. M-D to D.

Donald Waxman. *Quartet* (Galaxy 1966) 43pp., parts. Allegramente: SA; piano introduction; freely tonal but centers around D; subito trills; unusual coda; large span required. Adagietto: ABA, varied use of triplet figure, quintal harmony, flowing melody in mid-section. Introduction, Theme, Variations: chromatic figuration; piano gives out the bright theme by itself; 6 contrasting variations (piano is tacet in Var.4) with the final one extended by a coda. Gallic influence permeates this well-written work; a kind of Poulencian charm adds real interest to this basically Neoclassic-inspired composition. M-D.

Carl Maria von Weber. *Quartet* Op.8 1810 (CFP 2177 41pp., parts; IMC). Allegro: piano gives opening vigorous statement; second subject is given to strings while the piano weaves an intricate design around it; thorough development. Adagio: smooth beginning but soon becomes more agitated to a più moto e con fuoco; opening character returns but is disturbed by coda figuration. Minuet: highly agitated with some relief in the peasant dance trio. Presto: a versatile fugue subject that opens the movement is followed by a jaunty theme that takes on an operatic and potpourri character. Serene and sunny writing throughout. D.

Charles-Marie Widor. *Quatuor* Op.66 a (Durand 1892). Learned and accomplished writing, very much in the style of Saint-Saëns. Plenty of vitality. D.

Russell Woollen. *Quartet* A 1961 (CFE) 110pp., parts. Allegro deciso: freely tonal; octotonic; emphatic octaves; imitation; large span required. Andante: flowing; chantlike lines; more active mid-section that includes sweeping arpeggi. Allegretto: rondo; rhythmic hemiola lines; uses extremes of keyboard; pesante chromatic chordal section; basically thin textures; Neoclassic. D.

Iannis Xenakis. *Morsima-Amorsima (ST/4-1,030762)* 1962 (Bo&H) 28pp., parts. 10½ min. For violin, cello, double bass, and piano. Stochastic, pointillistic. Enormous dynamic extremes; every note has a dynamic mark attached. Avant-garde. D.

Quartets for Piano(s), Strings, and Winds

Jurriaan Andriessen. *Suite de Noel* 1944 (Donemus). For flute, violin, viola, and piano. Easy to listen to, uncomplicated, breathes something of the spirit of the 18th-century divertimento. M-D.

Theodore Antoniou. *Quartetto Giocoso* Op.26 1965 (Br) 15 min. For oboe, violin, cello, and piano. Ten short movements of ironic character, each of which is a miniature caricature of a well-known form, to be played amusingly, exaggerating the form. Explores abstract relationships between motivic ideas and the movements of sounds, possible combinations of dialogue, several ways of playing the instruments, and problems of space. Some of the pieces are Introduzione; Notturno; Duettino; Ostinato; Perpetuo; Rondoletto; Tollatino; Terzino; Finale. M-D.

Carl Philipp Emanuel Bach. *Quartet* W.93 a 1788 (Schmid—Nag 222) 19pp., parts. For flute, viola, cello, and piano.
——. *Quartet* W.94 D 1788 (Schmid—Nag 223) 19pp., parts. For flute, viola, cello, and piano. Allegretto: scales, dramatic figures, trills, alternation of hands. Sehr langsam und ausgehalten: more melodic, lovely harmonies. Allegro di molto: highly rhythmic, 16th-note figuration, driving conclusion. Represents a complete breakthrough to the Viennese Classical style, Beethoven-like. The keyboard part has freed itself considerably from the thorough-bass principles and shows fuller and richer writing. Bach probably meant this work to be performed on the Hammerklavier. M-D.
——. *Quartet* W.95 G 1788 (Schmid—Nag 224) 20pp., parts. For flute, viola, cello, and piano. Allegretto: many trills, arpeggiation. Adagio: chordal and scalar passages, effective ending. Presto: motoric, driving 16ths. M-D.
In all 3 *Quartets,* a violin may substitute for the flute, and the cello part is ad lib.

Johann Christian Bach. *Quartet* C (Ruf—Heinrichshofen). For flute, violin, viola, and basso continuo.
——. *Quartet* Op.6/8 E♭ (W. Radeke, F. Nagel—Schott 5989) 21pp., parts. For

flute, violin, viola, and basso continuo. Largo: chordal sonorities with some melodic interest. Allegro spirituo: rhythm emphasized, some development. M-D.

Johann Sebastian Bach. *Sonata à 3* (GS). For flute, violin, cello, and piano.

——. *Trio Sonata and Canon Perpetuus* ("Musical Offering") S.1079/8–9 c 1747 (H. Eppstein—Henle 294 1976, ISMN M-2018-0294-7, 23pp., parts; Br&H). For flute, violin, cello, and piano. Figured-bass realization for *Trio Sonata* in Henle edition is believed to be by Bach's pupil J. Ph. Kirnberger. Excellent Preface in Henle. D.

——. *Trio Sonata* S.1039 G (H. Eppstein—Henle 329 1980, ISMN M-2018-0329-6, 23pp., parts; Seiffert—Br&H). For 2 flutes, cello, and piano. Adagio; Allegro ma non presto; Adagio; Presto. Excellent Preface in Henle. M-D.

——. *Trio Sonata* b (Hindermann—Br). For 2 oboes, cello, and basso continuo.

Leonardo Balada. *Cuatris for Four Instruments* (Gen 1970) 18pp., parts. 8½ min. For flute or violin, clarinet or viola, trombone or cello or bassoon, with prepared piano or harpsichord. See detailed entry under quartets for piano and strings.

Niels Viggo Bentzon. *Mosaique Musicale* Op.54 (WH 3912 1951) 27pp., parts. One large movement with 3 contrasting sections. The following influences are felt: jazz, popular music, Hindemith, Schoenberg, and Bartók. Neo-Baroque style. Large span required. M-D.

Lennox Berkeley. *Concertino* Op.49 (JWC 1956) 33pp., parts. 11½ min. For recorder (or flute), violin, cello, and harpsichord (or piano). Aria I–Lento; Aria II–Andante; Vivace. Neoclassic style, especially apparent in outer movements. Aria I, for recorder and cello alone is built on a 12-note chaconne theme accompanied by serial melodic variations, 5 statements. This movement fits nicely in a work that has close ties with the 18th century. Traditional pianistic treatment. D.

Sebastian Bodinus. *Sonata* E♭ (H. Fischer—Vieweg 1939) 11pp., parts. For 2 oboes or violins, bassoon or cello, and piano. Adagio; Allegro; Siciliana; Allegro assai. Attractive, good realization. M-D.

Charles Boone. *Quartet* 1970 (Sal) 15pp., parts. For piano, violin, cello, and clarinet. Performance instructions in French and English; numerous directions in the score. Uses harmonics, clusters, stopped strings. "The end of each phrase is indicated by its time in seconds. The time of each individual phrase is proportional to its linear disposition of the notes, but the time-space ratio is not necessarily the same in all phrases" (from the score). Static sound blocks; extremes of instrumental timbre explored. Avant-garde. D.

Benjamin Britten. *Gemini Variations* Op.73 1965 (Faber F014) 37pp., parts. Twelve Variations and Fugue on an Epigram (musical piece) by Kodály. Quartet for 2 or 4 players. Written for 12-year-old twins, each of whom played the piano; one also played the violin, the other the flute. May be performed by 2 players (flute-piano, violin-piano) or by 4 players (violin, flute, and piano duet). Contains performance directions. The theme is No.4 of *Epigrams* (1954) by Zoltán Kodály. Written for varied combinations: Theme (piano duet with ad lib flute and violin); Var.I (piano solo); II (violin and piano); III (violin solo); IV (flute and violin); V (flute and violin); VI (flute and violin); VII (flute solo); VIII (flute and piano); IX (piano solo); X (piano duet with ad lib flute and violin); XI (piano duet); XII (piano solo); Fugue (flute, violin, and piano duet, with ad lib flute and violin). M-D.

Willy Burkhard. *Lyrische Musik* Op.88, in memoriam Georg Trakl (Br 2495) 23pp., parts. For flute, viola, cello, and piano. Poco lento; Allegro agitato; Lento; Allegro moderato; Allegro agitato. Highly linear and contrapuntal writing, neo-Baroque style. Large span required. M-D.

René de Castéra. *Concert* 1922 (Rouart Lerolle) 51pp., parts. For piano, cello, flute, and clarinet. Paysage; Intermède–Lent et Grave; Rondeau Varié. Folk song flavor noted in themes. Flexible style, fresh sounds for the time when they were written, tonal, mildly Impressionist. M-D.

George Crumb. *Eleven Echoes of Autumn* (CFP 1965) 11pp., parts. 16 min. For violin, alto flute, clarinet, and piano. Pieces to be performed without interruption: Eco 1. Fantastico (for piano alone). Eco 2. Languidamente, quasi lontano ("hauntingly"). Eco 3. Prestissimo. Eco 4. Con bravura. Eco 5. Cadenza I (for alto flute). Eco 6. Cadenza II (for violin). Eco 7. Cadenza III (for clarinet). Eco 8. Feroce, violento. Eco 9. Serenamenti, quasi lontano ("hauntingly"). Eco 10. Senza misura ("gently undulating"). Eco 11. Adagio ("like a prayer"). Each of the echoes exploits certain timbral possibilities of the instruments. A "bell-motif" generates much of the music played on the piano as 5th-partial harmonics. Descending whole-tone interval is important. Substantial musical material produces sonic effects and a ghostly atmosphere; improvisatory quality. D.

Carl Czerny. *Grande Sérénade Concertante* Op.126 E♭ (Musica Rara) 55pp., parts. For clarinet, horn, cello, and piano. Plenty of tricky turns in the elaborate piano part illuminate this extensive and delightful work. D.

Emma Lou Diemer. *Movement for Flute, Oboe, Clarinet and Piano* 1976 (Seesaw) 26pp., parts. 10 min. Serial influence, patterns are to be repeated varying the number of times and the order in which groups of notes are played; some sections are not to be synchronized. Varied sections, moods, and tempos. Glissandi on strings with finger and rubber eraser, harmonics, tremolo. Well constructed, avant-garde. D.

Gottfried von Einem. *Reifliches Divertimento* Op.35a (Bo&H 1974) 8pp., parts. For violin, viola, horn, and piano. Two short variations on a theme from Act

III of Von Einem's opera *Der Besuch der alten Dame* (The Visit of the Old Woman). Transparent and contrapuntal textures. M-D.

Elisenda Fábregas. *Portraits II* 1999 (Hidden Oaks). 17½ min. For clarinet or flute, violin, cello, and piano. I. Image, II. Capriccio, III. Cantilena-Dance, IV. Finale. Developed from *Portraits I* for solo piano, with which it shares the first movement. Contrasting sections with a broad range of musical pictures and dramatic gestures as suggested by the titles. Conventional writing packed with details. Extensive program notes in score. D.

———. *Summer Solstice* 2000/1 (Hofmeister). 18 min. For clarinet, violin, cello, and piano. One movement in 3-part free form. "The main motive developed throughout the piece consists of the first four notes of the melodic theme (its head); sometimes all four notes appear together, other times they appear in groups of two, as descending or ascending minor seconds. Other times, the theme is transformed in its entirety by changing its character, pace or rhythm" (from Program Notes, www.efabregas.com, Nov. 11, 2004).

Johann Friedrich Fasch. *Sonata* B♭ (W. Woehl—HM 26) 15pp., parts. For recorder, oboe, cello, and basso continuo. Largo; Allegro; Grave; Allegro. Efficient continuo realization. M-D.

———. *Sonata* D (R. Gerlash—HM 207) 20pp., parts. For flute, violin, bassoon, and basso continuo. Largo; Allegro; Largo; Allegro. Continuo realization is adequate and is only an editorial suggestion. M-D.

———. *Sonata à 4* (H. Töttcher, C. Spannagel—Sikorski 241) 11pp., parts. For violin, oboe, horn, and basso continuo. Andante; Allegro; Andante; Allegro. M-D.

Fasch's music shows the flowing and amiable handwriting of the Telemann school.

Morton Feldman. *Durations I* 1960 (CFP 6901) 5pp. For violin, cello, alto flute, and piano. Sonorities are the most important; technique is secondary. The duration of each sound is chosen by the performers. Numbers between sounds indicate silent beats. Low dynamics. Avant-garde. M-D.

Godfrey Finger. *Sonata* C (R. L. Minter—Musica Rara 1974) 18pp., parts. For trumpet, violin, oboe, and continuo. Fluent but traditional handling of the then-popular Italian idiom. M-D.

Ross Lee Finney. *Divertissement* 1964 (Bowdoin College Music Press) 70pp., parts. 25 min. For clarinet, violin, cello, and piano. Facsimile of composer's MS. Avant-garde techniques used for musical purposes. Allegro energico: much activity; pianist hits strings with flat of hand, plucks strings with hand or plectrum; dampens string with fingers. Adagio misterioso: sonority-oriented for piano; dynamic extremes; pianist produces rasp along string wiring with plectrum. Allegro giocoso: pianist scrapes wire of string with hard object, produces harmonics by touching string while striking key, and uses snare drum stick to pluck string (ad lib); pedal effects. Cadenzas: pianist may improvise discreetly using only sounds that can be produced inside the piano while the other instruments improvise freely following durations and contours suggested (the object is to achieve a virtuosity and rhythm that notation might inhibit, and to have fun!); Adagio misterioso returns and concludes with pianist playing a cadenza of harmonics only. Allegro energico: has much of the activity and excitement of opening movement. D.

Tommaso Giordani. *Quartet* Op.3/1 G ca.1775 (S. Sadie—Musica Rara 1966) 15pp., parts. For flute, violin, cello, and piano. Allegro; Rondo–Allegro. The piano's role is partly continuo and partly obbligato. This early example of a piano Quartet contains some charming Classical-style figurations and rhythms. Tommaso was the son of Giuseppe Giordani. M-D.

Arsenio Giron. *Quartet* 1963 (CF) 45pp., parts. For flute, clarinet, viola, and piano. Facsimile edition. Allegro; Largo; Presto. Serial, pointillistic, sudden dynamic changes, clusters, last 2 movements attacca. D.

David Gow. *Quartet* Op.28 1967 (Musica Rara) 38pp., parts. 13 min. For flute, oboe, cello, and piano or harpsichord. A one-movement work with varied tempos and changing meters, tremolo chords, rushing arpeggi gestures, broken chromatic chords, arpeggiated chords, alternating hands. Piano is used more for color and for its unifying capacity than melodically. Freely tonal. M-D to D.

Johann Gottlieb Graun. *Concerto* F (Schroeder—Moeck). For flute, 2 violins, and basso continuo. Expressive lines dotted with rests suggest more gallant style than Corelli sustained style. Some contrapuntal treatment. M-D.

Ray Green. *Holiday for Four* (AME 1949) 40pp., parts. 14 min. For viola (includes an alternate clarinet part in place of viola), clarinet, bassoon, and piano. Includes other suggested instrumentation. Fugal Introduction; Prairie Blues; Festive Finale. Contrasting movements, mildly 20th-century, many 7th chords, effective Suite. Blues and folk song elements permeate the second movement. M-D.

Jean Guillou. *Colloques No. I* (Leduc 1966) 17pp., parts. 13 min. For flute, oboe, violin, and piano. A one-movement, sectioned work. Lento: dotted rhythms in piano, harmonic 7ths and 9ths. Allegro: quick chromatic figurations in all instruments. Lento: character like that of opening movement; piano part ostinato-like. Allegro: rhythmic drive. Lento: ideas from both earlier Lentos. Moderato e misterioso: staccato right hand, *pp* line over sustained low chordal sonorities in left hand. M-D.

Jacques Guyonnet. *Polyphonie III* 1964 (UE 13550) 23pp., parts. For 2 pianos, flute, and viola. Explanations in French, German, and English, including placement of the instruments. Highly organized (pitch, dynamics, etc.), harmonics,

Expressionist, percussive treatment of the pianos, dynamic extremes, shifting
meters, pointillistic, avant-garde. D.

George Frideric Handel. *Concerto I* d (Zobeley—Schott). For flute, violin, cello,
and basso continuo.

———. *8 Psalmouverturen* (H. Monkemeyer—Pelikan 748-9) 2 vols. For oboe
(soprano or tenor recorder, or violin), 2 violins, and basso continuo. Contains
the overtures to Nos.1–5, 7, 10, and 11 of the *Chandos Anthems.* M-D.

———. *Water Music* (D. Burrows—Nov 90593 1991) 16pp., parts available separately. For 2 violins, bassoon (viola), and piano. The editor recommends a cello
double the basso continuo line in addition. Chamber Suite of 10 movements:
1. Air, 2. Minuet, 3. Boree, 4. Hornpipe, 5. [Menuet II], 6. [Menuet III], 7.
[Country Dance], 8. [Air Lentement], 9. [Boree II], 10. [Coro]. Extensive Preface considers historical setting, versions for performance, source, editorial
method, and commentary. M-D.

———. *Kammertrio* No.19 G (Br&H). For 2 flutes, cello, and piano.

———. *Kammer Trios* II d, IV F, VI D. For 2 oboes, bassoon (cello), and piano.
See detailed entry under quartets for piano and 3 woodwinds.

Charles Haubiel. *In Praise of Dance* (H. Elkan). For oboe, violin, cello, and piano.

———. *Masks* (Seesaw). For oboe, violin, cello, and piano.

———. *Partita* (Seesaw). For oboe, violin, cello, and piano.

Franz Joseph Haydn. *Quartet* Op.5/4 G 1770 (W. Upmeyer—Nag 129) 12pp.,
parts. For flute, violin, viola, and piano; cello ad lib. Vivace; Andante moderato;
Menuetto; Fantasia with 5 Variations. A little-known but charming and accessible work. M-D.

Johann David Heinichen. *Concerto* G (H. Fischer—Vieweg 1938) 11pp., parts.
For flute, 2 violins, and basso continuo. Vivace; Allegro; Largo; Allegro. M-D.

———. *Concerto* G (K. Janetzky—Hofmeister 1972) 16pp., parts. For flute (oboe),
cello (bassoon), cello, and basso continuo. Andante; Vivace; Adagio; Allegro.
This keyboard realization is more interesting than the Fischer realization
listed above. M-D.

John Heiss. *Quartet* 1971 (Bowdoin College Music Press) 10pp., parts. 7 min. For
flute, clarinet, cello, and piano. Combines nonstandard and standard notation,
pointillistic, numerous dynamic marks, proportional rhythmic relationships,
changing meters, many performance directions, varied tempos, Expressionist
and avant-garde. D.

Paul Hindemith. *Quartet* 1938 (Schott) 49pp., parts. For clarinet, violin, cello,
and piano. Mässig bewegt: SA; freely tonal around F; piano leads out with
main theme; lyric second subject follows in all instruments; dynamic climax
marks the beginning of the recapitulation. Sehr langsam: ABA; leisurely flowing melody, accompanied by subdued harmonies; dramatic, turbulent mid-

section rises to a *ff* climax, then a calm transition passage brings back the opening material. Mässig bewegt: 3 sections, each with different tempo markings, and a coda; first section is moderately paced; followed by a fast, brilliant, dancelike part interlaced with complex rhythms and counterpoint; tempo relaxes while piano has staccato figurations in the upper register; barbaric rhythmic figure in the piano introduces the coda, which moves to a swift conclusion. D.

Ilja Hurnik. *Sonata da Camera* 1952 (Artia). For flute, oboe, cello, and piano. Neoclassic style combined with Baroque forms and Czech folk music. M-D.

Johann Gottlieb Janitsch. *Sonata da Camera* Op.4 C (D. Lasocki—Musica Rara 1970 23pp., parts; B&VP). For flute, oboe, violin, and basso continuo. Andante e molto; Allegro; Allegro assai. Both editions are excellent. M-D.

——. *Chamber Sonata* Op.8 "Echo" (Wolff—Br&H). For flute, oboe (or violin or flute), viola, and keyboard. Fine counterpoint and unusual harmonies. M-D.

——. *Quadro 'O Haupt voll Blut und Wunden'* (K. Hofmann—Hänssler 1973) 26pp., parts. 2 pages of notes. For oboe, violin, viola, and basso continuo. Largo; Allegretto; Adagio; Vivace. A chorale melody in the oboe is used as a cantus firmus in third movement while other instruments are involved in separate dialogue. Editorial additions are identified. M-D.

——. *Quartet* c (Winschermann—Sikorski 617). For oboe, violin, viola, and basso continuo. M-D.
The influence of C. H. Graun is seen in all these works.

Tom Johnson. *Simultaneous Progressions* 1995 (Editions 75 1996) 11pp., parts. 10–12 min. For clarinet, trombone, cello, and piano. Four logical progressions for 4 instruments, each playing independently from the others, proceeding spontaneously in order from performance to performance. Tempos are unmarked. The piece ends when all 4 have completed their individual progressions. Extensive Preface and instructions for each instrument. M-D.

Heinrich Kaminski. *Quartet* Op.1B 1912 (UE 8333) 39pp., parts. For clarinet, violin, cello, and piano. Frisch; Ruthenisches Volkslied (4 variations on a charming folk song); Scherzo (Var.5); Finale (Var.6). Neo-Baroque style, polyphonically oriented, a few tangled spots. M-D.

Wilhelm Kempff. *Quartet* Op.15 (Simrock 1925) 74pp., parts. For piano, flute, violin, and cello. Andante–Allegro; Adagio con melancolia, semplice (based on an old Swedish folk song); Menuett; Introduzione e Finale. Smooth writing, technically facile, broad pianistic gestures. M-D to D.

Ernst Křenek. *Hausmusik* (Br 1959) 13pp., parts. Seven Pieces for the Seven Days of the Week. For piano, violin, guitar, and blockflöte (recorder). 1. Moderato: for piano, 4-hands. 2. Allegretto: for blockflöte and guitar. 3. Andantino: for 2 blockflöten and a third instrument. 4. Allegro: for violin and guitar. 5. Animato: for blockflöte and violin. 6. Andante con passione: for violin and piano. 7. Allegretto: for piano, alto blockflöte, and guitar. Minor problems for each instrument, logically worked out, intellectually satisfying. Int. to M-D.

Meyer Kupferman. *Infinities Thirteen* (Bowdoin College Music Press 1965) 54pp., parts. A Quartet for 8 instruments: flute, piccolo, alto flute, clarinet, bass clarinet, violin-viola, and piano. Part of a "Cycle of Infinities," all based on the same 12-tone row. Pointillistic, percussive use of piano, splashing dramatic gestures, flexible meters, complex ensemble problems. Requires 4 virtuoso performers. D.

Noël Lee. *L'Ami, L'Adoré* (Anecdotes) (AMC; CDMC) 15pp., parts. For horn, violin, cello, and piano. Allegretto con grazia; Largo. Neoclassic orientation, thin textures. Gallic wit and humor comes through; extreme ranges of keyboard exploited; ostinato-like figures. Large span required. M-D.

Gerhard Maasz. *Concertino* (Br 3331 1960) 23pp., parts. For piano, flute, violin, and cello. Fantasia: quartal harmony, freely tonal, arpeggi figuration. Allegro: light staccato in right hand over sustained single note in left hand; second half more chordal. Andante: peaceful and flowing. Rondo: thin textures; octotonic; cadenzas for flute, violin, piano; 20th-century Alberti bass treatment. Neoclassic. M-D.

Bohuslav Martinů. *Quartet* 1947 (ESC 1961) 12 min. For oboe, violin, cello, and piano. Rhythmic energy is in abundance. Wide harmonic range with simple progressions and harsh dissonances. D.

Toshiro Mayuzumi. *Metamusic* (CFP 6357). For piano, violin, saxophone, and conductor. See detailed entry under trios for piano, one stringed instrument, and one wind instrument.

Olivier Messiaen. *Quatuor pour la fin du temps* 1941 (Durand) iv+52pp., parts. For violin, clarinet, cello, and piano. Contains a condensed quotation from verses 1–6 of the book of Revelation, which was the inspiration for this piece. Study score, which includes an outline of the religious "programme of the work," is also available. 1. Liturgie de cristal: piano has an ostinato progression of 29 chords, repeated 5 times, while clarinet and violin have florid figurations. 2. Vocalise, pour l'Ange qui annonce la fin du Temps: ABA; B section has the "impalpable harmonies of the heavens" with a plainsong-like melody, accompanied by *pp* cascades of chords that represent drops of water in a rainbow. 3. Abîme des Oiseaux: ABA for solo clarinet. 4. Intermède: a scherzo, piano tacet. 5. Louange à l'Eternité de Jésus: piano and cello alone; calm, sweet chords of the piano accompany a ternary melody for the cello. 6. Danse de la fureur, pour les sept trompettes: all 4 instruments in unison; involved formal and metrical construction; gongs and trumpets are suggested. 7. Fouillis d'arcs-en-ciel, pour l'Ange qui annonce la fin du Temps: thematic references to first, second, and sixth movements; involved archlike form. 8. Louange à l'Immortalité de Jésus: piano and violin alone; related to fifth movement; a 2-part movement in 2 stanzas that begin identically and change directions halfway through; piano accompanies the violin's "expressif, paradisiaque" melody; sweet, succulent chords. Written while Messiaen was a prisoner of war; one of his most striking and beautiful works. Displays a wide range of instrumental textures and variety. D.

See Rebecca Rischin, *For the End of Time: The Story of the Messiaen Quartet* (Ithaca, N.Y.: Cornell University Press, 2003). David Stephen Bernstein, "Messiaen's Quatuor pour la fin du temps: An Analysis Based upon Messiaen's Theory of Rhythm and His Use of Modes of Limited Transposition," Ph.D. diss., Indiana University, 1974, 133pp. Contains an analysis of each movement.

Otto Mortensen. *Quatuor Concertant* (WH 3850a). For piano, flute, violin, and cello.

Ignaz Moscheles. *Fantasy, Variations and Finale* Op.46 (Musica Rara). For violin, clarinet, cello, and piano. Much decorative figuration, frequent empty gestures. M-D to D.

Johann Gottlieb Naumann. *Quartet* Op.1/5 E♭ (P. Bormann—Sikorski 275) 15pp., parts. For piano, flute, violin, and cello. Andante: flowing style. Grazioso; should have a dancing swing to it. Idiomatic keyboard writing in a conservative style. There is charm, a certain delicacy in the rhythmic treatment, and some originality in the piece that reminds one of Johann Christian Bach's works. M-D.

Stephen Oliver. *Ricercare* (Nov. 1973). For piano, clarinet, violin, cello.
See Jane Glover, "Stephen Oliver," MT 115, no. 1582 (December 1974): 1042–44.

Joseph Rheinberger. *Quartet* F 1857 (Musica Rara France MR 2225 1995) 27pp., parts. For oboe, horn (viola), cello, and piano. Adagio non troppo: stern *ff* opening by piano with marked rhythms quickly yields to *pp* and a gentle melody in oboe with imitative treatment followed by all. Allegro molto: opens again with piano and marked rhythmic melody before passing the thematic material to other instruments. Elements of neo-Baroque techniques are present through imitation, with the instruments rarely speaking homorhythmically except near the end. M-D.

Vittorio Rieti. *Sonata* 1924 (UE). For flute, oboe, bassoon, and piano. Lean textures; dance influence felt with much rhythmic motion. Key changes and frequent modulations are present along with strong lyrical lines. M-D.

George Rochberg. *Contra mortem et tempus* 1965 (TP) 39pp. 4 copies needed for performance. For flute, clarinet, violin, and piano. Uses open-score notation; basically unmeasured; permits maximum flexibility of performance. Notes to the performers explain other notation signs. Gradual changes of speed, harmonics on piano, arm clusters, long pedals, pointillistic. The performer with the best deep voice should sing-speak "con-tra mor-tem et tem-pus" at the very end. "Rochberg's most recent compositions incorporate Ivesian simultaneities of original and preexisting materials. The beautifully textured 'Contra mortem et tempus' juxtaposes snatches from Boulez, Berio, Varèse, and Ives as well as Rochberg's own somewhat Bergian 'Dialogues' for clarinet and piano (1958)" (Alexander L. Ringer, DCM, p.629). Avant-garde. D.

Alessandro Scarlatti. *Quartet* F (W. Woehl—CFP 4558) 10pp., parts. For recorder, 2 violins, and piano; cello ad lib. Untitled first movement; Allegro; Grave; Allegro. Basso continuo realization is somewhat bland and could be reworked. M-D.

Hans Ludwig Schilling. *Concerto Piccolo* 1964 (Br&H 6468) 37pp., parts. 14 min. For flute, English horn, viola, and piano. Proposta–sehr schnell; Ruhig (piano tacet); Rondo–lebhaft bewegt. Neoclassic, colorful chromaticism, freely tonal. Large span required. D.

Florent Schmitt. *Pour presque tous les temps (2/4 3/4 3/2 6/8 5/4)* Op.134 (Durand 1956) 25pp., parts. 10 min. For piano, violin, flute, and cello. Alerte; Au clair de la R-IV; Lent mais non languide; Vif. Sonorities and rhythms of intrinsic beauty, straightforward idiom, effusive lyricism, Impressionist influence. Requires large span. M-D to D.

Elliott Schwartz. *Soliloquies* 1965 (Bowdoin College Music Press) 26pp. 4 copies required. 9 min. For flute, clarinet, violin, and piano. Two untitled pieces. Four notes must be prepared on the piano by inserting objects (a metal screw or nail, a dime, some tightly wadded paper, bits of wood, rubber jar-lid liner, etc.), which should create a separate different sound. Requires a soft timpani stick for pianist to strike low strings. At times the piano itself is struck with the palm, not knuckles or fist, on described areas. Sonority-oriented with some unusual musical results. Sections marked "Free" indicate times when players are asked not to synchronize their parts with one another. Avant-garde. D.

Kazimierz Serocki. *Swinging Music* (Moeck 1970) 4 min. For clarinet, bassoon, cello or double bass, and piano. Strong rhythmic feel, nondoctrinaire use of compositional techniques, fluctuating dynamics. Some graphic notation allows a certain amount of interpretative freedom. M-D.

Akio Shiraishi. *Anagram* (Ongaku No Tomo Sha 1966) 18pp., parts. For clarinet, violin, cello, and piano. Four untitled pieces. Serial, pointillistic, dynamic extremes, tremolo, atonal. D.

Rick Sowash. *Daweswood* 1980 (Sowash) 48pp., parts. 15½ min. A Concertino for violin, clarinet, cello, and piano. I. "The Bud"–Allegro, II. "The Blossom"–

Andante, III. "The Berry"–Vivo. Composed while in residence at the Dawes Arboretum near Newark, Ohio, each movement reflecting the stages of growth for plants. Perky and spicy in the outer movements and languid in the center. M-D.

——. *Anecdotes and Reflections* 1989 (Sowash), parts. 38½ min. For violin, clarinet, cello, and piano. I. Allegro; II. Moderato, III. Allegro, IV. Larghetto, V. Lento, VI. Tempo di marcia. "Designed as three sets of 2 movements each, alternately an 'anecdotal' movement and a 'reflective' movement," in commemoration of the life of Louise Betcher. Elements of Eastern European and Klezmer influences, Gershwin, Tin Pan Alley, and others appear, all unified by a motif of "descending four-note musical shape—A-G-E-E flat—stated initially by the clarinet" (from Program Notes, *Chamber Music with Clarinet by Rick Sowash,* The Mirecourt Trio with Craig Olzenak, clarinet, compact disc, Gasparo 285, 1991). M-D.

——. *Cape May Suite* 1993 (Sowash) 57pp., parts. 23 min. For oboe, violin, cello, and piano. Morning at Seaside; Victorian Garden; Dinner at Louisa's; Ghostly Waltzes at Congress Hall. Inspired by the resort town of Cape May, New Jersey. Depicts scenes from the town and experiences of the composer in musical terms. Colorful. M-D to D.

Robert Starer. *Concertino* 1948 (Israeli Music Publications) 27pp., parts. For 2 voices or 2 instruments (oboe or trumpet, bassoon or trombone), violin, and piano. The 2 "voice" parts may be sung or they may be played by the suggested instruments. It is also possible to have one part sung and the other played. The concertante element dominates the entire work. The first movement (Cantamus) praises the joy of singing, the second is a tender lament, and the third a jubilant Allelujah. Mildly 20th-century with Judaic flavor. Octonic. Large span required. M-D.

William Sydeman. *Quartet* 1963 (Okra) 15 min. For flute, clarinet, violin, and piano.
——. *Quartet* (Seesaw). For clarinet, violin, cello, and piano.

Georg Philipp Telemann. *Concerto a 4* (Veyron-Lacroix—IMC). For flute, oboe, violin, and piano.
——. *Concerto* B♭ (EMT). For 2 flutes, cello, and piano.
——. *Concerto* D (Richter—Schott). For flute, violin, cello, and piano.
——. *Parisian Quartet I Concerto Primo* G (W. Bergmann—Br 1967) 34pp., parts. For flute, violin, viola da gamba or cello, and basso continuo. Grave; Allegro; Largo; Presto; Largo; Allegro. Written for 4 virtuosi in Paris with Telemann at the keyboard. Two different sets of figured bass, both Telemann's, from 1730 and 1736, present much contrast. One of Telemann's best pieces of chamber music. M-D.

———. *Quartet* b 1733 (E. Dohrn—Nag 24) 27pp., parts. For flute, violin, cello, and basso continuo. From "Nouveaux Quatuors en Six Suites," Paris. Prélude (with a B section "Flatteusement"); Coulant; Gay; Vite; Triste; Menuett. M-D.

———. *Quartet* b (Nag). For flute, violin, cello, and piano; second cello ad lib.

———. *Quartett* d (Tafelmusik 1733 II, No.2) (Seiffert—Br&H 1910) 19pp., parts. For recorder (bassoon or cello), 2 flutes, and basso continuo; cello ad lib. Andante; Vivace; Largo; Allegro (with a cantabile mid-section). Effective, if slightly over-edited. M-D.

———. *Quartet* D (Zimmermann). For flute, violin, cello, and piano.

———. *Quartet* e 1733 (E. Dohrn—Nag 10) 23pp., parts. For flute, violin, cello, and basso continuo. No.6 from "Nouveaux Quatuors en Six Suites," Paris. Prélude; Gay; Vite; Gracieusement; Distrait; Modéré. A highly interesting work. M-D.

———. *Quartet* e (Seiffert—Br&H). For violin, flute, cello, and keyboard.

———. *Quartet* G (H. Tsöttcher, K. Grebe—Sikorski 473) 24pp., parts. For flute, oboe, violin, and basso continuo. Part I, No.2 of Telemann's *Tafelmusik*, 1733. Largo; Allegro; Largo (with a Moderato section); Grave; Vivace. M-D.

———. Quartet G (Hinnenthal—Br 3534). For oboe or violin, violin, cello, and basso continuo.

Other works in these combinations are available from CFP; IMC; Foetisch.

Douglas Townsend. *8 × 8 Variations on a Theme of Milhaud* Op.3/1 (CFP 6094 1957) 7pp., parts. For soprano recorder or flute or piccolo, trumpet or clarinet or oboe, cello or bassoon, and piano. An alternate oboe part in C is provided. From the film *8 × 8* by Hans Richter. Theme, 4 contrasting variations and coda. Piano has a 2-line Interlude between Vars.3 and 4. Mildly 20th-century, attractive. M-D.

Ben Weber. *Variations* Op.11a 1941 (ACA) 16pp., parts. 5 min. For violin, clarinet, cello, and piano. Basically this theme and the 7 contrasting variations are conceived in a contrapuntal 12-tone idiom with strong tonal implications. Declarative gestures and corky rhythms give an air of witty exuberance. Requires a large span. D.

———. *Serenade* Op.39 1954 (ACA) 19pp., parts. 9 min. For flute, violin, cello, and piano or harpsichord. Alla marcia; Andante espressivo; Adagio teneramente; Moderato Allegro poco maestoso. Atonal and intense but not too harmonically complex. "Mr. Weber's *Serenade* is a hale and jolly four-movement piece . . . the work is neither agonizingly atonal nor harmonically complex. When it is not being playful, moreover, a highly selective romantic impulse chisels its lyric lines into a state of intensity that is always natural, never labored. In sum, the work is a fine one; it has gumption and it has charm. And it makes a lovely sound" (Jay S. Harrison, *New York Herald Tribune*, January 27, 1954). D.

Anton Webern. *Quartet* Op.22 1930 (UE 10050) 13pp., parts. 5 min. For tenor saxophone, clarinet, violin, and piano. Sehr mässig: motivic development by themes branching out, intertwining, moving forward and backward; canonic narrative in pointillistic application. Sehr schwungvoll: extreme, sparse texture that is characteristic of all Webern's later works; pointillistic; sense of wider-spread sonorities; more settled than first movement but still represents a rare-fied style. Carefully mixed instrumental colors. Canonic technique through-out. D.

Zbigniew Wiszniewski. *Quartet* 1972 (AA 1974) 21pp. 4 copies necessary for per-formance. For piano, flute, horn, and double bass. Explanations in Polish and English.

Quartets for Piano and Three Woodwinds

Leonardo Balada. *Cuatris for Four Instruments* (Gen 1970) 18pp., parts. 8½ min. For flute or violin, clarinet or viola, trombone or cello or bassoon, with prepared piano or harpsichord. See detailed entry under quartets for piano and strings.

Sebastian Bodinus. *Sonata* E♭ (H. Fischer—Vieweg 1939) 11pp., parts. For 2 oboes or violins, bassoon or cello, and piano. Adagio; Allegro; Siciliana; Allegro assai. Attractive, good realization. M-D.

Frank Campo. *Concertino* 1965 (WIM). For 3 clarinets (E♭, B♭, and bass) and piano. This work pits 2 instrumental groups against one another in a manner similar to that of the Concerto Grosso. The clarinets provide a strong color contrast for the piano. The work is in 3 motivically related movements performed without pause. The first movement is a Rondo in which both the rondo theme and the contrasting musical idea return each time in altered fashion (A-B-A′-B′-A″). A brief rhapsodic interlude for solo piano leads to the Tarantella finale, which utilizes various types of fugal imitation while maintaining the robust spirit of this southern Italian dance. M-D.

Jean Marie Depelsenaire. *Concertino* (Philippo—Combre 1972) 12pp., parts. For 3 clarinets and piano. Andantino; Larghetto; Andante–Allegretto. Octotonic, tonal with some chromaticism. Second movement is for the clarinets alone. Thin textures. M-D.

Peggy Glanville-Hicks. *Concertino da Camera* 1946 (L'OL) 24pp., parts. For flute, clarinet, bassoon, and piano. Allegretto; Adagio; Finale. Neoclassic, freely tonal, toccata-like rhythm in finale, mildly 20th-century. Large span required. M-D.

Ray Green. *Holiday for Four* (AME 1949) 40pp., parts. 14 min. For viola (or clarinet), clarinet, bassoon, and piano. See detailed entry under quartets for piano(s), strings, and winds.

George Frideric Handel. *Kammer Trio* I B♭ (Seiffert—Br&H). For 2 oboes, bassoon, and piano. M-D.

——. *Kammer Trio* II d (Seiffert—Br&H 1912). For 2 oboes, bassoon (cello), and piano. Adagio; Allegro; Affettuoso; Allegro. M-D.

——. *Kammer Trio* IV F (Seiffert—Br&H 1914) 15pp., parts. For 2 oboes, bassoon (cello), and piano. Adagio; Allegro; Largo; Allegro. M-D.

——. *Kammer Trio* VI D (Seiffert—Br&H) 17pp., parts. For 2 oboes, bassoon (cello), and piano. M-D.

——. *Kammer Trio* VIII g (Seiffert—Br&H). For 2 oboes, bassoon, and piano; cello ad lib.

——. *Kammer Trio* XIV g (Seiffert—Br&H). For 2 flutes, bassoon, and piano; cello ad lib.

The Seiffert realizations are somewhat thick but are always usable. There are 22 Chamber Trios in this series.

Vagn Holmboe. *Quartetto Medico* Op.70 (JWC 4069A 1962) 18pp., parts. 11 min. For flute, oboe, clarinet, and piano. Andante medicamento: bitonal implications, alternating hands, parallelism, octotonic, freely tonal, clean-edged lines. Allegro quasi febrilo: 7th chords, syncopation, chromatic scalar passages, patterns. Intermedico I (Andante senza pianisticitis): without piano. Intermedico II (sans marais): for solo piano; alternating hands, patterns similar to those in first movement, nontonal harmony, subtle dancelike rhythms. Allegro con frangula: alternating hands with broken patterns in right hand, tremolo, nervous vitality, thin textures, 16th-note patterns and scales, clever ending. Radiant woodwind writing throughout; luminous piano writing. Finely worked-out piece, Neoclassic style. M-D.

Arthur Honegger. *Rhapsody* 1917 (Sal 1923) 13pp., parts. For 2 flutes, clarinet, and piano, or for 2 violins, viola, and piano. Larghetto–Allegro–Larghetto. An early work with strong Impressionist tendencies in the outer sections. Tripartite structure, with the mid-section a rhythmic march. Rhapsodic more in the sense of sonorities than of form. Quartal harmonies, parallel 7th chords, octotonic, broken octaves. M-D.

Darius Milhaud. *Sonate* 1918 (Durand) 36pp., parts. For flute, oboe, clarinet, and piano. Tranquille: ABA, abstruse piano writing, pastoral. Joyeux: chordal, broken chords, widespread sonorities provide striking polytonal mixtures. Emporté: emphatic rhythmic treatment, free tonal exploitation, *ffff* climax. Douloureux: langorous; funereal; expressive; *pppp* closing; final C major tonic is meaningful. M-D to D.

Marcel Quinet. *Concertino* 1960 (CeBeDeM) 33pp., parts. 11 min. For oboe, clarinet, bassoon, and piano. Allegro giocoso; Sostenuto; Vivace. Seventh chords, chromatic, repeated open 5ths and 2nds in Vivace movement, Neoclassic in structure, freely tonal. Requires large span. M-D to D.

Georg Philipp Telemann. *Quartett* d (Tafelmusik 1733 II, No. 2) (Seiffert—Br&H 1910) 19pp., parts. For recorder (bassoon or cello), 2 flutes, and basso continuo; cello ad lib. Andante; Vivace; Largo; Allegro (with a cantabile midsection). Effective, if slightly over-edited. M-D.

———. *Quartett* d (Hinnenthal—Br&H). For 2 flutes, bassoon, and basso continuo; cello ad lib.

Antonio Vivaldi. *Sonata* g (G. F. Ghedini—IMC 1240) 19pp., parts. For flute (violin I), oboe (violin II), bassoon (cello), and piano. Allegro ma cantabile; Largo; Allegro molto. Unencumbered realizations. M-D.

Quartets for Piano, Woodwind(s), and Brass

Franz Berwald. *Klavierquartett und Klavierquintette* (Br 4913 1973) 233pp., parts. Vol.13 of the Complete Edition, edited by Ingmar Bengtsson and Bonnie Hammar. Includes *Quartet* for piano, woodwinds (clarinet, bassoon), and horn, Op.1 E♭. The *Quartet* is available separately (Br 43pp., parts; GM). Introduzione–Adagio, Allegro ma non troppo; Adagio; Finale. The piano part contains some moments of highly original and poetic writing, although Mendelssohn's influence looms large. The piano takes the lead through most of this work. Berwald replied to a critic, following the first performance of this work, "I had anticipated the rather unfavourable impression these works would make, written as they are in an altogether individual style"; this in particular since they are "experiments, based upon a rather unusual system, a new treatment of the instrumentation and its employment" (from the Preface of the Br edition, which is an Urtext edition with all editorial additions identified). M-D.

Charles Ives. *Scherzo—All the Way Around and Back.* See detailed entry under quintets for piano(s), percussion, and other instruments.

Robert Starer. *Concerta a Tre* 1954 (MCA 1966) 48pp., parts. 18 min. For clarinet, trumpet, trombone, and piano. Originally for clarinet, trumpet, trombone, and strings; reduction by the composer. Allegro: has elements of the Concerto Grosso in the juxtaposition of the winds against the piano. Andante: lyrical, treats the instruments more in their individual capacities. Finale: each instrument has its own thematic material derived from its own particular quality in sound and technique; in a cadenza-like section called Trialogue, they enter into purposeful conversation with each other. M-D.

Quartets for Piano(s), Percussion, and Other Instruments

David Amram. *Discussion* (CFP 1965) 20pp., parts. 10 min. For flute, cello, piano, and percussion. Theme and 4 variations. Jazz elements breathe naturally in this piece, which combines a strong lyric quality with genuine excitement and dissonant counterpoint. D.

Gilbert Amy. *Inventions* (2) (Heugel PH261 1965) 39pp., parts. 15½ min. For flute, piano/celesta, harp, and vibraphone/marimba. Directions in French and English. Serial, pointillistic, dynamic extremes, changing meters, improvisation required, traditional plus graphic notation, mobile form. Avant-garde. D.

Béla Bartók. *Sonata for Two Pianos and Percussion* 1937 (Bo&H). 2 (or 3) players required for the percussion ensemble: 3 timpani, xylophone, 2 side drums, bass drum, cymbals, suspended cymbal, triangle, tam-tam. Assai lento–Allegro molto: contains the most complexities. Lento ma non troppo: great color in this "night music" movement. Allegro non troppo: a lively dance movement that disappears in a C tonality. Traditional designs are used in the 3 movements (SA, ABA, and rondo), but they are given new dimensions and perspectives by the varied, colorful instrumentation. Percussive qualities of all instruments emphasized. The timpani and the xylophone have important thematic parts, while the other percussion provide colorful and somewhat heavy sonorities plus rhythmic emphasis. Thematic unification is not an aim of this work. Ensemble difficulties. D.

Luciano Berio. *Linea* (UE). For 2 pianos, vibraphone, and marimba. Opens slowly, soft with slipping overlaps, decorative. The title refers to the music's concern with lines and not to the struggle-game of Linus and Apollo in Xenakis's piece of the same name. M-D to D.

Antonio Gino Bibalo. *Autumnale* (Autumn Music) Suite de concert pour 4 instruments 1968 (WH 4261 1974) 36pp., parts. 20 min. For flute, piano, vibraphone, and double bass. 1. Musique nocturne (Prélude): 3 short sections; a short transition leads to the actual night music and a coda; bitonal; through-composed; piano opens with sustained arpeggi chords, virtuoso effects for piano; a little serenade is presented reminiscent of the night music movements in Bartók's string Quartets Nos.4 and 5. 2. Pas de quatre (pour insectes): scherzo, ABA, dancelike, bitonal, ostinato-like treatment in the piano's lower register, amusing, clever writing. 3. Melancolique (élégie): ABA; double bass has melody; pointillistically shaped transition; introductory material returns distributed between the double bass, flute, and vibraphone; coda. Dans les plateaux verts du Congo (On the Green Congo Meadows) (Invention): ABA; opening flute solo is a Congolese folk tune; "Invention" here is used in the sense of contrivance, not in the Bach context; A sections are treated like passacaglias; figurations derive from folk songs; double canon in B section between double bass and bass of piano part; piano is treated percussively. 5. Introduction et toccata (Etude–Finale): a brilliant tour de force in which all instruments are displayed in relation to each other; piano concludes movement with an octave chromatic cadenza. Well-written and highly interesting music. D.

Boris Blacher. *Two Poems for Jazz Quartet* 1957 (Bo&Bo) 11pp., parts. For vibraphone, double bass, drums, and piano. First *Poem* uses piano in chordal syncopation. Second *Poem* uses it more melodically with some chordal syncopation. Delightful sonorities. M-D.

Philippe Boesmans. *Sur Mi* (Jobert 1974) 7 leaves. 13 min. For 2 pianos, electronic organ, and percussion. Explanations in French. 4 copies necessary for performance. Percussion required: cymbals, tam-tam. Spatial and traditional notation, complex chords and rhythmic problems, pointillistic, dense textures, dynamic extremes. Contains almost insurmountable ensemble problems; only for the best equipped avant-garde performers. D.

Claude Bolling. *Sonata for Two Pianos, Percussion and Double Bass* (Les Editions Bleu Blanc Rouge 1973), parts. Piano I (classic) 30pp. Piano II (jazz) 34pp. Percussion required: cymbal, hi-hat, snare drums, small tom-tom, big tom-tom, bass drums. This *Sonata* "has been composed to allow two pianists of different styles to play together. It is not necessary for the classical pianist to be versed in jazz, nor the jazz pianist to have studied his classics. Even, it's heartily recommended that each of the two styles retain their individuality, and thereby accentuate the contrast" (from the score). The work is divided into 3 contrasting sections. The "classical" pianist's part has elements of Chopin and Rachmaninoff mixed with a Gershwin flavor. The "jazz" pianist's part reflects the influence of Duke Ellington, while the formal structure of the work depends on traditional forms and resources. The work holds together remarkably well in spite of its opposite styles. M-D.

———. *Suite* (Les Editions Bleu Blanc Rouge 1973) 70pp., parts. For flute, piano, percussion, and double bass. Percussion required: cymbal, hi-hat, snare drums, small tom-tom, big tom-tom, bass drums. 1. Baroque and Blue; 2. Sentimentale (pianist can improvise in this movement); 3. Javanaise (Java in 5); 4. Fugace (Allegro fugato); 5. Irlandaise; 6. Versatile; 7. Veloce. Bolling acquired a reputation in France as a jazz piano prodigy at the age of 14. He has had formal training and has performed with many jazz greats. "This Suite in 7 parts is composed for a 'classic' flute and a 'jazz' piano. The style of writing for each instrument is somewhat different. It should be interesting to bring out those oppositions in the interpretation. The first half of the 6th movement, 'Versatile,' is written for the bass flute. It is possible to play the whole piece with only flute and piano, but it is (more) complete with double bass and percussion" (from the score). Clever, effective amalgamation of the 2 styles that produces some surprising results. D.

Paul Bowles. *Music for a Farce* 1938 (Weintraub 1953) 34pp., parts. For piano, trumpet, percussion, and clarinet. Allegro rigoroso; Presto (Tempo di Tarantella); Allegretto (Tempo di Quickstep); Allegro; Lento (Tempo di Valse); Allegro (Tempo di Marcia); Presto; Allegretto. Clever, whimsical, mildly 20th-century. M-D.

Cesar Bresgen. *Bilder des Todes* (Dob 1973) 44pp., 19 min. Score and parts for 2 pianos and 2 players on kettledrums and percussion. Toccata: fast-moving, chromatic 16ths in both piano parts; mid-section becomes more lyric and sustained; an agitato section concludes the movement with a strong punch; large span required. Variationen: staccato and marcato figuration are contrasted with octotonic melody, syncopation, and triplet figuration in crescendo. Intermezzo I: melody is accompanied with secco chords; serious. Ricercare I: linear treatment of ideas. Intermezzo II: grace-note octotonic melody; short. Ricercare II: unraveling 8th-note figuration in one piano while the other comments and amplifies line. Epilog: free, long pedals, maestoso ending. Exciting writing in this Suite. D.

Dinos Constantinides. *Study II for Diverse Instruments* 1991 (Magni). 18 min. For clarinet, cello, percussion, and piano. Prelude; Scherzo; Fantasy; Finale. This Study "suggests the cycle of emotions a person experiences in his struggle for survival in a confused society . . . eclectic in nature and employs various styles. Quartal harmonies, clusters, polychords, and folk tunes are present throughout the work" (from Composer's web page: www.magnipublications.com).

George Crumb. *Dream Sequence* (Images II) 1976 (CFP). For violin, cello, piano, and percussion, including suspended cymbals, crotales, Japanese temple bells,

MUSIC FOR FOUR INSTRUMENTS

sleigh bells, maracas, Thai buffalo bell, glass harmonica (tuned crystal goblets). Crumb states that "The form might be described as cyclical movement within a prevailing stasis" and suggests that perhaps this is "indeed the proto-typical 'form' of dreams and nature." Characterization in the score reads "Poised, timeless, 'breathing': as an afternoon in late summer." Timeless effect created by ethereal drone of the glass harmonica, repetitive rhythms in piano and percussion, and free melodic fragments interpolated by strings. Forceful articulation in piano part terminates cyclical repetition. Short closing section fades away as goblets stop ringing one by one. D.

Edison Denisov. *Concerto* 1963 (UE 14301) 23pp., parts. For flute, oboe, piano, and percussion. Ouverture: flexible meters, octotonic, tritone important, light toccata-like passages, contrapuntal treatment of harmonic 7ths, shifting rhythms, fugal texture. Cadenza: flute cadenza; then oboe, piano, and finally the percussion follow, each with their own cadenza. Coda: pointillistic, changing meters, crescendo to end, *ffff* conclusion. Exacting writing. D.

Morton Feldman. *Four Instruments* 1965 (CFP) 6pp. For violin, cello, chimes, and piano. Durations of simultaneous single sounds are extremely slow. All sounds are connected without pauses unless notated. Dynamics are exceptionally low, but audible. Avant-garde. M-D.

Paul Fetler. *Cycles for Percussion and Piano* (Schott Bat 14 1973) 30pp., parts. Requires 3 percussion players and one pianist. Includes distribution, symbols, and notation instructions. Large percussive complement required. Also contains symbols for the percussion sticks. Piano part includes glissandi produced inside piano with thumbs or soft mallets and approximate pitches plucked inside piano. Widely spread sonorities, clusters, pointillistic treatment. Partially avant-garde. Large span required. M-D.

Lukas Foss. *Echoi* 1961–63 (CF and Schott). For clarinet, cello, percussion, and piano. A children's tune is introduced into this piece. Stochastic techniques. The work is controlled by the drummer striking the anvil to redirect the musical activity, banging on the strings of the piano to stop the pianist, etc. Avant-garde. M-D to D.

———. *Ni Bruit Ni Vitesse* ("Neither Noise Nor Haste") (Sal 1972) 21pp., parts. For 2 pianos and 2 percussionists. Careful explanations in English. Exploits sonorities on the keys and strings and requires in addition 2 cowbells, 2 Japanese bowls, and 2 triangle beaters. Percussionists play inside the pianos. Delicate percussive and timbre effects provide gamelan-like sonorities. Visual element of watching activity of performers provides much interest. Aleatoric. Hangs together remarkably well. M-D.

See Eric Salzman, "The Many Lives of Lukas Foss," *Saturday Review* 25 (Feb. 1967): 73–76.

Henryk Mikołaj Górecki. *Good Night* [=*Dobranoc*] 1990 (Bo&H 1994) 16pp., parts. 30 min. For alto flute, soprano, 3 tam-tams, and piano. See detailed entry under duos for flute and piano.

Juan Guinjoàn. *Cinco Estudios* (Alpuerto 1974) 17pp., parts. For 2 pianos and 2 percussionists. Explanations in Spanish, French, and English.

Donald Martino. *From the Other Side* 1988 (Dantalian 507 1989) 88pp., parts. 26 min. A Divertimento for flute (alto flute, piccolo, and maracas), cello (1 maraca), percussion, and piano (with bass drum beater). I. Introduction and Slow Dance, II. Tango dei Grulli, III. Dance of the Reluctant Flamapoo, IV. Ballad for a Blue Bill, V. Das magische Kabarett des Doktor Schönberg. Requires a highly detailed assortment of percussion instruments and beaters. Score contains detailed notes on notation, some notes on interpretation, and general program notes. Martino notes that the work "is a divertimento, sometimes serious, sometimes seriously satiric, sometimes silly, always, I hope, diverting, despite the rather depressing condition to which it owes its inspiration and to which its unfolding pays covert allegorical tribute." Expressionist, with angular melodies and abstractness. Accomplished performers are required to achieve the intended results. Movement V is a humorous and hysterical spoof on Arnold Schoenberg and what his music might "have sounded like had he retained his post as conductor at Wolzogen's Buntes Theater (1901) until his death in 1951," complete with stylistic interpretations of a tango, boogie-woogie, a hard-driving beat, blues, jazz, waltzes, and bebop, not to mention shouts by the performers! D.

Arne Mellnäs. *Capricorn Flakes* (CFP 1970) 4 large sheets. For piano, harpsichord, vibraphone, and glockenspiel. Aleatoric throughout. Twenty-two thematic fragments on one large sheet for each instrument constitute the score. Clever, funny directions in English such as "Nothing is too boring for you to tackle," or "Desire for Seclusion," "Produces the maximum effect with the minimum effort" (from instructions in the score). A fun piece. Avant-garde. M-D.

Francis Miroglio. *Réfractions* (UE 14796 1973) 6 loose leaves. For flute, violin, percussion, and piano. Reproduction of composer's MS. Explanations in French, German, and English. Percussion required: glockenspiel, vibraphone, temple blocks, bongos, caisse claire, ton grave, cimbale chromatique, cymbale clouée, cymbale aigu, cymbale grave, tam-tam, triangle, wood block, glass chimes. Extensive performance directions. Six sections are arranged in an interchangeable manner. The violin and flute play standing up and move according to the specifications given in one of the schemes provided. The instrument notated in the middle of the page and marked with a black line should be given prominence. Piano part includes clusters, playing on the string, rapid glissandi, pointillistic chords, long pedal effects. Aleatoric, avant-garde. D.

Marlos Nobre. *Canticum Instrumentale* Op.25 1967 (Tonos) 35pp., parts. 10 min. For flute, harp, piano, and percussion. Contains notation directions. Free rhythms; notes are to be played with irregular rhythms as long as the line lasts in the prescribed tempo. Long pedals, pointillistic, dynamics serialized, cascading gestures, harmonics, fascinating sonorities. Avant-garde. D.

Robert Parris. *Concerto* 1967 (ACA) 38pp., parts. 14 min. For percussion, violin, cello, and piano. Percussion required: xylophone, celesta, bells, tam-tam, side drum, bass drum, traps. Grave: freely tonal and dissonant; varied tempos; clusters; large and brittle chords move over keyboard; changing meters; toccata-like figuration; octave tremolo between hands; wide dynamic range; wispy staccati; requires large span. Allegro: virtuosic piano part with grand gestures moving over entire keyboard; conclusion subsides and fades away. D.

Urs Peter Schneider. *Kirchweih* (Moeck 1964–71) Five Reductions. I. Kreuge (1964–67), nach Heinrich Seuse, for xylophone, piano, flute, and harmonium. The other four *Reductions* are for different instrumentation.

Elliott Schwartz. *Multiples* (Cole 1975) 7pp. 4 scores necessary for performance. For piano, 3 percussionists, films, and tapes. Extensive performance directions. Pianist has special notational symbols. This piece is to be performed together with tapes, films, and slides of previous performances, not simply as a "live" piece on stage. For a first performance, make tapes, slides, etc., of rehearsals. Each percussionist has the following instruments: one capable of producing specific pitches; groups of instruments in "graduated" sizes offering 4 relatively "pitched" sounds from high to low; one or two middle-to-large-sized instruments capable of producing a sustained resonance. Each performer begins anywhere on the page and follows boxes in any circular path chosen. All performers are synchronized to a steady rhythmic metric pulse. Performance begins off-stage. In addition to other requirements, the pianist has to yell, scream into piano, and call out a name of a composer or an instrument. Avant-garde.

Milan Stibilj. *Condensation* 1967 (Br 6101) 25pp., parts. For 2 pianos, trombone, and percussion. Percussion required: 2 bongos, 3 tom-toms, bass drum, 2 cymbals, tam-tam. "Considered from a formal point of view, the composition is constructed on the principles of simple harmonic motion, which are represented in the note-values. Because the precisely determined rhythmic elements pass from one instrument to another, the underlying structure of the form remains fixed, despite the simultaneous use of improvised passages, which allow each interpreter to maintain his independence" (from Notes in the score). Pointillistic, serial, avant-garde. Extreme ensemble problems in precision. D.

Karlheinz Stockhausen. *Kreuzspiel* (Crossplay) 1951, rev.1960 (UE 13117) 32pp. 10 min. For oboe, bass clarinet, piano, and percussion. Pointillistic, "music in space." The idea of an intersection (crossing) of temporal and spatial phenomena is presented in 3 stages. Pitches are gradually shifted from one register to another. Careful directions are given for the grouping of the instruments and the heights at which players should stand or sit. Every note has a dynamic mark attached. The first of the composer's avant-garde pieces. D.

———. *Prozession* [No. 23] 1967 (UE 14812 1969) 2pp., parts. Minimum length: 23 min. For tam-tam, viola, electronium, piano, microphones, potentiometers, and possibly filters (4 instrumentalists, 2 assistants). Entirely indeterminate. "Each player begins with an event when he wishes. As soon as a player finishes an event, he reacts in accordance with the sign in his part either to the event he himself has just played (either immediately or after a pause), or else to the event of another player that is starting next, which he must hear out before reacting to it (hence trios, duos, and solos are formed)" (Composer's Note). "*Prozession* (process on its way) was written for Stockhausen's group to play on tours, and it presupposes a tremendous *rapport* and intelligence from the players, as the players' parts use only +, −, and = signs for 'form'" (Jonathan Harvey, *The Music of Stockhausen* [Berkeley: University of California Press, 1975], p. 109). Incorporates materials from earlier compositions. Extensive performance notes.

Morton Subotnick. *Serenade II* (McGinnis & Marx) 18pp., parts. For clarinet, horn, piano, and percussion. Performance directions concerning notation: bar lines indicate beats at the designated tempo; the spacing of the notes within the measure designates the way the notes fall in relation to the beat; notes are short unless otherwise indicated. The percussionist who works only inside the piano needs woven marimba mallets, using woven part for soft sounds, stick for hard sounds. All performers play from left to right together; however, they choose freely within each beat. A cadenza is made of 2 phrases, marked A and B, and the players decide on the patterns to use at each performance. The horizontal line indicates the middle of the range for each instrument. The number at the left of each group indicates the number of beats at 60 per minute for that group. The number to the right indicates the length of the pause between groups. The groups are chosen at random during the pause. Big notes indicate loud, small notes soft, etc. Clusters, pointillistic, avant-garde. D.

Stefan Wolpe. *Quartet I* 1950 rev. 1954 (McGinnis & Marx) 63pp., parts. For tenor saxophone, trumpet, piano, and percussion. Lento: loose, mournful and fanfare-like ideas, flexible asymmetrical meters, complex rhythms, cluster-like sonorities. Con moto: jazzy ideas and suave structures brought together; suspended conclusion. Intense Expressionist nontonal writing with numerous ensemble problems. Only for the most venturesome groups. Short and calculated attacks and timbres. D.

———. *Quartet* (McGinnis & Marx). For oboe, cello, piano, and percussion.

Hans Zender. *Quartet* 1964–65 (Bo&Bo 22027) 19pp., parts. For flute, cello, piano, and percussion. Directions for performance in German. Three movements with various directions for different realizations. Complex writing in a serial and strongly atonal style. D.

Music for Five Instruments

Quintets for Piano and Strings

[Piano, 2 violins, viola, and cello, unless otherwise specified.]

Charles Henri Valentine Alkan. *Rondo Brillant* Op.4 (Lemoine) 19pp., parts. Copy at LC. For piano, 2 violins, viola, and cello/double bass. Adagio (Introduction)–Largement; Rondo–Allegretto grazioso. Elegant salon style, all glitter and sparkle for the piano with the other instruments coming along only for the ride! D.

Anton Arensky. *Quintet* Op.51 D 1900 (USSR 1958) 67pp., parts. Allegro moderato: SA design. Andante: a set of variations on "Sur le pont d'Avignon," with shifting harmonies. Scherzo–Allegro vivace: SA with two scherzi. Finale–Fuga: free double fugue. Effective, full Romantic-style writing for the piano throughout. The fugue requires a fine octave technique. D.

Grażyna Bacewicz. *Quintet* I 1952 (PWM) 25 min.
——. *Quintet* II 1965 (PWM 3975) 57pp., parts. 18 min. Moderato–Allegro–Molto Allegro: the half-step and tritone are very important; alternating hands, bitonal figuration, glissandi, simultaneous trills in extreme registers, chromatic passagework, tremolo, clusters. Larghetto: sustained section, long pedal effects; large span required. Allegro giocoso: rhythmic figuration, chordal punctuation, repeated patterns; similar devices used in other movements. D.

Johann Christian Bach. *Quintet* Op.11/4 E♭ (Nag). For 3 violins (or flute, oboe, and violin), viola, and basso continuo; cello ad lib.
——. *Quintet* Op.11/5 A (Steglich—Br; Musica Rara). For flute or violin, oboe or violin, violin, viola, cello, and basso continuo.
——. *Quintet* Op.11/6 D (Nag). For 3 violins (or flute, oboe, and violin), viola, and basso continuo; cello ad lib.

Henk Badings. *Piano Quintet* 1952 (Donemus 1952) 53pp., parts. 24 min. Allegro; Scherzo–Presto; Adagio e mesto; Rondo–Allegro vivace. Strings often speak homorhythmically as if they were a choir juxtaposed to the piano. Limited interaction and imitation between instruments except in Scherzo. M-D.

Béla Bartók. *Quintet* 1904 (D. Dille—EMB 1970) 172pp., parts. Preface by editor in English, German, and Hungarian. Andante: freely tonal around C; chordal; flowing arpeggi figuration mixed with arpeggiated chords; chromatic scalar passages; tremolo; syncopated triplets; octotonic; broken figuration in triplets; long scalar passages used as dramatic gestures; fluent octave technique and large span required. Vivace–Scherzando: dancelike; centers around f♯; Hungarian gypsy flavor; spread-out Alberti bass figuration; imitation; lush Romantic chords in Moderato section; glissandi. Adagio: chromatic; lyric; syncopated chords lead to Adagio molto, where there is much instrumental reaction between piano and strings; sweeping arpeggi gestures, Romantic descending chromatic chords à la *Rosenkavalier;* some changing meters; leads directly to Poco a poco più vivace: Hungarian dance flavor; many octaves used to propel rhythm; tempo increases; concludes after a breathtaking pace in C. Virtuoso writing somewhat reminiscent in style of Bartók's *Rhapsody,* Op.1. D.

Leslie Bassett. *Quintet* 1962 (CFE) 50pp., parts. 20 min. Moderately slow: 12-tone; dramatic gestures; chordal punctuation; tremolo; requires large span. Fast: repeated harmonic 2nds; rhythmic drive; short chromatic lines. Slow: intense; varied figuration; low register of piano treated effectively. Slow–Faster: hammered chordal sonorities; widely spread texture; strong driving rhythms in final section. D.

Mrs. H. H. A. Beach. *Quintet* Op.67 f♯ 1909 (A. P. Schmidt) 47pp., parts. Adagio–Allegro moderato; Adagio espressivo; Allegro agitato. This dreamy, sensuous work in a Brahmsian vein contains effective writing for all the instruments, but the piano part seems by far to be the most important. The second movement has a rich Straussian melody, yet it has its own unique integrity and style. Many Romantic idioms, handled in a thoroughly crafted manner. Deserves reviving. D.

Franz Berwald. *Klavierquartett und Klavierquintette* (Br 4913 1973) 233pp., parts. Vol.13 of the Complete Edition edited by I. Bengtsson and B. Hammar. Preface in German and English, critical commentary in English. Includes *Quartet* Op.1 E♭ for piano, woodwinds, and horn, and *Quintet* Op.6 for piano and strings. The piano writing contains moments of highly original and poetic treatment, although Mendelssohn's influence looms large. The *Quintet* was composed during the 1850s, 1857 at the latest. Appendix: Larghetto and Scherzo for piano and string quartet from an earlier piano Quintet in A (composed during the latter part of the 1840s or about 1850). M-D.

Henrich Ignaz Franz von Biber. *Serenade* (P. Nettl—Nag 112) 12pp., parts. For 2 violins, 2 violas, and basso continuo; cello ad lib. Serenada; Allamanda; Aria; Ciacona (based on chorale "Der Nachtwächter"); Gavotte; Retirada. A fine Suite in period style. M-D.

Ernst Bloch. *Quintet* 1921–23 (GS) 129pp., parts. 35 min. Agitato; Andante mistico; Allegro energico. Quarter-tone usage. Picturesque exoticism, mildly 20th-century modal flavor, massive opening movement. D.

———. *Quintet II* 1957 (BB 1962) 40pp., parts. Animato: two 12-tone sections; the second is an exact transposition of the first, used only melodically; no other serial rules incorporated; the falling 5th outlines a tonic feeling; tritone frequently used. Andante: theme and variations; rich sonorities. Allegro; rondo with lyric interludes; bitonality plays an important part. Strong thematic ideas. Not as virtuosic as the first *Quintet.* D.

See Dika Newlin, "The Later Works of Ernst Bloch," MQ 33 (1947): 443–59. Contains a general discussion of Bloch's compositional style and an analysis of *Piano Quintet I.*

Luigi Boccherini. *Quintet* Op.57/1 A (S. Sadie—Musica Rara 1962) 27pp., parts. Allegro moderato; Menuetto; Andantino con un poco di moto; Allegro giusto. The Piano Quintet was a rare form when this work was composed. Interesting Classical figuration and some unusual harmonies are used. M-D.

———. *Quintet* Op.57/2 B♭ (GS; CFP B73; B&VP) 35pp., parts. Allegretto moderato; Menuetto tempo giusto; Finale. The piano part assumes some individuality. M-D.

———. *Quintet* Op.57/6 "Military Night Watch in Madrid" (IMC). Boccherini came close to Haydn's and Mozart's style in this work. Foreshadows some of the later developments of the Piano Concerto. M-D.

René de Boisdeffre. *Quintet* Op.11 d 1883 (Hamelle) 77pp., parts. Allegro con brio; Scherzo; Andante ma non troppo; Final. Undistinguished writing by today's standards. M-D.

———. *Quintet* Op.25 D 1890 (Hamelle) 85pp., parts. For piano, violin, viola, cello, and double bass. Allegro con brio; Intermezzo; Marche; Pastorale. Well written, pianistic. Traditional harmonic, melodic, and rhythmic treatment. M-D to D.

———. *Quintet* Op.43 B♭ (Hamelle).

Alexander Borodin. *Quintet* c 1862 (Br&H 5718; USSR 1968 55pp., parts). Andante: graceful flowing lines, cantabile and legato. Scherzo: large skips in left hand; chordal; some imitation; Trio uses octotonic writing and melody refers to the opening movement. Finale: short motifs contrasted with larger lines, broken-octave triplets, arpeggiation, syncopated chords, octave passages. M-D.

Siegfried Borris. *Quintet* Op.99/3 (Heinrichshofen/Sirius 1973) 33pp., parts. Photostat of MS. For piano, violin, viola, cello, and double bass. Allegro con brio; Largo; Largo–Vivace alla burlesca. Hammered repeated syncopated octaves, harmonic 2nds, 4ths, major 7ths, octotonic, chords in alternating hands, freely tonal, linear and thin textures, flowing lines in second movement, corky rhythmic subject for burlesca movement, shifting meters, Neoclassic orientation. M-D.

Johannes Brahms. *Quintet* Op.34 f (H. Krellmann—Henle 1971; Br&H; CFP 3660; GS L1646; Heugel 188; EPS). Henle edition (75pp., parts) uses the autograph and Brahms's own marked copy of the first edition as sources; contains fingering of piano part by H.-M. Theopold; includes brief remarks on each movement. Allegro non troppo; Andante, un poco Adagio; Allegro; Allegro non troppo. This work began as a String Quintet, the fifth instrument being a second cello. It was rearranged as a Sonata for 2 pianos (IMC), and finally emerged in its present form in 1865. This *Quintet* is probably one of the 10 greatest masterpieces in the chamber music repertoire. It is a big, muscular work for small forces and has features in common with Beethoven's *Quartet* Op.95. In both compositions the finales have slow introductions followed by long, binary main sections, which lead into faster, lengthy codas. Thematic metamorphosis takes place in the first and third movements. The slow movement is rather difficult to sustain. D.

See Thomas F. Dunhill, "Brahms' Quintet for Pianoforte and Strings," MT 72 (1931): 319–22—each movement is discussed and analyzed; Jae-Hyang Koo, "A Study of Four Representative Piano Quintets by Major Composers of the Nineteenth Century: Schumann, Brahms, Dvořák and Franck," D.M.A. diss., University of Cincinnati, 1993.

Frank Bridge. *Quintet* 1904–12 (Augener) 68pp., parts. Adagio–Allegro moderato: d; chord in right hand with fast chromatic figuration in left hand and the reverse is a pattern frequently found in this work; bold arpeggiated strokes; lyric second theme in F; tremolo. Adagio ma non troppo: B; nocturne-like in style; chromatic; Allegro con brio mid-section in d; works to great octave climax; opening section and mood return. Allegro energico: driving rhythmic figuration; legato and staccato triplets; frequent modulation; alternating hands; dramatic scalar and chordal gestures bring work to a close. Strong post-Romantic writing. D.

Adolf Busch. *Quintett* Op.35 (Br&H 5370 1927) 52pp., parts. Sostenuto; Adagio cantabile; Finale–Molto appassionato. Slight Reger influence, violent dynamic changes, some complex polyphonic spots. D.

Roberto Caamaño. *Quinteto* 1963 (IU) 72pp., parts. 19 min. Allegro: serial; opens with octaves in extreme registers that move close together and begin again, but moves directly into a sciolto figuration that embraces the main idea; triplet atonal (row) figuration spread over keyboard; punctuated chords (9ths and 10ths) and whole-note chords bring the movement to a close. Allegro: the row is run through quickly in pointillistic fashion. Lento: piano provides sustaining sonorities and marked chordal pulsation. Molto allegro: row is octotonically treated in various registers; chordal rhythmic punctuation. Thin textures throughout most of the work. D.

John Alden Carpenter. *Quintet* 1934 (GS) 60pp., parts. Moderato–Allegro: chromatic themes, pedal point under parallel moving chords, a few meter changes, Impressionist tendencies. Andante: sustained, low register exploited, broken arpeggi figurations, sweeping climax, 7th harmonies. Allegro non troppo: driving rhythms, chordal 2nds frequently used, dancelike syncopations, contrasting sections. D

Mario Castelnuovo-Tedesco. *Quintet* 1932 F (Forlivesi) 60pp., parts. Lento e sognante–Vivo e appassionato: chromatic broken-chordal figuration, grandiose chords, scalar. Andante: parallel chords; builds to a large climax then subsides; triplets are frequent. Scherzo: broken octaves, scales, repeated chords, contrary-motion figures. Vivo e impetuoso: alternating hands; sustained chords; arpeggi; dramatic piano part has a short quasi-recitativo section that leads to a Moderato (alla marcia funèbre) before returning to opening tempo and idea; brilliant conclusion. D.

———. *Second Piano Quintet* 1951 (Forlivesi).

Alexis de Castillon. *Quintette* Op.1 E♭ (Durand) 59pp., parts. Allegro; Scherzo; Adagio et Final. The spirit of Saint-Saëns hovers over this work. M-D.

Alexandre Cellier. *Quintette II* b (Senart 1922) 43pp., parts. Allegro ben moderato; Ben moderato e tranquillo; Lento recitativo; Allegro con fuoco. Strong Franck influence. M-D.

George W. Chadwick. *Quintet* E♭ (A. P. Schmidt 2569) 69pp., parts. Copy at LC. Allegro sostenuto; Andante Cantabile; Intermezzo; Final. Brahms and Franck influences are felt here, although the work does display a solid craft for the period. M-D to D.

Boris Chaikovsky. *Quintet* 1962 (USSR) 82pp., parts. Moderato: SA; proceeds almost from beginning to end in quarter notes; octotonic; modal; freely chromatic; dramatic development section leads to a mirror recapitulation with the climax at the beginning. Allegro: free rondo; lyrical refrain alternates with episodes; contrasting timbres of the piano and strings are underlined; abrupt tempo changes. Allegro: a poignant scherzo; toccata-like; SA characteristics; driving and impetuous; tense and dramatic main theme with a resilient rhythm. Finale: an Adagio in SA design without a development; progression of chords serves as the main theme, like a solemn procession; somber and melodious secondary theme. Emotions soar in this *Quintet,* but it gives an impression of being well knit, clear, and precise in its expression. A worthy work in a style best described as a mixture of Prokofiev and Khachaturian. M-D to D.

Camille Chevillard. *Quintette* Op.1 E♭ (Durand) 80pp., parts. Allegro ma non troppo; Tempo di Marcia; Molto vivace; Allegro molto appassionato. Traditional writing but exploits the piano admirably. M-D.

Barney Childs. *Music for Piano and Strings* (ACA 1965), parts. For piano, violin, viola, cello, and double bass. The solo piano part is composed of 27 individual sheets assembled in the order decided by the performer. There is no stipulated length on many of the sheets, this direction being left up to the soloist. A page turner is required. Soloist may rehearse with or without the strings—that is, a performance may be carefully worked out, so that all performers know just what will be happening when, or it may be completely spontaneous. Some of the directions for the pianist are: "This section is made up of these 4 chords (chords, 1 note) played in any order or repeated as you wish." "Using a piece of heavy aluminum foil or light sheet metal, crinkled or smooth, place over strings in middle register, after normal sound. Soft-drink bottle caps may be placed on top of the foil or metal if you wish. Music played during this section should be busy, linear, wandering." Contains unusual and original directions that produce some fascinating sonorities. The strings portion contains 6 "movements" to be played in any order. Four of them contain a solo for one of the string players. Requires a fine imaginative pianist to make this piece work, but the effort would be worthwhile. D.

Tudor Ciortea. *Cvintet Cu Pian* c♯ (Editura Muzicală 1961) 92pp., parts. Larghetto–Allegro non troppo ma deciso: introduction, SA, chromatic and interesting rhythmic structure, figuration in alternating hands. Molto vivace: Scherzo, ABA, coda. Adagietto: ABAB form, warm cantabile treatment of main A idea, contrasting B sections, coda. Vivace: rondo, freely tonal (but highly chromatic) and pianistic writing. D.

Halfdan Cleve. *Quintett* Op.9 E♭ (Br&H). In Brahms style and tradition. D.

Johann Baptist Cramer. *Quintuor* Op.9 E (Probst 321) 17pp., parts. Copy at LC. For piano, violin, viola, cello, and double bass. Largo–assai giocoso; Adagio; Allegretto vivo. Also available in an arrangement for piano and flute (or violin) by the composer. M-D.

Edison Denisov. *Quintette* 1987 (Leduc 1999) 77pp., parts. 24 min. Moderato: restless with proportional rhythmic relationships though lyric with strong touches of chromaticism; SA. Agitato: ABA with coda; chromatic perpetual mobile movement throughout A sections and pizzicati in B; proportional rhythmic relationships. Tranquillo: peaceful; imitation contrasted by brief homophonic passages in dense chordal structures; continual development of proportional rhythms; sustained chordal finish at *pppp*. An engaging piece. D.

Ernst Dohnányi. *Quintet* Op.1 c 1902 (Dob) 63pp., parts. Allegro; Scherzo; Adagio, quasi andante; Finale–Allegro animato. Written in the grand European tradition; sings and soars with the spirit that imbued the music of Dohnányi's masters, who closed the 19th century and ushered in the 20th. Brahms-like, broad, lyric, impassioned writing. Dohnányi played the piano part at his debut as a composer. D.

————. *Quintet* Op.26 e♭ 1919 (Simrock) 43pp., parts. 20 min. Allegro non troppo; Intermezzo; Moderato. One of Dohnányi's most impressive works. Strong contrapuntal techniques; form and drama interact closely; somber colors except for the scherzo (in the middle of the Intermezzo); Romantic but economical scoring. D.

Theodore Dubois. *Quintette* F. For oboe (or second violin or clarinet), violin, viola, cello, and piano. See detailed entry under quintets for piano(s), strings, and winds.

Johann Ladislav Dussek. *Quintett* Op.41 f (UMKR 39 1975 23pp.; Wollenweber), parts. For piano, violin, viola, cello, and double bass. Allegro moderato ma con fuoco; Adagio espressivo; Finale. Contains some interesting harmonic innovations through the use of chromaticism. Effective finale with some brilliant figuration. Concludes with ascending melodic form of scale. M-D.

Antonín Dvořák. *Quintet* Op.5 A (Artia).

————. *Quintet* Op.81 A (Artia; Simrock 59pp., parts; GS L1627; EPS 305) 28 min. The piano part is fuller than in Dvořák's *Piano Quartets*. First movement exploits submediant in the recapitulation and coda. National dance characteristics are found in the second movement (Dumka) and in the Furiant, which takes the place of a scherzo. A radiant rondo concludes the *Quintet*. Intoxicating melodies, vital rhythms, colorful scoring, and contrasts in mood are present in abundance. D

See Sir Henry Hadow, "Dvořák's Quintet for Pianoforte and Strings (Op.81)," MT 73 (1932): 401–404—an analysis compares the work and stylistic traits of Dvořák with those of Schubert and Beethoven; Jae-Hyang Koo, "A Study of Four Representative Piano Quintets by Major Composers of the Nineteenth Century: Schumann, Brahms, Dvořák and Franck," D.M.A. diss., University of Cincinnati, 1993.

Oleg Eiges. *Quintet* 1961 (USSR) 60pp., parts. Pesante–Moderato allegro: SA; theme of the introduction plays an important part in further development; driving and dynamic main subject is followed by a lyrical second idea; development builds on the introduction and main subjects; recapitulation presents the second subject and a coda based on material derived from the first subject. Andante con moto: SA; calm; melodious; first theme resembles a Russian folk song; second subject is in the nature of a slow march; an element from the first movement introduction is encountered in the more lively development section; the slower motion returns in the recapitulation. Allegro vivace: SA; combines a scherzo and fast waltz; an extensive coda is based on a theme from the introduction of the first movement; the finale lends its bright and vigorous coloring to the whole work. Idiomatic and kaleidoscopic writing. Mildly 20th-century. M-D to D.

Edward Elgar. *Quintet* Op.84 a 1918 (Nov) 67pp., parts. Moderato: chromatic, chordal, octotonic, arpeggi figuration, 16th-note octaves in left hand, 3 with 4. Adagio: broken-chordal figures move over keyboard. Andante–Allegro: sweeping arpeggi patterns, chorale-like section, wide dynamic range. Artistic writing but not always pianistically conceived. D.
See H. C. Colles, "Elgar's Quintet for Pianoforte and Strings, Op.84," MT 60 (1919): 596–600. A discussion of the work from a formal, harmonic, and developmental point of view.

Georges Enesco. *Quintet* Op.29 (Editura Muzicală Uniunii Compozitorilor 1968; Sal) 86pp., parts. Con moto molto moderato; Vivace, ma non troppo. Involved, highly chromatic although key signatures are present. Second movement is very long and includes varied tempos (Più tranquillo provides a needed contrast). Individual and unique style that includes some wild and impassioned writing. Requires thorough musicianship throughout. D.

Louise Farrenc. *Quintet I* Op.30 a 1839 (S. E. Pickett-Hildegard 1995) 84pp., parts. For violin, viola, cello, double bass, and piano. Allegro; Adagio non troppo; Scherzo; Finale. "Grounded on classical formal models: the first movement is in sonata-allegro form; the second is a slow rondo; the third is a scherzo-trio; the fourth is a rondo-sonata. But the work is thoroughly romantic in its soaring melodies, modulations to distantly-related keys, range of moods, sheer length, and virtuosic piano writing" (from Preface). Extensive notes and editorial comments. M-D to D.
———. *Quintet II* Op.31 E 1840 (S. E. Pickett—Hildegard 1996) 66pp., parts. For violin, viola, cello, double bass, and piano. Andante sostenuto–Allegro grazioso; Grave; Vivace; Finale. Composed only a year after the first *Quintet,* the 2 share similar characteristics, forms, pianistic, and ensemble requirements. Extensive notes and editorial comments. M-D to D.
These 2 *Quintets* provide delightful and fine alternatives to the standard literature with the use of the double bass.

Gabriel Fauré. *Quintet I* Op.89 d (GS 1907; Hamelle) 28 min. Molto moderato; Adagio; Allegretto moderato. Three movements of refined expression with a perfect sense of balance. The Adagio uses all instruments in a canonic workout with excellent effect and is the most successful movement. The finale develops from a single figure and is a masterpiece of delicate writing. D.
———. *Quintet II* Op.115 c 1921 (Durand) 76pp., parts. 30 min. Allegro moderato: 16th-note patterns, swaying dancelike chromatic movement, thin textures, imitation. Allegro vivo: scalar; broken octaves; broken double notes accompany melody in other hand; themes get tangled; triplets embedded with important bass line; flowing passagework; clever and vivacious. Andante mo-

derato: important half-step melodic idea; added-note and syncopated chords; rotary motion required; deeply emotional; arpeggi; melancholy mood. Allegro molto: triple-time bass with the piano accenting duple rhythm; long lines; octave-apart melodic writing; alternating hands; thematic transformation. A searching work of commanding proportions and great profundity. Shows the 71-year-old composer's fresh and youthful enthusiasm. D.

Richard Felciano. *Aubade* (ECS) 13pp., parts. For violin, viola, cello, harp, and piano. Sustained sonorities; long pedals; right foot is to come down hard on damper pedal from a distance of about 6 inches above, so that impact sounds. Sharp strokes on keys, pointillistic, glissandi, harmonics. Expressionist. M-D.

John Field. *Quintet* A♭ (Br&H 859) 17pp., parts. One beautiful movement that is Andante con espressione, nocturne-like throughout. The piano carries the largest part of the ensemble. M-D.

Ross Lee Finney. *Piano Quintet* 1953 (Henmar) 52pp., parts. Adagio sostenuto: chordal, sustained, leads to Allegro marcato: chords interspersed with octotonic disjunct figuration moving over keyboard; sustained slow section with references to the introduction interrupts from time to time, and these 2 basic ideas form the bulk of the movement. Allegro scherzando: continuous filigree figuration contrasted with rhythmic melodic idea; melodic idea is extended and accompanied by tonal repeated chords; long semi-chromatic runs; repeated A in piano part for final 4 bars concludes movement. Nocturne, Adagio sostenuto: freely flowing tonal lines. Allegro appassionato: serpentine chromatic right-hand triplets with 8th-note octaves in left hand; independent lines in both hands; much rhythmic push. Clear textures throughout. M-D.

———. *Piano Quintet II* (Columbia University Press 1974) 54pp., parts. Introduction–Larghetto: serial, dramatic, chordal, trills, quick melodic spurts in 32nds; uses most of keyboard. Allegretto moderato: secco style; piano has cadenza-like section that exploits runs, chromatic 3rds, and large skipping gestures. Allegro drammatico: piano has marked melodic line; octotonic; pointillistic effects; hammered repeated chords at end. Epilogue–Adagio cantabile: tranquil row unfolds; various layers of sound; final row statement heard in bell-like tolling tones; hypnotic conclusion. D.

Arthur Foote. *Quintet* Op.38 (H. W. Hitchcock—Da Capo) 6opp. Allegro giusto—appassionato; Intermezzo; Scherzo; Allegro giusto. Schumannesque and Brahmsian qualities. Whimsical themes throughout. Intermezzo (the finest movement) contains some real surprises in its instrumental color. Eminently worth reviving. M-D to D.

César Franck. *Quintet* f (CFP 79pp., parts; Hamelle; BMC; IMC; EPS) Molto moderato quasi lento–Allegro; Lento, con molto sentimento; Allegro non troppo, ma con fuoco. Although this is a fairly early work (1878–79), it is a fine, impassioned piece, full of Romantic sensibility. Economy of musical material and ability to create a coherent whole are beautifully illustrated in this dramatic work. One of the 3 or 4 greatest works in the form; represents the epitome in musical expression of which the combination is capable. D.

See Jae-Hyang Koo, "A Study of Four Representative Piano Quintets by Major Composers of the Nineteenth Century: Schumann, Brahms, Dvořák and Franck," D.M.A. diss., University of Cincinnati, 1993.

Peter Racine Fricker. *Concertante V* Op.65 (University of California at Santa Barbara) 28pp., parts. 9½ min. Declamato–Scherzoso: piano has much chromatic staccato activity in unisons 2 octaves apart; leads to a broader (Solemne) section, where the piano is treated more legato and chordally (Lirico); short accelerando moves into più mosso before a Molto allegro section juxtaposes long lines with short motivic ideas; cadenza for piano brings together much of the material already exposited; Alla marcia section brings back the Declamato–Scherzo material from the opening; a final accelerando brings the work to an exciting conclusion. The style is mainly linear with a transparent clarity, serially inspired, with free key centers lurking in the background. Fricker knows how to write idiomatically for instruments so they sound their best. M-D.

Ignaz Friedman. *Quintett* c (WH 1918) 66pp., parts. Allegro maestoso; Larghetto, con somma espressione; Epilog. Contains some fluent and beautiful writing, somewhat in a post-Brahms-Reger style. The second movement is highly eclectic with changes of mood and tempos. M-D to D.

James Friskin. *Quintet* Op.1 c 1907 (St&B) 79pp., parts. Allegro risoluto; Allegro molto; Adagio sostenuto; Molto sostenuto e maestoso. Written in a heroic Brahms-like style. M-D.

——. *Phantasy* f 1910 (St&B 1024) 43pp., parts. One large sectionalized movement in post-Romantic style. M-D.

Anis Fuleihan. *Quintet* 1964 (Bo&H) 71pp., parts. Allegro: flexible meters, serial, octotonic, trills; row is inventively treated. Andante con moto: more lyric, even in the Animato section; enfático added-note chords are effective. Allegro giusto: sempre staccato style, alternating hands; leads directly to Andante: long piano introduction moves through a Molto vivace and picks up rest of instruments; chords in 4ths and 5ths lead to a $\frac{7}{4}$ section, where the melodic idea is hammered out with arpeggiated accompanied chords; rhythmic pulsation increases to a subito Largamente coda that ends in A; *pp.* Clear textures. D.

Blas Galindo. *Quintetto* 1960 (IU; LC) 43pp., parts. Commissioned by the Sprague Foundation of the Library of Congress. Allegro; Lento; Allegro. Freely tonal writing that is at some points very tonal. Generally clear lines, some imitation and parallelism, alternating hands, cross-relations, 7th chords, and use of the tritone combine to make this Neoclassic work both accessible and exciting. D.

Edwin Gerschefski. *Quintet* Op.16 (ACA 1961) 54pp., parts. Maetoso; Allegro leggiero (rev. version); Adagio; Allegro con brio. Tremolo, octotonic, linear, glissandi, Neoclassic, hemiola. Low register of piano effectively exploited. Large span required. M-D.

Vittorio Giannini. *Quintet* 1932 (SPAM) 96pp., parts. Allegro con spirito; Adagio; Allegro. Virtuoso post-Romantic writing that constantly keeps the pianist involved. Extension of idiomatic pianism in the Brahms tradition. D.

Alberto Ginastera. *Quintetto* 1963 (Bo&H 19251) 52pp., parts. 16 min. Introduzione; Cadenza I per viola e violoncello; Scherzo fantastico; Cadenza II per due violini; Piccola musica notturna; Cadenza III per pianoforte; Finale. Strong, freely chromatic, wide dynamic range, clusters, tremolo, alternating hands. The piano cadenza is *ff* and dramatic, with large percussive chords; *ppp* figuration builds and leads (octotonically) to a large cluster that opens the Finale. Large span required. D.

Eugene Goossens. *Quintet* Op.23 1918 (JWC) 35pp., parts. One large movement with varied tempos and moods. Dramatic and flamboyant writing with chromatic octaves and figuration most consistently used. M-D to D.

Enrique Granados. *Quinteto en sol menor* 1898 (UME 1973) 41pp., parts. Allegro: SA; marcato unison opening; chromatic thirds; arpeggi; much statement and answer between piano and strings. Allegretto quasi andantino: chordal opening in piano while the violin has rhythmic figure, piano then takes this figure; undulating 3rds and 6ths. Largo–Molto presto: vigorous rhythmical figures alternate with more languorous idea from second movement. M-D.

Sofia Gubaidulina. *Quintet* C 1957 (USSR) 78pp., parts. Allegro: SA; austere and virile; short exposition is almost exclusively based on an intense development of the main subject from an initial motif; second subject, grotesque and full of restrained sarcasm, is stated polyphonically; abrupt and startling contrasts appear in the development; simple textures with scales in parallel and contrary motion. Andante: scherzo-like, simple timbres; based on a naive marchlike theme that, in further development, leads to combinations of weird, uncanny sonorities. Larghetto sensibile: warmly lyric; a cantabile theme flows like a calm narrative. Presto: rondo; toccata-like; full of energy; themes pursue one another in an irresistible torrent. Colorful writing in a mildly 20th-century idiom. M-D.

Reynaldo Hahn. *Quintet* (Heugel 28175 1923) 65pp., parts. Molto agitato e con fuoco; Andante; Allegretto grazioso. Flowing lines, Impressionist, beautifully pianistic. M-D.

Iain Hamilton. *Quintet* 1993 (TP 1999) 89pp., parts. Vivo; Adagio; Presto precipitoso. A true tour de force packed with energy and firecracker materials in outer movements contrasted by a peaceful, homophonically based middle which occasionally stretches the firmly rooted tonality. Piano cadenza in first movement. M-D to D.

Roy Harris. *Quintet* 1938 (GS) 74pp., parts. Strongly polyphonic, full of elaborate canonic devices and subtle thematic development, rich melodic invention. Passacaglia: not a true passacaglia, but has a strong central pattern that is used throughout; piano part develops into a quasi-toccata; 6 variations on the "theme." Cadenza: the piano is most effectively used in this movement, a multiple cadenza that employs sharp percussive writing, melodic passages in octaves, and intense polyharmonies; each instrument solos the "theme" rhapsodically. Fugue: a triple fugue on 3 subjects that has built-in toccata-like episodes. A strong spirit of Classicism permeates this entire work. Strongly polyphonic, full of elaborate canonic devices and subtle thematic development, rich melodic invention. D.
See Arthur Mendel, "The Quintet of Roy Harris," MM 17/1 (Nov.-Dec. 1939): 25–29.

Josef Matthias Hauer. *Zwölftonspiel (2. Juni 1948)* (Fortissimo 1971) 12pp., parts. Photostat of MS. For piano and string quartet, with a 12-tone row by Wolfgang Kammerlander.

Anthony Philip Heinrich. *The Yankee Doodleiad: A National Divertimento* 1820 (A. Stiller—Kallisti), parts. For 3 violins, cello, and piano (or string quartet and piano). Variations on the folk tune "Yankee Doodle." First printed edition.

Peter Herrmann. *Klavierquintett* (DVFM 8517a 1970) 57pp., parts. Allegro moderato; Lento; third movement untitled ($\downarrow$. = 80). Syncopated harmonic 2nds, octotonic, secco style, melody in lower register, chromatic 3rds and octaves, contrasting ideas and moods in all movements, traditional forms, bitonal. Finale contains fugal textures and figuration in alternating hands, *ppp* closing. Neoclassic Hindemithian style. D.

Heinrich von Herzogenberg. *Quintett* Op.17 C (Br&H) 58pp., parts. Allegro moderato, un poco maestoso; Adagio; Allegro; Presto. Masterly writing from the technical viewpoint and also intellectually interesting. Skillful use of the tone color of all instruments. Worth reviving. M-D.

Alun Hoddinott. *Quintet* Op.78/4 1972 (OUP 1973) 32pp., parts published separately. A one-movement work of 6 thematically linked sections. Sparse textures in all parts, nebulous clusters, much octave writing for the piano. M-D.

Alan Hovhaness. *Piano Quintet* Op.9 (CFP 6568 1963) 10 min. Andante: pianist must hold down pedal throughout the movement; short ornamental figures in upper register. Lento: mainly *p* arpeggio figuration mixed with short chromatic crescendo-decrescendo sections. Adagio: clusters, short chromatic runs, clusters return. Allegro molto: clusters in alternating hands. Allegretto: long pandiatonic chordal lines in the piano part. Very little drama, but interest is sustained by sheer continuity and evocative sonorities. M-D.

Johann Nepomuk Hummel. *Quintet* Op.87 E♭ (UWKR 25 41pp., parts; CFP; McGinnis & Marx; Wollenweber). For violin, viola, cello, double bass, and piano. Allegro e risoluto assai: SA; main theme martial; triplets; unusual tonal progressions; uneven number of notes in a bar of chromatic runs (à la Chopin); piano has melodic line part of the time. Menuetto: animation and exuberance mixed with melancholy; great fluidity in moving through keys; Schubert-like; scalar runs in the bright Trio. Largo: short; free cantabile style; almost a cadenza for the piano. Finale: agitated but cheerful mood prevails; driving rhythms; facile pianistic figuration; brilliant and effective closing. One of Hummel's greatest chamber works; great fun for the pianist. D.

Vincent d'Indy. *Quintette* Op.81 g 1924 (Senart) 42pp., parts. Assez animé: broken-chordal figuration; melody is taken by the piano in full-octave chords; fully worked-out development; un peu plus lent coda; *pp* closing. Assez animé: $\frac{5}{4}$; piano provides much syncopation; freely chromatic; strong *ff* closing. Lent et expressif: lightly flowing, sustained lines, rich harmonies. Modérément animé: 3 layers of sound in the piano opening, broken figuration in alternating hands, sustained mid-section, brilliant closing. D.

Charles Ives. *Adagio Cantabile* (The Innate) 1908 (PIC 1967) 5pp., parts. 3 min. For piano, string quartet, and double bass (optional). Chromatic, chordal, left hand over right, parallel chords. Concludes on quartet harmony. M-D.

——. *Hallowe'en* 1912 from *Three Outdoor Scenes* (Boelke-Bomart) 7pp., parts. 3 min. Contains 3 separate movements, all available separately: *In Re Con Moto Et Al* (PIC), *Largo Risoluto No. I* (PIC), *Largo Risoluto No. II* (PIC). The piano part is atonal in this cacophonic takeoff on Halloween and April Fools' Day jokes. It may be repeated 3 or 4 times; the last time a drum can be added to the general confusion, to be played "as fast as possible without disabling any player or instrument." M-D.

Frederick Jacobi. *Hagiographa* 1938 (Arrow) 59pp., parts. 26 min. A set of 3 musical biblical narratives. 1. Job: broken-chordal figuration; sustained section; at m. 14 piano has melodic idea supported with mild dissonant chords; syncopation; chordal f♯ closing. 2. Ruth: melodic; expressive; parallel chords; 16th-note figuration; syncopated chords; *ppp* dolcissimo ending; large span required. 3. Joshua: rhythmic and furious chordal opening; staccato broken octaves contrasted with long pedaled sonorities; flowing octaves in parts; climactic strepitoso ending. Tends toward seriousness and meditation. Colorful writing even if it sounds a little tame to today's audiences. M-D.

Ulysses Kay. *Piano Quintet* 1949 (ACA) 25 min. First movement: striking themes achieve a powerful climax; piano used contrapuntally. Second movement: slow; eloquent; derives its appeal from the slow rise of a beautiful melodic idea; resounding combination of instruments in vertical lines gives it life. M-D to D.

Kent Kennan. *Quintet* (GS 1940) 84pp., parts. Allegretto; Lento; Vivace; Andante–Allegro. Mildly 20th-century with strong melodic writing. Sweeping arpeggi, sturdy chords, quartal and quintal harmonies, octotonic, syncopated melodies, alternating hand patterns, feroce conclusion. Large span required. D.

Giselher Klebe. *Quintett 'quasi una fantasia'* Op.53 (Br 4150 1967) 32pp., parts. 16 min. Allegro molto; Andante mosso. Serial, atonal, pointillistic, Expressionist, concludes with same 6 bars that opened the work. Second movement has varied tempos and moods. Chords, chromatic figuration and arpeggi, repeated notes, varied tempos in last movement, unresolved final chords. D.

Erich W. Korngold. *Quintet* Op.15 E 1920 (Schott) 57pp., parts. 18½ min. Mässiges Zeitmass, mit schwungvoll blühendem Ausdruck; Adagio (9 variations on Korngold's "Lieder des Abschieds" Op.14); Finale. Extroverted writing that constantly moves the pianist over the keyboard. Accidentals are plentiful, à la Reger. D.

Hans Kox. *Memories and Reflections* 2002 (Donemus 2002) 36pp., parts. 20 min. Allegro furioso–Andante calmante; Allegro deciso–Andante cantabile; Allegro scherzando leggierissimo; Adagio molto–Allegro. Extensive passagework and interaction among instruments, packed with energy at times, then rapidly contrasted by contemplative melodies and harmonies. Deserves to be heard in the years to come. M-D to D.

Kenneth Leighton. *Quintet* Op.34 (Nov 1962) 98pp., parts. 29 min. Allegro con moto: chromatic; shifting meters; punctuated chords; quartal harmony. Adagio sostenuto e molto espressivo: octotonic; trills embedded in unwinding chromatic figures; works to a broad climax; large span required. Scherzo: fleeting, brilliant, syncopation, repeated chords, reiterated patterns. Passacaglia: quiet expressive opening builds and drops back; varied treatment of the passacaglia idea, including changed tempos, shifted meters, scalar intrusions, martellato figures in alternating hands, augmentation; *fff* conclusion in C. D.

Riccardo Malipiero. *Quintetto* 1957 (SZ) 35pp., parts. 18 min. Moderato: freely chromatic, changing meters, varied figuration. Molto veloce: octaves in alternating hands, chordal punctuation. Large span required. Adagio: piano has melodic and chordal treatment; animated section gives piano more rhythmic thrust; alternating perfect and diminished 5ths close the movement. Mosso: octaves, repeated chords, skipping left hand, dramatic conclusion. D.

———. *Sonata a Cinque* (Ric). For flute (violin), violin, viola, cello, and piano. See detailed entry under quintets for piano(s), strings, and winds.

Frank Martin. *Quintette* 1920–21 (Henn) 53pp., parts. Andante con moto; Tempo di Minuetto; Adagio ma non troppo; Presto. This piece is marked by Classical form, finely developed themes, and a predilection for delicately shaded sonorities. Idiomatic writing for all the instruments, chromatic melodies, ostinato-like patterns, and a rich mellow expressiveness make this a highly deserving work. The piano writing is a pleasure throughout. D.

Bohuslav Martinů. *Quintette* (La Sirène Musicale 1933) 28pp., parts. 18½ min. Poco allegro: octotonic, parallel chords, chromatic, scalar, varied use of triplets. Andante: scales; more sustained writing; large span required. Allegretto: changing meters; repeated octaves and notes; duplets into triple meter; alternating hands. Allegro moderato: chromatic chords alternate with scales; brilliant closing; good octave technique required. M-D to D.

———. *Piano Quintet II* 1944 (AMP) 60pp., parts. 18 min. Poco allegro: infectious; injects jazz into an old hymn tune "The Son of Man Goes Forth to War"; highly chromatic. Adagio: great serenity; staccato *p* repeated 16th-note chords. Scherzo–Poco allegretto: lively scherzo, much octotonic writing. Largo–Allegro: dramatic, opens with strings alone; in the Allegro the piano uses hand alternation and broken octaves. Engaging writing throughout. D.

See Joseph Kerman, "Current Chronicle: Princeton [The Chamber Music of Bohuslav Martinů]," MQ 35 (April 1949): 301–305. Includes an analysis of *Piano Quintet II.*

Toshiro Mayuzumi. *Pieces for Prepared Piano and Strings* (CFP 1957) 17pp., parts. 13 min. Prologue: Interlude; Finale. Materials required for preparation include pieces of rubber, a bolt, and a screw. Imaginative sonorities; uses variation of serial technique; neo-Impressionist; makes unique use of blending piano sounds with strings, especially in the repeated notes of the piano. A cadenza for prepared piano is included. Prepared and unaltered tones mixed. Mayuzumi is regarded as the Messiaen of Japan. D.

John McCabe. *Nocturnal* Op.42 (Nov 1967) 46pp., parts. 13 min. Introduction; Nocturne I; Cadenza I; Interlude; Cadenza II; Nocturne II; Epilogue. Strong 20th-century treatment of all instruments. D.

Nicolas Medtner. *Quintet* C 1950 (Zimmermann) 54pp., parts. Rachmaninoff influence is present in this strong idiomatic and articulate writing for the piano. It is an effective work, very playable, and it would be rewarding for performers who like their music to sound as though it were written in a comfortable and familiar style of the 1920s. Plenty to challenge the pianist. D.

———. *Chamber Music.* (USSR 4127) Vol.8 of *Complete Works.*

Olivier Messiaen. *Pièce* 1991 (UE 19 978 1992) 12pp. One of the composer's last works. Combines techniques of final decades, especially birdsong and sound-color relationships. Tends to juxtapose piano and string quartet in strongly contrasting sections. D.

Georges Migot. *Quintette, Les Agrestides* (Senart 1920) 85pp., parts. Un peu lent–Allegro; Rude, comme une danse agreste; Modéré. Difficult writing in Migot's unique style. Unusual harmonic shifts brought about by continuous superimposed melodic lines; moves over keyboard; flexible tempos; sudden dynamic changes permeated with a certain archaic flavor; architectural forms. All add up to an unusual work. D.

Darius Milhaud. *Piano Quintet* 1951 (Heugel) 36pp., parts. 16½ min. Avec vivacité; Avec mystère; Avec douceur; Avec emportement. Melodically oriented, but the themes are sometimes fragmented and juxtaposed amid much figuration. It is easiest to hear the themes and lines in the third movement. Small fragments build larger structures; homophonic and contrapuntal elements. Some polytonality, octotonic, quartal harmonies, parallel chords. Large span required. D.

Herman Mulder. *Kwintet* Op.71 1947 (Donemus 1951) 52pp., parts. Allegro moderato; Molto vivace; Adagio molto. M-D.
———. *Kwintet* II Op.188 1981 (Donemus 1983) 57pp., parts. 28 min. Andante sostenuto–Allegro; Allegro; Adagio; Allegro agitato. M-D.

Zygmunt Mycielski. *Five Preludes* 1967 (PWM 1973) 16pp., parts. Reproduction of the composer's MS.

Vítězslav Novák. *Quintet* Op.12 (Simrock 1904) 46pp., parts. Allegro molto moderato; Andante (based on an old Bohemian song from the 15th century); Slovakisch. Colorful writing with Bohemian folk song influence in a Brahms idiom. M-D.

Stephen Oliver. *Music for the Wreck of the Deutschland* (Nov 1972). An analogue that exploits the restrained sound of the String Quartet with the piano. Concentrated and complex writing. D.
See Jane Glove, "Stephen Oliver," MT (December 1974): 1042–43.

Juan Orrego-Salas. *Encuentros* Op.114 1997 (MMB 1997) 39pp., parts. Title and subsequent subtitle translates as "Encounters with Schubert on the 200th Anniversary of His Birth." Variations form in one continuous movement. Chordal theme of 19 measures commences Moderato in d and concludes in D. Nine freely treated variations follow in a Neoclassic vein emphasizing lyricism and phrasing within the context of shifting meters, a dance form, rapid passagework, and straightforward rhythms. Concludes with brief return to theme. Large span required. Score is copy of MS. D.

Tadeusz Paciorkiewicz. *Piano Quintet* 1972 (ZAIKS) 60pp., parts. Allegro ben moderato; Andante; Con moto. Linear, freely tonal, ostinato figures, harmonic

2nds and 4ths used in secco style, trills used extensively in final movement, tremolo, basically Neoclassic style. M-D.

Robert Palmer. *Piano Quintet* 1950 (CFP 6003) 61pp., parts. Allegro moderato; Scherzo; Aria; Lento Maestoso–Allegro. This entire work focuses mainly on rhythmic and metrical materials. Brackets are used to denote rhythmical groupings that depart from the normal meter. Highly saturated with rich dissonance. A cyclic theme appears in all movements. This work is consistent in style and substance and shows a highly developed craft. The Phrygian pastoral theme in the Aria is especially effective. Strong organic unity. D.

Vincent Persichetti. *Piano Quintet* Op.66 1954 (EV) 41pp., parts. 23 min. Reproduction of the composer's MS, easy to read. In one long, compactly organized movement but with frequent tempo and character changes. Economic style is austere, rhythmically vigorous, and contrapuntal. Piano textures are sparse and generally clear. Freely dissonant with some polytonal moments, yet the piece is tonally integrated. D.

Hans Pfitzner. *Quintet* Op.23 C 1908 (CFP 2923) 64pp., parts. Allegro, ma non troppo; Intermezzo; Adagio; Allegretto commodo. Strong influences of Wagner, Schumann, and Richard Strauss are felt in this work. It is Romantic and Germanic through and through and seems somewhat overblown today, but is superbly written for the pianist. Full of expansive lyricism and rich chromatic harmonies, the thematic transformations involve dissonant counterpoint and unconventional rhythmic intricacies. D.

Gabriel Pierné. *Quintet* Op.41 1916–17 (Hamelle) 93pp., parts. Moderato molto tranquillo; Sur un rythme de Zortzico; Lent–Allegro vivo ed agitato. Repeated chords, some shifting meters in the second movement, broad pianistic gestures, parallel chords, chromatic. D.

Willem Pijper/Jan van Dijk. *Zes Adagio's* 1947(?)/1992 (Donemus 2001) 21pp., parts. 8 min. Pijper's *Adagios* I–IV in an adaptation by Dijk into 6 *Adagios.*

Walter Piston. *Quintet for Piano and String Quartet* 1949 (AMP) 44pp., parts. 20 min. Allegro comodo; poetic; neo-Romantic mood; flowing harmonic figurations; main idea juxtaposed against this backdrop; more tension in the midsection which uses 4ths and 5ths, tonality is G. Adagio: light, dissonant harmonies over pedal point; bold dissonance of consecutive 7ths; *pp* to *ff* and back to *pp.* Allegro vivo: ABA; a Pistonian dance with a quasi-contrapuntal B section; opens with a tricky rhythmic figure; the A section has a coda in G and drops the 3rd in the final chord. Highly crafted writing with tasteful elegance. D.

Mel Powell. *Piano Quintet* 1957 (Bo&H) 49pp., parts. I. Fantasia: varied tempos, shifting meters, short motifs, controlled improvisation. II. Intermezzi: piano tacet. Presto figurato: chromatic figures in alternating hands; chordal punctuation; Alla stretta climax is capped with a glissando and quickly subsides to a Cantilena lento that contains much dialogue between instruments and finally diminishes to a *pp* closing. III. Allegro cantabile: figuration (chromatic, octotonic) moves over keyboard; additive meters ($\frac{3}{8} + \frac{2}{4}$). Entire work has serial overtones. Requires experienced performers. D.

Väinö Raitio. *Quintet* Op.16 (Fazer) 66pp., parts. Adagio espressivo–Allegro non tanto; Lento, ma non troppo; Finale. Impressionist influences, clear traditional forms, bold and dramatic gestures. Pianistic techniques are based on an extension of those used by Richard Strauss and Maurice Ravel. Mildly 20th-century. Large span required. D.

Günter Raphael. *Quintett* Op.6 c♯ (Br&H No. 1934a/g 1925) 72pp., parts. Allegro molto appassionato; Allegretto; Andante sostenuto; Allegro con fuoco. In Brahms-Reger tradition. Dramatic gestures for the piano. D.

Max Reger. *Quintet* Op.64 c (CFP 8853) 72pp., parts. Con moto e agitato; Vivace; Lento addolorato e con gran affetto; Allegro risoluto. Complicated harmonic system with great modulatory freedom. Shows a colossal craft. The pianist must constantly be moving from one complex situation to another. Slow movement is one of great beauty, in spite of its complexities. D.

Franz Reizenstein. *Quintet* Op.23 D (Lengnick 1948) 30 min. A noble 4-movement work with the piano writing by far the most interesting. Written in the tradition of Brahms, Fauré, and Elgar in a mildly 20th-century but effective style. The first movement is tense and stringently constructed; the second is slightly more relaxed and beautiful. An enchanting (if somewhat helter-skelter at places) scherzo is followed by a lofty finale. D.

Wallingford Riegger. *Piano Quintet* Op.47 1951 (AMP) 68pp., parts. 25 min. Allegro: octotonic, alternating hands, wide melodic skips, thin textures, large span required. Untitled second movement: 3 with 2, sustained with repeated chords, dramatic gestures. Untitled third movement: chordal punctuation; octotonic, repeated octaves; boisterous honky-tonk conclusion is unusual, even for Riegger. All 3 movements show an imaginative adventurousness, spiced with rugged and percussive use of the piano. Free 12-tone treatment in angular style with strong contrast of mood and materials. D.

Miklós Rózsa. *Quintet* Op.2 f 1928 (Br&H No. 1940a/f) 64pp., parts. 28 min. Allegro non troppo, ma appassionato; Molto adagio; Allegro capriccioso; Vivace. Freely tonal with strong pianistic gestures, sequences, large skips. Generally successful ensemble writing throughout. D.

Edmund Rubbra. *Lyric Movement* Op.24 (Lengnick 1947) 18pp., parts. Opens with undulating 3rds and octaves over widely spread triadic harmony in the left hand. Quartal and quintal harmony add a mildly 20th-century flavor in parallel chordal passages. Flowing melodies, hand crossings, rich sonorities through most of the work. A mid-section Allegro provides contrast. Big Romantic climax is reached, then subsides to a Lento *ppp* chordal close. M-D.

Anton Rubinstein. *Quintette* Op.99 g (Hamelle) 95pp., parts. Molto lento–con molto moderato; Moderato; Moderato; Moderato. Overflowing with 19th-century pianistic clichés and idioms. The piano has the most interest, and at places the strings seem almost superfluous. M-D to D.

Camille Saint-Saëns. *Quintet* Op.14 a 1855 (Leuckart; Hamelle 63pp., parts; UE). Allegro moderato e maestoso: opening theme is impatient; form is clearly crafted; tremolo; fluent triplet figuration. Andante: a broad liturgical motif opens the movement; light arpeggi in the piano; a hint of the coming Presto is heard near the end of the movement. Presto: strings engage in fugal acrobatics. Allegro assai, ma tranquillo: versatile pianistic patterns; brilliant scales in octaves round off work. Light textures with the balance between severity and heavier textures carefully observed. D.

Peter Schickele. *Quintet II* 1997 (EV 2001) 72pp., parts. 26 min. Flowing–A bit faster; Lively; Slow, serene; Lively. "Brahmsian gestures . . . in the first movement . . . Other aspects of the quintet, on the other hand, couldn't be more American: the square dance-inspired music of the finale, for instance, and the blues-inspired harmonies and boogie-woogie-inspired piano figures of the first trio-like section of the scherzo. The sort of lopsided waltz section of the scherzo—it's in $\frac{5}{4}$ time—certainly owes more to Celtic fiddle music than it does to the ballrooms of Vienna" (Composer's Note). Int. to M-D.

Franz Schmidt. *Quintet* G 1926 (Weinberger JW3761a 1954) 76pp., parts. Lebhaft, doch nicht schnell, Sehr ruhig; Sehr lebhaft. The piano part is written for the left hand alone, for Paul Wittgenstein (cousin of the famous philosopher, he was injured in the First World War and commissioned many notable composers to write works for him), but the work is also published in a version for 2 hands, made by Friedrich Wührer (Weinberger). Conservative and chromatic writing. M-D.

Florent Schmitt. *Quintette* Op.51 (Mathot 1910) 135pp., parts. Lent et grave– Animé; Lent; Animé. Tremolo chords, long lines accompanied by shorter chromatic figures, syncopated chords, large skips, brilliant passagework, chromatic octave runs, alternating hand figuration, long arpeggi. Requires 4 staves to notate piano part in some places. This work is a catalog of pianistic techniques in general use at the time it was composed. Difficult and involved writing with some moments of great beauty. D.

Arnold Schoenberg. *Weihnachtsmusik* 1921 (Belmont 1020), score, parts. For 2 violins, cello, harmonium, and piano. A tonal setting of the well-known Christmas tunes "Lo, How a Rose" and "Silent Night." This fantasy shows that the composer knew how to relax his contrapuntal craft when required. M-D.

———. *Die Eiserne Brigade* 1916 (UE 479 1974) 19pp. "'The Iron Brigade March' was composed for a gathering of one-year volunteers in [a] Vienna household regiment" (from Preface). This edition contains 2 authentic versions of the Trio, one with a "concert of animals" and one without. Shows Schoenberg on the lighter side in a short character piece. M-D.

See Arnold Whittall, *Schoenberg Chamber Music, BBC Music Guide 21,* 64pp. Includes analyses of Schoenberg's chamber music, with the exception of the *Fantasia* for violin and piano.

Franz Schubert. *Piano Quintet* (The Trout) Op.114 D.667 A 1819 (W. Haug-Freienstein, K. Schilde—Henle 463 1991, ISMN M-2018-0463-7 82pp., parts; CFP 51pp., parts; Br&H; Mercury; K; IMC 558 51pp., parts; EPS rev. ed. 118, 86pp.; Dover, in the *Complete Chamber Music for Pianoforte and Strings*). For violin, viola, cello, double bass, and piano. Allegro vivace; Andante; Scherzo–Presto; Tema–Andantino (and 6 variations); Finale–Allegro giusto. There is no happier or more playful music in all of Schubert than this work. The unusual combination of instruments was used before Schubert by Hummel in his *Quintet* Op.87. The piano part lies high because of the presence of the 2 low stringed instruments and tends to double its fluent passages in octaves. The fourth movement uses the song "The Trout" (Die Forelle), which gave the *Quintet* its popular name. The pastoral finale adds the exotic sound of a Hungarian or Bohemian dance. D.

Robert Schumann. *Quintet* Op.44 E♭ 1843 (Br&H 57pp., parts; Henle 355; UE; Litolff; GS L1648; Augener; IMC) 30 min. Allegro brillante: mainly a piano solo in which the strings double the piano part or fill in with isolated phrases. In modo d'una Marcia–Un poco largamente: combines different rhythms and is highly effective. Scherzo: resorts to much doubling, but the piano accompaniment provides a delightful substructure for melodic ideas provided by the strings. Finale: opens with a unison melody in the piano supported by repeated chords in the strings; a brilliant coda lets the pianist present the first subject from the opening movement in the right hand, while the left hand and the second violin bring out the first subject of the Finale; all instruments agree on a joyous conclusion. D.

See Jae-Hyang Koo, "A Study of Four Representative Piano Quintets by Major Composers of the Nineteenth Century: Schumann, Brahms, Dvořák and Franck," D.M.A. diss., University of Cincinnati, 1993.

Cyril Scott. *Quintet* (St&B 3048 1925) 85pp., parts. Andante con esaltazione; Allegro grazioso ma non troppo; Adagio con gran espressione; Finale. Traditional writing for all instruments, chromatic, chordal, with fluent figuration. M-D.

Giovanni Sgambati. *Quintuor I* Op.4 f (Schott 22575) 76pp., parts. Adagio–Allegro ma non troppo; Vivacissimo; Andante sostenuto; Allegro moderato (theme and 4 contrasting variations). Full-blooded Romantic writing littered with octaves, broken-chord passages, and numerous other 19th-century pianistic clichés. D.

Arthur Shepherd. *Quintet* 1940 (copy at LC) 53pp., parts. Andante: Andante con fermezza; Allegro spiritoso. Freely tonal, centers around f♯–F♯. Post-Romantic vocabulary, well-integrated writing, clear forms. D.

Dmitri Shostakovich. *Piano Quintet* Op.57 g 1940 (USSR 1941; CFP; MCA; IMC 2006 60pp., parts) 30 min. Prelude; Fugue; Scherzo; Intermezzo; Finale. A spacious, calm, and strange desolation is found in much of this lyrical piece. Compelling dramatic moments are contrasted with an austere repose. Limpid in texture, direct in appeal, and free from much of the bombast that mars numerous Soviet scores (including some of Shostakovich's). The Fugue is based on a traditional Russian song, while the Scherzo is one of the composer's happiest and most boisterous inventions. The Intermezzo has much diatonic serenity about it. The terse Finale is a blend of physical and spiritual energies, of lyricism and fleeting drama. The piano has some pure athletic lines that verge on the virtuosic. D.

Kaikhosru Sorabji. *Quintet* 1920 (London & Continental Music Publishing Co.) 64pp., parts. One movement, Modéré: beats are indexed underneath the score ($^{20}_8$); 3 staves necessary to notate the piano part. Highly chromatic with sweeping lines and fast-changing chords. Changing meters, harmonic 4ths in flowing figuration, tremolo. Enormous climax suddenly drops to *pp* and *ppp* with indication "Enigmatique equivoque." Complex and D.

Robert Starer. *Five Miniatures* 1996 (MMB 1996) 29pp. 7 min. Allegro moderato: dramatic rhythms; octotonic; playful. Andante: lyric; expressive; arpeggiation. Allegretto: $^5_8$ meter contrasted by $^2_4$; catchy rhythms; legato and staccato contrasts. Larghetto: pizzicati; octave jumps; mixed rhythmic patterns in melody. Poco presto: bouncy rhythms; motivic-driven; octaves; dynamic extremes. Short capsule-like pieces for less-experienced musicians. Score is copy of MS. Int.

Václav Stépan. *Les Premiers Printemps* Op.5 (Lerolle 1921) 73pp., parts. Joie et Jeu: light staccato chords; broken octaves; freely chromatic; arpeggi left hand; melody in 3rds in right hand; opening mood closes movement. Douleur et désir: lugubrious sustained chords; fast harmonic rhythm; agitato mid-section with alternating hand passages; triplets; Molto lento climax; *ppp* closing. Lutte et joie: march tempo; quick, repeated chords; curling chromatic figuration; intensity builds; tempo changes; thoroughly colorful writing with a brilliant conclusion; polyphonic. D.

Richard Stöhr. *Quintett* Op.43 c (R. Linnemann—Siegel 1914[?]) 66pp., parts. Un poco grave–Allegro con brio; Scherzo; Larghetto; Finale. Lyric, engaging work thoroughly rooted in 19th-century styles with modulatory effects. Broken-chord figurations, tremolos, octaves, and full chords typify piano score. Virtuosic-like at times without calling attention to itself. M-D.

Josef Suk. *Quintet* Op.8 g 1893–1915 (Supraphon 1973) 88pp., parts. Rev. by Vlastimil Musil. Allegro energico; Adagio (Religioso) scherzo; Finale. This tonal but freely chromatic work utilizes a late-19th-century pianistic, harmonic, and melodic vocabulary. D.

George Szell. *Quintet* Op.2 E 1911 (UE 3694) 61pp., parts. Bewegt: E; SA; sweeping post-Romantic lines; chromatic; 2 with 3; hemiola; alternating hands. Scherzo: C; octotonic; strings frequently play alone; piano also frequently plays alone. Mässig langsam: A♭; Brahmsian pianism; syncopated closing in G leads directly to Finale: E; rondo; bright and cheerful; rhythmic 16th-note figuration; contrasted chordal episodes; hand crossings; strong gestures in coda. Lyrical Romantic writing throughout. D.

Serge I. Tanieff. *Quintuor* Op.30 (Edition Russe de Musique) 101pp., parts. Introduzione–Adagio maestoso–Allegro patetico; Scherzo; Largo; Finale–Allegro vivace. Utilizes strong 19th-century virtuoso techniques and idioms. D.

Alexander Tcherepnin. *Quintette* Op.44 (UE 1927) 15 min. Allegro (SA); Allegretto (ABA); Allegro (Rondo). Written in a complex polyphonic style with a slightly Russian flavor. The Allegretto employs the composer's "interpoint" technique, in which vertical and horizontal elements are equal. The final Allegro is based on one theme that is treated contrapuntally. Highly chromatic. This piece is perhaps the culmination of Tcherepnin's chamber music. D.

Georg Philipp Telemann. *Suite* B♭ Telemann Werke Verzeichnis 55:B8 (A. Hoffman —Möseler 1975) 28pp., parts. 2 violins, viola, cello, basso continuo. Preface in French, English, and German. Ouverture; Scaramousches; Harlequinade; Columbine; Pierrot; Menuet I, II; Mezzetin en turc. Fine realizations. M-D.

Ernst Toch. *Piano Quintet* Op.64 1938 (Delkas) 75pp., parts. The Lyrical Part: bold lines. The Whimsical Part: ABA, antiphonal, muted strings. The Contemplative Part: ABA; strings alone in part A, piano alone in B; strings return; coda brings all together. The Dramatic Part: more writing for 5 instruments, contrapuntal. Programmatic titles, Romantic tendencies in an overall Neoclassic style. Lines and textures are generally clear and operate within freely tonal bounds. Strings are combined as one voice, the piano as another. D.

Joaquín Turina. *Quintette* 1907 (Rouart Lerolle) 58pp., parts. Fugue lente: piano embellishes fugue with full but *pp* sonorities; fugue is treated freely; broken-chord figuration; subject heard at end of movement. Animé: marchlike, strong rhythmic emphasis, fast harmonic rhythm. Andante scherzo: flowing; chromatic, undulating dolcissimo and cantabile; short figures evolve into longer ones; octotonic; moves through various keys. Final: recitative opening, sustained syncopated chords, Lento coda and *fff* ending. Does not sound like the later Turina that pianists know; a transitional work. M-D to D.

Louis Vierne. *Quintette* Op.42 (Senart 1924) 63pp., parts. Poco lento–Moderato; Larghetto sostenuto; Maestoso. Chromatic, many octaves, many triplets, arpeggi figuration. This work looks more impressive on the page than it sounds, although there are some lovely spots. M-D.

John Vincent. *Consort* (Belwin-Mills 1962) 95pp., parts. 26 min. Allegro con brio; Andante; Allegro vivo. Bitonal, secco bass, shifting rhythms, scalar passages, driving rhythms, flowing melody in Andante, repeated octaves in alternating hands, dancelike rhythms. Attractive, mildly 20th-century. M-D.

Anton Webern. *Quintet* 1907, rev.1974 (Boelke-Bomart) 30pp., parts. 12 min. Composed immediately before Op.1 and not included by Webern in his own catalog of works. A one-movement form in SA design. Strong early Schoenberg influence. Principal groups in C with subordinate group around the dominant! Themes include most of the 12 tones; series-like. The harmony is mainly triadic. Piano style is Brahmsian with octave doublings, thick chords, and subtle rhythmic shifts, but a few spots of thin textures and widely spread skips suggest future Webern techniques. A lyric work that would work well for groups not yet prepared to undertake later Webern. M-D.
See Dika Newlin, "Webern's Quintet for String Quartet and Piano," *Notes* 10/4 (September 1953): 674–75.

Moisei Weinberg. *Quintet* Op.18 1944 (USSR 1964) 87pp., parts. Moderato con moto: SA, Slavic theme for main idea, second theme animated and whimsical; develops naturally and effortlessly; closes with first theme diminuendo. Allegretto: in the nature of an intermezzo; piano has cadenza; *ppp* closing. Presto: scherzo with an irresistible drive. Largo: stirringly lyric and profoundly meditative; piano performs solo. Allegro agitato: fleeting and dynamic; based on the alternation of an austere ostinato theme and a gentle, lyrical one; at the climax (figure 142) the opening theme of the first movement is heard and serves to unify the cyclic work into an integrated whole; the progress of the finale resumes, but the music seems calmer, less impetuous, and the ostinato gradually melts away. Post-Romantic Russian style, mildly 20th-century, chromatic, and tonal. M-D to D.

Charles Marie Widor. *Quintette* Op.7 (Hamelle) 65pp., parts. Allegro; Andante; Molto vivace; Allegro con moto.
———. *Quintette* Op.68 (Schott 25731) 65pp., parts. Moderato; Andante; Allegro con fuoco; Moderato.

Malcolm Williamson. *Quintet* 1968 (Weinberger) 68pp., parts. 16 min. Adagio: chordal for piano, individual lines in other parts. Allegro molto: pointillistic, trills, extreme ranges exploited, large span required. Adagio: similar to opening Adagio but more developed. Dissonant, large formal blocks of organized material, harmonics, clusters, fluent and pianistic style. Writing is easy to follow with the ear. D.

Ermanno Wolf-Ferrari. *Quintett* D♭ 1900 (Rahter 1901) 60pp., parts. Tranquillo ed espressivo; Canzone; Capriccio; Finale. A large-scale work in late-19th-century styles. Full-chordal treatment.

Wawrzyniec Zulawski. *Kwintet Fortepianowy* 1966 (PWM) 102pp., parts. 20 min. Andante: quiet chromatic opening leads to a short piano cadenza, which leads to an Agitato; these tempos are juxtaposed against each other throughout the movement. Allegro vivace: a scherzo, chromatic chords and figuration, octotonic. Andante molto tranquillo: added-note chords, large climax à la Szymanowski, Lento *pp* close. Allegro moderato: tremolo, fast harmonic rhythm, broken left-hand figuration under right-hand octave melody, Allegretto episodes, *pp* closing, freely tonal around C. M-D to D.

Quintets for Piano(s), Strings, and Winds

William Albright. *Danse Macabre* 1971 (Bowdoin College Music Press) 31pp., parts. 14½ min. For flute, clarinet, violin, cello, and piano. Completed April 6, 1971, the day Igor Stravinsky died. Percussion required: 1 pair maracas, 2 pairs antique cymbals, 1 pair claves, 2 wood blocks, 1 large and 1 small triangle, bass drum, hi-hat, large tam-tam. Pianist also needs a brush, nail file, coin, glass ashtray, soft mallet. Piano part includes irregular tremolo on tritone, plucked strings, nail file on string, sudden tempo changes, glissandi, pointillistic treatment, low-sounding pitches to be played ugly and dry, improvisation on certain pitches, rambling with pitches ad lib, spoken words, tongue clicks, knuckles on lid and cross-beams, tempo di Valse section, soft irregular improvisation on insides of piano, Tarantella fantastica section. Piano must improvise and give the impression of "smothered virtuosity." Directions in Maniacal section to play crass, ugly, hammered, forearm clusters; all performers clap together at conclusion. Contains some awesome and startling sonorities. Avant-garde. D.

Milton Babbitt. *Arie da Capo* (CFP 66584) 14 min. For flute, clarinet, violin, cello, and piano. In one movement.

Johann Christian Bach. *Quintet* Op.11/1 C (Steglich—Br; Musica Rara 26pp., parts). For flute, oboe, violin, viola, and basso continuo. Allegretto; Andantino; Menuetto con variazione. M-D.
———. *Quintet* Op.11/2 G (Steglich—Br; Musica Rara). For flute, oboe, violin, viola, and basso continuo.
———. *Quintet* Op.11/3 F (Steglich—Br; Musica Rara 19pp., parts). For flute, oboe, violin, viola, and basso continuo. Andante; Rondo. M-D.
———. *Quintet* Op.11/4 E♭ (Nag). For 3 violins (or flute, oboe, and violin), viola, and basso continuo; cello ad lib.
———. *Quintet* Op.11/5 A (Steglich—Br; Musica Rara). For flute or violin, oboe or violin, violin, viola, cello, and basso continuo.
———. *Quintet* Op.11/6 D (Nag; E. Derr—Br&H 8544 1991). For 3 violins (or flute, oboe, and violin), viola, and basso continuo; cello ad lib. Br&H includes Postface and critical report in English and German.

———. *Quintet* Op.22/1 D (R. Ermler—HM 42; C. Gevet/B. Päuler—Amadeus 870) 27pp., parts. 16½ min. For flute, oboe, violin, cello, and continuo; realization by Walter Kraft. A charming work. Probably one of the first compositions of Bach's time to use an obbligato keyboard for chamber music with larger instrumentation. M-D.

———. *Quintet* Op.22/2 F (R. Erhardt—Schott 4167; C. Gevet/B. Päuler—Amadeus 872). For oboe, violin, viola, cello, and piano.

Arthur Berger. *Diptych* 1990, rev.1995 (CFP 67721 1999) 46pp., parts. 14 min. For flute, clarinet, violin, cello, and piano. Collage I; Collage II. "The collage-print was a genre that [Robert] Motherwell had developed, involving the use of each copy of one print as a background for different collages. This gave me the idea that I could do something analogous with certain works that I was thinking of transcribing for instruments other than those for which they were originally written. What would emerge would be not simply a transcription but virtually a new work. For me . . . it sufficed to produce one new 'collage' on the background of a given previous work, rather than the five or six that a prolific painter like Motherwell produced. *Diptych* is my first attempt. The background on which the 'collage' is mounted is my wind quintet of 1984. Since each of the two parts of the original work has certain subsistence, together they may be regarded as a diptych: two collages side by side having similar content . . . For both of them I draw upon the same materials—spread before me, so to speak, on my desk and ready to be 'pasted' on the one or the other background" (Composer's Notes). D.

Joseph Bodin de Boismortier. *Concerto* e (Ruf—Ric) 23pp., parts. For flute, oboe, bassoon, violin, and basso continuo. Figured-bass part is well realized. M-D.

William Bolcom. *Duets for Quintet, A Farce for Fun* (Bowdoin College Music Press 1971) 21pp., parts. For flute, clarinet, violin, cello, and piano (and stage manager for lights). Includes instructions for performance. "This is a 'theater-piece' but the 'theater' resides almost totally in the music . . . Each instrument has a sort of musical role, and a very *definite personality*, in his utterances. For the player, the object is to find his own 'profile' from (1) listening to his own part; (2) listening to the other parts, particularly the one he is 'in dialogue' with at the moment. The controlling idea is that of a duet-texture. 'Dialogues' are carried on between pairs of instruments; at some time a third instrument may interrupt" (from Notes in the score). Serial influence, pointillistic treatment, dynamic extremes, clusters, varied tempos. This is a fun piece but it requires thorough musicianship to bring it off. Avant-garde. D.

———. *Whisper Moon (Dream Music Number Three)* 1971 (Bowdoin College Music Press 1973) 22pp., parts. For alto flute, clarinet, violin, cello, and piano. Includes extensive instructions for performance. Requires improvisation, plucked and stopped strings. Pointillistic broken octaves and improvisation in this style, jazz rhythms, popular-music context with fragments of "Blue Moon" and "Louise" mixed in, sweeping glissandi inside piano, free time, skittery, half-pedals, clusters, harmonics. Violin and cello whisper words almost to themselves while playing ad lib; "everybody stops wherever he is when flute gives the little whoop signal." Delightful mixture of pop writing with avant-garde. D.

Roque Cordero. *Quinteto* 1949 (PIC 1967) 95pp., parts. For flute, clarinet, violin, cello, and piano. Vivace e con spirito: serial, piano lends strong rhythmic punctuation, varied tempos. Lento assai: chromatic figuration, strong octave gestures, octotonic. Allegro molto: requires a fine octave technique. Largo–Allegro molto: mixture of fugal and serial textures. Generally vigorous and robust writing. D.

David Diamond. *Quintet* 1937 (GS 1942) 52pp., parts. 13 min. For flute, violin, viola, cello, and piano. Allegro deciso e molto ritmico: SA; clear diatonic lines; strong rhythmic thrust; preference for 2nds, 7ths, and octaves in the piano part; white-key glissando in piano ends movement. Romanza: flowing melodies, more dissonant harmony; piano has sustained chords and some melodic emphasis. Allegro veloce: jig with folklike melody; piano has some polytonal treatment; upward white-key glissandi, strong propulsive rhythms. An economical and tightly constructed work with an overall brilliant effect. D.

Theodore Dubois. *Quintette* F (Heugel 1905) 58pp., parts. For oboe (or second violin or clarinet), violin, viola, cello, and piano. Allegro; Canzonetta; Adagio non troppo; Allegro con fuoco. Not of great musical worth but effectively scored for the instruments. Traditional turn-of-the century idioms and techniques. M-D.

William Duckworth. *Seven Shades of Blue* (Bowdoin College Music Press 1974) 10pp., parts. For flute, clarinet, violin, cello, and piano. Sections should be played without pause. Patterns are given that are to be repeated in specific ways (legato, rhythmically, diminuendo, etc.) for the indicated length of time. Piano part involves chords, single lines, arpeggi figuration, trills, long pedals, pointillistic treatment, sudden dynamic changes. Avant-garde. Requires a large span. M-D.

Donald Erb. *Quintet* 1976 (TP 144-400840), parts. 8 min. For flute, clarinet, violin, cello, and piano/electric piano. A one-movement work with four internal sections, based on motivic structure—according to the score, intervallic: the perfect 5th and minor 3rd. Unusual sonoric effects; mildly avant-garde. D

Morton Feldman. *Projection II* 1962 (CFP 6940) 10pp. For flute, violin, cello, trumpet, and piano. Graphic notation. Reproduced from holograph. Includes instructions for performance. Avant-garde. M-D.

Zdeněk Fibich. *Quintet* Op.42 (Supraphon 1973) 62pp., parts. For violin, clarinet, horn, cello, and piano. Preface and critical notes in Czech, Russian, German, and English. M-D to D.

Gerardo Gandini. *Música Nocturna* 1964 (PAU) 11pp. 5 scores required for performance. For piano, flute, violin, viola, and cello. Pointillistic, string glissandi, long pedals, experimental, avant-garde. M-D.

Walter Gieseking. *Quintett* B♭ 1919 (Adolf Fürstner) 54pp., parts. For oboe, clarinet, horn, bassoon, and piano. Allegro moderato: opens with flowing legato dolcissimo lines; broken octaves; arpeggiated chords; heroic quality in development; opening mood returns to close movement; large span required. Andante: syncopated accompaniment in piano to melody in other instruments; duplet and triplet figures prominent; interesting harmonic relationships; many added notes in chords; *pppp* closing. Vivace molto scherzando: scampering figuration, strong rhythmic emphasis in alternating hands, subito dynamics, dancelike, contrasting episodes. French sonorities; mildly 20th-century. M-D.

Donald Harris. *Ludus II* 1973 (Jobert) 20pp. 10½ min. For flute, clarinet, violin, cello, and piano. Five copies necessary for performance. Performance instructions in French and English. One movement. Freely chromatic, serial influence, extensive use of multiphonics for woodwinds. Taut organization, rhythmically complex, wide leaps, fast notes. Shows a strong craft. Requires virtuoso players with ensemble experience. D.

Franz Joseph Haydn. *Quintet* Hob.XIV:1 E♭ (W. Stockmeier—Henle 436 1987) 18pp., parts. For piano, 2 horns, violin, and cello. A spirited work composed no later than 1766, closely related to the early Piano Trios with the addition of horns. Moderato; Menuet; Finale–Allegro. This edition is extracted from the Complete Edition of Haydn, *Joseph Haydn Werke,* also published by Henle. M-D.
——. *Sonata* Op.4 E♭ (CFP MV1208). For 2 horns, violin, cello, and piano.
——. *Sinfonie Concertante* Op.84 (F. Sitt—Fr&H; Sitt—IMC 986 40pp., parts). For oboe, bassoon, violin, cello, and piano. Allegro; Andante; Allegro con spirito. Writing that endears itself to both performers and listeners. M-D.

Johann David Heinichen. *Concerto* G (H. Fischer—Vieweg 2152) 11pp., parts. For flute, 2 violins, cello, and piano. M-D.
——. *Sonata à 3* 1726 (Hofmeister) 22pp., parts. For 2 oboes, bassoon, cello, and keyboard. The bassoon is treated as a concertante instrument. M-D.

Paul Hindemith. *Drei Stücke* 1925 (Schott 3312). For clarinet, trumpet in C, violin, double bass, and piano. 1. Scherzando: bouncy rhythms; chromatic; grace notes add to gaiety. 2. Langsamer achtel: small intervals expand; rustling mood created in upper register for mid-section; effective syncopation. 3. Lebhafte halbe: martial quality; patterns prevalent; long chromatic lines provide contrast; dies away to *pp.* M-D.

Leopold Hofmann. *Concertino* A (A. Badley—Artaria 198 1998) 19pp. 20 min. For flute, violin, 2 cellos, and piano. Second cello generally doubles figured bass. Tempo giusto; Andante; Tempo di Minuetto poco vivace. Probably intended as a trio for flute, violin, and cello, the continuo realization is in good taste and herein gives the piano solo emphasis. Extensive notes by editor. M-D.

Ignaz Holzbauer. *Quintet* G (F. Schroeder—Br&H 2111) 19pp., parts. For flute, violin, viola, cello, and piano. Andante spiritoso; Menuetto grazioso—(5) Variations—Menuetto (Allegro). Classic style; refined and tasteful writing. The variations on the Menuetto and its return are unusually interesting. M-D.

Charles Ives. *Adagio Sostenuto* before 1912 (PIC 1969) 1p. (13 measures); parts. For English horn (flute), 3 violins (3rd violin ad lib or viola), cello ad lib, and piano or harp. Chromatic chords, extreme registers, quiet. Large span required. M-D.
———. *Scherzo—All the Way Around and Back* (PIC) 2pp., parts. For clarinet (flute), violin, trumpet, horn, and piano. Can be played by one or 2 pianists. Complex rhythms, chromatic, dynamic extremes, large span required if performed by one pianist. D.
For fuller description see quintets for piano(s), percussion and/or tape, and other instruments.

Friedrich Kalkbrenner. *Grand Quintet* Op.81 1826 (Br&H). For piano, clarinet, horn, cello, and double bass. Sounds like Schubert. Attractive melodies, lively rhythmic foundation. Somewhat like a Chamber Concerto; piano has by far the finest part. M-D.

Karl Kohn. *Capriccios* 1962 (CF) 12 min. For flute, clarinet, cello, harp, and piano. Three movements. Masterful manipulation of sounds; macro- and microstructures well shaped by a polyphonic discipline. Sustained cries of the final movement, which gradually climax in an instrumental dirge, are especially arresting. M-D to D.

Konradin Kreutzer. *Quintet* A (Musica Rara). For flute, clarinet, viola, cello, and piano. The piano dominates, but the themes are fairly distributed. Attractive material, especially the martial first movement and the engaging polonaise finale. Piano has much activity in the taxing florid lines of the finale. M-D to D.

István Láng. *Rhymes for Chamber Ensemble* (EMB 1972) 14pp. 5 copies necessary for performance. For flute, clarinet, viola, cello, and piano.

Elisabeth Lutyens. *Concertante for Five Players* Op.22 1950 (Belwin-Mills 1970) 24pp., parts. 10 min. For flute (piccolo), clarinet (bass clarinet), violin (viola), cello, and piano. Sectionalized; constantly changing sounds in a fascinating and always logically ordered serial manner. Subtle and convincing. M-D.

Gian Francesco Malipiero. *Sonata à Cinque* 1934 (Ric) 28pp., parts. 16 min. For flute (violin), violin, viola, cello, and piano. One large movement, varied tempos, chromatic coloration, large arpeggiated chords, open-5th sonorities, 4 octaves apart, glissandi. M-D.

Tomás Marco. *Albor* (Noli tangere meos circulos) (Editorial de Música Española Contemporánea 1972) 19pp. For flute, clarinet, violin, cello, and piano.

Wolfgang Amadeus Mozart. *Adagio and Rondo* K.617 c/C 1791 (H. Wiese— Henle 677 2001, ISMN M-2018-0677-8) 21pp., parts. For glass harmonica (piano), flute, oboe, viola, and cello. A one-of-a-kind setting in which the piano generally alternates with the other instruments, no doubt due to the soft nature of the original glass harmonica instrumentation. Mozart's last piece of chamber music, inspired by the blind Mariane Kirchgässner, a virtuoso of the glass harmonica, when she visited Vienna several months before the composer's death. M-D.

Thea Musgrave. *Chamber Concerto II* (JWC 1966) 59pp., parts. 15 min. Subtitled "In Homage to Charles Ives." One movement divided into sections. Metrical freedom for players. Incorporates popular tunes, as "The Keel-Row," "Swanee River," and "All Things Bright and Beautiful," which are placed in a dissonant environment. Highly dramatic and chromatic. D.

Pauline Oliveros. *Aeolian Partitions* 1970 (Bowdoin College Music Press) 5pp., 2pp. general directions, 2pp. directions for each performer. For flute (alto flute, piccolo), violin (viola), cello, clarinet (bass clarinet), and piano. "Composed for a proscenium stage with wings. Performers must be able to enter and exit from stage right and left during the performance and to get on to the stage from the house. A total house and stage blackout is necessary. If these directions cannot be met, abandon the performance entirely" (from the score). Prop list includes broom, newspaper, flashlight, transistor radio to be used by extra, page turner, megaphone, large gong, bow, suction cup, arrows and quiver, stage crew, 7 six-volt flasher lights, slide projector, slide of Star of David, 2 extras—preferably familiar to the audience, e.g., dean of the college, department chairman, mayor of the town, etc., who walk across performance on cue. Extensive directions help make this one of the funniest "theater pieces" this writer has seen. Climax of work arrives when audience is (may be) invited to join in the telepathic improvisation (with detailed instructions). Great fun for all! Avant-garde. M-D.

Robert Palmer. *Quintet* 1952, 1963 (PIC) 67pp., parts. 26 min. For piano, clarinet, violin, viola, and cello. Poco lento ma con moto: the most impressive movement in this large and ambitious work; modified SA design; develops 2 main melodic ideas over a broad time period; climax breaks off into a number of short cadenzas, followed by a recapitulation of the opening material. Allegro molto: a lively scherzo. Andante grazioso: contrapuntally conceived; each instrument unwinds its lyrical melodic lines. Allegro vivo: a frivolous finale; busy figuration and a frequently repeated Hindemithian melodic figure conclude the work. The piano and clarinet essentially frame the ensemble. D.

Juan Carlos Paz. *Dédalus* 1950 (Ediciones Culturales Argentinas—Impreso por Ricordi Americana 1964) 62pp., parts. For piano, flute, clarinet, violin, and cello. Expositio: serial, changing meters, pointillistic. Choral: sustained and chorale-like. Ostinato: row is run through all the instruments. Variacion I: cantus firmus. II: staccato chords contrast with sustained chords. III: light, fleeting. IV: ostinato and choral together. V: Fugato; canon in 4 voices; Reexpositio. VI: choral and ostinato varied together. VII: similar techniques to Var.II; piano Recitativo. VIII: cantus firmus and Recitativo together. IX: Fugato; Improvisatio; Reexpositio. X: Praeludium; canon perpetum; coda-cancrizans. This work is a catalog of serial and contrapuntal techniques. D.

John Christopher Pepusch. *Quintet* F (T. Dart—Schott 10688) 10pp., parts. For 2 recorders, 2 violins, and keyboard; cello ad lib. Largo; Allegro; Adagio; Presto. Delightful writing, excellent keyboard realization. M-D.
——. *Four Concerti* Op.8/1, 4, 5, 6 (D. Lasocki—Musica Rara 1974). For 2 treble recorders, 2 flutes or 2 oboes or 2 violins, and basso continuo. Score and parts available separately for each concerto. M-D.

Raoul Pleskow. *Three Movements for Quintet* (Of a November Morning 1970) 1971 (Bowdoin College Music Press) 25pp., parts. Reproduced from composer's MS. For flute, clarinet, violin, cello, and piano. Untitled movements, serial influence, pointillistic, chromatic, plucked strings, sudden dynamic changes, Expressionist, proportional rhythmic relationships, cluster-like sonorities. Complex writing. D.

Henri Pousseur. *Quintette à la mémoire d'Anton Webern* 1955 (SZ 5428) 63pp., miniature score, 14 min. For violin, cello, clarinet, bass clarinet, and piano. Highly organized, complex rhythmic ratios, pointillistic, intense, Expressionist, short pauses set off sections. Only for the most venturesome and experienced ensemble players. D.

Alan Rawsthorne. *Quintet* 1970 (OUP) 22pp., parts. 9 min. For clarinet, horn, violin, cello, and piano. One movement, divided into 5 sections (Andante; Allegro; Andante; Allegro; Andante); uses mirror form for the various sections. Austere writing, mildly dissonant with tonal and serial techniques. Piano part is the most difficult, with mainly chordal and chromatic scalar sections plus some martellato octaves in alternating hands. M-D to D.

Johann Heinrich Schmelzer. *Sonata* G "La Carioletta" (Musica Rara 1974) 12pp., parts. For cornetto (trumpet), violin, trombone, bassoon, and basso continuo.

Arnold Schoenberg. *Chamber Symphony* Op.9 (Webern—UE 12505) 97pp., parts. 22 min. Originally for 15 instruments. Arranged for flute (or 2 violins), clarinet, violin, cello, and piano. Constantly unfolds with varying tempos, dynamics, and moods. The piano part moves in a nonpointillistic manner and serves as a binding influence on the other instruments. Thematic variation takes place simultaneously rather than in succession. D.
See CCSCM, II, pp. 346–47 for a thorough analysis of the formal structure of this composition.
———. *Ein Stelldichein* 1905 (F. Cerha, R. Stephan—UE 493 1980) 16pp. For oboe, clarinet, violin, cello, and piano. Based upon the poem "Ein Stelldichein" (A Rendezvous) by Richard Dehmel. Unfinished, from the musical effects left at the composer's death. One movement in a slow tempo; tonally based with much chromaticism.

Robert Schumann. *Andante and Variations* Op.46 1843 (W. Wollenweber UWKR 11 1972) 33pp., parts. For 2 pianos, 2 cellos, and horn. Usually heard performed by only the 2 pianos, but the work is more effective in this, the original version. Filled with much dialogue between the instruments, this beautiful Romantic piece is pleasurable for performers and audience. One variation is more difficult than the others. M-D.

Elliott Schwartz. *Elan: Variations for Five Players* 1991 (GS/Margun) 15 min. For flute, clarinet, violin, cello, and piano. Performed from full score. "An 'homage' to French musical sources—appropriately, as the work was commissioned by a French ensemble. The variations all derive from the Machaut *Mass* and Debussy's *Pour le Piano.* Some minimalist gestures" (from Composer's letter to authors).

Seymour Shifrin. *In Eius Memoriam* (CFP 66479a 1976) 17pp., parts. 6 min. For piano, flute, clarinet, violin, and cello.
———. *Serenade* 1954 (Litolff 5853) 38pp., parts. For oboe, clarinet, horn, viola, and piano. Allegro molto, energico; Largo assai; Presto molto. Neoclassic orientation with clear structures, mildly pointillistic, freely tonal, fast harmonic motion, fragmentary lines; strongly contrasted ideas superimposed on each other produce dramatic tension. Flexible meters, especially in the last movement. Large span required. D.

Halsey Stevens. *Quintet* 1945 (GS 1949) 50pp., parts. 21 min. For flute, violin, viola, cello, and piano. Pastorale–Andante non troppo: harmonic 4ths and 5ths prevalent in the piano part; flowing; piano treated harmonically and melodi-cally. Scherzo–Vivo e ritmico: $\frac{5}{8}$; some changing meters; rhythmically driving; Poco meno mosso section is more lyrical; Tempo primo returns. Threnody–Lento: piano supplies rich chords that bind other melodically fragmented in-struments together. Fugue–Lieto: thoroughly worked out; elegant contrapun-tal technique displayed. Epilogue–Riflessivo: sums up work by echoing ideas from other movements; *ppp* ending. Clear counterpoint and tonalities mixed with infrequent dissonance. Displays extraordinary refinement in texture and melodious expressiveness. Contains no unnecessary notes. M-D.

Bruce J. Taub. *Quintet I* 1972 (ACA) 29pp., parts. For flute/piccolo, clarinet, vio-lin, cello, and piano. Also printed in *ASUC Journal of Music Scores*. Sectional, stopped strings, freely tonal, sudden extreme dynamic changes, sequences, trip-let figure important, secco style, chordal punctuation, thin textures, individual style. D.

Michael Torke. *Telephone Book* 1985–95 (Bo&H HPS 1263) 73pp., parts. 19 min. For flute, clarinet, violin, cello, and piano. The Yellow Pages; The Blue Pages; The White Pages. Blends key/color relationships and popular influences, par-ticularly swing and rock in the last 2 movements, into an individual, personal style. Movements can be performed separately. Preface by Composer. M-D.

Anatol Vieru. *Crible d'Eratosthène* 1969 (Sal) 32pp., parts. Variable duration. For clarinet, violin, viola, cello, and piano. Performance directions in French. Im-provisation mixed with traditional, avant-garde, and proportional notation. Fragments of the Beethoven "Moonlight" Sonata and a Rossini piece are in-terspersed with laughing and other sounds the performers are asked to make. This is a partially controlled "happening" and theoretically falls in the multi-media category. It could be very funny or a complete bore! Performers need a sense of humor. M-D.

Antonio Vivaldi. *Concerto* C F.XII/30; P.81 (Musica Rara) 15pp., parts. For so-prano recorder, oboe, 2 violins, and basso continuo. Adagio–Allegro; Largo; Allegro assai. M-D.

——. *Concerto* C, P.82 (Musica Rara). For flute, oboe, violin, bassoon, and basso continuo.

——. *Concerto* D, F.XII/9 P.155 (Musica Rara 1217) 22pp., parts. For flute, oboe, bassoon, violin, and basso continuo. (Allegro); Largo; Allegro. Valuable Pref-ace and critical commentary by the editor, David Lasocki. M-D.

——. *Concerto* g, F.XII/5; P.342 (Lasocki—Musica Rara 1185) 13pp., parts. For flute (violin), 2 violins, bassoon, and basso continuo. La Notte; Fantasmi; Il Sonno; Allegro. Helpful Preface. M-D.

——. *Concerto* g, F.XIII/6; P.360 (S. Sadie—Musica Rara 1184) 18pp., parts. For flute, oboe, bassoon, violin, and basso continuo. Allegro; Presto. M-D.

"P." stands for Marc Pincherle, *Antonio Vivaldi et la musique instrumentale,* 2 vols., Vol.II: *Inventaire thématique* (Paris, 1948).

————. *Concerto* g (Ghedini—IMC). For flute, oboe, violin, bassoon, and keyboard.

Matthias Weckman. *Sonata à 4* d (A. Lumsden—Musica Rara) 8pp., parts. For oboe, violin, trombone, bassoon, and basso continuo. One continuous movement: Moderato–Adagio–Allegro. M-D.

Lawrence Widdoes. *From a Time of Snow* 1970 (Bowdoin College Music Press) 21pp. For flute, clarinet, violin, cello, and piano. One movement, complex textures, fast-shifting pitches, cross-rhythms, many grace notes, random pizzicati performed by pianist. M-D.

Ellen Taaffe Zwilich. *Intrada* 1983 (Margun 1984) 27pp., parts. For flute, clarinet, violin, cello, and piano. In one movement, commencing ♩ = 132, for fast dramatic action. Explores coloristic possibilities of harmony and timbre. M-D.

Quintets for Piano and Winds

Josef Alexander. *Festivities* (PIC 1972) 52pp., parts. For trumpet, horn, trombone, tuba, and piano or organ. Separate parts are written for piano and organ. Piano part is well integrated with the brass ensemble. Moderato maestoso is the basic tempo and mood, but short contrasting sections are heard from time to time. Compositional language is mildly 20th-century and comes off remarkably well in this combination. M-D.

Seymour Barab. *Quintet* (Seesaw 2001) 55pp., parts. For flute, oboe, clarinet, bassoon, and piano. Allegro molto vivace; Andante sostenuto; Variations and Finale. Strongly tonal with invigorating rhythms, motivic development, and ensemble interaction. Cadenzas for piano and flute. M-D.

Henry Barraud. *Concertino* (Marbot 1955) 58pp., parts. For piano, flute, clarinet, horn, and bassoon. Vif et décidé; Dans un sentiment nostalgique; Avec entrain. Full of Gallic wit and glitter. Somewhat reminiscent of the Jean Françaix *Concertino,* but the Barraud work requires more piano technique and a larger span (10th). Thoroughly enjoyable for performers and audience. The piano part gets the most attention. M-D to D.

Ludwig van Beethoven. *Quintet* Op.16 E♭ 1796 (S. Kross, H.-M. Theopold—Henle 222 1971/1999, ISMN M-2018-0222-0 48pp.; CFP; Br&H; Boonin: Musica Rara; K; IMC 42pp., parts). For piano, oboe, clarinet, bassoon, and horn. Grave–Allegro ma non troppo; Andante cantabile; Rondo. Beethoven issued a quartet version of this work for piano, violin, viola, and cello at the same time that the wind version appeared with the same opus number. The style of this work is more like a piano solo with wind accompaniment, as the themes are usually stated by the piano and answered by the concerted winds. The Andante movement integrates all instruments more thoroughly. M-D.
See Eric Paul Ohlsson, "The Quintets for Piano, Oboe, Clarinet, Horn and Bassoon by Wolfgang Amadeus Mozart and Ludwig van Beethoven," D.M.A. diss., Ohio State University, 1980.

Franz Danzi. *Quintet* Op.41 d (CFP; Musica Rara 48pp., parts; GS; B&VP). For oboe, clarinet, bassoon, horn, and piano. Larghetto–Allegro; Andante sostenuto; Allegretto. "Danzi introduces in the piano part brilliant passages typical of late Beethoven, although always preserving the purity of Classical form. The present Op.41 Quintet is fully worthy to stand by the side of the famous works of Beethoven (Op.16) and Mozart (K.452) for the same combination" (from the Musica Rara Preface). M-D.

——. *Quintet* Op.53 (Musica Rara). For flute, oboe, clarinet, bassoon, and piano.

——. *Quintet* Op.54 (Musica Rara). For flute, oboe, clarinet, bassoon, and piano.

——. *Sinfonia Concertante* (Musica Rara). For flute, oboe, clarinet, bassoon, and piano.

Heinrich von Herzogenberg. *Quintet* Op.43 E♭ (CFP 2191, 72pp., parts; Musica Rara). For oboe, clarinet, bassoon, horn, and piano. Allegro; Adagio; Allegretto; Allegro giocoso. Effective and convincing late-19th-century style. This composer's works are worth reviving. M-D.

Léon Jongen. *Quintuor* 1958 (CeBeDeM) 72pp., parts. 22 min. For flute, clarinet, bassoon, horn, and piano. Moderato; Calme et Doux; Rondino. Written in a basically Impressionist style. Sectional tempo changes in all movements. M-D to D.

Noël Lee. *Partita* 1952 (AMC; CDMC) 20 min. For flute, oboe, clarinet, bassoon, and piano. Previously known as *Quintet*.

Charles Martin Loeffler. *Ballade Carnavalesque* 1902 (C. McAlister—MMP 2000) 32pp., parts. For flute, oboe, alto saxophone, bassoon, and piano. Commissioned and dedicated to Elise Hall. In one continuous movement with multiple sections. Reflects late-19th-century harmonic principles with long sweeping arpeggiation and lyrical melodies. Requires great sensitivity for successful ensemble performances. Richly expressive. One of the earliest chamber works to include the saxophone as a standard instrument. Extensive notes included. D. See Kathleen Schietroma, "Charles Martin Loeffler's *Ballade Carnavalesque:* For Flute, Oboe, Saxophone, Bassoon and Piano," D.M.A. diss., Temple University, 1990.

Nicholas Maw. *Chamber Music* (JWC 1962) 74pp., parts. 26 min. For oboe, clarinet, horn, bassoon, and piano. Introduction; Sonata; Complaint; Scherzo and Trio; Phrase; Dialogue and Lied; Variations (8)—Promenade; Invention; Berceuse; Recitativo espansivo; Pastorale; Canone all'quarto; Arietta; Perpetuum mobile. "All or any of movements 2, 4 and 5 may be omitted if so desired. Furthermore, the order of these 3 movements may be changed, but they should always be placed before and/or after the Scherzo" (from the score). Much thematic interplay between players and melodies. Romantic inspiration shows in fullness and opulence of harmonic texture. D.

Wolfgang Amadeus Mozart. *Sinfonia Concertante* K.297B, E♭ (Musica Rara). For oboe, clarinet, bassoon, horn, and piano. M-D.

———. *Quintet* K.452 E♭ 1784 (W.-D. Seiffert, K. Schilde—Henle 665 2000, ISMN M-2018-0665-5 43pp., parts; H. Federhofer—Br 43pp., parts; Leech-Hin—Musica Rara 31pp., parts; ST; IMC; Br&H 874 31pp., parts). For oboe, clarinet, horn, bassoon, and piano. Largo–Allegro moderato; Larghetto; Rondo–Allegretto. Each part becomes or may at any time become an equal partner in its own right. One of the greatest examples in this category. In a letter to his father shortly after the premiere, Mozart wrote, "I composed two grand concertos and then a quintet, which called forth the very greatest applause: I myself consider it [the *Quintet*] to be the best work I have ever composed" (from Henle Preface). Excellent Prefaces in both Henle and Br editions. D.

See Eric Paul Ohlsson, "The Quintets for Piano, Oboe, Clarinet, Horn and Bassoon by Wolfgang Amadeus Mozart and Ludwig van Beethoven," D.M.A. diss., Ohio State University, 1980.

Jean Papineau-Couture. *Suite* (CMC 1947) 26pp., parts. 15 min. For flute, clarinet, bassoon, horn, and piano. Prélude: displays elaborate contrast between 2 subjects, one rhythmical and one lyrical. Sérénade: bitonal; for horn and piano alone. Canon: in strict form, for clarinet and flute. Scherzo: all 5 instruments used; piano plays an important role; Trio features winds alone. Neoclassic. M-D.

John Christopher Pepusch. *Four Concerti* Op.8/1, 4, 5, 6 (D. Lasocki—Musica Rara 1974). For 2 treble recorders, 2 flutes or 2 oboes or 2 violins, and basso continuo. Score and parts available separately for each concerto. M-D.

Ignaz J. Pleyel. *Quintet* C (W. Genuit—Musica Rara 1969) 20pp., parts. For oboe, clarinet, bassoon, horn, and piano. Allegro; Adagio; Allegro. An exemplary work showing early Classical character. A fine addition to the otherwise scanty 18th-century literature of works for wind instruments and piano. M-D.

———. *Sinfonia Concertante* (Musica Rara; EMT). For flute, oboe, bassoon, horn, and piano.

Alan Rawsthorne. *Quintet* 1963 (OUP) 51pp., parts. 20½ min. For clarinet, oboe, bassoon, horn, and piano. Poco lento, languido–Allegro non assai: serial devices used but freely tonal; piano has a short cadenza-like passage that begins *ppp* and works up to *ff* before the final 2-line Meno mosso closes out the movement with *ff* marcatissimo octaves in the piano. Adagio: piano part unwinds chromatically to the affrettando, where cluster-like chords set off a new Più mosso section, in which the piano has some biting dissonances that soon subside to Tempo I and the opening quiet mood. Allegro non troppo, poco misterioso: the most serial of all the movements. Lento, poco tragico: dramatic octave gestures; chromatic runs lead to the Allegro risoluto: opens with a row; chromatic parallel chords soften this blow only to be followed by diverse figuration for the rest of the movement, with serial techniques permeating some of the writing. A highly effective piece in a personal style, thoroughly 20th-century, with terse and concise formal structures always present. The concept of preparation–tension–relaxation infuses this entire work. M-D.

Vittorio Rieti. *Sonata a Cinque* 1966 (Gen) 33pp., parts. For flute, oboe, clarinet, bassoon, and piano. Allegretto: open harmonies, strong rhythms, freely tonal. Allegro scherzando: dance character, flexible meters, moving chromatic lines over broken octaves, repeated chords. Andante alla croma: frequent modulations, key changes, fugal textures. Allegro: strong lyric lines with dancelike rhythms, sectional, perpetual motion figuration, Neoclassic. Delightful to play and hear. M-D.

Nikolai Rimsky-Korsakov. *Quintet* B♭ 1876 (USSR 88pp., parts; Bo&H; Belaieff; IMC). For piano, flute, clarinet, horn, and bassoon. Allegro con brio; Andante; Rondo. M-D to D.

Anton Rubinstein. *Quatuor* Op.55, published as a Quintet (Schuberth). For piano, flute, clarinet, horn, and bassoon. See detailed entry under quartets for piano and strings.

Giuseppe Sinopoli. *Numquid* (SZ). For oboe, English horn, oboe d'amore, heckelphone, and keyboards (piano, harpsichord, celesta). Only one keyboard player is required. Vivid writing, fragmentary, metrically notated. Oboes are treated melismatically. Keyboard parts bind the whole piece together. M-D.

Louis Spohr. *Quintet* Op.52 c 1820 (E. Schmitz—Br 2304 79pp., parts; Musica Rara; A. Broude; CFP) 26½ min. For piano, flute, clarinet, horn, and bassoon. Allegro moderato; Larghetto con moto (contains a surprising anticipation of *Tristan*); Menuetto; Finale. A lovely piece of scoring for this combination; some striking modulations. The piano has most of the dialogue, with the winds adding coloristic effects in the somber c hue. Facile and taxing if sometimes rambling writing, but this is first-rate Spohr. Running 3rds and octave passages have echoes of Clementi. M-D to D.

Quintets for Piano(s), Percussion, and Other Instruments

David Amram. *Discussion* 1960 (CFP) 20pp., parts. 10 min. For flute, cello, piano, and 2 percussionists. This work is a theme and 4 variations with the last variation extended to include a brilliant coda. The piano part completely shares the activity, and Amram's interest in jazz gives the rhythms a strong sense of vitality. Written in a generally 20th-century idiom with longer lines than many post-Webern composers. The variations are effectively contrasted. M-D.

William Bolcom. *Session 3* (Merion 1975) 27pp. 5 scores required. For E♭ clarinet, violin, cello, piano, and percussion. Percussion required: 4 tenor drums or tom-toms, 3 cymbals, glass chimes, glockenspiel. Contains a glossary, performance notes, and explanation of ideographic squiggles. Piano part includes clusters, plucked strings, pointillistic treatment, flutter pedal, wide dynamic range, harmonics, tremolo chords, improvisation. Avant-garde. Large span required. D.

Marius H. Flothuis. *Adagio* Op.74 (Donemus 1975) 43pp., parts. Photostat of MS. For 2 timpanists, percussion, and piano 4-hands. Explanations in English.

Arsenio Giron. *Vias* 1966 (CF 1972) 51pp., parts. Facsimile edition. For flute, clarinet, cello, piano, and percussion. Percussion required: glockenspiel, xylophone, vibraphone, tenor drums, suspended cymbals, 5 temple blocks. Serial, pointillistic, flexible meters, Expressionist. Interesting sonorities. D.

Peggy Glanville-Hicks. *Sonata for Piano and Percussion* 1951 (AMP) 10 min. Requires 4 percussionists. Allegro (based on an African folk melody); Lento sombreroso; Presto. Percussion required: xylophone, cymbals, tam-tam, tom-tom, timpani, and bass drum. Works well if the piano is loud and the xylophonist is first-rate. The style is somewhat like that of Hovhaness. M-D.

Lou Harrison. *Concerto in Slendro* (CFP 6610) 11 min. For violin solo, celesta, 2 tackpianos, and percussion. The title refers to the Indonesian gamelan tuning system of 5 pitches. This work has many extraordinary appealing and luxurious sounds. The Far East has inspired Harrison to write some of his finest music. M-D.

Charles Ives. *Scherzo—All the Way Around and Back* ca.1906 (PIC 1971) 5pp., parts. For clarinet (flute), violin, bugle (trumpet), middle bells (horn), piano I or right hand, and piano II or left hand. One of Ives's experimental works "in part made to strengthen the ear muscles, the mind muscles, and perhaps the soul muscles too . . . it had a reasonable plan to build on, from a technical standpoint" (Ralph Kirkpatrick, *Charles E. Ives Memos* [New York: W. W. Norton, 1972], p.63). Left hand (or piano II) has ostinato-like figures while right hand (or piano I) increases number of notes from one per measure to 11. Ends *ff*. Large span required. M-D for 2 pianists, D for one.

Jouko Linjama. *Fünf Metamorphosen für fünf Instrumente über fünf Canons von Anton Webern Op. 5,* Op.16 1963 (Finnish Music Information Centre) 7 min. For piano, harpsichord, guitar, celesta, and vibraphone. Serial canonic technique. Linjama said of this work: "It led to a tonal and total vacuum, where the rediscovery of the triad as the basis for a multidirectional pluristic tonality opened a road forward: backward."

Vincent F. Luti. *Mixed Quintet* 1967 (Bowdoin College Music Press) 19pp. 5 scores required. For flute/alto flute, clarinet/bass clarinet, violin/viola, cello, piano, and tape (optional). I. Invention, Toccata, Prelude, Fugue. II. Theme and Cadenzas. III. Chorale: "Lass, O Herr, dein Ohr sich neigen": built on chorale tune with the pitches sustained and overlapped with each other to form the harmonies. IV. Variation and Cadenzas. Inspired by Baroque forms and practices. "There is an option to play the second movement. It may be performed or omitted. However, it must be taped prior to performance and must then be played back during the performance of the fourth movement. Cues are notated in the score to get an approximate (closer the better) alignment of the 2 movements. Improvisational pitches should not be played in the order notated" (from the score). Piano part requires tack hammer, marimba stick, and long glass bottle. It utilizes harmonics, nonstandard notation, pointillistic treatment, fingernail tremolo on strings, and other effects with the glass bottle. Avant-garde. D.

Vaclav Nelhybel. *Quintetto Concertante* 1967 (Gen) 27pp., parts. For piano, violin, trumpet, trombone, and xylophone. Allegro marcato: samba rhythms with syncopated chords; alternating hands; changing meters; cross-accents; quartal harmony; imitation; highly interesting rhythmically; large span required. Slow: octotonic; harmonic 4th in alternating hands; Agitato section provides punctuated chords and an accented melody. Vivo: sweeping arpeggi; hammered repeated notes; extension of rhythm found in first movement with even more off-accents; octotonic; coda adds chords in the right hand for the pianist over the left-hand shifting rhythms; arrives at an exciting climax. The whole piece is a "rhythmic showcase." M-D.

Fred Noak. *Three Chicks and a Worm* (IU 1951) 12pp., parts. Humoresque for piano, 3 percussionists, and bass clarinet. 1½-p. narration. A clever story with instrumental writing that underlines every part of the action. Percussion required: temple blocks, 4 timpani, marimba, vibraphone. Twentieth-century harmonic, melodic, and rhythmic treatment; staccato chords; chromatic; clever ending. M-D.

Hans Osieck. *Variations Rapsodiques* 1982 (Donemus). 13 min. For clarinet, cello, electronic organ, piano, and snare drum. One of the most unique Quintets to be found. In 3 parts: Introduction, Blues, and Rondo. Spontaneous and light-hearted with spunk and joviality. Later transcribed for piano 4-hands. M-D.

Marta Ptaszynska. *Suite Variée* (Leduc 1973) 8pp., parts. For piano and 4 percussionists. Percussion required: suspended cymbal, triangle, maracas, wood block, tambourine, small and large timpani, xylophone, glockenspiel. Prelude; Dance chinoise; Polka. Piano provides melody, harmony, and some rhythmic interest. Traditional harmonic usage. M-D.

Elias Tanenbaum. *Chamber Piece I* 1956 (ACA) 71pp., parts. For flute/piccolo, clarinet, cello, piano, and percussion. Percussion required: 2 timpani, snare drum, suspended cymbal, crash cymbal, wood block, large triangle, xylophone, 4 temple blocks. Andante: chromatic chords, arpeggi figures, octotonic, rhythmic interest in Allegro molto section; large span required. Moderato: flexible meters; sustained cluster-like chords; leads to an Allegro molto dancelike section that is interrupted by a brief Andante before the Allegro molto leads to a stunning conclusion. Thin textures, Neoclassic. M-D.

Music for Six Instruments

Sextets for Piano and Strings

Tomaso Albinoni. *Sonata* a 5 Op.2/6 g (F. Giegling—Nag 189) 22pp., parts. For 2 violins, 2 violas, cello, and keyboard. Adagio; Allegro; Grave; Allegro. The final Allegro ($\frac{12}{8}$) is especially delightful and flowing. M-D.

Johann Christian Bach. *Sechs Quintette* Op.11 (R. Steglich—*Das Erbe Deutscher Musik* Vol.3 1953) 96pp. 1 C: Allegretto; Andantino; Menuetto con Variatione. 2 G: Allegro; Allegro assai. 3 F: Andante; Allegretto. 4 E♭: Andante; Menuetto; Allegro. 5 A: Allegretto; Tempo di Menuetto. 6 D: Allegro; Andantino; Allegro assai. All are M-D.
Available separately: Op.11/1 (S. Sadie—Musica Rara 1071 1962) 26pp., parts. Op.11/3 (S. Sadie—Musica Rara 1075 1962) 19pp., parts. Op.11/4 (Nag 123), for 3 violins or 3 flutes or 3 oboes, viola, cello, and keyboard. Op.11/6 (Nag 124; HM 42), for 3 violins or 3 flutes or 3 oboes, viola, cello, and keyboard.

Leslie Bassett. *Sextet* 1972 (CFP 1975) 30pp., parts. 19 min. For 2 violins, 2 violas, cello, and piano. In 4 movements. The strings of the piano are to be touched, plucked, or stopped. Stopped notes are muffled yet sonorous. "Stopping" directions are given. Most of the piano range is exploited; flat 5-finger tremolo on lowest 8–10 strings (inside piano); harmonics; long pedals in third movement. Serial-like but not always strict. Some sections are free and unbarred. Highly sophisticated writing that is well crafted throughout; effects called for inside the piano seem to be appropriate. Only for the most experienced performers. D.

William Sterndale Bennett. *Sextet* Op.8 f♯ 1846 (K&S1466; Augener 9240) 35pp., parts. For 2 violins, viola, cello, double bass, and piano. Allegro moderato; Scherzo; Andante grazioso; Finale. Much emphasis is placed on the piano writing with Romantic idioms and gestures and cantabile lines. The Andante grazioso, the outstanding movement, has an unusual subject of varied note values; however, the finale, although lively, seems to amble along in a very conventional way. M-D.

Ernest Chausson. *Concerto* Op.21 D 1891 (R. Lerolle 85pp., parts; IMC). For piano, violin, and string quartet. Décidé: $\frac{3}{2}$, $\frac{4}{4}$; sweeping scalar and arpeggi gestures with interwoven melody; trills; alternating hands; broken-chordal passages; chromatic; 3 with 4; fleet 3rds divided between hands; syncopation; large span required. Sicilienne: $\frac{6}{8}$; added-note chords; piano chordal sonorities provide binding effects; left-hand arpeggi include embedded chords; melodic line in piano often requires poetic interpretation; alternating hands in contiguous 5-note patterns; charming; Fauré characteristics. Grave: $\frac{3}{4}$; light chromatic lines with widely spread arpeggiated chords worked into the sonority; chromatic broken-octave triplets; fluid lines between hands; opening mood closes movement; wistful; melancholy. Très animé: $\frac{6}{8}$; opens with clever rhythmic figuration one octave apart; alternating chords and octaves between hands; syncopated melodic line; effective metrical division of $\frac{3}{2}$ into $\frac{3}{4}$; octaves forcefully employed; similar idioms from previous movements used; somewhat in the nature of variation form with highly successful rhythmic transformation. D.

Damiano Cozzella. *Discontinuo* 1964 (PAU 1966) 15pp. For 2 violins, viola, cello, double bass, and piano. Indeterminate writing constructed in box sets and interspersed with determinate sections. Spatial sounds and drastic dynamic changes are typical. Imaginative performers are essential to make the work coherent. Performance notes in Portuguese, Spanish, and English. M-D to D.

Manuel de Falla. *Pantomine and Ritual Fire Dance from El Amor Brujo* 1915, rev.1926 (JWC 60498 1995, ISBN 0-7119-5009-1) 40pp., parts. First publication of extracts arranged by the composer from his ballet. Parts correspond to those in orchestral version and show Falla's sense of instrumental balance in the 2 mediums parallel to one another. Wide span required. M-D.

César Franck. *Solo de Piano avec Accompagnement de Quintette à cordes* Op.10 1843 (J.-M. Fauguet—Editions Musicales du Marais 1991) 59pp., parts. For piano, 2 violins, viola, cello, and double bass. Based on a theme from the composer's choral work *Ruth*. Preface in English and French.

David Holden. *Music for Piano and Strings* 1937 (SPAM) 52pp., parts. For 2 violins, viola, cello, double bass, and piano. The double bass is optional. With virile accent; Veiled; Boisterously; Rota. Mildly 20th-century style. Third movement uses "Sumer is icumen in." Pleasant writing with Romantic and Impressionist influences. M-D.

Serge Liapounow. *Sextet* Op.63 (Zimmermann) 36pp., parts. Allegro maestoso; Scherzo; Nocturne; Finale. Traditional late-Romantic writing. The Nocturne is especially lovely, and the outer movements show the influence of Brahms. Elegant and polished. M-D to D.

Felix Mendelssohn. *Sextet* Op.110 D 1824 (Nov; Litolff 54pp., parts) 22 min. For piano, violin, 2 violas, cello, and double bass. Allegro vivace: bubbly writing, dazzling technical display. Adagio: muted strings. Minuet: notated in $^6_8$ for some strange reason. Allegro vivace: its merry frolic is interrupted with a statement of the minor minuet just before the conclusion. Flowing Mendelssohn style that is ever so pianistic. D.

Knudage Riisager. *Concertino* Op.28a 1933 (WH 24278) 16pp., parts. 8 min. For piano and 5 violins. Allegro: octotonic, changing meters, short motifs, chromatic. Lento: imitative, descending line. Allegro: scalar, chords, large span required. Neoclassic orientation. M-D.

Peter Tchaikovsky. *Allegro* c 1863–64 (Wollenweber 907) 7pp., parts. For 2 violins, viola, cello, double bass, and piano. Written during the composer's conservatory days. A brief, fast-action work characterized by scalar runs and large chords for the piano with string accompanimental figures. String parts could be doubled for use with chamber orchestra. Requires large span. D.

Joaquín Turina. *Scène Andalouse* Op.7 (Sal 1913) 19pp., parts. 10½ min. For viola solo, 2 violins, viola, cello, and piano. Crépuscule du Soir (Twilight): long preamble for the piano, evocative, song and dance elements in the Serenata and Habanera. A la Fenêtre (At the Window): strong Spanish expression; Impressionist influences permeated with ingenious variations on native rhythms. M-D.

Felix Weingartner. *Sextett* Op.33 e (Br&H 810/813 1903, 1917) 67pp., parts. For piano, 2 violins, viola, cello, and double bass. Allegro appassionato: undulating first subject catches attention immediately; contrasted with more delicate second idea. Allegretto scherzoso: two contrasted trios, one sentimental and the other more melancholy. Adagio ma non troppo: improvisatory; uses a canon and a waltz. Danza funèbre: interesting rhythmic treatment. This piece sounds good and is distinguished in a number of ways, but it is not a great work. Post-Brahms writing. D.

Sextets for Piano and Miscellaneous Instruments

Johann Christian Bach. *Sextet* C (Musica Rara). For oboe, violin, 2 horns, cello, and basso continuo.
——. *Quintet* Op.11/4 (Nag 123). For 3 violins or 3 flutes or 3 oboes, viola, cello, and keyboard.
——. *Quintet* Op.11/6 (Nag 124; HM 42). For 3 violins or 3 flutes or 3 oboes, viola, cello, and keyboard.

André Boucourechliev. *Anarchipel V* (Leduc 1972). For amplified harp, amplified harpsichord, electronic organ, piano, and 2 percussionists. Consists of 5 large sheets of notation laid out like maps, one for each instrument (both percussionists use the same page), which can be played simultaneously, depending on the performers' choice. Diverse materials. Piano part contains passages of single pitches and chords, clusters, trills, tremolos. Everything can be played at various dynamic levels; diagrams are patterns to be pursued and freely developed in the same character as long as one wishes. The score is not too helpful, but the reproduction of the autograph is original and fascinating! Avantgarde. D.

Raynor Brown. *Variations* (WIN 1973) 56pp., parts. For 2 trumpets, horn, trombone, tuba, and piano. Chromatic subject is heard octotonically in the piano to open the work. Followed by 11 variations, with the last one the most extensive. The piano is mainly treated to thin textures; unusual instrumental combination. Large span required. M-D.

Robert Casadesus. *Sextuor* Op.58 (Durand 1961) 91pp., parts. For flute, oboe, clarinet, horn, bassoon, and piano. Allegro con brio: $\frac{4}{4}$; syncopated chordal opening; scales in octaves and 10ths; arpeggi; octotonic; more sustained Grazioso second idea; repeated marcato chords; Molto quieto closing. Scherzo vivace: $\frac{3}{8}$; fleet movement over keyboard; dry staccato style; thin, widely spread textures; Trio en musette uses octotonic melodic writing. Andante: $\frac{3}{4}$; sustained long phrases use open 4ths and 5ths; alternating and crossing hands. Molto vivo: $\frac{3}{4}$;

sweeping gestures in 8th notes and triplets up and down keyboard; parallel chords; double notes; sustained passages contrast with fast-moving, staccato, chromatic lines; staccato style; grace notes add humor; effective broken-octave melodic writing at Tranquillo. Neoclassic style. D.

Niccolò Castiglioni. *Tropi* 1959 (SZ) 21pp., parts. 7½ min. For flute, clarinet, violin, cello, percussion (1 player), and piano. Serial: piano part separates sections and is heard by itself as well as in combination with the other instruments. Dynamic extremes, dramatic pauses, long pedals, spatial relationships, harmonics, pointillistic. Avant-garde. M-D.

Domenico Cimarosa. *Sestetto* G (A. Coen—Ut Orpheus 1998) 51pp., parts. For 2 violins, viola, cello, bassoon, and piano. Allegro maestoso; Siciliano; Rondo. A charming sextet retaining features of the Style Gallant well into the Classical period. Piano complements and interacts with the ensemble both independently and as a group. Deserves to be better known. Preface and critical notes in Italian. M-D.

Aaron Copland. *Sextet* (Bo&H 1948) 45pp., parts. 15 min. This is a 1937 arrangement of the 1932 *Short Symphony.* For piano, clarinet, 2 violins, viola, and cello. Allegro vivace: bold rhythmic style throughout; asymmetrical Hispanic-American rhythms; $\frac{3}{4}$ juxtaposed with $\substack{6\\8}$. Lento: modal, has characteristics of Latin American chants; solemnly eloquent. Finale–precise and rhythmic: rhythmic treatment similar to the Afro-Cuban danzon; piano part has jazz patterns. Written in an athletic style, full of irregular, stylized, and primitive rhythms and wide-skipping melodies; cast in a clarity and an economy of development. The harmonic idiom and textures owe a good deal to the Stravinsky of *Symphonies d'Instruments à vent.* D.

Damiano Cozzella. *Discontinuo* (PAU 1964) 15pp., parts. For piano, 2 violins, viola, cello, and double bass. Performance directions; separate directions for the piano. The 5 tempo signs are more an indication of density of sound per beat. A good example of sound-mass; individual pitches are not important or perceptible. Aleatoric. Avant-garde. D.

Johann Baptist Cramer. *Sextuor* Op.85 E♭ (Br&H 6057) 33pp., parts. For piano, 2 violins, viola, cello, and double bass. Allegro vivace; Andante quasi Allegretto (Marche funèbre 29 Juillet); Presto (Menuet); Finale. Facile writing. M-D.

Arthur Custer. *Sextet* 1961 (Joshua) 15 min. For flute, oboe, clarinet, horn, bassoon, and piano. Sinfonia; Cantilena; Finale. Ebullient; delightful and debonair writing with ironic tinges. M-D.

Peter Maxwell Davies. *Ave Maris Stella* (Bo&H 1975). For flute, clarinet, marimba, viola, cello, and piano. One of the composer's most poetic scores, yet it is full of sharp corners and sudden turns. A strange work of formidable exploration. M-D to D.

See Stephen Pruslin, "The Triangular Space: Peter Maxwell Davies's 'Ave Maris Stella,'" *Tempo* 120 (March 1977): 16–22. This excellent article throws much light on this complex work.

Emma Lou Diemer. *Sextet* 1962 (Seesaw 1976) 73pp., parts. 20 min. For piano, flute, oboe, clarinet, horn, and bassoon. With energy: 7th chords with quartal harmony, octotonic, driving rhythmic figures, staccato chords in alternating hands, strong bitonal implications. Slow: sustained, trills, longer lines, chromatic figuration, parallel chords, dramatic pianistic gestures in climax, incisive skips. Moderately fast: cadenza-like opening by solo piano moves to a $\frac{7}{8}$ faster fughetta section; thin textures interlaced with thicker chords in alternating hands; contrasting expressive section follows. Freely tonal, strong 20th-century writing. D.

Ernst von Dohnányi. *Sextet* Op.37 C 1933 (Lengnick) 106pp., parts. For clarinet, horn, violin, viola, cello, and piano. Allegro appassionato: $\frac{4}{4}$; sustained chords; parallel sonorities; rotating broken octaves; chromatic patterns in runs; arpeggio figuration; octotonic; 3 with 4; strong full chords. Intermezzo: $\frac{12}{8}$; full chords in various inversions; Alla marcia section with broken chords that evolve over the keyboard. Allegro con sentimento: $\frac{2}{4}$; tranquil, chromatic, legato chordal movement; octotonic runs; chordal punctuation; parallel broken-chordal accompaniment; alternating hands; chromatic arpeggi; opening idea returns in $\frac{6}{4}$ to close out movement and goes immediately to Finale: a marked cheerful figure opens the movement; chromatic double notes; other idioms from previous movements used; thin textures contrasted with thicker ones. Long, demanding writing. D.

Anton Eberl. *Sextet* Op.47 E♭ 1800 (W. Genuit, D. Klocker—Musica Rara 1969) 24pp., parts. For clarinet, horn, violin, viola, cello, and piano. Adagio–Allegro vivace; Andante molto; Menuetto; Rondo. Influence of Mozart is unmistakable. Delightful and highly interesting writing. Preface by the editors. M-D.

Donald Erb. *Three Pieces* (TP). For 2 trumpets, horn, trombone, tuba, and piano. Includes tapping or rattling the bell, muttering, hissing or yelling into instrument, kissing instrument, etc. Visual interest is greater than the musical interest. Avant garde. M-D.

———. *Mirage* 1977 (Merion 1978) 20pp., parts. 8 min. For flute, bassoon, trumpet, trombone, percussion, and keyboard. Keyboardist must be prepared to play piano, harpsichord, electric piano, electric organ, and harmonica, sometimes 2 simultaneously. Novel effects, such as turning off electric organ while sustaining pitches. M-D.

Blair Fairchild. *Concerto de Chambre* Op.26 (Augener 1912) 57pp., parts. For violin, piano, 2 violins, viola, and cello; double bass ad lib. Allegro; Andante; Allegro. Strongly chordal, chromatic lines, alternating chords, mildly Impressionist. M-D.

Morton Feldman. *Durations V* (CFP 6905 1962) 8pp., parts. For violin, cello, horn, vibraphone, harp, and piano/celesta. "The first sound with all instruments simultaneously. The duration of each sound is chosen by the performer. All beats are slow. All sounds should be played with a minimum of attack . . . Numbers between sounds indicate silent beats. Dynamics are very low" (from Notes in the score). Avant-garde, interesting sonorities. Performers must be super "counters"! Unbarred throughout. M-D.

———. *The Viola in My Life* (I) 1970 (UE 15395) 10pp., parts. 9½ min. For flute, violin, viola (solo), cello, piano, and percussion. Changing meters, cluster-like chords. Not a dynamic mark in entire score, only crescendo signs. Passing suggestions of tonality. A sonority study that uses the full range of the keyboard. Large span required. There are 4 pieces by Feldman with this same title, all separate and independent works, not single movements. M-D.

———. *Routine Investigations* 1976 (UE 21 049) 18pp., parts. For oboe, trumpet, piano, viola, cello, and double bass. Investigates timbre, harmonic, rhythmic, and spatial qualities within the context of constantly changing meters. Large span required. M-D.

Lukas Foss. *Tashi* 1986 (Pembroke PCB130 1987, ISBN 0-8258-2184-3) 56pp., parts available on rental. 18 min. For B♭ clarinet, string quartet, and piano. I. Lento, II. Allegro, III. Free, IV. Allegro commodo. Conventional notation with slightly unconventional use of instruments, especially muting the strings inside the piano, and finger noise with only the percussive sound of fingers on keys. Asymmetric rhythms, full chords, hints of minimalism. M-D.

Roberto Gerhard. *Libra* 1968 (OUP) 122pp., parts. 15 min. For flute/piccolo, clarinet, violin, piano, guitar, and percussion. Percussion required: glockenspiel, wood block, large and medium cymbals, large Korean block, vibraphone, timpani, castanets. Highly organized, sectionalized. Clusters, pointillistic, shifting meters, toccata-like martellato passages, ringing and unusual sonorities, dynamic extremes, fades away to nothing. Requires large span. D.

Lionel Greenberg. *Sextet* 1963 (CMC) 14½ min. For flute, oboe, clarinet, bassoon, horn, and piano. Allegro; Andante; Lento; Moderato: Largo. "The basic structural unit in this piece is the interval of the third. In a sense the entire piece is variations on that interval. The form of the first movement is free; second movement—canons, choral canons; third movement—free; fourth movement—giocoso—free; fifth movement is twelve-tone and is composed of two simul-

taneous three-part canons and their retrogrades over an isorhythmic bass"
(Composer's Notes).

Alexei Haieff. *Dance Suite—The Princess Zondilda and Her Entourage* (Belaieff
1965) 8pp., parts. For flute, bassoon, trumpet, violin, cello, and piano. Allegro;
Andante; Allegro. Octotonic, chordal punctuation, widely spread textures, ostinati, mildly 20th-century. Octaves in alternating hands; large span required.
M-D.

Talib Rasul Hakim. *Placements* 1970 (Bo&Bo 1975) 6pp. 6 copies necessary for
performance. For 5 percussionists and piano. Explanations in English.

Roy Harris. *Concerto* Op.2 1926 (AMP 1932) 58pp., parts. For clarinet, piano, and
string quartet. Fantasia: solid formal construction, much poetic beauty, interval of the augmented 4th important. Second Fantasia: effective scherzo, ABA
with B equaling one measure of very slow $\frac{12}{2}$ time. Third Fantasia: beautifully contrasted Adagio, quiet and contemplative. Fourth Fantasia: free fugal
form, impetuous and wild. Contrapuntal techniques are very important in this
work. D.

Edward Burlingame Hill. *Sextet* Op.39 B♭ (Galaxy 1939) 100pp., parts. For flute,
oboe, clarinet, horn, bassoon, and piano. Allegro non troppo, ma giocoso: rich
harmonic character with piano often taking the lead in imitative treatment;
expressive and rhythmic. Scherzo: light, bouncy theme at Molto vivace in E♭
with long trio in parallel minor. Lento con duolo: expansive ternary form in c♯
with extensive arpeggiation in middle section. Finale: witty, jovial character
with occasional $\frac{3}{4}$ measures thrown into $\frac{2}{4}$ meter; mad dash to the finish. Late-
19th-century stylistic writing. D.

Karel Husa. *Sérénade* 1963 (Leduc) 44pp., parts. 15 min. For piano, flute, oboe,
clarinet, horn, and bassoon. Also exists in another version for wind quintet
with string orchestra, xylophone, and harp or piano. La Montagne: trills, some
melodic function for piano although mainly rhythmic. La Nuit: some agitated
f chords for the piano, glissando, imitation, coda without the piano. La Danse:
staccato rhythmic octaves and chords, repeated notes, tremolo chords in upper
register, glissando at end. M-D.
——. *Concerto* 1965 (Leduc) 63pp., parts. 24½ min. For piano, 2 trumpets in C,
horn, trombone, and tuba. Quasi fanfara: much tremolo in piano, bold gestures,
widely spaced chords. Misterioso: harmonic 7ths and 9ths used frequently;
complex rhythms; spread-out octaves used in contrary motion; dissonance
colorfully exploited. Adagio: Impressionist *ppp* full chords; tremolos; staccatissimo rhythmic 2nds; trills; opposite dynamics between hands; bombastic conclusion. Requires experienced ensemble player with complete pianistic equipment. D.
——. *Recollections* 1982 (AMP) 58pp., parts. 21 min. For flute, oboe, clarinet,

horn, bassoon, and piano. Uses interior of piano, including paper under the dampers, cluster chords, and late-20th-century notational practices to achieve desired effects. In "six contrasting movements, each of which explores different aspects of the sonorities and virtuoso techniques of the individual instruments, as well as the new sonorities possible with the combination of piano and winds. Some passages are indicated in a relatively free notation to allow performers a certain freedom, but, in general, the music is precisely notated" (from the score). D.

Charles Ives. *Allegretto Sombreoso* ca.1908 (When the Moon Is on the Wave) (PIC 1958) 6pp., parts. For flute, English horn, 3 violins, and piano. Trumpet or basset horn may be substituted for the English horn. Long arpeggiated lines in $\frac{13}{16}$, a few chords in $\frac{11}{8}$, and a final arpeggiation in $\frac{18}{16}$. Words (by Lord Byron) are included for the English horn part. M-D.

Gordon Jacob. *Sextet* 1956 (Musica Rara 1962) 53pp., parts. For flute, oboe, clarinet, bassoon, horn, and piano. In 5 movements, 4 based upon the musical notes A, B, E, B, A, taken from the name Aubrey Brain, in whose memory the work was composed. Elegiac Prelude: dotted-8th–16th-note rhythm contrasted by triplets in largely early-20th-century homophonic setting. Scherzo: flowing passagework of octaves and scalar patterns in ternary form. Cortège: the only movement not based upon thematic pitches, set in the style of a slow march with increased independence among instruments. Minuet and Trio: short movement of staccato chords and scales. Rondo with Epilogue: rapid passagework in a spirited vivace with imitative rondo treatment leading to a false, explosive conclusion coupled to material from the Prelude at adagio to finish *ppp*.

Robert Sherlaw Johnson. *Triptych* 1973 (OUP) 22pp. for small complete score. For flute, clarinet, violin, cello, piano, and percussion (one player). Percussion required: vibraphone, marimba, Chinese blocks, cymbals, tam-tam. Catenary 1: serial; pointillistic; piano has a quasi-cadenza; clusters. Catenary 2: *pppp* trills; certain small sections are played out of time; quasi-tremolo; large span required. Procession: clusters, pedal instructions, unusual sonorities. Avantgarde. D.

Werner Josten. *Concerto Sacro I & II* (H. Elkan) 19pp., parts. For piano, 2 violins, viola, cello, and double bass. I. Annunciation; The Miracle. II. Lament; Sepulchre and Resurrection. Many short sections with titles that tell the story. Chromatic and picturesque writing. M-D.

Rudolf Kelterborn. *Adagio con interventi* 2000 (Br 8266 2000) 26pp., parts. 16 min. For flute, clarinet, violin, viola, cello, and piano. Extremely slow with frequent pauses and interventions. Uses an expanded Webernesque style with late-20th-century avant-garde techniques. Score is copy of difficult-to-read MS. D.

Karl Kohn. *Serenade* 1961 (CF 1972) 19pp., parts. Facsimile edition. For flute/ piccolo, oboe, clarinet, horn, bassoon, and piano. Moderato; Lento; Andante grazioso; Quasi adagio–in tempo rubato; Allegro non troppo. Serial, pointillistic. Small notes are to be played as fast as possible, chromatic clusters silently depressed. In those bars that lack precise conventional measurement, the notes are to be distributed in approximation of their graphic position between the bar lines. Strong Expressionist style with traditional and avant-garde idioms combined. D.

Hans Kox. *Sextet II* 1957 (Donemus) 23pp., parts. Reproduced from holograph. For piano, harpsichord, 2 violins, viola, and cello. Allegro: added notes, chromatic, syncopation, rhythmic shifting figuration, piano cadenza. Largo: piano is silent. Allegretto: running and chordal gestures. M-D.

——. *Sextet III* 1959 (Donemus). 10 min. For woodwind quintet and piano.

——. *Sextet IV* 1960 (Donemus). For woodwind quintet and piano.

Jean Yves Daniel Lesur. *Sextuor* (Amphion 1961) 36pp., parts. For piano, flute, oboe, violin, viola, and cello. Transcription by the composer of the *Suite* from *Trio à cordes et piano.* Nocturne; Ricercare; Berceuse; Tarentelle. Mildly 20th-century with Impressionist techniques. M-D.

Sergei Liapunov. *Sextet* Op.63 (USSR 1967) 100pp., parts. For piano, 2 violins, viola, cello, and double bass. Allegro maestoso; Scherzo; Nocturne; Finale. Traditional late-Romantic writing that displays a fine craft. The outer movements follow Brahms's lead. M-D to D.

Lowell Liebermann. *Fantasy on a Fugue of J. S. Bach* 1989 (TP 1998) 29pp., parts. 12 min. For flute, oboe, clarinet, horn, bassoon, and piano. Based upon the Fugue in b from *The Well-Tempered Clavier,* Book I. In one continuous movement with many tempo changes. Vigorous writing with sharp contrasts of dynamics and expressive qualities. Sets arpeggiated patterns in quadruplets which move to quintuplets, sextuplets, and septuplets. Central adagio develops opening fragment of fugal subject more thoroughly before a return to rapid speed but finishes in the final measures for the piano softly in B. D.

Donald Martino. *Notturno* 1973 (Dantalian 523 1998) 54pp., parts. 16 min. For flute (piccolo, alto flute), clarinet (extended bass clarinet), violin (viola), cello, percussion, and piano. Percussion required: glockenspiel, vibraphone, xylophone, marimba, 6 temple blocks, 3 tam-tams. Two large sections with smaller sectionalized portions. Colorful directions such as "Hyperdramatic; in an intensely anguished whisper." Strings plucked, damped, and struck with a bass drum beater. Expressionist, serial, dramatically imaginative. Requires fine pacing. Winner of 1974 Pulitzer Prize. D.

Bohuslav Martinů. *Musique de Chambre I* (ESC 7280 1966) 65pp., parts. 18 min. For violin, viola, cello, clarinet, harp, and piano. Allegro moderato: octaves in low register; harmonic 2nds and 9ths prevalent; alternating hands; chromatic; triplets both chordal and single notes; added-note sonorities; ostinati. Andante moderato: cluster-like chords; tremolo; chromatic figuration; arpeggiated octaves; short piano cadenza. Poco allegro: low-register chords; melodic clusters; fugal textures; piano provides much incisive rhythmic impetus. M-D.

——. *Sextet* 1929 (Br). For flute, oboe, clarinet, 2 bassoons, and piano. Displays Martinů's Classical style interlaced with jazz elements. M-D.

Shin-Ichi Matsushita. *Gestalt* 17 1969–70 (UE 15894) 14pp., parts. Reproduced from holograph. For 3 trombones, percussion, piano, and harp. Percussion required: vibraphone, xylophone, electric organ, 4 timpani, 12 campane tubolare, 3 tamburi piccoli, 2 tam-tams, 2 tom-toms, 3 piatti, 2 bongos, 2 congos, blocco di legno. Clusters, pointillistic, serial, dynamic extremes, Expressionist, avant-garde. D.

Francisco Mignone. *Sexteto* 1937 (Escola Nacional de Musica da Universidade do Brazil, Rio de Janeiro; Copy at LC) 61pp., parts. For flute, oboe, clarinet, horn, bassoon, and piano. Sostenuto–Moderato: dramatic chords; sweeping scales and octaves; long pedals; large span required. Lento: chordal, ostinati, builds to grand climax; moves directly into Allegro: chromatic figuration, varied tempos, driving rhythms to the end. Virtuoso writing. D.

Pauline Oliveros. *Variations for Sextet* 1960 (Smith 1974) 30pp., parts. 12 min. For flute, clarinet, trumpet, horn, cello, and piano. Theme of 9 measures emphasizes Webernesque techniques with touches of pointillism and rhythmic idiosyncrasies in a slow tempo. Complex meters occasionally jolt the flow and are derived from the theme where a $\frac{1}{4} + \frac{1}{8} + \frac{3}{4}$ measure appears in the context of $\frac{4}{4}$ and becomes the basis for development to follow. Variations are uneven in length and show a consistent development of tonal and rhythmic possibilities, including proportional rhythmic relationships sometimes realized in extreme registers under intense dynamic changes. Conventional notation for an avant-garde work of the late 20th century. Score is a photocopy of MS. D.

George Onslow. *Sextuor* Op.30 E♭ ca.1830 (Br&H) 35pp., parts. For piano, flute, clarinet, horn, bassoon, double bass. Largo–Allegro vivace assai; Menuetto; Andante con Variazioni (5 variations and a finale). Flowing, sometimes elegant and even clever writing from the pen of a second-rank composer. M-D.

——. *Grand Sextuor* Op.77bis a 1849 (Heugel 1972), parts. For piano, flute, clarinet, bassoon, horn, and double bass. Allegro spiritoso; Minuetto; Tema con (6) Variazioni; Finale. Elegant work suggesting early-19th-century styles. M-D.

Juan Orrego-Salas. *Sextet* Op.38 1954 (PIC 1967) 84pp., parts. For clarinet, 2 violins, viola, cello, and piano. Sonata: accented and punctuated chords; rhythmic subject of four 16ths and four 8ths; freely tonal; melodic and contrapuntal lines; alternating hands; octotonic chromatic scales. Differencias: full chords for chorale subject; 7 variations and closing; this movement is the "heart" of the work and is a catalog of variation techniques for all the instruments. Scherzo: variable meters; toccata-like in its drive; Meno mosso trio is expressive and cantabile; opening mood and slightly altered figuration return. Recitativo, Contrappunto e Coda: Lento clarinet opening; Tempo giusto section displays contrapuntal elements including single lines that evolve into 4-voiced textures for a climax; piano participates in chordal, 2-voice structures and finally in *pp* octaves in the lower register as the movement evaporates. Firm handling of formal structure and Neoclassic style throughout. M-D.

George Perle. *Critical Moments* 1996 (Galaxy 2000) 22pp. For flute (piccolo), Bb clarinet (Eb clarinet, bass clarinet), violin, cello, piano, and percussion. Percussion required: temple blocks, suspended cymbal, 3 tom-toms, bongo, snare drum, timpani, gong, crotales, marimba, xylophone, vibraphone. In 6 brief untitled movements. Dramatic action plays a key role with fast speeds in most movements making precision absolutely critical at all moments. Almost impossible for one percussionist as intended. D.

Hans Pfitzner. *Sextet* Op.55 g 1945 (Oertel) 48pp., parts. 25 min. For clarinet, violin, cello, viola, double bass, and piano. Allegro con passione, quasi minuetto; Rondoletto; Semplice, misterioso; Comodo. It is amazing that this work, composed in 1945, could be conceived in a Brahms-Reger style, but it is straight out of that tradition. M-D.

Willem Pijper. *Sextet* 1923 (Donemus) 35pp., parts. 15 min. For flute, oboe, clarinet, bassoon, horn, and piano. Lento; Andantino, quasi Allegretto; Comodo, alla ticinese; Vivo, con agrezza. Clear form and texture. Shows influence of Mahler, French predilections, and Dutch folk music. Beautifully contrasted movements. M-D.

Francis Poulenc. *Sextet* 1932–39 (WH 1945) 68pp., parts. 18 min. For piano, flute, oboe, clarinet, horn, and bassoon. Three movements of verve and wit. The outer movements are free in form and employ varied melodic and rhythmic gestures. The breezy middle movement, Divertissement, is in ABA design with a quicker mid-section that alludes to the opening idea in Mozart's *Sonata* C, K.545. A frivolous and delightful romp that blends the best of Chopin and the music hall! M-D.

Henri Pousseur. *Madrigal III* 1962 (UE 13804) 29pp., parts. For piano, clarinet, violin, cello, and 2 percussionists. Percussion required: vibraphone, 3 cowbells, cymbal, tam-tam, marimba, 2 bongos, 3 tom-toms. Directions in French, German, and English. Unusual notation, partly graphic. Piano has punctuated tremolo and pointillistic chords, long trills, dynamic extremes, half pedals. Unusual sonorities, avant-garde. M-D.

Anthony Powers. *Another Part of the Island* 1980 (OUP 1985) Rev.1994 57pp. 25 min. For flute (alto flute/piccolo), clarinet, piano (celesta), percussion, violin, and cello. Lentissimo; Allegro energico; Molto meno mosso; Lento moderato. Pianist plays celesta only at the beginning, end of third movement, and short passages in fourth. Extensive, uses indeterminate techniques, and complex rhythmic relationships. D.

Claudio Prieto. *Al-gamara, para conjunto de camara* (Editorial de Música Española Contemporánea 1973) 67pp., parts. 14 min. For piano, electric guitar, marimba, and wind, string, and percussion instruments. Avant-garde.

Serge Prokofiev. *Sextet* Op.34 g "Overture on Jewish Themes" 1919 (Bo&H 23pp., parts; USSR 1944; K; IMC) 8½ min. For clarinet, 2 violins, viola, cello, and piano. Prokofiev's only work based on folk material. Grotesque and lyric elements are worked out with brilliant craft. Alternating hands, secco style, tenuto chords, rapid finger passages, open 5ths and 6ths, dancelike quality, broken-chord figuration, syncopated soprano and bass melodic usage (at No.17, cantando), scalar passages, accented chords at conclusion. An unusual piece of writing. Large span required. M-D to D.

Bernard Rands. *Tableau* 1970 (UE 15416) 12pp., parts. 6-p. performance instructions. For flute/alto flute, clarinet/bass clarinet, viola, cello, piano/celesta, and percussion. Percussion required: 3 triangles, 2 cymbals, glockenspiel, vibraphone, 5 temple blocks, xylophone, bongos, 2 tom-toms, hard and soft sticks, brushes. Chance composition, duration variable from 10 to 20 min. Contains 5 sections: Monotone; Labyrinth; Epiphanies; Tutto è sciolto; Monologue intérieur. In any performance each section should be played at least twice, but not immediately follow itself. Written in proportional notation—absolute duration and rhythmic values are not indicated, but are suggested by relative tone proportions. Numerous other directions for each section. Piano has thick chords and is treated pointillistically. Dynamics are attached to most notes. Aleatoric, avant-garde. D.

———. *Déjà* 1972 (UE 16006) 10pp., parts. For flute/alto flute, clarinet/bass clarinet, viola, cello, piano, and percussion. Percussion required: 3 temple blocks, 1 pair bongos, 2 tom-toms, 2 triangles, 2 cymbals, 2 gongs, tam-tam, vibraphone. Extensive performance directions, including a diagram for arranging instruments. Several sections provide fine ideas to the performers. Choice of instrumentation and combination. Aleatoric. The piano part looks rather simple but demands the maximum of invention within the prescribed limits. M-D.

H. Owen Reed. *Symphonic Dance* (Belwin-Mills 1963) 19pp., parts. For flute, oboe, clarinet, horn, bassoon, and piano. Allegro giusto: chromatic; contrary figuration; chords used for rhythmic punctuation; chorale-like mid-section; opening ideas return; freely tonal; closing in C. M-D.

Hermann Regner. *Klangspiele* 1971 (Schott WKS5) 23pp., parts. For piano duet (4 hands) and 4 percussion players. Schnell; Langsam; Schnell. Twelve types of percussion instruments used (timpani, xylophone, metalophone, drums, 4 cymbals, wood blocks, 2 rattles, 2 bongos, triangle, tambourine). In Hindemith style. Short. M-D.

Verne Reynolds. *Concertare III* 1969 (CF) 27pp., parts. 17½ min. Facsimile edition. For flute, oboe, clarinet, horn, bassoon, and piano. Slow: serial influence, pointillistic, dramatic gestures, fast figuration. Fast: atonal fugues; syncopated chords; sudden dramatic extremes; closing section utilizes improvisation; long pedals; large span required. Very Fast: contrapuntal fast lines move to a long stopping position by holding one low key. Slow: brief reference to opening. Strong dissonances. D.

Josef Rheinberger. *Sextet* Op.191b (Edition Compusic 416 ca.1992) 50pp., parts. For flute, oboe, clarinet, horn, bassoon, and piano. Arr. by the composer from his Piano Trio Op.191a. Preface in English.

Wallingford Riegger. *Concerto for Piano and Woodwind Quintet* Op.53 1953 (AMP) 44pp., parts. For flute, oboe, clarinet, horn, bassoon, and piano. Allegro: octotonic, Neoclassic, triplets in alternating hands, quartal and quintal harmonies. Andante: rhythmic figure in lower register, chromatic 5ths, trills, staccato 16ths in octotonic treatment. Allegro molto: triplets in alternating hands, changing meters, tritone exploited, octaves in lower register as well as chromatic octaves, large skips, *p* smorzando closing. D.

Albert Roussel. *Divertissement* Op.6 1905 (Sal) 17pp., parts. For flute, oboe, clarinet, bassoon, horn, and piano. Animé: lively use of 7th chords, vigorous rhythmic treatment, broken-chord triplets, arpeggio figuration. Lent: sustained chords in left hand under broken-7th-chord figuration in right hand. En animant en peu: rhythmic emphasis in chromatic figures, octotonic scales. Lent: same ideas as in other Lent section. Animé: like opening. Fun for all; imaginative and racy writing. M-D.

Karl Schiske. *Sextet* 1937 (UE 11209) 47pp., parts. For clarinet, 2 violins, viola, cello, and piano. Schreitend; Schnell und lustig; Langsam; Sehr bewegt. Strongly chromatic, big chords, sweeping lines, post-Romantic characteristics. M-D to D.

William Schmidt. *Concertino* (WIM 1969). For piano, 2 trumpets, horn, trombone, and bass tuba or tuba. Allegro con brio; Largo; Allegro con spirito. A combination of Classical form with post-Impressionist harmonies and rhythms peculiar to American jazz. M-D.

Jonathan Clarke Schwabe. *Variations in Gallant Style* 1996 (Alfia 1997) 8pp., parts. For flute, oboe, clarinet, horn, bassoon, and piano. Commissioned by the

Northern Indiana Ballet Theater for a production of *Peter Pan*. Short, light-hearted, funlike fluttering in the air. M-D.

Elliott Schwartz. *RiverScape* 2002 (ACA) 14 min. For clarinet, string quartet, compact disc playback, and piano. Performed from full score. "A wandering melodic motive (derived from such 'watery' sources as Siegfried's Rhine Journey and Ol' Man River) becomes the subject of contrasting variations. Some aleatoric, unsynchronized passages, some minimalist repetition. The compact disc contains actual river sounds and quoted fragments from well-known 'river pieces' " (from Composer's letter to authors).

Johann Strauss/Arnold Schönberg. *Rosen aus dem Süden* (Belmont 1031 1974) 28pp. For string quartet, harmonium, and piano. Arrangement of Strauss's Op.388 for sextet by Schoenberg, 1921. Four waltzes with introduction and coda. M-D.

Morton Subotnick. *Serenade I* 1959–60 (McGinnis & Marx) 30pp., parts. For flute, clarinet, cello, vibraphone, mandolin, and piano. Three untitled movements. Serial influence, changing meters, pointillistic, sectional, some sections marked "Freely," Expressionist, broad chromatic arpeggi gestures, Webernesque. Piano has some solos. D.

——. *Play I* 1964 (MCA) 19pp., parts. For flute, oboe, clarinet, bassoon, horn, piano, tape, and film. Film by Anthony Martin available on rental. Includes performance directions. Graphic and traditional notation. Clusters; glissandi; pianist must clap, stamp, "whine," and "freeze" to end of tape. Aleatoric. A fun piece. M-D.

Georg Philipp Telemann. *Concerto à 6* F (I. Hechler—Pegasus 6009) 24pp., parts. For alto recorder, bassoon or gamba or cello, 2 violins, viola or third violin, and basso continuo. Largo; Allegro; Grave; Allegro. Displays Telemann's well-known preference for unusual instrumental combinations and tone colors. M-D.

——. *Concerto* G (K. Flattschacher—Müller 97) 20pp., parts. For 2 violas (concertata), 2 violins, viola, and basso continuo. Avec douceur; Gay; Largo; Vivement. The editor warns against too rapid a tempo. This work stresses most ingeniously the peculiarity of the viola continuo realization by G. Frotscher. M-D.

——. *Konzert* F (M. Ruetz—HM 130) 16pp., parts. For alto recorder, 2 violins, viola, cello, and basso continuo. Affettuoso; Allegro; Adagio (violins 1 and 2 and viola tacet); Menuett 1 and 2. Excellent realizations. The Adagio, for solo recorder and keyboard, is very beautiful. M-D.

——. *Suite* F TWV 55:F9 (A. Hoffmann—Möseler 1975) 24pp., parts. For 2 oboes, 2 horns, bassoon, and basso continuo. Preface in German, French, and English. M-D.

Ludwig Thuille. *Sextet* Op.6 B♭ 1891 (Br&H) 63pp. For flute, oboe, clarinet, horn, bassoon, and piano. Allegro moderato; Larghetto; Gavotte; Finale. Said to be "a rewarding vehicle for piano and wind ensemble with its expert instrumental balance and sweeping lyricism" (NGD). Richly harmonic from a mid- to late-19th-century perspective with doublings and thick chords, it is one of a handful of chamber pieces for 5 to 8 instruments from the era. A gem waiting to be rediscovered. D.

Carl Vine. *Café Concertino* 1984 (Chester 1987) 45pp., parts available separately. 10 min. For flute (piccolo, alto flute), clarinet, violin, viola, cello, and piano. "*Café Concertino* revolves around the treatment of a simple cycle of fifths. Although in a single movement, the work contains four distinct sections. The first interprets the series C–G–D–A–E–B as a C major tonality, and the following series (F♯–C♯–G♯–D♯–A♯–E♯) as an F♯ major tonality. The complementary series of E♭–B♭–F–C–G–D and A–E–B–F♯–C♯–G♯ give the remaining tonal centres of A and E♭ respectively. This approach to fifths and the consequent tritones (C–F♯, E♭–A) continues through each section, with an emphasis on creating tonal ambiguity through chord inversion and octave doubling. The tonal 'centre' of the second section is A, while in the third, F♯ major and E♭ minor are visited alternately. The final section is a recapitulation centring on the tritone and its derivation from the cycle of fifths" (from Composer's Note). D.

——. *Elegy for Peter Harthoorn* (Chester 1987) 18pp. 7 min. For flute (piccolo), cello, trombone, piano (4 hands; 1st player doubling organ), and percussion.

Volker Wangenheim. *Klangspiel II* (Litolff 1973) 45pp., parts. 14 min. For flute, clarinet, cello, piano, percussion, and unspecified melodic instrument. Each performer also plays a number of percussion instruments. The character of the work calls for atonal improvisation. Diagrammatic notation in part. M-D to D.

Robert Ward. *Night under the Big Sky* (CFP 67787 1998) 15pp., parts. 9 min. For flute, oboe, clarinet, horn, bassoon, and piano. Subtitled "A Nocturne based on themes from [the opera] *Lady Kate.*" Cast in one continuous movement marked Andante con moto with solos for all instruments. Occasional mixed meters, 3 with 2, octaves, and chromatic relationships within a largely diatonic work in E♭. Large span required. M-D.

Adolph Weiss. *Sextet* 1947 (ACA) 76pp., parts. 18 min. For flute, oboe, bass clarinet, horn, bassoon, and piano. Adagio: chordal; sustained, spread-out sonorities; requires large span; moves to Allegro moderato: rhythmic punctuation in upper register; contrary chromatic patterns; syncopated (almost jazzy) melodies; alternating hands with triplets and chords; legato, flowing, uneven rhythmic patterns (5 in the space of 4, etc.); wide-spread chromatic arpeggi; complex rhythmic conclusion. Andante: flowing, atonal lines; pointillistic chords. Allegro: chromatic triplets accompany atonal melody that evolves into a more rhythmic guise; one section uses 5 eighths in the space of 6; corky conclusion. D.

Stefan Wolpe. *Piece in Two Parts for Six Players* 1961–62 (British & Continental Music Agencies) 79pp., parts. 9 min. For violin, clarinet, trumpet, cello, harp, and piano. Part One: ♩ = 72; changing meters; pointillistic; serial; some long pedals. Part Two: ♩ = 120; similar characteristics to Part I; perhaps a little more sustained; builds to exciting climax. Highly organized, complex. D.

Charles Wuorinen. *Speculum Speculi* (CFP) 39pp., parts. Reproduced from holograph. 14½ min. For flute, oboe, bass clarinet, double bass, percussion, and piano.

Iannis Xenakis. *Eonta* 1964 (Bo&H) 78pp., parts. For piano, 2 trumpets, and 3 trombones. "Eonta (= "being"—the present participle of the Greek verb "to be") is so entitled in homage to Parmenides ... The work makes use of stochastic music (based on the theory of probabilities) and of symbolic music (based on logistics). Some of the instrumental parts, notably the piano solo at the opening, were calculated on an IBM 7090 Computer at the Plâce Vendôme, Paris. The Greek characters in the full score have nothing to do with performance; they indicate choice of particular pitches and of logical operations, and serve as an *aide-mémoire* to analysis" (from Notes in the score). The solo piano opens the first 30 bars with a static, complex, 12-chord arrangement all over the keyboard. Brass are stereophonically disposed by moving about the piano in 3 different positions. Increasing rhythmic involvement for brass while the piano retains its basic rhythmic structure. Enormously D.

Music for Seven Instruments

Septets for Piano(s) and Miscellaneous Instruments

Theodore Antoniou. *Events III* 1969 (Br) 20pp., parts. 12 min. For flute, oboe, clarinet, bassoon, piano, 2 percussionists, tape, and slides. Contains extensive performance directions. "Events, musical and otherwise, determine the technique, form, and general function of all elements of the piece. At some level musical and extra-musical ideas are integrated. The way the material is combined (relation, antithesis, chance, etc.) determines the character of each movement. I. Analoga: homogeneous, analogous, relatives, glissandi on strings, harmonics, clusters, spatial and graphic notation. II. Paraloga: of different meaning, of abstract relation, of actual events. Sound events with a cadenza character are developed in various ways, at the same time as others (in strict tempo; tapes or synchronized passages), controlled within the general tempo and the maximum possibilities which the ensemble can achieve. The continuous change between 'free' and synchronized situations gives the impression of 2 different ensembles" (from Preface). A catalog of avant-garde techniques. D.

Larry Austin. *A Broken Consort* 1962 (MJQ) 33pp., parts. For flute, clarinet, trumpet, horn, percussion, piano, and double bass. Intrada: random improvisation using suggested pitch and rhythmic motifs; varying dynamic levels; piano treated percussively. Fancy: tremolo chords, complex rhythms, pointillistic. Funke: piano has a motif to repeat several times, growing faster and softer; piano cues others for reentry; involved rhythmic structure. Blue: sustaining piano pedal is held down throughout for strings to vibrate sympathetically. Dumpe: in a hard, swinging, jazz tempo; movement is concluded with improvisation; directions given. Coda: Amarissimo, strong emphatic gestures in all instruments. An interesting "third-stream" work. D.

Carl Philipp Emanuel Bach. *Sonatina* C (Dameck—Bo&Bo). For piano, 2 flutes, 2 violins, viola, and cello.
———. *Sonatine* d 1764 (F. Oberdörffer—Br 2006). For 2 flutes, 2 violins, viola, cello, and keyboard.

————. *Sonatine* E♭ 1766 (F. Oberdörffer—Br 2007) 20pp., parts. For 2 flutes, 2 violins, viola, cello, and keyboard. Largo; Allegro di molto; Tempo di Minuetto. A good deal of ornamentation. Tasteful realizations. M-D.

Johann Sebastian Bach. *Musikalisches Opfer* S.1079 (K. H. Pillney—Br&H 3863) 93pp., parts. For flute, 2 violins, viola, 2 cellos, and piano. Based on a theme by Frederick the Great. Includes realizations of the canons in modern clefs for various instrumentations, and of the figured bass for the keyboard. D.

William Bergsma. *Changes for Seven* (Galaxy 1975) 20pp., parts. 9 min. For flute, oboe, clarinet, bassoon, horn, percussion, and piano. One continuous movement with 5 different sections, numerous other tempo changes, flexible meters, a few clusters, many octaves for the pianist, interpretative directions, dramatic writing. D.

Wallace Berry. *Divertimento* 1964 (EV) 36pp., parts. For flute, oboe, clarinet, bassoon, horn, piano, and percussion. Preludio: serial; unwinding figuration; pointillistic; strong percussive use of piano; large span required. Moto costante: 32nd-note figuration; broken 9ths; chordal punctuation; flowing lines; *fff* conclusion. Improvisazione: free opening; ostinato-like figures expand over keyboard; dynamic extremes; sonorous and rubato but quiet ending. Sensitive sonorities. M-D to D.

Konrad Boehmer. *Zeitläufte* 1962 (Tonos 7217 1968) 31pp., parts. 15 min. For 2 pianos, English horn, clarinet, bass clarinet, horn, and trombone. Highly organized, serial, pointillistic, extreme registers exploited, dynamics attached to most notes, flexible meters and tempos, piano parts are of equal difficulty. Somewhat in the style of Boulez's *Structures* for 2 pianos. D.

Henry Brant. *The Marx Brothers: 3 Faithful Portraits* 1938 (CF 5340 1996, ISBN 0-82580-2583-0) 44pp., parts available on rental. For tin whistles, flutes, oboe or accordion, viola, cello, harp, and piano; tin whistles may be played by pianist if desired (parts do not overlap). I. Chico: sentimental, mincing; opens "café schmaltz" with tin whistles; turns to Faster section where piano commences in "Chico Marx style" with glissandi and instructions to "poke with forefinger" one note. II. Groucho: furious, in ⁶/₈; full chords; oompah-pahs; extended trills. III. Harpo: "cadaverous," commencing with whistles in cadenza-like style; cadenza for harp; piano enters later with full chords, rolling arpeggiation, and "wild, fast black-key glissandos ad lib" using the palms of hands which finish with palm smashes. First performed "on the roof of the St. Regis hotel in New York at one of the 'HI-LO' concerts organized by Vladimir Dukelsky (Vernon Duke)" (from Preface). Score is facsimile of MS. M-D to D.

Jolyon Smith Brettingham. *O Rise* Op.6 1973 (Bo&Bo) 18pp., parts. For flute, trombone, 2 percussionists, harpsichord, piano, and cello. Explanations in German and English.

John Cage. *Seven* 1988 (Henmar 1988). Parts without full score for flute, B♭ clarinet, percussion, piano, violin, viola, and cello. "There are twenty time-brackets, nineteen of which are flexible with respect to beginning and ending and one, a different one for each part, which is fixed" (from Introduction).

Matthew Camidge. *Sonatina* (C. Bowen—SP 1974) 12pp., parts. 3 min. For piano, 3 violins (or 2 violins and viola), viola, cello, and double bass. From *Ten Easy Sonatas for the Pianoforte or Harpsichord.*

Dinos Constantinides. *Study I for Diverse Instruments* 1990, rev. 1994 (Magni). 7½ min. For flute, clarinet, bassoon, vibraphone, cello, double bass, and piano. Uses a harmonic language "based on the intervals of the fourth and fifth, which are constantly worked out in various ways creating new tonal possibilities" (from Composer's web page: www.magnipublications.com).

Roque Cordero. *Permutaciones 7* (PIC 1967) 36pp., parts. For clarinet, trumpet, timpani, piano, violin, viola, and double bass. Sectional, highly organized, serial, piano part treated pointillistically, numerous dynamic markings, frequent meter changes. Requires experienced chamber music performers. D.

Eric Ewazen. *Devil Septet* 1973 (Seesaw 1976) 14pp., parts. For 4 tubas, 2 percussionists, and piano. One movement consisting of 8 sections ranging in tempo from adagio to allegro. Late-20th-century notation requiring nontraditional use of instruments. With few exceptions, glissandi on strings and hand/arm clusters on the keys are the sole use of the piano. Includes 2 improvisatory sections of 15 and 20 seconds at end. D.

Richard Felciano. *Crasis* (ECS) 39pp., parts. 8½ min. For flute, clarinet, violin, cello, harp, percussion, piano, and tape. Written after Felciano had seen a performance of a Noh drama by a troupe from Japan. The sound substance of *Crasis* is related to the Noh. "The notation, which includes miniature mobiles, is both traditional and proportional. As the work progresses, the relation of the live instruments to the electronic sounds proceeds from complement to fusion, hence the title (crasis: the joining of two vowels into one)" (from Preface). Clusters, pointillistic, aleatoric, avant-garde. D.

Morton Feldman. *The Straits of Magellan* (CFP 1962) 9pp. For flute, horn, trumpet, amplified guitar, harp, piano, and double bass. Box notation. "Each box is equal to MM 88. Numbers indicate the amount of sounds to be played within the duration of each box. Arabic numerals indicate single sounds for all the instruments except the piano, which interprets the numbers given as simultaneous sounds." Contains other detailed directions. Avant-garde. M-D.

——. *False Relationships and the Extended Ending* 1968 (CFP) 15pp. For 3 pianos, cello, violin, trombone, and chimes. Durations for simultaneous and single sounds are extremely slow. All sounds are connected without pause unless otherwise notated. Dynamic level is extremely low, but audible. Specific metronome marks are listed for many measures. Avant-garde. M-D.

——. *The Viola in My Life* (II) 1970 (UE 15400) 14pp., parts. 12 min. For piano, flute, clarinet, violin, viola (solo), cello, and percussion. Only a celesta part is notated for keyboard. The entire piece is to be played extremely quietly, all attacks at a minimum with no feeling of a beat. Only crescendo and decrescendo signs are used for dynamics. Celesta has only a chord, octave, or single note. Flexible meters. Sonority study. There are 4 separate and independent pieces by Feldman with the title *The Viola in My Life*. M-D.

Mikhail Glinka. *Serenade on Themes from Anna Bolena by Donizetti* (USSR Vol.4 [Supp.] of Complete Works) 17pp., parts. For piano, harp, horn, bassoon, viola, cello, and double bass. Introduzione; Cantabile; Moderato; Variations 1 and 2; Larghetto; Presto; Andante cantabile; Finale. Sectionalized, combination of melodious and glittering writing. Elegant salon style. M-D.

Jean Guillou. *Cantilia* 1968 (Leduc) 40pp., parts. 15 min. For piano, 4 cellos, harp, and timbales. One movement. Chromatic marcato figuration spread in upper register, octotonic, 7th chords, syncopated chromatic chords, quartal harmony, many added-note chords, fast harmonic rhythm. A long climax is shattered by a subito Lento e molto espressivo: low chromatic chords in the piano add color, *pp* ending. The style is reminiscent of Messiaen, but a unique and individual voice is speaking. Colorful sonorities. Large span required. M-D.

Johann Nepomuk Hummel. *Septet* Op.74 d 1818 (CFP 1304) 75pp., parts. For flute, oboe, horn, viola, cello, double bass, and piano. Allegro con spirito: emphatic chords, florid chromatic and scalar figuration, tremolo, broken octaves, turns, triplets with melodic significance, sweeping arpeggi, some unusual harmonic usage. Menuetto scherzo: capricious triplets in right hand versus dotted 8ths and 16ths in left hand; written-out turns; large skips; clever grace note usage in Alternativo, where piano takes on more importance. Andante con variazioni: folklike sentimental theme; varied pianistic figurations, including fast repeated notes, are used in the variations. Finale: fugal textures, fast octaves, idioms similar to those in other movements, tempestuous climax. Facile virtuoso writing. D.

——. *Military Septet* Op.114 (Musica Rara; Lienau) 48pp., parts. 24 min. For flute, clarinet, trumpet, violin, cello, double bass, and piano. Attractive, imaginative writing with a brilliant piano part. The title reflects the fact that the trumpet, not normally used in chamber music at that time, is featured. Three contrasting movements. D.

Andrew Imbrie. *Dandelion Wine* (SP 1970) 4pp., parts. For piano, oboe, clarinet, 2 violins, viola, and cello. "*Dandelion Wine* is the title of a novel by Ray Bradbury concerning memories of a boyhood spent in a small town. It described the bottling of dandelion wine, with each bottle dated. These became symbols of memory, since each date recalls a particular summer day and its activities. My piece attempts to implant and then, at the end, recall certain musical ideas in new context to give, if possible, the effect of poignant reminiscences, all 'bottled' in a very brief container. It was written in Princeton, at a time and place quite conducive to a mood similar to that invoked in the novel" (Notes in the score). Freely tonal, a few pointillistic gestures, thoroughly contemporary idiom. M-D.

Leoš Janáček. *Concertino* 1925 (Artia; IMC 35pp., parts) 19 min. For piano, 2 violins, viola, clarinet, horn, and bassoon. Moderato: dialogue between piano and horn, chromatic motifs, alternating hands, trills, widely imitated intervals, whimsical. Più mosso: dialogue between piano and clarinet, repeated chords, skipping staccato left hand, trills over chromatic lines, chromatic chords. Con moto: full ensemble utilized; 2nds and 7ths become part of the chromatic fabric; arpeggi; moving chromatic chords; piano cadenza. Allegro: sweeping chromatic patterns, energetic octave melodic line, highly chromatic, forceful octaves in recitative passages, 5 versus 4, hammered conclusion. D.

Willem Kersters. *Septet* Op.37 "De drie Tamboers" 1966 (CeBeDeM) 48pp., parts. 14 min. For 4 clarinets, percussion, kettledrum, and piano. Allegro spiritoso: octotonic melody, chromatic runs and figuration, large marcato chords, glissandi. Andante con moto quasi allegretto: sustained, triplet and quick chromatic figures, shifting meters, rhythmic punctuation. Tempo di marcia: rhythmic chords; chromatic runs and octaves; "De drie Tamboers" tune is heard in the piano, accompanied by percussion; chromatic runs and chords return to finish the movement in a *p* closing. M-D.

Wilhelm Killmayer. *Schumann in Endenich.* Kammermusik No.2 1972 (Schott 6431) 11pp. 6 copies necessary for performance. 8 min. For piano, organ, and 5 percussionists. Percussion required: glockenspiel, bass drum, timpani, vibraphone, marimba, gongs, tam-tam, bongos. Long pedal passages for piano, upper register exploited, percussive triplets in left hand with hammered-out punctuated octaves in right hand, clusters, unusual sonorities. M-D.

Karl Korte. *Matrix* 1967 (ECS) 47pp., parts. For flute, oboe, clarinet, horn, bassoon (alto sax is optional), piano, and percussion. Percussion required: medium-sized suspended cymbal, small tam-tam, 2 bongos (high-pitched), snare drum, one side drum pitched lower than the snare, thunder sheet, marimba, vibraphone. Pairs of hard, soft, and medium rubber beaters. Snare sticks and soft timpani sticks. "Due to variations in frame construction not all pianos are capable of producing all effects as notated. In this case, pianist is to rearrange pitches as needed in order to come as close as possible to the effect as notated" (Note in the score). Piano part: pointillistic; serial; requires harmonics; clusters with palms; stopped strings; metal-tipped pencil to be moved across strings;

sudden dynamic changes; black-and-white-key contrary motion glissandi at same time. Interesting and subtle sonorities. Avant-garde. D.

Jos Kunst. *No Time, XXI:4* 1974 (Donemus) 28pp., parts. Photostat of MS. For 3 clarinets, bass clarinet, piano, and 2 percussionists. Explanations in English.

Edward Laufer. *Variations for Seven Instruments* (New Valley Press 1967) 24pp. For flute, clarinet, bassoon, trumpet, violin, cello, and piano. Score is a reproduction of the MS. Parts are supplied for transposing instruments only; others use full score. Includes 2 leaves of isolated measures to be pasted into scores to facilitate page turns. Originally an orchestral work. Serially derived mainly from 9 pitches. Long exposition followed by 6 complex variations that develop ideas, followed by a short conclusion. Imaginative writing that requires a first-rate group with ensemble experience. D.

Anne LeBaron. *Telluris TheoriaSacra* 1989 (MMB 1989) 115pp. 29 min. For flute, clarinet, violin, viola, cello, 1 percussionist, and piano. In 4 movements: Sea Horse Tails–Opalescence; Strange Attractors; The Devil's Polymer; Vortex Trains–Albedos–Gravothermal Collapse. "The title *Telluris TheoriaSacra* is derived from Thomas Burnet's *Sacred Theory of the Earth* (published in 1689). The frontispiece of Burnet's treatise suggested the principal organizational scheme for this composition. Both linear and cyclical progressions of time on the earth are depicted on the frontispiece illustration: an eternal divine presence straddles a circular arrangement of seven globes showing the earth's recurrent cycle of genesis and dissolution. The first globe represents the original, formless, chaotic earth which coalesces into the perfect earth of Eden's paradise—a smooth, featureless, second globe. A great flood then consumes the earth (third globe). When the waters recede, the cracked crust of our current earth remains (fourth globe). The earth is next consumed by fire (fifth globe) and then becomes smooth again (sixth globe) as the falling ashes reestablish spherical perfection. Finally, the earth, no longer needed for human habitation, becomes a brilliant star (seventh globe). Seven musical 'forms' are incorporated into the four movements of *Telluris TheoriaSacra,* each of which corresponds, respectively, to the seven globes of Burnet's illustration" (Composer's Note). D.

Daniel Jean Yves Lesur. *Sextuor* (Amphion 1961) 33pp., parts. Transcribed for 6 clarinets and piano by Armand Birbaum. Nocturne; Ricercare; Berceuse; Tarentelle. Effective transcription, mildly 20th-century with Impressionist characteristics, generally thin textures, unusual sonorities. M-D.

Peter Tod Lewis. *Septet* (TP 1967) 27pp., parts. For flute, clarinet, bassoon, violin, viola, cello, and piano. First movement untitled: serial; sudden dynamic changes; pointillistic; broken minor 9ths used as accompaniment; chordal punctuation; quotes from the Berg *Sonata,* Op.1; large span required. Lullaby: sustained, wide dynamic range with *pppp* closing. M-D.

Teo Macero. *One-Three Quarters* (CFP 66178 1970) 11pp., parts. 8 min. For 2 pianos, piccolo/flute, violin, cello, trombone, and tuba. One piano is to be tuned down a quarter tone; strings play up or down a quarter tone at specific indication. Tremolando, octotonic, dramatic arpeggiated gestures, syncopation, chromatic chords. Extreme registers exploited; short sections are repeated. Colorful sonorities. M-D.

Bruce Mahin. *By Departing Light* 1996 (Pioneer Percussion) 20pp., parts. For 6 percussionists and piano. Based upon an original poem by the composer, incorporated into the score for recitation by all performers. Indeterminate writing with pitch and motivic patterns to be repeated within controlled time segments. Requires large percussion ensemble. M-D.

Giacomo Manzoni. *Musica Notturna* 1966 (SZ 6562) 22pp., parts. 9 min. For flute, clarinet, bass clarinet, horn, bassoon, piano, and percussion. Picturesque, quiet dynamics, chromatic, pointillistic, tremolo, atonal. Study in quiet and quieter sonorities. Large span required. M-D.

Bohuslav Martinů. *Rondi* 1930 (Artia 1954) 24pp., parts. For oboe, clarinet, bassoon, trumpet, 2 violins, and piano. Six pieces. Poco Allegro: major 7th chords, accented 9th chords, octotonic in upper register, octaves. Poco Andantino: ostinato-like, chromatic chords, repeated harmonic 5ths. Allegro: broken octaves, expanding chromatic intervals, cluster-like chords, alternating hands, tremolo, glissandi. Tempi di Valse: parallel chords, left-hand melody under right-hand chromatic chords. Andantino: rotational figures such as broken 3rds and 5ths, syncopated chords. Allegro vivo: staccato and legato arpeggi, alternating chromatic octaves. Most of the pieces are strongly rhythmic. An attractive set. M-D.

———. *Fantaisie pour Ondes Martenot* 1944 (ESC) 15 min. For Ondes Martenot, oboe, 2 violins, viola, cello, and piano.

Ignaz Moscheles. *Septet* Op.88 D ca.1840 (Musica Rara) 39pp., parts. For piano, clarinet, horn, violin, viola, cello, and double bass. Allegro con spirito; Scherzo; Adagio con moto; Finale. Orchestral conception with the piano predominant. M-D to D.

Luigi Nono. *Polifonica-Monodica-Ritmica* 1951 (Schott), miniature study score 20pp. 12 min. For flute, clarinet, bass clarinet, alto sax, horn, piano, and percussion. Percussion required: gran cassa, cassa chiara, 3 tamburi, 4 piatti, tom-tom, xylophone. Polifonica–Adagio–Allegro: ideas unraveled between instruments with fragments tossed back and forth. Monodica–Largo: slower fragmented ideas; repeated notes lead directly to Ritmica–Allegro moderato: triplet figures play important role; piano has stopped strings and percussive chords; *pppp* closing. M-D.

George Onslow. *Septuor* Op.79 B♭ 1851 (Kistner No. 1831) 41pp., parts. For piano, flute, oboe, clarinet, horn, bassoon, and double bass. Allegro moderato; Scherzo; Andante; Finale. Chromatic, many early Romantic traits. M-D.

Vincent Persichetti. *King Lear* Op.35 1948 (EV 1977) 79pp., parts. 19 min. For flute, oboe, clarinet, horn, bassoon, timpani, and piano. In 9 sections, each with descriptive titles, and most to be performed without pause. Rhythmic, bitonal, and serene qualities permeate within a variety of expressive contexts. First performed as *The Eye of Anguish,* "the means by which the tragic protagonist achieves insight and self-knowledge and at the end, redemption" (from the score). Requires well-seasoned performers for precise ensemble playing. Commissioned by Martha Graham. D.

Willem Pijper. *Septet* 1920 (Donemus 1949). For flute/piccolo, oboe/English horn, clarinet, bassoon, horn, double bass, and piano. Largo: parallel chords, widely spread arpeggiated chords over keyboard. Pastorale: duple and some triple meter, rocking motion, hemiola, broken parallel chords. Pantomine: alternating hands in bitonal patterns, humorous quasi-Valse, glissando lands on a chord à la Debussy. Passacaille: freely tonal subject; low martellato octaves; sustained sonorities in middle register while upper octaves move in triplets in top register; large chords. Peripetie: alternating hands, left-hand octaves with contrary right-hand chords, syncopation, *pp* closing. Strong Impressionist influences. M-D.

Raoul Pleskow. *Music for Seven Players* (Seesaw). For flute, cello, violin, clarinet, harp, piano, and percussion. Characteristic of this well-proportioned piece is a continual crossing and recrossing of chromatic space, which produces a mercurial sequence of flashing figuration, lit here and there from within by such stabilizing factors as a discreetly held harmony. It throbs with restlessness, and constantly changes direction and intention with stimulating poetry. M-D to D.

Francis Poulenc. *Rhapsodie Nègre* 1917 (JWC) 27pp., parts. For flute, clarinet, 2 violins, viola, cello, and piano; voice ad lib. Prélude: right-hand parallel chords over left-hand moving 9th chords, octotonic melodic treatment. Ronde: staccato left hand, right-hand syncopated melody, bitonal, stringendo whole-tone run. Honoloulou: voice used here, but piano can play this solo; all 7th chords (lent et monotone) except for whole-tone usage at end of movement. Pastorale: rocking harmonic 5ths in left hand with melody in right hand; luscious chords at end. Final: octotonic scales, glissandi on white and black keys. A fun work. M-D.

Leonard Rosenman. *Chamber Music V* 1980 (GS 1984) 135pp., parts on rental. 19 min. For piano (solo obligato), flute, clarinet, 2 percussionists, violin, and cello. Mixed meters, tones bent one-third and two-thirds sharp and flat, plus extensive percussion. Maintains steady tempo throughout with only slight changes in a constantly evolving context of polyrhythms. Requires keen and perceptive performers, especially for piano, where the instrument is frequently treated in solo, with unconventional technical demands. No time to sneeze in this complex late-20th-century work. D.

Camille Saint-Saëns. *Septet* Op.65 (Durand 49pp., parts; IMC 35pp., parts). 16 min. For piano, trumpet, 2 violins, viola, cello, and double bass. Allegro moderato; Menuet; Intermède; Gavotte et Final. Displays enormously facile writing for the piano. Chords, scales, broken-arpeggiated figuration, octaves in alternating hands, all completely pianistic. M-D.

Peter Schat. *Septet* (Donemus 1958) 12pp., parts. For flute, oboe, bass clarinet, horn, cello, piano, and percussion. Variaties: various sections with the following titles—Pianissimo; Scherzino; Con fuoco; Presto; Adagio—use such devices as long pedals, clusters, tremolo, sudden dynamic changes, large arpeggiated chords. Allegro: conventional notation throughout; chromatic; extremes in registers exploited; works to large climax then ends subito *pp;* large span required. Mildly 20th-century. M-D.

Arnold Schönberg. *Suite* Op.29 (UE 1927) 111pp., parts. 32 min. For 3 clarinets and piano quartet. Overture: a sonata that is overly long for the material employed. Tanzschritte (Dance Steps): ideas are transformed and embroidered, rhythms exploited. Thema mit Variationen: mastery of this form, high degree of inspiration felt. Gigue: scintillating charm, free Sonata style. Transparent scoring throughout, 12-tone. The 3 types of instruments (strings, clarinets, and piano) provide great contrast possibilities. Broken chords in piano part are effectively used. A work of trenchant complexity that unravels itself only after thorough study. D.

Ludwig Spohr. *Septet* Op.145 a (Musica Rara 1145) 94pp., parts. For violin, cello, flute, clarinet, bassoon, horn, and piano. Allegro vivace; Pastorale; Scherzo; Finale. M-D.

Rudi Stephan. *Musik für sieben Saiten-Instrumente* (Schott), parts only. For 2 violins, viola, cello, double bass, harp, and piano. Score is facsimile of MS. In 2 broad movements reflecting a late-19th-century style. Full chords. D.

Johann Strauss/Arnold Schönberg. *Kaiserwalzer* (Belmont) 33pp. For flute, clarinet, string quartet, and piano. Arrangement of Strauss's Emperor Waltz, Op.437, by Schoenberg in 1925. Four waltzes with introduction and coda. M-D.

Igor Stravinsky. *Septet* 1953 (Bo&H) 29pp., parts. 12 min. For clarinet, horn, bassoon, piano, violin, viola, and cello. First movement: SA seething with contrapuntal treatment. Passacaglia: built on a 16th-note subject developed serially. Gigue: same subject as the Passacaglia worked out in various fugues and rhythmic transformations. Serial techniques prominent, but this piece is basically Neoclassically and tonally (A) oriented. D.

See Hilmar Schatz, "Igor Stravinsky: Septett," *Melos* 25/2 (February 1958): 60–63; Erwin Stein, "Strawinsky's Septet (1953)," *Tempo* 31 (spring 1954): 7–11.

Zsigmond Szathmary. *Alpha* 1968 (Moeck 5055) 16pp., parts. 8 min. For flute/piccolo, clarinet/bass clarinet, trumpet, violin, viola, cello, and piano/celesta. Harmonics, serial, clusters, pointillistic, dynamic extremes, tremolo, Expressionist, complex ensemble problems. M-D to D.

Georg Philipp Telemann. *Concerto* a (I. Hechler—Schott 4968) 18pp., parts. For 6 melody instruments and basso continuo. Preface in French, German, and English. Adagio; Allegro; Affettuoso; Allegro. Realization is only a suggestion, but it is a good one. M-D.

_____. *Concerto* B♭ (H. Töttcher—Sikorski 494) 27pp., parts. For 3 oboes, 3 violins, and basso continuo. Allegro; Largo; Allegro. Graceful and dancelike. M-D.

_____. *Concerto* D (Kölbel—Heinrichshofen). For 2 flutes, 2 oboes, 2 violins, and basso continuo.

_____. *Concerto à 7* F (F. Brüggen, W. Bergmann—Schott RMS 1262) 19pp., parts. For 2 treble recorders, 2 oboes, 2 violins, and basso continuo. Grave; Vivace; Adagio–Allegro. M-D.

_____. *Ouverture à 7* C (G. Kehr—Schott 5916) 46pp., parts. For 3 oboes, 2 violins, viola, and basso continuo. Grave–Allegro; Harlequinade; Espagniol; Bourrée en Trompette; Sommeille; Rondeau; Menuette I, II; Gigue. M-D.

Joan Tower. *Black Topaz* 1976 (AMP 1976) 31pp., parts. 13 min. For flute, clarinet, trumpet, trombone, 2 percussionists, and piano. "Tower's *Black Topaz* derives from a drawing she once did of color rays emanating from a black, piano-like object. This single-movement work examines a similar projection of color from its focal point, the solo piano (black), to a six-member supporting instrumental ensemble. Tower selected each ensemble instrument specifically for its ability to magnify and extend the piano's timbral essence . . . Even the title *Black Topaz* reflects the work's *raison d'être:* topaz is a structurally stable, yellowish mineral which can, however, transform into various hues. *Black Topaz* was one of Joan Tower's first compositions to move away from an earlier quasi-serial style in favor of a more fluid, organic style. Here a large-scale musical architecture reigns, emphasizing metamorphosis of color and musical time, and an ever-increasing level of harmonic consonance" (Program Notes in score). D.

Renier Van Der Velden. *Concertino* 1965 (CeBeDeM) 44pp., parts. 12 min. For 2 pianos, 2 trumpets, horn, trombone, and tuba. One movement with varied moods and tempos. Serial, octotonic, chordal, scalar, atonal, trills. Pulls freely toward b. Both piano parts are of equal interest. Effective combination. M-D.

Ivan Vandor. *Musica per Sette Esecutori* (SZ 1967) 50pp., parts. 10 min. For harp, celesta, piano, 2 percussionists, violin, and cello. *ffff* arm clusters, percussive single notes, chordal, long pedals. A study in loud and rhythmic sonorities. Large span required. M-D.

Stefan Wolpe. *Piece for Two Instrumental Units* 1962 (McGinnis & Marx) 56pp., parts. For flute/piccolo, cello, piano, oboe, violin, double bass, and percussion. Percussion required: vibraphone, glockenspiel, bongos, xylophone. One unit consists of flute, cello, and piano; the second consists of the other instrumentation. Chordal, motivic material carefully transformed, cluster-like sonorities, dynamic extremes, pointillistic, proportional rhythmic relationships, lines interchanged between instruments, stopped strings, cumulative form, traces of Beethoven's *9th Symphony* appear, extremely complex ensemble problems. Requires large span. D.

Charles Wuorinen. *Tiento Sobre Cabezón* 1961 (ACA) 36pp., parts. 4 min. For flute, oboe, harpsichord, piano, violin, viola, and cello. Based on the "Tiento del Primer Tono" from the *Obras de Música para Tecla, Arpa, y Vihuela* (1578). Piano part is varied, some parts sustained, others staccato; flexible rhythmic usage; some alternating hand octaves. Mainly diatonic style; wide dynamic range. Instrumental combinations provide some unusual sonorities. M-D.

Yehudi Wyner. *Serenade* 1958 (CFE/AMP) 40pp., parts. 14½ min. For flute, horn, trumpet, trombone, viola, cello, and piano. Nocturne; Toccata; Capriccio–Aria; Nocturne II. "*Serenade* is a lyric, poetic work, remarkable in no way for its structural devices. No preconceived schemes were used, no preliminary formal plans imposed; the piece grew in an almost improvisatory way, formal decisions being reached in the writing, imposing themselves retroactively as it were, then affecting my further progress" (from Composer's Note, *Yehudi Wyner*, Composers Recording CD 701 1995, p.5). Nocturne I: ternary with coda, piano has a quasi-cadenza at end with broken chords in alternating hands. Toccata: through-composed sectional form, ostinato-like figures and dance rhythms, spread-out figuration. Capriccio: ternary with codas for B and second A, serial-like, pointillistic. Piano is melodically treated in opening half of the Aria and more rhythmically projected in the second half. Nocturne II: through-composed, repeated broken figuration, quiet, lines in other instruments. M-D.

——. *Passage* I 1983 (AMP). 9 min. For flute, clarinet, trumpet, violin, viola, cello, and piano. Dark, introspective, with strident harmonies and tense relationships; shows influence of Ives. "*Passage* deals with vernacular elements, with utterly familiar musical materials. A small collection of ordinary harmonies is set in motion in a manner reminiscent of American popular music of years ago. The harmonic web is surmounted and penetrated by strands and patches of melodic stuff, none of it really self-sufficient or substantial, but all of it conventional. It might not be misleading to compare *Passage* with an ostensibly bland street scene by Edward Hopper or an 'American Flag' by Jasper Johns" (from Composer's Note, *Yehudi Wyner,* Composers Recording CD 701 1995, p.7).

Vasily Zagorsky. *Rhapsody* 1968 (USSR) 55pp., parts. For 2 pianos, violin, and 4 percussionists. Percussion includes: timpani, small drum, legni, bells, triangle, tom-tom, campane, piatti, cassa, tam-tam, crotali, gong. One large colorful movement, in the style of Khachaturian. M-D.

Music for Eight Instruments

Octets for Piano(s) and Miscellaneous Instruments

William Albright. *Caroms* 1966 (Jobert) 34pp., parts. 7 min. For flute/alto flute, bass clarinet, trumpet, double bass, piano, celesta, and 2 percussionists. Percussion required: vibraphone, marimba, glockenspiel, large triangle, 2 suspended cymbals (high and low), bass drum, gong, large tam-tam. Vertical lines spaced throughout the first part of the score represent seconds and should be used only as an indication of the approximate spacing of events. Notes are to be played according to their placement on the page and their spatial relationships to each other. Contains other performance directions. Pointillistic, many major 7th chords, dynamic extremes, tremolando, clusters. Pianist must whistle. Avant-garde, sonority-oriented. D.

Joseph Alexander. *Three Pieces for Eight* (Gen) 109pp., parts. For flute/piccolo, clarinet, trumpet, violin, cello, double bass, piano, and percussion. Percussion required: timpani, snare drum, maracas, triangle, tenor drum, xylophone, cymbal, small bass drum, wood block. Facsimile of the MS. Allegro brillante: bitonal syncopated chords, octotonic, strong rhythms. Presto gaio: vigorous, driving rhythms, contrary chromatic scales and arpeggi, parallel broken-chord figures, grazioso contrasting section. Moderato: mixed bravura and lyric writing, poco meno mosso section, strong marcato ending. More technical than interpretative problems. D.

Milton Babbitt. *All Set* 1957 (AMP) 50pp., parts. 8 min. For alto sax, tenor sax, trumpet, double bass, trombone, percussion, vibes, and piano. A sophisticated and brilliant serial work that uses cool, glossy jazz techniques. Breathless rhythmic vivacity and a good deal of intellectual stimulus are both brought out with the jazz-band instrumentation. M-D to D.

Mily Balakirev. *Octet* Op.3 c (Musica Rara; I. Jordan—USSR 1959 65pp., parts). For piano, flute, oboe, horn, violin, viola, cello, and double bass. In the USSR edition editor's notes and comments are in Russian and English. Editorial additions are given in square brackets. Only the first movement was completed by Balakirev. Allegro molto: SA, heroic theme, arpeggiation, chromatic scales, chords and octaves in alternating hands, tremolando; second tonal area introduced in e but quickly moves to f. M-D.

Lennox Berkeley. *Diversions* Op.63 1964 (JWC 1983) 41pp., parts on rental. 18 min. For oboe, clarinet, bassoon, horn, violin, viola, cello, and piano. Adagio; Vivace; Lento; Allegro. The piano is an essential instrument but is not played throughout. Textural and stylistic qualities are contrasted in this mid-20th-century work. Occasionally identified as Octet. M-D to D.

Earle Brown. *Novara* 1962 (UE 15383 1979) 4pp. 6–12 min. For flute, bass clarinet, trumpet, piano, 2 violins, viola, and cello. Chance music with graphic notation consisting of 5 events on each page. Requires a conductor. The composer notes: "For me, the concept of the elements being mobile was inspired by the mobiles of Alexander Calder . . . [and] the concept of the work being conducted and formed spontaneously in performance . . . by the 'action-painting' techniques and works of Jackson Pollock in the late 1940's." Extensive performance directions included in English and German. D.

Wen-Chung Chou. *Yün* 1969 (CFP) 37pp., parts. For flute, clarinet, bassoon, horn, trumpet, trombone, piano, and percussion. Reproduced from holograph. "Yün, from the expression 'ch'i yün,' foremost principle in Chinese art and poetry, means 'reverberations in nature'" (from the score). Large percussion battery, one page of symbol explanations. Piano participation is minimal but integral. The pianist is required to stop and pluck strings. Some pointillistic treatment, sensitive and usually thin textures throughout, fascinating sonorities. M-D.

Aldo Clementi. *Concerto* (SZ 1975) 16pp., parts. 8 min. For piano (2 or 4 hands), 3 violas, horn, bassoon, trumpet, and electric harmonium. The harmonium sustains a given tone cluster throughout the work by means of a wooden board held down by a weight. Instructions for performance in Italian and English. Avant-garde.

Henry Cowell. *A Composition* 1925 (CFP 6974 1988) 28pp., parts on rental. 9 min. For piano, oboe, clarinet, bassoon, and string quartet. In 3 untitled movements. Largo: piano plays entirely on the strings, plucking and gliding in proportional rhythmic relationships. Allegretto con moto: violin and piano only, the latter using both keys and strings, with the former almost exclusively in proportional rhythm. Presto: string quartet and piano only, requiring metal object and chisel to use inside piano. An intriguing piece requiring previous experience in the interior of the piano. D.

Paul Creston. *Ceremonial* Op.103 (GS 1973) 32pp., parts. 4½ min. For piano and 7 percussion players. Explanation of tone cluster symbols is given. A 12-bar introduction is followed by Allegro for the rest of the work. The piano part provides low chordal sonorities during much of the piece, although the upper register is shown off a few times. Effective ensemble writing for this unusual combination. M-D.

Paul Dessau. *Quattrodramma* 1965 (Bo&Bo) 31pp., parts. For 2 pianos, 4 cellos, and 2 percussionists. Serial, harmonics, pointillistic, subdivided rhythms, long trills, double glissandi, atonal, *ppp* closing. Three quotations from Sean O'Casey are given near the end. M-D to D.

Jacques Dupont. *Octuor* Op.4 1930 (Hamelle) 51pp., parts. For clarinet, bassoon, horn, 2 violins, viola, cello, and piano. One movement, ABA plus coda; chordal introduction (Très large); Allegro con fuoco has a syncopated rhythmic subject. Chromatic chords and figures, Impressionist, tremolando, *ppp* broken-chord conclusion. M-D.

Gottfried von Einem. *Steinbeis-Serenade* Op.61 1980/81 (UE 17452 1981) 30pp. 11 min. For oboe, clarinet, bassoon, horn, trumpet, piano, violin, and cello. Eight variations on a theme from Mozart's *Don Giovanni* with sharply contrasting characters, tempos, and textual treatment for each. Written for and dedicated to Hermann Steinbeis on his 70th birthday. D.

Morton Feldman. *Between Categories* 1969 (CFP 6971) 9pp., parts. Photostat of MS. For 2 pianos, 2 chimes, 2 violins, and 2 cellos. "Durations of simultaneous and single sounds are extremely slow. All sounds are connected without pauses unless otherwise notated. The dynamic level is extremely low, but audible" (from the score). Changing meters, unusual subtle chordal sonorities throughout, avant-garde. Requires large span. M-D.

Roberto Gerhard. *Concert for Eight* 1962 (OUP) 91pp., parts. 10½ min. For flute, clarinet, guitar, percussion, double bass, piano, mandolin, and accordion. "My intention was to write a piece of chamber music in the nature of a Divertimento, almost in the spirit of the *commedia dell'arte*. The eight instruments are introduced somewhat in the manner of *dramatis personae,* but the play itself consists of purely musical events, and must not be taken as evoking or illustrating any extra-musical parallels whatever. From the conventions of the *commedia* two have been adopted: that of extempore invention and, sometimes, that of disguise or masking—by which I mean unusual ways of playing the instruments. The piece falls into eight sections, which are played without a break" (from Composer's Note). Changing meters, extreme registers exploited, pointillistic, repeated notes, long pedals, unusual sonorities. M-D.

Ray Green. *Three Pieces for a Concert* (EBM 1958) 11pp., parts. For flute, 2 clarinets, 2 trumpets, trombone, percussion, and piano. Percussion required: snare and bass drums, cymbals, triangle. March; Quiet Song; Piece to End. Contrasting, mildly 20th-century, attractive, M-D.

Tibor Harsanyi. *L'Histoire du Petit Tailleur* 1939 (ESC 1950) 76pp., parts. 25 min.; with recitation, 30 min. For flute, clarinet, bassoon, trumpet, piano, violin, cello, and percussion. Thirteen short movements to go with Grimms' *Fairy Tales.* Requires a rather large percussion battery. Mildly 20th-century, chromatic style, attractive. Similar to Poulenc's *L'Histoire de Babar.* M-D.

Joaquin Homs. *Music for Eight* 1964 (Seesaw) 38pp., parts. For flute, clarinet, violin, viola, cello, trumpet, piano, and percussion. Passacaglia: serial; row evolves through various guises. Derivaciones: pointillistic, repeated notes, octotonic, octaves, syncopated chords. Poorly reproduced copy of MS. D.

Leoš Janáček. *Capriccio for Solo Piano (Left Hand) and Seven Instruments* 1926 (Artia 1953) 18½ min. For piano, flute/piccolo, 2 trumpets, 3 trombones, and tenor tuba. Four movements. Treatment of the parts causes this work to straddle the field of chamber and solo-accompaniment music. Virtuosity is avoided, thereby making the work more like a Sonata for concerted instruments. Originally called *Defiance,* moments of solemn disapproval are contrasted with intimate and quiet moods. "According to the correspondence and some authentic statements, *Capriccio* expresses a revolt against the cruel destiny" (Note in the score). Melodic treatment simulating speech and cryptic motifs stand out in bold relief. Tense, emotional writing. D.

Paul Juon. *Octet* Op.27a B♭ (Lienau 1905) 80pp., parts. For oboe, clarinet, bassoon, horn, violin, viola, cello, and piano. Allegro non troppo: SA, sequences, chromatic, octotonic, fast harmonic rhythm, scalar; large span required. Andante elegiaco: melodic and chordal. Allegro non troppo quasi moderato: triplets, staccato octotonic writing, sweeping chords. Moderato: chordal, octaves, in Brahms-Dohnányi tradition. M-D.

Karl Kohn. *Introduction and Parodies* 1967 (CF 1972) 23pp., parts. 23 min. Facsimile edition. For clarinet, horn, bassoon, string quartet, and piano. Largo: pointillistic; chromatic clusters silently depressed and struck with stiff, flat hand, crisp and staccato; coda for solo piano starts with instruments entering at specific points and then treats materials in aleatoric fashion; directions for performing Coda I are given; Coda II follows and quickly concludes the movement. Allegro con brio: piano not used until near the end of the movement; "Fragments and Cadenza" section also includes extensive notes describing entrances, etc. Aleatoric. Pianist must give many signals. For the adventurous who are especially looking for unusual sonorities. D.

Gail Kubik. *Divertimento II* 1958 (MCA) 44pp., parts. 10½ min. For flute/piccolo, oboe, clarinet, bassoon, trumpet, trombone, viola, and piano. Overture and Pastorale: bright; thin textures; cheerful tunes; slightly frantic; joined without break to the first of 2 Pastorales, both of which are leisurely, flowing, and meditative in character. Scherzino–The Puppet Show: fast and furious opening sets the scene; woodwinds have much dialogue suggesting Punch and Judy. Dialogue: a short, intimate conversation between oboe and viola. Dance Toccata: bright sounds and abrupt rhythmical changes; returns the divertimento to its happy and gay mood. Mildly 20th-century. M-D.

Jacques Lenot. *Solacium* 1974 (Amphion 339) 50pp., parts. For piano, flute/alto flute, oboe/English horn, clarinet/bass clarinet, harp, violin, viola, and cello. Highly organized (pitch, rhythm, dynamics) work, complex rhythms, pointillistic, strong dissonance. Only for the most adventurous and experienced group. Avant-garde. D.

John Lewis. *Sketch* 1959 (MJQ Music 1960) 15pp. 5½ min. For vibraphone, piano, 1 percussionist, double bass, 2 violins, viola, and cello. Blends jazz qualities with traditional string quartet. Piano part is largely improvisational on suggested chords. Int.

Peter Lieberson. *King Gesar* 1991–92 (GS). 60 min. For flute (piccolo), clarinet (bass clarinet), horn, trombone, percussion, cello, and 2 pianos. Requires narrator for text by Douglas Penick, inspired by Alexandra David Neel's *The Superhuman Life of Gesar of Ling.* King Gesar was a legendary 10th-century Tibetan ruler.

Donald Martino. *Serenata Concertante* 1999 (Dantalian 517 1998) 58pp., parts. 26 min. Octet for flute (alto flute, piccolo), clarinet (bass clarinet), flügelhorn (cornet), horn, percussion, piano, violin, and cello. I. Passeggiata, II. Scherzi (Intermezzo), III. Meditazioni, IV. Scherzo (Intrada), V. In Memoriam Earl Kim. Percussion required: 5 temple blocks, snare drum, 2 bongo drums, 2 timbales, 2 tom-toms, medium and large suspended cymbals, marimba, vibraphone, and glockenspiel. Expressionist with changing meters, dynamic extremes, and intricate parts. Requires considerably accomplished performers. D.

Francis Miroglio. *Phases* (UE 14691 1968) 15pp., parts. MS reproduced, easy to read. For flute, piano, violin, viola, cello, and 3 percussionists. May be played in the following 4 forms: 1. flute and piano; 2. flute, piano, and string trio; 3. flute, piano, and 3 percussion; 4. flute, piano, string trio, and 3 percussion. The order of sections A, B, C, D, and E may be varied. In version 4 it is left to the flutist to decide whether to move about the stage in accordance with the included diagram. Colored spotlights point up the changes of location and illuminate the accompanying groups. Numerous notational directions. Harmonics, tremolo, pointillistic, avant-garde. D.

Ottorino Respighi. *Suite della Tabacchiera* A♭ (Ricordi 1984) 34pp., parts. For 2 flutes/piccolo, 2 oboes/English horn, 2 bassoons, and piano 4-hands. Preludio; Minuetto; Finale. Atmospheric and conventional writing for piano duettists with parts stretching across the full keyboard in Preludio, contrasted by a classically oriented Minuetto, and a spirited Finale. M-D.

Ferdinand Ries. *Octet* Op.128 A♭ (Musica Rara) 25pp., parts in the original Probst edition (Leipzig). For clarinet, bassoon, horn, violin, viola, cello, double bass, and piano. Allegro; Andante; Rondo. Straightforward writing with brief Romantic intrusions; uses the traditional pianistic idioms of the day. Thematic material is frequently given to the piano in this attractive and unpretentious work. M-D.

Anton Rubinstein. *Octet* Op.9 D (CFP). For piano, violin, viola, cello, flute, clarinet, horn, and double bass. Beethoven influence noted. Each instrument has a share in the total work, but the conception of the piece is somewhat shallow, and a lack of integration is obvious. M-D to D.

Elliott Schwartz. *Octet* 1971 (ACA) 16pp., no separate parts. For flute, oboe, clarinet, violin, cello, percussion, and 2 keyboard players (piano, celesta, harpsichord, music boxes, and drum sticks). Performance directions included. A performance consists of 2 movements separated by the Interlude. Contains directions for aleatoric sections. Each notational section equals 15 seconds. Free entrances are selected by performers within duration of brackets. Uses clusters, loud whispers, string sweeping. Pianist must slap under the keyboard and strike strings with mallets, slam keyboard cover, snap and clap, finger trill on case. Avant-garde. D.

——. *Spirals* 1985 (MMB/Norruth) 15 min. For flute, clarinet, string quartet, double bass, and piano. Performed from full score. "A series of variations based on two different tone-rows (Stravinsky's *Variations* and Britten's *Turn of the Screw*, the latter alluded to in this work's title). Extreme style contrasts. Many of the performers double on simple percussion parts (bass drum, tom toms, etc.)" (from Composer's letter to authors).

Felix Weingartner. *Octuor* Op.73 G (Birnbach 1925) 112pp., parts. For clarinet, horn, bassoon, 2 violins, viola, cello, and piano. Allegro; Andante; Tempo di Menuetto; Allegro moderato. Clear forms, sufficient originality to make for some interest, composite style. M-D.

Charles Wuorinen. *Octet* 1962 (McGinnis & Marx) 111pp., parts. For piano, oboe, clarinet, horn, trombone, violin, cello, and double bass. Pointillistic, hand and forearm clusters, wide dynamic range, highly chromatic, glissandi, Expressionist, extreme ranges exploited, flexible meters, octotonic. Wide span required. D.

Anthologies and Collections

Piano and Violin

Böhmische Violinsonaten 2 vols. (S. Gerlach, Z. Pilková, H.-M. Theopold, K. Röhrig—Henle 334-5 1982–85). Contains 9 Sonatas by Bohemian composers from about 1730 to 1810. *I.* 45pp., parts, with basso. Wenzeslaus Wodiczka: G. Franz Benda: C. Johann B. Neruda: a. Johann Stamitz: D. Anton Kammel: A. Figured-bass realizations by Sonja Gerlach. *II.* 82pp., parts. Joseph Mysliweczek: D. Johann Baptist Wanhall: d Op.43/3. Joseph Anton Steffan: B♭. Johann Ladislaus Dussek: Op.69/1 B♭. Preface in German, English, and French. M-D.

Französische Violinmusik der Barockzeit 2 vols. (G. Meyn-Beckmann, S. Petrenz, E. Sebestyen—Henle 352-3 1991–92). Contains 14 Sonatas by French composers of the Baroque. *I.* 63pp., parts, with basso. Jean-Baptiste Senallié: g Livre V/9. Jacques Aubert: G Livre V/4. François Duval: b Livre VI/4. Jean-Joseph Mondonville: a Op.I/6. Pierre Miroglio: F Op.I/5. Etienne Mangean: e Op.4/2. Jean-Marie Leclair l'Aîné: G Livre IV/7. *II.* 63pp., parts, with basso. Jean-Baptiste Anet: e Op.III/3. Louis-Antoine Dornel: b "La Sauvion" Op.II/5. Jean-Baptiste Quentin: A Livre I/1. Antoine Dauvergne: E Op.II/11. François Francœur: g Livre II/6. Charles-Antoine Branche: F Livre I/2. Jean-Marie Leclair l'Aîné: b Livre II/11. Figured-bass realizations by Siegfried Petrenz. Preface in German, English, and French. M-D.

Hebrew Melodies (E. Wen—CF 2001 ISBN 0-8258-4447-9) 127pp., parts. Includes introductory notes. Joseph Achron: *Hebrew Lullaby* Op.35/2, *Hebrew Dance* Op.35/1, *Hebrew Melody* Op.33. Ernest Bloch: *Baal Shem, Abodah.* Josef Bonime: *Danse Hebraïque.* Eddy Brown: *Hebrew Folk Song and Dance.* Abraham Goldfaden: *Rozhinkes mit Mandlen* (trans. A. Collins). George Perlman: *Ghetto Sketches, Suite Hebraïque.* Lazare Saminsky: *Hebrew Rhapsody* Op.3/2. Jacob Koppel Sandler: *Eili, Eili* (trans. M. Elman). Joseph Sulzer: *Sarabande on the G-String* Op.8. Traditional: *Kol Nidre* (trans. M. Pilzer). Mark Warshawsky: *Oyfn Pripetshik* (trans. J. Belov). Leo Zeitlin: *Eli Zion* (trans. J. Achron). M-D to D.

Houslové Sonáty Českého Baroka (Violinsonaten des Böhmischen Barocks) Vol.18 in *Musica Viva Historica* (R. Tillinger—Supraphon 1981) 37pp., parts, including basso. Contains 3 Baroque Bohemian Sonatas. Jiří Čart: *Sonata* C. Antonín Kammel: *Sonata* B♭. Bedřich Ludvík Benda: *Sonata* G. Preface in Czech and German.

Italienische Violinmusik der Barockzeit 2 vols. (P. Brainard, S. Petrenz, K. Röhrig—Henle 350-1 1985–89), parts, with basso. Contains 25 works, all Sonatas unless otherwise noted below, by Italian composers of the Baroque. *I.* 83pp., Giuseppe Torelli: d Op.4/2; D

Op.4/11. Antonio Veracini: c Op.2/8; B♭ Op.3/6. Arcangelo Corelli: D Op.5/1. Francesco Geminiani: B♭ Op.1/5; C Op.4/3. Pietro Locatelli: c Op.6/5; d Op.6/12. Giuseppe Tartini: Sinfonia C; d. *II.* 107pp., Carlo Farina: d. Giovanni Battista Fontana: C. Giovanni Maria Bononcini: Allemanda, Corrente (La Fogliana) f Op.4; Aria, Corrente, Sarabande (La Fontana) F Op.4. Arcangelo Corelli: e Op.5/8. Michele Mascitti: E Op.2/10; g Op.2/14. Antonio Vivaldi: B Op.5/15. Tommaso Albinoni: A. Francesco Maria Veracini: b Op.1/3; B♭ Op.1/8; d Op.2/12. Carlo Tessarini: Allettamento G; Trattenimento A. Figured-bass realizations by Siegfried Petrenz. Preface in German, English, and French. M-D.

37 Violin Pieces You Like to Play (P. Mittell—GS 1943) 179pp., parts. Contains well-known classics by composers from the Baroque to the early 20th century. Alfredo d'Ambrosio: *Canzonetta* g. J. S. Bach: *Air on the G String* (arr. A. Wilhelmj). Luigi Boccherini: *Menuet* from *Quintet* E (arr. F. Hermann). Gaetano Braga: *La Serenata* (trans. A. Pollitzer). Johannes Brahms: *Cradle-Song* Op.49/4 (arr. F. Hermann). Max Bruch: *Kol Nidrei.* Claude Debussy: *Beau Soir* (arr. A. Hartmann). Franz Drdla: *Souvenir.* Riccardo Drigo: *Valse-Bluette* (trans. L. Auer). Gabriel Fauré: *Aurore* (arr. A. Hartmann). Rudolf Friml: *Chanson.* Jean Baptiste Gabriel-Marie: *La Cinquantaine (Air dans le style ancien).* Ernest Gillet: *Loin du Bal.* Benjamin Godard: *Berceuse* from *Jocelyn.* G. F. Handel: *Largo* G. Franz J. Haydn: *Serenade* C. Victor Herbert: *Canzonetta* B♭. Jenö Hubay: *Hejre Kati* (Scene from the Czárda). Kéler-Béla: *The Son of the Puszta* Op.134/2. Emil Mlynarski: *Mazurka* G. Moritz Moszkowski: *Serenata* (trans. F. Rehfeld). Jacques Offenbach: *Belle Nuit (Barcarolle* from *Tales of Hoffmann).* I. J. Paderewski: *Melody* G. Gabriel Pierné: *Sérénade* A. Fabian Rehfeld: *Spanish Dance.* Camille Saint-Saëns: *Le Cygne* (The Swan). François Schubert: *L'Abeille* (The Bee). Franz Schubert: *Ave Maria* (arr. A. Wilhelmj), *Serenade (Leise flehen meine;* arr. H. Sitt). Achille Simonetti: *Madrigale* D. Johan S. Svendsen: *Romance.* P. I. Tchaikovsky: *Canzonetta* from *Violin Concerto.* Henri Vieuxtemps: *Rêverie* (Adagio). Richard Wagner: *Träume (Dreams), Walther's Prize-Song* from *Die Meistersinger* (paraphrased by A. Wilhelmj). Henri Wieniawski: *Obertass (Mazurka), Romance* from *Second Concerto.* Int. to D.

Treasury of Music by Women before 1800 (W. Bauer—Ars Femina EAF 37-11 1994) 38pp., parts. For the young violinist, designed as a supplement to the Suzuki method, Vols. 1–3. Louise Duval: *Two Passepieds.* Sophie von Braunschweig: *Baurentanz.* Teodora Gines: *Son de la Ma Teodora.* Antonia Bembo: *Ballet, Menuet, Gigue.* Elisabeth-Claude Jacquet de la Guerre: *Air de Violon, The Trumpet, Air for the Athenians, March of King Nereus, The Shepherds, Rondeau* (for 2 violins), *Bouree* (for 2 violins). Elisabeth Ahlefeldt: *Canary Trio.* Wilhelmine von Bayreuth: *Gavottes I, II.* Int. to M-D.

Unbeaten Tracks (E. H. Jones—Faber 1999 ISBN 0-571-51914-8) 34pp., parts. Eight contemporary pieces with Preface and short biographies. The collection "springs from the need—felt by many players, teachers, and composers—for real 'new music' for less advanced players ... who perhaps have a limited technique. At the same time the composer's own distinctive language has not been comprised or watered down" (from Preface). Graham Fitkin: *Glass.* Christopher Fox: *Crossing the Border.* Michael Zev Gordon: *Grace.* Eddie McGuire: *Reflection.* William Sweeney: *The Ballad of the Cat and the Ram.* Dominic Muldowney: *Lear's Fool.* Errollyn Wallen: *Woogie Boogie.* John Woolrich: *Midnight Song.* Int. to M-D.

Venezianische Sonaten (C. Schneider, G. Hambitzer—UE 17-595 1998, ISMN M-008-05877-6). For oboe or violin. See details below under piano and oboe.

Piano and Viola

Cztery utwory Kompozytorów polskich (J. Kosmala—PWM 8208) 31pp., parts. Contains 3 works for viola and piano by Polish composers. Henri Wieniawski: *Legenda* Op.17. Karol Szymanowski: *Taniec z 'Harnasiów'*. Arthur Malawskí: *Siciliana: Rondo na tematy Janiewicza*. Also includes Grażyna Bacewicz: *Kaprys polski* for solo viola. M-D to D.

The Virtuoso Violist (W. Primrose—GS 1995) 78pp., parts. Contains 2 original works: Boris Myronoff's *Caprice* and Efrem Zimbalist's *Sarasateana*, and transcriptions of works originally for other instruments, notably Henryk Wieniawski's *Caprice* (originally for violin). M-D.

Piano and Cello

Frauen Komponieren/Female Composers: 14 Stücke/Pieces (B. Heller, E. Rieger—Schott 8628 1999 ISMN M-001-11596-4) 94pp., parts. Contains 14 short to medium-length pieces by 12 European female composers of the 19th to 20th centuries. Marie Wieck: *Fantasie über Skandinavische Volkslieder*. Luise Adolpha Le Beau: *Romanze*, Op.24/1. Clara Faisst: *Melodie nach einer alten Ballade*. Johanna Senfter: *Drei Stücke*, Op.25. Lucie Vellère: *Nocturne*. Verdina Shlonsky: *Dialog*. Myriam Lucia Marbe: *Prophet und Vogel*. Barbara Heller: *Lalai*. Lucie Robert-Diessel: *Lamento*. Elena Firsova: *Album- blatt*, Op.67. Violeta Dinescu: *flash across*. Caroline Ansink: *Water under the Bridge*. Int. to D.

The Great Cello Solos (J. L. Webber—JWC 1992, ISBN 0-7119-2998-X) 39pp., parts. Con- tains 7 original and/or adapted works by 5 French and German composers from the Baroque through the 19th century. "The purpose of this collection is to bring the es- sential short pieces for the cello together in one attractive volume. Great care has been taken to make use of the composers' original editions, and editorial markings have, I trust, been kept to a helpful minimum" (Note by Editor). Camille Saint-Saëns: *Allegro Appassionato; The Swan*. Gabriel Fauré: *Après un rêve; Elégie*. Johann Sebastian Bach: *Arioso*. Max Bruch: *Kol Nidrei*. Felix Mendelssohn: *Song without Words* (D; an original work). M-D.

Violoncello Classics: A Collection of Original Pieces and Arrangements for Violoncello, with Accompaniment of Piano 2 vols. (L. Schulz—GS 1900), parts. Contains 32 works by European composers of the 19th century. Includes some operatic transcriptions. Vol.I, 71pp. Woldemar Bargiel: *Adagio* Op.38. Carl Davidoff: *Romance sans paroles* Op.23. Jean Gabriel-Marie: *Sérénade badine*. Benjamin Godard: *Berceuse* from *Jocelyn*. D. van Goens: *Scherzo* Op.12/2. Georg Goltermann: *Cantilena*. Jules Massenet: *Mélodie* Op.10/ 5. C. Matys: *Romance* Op.32. Jacques Offenbach: *Musette*. David Popper: *Widmung*, Op.11/1. Camille Saint-Saëns: *Romance* Op.51. Franz Schubert: *Moment Musical* Op.94/ 3. Leo Schulz: *To the Evening Star* from *Tannhäuser*. Robert Schumann: *Adagio* from *Concerto* Op.129. Peter Tschaikowsky: *Andante cantabile*. L. Zeleński: *Berceuse* Op.32. Vol.II, 75pp. Max Bruch: *Kol Nidrei* Op.47. Adolph Fischer: *Romance* Op.5. Jean Gabriel- Marie: *La Cinquantaine*. Benjamin Godard: *Sur le Lac*. D. van Goens: *Romance sans paroles* Op.12/1. Georg Goltermann: *Romance* Op.17; *Saltarello* Op.59/2. Sebastian Lee: *Gavotte* Op.112. A. Nölck: *Wiegenlied* Op.2. David Popper: *Sarabande and Gavotte* Op.10; *Herbstblume* Op.50/5. Bernhard Romberg: *Andante* from *Concerto No. 2*. Xaver Scharwenka: *Mazurek*. Francis Thomé: *Andante religuoso*. B. Triebel: *Ein Albumblatt* Op.5. Leo Schulz: *Andante* from *Orpheus and Eurydice*. Int. to M-D.

Willeke's Violoncello Collection: Thirty Solo Pieces for Violoncello with Piano Accompaniment 2 vols. (W. Willeke—GS 1939), parts. Contains 30 original and trans. works by European composers from the late Baroque to the early 20th century. Vol.1, 64pp. Frédéric Chopin: *Largo* from the *Violoncello Sonata* Op.65. Archangelo Corelli: *Sarabanda.* Rudolf Dietrich: *Konju-Raku (Old Chinese Dance).* Friedrich Grützmacher: *Fantaisie Hongroise* Op.7; *Notturno* Op.32/1. Georg Frideric Handel: *Largo* from the *Sonata F* (trans. by Willeke). Samuel de Lange: *Andante.* Padre Martini: *Gavotta.* Wolfgang Amadeus Mozart: *Larghetto.* Pietro Nardini: *Larghetto* (arr. C. von Radecki). David Popper: *Erzählung (A Story).* Wilhelm Popper: *Mazurka* Op.3. R. Renard: *Berceuse.* Anton Rubinstein: *Melodie* Op.3/1 (trans. D. Popper). Robert Schumann: *Abendlied (Evening Song)* Op.85/12; *Träumerei* Op.15/7 (trans. D. Popper). Vol.2, 63pp. Georg Goltermann: *Andante* Op.30. H. Gottlieb-Noren: *Lullaby* Op.12. Edouard Lalo: *Intermezzo.* David Popper: *Mazurka* Op.11/3; *Vito* Op.54/5. Wilhelm Popper: *Impromptu* Op.6. Jean-Philippe Rameau: *Gavotte.* Louis Schnitzler: *Evening Song (Abendlied)* Op.5. Joz Schravesande: *Elégie* Op.5. François Servais: *Andante.* Hans Sitt: *Serenade* Op.33/2. B. A. Verhallen: *Gavotte-Impromptu* Op.19. Th. H. H. Verhey: *Andante* Op.5/1. Int. to M-D.

Piano and Double Bass

Album Kontrabasisty 2 vols. (T. Pelczan—PWM 7573 7775, ISBN 83-224-2107-9), parts. Transcriptions of works by Baroque and Classical European composers. Vol.1, 20pp. Jean-Baptiste Lully: *Aria* from *Armida.* Archangelo Corelli: *Adagio.* Henry Purcell: *Aria* (trans. D. Popper). Antonio Vivaldi: *Largo* from *Concerto Grosso* Op.3/11 d. Jean-Philippe Rameau: *Les Tendres Plaintes* from *Suite* (*Pièces de Clavecin*). George Frideric Handel: *Menuet* from *Suite* d (Keyboard). Johann Sebastian Bach: *Siciliana* from *Flute Sonata* E♭. Vol.2, 26pp. Joseph Haydn: *Adagio cantabile* from *Symphony 13* D; *Presto* Op.33/3. Wolfgang A. Mozart: *Andante* from *Piano Sonata* K.330; *Adagio* K.261 E. Ludwig van Beethoven: *Menuet* G; *Rondo* Op.51/1 C. M-D.

Drabiazgi Kontrabasowe/Short Pieces for Double Bass with Piano Accompaniment (S. Bukalski—PWM 4391, ISBN 83-224-1724-1) 19pp., parts. Nineteen 1- to 2-page pieces transcribed from the Baroque through the 19th century. Robert Schumann: *A Short Piece* Op.68/5; *The Merry Peasant* from *Album for the Young* Op.68/10. Piotr Czajkowski (Tchaikovsky): *Old French Air* Op.39/16. Ludwig van Beethoven: *Sacrificial Song; Lovely Flower* from *Acht Lieder* Op.52. Johannes Brahms: *Cradle-Song* Op.49/4; *The Hen* from *Volkskinderlieder* 3. Michail Glinka: *Elegy; The Wind Soughs.* Nicolai Rimski-Korsakow: *Song.* Wolfgang A. Mozart: *French Song (Ah, vous dirai-je maman)* K.265; *May-Song* K.596. Archangelo Corelli: *Sarabande.* Johann Sebastian Bach: *Menuet* from *Notebook for Wilhelm Friedemann Bach; Musette* from *Notebook for Anna Magdalena Bach.* Corelli: *Gavotta* from *Violin Sonata* 10. Leopold Mozart: *Aria.* Franz Schubert: *Ecossaise* from *8 Ecossaisen for Piano.* Carl Maria Weber: *Vivace.* Int. to M-D.

Four Russian Pieces (MMP) 36pp., parts. Four early-20th-century works by Russian composers. Aram Khachaturian: *Lyric Poem* (arr. R. Azarkhin). Reinhold Gliere: *Romance* from *The Red Poppy* (arr. Azarkhin). Rodion Shchedrin: *Final Dance* from *The Humpbacked Horse* (arr. F. Galkin). E. Plutalov: *Humoresque.* M-D.

Młody Kontrabasista (J. Marczyński—PWM 7701, ISBN 83-224-1031-X) 19pp., parts. Seven transcriptions of works by 4 European composers. Archangelo Corelli: *Preludium* from *Sonata* Op.5/8 e; *Gavotte* from *Sonata* Op.5/9 A; *Sarabande* from *Sonata*

Op.5/8 e. Johann Sebastian Bach: *Aria* from *Orchestral Suite* BWV 1068 D. Stanislaw Moniuszko: *Pieśń wieczorna; Aria Stanisława* from *Verbum Nobile*. Camille Saint-Saëns: *The Swan* from *Carnival of the Animals*. M-D.

Solos for the Double Bass Player (O. Zimmerman—GS 2657 1966) 77pp., parts. Sixteen works by composers from the Baroque to the 20th century. Most are transcriptions. Johann Sebastian Bach: *Bourrée* from *Cello Suite* III. Evaristo F. dall' Abaco: *Grave*. Antonio Vivaldi: *Concerto* from *Violin Concerto* a (first movement). Jean François d'Andrieu: *Prelude* and *Allegro* from *Sonata* G. George Frideric Handel: *Sonata* c. Ludwig van Beethoven: *Sonatina* g; *Minuet* C. Giovanni Bottesini: *Elegy; Andante* from *Concerto* II. Giuseppe Verdi: *Aria* from *Rigoletto*. Johann Geissel: *Adagio* from *Concerto for Contrabass* Op.32. Sergey Vassilievitch Rachmaninoff: *Vocalise*. Sergey Sergeyevitch Prokofiev: *Romance* from *Lieutenant Kijé*. C. Franchi: *Introduction and Tarentelle*. Thomas Beveridge: *Serenade* from *Sonata for Bass Viol*. Armand Russell: *Chaconne*. M-D.

Piano and Flute

Flötenmusik 2 vols. (P.-L. Graf, E.-G. Heinemann, S. Petrenz—Henle 368 1985, ISMN M-2018-0368-5, Henle 369 1993 ISMN M-2018-0369-2), parts, including basso. Vol.1 Barock (Baroque), 74pp.: Daniel Purcell: *Sonata* F. Johann Christoph Pepusch: *Sonata* F. Johann Christian Schickhard: *Sonata* Op.17/3 a. Johan Helmich Roman: *Sonata* b. Jacques Loeillet: *Sonata* Op.5/1 e. Thomas Roseingrave: *Sonata* G. Michel Blavet: *Sonata* Op.2/4 g. Giuseppe Sammartini: *Sonata* Op.2/6 a. Johann Philipp Eisel: *Divertimento* d. Giovanni Chinzer: *Sonata* Op.5/6 G. Vol.2 Vorklassik (Pre-Classical), 106pp.: Johann Samuel Schröter: *Sonata* F. Johann Baptist Wendling: *Sonata* Op.4/5 e. Johann Gottlieb Nicolai: *Sonata* Op.6/1 G. Johann Baptist Vanhal: *Sonata* Op.10/4 A; *Sonata* Op.17/1 D. Friedrich Wilhelm Heinrich Benda: *Sonata* Op.5/3 E. Franz Anton Hoffmeister: *Sonata* Op.21/1 D. François Devienne: *Sonata* Op.58/5 G. M-D.

Flute Music by French Composers (Moÿse—GS 2699), parts. Ten compositions by French composers or composers who made their home in France from the 19th through 20th centuries. Henri Büsser: *Prélude et Scherzo* Op.35. Cécile Chaminade: *Concertino* Op.107. Alphonse Duvernoy: *Concertino* Op.45. Georges Enesco: *Cantabile et Presto*. Gabriel Fauré: *Fantasie* Op.79. Louis Ganne: *Andante et Scherzo*. Philippe Gaubert: *Fantaisie; Nocturne et Allegro scherzando*. A. Perilhou: *Ballade*. Paul Taffanel: *Andante Pastoral et Scherzettino*.

Flute Music by Soviet Composers (Lozben—GS 3824), parts. Ten compositions by composers who lived all or part of their lives in the former Soviet Union. Elena Firsova: *Two Inventions*. Mikhail Burshtin: *Pastorale*. Sofia Gubaidulina: *Sonatina*. Vasily Lobanov: *Modulation and Solfeggio*. Vyacheslav Artyomov: *Recitative III*. Vladislav Shut: *Sonata Breve*. Peteris Vasks: *Landscape with Birds*. Yury Obyedov: *Andantino*. Georgy Dmitriev: *The Shape of Motions*. Sergei Pavlenko: *Sonata* (ed. Lozben).

Flute Music of the Baroque (L. Moÿse—GS 2531 1967) 129pp., parts. Selected, revised, and annotated by Louis Moÿse. Thirteen compositions by Baroque composers from Germany, France, Italy, and England. Carl Philipp Emanuel Bach: *Allegro* from *Concerto* A. Luigi Boccherini: *Allegro moderato* from *Concerto* Op.27 D. Frederick the Great: *Sonata* XI d. André E. M. Grétry: *Allegro* from *Concerto* C. Jean-Marie Leclair: *Adagio* from *Concerto* Op.7/3 C. Jean-Baptiste Loeillet [London]: *Adagio, Gigue* from *Sonata* G. Johann Christoph Pepusch: *Sonata* F. Giovanni Batista Pergolesi: *Allegro spiritoso* from *Concerto* G. Giovanni Platti: *Sonata* II G. Johann Joachim Quantz: *Arioso* from

Concerto G. Karl Stamitz: *Concerto* G. Guiseppe Tartini: *Concerto* G. Antonio Vivaldi: *Concerto* (*Il Cardellino*) Op.10/3 D. M-D.

24 Short Concert Pieces (R. Cavally—Southern B435 1969) 97pp., parts. Contains 22 original and trans. works by European composers from the Baroque to the early 20th century. Joachim Andersen: *The Mill* Op.55/4, *Scherzino* Op.55/6. J. S. Bach: *Suite* b (Rondeau, Polonaise, Badinerie, trans. H. Altès). Georges Bizet: *2nd Menuet* from *L'Arlésienne.* René de Boisdeffre: *Orientale* Op.31. Léo Delibes: *Waltz of the Flowers.* Johannes Donjon: *Pan: Pastorale* and *Offertoire* Op.12. Gabriel Fauré: *Sicilienne* from *Pelléas et Mélisande* Op.78. Benjamin Godard: *Idylle* and *Allegretto* from the *Suite,* Op.116. Christoph Willibald Gluck: *Minuet and Dance of the Blessed Spirits* from *Orpheus.* Georges Hüe: *Sérénade.* Victorin Joncières: *Hungarian Sérénade* (trans. A. J. Andraud). Jules Massenet: *Mélodie-Elégie* Op.10. Wilhelm Bernhard Molique: *Andante* from *Concerto* Op.69 d. W. A. Mozart: *Adagio Religioso* from *Concerto for Clarinet* K.622. A. Périlhou: *Ballade.* Emile Pessard: *Andalouse.* Johann Joachim Quantz: *Arioso and Presto.* Franz Schubert: *Ave Maria.* M-D.

Unbeaten Tracks (P. Davies—Faber 1999, ISBN 0-571-51915-6) 32pp., parts. Eight contemporary pieces with Preface and short biographies. The collection is designed "specifically for the intermediate player" (from Preface). Carl Davis: *Beatrix.* Daryl Runswick: *Blue Six.* Colin Matthews: *Little Pavane.* Christopher Gunning: *Waltz for Aggie.* David Matthews: *Pieces of Seven.* John Woolrich: *A Sad Song.* Eddie McGuire: *Caprice.* Fraser Trainer: *Outside Lines.* Int. to M-D.

Piano and Oboe

Venezianische Sonaten (C. Schneider, G. Hambitzer—UE 30-499 1998, ISMN M-008-05881-3) 20pp., parts, with basso. For oboe or violin. Two Sonatas from Venice at the end of the Baroque. Antonio Vivaldi: *Sonata* RV28 g. Tomaso Giovanni Albinoni: *Sonata* C. Preface in German, English, and French. M-D.

Piano and Clarinet

Masterworks for the Clarinet (Simon—GS LB1747), parts. Six major 19th-century works by 4 German composers. Carl Maria von Weber: *Grand Duo Concertant* Op.48; *Variations* Op.33. Robert Schumann: *Fantasy-Pieces* Op.73. Felix Mendelssohn: *Sonata.* Johannes Brahms: *Sonata* I Op.120/1; *Sonata* II Op.120/2. M-D to D.

Sixteen Grands Solos de Concert (D. Bonade—ST B-109) 147pp., parts. Sixteen works by 14 European composers from the Baroque to the early 20th century. Charles-Marie Widor: *Introduction and Rondo* Op.72. Charles-Edouard Lefebvre: *Fantaisie-Caprice* Op.118. Max d'Ollone: *Fantaisie Orientale.* George Marty: *1st Fantaisie.* André Messager: *Solo de Concours.* Carl Maria von Weber: *Concertino* Op.26. H. C. L. Stocks: *A Wessex Pastorale.* Paul Jeanjean: *Deux Pièces: Andantino; Scherzo Brillante.* François Francœur: *Sicilienne; Rigaudon.* Gabriel Pierné: *Canzonetta* Op.19. Nikolai Rimsky-Korsakoff: *Flight of the Bumble Bee.* Philippe Gaubert: *Fantaisie.* Arthur Coquard: *Melodie and Scherzetto* Op.68. Reynaldo Hahn: *Sarabande et Thème Varié.* M-D.

Piano and Bassoon

Contemporary French Recital Pieces (IMC 1835 [1954]) 15pp., parts. Reprints of 6 original pieces by early-20th-century French composers published in 1953 by Pierre Noël. André Bloch: *Drolleries.* André Lavagne: *Steeple-chase.* Jacques Ibert: *Carignane.* Marcel Bitsch: *Passepied.* Fernand Oubradous: *Divertissement.* René Duclos: *Quadrille.* M-D.

Piano and Horn

Contemporary French Recital Pieces (IMC 1837 1954) 12pp., parts. Five short 20th-century works originally published by Pierre Noël in 1953. Joseph Canteloube: *Dance*. André Ameller: *Gavotte*. Henri Martelli: *Waltz*. Emile Passani: *Vesperal*. Jean Français: *Canon in Octave*. M-D to D.

Solos for the Horn Player (M. Jones, V. Sokoloff—GS 2462 1962) 96pp., parts. Original and transcribed works by 14 composers from the 17th to 20th centuries. Felix Mendelssohn: *Andante* from *Symphony No. 5*. Alessandro Stradella: *Aria* (Kirchen Arie). Henry Purcell: *I Attempt from Love's Sickness to Fly*. George Frideric Handel: *I See a Huntsman* from *Julius Caesar*. Arthur Frackenpohl: *Largo and Allegro*. Maurice Ravel: *Pavane pour une Infante Défunte*. Alexander Glazunov: *Reveries* Op.24. Charles Lefebvre: *Romance* Op.30. Camille Saint-Saëns: *Romance* Op.36. Wolfgang Amadeus Mozart: *Rondo* from *Horn Quintet* K.407. Ludwig van Beethoven: *Scherzo* from *Septet* Op.20. Johannes Brahms: *Scherzo* from *Serenade* Op.11. Joseph Labor: *Theme and Variations* Op.10. Paul Dukas: *Villanelle*. M-D.

Piano and Trombone

Three French Pieces (Well-Tempered Press/MMP) 27pp., parts. Three late-19th- to early-20th-century works by French composers. Jean Guy Ropartz: *Pièce* E♭. Henri Büsser: *Cantabile et Scherzando* Op.51. Théodore Dubois: *Solo de Concert*. M-D.

Piano, Violin, and Cello

Chamber Music Sampler 3 books (J. Haroutounian—Kjos WP324-6 1992), parts. Accessible chamber music for the young musician. Short works organized in progressive levels of performance difficulty. Appropriate for junior and senior high school students. Includes rehearsal suggestions and cueing directions. Separate notes to pianists and string players. *Book 1* 28pp. (ISBN 0-8497-9461-7). Pius Köhler: *Scherzo* from *Trio* Op.49/2 B♭. Julius Klengel: *Allegro* from *Kindertrio* Op.35/2 G; *Finale* from *Kindertrio* Op.39/1 F. Muzio Clementi: *Allegretto* from *Trio* Op.22/1 D. *Book 2* 54pp. (ISBN 0-8497-9462-5). Franz Joseph Haydn: *Finale* from *Trio* Hob.XV:29 E♭; *Finale* from *Trio* Hob.XV:20 B♭. Julius Klengel: *Andante* from *Kindertrio* Op.39/2 G. Muzio Clementi: *Allegro* and *Rondo* from *Trio Sonata* Op.35/2. *Book 3* 45pp. (ISBN 0-8497-9463-3). Franz Joseph Haydn: *Rondo all' Ongarese* from *Trio* Hob.XV:25 G. Wolfgang Amadeus Mozart: *Allegro Assai* from *Trio VI* K.254. Franz Schubert: *Scherzo* from *Trio* Op.100 E♭. Ludwig van Beethoven: *Trio VIII* op. posthumous. Int.

A Christmas Tableau of Piano Trios (E. R. Rocherolle—Kjos GP376 1994, ISBN 0-8497-6191-3) 40pp., parts. Familiar carols well arranged for this medium by Eugénie Ricau Rocherolle. Includes: Bring a Torch, Jeanette Isabella; The First Noel; A Holly Jolly Christmas; It Came upon a Midnight Clear; Jingle Bells; O Holy Night; Rudolph, the Red-Nosed Reindeer; Silent Night; What Child Is This? Program notes included. Int.

A Tableau of Piano Trios (E. R. Rocherolle-Kjos GP374 1995, ISBN 0-8497-6189-1) 22pp., parts. Original pieces for young musicians by Eugénie Ricau Rocherolle. Appropriate for advancing upper elementary to junior high school students. Includes: Antique Lace; Daydreaming; Indian Lore; Parade; The Setting Sun; Swing Your Partner! Int.

Piano with Mixed Ensembles

American Chamber Music (J. Graziano—G. K. Hall 1991) 355pp. In the collection "Three Centuries of American Music," Vol.8. Includes a piano duo and trio by American composers as well as chamber music without piano. Bibliographical references provided. Edited primarily from printed and MS sources. Literature for piano in chamber ensembles includes: Raynor Taylor: *Sonata* for piano and violin and Arthur Foote: *Trio* I Op.5 for violin, cello, and piano (reprinted from the Schott edition published in 1884). Also included are chamber music works without piano by Charles Hommann, Léopold Meignen, William Henry Fry, Horatio Parker, and Amy Marcy Cheney Beach.

Annotated Bibliography

This section is an extension of the suggested readings that appear after individual composers or single compositions. It concentrates on English-language books, periodicals, and, particularly, dissertations. These sources are most helpful when used in conjunction with the musical score. Biographies have been excluded except when they appear as a part of a larger work.

Paul G. Anderson. *Brass Ensemble Music Guide.* Evanston, Ill.: Instrumentalist Company, 1978. 259pp.

Willi Apel. *Italian Violin Music of the Seventeenth Century.* Bloomington: Indiana University Press, 1990. 320pp. Narrative description of the development of Italian violin literature during the first two-thirds of the Baroque.

Yvett Bader. "The Chamber Music of Charles Ives." MR 33 (November 1972): 292–99.

Stephen Banfield. "British Chamber Music at the Turn of the Century." MT 115 (March 1974): 211–13. Mainly a discussion of the chamber works of Parry, Stanford, and Mackenzie.

John H. Baron. *Chamber Music: A Research and Information Guide.* New York: Garland Publishing, 1987. An annotated bibliography of chamber music resource materials in English and other European languages. 500pp.

BBC Music Library Catalogues: Chamber Music. London: British Broadcasting Corp., 1965.

William Charles Bedford. "Elizabeth Sprague Coolidge—The Education of a Patron of Chamber Music; the Early Years." Diss., University of Missouri, 1964. 350pp.

Melvin Berger. *Guide to Chamber Music.* New York: Dodd, Mead, and Co., 1985.

Heidi M. Boenke. *Flute Music by Women Composers: An Annotated Catalog.* Westport, Conn.: Greenwood Press, 1988. 202pp.

Helmut Braunlich. "Violin Sonatas and the Standard Repertoire." AMT 25 (April-May 1976): 19–21.

A. Peter Brown. "Critical Years for Haydn's Instrumental Music: 1787–90." MQ 62 (July 1976): 374–94.

———, in collaboration with C. V. Brown. "Joseph Haydn in Literature: A Survey." *Notes* 31 (1975): 530–47. A fine introduction to any facet of Haydn research.

Elizabeth Bankhead Buccheri. "The Piano Chamber Music of Wallingford Riegger." D.M.A. diss., University of Rochester, 1978.

M.-D. Calvocoressi. "Charles Koechlin's Instrumental Works." ML 5 (October 1924): 357–64.

Chamber Music: A Research and Information Guide. New York: Garland Publishing, 1987.

Chamber Music by Living British Composers. London: British Music Information Centre, 1969. 42pp. A listing of the chamber music holdings, both published and unpublished, of 20th-century British composers.

Joan Chissell. "Style in Bloch's Chamber Music." ML 24 (January 1943): 30–35.

James Christensen. *Chamber Music: Notes for Players.* Plantation, Fla.: Distinctive Publishing Corp., 1992. Descriptive comments on chamber music with piano by principal composers from the Classical period through the early 20th century. 244pp.

John Clapham. "Martinů's Instrumental Style." MR 24 (1963): 158–67.

Classical Keyboard Music in Print: 1993. Palo Alto, Calif.: Accolade Press, 1993. Includes chapter identifying chamber music for piano and nonkeyboard instruments.

Walter W. Cobbett. *Cobbett's Cyclopedic Survey of Chamber Music,* with supplementary material edited by Colin Mason. 2nd. ed., 3 vols. London: Oxford University Press, 1963.

Arthur Cohn. *The Literature of Chamber Music.* 4 vols. (Chapel Hill, N.C.: Hinshaw, 1997). An annotated listing of chamber music with and without piano. Arranged alphabetically by composer. 3075pp.

Henry Cope Colles. *The Chamber Music of Brahms.* London: Oxford University Press, 1933. Reprint, New York: AMS Press, 1976.

Karen L. Dannessa. "An Annotated Bibliography of Trios for Clarinet, One String Instrument and Piano Composed between 1978 and 1990 by Composers Active in the United States." D.Mus. diss., Florida State University, 1994. 117pp.

Archibald T. Davison and Willi Apel, eds. *Historical Anthology of Music.* 2 vols. Cambridge, Mass.: Harvard University Press, 1947, 1950.

Mary Anne Dresser. "Twentieth-Century Russian Cello Sonatas." D.M.A. diss., University of Texas, Austin, 1983.

John Robert Drew. "Classic Elements in Selected Sonatas for Trombone and Piano by Twentieth-Century Composers." D.M.A. diss., University of Kentucky, 1978. Includes works by Halsey Stevens, Richard Monaco, Klaus George Roy, John Davison, Paul Hindemith, George F. McKay, Robert W. Jones, Walter Watson, and Henry Cowell.

Arno P. Drucker. *American Piano Trios: A Resource Guide.* Lanham, Md.: Scarecrow Press, 1999. An annotated guide to the literature for piano, violin, and cello by composers in the United States. 405pp.

Angelo Eagon. *Catalog of Published Concert Music by American Composers.* Metuchen, N.J.: Scarecrow Press, 1969. 348pp. Also Supplement to the 2nd ed., 1971 (150pp.) and Second Supplement to the 2nd ed., 1974. 148pp.

Edwin Evans, Sr. *Handbook to the Works of Brahms.* 4 vols. London: W. Reeves, 1933–35. Vol. II, *Chamber Works.*

Thomas G. Everett. *Annotated Guide to Bass Trombone Literature, Third Edition* (Revised and Enlarged). Nashville, Tenn.: Brass Press, 1985. Descriptive guide to literature, methods, studies, etc., on bass trombone. 95pp.

William A. Everett. *British Piano Trios, Quartets, and Quintets, 1850–1950: A Checklist.* Warren, Mich.: Harmonie Park Press, 2000. A listing of literature for piano and strings in combinations of 3, 4, and 5 instruments by British composers. 234pp.

Patrice R. Ewoldt. "'La bande à Franck:' Chamber Music for Piano and Violin." D.M.A. diss., University of Maryland, College Park, 2000.

David Edward Fenske. "Texture in the Chamber Music of Brahms." Ph.D. diss., University of Wisconsin, 1973. 540pp. A statistical study of each of the movements of Brahms's 18 chamber works.

Donald N. Ferguson. *Image and Structure in Chamber Music.* Minneapolis: University of Minnesota Press, 1964. 339pp.

Robert Fink and Robert Ricci. *The Language of Twentieth Century Music.* New York: Schirmer Books, 1975. 125pp. A dictionary of terms.

Ella Marie Forsyth. *Building a Chamber Music Collection: A Descriptive Guide to Published Scores.* Metuchen, N.J.: Scarecrow Press, 1979. Identifies and describes well-known chamber music literature with piano up to 7 instruments.

Hubert Foss. "The Instrumental Music of Frederick Delius." *Tempo* 26 (winter 1952–53): 30–37.

Robert Eugene Frank. "Quincy Porter: A Survey of the Mature Style and a Study of the Second Sonata for Violin and Piano." D.M.A. diss., Cornell University, 1973. 303pp.

Floyd Donald Funk. "The Trio Sonatas of Georg Philip Telemann (1681–1767)." Diss., George Peabody College for Teachers, 1954. On 64 of the trio sonatas.

Diane Carol Gee. "Flute Chamber Music by Twentieth Century American Women Composers." D.M.A. diss., University of Washington, 1994. 184pp.

Janelle Magnuson Gelfand. "Germaine Tailleferre (1892–1983): Piano and Chamber Works." Ph.D. diss., University of Cincinnati, 1999. 393 pp.

Virginia Snodgrass Gifford. *Music for Oboe, Oboe D'Amour, and English Horn: A Bibliography of Materials at the Library of Congress.* Westport, Conn.: Greenwood Press, 1983. A listing of 5,600 works for various combinations of oboe, oboe d'amour, and English horn at the Library of Congress. 431pp.

Eugene Gratovich. "The Sonatas for Violin and Piano by Charles E. Ives: A Critical Commentary and Concordance of the Printed Editions and the Autographs and Manuscripts of the Yale Ives Collection." D.M.A. diss., Boston University School of Fine and Applied Arts, 1968. 242pp.

Elizabeth Remsberg Harkins. "The Chamber Music of Camille Saint-Saëns." Ph.D. diss., New York University, 1976. 216pp.

Elaine Atkins Harriss. "Chamber Music for the Trio of Flute, Clarinet, and Piano: A Bibliographical and Analytical Study." Ph.D. diss., University of Michigan, 1981. 160pp.

George Hart. *The Violin and Its Music.* Boston: Milford House, 1973. Reprint of the 1885 edition, London: Dulau.

John Riley Haws. "Henri Dutilleux's Early Chamber Works With Piano: An Analysis of a Formative Style." D.M.A. diss., Peabody Institute of the Johns Hopkins University, 1990. 340pp.

Christopher Headington. *The Listener's Guide to Chamber Music.* New York: Quarto Marketing, 1982.

Stephen E. Hefling, ed. *Nineteenth-Century Chamber Music.* New York: G. Schirmer, 1998. 389pp. A historical and analytical study of chamber music in the 19th century with concentration on the principal literature. Focuses on Beethoven, Schubert, Spohr, Weber, Mendelssohn, Schumann, Brahms, Smetana, and Dvořák, and includes comments on works by other composers.

Eugenia K. Hinson. "Arthur William Foote: His Contribution to Chamber Music in Boston and Analyses of Selected Piano Chamber Works." D.A. diss., Ball State University, 1994.

Anthony Hoboken. *Joseph Haydn, thematisch-bibliographisches Werkverzeichnis.* Mainz: Schott, 1957–. Vol. I. Instrumental Works.

Donald Homuth. *Cello Music since 1960: A Bibliography of Solo, Chamber, and Orchestral Works for the Solo Cellist.* Berkeley, Calif.: Fallen Leaf Press, 1994. Identifies more than 5,200 works for solo cello written by 3,100 composers over roughly the final third of the 20th century. 451pp.

Aaron Horne. *Keyboard Music of Black Composers: A Bibliography.* Westport, Conn.: Greenwood Press, 1992. Identifies literature for piano in chamber ensembles up to 12 instruments by Black composers.

John Horton. *The Chamber Music of Mendelssohn.* London: Oxford University Press, 1946. 65pp. The Musical Pilgrim series.

Charles Williams Hughes. "Chamber Music in American Schools." Ed.D. diss., Columbia University, 1933. 62pp.

A. J. B. Hutchings. "The Chamber Music of Delius." MT 76 (1935): 17–20, 214–16, 310–11, 401–403.

Eileen Joan Hutchins. "The Performance of the Piano and Chamber Music of Claude Debussy." D.M.A. diss., University of Maryland, College Park, 1996. 56pp.

Milan R. Kaderavek. "Stylistic Aspects of the Late Chamber Music of Leoš Janáček: An Analytic Study." Diss., University of Illinois, 1970. "A critical study of Janáček's mature style, based on the chamber works of his last 5 years. Provides an analysis of the stylistic aspects of these works and demonstrates the influence of his native folk song on the instrumental compositions. A summary of his stylistic traits is based on a systematic examination of each work. Melodic design is given special attention, since it was perhaps most influenced by folk music and by Janáček's concept of what he called *napevky mluvy* (generally translated as 'speech melody'). Janáček's harmonic procedures, also folk-influenced, are illustrated by graphs using a modified form of the linear reduction technique developed by Heinrich Schenker. The unique and original aspects of Janáček's music are described" (author).

Hortense Reid Kerr. "The Chamber Music for Piano and Strings of Three African-American Composers: The Chevalier de Saint-Georges, William Grant Still, and Roque Cordero." D.M.A. diss., Catholic University of America, 1996. 350pp.

Ivor Keys. *Brahms Chamber Music.* London: 1974; Seattle: University of Washington Press, 1974. 68pp., BBC Music Guides series.

Ronald R. Kidd. "The Emergence of Chamber Music with Obbligato Keyboard in England." AM 44 (July 1972): 122–44. "The sonata for obbligato keyboard and accompanying instruments in England acquired characteristics which distinguished it from the Parisian varieties. Especially notable in English works is the borrowing from the Italian concerto. Beginning with Giardini's Op.3, thematic material is often presented in a concertante exchange between instruments, comparable to the tutti/solo opening of a concerto. The English practice of printing accompanied sonatas in score led to greater independence in the added parts but did not eliminate the option of a solo keyboard performance. In the 1760's a number of Italians, Germans, and Englishmen produced sonatas that vacillated between optional and obbligato scoring. Towards the end of the decade, superfluous accompaniments became the more frequent owing to influence exerted by the imported works of Schobert. Examples of sonatas with concertante treatment remained isolated until the end of the century when that style became predominant" (author).

A. Hyatt King. *Chamber Music*. New York: Chanticleer Press, 1948. 72pp. An overall survey, particularly notable for its outstanding illustrations.

Elise Kuhl Kirk. "The Chamber Music of Charles Koechlin (1867–1950)." Ph.D. diss., Catholic University of America, 1977.

Bjarne Kortsen. *Contemporary Norwegian Chamber Music*. Fyllingsdalen, Norway: Edition Norvegica, 1971. 235pp.

Chang-Yi Lai. "An Analytical Study of Nine Selected Sonatas for Trombone and Piano." Master's thesis, Lamar University-Beaumont, 1993. Analyzes selected sonatas, including transcriptions, by J. S. Bach, Leslie Bassett, Newell Kay Brown, Francesco Corelli, Johann Friedrich Fasch, Walter Hartley, Paul Hindemith, Richard Monaco, and Donald White.

G. B. Lane. *The Trombone: An Annotated Bibliography*. Lanham, Md.: Scarecrow Press, 1999. An all-purpose general reference guide to the trombone with biographies, literature, performance practice, pedagogy, etc. 425pp.

Jerome Leonard Landsman. "An Annotated Catalog of American Violin Sonatas, Suites, and Works of Similar Character, 1947–1961, with a Survey of Traditional and Contemporary Technique." D.M.A. diss., University of Southern California, 1966. 488pp.

Marlene Joan Langosch. "The Instrumental Chamber Music of Bernhard Heiden." Ph.D. diss., Indiana University, 1974.

Nadia Lasserson. *Piano Needn't Be Lonely: It's Fun Playing with Friends*. 2nd rev. ed. Published independently; available from: 34 Carver Road, London SE24 9LT, United Kingdom, Tel: (44) 20.7274.6821.

Jeffrey Jon Lemke. "French Tenor Trombone Solo Literature and Pedagogy since 1836." D.M.A. diss., University of Arizona, 1983. See entry for J. Mark Thompson and Jeffrey Jon Lemke's *French Music for Low Brass Instruments*.

Abram Loft. *Violin and Keyboard: The Duo Repertoire*. New York: Grossman Publishers, 1973. Vol. I: *From the Seventeenth Century to Mozart*. 360pp. Vol. II: *From Beethoven to the Present*. 417pp.

Jean Marie Londeix. *150 Years of Music for Saxophone: Bibliographical Index of Music and Educational Literature for the Saxophone: 1844–1994*. Cherry Hill, N.J.: Roncorp Publications, 1994. In French and English. 438pp.

German Eduardo Marcano. "A Catalog of Cello Music by Latin American Composers." D.M.A. diss., University of Wisconsin, Madison, 2001.

Colin Mason. "The Chamber Music of Milhaud." MQ 43 (July 1957): 326–41.

———. "Some Aspects of Hindemith's Chamber Music." ML 41 (April 1960): 150–55.

———. "Webern's Late Chamber Music." ML 38 (July 1957): 232–37.

Daniel Gregory Mason. *The Chamber Music of Brahms*. New York: Macmillan, 1933.

James McCalla. *Twentieth-Century Chamber Music*. New York: Schirmer Books, 1996. 274pp. A historical introduction to chamber music of the past century with brief analytical studies of individual works. Concentrates on principal composers, commencing with Impressionism, Expressionism, and Ives, and concluding with Minimalism.

William Wallace McMullen. *Soloistic English Horn Literature from 1736–1984*. Stuyvesant, N.Y.: Pendragon Press, 1994. A thematic catalog with descriptive comments on composers and compositions. 257pp.

Samuel Midgley. *Handbook to Beethoven's Sonatas for Violin and Pianoforte*. London: Breitkopf & Härtel, 1911.

Patrick Miles. "A Bibliography of Trios for Horn, Violin, and Piano Composed 1945–1985 with Selected Annotations." *Horn Call Annual* no. 6 (1994): 18–31. Provides descriptive comments about the ensemble combination and its compositions during the 40-year span. Includes unpublished as well as published works.

R. Winston Morris and Edward R. Goldstein. *The Tuba Source Book*. Bloomington: Indiana University Press, 1996. Identifies tuba literature by ensemble type, including 1,900 pieces for tuba and keyboard, plus numerous other combinations. 656pp.

Brian Morton and Pamela Collins. *Contemporary Composers*. Chicago: St. James Press, 1992. Contains biographical information, a listing of principal works, and descriptions of compositional style for over 400 composers whose careers were in the second half of the 20th century. 1019pp.

William S. Newman. *The Sonata in the Baroque Era*. Chapel Hill: University of North Carolina Press, 1959; rev. ed., 1966. 3d ed., New York: W. W. Norton, 1972.

——. *The Sonata in the Classic Era*. Chapel Hill: University of North Carolina Press, 1963. 2nd ed., New York: W. W. Norton, 1972. 897pp.

——. *The Sonata since Beethoven*. Chapel Hill: University of North Carolina Press, 1969. 2nd ed., New York: W. W. Norton, 1972. 854pp.

Christie Blanche Nigro. "The Chamber Music of George Whitefield Chadwick." Ph.D. diss., University of Massachusetts, 1998. 451pp.

Orval Bruce Oleson. "Italian Solo and Chamber Music for the Clarinet—1900–1973: An Annotated Bibliography." D.M.A. diss., University of Missouri, Kansas City, 1980.

Juan A. Orrego-Salas, ed. *Music from Latin America*. Bloomington: LAMC, Indiana University, 1971. 412pp. A listing of scores, tapes, and records available at the LAMC of Indiana University.

Thomas Montgomery Osborn. "Sixty Years of Clarinet Chamber Music: A Survey of Music Employing Clarinet with Stringed Instruments Composed 1900–1960 for Two to Five Performers." Diss., University of Southern California, 1964. 388pp. Chapter 2, "Traditional Instrumental Combinations," includes a discussion of works for clarinet, strings, and piano as well as for clarinet, strings, winds, and piano. Chapter 3, "Novel Instrumental Combinations," is devoted to works for clarinet, strings, and piano as well as for clarinet, strings, other winds, and piano. A number of appendixes give more detailed information on each work.

Dorothy Pachard. "The Joys of Chamber Music." *Clavier* (Nov.-Dec. 1964): 14–17.

James J. Pellerite. *A Handbook of Literature for the Flute*. Bloomington, Ind.: Zālo Publications, 1963. 408pp. Provides an annotated listing of solo and ensemble literature for flute, alto flute, bass flute, and piccolo with piano from duos to quintets. Also identifies exercises, etudes, and pedagogical materials for flute.

Harry B. Peters. *Woodwind Music in Print*. Philadelphia: Musicdata, 1997. Lists music in print for flute, oboe, clarinet, bassoon, and saxophone in solo, chamber music, and orchestral settings. 743pp.

Roger Paul Phelps. "The History and Practice of Chamber Music in the United States from Earliest Times up to 1875." Ph.D. diss., University of Iowa, 1951. 2 vols., 991pp.

Nancy Ping-Robbins. *The Piano Trio in the Twentieth Century*. Raleigh, N.C.: Regan Press, 1984.

Victor Rangel-Ribeiro and Robert Markel. *Chamber Music: An International Guide to Works and Their Instrumentation*. New York: Facts on File, 1993. A master index of 8,000 chamber music works by title and instrumentation from the 16th century to the present. 271pp.

Alec Robertson, ed. *Chamber Music.* Baltimore: Penguin Books, 1957. 423pp.

Ruth Halle Rowen. *Early Chamber Music.* New York: King's Crown Press, 1949. Offers interesting information concerning chamber music before Haydn.

Harold Duane Rutan. "An Annotated Bibliography of Written Material Pertinent to the Performance of Brass and Percussion Chamber Music." Ph.D. diss., University of Illinois, 1960. 368pp.

Stanley J. Sadie. "British Chamber Music, 1720–1790." 3 vols. Diss., Cambridge University, 1957.

Edith A. Sagul. "Development of Chamber Music Performance in the United States." Diss., Columbia University, 1952. 221pp.

Otto Schumann. *Handbuch der Kammermusik.* Wilhelmshaven, Germany: Heinrichshofen's Verlag, 1956. 557pp.

D. A. Shand. "The Sonata for Violin and Piano from Schumann to Debussy." Diss., Boston University, 1948.

Robert Virgil Sibbing. "An Analytical Study of the Published Sonatas for Saxophone by American Composers." Ed.D. diss., University of Illinois, 1969. 179pp.

Thomas Siwe. *Percussion Ensemble and Solo Literature.* Champaign, Ill.: Media Press, 1993. A listing of percussion literature by composer with ensemble requirements and publishers. 611pp.

Otakar Šourek. *The Chamber Music of Antonín Dvořák.* Prague: Artia. 177pp. English version by Roberta Finlayson Samsour.

Alfred Sprissler. "Piano Trios and the Student." *Etude* (Oct. 1925): 747.

James Gwynn Staples III. "Six Lesser-Known Piano Quintets of the Twentieth Century." D.M.A. diss., University of Rochester, Eastman School of Music, 1972. 295pp. UM 73-984. Investigates the use of the piano quintet medium by each of six 20th-century composers chosen to represent a wide diversity of countries and dates of composition as well as of compositional style and idiomatic treatment. Discusses quintets by Elgar, Ross Lee Finney, Martinů, Medtner, Vierne, and Webern.

Giuseppe Tartini. "Treatise on the Ornaments of Music." Translated and edited by Sol Babitz. *Journal of Research in Music Education* 4 (fall 1956): 75–102.

Telemann Werke Verzeichnis. Kassel-Wilhelmshöhe: Bärenreiter, 1950–. A complete catalog prepared in conjunction with the Telemann *Musikalische Werke.*

J. Mark Thompson. "An Annotated Bibliography of French Literature for Bass Trombone, Tuba, and Bass Saxhorn including Solos and Pedagogical Materials." D.M.A. diss., University of Iowa, 1991. See entry for J. Mark Thompson and Jeffrey Jon Lemke's *French Music for Low Brass Instruments.*

J. Mark Thompson and Jeffrey Jon Lemke. *French Music for Low Brass Instruments: An Annotated Bibliography.* Bloomington: Indiana University Press, 1994. 178pp. Identifies and briefly evaluates French duo literature for tenor trombone, bass trombone, tuba, and bass saxhorn with piano. Also includes pedagogical materials. This text comes primarily from a combination of the authors' doctoral dissertations.

Donald Francis Tovey. *Essays in Musical Analysis; Chamber Music.* London: Oxford University Press, 1944.

Bruce Clarence Trible. "The Chamber Music of Henry Cowell." Diss., Indiana University, 1952. 116pp. Includes a chapter on general stylistic analysis. Chapter 3 is devoted to Cowell's compositions for solo instrument and piano. Includes a discussion of Suite (violin and piano), 6 Casual Developments (clarinet and piano), 3 Ostinati with Chorales (oboe and piano), How Old Is Song (violin and piano), Hymn and Fuguing Tune No. 7 (viola and piano), and Fuguing Tune (cello and piano). Also contains chapters on compositions for stringed instruments, wind instruments, and miscellaneous combinations.

Burnet C. Tuthill. "Sonatas for Clarinet and Piano: Annotated Listings." *Journal of Research in Music Education* 20 (fall 1972): 308–28.

Homer Ulrich. *Chamber Music.* 2nd ed. New York: Columbia University Press, 1966. 401pp.

Frans Vester. *Flute Music of the 18th Century: An Annotated Bibliography.* Monteux: Musica Rara, 1985. Lists literature for solo flute and flute in chamber ensembles by composers. 573pp.

———. *Flute Repertoire Catalogue.* London: Musica Rara, 1967. Over 373pp.

John Vinton, ed. *Dictionary of Contemporary Music.* New York: E. P. Dutton, 1974. 834pp.

Himie Voxman and Lyle Merriman. *Woodwind Music Guide: Ensemble Music in Print, 1982 Edition.* Evanston, Ill.: Instrumentalist Company, 1982. 498pp.

Therese M. Wacker. "The Piccolo in the Chamber Music of the Twentieth Century: An Annotated Bibliography of Selected Works." D.M.A. diss., Ohio State University, 2000.

Jae-Wook Kim Wager. "Chamber Music for Pianosolo and Seven Players." D.M.A. diss., University of Maryland, College Park, 1998.

Helen Walker-Hill. *Piano Music by Black Women Composers: A Catalog of Solo and Ensemble Works.* Westport, Conn.: Greenwood Press, 1992. Identifies by listings and descriptions many ensemble works with piano by Black women composers.

Hsiu-Hui Wang. "Tracing the Development of the French Piano Trio." D.M.A. diss., University of Maryland, College Park, 1999. 69pp.

J. A. Westrup. *Schubert Chamber Music.* Seattle: University of Washington Press, 1969. 63pp. BBC Music Guides series.

Un-Yong Whang. "An Analysis of Dello Joio's Chamber Music for Piano and Strings with Performance Suggestions." Ed.D. diss., Columbia University Teachers College, 1986.

G. Larry Whatley. "Donald Francis Tovey: A Survey of His Life and Works." AMT 25 (April-May 1976): 9–12.

Arnold Whittall. *Schoenberg Chamber Music.* Seattle: University of Washington Press, 1972. 64pp. BBC Music Guides series.

David Wilkins. "Recitalectics No. 2: The Role of the Pianist." AMT 25 (January 1976): 24, 26. Discusses the role of the pianist in a chamber ensemble.

Wayne Wilkins. *The Index of Flute Music Including the Index of Baroque Trio Sonatas.* Magnolia, Ark.: Music Register, 1974. 131pp.

———. *Index of Violin Music (Strings).* Magnolia, Ark.: Music Register, 1973. 246pp.

———. *1974 Supplement to Index of Violin Music.* Magnolia, Ark.: Music Register, 42pp.

Michael D. Williams. *Music for Viola.* Detroit: Detroit Studies in Music Bibliography, 1979. Lists works for viola solo, with keyboard, and in chamber ensembles. 362pp.

Index of Works for Two or More Pianos and Other Instruments

Index of Works by Female Composers

Index of Composers

Maurice Hinson, one of the foremost authorities on piano literature, is Senior Professor of Piano at the Southern Baptist Theological Seminary. Author of *Guide to the Pianist's Repertoire* (Indiana University Press), he has performed and given master classes worldwide.

Wesley Roberts is Professor of Music at Campbellsville University. He has presented concerts as pianist and organist throughout the United States and Europe, including programs in New York City, Los Angeles, London, Paris, Lyon, Amsterdam, Copenhagen, Prague, and Zurich.